30th Anniversary

1976 Deluxe Edition

EDITED BY JOHN T. AMBER

DBI BOOKS, INC., NORTHFIELD, ILL.
(formerly Digest Books, Inc.)

The covers for this 30th edition of GUN DIGEST, *front and back, are once again the work of artist James M. Triggs—his superb portrayals of firearms need little introduction to our readers.*

The front cover reveals the handsome Creedmoor or long-range styled Ruger No. 1 Single Shot rifle that was custom made and profusely engraved for presentation to your editor in celebration of his twenty-five years with this widely-distributed annual, a volume devoted to guns and shooting.

Bill Ruger called on two of the world's best engravers to embellish this 34-inch barreled near-replica of a late 19th century type—Winston Churchill of Vermont and Lynton McKenzie of Louisiana. You'll find an account of the rifle's long preparation elsewhere in this issue, plus an explanation of why the Triggs painting doesn't conform exactly to the completed rifle!

Our back cover shows two views of the Ruger Model 77 bolt action rifle, the cutaway drawing clearly exhibiting Jim Triggs' mastery of this difficult technique. The Model 77 pictured is the Magnum version, as the 458 Winchester cartridges seen will indicate.

Townsend Whelen Award

We had not intended that our annual award honoring the late Colonel Whelen should go the the same author more than once, but that's happened this year. The 10th presentation of the Award goes to Mr. M. L. Brown for his "Firearms in Frontier America," a deeply researched and truly unique study of the economic impact of firearms on the 200-year history of the United States—an approach not previously attempted!

This annual $500 award is given to the author who, in the opinion of our judges, made the best contribution to the literature of firearms, as published in this edition. The criteria are originality, clarity, readability and lasting value.

Our thanks to Mr. Brown and our sincere congratulations.

The views and opinions contained herein are those of the authors. The editor and publisher disclaim all responsibility for the accuracy or correctness of the authors' views.

Manuscripts, contributions and inquiries, including first class return postage, should be sent to the Gun Digest Editorial Offices, 540 Frontage Rd., Northfield, Ill. 60093. All material received will receive reasonable care, but we will not be responsible for its safe return. Material accepted is subject to our requirements for editing and revisions. Author payment covers all rights and title to the accepted material, including photos, drawings and other illustrations. Payment is made at our current rates.

ISBN-0-695-80598-3 Library of Congress Catalog #44-3588

IN THE BLACK

Outstanding Handgun Award

This year's winner of the Outstanding American Handgunner Award—and the handsome bronze statuette that goes with the honor—was William B. Ruger. No one, I feel, better deserved it, for Bill Ruger has contributed immeasurably to the rapidly growing sport of handgunning. Initiated in 1973, almost entirely through the efforts of Lee Jurras (formerly head of the late Super Vel Corp.), this important and prestigious Award is intended not only for those who have or do excel in handgunning as such, but to those people who have strongly brought the use and acceptance of the one-hand firearm to the attention of the public. Bill Ruger has been notably "outstanding" in just that area, and our warmest, most sincere congratulations to him.

Outdoorsman of the Year

Warren Page, president of the National Shooting Sports Foundation, and a leading outdoor writer, sporting firearms authority and veteran hunter, was presented with the Winchester-Western Outdoorsman of the Year Award for 1974 during the 1975 National Sporting Goods Association Show in Houston, Texas. The presentation, made by Winchester president George A. Chandler, consisted of a scroll and a custom-built Winchester Super-X Model 1 autoloading shotgun.

Our heartfelt congratulation to Lefty, and our best wishes for his full recovery from a serious illness.

Questions and Answers

Letters to the editors *must* include a stamped, self-addressed envelope. We try to answer all communications, but it often takes a long time. Patience!

NBRSA Gun Digest Trophy

Old friend Neal Knox—editor of *Handloader* and *Rifle* magazines—was the 1974 winner of the Heavy Varmint Rifle National Championship and, with it, the GUN DIGEST TROPHY. Nice going for a relatively new shooter.

Neal's score in the Grand Aggregate was 0.2980 MOA for the 50 shots—25 each at 100 and 200 yards. His rifle consisted of a Shilen DGA action and Shilen barrel, caliber 222, and his handload was 21.1 of Reloder 7 powder, CCI BR4 primers and 53-gr. bullets he made himself in Simonson dies.

Ray Riling 1896-1974

Raymond L. J. Riling, arms collector, author, publisher and founder of Ray Riling Arms Books Co. He was one of the country's foremost authorities on antique firearms and their accessories, the author of *The Powder Flask Book* and *Guns & Shooting: A Bibliography,* two major works in his specialized field. He was the compiler of "The Arms Library" of the GUN DIGEST for the past sixteen years and a contributor to many other publications in the arms field. The Ray Riling Arms Books Co. is being carried on by his two sons.

IBS Heavy Varmint Trophy

The winner in 1974 of the H.V. championship—and the GUN DIGEST TROPHY—was Jim Stekl (right) of Mohawk, N.Y., a veteran benchrester. His Grand Aggregate for the match was 0.3245-minute of angle (MOA)—not a new record but mighty nice shooting for the 50-shot contest—five 5-shot matches at 100 yards, 5 at 200.

Stekl used a Remington 40XB-BR rifle in 222 caliber, his scope a Unertl 24x. His handload was 24.5 grains of 4895 with Remington Bench Rest 52-gr. bullets.

CONTENTS

FEATURES

DEPARTMENTS

Firearms in Frontier America

The Economic Impact

Part I

1560 to 1800

Firearms exerted a powerful influence on the complex political, economic and technological aspects of the North American colonies. Nowhere was that pervasive influence more apparent than in the region which subsequently became the United States.

by M.L. BROWN

FIREARMS, by the very nature of their existence, exerted a powerful influence on the complex political, socio-economic and technological factors profoundly affecting the wealth and welfare of all nations and, consequently, transformed the entire structure of civilization. Nowhere was the pervasive influence of firearms more discernibly apparent than on the inexorably expanding frontiers of North America; particularly that region which subsequently became the United States.

When Genoese navigator Christopher Columbus rediscovered the Western Hemisphere in 1492, firearms designed for individual use had seen nearly two centuries of gradual development. The primitive 14th century hand cannon emerged as the more advanced matchlock—the first firearm using mechanical rather than manual ignition—and the evolutionary process continued unabated, creating even more sophisticated and effective firearms.

In the wake of discovery came the inevitable collision of Old World culture with that of the New World inhabitants. As history tragically records, the Indians lost more than they gained in the violent exchange and were inextricably drawn into the sanguinary European power struggle which ravaged the Americas for nearly three centuries. Following the birth of the United States, the Indians were involved in an equally savage contest as an infant Republic attempted to wrest a nation from the vast, hostile wilderness.

Old World powers generally pursued a policy of subjugation, exploitation and extermination in dealing with the Indians; a policy endemic to the fledgling Republic. Of all the European invaders, only Spain refused to provide the Indians with firearms. This unrealistic approach ultimately contributed to her decline in North America since her emerging French, Dutch and English rivals bolstered their military strength and economic interests by encouraging an extensive arms trade among the various tribes.

Acutely aware of the enormous sums requisite for exploration and colonization, Spain early admonished her administrators to economize; a practice more observed in the breach than otherwise, though there were such exceptions as Luis de Velasco, Viceroy of New Spain. Distressed by events at the later-abandoned Pensacola (Fla.) settlement, Velasco expressed his concern to colonial administrator Tristan de Luna in correspondence dated 6 May 1560:

"...that your captains do not take proper care to keep their men well disciplined...and their arms in proper condition pains me much, and they ought not to permit this; for they can see that they are in a land where arms are needed and cost a great deal of money."[1]

Though there is no way to determine the value of the 16th century Spanish *ducado* (ducat), some idea of the cost of the arms during this early period can be calculated by comparing prices of various items available in 1565 at St. Augustine, Fla., the first permanent European settlement in North America, and established by Adelantado Pedro Menéndez de Avilés that year.

Ship biscuits (600 lbs)	3 ducats
Beef (½ side)	5 ducats
Beer (bbl.)	3 ducats
Swords	1 to 3 ducats
Arquebus (matchlock)	3 ducats
Bow & 24 arrows	2 ducats
Crossbow	2 ducats
Cutlass (gilded)	4 ducats
Coat of mail	50 ducats
Harpoon w/cord	1 ducat

Early Firearms

Conflicting territorial claims often erupted into open warfare as the Old World powers expanded their imperialistic prerogatives and, throughout the early period of conquest and colonization, there was continuous development in firearms evolution.

By about 1520, wheel-lock arms were introduced in Europe and subsequent refinements of the ignition mechanism produced the first practical pistols. Archaeological and documentary evidence leaves no doubt that, by the late 16th century, various types of wheel-lock arms were used in limited numbers throughout the Spanish possessions and by English settlers at Roanoke Island, these guns performing a more important role in Colonial America than is generally supposed.

A simplified, more advanced ignition device appeared in the Netherlands about 1550. Known as the snaphaunce, it was the first of various snapping-type flintlocks emerging in Europe. Yet another flintlock originated in Spain about 1575. The Spanish lock, or *miquelet,* differed radically from the snaphaunce. A distinct improvement, it appeared in various forms.

The dawn of the 17th century saw the Spanish position in North America challenged by the militant colonialism displayed by the great mercantile houses of England, France and the Netherlands. The unlimited financial backing and monopolistic trade concessions granted by those affluent merchant associations, supported by military force when required, inspired increasing colonization attempts, as did the intolerable socio-economic conditions then flourishing throughout Europe.

Centuries before the white man arrived the Indians had established an extensive fur trade. With the advent of the Europeans, the fur trade quickly assumed paramount economic significance. French fur traders established themselves on the islands off the Canadian coast by 1600 and, on 10 April 1606, the London and Plymouth Companies were chartered by James I. On 14 May 1607, 144 "gentlemen adventurers" of the London Company began the first permanent English settlement in North America at Jamestown, Va.

In 1613 Adriaen Block and Hendrick Christianson established a Dutch fur trading post on Manhattan Island and, on 11 October 1614, the New Netherland Company was formed, giving Amsterdam merchants a 3-year fur trade monopoly. Meanwhile, the Leyden Separatists were granted permission by the Virginia Company to settle within its territory and, on 11 November 1620, the *Mayflower* deposited its cargo of Pilgrims on New England shores.

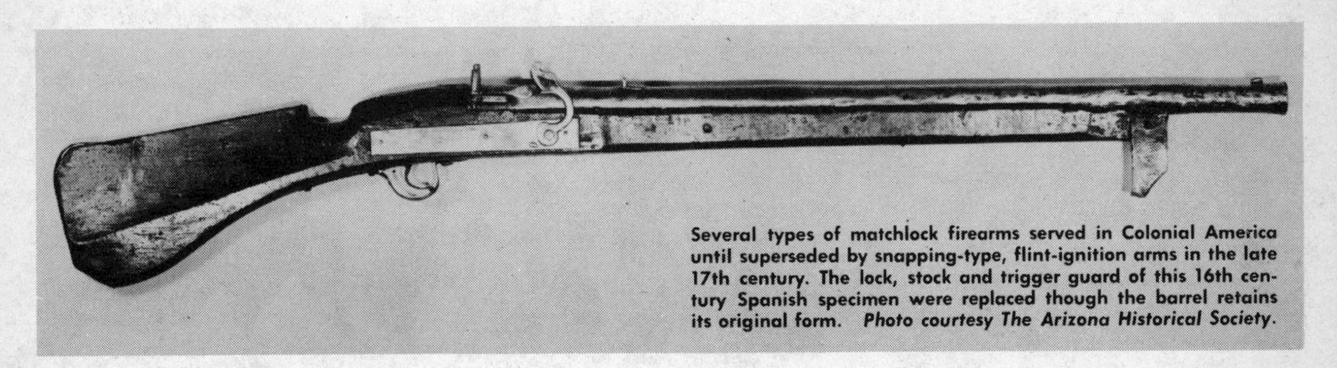

Several types of matchlock firearms served in Colonial America until superseded by snapping-type, flint-ignition arms in the late 17th century. The lock, stock and trigger guard of this 16th century Spanish specimen were replaced though the barrel retains its original form. *Photo courtesy The Arizona Historical Society.*

First True Flintlock

By this time the Dutch snaphaunce and Spanish lock had seen gradual refinement. Each was an effective ignition mechanism, yet it remained for a French gunmaking genius, Marin le Bourgeoys, to extract their best features and combine them with his own innovations to create a superior, hybrid flintlock about 1615. This was the first *true* flintlock. Numerous variations subsequently appeared, emerging to serve as the primary form of ignition for nearly 200 years.

Developed concurrently in Britain was a snapping-type flintlock appropriately called the English lock, one of several mechanisms referred to as "dog" locks. These locks quickly supplanted the snaphaunce in England and, in conjunction with the still predominant matchlock, arms of this type were early employed by the English colonists in America.

As Charles Winthrop Sawyer sagaciously noted in *Firearms In American History, 1600-1800,* "The Colonists in America were the greatest weapon-using people of that epoch in the world." The colonists and traders arriving in North America during the 17th century demanded, regardless of cost, the most reliable firearms available since, like the ax and plow, the gun was a primary tool for survival.

In 1609 Capt. John Smith reported that the Jamestown settlers had on hand 300 firearms, including matchlock muskets, snaphaunce muskets and muskets with English locks. Though most Pilgrims were armed with matchlock muskets, Capt. Miles Standish and an anonymous companion had flintlock arms of some undetermined kind, using them advantageously in a brush with the Indians when exploring Cape Cod and, incidentally, pilfering the winter food supply of those "heathen selvages."

By 1630 matchlock arms had been practically abandoned in Virginia and New England. A Virginia arms inventory of 1625 disclosed 981 "peeces fixit" and snaphaunces, 47 matchlocks, 55 pistols and 6 petronels. A year later, settlers sailing for the Massachusetts Bay Colony brought with them 80 snaphaunce muskets, 10 snaphaunce fowling pieces and 10 matchlock muskets.

Matchlock arms had been largely supplanted in North America by 1675 except among the Indians and in the Spanish settlements. The first flintlock arms arrived at St. Augustine from Mexico in December, 1668, when Gov. Francisco de la Guerra received 24 *escopettes,* purchased for the garrison at 22 *pesos* (roughly $35) each. By 1680 most of these had disappeared, probably through normal attrition.

The matchlock musket remained the standard Old World military arm until the end of the 17th century more as a matter of economy than through traditional opposition to change; then as now, extensive rearmament and retraining programs placed an enormous burden on national treasuries.

Spain did not abandon the martial matchlock until 1703, but the transition to flintlock arms was not complete in her virtually orphaned Florida provinces until 1740. This inordinate delay proved disastrous, seriously undermining Spain's position; for since 1670 Indians supplied with superior English and French flintlocks had continuously encroached upon Spanish territory, disrupting commerce and destroying numerous missions.

The fur trade early assumed paramount economic importance in Colonial America and the Indians willingly parted with pelts to procure arms and ammunition. French traders contacted the Mandans (above) on the Missouri in 1738. This Carl Bodmer engraving from Maximilian's, Prince zv Wied, *Atlas* (London, 1820) depicts the Mandan Bull Society Bison Dance. *Photo courtesy The American Museum of Natural History.*

Since the Indians were the primary source for furs in the colonies, most European traders eagerly catered to their demands. The mere possession of a firearm elevated the status of the Indian hunter-warrior to undreamed-of tribal heights and transformed many of the sedentary and semi-sedentary tribes into aggressive nomads preying on their less fortunate neighbors.

Early demonstrating a political acumen of Machiavellian dimensions, the Indians quickly learned to manipulate the Europeans, frequently using transitory promises of peace, trade and military alliance to procure firearms, ammunition and other trade goods. The high cost of arming the Indians was not entirely an economic problem, for on the frontier the price was often paid in terror and bloodshed.

The Indian Gun Trade

The French had few qualms about trading firearms to the Indians, nor had the Dutch, who supplied the Mohawk in 1614 and the Pequot in

1621, despite contrary official policy. Plymouth Colony early proscribed selling or trading guns to the Indians and, in 1628, deported Thomas Morton for that offense, yet economic and military considerations quickly erased the stigma in most regions under English control.

Iroquoian tribes along the Hudson had received at least 400 matchlock muskets from Dutch and English traders by 1634. The Susquehanna Indians were so well armed by Virginia traders in 1647 that they offered the Huron tribes 1,300 warriors—trained in European tactics by the Swedes—for use in their perpetual wars with the Iroquoian Confederacy. In 1663 Maryland colonists presented the Susquehanna with a small cannon, two barrels of gunpowder and 200 lbs. of lead.

Though the Indians never learned to make gunpowder or smelt lead, they moulded bullets and repaired their arms in crude forges which became prime military targets during the many colonial conflicts. The influx of firearms among the powerful Eastern Woodland Indians left many of their traditional enemies vulnerable, driving them westward in a monumental, involuntary migration beginning about 1630 and continuing sporadically thereafter.

England expelled the Dutch from New Amsterdam in 1664 and, in 1670, Charles II chartered the Hudson's Bay Company, granting English fur traders a monopoly in competition with the French. Five years later King Philip's War (1675-78) ravaged New England, the victorious colonists virtually annihilating the allied Narraganset, Nipmuc and Wampanoags.

The rapid expansion of the fur industry during the latter half of the 17th century intensified European rivalry and stimulated Indian demands for firearms. Before about 1680 a potpourri of obsolete matchlocks, obsolescent flintlocks and inexpensive versions of contemporary flintlock muskets and fowling pieces were traded to the Indians. Sensitive to Indian desires. European armsmakers had developed distinctive trade arms by the beginning of the 18th century. Of whatever origin, these firearms displayed several common characteristics. Most specimens had slender, 48-to-54-inch barrels of 50 to 60 caliber with brass furniture and full-length, fish-belly stocks.

The lightweight flintlock trade fusil, subsequently known as the "Northwest gun," emerged as the single most important article of commerce among the Indians and received wide distribution. Indian trade fusils were made in large numbers and various patterns by English, French, Dutch and Belgian makers during and after the colonial period. American gunmakers entered the business late in the 18th century.

The Hudson's Bay Company set the value of trade fusils, gunpowder and lead at its scattered wilderness trading posts or "factories," about 1680, along these lines: Long-barreled fusils sold for 12 pelts or "plews," medium-barreled specimens went for 10 skins and short-barreled models brought 8 pelts. One plew purchased a half-pound of gunpowder and two bought 4 pounds of shot. Prices were reasonable and competitive. By 1700 the value of furs exported from the English colonies exceeded £16,000 and by 1775 totaled £53,709.

Since firearms were at a premium in the colonies, they often served in early real estate transactions and treaty negotiations with the Indians. The Rev. John Woodbridge of Newbury, Massachusetts Bay Colony, moved to the New Jersey Colony in 1664, purchasing the entire vast Elizabethtown tract from three Indians for "...20 fathom of trayden (trading) cloth, 2 cotes (coats), 2 Gunnes, 2 Kettles, 10 barrels of Lead, 20 handful of Powder, 400 fathom of white Wampum or two hundred fathoms of Black wampum."[2]

During most of the 17th century there was never enough currency in the English colonies to stabilize the

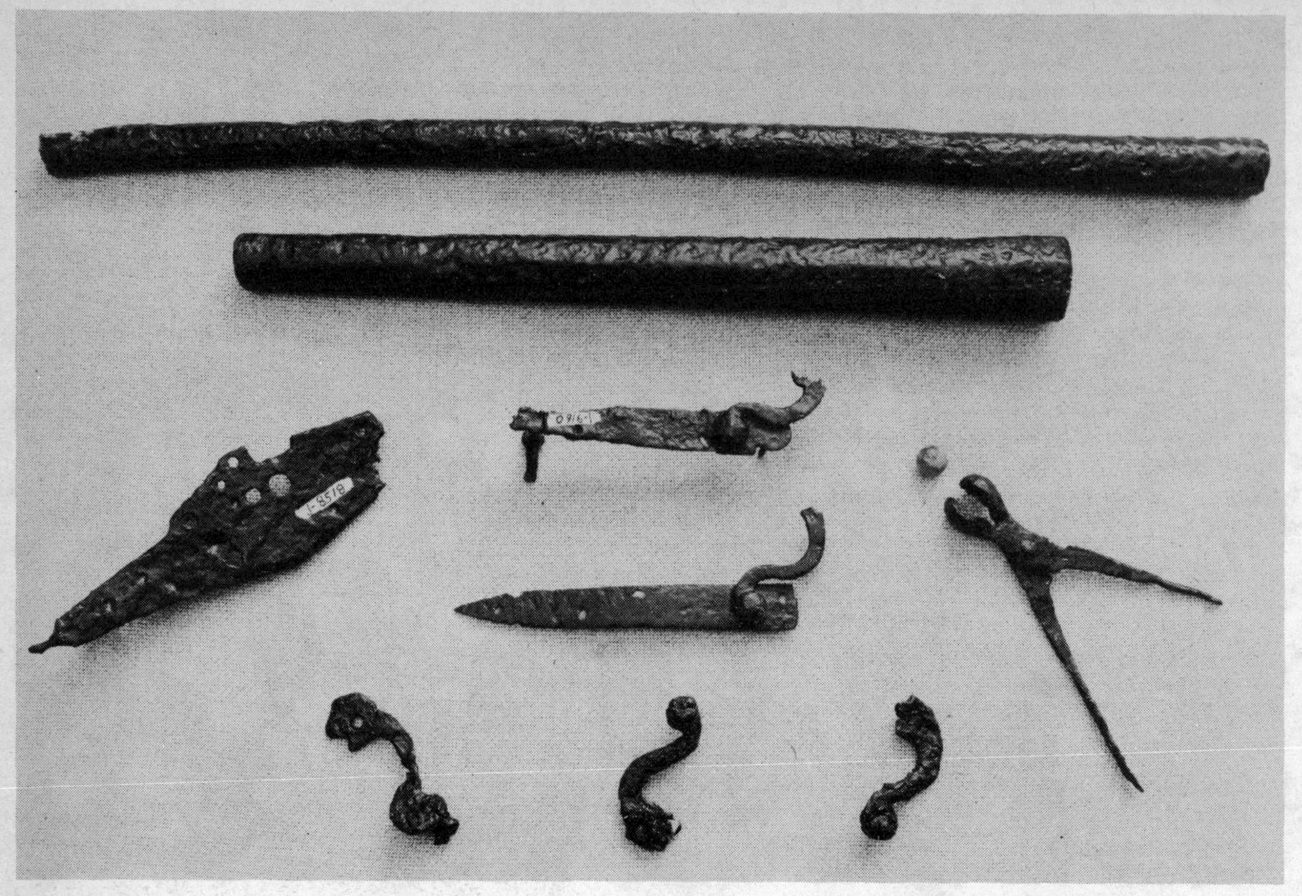

These artifacts excavated at Jamestown, Va., illustrate the various types of firearms and accouterments used by early 17th century English settlers. Top—Musket barrels. Center, from left—fragmented wheel-lock lockplate; a pair of fragmented matchlocks; single-cavity scissor mould and musket ball. Bottom—three matchlock serpentines. *Photo courtesy Jamestown Colonial National Historical Park; Thomas L. Williams, photographer.*

chaotic money situation and the settlers bartered furs, Indian wampum, farm products and various other items including musket balls. Since practically all lead, like gunpowder and gunflints, was imported and consequently expensive, musket balls served as a convenient exchange medium; each was worth a farthing, though tradesmen were not required to accept more than a dozen per purchase.

First Gunmakers

Among the numerous English settlers disembarking on hostile shores were the first craftsmen; artisans who were to create the foundation upon which rests one of the greatest technological cultures the world has ever known. From armorer to wheelwright, those skilled individuals contributed immensely to the building of America, yet the influence of the gunsmith and the production of firearms on nearly every phase of American endeavor can hardly be overstated. Still, armsmaking remains one of the most neglected fields of study in the broad development of the successful American technomic* system.

*Coined word combining *(tech)*nology and ec*(onomic)*, describing an economic system based on technological achievement. MLB.

For a considerable time all firearms and components had been imported, either as personal possessions or held in common trust by civil and military authorities. Few, if any, gunsmiths were active in the English colonies before 1630. Damaged firearms posed a serious problem and, when possible, colony blacksmiths or military artificers performed the needed repairs. Blacksmith James Read served in this capacity at Jamestown in 1607, while Moses Fletcher of Sandwich was the first Pilgrim blacksmith, arriving with the *Mayflower*.

There were 4,646 whites and negroes in the English colonies by 1630; their number had swelled to 50,368 by 1650. Increasing population, the expanding fur trade and accelerated rivalry with the Spanish and French stimulated the demand for firearms, demonstrating the need for gunsmiths to make and repair arms for both settlers and Indians.

The first English gunsmith of record to appear in the colonies was Eltweed Pomeroy of Devonshire. In 1630 he founded a gunsmithery at Dorchester, Mass., and was active there until 1635 when he moved to Windsor, Conn. Pomeroy relocated in Northampton, Mass., in 1670 and died there a year later. His sons, Eldad and Medad, continued in the trade as did most Pomeroy males thereafter. The Pomeroy gunsmithing dynasty, one of many to emerge in the colonies, terminated with the death of Lemuel Pomeroy, Jr., at Pittsfield, Mass., in 1849.

English gunsmiths Bennet and Packson made arms for the Maryland Colony and repaired Indian trade fusils at a gunsmithery on Kent Island in 1635. That same year Richard Waters established a shop at Salem, Mass. In 1640 gunsmith Thomas Nash served as town and colony armorer at New Haven, Conn., while in 1643 James Phips started a gunshop on the Kennebec to handle the growing Indian trade.

Covert Barent was active as a gunsmith at New Amsterdam from 1646 to 1650 and Francis Soleil established there in 1655. By that time Boston could boast at least three gunsmiths of record: William Davies, Herman Garret and Richard Leader. Numerous gunsmiths were active from New England to the Carolinas by 1700, proliferating rapidly thereafter.

Aside from the fur trade, ironmaking was one of the first, most important, colonial industries. Since large quantities of wrought iron were essential to the manufacture of firearms and other goods, and while imported iron was expensive and therefore relatively scarce, English colonists early sought to produce their own.

Early Iron Making

Crude bog iron was made at Jamestown in 1607 and in 1619 a large furnace was established at nearby Falling Creek. The Falling Creek Furnace, or "bloomery," produced a poor grade of wrought iron and, in 1622, it was destroyed, along with the ironmongers and their families, during the savage Powhatan uprising in which 349 of Virginia's 1,250 colonists were slain.

The first fully successful colonial furnace was the Saugus Iron Works, located near Boston and established by gunsmith Richard Leader and John Winthrop, Jr., a saltpeter manufacturer. Operations began in 1648. A lack of skilled workmen and raw materials closed the furnace in 1670. Other furnaces were started before 1700, including the Braintree Furnace south of Boston (1646-53), the New Haven Furnace (1658) and the Shrewsbury Furnace (1682) in New Jersey.

Castiron, charcoal iron and wrought iron were the only ferrous metals readily available and easily worked by colonial 'smiths. Of those, only wrought iron was suitable for gunmaking, even though slag inclusions made it weak and it lacked carbon for hardness. This latter defect rendered it unsuitable for making springs, a primary component of the gunlock. Until about 1770 when "crucible" or "cast" steel became available, colonial gunsmiths made springs from scrapped sword or saber blades and recarburized wrought iron, an expensive and unreliable product termed "blister" steel. In 1784 Henry Cort's "puddled" iron was introduced in England, but this high-grade wrought iron was not accepted in the U.S. until about 1870, by which time it had already been superseded by a superior steel-making process.

Parliament, early aware that a large colonial iron industry presaged a potentially dangerous war machine, passed the infamous Iron Act of 1750, attempting to curtail the manufacture of iron products in America and limiting the establishment of tilt hammer forges and rolling and slitting mills. The colonists ignored the Iron Act and in 1769 little more than six tons of bar iron were imported while thereafter imports and exports sharply declined. By 1775 the English colonies were self-sufficient, producing 30,000 tons of iron as compared to a worldwide figure of 210,000 tons.*

Colonial population had increased to 250,888 by 1700 and jumped another 180,883 by 1710, many of that number arriving from Central Europe. Among them were a group of German and Swiss gunsmiths settling in southeastern Pennsylvania. The first of those craftsmen is believed to have been Swiss-born Martin Meylin,

*From *Historical Statistics of the United States*, Bureau of Census, Washington, D.C. 1961.

Wampanoag chief King Philip, son of Massasoit, was slain 12 August 1676 during the New England Indian war bearing his name. Contemporary engraving by Thomas Church also depicts an English flintlock fowling piece with cumbrous butt and brass heelplate typical of arms traded to the Indians during the early colonial period. *Photo courtesy The Smithsonian Institute.*

who lived in West Lampeter Township, Lancaster County. In 1719 he built a gunsmithery with the first barrel-boring mill in the region and was active there until his death in 1749.

The most significant technological achievement in the English colonies during the first half of the 18th century was the creation of Lancaster area gunsmiths working in concert with the lone hunter of the Appalachians. Together they produced a reliable, lightweight, accurate flintlock rifle suited to the game and terrain of the region. This was the American rifle or, as it is more commonly termed, the "Kentucky," for its enviable reputation was established in that "bloody ground" by the restless hunters and pioneers moving ever westward.

The mainstay of the 18th century weapons system was the muzzle-loading flintlock musket with bayonet exemplified by these 75-caliber British specimens: the Long Land Pattern Musket ca. 1762 (at right) and the short Land Pattern Musket made in 1747 by Jordan (fl. 1733-62). *Photo courtesy West Point Museum.*

The American Rifle

The American rifle traces its ancestry to the alpine region of Central Europe where, since 1580 in wheel-lock form, it was known as the *Jäger* (hunter's) rifle. By 1665 the transition to flint ignition had begun and it was in this form that the Jäger rifle appeared in Pennsylvania with the influx of German and Swiss settlers. Between 1725 and 1760 it was gradually transformed into the American rifle, reaching the pinnacle of perfection shortly after the War of Independence (1775-81).

Prior to the mid-19th century gunmaking in America was primarily an individual, household enterprise. Each firearm made was a distinct individual entity, though displaying common characteristics as to type, since it reflected the idiosyncracies of the individual craftsman. Most gunsmithing was manually performed, although some crude machinery was used, principally the bellows, rifling bench and pole lathe. Power was supplied by the hand crank, foot treadle, water wheel, windmill and several types of treadmills operated by humans or animals.

The common 18th century gunsmithery consisted of a small, single-story wood, stone or combination structure containing a brick or field stone forge, though the forge was often separate from the building and usually covered. The work area frequently doubled as a retail shop or store, and many times also served as living quarters. There was no guild system, such as had early evolved in the Old World, nor were colonial gunsmiths required to submit their work to a proof house for approval; this is still characteristic of the U.S. firearms industry today, though all, it is believed, conduct their own "proof" testing.

Members of the family or relatives usually supplied the work force in small shops. The more affluent gunsmith with a larger shop frequently formed a partnership, hired experienced help or employed an apprentice or two. The apprentice was often an illegitimate child or orphan whose term and conditions of indenture were governed by law, some colonies requiring a 7-year term. Upon completion of their term, apprentices were generally provided with a suit of

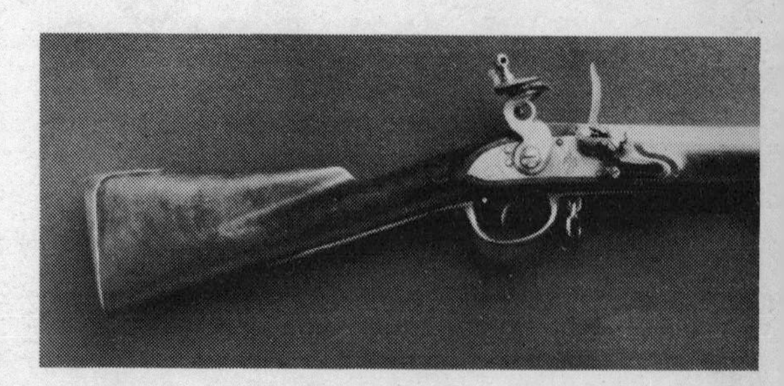

clothes, a set of gunsmithing tools and a small stipend; they then served as journeyman gunsmiths for three years.

A number of large gunsmitheries which could be properly called factories were established in the colonies before 1750. A contemporary description states that each contained "...3 or 4 barrel forges, a grinding mill for grinding and polishing barrels, a lock shop with 7 forges, and benches for 40 filers, 10 benches for gunstock makers, a brass foundry for mountings with several finishing benches, a couple of forges for bayonets and ramrods, together with a mill for grinding and polishing them, another forge for fittings, and an assembly shop."[3]

Gunsmitheries similar or equal to that described were operated by at least two industrious and reputable colonial figures, Hugh Orr (1717-98) and William Henry (1729-86). A trained gun-and-locksmith, Orr emigrated from Scotland to Easton, Pa., in 1737 and, a year later, moved to Bridgewater, Mass. There he erected a large scythe and ax works, incorporating the first trip-hammer or drop forge in New England. In 1748 he made 500 muskets for the Massachusetts Militia, and he avidly supported the patriot cause during the Revolution. Henry, born in Lancaster, Pa., started a gunsmithery there in 1745, making Kentucky rifles and pistols. In 1755 he served as an armorer with Gen. Braddock's ill-fated expedition. During the Revolution his works produced muskets and bayonets for the patriot cause. His sons continued in the trade and the last Henry active as a gunsmith, Granville, retired in 1891.

Thousands of French arms served in patriot ranks during the American Revolution. This M1763 French martial musket and the later M1768 served as prototypes for the first U.S. military shoulder arm, the M1795. *Photo courtesy the Smithsonian Institute.*

Even before the Revolutionary War a great deal of specialization emerged in the gunsmithing craft. Some artisans devoted themselves to barrel-making, erecting mills exclusively for that purpose; others engaged in lock-making, though most quality flintlocks were imported prior to hostilities; still others confined themselves to stockmaking. This division of labor was particularly evident in the larger gunsmitheries and factories, these expanding rapidly after the Revolution.

Colonial population had grown to 1,170,760 by 1750. Increasing French incursions into the fur-rich Ohio and Mississippi Valley posed a serious economic and military threat to the Crown, inexorably drawing the English and French into the devastating global conflict known as the French and Indian War (1754-63). That bloody confrontation terminated with England gaining nominal possession of North America east of the Appalachians except for East Florida and other areas under Spanish control.

Warfare in the Colonies

Warfare in Colonial America had been generally conducted in the orthodox European fashion since the initial invasion though characterized by linear tactics since 1700. The smoothbore, muzzle-loading flintlock musket and bayonet was the mainstay of the 18th century weapons system and remained predominant on both sides of the Atlantic until well into the 19th century. The American rifle was in its infancy during the French and Indian War, but by 1765 virtually every frontiersman was familiar with it and equally well versed in the unorthodox, guerilla-style tactics employed by the Indians.

The cataclysmic events at Lexington and Concord on 19 April 1775 found rebellious English colonists as unprepared for war as their descendants have been in the 200 years since that bloody struggle. The procurement of arms and munitions was paramount if patriot efforts were to succeed. Con-

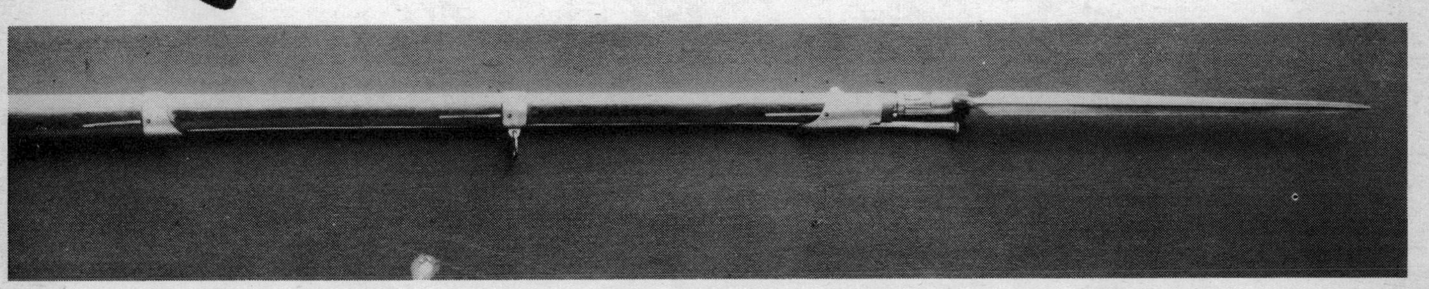

U.S. musket, M1795. These arms were produced at both national armories and by private contractors. The 69-cal. barrel averaged 44⅝". Over-all length was about 59.5", and weight averaged 8 lbs., 14 ozs. *Photo courtesy The Smithsonian Institution.*

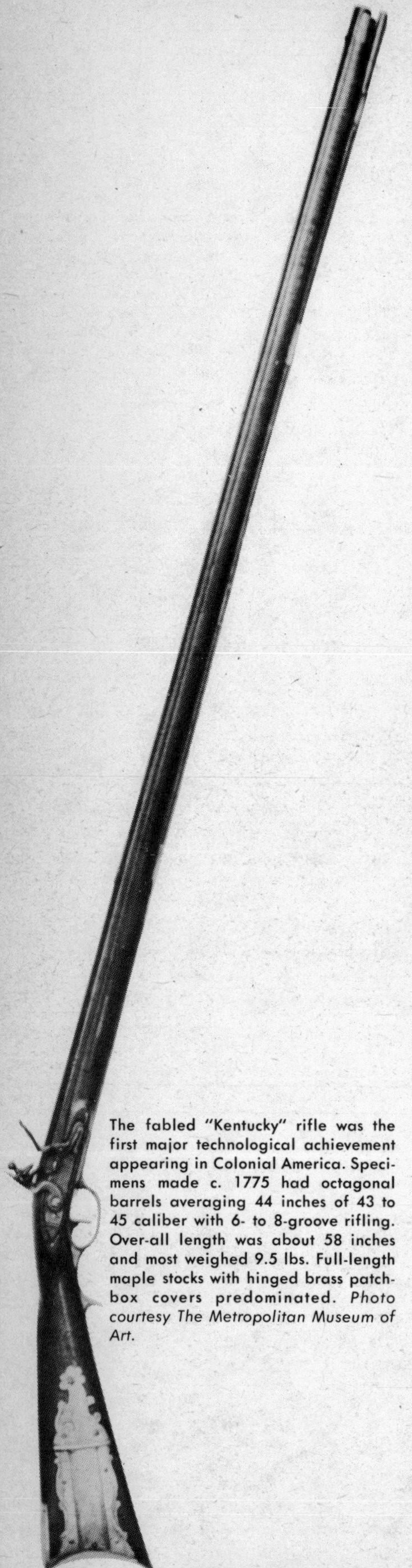

The fabled "Kentucky" rifle was the first major technological achievement appearing in Colonial America. Specimens made c. 1775 had octagonal barrels averaging 44 inches of 43 to 45 caliber with 6- to 8-groove rifling. Over-all length was about 58 inches and most weighed 9.5 lbs. Full-length maple stocks with hinged brass patchbox covers predominated. *Photo courtesy The Metropolitan Museum of Art.*

fiscated and captured British arms filled patriot ranks at the beginning and rebel gunsmiths responded enthusiastically to the demand for arms.

Committees of Safety in the 13 colonies contracted for arms from many gunsmiths, as did the Continental Congress. Colonial authorities established their own armsmaking and repair facilities. Patriot statesmen like Benjamin Franklin found numerous European nations, especially France, sympathetic to the revolutionary cause if only to profit from Britain's discomfiture and the lucrative arms trade. Dummy corporations such as Hortalez et Cie, a French-Spanish concern, covertly funneled arms and more than 80 percent of patriot gunpowder into the colonies via the Dutch West Indies, Bermuda and Spanish Louisiana, while American privateers and French vessels regularly breached the British blockade.

New England was the hub of colonial gunmaking at the outset of hostilities, though Pennsylvania soon emerged as the "Arsenal of America." The Continental Congress appropriated $10,000 for the manufacture of muskets in March, 1776, while Franklin purchased 80,000 French muskets in 1777. The average price of a musket, complete with ramrod and bayonet, was $12.50 shortly after the war began, though rampant inflation soon raised prices. Rifles sold for as much as $16.00 when available, but the American rifle performed a minor role in Continental ranks. However, in the hands of the frontiersman it kept England's Indian allies from invading the populous eastern settlements and disrupting patriot supply lines.

Military action destroyed many armsmaking facilities during the Revolution, while shortages of funds, raw materials and skilled artisans disrupted others. When the conflict ended, so too did the inordinate demand for arms; numerous contractors as well as state installations terminated operations. It was apparent, nevertheless, that the infant Republic needed a "regular" army and the means to provide it with the requisite arms, munitions and related ordnance materiel. Thus was born the concept of a system of Federal armories and arsenals.

In 1777 the Continental Congress established an arsenal and powder magazine at Springfield, Mass. In 1781, after hostilities terminated, that facility became the Massachusetts State Armory. On 2 April 1794 George Washington, as president of the new nation, was authorized by Congress to establish two Federal armories and appropriated $340,000 for the project. Washington selected the Springfield site and Harpers Ferry, Va. This decision placed Federal ordnance installations in widely separated areas, easing distribution problems and effectively decentralizing the system in the event of war.

After expanding existing facilities and adding others, the Springfield Armory began making flintlock muskets in 1795, producing 245 that year. These were the first U.S. martial arms, patterned after the French "Charleville" muskets of 1763 and 1768, many of which had served patriot forces during the Revolution. Robert Orr, son of Hugh, was the first master armorer there and David Ames, son of colonial gunsmith John Ames, served as superintendent from 1795 to 1802.

Harpers Ferry

Construction on the Harpers Ferry Armory began in 1796, and 293 U.S. M1795 flintlock muskets were produced in 1801 under the direction of James Stubblefield, supervising the works from 1800 to 1807. In 1803 the armory made 780 flintlock rifles. Between 1807 and 1808 4,088 M1806 flintlock pistols were produced. In 1814 10,400 flintlock muskets and 1,600 rifles were made.

Both Federal armories, from the time operations began, were unable to supply the increasing demand for martial arms, particularly during war years. This chronic condition persisted even though additional Federal facilities were subsequently established. To solve this problem the War Department awarded arms contracts to commercial enterprises and individual gunsmiths. This arrangement proved generally satisfactory over the years and remains a standard practice.

The closing years of the turbulent 18th century witnessed the introduction of the two greatest technological contributions ever made to American industry. It was then that the radical concepts of interchangeable parts and mass production methods were initially and successfully applied to firearms manufacture in the United States. Those novel techniques, subsequently adopted the world over, came to be known as the "American system" of manufacture, delivering an economic impact which remains both phenomenal and incalculable.

The singularly profound concepts of mass production with interchangeable parts originated in France about 1717, though most other efforts were unsuccessful. An inventor in his own right, Thomas Jefferson, while American minister to France, visited a musket factory there in 1785 and was thoroughly impressed by the application of those techniques. Returning to America, he failed to arouse commercial or government interest.

In England, meanwhile, identical techniques were used to make pulley blocks for the Royal Navy by a tool and machine-designer genius, one Joseph Bramah, and a Royalist officer —an exile from the French Revolution (1789-95)—Marc Brunel. Official prejudice, poor management and lack of sophisticated tools and machines thwarted the practical application of those techniques on a large scale abroad. It remained for two unrelated Connecticut Yankees, Eli Whitney and Simeon North, to overcome those obstacles and make the system work.

Eli Whitney (1765-1825), practically destitute and disenchanted from numerous court battles involving patent infringements on his famous cotton gin, channeled his energetic genius into firearms manufacture. On 14 January 1798 he obtained a Federal contract for 10,000 M1795 flintlock muskets at $13.40 each; 4,000 to be delivered by September, 1799, and the rest in 1800.

Whitney made his first delivery in 1809, defaulting his contract by 9 years. The lengthy lapse was not unproductive since the time was spent constructing a factory at East Rock (Whitneyville), near New Haven, Conn., and inventing and perfecting the tools and equipment needed before the first workmen were hired. In addition to jigs, fixtures and other equipment, Whitney designed a power-driven drill press and devised the first fixed-spindle milling machine or "slabber." Despite the delay the War Department accepted Whitney's muskets and radical methods, subsequently awarding him additional arms contracts.

Meanwhile, Simeon North (1765-1852) received a Federal contract on 9 March 1799 for 500 M1799 flintlock pistols at $6.50 each. These were patterned after the M1777 French army pistol and were the first U.S. martial pistols made. North, an established scythe-maker located at Berlin, Conn., enlarged his factory and, like Whit-

Eli Whitney, born in Westborough, Mass., revolutionized the U.S. firearms industry with the daring concepts of interchangeable parts and mass production methods. A Yale graduate (1792), Whitney's arms factory remained in family hands from 1798 until purchased by the Winchester firm in 1888. *Photo courtesy Yale University Library.*

Eli Whitney's Armory at East Rock on the Mill River near New Haven, Conn., c 1815. The Whitneyville complex served as a model for several national armories established early in the 19th century. *Photo courtesy Yale University Library.*

To implement his radical manufacturing methods, Eli Whitney designed and built various tools and fixtures, including the first practical milling machine or "slabber" (right). Many of the machines initially designed for the firearms industry were subsequently adapted for other complex products. *Photo courtesy The Smithsonian Institution.*

Simeon North, Whitney's contemporary, also made firearms using mass production techniques and interchangeable components. Each worked independently to pioneer a system of manufacture emulated internationally. Their efforts radically altered the socio-economic structure of the U.S. *Photo courtesy The Smithsonian Institution.*

In 1794 the first national armory was established at Springfield, Mass., site of a Revolutionary War arsenal. The armory, depicted above c. 1855, served continuously until a Department of Defense economy move halted operations in 1964. It has since become an arms museum. *Photo courtesy J.E. Morgan.*

ney, set about creating the requisite equipment. Before completing his initial contract, North was given another on 6 February 1800 for 1,500 M1799 pistols at $6.00 each, delivery due two years from acceptance. He finished this contract on 11 September, 1802. Though North also defaulted, he subsequently received additional contracts from the War Department.

Neither Whitney nor North can be credited with conceiving the "American system" of manufacture, but each proved that, given the proper equipment and procedures, unskilled laborers could make large quantities of firearms or other complex products faster and more economically than skilled artisans could using the time-consuming, hand-finishing methods of the past. In essence, this was the beginning of the end of an era and the solid foundation upon which all modern industry rests. ●

Notes

[1] Herbert Ingram Priestly (ed. and trans.), *The Luna Papers,* Vol. I (DeLand, Fl.: 1928), p. 107.

[2] Earl Schenck Miers, *Where the Raritan Flows,* (New Brunswick, N.J.: 1964) p. 9.

[3] James E. Serven, "Massachusetts, Cradle of American Gunmaking," *The American Rifleman:* Vol. 116, No. 3, p. 26.

Bibliography

Carey, A. Merwyn, *American Firearms Makers,* New York, N.Y., 1953.

Gardner, Robert E., *Small Arms Makers,* New York, N.Y., 1962.

Gluckman, Arcadi, *United States Muskets, Rifles and Carbines,* Buffalo, N.Y., 1948.

——————, *United States Martial Pistols and Revolvers,* Harrisburg, Pa., 1956.

Kauffman, Henry J., *Early American Gunsmiths 1650-1850,* Harrisburg, Pa., 1952.

——————, *The Pennsylvania-Kentucky Rifle,* Harrisburg, Pa., 1960.

Miers, Earl Schenck, *Where the Raritan Flows,* New Brunswick, N.J., 1964.

Peterson, Harold L., *Arms and Armor in Colonial America 1526-1783,* New York, N.Y., 1956.

Priestley, Herbert Ingram, *The Luna Papers,* DeLand, Fl., 1928.

Russell, Carl P., *Guns on the Early Frontiers,* New York, N.Y., 1957.

Willison, George F., *Saints and Strangers,* New York, N.Y., 1965.

Wilson, Mitchell, *American Science and Invention,* New York, N.Y., 1960.

Woodward, William E., *The Way Our People Lived,* New York, N.Y., 1965.

Monographs

Arnade, Charles W., *Florida on Trial,* Coral Gables, Fl., 1959.

Cotter, John L. & Hudson, J. Paul, *New Discoveries at Jamestown,* Washington, D.C., 1957.

Periodicals

Brown, M.L., "Early Gun Makers Met War Woes," *The American Rifleman,* Vol. 119, No. 1.

——————, "Muskets, Powder and Patriots," *The Gun Digest,* 1973.

Gordon, Robert B., "Early Gunsmiths' Metals," *The American Rifleman:* Vol. 107, No. 12.

Keim, Charles J., "Beaver Pelts and Trade Muskets," *The American Rifleman,* Vol. 106, No. 2.

Serven, James E., "Massachusetts, Cradle of American Gunmaking," *The American Rifleman,* Vol. 116, No. 3.

Reports

U.S. Census Bureau, *Historical Statistic of the United States, Colonial Times to 1957,* Washington, D.C., 1957.

A Solid Shooting Stance

Here's a two-handed combat shooting system that offers increased stability in all positions, better gun control and enhanced accuracy. New? It derives from an ancient art—Karate!

by VALVERT LUCIUS FOX

SHOULDERING the old 12 gauge LeFever, I didn't really know what to expect. So, I stood there with my feet close together, leaning backwards to balance the awkward weight of the old cannon. Looking down the long rib of the 32-inch barrels, I pulled the trigger. The roar scared the blazes out of me! The glass jug shattered into oblivion and the recoil drove my fragile little 10-year old body five steps to the rear. Since dad never met with such a violent reaction, I surmised that shooting must have something to do with stance—or that stance must have something to do with shooting!

I can still shatter a glass jug, but I never became much of a shotgunner. Most of my time and effort has been directed at perfecting combat shooting techniques with handguns. Quite a lot of that energy has gone into thought and experimentation with this thing called stance.

This research has revealed weaknesses in many of the combat techniques often subscribed to—especially when applied to practical situations encountered in actual combat.

The stance I finally settled upon is not new! It evolved through centuries of study and application by ancient masters of an oriental martial art—Karate.

These wise old gentlemen concluded that, unless students learn techniques on a scientific basis—employing a systematic and properly scheduled training program—their efforts will be in vain. They elaborated further, saying that training in stance can be considered scientific only when it is conducted on the basis of correct physical and physiological principles. Karate strives for optimum utilization of the human body while embracing these principles. For only by making your body into a solid platform can a strong technique be achieved. If your body lacks balance and stability, your technique will not be effective!

This same concept applies to combat shooting as well as Karate. We must constantly strive to make our body into a solid platform from which to shoot a handgun. Why? Because our shooting is much more effective from a strong and stable base.

A Stable Stance

The stability of your stance depends to a great degree on the area included within its base. For example, standing with your feet close together places you in a precarious position from every angle. Spreading your feet to shoulder width gives you good lateral stability. It does not, however, assist your stability to the front or rear. What we need is a stance offering good balance and stability to the front, rear and both sides.

Front view of the zenkutsu-dachi position as developed in Karate.

The answer to this problem is known in karate as *zenkutsu-dachi* or, front stance. Your feet are spread about 32 inches from front to back while maintaining a width between them equivalent to the width of your hips.

Actually, for shooting it is more convenient to assume a half-front facing stance. In this, your feet and head are facing front as explained, but your hips and shoulders are at a 45-degree angle to the front. You'll see why later!

But let's get back to the mechanics of our stance. If you are shooting right-handed, your left foot will be out front and your right foot to the rear—about 32 inches between them. Your feet are hip width apart. Now, point the toe of your front foot slightly in-

Pointing your leading toe inward places the knee of your front leg just to the inside of the ball of your foot. Your feet are about hip-width apart.

By spreading your feet about 32 inches apart and bending your knees you have good stability fore and aft and a lower center of gravity.

Leaning the upper part of your body this far forward places your balance too much to the front. This reduces your turning radius greatly.

ward, otherwise your front leg will tend to fall outward, creating unsteadiness.

Pointing your front toe inward places the knee of your front leg in such a position that a plumb line dropped from its center will fall just to the inside of the ball of your foot. This gives you more lateral stability and the ability to turn from side-to-side much faster.

Distribute your body weight so that your front leg supports about 60% and your rear leg about 40%. From this position you'll never have to worry about losing your balance to the rear no matter what handgun you are shooting.

In assuming this stance there are a number of faults that can crop up: 1) One foot is placed directly behind the other, reducing the distance between the feet to less than the width of your hips. This lessens stability and balance to the side. On the other hand, balance to the front and rear will be weakened if your feet are placed wider apart than the distance of your hips; 2) The front foot points outward instead of slightly inward, or your rear foot points outward rather than forward; 3) The front knee is straight instead of being bent. This raises the level of your hips and reduces stability; 4) Leaning the upper part of your body forward, placing your balance too much to the front.

Aside from avoiding the above errors, there is one other essential consideration—your center of gravity. As your center of gravity is lowered, your stability increases. Your stance gains or loses stability as your center of gravity is lowered or raised. From this you can see that it is very beneficial to *bend your knees*.

One caution, though. You can bend your knees and lower your center of gravity to the point where mobility suffers. Experiment a bit. You will feel the difference. Once you get too low, you will be slow and awkward getting out of your stance.

After digesting the foregoing points, begin actual training in developing your stance. A mirror is helpful in correcting faults that may appear initially. A couple of minutes a day for the first week or so will probably be enough. You'll discover muscles you never realized you had!

Hands and Arms

Now that we know what to do with our feet, legs, trunk, and head, what about our hands and arms?

Somehow, the tales of Ned Buntline and other writers of our glorious early West have instilled in the American male the idea that it is unmanly to use two hands when shooting a handgun. Let's analyze this plight in some detail.

One hand offers little stabilization for the gun. Using only one hand leaves you susceptible to the influences of gravity, weight and wind on the gun. Neither does it offer any great control of recoil nor facilitate quick pointing.

Granted, there are good shooters who fire fantastic scores using the one-handed method. But they shoot well in spite of it—not because of it! As a matter of fact, competitive pistol shooting and actual combat shooting are about as much alike as steak and hotdogs.

There is a world of difference between knowing how many seconds you have to fire a specified number of shots at an inanimate target that is not shooting back and, in the heat of battle, trying to get a shot off in a split-second—wondering all the time if the other guy is going to get you before you can get him. Real combat causes your guts to knot up. The blood pounds in your head. Your breath comes in short gasps that burn on the way to your lungs. Your adrenalin pumps through your body and your hands shake! For all but ultra-close ranges—nothing to 4 feet or so—you need two hands on your gun.

Though there are many ways of using both hands on a handgun, here's a method that's worked well for me over the years.

Grip the gun with your strong hand using the accepted double-action grip—thumb drawn down and exerting pressure. Now bring the index finger of your supporting hand up just *under* the trigger guard, clasping your shooting hand tightly with your supporting hand. When executed from the leather this action is much like slamming your fist (gun hand) into your open (supporting) hand.

So far we have a pretty good grip, but still have the thumb of our supporting hand unoccupied. What do we

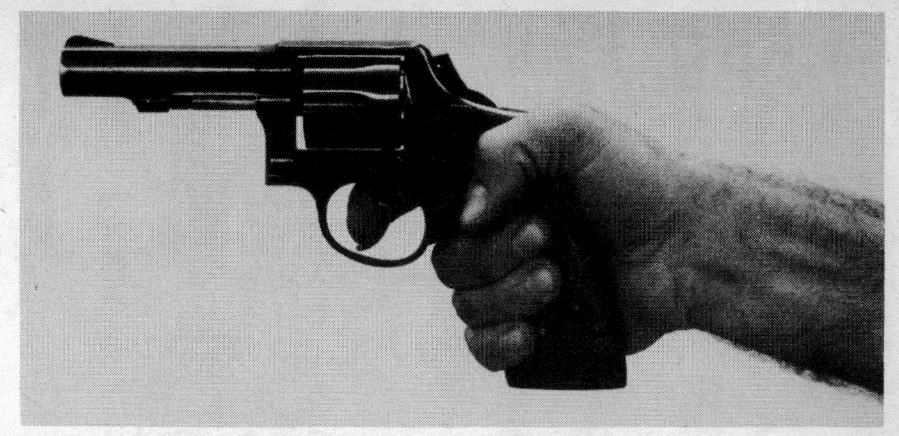

Grip your gun using the accepted double action grip—thumb drawn down and exerting pressure.

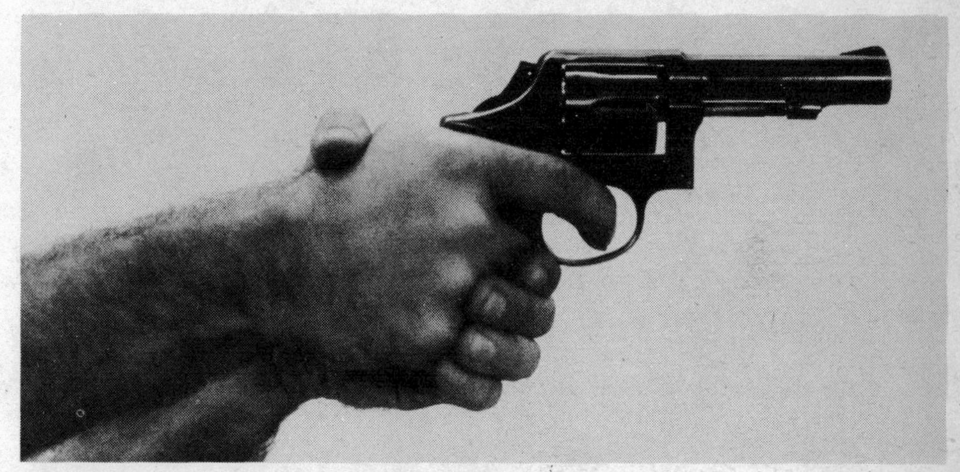

Bring the index finger of your supporting hand up just *under* the trigger guard.

Clasp your shooting hand tightly with your supporting hand.

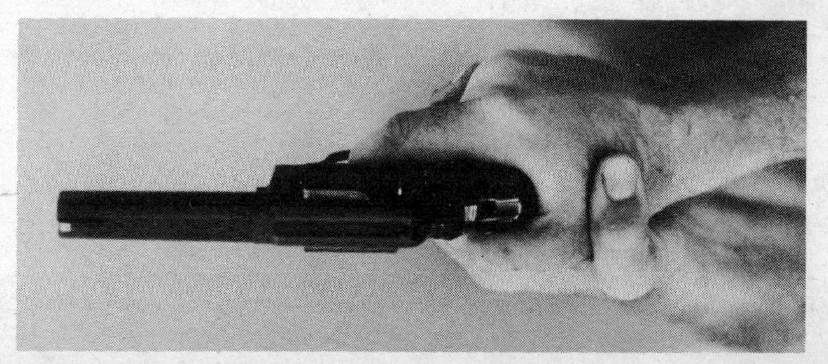

Placing your other thumb across the web of your shooting hand gives extra mass and added strength to the weakest point.

Bending your shooting arm slightly brings more muscles into play, giving you greater control.

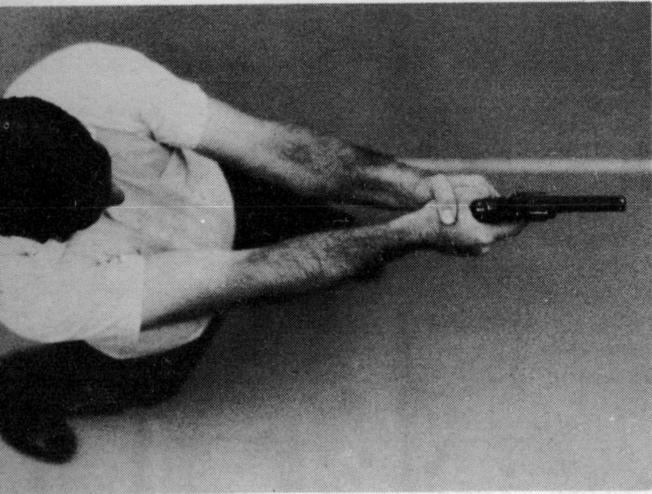

Both arms together form a lateral triangle which gives good pointability and control when swinging on multiple targets.

do with it? I have seen many good shooters place it parallel with the thumb of their shooting hand. This doesn't hurt anything, but it doesn't help anything either. Some clasp the supporting thumb over the other thumb.

The weakest point in your shooting hand is, I think you'll agree, the web between your thumb and index finger. There is little muscle here. Because a handgun muzzle bucks in recoil, the web of the hand takes the greatest recoil impact. Consequently, this is where our other thumb will do the most good. It gives us a little extra mass and strength at the weakest point. This applies to revolvers. (Do it with an automatic and you'll come up short on thumb.)

Thumb Placement

You'll have to work out the exact placement of *your* thumb for yourself, but here is a guide. Try placing it over the web of your shooting hand about ½-inch back from the pistol stocks. If it is closer than this it doesn't offer optimum strength. You may also discover that closer placement interferes with the rearward movement of the hammer, unless you've amputated the spur. Also bear in mind that this supporting hand must strongly grip your shooting hand if it is to serve its purpose. Using both hands properly lessens the recoil of even the mighty 44 Magnum, making successive shots possible and accurate.

As I said, there are other ways to use two hands for gripping a handgun, but they generally fall short of helping control recoil under conditions where it is paramount to control it—full service and magnum loads, excitement of combat conditions, etc.

There is a song about the head bone being connected to the neck bone, which all books of anatomy verify. It follows, then, that your hand bones are connected to your arm bones. So, let's see how our arm bones can best be employed to improve our shooting through proper and scientific positioning.

Construction engineers will tell you there is more structural strength in a triangle than in any straight span. It stands to reason, then, that by using your arms in a triangular formation, you'll strengthen the position of your hands, give them more rigidity.

Do this by bending your shooting arm ever so slightly. To an observer this is almost imperceptible, but you can feel the difference. Your bicep, tricep and radial muscles will be exerting more strength. Actually, this is accomplished by drawing your *right elbow under,* flexing it only slightly. The point of your elbow is pointing at the ground. Bend your supporting arm sharply at the elbow. It will form about a 45-degree angle. Bring the elbow of this arm in toward your belt buckle. This supporting arm forms a nearly vertical triangle. Thus you have a double triangular formation. First, you have a lateral triangle giving you good pointability and good control for swinging on multiple targets. Secondly, you have a vertical triangle formed by your sharply-bent supporting arm giving you good vertical control and, more importantly, good recoil control.

An added advantage is gained in bending *both* your arms. It brings more muscles into play, and the more muscles in use, the stronger your

A vertical triangle is formed by your sharply-bent supporting arm, giving you good vertical and recoil control.

position, the greater your control. Don't, though, bend your shooting arm *too* much. This forces you to cock your wrist, relaxing your shooting hand.

One-hand shooting doesn't offer these advantages, doesn't even bring all the muscles of your upper arm into play. The shoulder muscles support most of the weight. Your bicep, semi-relaxed, isn't used to anything like its fullest advantage.

The two-fisted method averts these shortcomings. Chances are you won't really appreciate the desirability of the two-handed grip shooting little wadcutter loads, but you will when shooting full service loads under combat conditions. Particularly if you're using the new hot 38s or magnums. It makes them manageable. Remember, if you can't manage them for quick successive shots, perhaps you shouldn't be shooting them.

Let's see how this Karate stance stacks up in some of the other areas. How much turning radius do you have without moving your feet? In other words, how wide is your field of fire? How does it relate to barricade, kneeling and prone shooting? How much over-all mobility does it offer?

Let's consider turning radius. Because you bend your knees in this position you have a much, much greater turning radius than with any position where your knees are straight. Since this stance includes a great degree of area within its base you can turn your upper body without having to move your feet. It gives you up to 135 degrees of turn to the left and 180 degrees to your right without having to change position of your feet. Do your turning with your hips and legs, rotating your entire upper body as one unit. Keeping your upper body in one integral unit also means keeping your arms in the same relationship to your chest, turning or shooting straight to the front. Your gun remains nearly the same distance from your eyes, your sight picture doesn't change as you turn. Your field of fire is more than equal to the full radius of your peripheral vision if you shoot with both eyes open. Very useful in actual combat!

Barricade Shooting

The long-accepted method of barri-

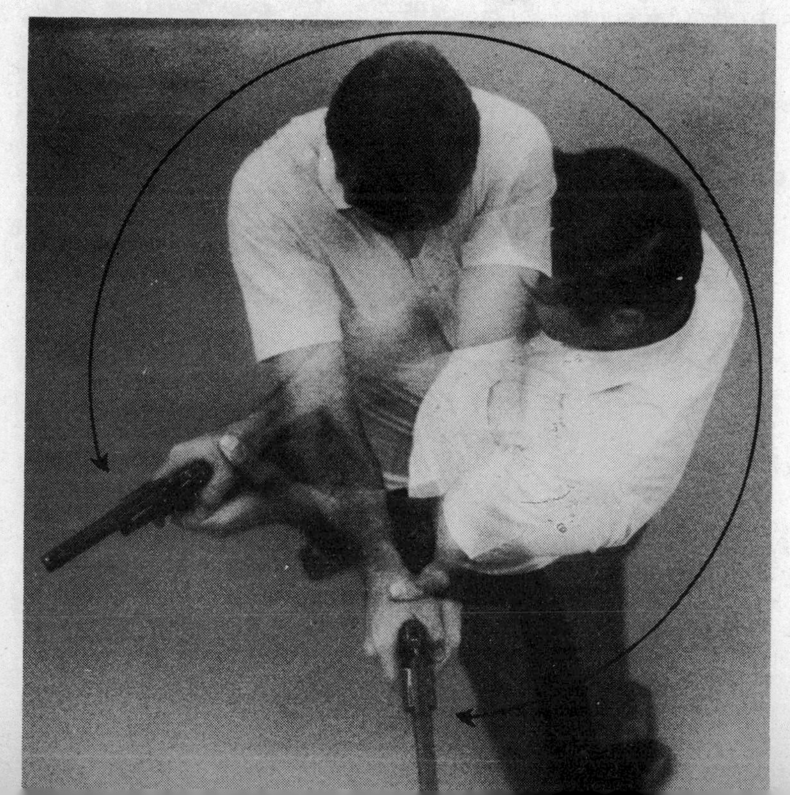

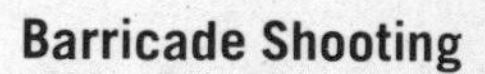

This stance gives you up to 135 degrees of radius to the left and 180 degrees to your right.

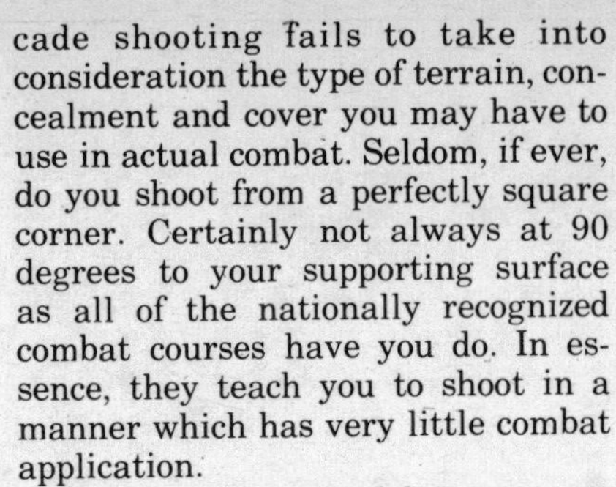

cade shooting fails to take into consideration the type of terrain, concealment and cover you may have to use in actual combat. Seldom, if ever, do you shoot from a perfectly square corner. Certainly not always at 90 degrees to your supporting surface as all of the nationally recognized combat courses have you do. In essence, they teach you to shoot in a manner which has very little combat application.

The present method has you rest your supporting hand against the barricade, holding your shooting arm in the web between your thumb and forefinger – or fingers. Such a position does little more than assist you in holding up the weight of your gun. It offers no support whatsoever in helping you control recoil. Personally, I feel you shouldn't be shooting at all if you can't hold the gun up with one hand! If you can hold it up with one hand, you don't need the supporting hand to hold it up, you need it to help control recoil and help steady your shaking hand. Remember, we're talking about combat – *the real thing!*

To get the added strength out where it's needed, we have – in our modified Karate stance – superimposed the fingers of our supporting hand directly over the top of our shooting hand.

We don't need to change a thing

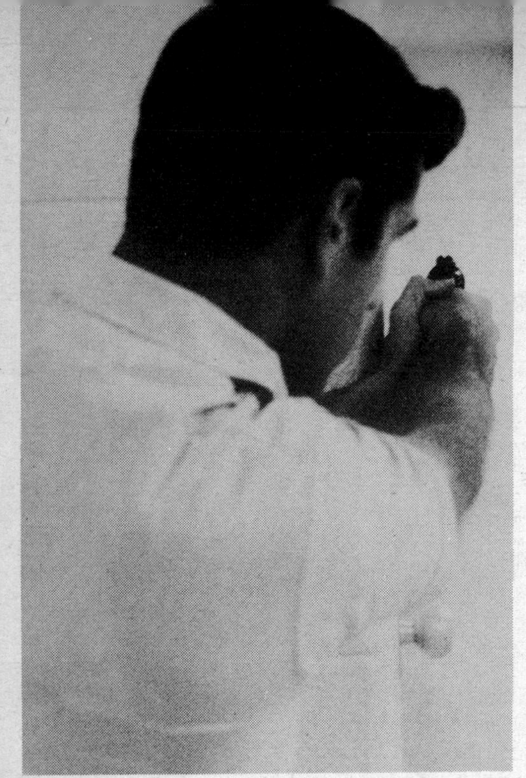

This grip allows you to rest the back of your supporting hand comfortably against most any surface at most any angle. Thus you can use buildings, trees, or other obstacles for cover without hampering your shooting.

This kneeling position gives you greater mobility and good accuracy too.

Nearly all combat situations that require kneeling preclude the possibility of resting your elbow on your knee.

when shooting from a barricade. Merely rest the back of your supporting hand against the barricade. I might add, the back of your supporting hand can be rested comfortably against most any character of surface. Thus you have a sturdy position incorporating all of the advantages mentioned previously—good recoil control, good control and pointability on multiple targets and the added strength of the triangular formation of your arms.

Our new position does expose more target area—about one inch of your hands. If you object to this small added exposure, look at it this way. There is no question but that you can shoot more accurately from this position, so you should be able to accomplish your job much more quickly than with the old method. Your total exposure is less from the new stance, even though your initial exposure is greater. Really it's a small price to pay for the dividends you get in greater accuracy.

Assuming a kneeling position from our new stance is no problem at all. Bend your rear leg at the knee until it is on the ground. Maintain your upper body in the same relative position as regards the placement of your arms and hands.

Don't try to place your supporting elbow on your knee. This rifle shooting position is not really applicable to handgun shooting. With a handgun this changes your sight picture, puts your gun on a different plane, causing you to bend your head down and cutting off the flow of oxygen to your lungs. At the same time it greatly reduces your ability to change positions rapidly.

Kneeling and Prone

You may also be interested in knowing that you can actually shoot more accurately from a kneeling position if you use your arms and hands in the unsupported position. Besides being able to direct your fire better, all of the situations I've ever encountered that call for kneeling preclude the possibility of resting your elbow on your knee. I'm referring to window sills, over automobile trunks and hoods, and in high weeds.

As for the prone position, it is much the same as the one currently taught except that you maintain your hands in the same relative relationship. It might also surprise you that prone is one of the poorest combat positions. Not only does it limit your field of fire and hamper your general mobility, it's also poorer than supposed from the standpoint of accuracy. Perhaps because of the eye strain created by looking at your sights through severely angled eyes, perhaps through impairment of your breathing by supporting much of your weight on your chest, maybe by the extreme contraction of your major back muscles. Or maybe a combination of all of these that results in poorer results from this position than you might suspect.

There is another consideration which makes me rate prone as a poor combat position. Ricochet shots seldom angle more than a foot off the ground, so there's a good possibility you may be struck by a bullet that fell short of its mark and ricocheted. Too, a bullet entering a body and traversing a path from head to foot will most certainly do much more extensive damage than one passing straight through a standing body.

The Karate stance greatly simplifies and speeds the learning process. Having only one stance to learn gives you more time to perfect your movements and become accustomed to them. Consequently you'll become much more adept at them.

Benefit by the years of knowledgeable study and practice the ancient Karate masters devoted to the perfection of this stance. Benefit and use it to your advantage as a shooter—it offers good mobility, wide field of fire, excellent stability, a solid base of support and, most importantly—it will improve your shooting! ●

Maintain your arms and hands in the same relative position when shooting prone.

William

by JAMES E. SERVEN

One of the most historic of pistols in the Renwick Collection is this Gabbetas flintlock, given to George Washington by General Braddock. Appropriately, it now is housed in our national museum, the Smithsonian.

RECORDS WERE established in auction rooms in 1972 when a Louis XIII flintlock gun was sold for about $300,000 and a pair of repeating flintlock pistols were bid up to about $140,000. These choice items were but two of the many rarities from the extensive William Renwick collection, formerly housed at Tucson, Arizona.

During the past several decades it has been my good fortune to know as friends many of the prominent American arms collectors. Major Bill Renwick was one of these; our paths first crossed in the 1930s. By a combination of residential proximity, mutual interests, similar backgrounds and general concord, we became close friends.

Among the many enjoyable features of this friendship was mutual study and discussion of what has been acclaimed one of the greatest privately owned arms collections of all time. However, access to the collection could not be a privilege placed higher than that of sharing the invigorating and gracious companionship of the man himself.

In all the years I knew Bill Renwick, I have never heard a critical word against him and, in the sometimes fiercely competitive field of arms collecting, that speaks well of the fair-minded spirit of this keen but considerate man. The best way I can describe him is that he had Irish wit, the conservatism and canniness of his Scots ancestors and the courtly manner of a southern gentleman.

It is reasonable to ask: "How did a man like Bill Renwick assemble such an extensive collection of beautiful and rare guns?" There are, of course, no simple answers. Briefly stated, it involves goodly measures of time, money, dedication, and ability plus a slight dash of luck. This was a combination of factors which Bill Renwick possessed at the most favorable period in collecting history. To present the story in proper perspective we must paint in a bit of the background.

Renwick's Background

When William Renwick died in 1971 at 85 years of age, he had been a winter resident of Tucson for many years and a year-round resident since 1958. Mrs. Renwick's frail health and the necessity of a mild, dry climate had been factors in their selection of southern Arizona. It must be said that the arms collection had been rather completely assembled before the Renwicks made Arizona their permanent home. The 1920s through 1940s had been the years of Bill Renwick's greatest collecting activity.

As a young man, exposure to the flea markets, museums and various antique and arms shops of Europe had come during summer vacations abroad. He was bitten by the collecting bug early in life. This exposure gradually ripened over the years into acquaintance with some of the leading dealers and arms experts of England and the Continent—men like Keith Neal and Howard Blackmore of England, Robert Jean Charles of France, Torsten Lenk of Sweden, Arne Hoff of Denmark and many others. An equal acquaintance was gained with prominent Americans in the arms field.

The Renwick propensity to travel was not limited to England or Europe. He was one of the first to drive a motor car cross-country (1907) when road maps were practically unknown and many roads in the West were little better than old wagon trails.

After Bill graduated from Harvard law school, the Renwicks (married in 1908) moved into a spacious old home at Weston, Mass., near Boston. Here the gun collection slowly began to grow. But World War I brought that to an abrupt halt and it was not long before Bill Renwick was off to the Air Force at Kelly Field near San Antonio.

We need dwell but lightly on the Renwick military career, and it will suffice to say that he served well and honorably; when discharged he held the rank of major in the Military Intelligence Division.

It was in the post World War I period

Goodwin Renwick

A story of one of the world's great arms collectors.

that Bill Renwick's collecting opportunities really opened up. There was a severe economic crisis in England and Europe after that devastating war. Many of the old and once wealthy families and institutions were hard pressed for cash. The sale of treasured old arms became a means of raising funds to tide them over the postwar depression.

In the fortunate position of having the time and the money, Bill Renwick also had the foresight and the courage to venture his funds in what he considered both a pleasant pursuit and a sound investment. It is regrettable that he could not have lived to see just how wise were the arms investments he had made, but certainly he was aware of the great appreciation in value over the years when fellow collectors made increasingly tempting offers for some of his guns.

I know of only one instance of sales from the Renwick collection in the past 10 or 15 years other than the final sale of Sotheby-Parke Bernet. That earlier sale was when he moved his entire collection from Weston, Mass., to a new large gunroom wing he had had constructed at his home in the Tucson foothills. At that time he sold a small group of what he considered lesser specimens rather than move them.

Backtracking a bit, it should be told here that as the collection had grown in size and value, Major Renwick had built a concrete vault which might be entered from his gunroom in the Weston home. This vault had soon become somewhat crowded.

William Goodwin Renwick—
soldier, lawyer, collector and, most of all, a thorough gentleman.

The Biter Bit

When fellow gun collectors visited Bill would fetch from the vault some of the special types in which his visitors were interested. One day some prominent gun collectors from the Philadelphia area called to see

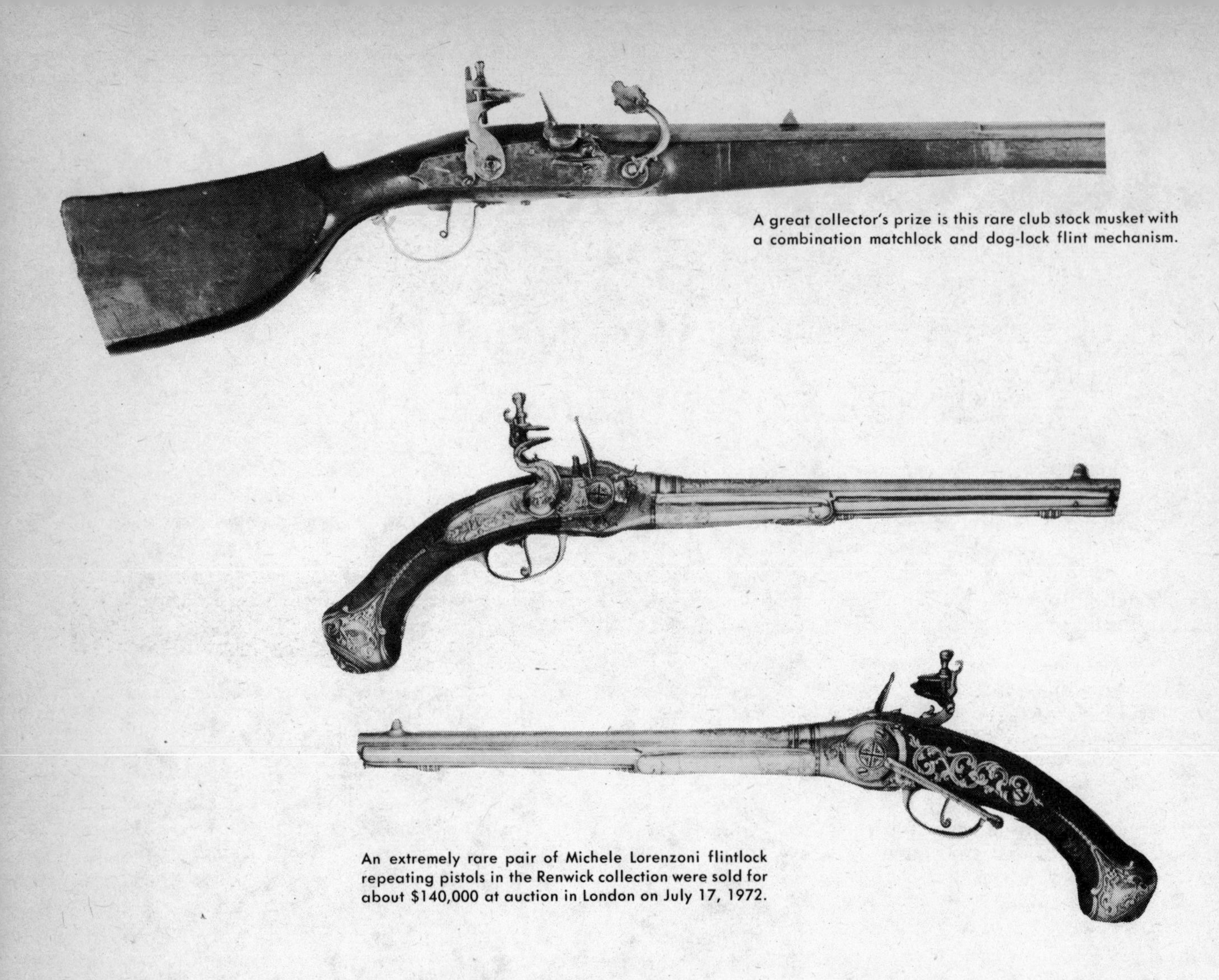

A great collector's prize is this rare club stock musket with a combination matchlock and dog-lock flint mechanism.

An extremely rare pair of Michele Lorenzoni flintlock repeating pistols in the Renwick collection were sold for about $140,000 at auction in London on July 17, 1972.

him. These were old hands at collecting and one of the visitors had a rather high estimate of his own knowledge and standing in the field; his attitude indicated that he considered Bill somewhat of a novice in collecting. The Renwick group of cylinder rifles (illustrated in my book *The Collecting of Guns**) was even then reasonably well-known and the visitors had gotten around to inquiries about this type of gun. After Bill had shown them four or five of the rare Paterson Colt cylinder rifle models the pompous visitor remarked, rather superciliously, "I don't suppose you have one of the Whittier rifles." These were made in Enfield, New Hampshire, and are exceedingly rare.

I am sure a twinkle must have come into Bill's eyes as he pondered the question for a moment and then answered: "Ah yes, which model would you like to see?" There may not be a dozen surviving Whittier cylinder rifles today, and possibly nowhere else in the world would one have found both of the two known models in the same collection. There were no more baited questions from this visitor!

When the Renwicks first started spending the winter months in Arizona Bill brought out for study a fine group of Colt and Smith & Wesson revolvers; the major portion of the general collection stayed in the locked vault at Weston. This was about the time (1934) that Bill published his monograph titled *The Folding-Trigger Paterson Colt.** This monograph was the result of a very exacting study and was the first definitive work on these rare first models of the Colt pistol line. It proved to be of help to me 20 years later when I dug out material for my inclusive Colt book titled *Colt Firearms—From 1836.*†

When the Renwicks returned to Weston for the summer, they customarily put their most valuable things from the Tucson house in storage. In this connection a rather tragic thing occurred in the late 1930s. In packing the Colt and Smith & Wesson pistols for storage at Tucson, Major Renwick's chauffeur, recalling that moth crystals help to keep silverware from tarnishing and that a few of the arms had some silver plating, sprinkled moth crystals throughout the boxes sent to storage. Moth crystals contain an active ingredient with the hard to spell and pronounce name Paradichorobenzine.

Costly Crystals

It chanced that the Renwick boxes were stored on the ground floor of the storage warehouse, and during that summer the rains were unusually heavy, causing the first floor of the warehouse to flood. At that time I was living on my ranch in the Sonoita valley south of Tucson, and one day I received an urgent telegram from Bill requesting that I go in to the warehouse and check any damage to the pistols.

A disheartening sight awaited me when I opened those boxes. The water would not have been so bad, but combined with the moth crystals an acid had been set up that picked off great patches of blued finish from Paterson Colts, flat-top Frontier Colt target pistols and all the other fine and rare

*Stackpole Books, Harrisburg, PA 1964.

*Small 4to, 24 pp., paper. No place of publication given.

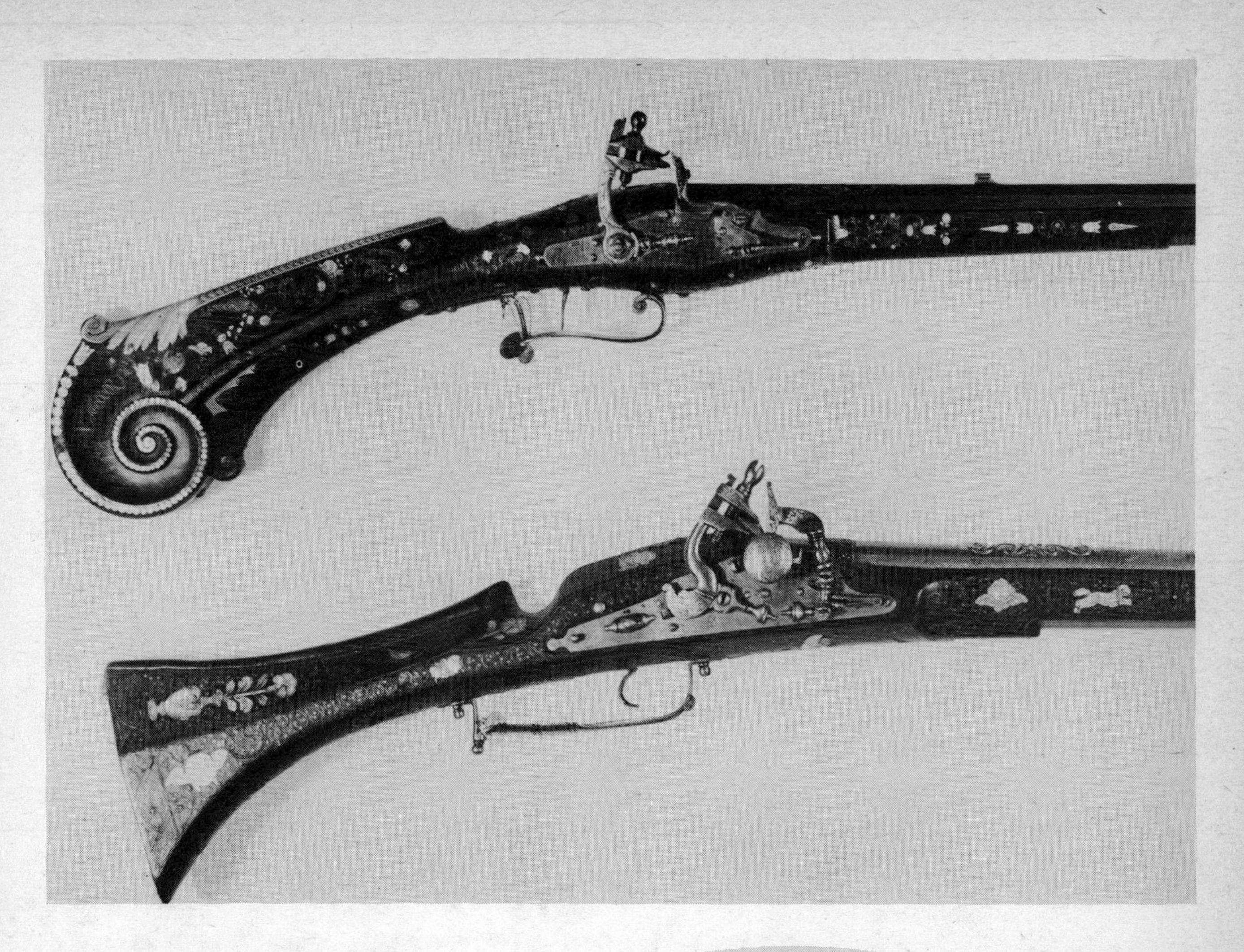

Two extremely valuable guns from the "Cabinet d'Armes" of Louis XIII. The top gun was recently bought by the Metropolitan Museum of Art (New York) for a price close to $300,000. The lower gun, an English snaphaunce dated 1622, was bought by a California collector for about $50,000. ● Left side of the Louis XIII gun. The royal cipher helped in bringing one of the highest prices ever paid for an antique firearm.

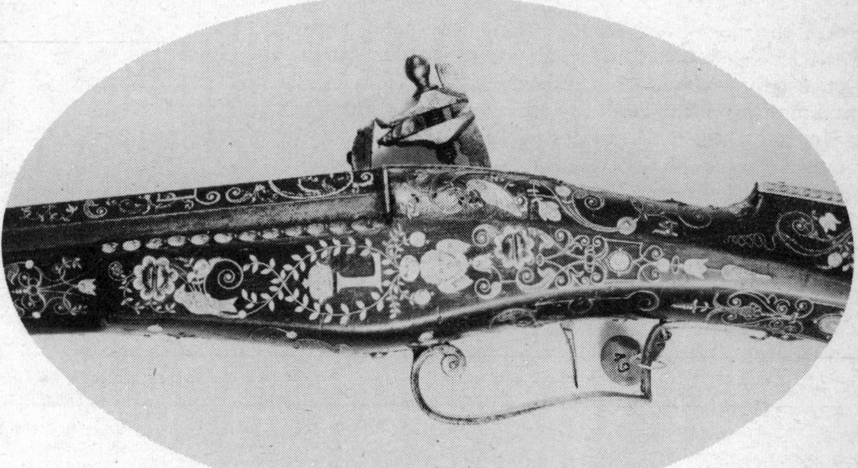

pistols of that valuable group. It was sickening!

I dried and oiled the pistols and repacked them in the best manner possible, but I knew what Bill's reaction would be when he returned to Tucson in the fall. As I had expected, when he looked at the havoc that acid had wrought, he said, "Jim, will you take these pistols and get rid of them for me as best you can?"

The pistols found new homes, and I presume some of the new owners had them refinished or were content in having a rare item regardless of the condition. But that was not Bill Renwick's way. Inferior quality was contrary to his nature in all things.

Renwick's Writings

The Renwick monograph on Paterson Colts, mentioned previously, was but one of the many deep studies Bill pursued, although it is one of the very few that ever saw print. In some studies he collaborated with Dr. Thomas T. Hoopes, curator of arms at the City Art Museum of St. Louis, Missouri. One such effort was titled *Three Essays on Firearms*. These technical papers were printed in a booklet and inscribed "Presented by Fellow Members of the Armor and Arms Club to Bashford Dean in honor of his Sixtieth Birthday, October 28, 1927." A yet unpublished work by Hoopes and Renwick is tentatively titled *A History of Firearms*. The prospectus

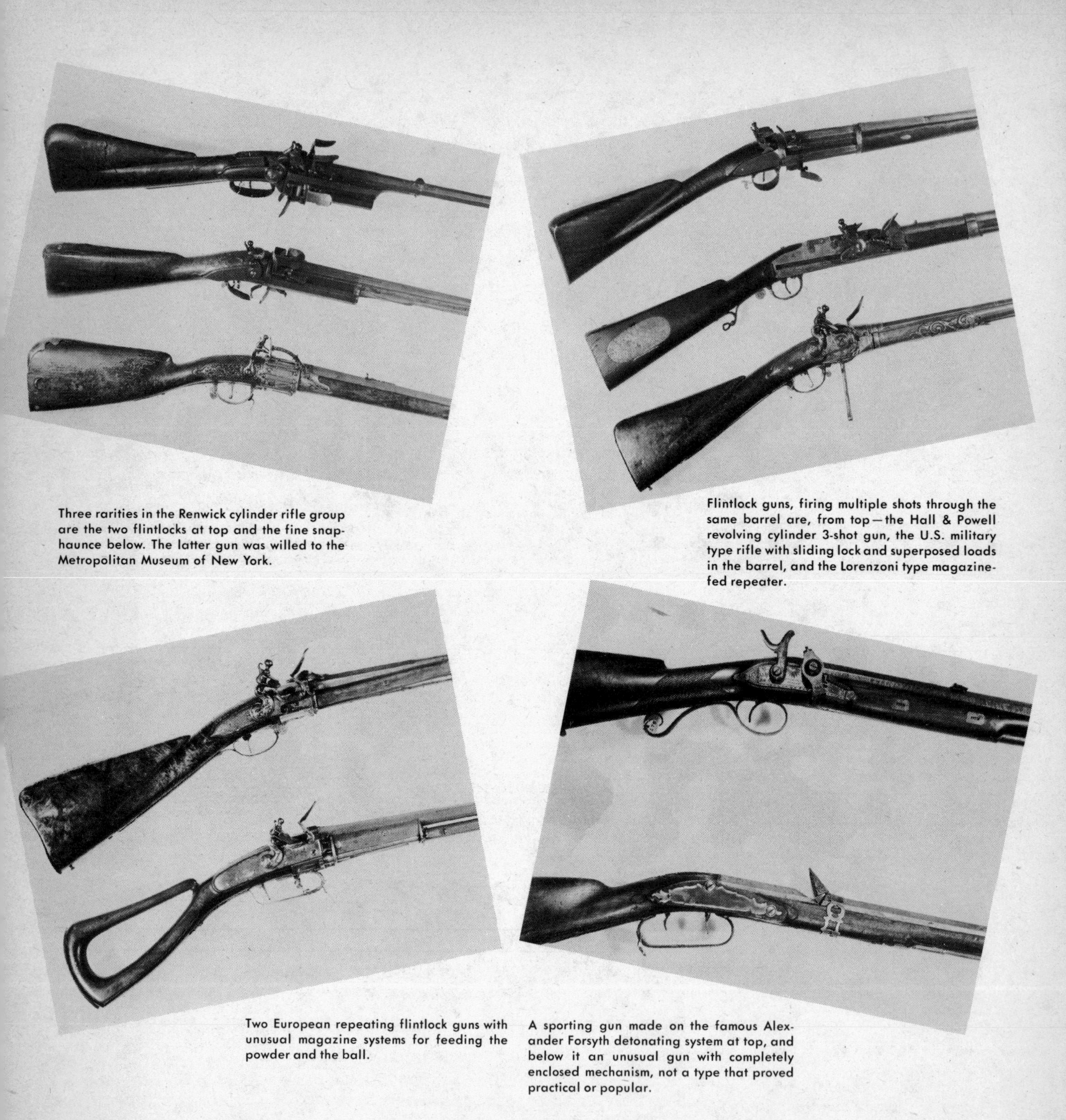

Three rarities in the Renwick cylinder rifle group are the two flintlocks at top and the fine snaphaunce below. The latter gun was willed to the Metropolitan Museum of New York.

Flintlock guns, firing multiple shots through the same barrel are, from top—the Hall & Powell revolving cylinder 3-shot gun, the U.S. military type rifle with sliding lock and superposed loads in the barrel, and the Lorenzoni type magazine-fed repeater.

Two European repeating flintlock guns with unusual magazine systems for feeding the powder and the ball.

A sporting gun made on the famous Alexander Forsyth detonating system at top, and below it an unusual gun with completely enclosed mechanism, not a type that proved practical or popular.

indicates that if published this may indeed be a very scholarly work.

A Renwick loan exhibition at the St. Louis museum was accompanied by an interesting bulletin put out by Dr. Hoopes in January, 1940, and entitled *Firearms of the Princes.* This features arms from the Renwick collection associated with Louis XIII, Louis XIV, the Prince of Schwarzburg-Rudolstadt, Christian II of Saxony, Frederic I of Sweden, Russian Czars, and Napoleon I. The periods run from 1560 to 1804. It may be recalled by some that my article *"Elegant Arms of the Favored Few"* in the 1969 GUN DIGEST illustrated a few of the Renwick arms featured at the City Art Museum of St. Louis.

Another very exhaustive study undertaken by Major Renwick was devoted to the evolution of the Pennsylvania-made Kentucky rifles. I recall that he had a notebook filled with pages of strip photographs which showed the gradual development from the bulky early *jäger* type to the more graceful guns made during the "Golden Age" period of the late 18th century and into the early 19th century. He was, indeed, a serious student, and this combined with natural astuteness and keen observation con-

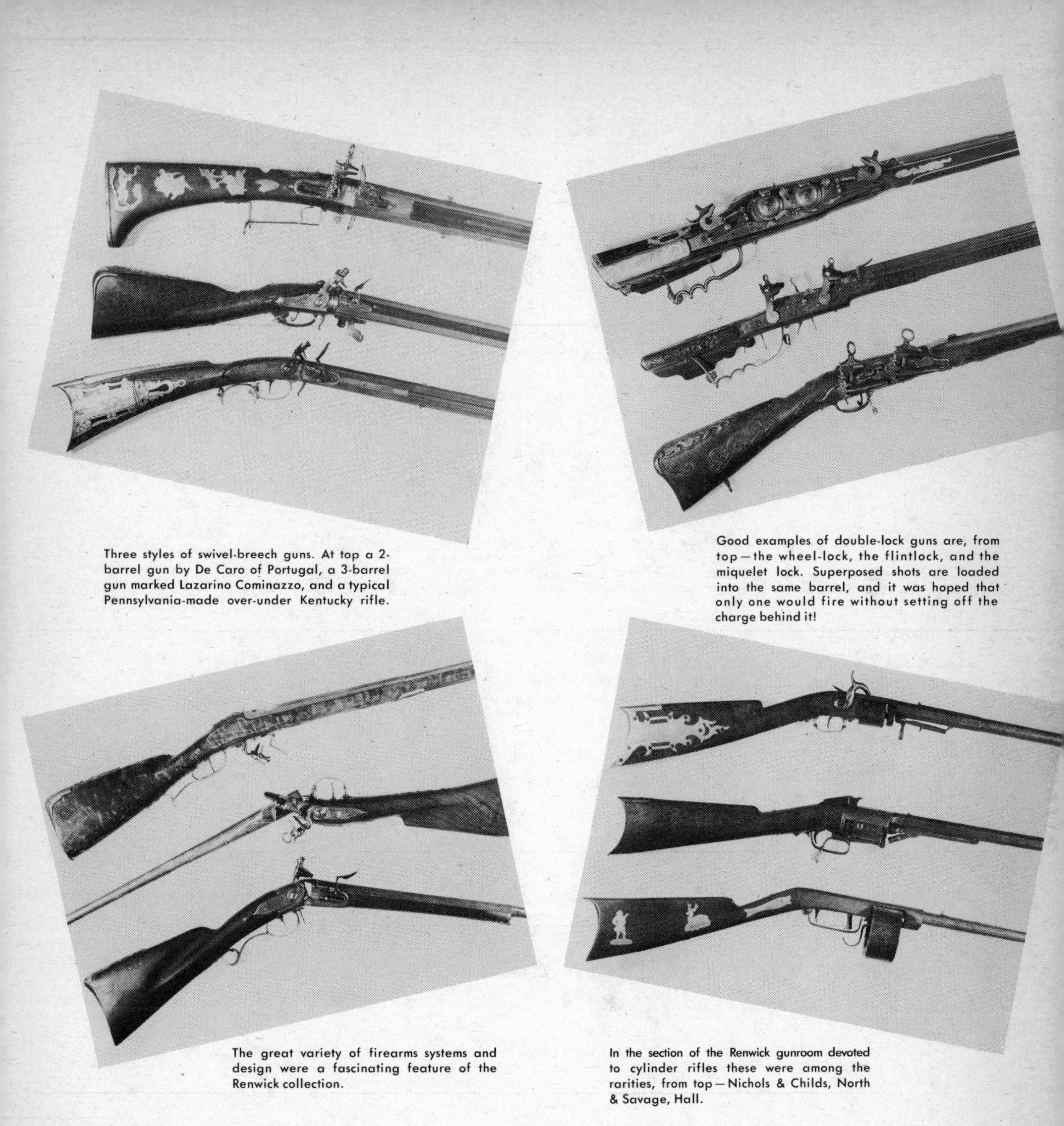

Three styles of swivel-breech guns. At top a 2-barrel gun by De Caro of Portugal, a 3-barrel gun marked Lazarino Cominazzo, and a typical Pennsylvania-made over-under Kentucky rifle.

Good examples of double-lock guns are, from top—the wheel-lock, the flintlock, and the miquelet lock. Superposed shots are loaded into the same barrel, and it was hoped that only one would fire without setting off the charge behind it!

The great variety of firearms systems and design were a fascinating feature of the Renwick collection.

In the section of the Renwick gunroom devoted to cylinder rifles these were among the rarities, from top—Nichols & Childs, North & Savage, Hall.

tributed to building his outstanding collection. Certainly it did not grow by chance.

A few years past, when advanced age had put an end to Major Renwick's interest in active arms research and knowing of my pursuits in this field, he graciously permitted me to purchase his library of gun books. As might be expected, there were first editions of Thierbach, Meyrick, Grancsay, Pollard, Laking, Lenk, Dean, and other fine reference works, many out of print.

The Elegant and the Simple

While the elegant arms of the Old World provided spectacular beauty through the highly decorated wheel locks, flintlocks, etc., Bill Renwick also had a great eye for plain rarity as many of the American pieces in the collection will demonstrate. In the early days my own inexperience and his experience were demonstrated when I sold him a very plain but rare Hawken rifle for $50 (my price). I learned from him and by hard experience. Recently I refused $1500 for a similar gun.

It may be that Bill sold guns in his earlier collecting days to upgrade the collection, but by 1935 the upgrading

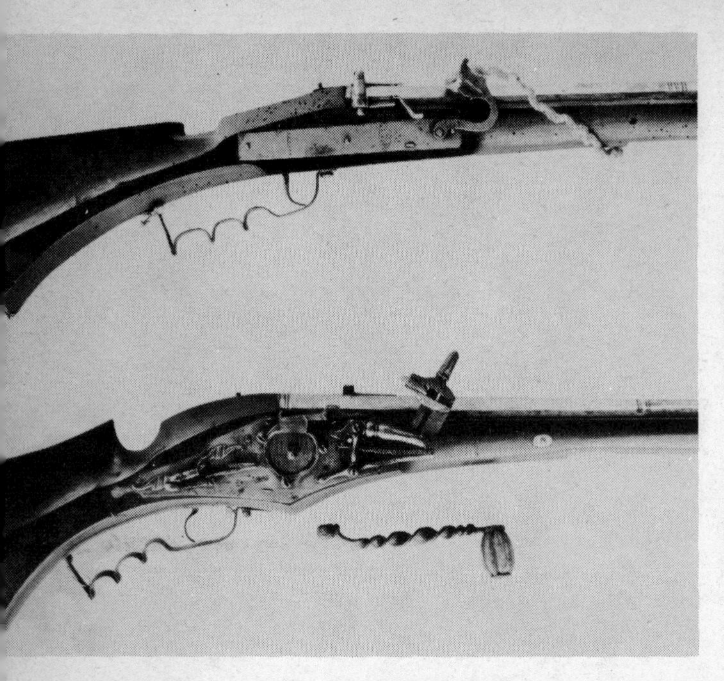

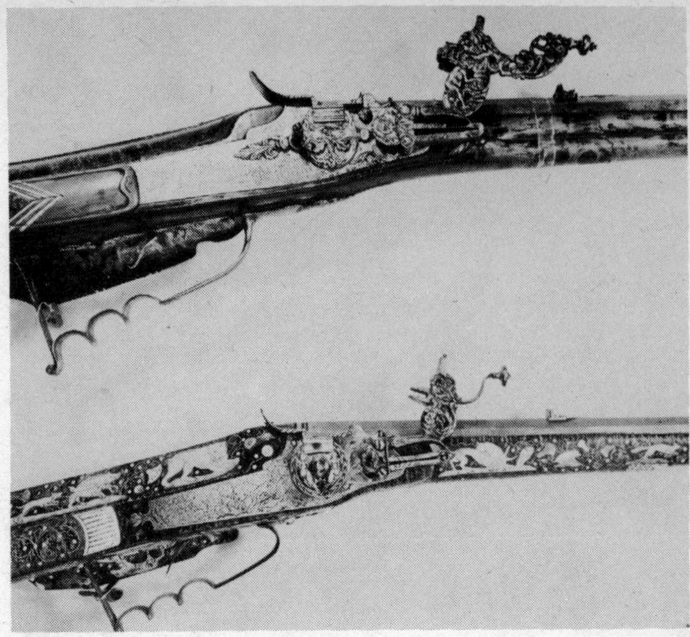

Left—among the earliest military arms in the Renwick collection, the matchlock gun (top) and the wheel-lock gun, shown with its cocking crank, are in excellent condition considering their great age. • Right—two of the rare wheel-lock guns which will be displayed at the Smithsonian.

had been completed and, while I know of several trades where duplicates were involved, I know of no individual gun sales after that time except the acid-damaged guns mentioned earlier. During his residence in Arizona he did add to what he liked to call his small group of "Covered Wagon Guns." As the name implies, this involved guns used on the early western trails such as the Hawken rifle. This Hawken rifle, incidentally, has been given to a close friend of the two Renwick heirs (a devoted niece and nephew) and he is placing it on loan at the Arizona Historical Society. The gun has historic Arizona association. Earlier, a gift of 28 firearms to the Arizona State Museum was made by Major Renwick. This group of arms tells the story of firearms evolution with the major emphasis on the Spanish influence in the Southwest.

As is the usual case when the builder of a great arms collection dies, there was great interest and speculation concerning the collection's future fate. There are several schools of thought on the proper way a collector should will the guns that have given him so much pleasure in life. The matter is simplified if there is an interested heir, but in the absence of that, what is the best course?

Dispersion of the Collection

I know of no better solution than that followed by Bill Renwick in the light of his personal situation. He had no direct or seriously interested heirs. He was conscious of the fact that if everyone had put all his guns in the permanent possession of museums he could never have had the purchase

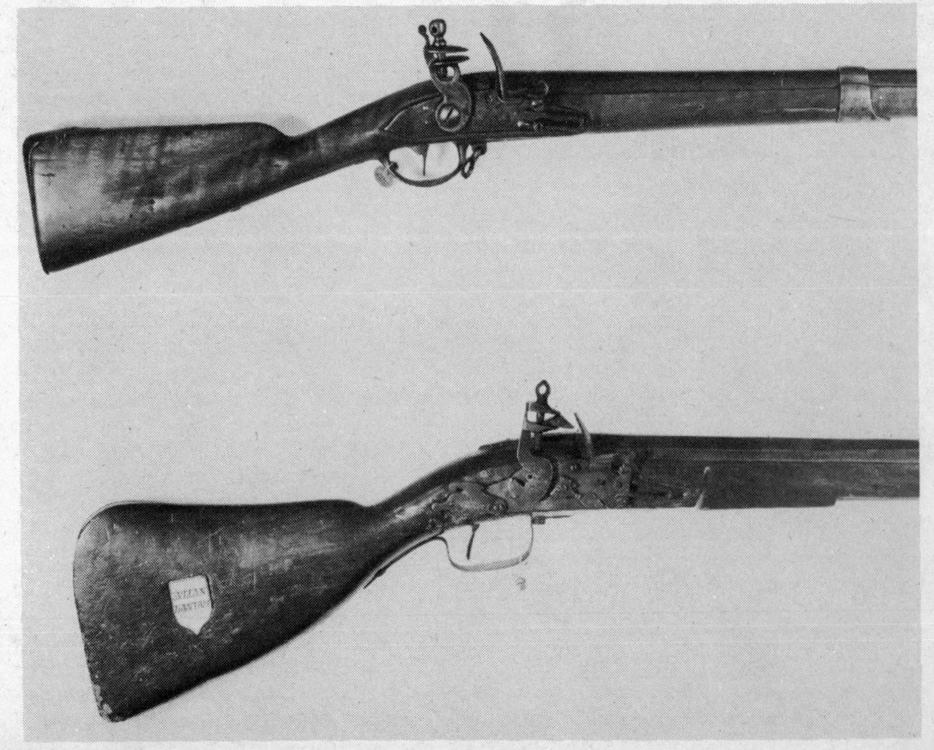

At top is an example of the Revolutionary War musket used by the American Colonists, and below a very early dog-lock gun once owned by the Sultan of Bantam.

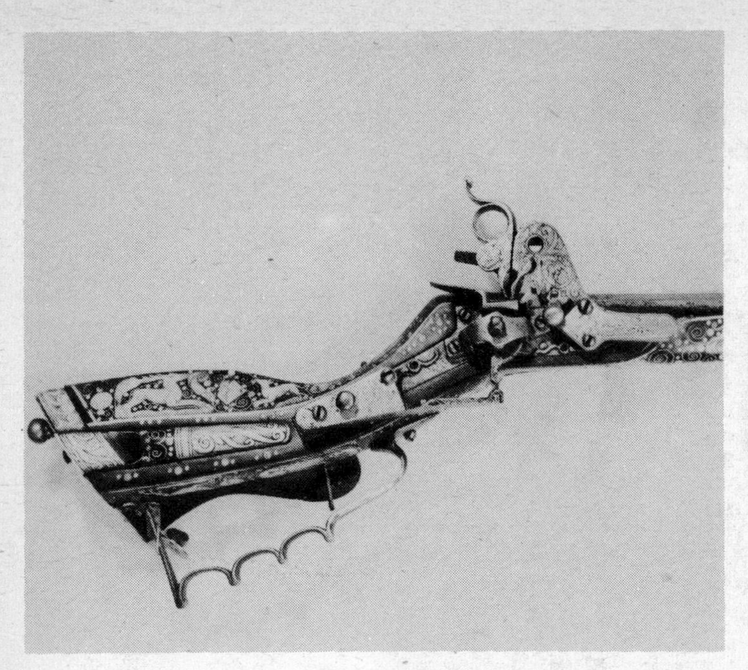

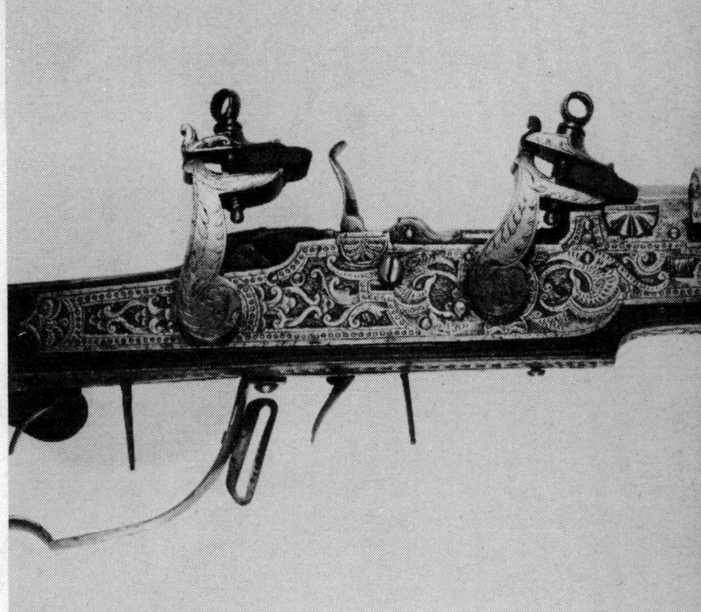

Left—this form of wheel-lock gun is known as a tschinke, the specimen seen here elaborately inlaid with animals of the chase. • Right—close-up view of a double-lock double-barreled gun, illustrating not only the very unusual mechanism but also the extensive decorative treatment in a style sometimes called Gothic.

opportunities and consequent personal enjoyment that had come to him. Therefore, he wished to put a good portion of the guns back into circulation, a decision reached in his case for moral rather than financial reasons.

On the other hand, Bill Renwick was conscious of several other considerations. He knew through his good friend Stephen Grancsay, curator emeritus of arms at the Metropolitan Museum of Art, that the museum was greatly interested in acquiring his rare revolving cylinder snaphaunce gun. He knew, too, that our national museum, the Smithsonian, was lacking in European arms of the "high art" type. He also knew that sometimes fine arms given to a museum end up in the basement or "somewhere else," so while he decided to donate arms of a type the Smithsonian needed, he accompanied the grant with rigid conditions.

The snaphaunce gun went to the Metropolitan, and the Smithsonian, represented by Mr. Craddock R. Goins, Jr. of the Division of Military History, was permitted to select 149 items (32 of which were pairs) with the strict provision that all must be placed on *permanent* display—no cellar storage for them! The balance of the collection was sold to Sotheby-Parke Bernet to be put back into the mainstream of collecting through periodic sales in London and Los Angeles. European guns were to be sold in London, American guns in Los Angeles. In this connection the auctioneers are issuing excellent catalogs for each of the sales. These catalogs are beautifully illustrated and contain valuable

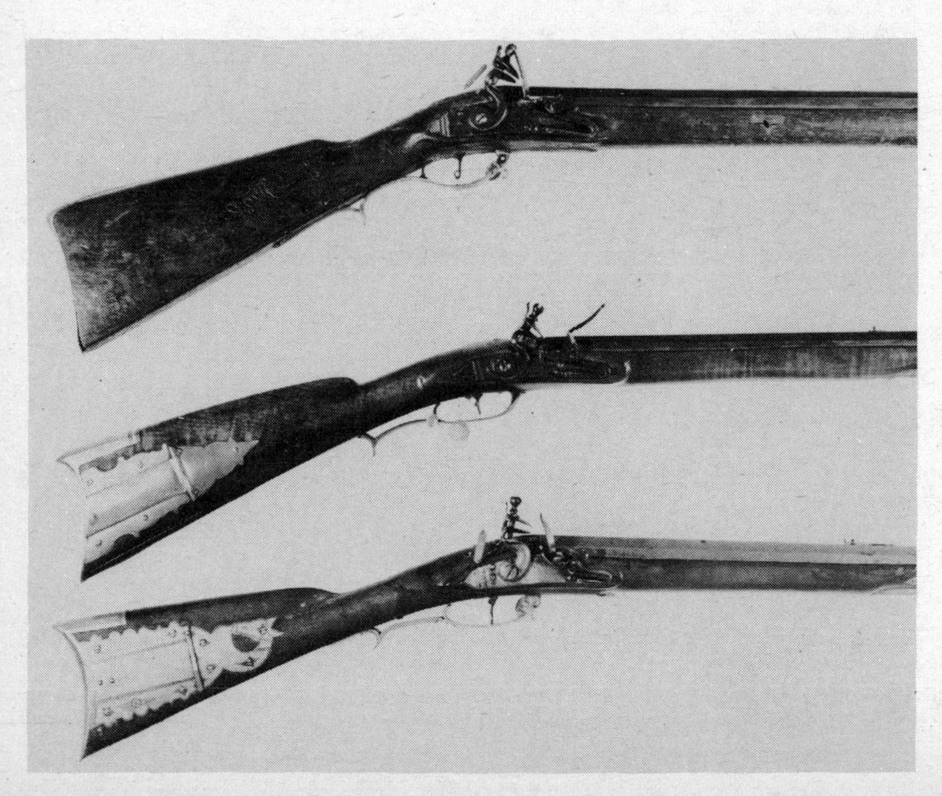

The Renwick Kentucky rifle section contained specimens from the earliest workmanship, as exemplified at top, to models throughout the entire period of these great Pennsylvania gunmakers.

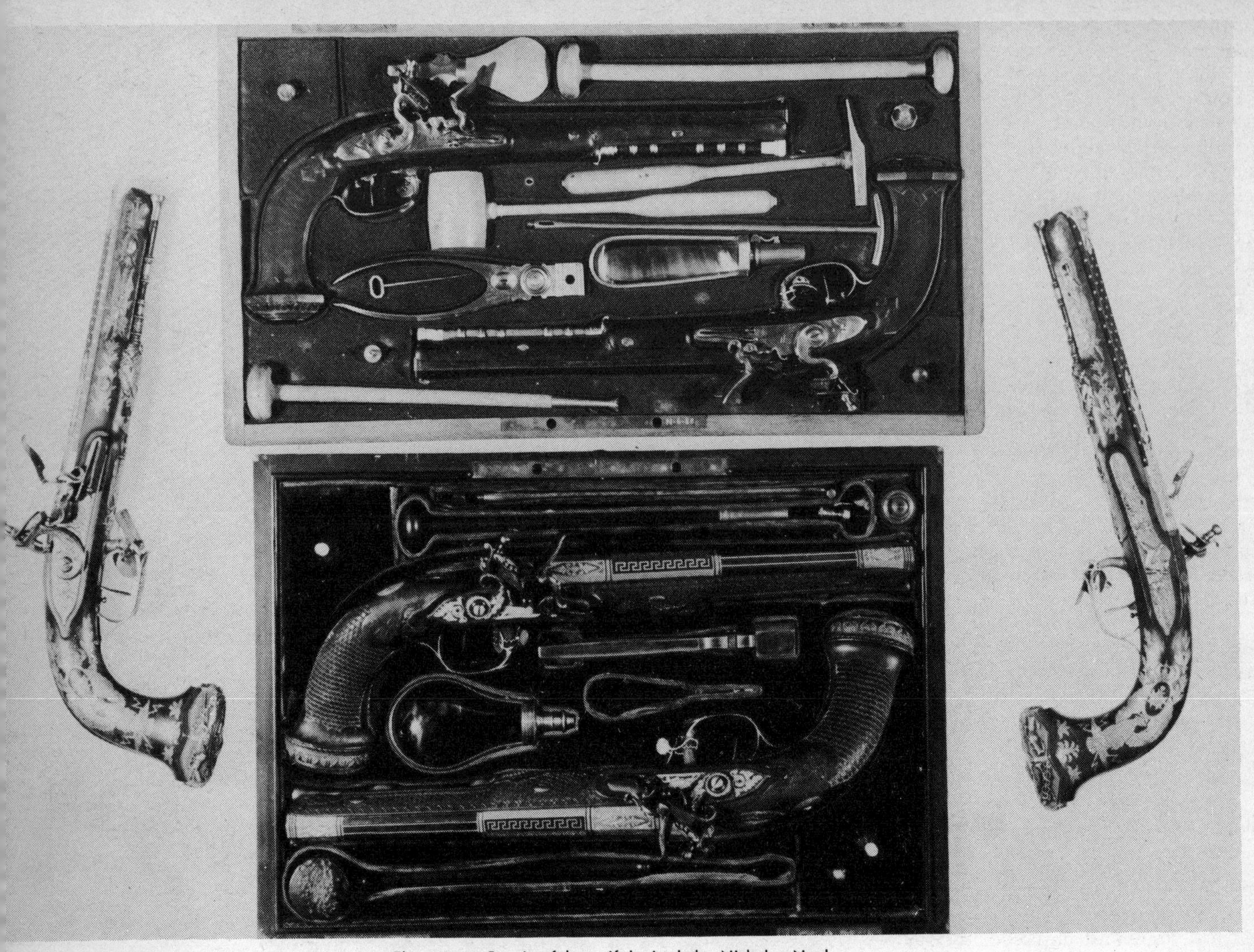

There were 5 pair of beautiful pistols by Nicholas Noel Boutet among the Renwick displays, all showing the great skill of France's "Directeur Artiste" for Napoleon 1st.

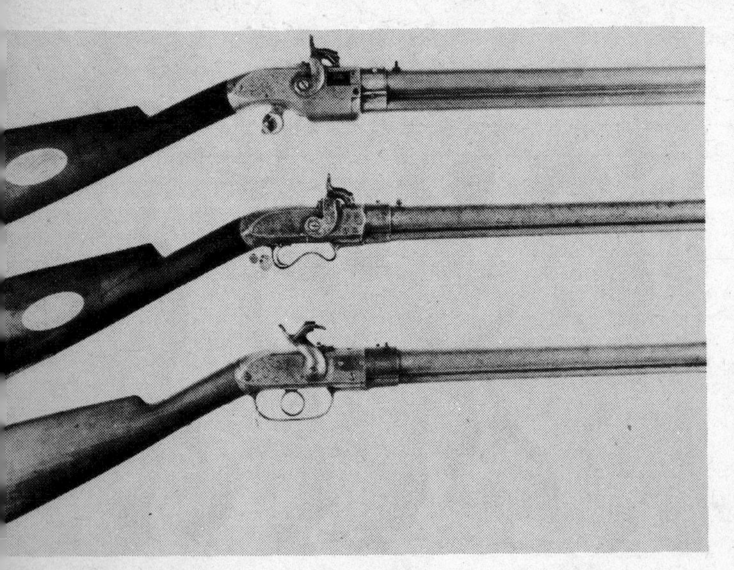

The Jennings rifle is said to have been the gun that led eventually to the Volcanic, Henry and Winchester rifles with their then innovative fixed ammunition. Three varying types of this rare gun came to rest in the Renwick gunroom.

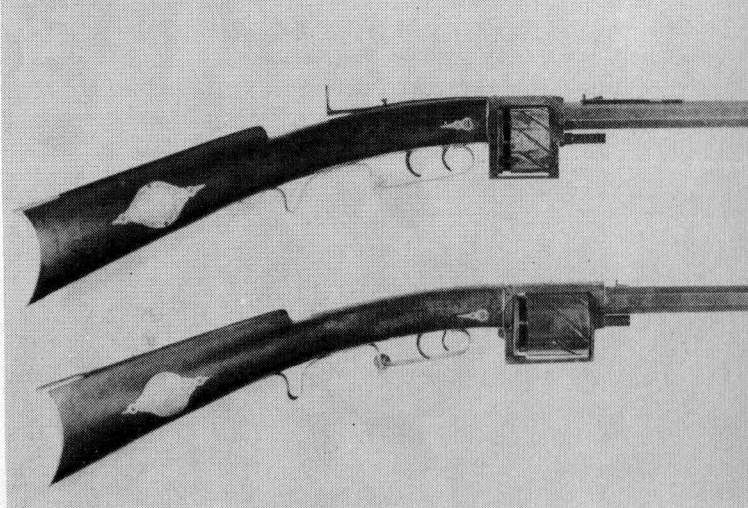

The Renwick collection held one of the most outstanding groups of revolving-cylinder guns ever assembled. It is unlikely that any other collection of Major Renwick's day had both models of the extremely rare Whittier guns shown here.

information. I recommend them for information and general reference. But even experienced auctioneers overlook a vital point sometimes. As an illustration one of the extremely rare Whittier rifles of the Renwick collection offered at the October 1, 1972 sale in Los Angeles was merely described as "An unusual Kentucky Percussion Cap Sporting Gun." Apparently most of the buyers present were asleep or unacquainted with the great rarity of the gun for it was worth five times the price at which it was sold. This illustrates that while the record high prices at auctions get the most publicity, occasionally there are "sleepers" to be found there, too.

Despite the elimination of 151 very rare items by grant, the Sotheby-Parke Bernet sales brought over seven figures and was one of the highest priced antique arms purchases of our time.

Thus far the Renwick guns have been referred to in generalities, knowing that the illustrations would provide some of the specifics. A quick trip around the gunroom may give an idea of the major categories which Bill Renwick favored.

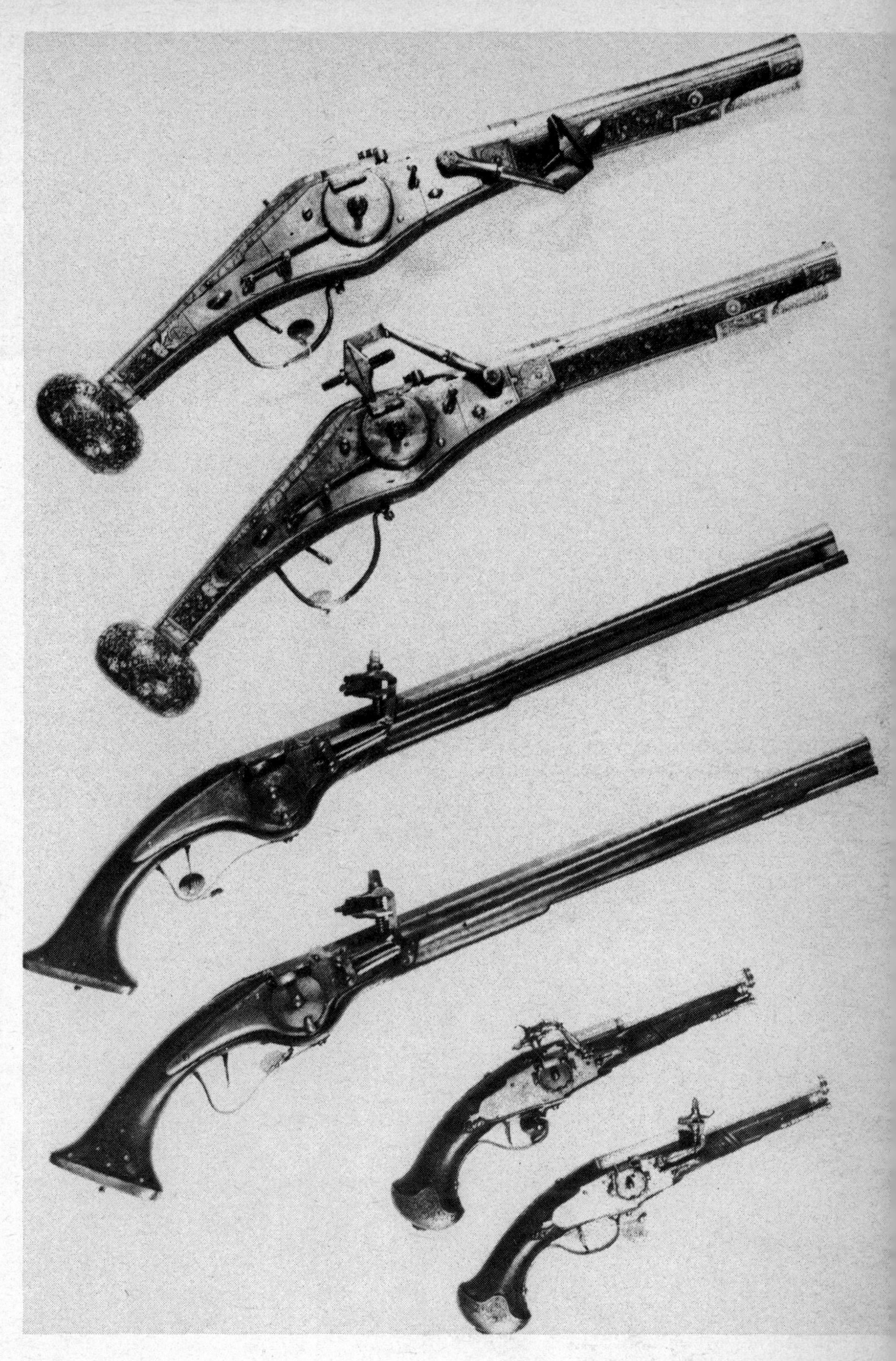

Three pairs of wheel-lock pistols which illustrate differences in design and country of origin. At top the ornate ball-butted dags of Saxony; the plain military pistols of England and the Continent, and the sculptured and engraved pistols of Brescia.

The Tucson Gunroom

The Tucson gunroom itself was a windowless rectangular room as large as an average ballroom. Entrance was gained from an adjacent study through a steel door of the bank vault type. The door itself was concealed behind a handsome tapestry featuring early-day guns and hunting, which could be swung to one side to reveal the door. As one entered he was conscious of soft lighting which revealed not only gun covered walls to the right and left but two-sided floor racks in which guns stood like soldiers in a row. There were oriental rugs on the floor, heavily carved furniture, some of the tables stacked with gun and pistol cases.

At the far end of the room were displays of armor, pole arms, etc., against a background of carved chests and a great wall tapestry. The guns lining the side walls were mostly in three categories: 1) Highly decorated wheel-locks, flintlocks, etc., 2) Guns with unusual mechanisms, 3) Guns of early or special historic provenance.

Running almost the length of the room on the left and on the right were A-shaped racks which supported shoulder arms on either side. Here one would find the large section devoted to cylinder rifles (of which there were great rarities) and the lever action section which included such arms as Volcanics, Henrys, and Winchesters (some richly engraved). Then there was a section devoted to Kentucky rifles, from the earliest form to the latest. Beyond this there were sections devoted to European or American arms of such rarity and unusual

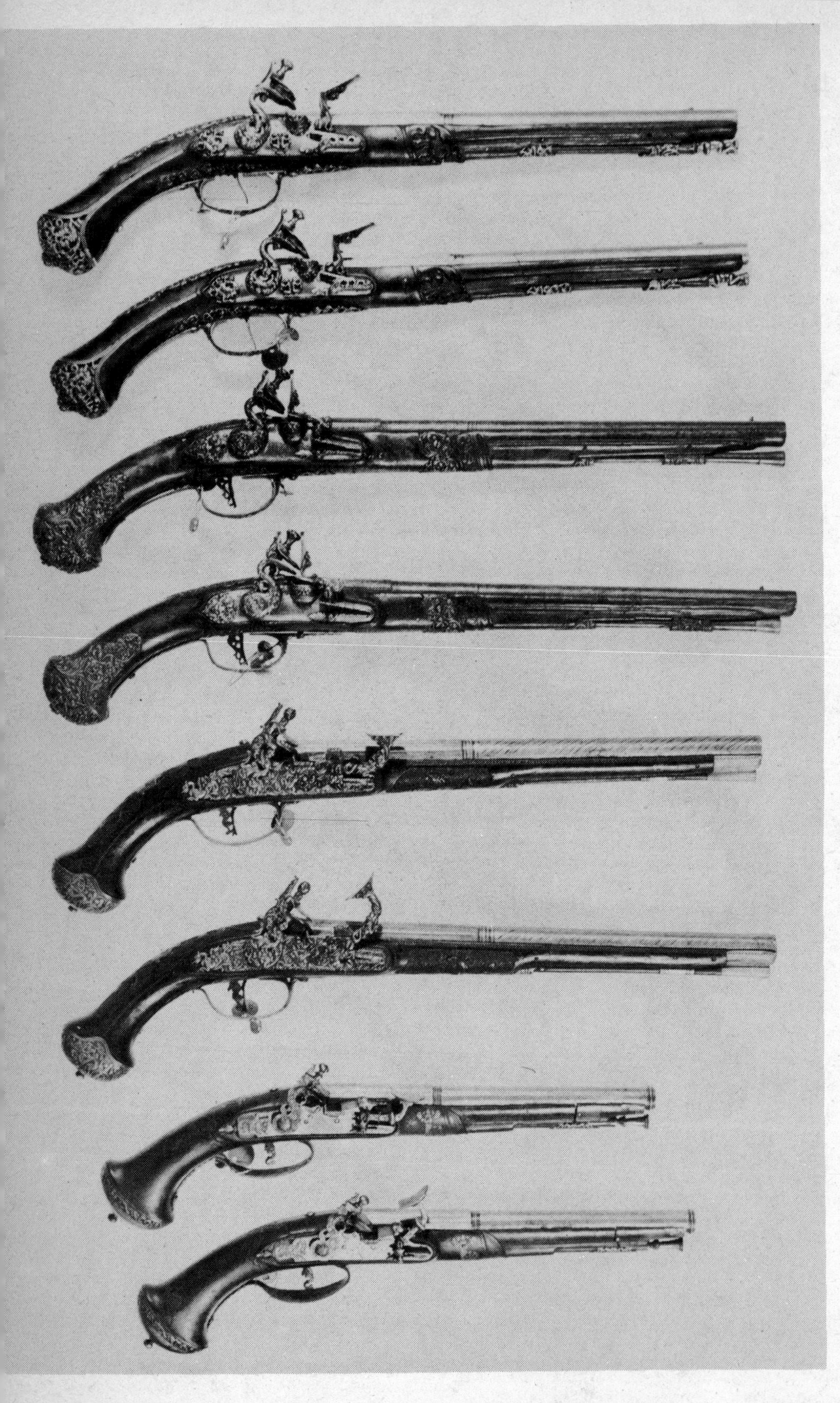

design as to be almost unique. Finally, the guns of the frontier and Indian guns in what Bill called his "Covered Wagon" section.

On either side of the doorway as one entered were rows of wide but relatively shallow drawers. There were one hundred of them, lined with thin foam rubber. As to the handguns themselves, there were selected specimens (many in pairs) of the all-metal Scottish type; beautifully sculptured Brescian flintlock and snaphaunce pistols; wheel-locks of many varieties; matchlock, flintlock, caplock, tubelock, and patent-ignition pistols of varied types and from many countries; and many pistols with unusual mechanisms or design, generally classified as "firearms curiosa." There were early powder flasks, horns, powder testers, spanner wrenches and gunlocks with rare mechanisms.

Among this great array there were relatively few American-made handguns—a small scattering of Colts, some Smith & Wesson and Volcanic magazine pistols, and a nice group of pepperbox pistols. There were, however, such rarities among the American pistols as a Cochran turret pistol, a pair of Wm. F. Cody derringer pistols, and pistols believed to have belonged to Confederate General J. E. B. Stuart and to Henry Clay. Though it is an English flintlock pistol, the most interesting piece pertaining to American history was one presented to George Washington by General Edward Braddock when Washington was a colonel serving with the British against the French. This pistol may be seen at the Smithsonian when the Renwick collection is prepared for display. By coincidence, there is another Renwick of special significance at the Smithsonian—James Renwick. He designed a building within the Smithsonian complex, and the Renwick Gallery there is named for him.

The Cupboard is Bare

Now the Renwick gunroom at Tucson is bare; the house will be sold and the sixty acres of very scenic land surrounding it will be subdivided. Where will be the new homes for those hundreds of fine arms William

Examples of top quality in Brescian pistols are the two pair of flintlocks above and the two pair of snaphaunce pistols below. The Lazarino Caminazzo family of gunmakers, leaders in this field, are well represented in the Renwick arms.

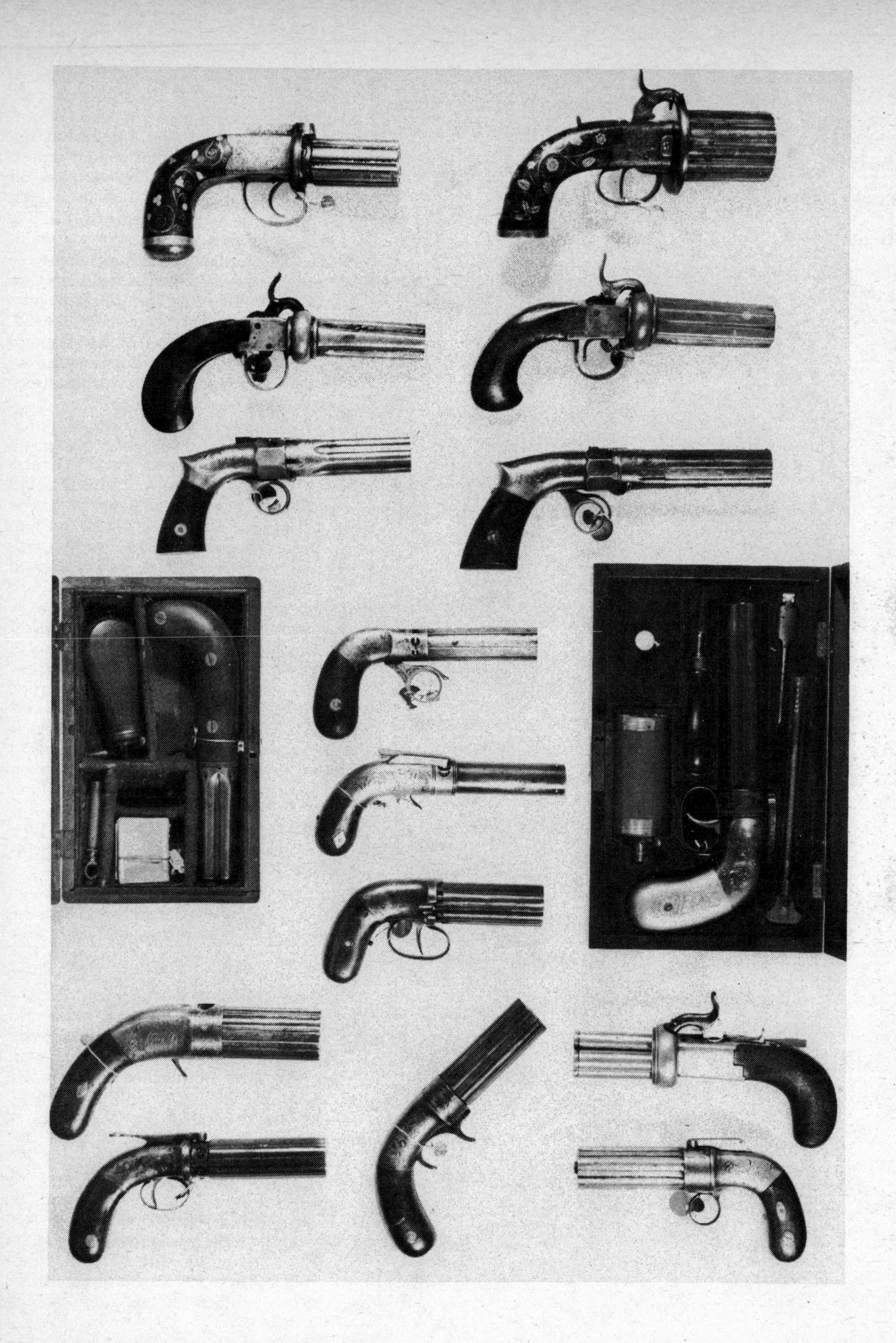

The collecting of pepperbox pistols has become popular in recent years. Here are some of the rare American and English models in the Renwick collection.

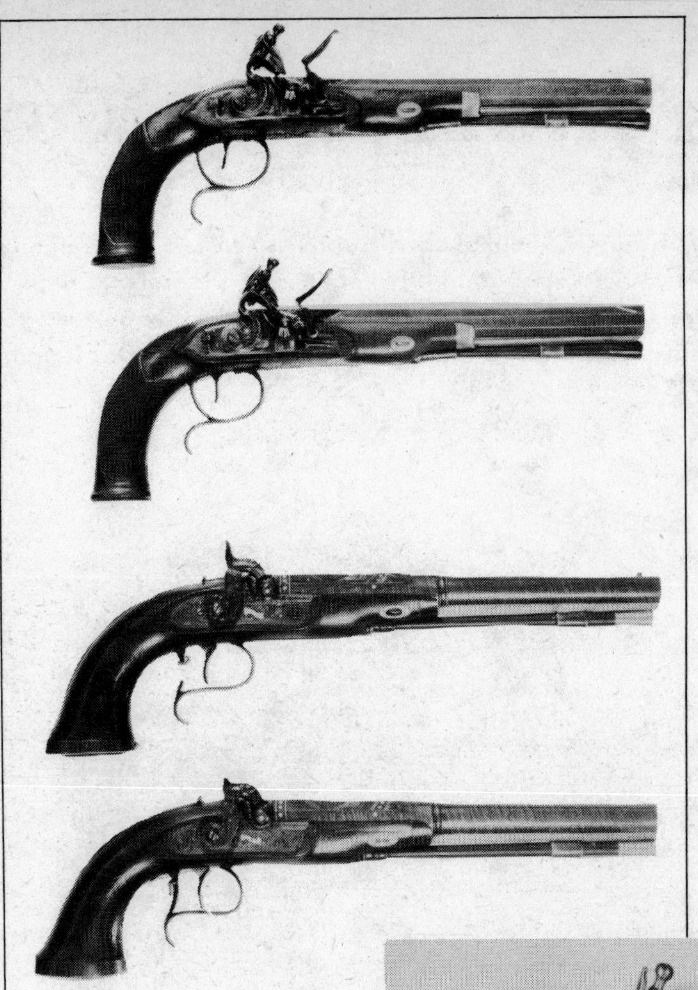

Goodwin Renwick so zealously and laboriously assembled? It is impossible to tell the final destinations of many of the guns sold at auction for these are often bought in the name of agents and not the actual buyer.

We do know that 149 choice items eventually will be on permanent display for collectors and others to enjoy at the Smithsonian; we do know that, except for the snaphaunce cylinder rifle and the Hawken mountain rifle which will go on display at the Metropolitan Museum and the Arizona Historical Society, all the remaining arms will be offered at auction for other collectors to treasure and enjoy.

The shifting fortunes of life tend to assemble and disperse men's possessions. At best we are only the temporary custodians of our treasures. But a distinguished, honorable record in any field of endeavor long outlives the man who makes it. I believe that William Goodwin Renwick has made the kind of personal record his many friends and gun collectors everywhere will unanimously applaud and long remember. ●

Two pair of top quality American-made pistols. The flintlocks at top were made by Haslett of Baltimore; the percussion pistols, which bear no maker's name, are inlaid in gold and carry the American eagle and shield atop the barrel.

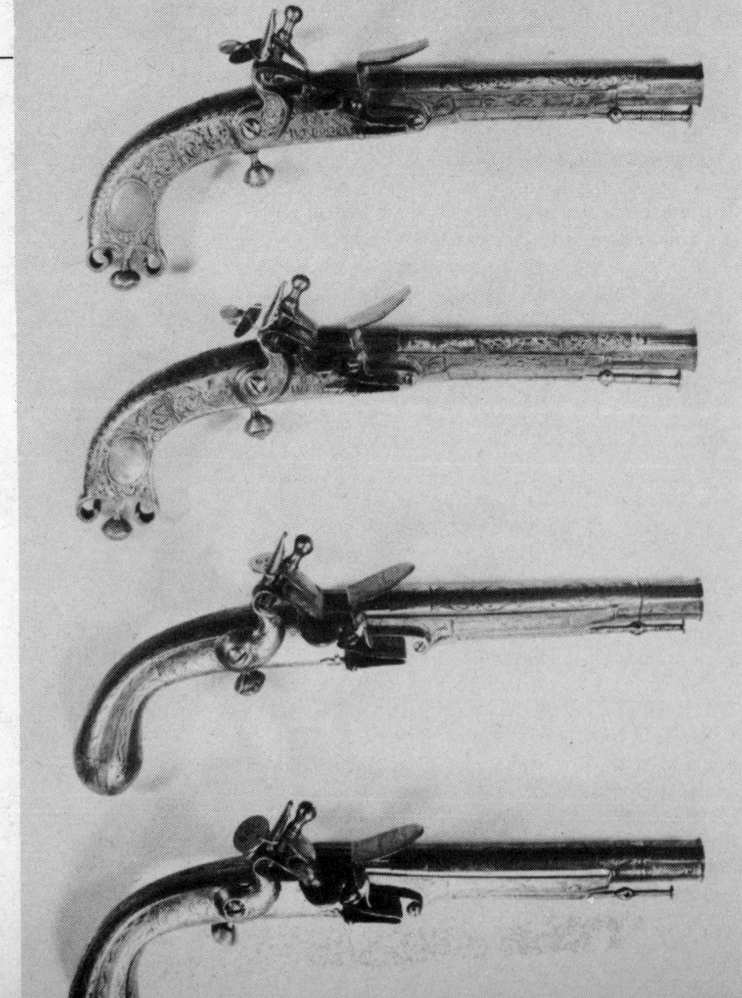

All-metal Scottish pistols were well represented in the Renwick collection. Here are two of their various forms.

Sporting Arms of the World

The manufacturers of firearms, the makers of products related to the hunting and shooting sports, have been generally cautious about making major changes in their lines. Yet there are numerous new products of interest to the firearms enthusiast, and they're reported on here, briefly or at length.

by LARRY STERETT and the editors

THERE'S ONLY one word to describe the sporting arms makers' field during 1975—"caution." Some new arms have been introduced, but a lot of the firms that have been in the field for many decades have held to a wait-and-see line. This consists of not introducing any new guns, or of simply coming out with modifications of an arm or arms already in production. One problem bothering all manufacturers to one degree or another is raw material availability. On a visit to several of them in mid-1974, the most heard comments were about materials not arriving when scheduled or sub-contracted parts behind in delivery. Even many imported arms failed to appear—the Beretta BL-2/S introduced early in February 1974 didn't arrive until after the 1974 hunting season. Similar delays were noted on arms of other firms. In early 1975 one importer told this writer that he simply did not have some rifle models available because the Austrian maker was 6 months to a year behind. However, despite the delays and other inconveniences, most of the sporting arms and accessories that have been introduced, or finally appeared, are worth the wait. LSS

Savage

This firm has the largest number of modified and new models of any of the arms manufacturers. Biggest news is the Model 2400 shotgun/rifle combination gun. Priced at $399.50, and available in 12 gauge over a choice of 308 or 222 barrel, the 2400 is based on the Finnish-made Valmet O-U action. Valmet has manufactured such a combination gun for European use for many years, chambered for the 16 gauge over the 25-35 rifle cartridge. The Savage version is an Americanized model in the stock department and definitely better looking than its Continental parent. Barrel lengths are 23½" and a fold-down rear sight fits into the barrel rib, which has a section milled for scope mounting. Since the 2400 uses the same receiver as the 330 and 333 O-U shotguns, the barrel selector is the same—housed in the single trigger. Weighing about 7½ pounds, and measuring only 40½" over-all, the 2400 is a handy combo for those shooters desiring a shotgun/rifle combination with a bit more power than the 24-V model. This writer first saw the 2400 prototype in mid-1974, and it was a gem; the production gun is even better.

Next is the 112V Varmint Rifle. Using the 110 action, but without a magazine cut, the 112-V is a single shot bolt rifle with a 26" tapered barrel chambered for 5 different varmint cartridges, including the 220 Swift. Furnished without iron sights, the receiver is tapped for scope mounts and target scope mount blocks come with the rifle. The American walnut stock is plain, without Monte Carlo, but with a full pistol grip, hand checkered grip panels (20 lines-to-the-inch), and a Wundhammer swell on both sides to benefit right- or left-hand shooters. A recoil pad and 1¼" target swivels are standard equipment on this $219 rifle.

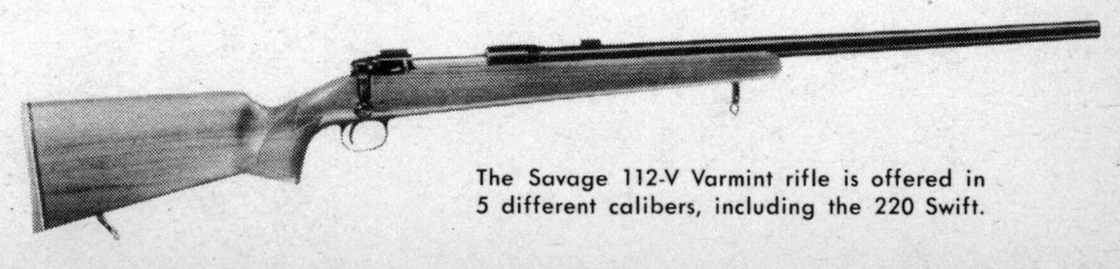

The Savage 112-V Varmint rifle is offered in 5 different calibers, including the 220 Swift.

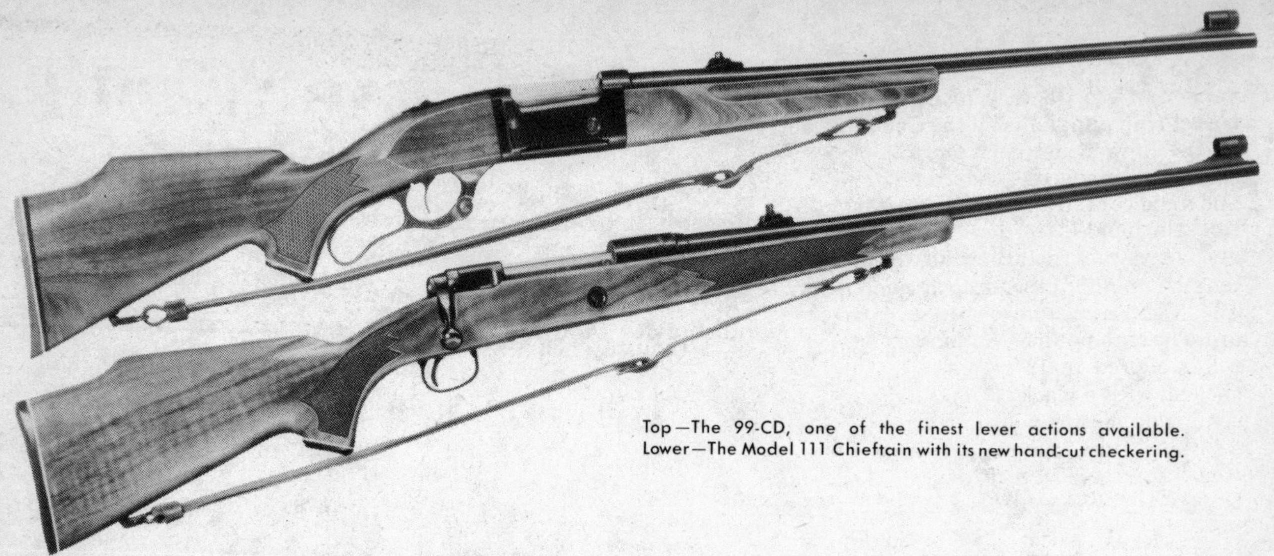

Top—The 99-CD, one of the finest lever actions available.
Lower—The Model 111 Chieftain with its new hand-cut checkering.

Also new is the Model 99-CD, a truly deluxe version of this time-tested lever action. It has the best looking stock to appear on the 99 in many years (except possibly for the 99-A), made of select walnut with Monte Carlo, well fluted comb, pistol grip cap, finger-grooved beavertail-style fore-end, and some excellent hand checkered panels on the grip and bottom of the forearm. Made only with a 22" barrel chambered for the 250-3000 or the 308 Winchester, the 99-CD has a Williams rear sight adjustable for windage and elevation, plus a hooded ramp front. A rubber butt pad and quick detachable sling swivels, with leather sling, are included in the $219.95 price tag.

Other changes in the line include the return of the Model 340 rifle chambered for the 22 Hornet cartridge. Before the 222 Remington came on the scene the 340 was chambered for the Hornet, but then it was dropped in favor of the hotter rimless cartridge.

The 99-E has new skip-line checkering, plus a folding leaf rear sight. The 110-E has a similar rear sight, and the 111 Chieftain has 20 lines-to-the-inch hand checkering.

All in all, Savage's current line is impressive, when most of the other firms are busily trimming, or holding, the line.

LSS

Harrington & Richardson

The 243 Winchester chambering has been added to the Models 300 and 301 rifles, but the Models 322 (222 Rem.) and 333 (30-06 and 7mm Mag.) rifles have been discontinued. The S.A.M. Silver-Plated Model 172 and the Officer's Model 173 45-70 Trapdoor Springfield rifles have been dropped also, but the Custer Memorial Collection was still available at the time this was written (spring '75). Otherwise, this is the sporting arms situation on Industrial Rowe. H&R now distributes the "GB" Lin-Speed oil gunstock finish and, when this writer visited the factory, an entire section was being set up for the production and bottling of this excellent product.

LSS

Omega Arms

Omega, we learned in mid-March, has been sold to the Hi-Shear Corp. (2600 Sky Park Dr., Torrance, CA 90509), but the new owner won't be producing Omega rifles until 1976. Homer Koon, former designer-owner of Omega, remains as a consultant for a brief time.

J.T.A.

Browning

The Citori O-U, introduced last year in 12 gauge, is now available in a 20 gauge Skeet version, Grade 1 only, with choice of 26" or 28" barrels. Priced at $405, the latest Citori has a stock dimensioned for the sport, and comes with a Skeet-style recoil pad. The B-SS 12 gauge shotgun, which is one of the best handling doubles this writer has used, is now available for $319.50 with 30" barrels chambered for 3" shells, and is choked full and full, or modified and full. Several knives have been added to the Browning line, including a folding model with 10 tools. One other useful accessory for the hunter is the tapered carrying sling. Priced at $13.95, this basketweave-stamped strap is lined with suede and tapers from 2" in width to 1". An unusual feature of the strap is the two quick-detachable swivels sewn into the strap, permanently, and a choice of swivel styles is available.

LSS

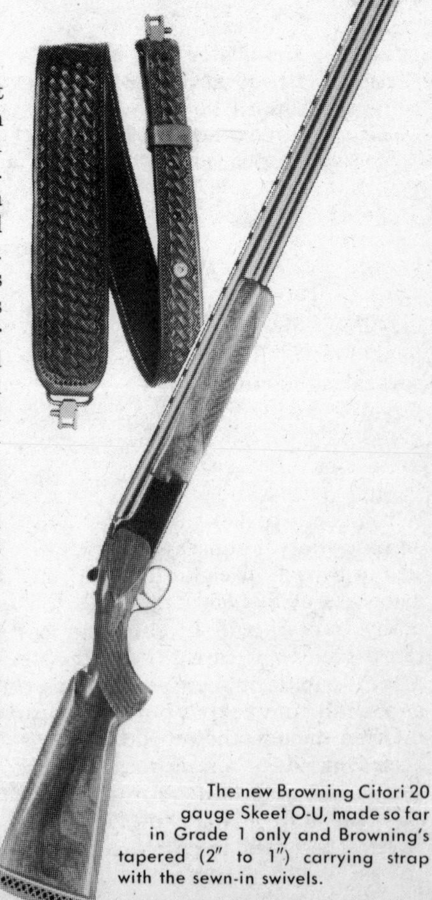

The new Browning Citori 20 gauge Skeet O-U, made so far in Grade 1 only and Browning's tapered (2" to 1") carrying strap with the sewn-in swivels.

Ithaca

This old-line firm is really moving. In late 1974 it introduced an improved version of the Century model single barrel trap gun. Labeled the Century II, the new model goes for $599.95, and features a wedge-shaped fore-end and a choice of straight or Monte Carlo stock in hand-fitted, hand-checkered and hand-rubbed French walnut—length of pull is 14⅛", drop at comb is 1½", with a trap-style recoil pad standard. The chrome-lined Rotoforged barrel is offered in 12 gauge only, full choked, with a black chrome exterior, semi-wide matted ventilated rib with a Bradley-type front sight and middle bead, and in 32" or 34" length. The boxlock action uses double-locking for added strength, a one-piece extractor, and carefully polished hammer and sear for excellent trigger pulls. The silver-finished steel frame is covered with elaborate English-scroll etching, and the trigger is gold-plated.

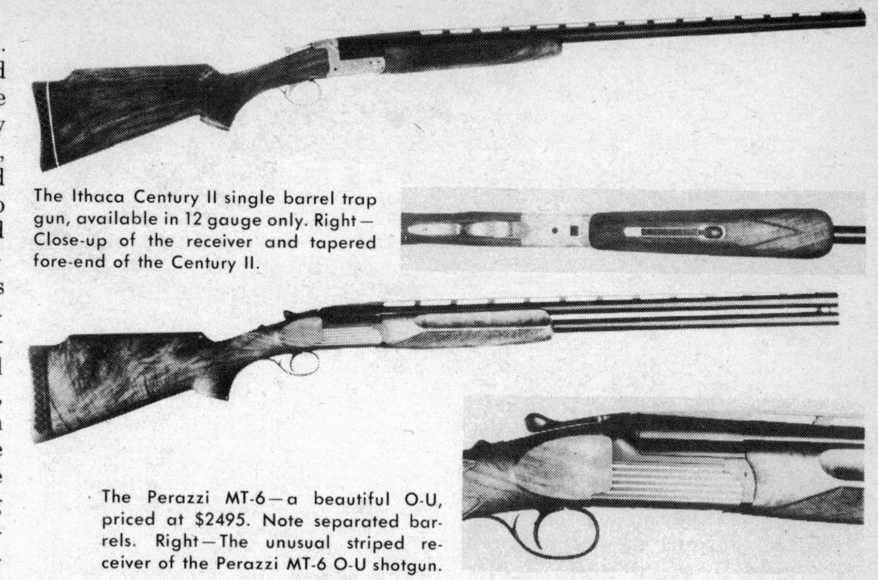

The Ithaca Century II single barrel trap gun, available in 12 gauge only. Right—Close-up of the receiver and tapered fore-end of the Century II.

The Perazzi MT-6—a beautiful O-U, priced at $2495. Note separated barrels. Right—The unusual striped receiver of the Perazzi MT-6 O-U shotgun.

The Mag 10 autoloading shotgun finally started to arrive in retail outlets at the end of 1974, although I observed the massive receiver in production during a visit to the plant 6 months earlier. Every new design requires time to get the bugs ironed out, and the production flowing smoothly. The Mag 10 was no exception, but it is worth the wait.

The German-made Model 72 Saddlegun is now chambered for the 22 WRM cartridge. Priced at $134.95, the excellent 72 has an 18½" barrel and an 11-round tubular magazine. Weight of the magnum version is about 5½ pounds, and, like the 22LR model, the American walnut stock is adult-sized with a 14" pull. Suitable for right- or left-handed shooters, the 72 magnum is a side ejector, so the use of a scope is almost automatic.

Probably the biggest news at Ithaca is the Perazzi MT-6 over-under shotgun, which should be available about mid-1975 or so. Housed in its own special luggage-style case, the MT-6 lists at $2495, and has, of course, all the quality expected of a Perazzi. Designed for the '76 Olympics, the MT-6 offers a unique striped receiver, a single selective trigger operated by the safety/barrel selector mechanism, and fully-separated barrels (no side plates) in a choice of 30" or 32" length. The barrels have interchangeable choke tubes (5 of them come with the shotgun), and the bottom barrel can be adjusted for point of impact. The top barrel has a high, wide ventilated rib. The fore-end has finger grooves along the upper portion, and a new latching system to compensate for changes due to humidity. It and the buttstock are hand checkered 24 lines-to-the-inch. Four buttstock styles are available, but a Monte Carlo is generally considered standard. All in all it appears to be quite a shotgun. At that price it should be!

LSS

Bushnell

Myron Stolp, old friend and new president of Bushnell, showed me several of their just-announced optical products during the NSGA show, and here's a brief rundown on them, pending arrival of test samples.

First, a fresh and welcome design in a compact, pocket-sized rifle boresighter—only 4 ounces and about the size of a pack of cigarettes, the cost moderate at $24.95. I feel sure that many hunters will be carrying this latest borescope, called the TruScope Model 74-4001, into the hunting camp as a small but vital piece of insurance.

Often enough the scoped rifle has been carried by air or shipped, and you wonder if it's still on zero. Maybe the rifle fell or was knocked over. Sure, a test shot in camp could give you the answer, but the game might be spooked for miles around. You never know.

Here's a way to lick the problem—before leaving home, use the TruScope rifle and bullet reference chart (furnished with the unit) to record your zero-in position. Then, in the field, if you have reason to suspect some misalignment, use the TruScope to re-align the scope—without firing a shot.

The gift-boxed TruScope comes with one adjustable arbor, and two others are available, the caliber range 22 to 45.

Bushnell recently announced two wide-angle 7x35 Sportview binoculars with a new and improved version of their Insta-Focus. This patented and unique lever-action focusing delivers three times faster focusing than conventional center-focus binoculars give. The quick finger-tip action lets the hunter follow his game without losing focus. All this and a low price tag, too, for these new Insta-Focus glasses in a wide field type (10° angle and 11° angle), sell for $54.50 and $59.50 respectively.

Bushnell's patent covers a unique rocker arm that replaces the usual center-focus wheel. Now the user's finger-tips, dropping naturally on to the fast-focusing lever, let the picture snap effortlessly into focus. Both models come with roll-down rubber eyecups, a convenience for eyeglass wearers, a deluxe carrying case with strap and, of course, Bushnell's 1 year warranty for quality and workmanship.

J.T.A.

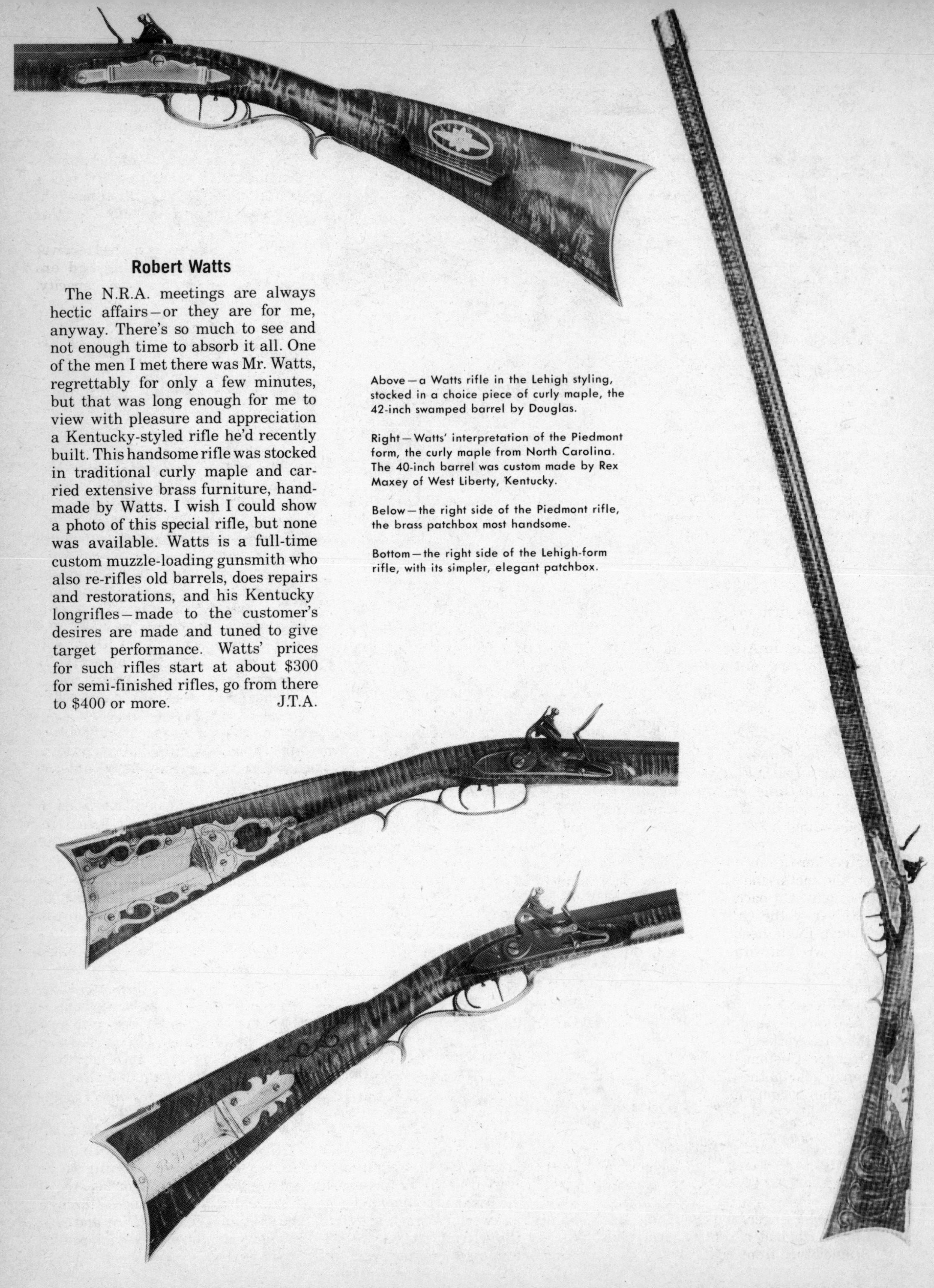

Robert Watts

The N.R.A. meetings are always hectic affairs—or they are for me, anyway. There's so much to see and not enough time to absorb it all. One of the men I met there was Mr. Watts, regrettably for only a few minutes, but that was long enough for me to view with pleasure and appreciation a Kentucky-styled rifle he'd recently built. This handsome rifle was stocked in traditional curly maple and carried extensive brass furniture, handmade by Watts. I wish I could show a photo of this special rifle, but none was available. Watts is a full-time custom muzzle-loading gunsmith who also re-rifles old barrels, does repairs and restorations, and his Kentucky longrifles—made to the customer's desires are made and tuned to give target performance. Watts' prices for such rifles start at about $300 for semi-finished rifles, go from there to $400 or more. J.T.A.

Above—a Watts rifle in the Lehigh styling, stocked in a choice piece of curly maple, the 42-inch swamped barrel by Douglas.

Right—Watts' interpretation of the Piedmont form, the curly maple from North Carolina. The 40-inch barrel was custom made by Rex Maxey of West Liberty, Kentucky.

Below—the right side of the Piedmont rifle, the brass patchbox most handsome.

Bottom—the right side of the Lehigh-form rifle, with its simpler, elegant patchbox.

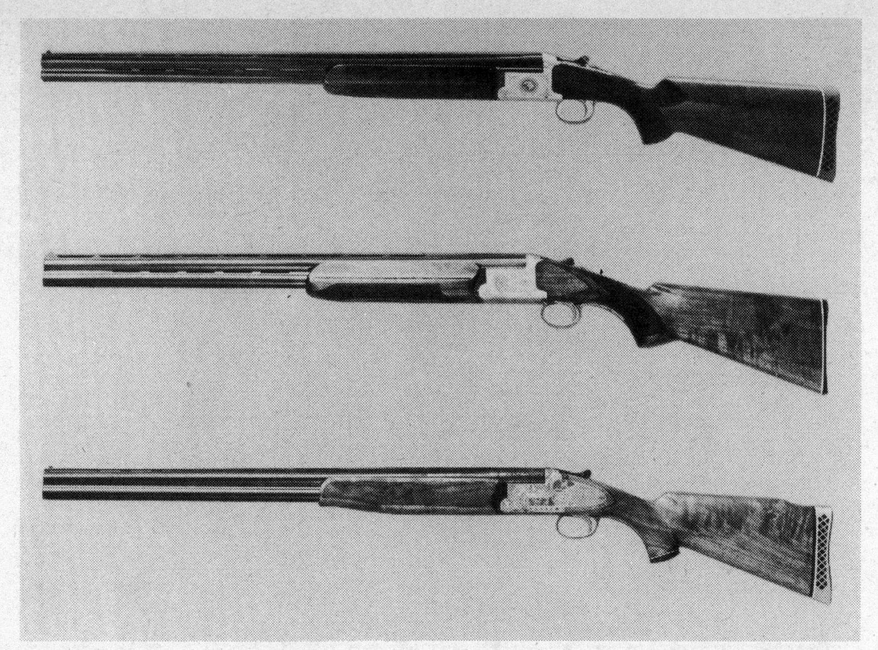

Top to bottom — Nikko Golden Eagle Grade I; note the eagle head in relief on the receiver. Golden Eagle Grade II; note ventilated side ribs. Golden Eagle Grade III Grandee Custom O-U shotgun with hand-engraved false sideplates. This model has a pistol grip cap, other models do not.

Nikko

Another firm made its appearance in late 1974 – Kanematsu-Gosho USA Inc., located in Arlington Heights, IL 60005, makers of the Nikko line. An O-U shotgun is the first of a series of classic sporting arms that will eventually include pump and automatic shotguns, centerfire and rimfire rifles, and rifle scopes. The Model 5000 Golden Eagle O-U is made in 12 or 20 gauge in three grades – starting at $699.50 for the Grade I Field Model and ending at $2299.50 for the Grade III Trap or Skeet models. Several of these were examined and the finish on the metal and wood surfaces was excellent. On each side of the blued receiver of the Grade I models is a Golden Eagle head within a sterling silver wreath, while the Grade II has an eagle in flight within a sterling silver wreath, in the same location. These eagles are the creation of the "Alaskan silversmith" Sid Bell, and they are works of art. The Grade III Grandee Custom examined was inlaid in gold on the left side of the barrel, the trigger, and fore-end latch were gold plated, and a golden eagle head was in relief on the axis of the top lever. The false sideplates were also fully engraved. The trigger on this $2299.50 O-U was twisted slightly to the right for ease in positioning the trigger finger, and the 11mm ventilated rib had a center bead, plus Bradley-type front bead.

All shotguns have chrome-lined barrels, are chambered for 2¾″ shells, and barrels range from 26″ to 32″, with chokes accordingly. Three ventilated rib widths are available – 8mm, 11mm or 15mm – depending on model and barrel. The side ribs on the Grade II trap and Skeet guns are ventilated also. The underlug boxlock action tends to produce a greater receiver depth, but it is a time-tested design still in use by Browning, Franchi, and a host of others.

Weights vary from about 6¾ pounds for 20s to some 8½ pounds for the 12 bores. Checkering runs from 18 lines on Grade Is to 28 lines on Grade III and IV. There is also a little castoff on each stock. Drops at the comb vary from 1$^{15}/_{16}$″ on the Grade III trap to 1½″ on the Skeet. The heel drops range from 1⅞″ on the Grade II trap gun to 2½″ on the field guns. On all grades (I, II, and III) the dimensions, including the 14″ pulls, were about perfect for handling qualities – at least for this writer.

A Grade IV true sidelock in 12 gauge trap and Skeet is $2499.50, with barrel lengths of 29¾″ and 27½″ respectively, with 11mm ventilated rib. The receiver is fully hand engraved, and the lock mechanism is the inertia type, meaning light loads might not set it for firing the second barrel. (The boxlock models have mechanical lockwork.) A single selective trigger – the selector coupled with the safety mechanism on the upper receiver tang – coil springs, and selective ejectors are standard, as they are on the Grades I, II, and III.

Nikko now manufactures the Weatherby Centurion and Patrician shotguns, plus the 22 Weatherby autoloading rifle, so the new KG pump, priced under $200, will resemble the Patrician, as will no doubt the other models. Available in 12 or 20, for 3″ shells, the pump has a steel receiver with golden eagle inlay and engraving, a 5-round magazine capacity, interchangeable chrome-lined barrels in 26″ to 30″ lengths, with screw-in choke tubes, ventilated rib, center and front beads, a slug barrel for deer hunting, and American walnut stocks with hand checkering. The pump 12 will weigh about 7 pounds, the 20 corresponding lighter. The gas-operated semi-automatic will be offered in the same gauges and barrel lengths, priced under $240. Like the pump it is chambered for 3″ shells and will have interchangeable choke tubes. Weight, in 12 gauge, about 7½ pounds.

The planned big game bolt rifle, weight about 7½ pounds, will have a stock shape similar to the Weatherby rifles. Barrels will have a Weatherby #2 contour, the receiver drilled and tapped for scope mounts (there will be no iron sights), the bolt will fully enclose the case head, and the magazine may be usable as a detachable or in-action type. A fully adjustable trigger and shotgun-type safety will be standard. Calibers include all popular ones, including the 300 Weatherby Magnum.

The rimfire rifles will be made in semi-automatic and bolt action repeating types with choice of tubular or box magazine.

The riflescope line includes five models at present – a 4x model for rimfire rifles, and a 4x standard in regular and wide angle, plus a 3x-9x variable in regular and wide angle for centerfire rifles.

The rimfire version lists at $34.95, the top of the line 3x-9x variable is $104.95. The scopes are nitrogen-filled, have coated lenses, plus an "eagle-eye" reticle (sort of a duplex with heavy and light crosshairs).

A complete network of dealerships and warranty stations is being set up throughout the US and, from what this writer saw, it looks like the Golden Eagle line is going to be around for awhile. Major repairs, if ever needed, will be handled through the Arlington Heights office, and each warranty station will be equipped for minor repairs. L.S.S.

Ruger

Nothing really new at Southport in the long arm line, except the No. 3 carbine in 22 Hornet caliber is now tapped for target-type scope mount bases. (The 30-40 Krag and 45-70 models are not so drilled.) The 22 rimfire carbine with the "international" stock has been discontinued, but the de luxe and standard stock models are still being produced.

Stainless steel handgun models have been increased to 9 at present, including the Security-Six, Speed-Six, and the latest—the Police Service-Six, which is offered in 38 Spl. or 357 with 4" barrel and fixed sights, or with a regular blued finish and a choice of 2¾" or 4" barrel.

The Ruger O-U shotgun is not included in the 1975 catalog, nor the Mini-14. But the Mini-14 is in production, though, most of them going to police departments and foreign governments. A few have been available to some dealers. (See the "Testfire Report" section in this edition for a report on the Mini-14.) L.S.S.

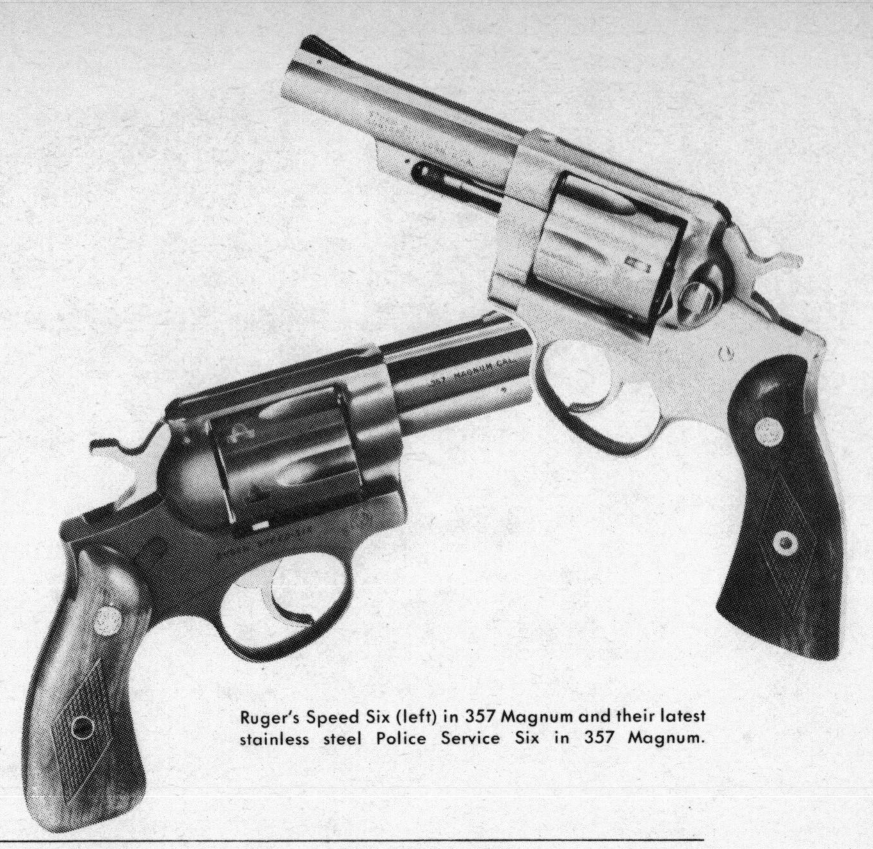

Ruger's Speed Six (left) in 357 Magnum and their latest stainless steel Police Service Six in 357 Magnum.

Smith & Wesson

Although still very much in the shotgun business with their 916 pump gun and 1000 autoloader, S&W terminated production of all loaded shotshells in November 1974, but will continue to offer components for reloaders. The Alton, Illinois (old Alcan) plant will be phased out and all manufacturing of centerfire rifle and pistol ammunition, plus 22 rimfire ammunition and shotshell reloading components will be at the Rock Creek, Ohio, plant. The High Precision Manufacturing Co. of Orange City, Iowa, has been bought by S&W from the former owner, Al Hancock. To be known as the S&W Ammunition Co. Projectile Division, this facility will produce the bullets for the S&W centerfire line of rifle and pistol cartridges, plus an expanded line for reloaders.

The S&W designed centerfire rifle introduced a couple of years ago, but never produced, has been shelved for good. Possibly a new rifle design may become available in the future, but during this writer's visit to the Massachusetts factory, he was informed the original rifle design will not be manufactured. S&W will, of course, continue to manufacture their extensive line of quality handguns, including the Model 29 with 8⅜" barrels in blue and nickel versions. LSS

New Weaver Mount

The twin mounts pictured here are Weaver's latest development—their See-Thru system. They're light and reasonably compact, sized to accept any 1" scopes, and designed to take the thrust of the heaviest recoil.

As Weaver says, "...shooters will appreciate the instant use of either scope or iron sights. There's *nothing to take off*, nothing to fiddle with." I've added the emphasis because, in another part of the same Weaver release, it is pointed out that the new See-Thru mount "can be removed instantly with a quick twisting motion," and as quickly replaced, with exact zero alignment.

Question—if the scope/mount combo is instantly removable for iron sight use, who needs the See-Thru aspect, which places the scope in a too-high-for-comfort position and produces a high mount that can hardly be called handsome or one that adds anything to the appearance of the rifle.

On the other hand, assuming that the snap-off/snap-on feature works well, the See-Thru construction could well be abandoned. I wonder if any attempt was made to design the QD feasibility into Weaver's regular and long-popular low mounts, or to design the fast off-on system for a new low mount? J.T.A.

Weaver's new See-Thru scope mounts offer a degree of redundancy—if the iron sights cannot be seen with the mounts in position, yank the scope and mounts off together for a full view.

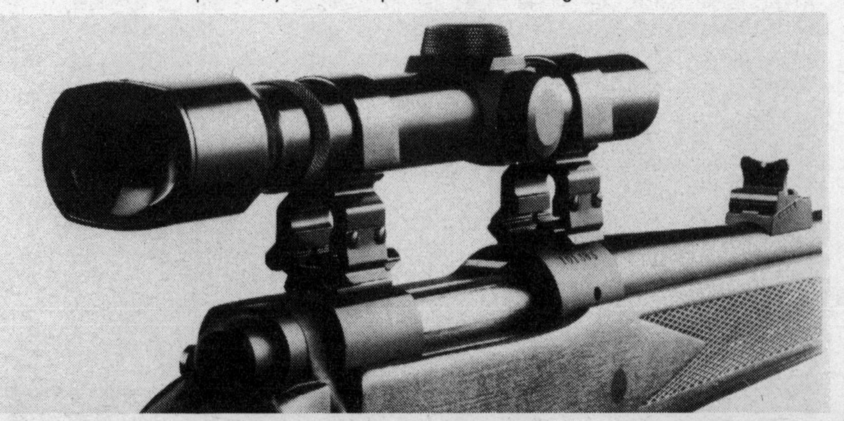

LENARD M. BROWNELL
Master Gunsmith

As our faithful readers know, Mr. Brownell is no stranger to these pages. He's been building custom rifles for some years, and he continues to do so—all masterpieces of the classic form.

Way back then Len soon learned that the metalsmithing he required to let him make a quality rifle—special floorplates, guards, and the like—was hard to obtain, slow in reaching him, and it wasn't always exactly as he wanted. So he became a metal worker as well, and a very much first class one—take a look at the quarter-rib and the grip cap on the beautifully-done rifle seen here, plus the 3-leaf express sight, all from Len's talented hands.

Len Brownell calls this Ruger No. 1 single shot "one of the nicest rifles" he's ever done, and I agree completely—it is a brilliant and perfectly integrated effort. The wood is a fancy piece of European walnut, fine-line checkered, and the extensive engraving is by John Warren of Cape Cod, a renowned master of this demanding art.

The rifle was made for Donald R. Glaser, an accomplished amateur engraver himself and, with John Rohner, the developers of the Gravermeister tool for engraving.

Photographs by Dick Kernwald, Wyarno, Wy.

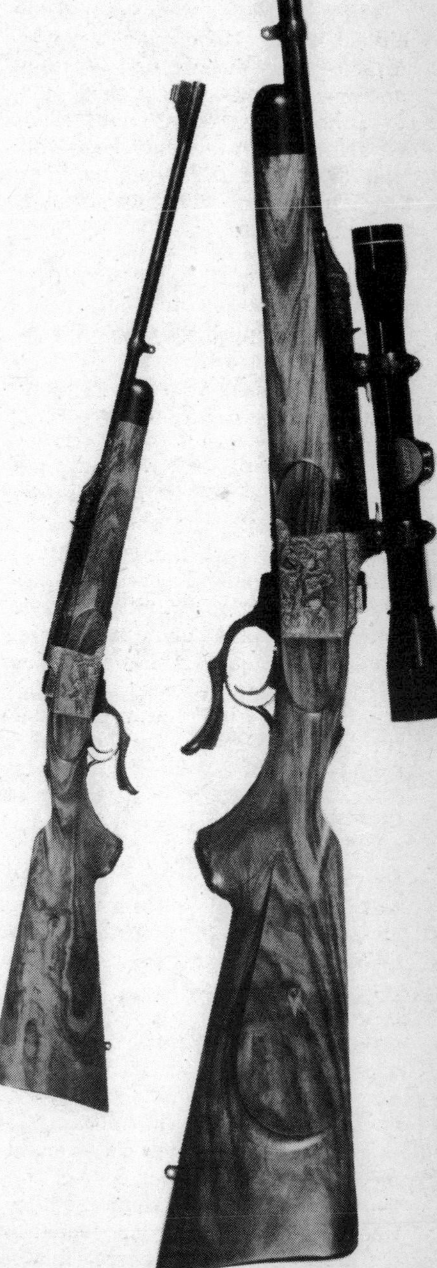

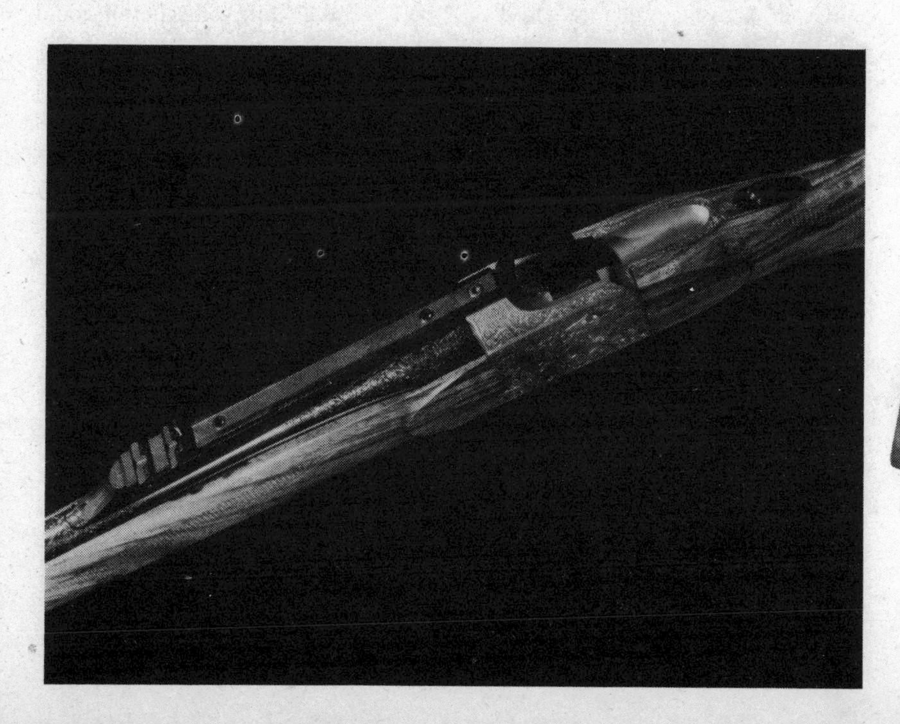

L.E.S.

This Skokie, Illinois, firm has an extensive line of law enforcement arms, plus being the distributor for the world renowned Steyr-Daimler-Puch line of sporting rifles. (New in the Steyr rifle line is the Steyr-Mannlicher Model M in a left-hand version. Calibers available include the 270, 30-06, 243, and other popular U.S. cartridges. In recent years arms manufacturers have finally realized there are left-handed shooters, and Steyr is one of the first European manufacturers to get the word.) Now a couple of side-by-side shotguns have been added to the L.E.S. line. Labeled the Sabel and the Silver Sabel, and currently available in 12 and 16 gauge versions (a 20 gauge may be available later) with 26" or 28" barrels, both shotguns feature double triggers and Holland-type extractors. The low-priced Sabel at $235.00, has an Anson & Deeley boxlock action with Purdey bolt, straight English-style hand checkered walnut stock and splinter fore-end. The safety is the automatic-type which goes "on" as the top lever is operated. All parts are hand-fitted, and on the model examined the wood-to-metal fit and finish was good. The Silver Sabel, priced at $435.00, is a true sidelock with Purdey bolt, and double safety sears. The receiver has a brushed silver finish to complement the blued side-plates, and a bit more engraving appears on the action areas. The hand-checkered walnut stock has a Monte Carlo comb, and a beaver-tail fore-end is standard. The top rib on this sidelock model is higher than usual, while the top rib of the standard Sabel has a concave or "swamped" sighting surface.

Above—The Steyr-Mannlicher Model M in left-hand version. Below—The Steyr P-18 semi-automatic pistol is chambered for the 9mm Parabellum cartridge.

The big news at L.E.S. is the Steyr P-18 semi-automatic pistol. Manufactured in Illinois, the Austrian-designed pistol is chambered for the 9mm Parabellum or Luger cartridge and has an 18-round capacity. It features a 5½" barrel permanently welded to the frame, and is a gas-retarded blowback design. The chief function of the burning gases is to reduce recoil greatly. See John Amber's shooting report on this unique pistol elsewhere in this section. It can be fired double-action with a 9 pound trigger pull, or cocked using the outside hammer, for single action firing with a pull of less than 2 pounds. A slide-mounted safety—a la Walther P-38 or S&W M39 style—will be familiar to many shooters. Currently priced at $175.00 or so, it is one of the most unusual pistols to come down the pike in many years.

LSS

Ranger Arms

Our annual form letter failed to elicit a reply from Ranger so we phoned—or tried to. The line had been disconnected, the office equipment moved, but the factory machines remained.

J.T.A.

Game Management Success

Many sportsmen are aware that hunter-financed wildlife management programs have been responsible for restoring to healthy population levels such popular game species as the white-tailed deer, pronghorn antelope and elk. Less known is the fact that *hunter dollars* have supported management efforts directed at restoring a variety of nongame species. Here are a few historical comparisons:

Egrets and Herons: In 1910 several species were on the brink of extinction. Today most species are common to abundant over most of the United States.

Trumpeter Swan: In 1935 there were only 73 survivors south of Canada on one wildlife refuge. Today there are thriving populations in two national parks and several national wildlife refuges. These swans were removed from endangered status in the late 1960s.

Sea Otter: Nearly extinct in 1907, there were a few survivors in Alaska's Aleutian chain and in coastal California. Today, there's a minimum of 50,000, successfully restored to the waters of mainland Alaska, Oregon, Washington, and British Columbia.

Brass Extrusion Laboratories Ltd.

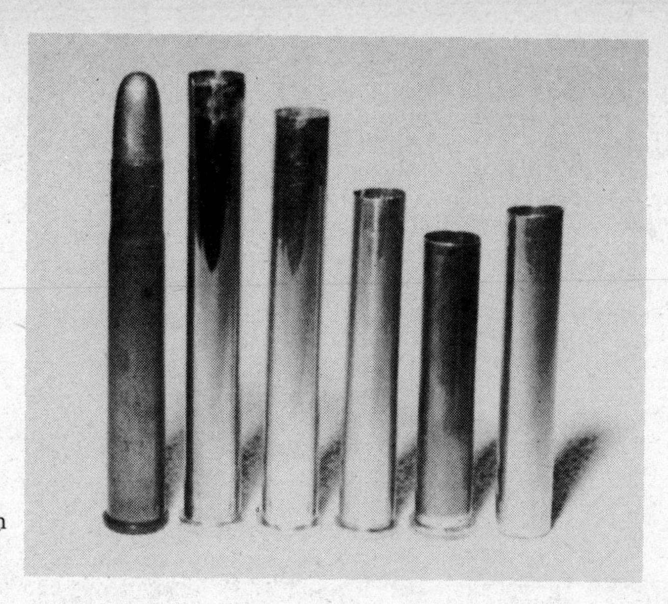

Several steps in making B.E.L.L. cases. The third case from left is finished except for trimming to length. The next two cases are drawn out to show the lengths possible. Last, an original Kynoch 475 No. 2 Jeffery.

Do you have a 577 double rifle in your rack that you need cartridge cases for? Or maybe a 475 No. 2 Jeffery? How about a 280 Ross for which no U.S. ammunition has been produced since about 1939? If you do, take heart. Such cases will eventually be available in due course from a new firm located only a few miles from the GUN DIGEST general offices.

Back in December 1973, a chance inquiry by Jim Bell of Bell's Gun & Sport Shop Inc., in Franklin Park, IL, led to what has become Brass Extrusion Laboratories Ltd. Although this firm will eventually produce such modern bread-'n-butter calibers as the 45 ACP, 38 Special, 41 Magnum, 44 Auto Mag, and 9mm Parabellum, the plant was built to manufacture limited lots of the larger caliber cases needed to put the old American single shot buffalo rifles and double barrel English elephant rifles back into operation.

In the past a few such cases have been lathe turned from brass bar stock. For low power loads such cases work so-so, but they cannot be readily resized or used for high powered nitro or smokeless powder loads. (This writer has used such turned cases in a 577 Snider, and in this caliber they at least provide a means of shooting a rifle for which cases are almost nonexistent.) The problem with turned cases lies in the work hardening of the brass in the fabrication process. In addition, the brass grain structure in the cartridge head needs orientation to produce a strength factor known as *hoop* strength.

When this writer visited the factory in late March 1975 a number of the first cartridge cases had already been subjected to pressure tests of at least 61,000 psi, which is more than most of the rifles the cases are intended for will handle. During one test a single case was loaded to the capacity limit with #4198 powder behind a 500-gr. bullet for 5 successive firings. The case head never did fail, although the case finally split longitudinally on the fifth shot. Several cases were examined that had been used in these pressure tests and, though the primers were flattened and the firing pin impressions slightly cratered, the case heads showed no signs of weakening.

It has taken time to accumulate a quarter-million dollars worth of equipment, consisting mainly of used arsenal presses. These presses, which have arrived from such distant points as California, New York, and even the Virgin Islands, have been disassembled, cleaned, rebuilt and modified in almost every instance for their new jobs, painted—white with "international orange" on all moving parts to conform to safety regulations—and reassembled. In addition to the required heavy duty presses, there was the obtaining of pressure barrels, plus the necessary dies and tools to perform the 5-step forming operation, not to mention a new brick building, and laboratory equipment, including a Rockwell hardness tester, and an optical comparator.

Although the presses could be adapted to produce cartridge cases over 5″ long, no known sporting rifle cartridge required such a case. The longest cases for which rifles have been chambered measure 3½″; an example is the 475 No. 2 Jeffery. Most of the other big bores use cases measuring 3¼″ in length (50 Sharps) or less. As a result, the first case from B.E.L.L. is the 500 RCBS Basic, which can be used to form the 470 Nitro Express, 500/465, 500/450, and the 475 No. 2—all English double rifle calibers. Others planned include the big Sharps, such as the 50 Sharps 3¼″, the 577, and eventually the 280 Ross.

On the day this writer visited B.E.L.L., Jim Bell had been out to the range during the morning testing some of the initial ammunition using 5 different double rifles. He and an assistant had put 100 rounds through the rifles without any problems—enough to verify that the new cases were up to par and to produce a couple of black-'n-blue shoulders.

In time the plant will be fully automated so far as the machines go, and will employ about 8 persons. Capacity will be some 10,000 cases per day when everything is completed. That may sound like a lot of cases, but it is not when you consider that the minimum number of cases a factory like Norma will make is 100,000, and often the introduction of a new case can only be justified if the sales are in the millions. The operation of drawing a cartridge case is well known, but it is involved and expensive, and for this reason large factories will not tie up their equipment for a "small" quantity of cases. Their overhead is just too large, and the quantity of cases sold too small to warrant their production. This was the reason Kynoch (IMI) discontinued production of most of the big English calibers, such as the 475 No. 2 Jeffery, in 1963.

The B.E.L.L. process, a slightly modified version of the regular process, will permit the manufacture of a smaller lot of cases. Even so the cases will not be cheap, but what is these days? Prices had not been set when this writer visited the plant, but I think the price will probably be somewhere around $1.00 per case for the large calibers. If this seems a bit steep, consider that turned cases from bar stock were costing $1.00 to $2.00 per case over a decade ago and they could not begin to equal the quality of the B.E.L.L. cases in finish, strength, or durability. Kynoch cases, when a few can be found, cost as much or more, and require odd-size Berdan primers, which are also difficult to locate. The B.E.L.L. cases take regular, readily-available, .210″ Boxer primers, which alone makes them a good buy.

LSS

Winchester

No longer cataloged are the bolt action Models 310 and 320 rimfire rifles introduced earlier in this decade. This is too bad, as they were good rifles. In the shotgun line the Super-X Model 1 comes only with ventilated-rib barrel now, although the field grade plain barrel is available as an extra for $62.95. The 3" chambering has been dropped, as have all the 20 gauge models. Apparently sales were not high enough to warrant keeping them in a line that was already an expensive autoloader. (Early 1975 price of the Field Grade Super-X Model 1 was $330.) The Model 12 is still in the lineup, but only the Trap Grade is on the current price list, so don't expect to see many field or Skeet grades around. Also discontinued are the air rifles and air handguns, along with the regular and match pellets.

For small bore target shooters the good news is a new Model 52 International Prone Target rifle and 22 Long Rifle Super-Match Gold cartridges. Even the Super Match Mark III cartridges have been improved. The new rifle is available on special order only, the price dependent on when the rifle is shipped; in any event you can bet it will be an expensive rimfire. Weighing 11½ pounds, this latest Model 52 has a removable full roll-over cheekpiece and a 28" straight taper barrel.

So much for the sporting arms. The boys at the big red W have been busy on handloading components, and a couple of new powders should be out by the time you read this, plus some match grade centerfire primers, a new reloading manual and some match quality bullets. LSS

Jeffredo Gunsight Co.

This new firm offers several interesting shooters' items, among them a new Bridge Type Scope Mount, made of solid steel throughout, that uses an unusual screw-cam system to attach the rings to the base—these hardened steel No. 10 hex-socket machine screws. As our picture shows, here's a handsome, cleanly-made mount, free of projections and with base and rings line-bored for optimum scope alignment. Made for most popular rifles, the cost is $40 (1" rings only), or $10 extra for a quick-detachable version that mounts on a dovetailed rail.

Jeffredo also produces a scope mount they call the Windage and Elevation Adjustable model, this one intended for those shooters who prefer to use the non-adjustable B&L rifle scopes—though any 1"-tube scopes can also be accommodated. Made from aircraft-type alloys and tool steel, the front screw thimble is used for elevation, the rear one for windage adjustment. The scope so-mounted can be rotated leftward for instant use of iron sights, with no failure to return to zero. Made for popular rifles (and special jobs), the rings cost $25 each; an adjustable base, which permits using one scope on one or more rifles (if these have the adjustable base)is $30. A non-adjustable base is $17.

Other Jeffredo products are: a Recoil Pad-Cartridge Trap, designed for safe storage plus instant access to the cartridges. Made from strong steel (silver brazed to allow high heat blueing) combined with a Pachmayr 880 or 750 pad, the Kit sells for $32.50, or Jeffredo will install it for about $45. Jewelling is $7.50 extra.

There's also a one-piece firing pin and 3-position safety for Springfield bolt rifles at $50, factory adjusted for easy installation, and the price including a high-speed mainspring.

Write to Jeffredo (1629 Via Monserate, Fallbrook, CA 92028) for full data on the foregoing useful items, and ask about their soon-to-be-ready "45 ACP High Performance Kit," designed for use with a new Jeffredo 45 Magnum cartridge. Briefly, a new barrel (part of the $85 Kit) is required to handle a 45 auto case 1.050" long instead of the .898" standard 45 ACP length. Muzzle velocity can be stepped up to about 1400 fps, using 185-gr. bullets, with operating gas pressures about normal. At the same time, regular 45 ACP ammo can be used in the revised pistol, a nice plus. J.T.A.

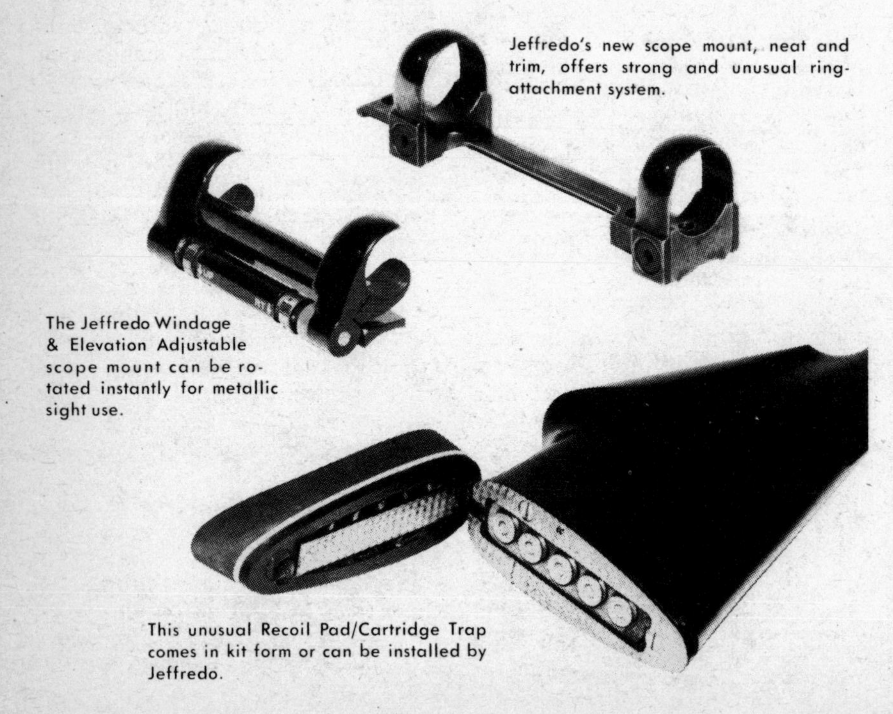

Jeffredo's new scope mount, neat and trim, offers strong and unusual ring-attachment system.

The Jeffredo Windage & Elevation Adjustable scope mount can be rotated instantly for metallic sight use.

This unusual Recoil Pad/Cartridge Trap comes in kit form or can be installed by Jeffredo.

Thompson/Center

The Contender Hot Shot barrels with ventilated rib and screw-in chokes have not materialized yet in any quantity, but they should be available by the time this edition is on the stands. New this year is a plain 54 caliber muzzle-loading rifle called the Renegade. Priced at $165, the Renegade has all steel trim, including the trigger guard and buttplate, a wooden ramrod, hooked-breech system, and adjustable sights, plus double set triggers. Designed to handle a new 400-gr. Maxi-Ball for serious hunting of big game, it can be loaded to provide a muzzle velocity that gives 446 ft. lbs. greater energy than the factory 45-70 load. An accessory pack is $12.35, including a box of 20 cast 54 caliber Maxi-Balls, powder measure, Maxi-Lub, bullet starter, extra nipple, and nipple wrench. Like the T/C Hawken and the Seneca, the Renegade is a quality arms and worth every cent of its price. LSS

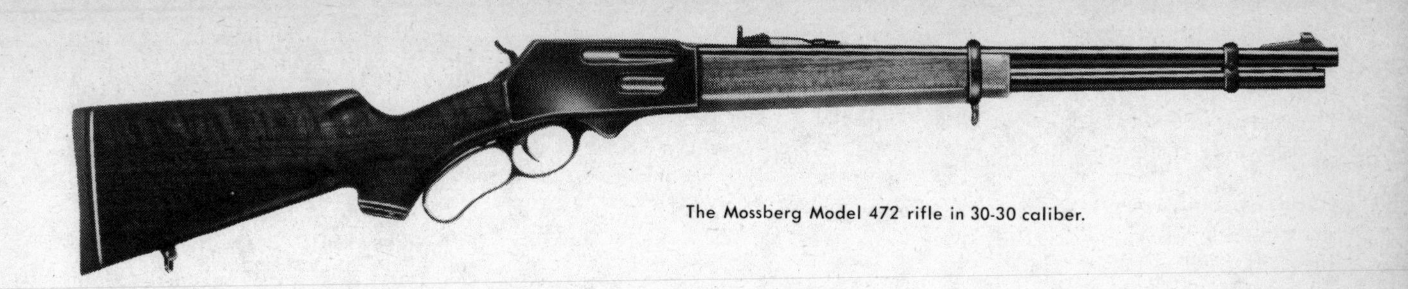
The Mossberg Model 472 rifle in 30-30 caliber.

Mossberg/Pedersen

The name of the game at 7 Grasso Avenue is similar to that of other firms—trim the line and hold on the main movers. The 16 gauge chambering has been discontinued in the entire line, along with the field-grade, slide-action Model 500AMR 3" magnum version. The 500AMR Super Grade and the 500APR in a 12 gauge are available in Skeet, trap and field grades. In the rifle line the detachable box magazine has been dropped from all calibers in the Model 810 series, and the 222 chambering introduced just last year has been dropped from the Model 800 series in all three grades. There have been no changes in the 472 line, and although the writer was informed during a visit to the plant in mid-1974 that the 472 manual safety on the left side of the receiver would be discontinued, it's still there. The rimfire line remains as it was last year with the exception of the 321B (with peep sight) being dropped.

There are no new basic designs, but there has been an addition to the 500 series. This is the Model 500DSPR Limited Edition Commemorative Pigeon Grade shotgun with "steel-shot" barrel. Only 1000 of these shotguns will be manufactured, all with a 30" full choke ventilated-rib barrel chambered for 3" shells and especially designed for steel shot. A wood duck is etched on the right side of the receiver and a pair in flight is etched on the left side, while a 1974-75 duck stamp is affixed to the walnut-finished plaque which accompanies the shotgun; the shotgun and plaque are serial numbered the same, and registered as a commemorative sporting arm. The barrel, offered separately, is marked with a duck's head and the words "steel shot." It should be available by the time this appears in print.

The Pedersen line is basically the same, although the Grade III Model 1000 O-U shotgun is no longer being listed. This was the plain member of the family, without engraving, and apparently a shooter paying the Pedersen price was willing to add a bit more for some engraving. LSS

Dixie Ashmore Lock

Dixie Gun Works now offers this exceptionally well made flintlock of pre-Revolutionary War styling. Measuring 4½ inches long and ⅞-inch across at its widest point, this lock is well suited for use on any early styled flintlock rifle, pistol or fowling piece. The inner workings of this high quality Italian-made lock are comparable to any other top quality lock now on the market, many of which are considerably higher priced. The frizzen has been well hardened to insure a shower of hot sparks into the pan. The remainder of the lock has been left unfinished to that the metal may be completed in whatever manner preferred. The plate is clearly marked "ASHMORE WARRANTED" and dated "1776." Although Ashmore was a well known London lockmaker, many of his locks can be found on early American made guns, such as those produced by L.M. Leland of Augusta, Maine, and M. Mater of Chippawa, Ontario.

Available from Dixie Gun Works, Inc., P.O. Box 130, Union City, TN 38261, this modern made copy of the Ashmore lock is priced at $29.95.

Dixie Gun Works, Inc. now offers the Italian-made Ashmore lock for flintlock pistols, rifles and fowling pieces.

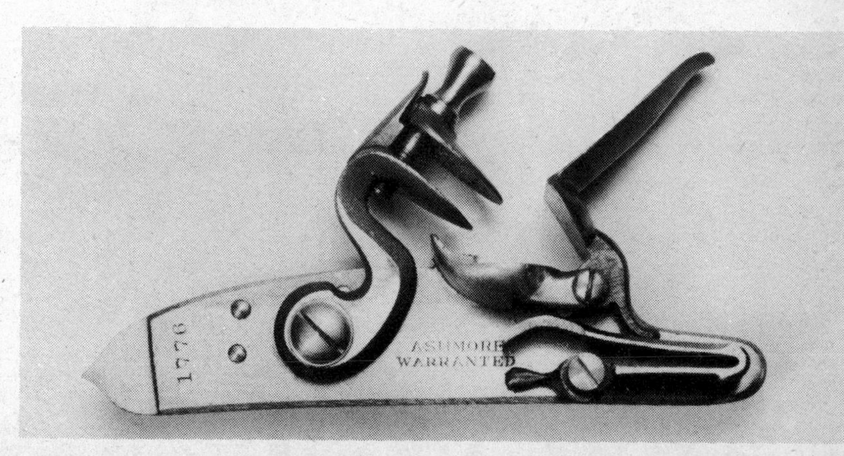

Mandall Shooting Supplies

This firm handles a line of imported sporting arms not often seen elsewhere. Included are the custom Alpine centerfire sporting rifles from England, several versions of the 22 WRM JGL rimfire autoloader from Germany, some German riflescopes, the excellent Finnish Valmet Lion target rifle, an Italion O-U rifle/shotgun, double barrel shotguns with internal or external hammers in 12, 20 and 10 gauges, plus some black powder arms. Available later may be the Voere-made AM-180 in a semi-automatic version. (A full-auto version of this 22 long rifle rimfire with a 180-round magazine has been used by some police departments.) Of the arms examined the Finnish Lion is a target rifle of excellent quality; the JGL rifles are not fancy but they're among the few autoloaders chambered for the 22 WRM cartridge. The M72 with one-piece stock is cramped in the grip area due to the receiver extension, but the stock is well shaped, and comes complete with buttplate and 1" sling swivels. The buttstock and forestock on the M102 and M104 versions are slab-sided, without buttplate or swivels, which makes them look unfinished; on rifles costing $200 there should be a bit more value. However, accuracy was good on three different rifles examined, with 5-shot groups at 25 yards averaging just under ½" when using a 4x Bushnell scope. LSS

Remington

The 3200 O/U introduced in 1973 is now available in a 12 gauge magnum model with 30" barrels chambered for 3" shells. This boomer is designed to handle steel and lead shot loads in 2¾" and 3" sizes. It does so by use of a special barrel steel and by thickening the barrels for the last 3" approaching the muzzle. This thickened area, only slightly noticeable, is necessary to prevent the less compressible steel shot from enlarging the muzzle. Weight of the magnum is about 8¾ pounds, and chokes of modified and full, or full and full are available. A trap model with 32" modified and full barrels is also offered plus a special trap model, either with regular or Monte Carlo stock.

The Model 788 rifle can now be had in 223 Remington caliber. Since this cartridge is the sporting counterpart of the military 5.56mm load, and military brass can be easily reloaded, this is a welcome addition to the line. (It is also available with a 4x scope mounted.)

For those who want something different and can afford it, the 742F autoloader and the 760F pump rifle are available with gold inlay for $2400. This writer visited the engraving department of the Remington factory a few months ago, and the quality of the work is excellent. There is even a de luxe rimfire sporter available—The Sporter, 22 long rifle version of the Model 700 C Custom, at $425.00.

Remington, in recent years, has developed a great array of new sporting arms and cartridges. While this year's releases may not be quite as impressive, look at the variations offered in the current Remington line—191 different shotguns, 207 centerfire rifles, 21 rimfire rifles, 112 shotgun loads, 136 centerfire pistol and rifle loads, and 15 rimfire cartridges, all of which is a lot in anyone's language. LSS

The Remington 3200 O-U (upper) is now available in a 12 gauge magnum model with 30" barrels. Their Model 788 rifle (lower) can now be had in 223 Rem. cal.

Springfield Armory (Illinois)

This is not the Museum in Springfield, Massachusetts, but an Illinois firm that is building semi-automatic civilian versions of the M14. While many of the parts are government surplus or overruns from H&R, Thompson, etc., the receivers are of new manufacture. The 8-lb. block of 8620 alloy steel requires 89 machining operations, plus heat treating, before it is completed, and inspection includes "magnafluxing" to spot any fissures. Labled the M1A, the completed rifle is available in two basic models—the standard with issue sights and stock lists at $297.50, with a specially-bedded National Match barrel model costing $397.50, complete with match sights—both with new barrels. A special heavy weight premium grade 6-groove Douglas barrel will be available—possibly by the time you read this. The only caliber made now is the 308 NATO, but prototypes in 243 and the 358 Winchester cartridges are under development. (For those shooters wanting to build their own rifles, receivers are $147.50, and barreled receivers at $197.50.)

M1A stocks are walnut or birch, although a fiberglass model is available if desired, as is the M14E2 with extended pistol grip. A 20-round magazine comes with each rifle, but new 5-round and 10-round magazines are also available. The rifle, with empty 20-round magazine, weighs 9 pounds 10 ounces. Measuring 44⅜" over-all, the same rifle weighs 10 pounds 12 ounces when topped with a 4x Bushnell Scopechief IV Lite-Site in the S&K Quick-detachable mount. (The Leatherwood Bros. also have a mount that fits the M1A.)

When the author visited the Armory in mid-spring '75, rifles were being assembled, and orders shipped. (Orders have been shipped as far away as Australia and Hawaii, plus Alaska and many of the other states—through dealers, of course.) LSS

The Springfield Armory M1A with a Bushnell 4x Lite-Site installed using the S&K scope mount, which fits perfectly without any drilling or tapping.

Richland Arms Co.

Richland Arms Co.'s new caplock "Michigan Carbine" offers a refreshing change from its longer and heavier ancestors. It weighs less than 6 pounds and has a barrel of just 26". The ⅞" octagon barrel, made of ordnance steel, is precision rifled for a 45-caliber round ball. Over-all length is 41⅜".

The new carbine/short rifle has adjustable double-set triggers and the lockplate is color case-hardened. The fittings—buttplate, trigger guard, front and rear sights, fore-end tip and patchbox—are of polished brass. The stock, made from select American maple, is hand-finished. Price, about $144.

I'm afraid I can't call the Michigan Carbine the handsomest muzzleloader I've seen, but *de gustibus*..., I guess, and I think there's a need and a market for lighter, handier front feeders. J.T.A.

Greyhawk Arms

This firm is all new, but the rifle originally was on the market about 4 years ago for a brief time. Now even the rifle has been changed. Tabbed the Model 74 Rolling Block, the modern replica of an old design is available in 7 calibers, ranging from the 22 Hornet to the 44 Magnum. The receiver is a one-piece investment casting, with it and all internal parts made of 4130 alloy steel. Stocks and fore-ends are of American walnut with hand-rubbed oil finish. Sights consist of a post front and an adjustable folding rear, with a peep sight and scope mounting provisions available as extras. Total length of the Model 74 is 40", and the weight varies from 6¼ to 7 lbs. depending on the caliber. Price for the basic rifle is expected to increase by mid-year, but in early 1975 it was $129.00. A life-time guarantee goes to all original Model 74 purchasers, and this alone is worth a bit extra. LSS

High Standard

Nothing new at 1817 Dixwell Avenue except that, as with most other firms, prices have moved upward. According to the HS brass 1974 was the best year the firm has had since 1959; when the author visited the plant in July '74, things were going full blast. The Shadow shotgun line introduced last year is doing well. The steel frame Sentinel Mark IV 22 WRM revolver is just becoming available in quantity (early '75), and the 4" barrel version should be on sale by the time you read this. LSS

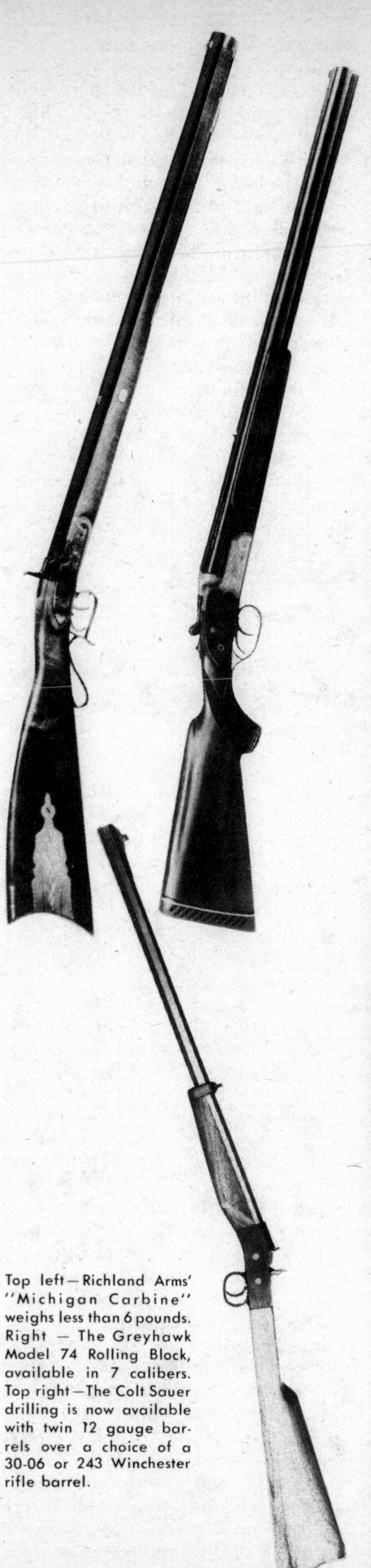

Top left—Richland Arms' "Michigan Carbine" weighs less than 6 pounds. Right — The Greyhawk Model 74 Rolling Block, available in 7 calibers. Top right—The Colt Sauer drilling is now available with twin 12 gauge barrels over a choice of a 30-06 or 243 Winchester rifle barrel.

Colt

A couple of new calibers in the sporting arms line were the only additions offered by the "Rampant Colt" firm. The 300 Weatherby Magnum is now available in the Colt Sauer rifle, and the 243 Winchester caliber is an alternate choice for the Sauer drilling (3-barrel gun), previously chambered only for the 30-06. Otherwise, the line remains the same as last year. LSS

El Monte International Shooting Vest

Because there seems to be a strong interest in international style shotgunning, Bob Allen has developed the handsome shooting vest shown here. The "El Monte International" features a full length glove-leather gun pad, pocket trim and western-style yoke. Extra large lower pockets offer ample room for back-up shots in trap and Skeet doubles. The body fabric is 65% Dacron polyester/35% combed cotton in a mid-weight, hard finished, gabardine. Rights and lefts in S-M-L-XL sizes are available in a dark, forest green color that helps to hide soil. Priced at $29.95, these new No. 102 vests are at your dealer, most likely, but if not write to Gun Club Sportswear, P.O. Box 477, Des Moines, IA 50302. J.T.A.

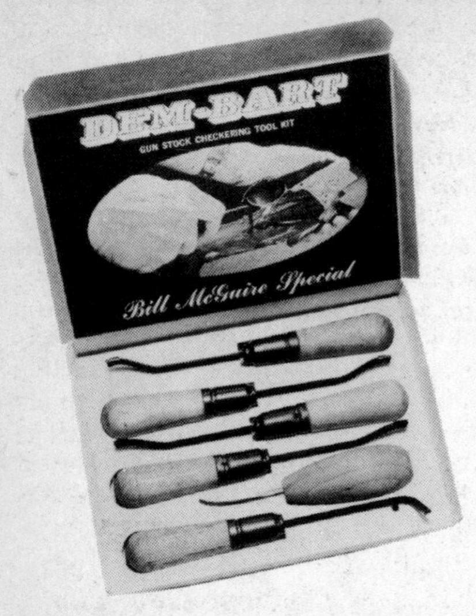

The Dem-Bart "Bill McGuire Special" kit contains everything the checkerer needs to dress up his favorite sporting arm.

A flick of the forward thumb and a push with the rear thumb release the Supreme lens covers, and it can be done while the rifle is being shouldered.

Accessories

Rifle and shotgun owners can often do much to dress up the functional and decorative properties of their favorite sporting arm by cleaning up the checkering. At its simpiest this consists of going over the original checkering, which often has been filled in with finish at the factory. Or, maybe the stock is plain and the owner would like to add a bit of checkering. Dem-Bart produces a "Starter's Special" kit of 3 complete tools for $11.50 and a 6-piece "Bill McGuire Special" kit for $17.50. Beginners would also do well to obtain a copy of *Fundamentals of Gunstock Checkering* by Bill McGuire, cost $2, before tackling their project.

Any shooter who has ever had a scope lens covered with rain or snow while hunting will appreciate a set of lens covers. The Butler Creek Corp. (Jackson Hole, WY) produces the Supreme lens covers which feature quick-opening hinged lids for the eyepiece and objective lens. Available for most riflescopes, the price is only $7.50.

Need a good paperweight for your gun room, and an informative one? *Jane's Infantry Weapons 1975* is a 7¾ lb. tome containing 860 pages on small arms, ammunition, area weapons, and some of the larger military weapons. Though the latter types are not exactly of interest to hunters and collectors the small arms and ammuition are, since military cartridges often later become widely used as commerical sporting cartridges, and military designs are adapted and modified for sporting use. (As an example, look at our own Krag, our Springfield, plus the German Mauser, the British Enfield, and a host of other lesser known designs.) Most arms are illustrated with one or more photographs—some of which are not high quality—and often there are sectionalized drawings illustrating the parts relationship during operation. Without counting, there must be at least 2000 such photographs and drawings. At the end of the book is a listing of the arms in service for 59 countries—Communist and non-Communist—plus a 12-page index. Printed on heavy-weight slick paper, *Jane's...* is a large—8¾"x12⅞"—text, and relatively expensive at $55. But it does contain information not readily available elsewhere on some of the arms currently in use, including some of the prototype arms currently being considered.

Now there's a trio of books that will answer most questions about cartridge or chamber dimensions. Published in German, and available from Frank Mittermeier, Inc., *Patronen u. Patronenlager-Massblätter* by R. Triebel consists of a 3-volume set of chamber and cartridge dimensional drawings for most of the world's more common and some not-so-common calibers. Vol. I consists of 90 drawings (one cartridge and chamber per page) of rimfire and centerfire handgun cartridges, plus shotgun shells, for $8.95. Vol. II holds 94 drawings of metric rimmed and rimless rifle cartridges ($9.95), and Vol. III has 120 drawings of American and British rimmed and rimless rifle cartridges, including such big boys as the 475 No. 2 Jeffery. The three books can also be bought together for $29.95. Looseleaf bound with vinyl covers, the line drawings are easily understood. The one minor drawback is that all dimensions are in the metric system, and any text in German, but a brief glossary of translated terms is included and the metric system is going to be "our thing" before long; just divide any linear metric measurements by 25.4 millimeters to get inches. (Better yet, get a Metric/English Converter—there are several on the market for about $1 or less.) As far as this writer is concerned *Patronen* is one of the handiest sets of material he has seen in a month of gunshows.

What's the most popular centerfire rifle cartridge? The 30-06, and that's the name of a new plastic bound source book by Lynn Godfrey, a registered engineer and big game hunter. Selling for $8.95, and containing some 426 pages, this manual covers the 30-06 in a way it has never been covered before. Reloading data is provided for a wide assortment of powders, and for the following bullet weights: 50, 77, 110, 150, 180, 220, 250, and 300 grain. Velocities are listed, and pressures in psi, via strain gauges, for almost every load. Absolute pressures and muzzle velocities are graphed, and oscilloscope photos show the pressure peaks. There are also photos of each powder used, on a grid background, plus comments on many of the loads relating to interpretation of the graphs. Available from Elk Mountain Shooters Supply, *The 30-06* contains more solid data on this one specific cartridge than any other loading manual.

Owners of rifles chambered for the 22-250 Remington cartridge can now fire 22 rimfire long rifle and WRM cartridges in their rifles, or even the 22 Hornet, via the use of one of the latest adapters available from Sport Specialties.

These are the latest adapters from Sport Specialties.

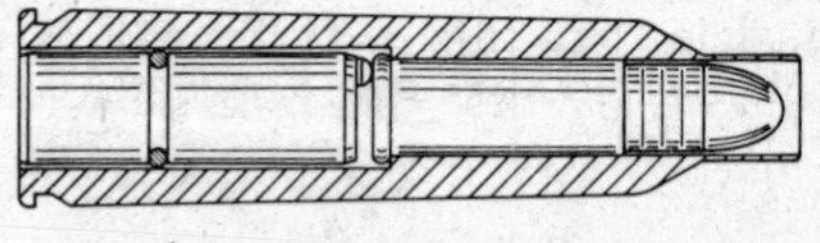

.22LR/.22-250

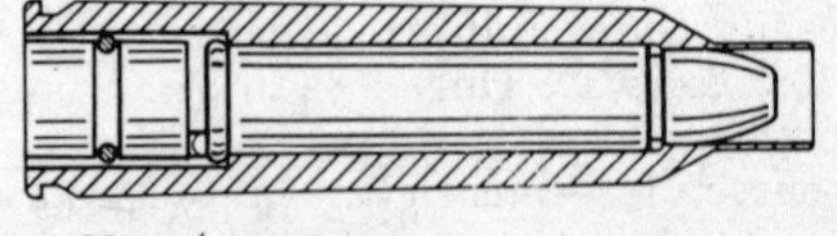

.22WMR/.22-250

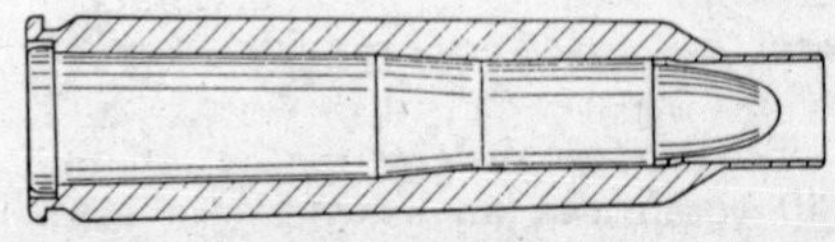

.22 HORNET/.22-250

Chubb Multigauge

Early in 1973 I inquired of several people—and sources—whether there existed somewhere a tool that could measure shotgun bore internal diameters full length. "Full length" was the operative term, for there are gauges that permit such measurement some lesser distances into the bore, whether from breech or muzzle. Proof houses abroad, in fact, have used such gauges, which measure up to 9 inches; the standard distance for proof house gauging to determine the true cylinder section diameter, that distance being behind the choke area or forward of the chamber-forcing cone area. None I talked to knew of the type of gauge I wanted.

Then, by coincidence, I learned about the tool about to be described. My interest in wanting a tool that would measure a bore full length had been raised by examination of a top grade Darne 12 bore double gun, one recently bought and which I described at some length in our 27th edition. Among the proof marks on this fine smoothbore were the figures 18.2, these numerals indicating the gun's cylinder diameter in millimeters. That diameter, 18.2, is equal to 0.7185-inch, and that indicates a pretty tight cylinder measurement. I wanted to determine if such was the case, and when the Chubb instrument arrived I did just that.

The Darne 12 has a cylinder diameter of .7185″-.7188″ in both barrels; the choke section is rather long, tapering from .719″ to .687″ in one barrel, to .700″ in the other, the decrease starting at 6¼″ from the muzzles. Thus the total construction in the right barrel is .719″ minus .700″, or 19 points net. The extreme muzzle end opens, slightly, to .703″. The left barrel is cut in the same fashion, the tightening starting 6¼″ from the muzzle, but this choke shows 32 points—.719″ less .687″. The muzzle of this barrel also opens a little, this one to .691″.

These chokes would, nominally, be considered improved-modified and modified, though the left barrel might easily throw full choke patterns, or 70% anyway. Only shooting at the pattern board will tell the tale, of course, for constriction as such is relatively meaningless. The length of the choke section, the length of the ultimate diameter (here quite short), and the choke-area quality—smooth or not-so-smooth—have their effect.

The Chubb Multigauge (12, 16 and 20) comprises an assembly of steel tubes, 22¾″ over-all from the knurled rotating handpiece to the end of the cap nut that finishes off the other end. Weight is about 21 ounces.

The working end (see photo) consists of a 3½″ long section, split nearly its full length into 3 fingers 120 degrees apart. Each finger, at its forward end, terminates in a raised section—roughly a truncated triangle, integral with the finger. These ends are about 3/32″ at their tips, the tips round and radiussed for smooth bore contact.

A 0.001″ dial indicator is mounted near the other end of the instrument. Half-thousandths can be easily read, too. Rotating the knurled handpiece propels the DI spindle, this motion driving a small upright which, in its turn, drives an interior rod rearward or forward. The interior rod serves to actuate or move the spring-steel fingers described, spreading them outward and into contact with the barrel interior.

The outward movement or splaying of the 3 finger ends is achieved thus: each finger moves, in or out, as a triangular piece of steel, rather like a 3-sided pyramid, is pushed or pulled by the DI spindle. The corners or edges of the steel triangle, nicely radiussed, ride in the round opening formed by the inside shape of the 3 finger ends.

Three steel rings, mounted in a wood retaining block, are furnished, these letting the Chubb gauge be rezeroed when and if necessary. These steel rings, carefully made to close tolerances, measure 0.729″, 0.665″ and 0.615″, or 12, 16 and 20 gauge respectively. To check for error, the measuring tips of the Chubb tool are placed in the chosen gauge ring and a measurement made. If a discrepancy is revealed, the DI is readily readjusted to read 0.729″ or whatever.

Once the Chubb tool is known to be adjusted, bore dimensions can be quickly and accurately made. The working end of the instrument is inserted into the breech end or muzzle, located lengthwise as desired, and rotation of the knurled knob clearly shows the bore or choke diameter(s) on the DI.

The Chubb Multigauge could be made more useful, I think, if the cylindrical sections, at least, were marked off in inches or centimeters. As it is, one can only guess at the distance from the muzzle or breech of the bore being measured, unless a rule is applied to the tube section not inside the shotgun barrel. To aid this ability, I obtained a length of calibrated plastic rule and pasted it onto the steel tube, making allowance for the 3½-inch length of the steel-finger section.

The Chubb Multigauge came in sturdy wood case, the all-steel tool well-protected and locked in when the cover is closed. 12, 16 and 20 bores, to 30″ long, can be accurately measured. Bob Steindler examines the tool.

The 3 tip ends that make bore contact are not quite as smooth as I'd prefer to see them. Light tool marks can be seen in them, these travelling circumferentially. A light stoning-polishing of these tips—which I did not attempt—would smooth them for improved metal-to-metal contact inside the barrel. A minor point, to be sure, and perhaps the change would be a more cosmetic one than anything else.

This is a well-made precision tool, doing just the job it claims to do. Who needs it or may want it? Well, not the average shotgunner certainly, but I think those gunsmiths working on shotgun barrels would find it highly useful, particularly where chokes are being recut or altered. Gun and shotshell makers? Yes, as an auxiliary gauge to supplement the gauges already used in production, such as the air types made by Sheffield. Ballistics labs—such as H. P. White—and police firearms labs ought to find the Chubb Multigauge quite useful.

Cost of the Chubb Multigauge, including a sturdy wood case, dial indicator, 3 test gauges and an Allen wrench, is $175. J.T.A.

The Editor's New Gun

by ROGER BARLOW

An apt background for the Castore double is this drawing of a Rolls Royce Silver Ghost tourer circa 1910, one of many made by Lewis Brown for Jose Ortega y Gasset's book, *Meditations on Hunting*.

No, not a shooters' version of the Emperor's New Clothes, but a close look at, and a field test report on, the Armi Famars Castore hammer gun—*con amore e espressione.*

IT ISN'T VERY often that one gets an assignment to road test a new 12 gauge double barreled shotgun having running boards, a real honest-to-God radiator and the two spare wire wheels carried forthrightly on side mounts!

The writer feels doubly honored, for not only is the unusual shotgun in question the recent acquisition of the hospitalized Editor himself, but it is, indeed, very much like being invited to drive a spanking new replica of a fine 1912 English touring car, complete with wicker picnic hampers—all very much like the Rolls-Royce Silver Ghost in which King George V might have ridden on his way to a weekend shooting party.

This comparison between the Editor's new shotgun and a historic motor car might legitimately be carried a bit further, for this gun is also very much like those with which George V did his shooting.

Although the Silver Ghost touring car,* in which the Royal Person traveled on his way to shoot partridges or pheasants, may have been the latest in automotive design of that day, the royal shotguns were unusual in *not* being the newest examples of firearms design, such as the hammerless ejector guns already so popular with other shooting men, aristocrats as well as less exalted sportsmen.

Because King George V apparently liked the feel of a hammer beneath the royal thumb, as well as preferring the appearance of the traditional gun with hammers, he was loth to give them up in favor of the new hammerless ejector guns which, admittedly, were more suitable for use when driven birds were streaming past overhead; largely because they were easier and faster to reload.

The solution was, of course, a simple and logical one—a hammer gun with ejectors! In 1894 James Purdey built a pair of such guns for Earl de Grey, Marquess of Ripon, widely acknowledged as the greatest game

Although the Castore came into Barlow's hands after the close of the hunting season in Virginia, and with only a couple of days of the preserve season left, enough experience was gained to convince him of this gun's effectiveness in the field. He also makes the point that a gun like this provides pleasure and satisfaction by its beauty and workmanship even when there is no game to be shot.

*Daimlers were the ceremonial cars of the English royal family, but various members owned and used Rolls-Royce cars for less formal occasions.

shot of that period. This pair of guns was based upon the older back-action locks, the type in use since the 1860s, and were *not* self-cocking. Nor were the hammer guns Purdeys made for George V self-cocking, although I have heard of some such guns having been made in England around the turn of the century. Actually Purdeys made a number of ejector hammer guns for King George right up to 1930, so perhaps some of these had the more modern bar-action locks.

The Armi Famars Castore

In any event, the Editor's new/old gun *is* a self-cocking, ejector hammer gun—the Brescian-made Armi Famars' Castore, almost as unique in this day as would be a genuine modern replica of a Silver Ghost or a 1925 Locomobile.

(Famars guns are named for certain stars and planets—the Castore for one of two Gemini stars, the other star being Pollux.)

Whenever I encounter a restored 1932 Chrysler Imperial, a 540K Mercedes, a Lincoln of the late 1920s or most any car of quality in the classic configuration, they make the vehicles of today—with their slab sides, look-alike grilles and disc wheels—appear to be revolting, stamped-out-of-tin boxes and almost characterless. Just what the hell have we received in return for giving up that classic elegance of the great motor cars of the 20s and early 30s? What do we have now that is supposed to be more pleasing to the eye or more functional than those sweeping fenders, the architectural dignity of those honest radiators and the airy grace of large wire wheels?

It wasn't engineering advances that dictated the changes, for those cars all had 4-wheel brakes while some had V8, V12 or V16 engines and one or two had already adopted independent front suspension. Every one of them could have accepted power steering, automatic transmission and air conditioning with little if any difficulty.

And don't tell me people don't appreciate these cars, for a lean L29 Cord attracts more attention and admiration on the street than does an overblown Eldorado. Each year literally millions of Americans pay good money just to look at classic cars in collections all over the country.

The Classic Concept

Well, just as there are lovers of the classic car, so are there devotees of the *classic* firearm, enthusiasts ready and willing to put their money where their hearts are. When Bill Ruger, who appreciates cars of this character as well as classic guns, went way out on a commercial limb by putting a modern but classic-styled version of the Victorian-era single shot rifle into production the industry shook its collective head and thought he was off his rocker. That the Farquharson-like Ruger No. 1 and No. 3 rifles are still selling in ever increasing numbers is some proof of the modern shooter's appreciation for the truly great products of the past. I'm sure I needn't dwell on the classic elegance of Ruger's Model 77 bolt rifle.

In the shotgun field there is the Italian firm of Armi Famars, and long may they prosper, for this is a relatively small firm enterprising enough to build the shotgun equivalent of a fine classic car, one incorporating many worthwhile modern engineering developments and materials.

This is the truly elegant Castore double which John Amber, also a classic car admirer, has entrusted me to field test. In case you haven't already guessed it I, too, would take more pride in owning a Lancia Dilambda or Stutz Blackhawk than a fat modern luxury sedan—and I would rather hunt with this gun than any ultra modern gas-operated autoloader.

There are, of course, other double barreled hammer guns being made today in Spain, Belgium, the USSR, Brazil and Italy but these are mainly simple and inexpensive "work" guns.

Just as running boards, fenders and a radiator define the outline of the classic motor car, so do the graceful external hammers and the decorative, fluid lines of the fences surrounding the firing pins define the external form of the fine 19th century shotgun.

What makes the Armi Famars hammer guns so intriguing is that this highly creative Italian gunmaker—Mario Abbiatico—chose *not* to make a simple copy of the Victorian hammer gun, good as it was, but to build with 20th century technology a double in the classic hammer gun configuration, and to do so with that special Italian skill and artistry with metal which has dazzled the world from the time of Cellini to Pinin Farina.

Just examine the close-up views of the standing breech and fences of the Castore—these flowing lines would do credit to the modern sculptor, Brancusi! By comparison, I'm afraid the hammers may seem a bit stodgy and . . . well, rather un-Italian and not quite the equal of those truly elegant fences. However, it may well be that the traditional form of those hammers actually serves to *set off* the form of the fences in a way that more sweeping hammers might not do. One would have to see a direct comparison of the different hammers on the gun to be certain.

A most intriguing aspect of the Famars Castore hammer gun are the unusual oval fences, their polished surfaces contrasting effectively with the scroll engraving. The crown on the top lever is gold as are the lines at the breech and muzzle end of the barrels. The polished lockplates are also outlined in gold.

Because this is a gun of today in the mode of the 19th century, it has modern steel barrels proved for today's nitro loads. However, these barrels are not blued in the conventional way but are *browned!* This soft, warm and gentle coloration of the barrel metal so perfectly complements and enhances the cool purity of the polished steel of the fences and lockplates that one can only wonder how and why we shooters of today have deluded ourselves into believing that a blued barrel and action is the only way to go.

Handling and examining this gun

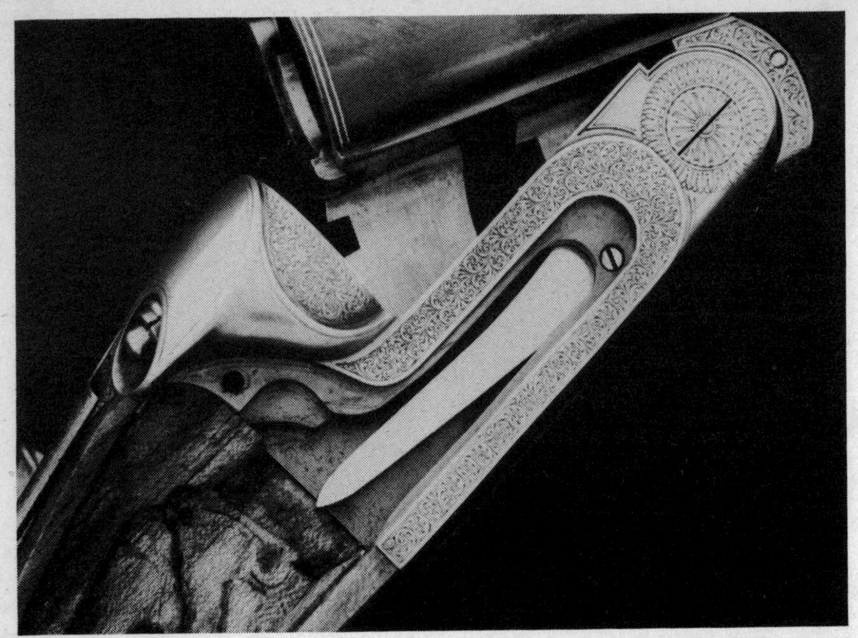

The hammers of the Castore are not cocked by rods moving in a fore-and-aft direction but by pivoted lifters raising the extensions on the tumblers as the gun is opened. The cocking of both locks and ejectors requires appreciable effort in the opening of the gun, although with continued use one becomes much less conscious of this. Cocking the hammers manually reduces the opening load.

makes it easy to understand why many Victorian shotgunners were reluctant to give up their Damascus-barreled guns, the beauty of which—and the lovely figures—was brought out by browning, and the actions color case-hardened in warm tones with only touches of blue.

Indeed, some gentlemen of means in the 1890s when they did order new guns of the hammerless type, still insisted upon having them made with high grade Damascus barrels. Many such guns were made well into the 1920s. These shooters often maintained they preferred Damascus because the new fluid steel barrels "rang" to a discomforting degree when fired, sometimes producing headaches. However, I suspect they simply thought that a browned, well-figured Damascus barrel was far more beautiful, but were ashamed to admit to such strong esthetic feelings!

Be that as it may, even though those browned steel barrels of the Castore lack a Damascus figure, they are a welcome surprise and a delight and will probably prove a revelation to those seeing such barrels for the first time.

Shooting and Handling

But how does this Italian beauty handle and shoot? That is also what ye disabled Editor mainly wanted to know. When I got it home there was a week of winds far too strong to permit me to hang paper and shoot patterns, so I went out and broke 30 straight clay targets—enough to suggest that perhaps I should adopt the Editor's ideas on stock dimensions as my own! While one can adapt to shoot almost any gun with reasonable success, it is always gratifying to encounter a new gun that comes up and aligns to break targets or drop birds seemingly without conscious effort on the part of the shooter. That the Famars Castore did this for me was something of a surprise because it is choked modified and full. I freely admit to shooting more effectively with a gun bored improved cylinder and modified or, better yet, cylinder and IC for quail and grouse as I have to take them at 15-30 yards.

Patterns, when finally shot, were as the barrel markings indicated as well as being commendably even and regular with 4 different brands and loads, as you can see by some of them illustrating this report. They also show that this gun was throwing a pattern too dense for my taste when using 1⅛ ounces of 7½s with a plastic wad column. Therefore, I also tired some light Eley loads of ⅞-oz. 7s and Crudgington 1-oz. 6s (these being 7½

The escutcheon for the Editor's initials is part of the handsome gold Famars trademark. The very fine checkering reminds one of what an abomination is the pressed-in variety.

The breech face of the Famars Castore is clean and uncluttered, no doll's head, crossbolts or other such locking elements obtruding. Lockup is handled by double underlugs.

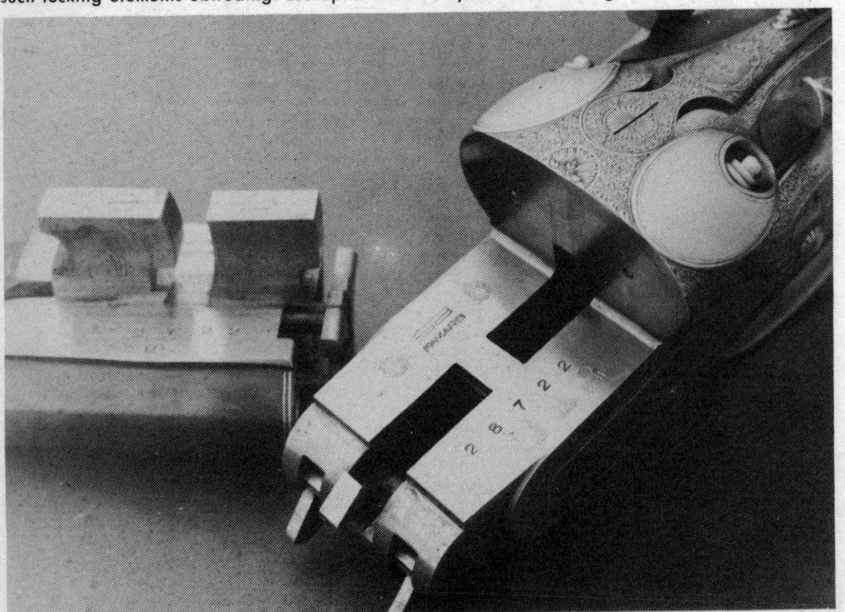

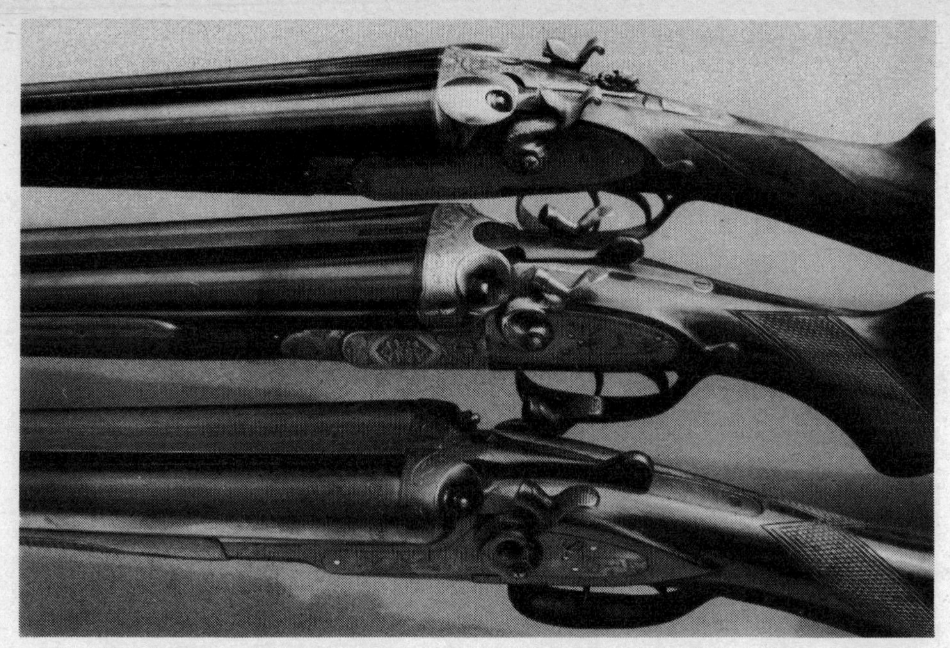

At the bottom is a $40 simple work gun with hammers, as made in the Soviet Union and widely used by their professional hunters. Next is the best of the Bernardelli hammer guns, which is very well done and sells for about $400; at the top, where it rightfully belongs, is the Famars Castore with a current price tag of around $3500. But note that even the cheapest of these guns has a certain elegance bestowed by the shape of the fences.

and 7 size shot) these being loaded in paper hulls using old fashioned felt and card wads with *no* shot cup. You can see by the photos of these patterns that the very light loads are far less likely to ruin grouse or pheasants for the table, while still having adequate pattern density to beyond 40 yards. Indeed, if I were to hunt with this gun, choked as it is, I would usually carry a load of FN *cube* shot in the full-choked left barrel and use that one first on 20-30 yard birds, reserving the modified right barrel for shots at around 30-40 yards. The double triggers on the Castore give me that instant choice of barrels not possible with a single trigger and barrel-selector button.

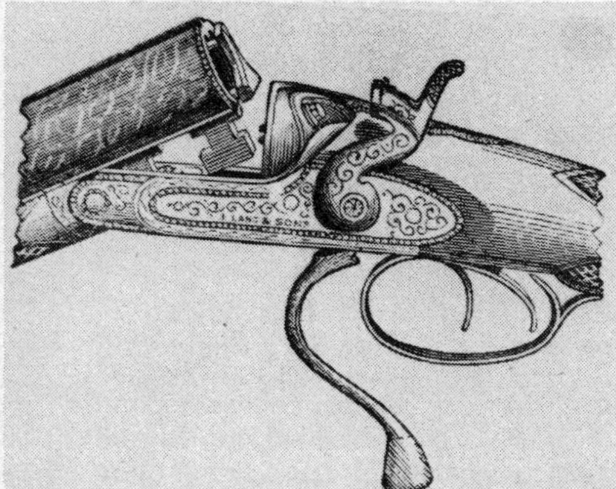

Self-cocking hammer guns came into being in the mid-1870s. The Joseph Lang (above) and the Woodward (not illus.) were two of the best of these lever-cockers. Holland & Holland's approach was both simple and practical but not at all attractive with that cocking-rod poking up through a hole in the action!

So this gun, as it is now choked, throws patterns far too dense for it to be ideally suited for hunting eastern upland game. But out West the Editor can let the pheasants, sharptail grouse and sage hens get out to 30 yards or so before shooting.

The Castore feels only slightly lighter than the just-over 7 pounds the scales say it weighs, but I would prefer it to weigh about a half-pound or so less if I am to carry it for several hours in the field after quail or grouse. I wonder if Famars can build these guns to 6¼ or 6½ pounds if asked to do so? The balance is somewhat more forward than, say, a Franchi Falconet or a Darne, but 3-3¼ pounds of its weight on the left hand is appreciably less than any of the gas-operated autoloaders and even many other 12 gauge doubles.

The Traditions of Hunting

Hunting is a sport rooted deep in tradition. We enjoy it most, I feel, when we are conscious of a link with the past—hunting where our father or grandfather hunted; in country where Daniel Boone, Lewis and Clark, George Washington or Teddy Roosevelt hunted. Perhaps, above all, hunting with guns themselves having roots in the past. Pumps, autoloaders and, yes, sleek modern over-under doubles may kill birds like crazy but they offer only the most tenuous link with our rich heritage of the previous 200 years. Unfortunately, few of us can hope to go afield with a flintlock of the 1790s, an 1845 pinfire or even a breech-loading hammer double of the 1870s. In any event, many shooters would today object to the use of black powder even if such old guns were readily available.

This is why the *modern* hammer gun, plain or fancy, has so much to offer the perceptive shooting man—for with its ability to handle modern nitro shells there is no longer a problem with smoke or of messy cleaning after every use, despite its basic configuration and mechanical design being, in many instances, identical with the guns of the second half of the 19th century, that Golden Age of the shotgun.

Thus a gun like the Famars Castore, with its unique blend of traditional form with the convenience of automatic ejectors and self-cocking locks, gives us, it strikes me, the very best of both shooting worlds—ours of today and that of a century ago. ●

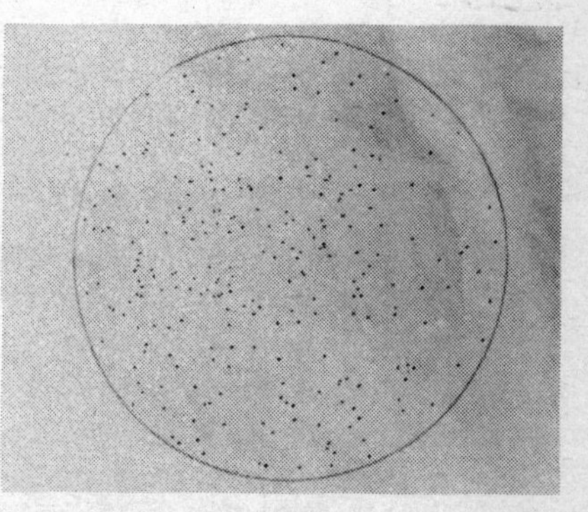

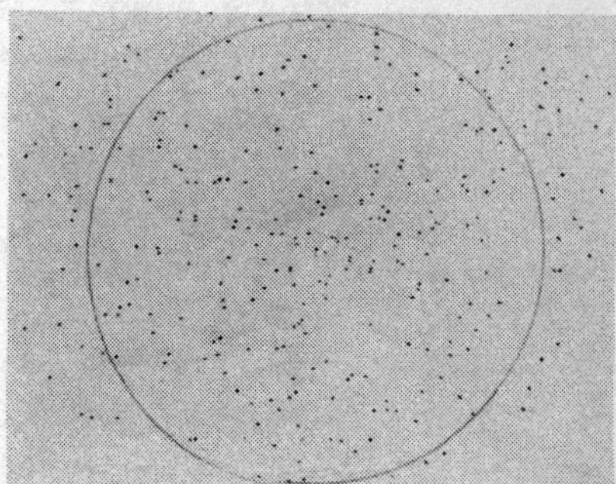

40 yard patterns (left barrel above) with factory 1⅛-oz. loads of 7½s (one-piece plastic wads) gave excellent regularity but would have put a bit too many pellets into grouse or pheasants even at that range, and certainly so at the more normal 30-35 yards maximum range these birds are killed. Lighter loads or larger shot would do less damage yet score clean kills. (Right barrel below.)

Buffered Shot Loads

The Ultimate Step

They're not easy to put together, and there is a dearth of factory data available on their assembly, but buffered shot loads offer the skybuster the last word in ultra long range performance. Field-tested load data, extensive in scope, are shown here for the first time.

by WALLACE LABISKY

SINCE SHOTGUNNING'S infancy shooters have sought ways to give the smoothbore a few additional yards of effective range. Most major developments in the shotshell field in recent times have been in this direction.

The modern, fold-crimp closure contributes to better performance by eliminating top-wad interference at that crucial point when the pattern is taking form. Plastic wads increase pattern efficiency through better gas sealing and, in some forms, by protecting the shot charge against pellet-damaging bore scrub. Slower-burning propellant powders permit heavier shot charges at acceptable velocities without running chamber pressure to a level that threatens both the gun and personal safety.

All of these avenues are wide open to the handloader, if he desires to travel in the direction of improved effectiveness at long range, and many do. Yet the quest for even better load performance continues, particularly among those waterfowlers who do a great deal of long-range pass shooting. If the gun/load combination does a crisp job at, say, 60 yards, the chap behind it often pines for similar performance out at 70 yards.

What appears to be the last remaining step in load improvement is that

A pair of blue geese that were dumped from a cloud-dusting flock during Labisky's early work with buffered shot loads. The gun is a Richland Arms M-711 side-by-side 10-ga. Magnum.

This cut-away view of W-W's XX Magnum load (compression-formed plastic shell) shows how granulated polyethylene is mixed with the shot charge to eliminate pellet deformation caused by jamming when the charge first begins to move.

of using a buffering agent distributed throughout the entire shot charge. By filling the pellet interstices with a non-combustible material of fine granulation, each of the individual pellets is cushioned to some degree. As such, they cannot jam against one another quite so violently during the initial accelerating thrust of the expanding powder gases. This elimination of severe jamming means fewer deformed pellets, or at least deformation to a much lesser degree. Leaving the muzzle, the flight of the undeformed pellet is much more true than that of the misshapen one; the end result is an appreciably tighter pattern that registers the required density at increased range.

Incidentally, it is believed that the jamming action, occurring as the inertia of the resting shot charge is overcome, causes far more pellet damage than does bore scrub. In passing through the barrel, only the outer layer of pellets are subject to bore abrasion. But on the violent inertia setback at least 50% of the charge (the lower portion, of course) takes a pretty rough beating.

Another benefit that is thought to accrue through the use of a buffering agent is that it makes the shot charge more responsive to the choke, particularly with pellets of No. 4 size and larger.

The idea of mixing in a buffering agent with the shot charge is not new. Old literature on shotgunning informs us that back in the middle 1800s (and possibly earlier) the British used bonemeal to tighten the patterns tossed by their cylinder-bored guns. It remained, however, for Winchester-Western to revive this old practice, and to do so with a modern twist, when the Mark 5 Super Buckshot loads were introduced in 1963.

It is my understanding that W-W experimented with a number of different materials, the final nod going to granulated polyethylene as a bedding material for the "blue whistlers." Before this most shotguns performed pretty sadly with buckshot, regardless of how they were choked. But now, with this new method of loading, most any full-choke 12-ga. barrel will place the entire charge of 0B or 00B in a 30" circle at 40 yards. The smaller sizes of buckshot generally will not stay in such a tight cluster, patterning more on the order of about 85%.

It wasn't long before Remington adopted this same practice of bedding buckshot in granulated polyethylene. More recently, Smith & Wesson and Browning have followed suit.

But W-W took the matter one step farther in 1968, bringing out a 1½-oz. 12-ga. load in the 2¾" shell, designated at first as the HD (High Density) Magnum, but known today as the XX Magnum (see GUN DIGEST, 25th ed.) Like the buckshot loads, the shot charge (Nos. 2 and 4 only) is buffered with plastic "sawdust," and patterns running as high as 90% are not unusual from tightly choked barrels. Many shooters are not aware of this, but the XX Magnum loading moves the standard 12-ga. gun up into the 3" magnum class. Some standard guns, in fact, will actually surpass typical 1⅝-oz. performance levels.

Early Trials

My experience with buffered loads on waterfowl preceded the appearance of W-W's XX magnum loading by some two years. I had then recently acquired a 10-ga. magnum but was thoroughly dissatisfied with its pattern performance with factory loads. My handloads with a plastic over-powder (O/P) wad and a plastic sleeve around the shot charge did markedly better than the factory fodder, and the use of Lubaloy shot sweetened things a bit more. But I decided that if my Big Ten was going to earn its keep as a specialized gun for pass shooting, it would have to deliver really outstanding patterns. Having had limited experience using Cream-of-Wheat as a buffer material in buckshot loads, I gave it a trial with 2⅛ ozs. of 2s, and the pattern percentage jumped dramatically to a 77% average. This was in contrast to a 58% level with factory ammo.

About this time Robert W. (Bob) Evans, who headed Alcan's ballistic research department (now S&W Ammunition Co.) told me he had been getting patterns running around 90% using a grade of granulated polyethylene known commercially as E2010-46AA and manufactured by Eastman Chemical Products, Inc. (Kingsport, Tenn.). Bob sent me a supply for trial and I found it quite similar in granulation and density to the material used in the W-W buckshot loads, but not identical.

At any rate, using 30 to 32 grs. of E2010-46AA with 2 and 2⅛-oz. shot charges did a terrific job. With chilled 2s, the right barrel of my Richland Arms M-711 double gun printed an 84% average at 40 yards (a 26% increase over factory loads), while the left barrel digested the same charge of No. 1 shot for better than a 90% average.

As for the details of loading, I used new Alcan 3½" paper-tube shells, the 220 Max-Fire primer, and 52 grs. AL-8 behind the 2⅛-oz. payload. Wadding consisted of a PGS topped with a ⅜" Feltan-Bluestreak filler and the Alcan Kwik-Sert plastic shot sleeve. A one-inch square of thin paper was used over the shot charge to help retain the granulated polyethylene, and the crimp was a 6-point fold.

Later, I shipped 5 rounds to the Alcan lab for a check on the ballistics. Average velocity was 1,308 fps (feet per second) with a maximum variation of only 36 fps. The chamber pressure leveled off at 11,400 lup (lead units of pressure). As such, the load is slightly on the *hot* side, but certainly not hazardous if used in strongly-built guns of fairly recent manufacture.

For the past couple of years I have been using the Alcan Type CM plastic shell for this same load, all details being the same as outlined above except that two fillers of ¼" thickness are used in place of the single ⅜" wad. The wadding change is the result of thinner tube walls which increases case capacity, and I suspect that the extra wadding eases the pressure by a small amount. Using 2⅛ ozs. of Lubaloy 2s, this load in the plastic shell averages nearly 92% from a Richland M-810 over-under, with an extreme variation of only 5 pellets for a 5-shot string. When a goose doesn't crumple, I can't blame load performance; it's my own proficiency at fault.

My initial work with buffering agents in 10-ga. magnum handloads was reported in some detail in *Handloader's Digest,* 4th ed. We didn't want to get readers all fired up, only to have them run into a stone wall, so before writing that article I made some inquiries regarding availability of the E2010-46AA material. A sales representative of Eastman Chemical assured me that company would be happy to sell the material in any quantity, large or small. That, indeed, was good news, and the price I was then quoted of less than 50c per pound made it all the more attractive, as a pound of this plastic "sawdust" goes a long, long way. At 30 grs. a throw, for example, a pound is enough to handle nearly 250 rounds. And considering that the expenditure of these specialized loads would be relatively limited, a 5-pound supply would keep the average handloader going for years.

Eastman Renigs

After that article appeared Eastman Chemical was nearly flooded with orders for the E2010-46AA material. But as far as I know, not one of these many orders was filled, my own included. To this day, the company's policy to not release the material for handloading purposes remains firm. The whole affair can be written off as a classic example of the right hand not knowing what the left hand is doing.

The explanation offered by the home office to editor John Amber and yours truly was that the company did not wish to become legally liable for personal injury or gun damage that could conceivably result through the use of the product in an area of application for which it was not originally designed. E2010-46AA, by the way, was designed for certain industrial applications, such as carpet backing.

What Eastman Chemical was saying, in effect, was that there had been no laboratory tests with this product to determine the possible hazards connected with its use in shotshells. In other words, the ballistical factor, or the effect of the material on chamber pressure, was very much an unknown in handloading circles. Even today the situation remains pretty much the same. In fact, I'll wager a few canisters of powder that the ballistic tables which accompany these remarks are the first ever to appear in the firearms press.

Surely the big ammo companies could provide some guidelines in the use of buffering agents, but this is not likely to happen unless the material they themselves are using is released to handloaders. At the moment, there is precious little promise of that. A recent rumor had it that W-W intended to turn loose the granulated polyethylene used in the XX Magnum load. But in following up on this I was informed that "...we most definitely will not be offering it as a handloading component."

Other Materials

Herter's, Inc. (Mitchell, S. Dak. 57301) sells a material designated as GP1 and which is described in the firm's catalog as "perfectly ground plastic" for use with either buckshot or birdshot. I obtained a supply of GP1 only to find that no loading data is supplied with the material. So again, the handloader is strictly on his own.

This GP1 material is quite dissimilar to Eastman Chemical's E2010-46AA and to the material used by W-W, Remington and S&W. It is not granulated polyethylene at all, but an expandable polystyrene used by the plastics industry for making styrofoam products. Physically, GP1 is a somewhat coarse, globular type material with a considerable variation in granule diameter. As such it does not lend itself to optimum occupation of the pellet interstice area. This is true even with coarse shot such as 2s and BBs. However, I would speculate that for use with buckshot the Herter material should work out very well.

There are, of course, other materials that will do a respectable job of buffering the shot charge, and with no problem of availability. As I've already mentioned, Cream-of-Wheat works quite well. So does ordinary household flour. Even some of the laundry detergents probably could be pressed into service, though a tongue-in-cheek observation would be to avoid these for rainy-day use. Interestingly, a West Coast handloader told me he'd used powdered oatmeal with excellent results, some 40-yard patterns running as high as 97% with 1¼ ozs. No. 4 shot.

So that I could explore this matter of buffering agents more fully, S&W graciously supplied me with a couple

Putting the shot-buffered handload together requires extra time and effort, but this method of loading pays handsome dividends in the form of high-density patterns for greater effective range.

BALLISTICS TABLE I

12-gauge 2¾" shell/1⅛ ozs. No. 4 shot

Case & Primer	Powder Charge/grs.	Wad Column	Average Velocity fps	Average Pressure lup	Maximum Pressure lup
W-W UPLAND Plastic WW209	HS-5 28.0	White ARRO-WAD + 15 grs. E2010-95DA gran. poly.	1,300	9,366	9,700
W-W UPLAND Plastic WW209	HS-5 28.0	White ARRO-WAD + 30 grs. Cream-of-Wheat	1,326	10,333	10,800
W-W UPLAND Plastic WW209	HS-5 28.0	White ARRO-WAD + 25 grs. household flour	1,295	9,333	9,900

Comments: Ballistic tests courtesy Hodgdon Powder Company, Inc. Velocities and chamber pressures listed represent a 3-shot average fired from a 30" full-choke test barrel. Velocities are instrumental at 75 inches from the muzzle. Powder, shot and buffer material weighed for all loads. Wad seating pressure 30 pounds; crimps, 6-point fold.

BALLISTICS TABLE II

12-gauge 2¾" shell/1¼ ozs. No. 4 shot

Case & Primer	Powder Charge/grs.	Wad Column	Average Velocity fps	Average Pressure lup	Maximum Pressure lup
Fed. FIELD Plastic 220 Max-Fire	AL-5/31.0	A-W + 5/16" FBS + Fed. 12SC114 shot cup	1,187	8,600	9,000
Fed. FIELD Plastic 220 Max-Fire	AL-5/31.0	A-W + 5/16" FBS + Fed. 12SC114 shot cup + 17.0 grs. E2010-46AA gran. poly.	1,185	9,500	9,800
Fed. FIELD Plastic 220 Max-Fire	AL-5/29.0	A-W + 5/16" FBS + Fed. 12SC114 shot cup + 17.0 grs. E2010-46AA gran. poly.	1,117	8,600	8,800
Fed. FIELD Plastic 220 Max-Fire	AL-7/32.0	A-W + ¼" FBS + 1" plastic sleeve + 20.0 grs. Herter's GP-1	1,283	11,600	12,300
Fed. CHAMPION II Fed. 209	HS-6/32.0	Power Piston W29926 + 15.0 grs. E2010-95DA gran. poly.	1,354	11,300	11,900
Fed. CHAMPION II Fed. 209	HS-6/32.0	Power Piston W29926 + 20.0 grs. S&W gran. poly.	1,396	13,500+	13,500+
Fed. CHAMPION II Fed. 209	HS-6/32.0	Power Piston W29926 + 35.0 grs. Cream-of-Wheat	1,390	13,500+	13,500+

Comments: Ballistic tests for Alcan powder loads courtesy S&W Ammunition Company; for Hodgdon powder loads courtesy Hodgdon Powder Company, Inc. Velocities and chamber pressures listed represent averages fired from a 30" full-choke test barrel. Velocities shown for the loads with Alcan powders (based on 5 shots) are instrumental at 15 feet from the muzzle; for the Hodgdon powders (based on 3 shots), at 75 inches. Powder, shot and buffer material weighed for all loads. In all instances, the Federal shot cup was modified to regulate crimp space by trimming off the base flange and perforating the floor with a .410 wad punch. A-W = Alcan Air-Wedge over-powder wad. FBS = Alcan Feltan-Bluestreak fiber filler wad.

BALLISTICS TABLE III

12-gauge 2¾" shell/1⅜ ozs. No. 4 shot

Case & Primer	Powder Charge/grs.	Wad Column	Average Velocity fps	Average Pressure lup	Maximum Pressure lup
Fed. CHAMPION II WW209	HS-6/31.0	W-W Universal O/P cup + ¼" W-W fiber + 1" plastic sleeve + 22.0 grs. S&W gran. poly.	1,321	13,500+	13,500+
Fed. CHAMPION II WW209	HS-6/31.0	W-W Universal O/P cup + ⅜" W-W fiber + 22.0 grs. S&W gran. poly.	1,276	10,500	10,900

Comments: Ballistic tests courtesy Hodgdon Powder Company, Inc. Velocities and chamber pressures given represent a 3-shot average fired from a 30" full-choke test barrel. Velocities instrumental at 75 inches from the muzzle. Powder, shot and buffer material weighed for all loads. Wad seating pressure 40 pounds; crimps, 8-point fold.

of pounds of the very same granulated polyethylene used in their excellent buckshot loads. (Wouldn't it be a great day in the morning if this material were added to the Alcan line of shotshell components? Think about it, S&W!)

The granulation and density of the S&W poly is such that it will easily "settle in" with shot of No. 4 size and larger. With a shot scoop set on the ⅞-oz. mark, dipped full and struck off level, I came up with a weight of roughly 29.5 grs.

The weight-to-volume picture for Eastman Chemical's E2010-46AA is almost identical at 29.3 grs. The granulation, however, is slightly finer than the S&W poly—about on the order of table salt. Another Tenite polyethylene powder designated as E2010-95DA (from the same company) is slightly more coarse, weighs out less at 20 grs., but being more fluffy it does not settle in quite as readily. While it has the advantage of adding less weight to the ejecta, it doesn't seem to be as effective as E2010-46AA in tightening patterns.

Tide, a laundry detergent, appears to be of useful granulation, and with the ⅞-oz. scoop setting it runs 21.5 grs.—about the same as E2010-95DA.

For the same bulk, Herter's GP1 averages 40.2 grs., making it substantially heavier than the S&W poly. The same is true of Cream-of-Wheat, which runs a fraction over 52 grs.

In contrast, ordinary household flour runs 30.5 grs. It completely fills every last nook and cranny of the pellet interstices, and it seems to do a very creditable job of increasing pattern density. But it does have a disadvantage when used in conjunction with plastic shot-protector wads. Because of its extremely fine granulation, flour will work through the slits in the shot cup and will be over-ridden by the wad. This over-riding action, plus high-temperature powder gases, tends to "bake" the flour to the heat-roughened interior walls of plastic shells. The result is a crusty and tenacious accumulation that has to be brushed out before the hull can be loaded again.

Buffer Selections

Writing on this method of loading in another publication, a colleague stated that a buffering agent of somewhat coarse granulation which does not completely fill the pellet interstices appears to be a better bet than a material of fine granulation. With this, I cannot agree. My own experience dictates that a granulation which fills every void produces far and away the better results in terms of high-count patterns. Also, the coarse material has the distinct disadvantage of adding more bulk to the shot charge and this will demand, in turn, that the wad column be slightly reduced in length. And a reduction in the wadding almost always results in an increase in chamber pressure.

The amount of buffering material needed per individual load will be governed not only by the weight of the shot charge, but also by the size of the shot pellets. A heavy shot charge will call for more material than a light one; and for a given weight of shot, the larger shot pellets will swallow up more material than smaller sized pellets. By referring to the accompanying ballistic tables, the reader will get an idea of the amounts required with the various materials mentioned above.

While it is the lower half of the shot column that derives the greatest benefit from a buffering agent, it is important that enough material be used to accommodate the entire shot charge. If not, the material will have a tendency to shift about during normal shell handling. It will then become thinly distributed or, worse yet, become concentrated near the crimp end of the shell. This, plus any appreciable variation in the amount used for a given load, will result in pattern irregularity. Which is to say that in a series of five, 10 or more shots, we will end up with wide and unwanted fluctuations in both pattern percentage and pellet distribution. As in any phase of handloading, uniformity is the key to top-flight performance.

Buffer Ballistics

One of the foremost questions relative to the use of a buffering agent revolves around the matter of ballistics. Does it increase chamber pressure? If so, how much, and what can be done to prevent it?

It most definitely does contribute to a rise in pressure; sadly, in many instances the rise is of such magnitude that the load becomes downright dangerous.

One rule of thumb currently making the tour is that the shot charge weight be decreased by the amount of buffer material added, so as to keep the ejecta weight the same. Another rule sometimes offered is that the powder charge of any load that is already at, or very near, maximum be reduced by two grains.

My experience with buffered loads will not permit me to take either of these approaches at face value. Although they are applicable in some

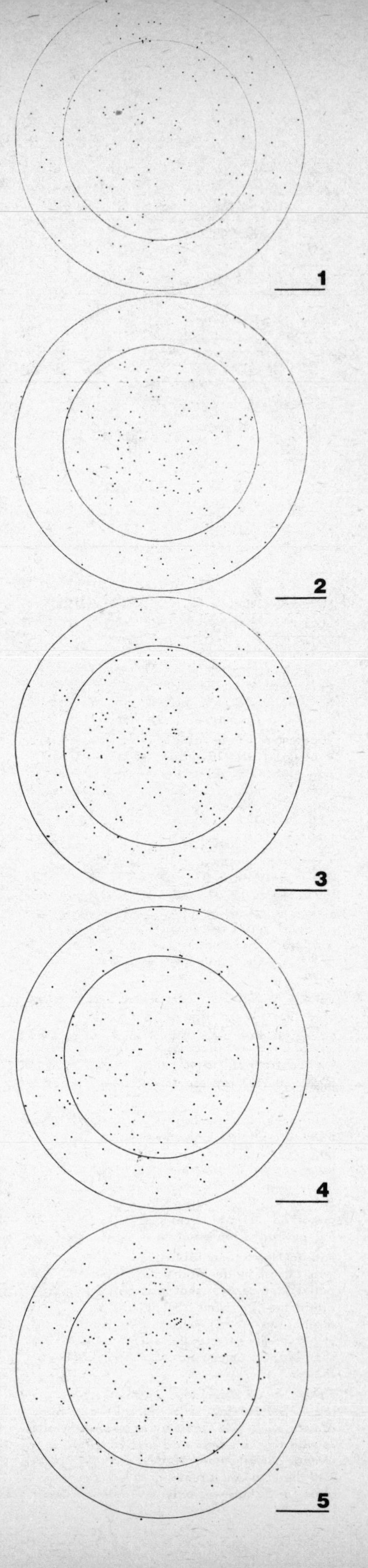

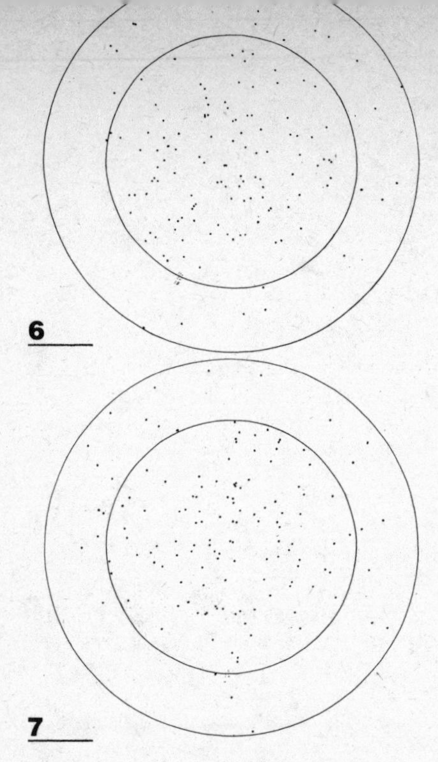

Pattern No. 1 (See Table A). The 1⅛x4 control load with 29/HS-5 and White Arro-Wad averaged 76.6% from the full-choke barrel of a Dakin S/S double gun. Pellet distribution was balanced, but much patchiness was in evidence, along with a rather high extreme variation in density. This 76.8% pattern is typical of the 40-yard performance.

Pattern No. 2 (See Table A). Buffering the 1⅛x 4 payload with 18 grains of S&W granulated polyethylene boosted the 40-yard average to 88%—a gain of better than 11% over the "straight" load. This pattern counts out to 85.5% and the strong center density is representative.

Pattern No. 3 (See Table A). The gain in density when using household flour as the buffering agent matched that given by the S&W poly—this string of 1⅛x4 loads also averaging 88%, with a duplication in center density. In this series of tests, the loads buffered with flour produced the smallest extreme variation in density—only 5 pellets. Shown here is an 89.3% pattern.

Pattern No. 4 (See Table B). Full-choke barrel of author's 12-ga. Dakin S/S double averaged a fraction over 70% with a "straight" load of 1⅜ ozs. No. 4 chilled. Pattern width at 40 yards ranged from 36" to 46", and the one pictured here (70.2%) represents the norm for pellet distribution.

Pattern No. 5 (See Table B). When 22 grains S&W granulated polyethylene was added to the 1⅜x4 payload, the Dakin full-choke barrel averaged better than 87% at 40 yards, this being a gain of 17% over the unbuffered load. Pattern width was substantially less, along with a marked increase in center density. At 87.6%, this pattern is representative.

Pattern No. 6 (See Table C). This 40-yard pattern almost made history. Except for a single pellet, the entire shot charge is contained within the 30" circle. Twenty-two grs. of S&W granulated polyethylene protected the 1½-ozs of No. 2 chilled shot, powered by 35/Blue Dot. The 20-inch core contains 82% of the total charge.

Pattern No. 7 (See Table D). Another outstanding handload in the author's Breda Mark II consists of 35/SR-4756 behind 1⅝ ozs. of chilled 2s with the Flite-Max wad and 25 grains granulated polyethylene. This is a 94% pattern, with the core count running 76%. Extreme variation for 5 shots was only 4 pellets.

instances, they should not be regarded as final, catch-all solutions to the maintaining of safe chamber pressure. The matter is much more complex than that.

Even the practice of selecting a powder and charge weight recommended for a payload that is ⅛ oz. *heavier* than what you're actually using isn't always the answer either, though this approach does show promise.

Let's look at some examples. In Ballistics Table II are detailed a trio of 1¼-oz. loads using HS-6 powder. For both grades of granulated polyethylene the increase in the ejecta was less than 1/16 oz., while with Cream-of-Wheat the total combined weight of the shot and the buffering agent remained 20 grs. short of 1⅜ ozs.

Hodgdon's No. 21 manual recommends 33/HS-6 behind a 1⅜-oz. payload in the 12-ga. 2¾" AA plastic shell, with the WW209 primer and Power Piston W29928 wad. Velocity and chamber pressure are listed at 1,306 fps and 10,700 lup. Because I used Champion II shells and Federal 209 primers instead and, in the interest of crimp space with the Power Piston W29926 wad, I wanted to be on the safe side, I thus elected to reduce the powder charge to 32/HS-6.

The results were interesting. With 15/E2010-95DA the load turned out to be a *hot* one at 11,300 lup. However, a further reduction of one grain of powder would drop the pressure to a safe level; and in view of the extra-high velocity, the powder charge could be cut even more.

With 20 grs. of the S&W poly (a mere 5.0-gr. increase in the ejecta weight), the chamber pressure zoomed to over 13,500 lup, as it did with 35/Cream-of-Wheat. Both of these loads can be classed as *hazardous*. That's just too much chamber pressure to play with, even when a very strong compression-formed hull such as the Champion II is used.

Seen in this trio of loads is a substantial spread in chamber pressure; I believe we can attribute this, for the most part, to differences between the buffering agents rather than to differences in the ejecta weight. Apparently the lighter and fluffier E2010-95DA material creates less drag or friction within the shell and bore. I might add at this juncture that, in my opinion, when any buffering agent is used there is increased friction, and I believe this extra resistance to the expanding powder gases is a much greater factor in upping chamber pressure than is the relatively small increase in the ejecta weight.

Still looking at Table II, we see something of a paradox in the 1¼-oz. loads with AL-5 powder. This is one of the propellants that helped launch the revival in shotshell handloading and it has remained a highly popular one for engineering heavy field loads. S&W's most recent charge table shows the top 12-ga. loading to be 31 grs. when using a plastic O/P wad and fiber fillers in Alcan, S&W or Federal plastic shells with a paper basewad. The listed velocity for a 1¼-oz. shot charge is 1,230 fps when ignited by the 220 Max-Fire primer—not 1,330 fps as frequently stated by optimistic typewriters.

Obviously, AL-5 in this capacity does not generate nearly as much chamber pressure as many of us believed. Even with the addition of a shot cup, which in itself usually promotes a pressure build-up, the 31.0-gr. loading is a mild one. Adding 17 grains of E2010-46AA boosted the average pressure by 900 lup, yet an excellent safety margin still remains.

Load Guidelines

Is this, then, the sought-after guideline to the use of a buffering agent—that of selecting a low-pressure load as a starting point? Certainly it's a step that has merit. But I think that when we move up to heavier shot charges an equally good approach is to choose a powder and charge weight that is recommended for payloads running at least ⅛ oz., and preferably ¼ oz., heavier than the intended load. In other words, we will profit by using a propellant which normally would be considered too slow burning for the payload in question, because it will enable us to maintain respectable velocities with less chance of exceeding pressure limits.

Most of the 1½-oz. 3" loads shown in Table VI illustrate this. Note in particular the two 33/HS-6 loads which use the W-W compression-formed plastic shell. For this very same hull Hodgdon recommends the same 33.0-gr. charge behind a 1-⅝-oz. shot weight, listing the velocity at 1,231 fps and the pressure at 10,800 lup—a *max* loading to be sure.

Adding 22 grs. of the S&W poly material to 1½ ozs. of 2s and sticking to the 33-gr. powder charge resulted in a fine load at 1,242 fps, with a pressure that exactly matched the Hodgdon prescription.

Also note that when the plastic shot sleeve was dropped from a duplicate loading, both the velocity and pressure faded to a considerable extent. This supports what was pointed out previously, that the use of

BALLISTICS TABLE IV
12-gauge 2¾" shell/1½ ozs. No. 2 shot

Case & Primer	Powder Charge/grs.	Wad Column	Average Velocity fps	Average Pressure lup	Maximum Pressure lup
Fed. HP Plastic 220 Max-Fire	AL-7/34.0	PGS + ⅜" FBS + Fed. 12SC112 shot cup	1,278	13,700	14,200
Fed. HP Plastic 220 Max-Fire	AL-7/34.0	PGS + 5/16" FBS + Fed. 12SC112 shot cup + 20.0 grs. E2010-46AA	1,300	15,900	16,700
Fed. HP Plastic 220 Max-Fire	AL-7/32.0	PGS + 5/16" FBS + Fed. 12SC112 shot cup + 20.0 grs. E2010-46AA	1,262	14,600	15,100
Fed. HP Plastic 220 Max-Fire	AL-7/32.0	PGS + 5/16" FBS + Fed. 12SC112 shot cup + 30.0 grs. Cream-of-Wheat	1,243	14,600	14,900
Fed. HP Plastic 220 Max-Fire	AL-7/32.0	PGS + ¼" FBS + Fed. 12SC112 shot cup + 25.0 grs. Herter's GP-1	1,260	14,700	15,100

Comments: Ballistic tests courtesy S&W Ammunition Company. Velocities and chamber pressures shown represent a 5-shot average from a 30" full-choke test barrel; velocities instrumental at 15 feet from the muzzle. Powder, shot and buffer material weighed for all loads. To regulate crimp space, the Federal 1½-oz. shot cup was modified in all instances by trimming off the base flange and perforating the floor with a .410 wad punch. Wad seating pressure 50 lbs.; crimps, 6-point fold. PGS = Alcan plastic gas seal.

BALLISTICS TABLE V
12-gauge 3" shell/1⅜ ozs. No. 4 shot

Case & Primer	Powder Charge/grs.	Wad Column	Average Velocity fps	Average Pressure lup	Maximum Pressure lup
Fed. HP Plastic Fed. 209	Blue Dot/42.0	A-W + ⅜" Fed. fiber + 1" plastic sleeve + 22.0 grs. S&W gran. poly.	Lost	12,900	12,900
Fed. HP Plastic Fed. 209	Blue Dot/40.0	A-W + ⅜" Fed. fiber + 1" plastic sleeve + 22.0 grs. S&W gran. poly.	1,436	11,600	12,300

Comments: Ballistic tests courtesy Hodgdon Powder Company, Inc. Velocities shown are instrumental at 75 inches from the muzzle. Regarding the 42/ Blue Dot load, only one round was fired for test. Powder, shot and buffer material weighed for all loads. Wad-seating pressure 60 lbs.; crimps, 6-point fold. A-W = Alcan Air-Wedge over-powder wad.

BALLISTICS TABLE VI
12-gauge 3" shell/1½ ozs. No. 2 shot

Case & Primer	Powder Charge/grs.	Wad Column	Average Velocity fps	Average Pressure lup	Maximum Pressure lup
W-W C/F Plastic WW209	HS-6/33.0	A-W + ⅜" W-W fiber + 1" plastic sleeve + 22.0 grs. S&W gran. poly.	1,242	10,800	11,200
W-W C/F Plastic WW209	HS-6/33.0	A-W + ½" W-W fiber + 22.0 grs. S&W gran. poly.	1,200	9,366	10,000
Rem. SP Plastic Alcan G57F	HS-6/39.0	.135" NC + ½" W-W fiber + 1" plastic sleeve + 22.0 grs. S&W gran. poly.	1,196	11,450	11,500
W-W P/F Plastic WW209	HS-6/40.0	.135" NC + ½" W-W fiber + Fed. 12SC112 shot cup + 22.0 grs. S&W gran. poly.	1,182	10,666	11,200
W-W P/F Plastic WW209	HS-6/39.0	.135" NC + ½" W-W fiber + 1" plastic sleeve + 40.0 grs. Cream-of-Wheat	1,194	10,466	11,100
Fed. HP Plastic Fed. 209	Blue Dot/35.0	A-W + ⅜" Fed. fiber + Fed. 12C112 shot cup + 22.0 grs. S&W gran. poly.	1,274	10,166	10,900

Comments: Ballistic tests courtesy Hodgdon Powder Company, Inc. Velocities and chamber pressures shown represent a 3-shot average from a 30" full-choke test barrel; velocities instrumental at 75 inches from the muzzle. The Federal 12SC112 shot cup was modified by trimming off base flange and perforating floor with .410 wad punch. Wad-seating pressure 70 lbs. for nitro card loads; 80 lbs. for A-W in C/F plastics; 60 lbs. for Blue Dot load. Powder, shot and buffer material weighed for all loads. Crimps, 6-point fold. A-W = Alcan Air-Wedge. NC = Alcan nitro card. C/F = Compression-formed. P/F = Poly-formed plastic shell.

BALLISTICS TABLE VII
12-gauge 3″ shell/1⅝ ozs. No. 2 shot*

Case & Primer	Powder Charge/grs.	Wad Column	Average Velocity fps	Average Pressure lup	Maximum Pressure lup
W-W P/F Plastic WW209	SR-4756/37.0	Flite-Max No. 1 + 25.0 grs. S&W gran. poly.	1,317	11,950	12,200
Fed. HP Plastic Fed. 209	Blue Dot/39.0	PGS + .070″ NC + ⅜″ Fed. fiber + 1¼″ plastic sleeve + 25.0 grs. S&W gran. poly.	1,480	13,500+	13,500+
Fed. HP Plastic 220 Max-Fire	AL-8/37.0	Flite-Max No. 1 + 25.0 grs. Herter's GP-1 poly.	1,125	10,500	10,800
Fed. HP Plastic 220 Max-Fire	AL-8/38.0	Flite-Max No. 1 + 25.0 grs. Herter's GP-1 poly.	1,146	10,900	11,200
Fed. HP Plastic 220 Max-Fire	AL-8/39.0	Flite-Max No. 1 + 25.0 grs. Herter's GP-1 poly.	1,162	11,000	11,700
Fed. HP Plastic 220 Max-Fire	AL-8/37.0	Flite-Max No. 1 + 40.0 grs. Cream-of-Wheat	1,105	11,200	11,500
Fed. HP Plastic 220 Max-Fire	AL-7/33.0	A-W + "B" card + ⅜″ FBS + 1″ plastic sleeve	1,203	10,100	10,600
Fed. HP Plastic 220 Max-Fire	AL-7/33.0	A-W + ¼″ FBS + 1¼″ plastic sleeve + 25.0 grs. E2010-46AA gran. poly.	1,221	12,700	13,000
Fed. HP Plastic 220 Max-Fire	AL-7/33.0	A-W + 5/16″ FBS + 1¼″ plastic sleeve + 30 grs. Cream-of-Wheat	1,218	12,900	13,600
Fed. HP Plastic 220 Max-Fire	AL-8/41.0	PGS + 5/16″ FBS + 1¼″ plastic sleeve + 40.0 grs. Cream-of-Wheat	1,298	14,200	14,700

Comments: Ballistic tests with SR-4756 and Blue Dot powders courtesy Hodgdon Powder Company, Inc., the results shown representing a 3-shot average from a 30″ full-choke test barrel; velocities instrumental at 75 inches from the muzzle. Tests with AL-7 and AL-8 powders courtesy S&W Ammunition Company, the results shown an average of 5 shots with the velocities instrumental at 15 feet from the muzzle.
*The last 4 loads listed in this table contained No. 4 shot. Powder, shot and buffer material weighed for all loads. The Flite-Max wad was seated so as to make firm powder contact; all other loads 50 lbs. All loads closed with 6-point crimp. HP = Hi-Power. A-W = Alcan Air-Wedge over-pow er wad. PGS = Alcan plastic gas seal. FBS = Alcan Feltan-Bluestreak fiber filler wad.

BALLISTICS TABLE VIII
12-gauge 3″ shell/1¾ ozs. No. 2 shot*

Case & Primer	Powder Charge/grs.	Wad Column	Average Velocity fps	Average Pressure lup	Maximum Pressure lup
Fed. HP Plastic 220 Max-Fire	AL-8/38.0	PGS + ¼″ FBS + 1¼× plastic sleeve + 25.0 grs. Herter's GP-1 poly.	1,084	11,600	11,900
Fed. HP Plastic 220 Max-Fire	AL-8/38.0	PGS + 5/16″ FBS + 1¼″ plastic sleeve + 40.0 grs. Cream-of-Wheat	1,102	12,200	12,700
Fed. HP Plastic 220 Max-Fire	AL-8/39.0	PGS + ¼″ FBS + 1¼″ plastic sleeve + 25.0 grs. Herter's GP-1 poly.	1,158	11,500	11,800
Fed. HP Plastic 220 Max-Fire	AL-8/39.0	PGS + ¼″ FBS + 1¼″ plastic sleeve + 25.0 grs. Herter's GP-1 poly.	1,158	12,300	12,500
Fed. HP Plastic 220 Max-Fire	AL-8/41.0	PGS + 5/16″ Sacork + 1¼″ plastic sleeve	1,266	11,200	11,800
Fed. HP Plastic 220 Max-Fire	AL-8/41.0	PGS + ¼″ Sacork + 1¼″ plastic sleeve + 25.0 grs. E2010-46AA poly.	1,284	13,300	13,600

Comments: Ballistic tests courtesy S&W Ammunition Company. Results shown are an average of 5 shots, the velocities instrumental at 15 feet from the muzzle.
*The last two loads listed in this table contained No. 3 shot. Powder, shot and buffer material weighed for all loads. Wad-seating pressure 50 lbs. for all loads; 6-point fold crimps. HP = Hi-Power. PGS = Alcan plastic gas seal. FBS = Alcan Feltan-Bluestreak fiber filler. SACORK = Cork filler wad, now discontinued.

either sleeves or shot cups will strengthen the ballistics.

An example of how easily rules can be gunned down is seen in Table VII which details 1⅝-oz. payloads in 3" hulls. The *Lyman Shotshell Handbook* shows a SR-4756 loading for 1⅞ ozs. of shot in the W-W poly-formed plastic shell. The recommended charge is 36.5 grs., with the Remington 97* primer and the Flite-Max wad rounding out the picture. Velocity and pressure are listed at 1,185 fps and 10,500 lup.

This looked like a good bet, because when 25.0 grs. of the S&W poly material was added to a 1⅝-oz. charge of 2s, the combined weight was well under 1⅞ ozs. In fact, it was 29.0 grs. under 1¾ ozs. I decided to substitute the WW209 primer and hike the powder charge to 37.0 grs. This combination, as you will note, turned out to be a *hot* "recipe" at close to 12,000 lup. I think it would have been hot even without the component substitutions.

However, at 1,317 fps it was definitely a fast-stepping load, and one that could easily stand a powder reduction to drop the pressure into a more normal range. So I cut the charge to 35.0 grs. and ran a string of patterns from my Breda Mark II Magnum. The performance was truly outstanding, as can be seen in Table D, with an average of 93.8%. In comparison with a 1⅞-oz. factory loading, the buffered handload with ¼ oz. less shot was ahead on all counts—efficiency, density and extreme variation.

A Different Approach

Another approach that promises to have some merit is to take data for a 2-¾" case and apply it to the 3" shell. This can be seen in the Blue Dot loading detailed in Table VI.

For the 2-¾" Federal plastic shell (paper basewad), Hercules says that 36/Blue Dot behind the Filter-Max wad and 1½ ozs. of shot will produce a velocity of 1,275 fps at a pressure of 9,800 lup. Using a built-up wad column and 22.0 grains of S&W poly in Federal's 3" plastic shell, I cut the powder charge back to 35.0 grs.

By happy coincidence the buffered handload produced a matching velocity, while the pressure increased but slightly to just over 10,000 lup. At the pattern board the load also did itself proud (see Table C), averaging 92% for 5 shots. In fact, this Blue Dot prescription very nearly made history, as there was one pattern in the string which went 99.2 percent! What has long been regarded as the impossible would have been achieved had it not been for that lone pellet which failed to register within a 30" circle at 40 yards. But, alas, no witnesses!

I could go until the moon turns blue in hashing over the many loads shown in the tables, but doing so would really serve no useful purpose. The issue seems tangled enough as it is, and one cannot help but wonder whether there really are any clearly defined rules to follow when using a buffering agent with the shot charge. Perhaps the truth is that each

TABLE A
40-yard Pattern Tests/1⅛ ozs. No. 4 shot
Dakin 12-Ga. side-by-side double, 30" full-choke barrel, bore .724", choke .029"

Load	Density 20" circle	Density 30" circle	Efficiency 30" circle	EDV 20" circle	EDV 30" circle
29.0 grs. HS-5 White ARRO-WAD	69	122	76.6%	30	29 (18.1%)
28.0 grs. HS-5 White ARRO-WAD 15.0 grs. E2010-95DA	82	129	81.0%	24	14 (8.8%)
28.0 grs. HS-5 White ARRO-WAD 30.0 grs. Cream-of-Wheat	84	125	78.1%	26	22 (13.8%)
28.0 grs. HS-5 White ARRO-WAD 25.0 grs. Flour	97	140	88.0%	22	5 (3.1%)
28.0 grs. HS-5 White ARRO-WAD 18.0 grs. S&W granulated polyethylene	96	140	88.0%	16	12 (7.5%)

Comments: All loads assembled in W-W UPLAND compression-formed plastic shells and the WW209 primer used throughout. The shot was W-W brand, counting 160 pellets to the 1⅛ ounce charge. Crimps were 6-point fold using a Versamec 700 tool. Wad-seating pressure 30 lbs. in all instances; all powder and shot charges weighed. The results shown represent an average for 5 shots. EDV = Extreme variation in pellet density.

TABLE B
40-yard Pattern Tests/1⅜ ozs. No. 4 shot
Dakin 12-Ga. side-by-side double, 30" full-choke barrel, bore .724", choke .029"

Load	Density 20" circle	Density 30" circle	Efficiency 30" circle	EDV 20" circle	EDV 30" circle
31.0 grs. HS-6 W-W Universal + ½" W-W fiber	76	137	70.2%	24	8 (4.1%)
31.0 grs. HS-6 W-W Universal + ⅜" W-W fiber + 22.0 grs. S&W poly.	123	171	87.6%	10	16 (8.2%)

Comments: All loads assembled in Federal Champion II plastic shells and the WW209 primer used throughout. The shot was W-W brand, counting 195 pellets to the weighed-out 1⅜-oz. charge. Crimps were 8-point fold using a Versamec 700 tool. Wad-seating pressure 40 lbs. Powder, shot and buffer material weighed for all loads. The results shown represent an average for 5 shots. EDV = Extreme variation in pellet density.

An adjustable powder/shot dipper, such as the old Ideal shown here with Cream-of-Wheat, can be pressed into service for measuring the buffering agent. The setting should be arrived at, of course, by weighing sample charges on a powder scale.

specific set of components is strictly a law unto itself.

Vital Notes

Shown in these tables are a number of safe loads, as well as many that are not. Those which do not exceed an average pressure of 11,000 lup can be classed as SAFE loads. Those falling within the 11,000 to 12,000 lup range, however, should be regarded as *hot* loads, but these can be safely used if the powder charge is reduced accordingly. Those, of course, which exceed an average pressure of 12,000 lup are definitely *hazardous*. Their use could easily result in gun damage and even injury to the shooter.

Pulling the teeth from a buffered load which is *hot* can usually be accomplished without cutting the powder charge, providing there is a built-up wad column topped by a plastic sleeve or cup. The simple expedient of eliminating the plastic "guard" will serve to sufficiently tame the pressure.

The same step will *sometimes* work for a hazardous load. Table III, for example, gives the dope on a pair of buffered 1⅜-oz. loads powered by 31/HS-6. The sleeved load churned up in excess of 13,500 lup, while the unsleeved load showed a pressure drop of at least 3,000 lup. Part of this decrease, of course, can be attributed to the extra ⅛" of filler wadding.

But the pressure drop can easily vary, so don't bank on this trick as an infallible rule. In Table VI, for example, the pressure difference between the sleeved and unsleeved 3" loads (33/HS-6, 1½ ozs. No. 2) amounted to less than 1,500 lup.

TABLE C
40-yard Pattern Tests/1½ ozs. No. 2 shot/3" shells

Breda 12-Ga. Magnum Autoloader/⅛ choke, 29½" barrel, bore .720", choke .032"

Load	Density 20" circle	Density 30" circle	Efficiency 30" circle	EDV 20" circle	EDV 30" circle
Factory (Control) W-W Super-Speed Mark 5 1⅞ Ozs. No. 2 (166)	89	133	80.4%	22	9(5.4%)
33.5 grs. HS-6 Air-Wedge + ½" W-W fiber + 25.0 grs. S&W poly.	91	119	85.6%	31	16(11.5%)
33.0 grs. HS-6 Air-Wedge + ⅜" W-W fiber + 1" plastic sleeve + 25.0 grs. S&W poly.	92	125	89.9%	25	12(8.7%)
35.0 grs. BLUE DOT Air-Wedge + ⅜" Fed. fiber + Fed. 12SC112 shot cup + 22.0 grs. S&W poly.	98	128	92.0%	31	18(12.9%)

Comments: The loads with HS-6 powder were assembled in the W-W compression-formed plastic shell, using the WW209 primer. The Blue Dot load used the Federal plastic shell and Fed. 209 primer. The shot was Lawrence brand, counting 139 pellets to a weighed-out 1½-oz. charge. Crimps were 6-point fold using a Versamec 700 tool. Wad-seating pressure was 80 lbs. for the HS-6 loads; 60 lbs. for Blue Dot. Powder, shot and buffer material weighed for all loads. The results shown represent an average for 5 shots. EDV = Extreme variation in pellet density.

TABLE D
40-yard Pattern Tests/1⅝ ozs. No. 2 shot/3" shells

Breda 12-Ga. Magnum Autoloader/¾ choke, 29½" barrel, bore .720", choke .032"

Load	Density 20" circle	Density 30" circle	Efficiency 30" circle	EDV 20" circle	EDV 30" circle
Factory (Control) Federal Hi-Power Long Range shot cup 1⅞ ozs. No. 2 (163)	91	138	84.8%	13	8(4.9%)
35.0 grs. SR-4756 Flite-Max No. 1 25.0 grs. S&W poly.	112	140	93.8%	17	4(2.6%)

Comments: The handload with SR-4756 powder was assembled in the W-W poly-formed plastic shell, and the WW209 primer was used. The shot was Lawrence brand, counting 150 pellets to a weighed-out 1⅝-oz. charge. Crimp was 6-point fold on Versamec 700 tool. The Flite-Max wad was seated to make firm powder contact. Powder, shot and buffer material weighed. The results shown represent an average for 5 shots. EDV = Extreme variation in pellet density.

When a buffering agent is used without a plastic sleeve or cup, pattern efficiency is likely to fall off a few percentage points. Nonetheless, it is almost a certainty that the performance will still surpass that given by the sleeve alone.

Speaking of patterns, those delivered by the buffered load are invariably characterized by unusually high center density. In fact, when patterns reach the 85% to 95% plateau, 65-70% of the total charge often registers in a 20″ circle at 40 yards. This high center density is the hallmark of a long-range pattern, and it will extend effectiveness several yards beyond that of a pattern of matching percentage which has balanced pellet distribution. As an extra bonus, those pellets comprising the core of the pattern are the least damaged, are traveling a bit faster and therefore will deliver more energy on the target than those in the pattern fringe.

It should be obvious that the buffered load is not for everybody. The pattern width at 40 yards is such that it imposes a heavy handicap, and any bird hit squarely at that range would almost be reduced to pulp. And even out at 50 yards an overkill situation will exist with the heavier shot charges. It is out at the long yardages encountered in pass shooting ducks and geese where the buffered load pays its way. It is a specialized tool engineered to step in and kill cleanly at those distances where the ordinary load fails.

Loading Techniques

Nor is it a load that lends itself to high output at the loading bench. Extra time and effort are required to crank out these "specials." I usually spend an hour or more producing a single box of 25 rounds—but in my estimation it is time well spent.

The most time-consuming part is that of blending the buffering agent into the shot charge. If maximum benefit is to be derived, the agent has to be distributed evenly throughout the shot column. Materials such as Cream-of-Wheat and the S&W granulated polyethylene are best handled by adding them in small amounts at a time.

The practice I follow is to place both the shot charge and the buffering agent in separate plastic vials (the kind your druggist uses in putting up prescriptions). First, a layer of shot is poured into the shell, then enough of the buffering agent to just cover those pellets. Then more shot is added, followed by more of the agent—both being trickled in always in small amounts. Continuously tapping the shell rim against the loading bench is recommended. This provides a large assist in getting the material to completely fill the voids between the pellets.

With a more coarse material, such as Herter's GP1, the above method doesn't work. Even with a shot size as large as No. 2, the individual granules are too large (most of them) to work into the pellet interstice area, and jiggling and tapping the shell doesn't help either. The best way I've found is to place the shot charge in a vial and then simply pour the entire amount of GP1 on top of it. By closing the container and giving it a few vigorous shakes, the material seems to distribute itself quite uniformly throughout the shot charge. The mixed charge is then dumped into the shell. This is a much faster method than the other but, unfortunately, it will not work well with the other materials.

Herter's GPI, a globular-type buffering agent, can be mixed by placing the material on top of the vial-contained shot charge, as shown at left. Giving the vial a few shakes will distribute this rather coarse agent quite uniformly, as seen at right, after which it is poured into the shell.

Any shell used for hunting purposes is usually subjected to a fair amount of handling, including considerable jiggling about in hunting coat pockets and shell bags. With the buffered loads this will invariably result in some loss of the agent (except for the GP1 material), as it will tend to sift out through the tightest of crimps. To help solve this problem, I place a piece of thin paper over the shot charge before crimping. A one-inch square works well for both 10 and 12-ga. loads.

The paper shield will only retard the loss of the buffering agent—not block it completely. So it is a good idea to give the fold crimp a coating of candle wax or household paraffin. Placing a dab of this sealant in the center where the crimp folds meet is not enough; the entire recessed part of the crimp should receive a thin coating. This also makes the plastic-cased load virtually waterproof.

There is no doubt about it. Producing the buffered load is something of a chore. But the vast improvement in pattern performance is definitely worth all this extra fussing around—assuming, of course, that there is a genuine need for extra performance. When properly put together, the buffered load practically guarantees an increase in pattern efficiency of at least 10% to 15%; and increases of 20% to 25% are not uncommon. This is the same as adding one to two degrees of choke. A modified barrel will move up to the full-choke level, and a full-choke tube moves right into never-never land.

Another big selling point for the buffered load is that we can make a lighter shot charge do an equally effective job (if not a better job) than one which is substantially heavier. The advantage in this should be obvious—greater economy and lessened recoil, and with no sacrifice in reaching power.

The biggest obstacle facing those who want to try this method of loading is the difficulty in obtaining a really good buffering agent, such as that used by the big loading companies. That, plus a lack of published data from them. But if enough of us make our wants known, the situation may change. ●

SHOOTING EDITOR

by JACK O'CONNOR

There are many routes to a gun editorship—one of my colleagues was a cowboy, a forest service packer and a guide. Another was a former naval officer and later an ammunition company ballistician. A third was a Harvard graduate and a teacher in a boys' school. This is the rags to riches story of how I became one.

O'Connor wears this stern and noble look because he managed to make a pretty good running shot on this Coues whitetail (Arizona whitetail) in Sonora.

TO ANY WRITER the most fascinating subject in the world is himself—his glorious deeds, his wise and witty sayings, his triumphs and his defeats, even his corns, his back aches and his acid stomach.

This is a piece about me—or at least how I became a gun editor. I am doing this partly because writing about himself in one way or another is a good part of any writer's stock in trade, and partly because a great many young men would like nothing better than to get a job like the one I held on *Outdoor Life* for 31 years.

I haven't kept a record of the number of letters I have received from aspiring gun editors and outdoor writers, but in the years I was with *Outdoor Life* I am sure I received several thousands. I used to get at least 100 requests for such information a year and often I received several such queries in one week.

Many of the letters were from earnest and gifted young men who would probably become good outdoor journalists. Others were from unimaginative lads to whom the job simply looked like a very soft way to make a living. I got some letters that began: "Please tell me how you got your job, how much you make, how many hours a week you work, what vacations you get." Likewise, I get many letters from high school and college students wanting to know what courses to take in order to become gun editors.

There are plenty of routes to a gun editorship. One of my colleagues was a cowboy, a forest service packer, and a guide. I doubt if he finished high school. Another was a former naval officer with an Annapolis background who was for a time a ballistician for one of the big ammunition companies. Yet another was a Harvard graduate and a teacher in a boys' school.

Of the old time gun editors I read when I was growing up, one had been an advertising man, another an oil company executive, another an army officer. Still another was, I believe, a dog trainer and market hunter. Yet another was a sort of society play boy.

None of the practioners of the trade took college courses in gun editing and outdoor writing—such courses didn't exist then. Most of them simply happened to fall into their jobs. One gun editor I know had long been a fishing enthusiast, but was not particularly mad about either guns or hunting. He went to a magazine office, asked for a job as a fishing editor. He was hired as a gun editor instead, and since he is an intelligent and adaptable person, he speedily learned a great deal about guns.

Writing and editing a shooting department or any other department in an outdoor magazine is a branch of the very wide field of journalism—or "communications" as it now seems fashionable to call it. A good gun writer or, for that matter, any kind of writer in the outdoor field is primarily a journalist who knows a good deal about his specialty. But first and foremost, he is a *writer*.

Sports Specialists

The world is full of fine big-bore and small-bore target shots, crack Skeet and trap shots, expert big-game guides, champion bait-casters, erudite ballisticians, shrewed optical engineers. It is also full of excellent writers. But the world is not exactly full of people who know something about rifles and rifle shooting, shotguns, big game hunting, elementary optics, reloading and A.B.C. ballistics, and who can write about these things interestingly, entertainingly, and clearly.

Few genuine specialists in the sports world are able to write well about their specialties. Boxers, golf players, jockeys, baseball pitchers, professional halfbacks, are seldom articulate and the stuff that appears under their by-lines is generally written by ghosts—usually facile newspapermen trying to pick up an extra buck. One big league pitcher is a highly articulate person and an excellent writer, but he is regarded by his fellows as being exceedingly odd if not actually subversive.

Ballisticians, optical engineers, and biologists write for other optical engineers, ballisticians, and biologists. The stuff they turn out would bring the average reader down with chills and fever. If their stuff is presented to the public in understandable form, it generally must be put into English by a journalist.

In some ways, outdoor journalism differs from other forms of sports journalism. The average sports writer cannot throw a down-field block, hit big-league pitching, break 90 at golf, or last one round in the ring with even a third-rate welterweight.

But the outdoor journalist must be able to perform reasonably well and, if he can write, the more he knows about his field the better off he is. He can't tell others how to shoot unless he knows how to shoot himself, how to outwit a whitetail buck unless he has hunted whitetail long and intelligently, how to load ammunition or sight in a rifle unless he himself has worked out the angles. Most outdoor writers are reasonably good at what they write about. If they were not they wouldn't last—their stuff is read by a highly critical, often very well informed, audience of enthusiasts.

But even more than the ability to write, even more than knowledge of the subject, the important thing is enthusiasm. The longer I write, the more convinced I am that no amount of writing skill or knowledge of a subject can make up for a lack of enthusiasm. No man can do well with a subject that bores him, and any writer is most successful when he writes about something about which he feels deeply.

Many people have a great deal of enthusiasm for guns, for hunting, and for fishing, but are they writers? I would say that if a young man has reached the age of 21 and has never written anything he did not have to write, he is probably not an instinctive writer. The man whom God intended to write plays with words as naturally as a Brittany spaniel or a setter points birds or a hound follows a trail. I have a daughter who, I believe, will eventually be a professional writer. When she was 10, she wrote and illustrated a "novel" about a horse and a little girl who by some odd coincidence was also 10 years old.

But first, let us see how I got into this business of being what used to be called gun editor or arms and ammunition editor, but which is now generally called shooting editor.

Early Days in the West

I can hardly remember when I was not a gun nut. I probably became one because I grew up in an atmosphere of guns. My maternal grandfather, who had come west from Kentucky in the 1870s was a big-game hunter, a bird shot, and something of a gun nut himself. When he started a cattle ranch in the Rocky Mountains along the New Mexico-Colorado border, he hunted bighorn sheep, mule deer, black bear, mountain lions, and grizzlies. When he moved to Arizona, he hunted desert bighorn sheep in the mountains around the Salt River Valley and mule deer out on the flats. He was a passion-

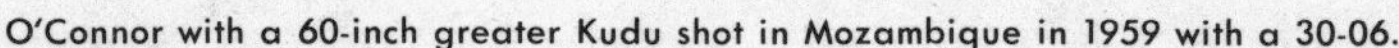
O'Connor with a 60-inch greater Kudu shot in Mozambique in 1959 with a 30-06.

O'Connor with urial ram (Iran, 1958).

ate bird hunter, shooting whitewing and mourning doves and Gambel quail. As I've said, he was also something of a gun nut – meaning that he really had more firearms than he had use for. I can remember that he had an old Model 1876 Winchester for some now-obsolete black powder cartridge, a Model 1886 for the 45-70, and a Model 94 Winchester in 30-30. But in his declining years James Wiley Woolf, my grandfather, was more of a shotgun nut than a rifle nut. He had a Parker of good grade, an Ithaca, and a Purdey with two sets of barrels in a fitted oak-and-leather case lined with billiard cloth. All his guns were 12 gauge. He looked upon 20 and 16 gauge guns as playthings for women and children and weaklings, and on pumps and automatics as inventions of the Devil.

My uncle Bill Woolf, his son, was a crack rifle shot and a fine shotgun handler. He competed at Camp Perry. Another uncle is reputed to have awakened one morning to see a desert bighorn ram staring at him from a rocky hillside a couple of hundred yards away. He rolled over in his bedroll, grabbed a 30-30 and bumped the ram off. Another uncle told me in later years that when he'd had a ranch in Nevada he used to shoot desert rams with a 30 caliber Luger pistol. There were a good many sheep in the Southwest in those early days.

Yet another gun nut uncle was from the Irish side – Jim O'Connor, a lawyer, superior court judge and rancher. He owned a whole flock of rifles and shotguns including a Model 92 Winchester 25-20 with which I shot my first coyote, and a 10 gauge Model 1910 Winchester lever action shotgun that I used to sneak out and shoot.

If I had not been allowed to acquire the air rifle I wanted when I was 5 years old, I may not have turned out to be a gun nut. But at that time, my mother was pretty sour on guns. She had just divorced my father and one of the things she held against him was that he was a sucker for good guns and fine watches and he had been known to come home without his pay check but with a new top-grade Uncle Dan Lefever shotgun or a watch that had a filigreed solid gold case, struck the hours, and could even be set to go off like an alarm clock. My good mother was convinced the my precocious interest in air guns was proof that, unless she watched me, I was destined to go waltzing down the primrose path just like my old man. I would have, she thought, a rifle in one hand, a shotgun in the other, a $200 watch in my pocket, but not a dime in cash to my name. She told me that it would be over her dead body if I ever got that air rifle.

But I fooled her. Later on I sold copies of a wild newspaper full of murder, jewel robbery, rape and assorted chicanery called (if my memory serves me correctly) *The Chicago Blade and Sunday Ledger*. I peddled it in Tempe's two saloons, in the pool halls, to my mother's friends, and in what I now know was a house of ill fame in Mexican Town. I got the air gun. It was a break open single shot. It retailed for $1.50. It cocked by breaking and I loaded one BB at the muzzle. With it I shot black birds, sparrows, spun clothespins on my mother's clothes line, and I also shot some of my pals in their derrieres.

Starting at the age of 5, I went along with my Grandfather Woolf to shag birds and when I was 8, he bought me a 20-gauge Iver Johnson single shot. Later I got a Marlin 22 pump. I shot my first deer with a 30-40 Krag army rifle that I bought for $1.50 from a bindle stiff who had a camp down in the river bed. He was at the time in grave need of a quart of sour-mash bourbon.

My grandfather was a devoted reader of *Outdoor Recreation, Field & Stream, Outdoor Life,* and *Hunter, Trader, & Trapper.* So was I. I sent off for gun catalogs of European importers and American manufacturers. I read all the stories of hunting bighorn sheep and elk in Wyoming, Dall sheep and grizzly bears in the Yukon, giant moose and brown bears in Alaska, Stone sheep and caribou in the Cassiar section of British Columbia. I saw the African movies of Paul J. Rainey and read about Teddy Roosevelt's heroic feats in British East Africa.

I also read the early stuff of Capt. E. C. "Ned" Crossman, Col. (then lieutenant) Townsend Whelen, Charles Askins Sr., and Chauncey Thomas. I longed to own a Model 1910 Ross straight-pull rifle or a Newton. Later, by heroic toil and spartan savings, I acquired enough money to buy a deluxe grade 256 Newton. This, I believe, was in 1916, when I was 14. Those were the days when a dollar was a dollar – and mighty hard to come by, I might add. My Newton cost me either

$40 or $45, if I remember correctly. It had a little engraving, a Lyman 1-A cocking piece rear sight, a stock with cheekpiece which was supposed to be made of French walnut. I also bought 100 rounds of ammunition at a cost of about $6. My mother was absolutely certain that I had lost my marbles.

I shot a couple of mule deer and a javelina with the 256. I sold it at a time when I could get no more ammunition and when I was also broke. I hunted later with a remodeled Springfield 30-06, with a Model 95 Winchester lever action in 30-06, with a Model 8 Remington auto in 35 Remington caliber that I bought for $5. Its sheepherder owner had inlaid about 65 coins in the stock. He had hocked it for $5 in Holbrook, Arizona.

I went to college, worked on newspapers, did P.R. work, got a master's degree, fell in love with a cute little broad, married her, got a job teaching and doing publicity at a college in Texas. At the time, I had a Winchester Model 54 in 270, a 12 gauge Winchester Model 12 shotgun with a 30-inch full choke barrel. I got my bride a Model 30 Remington bolt-action rifle in 25 Remington rimless caliber and an Ithaca 20-gauge shotgun. Between us we had a Winchester Model 75 bolt-action 22.

The Writing Begins

I tried my hand at a few short stories and sold most of them. I wrote a novel called *Conquest* and it was accepted by Harpers about the time of the 1929 stock market crash. It came out a year later. It created something of a scandal there in Texas because in it one of the characters called another a son of a bitch. At that time down in Texas the phrase son of a bitch was very useful. It could be used as a pronoun as in "I told the SOB (for him) what he could do with it", or "Don't bother me. Just put the SOB (for it) on the table and get the hell out of here." You could even use it as part of an adverbial phrase as in "as cold as a son of a bitch." But, by golly, you couldn't write it without getting your tail in a crack. I didn't exactly get fired because of that word in the novel, but I beat them to the draw and resigned.

At 29, I had a wife, a baby, a few hundred dollars and a 1929 Chevrolet coupe. No job. The Depression had really struck in the East in 1931, but conditions were not quite so desperate in the West. I returned to my home state of Arizona and luckily managed to get a job teaching and doing publicity at what is now called Northern Arizona University at Flagstaff.

I could hunt mule deer and wild turkey within a few miles of town, shoot quail in the Verde Valley an hour and a half away. My salary was $2,500 a year, and even in those days that was poor pickings. I got a check for a few hundred dollars for English and American royalties on my novel. A bank failure gobbled it up. At the end of my first year at Flagstaff I, along with the other members of the faculty, got a 10 per cent salary cut, and at the end of my second year, I got another 10 per cent cut. The state couldn't collect its taxes and instead of cash we state employees got warrants. Magazines were not buying fiction. All of them were almost broke and were living on the stuff they had bought previously.

The O'Connors were pretty hard up for cash. What to do? Since I had been a hunter and a gun nut all my life, I decided to try my hand at the outdoor field. I wrote a piece called "Rifles & Cartridges for Southwestern Game." Turned down by *The American Rifleman*, it was bought by *Sports Afield*. I wrote a piece on mule deer and sent it to *Field & Stream*. Ray P. Holland, then editor, liked it, bought it, sent me a check for $50. The check was printed on buff-colored paper and had a wild duck on it. Ah, a lovely thing! In those days, 50 bucks was like 500 today. I was launched in a new and supplementary career. By today's standards, the checks I got were not big, but they enabled me to balance the budget and to buy a new rifle now and then.

I wrote for *National Sportsman* and *Hunting and Fishing* as well as for *Sports Afield, Field & Stream,* and *Outdoor Life*. Popular Science Publishing Company then bought *Outdoor Life* and the new editor, Ray Brown, encouraged me to write some gun stuff for the front of the magazine.

The Old Magazines

Today it is hard to turn around without falling over a magazine that publishes articles about guns and shooting, but in those days such magazines were scarce. Capt. Paul Curtis was the gun editor of *Field & Stream*. For a time, Major Charles Askins (father of Col. Charles Askins Jr.) and Col. Townsend Whelen wrote shotgun and rifle stuff for *Outdoor Life*. Capt. E. C. "Ned" Crossman was freelancing when I first got into the business, but sometime in the 1930s he was hired to do gun departments in *Hunting & Fishing* and *National Sportsman*. Both magazines are now unhappily defunct, largely because the publisher could never convince himself that he ought to pay anything more than a pittance for contributions. I sold a few pieces to Bill Foster, the editor and, incidentally, the guy who invented Skeet, for $35. Then he sent me a check for $15 for a piece. I sent the check back to Foster and told him to return the manuscript. He did so and explained that the owners of the magazine had told him he could pay no more than 15 bucks for anything. Eventually, the two magazines bought

O'Connor (right) and his son Bradford, with trophies taken by their party in northern British Columbia in 1967.

no material at all. Instead, they simply published letters from readers. When they were in their death throes, they were dreadful to contemplate.

Back in the 1930s, Russell Annabel, who was and is a very good writer, was getting some of those little checks. Archibald Rutledge killed a monster South Carolina buck or a wild turkey regularly in *Field & Stream.* Askins and Whelen both wrote regularly for the *American Rifleman.* Bob Nichols replaced Capt. Paul Curtis as gun editor of *Field & Stream.* Monroe Goode edited a very interesting shooting department for *Sports Afield.* Elmer Keith was writing for the *Rifleman* and now and then he had a piece in *Outdoor Life.*

By 1934, I was to some extent getting established as an outdoor writer. *Field & Stream* was putting my name on the cover and had raised my remuneration to $75 a story. The market for short stories had opened up and I was peddling one now and then.

Hundreds of people have written me asking how to get a story in an outdoor magazine. The only way I know of is to write the tale up and send it to the editor with suitable pictures. It helps if the story is neatly typed, the sentences make sense, and the pictures are good. Most magazines have a story read by about three sub-editors. These write reports on each manuscript. If the verdict is unfavorable, the story is returned. If the sub-editors like the yarn, it goes to the editor's desk. He either buys it or turns it down.

Selling a Story

An editor turns down a manuscript for various reasons: (1) It isn't any good. (2) He has bought something too much like it. (3) He is running out of budget money and he would have to hold the script too long before he published it. (4) Or he is hung over and feels like hell.

If, on the other hand, the editor buys it, the reason may be that (1) it is a good story and he likes it, (2) that he is short of whitetail stories and this will fit in, (3) he hopes to encourage the writer, (4) the story stinks but the writer has a following, (5) the story stinks but the poor bastard who wrote it needs the money.

In the fall of 1934, I went to the University of Arizona as professor of journalism and promptly incurred the enmity of my immediate superior when he found that I had got the then fabulous sum of $750 for a short story that came out about that time in what was then known as a Big Slick.

O'Connor (right) with his last ram, a Stone shot in northern B.C. in 1973.

At the same time, I was doing a lot of hunting in Mexico, working on a novel and balancing the budget by writing outdoor stuff. In 1936, I got a proposition to write for no other outdoor magazine except *Outdoor Life.* I accepted it. That same year, Townsend Whelen resigned as rifle editor for *Outdoor Life* and Ned Crossman was hired to take his place. By this time I had written perhaps a dozen gun and shooting articles for the front section of *Outdoor Life.* Then, in 1939, Ned Crossman committed suicide. Ray Brown put me in his place as a columnist and in 1941, he promoted me to Arms & Ammunition Editor, as the job was then called, and Major Charles Askins Sr. went to *Sports Afield.*

The Hardy Perennials

I once told an aspiring outdoor writer that I had told all I knew in my first four or five articles as a gun columnist and had been repeating myself ever since. That was jest to some extent, but the number of suitable shooting department subjects is limited. Perennial subjects include: How to Sight in a Rifle, Cartridges for Whitetails, What Choke in a Shotgun Is, How to Lead Birds and Clay Targets. All of these subjects are old and all the gun writer can do is to dish them up in a frisky and ingratiating manner. He should attempt to write so he can be understood by those who are just beginning and know little and entertain those who know as much or more than he does. I have probably written How to Sight in a Rifle a dozen times. The gun editor should not forget that he writes for an ever-changing audience. Old readers die off or quit. New ones come in!

Bill Rae, the former editor of *Outdoor Life,* and I were having lunch not long ago, and Bill commented that he had been the editor of an outdoor magazine for 20 years and that there were fewer good outdoor writers now than there were when he got into the business. I am inclined to agree with him. For that reason of little competition and many magazines, I think it is even easier to break into the field now than when I was starting out.

I read the young gun editors with considerable interest. Some, alas, can't write their way out of a paper bag. Others have had almost no experience, don't know much, and try to cover their ignorance with bluff and baloney. But now and then I bump into the writings of some youngster who can write, who knows something, and who can communicate his experience.

Such a lad can go a long way and lead a good life if he works hard and is smart. He should curb his natural tendency to larceny and fat headedness, be honest with himself, remember that he is working for the magazine and only incidentally for himself. If he does all this, he may pick up some extra bread by writing books. He will be able to charge the hunts that produce his copy off on his income tax. Men will admire him and beautiful maidens will warm him with their smiles. It's a good life for the industrious and gifted. ●

Testfire Report

A concise and critical review of new and recently-introduced firearms — covered are Iver-Johnson's Silver Shadow O-U, the Beretta BL-2/S, the Savage Model 2400, the Mannlicher-Schonauer Model 72, the Ruger Mini-14 Carbine and the Valmet M-62/S

by LARRY S. STERETT

Iver Johnson's Silver Shadow O-U

Thirty-five years ago Iver Johnson turned out an excellent line of break-action shotguns, both single barrel and side-by-side doubles in gauges from the 410 bore to the 12. A hurried check revealed that in 1939 the line included 3 field guns, two trap guns, and a Skeet gun. The low price model was the single barrel, plain Champion Grade with automatic ejector, at $9 in 410, 28, 20, 16 or 12 gauge with barrel lengths from 26" to 32", or $1 more for the 36" barrel. Hand checkering on the grip and forearm, and a matted top rib on the barrel, upped the price to $12.50. A Special Trap gun used the same action, but was available in 12 gauge only, with a 32" vent rib barrel, ivory beads, and checkered wood with special trap dimensions, all for $18!

There was also the Hercules Grade field double with a plain extractor or ejectors, at $32 to $42. Good wood with checkering, double triggers, and barrel lengths up to 32" were available. For $14 or $17.50 additional, an option was the Miller single trigger, non-selective or selective. The Super Trap gun, 12 gauge only at $49.50, came with a select walnut stock and beavertail forearm, deluxe checkering, recoil pad and pistol grip cap, ivory beads, special trap stock dimensions, with the single trigger an optional extra. Top of the line then was the Skeet-Er Model, available in all 5 gauges. Priced at $55 for the ejector model, it had a fancy-figured walnut stock and beavertail forearm, with a straight-grip stock optional. The standard barrel was 28", with 26" as an option, both bored for Skeet or upland field use. Options offered with the other models cost extra.

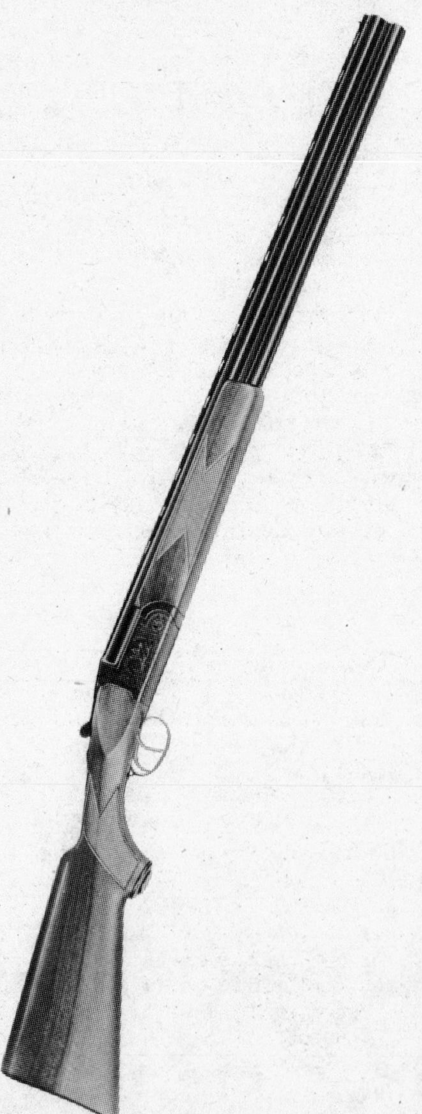

Iver Johnson's Silver Shadow is available in 12 gauge only. Barrel lengths available are 26", 28" and 30".

Today Iver Johnson Arms & Cycle Works, Inc., produces two shotguns. The plain Champion was reintroduced about 3 years ago after an absence of several years. It is made in 12, 20, or 410, cost $44.95. In 1974 an imported O-U was introduced in 12 gauge only.

The new shotgun, which has a single non-selective trigger, is manufactured in Italy. Weighing 7¼ pounds, it measures 45" over-all, and only one barrel length — 27¾" — is available. The barrels, with solid side ribs, are topped by a ventilated rib. The serrated top does an excellent job of breaking up light reflections. The rib, starting out as a solid rib, was ventilated by milling a groove down each side — apparently freehand, as the grooves don't exactly follow a straight line.

Breaking the boxlock action cocks both hammers but sets the sear only for the lower barrel. Recoil of the lower barrel sets the sear for the upper barrel, via a weighted pendulum. Both hammers are powered by coil springs, as is the top lever. Modern manufacturing methods, combined with hand fitting, are evident; roll pins are used to hold many parts together, a hairpin spring is used on the non-automatic sliding safety, and both the upper and lower tang show bright metal due to hand filing after these parts were blued. The buttstock covers the bright metal, but a quick touchup would not be asking too much.

The stock wood is apparently beech, as the bare wood is almost white, without figure, and with close pores. The outside surfaces have had the pores sealed with a dark stain, which appears to have then been wiped off, followed by a hard plastic finish. The result is similar to that obtained when the do-it-yourselfer buys an antique finish kit and uses it on a piece of old furniture. The outside surfaces are smooth and hard but underneath some of the rasp marks are evident. The inletting is excellent, and the wood-to-metal fit good. However, the wood under the buttplate is not finished, nor is the inletting around the action; the inside of the forearm has been sealed. The forearm shape is a modified U, the top half slanted slightly inward. The lower half of the forearm shows crude checkering of about 20 lines-per-inch. Checkering on the grip goes about 16 lines and it's of somewhat better quality. All checkering seems to have been done before finishing was done, so it is almost smooth, thus more decorative than functional. A two-line border is used but runouts are evident, and some of the checkering on the forearm is ragged.

The buttstock, attached to the receiver by a hex-head through-bolt, is cut away to make a rectangular 11/16" by 2" hole, with a circular center area—large enough to hold some emergency supplies, and even a spare 12 gauge shotshell. A checkered black plastic buttplate shows Diana (?) with her bow. The pistol grip has a black plastic cap with red I.J. on it. Length of pull is 14¼", drops at comb and heel 1 7/16" and 2⅜" respectively. The I.J. handles well, and the non-fluted comb is wide and comfortable. The bottom of the grip is rather thick and bulky.

The plain extractors raise the shells, or empties, about ¼" for removal. The non-automatic safety should be placed "on" before loading. The lower barrel fires first. The trigger, smooth and heavily chromed, shows a pull of about 5½ pounds for the bottom barrel, and 8½ for the upper.

After looking the I.J. over I went to the patterning board, wanting to make a check before using the gun on clay birds and game. The barrels, though not marked as to choke, are stamped with their cylinder diameters—18.5mm and 18.6mm respectively.

The lower barrel, using Herter's trap load (2¾-1⅛-7½) gave an average for 5 shots of 55.9%, about modified for that particular load. Switching to the S&W Heavy Field shells (3¾-1¼-6) for the upper barrel, its 5-shot average in the 30" circle at 40 yards was 61.2%, or about improved-modified.

The patterns were quite good in density, but a surprise came when the I.J. was used on clay birds. Using Federal loads (3¼-1⅛-7½), Federal Champion II (2⅝-1⅛-8½), and Remington All American loads (2¾-1⅛-8) and alternating barrels, there was no difficulty in regularly breaking the birds—usually in a puff of black dust.

The I.J. comes up well and should do well in the field, although the season had passed before an opportunity came to try it on game. It does seem slightly overpriced, in view of the stock quality, at $259.95 for the two-trigger model and $272.25 for the single trigger, but it handles well and, more importantly, it puts the shot charge where it is supposed to be—right on target at 40 yards and slightly beyond. If all the new O-Us from I.J. do as well as we should see many of them afield this fall. LSS

Beretta BL-2/S

This writer first saw and handled the Beretta BL-2/S in early February 1974, but it was nearly 1975 before this unique trigger O/U was available for use in the field. The trigger, which pivots in the middle, is shaped with two concave surfaces on its forward edge; a pull on the upper surface fires the bottom barrel, with a pull on the lower surface firing the upper barrel. (The trigger is marked on the left side with a "B" (bottom) and a "T" (top) to indicate the correct barrel, in case you forget.) Sounds simple, and it permits the hand to remain in the same position on the grip. Another advantage lies in the trigger finger having instant barrel selection available without having to push a button or lever, or move to a different trigger as with a two-trigger shotgun. The only disadvantage is getting use to moving the finger up or down on the trigger, but practice will soon overcome this problem.

The BL-2/S is 43 5/16" over-all, its 26⅜" barrels topped with a .275" matted-surface ventilated rib having a .115" aluminum bead. The barrels are joined only at the breech and muzzle—there are no side ribs. The action is the same as Beretta has used on their boxlock O/Us for many years—twin truncated locking bolts from the standing breech projecting into abutments on the barrel breech. The new O/U weighs 6 pounds 10 ounces, or 10 ounces lighter than a previous Beretta which had 27 15/16" barrels. Part of this weight decrease is due to the lack of side ribs, and the shorter barrels, but the remainder is apparently due to the stock wood, which appears to be beech stained a dark walnut color and given a glossy finish, instead of being European walnut.

The barrels are finished a non-

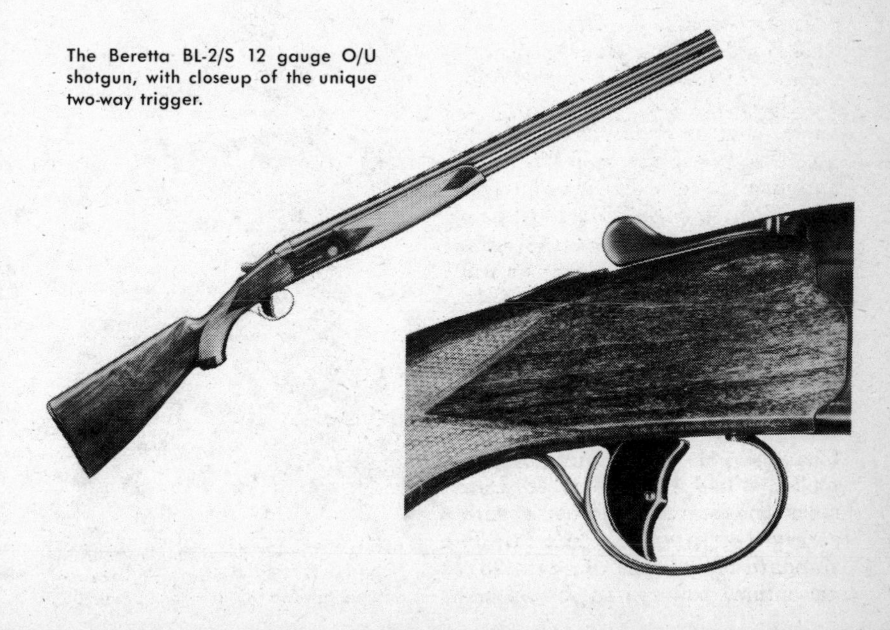

The Beretta BL-2/S 12 gauge O/U shotgun, with closeup of the unique two-way trigger.

glossy brushed blue, while the top of the receiver, trigger and the trigger guard have a high luster blue finish. The receiver sides are not as highly polished as the top, but do have more luster than the barrels. Over-all the metal finish is up to the usual excellent Beretta standards. Decoration on the BL-2/S consists of the Beretta trademarks on the receiver sides and bottom, plus some good quality scroll and floral designs on the barrel breech, receiver bottom, and top lever. All markings are uniform in depth and very evenly done, with the one exception of the "P. Beretta Gardone V.T." on the left side of the barrel being double stamped. If decoration is to be used, this writer prefers good quality stamped (rolled-on) designs to poor quality engraving, and the Beretta quality is good.

The cross-grooved safety button is automatic. Contoured slightly to match the thumb shape it could still be improved a bit.

The between-the-barrels extractor raises both shells—fired and unfired—about ¼". Ejectors are not available.

The lower edge of the buttstock has the European fish-belly shape, and the fore-end is similarly curved. The comb on this O/U is perfect for the writer—fluted on both sides—and much better than the narrow combs on the older Beretta O/U shotguns. Drops are 1½" and 2½" at comb and heel respectively, with a 14⅜" pull. The pistol grip has a black plastic cap with the Beretta trademark, as does the black plastic buttplate. The wood to metal fit is good, with only a minor amount of wood projecting above the metal. The stock finish is excellent on the outside surfaces, but some inner wood surfaces are not finished. The grip and fore-end are checkered 18 lines-per-inch, with a narrow two-line border. Runouts are few, the diamonds are complete for the most part, and the lines are generally straight where they are supposed to be straight. However, because the stock finish was applied after the checkering was done the checkering is more decorative than useful.

The fore-end latch, a circular-type located in a small dished-out area on the fore-end bottom, is grooved at the rear portion for non-slippage. Rotating it forward against the stock permits the fore-end's removal.

The BL-2/S is marked "modified" on the top barrel and "improved cylinder" on the lower barrel, which means it should pattern about 45-55% and 35-45% respectively. To verify this it was patterned with 4 different loads in the top barrel and one in the bottom barrel, prior to trying it at the trap range and in the field. Averages were based on 5 shots at the 40 yards distance. Starting with the Winchester-Western dove load (3-1-8) top barrel averaged 42.4%, or just a bit lower than modified. (The dove load is a paper-cased load without a pellet protector, and using a conventional molded fiber wad column.) Switching to the all plastic Herter Inter-Nation load (2¾-1⅛-7½) with its plastic wad column and plastic top wad brought the pattern averages up to 52.9% in the 30" circle. A further increase was provided by the excellent Federal Champion II (2¾-1⅛-8½) load, average 60.2%. (In some full-choke shotguns this same load has averaged 80-90% patterns for me.) Most shotguns pattern tighter with larger shot sizes, and the BL-2/S was no exception. With the Winchester XX Magnum Mark 5 load of 1½ ounces of No. 4 shot the average jumped to 73.6%, which should more than take care of ducks and pheasants at conventional ranges. The Herter load was also checked in the bottom barrel, where it averaged an even 38.0%. All the patterns provided by the BL-2/S were well within the generally accepted standards for the choke, and well above average for some shot sizes, indicating the Beretta may well be choked tighter than marked.

When checked on flying targets—Remington Blue Rocks and such quail as would cooperate—the BL-2/S performed like a trooper. The center-of-gravity is right at the hinge area, and the shotgun swings easily and aligns perfectly on the bird when the butt touches the shoulder—at least for this shooter. The trigger pulls checked out at 3½ and 6¼ pounds respectively for the lower and top barrels, or about average for field model O/Us. The let-off is crisp, and when shooting at moving targets the pulls seemed lighter than they actually were. As mentioned the shifting of the finger on the trigger takes some getting used to (concentration), but the BL-2/S offers a fast and handy system, and should be seeing a lot of field use. I suppose there were design difficulties, but how much more convenient it would have been if the top of the trigger fired the top barrel—and vice versa.

LSS

At presstime Garcia announced that they will no longer distribute the Beretta guns.

Mannlicher-Schonauer Model 72

Mannlicher-Schonauer carbines and rifles have been around in military or sporting form for some 75 years. Their outstanding feature was the rotary magazine, which proved entirely reliable over the years. Thus, when Steyr finally put the time-tested design out to pasture that decision was resented by many shooters. The Austrian firm apparently felt something also, for it wasn't long before a redesigned Mannlicher-Schonauer was introduced. Labeled the M72, the new model retained the best features of the old—the rotary magazine, excellent finish, and slim fore-end—and coupled them with an entirely

The Mannlicher-Schonauer M72 rifle, the bolt partially retracted to show the locking lugs.

The M72 as tested in 6mm caliber had double set trigger and the Europa quick-detachable scope mount—shown here with the scope ready to be lifted off. The bolt sleeve safety is depressed to the left so it is in the "firing" position, and the spiral form of the barrel can be seen below the objective end of the scope.

new receiver assembly.

The test piece—a Model L/M in 6mm Remington caliber—is 40⅛" over-all with a 19⅞" barrel. The barrel, cold-forged via multiple hammers, has a twisted appearance on the outside. Steyr, instead of grinding the outside surface fully round, as Sauer does with the Weatherby barrels, leaves the outside surface as it comes from the forging machine.

The barrel has a ramp.mounted front sight having a .085" German-silver bead, and a single square-notch rear leaf is dovetailed into a base fastened to the top of the barrel. Being dovetailed, both sights can be moved for windage, but not for elevation. The sight radius is 14½", and the sights are mounted high in order so they can be seen above the mount bases when the scope is removed, and to align with the Monte Carlo stock. The Redfield 2x-7x scope was mounted in a Steyr-made quick-detachable "Europa" model mount, quite similar in use to the Redfield JR type.

The walnut full length stock has the characteristic blued steel nosecap, slim fore-end, full pistol grip with white spacer and rosewood cap with white diamond inlay, a Monte Carlo comb with cheekpiece, and brown rubber recoil pad with black base and white spacer. The comb is reasonably wide, fluted on both sides, and the correct compromise height for use with the iron sights when cheeked tightly, and the scope when cheeked a bit more loosely. The grip and fore-end are 20 line hand checkered inside a wide two-groove border. The checkering was good, with few runouts, but there were a few flat diamonds and the top edge of the fore-end pattern on the left side was a bit wavy. Non-detachable ⅞" sling swivels are standard equipment.

Unlike the original Mannlicher-Schonauer, which had a split receiver bridge and a bolt handle that turned down in front of the bridge, the M72 has a Mauser-type action with a bolt handle that locks down behind the bridge. The bolt is a bright-finished cylinder .787" in diameter at its maximum (the rear portion is relieved slightly and blued). Locking is via 3 sets of dual locking lugs forward on the bolt. Spaced 120 degrees apart, and of the same diameter as the bolt body, they lock into corresponding recesses in the receiver ring. The left side of the bolt head is slotted for a Mauser-type ejector, and a sliding extractor (something like a M70 Winchester) is recessed into the front lug on the right. About ⅓ of the cartridge head is enclosed by the bolt face on the upper left, and about the same amount is enclosed by the rather large extractor. The bolt body has .080" gas ports to vent any escaping gas to the right out of the ejection port. The bolt stop is a steel cylinder projecting up thru the bottom of the receiver behind the mazagine; it also acts as a guide by sliding in a groove in the bottom of the bolt body. Pulling firmly back on the front trigger lowers the bolt stop, permitting withdrawal of the bolt.

The bolt handle is the butterknife-style, deeply grooved on the underside. The streamlined bolt sleeve is a combination sleeve and safety. The cocking piece projects about ¼" beyond the bolt sleeve when the rifle is cocked, with a bright red dot then visible on top. In addition the bolt sleeve has a bright red rectangular area on its right side behind the bolt handle, visible when the safety is not on. The sleeve has wings projecting from both sides; when the right wing is pushed down the rifle is on "safe"—the sear is blocked and so is the bolt handle—and a white mark on the sleeve lines up with a white "S" on the left side of the receiver to so indicate. Pushing the left wing down exposes the red area on the right of the sleeve, and lines up the white mark with a red "F" on the receiver to indicate the rifle is now in firing condition.

The test rifle had a double-set trigger. Pulling the rear trigger sets the front trigger for firing. The front trigger will also fire the rifle without being set, and the amount of pull is adjustable by means of a setscrew located between the triggers. Right out of the box the unset pull measured an even 2 pounds and a clean 8 ounces when set, without any creep.

Removing what appear to be the guard screws on the M72 only removes the trigger guard and the magazine floorplate—the barreled action is still retained by additional screws beneath. The floorplate appears to be machined from solid stock but is actually a highly polished steel stamping. The skeletonized magazine body is a non-ferrous casting, while the rotor is black plastic. To load the magazine —capacity 5 rounds— the cartridges are simply pushed down against the rotor; a lip projecting from beneath the right receiver rail retains the cartridges. Pushing down on a grooved lever or button in the right receiver rail withdraws the retainer, and the cartridges in the magazine pop up into your hand, powered by the rotor spring. It's a simple and rapid way to empty a magazine.

At the range the action was quite stiff, and it was impossible for the writer to cock the rifle while it was at the shoulder. After some 30 rounds, however, the mechanism loosened a bit and from this point on it was reasonably easy to cock the rifle at the shoulder. Three-shot groups were fired at 100 yards from the bench, with the Redfield set at 7x. Norma, Remington and Western factory cartridges loaded with 100-gr. bullets were used, plus the new Western Super-X 80-gr. load and some Gevelot cartridges loaded with 87-gr. PSP bullets. All groups averaged just over 1⅞" with the smallest 21/32", using the New Western Super-X cartridges loaded with 100-gr. Powerpoint SP bullets. None of the Western or Norma loads shot over 2", and the 80-gr. Super-X load made one group for an even 1". Since the rifle had done so well with the scope, I checked the open sights using the Super-X 80-gr. and 100-gr. loads. The results were discouraging with none of the groups going under 7" at 100 yards. The rifle/ammunition combo is accurate—with the scope—so apparently the open sights leave a bit to be desired since with another rifle using iron sights the writer shot several 1"-2" groups during the same session.

At $650 with the open sights the M72 is a handy rifle, but certainly not low or medium priced! With the Redfield 2x-7x scope it weighed an even 8 pounds but, perhaps because of the slim fore-end and short total length, it seemed much lighter. LSS

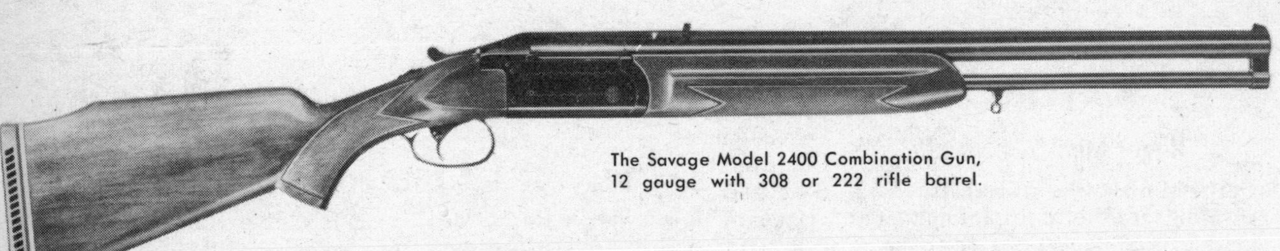

The Savage Model 2400 Combination Gun, 12 gauge with 308 or 222 rifle barrel.

Savage Model 2400

Combination guns, made over the years by Savage, Marlin, Stagg and some others, have not—excepting the Savage M24 series—sold very well. In their latest 2400 Savage has one of the best looking, best handling combo arms seen in a long time.

Made by Valmet of Finland (as are the Savage 330 and 333 O/U shotguns), the 2400 has a 12 gauge barrel over a choice of a 308 or 222 rifle barrel. (This test gun has the former combination.) Measuring 40½" overall with 23⁹⁄₁₆" barrels, the 2400 weighed 7 pounds 8 ounces as it came from the box.

The shot barrel has a .315" solid rib, its top non-reflective, and a .090" blade front sight, dovetailed in from the muzzle. The rear of the rib is wider, and milled to take a Sako-type scope mount. A rear sight with square notch, attached to the front of the scope mount base portion, folds down into the rib, presenting an uninterrupted sighting plane for shotgun use. The open sight radius is an even 18".

The 2400 uses the same action as the 330 and 333 Savage shotguns, and the 12 gauge barrel is assembled in the mono-block of the 2400 as it is on the shotguns. The 308 barrel of the test gun is assembled in the same fashion, but immediately on leaving the mono-block it tapers to a diameter of .530". It is not rigidly attached to the shotgun barrel, but is free to move longitudinally through two adjustable barrels bands. The first band, located between 11" and 12" from the muzzle, uses a sloping dovetail arrangement parallel to the barrel for deflecting the barrel up or down to alter the point of impact in a vertical plane, while another band at the muzzle has dovetails which can move only to the right or left and thus move the point of impact in a horizontal plane. It's simple and it works. A lug silver-soldered to the bottom of the rifle barrel secures the fore-end.

The 2400 barrel selector is the same as on the shotguns—if the button is pushed in on the right side where the arrow points "down" it readies the rifle barrel; pushing it in from the left will ready the shotgun barrel. The single trigger mechanism is mechanical—after the first barrel is fired pulling the trigger again fires the other barrel, even if a light load is used.

The fore-end and buttstock are European walnut, not fancy, but well finished, even on the inletted areas. The fore-end is a U-shaped semi-beavertail type with finger ledges along the top edge. Two large panels on the grip and the fore-end are checkered—16 lines-per-inch on the latter, 18 lpi on the grip. It's of good quality, with only a couple of very brief runouts, and the lines are almost perfectly straight where intended. However, like many other sporting arms, the checkering is filled with the stock finish, making it more decorative than functional.

The pistol grip has a flat bottom, but no cap; an initial cap could be installed to personalize the arm. The black rubber recoil pad has a white spacer. Nondetachable ¾" sling swivels are fitted, a size not readily found in the U.S. Savage has asked Valmet to put standard 1" swivels on the 2400, but little things take time.

The wood-to-metal-to-metal fit is excellent—not always seen on mass-production arms.

Length of pull is 14", with drops at the comb, heel of Monte Carlo, and heel, of 1½", 1¾", and 2½" respectively. The Monte Carlo is not pronounced, and there is no cheekpiece. The medium-wide comb is not fluted. This writer prefers a fluted and wider comb, but this one is decidely more comfortable than many found on other European shotguns and rifles.

To check the 2400's improved-modified choke marking, 4 loads were patterned for an over-all average of a surprising 75.5%. Individual 5-shot averages ranged from 58.4% for S&W's Hi-Velocity (3¾-1¼-6) load to 96.3% for Remington's Express 00 Buck load. (It was expected that the larger shot size would provide the highest pattern percentage, although I-M chokes are supposed to pattern in the 55/65% range.) Winchester Upland (3-1-5) loads gave a 62.9% average; Winchester XX Magnum load, with 1½ ounces of 4s, came through with a well-distributed 84.1%. The smaller shot sizes were not patterned but, when the 2400 was tried on clay birds—the season was over on live birds—the results certainly indicated good target-breaking patterns.

Scope mounts were not available for the 2400 during my time with it, but most major mount makers will have them in due time, I understand. As a result all firing was done using open sights, which are not adjustable for windage or elevation. Thus, without a scope, it would be advisable to find one load that would print at the point of aim and stick to it for all shooting with the rifle barrel. Three-shot groups were fired at 100 yards from the bench, using sandbag fore-arm and butt rests. Dominion and Federal 308 ammunition was used, with bullet weights ranging from 130-gr. to 180-gr. All printed over 4", and bullet weight didn't seem to make much difference—other loads might make smaller groups, but in a combination gun of this type iron-sight groups around 4½" were not unexpected.

A few rounds were fired offhand to see how the 2400 would handle afield. When the butt touched the shoulder, and the cheek settled on the comb, the front blade was perfectly aligned in the square notch. So this shooter, at least, would have no excuse for missing.

The metal of the 2400 shows a high-polished blue-black finish. There is no decoration on the metal other than the Savage name on the bottom of the receiver, and a simple line stamping on the receiver walls.

The 2400 has an automatic safety, a thing this shooter has never cared for—unless he puts it "on" he forgets to take it "off." However, the tang safety is large and deeply grooved so it can be operated easily, even with gloves on.

The 2400 is one of the most versatile guns to appear on the market in several years, and it handles better than others of this type that have been tried. Priced at $399.50, the 2400 is equal to or better in quality than other arms in that range. L.S.S.

Ruger Mini-14 Carbine

The Mini-14 was shown on the back cover of the 28th ed. GUN DIGEST and described in that same issue. But it wasn't until late 1974 that they started to become really available. Because basic specs and dimensions are shown in the table, I won't cover them here. Beside the 5-and 20-round magazines available, a 30-round version for police use will soon be available.

The action appears to be a miniature M-14, and the operation is similar in locking, safety, and takedown. But it is not a scaled-down copy of the M-14. The gas-operating system is entirely different. Instead of a tubular operating rod, the Mini-14 uses a heavy, investment-cast operating slide housed in the fore-end, which is lined with sheet steel. The front of the slide is hollowed to fit over a gas nozzle fixed to the barrel. Gas bled from the barrel drives the slide to the rear, operating the mechanism, with any excess gas exhausted into the steel-lined fore-end.

The trigger/hammer assembly is based on a Browning design in use for well over 50 years, and the manual safety is similar to that found on the M1 Garand and later M-14. Located to the left of and in front of the trigger guard, the safety lever protrudes into the trigger area when "on," where it is easily felt. Blocking the hammer and the trigger, it must be "on" before field-stripping of the rifle is possible. To ready the Mini-14 for firing requires only a forward push of the safety with the trigger finger to the "off" position—it's fast and simple.

Takedown is almost identical to

Ruger 223 (5.56) Mini-14 Carbine

Technical Data

Weight (mag. empty)	6.4 lbs. (2.9kg.)
Length	37.25" (94.6cm)
Length, std. barrel	18.5" (47cm)
Rifling—6 grooves, right twist, one turn in	12" (30.5cm)
Sighting radius (100 yd. setting)	22.10" (56.1cm)
Sight gradations (adj. for windage and elev.)	One MOA
Stock	Steel-reinforced American walnut
Mechanism	Gas-operated—fixed piston
Feed (5 or 20 round)	Staggered box magazine
Trigger pull	4.5 lbs. (2kg.)
Caliber: 223 (5.56mm)	Standard U.S. Military ball or commercial cartridges
Chamber pressure (max. ave.)	51,500 psi (3504at.)
Maximum range (approx.)	3000 yds. (2740m)
Mizzle velocity	3300 fps (1005m./sec.)
Muzzle energy	1330 ft. lbs. (183.9kg./m)

Note similarities between the Mini-14 (foreground) and the 308-cal. M-14 (M1A). Locking is basically the same, as is the take-down. The M-14 has a stripper clip guide ahead of the rear sight, the Mini-14 does not.

Left—The author fires the Mini-14 offhand, finding the carbine light, fast on target, a pleasure to shoot.

Below—Cutaway view of the Mini-14, showing the gas-piston beneath the barrel and the Garand-style trigger assembly. The magazine is the 20-round version.

that of the M1 Garand; remove the magazine, cock the action, put the safety "on," spring the rear of the trigger guard out with a bullet tip and pull the guard down and forward. The rifle can now be separated into three units—trigger assembly, barreled action and stock assembly—and all in about 5 seconds.

The walnut-finished stock, plus handguard, is better shaped than the famous M1 carbine. The grip area is smaller, and the Ruger buttplate (found on the 22 and 44 Ruger carbines also) tends to center the butt on the shoulder, making it fast to get on target. Inletting of the upper handguard carries no finish, but the action area of the stock does, as is true also of the steel-lined fore-end.

The 5-round sheet steel magazine has a heavy plastic floorplate that bears the Ruger name and trademark. The molded follower is of the same material. To insert the magazine it is slid in against the front edge of the magazine well and rocked back until it "clicks" in place, flush with the bottom of the stock. To remove, the release at the rear of the magazine is pushed forward and the magazine literally jumps out.

Sights on the Mini-14 consist of a .070″ brass bead dovetailed into a muzzle band, plus a rear peep resembling the Garand version, but not the same. (See table for click values and sight radius).

The Mini-14 has no provisions for mounting a scope, though one could be attached to the left receiver wall. Shooting with the standard open sights, 3-shot groups were fired at 100 yards from the bench using GI Hard Ball, Federal, Norma and Remington sporting loads. Group sizes ranged around 3″, which is darn good with open sights and a mixture of ammunition. The smallest group measured 1¼″, and was obtained with some of Interarm's 5.56mm Hard Ball. (This excellent ammo, manufactured in Singapore, is Boxer-primed, loaded with 55-gr. FMJ bullets, and *did* retail at $12.50 per box of 50 rounds.) This ammo made several other excellent groups, average about 1$\frac{5}{16}$″, indicating the quality of the Mini-14 and the ammunition.

The Mini-14 was fired offhand to check handling qualities, and it felt entirely suitable for running targets. Ejected cases weren't as hard to locate as expected, for they fall just to the shooter's right, usually within 6 feet. The 2-stage trigger pull checked out at 5¾ pounds.

Only factory ammo was tried in the Mini-14, but not because of any strength factor. Gas-operated guns require cartridges be loaded to a certain pressure level, and we didn't have time to tailor a suitable handload, one that would operate the mechanism reliably all the time.

The Mini-14, though military in appearance, could make a very handy small bore rifle for varmints and various small game. Retailing for $200, it should find a host of buyers. LSS

Valmet M-62/S

The current Soviet family of small arms appeared right after World War II, but it wasn't until the past decade that many Americans became aware of the AK-47 and related versions produced in the satellite countries. The AK-47 is a full-automatic arm, and as such its ownership is frowned on, not to mention the expensive $200 tax. Now there is a semi-automatic version available from Interarms labeled the M-62/S and made in Finland by Valmet—the firm that produces the Savage's 330 and 333 O/U shotguns, plus their new 2400 combination gun.

Measuring 37″ over-all with an 18″ barrel, including the flash suppressor, the M-62/S weighs about 8¾ lbs. with an empty 15-round magazine. Except for the sear mechanism, the walnut grip and buttstock, and some external features, it is a good copy of the arm used by the Finnish armed forces (a model with a tubular metal buttstock is also available). The walnut buttstock has a 13¾″ pull and a black plastic buttplate. The pistol grip is also walnut, the perforated fore-end is a synthetic, and there's no upper handguard. The metal shows a dull gray "parkerized" finish, except on the magazine.

Priced at $300, the M-62/S is a solidly-machined arm, the only notable stampings being the receiver cover, magazine, safety and the trigger guard/magazine catch assembly. The magazine is constructed of spot-welded ribbed stampings, with one

Left—The author shooting the Valmet M-62/S. Below—Closeup of the Valmet M-62/S in the foreground, the safety "on," with a M1A National Match rifle behind it. The M1A can be loaded with stripper clips, but there is no such provision on the M-62/S.

machined part, and it has a removable floorplate for ease in cleaning.

Unlike the AK-47, which has the front sight mounted on a high band at the muzzle, the front sight on the M-62/S is dovetailed on top the gas block. The sight is a hooded .10" round post, which can be moved for windage via opposing screws. There is also a .20" wide night sight, with a white dot, that can be flipped up in poor light. On the various AK-47 rifles the rear sight is an open notch, Mauser sliding tangent type, mounted on the barrel just ahead of the receiver, and calibrated from 100 to 800 meters. These have a sight radius of about 15". The M-62/s rear sight is a similar Mauser-type, but marked from 100 to 600 meters, and with a vertically-adjustable rear aperture of .060" diameter. The rear sight is spot welded to the top rear of the stamped receiver cover, the sight radius 18½". The cover is rigidly attached so there is no apparent wobble of the rear sight.

In operation a loaded magazine is inserted by rocking it upward and back until a "click" is heard; to remove it, grasp it in the right hand, pull the release forward with the right thumb, and rock it down and forward. With a full magazine in place, pull back on the cocking handle, which is permanently fixed to the right side of the bolt carrier and travels with it during firing. When the handle is released the bolt will move forward, chambering a cartridge. When the magazine is empty, a hold-open device keeps the bolt from moving forward until the magazine is removed and the bolt retracted slightly, then released.

When the trigger is pulled a hammer strikes the floating firing pin, which then strikes the cartridge primer. The generated gas pushes the bullet up the barrel, with some of it diverted into the gas cylinder on top of the barrel. There is no gas regulator. The piston is driven back and the bolt carrier, built into the piston extension, has about ⅓" free travel while the pressure drops to a safe level; the gas is bled off through eight .120" holes in the gas cylinder. A cam slot in the bolt carrier engages the cam stud on the bolt and the bolt is rotated 35 degrees to unlock it from the receiver. There is no primary extraction to unseat the case during the bolt rotation, so a large claw-type extractor is fitted in the upper right portion of the bolt face. This holds the case securely until it strikes the fixed ejector formed in the left guide rail and is thrown out of the gun to the right; and it is thrown—about 25 feet to the right and forward. As the bolt travels to the rear it cocks the hammer and compresses the recoil spring, before coming to a halt against the solid end of the receiver. As the bolt returns forward it chambers a round from the magazine, the extractor grips the canellure of the case and the bolt stops; the carrier continues onward for about ⅕" after locking is completed, and during this movement the carrier safety sear is released and control of the hammer taken over by the trigger sear.

The trigger and firing mechanism is based on that of the time-tested M1 Garand rifle, indicating that it is difficult to improve on a good design. The safety lever—one of the largest on any current rifle design—is a stamped bar pivoted at the rear, applied by the firer's thumb, and mounted on the right side of the receiver. The top position is "safe," where it blocks the trigger, closes the slot where the cocking handle would normally slide, and physically prevents the bolt from coming back far enough to pass beyond the rear of a cartridge in the magazine; but far enough to see whether there is a cartridge in the chamber. In the down position it is "off," permitting the trigger to be pulled and the rifle fired. Operated normally, the safety is noisy, but it is reliable.

To disassemble the M-62/S remove the magazine and be sure the chamber is clear. Then press the rear of the recoil-spring guide into the rear of the receiver cover and lift the cover up and off. Push the recoil-spring guide forward to clear its rear housing and remove. Pull the cocking handle to the rear and remove the bolt carrier and bolt; the gas cylinder will slip out of its dovetail at the rear and can be removed at the same time. Separate the bolt from the carrier, and basic disassembly is completed. Assemble in reverse order.

To check the functioning and accuracy the M-62/S was fired from the sandbag bench at 100 yards. Several 3-shot groups were fired using the only 7.62x39mm ammunition currently available—the Finnish-made loads imported by Interarms. Firing a 123-gr. FMJ bullet to a velocity of 2070 fps, this ammo—a product of Lapuan Patruunatehdas—fed perfectly and groups averaged around 3". The Lapuan cartridges are Berdan-primed, making reloading them a chore, but it can be done. The cases are well heat-treated for long life. Feeding and ejection were excellent, but ejection was violent—fired cases landed 20-30 feet from the firing point—not exactly a handloader's delight.

Para-military arms such as the M-62/S may be considered sporting arms if they provide enjoyment, diversion, and/or a pastime for the shooter, but they're not the style of arm this writer likes to see afield during the hunting season. As for quality the M-62/S is one of the best of its type. Finishing of wood and metal is good to excellent, with wood-to-metal fit better than on many more conventional sporting rifles. There was one surprise; the left side of the gas block has a fixed 15/16" sling attachment, but there is no sling swivel or any provision for one anywhere on the buttstock, although one could be attached in a few minutes. LSS

The H&R Free Pistol

by LADD FANTA

Made for a relatively short period, and not in large numbers, the U.S.R.A. Model single shot was an excellent and accurate pistol in its ultimate version.

KNOWN AS THE U.S.R.A. model, this single-shot target pistol rapidly became the most famous—and most expensive—that Harrington and Richardson ever produced. Discontinued in 1941 and seldom seen today, those fortunate enough to own a good specimen should cherish it as one of the finest U.S. made pistols.

Since we cannot set the clock back 30 years or so, many manufacturing details are getting to be hazy and the H&R factory has only the most meager of general information to furnish. No more than 3500 of these U.S.R.A. pistols were made, and serial numbers starting with No. 1 ran consecutively through all modifications.

Historically, most gun buffs have heard or read something about the early day Creedmoor rifle matches, beginning in the early 1870s, but it is not generally known that handgun target shooting was a well-established competitive sport in the U.S. well before the beginning of this century. In 1886 pistol match shooting was done with such large-caliber revolvers as the 45 Colt and the 44 S&W Russian. Improvements in 22 Long Rifle cartridges and the advent of the Stevens single-shot pistols in that caliber were bettering the early records by 1888.

In 1900 the United States Revolver Association (USRA) was formed to foster and develop revolver shooting. This organization set down certain rules, some of which were important in the development of single-shot pistols.

The choice of a single-shot pistol in the early years after 1900 lay among the Remington rolling-block,

the S&W model 1891, and the Stevens pistols in their four different qualities and weights—the Lord, Gould, Conlin and Diamond models. In the following years, to supply suitable pistols for the USRA, the S&W Olympic and Colt Camp Perry models were produced. In 1928 Harrington and Richardson entered the target pistol field with a single-shot 10″ barrel fitted to one of their hinge-frame tip-up revolvers. With the able assistance of the late designer, Walter Roper, the later H&R U.S.R.A. models incorporated refinements that were truly outstanding for their day. Some of the salient features were, for example, a very light hammer with short throw or fall. This was the first real speed-lock action on an American-made pistol. The bore diameter was held to a small .217-inch and the barrel was chambered to seat bullets 1/32-inch into the rifling. The sights were of deep Patridge* type, with an undercut front sight with vertical adjustment; the rear sight was laterally adjustable, sloping rearward and shaded from side light. The trigger guard with integral rear spur gave a point of support for the shooter's second finger, enabling a very light hold. The

*Because of the problem of cost, I suppose, few so-called Patridge sights conform to Mr. Patridge's original design, now or at the time of the U.S.R.A. pistol. All such sights lack an essential element of his design, which was the use of a taper. Looking down upon a true Patridge front sight, one sees the blade tapering from its rear face forward. The square opening of the Patridge rear sight also tapers, the side walls becoming wider toward the muzzle.

The advantages of such tapering is obvious—one sees a sharply-defined, crisp opening in the rear sight, and an equally sharp-edged front blade.

Challenge of the Single Shot. Single shot firearms are often the recommended choice for beginner training, mainly because of safety. In general, economy and simple maintenance are also important factors to be considered. Many advanced shooters enjoy the deliberation of single shot firing since it has a way of instilling confident self-discipline to make that one shot count.

Unlike rifles and shotguns, few single shot 22 pistols are made today. For a few years the fine Webley "Match Invader" was offered here, but faded away. Aside from the costly Hämmerlis, there is the versatile, caliber-selectable T/C Contender. For about $40 a well-made German copy of the Stevens Favorite is currently available, with optional rosewood grips at a few dollars more.

The fired case (not pictured) remains chambered until the action is fully opened, whereupon it is forcibly ejected about 10 feet rearward. Note the almost straight "spur" trigger, a form best suited to be merely touched-off rather than conventionally pulled.

The relatively lightweight hammer describes only a very short arc, producing almost no inertial disturbance to the rest of the gun. Compare this short and fast fall with the typical sixgun's hammer travel!

The radiused grip frame—an excellent and simple design—permitted quick interchangeability of cheaper-to-make stocks in various forms. A single screw holds these one-piece grips securely; a metal insert within the grip accepts the screw. The trigger adjustment screw is in the upper front of the trigger guard.

The Stevens Lord Model (No. 36) weighed 44 ounces with its standard 10" barrel, sold for $16.50 around 1910. Compare frame form, frame length and spurred guard with the Conlin pistol shown.

The Conlin Model Stevens (No. 38) was identical to the Gould type except for the former's spurred guard, and sold at the same $16.50 price.

The cutaway view on the facing page shows the U.S.R.A. pistol fully cocked, the new double-point sear insuring that, should the hammer "slip from the thumb when being cocked," no damage to the full cock sear could result. The picture alongside illustrates the "safe" position of hammer and sear. These views were taken from an H&R leaflet published about 1934, which shows 5 different stocks available (not pictured here). The U.S.R.A. pistol was then priced at $30, extra grips were $2.20 to $2.75, and a fitted trunk-type case was $5. A 1939 H&R catalog, so-dated, shows the same prices. The 5-shot full-size targets shown, taken from the same 1934 H&R leaflet, were fired from machine rest at 50 yards with a U.S.R.A. pistol. The leaflet reads further, "Each pistol machine-rest tested, and target sent with the arm."

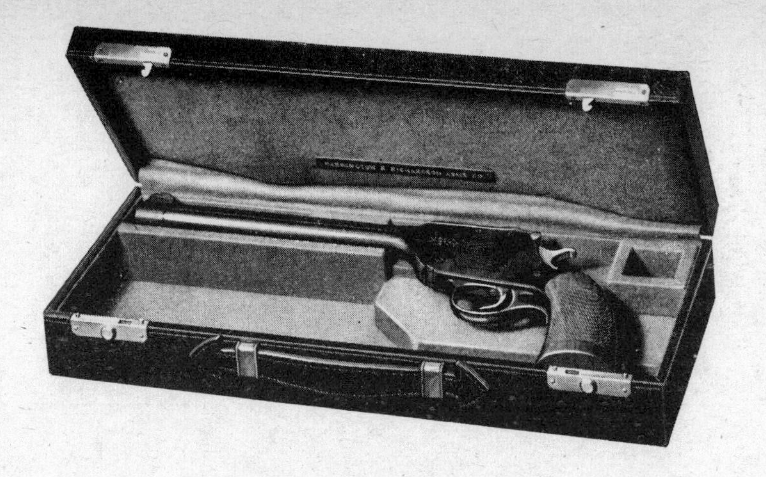

SPECIFICATIONS

The barrel—Either 7″ or 10″. Super accurate heavy type with thick top rib matted full length. Specially bored, rifled and chambered for the modern non-corrosive, smokeless 22 long rifle cartridge. New extra strong square barrel catch. **The action**—New type H. & R. Speed Action, with double point trigger, and non-jarring, rebounding hammer. Working parts made of hardened tool steel. Hammer and hinge joint bearings, large keyed bushings. **The sights**—Front sight, 1/10″ undercut Patridge adjustable for elevation. Rear sight, streamlined, square notch, undercut and side shaded, adjustable for windage and elevation by large interlocking screws. **The stocks**—Choice of five different shaped, interchangeable one-piece stocks of beautifully grained butt log walnut, finely checked on back and sides and finished in oil. **Adjustable trigger pull. Automatic ejector. Length over all** with 10″ barrel—13¼″. **Sight radius**—9″. **Balancing point** slightly forward of the hinge joint. **Weight** with 10″ barrel—31 oz., with 7″ barrel—28 oz. **Finish**—High polish, dark blue.

The New American Free Pistol Record!
532 x 600!

60 shots at 50 meters on international target (8″ bull's-eye small ring count). Made by R. C. Bracken, Columbus, Ohio, Sept. 18, 1932, with U. S. R. A. Model Pistol.

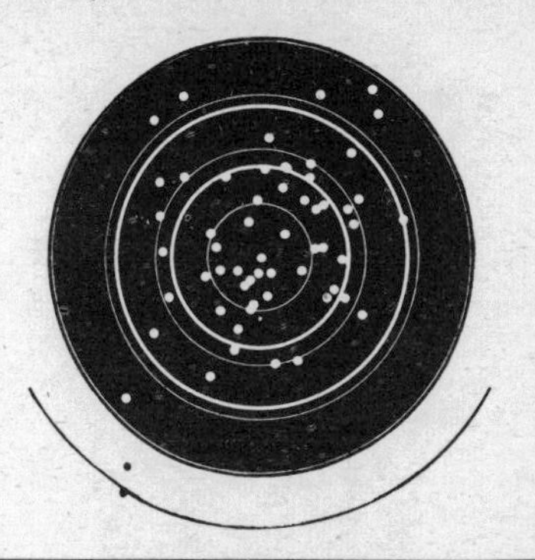

The New Intermediate Pistol Record!

Made by G. W. Bassett, East Longmeadow, Mass., April, 1933, with an H. & R. U.S.R.A. Model Single Shot Pistol. Standard American target, 2.72″ bull's-eye.

Range 20 yards
Score, 475 x 500!

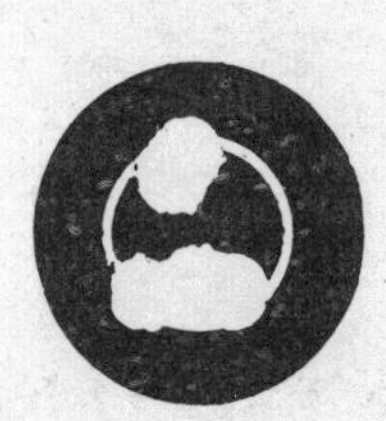

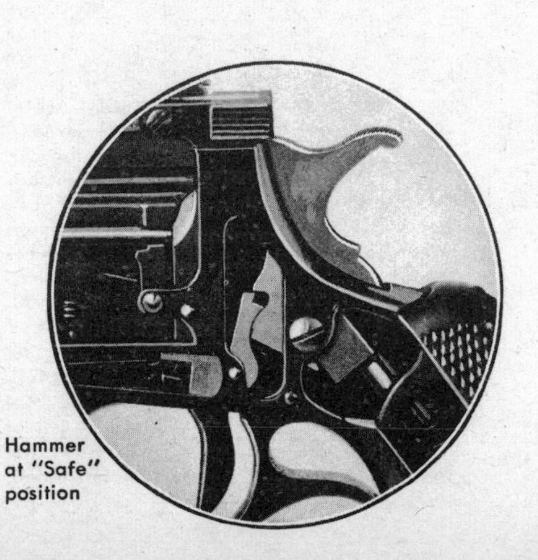

Hammer at "Safe" position

Cocked

Harrington & Richardson Arms Co.
WORCESTER, MASS., U. S. A.

H. & R. "Single Shot" Pistol (New)

The H&R "Single Shot" pistol shown here is reproduced from a 1929-dated small H&R catalog, No. 17. Though obviously the basis for the later U.S.R.A. type, several differences exist—the earlier ribbed barrel, made then in 10" length only; a well-curved trigger, the gurad without integral second-finger rest, and a hammer of different profile. The accompanying catalog copy does not mention the short trigger fall and fast lock time of the later U.S.R.A. pistol, and no model number is listed. The stocks pictured were not, I think, ever offered for the U.S.R.A. pistol, but they would have fitted, certainly. That seems to make 13 grips offered at one time or other.

Stocks Available
For Models 777 - 199 - 999 - 944

No. 1 — For small or thin hands.

No. 2 — Like No. 1, except thicker and more rounding.

No. 3 — Same as No. 2, but with lip at top.

No. 4 — Frontier type.

No. 4-O — Same shape but thicker.

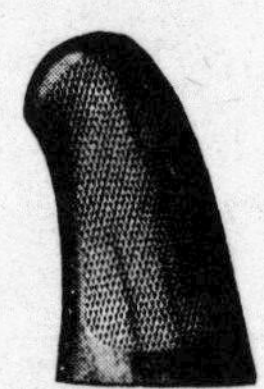

No. 5 — Free Pistol type.

No. 5-O — Same shape but thicker.

No. 4TR — Thumb Rest.

No. 4, 4-O, 5, 5-O may be had with Thumb Rest Feature.

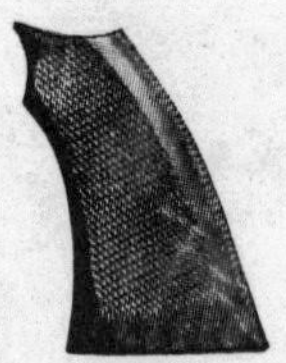

These are the 6 basic stocks offered for the H&R U.S.R.A. pistol in 1939, our reproduction made from the H&R catalog 22 of that date. As the catalog notes, thumb rest grips could be had for Nos. 4, 4-0, 5 and 5-0, in addition to No. 4TR, which was standard with thumb rest, though not illustrated here. This makes by my count a total of 12 different stocks, yet on page 13 of the same 1939 catalog it is stated that 11 grips are available.

trigger was adjustable for a crisp, uniform and unchanging let-off of less than one pound. Clever frame design permitted the buyer to choose from at least 6 basic styles of interchangeable once-piece grips—and I believe a total of 11 or 12 styles were offered at one time or another.

In 1931 the H&R U.S.R.A. Model became available in a 7-inch barrel length, its weight 26½ ozs. Some were also made in an 8-inch barrel length. The 10-inch barrel models weighed 31 ozs.

The original H&R 22 pistols had a barrel of different section than was later used on the shorter barrels. The 10-inch barrels were essentially round, topped by a flat rib; these looked something like a flat-topped figure 8. The later barrels appear, in section, like a truncated teardrop, thus such barrels are heavier for a given length than the earlier type.

Shooting one of these early day match pistols can be a revealing and enrapturing experience. True, you can't shoot a rapid fire course, but then again you are not plagued by cylinder misalignment or bullets battered and shaved by a harsh magazine during autoloading cycles.

Years ago shooting notable Bill Toney, in preparation for ISU free-pistol shooting, changed from his Colt Woodsman to a 10-inch H&R U.S.R.A. Model. After shooting both guns for a few days, he found that he was netting about one point more per 10 shots on the International Target with the H&R. In another instance, a remarkable record was shot over the Olympic ISU course by E. A. Hatmaker of Florida using an H&R U.S.R.A. Model. Even today, specimens in good condition can hold their own against target grade U.S. made 22 caliber handguns. This is an excellent tribute to the skill and care which went into the manufacture of these fine pistols. ●

A History of Proof Marks

Military Proof Marks

This new "History of Proof Marks," begun in our 22nd edition, has been deeply researched by the author. Military arms from the late 18th century are covered in this 9th installment.

by Lee Kennett

IT USED TO BE said that the military were conservative in the matter of armament, adopting new types of weapons long after they have come into use in the civilian market. While this may have been true in many instances, it was certainly not the case with proof. While information on civilian proof is very scarce in the sixteenth century, and procedures rather haphazard, proof of military arms is frequently mentioned, from the heaviest cannon down to handguns. Though most armies in that period obtained their weapons from private sources, the contracts in almost every case laid down specific rules for proof before acceptance, this being administered in the presence of the accepting officers.

The usual proof charge in those early days was a charge of powder equal to the weight of the ball. This charge, which seems very heavy, was probably used for a very simple reason. In the excitement of battle soldiers frequently overloaded their arms, ramming home two or three charges before firing (muskets picked up on Civil War battlefields frequently contained two or more charges). Thus it was of great practical importance for these arms to withstand heavy overloads.

Governments took the matter of proof very seriously. Peter the Great would from time to time assist personally in the proof of musket barrels for his army. If a barrel burst, the Czar invariably sentenced its maker to undergo a whipping in the town square. Artillery officers conducted every conceivable test with firearms in the course of the eighteenth century. The first mention of interchangeable parts dates from 1723. In addition to ordinary proof, selected muskets were subjected to very heavy loads to ascertain their bursting point, which was sometimes surprisingly high. A French model 1777 musket tested in this way did not split its barrel until it had been loaded with a quarter pound of powder and eight balls to caliber.

During the 19th century the proof of military arms continued to be perfected, often being in advance of civilian proof procedures in this regard. In Napoleon's time French military small arms were already proved according to tables of charges, while the old powder-ball weight ratio still prevailed in most civilian proof houses.[1] The Jonkopping Arsenal in Sweden was using both provisional and definitive proof of musket barrels by 1830; provisional proof was designated by the stamp "P^1", definitive proof by "P^2". The artillery, the arm of the service charged with arms procurement in most armies, played a great role in the development of ballistics; both Le Boulengé and Rodman were artillery officers.

Though military proof has a long history, methods and procedures soon began to vary from those in civilian proof houses. Military arms rapidly became a distinct type, manufactured by governments themselves and proved as part of the manufacturing process. Here proof is no longer a protective barrier that keeps arms of doubtful or unknown quantity out of the hands of unwary users. It is but one small phase in a long series of tests and controls that begin with the chemical and physical properties of the steel used, and end with the accuracy tests given to the finished rifle. Here, for example, is a description of some of the quality controls involved in the manufacture of the Model 1893 Spanish Mauser:[2]

"The barrel material, which is the object of particular attention, must offer a complete guarantee. After its reception, one percent of each lot of barrel blanks undergo the following tests: Half the selected blanks undergo physical and chemical tests. The chemical tests consist of an analysis in which are determined the proportions of phosphorus, silicon, carbon, sulfur and manganese which the steel contains. These must conform to established formulae, with only the absolutely indispensable tolerances. Mechanical tests are made by breaking the blanks under traction... Solid bars one square centimeter in section must not lose their elasticity before being subjected to a strain of 11,000 lb., nor break under a strain of less than 16,500 lb. Moreover, in order to obtain information on what will occur when powder is fired in the arm, hollow tubes are made and filled with oil under very high pressure... until they rupture. The readings which result from these tests must exceed limits previously set. The second one-half percent of the blanks are made into barrels and submitted to a firing test with smokeless powder which produces

Military Proof Marks

Great Britain:

About 1830, view and proof

About 1850, view and proof

About 1905

Note: The crossed pennants proof mark, first used about a hundred years ago, has become standard. Early marks of this type are often found in pairs, with "1P" and "2P", for provisional and definitive proof. The royal cipher changes with each reign; VR meant Victoria Regina, ER meant Edwardus Rex, etc. The letter "I" was added to the cipher for arms made in India; thus ERI, Edwardus Rex Imperator, etc.

United States:

VPL	VF	V P	P Ⓟ	P Ⓟ Ⓟ
1799	1802	1862	1903	1934

Note: These are as given by Goddard in his *Proof Tests and Proof Marks.*

France:

E

Saint Etienne

Sailleville

Mutzig

Chatellerault

Tulle

Note: These marks, adopted about a hundred years ago, are both arsenal and proof marks.

Russia:

ПK

Pre 1917

Switzerland:

1900–

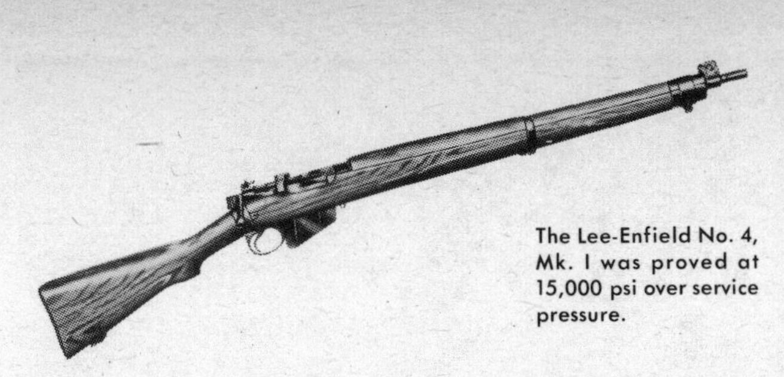

The Lee-Enfield No. 4, Mk. I was proved at 15,000 psi over service pressure.

Rifle	Service Pressure (psi)	Definitive Proof Pressure (psi)
Austr. Mannlicher M1895	44,800	57,000
Brit. Lee-Enfield No. 4 Mk. I	43,000	58,000
German Mauser M1898 (pre-1914)	42,500	57,000
Ital. Carcano M1898 (6.5mm)	36,000	42,000
Ital. Carcano M1938 (7.35mm)	38,000	47,000
Swiss Schmidt-Rubin M1931	45,000	64,000
U.S. Springfield M1903	50,000	70,000

a pressure of over 80,000 p.s.i.; and for the lot of blanks to be accepted, no barrel may have an enlargement of more than .05 mm. Finally, to prevent the possibility of a bad barrel finding its way among the good ones, through invisible defects, all rifles are proved with two shots of smokeless powder (2.85 grams of Nobel Smokeless), which produce a pressure never lower than 57,000 p.s.i. In addition, before leaving the factory, at least four shots are fired in each rifle with service cartridges to test accuracy and correct any defects in this connection." [2]

It goes without saying that all other materials and parts of the Model 1893 rifle were subjected to similar tests. These procedures, with various minor modifications, were those employed in most European arsenals.

Any researcher in the field of armament soon runs into the obstacle of official reticence, which is happily less pronounced in our own country than in Europe. Figures and specifications on military arms are not easily come by in Europe. Governments sometimes go to rather extreme lengths in keeping them confidential; a French arms expert was recently refused information on the production figures of the French Model 1873 revolver! For this reason information on proof pressures is very difficult to find. Reproduced above are official proof and service pressures for several types of military rifles, gleaned from various official and semi-official sources. In no case should they be used as a basis for devising loads for any rifle of a particular type. The quality and condition of surplus military rifles vary greatly; there was also variation in proof and service pressures, one or both being changed from time to time.

The carefully supervised manufacture of military arms renders firing proof less important; very few rifles indeed fail at proof. Even in the case of the old British Peabody-Martini, not one barrel in 50,000 burst at proof, though this was done with a double charge of powder and a projectile weighing fifty percent more than the service bullet. Such a large safety margin might well lead to the conclusion that firing proof of individual rifles could be omitted, and in some cases this was done. For the 1898 Model U.S. Krag, for example, barrels were tested *before* rifling or breeching at 70,000 and even 100,000 p.s.i., but after attachment of barrels to actions and completion of the rifles, the only firing seems to have been with service rounds, to check accuracy. The service pressure of about 38,000 p.s.i. was only 3,000 p.s.i. or so less than the maximum pressure that the relatively weak action could withstand.

Recognizable or distinctive proofmarks are uncommon on military arms, generally speaking, but there are some exceptions. In Belgium military weapons receive the same marks as civilian arms, but Belgium is unique in this regard. British and American arms have usually borne clearly discernible proofmarks. French military proofmarks are distinctive but not easily visible. They are impressed on the underside of the barrel, and the entire rifle has to be dismantled in order to see them. For most other countries there are no proofmarks *per se*.

Military arms do bear marks of all kinds, sometimes great numbers of them (a Model 1871 Dutch Beaumont rifle in the author's collection bears nearly a hundred, affixed to every part of the gun, including screw heads). The great majority of these marks are in most cases inspectors' marks, indicating that the part for which the particular inspector was responsible was found satisfactory by him. In most cases these marks are composed of letters, the initials of the various inspectors. Among these is the barrel inspector's mark, which often takes the place of a proofmark. Also customary is a government property mark, a coat of arms or a representative symbol such as the British broad arrow. This mark is often the last to be affixed, and indicates acceptance of an arm that has passed all tests, including proof. Still another category is composed of arsenal marks; these were simply the arsenal name, as was the practice in Germany for a long period of time, or a special symbol such as the crowned "E"s used in France or the arrows used in Russia. In recent years arsenal marks have tended to become more cryptic, in part for security reasons; an excellent case in point are the German letter codes used in World War II. The serial number remains a standard mark affixed to arms; unit designation is much less used than formerly, probably once again from security reasons. Unit designations were most often composed of a string of letters and numbers. Thus the stamping "B-1 R.C.2. 30" on a Mauser carbine meant "First Bavarian Reserve Cavalry Regiment, Second Squadron, carbine no. 30." ●

Footnotes

[1]These tables of proof charges may be found in H. Cotty, *Memoire sur la fabrication des armes portatives de guerre* (Memoir on Military Small Arms) Paris, 1806, p. 146.

[2]Jose Boado y Castro, *El fusil Mauser espanol, modelo de 1893* (The Spanish Mauser Rifle, Model 1893), Gijon, Spain, 1896, pp. 144-146.

PRESENTATION CREEDMOOR RIFLE

In celebration of John Amber's twenty-fifth year as editor of this annual publication, Bill Ruger—with the close collaboration of famed engravers Winston Churchill and Lynton McKenzie—has created for his old friend a superb long range target version of the Ruger Number One Single Shot rifle.

I'm going to try describing a rifle here that I haven't seen, one that is not yet—as this is written—quite finished. Why the unseemly, perhaps, haste? Good question, and one I'll answer in a moment, but first some background information.

As you've seen via the cover drawing—handsomely executed by Jim Triggs—John Amber is being saluted in honor of his twenty-five years as editor of GUN DIGEST. I'm sure that virtually everybody will recognize the artist-embellished rifle as a Ruger Number One Single Shot, the engraving depicting the editor's head amidst the scrollwork.

As regular readers of this publication know, Bill Ruger and Amber have been friends for a quarter-century. Both share and enjoy an interest in firearms of all kinds, but with a special attachment to quality rifles of whatever period—flintlock to metallic cartridge types, multi-shot or single shot, plain and fancy. Both men have acquired, over a long time, collections of rifles that are similar in most respects, and a high percentage of their rifles are of the Creedmoor and Wimbledon type—the long range competition rifles, muzzle-loading and breech-loading. Used for a rather short period relatively, these long-barreled single shots saw their heyday from about 1860 in the British Isles to about 1890 there and in the United States.

As everyone also knows, Ruger's single shot rifle is close in spirit and the externals to the far-famed—and much sought for in the originals—rifle developed and patented by John Farquharson.

In the goodness of his heart, and as a worthy token of their long friendship, Bill Ruger decided on a generous gesture to commemorate Amber's 25 years at the helm—he'd have prepared a specially engraved, custom built No. 1 rifle as a presentation piece to the editor, a rifle highly personalized as well.

But Bill Ruger doesn't do things by halves or in conventional fashion—not being a very conventional fellow himself. Rather than present Amber with a *fait accompli,* a rifle designed and constructed as Bill might like to have seen it done—much as that one would certainly have been an assured masterpiece—Ruger invited Amber to participate in the design, to even, indeed, plan and direct the operation.

The inlaid gold oval plate (facing page) is about two inches long, the engraving and period lettering by Winston Churchill.

Right—the left side of the Ruger No. 1 action carries John Amber's initials inside an inlaid gold oval, the background blackened. The surrounding engraving—best English scroll—was cut by Lynton McKenzie, as was the receiver top shown below.

A noble and gracious touch.

After several discussions between them on various aspects of the rifle to be, the project got under way in late 1974, but engravers, notably, don't work all that fast, so the rifle could not be completed in time for the 30th edition cover, which has to be readied long before the body of the book. That, then, is the reason for the simulation by Triggs of the actual, unseen, not-yet-completed rifle. By much the same token, as indicated above, this material has to be prepared well before publication date of this year's GUN DIGEST. On the other hand, photographs can be managed quickly, and I'm hopeful that some will be delivered in time to accompany this piece.

Here then, after the preamble, is at least a rough outline of what the finished rifle will look like. I've had several talks with Amber about this—though he has yet to glimpse the rifle—and here's what his plans called for.

First, the action, the heart of any rifle. Standard in form, of course, but its embellishment will be the work of two great engravers—a decidedly unusual collaboration—artists and craftsmen both, and both regarded everywhere, the world over, as pre-eminent in their specialties.

Winston Churchill, a native of Vermont, is famous for his command of scenic treatments. He has created a portrait head of John Amber, done in low relief and set inside a gold inlaid border on one side of the receiver. The other side carries John's initials, again within a gold border.

Lynton McKenzie—an Australian who spent some 5 years working in London for the gun trade, and now lives in New Orleans—is equally renowned for his superb engraving. Lynton now has the action and barrel, on both of which he will cut the background embellishment for Churchill's work. This will include large English scrollwork on the guard and lever, the tangs, the receiver—all with black backgrounds—barrel, back and front. A very intricate double-leaf border graces both sides of the action. He will also engrave the caliber markings on the barrel. I've seen a rubbing of the barrel work, and it was beautiful. The action will be finished in French gray, not blued.

The barrel is a special one made by Sharon Rifle Barrel Co. of Montana,

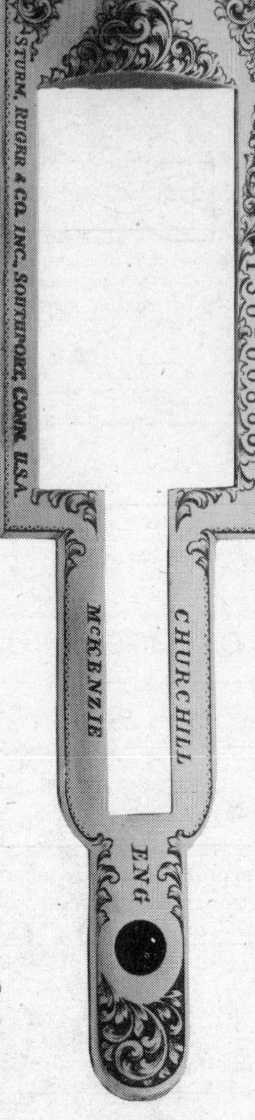

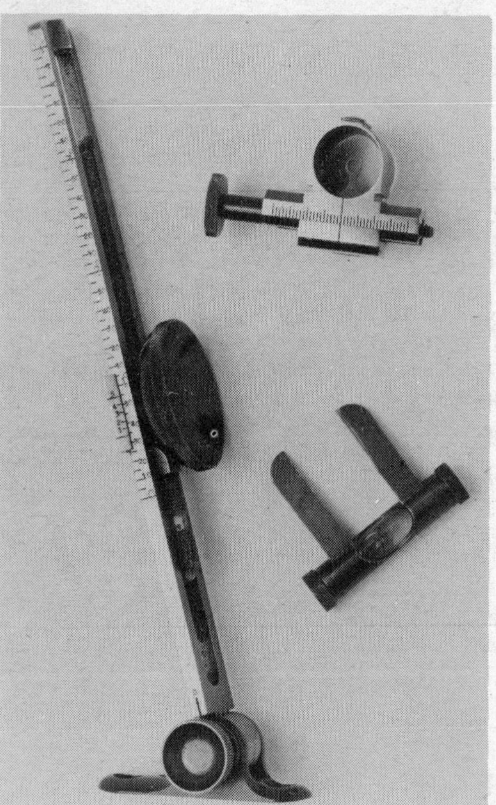

Above left—as on the left side of the action, Churchill sunk a gold oval to surround the head of John Amber, set against a black ground.

Above right—the bottom of the No. 1 receiver carries the engravers' names.

Left—modern replicas of a Sharps-Borchardt long range Vernier-scaled tang rear sight and a windgauge spirit-level front sight.

Below—the top rear flats of the 34-inch octagon-round barrel, made by Sharon Rifle Barrel Co. in 45/2.6-inch caliber, are decorated with McKenzie's scroll engraving, as is the muzzle.

a half-octagon 34 inches long, the caliber 45 with a 2.6-inch chamber, the long reamer supplied by Fred Huntington of RCBS. That barrel length was pretty much standard on Creedmoor rifles, and 2.6-inch cases were introduced by Remington for the 1874 International Matches held on the Long Island (N.Y.) range.

The buttstock and fore-end are of regular Ruger make, the wood well figured, and the fore-end of the shorter Alex Henry form. On the right side of the stock Winston Churchill inlaid a gold oval plate, about two inches long and carrying the presentation inscription. I don't know the exact wording or I'd put it down, but Winston cut it using appropriate old type faces and engraved a handsome single-leaf border around its perimeter. There wasn't time for a custom stock, either, but one will be made up later, says John, perhaps the work of a third craftsman.

That's the presentation rifle, then, as far as I can describe it in the circumstances. I envy John, but God knows he needs something to lift his spirits, as this masterpiece surely will. He suffered a series of body blows over the past few months—literally! A run of serious medical-surgical problems beset my old friend and shooting partner, but he's back at his desk now.

A.M. Wynne, Jr.

Pistols and Revolvers

Domestic and Foreign

A searching survey of the handgun scene as it exists today, with a close look at the scarcity situation now prevailing.

by GEORGE C. NONTE, Jr.

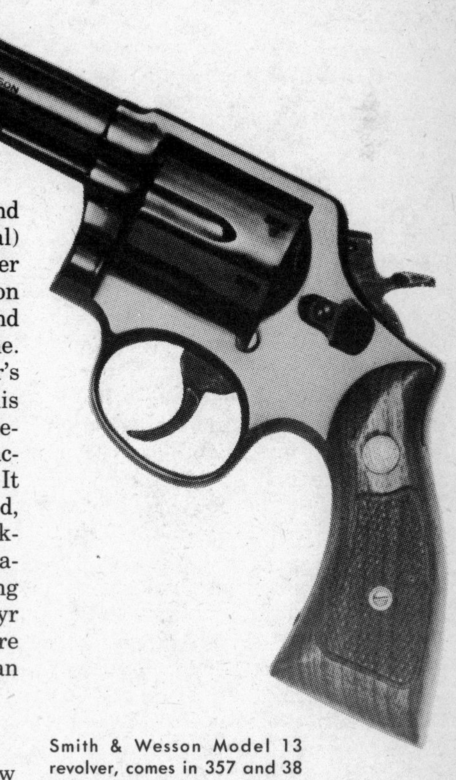

Smith & Wesson Model 13 revolver, comes in 357 and 38 Spl. calibers, with heavy barrel, K-frame and square butt.

WELL, IT'S THAT time again; the time when we look at what we can see, interpret what we can hear, add speculation, conjecture, and a bit of guesswork—and then try to give you the over-all handgun picture. Believe me, it ain't easy, though one would expect it to be. Simply repeating press releases, cocktail party statements by company executives, and catalog dope won't do it.

Those things do help a lot, though. For example, and without fanfare, Smith & Wesson finally introduced—and more important, shipped to the trade—a heavy-barrel version of the fixed-sight M10 square-butt revolver in 357 Magnum caliber. This gun has been wanting for many a year, and it's long overdue. It is listed as the M65 in stainless, M13 in plain, blued steel.

The new SIG/Sauer pistols (P220, P230) mentioned here last year are still not available, as was anticipated. We have, though, had an opportunity to examine samples brought here by a SIG representative. We've been told that a few P230s may be available late this year, and that the P220 will come in '76. Tentatively, Hawes Firearms has been appointed the principal importer, at last report.

During the 1975 NSGA show in Houston's Astro Hall, we saw a new 5-shot, 38/357 Magnum revolver in pre-production form. Produced by Security Industries, this design is superficially similar to the basic S&W series and is roughly the size and weight of the J-frame (Chiefs Special) line. Since then, ye editor John Amber has obtained samples of production guns and reports on their quality and performance elsewhere in this tome.

Likewise, you'll find friend Amber's report on the P18 9mm pistol in this edition. This Steyr-Daimler-Puch design, from Austria, is to be manufactured by L.E.S. of Skokie, Illinois. It features gas-assisted, but unlocked, breech closure, double-action lockwork, and 18-cartridge magazine capacity. John was fortunate in being able to shoot this gun at the Steyr plant in Austria last year, so has more background information on it than anyone else I know.

Star PD 45

Last year we mentioned the new Star PD 45 auto pistol. It's the smallest and lightest 45 auto ever produced commercially, and should appeal to many pistoleros. This scribe was able to obtain a sample (none have been sold yet, at this writing) and elsewhere in these pages you'll find a detailed report on it.

There is little new from Colt. The updating of the revolver line begun with the new 1972 Detective Special continues, but no *new* models have been added. Of special interest, though, to muzzleloading buffs is the fact that a few of the "New Dragoon" reproduction of the original percussion cavalry revolver have finally been shipped. This gun was introduced quite some time ago, but release of *production* guns was much delayed.

The Ruger handgun line shows little change since introduction of the Security Six series and the change-over to the new transferbar lockwork in all the single-action revolvers. Stainless steel 357 Blackhawk and 22 RF Single Six revolvers are now avail-

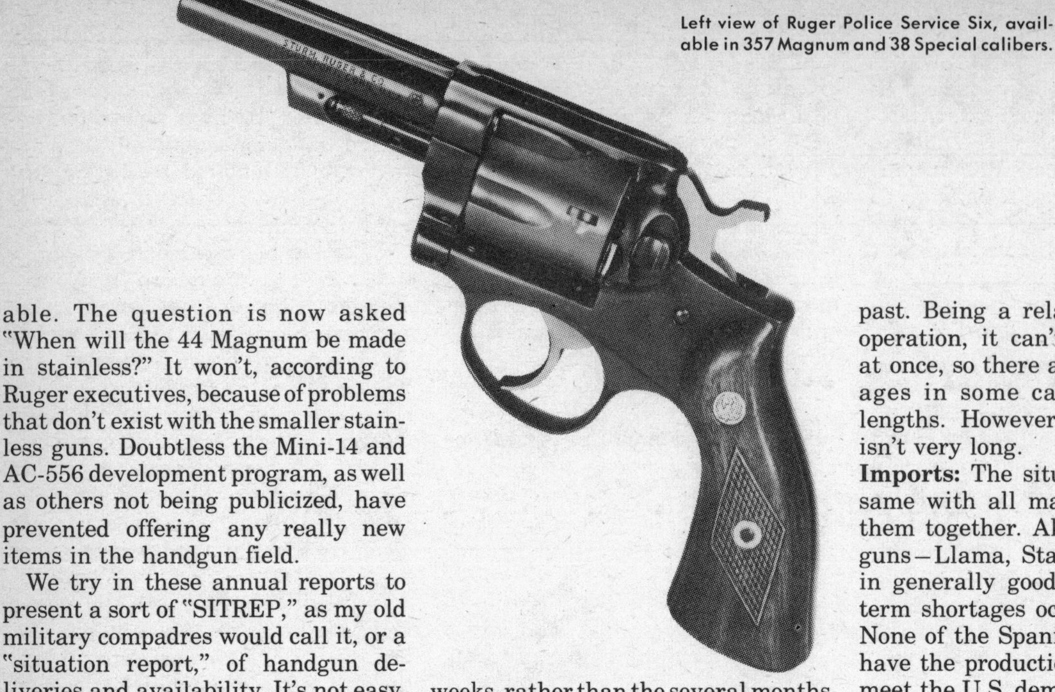

Left view of Ruger Police Service Six, available in 357 Magnum and 38 Special calibers.

able. The question is now asked "When will the 44 Magnum be made in stainless?" It won't, according to Ruger executives, because of problems that don't exist with the smaller stainless guns. Doubtless the Mini-14 and AC-556 development program, as well as others not being publicized, have prevented offering any really new items in the handgun field.

We try in these annual reports to present a sort of "SITREP," as my old military compadres would call it, or a "situation report," of handgun deliveries and availability. It's not easy, and we won't be right all the time, but here is what our phone calls and discussions have produced.

Smith & Wesson: All N-frame and all stainless revolvers are still in short supply, with some dealers reporting backorders of 6-12 months. There is thus a thriving premium-price market for the magnums, with some affluent (or foolish) buyers paying up to *double* the current list price for some variations and calibers. The M59 auto remains virtually unobtainable on the open market (due to heavy police orders, we're told), but M39s are much less difficult to obtain than a while back. S&W parts seem fairly easy to obtain.

Colt: Here the situation seems confusing, for one dealer will say he can't get guns while another has no complaints. There are periodic recurring shortages of most models except the bread-and-butter revolvers. Standard 45 Government Models seem fairly plentiful, but the 38 Super and 9mm versions are hard to come by. Lightweight Commanders are also scarce, as are Combat Commanders to a lesser degree. Parts are a problem, with one distributor reporting he had to wait 6-12 months for common replacement parts.

Ruger: Deliveries may be slow on some Ruger models, but don't believe that they aren't turning out more guns than ever before. I've seen the production schedules there, and the quantities of the more popular models being made would amaze you. Some models are in short supply, but delays are usually no more than a few weeks, rather than the several months of some other makers.

Indian Arms: As is often the case with a new gun and new production facility, this outfit has fallen far, far behind its planned production schedule. Its stainless-steel copy of the Walther PPK is quite difficult to find, and will surely remain so for quite a while. Nevertheless, guns are coming off the Indian Arms line as this is written, and more will be available soon.

NORARMCO: Producers of the very fine stainless-steel Budischowsky TP-70, a double-action 25 ACP auto, this company is also far behind schedule. Though production guns began coming off the line early in '74, their numbers are far too few to meet demand. Consider yourself very fortunate if you can obtain one. Also the 22 LR version of this gun, intended for production over a year ago, is not available yet.

High Standard: Deliveries here are fairly good, with only spotty and temporary shortages of certain models.

Auto Mag: Contrary to some reports, this outfit is still going and is producing more guns now than ever in the past. Being a relatively low-volume operation, it can't make everything at once, so there are recurring shortages in some calibers and barrel lengths. However, the wait usually isn't very long.

Imports: The situation is much the same with all makes, so we'll lump them together. All the good Spanish guns—Llama, Star, Astra et al—are in generally good supply, but short-term shortages occur now and then. None of the Spanish makers seem to have the production capacity to fully meet the U.S. demand, but they don't get far behind. Such new models as the Star D and PD are in scarce supply, as is usual with *new* items. German makers, mainly Walther and Mauser, keep up fairly well with the U.S. demand and, in fact, there is a surplus of some models and calibers in U.S. warehouses. Italian makers seem a bit slow, and don't appear to worry much about fulfilling U.S. requirements. As a result, there are shortages, especially so in the newer models.

Colt 3rd Model Dragoon black powder revolver, cal. 44 (for .457" round ball).

Finding Scarce Types

Generally speaking, the best way to obtain *any* scarce model at the standard price is to approach a large retailer, who will accept a bonafide order (with a cash deposit for encouragement), then follow through on it. It's obvious that a small, local shop selling only relatively few guns isn't going to get any special treatment by distributors, nor can he expect to automatically receive scarce guns. Simply checking shops periodically is the worst possible way to obtain a scarce gun. In fact, it's almost totally unproductive unless you're just lucky enough to arrive as a shipment containing what you want is opened—even then there may be an existing order for the item, so you can't have it.

On the other hand, if you simply *must* have an 8⅜-inch S&W M29 or other scarce item and can spare the loot, shop the open mail-order market. Quite a few dealers specialize in hard-to-get guns and can supply virtually any item you want at a premium price. Go this route if you like, but please don't pay double for something, and then write to me (as many have done), asking that we "do something about the black market." First of all, it's not a "black" market, but a legitimate *free* market operating under the well-known and irrefutable law of supply and demand. The word "black" connotes an unlawful market. which it is not. If people weren't willing to pay premium prices, the market wouldn't (couldn't, in fact) exist. Incidentally, one fellow I know seems to be able to supply almost any scarce S&W gun—that's Joe DeSaye, out in Turner, Montana 59542.

Combat Conversions

The field of "combat" and "combat competition" conversions continues to grow. Combat conversions are generally applied to big-bore autos, reducing their weight and bulk while increasing accuracy, reliability (especially with high-performance ammunition), and handling speed and ease. Such conversions are intended for serious, urban combat with human targets by professional gun handlers.

The most recent combat conversion I've tested is the "Devel," a much-altered Smith & Wesson M39 turned out in Cleveland, Ohio. The maker asks to remain anonymous until preparations are completed for prompt, production-line service on customer's guns. He says he has no intention of accepting any orders until prompt delivery can be guaranteed—certainly an admirable and rare attitude these days.

On the other hand, combat competition conversions are usually applied to 38 and 357 revolvers intended for formal PPC (police pistol combat) or similar combat-type police competitions. The features usually added are ribs and better sights, muzzle-heavy balance, sometimes thicker and heavier barrels, special grips (nothing new in that) and meticulous action tuning. Actions are often converted to double-action only, and are invariably regulated to the lightest DA trigger pull that will produce reliable ignition.

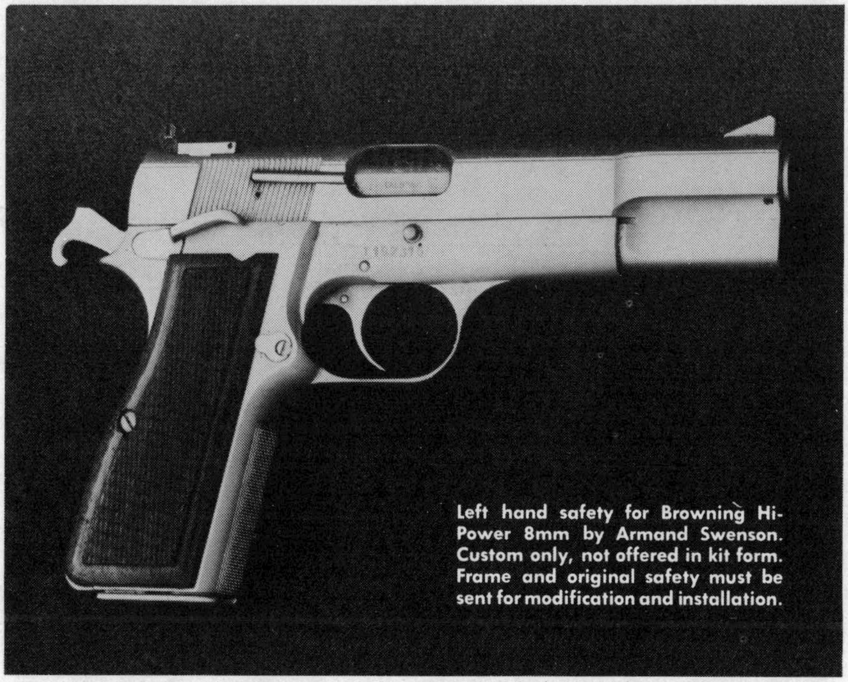

Left hand safety for Browning Hi-Power 8mm by Armand Swenson. Custom only, not offered in kit form. Frame and original safety must be sent for modification and installation.

Of this type conversion, I own the one pictured, made up by Austin Behlert (Custom Gun Shop), and it performs beautifully. The lockwork is stock, though much smoothed and polished. I've also tried the DA-only conversion of Fred Sadowski (300 Gunsmith Service) and it is superb.

Prices of conversions continue to soar. Several range from $400 to $500 or more, and one maker now charges well over $700 for a full-house combat conversion of the 45 auto. Whew!

We've discussed it with the maker and have examined photographs, but haven't yet had an opportunity to try the gun. It is a *true* double-action conversion of the justly-famed Browning/FN High Power 9mm P. autoloader. Louis Seecamp, who designed and now produces his excellent DA conversion of the Colt Government Model, has been working on a Browning conversion for several years. It is now fully developed and will be offered soon, perhaps in limited quantity by the time these words are in print.

We can't give any details until we try the gun, but Seecamp has an excellent reputation for both design and workmanship. There has long been a solid demand for a double-action variation of the 13-shot Browning and, oddly enough, the availability of the big-capacity, double-action Smith & Wesson M39 hasn't abated it. We predict Seecamp's Browning conversion will do well.

New Models

As usual, we've been bombarded this past twelvemonth with new handgun designs, most of them autos, most double-action, and most of them attempts at making the gun as small and compact as possible. Most of them are also intended for manufacture from stainless steel. Few, if any, of these guns exist except in prototype or working model form. They aren't in production now, and aren't likely to be for several years at best. Naturally, the designers plan on production, else they wouldn't spend great amounts of time and money on design and testing. However, making and selling a new gun in quantity—and making it at a practical price—is a complex and very costly proposition. Designers seldom

Combat conversion by Armand Swenson of full length 45 ACP has checked strap, squared guard, combat safety and S&W rear sight. Ten-shot machine rest group, fired after 6,000 rounds went through this pistol, measures ⅝" on centers, was made at 25 yards.

are able to finance such operations alone, so they must go on the open market for money, lots of it. And these days investors don't get very excited about handguns, no matter how good they look. The track record for new handgun companies looks pretty poor from the investor's point of view, with return slow in coming, even from a successful operation. Many new handgun companies have been attempted since the middle 1940s and several still exist, but only two, Sturm, Ruger and Charter Arms, can be judged genuinely successful.

The result of all this is clear—even though quite a few good-looking, new designs are in existence today, we won't see any of them in production soon if ever. New guns have a hard row to hoe, and the survival rate is very low except for those developed by big, long-established companies.

Accessories

Through the popular practice of installing sight-bearing ribs on some revolvers for competitive combat matches, Bo-Mar (Box 168, Carthage, TX 75633) has introduced a new rib for the S&W M10 HP four-inch revolver. Called the "Combat Rib With Wings," it is just that—a rib with protective wings on either side of the front sight blade. Blade and wings are a separate unit, secured to the rib top by a socket-head screw. This not only simplifies manufacture, but allows front sight height to be varied by removing or adding metal at the joint. The blade is exceeded in all dimensions by the wings (in military rifle fashion) so that nothing will strike or rub the blade. This serves to protect its original matte-black finish and/or any sight blackening that might be applied. Even when holstered, the blade is fully protected—which further allows any blade shape, even one deeply undercut, without fear of sight hangup in the holster.

The Bo-Mar rib is attached by two countersunk, socket-head screws, one into the barrel and one into the top strap. Factory installation is recommended, but it's an easy job at home if you're careful and possess a good drill press. The all-steel unit, which adds several ounces to the gun's weight, carries the standard Bo-Mar target rear-sight leaf inletted at the back.

An item of particular interest was the termination of all operations of the Super Vel plant last November. Few handgunners are not aware of the tremendous impact Super Vel president, Lee Jurras, had on handgun ammunition development. Jurras alone, by his designs, production, and wide sales of light high-velocity expanding jacketed bullets, forced all the old-line companies to develop competitive loads. Ten years ago, the *only* true high performance, factory-loaded revolver and auto cartridges carried the Super Vel headstamp. Today, every maker offers similar (but not better) loads in at least the most popular calibers.

Seecamp double-action conversion on Colt Combat Commander.

4-gun Case Master case accomodates any size pistol, revolver or spotting scope and has built-in wind-proof clip for holding lid securely.

In discussing the door-closing of Super Vel with me, Jurras said "Lack of sales was never any problem. We had bonafide back orders for millions of rounds. We had to close because of tremendously inflated prices for vendor-supplied items, material shortages, and poor and uncertain delivery of almost everything that went into our ammunition. It just wasn't economically feasible to buy components from the outside and load our type of ammunition. Anyone who tries it now had better have his own case and bullet production facilities or he'll never make it."

Super Vel's closing leaves several gaps in the high-performance ammunition field. We hope the other makers will fill them soon.

Now, with fair pertinency to the foregoing, is some good news. One new company, C.A.S. (P.O. Box 15531, Santa Ana, CA 92705) is producing standard, popular-caliber handgun loads. According to our best information this plant is a complete in-house operation, manufacturing its *own* cases and bullets, only powder and primers being procured on the open market. The most interesting facet of this new operation is that published retail prices run 20-25% *less* than those of the big three, at least as of this writing. If this carries forth into the future, it will be very important to those who shoot mainly factory ammunition.

The P18 pistol mentioned elsewhere in these pages was designed around a high-pressure, 9mm Parabellum loading. This load reportedly develops pressure in the 40-45,000 CUP range and produces comparably increased velocity. To date no such ammunition is currently available here as a commercial item though John Amber shot some in Austria. Perhaps that's a good thing, because many neophyte shooters might try to magnumize other 9mm guns, pistols that can't stand such pressures. However, we hear rumors (nothing more) that the maker of the P18 *may* produce (or have produced) this special load *for that gun only*. If this occurs, beware, and *don't* try to use it in any other gun. The results could well be disastrous! ●

Security Industries of America

A new 38 Special revolver, made entirely of stainless steel, was introduced at the NSGA meeting in Houston, Texas early in 1975. Weighing 19 ozs. with its nominal 2-inch (full ejector-rod shroud) barrel, the barrel measures 1.821 inches. This 5-shot handgun may be fired single-or double action, has a ⅛-inch wide grooved trigger, checkered walnut grip panels, and an inertia-type firing pin. Repeated dry firing, it is said, won't damage or break the firing pin. The hammer spur is nicely checkered across its ¼-inch width.

A "rotary action hammer block," which does *not* work in conjunction with the removable sideplate, allows custom fitting of each action. This safety device (patent pending) is in position up to the instant of "full hammer block release . . . reducing the possibility of accidental discharge to zero."

Unusual among such things is a "100%, 5-year warranty, with no service charges," which we'll return to later. Cost is $150 at retail.

Our sample, a Model 1S28 Police Security 38 Special (SN 06043), appeared to be in excellent working order as received in late March. Trigger pull single action was crisp and clean at 4 lbs., the 10-lb. double action pull smooth and quite uniform. The gun handles well with the standard-size grips, but a second-finger adaptor or grips so made would improve control. Exterior finish is in a matte or satin effect, quite attractive.

This drawing shows a gas-operated, rotary-bolt autoloading pistol, calibers 357-44 Magnum, in prototype configuration. All stainless steel, various barrel lengths are planned, projected price less than $300. Called the Wildey System, development was by W.J. (Will) Moore of Newburgh, NY 12550.

The square-notch rear sight is 0.120″ wide, the streamlined ramp front blade (integral with the barrel) 0.100″.

Our test firing of the new S.I.A. revolver was frustrating from the beginning, and hence ended prematurely. We meant to expend 50 factory cartridges and the same number of handloads—2.7 Bullseye and 150-gr. semi-wadcutters—but the revolver wouldn't cooperate.

Mike Bigalke, a personable and helpful young man who collects S&W handguns, did the actual firing of the Model 1S28 because my doctor says I can't shoot for several months—I had eye troubles early in the spring.

Mike fed the gun 5 of the handloads and fired them single action with no trouble. Accuracy at 10 yards was good, the 5 going into a couple of inches—offhand. The next 5 rounds, same ammo, saw only two shots letting go in double action. The primers of the 3 not discharging were dented, but obviously only lightly. These same 3 rounds failed to fire in spite of some 4-5 blows from the firing pin in double action mode, but they did fire when shot single action.

Were Mike's handloads at fault, perhaps? No—10 of them fired perfectly in another revolver, a Smith & Wesson promptly borrowed to make the check.

Ordinarily I'd have concluded that this unsatisfactory performance might have happened because our sample gun had—some way—slipped through factory inspection, but soon after I received a report that another such S.I.A. revolver had acted exactly the same way.

On the face of it, certainly, this hardly reflects adequate quality control/inspection at the factory.

On calling the factory about these problems, we were told that *every* S.I.A. revolver is test-fired with 5 rounds of live ammunition, in double action mode, and at a target.

All of this took place only a few days ago (8-9 May '75), and the second sample S.I.A. revolver hasn't arrived yet for a resumption of the test. Until then...

The second S.I.A. revolver arrived a few days ago and, not unexpectedly, fired without a hitch in double action and single action shooting with Mike's handloads (from the same batch as before) and with Remington factory loads. During this latest shooting (of 35 rounds) the trigger stuck again in the rearmost position, but only once. J.T.A.

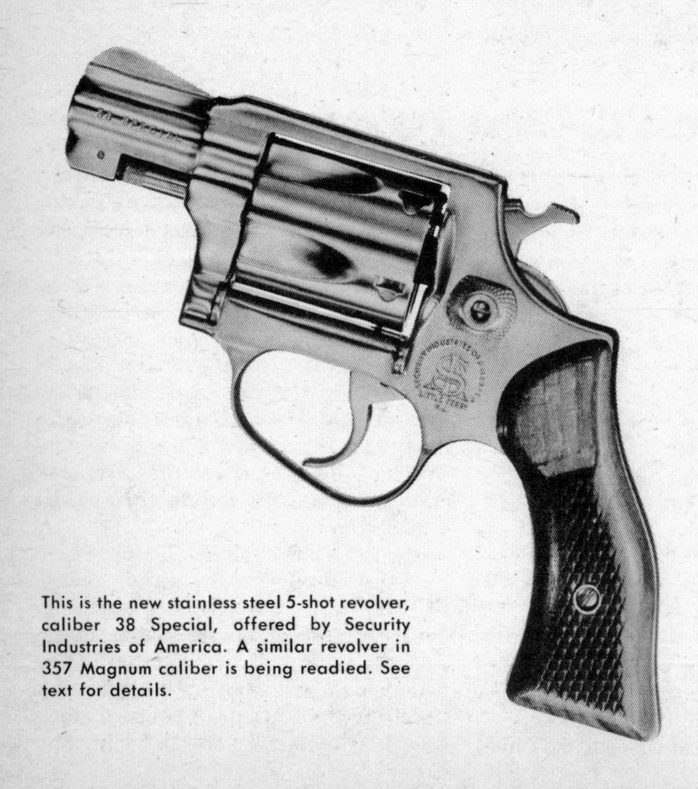

This is the new stainless steel 5-shot revolver, caliber 38 Special, offered by Security Industries of America. A similar revolver in 357 Magnum caliber is being readied. See text for details.

Case Master

Particularly intended for competition handgunners, the latest Case Master is made in 3-, 4-, or 5-gun versions, prices $58, $85 and $96 respectively. All have durable genuine Formica exteriors in a choice of several wood-grain finishes from a light colored Dovetree to a rich dark walnut. The piano-hinged lid has a wind-proof, built-in clip, and is locked when closed by double side locks. The tote strap is fully adjustable for shoulder or hand carrying. The larger sizes come with two slide-out trays of ample capacity—no back doors to bother with. The popular 4-gun case, 18″ long by 9″ wide and 13″ high, weighs about 12½ lbs.

A just-released brochure is yours for the asking. Write to Case Master at 4675 E. 10th Ave., Hialeah, FL 33013 J.T.A.

The Dodge Ramcharger/Plymouth Trail Duster come without a top, and offer options of either a rag top or hard top. The fabric top is cheaper and lighter, resulting in a lower center of gravity—a real asset when negotiating a steep sidehill—but it affords less protection from the elements, and is noisy on the road. Similar optional tops are offered by Jeep, Toyota, Blazer, etc.

FOUR WHEEL DRIVES--
they'll take you where the hunting is.

by JOHN LACHUK

The modern 4WD has come a long way since the days of the rugged but stark wartime Jeep. This detailed and critical review of the newest models offers valuable data and information to the potential buyer.

WITH "HUNTING" becoming more and more a matter of *hunting a place to hunt,* the ability to escape civilization is becoming more a matter of necessity rather than mere convenience. A four-wheel drive (4WD) vehicle can become the modern hunter's magic carpet to the outback.

As its title implies, 4WD provides four points of traction instead of just two. Instead of trying to *push* the front wheels through sand and mud, or over rocks, you let them *pull* you through and over obstacles. This factor becomes most evident when cornering. Rather than sliding outward on hard surfaces or plowing a furrow in mud and sand, the front wheels draw the vehicle along its intended path. An adequately-powered 4WD has the traction to climb precipitous slopes that would stop most two-wheel drive pickups and cars in their tracks.

It's the ability to slog through mud and snow, straddle rocks and cut cross-country off the road, that sets a 4x4 apart from conventional vehicles, and offers the hunter access to the deep woods and high mesas. Actual off-road driving is seldom required to reach even the most remote areas. Well-tended maintenance roads parallel high tension power lines. Logging and mining roads (*not* so well tended!) extend through the dim recesses of most mountains and across tractless desert wastes. If you've been singing that frequently-heard refrain, "Where can I go to hunt?" you're ready for a 4-wheeler now!

The off-road vehicle, though, is a different breed of cat from what you're used to. To gain sure-footedness and agility you must sacrifice some creature comforts and eye appeal. Long wheelbases and hoods to match are liabilities, not assets. All else being equal, the shorter the vehicle the tighter circles it can turn. A long hood obscuring the road ahead makes topping even a small rise pretty spooky. I often get out and scout ahead before cresting a blind ridge. That precaution once saved me and my Jeep from nosing over a sheer embankment!

The Jeep

The Jeep CJ-5 (Civilian Jeep Mark V) comes closest to the ideal off-road vehicle. Simply by virtue of being smallest, it can penetrate the densest cover and tame the most rugged terrain. It has the most desirable attributes for rough travel, including maximum ground clearance, short wheelbase, minimal overhang fore and aft, and is narrow enough to slither through a dense stand of timber or thread its way between a rock and a hard place!

The plucky little bobtailed CJ-5 is directly descended from the father of them all, the G.I. Jeep of World War II.

For many years after the war, the commercial Jeep echoed the relative austerity of the G.I. Jeep. In 1970, American Motors, having acquired the Jeep Corporation, updated the Jeep to catch up with the competition, lengthening the wheelbase from 81″ to 84″, with a commensurate increase in frame and body length, to accommodate the 304 cubic-inch (c.i.) V-8 that displaced the old Buick V-6. Axles and springs were beefed up to higher GVW (gross vehicle weight) ratings. With a standard 3.73 rear end ratio, the new V-8 gave the CJ-5 good highway speed (without excessive rpm's) and power to spare for the tallest hill. Part of the package were new synchromesh 3- and 4-speed manual transmissions, and an improved Dana 20, 2.03:1 transfer case. The tightest turning circle of any 4x4, 32.9 feet, resulted from adopting the Dana 30 open-end, live-axle front end, with a wider track of 51.5″ instead of the old 48.4″. A new 24:1 recirculating-ball manual steering and optional Saginaw 17.5:1 power steering put driving the Jeep within the muscular means of a woman, too. Larger drum brakes, with power assist, and a bigger manual clutch rounded out the picture.

The 1974-75 CJ-5 remains much the same, except for a luxury version called the "Renegade," with such niceties as carpeting, forged aluminum wheels, etc. The Jeep Commando (formerly the Jeepster) is gone, replaced by the Jeep Cherokee, AMC's answer to the Blazer. The Cherokee has received the most effusive "press" of any 4x4 to hit the market, I think

Being the smallest, the CJ-5 Jeep turns tighter circles, penetrates more inaccessible areas than its competition. Although somewhat refined it closely resembles the old G.I. Jeep.

Jeep Renegade, a luxury version of the CJ-5, comes with such niceties as carpeting and forged aluminum wheels.

Jeep Wagoneer was introduced in 1962; current version has power steering, automatic transmission and Quadra-Trac as standard equipment.

The Cherokee is Jeep's answer to the Blazer, but it looks too "car-like" to please the real off-road buffs. However, with full-time 4-wheel Quadra-Trac, it is an efficient 4x4. Major flaws are an inability to accept wide tires, and poor ramp-breakover and departure angles.

mainly because it is equipped with "Quadra-Trac," the Warner Gear Co. *full-time* 4-wheel drive system, possessed of a *limited-slip* differential in the transfer case. In effect, power is delivered to all 4 wheels, all of the time, with the differential allowing for variations in the turning speeds of front versus rear wheels. However, if one end loses traction the limited-slip feature takes over, sending power to the end that retains firm contact. Given a limited-slip *rear end* differential (a $60 option), the vehicle will retain headway so long as one rear wheel can get a grip on the road. By contrast, the "New Process" full-time 4x4 drive used by General Motors and Chrysler has an "open" differential in the transfer case, without the limited-slip feature. Thus if one wheel breaks loose and spins the other three are powerless. That's why the Blazer, etc., have a lock-out lever, converting the vehicle to a conventional 4WD mode.

Despite saturation publicity declaring the Cherokee "all new" it is obviously just a two-door version of the 4-door station-wagon-styled Jeep Wagoneer introduced in 1962, sharing its eye-appeal, comfort, and generous load capacity. Power steering and Turbo Hydramatic auto-trans are optional on the Cherokee, standard on the Wagoneer. The Cherokee/Wagoneer turning circle of 38.4 feet is only slightly larger than the Blazer's. Engine options range from an in-line 6 to a 401 c.i. V-8. Both have full instrumentation (no idiot lights), and power brakes, with discs up front.

Blazer-Jimmy

The Chevrolet Blazer and its identical partner, the GMC Jimmy, are highly favored by big game hunters because they offer ample load capacity, plus seating for 5 brawny nimrods. The Blazer/Jimmy provides a limousine highway ride, combined with excellent off-road capability, limited only by its width. GM evolved the Blazer/Jimmy by bobbing the tail of their ½-ton pickup, and extending the cab rearward, hence the term "bobtail." The high-riding body offers ample ground clearance, and yawning wells accommodate 12" wide flotation tires with room to spare. GM introduced the off-road crowd to such refinements as built-in air conditioning, power steering, disc brakes, etc. Full-time 4WD is standard with the 400 c.i. V-8. A Hurst shifter offers "high" and "low" drive, plus "high-lock" and "low-lock."

Ramcharger-Trail Duster

The transfer case used by GM is supplied by New Process Gear, a division of Chrysler Corp., which is using the self-same NP-203 unit on its new Dodge Ramcharger and Plymouth Trail Duster, identical except for grills and nameplates. The new Dodge/Plymouth offering has the bulk of the Blazer, but is more agile, with a turning circle of just 35.4 feet. At the front of the 106" wheelbase is a rugged 3500-lb. capacity Spicer open-end 44F-BS front axle. A 3600-lb. Chrysler 9¼ brings up the rear. Front stabilizer bar is standard, along with power brakes, discs up front. Four engines are available, topped by a burly 440 c.i., with an impressive 235 net horsepower. Chrysler introduced electronic ignition to 4x4s in 1974. For 1975, breakerless ignitions are standard with GMC, Chevrolet, and Jeep, as well.

Ford Bronco

Ford was first of the "Big Three" automakers to enter the bobtail field,

Easily the most popular 4WD is the Chevrolet Blazer—GMC Truck Division's "Jimmy" is identical, except for grill and name plates. GM evolved the vehicle by bobbing the tail of their ½-ton pickup and extending the cab rearward.

Cutaway view of the Ramcharger shows the drive train setup and standard disc brakes.

During press unveiling of Ramcharger/Trail Duster, one writer almost tipped this rig over on test course. The fact that it stayed upright is a tribute to its suspension system!

when they introduced their Bronco in 1966. Earlier I dubbed the Jeep CJ-5 the nearest thing to the ideal off-road vehicle. The Ford Bronco is certainly a close runner-up. The Bronco's 92" wheelbase, although 8" longer than the CJ-5, is shorter than any other American-made 4WD. Even though almost 10" wider and over a foot longer than the CJ-5, the Bronco boasts a turning circle less than 12 inches longer and, with optional 7.00x15 tires, the Bronco rivals ground clearance, approach, departure, and ramp breakover angles of the Jeep bobtail. These are the really telling statistics for an off-road rig! The relatively slight increase in size has blessed Bronco owners with a big increase in highway and off-road comfort.

The Bronco was born as a spartan 4x4, and little has happened to change that. It wasn't until a year ago that Ford grudgingly added power steering and automatic transmissions to 4x4s. Now integral power steering and Ford Cruise-O-Matic transmissions are optionally available with the 302 c.i. V-8. Bronco body lines are still identical to the original, even to the rear fender wells, which must be cut out to accommodate wide flotation tires. The Bronco's dinky 12.2-gallon fuel tank is inadequately supplemented by an optional 7.5-gallon auxiliary tank.

Ford is alone among American makers in offering coil spring front suspension on a 4x4, with forged steel radius rods for axle alignment. Bronco's front coils have been praised as the only 4x4 suspension that provides both comfort and superior front-wheel road contact, and damned as too soft for rugged off-road use. True, most Bronco owners who really use their rigs off-road end up by adding coil spring booster shocks for extra stiffness. Bronco offers another feature, the optional Dana 44-1F limited-slip front differential. Many consider this a mixed blessing, better done without! Even experts sometimes find a limited-slip front axle too hot to handle, especially when crossing a sidehill with spotty traction. Ford has yet to come around to front disc brakes on the Bronco, but the 11"x2" front and 10"x2½" rear drums are adequate.

Beginning with the 1975 models the Bronco is available with the 302 c.i. V-8 only. With a standard GVW of 4300 pounds, it falls well within the limits prescribed for the requirement of catalytic converter (that is, under 6001-pound GVW). The requirement for using unleaded fuel only may hobble the frisky Bronco somewhat! The Bronco is now available with air conditioning as well, and electronic breakerless ignition is now standard.

Ford Bronco comes close to the agility of the Jeep CJ-5 but offers more load space and rider comfort, plus recently introducing power steering, automatic transmission, etc. Functional body lines are unchanged since the Bronco's introduction in 1966.

Scout II

International's Scout II offers two V-8s (in addition to its standard inline 6 cylinder), a 304 c.i. and a 345 c.i. With smog regulations continually sapping strength from internal combustion engines, the 345 looks more realistic for off-road use. While retaining the original 100" wheelbase, the Scout II body is about a foot longer, and has a wider track (from 55.7" to 57.1"), with a slightly broader body to match. Height is the same, 66.2". Increased cargo space of the Scout II allowed mounting the spare tire inside, flat against the left-rear body panel, behind the fenderwell. A new open-end front axle compressed the turning circle from 42 to 37 feet.

The Scout II is not offered with a "rag" top, but comes rather with a pickup-styled Cab Top or the sporty-looking full-length steel Traveltop. Fender well size allows use of big tires if desired. Power brakes, with discs up front, are standard. The standard 3-speed all-synchro-mesh manual transmission is backed by an optional 4-speed manual or 3-speed automatic with center console shifter. Note however, that the standard 4x4 transfer case is *single speed!* If you want the TC-145 2-speed transfer case, you have to order it as an option! A single 19-gallon fuel tank nests between the frame rails under the tail. Scout II offers luxury interiors, with ample color options to suit any taste. Gauges grace the dash, not idiot lights.

Without sacrificing ruggedness or maneuverability International made the Scout II into a stylish-looking 4x4, capable on-road or off. It strikes a happy medium between the ponderous Blazer and the choppy-riding Jeep CJ-5.

Toyota

Before World War II the Japanese were reputed to be the greatest "copiers" in the world. They're still copying but, having developed some technology of their own, they are also doing a bit of innovating. The Toyota Land Cruiser, slightly longer than the CJ-5 with its 90" wheelbase, is wider and taller too, and built like a brick outhouse! Under the hood is a 138 HP overhead-valve inline 6-cylinder 236.7 c.i. 2-bbl. engine. The low 7.8:1 compression ratio really should be coming into its own now, with smog regulations pushing gasoline octanes ever downward. A 4-speed manual transmission is standard. Also standard are skid plates for the oil pan, transmission, and transfer case; a heavy duty 70 ampere-hour battery; foldout rear passenger seats, and 7.60x15 tires. Land Cruiser wheel wells are cavernous, offering ample clearance even for tractor tires if need be.

The Land Cruiser offers more load space than the CJ-5, with about the same degree of off-road mobility, even though it may not be the plushiest rig for cruising concrete. It comes with soft top or steel hard top, and a 106.3" wheelbase station wagon is also available.

Land Rover

The British-made full-time 4WD Range Rover, acclaimed as "the best 4WD ever made," will likely never see our shores. Its cousin, the Land Rover, has proved to have been only a visitor. Leyland Motors is peddling their slab-sided, aluminum-paneled 4x4s where they're more appreciated!

The Big Wagons

If added load and passenger space is more important to your hunting plans than the ability to penetrate the deepest depths of the forest, you might want to pass over the bobtails in favor of a magnum-sized station wagon, such as the Chevrolet/GMC Suburbans (identical except for grills and name plates). Built on light-duty truck frames, these two come in ½-ton and ¾-ton versions—K-10 and K-20 from Chevrolet, K-1500 and K-2500 from GMC. Both have 129.5" wheelbases and bodies to match. The Suburban, with optional 3rd rear seat, can carry as many as 9 people. Or it

The International Scout II is a second generation off-road vehicle with additional wheel base which has been well-used to provide extra load space and more passenger comfort. With engine options up to 345 c.i., the Scout is powerful, rugged vehicle for hunters interested in reaching the remotest areas. With the rear seat folded down, the Scout II doubles as a small pickup truck.

The Japanese-made Toyota Land Cruiser is, in essence, a beefed-up Jeep, reflecting near-wartime austerity in its interior appointments. However, it is an able and tough back-road vehicle. The Toyota is available with rag top or steel hard top.

Battered old G.I. Jeep enabled author to reach lofty mesa that harbored this huge old cactus buck. The Jeep Gladiator pickup truck provided comfortable quarters, and towed the smaller 4WD for ultimate in mobility.

Other Options

There is yet another means to travel the outback in style. In 1969 I bought a short wheelbase Jeep Gladiator 4x4 pickup truck, and added a rugged steel-skinned camper from Pullman, of Downey, CA. This camper cap, slightly taller than the truck cab, has enough head room to let me sit comfortably on its full-width cushioned seat. Using a Coleman butane stove, I can cook and eat inside during the rough weather that usually accompanies deer season. At night, the seat becomes a bed. I added a 20-gallon auxiliary fuel tank and a set of Dick Cepek's big Norseman tires, and the rig gets me almost anyplace I want to go.

If you opt for a truck-camper, steer clear of those tall models with everything including the kitchen sink. With all of that weight, that's just what they'll do, sink you in the nearest muddy pothole! They're top-heavy too, whereas your 4x4 should have the lowest possible center of gravity, a must for those steeply-angled hills.

Jeep still makes 4x4 pickups, updated to include such options as Quadra-Trac full-time 4WD, and a 401 c.i. V-8, both of which I highly

offers 40 square feet of cargo area with the 2nd rear seat folded flat. You could camp in the back! Power and drive trains are those of the Blazer, interiors sumptuous. On-road comfort is laudable, but off-road the Suburban is hampered by its length and wide turning circle. A wide range of comfort options are available, including *twin* air conditioners!

The International Harvester Travelall, of more modest dimensions, offers 124 cubic feet of cargo space. The Series 150 has a 6200-lb. GVW, the Series 200 has 6900 GVW. Standard engine for both is the 392 c.i. V-8 with 179 net HP, with the 400 c.i. 210 net HP optional. Besides the standard 3-speed manual transmission, IH offers two 4-speed gearboxes, one a close-ratio type, the other with wide gear spacing, plus two 5-speed manual transmissions. Both start at 6.21:1, but one ends with a 1:1 top gear, the other with an 18% overdrive, which should provide some welcome relief for gas pains! A 3-speed automatic is also available. Travelall has the conventional 4x4 system, not full-time 4WD. Many of us prefer it that way! Power disc brakes up front are standard.

The author's 4WD Jeep Gladiator, a short wheelbase pickup with a lightweight but sturdy Pullman Camper to provide night quarters and cooking space in bad weather. A 20-gallon auxiliary fuel tank, plus two 5-gallon Jeep cans on the rear, gives the rig a 500-mile range. The camper is low, easily clears low-hanging limbs of trees.

A Toyota got this pair of rabbit hunters out where that cactus is in bloom. Narrow tires seen here are not considered assets by most desert travelers, because such treads sink into the sand too easily.

Another vehicle popular with hunters is the Toyota Station Wagon, combining the toughness of the Land Cruiser with a stretched out body for added cargo space, and some added luxury items.

recommend! The 6025 GVW J-10 with 119″ wheelbase, turns tighter (41.9′) than the 6500 GVW J-20 (45.4′). I had to beef up the springs on my rig (6000 GVW), but I'd do it over again to gain the added maneuverability.

International makes two 4x4 pickups—the agile Series 150 with 115″ wheelbase, boasting a tight 40.5-foot turning circle, and the Series 200 with 132″ wheelbase. Standard GVWs are 6200 and 6900 respectively. Transmission options resemble those of the Travelalls.

The Chevrolet K-10 ½-ton 4x4 pickup with 117.4″ wheelbase looks and acts much like a Blazer, but with almost a foot of extra length between hubs, it's less nimble. The ¾-ton K-20 with 131.5″ wheelbase further inhibits backwoods access, in exchange for more load space.

Dodge 4WD "Power Wagons" have been favored by hunters since their introduction shortly after World War II. In 1974, Dodge made big news by developing their "Club Cab," stretched 1½ feet rearward, in both their ½-ton W-100 and ¾-ton W-200 models. Adding 34 cubic feet of *inside* storage space should help discourage casual rip-offs in the field. These cabs also provide fold-down seating for two extra hunting companions. Both rigs come with 8-foot boxes on 149″ wheelbases. A better bet for hinterland hunters would be the W-100 with 6½-foot bed, on a 133″ wheelbase. That shrinks to a more manageable 115″ with the standard cab. Engine and trans options resemble those of the Ramcharger, but with conventional 4WD. Manual locking hubs are standard.

For those desiring maximum ground clearance for spring-supported components, Ford offers a high-riding body on their conventional 4x4 pickups. The ½-ton F-100 comes either with 6¾-foot Styleside box on a 117″ wheelbase, or with an 8-foot box on 133″. The F-250 is available *only* with an 8-foot box and 133″ between hubs. Engines include standard inline 6s and an optional 360 c.i. V-8. Manual 4-speed trans is standard, with 3-speed Cruise-O-Matic optional.

Admittedly no pickup can follow a Jeep CJ-5 through the boondocks, but they can likely get you within walkin' distance. Or you can team up with a buddy who has a bobtail, and tow it behind your camper, as I did the time I nailed that craggy buck in Utah. You can use the camper as base camp, and probe surrounding areas with the bobtail.

Optional Equipment

The bare-bones offerings of most 4x4 makers are base-priced well under $4000. So why do the vehicles deliver at closer to $6000? The answer is, "options!" The list of options offered makes you wonder if the standard rig even comes with wheels! Fact is, it does – wheel/tire combos suitable only for a foreign compact. The makers say that they can't know what you want, so they provide the bare minimum and let you choose what you want. That rationale is at least partially justified, inasmuch as no two individuals will subject a vehicle to exactly the same use. But you have to wonder a little when you discover that Jeep's Wagoneer/Cherokee and International's Scout II come standard with *single-speed* transfer cases, surely poor equipment for off-road travel! If you want a two-speed transfer case it's an extra-cost option!

One option that is virtually a necessity is a limited-slip rear differential. This allows each wheel to rotate at its own rate while cornering, but locks when one wheel loses traction, and drives the other wheel. This feature is best confined to the rear end – limited slip up front makes a vehicle tricky to control, even for an expert driver.

Vehicles without full-time 4WD normally have front hubs bolted directly to the axle flanges. Thus even with the 4x4 lever disengaged, the wheels turn the front axles and drive train, resulting in unnecessary wear and frictional drag. Locking hubs, such as standard Warn type, allow the wheels to rotate independent of the axles, via the usual twist of a clutch disc in each hub. Warn Lock-O-Matic hubs are free-wheeling until the 4x4 lever is engaged, at which time they automatically lock the wheels and axles, in forward or reverse gear, providing 4x4 power when needed; the driver doesn't have to leave the cab to engage the hubs manually – most appreciated in a driving rain! Lock-O-Matics may also be *manually* locked, to provide enhanced braking with the front wheels on downhill runs. Warn and other hubs are available as dealer options, if not as standard equipment.

Lesson number one for off-road drivers: when you leave the blacktop, *lock those hubs!*

Another optional must is power steering. Because less muscular effort or leverage is required, power steering ratios are faster than manual, enabling you to respond quicker to emergencies. Also, if you hit a rock or hole, it won't yank the steering wheel from your hands and send you off into a ditch. And a soft shoulder won't pull you off of the road, as it can with manual steering. Also, in sand or mud, hydraulic power helps you turn the wheels against heavy resistance.

Vacuum power-assisted brakes are becoming standard rather than optional. If not, be certain to order them, with discs up front if possible! Disc brakes offer improved stopping on pavement and off, plus shrugging off heat and deep-water immersion without fading.

Oversized or accessory fuel tanks have always been essentials for off-roaders. Service stations are few and far between in the boondocks! Jeep cans should *never* be carried inside a vehicle, but with proper hangers, are OK on the outside.

"Idiot lights" often warn you of overheating *after* your engine has burned up. Dial instruments showing actual engine temperature, oil pressure, and battery charging rate should be ordered if not standard. I also like an intake-manifold vacuum gauge as a guide to better mileage, and a tachometer showing engine rpms, to avoid lugging the engine. A handy navigational instrument is a trip odometer, which can be zeroed at the beginning of a given leg of your journey, to indicate when you're approaching a turn or fork in the road, as shown on your map.

Heavy duty springs and shocks, HD cooling, HD battery and alternator are all low-cost options that are needed off-road. But HD suspension makes a rig rough-riding on pavement when not loaded, so I carry 100 pounds of lead in the rear of my Jeep Commando to ease the bumps. A Bostrom suspension seat, cushioned by air or a torsion bar, takes the backache out of the stiffest suspension. (Write: Bostrom, 133 W. Oregon St., Milwaukee, WI 53201.)

Such optional luxury deals as the Blazer's Cheyenne package or Ramcharger's SE package often link desirable practical features – hood insulation, foam bucket seats, center console, et cetera – with exterior wood-grained finish and decorative metal moldings that are highly vulnerable to damage from rocks and tree limbs when negotiating narrow passages off-road. What might be merely a paint scratch with a bare body becomes an expensive replacement. If possible, leave the chrome at home!

Air Conditioning

Air conditioning is less a luxury than some people imagine. It allows you to button-up your vehicle and exclude dust from your lungs and equipment during hot runs down dry dirt roads. You'll reach the hunting area less tired and better able to make that long shot count! Vehicles with air ducts in the dash are best ordered with factory AC. Those, such as the Jeep, which use add-on units under the dash can be ordered with HD cooling, and a commercial air conditioner added later at much less cost.

Wide tires, on the order of 10" to 12" wide are a necessity for off-road travel. Best traction in mud, snow or sand requires what is called a "flotation tire." Shown here is the Norseman, a popular, rugged, steel-belted tire.

Choosing the proper engine is complicated by today's maze of smog regulations, which have brought with them poor efficiency, low compression ratios, high fuel consumption and reduced engine life, leading many makers to introduce bigger bore motors to offset some of the power loss. In general, a big-bore engine with a flat torque curve is best for off-road use. Their only contraindication is low miles per gallon in this day of fuel shortages and exorbitant prices. On the other hand, a small engine struggling to do the job often uses more fuel than a big-bore-block hardly working up a sweat.

Inextricably linked to engine displacement is the question of differential ratios. On the highway a tall gearing, say 3.07:1, makes a lot of sense in terms of fuel economy and quietness, but off-road it might severely handicap your engine. With a powerful engine, a middle range gearing, perhaps 3.55:1 might be a good compromise, with 3.73:1 tilted more to off-road use. Differentials geared 4.10:1 would be most at home off-road, with high rpm engine noise likely to prove objectionable on the highway. Transmission gear ratios also enter the equation. If you like a stick shift, choose a 4-speed with a wide ratio that provides really low bottom range for inching through the rough, or perhaps an overdrive gear at the top end for highway economy. Most Blazer/Jimmy vehicles are sold with automatic transmissions, and the trend is becoming evident among other makes as well. The auto trans, with its fluid coupling multiplying torque, can deliver power to the wheels gradually without breaking traction and digging in the way a solid clutch often does.

Perhaps the potentially most useful single aftermarket item that a hunter can buy is a winch, such as this Warn M-8200. The electrically-powered Warn can tug you through a stream, even after your motor has stalled. The power-takeoff winch must have the motor running in order to function. A winch can pull you up an impossible hill, get you out of a bog, or pull your fallen deer up a hill and finally up into a tree for cleaning and skinning.

It is possible to have high-number differentials and still enjoy low engine rpms and good mileage on the highway—by adding an aftermarket overdrive. Note, though, that most such units can't be used with full-time 4WD rigs. One of the oldest, made by Rancho Jeep Supply, 6309 Paramount Blvd., Long Beach, CA 90805, is the Borg-Warner OD unit for the Jeep CJ-5. The Warn All-Range Overdrive for Jeeps and Scouts fits into the power takeoff opening in the transfer case, and can be used in 2WD and 4WD mode in contrast to most units, which work in 2WD only. Most widely adaptable are the Hone-O-Drive units from Hone Mfg., 11748 E. Washington Blvd., Santa Fe Springs, CA 90670. One version bolts directly to the transmission, the other bolts to the rear differential. Both function in 2WD only. All OD units are basically alike—planetary gears reduce the final-drive ratio from 25% to 30%.

Tire Options

Differential ratios are always calculated with standard tires, which are next to useless off-road. Substituting wider, larger-diameter tires reduces the ratio, though not enough to worry about. 4x4 makers offer many tire and wheel options, but it is difficult for the buyer to make a good choice from a list of often meaningless numbers. Vehicle dealers seldom have the knowledge or patience to explain tire options, and rarely have them available to show the customer. I suggest buying your rig with the maker's standard "bicycle" tires and then obtain the tires you want on the aftermarket, where the choice is broader and easier! Easily the most famous name in off-road tires is Dick Cepek, 9201 California Ave., South Gate, CA 90280. Dick's free catalog is a college education on tires and oversized wheels, and it offers the widest selection of off-road goodies known to man! Dick considers Armstrong Norseman tires outstanding for practical on/off road travel. The Norseman LR78-15 tire, 10.1" at its widest point, has adequate flotation in all but the most liquid of silty sand; its 7¼" wide, self-cleaning tread gives ample traction under severe mud/snow conditions, yet on the highway it is relatively quiet. Where glare ice is a problem Norsemen tires will accept steel studs, all but eliminating the need for chains. Mounted on Cepek's 15"x 8" steel wheels the Norseman's 29.5" outside diameter makes it tall enough to provide good ground clearance for axles, differentials, etc. New Norseman steel-belted radial tires have thicker sidewalls, are quieter on the road, and afford better traction and mileage. They greatly improve vehicle handling and they're all but impervious to ordinary punctures.

Advance Adapters, Inc., 12120 Woodruff Ave., Downey, CA 90242, makes adapter units that enable the use of other 4-speed and automatic transmissions, plus adapters for switching engines. AA also vends add-on disc brakes, roll bars, fender cutout kits, skid plates, exhaust headers, swing-away tire carriers, etc.

Winches

Hickey Enterprises, Inc., 1645 Callens Rd., Ventura, CA 93003, offers the most complete stock of aftermarket high-performance items—HD shocks and springs, large-capacity replacement and auxiliary fuel tanks, directional-stability kits, and his unique Sidewinder winch.

The Sidewinder, remarkable for its relative lightness, tucks *under* the front bumper of most 4WDs not sticking way out in front. On the Scout it mounts between the frame rails, under the driver's seat, the cable routed out through the center of the front bumper. It has been said of a 4WD, "The only difference from a 2WD is that a 4x4 allows you to get stuck in worse places!" If you should ever have the misfortune to confirm that, your best friend by far will be a winch.

If you can find an anchor, a winch will get you out of most messes. It'll retrieve a downed deer from a deep canyon, and it will haul that deer up a tree for dressing and skinning.

Notes and Tips

Co-existing with a 4x4 rig requires a certain amount of expertise, which could be the subject of another long article, but a few hints are in order. First and foremost, when you leave the blacktop, *get out and lock the front hubs* (unless you have full-time 4WD or Warn Lock-O-Matics). You don't have to engage the 4WD until needed, but you *can* pull the transfer-case lever back into 4WD mode as soon as you enter loose dirt, which provides the necessary slippage so that front and rear wheels, running at different speeds in turns, etc., won't introduce unwanted stresses into the drive train. I recommend locking the front hubs whenever possible, if only to exercise the front drive train. When the going gets steep or rough, shift into low range, to deliver twice the torque to the wheels, and provide slow, precise control of speed and direction. Use low range on downhill runs also, to double braking effect of engine compression.

When you buy a 4x4 you'll find yourself at loggerheads with ecofreaks opposed to off-road travel. Such well-funded organizations as the Sierra Club feel that only stout young lads with backpacks have any rights in the outback. Finding both "stout" and "young" highly transient conditions, long behind me, I of course disagree! Certainly irresponsible off-road use can damage local ecology, but irresponsibility anywhere is damaging! Most 4WD users travel primitive roads rather than charging off across virgin ground, where their tire tracks could cause erosion.

Use common sense in the wilderness. Don't litter—haul out your trash or bury it well.

As a 4WD user, your reward will be hunting in areas where the game is still abundant, and competition from other hunters often small or nonexistent. ●

Latest Remington and Winchester Seminars

by GEORGE C. NONTE, Jr.

OVER 16 YEARS ago a new shooting industry institution was born. At that time young Jim Rikhoff, then PR man for Winchester Western, invited a handful of the best-known gun writers to a combination hunt and preview of the next year's new arms and ammunition products. The event was a resounding success with much benefit derived by both the scribes and W-W. For the first time writers had an opportunity to view, fondle, and use new products *before* they were actually on the market. On the other hand, W-W gained a face-to-face contact and rapport with writers that had never before been achieved. Further, industry sometimes gained the valuable reactions of some of the world's most experienced gun buffs to new products before those products were committed (expensively) to production. We might say that in one fell swoop, W-W gained the part-time services of the large panel of the top consultants in the sporting arms and ammunition field.

Unfortunately, the long lead times and other problems attending the introduction of new models being what they often are, the assembled writers were faced with new firearms that were in full production. Some of these made it in the market place, others did not. Some years ago, I remember, a handful of writers were asked to view privately and critique a group of prototype rifle stocks, most of whom chose a classic form. But it wasn't adopted—W-W sent the same several stock styles to a group of jobbers, and their choice was put into production!

Winchester-Western has repeated the performance every year since, with the 1974 gathering at Belmont Plantation being the 16th in the series, without any gap.

Of course, where one leads successfully, others can't help but follow. In 1962 Remington launched its first writers and editors seminar on the same plan, and hasn't missed a year since. The 1974 gathering at Remington Farms was the 13th. In later years Colt and Ruger have held similar gatherings, and other companies have conducted lesser gatherings for the same purpose.

If you've read these pages (and others) regularly for 16 years, you know what makes up the seminars. If not, well, they range from simple, low-key gatherings at the respective companies' game preserves (Remington Farms; Nilo Farms) to bird and big game hunts in the western U.S.A., to exotic Mexican, European, and African hunts. Generally, though, they are three-day gatherings of about half hunting and shooting afield and half discussion of new products, marketing, development trends, and mutual brain-picking. The companies send their top engineers, designers, and sales people to rap with us pencil pushers and keyboard pounders. Everybody benefits, not only us and the manufacturer, but you readers even more—for without this rapport and mutual information exchange, we'd have a lot less to tell you.

The man-sized Winchester Model 490 autoloading 22 rifle was delayed a while but it's here now.

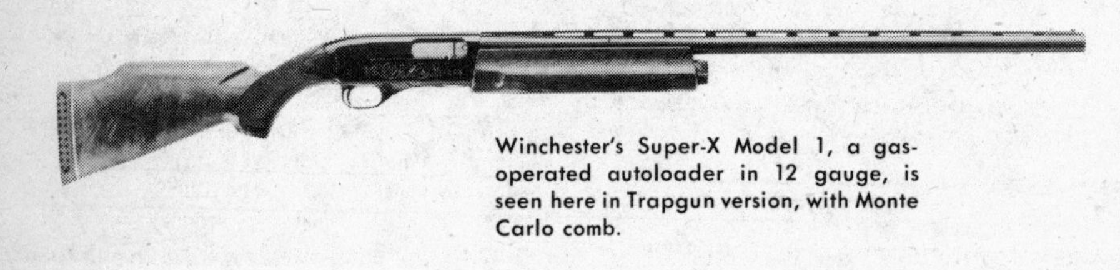

Winchester's Super-X Model 1, a gas-operated autoloader in 12 gauge, is seen here in Trapgun version, with Monte Carlo comb.

Sure, it costs the arms companies quite a few shekels to ferry us all in from all over the country, and to put on the show, but they feel its worth it or they wouldn't do it. But don't get the idea this is unique to the shooting industry—it isn't. Almost all industries do the same, usually on a more elaborate and costly scale. All the auto, aircraft, and boat producers host large gatherings of writers and editors at new-product times. It's the best way they know to get the word out to enthusiasts and customers.

Winchester's 16th Session

Anyway, in 1974 the Winchester-Western gathering was held at Belmont Plantation near Garnett, South Carolina. This old plantation, with its quail cover, deer, and bass ponds, is now operated by the State as a hunting/fishing preserve under the auspices of the South Carolina Wildlife and Marine Resources Commission. The commission chairman, Joe Hudson and his staff, went all out to make us welcome—I think I'll go back soon.

It wasn't a big, new-product show, for Winchester's major recent effort (1973) went into the fine new Super X auto shotgun. Those things are cyclic, and any major, multi-million-dollar development like that is followed by a sag in new items while everyone catches his breath.

Bill Steck, head of Weaver Division, introduced a new line of all-steel, bridge-type scope mounts for those who prefer this type of the time-proven, basic Weaver design. It features a very secure method of clamping the detachable rings to the base. Also shown was a new, see-through mount scheduled to be available later in '75. Steck also announced that all of 1974's production delays have been overcome and that the entire current line of Weaver scopes are in good supply.

The new M490 22 autoloader announced last year was delayed, but we were assured it will be on dealer's shelves before 1975 is out.

New items are coming out of the East Alton ammunition plant. Gold Label is the name of the new select-quality version of the Super Match 22 rimfire match ammunition. Cartridges in the gold boxes will shoot just a bit more accurately than regular Super Match. There are also new "match grade" jacketed bullets in 22, 6mm and 30 caliber for the benchrest clan. A new, slow-burning, ball

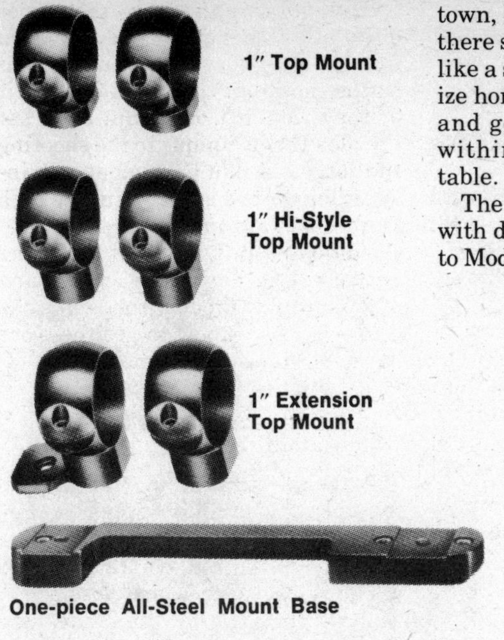

Weaver's new all-steel top mounts and base.

town, Maryland. Most of us have been there so many times now that it seems like a second home—if you can visualize home with some of the finest duck and goose shooting in the country within five minutes of the dinner table.

The shooting was great this time with ducks and geese falling like rain to Model 870s, Model 1100s, and a few

The excellent—but low cost—M788 rifle with its unique multiple-lug, rear-locking bolt and unusually fast lock-time has been expanded to include another caliber. It may now be obtained for the 223 Remington cartridge, which every gun buff knows is simply the sporting version of the U.S. 5.56mm service cartridge used by the M16 assault rifle. The flat-shooting

Remington's Model 788 bolt rifle can now be had in caliber 223 centerfire (which is to say the 5.56mm U.S. service cartridge), among others.

powder for hot magnum rifle loads has been under development for several years. To be called #785, we'll see it this year, and it will *not* require a "magnum" primer for proper ignition.

International Skeet is a fast game, with fast birds, so a new, high-velocity, 12-bore load is now offered for it.

We were also advised by Ed Matunas that a concentrated effort will be made to get more W-W handloading components into dealer's hands and thus more available to individuals. He also told us of closer-tolerance primers and a new primer for heavy handgun loads. A new handgun powder, #231, will take the place of #230, and a bigger W-W Loading Manual should be ready as you read this.

Winchester's "Trailblazer" division has also introduced many new items of camping equipment, along with new "Comfy" sleeping gear. There is also a new line of excellent Winchester hunting clothing.

Aside from that, I had great quail shooting, but no luck on deer. Things were reversed for some scribes, and others got skunked in both areas.

Of memorable note, though, were the bushels of succulent oysters and shrimp, along with all that other fine southern cooking. After a little practice, I proved I can shuck oysters fast enough to feed both Elmer Keith and myself all we can hold.

Remington's 13th Meeting

Remington's gathering was back at the old familiar and much-loved Remington Farms preserve near Chester-

Model 3200 stackbarrels. For a change, I was hitting feathered targets well, so didn't have to send back for more of those excellent green-case waterfowl loads. The weather was fine, too—no cold, watery deluge as in some past years.

Remington, too, didn't have a great many new products to show—and for the same reasons as W-W. The recent

223 makes this a first-class, medium-range varmint combination at relatively low cost.

All in all, Remington's conservative and more-or-less traditional approach to new products has paid off in two ways—better products for the shooter, and very, very few items that have not achieved remarkable market success. That way everybody wins.

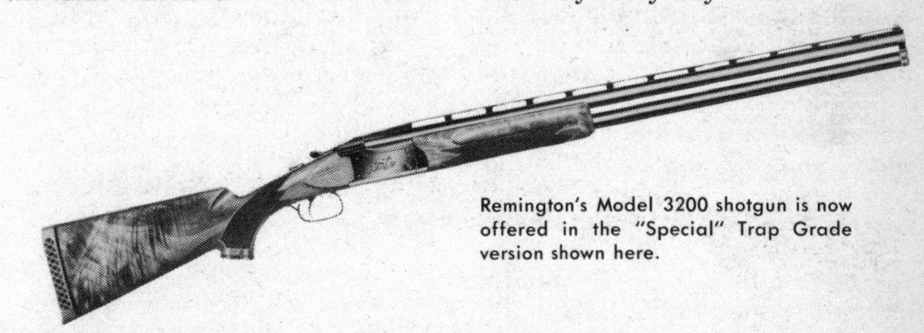
Remington's Model 3200 shotgun is now offered in the "Special" Trap Grade version shown here.

development of the very fine M3200 over-under scattergun absorbed most R&D efforts, so it will be a while before there are any major new items.

We were shown a new variation of this gun, the M3200 Magnum. Chambered for three-inch shells (12-bore only), it is factory fitted with a recoil pad, and with the standard 30-inch tubes and ventilated rib, tips the scales at 8 pounds 12 ounces. Stock dimensions are 1½"x2⅛"x14" for comfortable shooting and good pointing. Bored F&F or M&F.

Another new offering is the M3200 Trap with 32-inch barrels bored F& IM. This combination is available on both regular and Special Trap models with or without the optional Monte Carlo stock.

In summary, we can say that the two major seminars do reflect the current economic situation to some degree. Because of the tremendous costs of developing major new products, we expect to see fewer of them in the future—sort of a return to the old days when a really *new* rifle or shotgun appeared only every decade or so. Instead, we expect to see evolution rather than revolution; refinement of existing items more than development of entirely new models; more small less complex, new items which cost less in development and tooling.

Rest assured, though, that the shooters' interests will be looked after. They are the people who make the shooting industry profitable. ●

RELOADING TODAY

Though the spate of new products useful to the handloader is not, perhaps, as great these days as it was in the recent past, there's still a lot of interesting stuff coming along.

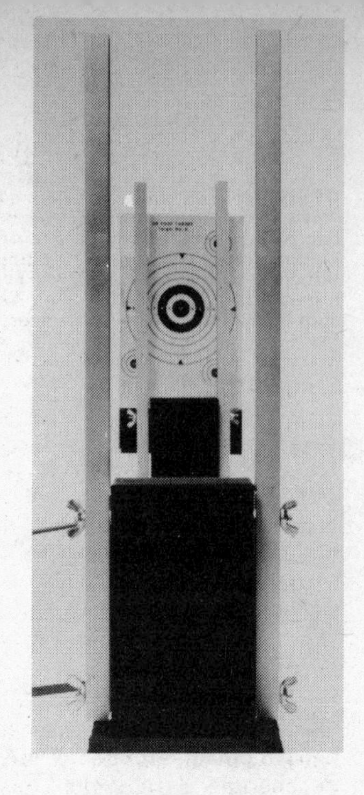

by JOHN T. AMBER and the editors

Telepacific Chronographs

The excellent Model TPS-02-E chronograph system, which uses their ambient-light Electroscreen Detector screens—Model TS-E—was described at some length in our 29th edition (p. 216). I pointed out at the time that Telepacific Electronics Co. (Box 2210, Escondido, CA 92025) should be praised for holding the line on prices, the TPS-02-E System being priced last year at exactly the original 1972 figure—$270. It's still true—$270 is the price for 1975, and that's an attractive figure—inflation being what it is—for a professional-quality chronograph that reads out in foot seconds, and comes with the highly convenient Electroscreen Detectors.

Telepacific has two interesting new products for 1975. A new instrument (or chronograph display unit) is the Model TPB-03, which will have a numerical digital display instead of the coded-light readout used in the TPS-02-E system, and it will be powered by rechargeable Nicad batteries. Furnished with a pair of the Electroscreen Detectors, the new system is coded TPS-03-E and will retail at $330 or, with an expanded MV range of 90 to 5,000 fps, $365. The basic TPB-02 instrument will *not* be discontinued.

Telepacific's Model TS-Y system—a brand new detector-screen technique throughout—forms the exciting news for me, and I'm sure for many of you reading this. Here is what Peter A. Cooke, president of Telepacific, had to say about these interesting devices: "They detect the approach of the bullet by a method of Doppler radar, emitting a trigger pulse at the instant that the bullet ceases to move *toward* the detector and starts to move *away* from it. They have the advantage of providing a much larger area of sensitivity than (our) photo-screens and also of *requiring no light source*. They will be directly interchangeable with Electroscreens for use with any of our chronograph instruments." That emphasis on "no light screens" is mine.

This Doppler Screen system, when supplied with a Telepacific system in place of the Electroscreen Detectors, will sell for $45 additional. As a separate unit, for use with other makes of chronograph instruments, the Doppler Screens will cost about $165.

A picture of this new system is shown here, but I've had no opportunity to try either—they're not ready!

A Telepacific unit that can be bought now, and not previously described here, is called TS-EK. This Kit comprises a set of TS-E Electroscreen Detectors with a type TS-K adaptor unit (see photo) to permit use with most types of "break-wire" chronograph instruments. (The TS-E Electroscreens *alone* were developed specifically for use with our Chronograph Instruments and are not directly compatible with any other make of instrument.)

Price of the Model TS-EK system (TS-K Adaptor Unit and a set of TS-E Electroscreen Detectors) is $115 complete. J.T.A.

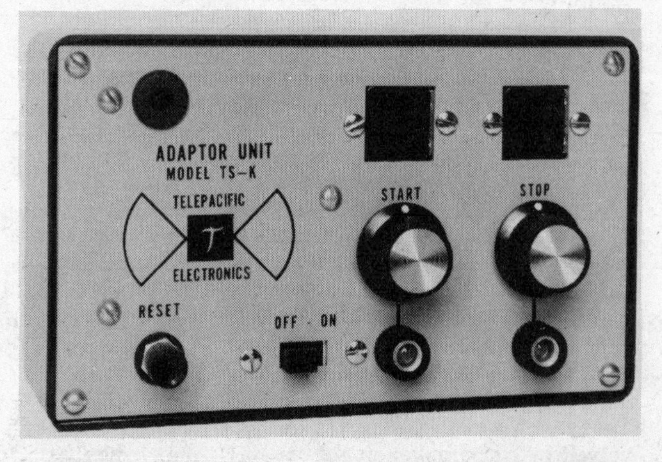

Above—Telepacific's latest chronograph "Radioscreens" (code TS-Y) require no illumination whatsoever, and offer a 3.5" opening between the alloy rods seen, projecting 10" above the electronic black boxes. The rods, attached by wing nuts, can be quickly replaced if struck, their cost low. Below—new Telepacific TS-K adaptor unit. See text for detail.

New Hercules Smokeless Powder Guide

BULLETIN: Hercules announced in early April that the new *Guide* described below contains an error—the second entry on page 17, under the heading "20 Gauge, 3-Inch Winchester-Western AA Type Shell," shows a load with 1⅜ ounces of shot. The correct shot load should read 1³⁄₁₆ ounces. Copies of the *Guide* released subsequent to this announcement have been corrected.

Early in January of this year a new, revised edition of the Hercules Smokeless Powder Guide was published. Unfortunately, a copy of the new booklet didn't arrive in time for inclusion of a review of it in *Handloader's Digest 7*.

This current edition, the latest in the series, is the result of an exclusive testing program carried out in the Hercules ballistics laboratory. These facilities use the most modern equipment available to provide the dependable data which has been a Hercules standard for many years.

Reloading data for all of those Hercules smokeless powders available to handloaders are included, but please note that no rifle loads are published—only those for shotshells and handguns are listed.

The powders are: Red Dot, Unique, Bullseye, Blue Dot, Green Dot, Herco, and 2400.

The most extensive changes are seen in the shotshell section, which has been completely revised to encompass data with the latest components of all major manufacturers. Loads from light target to heavy magnum, with many alternate powder, wad and primer choices, are listed.

The pistol and revolver section has been revised and enlarged. It now contains many new loads, including magnum loads with Blue Dot.

Hercules "strongly advises that all previous editions of the Hercules Smokeless Powder Guide should be destroyed." I wonder why.

Copies of the 1975 Guide should be available at your distributors and dealers, but single copies may be obtained by writing: Advertising Dept., Hercules Inc., 910 Market St., Wilmington, DE 19899.

Black Powder Limit Lifted

Legislation raising the limit on the purchase of commercially produced black powder from 5 to 50 pounds for muzzle-loading enthusiasts was passed by Congress in February of this year. Authored by Senator Birch Bahy (D-Indiana), this legislation should remedy the severe problems of availability to legitimate users of black powder caused by the 5-pound limitation.

The 50-lb. limit on purchases of black powder for sporting, recreational or cultural purposes will not alter in any way the strict criminal penalties for the misuse of explosives, including black powder and igniters. According to the National Bomb Data Center, black powder is used in an insignificant number of bombings. From July 1970 through June 1971, the Center recorded 2,353 bombings, of which only 96 involved black powder. Even if black powder were used in more bombings, it would still be difficult to control because it can easily be made from commonly available ingredients.

Only commercially manufactured black powder is suitable for muzzle-loading rifles and antique cannons. Today, some 500,000 people are involved with the increasingly popular sport of collecting and shooting muzzle-loading antique and replica firearms. Thousands gather at numerous competitive target shooting events all over the country, the largest of which—at Friendship, Indiana—attracts over 15,000 participants and spectators each year. Additional thousands have been drawn by the challenge of hunting with muzzle-loading rifles and shotguns—so many that 39 states now permit hunting with black powder guns.

Warning!

It appears that some handloaders are not doing their homework. I've had a gaggle of letters over the past few months, their writers complaining that IMR 4831 has been giving them trouble—loosened primer pockets, heavy bolt lift, and the like. Judging from their comments to me, these fellows blithely assumed that IMR 4831 could be loaded, grain for grain, with Hodgdon 4831. *That is not so,* but even if it were, what the hell were those guys thinking of when they didn't reduce their initial trials of the new powder by at least 5%? Inexcusable, of course, and particularly so because the DuPont leaflet on IMR 4831 powder has been available for many months. This sheet shows the suggested load level for every factory cartridge offered in the U.S., and with 2 or more bullet weights for many of them. J.T.A.

Marmel Products

Reloaders who cast bullets will be interested, I think, in two new Marmel items. One is a new thermometer, accurately calibrated to show lead-mix temperatures, the highly legible dial reading from 200° to 1000° Fahrenheit.

Apart from some of the electric lead melters, it is impossible to know, except rather vaguely, what the lead heat temp may be at a given time. One can and does, of course, lean on experience to reach a working temperature, one that results in satisfactory cast bullets. That usually takes a bit of fiddling with the heat control, if any. More importantly, at subsequent casting sessions, it is difficult to reach that same desirable heat without further trial-and-error adjustments. The new Marmel thermometer fixes that problem.

Just insert the tip of the long (8½") stem into the heated alloy and, in a moment or so, read the prevailing temperature, *accurately*. Too low, too high? Adjust the controls until the bullets are casting to suit you, then record the reading and setting.

I'll admit I held the Marmel's wide dial gingerly, fearing I might burn my mitt, but nothing at all happened—the upper dial portion of the device stays quite cool.

Though it is not exactly cheap at $25, this is a quality instrument and, as far as I can learn, the first such tool for the job ever offered.

Marmel's Marvelux is a lead-alloy flux compound that differs markedly from such homely dross-clearing and alloy-smoothing materials that bullet casters have long used—small gobs of beeswax, grease and bullet lube. Marvelux is non-corrosive to iron and steel, and its continued use will, in fact, keep the lead pot free of rust. No obnoxious fumes are given off, either, and I found that a small bit of the stuff goes a long way. It keeps the mix flowing more freely for a longer time. Cost? A ½ lb. can is $2 and a pound is $3.75, both ppd. $10 buys 4 lbs., 8 lbs. costs $16, both plus postage for 6 and 10 lbs. respectively. J.T.A.

MTM Molded Products

MTM, makers of the excellent Case-Gard all-plastic containers, which we've covered in this section before, has several interesting new items worth your attention.

While not 100% new, the latest Case-Gard 60 is sure to be welcomed by handloaders, as was the earlier Case-Gard 50. Both are rugged, latest one because it will hold 60—rather than 50—pieces of brass. That means, of course, that it will take the contents of three 20-round ammo cartons, not leaving the other 10 out.

Case-Gard 60s are made in two sizes—one for 22-250 to 308 and similar lengths, the other for lengths up to the 458. Price, $2.50 each, only a little more than the $2.20 cost of the Case-Gard 50 rifle ammo boxes.

Brand new is the MTM "Under-Cover," a wallet-size black plastic case, and one which is intended primarily for law enforcement people. Made in 5 sizes for all popular handgun ammo, each holds 18 cartridges. After each round is snapped into its individual compartment, a touch of firm finger pressure on the bullet end quickly effects their release. This new Case-Gard 18 has a Press-Lok release system, once closed, that frustrates kids, an excellent safety measure, and it won't pop open if dropped.

Small enough to slip easily into the pocket, Case-Gard 18 is $1.95.

The MTM Case-Gard 100—introduced a year ago or so, and widely accepted—has been further improved by the use of a new tacklebox latch for faster, easier opening/closing.

Each of the two stacking trays furnished holds 50 shotshells—or empties, of course. This compact container (7"x9"x11"), has top and bottom halves made of one smoothly-rounded piece, and they're virtually waterproof when closed. The Case-Gard 100, including two trays, is $8.50, in 12, 16 or 20 gauge. Extra trays, $1.80 each in all gauges, also make excellent shellholders for the reloader.

Last of the latest MTM products for 1974 is their Handloader's Log, a sturdy 3-ring vinyl binder, furnished with 50 printed charts that have room enough for 1,000 entries. These charts ($3.50 for 50 more) show rifle model, serial number, date, yards, charge weights, etc. A handy item, ready for fast use. Price, $5.95.

All MTM products carry a 3-year guarantee in normal use, and the hinged MTM containers are warranted for one million open-close cycles! J.T.A.

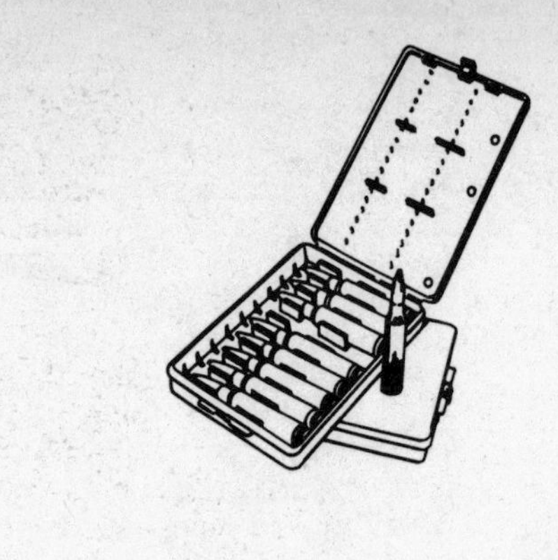

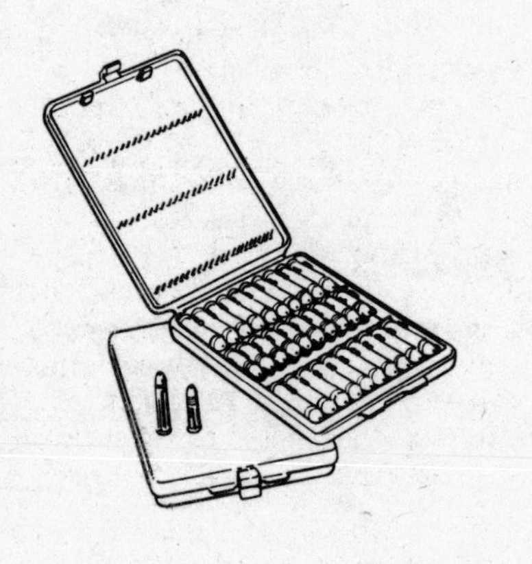

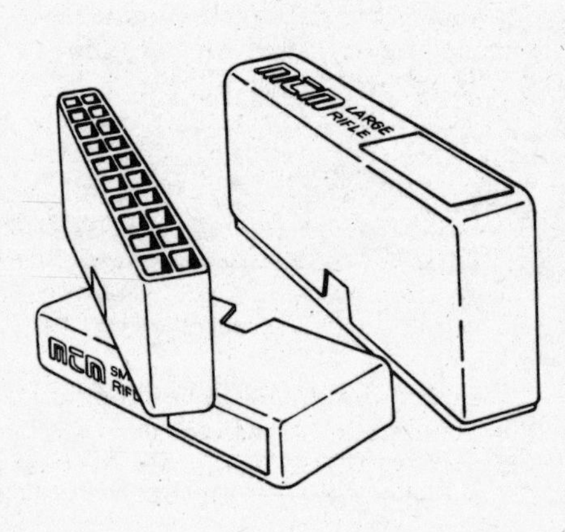

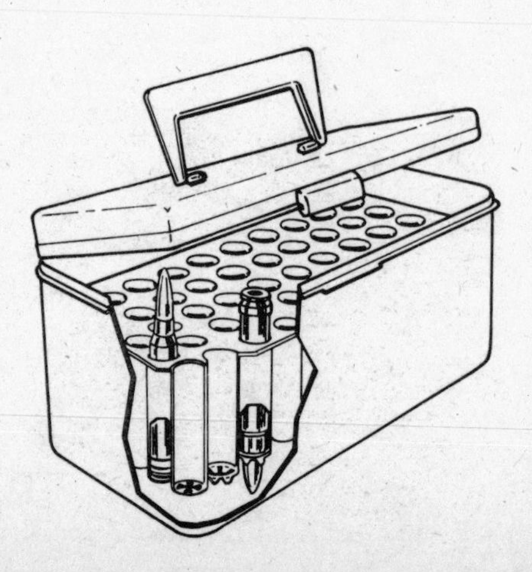

Federal Nickel Cases

Benchrest shooters place special demands on rifles and ammunition. For them, minor details can make the difference between first and last place. Thus, benchrest competitors demand highly uniform components for handloading ammunition to obtain the best possible performance from their individual rifles. Cartridge cases have always presented a problem. Competitors had to sort once-fired cases from factory ammunition or rework standard cases for their match loads.

Federal Cartridge has come to their assistance by introducing unprimed, unfired match-grade cases in calibers 222 Rem. and 308 Win. Designed specifically for the precision handloader, these cases feature uniform neck concentricity and minimum weight variation. In addition, they are nickel plated to reduce the buildup of tarnish and residue both in the primer pocket and on the case body. The need to clean dirty cases by soaking is completely eliminated. Resizing is also made easier.

Order numbers and list prices for these new items are 222MX and 308MX, each box of 20 $2.94 and $3.96 respectively.

A hasty check of the nickeled Federal cases showed excellent uniformity in neck-wall dimensions and case weight. A random 222 sampling (10 cases from a box of 20) gave average weight of 84.8 grains, with a low of 83.8 and a high of 85.8. Neck walls of the same ten 222 cases ran very close—most varied .0005" to .001", with two having zero tolerance, and only one with .002" difference. Total range was .0011"-.0014", with no single case over .002".

The nickeled 308s were equally good—another random 10-round sample showed 164.95 grains average weight, the low-high 162.5/166.7. Six of these went 165.0-166.2. The 308 necks showed remarkably low tolerances—most were under .001", with only a couple at .002". Total range was .0140"-.0168", but no individual cases went over .002". J.T.A.

Latest MTM products, from the top, include Case-Gard 9, made for 222 to 30-30 and 22-250 to 375, offers a safe, silent case; $1.95 each. Next, Case-Gard 30, light and compact, holds 30 rounds of any 22 rimfire ammo, including 22 WRM. Third, 20-round cartridge boxes, $1 each. Last, Case-Gard H50 handled box has greater hole-spacing for easier finger grasping, built-in grippers to prevent case rattle, and cases/cartridges can be inserted point-up or down. Four sizes, for virtually all calibers, $2.95 each.

16th Winchester Seminar

Having nothing new in rifles or shotguns to offer for 1975, the Big Red W will bend its efforts to promote W-W components next year—or this year as you read this.

Highly aggressively, too, we were told during the 5 to 8 December get-together in South Carolina. The reloading line is total and complete now, including bagged shot, match bullets in several calibers, and the long-awaited slow-burning powder, its number 758. I'll show a few typical loads here using 758 (and a new handgun powder, No. 231, which replaces No. 230) if I get the data in time.

Ed Matunas, head of Winchester's components division, just phoned and gave me some recently developed load data using *pilot lots* of Ball powder. For that reason, he said, "It is possible that the exact data and final ballistics might vary slightly" when published. Here are the data which, you'll note, cover the two new powders:

785 Powder/44 grains/100-gr. bullet in 243 Win. for:
A—2957 fps, 45,200 psi.
B—2955 fps, 44,800 psi.

Load A used a standard primer (0.5-gr. pellet); load B carried a magnum primer, pellet weight 0.6-gr., yet ballistics are almost identical.

785 Powder/58.6 grains/130-gr. bullet in 270 Win. for:
C—3018 fps, 45,500 psi, standard 0.5-gr. primer.
D—3018 fps, 45,500 psi, magnum 0.6-gr. primer.

The following loads don't compare primers; they are loads that will appear in the forthcoming W-W *Data Book,* subject to the comments made in our opening paragraph. All 4 used **No. 231** Ball powder.

2.6 grains/38 S&W 148-gr. bullet/675 fps/11,500 psi.

5.1 grains/9mm Para./115-gr. bullet/1125 fps/30,500 psi.

6.7 grains/357 Mag./158-gr. bullet/1275 fps/42,500 psi.

6.9 grains/357 Mag./150-gr. bullet/1305 fps/42,000 psi.

Winchester will not introduce magnum primers, rifle or handgun. Lab tests, we heard, showed that Ball powders perform equally well—or better—with their standard primers versus those of magnum type. Muzzle velocities and pressures were on a par with either primer form, and in rifle or handgun.

The new match grade bullets include two 22s; a 52-gr. HPBT and a 53-gr. HP. There also is an 85-gr. HP in 243, and a pair of 30-cal. bullets—a 168-gr. HP and a 190-gr. HPBT. We saw a lot of ultra tight groups shot with the 22 and 243 bullets, easily small enough to have won benchrest matches.

New W-W bullets—5 new "superaccuracy bullets, designed to offer the bench rest and varmint shooter the best quality bullets obtainable for handloading," should be on the dealers' shelves as you read this. Packed 100 to the box, the new match bullets come in white boxes carrying the big red W.

The new *Winchester Ball Powder Data Book* is not, regrettably, ready as I write this in mid-December, and it probably won't appear until May of 1975. I do know that it will be bigger and more comprehensive in its coverage—more calibers, more loads and the latest powders, 785 and 231, will be included. J.T.A.

Lyman Black Powder Catalog

Lyman's latest is their *Black Powder Handbook,* a 240-page volume that includes 60 pages covering trajectory and wind drift tables on round balls and conical bullets. Over 20,000 shots were fired to obtain valid and valuable load data for muzzle-loading rifles, handguns, muskets and shotguns. Virtually every caliber, barrel length ball or bullet type available today is included. There's much more, of course, in the $6.95 book.

Free from Lyman is their Black Powder Catalog, 16 pages of good stuff for the front-feeder fan—everything needed by the muzzleloader.

Lee Jurras Assoc. AMP Ammo

Many if not most handgunners know that Auto Mag pistol availability has been an on-again, off-again affair. That unsatisfactory situation has, it now appears, been remedied. Lee Jurras (former head of the now defunct Super Vel Corp.), an early enthusiast for the Auto Mag concept—and a master hunter with one—has taken on national and international distribution of all Auto Mags to be produced. Harry Sanford, designer of the pistols, continues as production chief at the factory in California.

However, the news for handloaders is this: L. E. Jurras will offer 357 and 44 AMP ammo, now loaded to improved and reliable standards of performance. The original production cartridges, made in Mexico by CDM, gave unsatisfactory results in many AMP pistols—breech pressure was too low to operate the gun reliably. Not so the new Super Vel loads—a 6½-inch barreled 357 AMP will give about 1900 fps with 137-gr. JSP bullets, and 2000 from an 8-inch barrel. In the 44 AMP the numbers are, with a 180-gr. JSP bullet, MVs of 1850/1950 fps from 6½- and 8-inch barrels.

The Jurras AMP ammo, including a new development—the 41 JMP cartridge—will be manufactured at a new plant in Roswell, New Mexico. Prices will be around $18.50 for 50 of either. J.T.A.

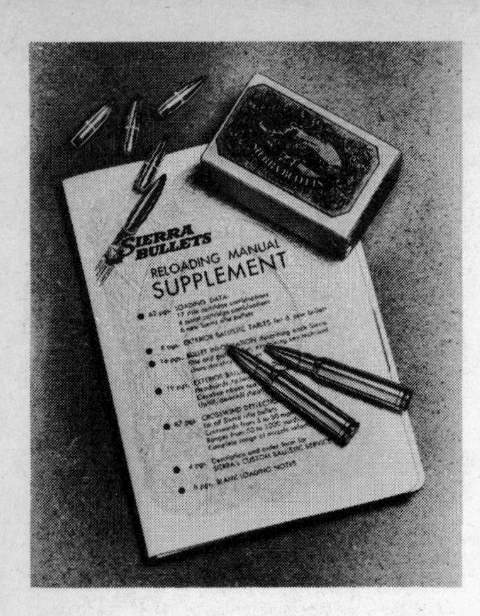

Sierra Bullets
Reloading Manual Supplement

Those discerning handloaders wise enough to buy the 1st edition Sierra *Manual* will certainly want to obtain the new Supplement.

The Supplement has 208 pages, each numbered to let it be readily inserted in correct sequence. This easy interleaving is feasible because the Sierra *Manual* is of loose-leaf form—which style has multiple advantages. It allows Sierra to offer its Supplement at a nominal price, in that these are a simple collection of sheets. This saves the original *Manual* buyer money, for he doesn't need to buy the 2nd edition—which is also available from Sierra (including the new Supplement) at $9.20 plus 25¢ postage.

The new data offered is extensive, and two of the sections offer fresh and original material. There are 19 pages of exterior ballistic tables (head winds, up- and down-hill shooting, etc.), plus a big 87 pages giving crosswind deflection for all Sierra bullets, the wind velocities running from 5 to 30 miles per hour at 50 to 100 yards, and for a complete range of muzzle velocities.

Sixty-eight pages cover new cartridges—17 rifle and 4 handgun, plus 6 new Sierra bullets and the exterior ballistic tables for them.

Also described is Sierra's new Custom Ballistic Service. The details are too lengthy to go into here, but in essence you can send Sierra your loads and receive from them a thorough report on their performance. The fee is nominal.

All in all, 208 pages of highly valuable, useful and up-to-the-minute data. Cost of the new Supplement is $3.45 or, if ordered from Sierra Bullets, add 25¢ for postage. J.T.A.

4831 Powders

The Hodgdons very generously ran some tests for *Gun Digest* using newly-made (in Scotland) H-4831 *versus* Du Pont IMR 4831. Here are the firing results for two calibers, using 26-inch pressure barrels.

In the 25-06, 56/IMR 4831 (Lot 73S9B) behind the 100-gr. Speer bullet gave a muzzle velocity of 3282.6 fps, and a CUP figure of 50,340, these for a 5-shot average. In the same 25-06, this time with 56.0/H4831 of new manufacture, MV was 3160.8, CUP at 46,980. Hodgdon's 4831 would seem to be a bit slower and more efficient—pressure is lower by 3360 CUP and MV down only 121.8 fps.

Much the same results were seen when shooting the 270 Winchester and the 150-gr. Hornady bullet. Average MV was 2986.6 using 58/IMR 4831, same lot as before, with 54,300 CUP for the 5 rounds. With 58/H4831, MV was 2855.4, CUP showed 48,760; thus IMR 4831 gave an increase of 130.2 fps, but at a pressure average 5.540 CUP more.

How much more H4831 might it take to reach the IMR 4831 velocity shown here? I don't know, but I'd think not enough to boost pressures to those listed for the Du Pont powder.

New Hodgdon Manuals

Bruce Hodgdon's latest smokeless powder *Reloading Data Manual* is No. 22, now hardbound in standard style (not spirally) and up from a previous 144 pages to today's 192 and costing $2.95 postpaid. New loads are listed in this fully-revised and updated volume, among them more potent 45-70 recipes for such rifles as the Ruger No. 1 single shot, and loads for the 44 Auto Mag. As before, the new Manual also shows numerous lead-bullet loads, almost as many as there are for jacketed bullets.

Also new are several powders, these made for Hodgdon in Scotland—HP38 for handguns; X58, Trap 100 and HS7, all for shotshell loads, plus H205 (guess what that duplicates) and newly-manufactured 4831.

Several other new powders, these not shown in No. 22, will soon be offered by Hodgdon—H3031, H4320, H4064 and H4350.

Though No. 22 lists extensive load data for rifles, handguns and shotshells, also available is the Hodgdon *Shotshell Data Manual,* fully revised, and there's a new 2nd edition of their *Black Powder Data Manual,* brought completely up to date and costing 50c postpaid. J.T.A.

Lyman 100 SL Shotshell Press

We've been giving Lyman's latest shotshell press—the 100 SL—a workout recently, and the end products have been excellent—the crimps are tight and well rounded for sure feeding in autoloaders and pumps—some 30 rounds were fired in the new Winchester Super X 12 bore auto. This new press is also one of the fastest single-station presses I've used.

The 100 SL shotshell press consists of a free-rotating drum that insures consistent and accurate powder and shot charging. It offers full length sizing of high or low brass, 2¾" or 3", with a smooth cam-actuated ejection of all types and sizes without adjustment. A primer feed activates the optional primer reservoir, which holds 100 primers and feeds them to the primer drop tube.

A floating wad guide offers easy alignment in the case mouth during wad insertion. The floating crimp starter aligns automatically and works with a newly designed crimping die to give those uniform, tight crimps I spoke of. The "Quick Dump Reservoirs" are emptied by activating

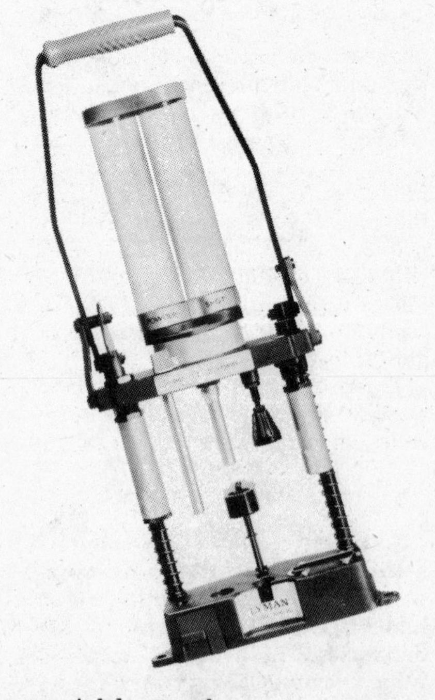

a special dump valve.

The 100 SL shotshell press, available in 12 and 20 gauge, lists at $79.50. Conversion kits (12-20 or 20-12 gauge) are $19.50. The optional primer magazine is $8.50. J.T.A.

Brief Notes

Bahler Die Shop can now furnish a few sets of dies for making handgun bullets, but please note that these are made *only* for use in RCBS Rockchucker presses.

Simple to use, and making a bullet with every press stroke, these Bahler Die sets make any reasonable bullet weight, and any nose shape wanted can be furnished. Solid point die sets are $60, HP sets are $65, and bullet jackets (½ and ¾ in 38 or 44) are $12-$15 per thousand.

Bahler continues to supply 17-cal. bullets and rifle die sets, of course, prices and full data on application.

RCBS will soon be supplying an extensive line of bullet moulds and related products—ingot moulds, lead pots and dippers, top punches to match the moulds, etc. Fred Huntington has taken over the manufacture of these items from Ohaus, though the latter firm will continue to market its well-known powder scales and measures, etc. RCBS has also been negotiating with LEC (Lachmiller Engineering), so maybe some LEC products will be offered by RCBS in the near future.

J & G Rifle Ranch continues a prime source for case/cartridge cleaning and polishing machines. These motorized rotaters, all consisting of original Thumler Tumblers, come in a variety of sizes and capacities. The Model A uses one 15-oz. bag of polishing media; others handle up to four pounds, and will clean up to some 225 rifle cases or 400-500 handgun hulls. Prices run from $22.95 to $49.95, all ready to work as received, and all guaranteed.

This is good equipment—I've used a couple of J & G tumblers for several years, and with full satisfaction. J.T.A.

Echo products, an old name in shooting-reloading circles, has been sold to a Canadian group—Quaco Industries, Ltd., St. Martins, St. John County, New Brunswich EOG 2Z0. E. C. Herkner owned and operated Echo for 28 years—my first Model 70 Winchester wears an Echo scope mount—and we're sorry to see the end, at least in the U.S., of the firm.

Hornady/Pacific Sure-Loc Die Rings

Made for use with all standard 7/8"x 14 thread dies, these new rings, of solid steel, provide a positive grip around the entire circumference of the die threads.

Each Sure-Lock ring comes with an allen wrench for pulling the collar tight uniformly and evenly around the threaded die, preventing possible damage to the die's threads. There is no seizing of the ring—it is easily and quickly loosened when adjustment is required.

The blue-finished lock ring won't flex under pressure. Cost is $1.00 each.

G96 Ammo Brightener

Among the numerous and good G96 products offered by Jet Aer Corp. (Paterson, NJ 07524) is their new Brass Ammo Case Polisher. This 2-part system—a 7"x11" treated polishing cloth and a like-size buffing cloth—works very well, as I recently learned.

I grabbed a few well-tarnished 30-06 cases, some old GI stuff, and in a few minutes they were gleaming—the G96 polishing cloth soon became blackened, but that's OK, for the instructions say the cloth gets better as it gets blacker! Time will tell, of course, but Jet-Aer says the polishing cloth will last for years, until it wears out. The abrasive action, if any, seems minimal.

To speed the case cleaning I chucked a tapered steel rod in my drill press, then pushed empty cases onto it and applied the polishing cloth to the spinning case. That worked a lot faster on most of my brass, but I also discovered that heavily-tarnished cases took a bit more time and effort, of course.

A good product, and worth its cost of $1.98. J.T.A.

Texan Reloaders, Inc.

I've always found the several Texan shotshell loaders excellent values—even the lower-cost tools do a first class job. My Model FW (about $85) in 20 gauge produces loads that can't be faulted, though it isn't the fastest press made.

The latest Texan is the GT, only $69.95 (12, 16, 20, 28 or 410, with conversion kits $24.95), and made with extra leverage that eases every operation. All steel frame and 2-post design for long life and positive alignment, the 4-station GT offers full case resizing/depriming (without cupping the case head), a self-lowering wad guide and charge-bar programming for correct load sequence.

Our sample GT, set up for 16 gauge cases, has performed smoothly and efficiently. I particularly like the simplified station 2 operation—the unique design combines primer seating, wad insertion, wad pressure and charge-bar programming. The nylon crimp starter avoids case mouth damage and locates itself on the crimp folds accurately. Final crimping produces a tight taper (adjustable for *your* gun), and uniform-length cartridges. J.T.A.

Redding-Hunter

A number of improvements in the Redding line were announced in late 1974, plus some new items and a promise of others to come. Their No. 7 C-press now has a stronger steel alloy frame, and the throat is shallower to avoid deflection or bending under stress. The lower linkage is now stouter, too, being of alloy steel, and a rear mount-lug has been added to prevent springing of the tool.

The No. 3 Master Powder Measure now comes with either a Universal or a Pistol Measuring Chamber (or both, if you like). These chambers are micrometer set, and they quickly interchange.

New for 1975 is the Redding Master Case Trimmer, handling all rifle and handgun cases. It differs from other trimmers in that it chamfers and deburrs the case during the trimming—if desired. A straight cutter blade is also furnished at no extra cost. A case-cleaning brush and a primer-pocket cleaner are attached to the frame—both worthwhile and handy.

Send for the 1975 Redding catalog. It will show the items described here plus the rest of their line—turret press, shotshell press, dies, etc. J.T.A.

New Schmidt-Weston Standard Chronograph

We've just received a most interesting and decidedly different chronograph, one that has unique aspects, I believe. Unfortunately, it has arrived too late for a thorough Testfire Report, but we'll give it a full check for function and performance, of course. First, though, a description. The readout unit, 4"x9¾"x9⅛" deep, weighs about 10½ lbs. with battery, and is constructed in a highly professional manner of 16-gauge steel. Readout is in foot seconds to 4 decimal places via LEDs (light emitting diodes) for long life and reliability.

Screen spacing may be 2, 5 or 10 feet; a rotating switch lets the user choose whichever he wants. The crystal clock frequencies are 5 Mhz (5 million cycles) at 2 feet; 2 Mhz at 5 feet and 1 Mhz at 10 feet. Accuracy is guaranteed to be plus-0 to minus-1 foot second at a 3,000 fps level, whichever screen spacing is in use—and assuming a careful screen setup preparation. Velocities from 150 to 9,999 foot seconds can be measured—a great range indeed, one that lets BB or air guns be checked.

The Standard Chronograph is dual powered—110 V AC or nicad internal batteries. Plug the unit into the line and a built-in charger begins to build up the battery; take the instrument into the field and operation is via the nicad battery. A simple and highly desirable system. The charged nicad will operate the chronograph for an hour, enough time to test 100-120 rounds.

Two screen systems are offered, either immediately usable. Conventional break-type screens can be used (details and prices below), or a pair of Auto-Setting Lite Screens, supplied by Schmidt-Weston as part of one package. These ambient light screens are quite unusual in operation and function—either may be used as a front or back screen, and either may also be positioned to let the bullet pass over in either direction.

As the makers point out, using this new system is virtually a "hands off" operation. Here's why—on firing the first shot over the Lite screens, the foot-second reading appears instantly, and it remains on view until the next shot is fired. There's nothing to touch or manipulate; just shoot, record and shoot again, about as fast, too, as you'd like! The Lite screens are powered by 9-volt batteries (2), each good for about 20 hours of useful life.

The Lite screens can also be used indoors or out, being triggered by ambient light outside or by incandescent light sources indoors.

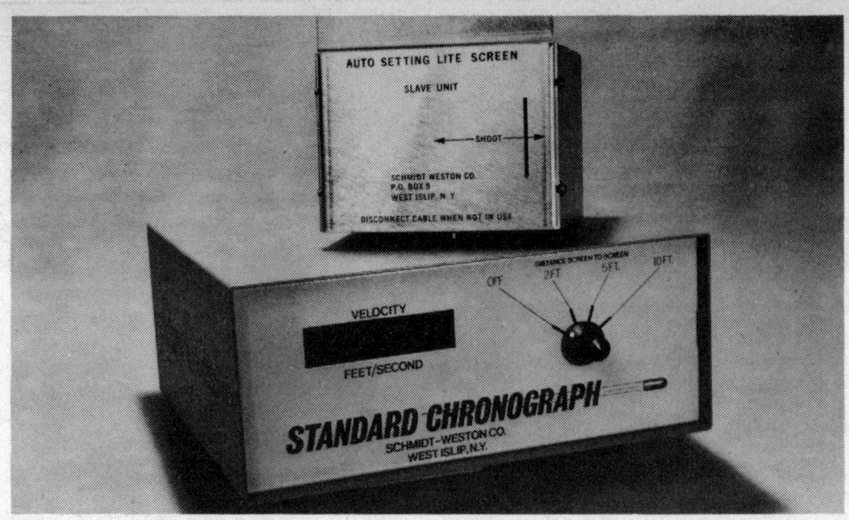

The shooting area over the Lite screens is a generous one—the shape is that of a keystone or inverted triangle, about 18 inches high by 12 inches wide at the top, the sides tapering to 1½ inches at the bottom. Under optimum light conditions outdoors the height can be as much as 3 feet.

The makers define "optimum" ambient light condition as those existing on overcast, dull days. Presumably the light on such days has less tendency to vary in intensity, but I was told that their design allows for wide alterations in light intensity, provided the changes are not rapid.

The S-W instrument may be used at extended ranges as well; a terminal strip at the rear accepts cables (the user's) of any feasible length.

Shotshell velocity can be tested, too. Using the 2-foot screen separation, the pellet pattern is small enough to be detected as a single unit.

An ingenious technique is used in the all-digital Standard Chronograph to indicate trouble or correct hookup. Each LED position reveals a lighted decimal point when A) the chronograph is running "over-range," meaning a too-slow shot or B) when the screens are properly connected, and C) if the battery(s) is low.

Connecting the Standard Chronograph to the Lite screens was only a moment's work, and a check of function and readout was equally quick. Turning the switch from "Off" to any of the 3 screen-spacing points lights up the LEDs in a more or less random readout. Waving my hand rapidly over both screens produced readings between 160-190 foot seconds at the 2-foot position, satisfactory results considering the less-than-ideal condition of the test.

The Schmidt-Weston system, using the Auto-Setting Lite screens, seems to work excellently, and the shoot/read-read functioning is beautiful.

My only chance to field test the S-W chronograph came on a gloomy cold day—"optimum light conditions," per Mr. Weston, and so it proved.

I had mounted the twin A-S Lite units, by means of their drilled steel flanges, to a 2x4, carefully spacing them two feet apart. The assembly was positioned at my outdoor chrono bench, the first screen about 5 feet from the muzzle of an old Winchester M52 target rifle. I wanted to check 22 LR ammo first to get a comparative readout.

Lining up the rifle with the screens was no problem this time; the short spacing helped. But with a scoped rifle I'm going to arrange an aiming point above and behind the second screen.

I shot 20 rounds of fresh Winchester Super Match Mark III ammo over the Lite units. Nominal MV of Mk IIIs is 1120 fps, and these 20 shots came close—1083.5 on average, with a low and high of 1061/1099, about right for a muzzle distance of 5½ feet and a 28-inch barrel.

Another 20 shots were made with Winchester's 22 LR High Speed solids, factory MV of 1285 fps. These were not quite as uniform, lows and highs running 65 fps apart, with the average at 1291, a bit higher than the published figures!

There wasn't time for further testing, but the chronographing managed was easily and quickly done, without a bobble. I held some 6-8 inches over the screens for the 40 cartridges shot.

Costs? The Standard Chronograph, with frangible screens, holders and cables, is $185. With the Auto-Setting Lite screens, but not including the breakable-screen system, $250. 100 break screens, including holders and cables, are $15 per pair. The A-S Lite screens, if ordered later, are $85 a pair. Break screens per 100 (each 4½" x2¾") are $4.90. J.T.A.

The 6.5x55 an old Swede

After long study and careful weighing of the ballistic facts and figures, the author selected the old and respected Swedish military cartridge for his all-purpose rifle. He presents well-reasoned arguments, good results, but . . .

by EMIL S. PIRAINO

TODAY CULMINATES four years of research and testing, a happy occasion for me because it marks the end of a long search, a hunt for the ideal rifle-cartridge combination for my purposes and the beginning of a novel chapter in shooting adventure. I have finally found what is, for me, the "all-purpose rifle."

The thought of using one rifle exclusively for all my hunting and shooting needs began to intrigue me some years ago when my wife and I thought of moving to British Columbia—though we later changed our minds and settled for Oregon instead. But, once kindled, the desire for an all-purpose rifle became an obsession. I strongly desired an arm that would be carried on any and all my hunting trips—one that could dispatch, if necessary, just about anything found in the North Woods, and would accomplish this with the least amount of blast and recoil.

The shooting game was relatively new to me then, and I failed to appreciate the magnitude of the task that confronted me. Selecting a cartridge-rifle combination for all-round use requires at least a rudimentary knowledge of modern arms and ammunition capabilities, and some understanding of ballistics. Shooting literature points out repeatedly that the all-purpose rifle simply does not exist; that it is only a myth. I was resolved to have one, though, but if such a rifle could not be produced, I'd at least have found why not!

Consequently, every bit of shooting literature I could obtain was read avidly. The many complex and contradictory statements became a source of constant frustration and bewilderment. In the ensuing years I accumulated and digested a voluminous amount of material, always with one thought in mind—that all-elusive, all-round rifle. Needless to say, much that I read lacked objectivity and was therefore of little use.

Slowly the fog began to lift, however, and out of the seemingly endless maze of personal opinions, fancy and fact, the basic element of the problem came sharply into focus: the choice of an all-purpose rifle is governed by two sets of criteria, one subjective, the other objective in nature.

The subjective factors relate to the individual's tastes, needs, skills, temperament and interests. Objective considerations concern the technical aspects of rifle and cartridge design and their performance under varying conditions and circumstances. Since the effectiveness of a given rifle cannot be entirely evaluated apart from the person who uses it, any "all-round" rifle must be, to some extent, the product of an individual's opinion. Most inveterate shooters will, soon or late, develop a strong preference for a certain cartridge. More often than not this preference is dictated more by personal likes and dislikes than by a judicious and impartial analysis of the cartridge.

In arriving at my choice, however, personal considerations were eliminated as far as possible—my attention was concentrated on those factors that were demonstrable and capable of being tested. Still, the subjective criteria had to be clearly defined and stated before an objective could be formulated. I

Testing the 6.5x55 rifle at 100 yards, the author shooting. The new 10" twist barrel proved more accurate than the original one of 1-in-9. The scope mounted is a B&L 2x-8x Balvar.

posed myself the following questions:

1. What will be the smallest and the largest game animals likely to be hunted with this rifle?
2. Over what type of terrain will most of the shooting take place?
3. What will the rifle be used for most of the time?
4. How much shooting skill do I possess, or am I willing to acquire?
5. What are the legal requirements for game shooting in the territories I'll be hunting?
6. How much recoil can I tolerate for pleasant shooting?
7. Is the rifle to be used for competitive shooting also?

Answering these questions was no problem, but making a rifle versatile enough to meet them had yet to be pinpointed.

To qualify for all-round use, a rifle-cartridge combination must adapt itself readily, within a predetermined latitude, to any shooting situation that may come up. This may be a large order indeed if the rifle must perform satisfactorily over a wide range of conditions. It must first of all be accurate, not only with bullets for heavy game, but above all with light, varmint bullets. For consistent hits on squirrels or woodchucks at ranges beyond 200 yards, these bullets must strike within a one-inch circle at 100 yards, or 1 minute of angle.

Rate of Twist?

One aspect soon became paramount—a given rate of rifling twist will stabilize bullets of a certain weight and length better than some others. For example, a rate of twist suitable for the 30-06/180-gr. bullet will spin the 110-gr. bullet more than necessary to stabilize it in flight. The consequent overspinning results, we've been told, in reduced accuracy, although it must not be inferred that overspinning itself is the sole cause of reduced accuracy. There are other factors involved, as Franklin W. Mann discovered many years ago.

Selecting that rate of twist which will bring out the highest degree of accuracy to the widest selection of bullets is the problem.

To keep the overspinning of light bullets at a minimum, such a barrel must stabilize the heavy bullets just enough to insure good accuracy at game ranges and no more. Many rifles, especially of military type, are made with faster rates of twist than are necessary to stabilize the bullets most commonly used in them. Notable among these are the rifles (military and sporting) chambered for the 30-06. Their barrels are made with a rifling twist of 1 turn in 10 inches, which overstabilizes the 150-gr. bullets used by the army. In fact this 1-10 twist is a bit fast for hunting bullets, at least at usual game ranges. The Swedish and Japanese 6.5mm military rifles have sharp twists—1 turn in about 8 inches. The tendency has been toward overstabilization rather than in the opposite direction—and for good reason. Sporting gunmakers want to be sure that the heaviest bullets likely to be used in their rifles will be stabilized. Military considerations demand that bullets be stabilized all the way out to extreme ranges. A sporting barrel, however, can be chosen with that rate of twist which best serves the needs of the discerning hunter-rifleman.

Because the choice of caliber necessitates a compromise, any all-purpose cartridge must be on the modest side of the energy scale for the largest game and on the plus side for the smallest varmints. This consideration merits careful attention. A slightly heavy bullet for varmint shooting is not a disadvantage, provided it is accurate and pleasant to shoot. The big drawback lies in having only a minimum of power for the humane killing of the largest game that must be taken. This disadvantage can be greatly offset, however, by three factors: 1) the use of bullets with the highest feasible sectional density and ballistic co-efficient values; 2) a knowledge of the capabilities of the weapon and its judicious use on game, and 3) good marksmanship. That last aspect is probably more important than the other two.

SD and BC

Sectional density (SD) is the ratio of the cross-sectional area of a bullet to its weight; ballistic co-efficient is a measure of the bullet's efficiency in overcoming air resistance; both terms are expressed numerically. The higher the SD number of a bullet, the better will be its penetrating characteristics; the higher the ballistic co-efficient number, the less pronounced is its velocity loss during its flight to the target. Unless made for long range use, bullets lose as much as 16% of their speed every 100 yards. Round-nosed bullets lose speed very rapidly, hence are suitable only for short and medium ranges. A well-designed long-range bullet will lose speed at the rate of about 7% or less. This fact becomes highly significant considering that kinetic energy, the criterion used for killing power, is more a product of speed than mass weight. For example, a 100-gr. bullet at 2800 fps develops 1740 foot-pounds of energy. By decreasing it to 50 grains, its energy at the same speed will be 870 ft. lbs., or half of 1740; its energy has decreased in the same proportion as the weight of the bullet. But reduce its speed—rather than its weight—by half, and at 1400 fps the 100-gr. bullet generates a mere 435 fp of energy. A streamlined bullet is a decided asset for long-range shooting, because it will have a great deal more sustained energy when reaching the target than a bullet of inferior design. Many cartridges, loaded with low sectional density bullets, start out like a whirlwind but soon dwindle to a mere whisper, thus making them ineffectual on large game beyond relatively short ranges. Tabulated below are sectional density and ballistic coefficient figures for some popular calibers and Speer bullets. Unless preceded by RN, indicating a round nose, the values apply to sharp-pointed bullets.

SD/BC Table

Bullet/Dia.	Wt./grs.	SD	BC
.224"	55	.157	.209
.243"	90	.217	.323
	105	.254	.395
.257"	87	.188	.294
	100	.216	.354
	120	.258	.423
.264"	87	.179	.280
	120	.247	.405
	140	.289	.482
	160	.329	†
.277"	100	.186	.291
	130	.241	.395
	150	.278	.463
.284"	130	.230	.365
	145	.257	.425
	160	.284	.469
.308"	110	.165	.261
	150	.225	.387
	180*	.270	.288
	180	.272	.435
	200*	.301	.425
	200	.301	.502

*RN, round nose †Not Speer

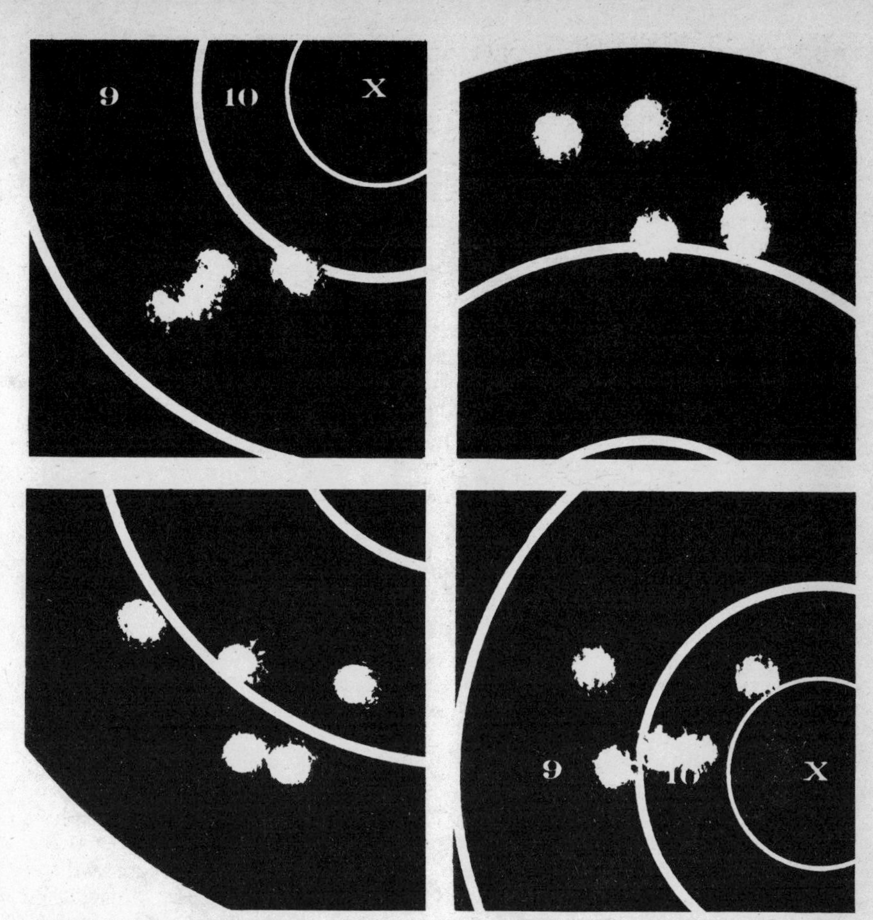

The four 5-shot groups shown here were fired at 100 yards, bench rest, the rifle the author's 6.5x55, a custom Mauser with 26" barrel, rate of twist 1-in-10". Upper left, 46.0/4350/100 Sierra HP. Upper right, 40/3031/85 Sierra HP. Lower left, 43/4350/156 Norma SP. Lower right, Norma factory load, 139-gr. SP. All targets are shown life size.

Bullets with SDs less than .200 rate poor when used on big game; .250 to .300, generally very good; over .300, superior. The preponderance of evidence favors the bullet of good construction and design, one that starts out at a fairly good speed and maintains it over its range of flight with a minimum of loss. Such a bullet will also show good performance over a relatively long range. Obviously, therefore, in selecting a cartridge for a given use the variety of bullets that can be used with it becomes of vital importance.

For my particular wants the rifle had to be highly accurate with both heavy game bullets and light varmint bullets. The rifle would be used for varminting as often as conditions permitted, so I wanted minute of angle accuracy with lightweight bullets. The largest animal to be hunted would be elk, with deer and black bear in between, and perhaps an occasional antelope. The rifle would be used mostly for long range shooting in open areas, but would have to perform satisfactorily in woods country. To meet the legal requirements for taking elk in Oregon, the cartridge could not be less than 25 caliber and had to be capable of delivering at least 1200 ft. lbs. of energy at 100 yards. In the matter of recoil, suffice it to say that anything more violent than the 270 would cease to be fun for varmint shooting. My preference has been for rifles of relatively light recoil. I also wanted to use the same rifle at turkey shoots. Once these requirements had been settled, a number of possible candidates was indicated.

From the standpoint of accuracy and light recoil, the 250 Savage seemed a good choice, as did the 257 Roberts and the very popular 243 Winchester, all three ideal for long-range varminting.

The 250 and 257

The 250 Savage has been regarded generally as an excellent medium-power cartridge. With an 87-gr. bullet starting out at the then amazing speed of 3000 fps, it made sensational news back in 1915. For deer-sized game, it is factory loaded with a 100-gr. bullet. Unlike the 257, it has not been loaded with heavier bullets because 250 Savage rifles are made with slow rifling twists. The gain with heavy bullets, even if usable, though, would be negligible, except perhaps for hunting in heavy cover. The small-capacity case would be unable to impart sufficient velocity to a bullet of about 120 grains to make it serviceably effective on elk-sized game. Designed primarily for long-range varmint shooting, the 250 does its best work with the 87- and 100-gr. bullets.

The 257 Roberts seemed better adapted for all-round use because of its larger case, which will naturally handle bullets of higher sectional density at higher speeds and with less pressure than would be possible in the 250 Savage case. The factory 117-gr. load has an advertised velocity of 2650 fps, which does not quite develop its full power potential. In a good rifle this speed can be increased to make this a more effective round on large-size game. The higher speed might even improve accuracy with this bullet, which comes close to being marginal in barrels having a twist of 1 in 10. It might also permit the use of 125-gr. bullets. In

Norma's 139-gr. boat-tail loading of the 6.5x55. Norma bullets, from left—77-gr. semi-pointed SP; 93-gr. full jacketed pointed; 139-gr. semi-pointed boat-tail; 156-gr. round nose SP; 139-gr. full jacketed boat-tail. All are shown life size.

any case, the 257 Roberts cannot be entirely excluded from the class of the 250 Savage and the 243 Winchester, for its limitations for game larger than deer are not unlike those of the latter two.

Choosing the 243 Winchester, of course, would have meant giving up elk hunting, since its use on this game animal is unlawful in Oregon as well as in some other states. In this class of cartridges, however, another possibility was still open.

By chambering for the 257 Improved, speeds with the heavier bullets could be stepped up considerably over factory figures. Since cases are made by firing standard 257 cartridges in the larger chamber, readily obtainable factory ammunition could be used at any time. With a 125-gr. bullet and 43-44 grains of 4350 powder, some 2900 fps is obtained in a 24″ barrel using the standard 1 in 10 twist. A 25-cal. sharp nose bullet in this weight has ballistic properties highly suitable for long-range shooting. The above load would have the flat trajectory of the 270, and would even approach it in effectiveness on game. The 125-gr. 25-caliber bullet has a higher sectional density than the 130-gr. 270 bullet. For hunting in heavy brush and woods, the combination of high velocity and *relatively* light bullets is subject to blow-ups and deflections. If slower speeds were resorted to, heavier bullets (to help offset the reduced energy) could not be used. The 1 in 10 twist would not stabilize them.

The idea of using a faster twist—say, 1 in 9—came to mind. The possibilities with this rate of twist become more far reaching. Since the 1 in 10 twist will stabilize 125-gr. bullets, might not the sharper twist handle 140-gr. bullets? The high sectional density needed for effectiveness on big game would be amply fulfilled with such a bullet. With a round nose at about 2600 fps it would be a decided improvement for woods hunting. Changing it to a spitzer bullet weighing about 130 grains at some 2900 fps, and the long range possibilities become very interesting. Such a bullet, with its high ballistic coefficient, would shed the barest minimum of its speed during flight. How well varmint bullets would perform in the 1 in 9 twist is open to question. Certainly, the faster twist would not *improve* their accuracy. All this, of course, would have to be put to the test, which, because of heavy expense, is not always practical. Besides, since bullets would have to be custom made, their availability could not always be depended upon.

What about the heavier calibers?

The 30-06 and 270

The 30-06 has been repeatedly upheld as "the all-round medicine" for North American game. As a varminter, however, it leaves much to be desired. It is much too formidable for the smallest game; whether varmint loads would deliver the desired accuracy is highly questionable. In fact, it is regarded by many as being unnecessarily heavy for deer. Shooters who enjoy the sensation of overwhelming power might find delight in blasting small game to smithereens with it, but I am not one. No, the historic 30-06 must be rated primarily as a big game cartridge, and only accidentally would it fulfill the requirements for varminting, which is not what was being sought.

The possibility of adapting the 270 Winchester for all-purpose use occurred to me, of course—its excellent record for game-getting cannot be disputed. Best accuracy has been obtained with the 130- and 150-gr. bullets, and much of the game hunted is stopped with these bullets. In the right hands this cartridge has proved very deadly—even on polar bear. It was designed with a special purpose in mind: that of long range big game shooting in open country. Its most outstanding characteristic is the flatness of its trajectory. It was intended therefore for the wide open areas of the West and for the vast North American mountain ranges where sheep are hunted. Handloading it with the 150-gr. soft point boat-tail bullet gives it about 2900 fps, and develops its power potential most fully. For varminting, good accuracy has been reported with 90-gr. hollow point bullets, and with devastating results. Because of its specialized nature, however, the 270 leans too far on the power side of the scale, without which a flat enough trajectory could not be achieved to justify its adoption. Having the same case capacity as the 30-06, both are definitely in the same class, energy-wise. For year-round varminting, though, it did not appeal strongly enough. Its large capacity case would be a needless waste, and blast and recoil would not be conducive to many hours of pleasurable shooting. The late Colonel Townsend Whelen used the 270 Winchester for big game hunting from 1928 until his death, having found it more reliable than the 30-06; but with all his experimenting, minute of angle groups were achieved very rarely. Admittedly, bullets available to him, we now know, were much inferior to today's best quality.

Some wildcats were considered

besides the 257 Roberts Improved, but these are not desirable when one must depend on one rifle because they must be assembled at home; components may not always be readily available. In remote areas, obtaining ammunition would be impossible.

The 6.5x55

My final choice rested with the Swedish 6.5x55 cartridge. Using bullets of .264″ diameter, this comes closest to approaching the ideal for all-purpose use. It possesses, to the highest degree possible, the best features of our most popular cartridges: namely, sufficient power for big game, flatness of trajectory, outstanding accuracy with both big game and varmint loads, very mild recoil, plus bullets of excellent shape in a wide assortment of weights. Its most publicized feature has been its distinguished record for unsurpassed accuracy among cartridges of the same class, which has served to put the 6.5x55 in the forefront among Olympic match shooters—who have amply developed its possibilities for long range precision shooting. Since 1894, when it was adopted by Scandinavian armies, its case design has remained unchanged.

Among European shooters, notably Scandinavians, the 6.5x55, like the 30-06 in America, has enjoyed wide popularity, being regarded as a sort of national cartridge. The number of rounds fired and reloaded by civilian shooting clubs runs into an impressive figure. In Sweden alone, more than 2300 shooting clubs fire more than 40 million rounds of this cartridge per year. Swedish and Norwegian hunters use it extensively to bag their yearly quota of moose and other game—even the formidable polar bear.

Until recent years, 6.5mm ammunition was little known in this country. With the influx of foreign military arms during the late 1950s, however, there has been a growing interest shown. The 6.5x55, along with other foreign 6.5s, has often been dismissed as being in the same class as our 25-cal. sporting cartridges. Responsible for this unfavorable comparison have been a number of features inherent in the military arms and ammunition that appeared here, features which impose marked limitations on their use for the hunting of various game.

The actions in Swedish military rifles and carbines were designed to operate at pressures of about 47,000 psi, mild compared to those generated by modern sporting cartridges. Not knowing how much use, and abuse, these rifles have been subjected to, the reloader must approach full power loadings with the greatest caution. Another disadvantage for sporting use is the very fast twist in the barrels, which, besides increasing pressures, gives generally poor accuracy with all but the heaviest bullets. In addition to these limitations, Swedish carbines (not rifles) have extremely short barrels, further reducing the effectiveness of the cartridge. The net result, of course, is a far cry from the full power potential and flexibility of the 6.5x55 when used in a modern rifle.

The cartridge is currently manufactured by Norma of Sweden and exported to this country. The high quality of Norma ammunition is attested by all who have used it. Reloading components have been developed to meet the exacting requirements for Olympic match shooting. For the reloader, a wide assortment of domestic bullets is readily available. These range in weight from 85 to 160 grains. Of special interest are the Nosler Partition bullets in 125- and 140-gr. weights, which extend the usefulness of the cartridge for big game hunting. These bullets have proven their ability to hold together and smash through bone and muscle under almost any circumstance. Norma bullets are in 77-, 93-, 139-, and 156-gr. weights, making this a remarkably versatile cartridge. The 93-gr. bullet is made with a full jacket to minimize tissue destruction on edible game downed with soft point bullets, which must be finished off. A table shown below published by Norma Projectilfabrik, shows factory ballistic values.

Barrel length used to obtain the above figures is not known. Swedish military rifles were made with 29.1″ barrels, and professional shooters there commonly use barrels of about the same length, with a twist of 1 turn in 8½″. Long barrels and long sight separation lets shooters place shots with more precision in matches where scopes are not permitted.

Since we are dealing with a medium capacity case, however, it becomes questionable whether a barrel longer than 24″ would improve ballistics appreciably. In deciding on the barrel length for my rifle, therefore, it seemed reasonable that the published figures could be duplicated very closely with a 24″ barrel—at the most, 26″.

Once my cartridge choice had been decided, selection of a suitable rate of twist became a critical decision. A twist permitting minute of angle accuracy with bullets from 85 to 120 grains, and one that would also stabilize the heavy 160-gr. bullets, was desired. Attaining this goal would have presented little problem in a larger bore for these reasons: overspinning or underspinning of bullets of like composition, when fired through a barrel with a given rate of twist, is affected markedly by their length. .01″ is significant in the length of a bullet, and may spell the difference whether such a bullet will be stabilized or not. In a 6.5mm bullet, a 40-gr. increase results in a much longer projectile than in 30 caliber, causing a sharper reaction in the barrel. Therefore, as the caliber decreases, so must the latitude between the heaviest and the lightest bullet that can be fired accurately through the same barrel.

From all available information on the subject, the 1 in 9 twist seemed to be the best choice. Accordingly the rifle was assembled with the following specifications:

Action	F. N. Mauser
Barrel	Douglas, 26″, medium weight
Twist	1 in 9 inches
Stock	Maple, with cheek rest
Sights	Balvar 2x-8x variable scope
Pull	13¼″
Weight	8 lbs. (without scope)

Norma 6.5x55 Ballistics

Bullet		Velocity—ft. per sec.				Energy—ft. lbs.				MRT—ins.		
Wt./grs.	Type	Muzzle	100	200	300	Muzzle	100	200	300	100	200	300
77*	SPP	3116	2730	2370	2040	1664	1275	961	712	.0	1.9	5.6
93*	FJP	3150	2705	2292	1920	2050	1512	1085	762	.0	1.9	6.0
139	SPBT	2788	2630	2470	2320	2402	2136	1883	1662	.1	2.0	5.6
156	SPR	2493	2271	2062	1867	2153	1787	1473	1208	.3	2.9	7.9

*These loads not currently available from Norma-Precision. MRT—Mid-Range Trajectory, scope height 0.7″ above bore.
SPP—Soft Point, pointed FJP—Full Jacket, pointed SPPBT—Soft Point, Boat Tail SPR—Soft Point, Round Nose.

Comparative Ballistic Table

	Bullet/grs.	Velocity/fps Muzzle	100	200	300	400	Energy/fp Muzzle	100	200	300	400	Energy Loss*
250 Sav.	100	2820	2510	2220	1960	1673	1765	1400	1095	850	622	286
257 Rob.	100	2900	2590	2290	2020	1727	1865	1485	1165	905	663	300
	120	2645	2405	2180	1960	1732	1865	1540	1260	1030	800	266
6.5x55	139	2790	2630	2470	2320	2163	2395	2130	1880	1650	1453	236
270 Win.	130	3140	2885	2640	2405	2160	2835	2390	2000	1660	1444	348
	150	2800	2615	2435	2260	2080	2605	2270	1970	1700	1440	291
30-06	150	2970	2680	2400	2140	1923	2930	2385	1915	1520	1231	425
	180	2700	2490	2295	2110	1913	2895	2470	2095	1765	1463	358

*Per each 100 yards.

New Rifle Flops

The rifle was taken to the range for trial. Over 400 rounds were put through the barrel with bullets ranging in weight from 100- to 160 grains. Over-all results were most discouraging. None of the loads tested, with few exceptions, gave satisfactory groupings. Best accuracy was obtained with the heavy bullets when loaded much below full capacity. 160-gr. Hornady bullets made fair groups, averaging about 2 inches. 140-gr. Centrix bullets gave best accuracy; five-shot strings ran around 1″; Sierras grouped slightly under 2 inches. When loaded to full capacity, the smallest groups made with 140-gr. bullets measured just over 2 inches. The 120-gr. bullets tested gave poorer results than Hornady's 100-gr. ones, although none were sufficiently tight to merit use.

Powder/grs.	Bullet/grs.	MV
4831/45	160	2466
4831/43	140	2422*
4831/48	140	2707
4831/50	120	2920
4350/50	100	3225

*Most accurate load

After initial testing, the rifle was worked over to see if accuracy could be improved. The action and barrel were glass-bedded and the same loads tested again; no improvement. The glass bedding was next gouged out from the fore-end and the barrel left free floating from action to muzzle. Testing was resumed once more with the same components, this time with noticeable group improvement with all bullets so far tested. The rifle was subsequently taken to RCBS of Oroville, Calif., where several loadings with bullets of varying weights were chronographed; see RCBS Test table.

The increased accuracy gained after tuning the rifle still didn't satisfy me. It was highly desirable to gain, if possible, excellent accuracy with the 120-gr. bullets at a speed of about 3000 fps for long-range shooting. Such a speed could be had with 48 grains of 4350, without too much pressure. The resulting flat trajectory would be advantageous for plains shooting.

Accuracy results thus far seemed to show that the 1 in 9 twist would not fulfill this requirement. The barrel was scrapped in favor of one having a 1 in 10 twist and a length of 24″. I thought that the slower rate of twist might produce the desired accuracy with the lighter bullets while giving reasonably good results with the 140-gr. ones. Popular opinion and authoritive sources were unanimous in pointing out that I would be unable to use bullets heavier than 140 grains because the slower twist would not stabilize them. But here a pleasant surprise was awaiting me.

New Barrel

The 1 in 10 twist proved by far the better choice. The first 140-gr. bullets tested made remarkably tight groups. Factory ammunition with the 139-gr. boat-tail bullets registered consistently within 1″, with no fliers. The 120-gr. bullets also did very well; groups with these measured 1¼″ to 1½″, lower speeds producing the tighter groups. 100-gr. Hornady spire point bullets registered within 2½″. Then, with nothing but sheer curiosity in mind, three 156-gr. Norma bullets were tried, and—lo and behold—they grouped within ¾″! Inspired by this performance, I made up more of the same loads, varying the seating depth of the 156-gr. bullets in groups of three. The same satisfactory accuracy was produced with all of them.

There could be no doubt about it: this bullet was inherently accurate with this barrel. This performance, unexpected because it defied everything I'd heard and read about twist, was most gratifying. It extended the usefulness of this rifle and entrenched it more firmly in the all-round class. Subsequent testing with Hornady's 160-gr. round nose bullets established them as marginal for the heavyweights. At a muzzle velocity of 2580 fps these bullets scored 2″ groups.

Up to this point attention had been given only to the big game bullets. These proved their accuracy from the very first; extensive testing with them was not necessary. The first serious experiments with the varmint bullets were disappointing, to say the least. Bullets tried were Hornady's 100-gr., and Speer's 87- and 100-gr. weights. None gave the minute-of-angle accuracy necessary for long range varminting, no matter what the type of powder used or how reduced the loads. Various bullet seating depths were tried, but with no change. Best groups were made with the 100-gr. bullets, which averaged just under 2″ at mild speeds.

When Sierra recently introduced their hollow point bullets in 85- and 100-gr. weights, they answered a longfelt want. With their 100-gr. HP bullets, groups under 1″ were not unusual. The 85-gr. bullets grouped most consistently in about 1″ at a speed of 3015 fps. These proved excellent and effective loads for long-range shooting of either squirrels or woodchucks. The above speed, incidentally, is obtained with a relatively low powder charge (see RCBS Test table), resulting in exceptionally pleasant shooting. The recoil is very mild; pressures are kept to a minimum and the life of cartridge cases is extended considerably. All this adds up to a great deal of enjoyable shooting with a minimum of wear on the barrel.

RCBS Tests

Various loads were shipped to RCBS, along with my rifle, and the results in velocity and accuracy will be found in the accompanying table

It will be noted that the 24″ barrel did more than duplicate the advertised velocity of 2788 fps with the factory cartridge using the 139-gr. bullet. This excellent factory load can be slightly bettered with 46 grains of 4350 powder for 2850 fps. 47 grains of this powder produces a velocity just short of sensational for the size of case used, but accuracy suffered. This load also shows signs now of high pressure, revealed in an enlargement of primer pockets after a few reloadings; for practical use it should be considered maximum.

An appreciation of the full power potential of the 6.5x55 and its suitability for long-range shooting of game cannot be entirely gained without a comparison of its ballistics with those of other cartridges of known performance. Our table shows factory-published figures, except for the 400-yard velocity and energy values. These were obtained by taking the average velocity loss per 100 yards up to 300 yards and subtracting this average from the 300 yard value. This method gives a reasonably accurate figure since the loss of speed is fairly consistent.

As indicated, the 139-gr. bullet is outstanding for its sustained energy at long ranges. The combination of high sectional density and a beautifully executed, streamlined design makes this bullet unbelievably efficient. If the table were extended beyond 400 yards, its superiority in this respect would become increasingly more pronounced, as it would surpass all other bullets listed, all of them boat-tail types also.

What about trajectory?

In order to obtain a fairly accurate idea of the trajectories made with bullets of varying weights and to determine the longest possible pointblank range for big game shooting, four bullet weights were tested for drop at ranges up to 400 yards. For each bullet weight, 5-shot strings were fired at 200, 300 and 400 yards after initial sighting at 100 yards.

To facilitate comparison, the rifle was sighted to put all bullets, except the 85-gr., 3 inches above point of aim at 100 yards. The 156-gr. bullet, for obvious reasons, was not tested beyond 300 yards. The Trajectory Table shows the result of this shooting; each figure represents the average of a 5-shot group. If the 120-gr. bullet is used, this range is extended to slightly beyond 300 yards.

Another interesting development was seen, when different bullets were fired at the 100-yard target with one sight setting. Except for the varmint bullets, all struck extraordinarily close to one another. 5-shot groups with the 120-, 139- and 160-gr. bullets (15 shots) landed within a circle less than 3" wide. The 156-gr. bullets registered just a little lower than the 160-gr. ones. With this rifle, at least, it seems practical to carry these three loads and to use them as the occasion requires without any change in sight setting. It is also, perhaps, possible to develop a varmint load that shoots to the same point of impact, as say, the 120-gr. bullet. What a boon this would be! The need for changing sight settings every time a different bullet is used would be obviated forever.

The 6.5x55 cartridge has many points to commend it, and the sportsman who is interested in owning one rifle should not overlook its great versatility and overall efficiency. I look forward with keen anticipation to future hunting trips and to many hours of pleasurable and absorbing shooting with my all-round rifle. ●

6.5x55 Handloads—RCBS Tests

Custom 6.5x55 rifle, 24" Douglas barrel, 1 in 10 twist

Powder/grs.	Bullet/grs.		MV	Group/ins.
40/3031	Sierra	85 HP	3015	1
44/4895	Sierra	85 HP	3191	1½
42/4895	Sierra	100 HP	2921	2
48/4350	Sierra	100 HP	3016	1¼
45/4350	Speer	120 SP	2728	1¼
48/4350	Speer	120 SP	3038	1½
45/4350	Norma	139 BT	2778	1½
46/4350	Norma	139 BT	2850	1¼
47/4350	Norma	139 BT	2933	2½
43/4350	Norma	156 RN	2585	1¾
45/4350	Sierra	140 BT	2766	1
43/4350	Hornady	160 RN	2580	1½
Coml.*	Norma	139 BT	2789	1½

*Commercial factory load, Norma.
HP—Hollow Point SP—Spitzer BT—Boat Tail RN—Round Nose
Norma cases and CCI primers used in handloads.

6.5x55 Trajectories

Bullet/grs.	Type	MV/fps	Point of Impact 100 yds.	200 yds.	300 yds.	400 yds.
120	Pointed	3038	+3.0"	+3.2"	−2.3"	−15.3"
139	Pointed BT	2850	+3.0"	+3.0"	−4.1"	−16.0"
156	Round Nose	2580	+3.0"	−0.6"	−12.7"	
85	Hollow Point	3015	+3.4"	+3.3"	−6.3"	−27.5"

The first two bullets shown above gave strikingly similar results at the 400-yard range and were therefore subjected to a second test on a different occasion, when the air was exceptionally calm. There was, however, no significant change in trajectory, and the above figures must be conclusive. Note that there is no appreciable difference between the two sets of figures. The 120-gr. bullet, which was desired so much for open country shooting, has only a marginal advantage over the more efficient 139-gr. bullet. The latter is definitely the better choice for long range shooting, not only because of its unerring accuracy, but because its retained energy is much greater at the longer ranges. Its maximum range for "point-blank" shooting of deer-sized game would appear to be about 280 yards. If the 120-gr. bullet is used, this range is extended to slightly beyond 300 yards.

bluing and browning Antique Arms

Before restoration was started, the top surface of the hammer on this 1851 Navy Colt was welded-up and recontoured to its original shape.

The antique gun restorer treads a thin and sometimes wavering line between acceptable practices and those condemned. Here are solutions with solutions.

by ROBERT E. COLBY

SURE, SLAP A COAT of rust or mottled cold blue on that repaired or replaced part. Worse yet, scrape off all that handsome old patina and refinish the whole gun so that everything gleams and glares.... That's "restoration," or so you would believe after seeing many so-treated antique firearms displayed and offered for sale. In reality, there goes another potentially valuable antique ruined by unknowing and inexpert attemps at restoration.

Proper restoration of antique firearms is quite legitimate and desirable, especially those relatively unaltered, genuine antiques missing a part or in need of minor repairs. (We do not refer to those obviously cut-down and put-together conglomerations of parts represented as genuine antiques.) Proper restoration is especially valid today, with the majority of better guns already in collections or commanding very high prices. With this the case, the less desirable guns—those most often in need of restoration—are becoming more valuable and sought after as collector's items, display pieces or just plain shooters. With a thorough understanding of how and when to refinish, plus the proper tools and materials, and above all care and considerable patience, you can give to replacement parts that antique finish developed through years of use and misuse. Very often recreation of this finish is the difference between a good and bad job of firearms restoration.

But where do you draw the line between ethical restoration and creation of an ungraded antique, a much-altered gun that does not reflect its true history or value? This question is quite important because of the high dollar value placed on many antique weapons, and the current unethical practices of counterfeiting antiques by such means as renumbering mixed parts, removing signs of age, refinishing entire guns to "near-mint" condition, and the aging of restamped replicas.

Perhaps the best answer to the question is that ethical restoration be limited to repairing broken parts, replacing missing parts without which the firearm would be incomplete or nonfunctional, and then refinishing these parts to match the existing overall finish on the firearm. Beyond the actual restoration, moreover, good ethics demand that a potential buyer be informed about all aspects of the restoration, and that the firearm be priced accordingly.

Most old finishes on iron and steel gun parts are combinations of blue, brown, gray, or black colors caused by oxidation (rusting) during the original finishing process or by handling through the years. However it was formed, restoring the finish to a replacement part or a repaired original part requires matching both texture and color.

Modern hot- and cold-bluing compounds are seldom suitable for such restoration since they are chemically different from the old-time solutions, and the techniques of using them are usually quite different also. Successful antique finish restoration lies in the application of old-time solutions, as they were used years ago, but with several modifications to produce an aged finish in a short period of time. The actual procedure has seven steps: degreasing, texturing, applying the solution, rusting, darkening, brushing, and fixing. With the exception of texturing and fixing, the steps are repeated and varied until the desired depth and color of finish are achieved. The best finish is achieved little-by-little rather than all at once.

Degreasing must remove all oil and grease from the part. From first to last, do not touch the part with ungloved fingers.

First, a few words of caution. This procedure described is for use on iron and mild steel surfaces whose current finish is due to oxidation. It will have little effect on stainless steel or hardened surfaces. Some of the chemicals are too corrosive for use in inlaid surfaces and may produce unexpected effects on twist or Damascus barrels. Experiment on scrap metal or junk parts to determine what variations of the procedure will produce the desired result. Each job presents its own problems, and mistakes on the real item are often permanent. Handle the degreasing agents, acids, and oxidizing solutions with care. They are toxic, corrosive, or flammable. Rubber gloves must be used at all times and non-metallic containers (rubber, glass or plastics) should be used with acids. Needless to say, any part must be completely disassembled prior to refinishing, and do *not* use acid or bluing solutions on springs, flat or coiled.

The hammer after recontouring and before starting the restoration procedure to match the somewhat mottled, brownish-black finish remaining on the lower part of the hammer.

The necessary tools and materials are few and easily acquired. They include: rubber gloves, cleaning solvents, cotton rags, corks, metal foil, a boiling pot, and various abrasives from fine steel wool to a wire buffing wheel. A wide variety of oxidizing (bluing or browning) solutions can be used. Two that give good results and are easily available, are Dixie Gun Works Antique Browning Solution and Stoeger Gunsmith Bluer. Both are very similar to the old-time solutions. However, if you choose to mix your own from chemicals available at a drugstore, a very excellent source is *Firearms Blueing and Browning* by R. H. Angier. This book not only lists solutions and their preparation, it also describes their use and the preparation of metal surfaces.

Degreasing

Successful refinishing probably depends more on thorough degreasing than on any other factor since the finish will not adhere to the metal if any oil or grease remains. Degrease by either washing the part in alcohol, acetone, gasoline or a similar solvent. You also can boil it for 20 minutes in a solution of soda or lye and water, then boil it in clear water for a few minutes. Very oily parts can be boiled and then coated with a soda or lye paste, brushed off when dry. Once degreased, do not touch the part with the bare fingers. Degrease the entire part so that oil cannot seep onto the clean area during succeeding steps. To prevent internal rusting, coat bores and cylinder chambers with a good gun grease or oil, and tightly seal with corks or wood plugs. Then degrease the external surfaces.

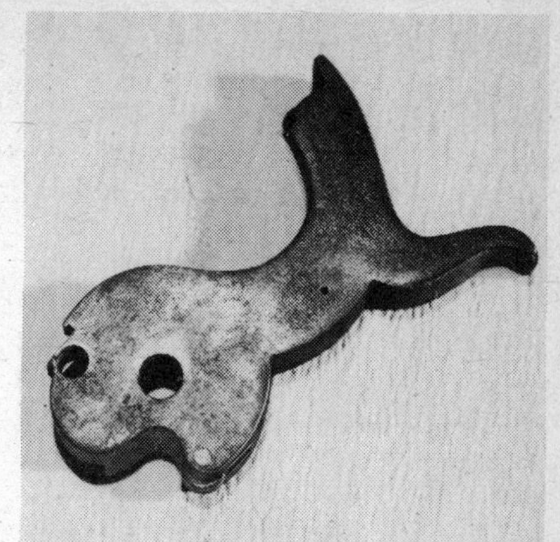

The restored finish, obtained by darkening the first run to get black tints, but not darkening the second run. This gave brown tints desired.

Texturing

This step matches the surface texture of the new or repaired part to the surface condition on the rest of the gun, when the latter shows etching through prolonged handling and use. The metal surface is first polished and then etched with acid. The type and strength of the acid, as well as the period of application, depends on the metallurgy and hardness of the surface. Concentrated muriatic acid applied for several minutes with a cotton swab or by dipping, will create the finely etched surface so typical of many antique firearms. Strong acids, such as sulfuric, may be required to duplicate deeply etched surfaces. After texturing, neutralize the acid by rinsing the part in a diluted solution of soda water.

The muriatic acid is 35% to 38% concentration, the kind you can buy at the drugstore. I use it without dilution. I very seldom use the stronger acids. I buy sulfuric acid in concentrated form, then dilute it to suit the job, usually around 5-10%. The same percentages of nitric acid also do the job. For the soda/water bath put a tablespoon of baking soda into about two gallons of water.

When only a portion of a part is being refinished, coat the area not being textured with oil. This helps prevent the fumes generated by the acid-metal reaction from removing any finish on the portion not being

Texturing the restored part in muriatic acid reproduced the finely etched metal surface found on the rest of the hammer. Ordinarily the entire area would be submerged in the acid to obtain an even finish, but here only the darker portion has been submerged to show the effect of texturing on the metal. Note rubber gloves and non-metallic container.

textured. Be sure to degrease the part again after etching.

Bluing & Browning

Before applying the oxidizing solution, slightly heating the part will help the solution adhere to the metal. Immediately apply the solution with a clean cotton swab and watch closely for the metal to darken or for color tints to appear. These effects indicate that the chemicals are reacting with the metal surface and that no more solution is needed.

With the exception of the texturing step, the refinishing procedure up to now has been the same as is used for normal bluing. At this point, however, the techniques of applying the solution can be varied to produce significantly different results. If a smooth, uniform finish is required, apply a minimum of solution, so that no droplets remain on the metal. Apply in one direction, usually parallel to the long axis of the part. If a mottled finish is required, apply excess solution in an irregular motion, leaving droplets on the surface.

A slight excess of oxidizing solution is applied in an irregular motion to create the required mottled finish. Other finishes require different application techniques.

Rusting

Hang the parts on a hook made from a wire clothes hanger or, if there are no holes in the part, stand it on end in a small box made of foil. The rate of rusting depends on humidity, type of metal surface (hardened, polished, etc.), and strength of the oxidizing solution. Where the outdoor humidity is high hang the part overnight where moisture cannot precipitate directly on the metal. Where humidity is low or when rusting must be hurried, a steam chamber can be used. This can be specially constructed, as described in *Firearms Blueing and Browning,* or it can be the bathroom shower. When the shower is used, place the part high in the room, turn on the hot water and close the door. Once a heavy cloud of steam is generated, turn off the shower, and leave the part in the closed room until a fine coat of rust has formed over the treated area.

At this point the basic refinishing procedure can be varied to produce different finishes. Most bluing instructions warn against letting droplets of water form on the metal surface through prolonged exposure to dense steam. If a smooth, uniform finish is desired, follow these instructions, keeping the part outside the shower stall and limiting the time it is exposed to the steam. If a mottled finish is required, however, place the part close to the steam source and let it remain until droplets form.

Whatever the desired finish, permit only a light coat of rust to form during each rusting period. This usually requires 1 to 3 hours. The purpose of rusting is to create a very thin layer of color which adheres tightly to the metal. Thick rust will not produce more or deeper color, but only hard work and often a poor finish. Repeated coats of thin rust produce the desired effect with a minimum of effort.

A yellowish brown, spotty rust, required to produce the mottled finish, was achieved by placing the part close to the steam source. A more uniform finish would require placing the part farther away. About 20 minutes boiling in distilled water is often used to darken the rusted part, producing the black tints found in many antique finishes.

Darkening

Darkening involves boiling the part in water or exposing it to a steam jet for about 20 minutes to change the brown ferric-oxide rust to black ferro-ferric oxide. Distilled water is recommended as hard water tends to reverse the process, but unless the water is unusually hard, tap water is usually satisfactory. Add a teaspoon of baking soda to the water to neutralize any acid residue from the oxidizing solution and to stop the rusting action. Neutralization also retards any incidental alteration of those portions of the part not being refinished. This can be quite important if boiling loosens the plugs in bores and chambers, permitting seepage of acid residue diluted by boiling water.

If the finish to be matched has no gray or blackish colors, a lighter brown finish can be developed by omitting the darkening step altogether. Mildly brush the rust coat and then lightly rust and brush the part several more times, each time omitting the darkening step. For a brownish-black finish darken the first coat, but not succeeding coats. For that steel-gray finish typical of many well-used antique firearms, heavily brush one or more coats of darkened rust, almost to the bare metal.

Brushing

Brushing involves nothing more than removing the loose rust scale with such abrasives as razor blades, then steel wool, emery paper, wire brushes and wire wheels. *The idea is to remove the scale while leaving a very thin layer of color.* Select the finest abrasive that will do the job with moderate effort, then use successively finer abrasives until the rust coating remains only as color.

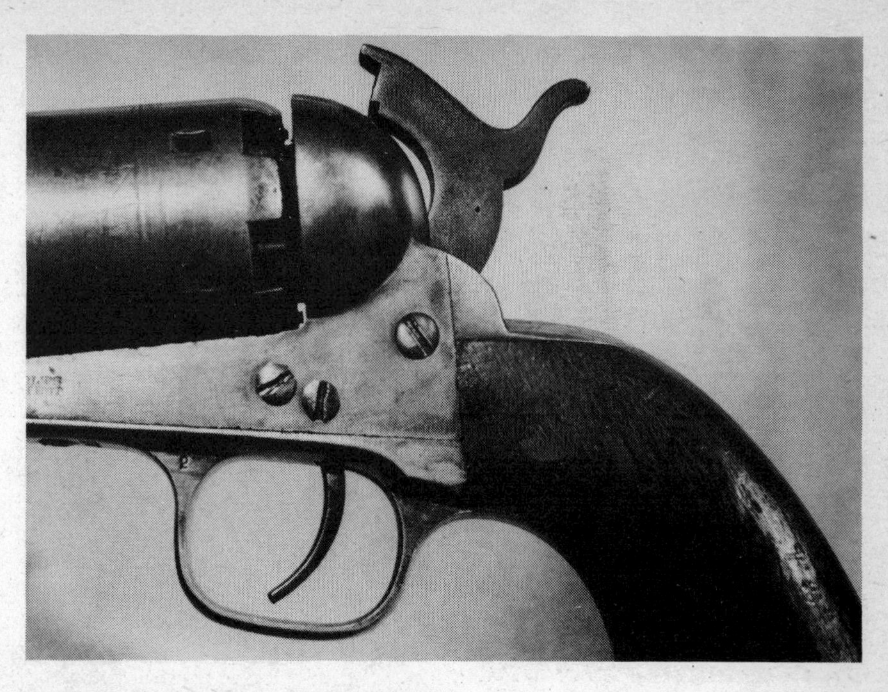

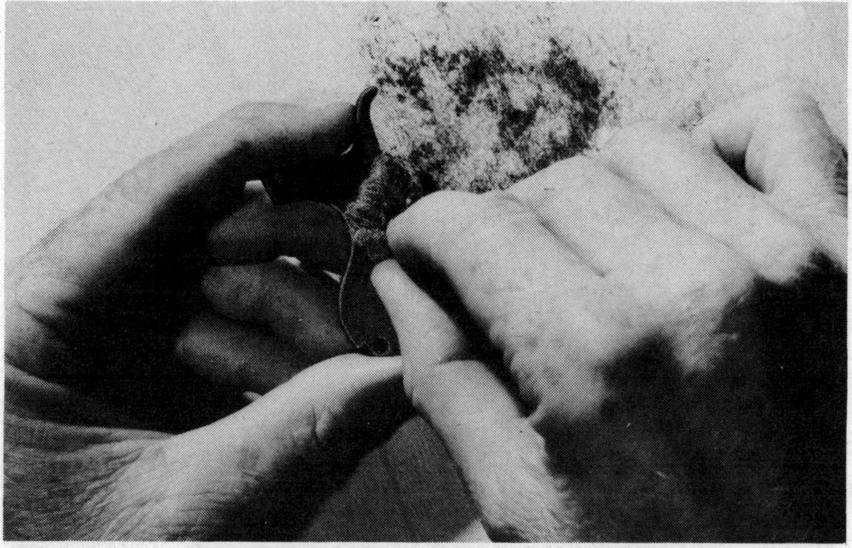

At the left: The finest abrasive that will remove the rust scale without excessive work is used to brush the part. Take it slow so that the new finish is not completely removed, especially around corners and edges. After the desired finish is achieved, coating the part with oil will help preserve it and stop any further oxidation. Remember that the oiled finish will be somewhat darker than the dry finish. Above: After restoration, which took about 3 days, the hammer matches the rest of the revolver.

Brush the part between each application of rust, either after the darkening step or immediately after the rusting step, if the darkening step is omitted. Work lengthwise on the part, then crosswise, using a light touch to avoid removing all of the color, especially on sharp edges and after the initial rust coats.

While the basic texture of the finish is created by the texturing step, the manner in which abrasives are used can help match the texture of the refinished area or part to adjacent areas. For instance, after the part is brushed to a relatively smooth surface, a hard stick, a piece of leather or coarse cloth, or even the fingers can be used to rub the metal to that shiny well-handled patina so typical on many antique firearms. If a dull or rough finish is required, this rubbing is omitted.

In most cases, the refinishing procedure must be repeated several times to closely match an existing finish. Degrease the part after each brushing and before applying more oxidizing solution. If a brown, undarkened finish is desired, degrease with a solvent, not a boiling-soda or lye solution. Do not repeat the texturing step since the acid will remove the finish previously applied.

Fixing

After the desired color is achieved, coat the brushed finish with a *non*-rust-solvent oil or a silicone rust preventive. Then heat the part in an oven to 250°-300°F until any oil residue evaporates. Waxing or lacquering can be substituted for oiling, but do not heat in these cases.

In some cases, especially when rusting is not followed by boiling to darken the rust coat, delayed rusting may cause small rust spots on the refinished area. Lightly brushing off the rust and re-oiling will usually stop this rusing in a few days. If it does not, soak the part overnight in a cold solution of 30% baking soda and water.

Many "experts" have stated that you simply can't reproduce that patina. Granted a genuine 100-year-old patina can't be recreated in 3 days, nearly any oxidized finish can be closely duplicated—to the point where it is difficult to tell whether restoration was involved. This procedure is one of the few satisfactory ways to accomplish this on repaired and replaced parts of antique firearms. Used with judgment and care it can make the difference between a valued collector's piece and just another busted old gun. ●

GUNS GADGETS GIMMICKS

Displays of trapshooting accessories at the larger tournaments are dazzling enough to catch the eye of the most jaded shooter. If you've garnered a gaggle of these gimmicks and gadgets – and they haven't helped your scores...!

by CLARENCE MASSEY

HE CONSIDERED HIMSELF an experienced trapshooter. He listened carefully to the loudspeaker as the squads of shooters were called up to the trapline. Before his squad was called to the traps, he prepared himself for the 100 target grind that lay just ahead.

From the trunk of his car he carefully put four boxes of meticulously reloaded shotgun shells into a specially made metal shotshell carrier. His name was handsomely engraved on the front of the shell carrier, repeated in gold on the receiver of his expensive, custom made shotgun, once again on the front of his shooting jacket and finally emblazoned on the back of his shooting vest along with a brief statement referring to a shoot in which he had once emerged victor.

Slipping into his handsome jacket, our trapshooter hastily felt through the pockets for his custom-made ear plugs. These were specially-made soft rubber plugs, moulded to fit his ears and, as in most of his other shooting accessories, at a very expensive fee. Fitting the delicately skin-colored plugs into his ears, he looked over his array of shooting glasses. Turning in a 360° circle, he took a careful look at the weather, taking into consideration such things as the brightness of the sun, the background behind the clay targets, color of the targets, and the possibility of a change in weather or lighting conditions. Since it was a generally cloudy day, he chose a medium-yellow colored pair of shooting glasses that, in reality, looked more like goggles than they did glasses. They had huge lenses and, when he put them on, they rode high upon his nose, leaving no doubt at all they they were special-order glasses.

Then, after another thoughtful look around the horizon, our trapshooter picked up a second pair of shooting glasses. These were of a dark green color, and he put them in a special bracket built on the side of his shell carrier to hold the handsome leather case. After all, maybe the sun would come out and he'd need to change glasses in the middle of the event. He did want to be prepared. It would be tragic to lose a target just because he was wearing the wrong pair of colored shooting glasses.

A rather gusty wind was beginning to pick up particles of dust and blow them across the parking lot. Our careful shooter noted this and removed his shooting glasses. He carefully selected a pair of cardboard "blinders" from a half-dozen pair lying in the back of the car. He slipped them onto the

curved wires forming the ear pieces and shoved them gently up against the lens frame. He didn't want that dust blowing into his eyes. No Sir! This was an important shoot and all these little possibilities had to be given consideration and the proper precautionary measures taken.

After putting the shooting glasses back on, he fumbled with them a bit, took them off again and selected a different shaped pair of blinders. Attaching these, he put his glasses on again and seemed satisfied.

Although the weather was cloudy and a breeze was picking up, it was quite warm. Our shooter looked thoughtfully at a "sweat band" consisting of an elastic head band with a soft, absorbent piece of sponge rubber in the center. It was used as a sort of mop on his forehead when he began to perspire on a hot day. A handy little gadget, he thought, as he put it into the shell carrier. Never can tell, it might turn hot before he finished, and he just might need it.

He looked over a selection of three or four caps and hats, finally selecting a jaunty, green felt model complete with a couple of bright feathers in the hatband. Actually, he preferred a wide brimmed hat but with this gusty breeze blowing, well ... it just might turn into a wind. He sure didn't want to be worrying about his hat blowing off while he was shooting. Yes Sir, a fellow had to think of all these little details if he was going to be a really good trapshooter. You just can't be too careful in preparing for an important trapshooting tournament.

As he stood at the back of the car, he rocked thoughtfully on his heels. There was a bit of gravel scattered across the sidewalks in the shooting area, and those leather soled shoes he was wearing just might slip on that gravel. Maybe he had better change to those soft, crepe soled loafers that were also reclining in the trunk of the car. Balancing about on one leg, he quickly changed shoes and again looked into the trunk of the car to see if he had thought of everything.

His gold inlaid shotgun was lying in its case and would, of course, be the last item he picked up before walking out to the shooting area. As he looked at the gun he fingered a specially built pocket high up on the left side of his shooting jacket. This little pocket had compartments for two extra shells just in case he should have a malfunction of his gun or a defective shell while shooting in the match. One compartment was empty and he nervously tore open a new box of shells to get the one shell needed to fill the pocket.

He carefully lifted the handsome shotgun from its case and, picking up a special dust-collecting gun wiper, he carefully wiped the gun from its muzzle to the specially fitted and adjustable recoil pad. Replacing the gun wiper in its box, he quickly put the gun to his shoulder and made a couple of quick points with it at imaginary targets. Seemingly, all was well and our shooter took a final searching glance into the trunk of his car and slammed the lid shut.

Feeling a little like a gladiator marching into the arena, our shooter strode purposely up to the long line of traps. Although he wasn't the least bit thirsty, he paused at the drinking fountain for a quick gulp of water. He reached his designated trap just as the previous squad finished their round of 25 targets.

Removing his glasses, he took out a clean handkerchief and suddenly realized that he had forgotten the little tube of special glass cleaner that he always used to clean his shooting glasses. With a hurried word to his fellow squad members, he rushed back to his car to retrieve the special cleaner. Hurrying now, he quickly cleaned his glasses, grabbed his shotgun, dumped a box of shells into his jacket pocket and hurried to his post, apologizing profusely to the other squad members.

Lures in Profusion

So we leave our trapshooter to his predictable fate. Already burdened with an awesome array of specialized shooting equipment, he is probably one of the best equipped participants in any sport and yet, as he strolls down the trapline at any big trap tournament, he is constantly aware of still more new gadgets and gimmicks to further his shooting pleasure. "Shooting pleasure," of course, is virtually synonymous with "high score" in the trapshooting world.

Displays of trapshooting accessories at any large tournament are enough to catch the eye of even the most casual, jaded shooter. Custom stockmakers display a tantaliz-

ing array of artfully designed stocks to fit your shotgun. The beautifully figured and smoothly polished wood on these flossy shotguns feels like the soft caress of a vestal virgin's cheek as you snuggle one of these exquisite examples of the stockmaker's art to your shoulder. Surely, you think, one of these perfect feeling stocks would help you shoot a higher score.

Or perhaps your taste runs to fine clothing. Racks of shooter's garments, manufactured by specialists in the game, offer a wide and wondrous variety of apparel, all designed to help the gunner maintain the inward calm and outward appearance of the suave, professional shooter. It's all there from special shooting caps to windproof, lightweight trousers to protect the sometimes shaky knees of the nervous trapshooter from the sudden, chilling blasts of winter winds.

Shrewd designers and inventors have rightly pegged the average, serious trapshooter as an easy mark for any kind of shooting gadget, just as long as it holds out some hope for improvement in his score. No matter how nebulous or transparent the claim might be, if there is even a psychological advantage to its use, there'll be some trapshooters who'll buy it. Speaking of psychology, it's pretty well known that if a championship is won by a shooter using some bit of equipment that is just a little different from the ordinary, there'll be a flock of shooters immediately switching to its use.

For instance, some years ago I observed a state shoot in which the match was won by a shooter who carried a small sponge fastened to a piece of string tied onto his belt. The weather was very hot, and this shooter would wet his sponge before the start of each round of 25 targets. As he finished his five targets at each post he would wipe down his hot gun barrel with the damp sponge as he walked to the next post. Now that precaution may have cooled the rib on his barrel and prevented heat waves. I don't know. But the interesting thing is this. The next day there were at least six other shooters with sponges dangling from their belts!

Take a stroll around the grounds at any large gun club during a state or regional trapshoot. Retailers of shooting accessories will be displaying an infinite variety of stuff, lures that run the gamut from cynically printed "crying towels" to some kind of a gadget, gimmick or gun alteration that is a semi-plausible Rx for whatever shooting ailment made you miss a few too many targets in your last event.

Concentration's the Secret

It seems to be a weakness of us ordinary humans to search for a mechanical or inanimate cause of our failures at any endeavor. But the human trapshooter is not a mechanical device, and the errors that make him miss targets are rarely caused by the omission of some minor accessory. Indeed, the really proficient or natural trapshooter has trained himself in concentration and as any honest and knowledgeable trapshooter knows, concentration is the real key to consistently high scores.

The shooter who regularly shoots high averages is apt to be unaware that he is wearing glasses of a color that might not be technically correct for the prevailing light conditions. Or he may lug his boxes of shells in his arm as he goes from one trap to another, not realizing—or caring—that it might be more convenient to use a fancy leather or metal shell box. He isn't distressed because he forgot a minor item of equipment on his way to the trapline. In truth, while he's shooting, he thinks of nothing except breaking each target when he calls for it. Even if he misses a target, this high scoring trapshooter is not unduly upset, he doesn't search for an obscure bit of equipment to blame for his miss. He is thinking only about breaking his *next* target.

So, if you should find yourself acquiring quite a collection of trapshooting gadgets and your scores show no real improvement, cast a quizzical eye on that treasure trove. It could be that you're subconsciously debating the merits of a new gadget or worrying about the one you forgot to bring along when you should be concentrating on that next target—and the *next* one.

If there is one thing trapshooters agree on, it is that a good trapshooter concentrates on *every* target . . . but *one at a time.* Everything else is blotted out, and that includes all his trapshooting equipment, whether it be gun, shells, glasses or whatever. Give it some thought. Perhaps you're so wrapped up in preparations for shooting that your mind cannot forget all that gadgetry and concentrate on why you're on the trapline in the first place. ●

NOTHING IN FIREARMS is more American than the solid-frame single shot rifle. From its earliest beginnings to its current high degree of excellence it has to rank as a rifle that can tickle the imagination of the most stoic citizens. Its straightforward practical form, its beauty and simplicity of line, are a joy to behold. Granted, for those who want to unload 5 fast shots in a hurry, it has its shortcomings.

The rifles pictured here are stocked with California walnut—one dark variety and three of light or English walnuts.

which grows from Arizona to west Texas, but not in California. These true species have been crossed in many ways, such matings often called hybrids. These have such local names as Claro, Bastogne, Paradox, et al. Where such names originated is not important, but let's say you have a rifle stocked with California laurel or *Umbellaria Californica*. What's that? Simply myrtle, another example of a local name.

English walnut also has a lot of varieties—Mayette, Frankette, Hartley, Paine, Eureka, and others. Con-

It takes fine checkering and many gunsmiths like it for its fine working qualities. Unfortunately, the trees are short and of small diameter. The quality of the plain wood is just as good as the fancy wood, but I can hardly give it away. It air dries a little faster than the black walnuts, which is another plus for it, and it can be checkered to very fine lines. In a beautiful stick it is about the best in the world today.

The black walnuts here in California should usually be checkered in a little coarser pattern, although

SINGLE SHOT RIFLES

and Juglans Variorum

An expert views and rates the wide range of walnut woods. Like whiskey, some are better than others, but none is bad!

by JACK BURRES

While the basic design of these rifles was being developed in the 1800s, walnut trees were also being planted that would enhance the beauty of these and many other firearms. Alas, these fantastic woods are now being exported at a rate their growth cannot stand. (Take 5 minutes to write your elected officials to stop this export of walnut or the next generation will be using arms stocked in plastic or the like.) Some of these trees, 100 years old or more, are just not replaceable.

Let's see if we can't clear up some of the confusion about the walnuts, especially the wood from California. Let's assume that a walnut tree with a scientific name is a true species. Examples—black is *Juglans Nigra*. English is *Juglans Regia*. Hind's is *Juglans Hindsii*. California is *Juglans Californica*. Arizona is *Juglans Major*,

fused? I don't blame you. I have a solution. Let's just use the term "black walnut" for the dark traditional looking wood, and "English walnut" for the light-background stuff with the black lines, which has a marblecake effect in its fanciest form. Maybe some of the dark walnuts could be hard to differentiate, but none could ever be mistaken for English walnut once the differences are pointed out. English walnut grown in California is also called English Circassion or just Circassion, though it has never seen any part of Circassia. It has the same characteristics as the best French wood and its beauty is superior to any recent French wood I've been seeing. It has more contrast but it's without the reddish-brown hue of imported walnut, its color more black-and-white or black-and-cream tones.

some blanks get as hard as flint and take fine checkering. I never really know what some of these hybrid trees will come out like. There is nothing like California walnut for sheer weird colors—sometimes 4 or 5 different and distinct colors can be seen in one blank. Maybe, another time, we can discuss the taking out of trees, sawing the logs into slabs, drying the wood and finally making blanks. If you are a woodaholic, as I am, it's a fascinating subject, though I've never found anything in the library that has shed much light on the subject. Sawmilling a walnut log that you suspect might have some beautiful wood in it is just like pulling a lobster trap. The anticipation can get the juices flowing before you ever see what's in it.

The three gunsmiths mentioned

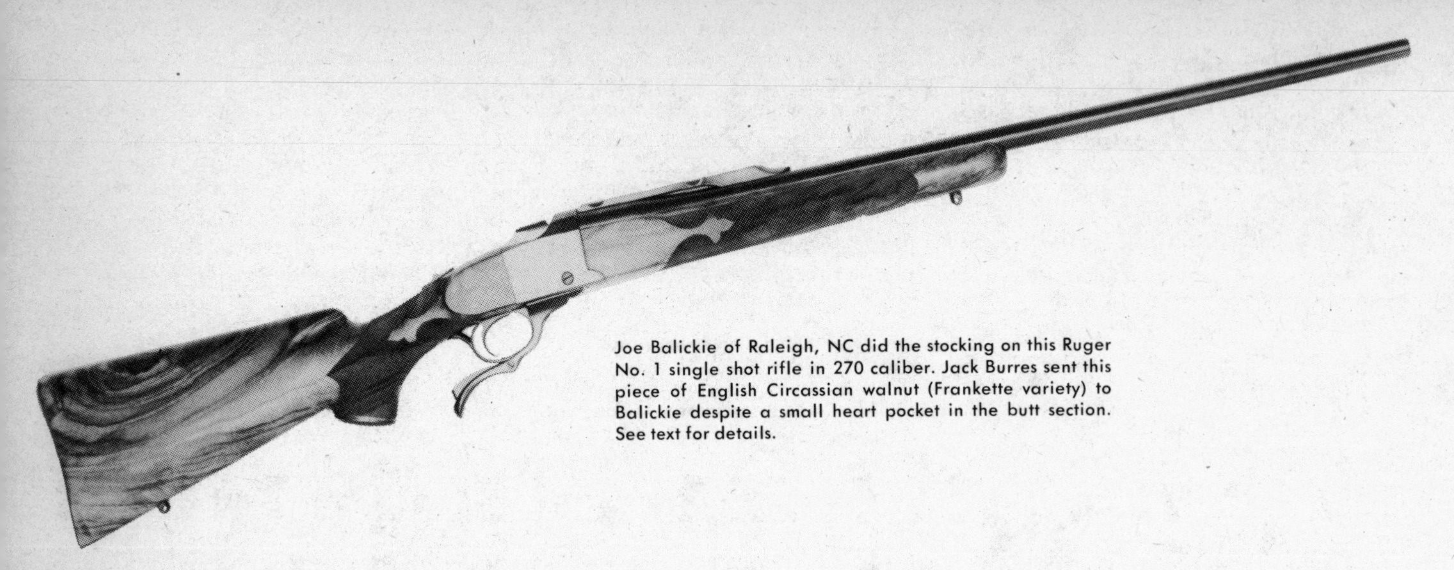
Joe Balickie of Raleigh, NC did the stocking on this Ruger No. 1 single shot rifle in 270 caliber. Jack Burres sent this piece of English Circassian walnut (Frankette variety) to Balickie despite a small heart pocket in the butt section. See text for details.

here did excellent work. I sent them the wood and the barreled actions, telling them to use their own judgement, to build the rifles as if they were building them for themselves. Except for a standard length of pull I requested nothing.

All of the work was top grade, and none took longer than 8 months. When the first rifle came in a fellow gun nut looked it over with me. His comment was that it was handsomely made and fitted and checkered beautifully, but that I was probably getting a special price because I sell blanks to the gunsmiths, and they're hopeful of getting gem blanks. Plain B.S.! First rate craftsmen don't do a lousy job for one customer and a beauty for the next one. It's just not in their makeup. They are all trying to throw a no-hitter, and the good ones have too much pride to do otherwise.

Joe Balickie of Raleigh, N.C., sent in the first, a Ruger No. 1 in 270 caliber. I'd sent Joe a piece of English Circassion in the Frankette variety. It had a heart pocket about three inches from the pad which, of course, did not affect the grip or entry into the iron. A heart pocket runs the center of the log lengthwise, and is about the diameter of a welding rod. I saw-mill some fantastic wood at times that will have various flaws, and I never send it to a customer unless he knows what he's doing. Flaws in English walnut can be filled with a black epoxy that looks just like the black grain of the wood. Some of the purists tell me they won't have a flaw in any blank. If it is away from the grip or fore-end area I can live with it. Much of the really beautiful wood cut has minor problems. It's the straight ugly ones that are perfect. With the scarcity of good wood these days a beautiful piece cannot be cast aside because of a non-critical flaw.

The swirling pattern in this blank made for a different and beautiful stock. Joe used 26-line checkering and it is perfect. The steel buttplate is gloved into the wood. Inletting around all the iron is, of course, precise.

The thing you will notice about these three gunsmiths is their love of the classic stock form. Leaping leopards and inlaid diamonds are not their style. Joe put this gun on exhibit at a couple of gun shows and no one detected the flaw.

Another Ruger No. 1 Joe made into

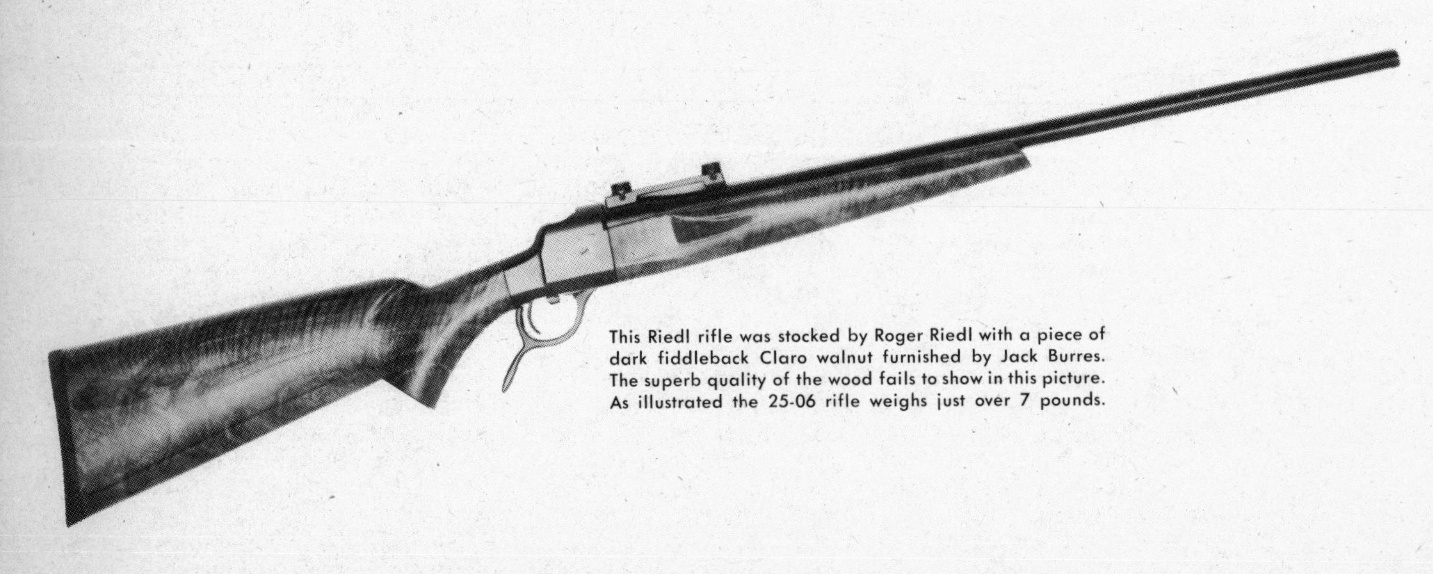
This Riedl rifle was stocked by Roger Riedl with a piece of dark fiddleback Claro walnut furnished by Jack Burres. The superb quality of the wood fails to show in this picture. As illustrated the 25-06 rifle weighs just over 7 pounds.

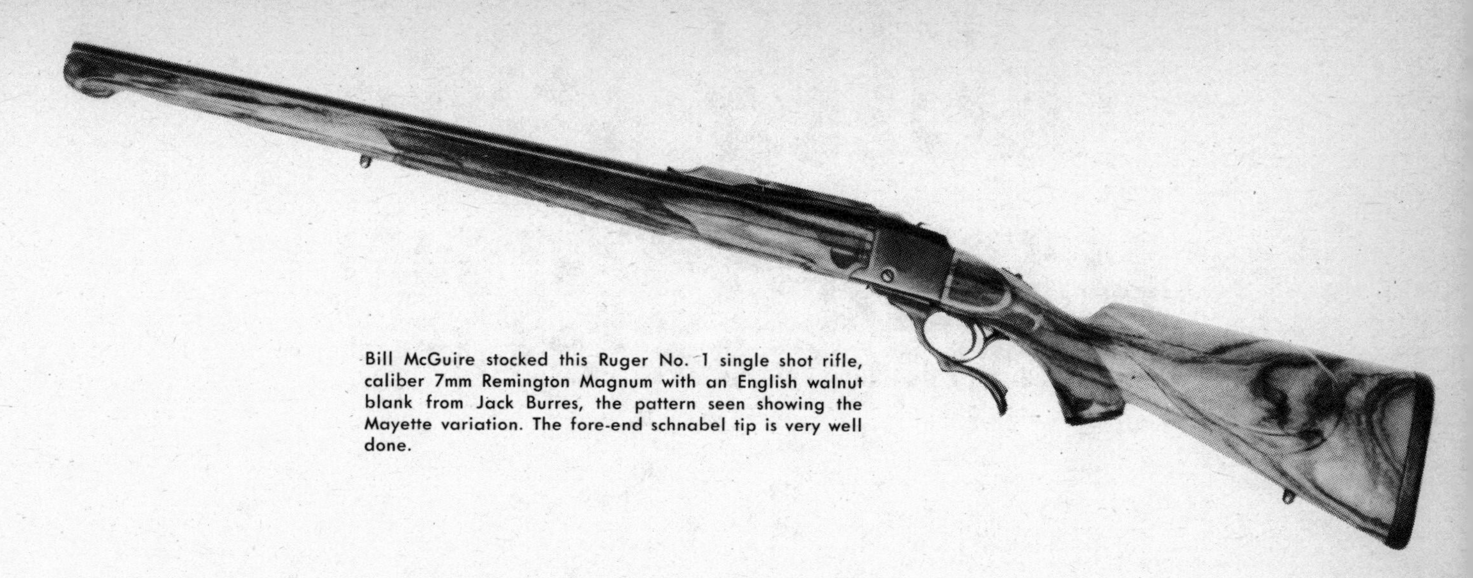

Bill McGuire stocked this Ruger No. 1 single shot rifle, caliber 7mm Remington Magnum with an English walnut blank from Jack Burres, the pattern seen showing the Mayette variation. The fore-end schnabel tip is very well done.

a 45-70, using a piece of burl I'd sent to him—occasionally I cut a few burls into two-piece sets with solid wood in the grip area. Burl is all that the name implies—wild, weird grain full of tiny knots, and I knew the piece I'd sent Joe would open in the drying, which it did. But Joe made a fine job of filling it, considering what he started with. I don't recommend wood of this kind to anyone unless he likes something really different.

Jim Riedl sent in the third rifle, based on his single shot action. He used a fiddleback Claro blank of classic beauty. You will notice there is no fore-end tip or grip cap and no checkering on this rifle. Roger Riedl, who does the stock work, put a plain black pad on the gun and that's it. The lines are rather severe and the fore-end is what one might call a modified beavertail style. To carry off this style of design one must have a really beautiful stick of wood. I fell in love with this little 25-06 rifle, which weighs 7 pounds one ounce with mount but no scope. Jim sells this rifle with a standard grade stock at $279. I have offered to supply Jim with a stock like the one on the gun at $50 for any customer who wants fancy wood.

Bill McGuire sent me another Ruger No. 1 in 7mm caliber, the full length or Mannlicher-style stock made from an English blank of Mayette variety. Bill does some scrumptious things with stock wood, and if he makes a gun for you it will have as good a piece of wood as there is available. Bill carried this difficult job off in grand fashion, what with the schnabel tip and the fleur de lis checkering. Full stocks are hard to do.

Both Joe Balickie and Bill McGuire charged $400 for their labor, which includes any checkering pattern wanted, plus a steel grip cap and buttplate, with dimensions to order. Bill charged $100 extra, however, for the Mannlicher length.

I'm having 8 of these rifles made by various craftsmen around the country, using the different kind and varieties of walnut I sawmill. Walnut is the king of woods, in my opinion, so I cut nothing else nowadays, though I have cut in the past maple, myrtlewood, mesquite, sycamore, and many others. Nothing, but nothing compares with walnut! ●

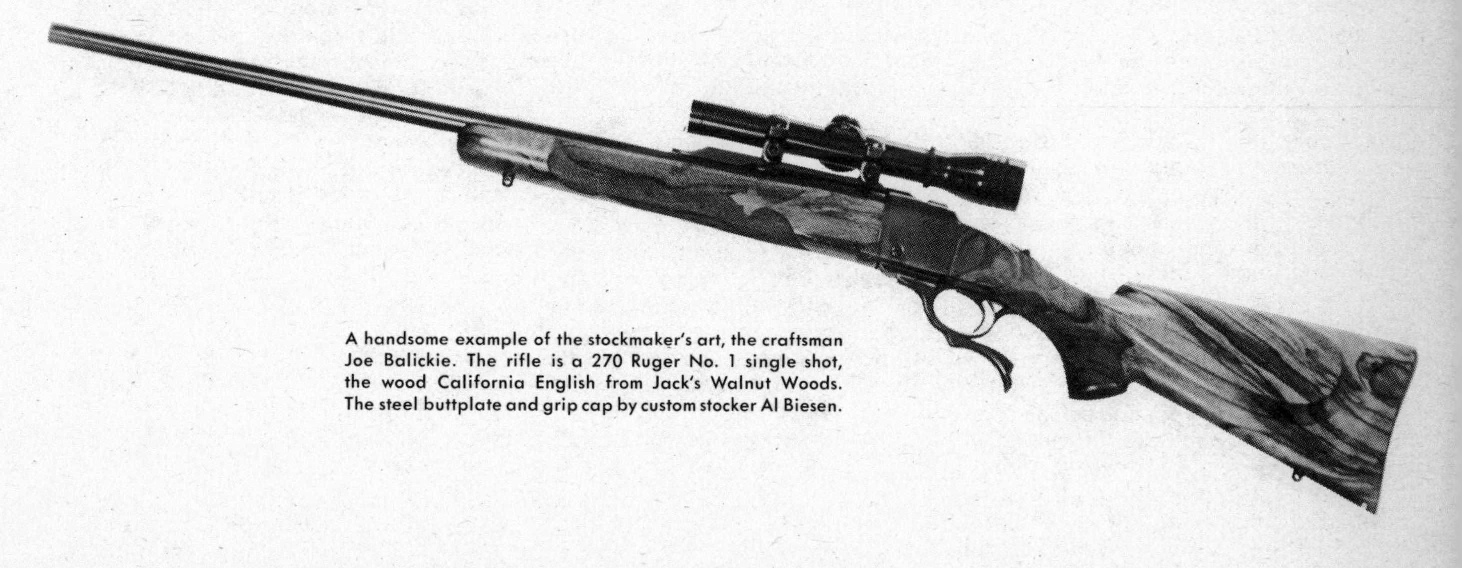

A handsome example of the stockmaker's art, the craftsman Joe Balickie. The rifle is a 270 Ruger No. 1 single shot, the wood California English from Jack's Walnut Woods. The steel buttplate and grip cap by custom stocker Al Biesen.

NOTES FOR HANDLOADERS

Hints and tips for better, safer, more accurate loads, ideas and suggestions you won't find in the average manual.

by GEORGE C. NONTE, Jr.

LATE ONE NIGHT—we always work into the small hours—your editor called me, suggesting I dig through the files for some handloading hints or techniques, for solutions to problems that readers from all over the country have described to us. The odds and ends that follow are the careful gleanings of a couple evenings I spent going over the past two years' correspondence and columns.

GI cases If you find yourself without something to ream out military-primer crimp, try this: pick up a low-cost 45° or 60° countersink at the hardware store; then grind its point back until it enters the primer pocket deeply enough to cut away the crimp. The end then acts as a stop to prevent cutting too deep. Used by hand it will do a good job, leaving a clean bevel at the pocket mouth to facilitate entry of a new primer.

It can also be used under power (as can a Lyman or other primer pocket reamer) in a variable-speed drill press or electric hand drill. Run at lowest speed and press cases over the cutter by hand. You might find this handier than other methods.

Primers Rifle primers in handguns? It isn't a good practice for several reasons: rifle primers require a heavier firing pin blow for proper ignition; the greater amount of priming compound may increase pressures (not necessarily dangerously); and handgun-case primer pockets aren't always deep enough for rifle primers.

Big, heavy frame revolvers (S&W N, Colt New Service, Colt & Ruger SA, etc.) have heavy hammers, strong mainsprings, and long hammer travel. In my experience they will reliably ignite rifle primers. During wartime periods of component shortages I used thousands of rifle primers in such handguns without any ignition problems at all.

On the other hand, I've yet to encounter an autoloader, even the 45 Government Model, which would ignite rifle primers reliably. As for small- or medium-frame revolvers, the latter will *sometimes* do well with rifle caps, the former hardly ever.

Recognize these limitations and be guided accordingly, should you be tempted to use rifle primers in handgun loads simply because they are available or cheap.

Note well! Never take primers out of their compartmented containers until ready for use; never store loose primers in bulk, and never agitate or shock loose primers. To do any of these things can set up a dangerous condition, one which might produce an explosion.

Berdan Primers

In spite of Boxer primers being far more widely used today than ever before, someone will occasionally find it necessary to shoot—and eventually reload—Berdan-primed cases. With

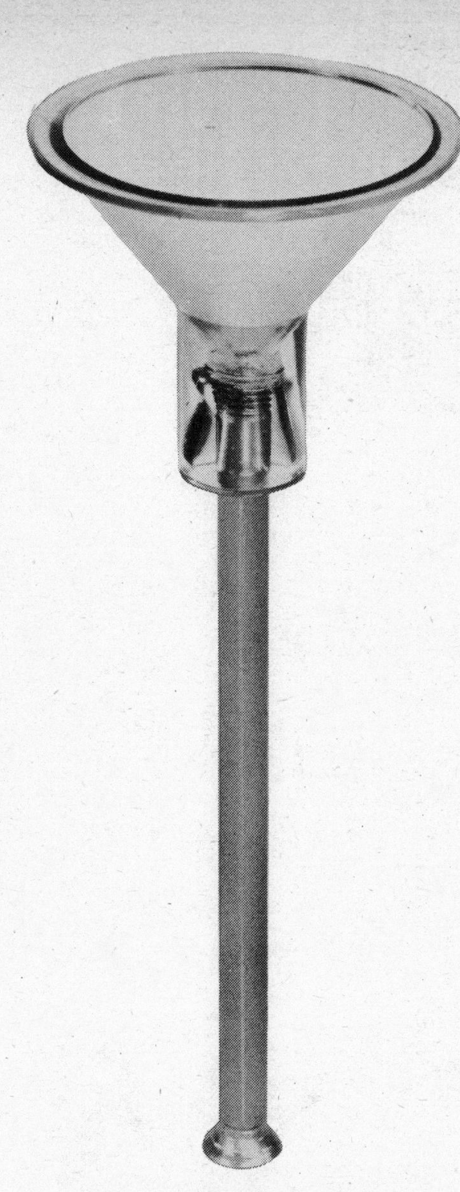

This long-tube Bonanza funnel will serve to get more powder in the case—greater falls of granules help compaction.

many of the older British and metric calibers now or soon-to-be discontinued, we have no choice but to hoard such ammo and cases as are available against future needs. Such ammunition is Berdan-primed, and no more will be produced. So long as you save the cases in good condition, you can generally find powder and bullets suitable for reloading them.

Primers, though, could be a problem in the future. The more common Berdan sizes suitable for fairly modern metric cases will likely be available for a long time. The principal sizes, .177-inch, .217-inch and slight variations thereof, are available. The .250-inch and .254-inch can still be had, but are getting scarcer. These basic metric sizes can be obtained through dealers from Godfrey Reloading Service, Box 12, Alton, Illinois 62002, and Stoeger Arms, 55 Ruta Court, South Hackensack, New Jersey 07606, in modern non-corrosive, non-mercuric form.

Berdan primers for the various big-bore British cartridges are of different sizes and harder to obtain. Further, they aren't likely to be available much longer. Some sizes are still available from Oregon Ammunition Service, Box 19341, Portland, Oregon 97291, but not in especially great quantities.

The solution to being able to shoot those odd calibers in the future is to lay in a supply of the primers you need now. Don't get greedy, though—you won't really shoot that 10.75x 68mm or that 475 No. 2 Nitro more than a few hundred times at most over the rest of your powder-burning days. So don't try to corner the Berdan primer market—a thousand will surely do in each of the sizes you'll need.

It may be quite a while, though, before you'll use all those primers. How to keep them from deteriorating so that a decade or so from now they'll perform properly? First, make sure the original containers are sealed and in good condition, then separate into batches of two or three hundred each (British are packed 250 per sealed tin). Obtain small containers that can be sealed air-tight and seal up each small batch separately, putting a few dessicant pellets in with each. Label and date, then store in a safe dry place where temperatures won't go above about 80 degrees. Don't mess with them and 10 years or more from now they'll still be perfect.

As for containers, I'm partial to half-pint glass Mason jars with gasketed, screw-on lids. I spray them with black paint after sealing to keep out light which will fade primer carton labels—not really necessary, but convenient.

Flash Holes As long as these are located reasonably near the center of the pocket, there'll be no measurable effect on accuracy. Hole size also has very little effect except when very wide variations exist within the same lot. However, size can be controlled, location can't. In any given lot of cases, simply check flash holes with a set of small-size twist drills. Then pick the drill size matching the largest hole, and use it to open all others to match.

A variation of this is to use a set of taper-pin reamers. Fit a stop on the reamer that enters the largest hole about half its length, then run it into all others. The stop will limit reamer travel and insure uniform hole diameter.

Corrosive Primers This question comes up frequently—how do you tell which military ammunition is loaded

Non-Corrosive Primers
U.S. Military Ammunition
30-06 and 45 caliber

Headstamp	Maker	Changeover date	Safe Headstamps
FA	Frankford Arsenal	Oct. 1951 (30) July 1954 (45)	FA 52, 53, 54, etc. FA 55
FCC	Federal Cart. Corp.	Nov. 1953 (45)	FCC 54
DAQ	Dominion Arsenal*	All non-corrosive	
VC		All non-corrosive	
WRA	Winchester	Aug. 1951 (30 Ball) June 1954 (30 AP) Nov. 1951 (45)	WRA 52 WRA 55 WRA 52
WCC	Western	June 1951 (30) Nov. 1952 (45)	WCC 52 WCC 53
TW	Twin Cities Arsenal	Dec. 1950 (30 Ball) Feb. 1952 (30 AP)	TW 51 TW 53
SL	St. Louis Ordnance Plant	May 1952 (30 Ball) July 1952 (30 AP)	SL 53 SL 53
RA	Remington	Nov. 1951 (30 Ball) Sept. 1952 (45)	RA 52 RA 53
LA	Lake City Arsenal	June 1951 (30 Ball) April 1952 (30 AP)	LC 52 LC 53

All 30 Carbine, 9mm Luger, 38 Special with U.S. headstamps were loaded with standard commercial non-corrosive primers. All 7.62mm (308) and 5.56mm (223) is non-corrosive.

*Canada

with corrosive or non-corrosive primers? The best answer available, insofar as domestic ammunition is concerned, is found in the chart reprinted here from *Modern Handloading,* available from Winchester Press:

Foreign military surplus ammunition is another problem entirely, and accurate information is almost impossible to obtain. During WW II and immediately following, only very small amounts of foreign military ammunition were assembled with non-corrosive primers. The most notable exceptions are the Boxer-primed Canadian production of 9mm Parabellum and 30-06. Beyond that the only safe assumption is that *any* foreign military surplus manufactured before the late 1950s and early 1960s is probably assembled with corrosive chlorate primers and clean your guns accordingly.

Powder/Cases

We often hear complaints about an inability to get certain recommended powder charges into the case in question. For example, the *Speer Reloading Manual No. 8* lists a charge of 59 grains of H4831 powder with a 180-gr. bullet. Shooters without a great deal of experience in this particular area choose this load, set up the powder measure, check it out, and then go into a sizzling sweat when they discover that *as dropped from the measure,* that charge overflows the case—you just can't get that much *loose* 4831 into the case. They immediately suspect that load of being erroneous—and naturally, that perhaps other data in the manual might also be incorrect. Now they're afraid to use any of the dope in their particular manual—and it may be the only one at hand.

All this is understandable, but just a wee bit more knowledge would save the day. Like any other granular material, propellant powders can be made to occupy a lot less space than they do when simply dumped loosely into a container. You think nothing of jarring or vibrating a container of other physically similar materials to settle the contents into less space, so why not powder?

The old-timers whipped this problem with black powder by using a long drop tube or loading tube, which caused the powder to fall as much as three feet before it entered the case, thus compacting itself. If no great amount of compaction was required to get the charge in the case, they simply compressed the powder during bullet seating. Both methods will work today, but the use of a long loading tube is a considerable inconvenience and compressing the charge with the bullet can result in the fracture of a good many powder granules, causing ignition and burning rates to vary. By far the best method I've found is to simply put the case fully up into the conical mouth of the measure drop tube, throw the charge, then rap on the head of the case with a length of ¼″ brass rod to settle the powder. Depending on which powder is involved, this method settles the charge as much as 10-20% of its normal as-dropped bulk.

Autoloaders and Loads

Next time you have extraction or ejection difficulties with handloads in any auto shotgun, check the gun closely before blaming the ammunition. That the gun works OK with factory ammo doesn't mean it's perfect.

First, thoroughly clean the gas cylinder and piston (if present), all recoiling parts, and especially the chamber. Examine all moving parts carefully for burrs, deformation, or excessive wear that produces extra friction. Examine the chamber carefully for evidence of rust pitting, scratches and gouges, burrs, reamer marks, or hard-caked fouling patches. Make certain the gas port isn't partially clogged.

The chamber is especially important. In some guns functioning may be OK with factory loads, then erratic when same cases are handloaded to the same performance. Handloaded cases may cling just a little more to chamber walls—enough to slow down extraction and cause a bit of trouble.

Getting the chamber absolutely clean and then polishing away any roughness should cure the problem. But be sure you *polish only;* don't grind the chamber oversize. It only needs smoothing, not enlargement.

As a last resort—when you've a batch of handloads that just don't quite give full cycling—the situation can be salvaged by lubricating the cases. Hang me in effigy if you like for such a heretical suggestion, but it does often allow proper functioning *without* apparent ill effects. Just a trace of lube, though, or it will build up in the chamber. I've had good results with wiping cases lightly with a cloth into which has been rubbed a good paste wax. Other times I've rubbed just a trace of resizing lube on with my fingers.

As for handguns, it has long been the practice of many first-class competitive shooters to literally drench lightly-loaded cartridges with oil to insure reliable feeding. Many a 45 auto that won't work at all well with 3.2 or 3.3 grains of Bullseye in *dry* cases, will perform flawlessly when the same cartridges are well oiled. The usual procedure is to just squirt oil into the magazine after it is charged.

In the final analysis ammunition lubrication can be safe and worthwhile. Generally speaking, it becomes dangerous only when very high chamber pressures are combined with *excessive* amounts of lube.

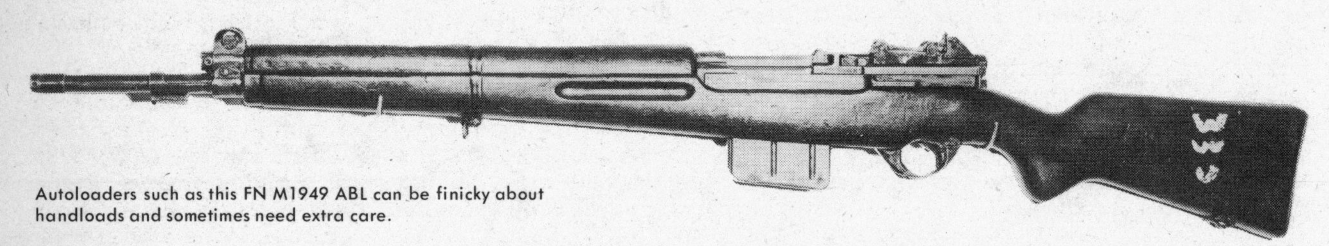

Autoloaders such as this FN M1949 ABL can be finicky about handloads and sometimes need extra care.

Defense Loads

Much has been said about the use of lead, hollow-base wadcutter bullets in 38 Special for defense purposes. The 146/148-gr. full wadcutter bullet loaded by all ammunition manufacturers is a pretty fair manstopper in its own right, if its velocity is stepped up a bit. The current factory-load velocity of about 770 fps (in a 6″ test barrel) dribbles off badly in barrels under 4″ long, so it doesn't have much smash—but even so, it's more effective than the smaller revolver cartridges and most auto-pistol calibers under 9mm.

This current loading is labeled "mid-range," thus its mild disposition. There was once a "full-charge" wadcutter load, now discontinued, with a good deal more authority, delivering the same bullet at 870 fps. On paper it was nearly as good as the standard 158-gr. round nose load, but in practice it was far superior.

That flat-ended, soft-lead slug

To insure higher accuracy and safety, all cases should be checked frequently, particularly those for rimless autoloaders. The 9mm Luger is shown. Every handloader should own good measuring instruments—a micrometer first, a 4″ or 6″ caliper like this as well.

penetrated far less, thus transfered more energy to the target; it created a larger wound channel and more secondary projectiles; it was generally bad news to any animated target.

If you want to use the HB wadcutter in your defensive handloads, by all means copy the full-charge load of yesteryear. Bullseye powder does the job well, with 3.5 grains giving about 880 fps; 4.5 grains of Unique will do about the same.

Going higher, 4.4 grains of Bullseye or 5.6 grains of Unique will churn up just over 1000 fps for particularly deadly results. But at this MV level accuracy may go to pot unless bullets are cast quite hard. The walls of the bullet base, around the cavity, are thin and weak, and they may be badly deformed by gas pressure as the bullet leaves the muzzle.

Of course, *all* commercially available HB wadcutters are made from very soft lead, so they don't take kindly to being souped-up much past the old full-charge velocity.

There's also the practice of loading soft HB wadcutters *inverted* to produce what looks like a massive hollow point. Even at low velocities this will produce considerable expansion in tissue; at higher velocities it will fragment, throwing off pieces which add to the destruction it causes.

While the modest load of 3.5/Bullseye and the inverted HB is highly favored by some; others complain about its accuracy. The problem arises in the degree of accuracy required. Generally, it's recommended as a defense load in 2″ guns at across-counter ranges where minimum blast and recoil are desired.

Micrometers No serious handloader can consider himself properly equipped if he doesn't own a first-class zero-to-one-inch micrometer and a four-inch or larger capacity vernier caliper of comparable quality. They aren't exactly cheap, but the assurance that accurate measurements give you, and the hazards they help you avoid, are worth many times the cost. If you live in a highly industrialized area, you'll find excellent buys in good used tools in hock shops and second-hand stores. If not, any good hardware or tool store can fix you up, or you can use one of the many mail-order tool catalogs.

First-class domestic brands will cost in the $25-40 range, but adequate less expensive models are available. Some importers offer excellent imports for substantially less—but don't get the idea one of those "Super Precision" $2.98 mikes advertised in the pulp magazines will serve your purpose. It won't, and it might be so far off as to lead you *into* trouble.

A measuring tool is a precision instrument. If it doesn't *look* like it's made with precision, it likely isn't. Free but firm movement without backlash, smoothly finished parts, neat and mar-free assembly, clear and easily-read scales and graduations indicate good quality. If they aren't present, look elsewhere. A good mike or vernier will last all your life if properly used and cared for, so don't try to save fifty cents a year from now on by buying junk.

Case Annealing

The best method for annealing case necks is immersion in molten lead. It produces the most consistent case-to-case results, and it's simple and easy to do.

Fire up your electric bullet-casting furnace and generate a ⅔-pot of molten lead; turn the heat as low as possible and still keep the lead completely fluid; skim off the dross, but *do not* flux the mixture.

Pick up a case—either in fingers or pliers or some secure holding device—and dip case neck/shoulder area in light oil or finely powdered graphite. Give it a quick flip to throw off the excess, then immerse neck and shoulder *vertically* into the molten lead. Leave it there four or five seconds—

Best way to anneal cases is in molten lead, using a thermostatically-controlled electric furnace.

thick brass may require a bit longer. Then draw out the case, give it a quick flip to throw off any clinging lead, and quench by dropping it into a bucket of cold water.

That completes the job, and it can be done just as quickly as you can pick up and dunk cases—even faster if you want to make a holding fixture that takes several cases. I've used perforated plates or strap hinges drilled to accept as many as 10 or 12 cases for simultaneous dunking. In fact, I once used a battered old serving fork whose tines would hold a half-dozen 30-06 cases by their extractor grooves.

Experiment with the time of immersion. Keep it as short as possible to still produce the degree of softness required, but don't overdo it and get necks so soft they crumple. Just enough to produce a bluish-brown surface color on the brass is about right. If you're worried about overdoing it, hold cases between thumb and forefinger. That way, you'll feel the head getting hot and pull and quench the case before your fingers get burned. It's a fail-safe system, but warm on the hands.

Dirty Shotshells Ever wind up with a batch of really dirty fired shotshells? If they are one-piece plastic like the Winchester AA, just wash 'em. Dump them into mama's automatic washer with any good detergent, set water temperature to cold or warm (if the latter, check first to make sure it doesn't get hot enough to soften or warp cases), set for the shortest cycle available, and switch it on. It's a good idea to place these in an old pillow case or mesh bag to make sure the inside of the washer drum doesn't get chipped, and this also makes handling them easier. Cases will come out clean as a whistle, though the inked-on markings will probably be removed.

To dry quickly, tumble in mama's dryer, with heat turned off or at least set as low as possible. The dryer will also serve to dry out paper or built-up plastic cases you might pick up on the range after a shower or heavy dew. Just make sure you don't run it too hot. The "nylon" setting usually works fine, without damage to cases.

Waxing Shotshells

If you're having trouble with hard shotshell resizing, first check the die. It may have some annular reamer marks or other roughness (maybe from rust you allowed to accumulate) causing most of the trouble. If polishing the die doesn't cure the problem, try a little wax to lubricate both die and cases. A trace of beeswax rubbed on a few cases now and then may do the job. If not, give all cases a shot of aerosol wax. Make sure this is a hard wax, not just an oily furniture polish. In a few minutes the volatile spray vehicle will evaporate, leaving just enough wax on the cases so they'll run smoothly through the die.

Revolver Case Extraction How often have you been told that so long as a revolver load extracted easily, it didn't produce excessive pressures? Don't believe that. We've seen 357 Magnum cases fired at 55-60,000 psi literally fall out of a test barrel of their own weight. On the other hand, I've seen cases fired in a *new* revolver that required being *driven* out of the chambers after firing at a conservative 15-20,000 psi.

Chamber finish and case hardness gradient are what really control extraction effort, far more than chamber pressure. Take a revolver with smooth, slippery chambers (like S&W used to burnish them) and keep running pressures up—you'll blow the gun before extraction effort becomes excessive. On the other hand, take a recently-made gun of a make and model with all-too-common rough chambers, and even light factory loads may hang cases up solidly in chambers. I've seen lots of *new* guns the past few years that required polishing of the chambers before cases could be gotten out without the aid of a mallet or boot heel.

Don't take easy extraction as an indicator of safe pressures; instead, stick with known safe loads, and you're a lot less likely to wreck a good gun or your shooting hand.

Cartridge Corrosion If you carry handgun loads in a typical looped leather cartridge belt, you'll eventually encounter corrosion problems. Brass cases will invariably develop greenish verdigris from contact with residual acids or moisture in the leather. The only way to prevent this with naked brass is to keep the leather as dry as possible and to remove and wipe the cartridges clean daily. Some police officers, not particularly gun-wise, coat their belted cartridges with clear lacquer or varnish. This will hold off corrosion, but unless very carefully done, it can cause chambering difficulties—especially with handloads whose cases aren't resized quite down to original dimensions. The lacquer may be thick enough to prevent chambering, especially if it runs or drips. A thin, well-buffed coat of hard paste wax will protect from corrosion for a while, but requires occasional renewal.

Your best bet is *unscratched, unmarred,* nickeled cases. The nickel must be unbroken, not scratched by resizing, so new cases are best for loads to be belt-carried for a long time.

Bullets will also corrode from contact with leather, whether lead or jacketed. Frequent wiping will do the trick, and so will a wax coating. However, lacquer *can* be safely used on bullets if not allowed to lap over onto the case. Dipping is okay if the lacquer is quite thin and the cartridge is hung point down by its rim to drain dry.

By far the worst method of avoiding or removing cartridge corrosion is buffing. Many a cop with a blitz cloth shines his belt ammunition by hand. That's OK because no metal is removed. But if this is tried on a powered buffing or polishing wheel, half the vital wall thickness can disappear in a flash. If the same rounds get another treatment later, they may be paper-thin, and rupture when fired. The rupture won't hurt the shooter, but if he's in the middle of a shooting encounter when it happens, the consequences might well be fatal.

7.62x39mm Cartridges

We continue to get many queries for a source of ammunition and/or components for the Soviet 7.62x39mm M-43 service cartridge for use in SKS carbines and its various copies. At least we hope they're for use in the semi-automatic SKS, for all the other guns chambered for that cartridge are full-automatic and thus prohibited by Federal law.

You won't find this ammunition in the average gunshop, but some surplus vendors occasionally have a supply of military loads. They are Berdan primed, but usually non-corrosive, and of good quality. What I've shot has been quite accurate in a Sako Vixen sporter.

Boxer-primed ammunition is, for all practical purposes, non-existent—though many millions of rounds have been loaded at the Lake City ammunition plant for the U.S. government. While you just might run across some of this loaded ammo, I'd recommend extreme caution. NONE has been legally released, and any you might encounter is most certainly "liberated" (for which read stolen) and possession thereof is frowned upon.

The only other source of ready-made Boxer-primed cartridges I know is George Spence, Steele, Missouri. George custom-loads it, forming the cases from C.I.L. 6.5x54mm Mannlicher-Schoenauer primed cases he seems to have in plenty. He can also

These three 7.62x39mm loads for Soviet SKS rifle are assembled in cases reformed from 6.5x54mm Mannlicher-Schonauer brass.

supply, at less cost, Berdan-primed loads made from reworked Italian 7.35mm ammunition of WW II vintage. Corrosive-primed, of course, but if you are too lazy to clean your guns, you deserve no better.

As a last resort for your own loading, use Norma unprimed cases in 6.5x54mm M-S or 6.5mm Carcano caliber and a set of 7.62x39mm forming dies, obtainable from RCBS, Inc., Box 1919, Oroville, California 95965. After resizing, trimming, neck-reaming, base-swaging, and annealing, you'll have excellent Boxer-primed cases which will serve for many, many reloadings if given proper care.

Though Russky and Chicom 7.62mm barrels usually run about .310" groove diameter, I've had fine results with standard .308" diameter 30-cal. bullets. Best were the 125/130-gr. weights, with fairly sharp points, ahead of IMR 4227 powder. Start at about 22 grains and work up until the gun in question gives reliable semi-auto functioning, then stop. This isn't a magnum, and even a smidgin more powder past the optimum level raises pressures sharply.

Black Powder

Having trouble getting enough black powder? Maybe it isn't as bad as it looks. The "User-Limited" purchase permit allows buying more than the picayunish 5 pounds normally allowed by Federal law, and also permits you to buy outside your state of residence.

In effect, a "User-Limited" permit enables the purchase of enough black powder at one time to make the often-necessary long drive pay off. A buying trip not worthwhile for 5 pounds isn't so bad if you can pick up 50 pounds, or if you can get together with several friends and send one man after enough powder for the whole lot.

Ask your local ATFD office for form #4707, execute it properly, then turn it in with the prescribed $2 fee. Eventually—there may be some delay—you'll receive a one-time purchase permit (Form #4709) which must be presented when and where your purchase is to be made. When making the purchase you'll also be required to execute a purchase record and to properly identify yourself.

Form #4709 is strictly a one-shot deal, and it's made out for a specific amount of powder. You can't buy more than the permit specifies—and if for some reason you buy less, you can't go back later and try to pick up the balance. *Every* individual purchase must be made under a new permit.

In some instances it might not be all that simple, depending upon *your* state and local laws and the state and local laws in force where you want to do the buying. Federal regulations specify that the permit will not be honored if the purchase or the transportation of the black powder will be in violation of state and local laws in the areas concerned.

Short Pistol Cases

A fellow dropped in the other day with his pet auto pistol and three or four boxes of cases fired in it—and with a problem. For years he had loaded straight rimless auto-pistol cases without any concern for case length. He knew that any case which had been fired successfully in that gun *couldn't* be too long—and he'd also felt that factory cases weren't likely to be too short.

He was a little shocked when he—for some reason—measured a few cases and found them much shorter than he'd expected. This prompted him to check quite a few cases—and none of them were long enough to headspace solidly on the chamber shoulder!

His first question was why the cases were generally a good bit shorter than published length. Well, there is no industry-standard minimum length for such cases, though maximum length is specified in SAAMI minimum-chamber/maximum-case drawings. Individual manufacturers set their own minimums compatible with tooling and production methods. So, since auto pistols are unusually tolerant of short cases and excess headspace conditions, tolerances are set rather loosely.

How loose? That information isn't released by the manufacturers, but a fair idea can be obtained by measuring a handful of cases from every make and lot you can find in one caliber. I once did this when a good many lots of commercial 45 ACP ammunition were handy. In one make alone I found a spread of .040'' between longest and shortest cases. Other makes and lots showed a bit less spread, but still more than one might expect.

This doesn't mean that the cases or the makers are bad. As already mentioned, auto pistols are quite tolerant in this respect. Most autos have virtually unlimited firing pin protrusion, so will ignite a primer, even if the cartridge be rammed 1/16", or even 1/8", deeper than normal in the chamber. So long as primers are ignited properly, the cartridges will function normally.

When it comes to producing maximum accuracy, though, those short cases can cause trouble. Uneven lengths will cause variations in ignition—which in turn produce greater velocity variations and a poorer degree of accuracy. The difference may not be much, even in a first-class target gun. But a half-inch in 50-yard group size can cost you a match just as easily as if it were a furlong.

To avoid such fuss and feathers,

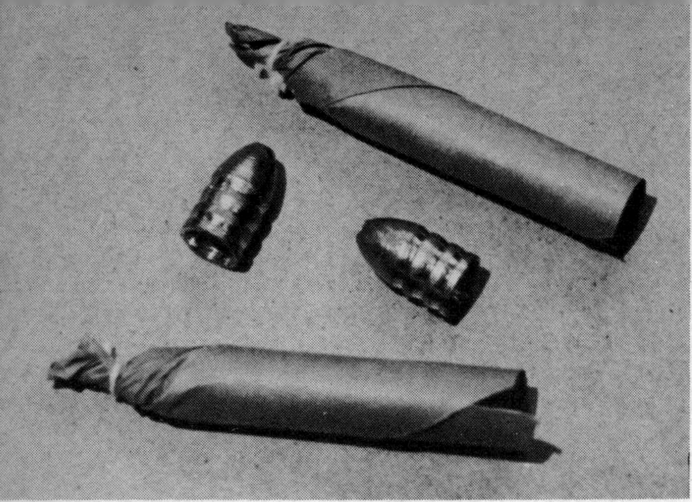

Minie bullets — and some others — can be rolled to size if overlarge for your barrel. See text for details.

sort your once-fired cases by length. While a set of case gauges made up in .005" or .010" steps would be handy, I use a low-cost vernier caliper. Set aside for match use those cases no more than .010" shorter than breech-face/chamber-shoulder distance of the gun. The rest can be lumped together for general use, but you might want to split them into two batches, one for service use and the other for plinking where accuracy requirements are least stringent of all.

Minie Balls Maybe you've acquired a muzzle-loading rifle of some sort (probably a 58) and want to use minie bullets in it. That presents no problem if your bore is of standard diameter. Lately, though, I've seen a few 58s with undersize bores—and standard minies are too large for easy loading. Of course, you can buy a new .575" or undersize mould, but that's expensive.

Try this instead. Take the standard too-tight minie bullets (unlubricated) and lay them on a smooth, *hard* surface. Steel plate is best, but smooth hardwood, glass, formica, masonite, etc., is O.K. Lay a strip of hardwood or steel over the bullet(s), bear down equally with both hands, and roll it on them a few turns. Experiment with pressure and don't overdo it. You'll find you can reduce bullet diameter a small amount quickly and easily. With a little care, you can reduce them quite uniformly.

Greasy Cases When your handloads finish up a bit greasy—whether from bullet lube, sizing lube, or greasy hands and dies—it's best to clean and dry them before use, or before boxing and storage.

A power-driven tumbler is great for this, but if you don't have or can't afford one, you don't have to wipe off individual cartridges slowly and tediously. Just dig out a large, thick-napped bath or beach towel and sprinkle it lightly with lighter fluid or some similar grease-cutting solvent that evaporates quickly. Dump a couple hundred 38 Specials—or whatever it will hold conveniently—fold the towel over lengthwise, grasp it by both ends, and rapidly shuffle the loose rounds from end to end for a couple of minutes. The long nap and solvent will clean the cartridges, leaving them dry and bright. No more messy handling, and no oil-produced misfires.

When Seating lubed lead bullets, especially if you're loading lots of 'em, lubricant often accumulates in the hollow of the seating screw, gets packed there tightly, and progressively forces bullets deeper into the cases. That causes wide velocity variations and consequent vertical stringing on the target.

Some dies are vented through the seating screw to allow excess lube to escape. That works part of the time, but the necessarily tiny vent is easily clogged and hard to clean.

Lube-free bullet noses will help a lot, even though some grease will occasionally be forced up along the bullet by the case mouth. The only sure solution is to swab out the die and the punch cavity now and then with a solvent-wet wad of cotton on a stick. If bullets are clean-nosed, doing this every hundred rounds or so will insure uniform seating depth and clean loaded cartridges.

Straight Cases When loading such old long straight cases as the 45-70 and 45-90 for maximum performance in modern guns, the powder charge usually fills the case pretty well. Loading to original factory ballistics for the older guns, on the other hand, means the charge may occupy no more than ¼th to ⅓d of the available powder space.

Most of today's handloaders hold the charge to the rear of the case with a loose ball of toilet tissue, kapok fluff, Dacron or some other light material. They all work, but none actually secures the powder's position quite as well as what the factories used in years gone by.

In straight cases an ultra-light ball of fluff will shift inside the case under the weight of the powder through handling and recoil impacts. When that happens, you aren't much better off than without it.

A tight-fitting card wad will grip the case walls better and will not shift nearly so easily. Hard, stiff, smooth cardboard at least 1/32-inch thick is best, and the wad must be large enough to fit quite tightly. It is tight enough when the edges are forced up slightly as it is rammed solidly onto the powder charge with the largest dowel the case will accept. Start the wad squarely by thumbing it into the case mouth, then seating it with a single smooth thrust of the dowel. Check afterward to make certain the wad hasn't scooped up part of the powder charge.

45 ACP load at left is shown with bullet seated correctly. The case at right has had the bullet driven too deeply by grease and dirt compacted in seating die.

A dry wad will normally do the trick, but dipping it first into melted beeswax may improve accuracy, and will sometimes help with any leading problem that occurs. Adding a 1/16-inch wax or grease wad directly under the bullet may also help. Just make up a sheet of lube or wax, then thumb it over the case mouth, and seat the bullet directly over the resulting wad.

A source of such wads, offered in sheets of colloidal-graphite wax (.033", .046" and .064" thick) is IPCO, Box 14, Bedford, Mass. 01730. These are $1.25 a box. Their stick lubes, hollow core or solid, are $1.25 for two sticks. ●

The most commonly used 9.3s. From left—9.3x57 Norma 285-gr. • 9.3x62 DWM 293-gr. Brenneke TUG • 9.3x62 RWS 285-gr. • 9.3x64 DWM 285-gr. full jacket • 9.3x72 Norma 200-gr. soft point • 9.3x74R DWM 293-gr. Brenneke TUG • 9.3x74R Norma 232-gr. hollow point boat-tail.

The 9.3mm Cartridges—all but forgotten!

Well and favorably known in Europe and Africa for many decades, none of the several 9.3mm loadings ever gained great popularity in the United States. Here's a comprehensive survey of them, their capabilities, their ballistics.

by D.C. COLE

Photos by Jack Heyn, Des Moines, Iowa.

CARTRIDGE FADS, like women's fashions, are changeable, but seem to run in recurrent but unpredictable cycles. For several years there's been considerable interest in the calibers which are classed together as the medium bores.

Older sportsmen may remember an earlier wave of interest in the mediums. During the 1920s many a 30-06 became a 35 Whelen. Custom arms from Newton in 33 and 35 caliber and from Hoffman in 375 adorned many gun cabinets. Even a few European 375s by Holland & Holland, Rigby, and Purdey could be found in the hands of discriminating—and well-heeled—sportsmen. By the mid-1930s Winchester had joined the movement, bringing forth the Model 70 in 375 H&H Magnum.

The recent "medium wave" has carried on its crest such cartridges as the 338 Winchester, 350 Remington, and the 350 Norma. Less popular, but with some following, are the 358 Winchester, the 35 Remington, plus the wildcat 33s and 35s by various custom gunmakers.

Overlooked in this rush to the medium bores have been several fine standard cartridges. Widely used and acclaimed in Europe, Africa, and Asia, these cartridges are members of the German-designed 9.3mm family. Most commonly encountered today are the 9.3x72R, 9.3x57, 9.3x62, 9.3x64, and 9.3x74R. These cartridges span a range of use covered in the U.S.

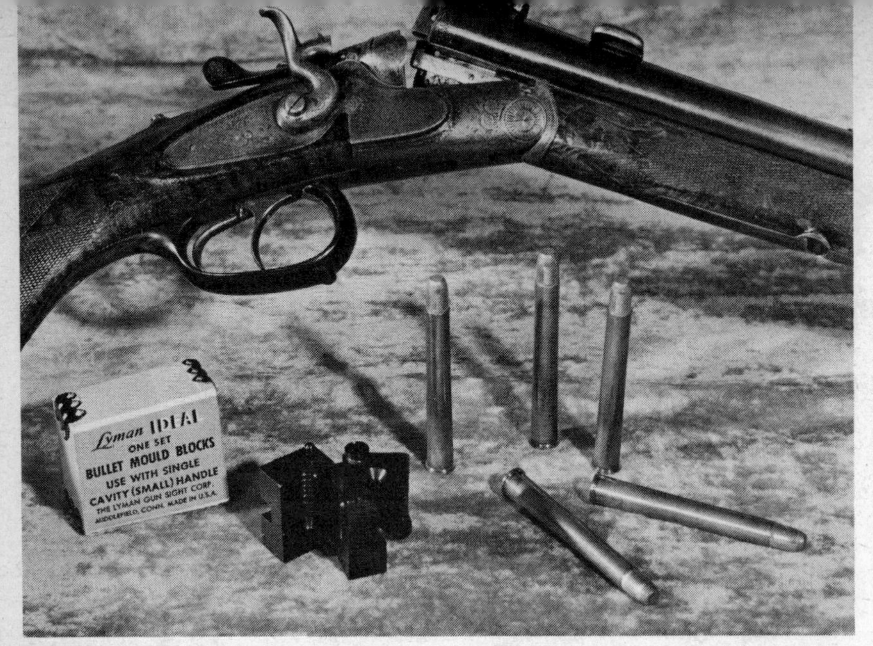

The Loffler drilling in 9.3x72R. In spite of the rabbit ear hammers, the gun was made in the 1930s.

by chamberings from 35 Remington to 375 H&H.

The various 9.3mm cartridges use bullets of .365"-.366" diameter. A multitude of bullet designs are available in weights from 192 to 297 grains. Velocities range from 2000 to 2800 feet per second, depending on the cartridge chambering and case type. Wide use of break-open actions in Central Europe has resulted in many rimless cartridges being duplicated in rimmed case chamberings. As a general rule, the rimless cases were used in bolt action rifles, the rimmed cases in hinged breech guns. Early experimenters with bolt guns turned out some beautiful long-barreled rifles in the 9.3mms. Many of these are superbly crafted arms, stocked and balanced like our American "Kentucky" or Pennsylvania rifles.

Rimless cases were, in later years, adapted to double rifles and combination guns, but such guns were prone to extraction problems on occasion. They were considered unreliable by many hunters and gunsmiths. Most of these complaints related to African experiences, instances when rifle extractors either slipped out of the case groove or pulled through a perhaps soft brass case. The probable culprit in many of these cases was the African sun, which heated ammo in safari boxes, boosting already high pressure loads, such as the 9.3x64mm, to the degree that the case stuck in the chamber.

For several years I used a Sodia (Austrian) combination gun in 9.3x62mm for elk in Arizona and New Mexico, and I was never bothered with extraction problems. A colleague using a Sodia double 30-06 had several failures to extract during his hunts at the same time. As usual, this doesn't prove anything except that no two rifles are ever identical.

Like other cartridges, the 9.3mms were developed for specific purposes and pressures. Reloaders should consider the original pressure and loading data when working with new loads.

The 9.3x72R

The mildest of the clan, the old 9.3x72R, originated as a black powder cartridge of about 38-55 performance. Generally the 9.3x72R is found in combination guns and double rifles, often of very high quality and fine workmanship. Such guns were made well into the 1930s by various European makers on both a volume and a custom basis. Single barrel rifles of falling block or break-open action are encountered less often. Rarely an early bolt action in 9.3x72R may come to light.

Until a trading session developed a year ago I used a bolt action 9.3x72R single shot by Hamer. The gun was graceful, light as a feather to carry, and quite accurate at the 100 yards or so of normal woods ranges. My other 9.3x72R is a Loffler hammer drilling assembled in 1932. Factory loads in this drilling will sometimes print groups less than one inch, although 1.5" is average. Pick the right load for the 72R and consistent accuracy is possible, at least with most barrels. Many shooters find 9.3x72R ammo hard to find and so buy several varieties and shoot a little of each. Different makes and velocities will almost always shoot to different points of impact on targets or game.

Commercial loadings for the cartridge vary from 193-gr. bullets at 2000 fps (feet per second), about 38-55 class, to those of 200 grains at 2250 fps. This last loading, by Norma, shades the 35 Remington. It's superb for woods use on such game as whitetail deer and black bear. Cartridge pressures are mild, about 25,000-30,000 psi (pounds per square inch), and recoil is moderate even in relatively light combination guns. The cartridge reloads easily, performs very well with cast bullets, and would be a fine chambering for any of the older smokeless single shot actions, if barrels, bullets, and cases were readily available.

Shooters planning to reload the 9.3x72R are in for a number of problems. Cases are often hard to get. Norma stopped the sale of their excellent 9.3x72R cases in the U.S. several years ago. RWS and DWM cases could be had from distributors on special order, but DWM was in trouble in

Luftwaffe Sauer M30 drilling in 9.3x74R used by the German air force in WW II. The Pak Tool, made by English, is shown.

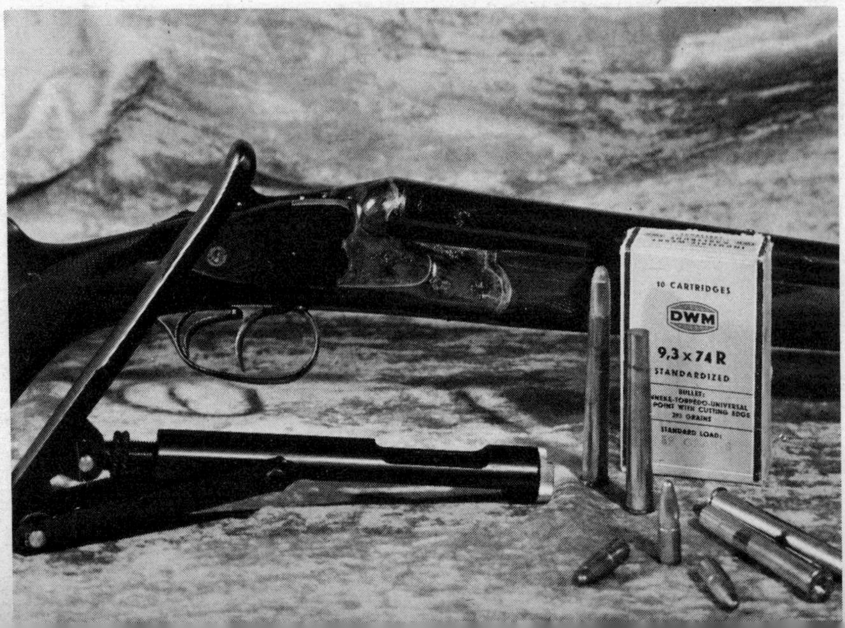

Classic Mannlicher-Schoenauer carbine was available in 9.3x57 and 9.3x62. Lyman dies are shown.

1972, and RWS bought their assets. Whether DWM cases in 9.3x72R will be made again...? These cases, usually Berdan primed, are more trouble in reloading than U.S. brass. A few reloaders have made cases by swaging 30-06 cases or drawing out 30-30 brass. Both processes test patience, skill, and perseverance.

Jacketed bullets are at times available for the 9.3x72R, but most reloaders use cast bullets in this case. Lyman's #366408 mould casts a plain base bullet designed especially for the 9.3x72R, and one that works quite well.

When working up loads it is wise to keep pressures down in most European actions. Almost any loadings for the older 38-55 rifles will be OK. Remember that most of these rifles were intended for black powder or very mild smokeless loads. 9.3x72R barrels vary a great deal, so it is best to start working up loads on the light side, then gradually increasing them until you obtain the best accuracy for your barrel consistent with safe pressures. Slugging the barrel is always a good idea, too, letting you know just what bore and groove dimensions are.

Late Nazi-proofed 9.3x72R rifles or those from the post-World War I period can be loaded considerably higher if the guns are in good condition. 43 grains of 3031 will give performance in the 35 Remington class. So loaded, the 9.3x72R is an excellent woods cartridge for whitetail deer.

The 9.3x74R

Big brother of the rimmed 9.3s is the powerful 9.3x74R. This bottlenecked cartridge has been widely used in Africa and Europe for heavy, dangerous game. Such diverse authorities as Jack O'Connor, Elmer Keith, and John Taylor have endorsed the 9.3x74R in books and articles in widely circulated magazines.

Before World War II, Sauer, Merkel, Sodia, and others produced drillings and combination guns for the 9.3x74R. The Sauer M30 was even adopted by the Luftwaffe during the war for survival and recreation use. Combination guns in this chambering are made at present by Buhag (East Germany), Sodia, and Krieghoff.*

Most 9.3x74Rs were and are double rifles. Superb over and under rifles from Merkel and Sodia were highly prized before the war. Purdey, H&H and Rigby made side-by-side rifles on order. Currently Dumoulin, Sodia and FN, among perhaps others, produce fine double rifles in 9.3x74R in the thousand dollar and up class.* Fine single shots and a few bolt action Mausers are sometimes encountered.

Commercially loaded by Norma, DWM, RWS, and ZB, the 9.3x74R may be the most ballistically versatile of its family. Norma loads a 232-gr. hollow point at 2650 fps. The Norma loading is fine for light, thin-skinned game, such as antelope and mule deer. A 232-gr. solid was loaded at the same velocity but does not seem to be currently available. A 285-gr. soft point bullet at 2350 is intended for larger game. An identical weight solid performs the same function in the 9.3x74R as the 300-gr. solid in the 375H&H.

RWS offers two fine 257.7 grain H-Mantel loadings for the 9.3x74R, a design similar to that of the American Nosler bullet. One, a copper hollow point bullet, opens quickly yet penetrates well on game of medium size. The other H-Mantel has a lead tip and performs admirably in brush or open country and is especially fine for jaguar, boar, or elk. Both RWS bullets travel at 2650 fps and deliver over 3900 ft. lbs. at the muzzle.

DWM had a 262-gr. bullet at 2530 fps, a 285-gr. soft point at 2350, and the excellent 293-gr. TUG Brenneke bullet at 2360. This last loading made the 9.3x74R fully the equal of

---

*Over-unders and drillings (3-barrel guns) are currently available from Krieghoff, Heym, Franz Sodia and Waffen-Frankonia (Wurzburg, West Germany) in their Suhler Model in various 9.3mm calibers, but not including 9.3x72R. Bolt action rifles by Waffen-Frankonia, BRNO, Mauser, Steyr-Mannlicher and others were offered in the 1972 Waffen-Frankonia catalog in 9.3x62 and 9.3x64.

This W-F Catalog, 280 pages and very well put together, is worth seeing, even if your German is poor. Profusely illustrated, you can have a copy, postpaid, for $2.00.

*Firearms Center, Inc., are importing *some* Dumoulin rifles (as well as Darne shotguns, Dschulnig (Austria) bolt and O-U rifles, and other arms). Ask about Dumoulin double rifles and their availability on special order.

Author's favorite elk rifle: Husqvarna M1950, 9.3x62mm, with RCBS dies. DWM cartridges, left, have "Starkmantel" bullets.

A variety of 9.3mm loads, tools and components.

the 375 H&H for any practical purpose. Brenneke's design incorporates a combination of lead core materials, a complex jacket, and a boat-tail. The bullet loses velocity slowly and performs well on dangerous, thin-skinned game. Scandinavian hunters seem to prefer the 293-gr. Brenneke for polar bear, while African sportsmen use it with great success for lion and larger antelope.

RCBS dies for this cartridge are available. English made a fine Pak Tool on request for the 9.3x74R. Cases are readily available from Norma, RWS and, once, DWM. 9.3x74R cases would be almost impossible to form out of others. Fortunately, it is a case widely used to form more exotic calibers and is a favorite with wildcatters using rimmed cases.

Bullets may be obtained in weights of 232, 257, 286 and 297 grains from manufacturers or jobbers, but only through a federally licensed dealer. Waiting time is on the order of 3-6 months. Lyman mould #366408 can be used for light loads in the 9.3x74R, as it can in any 9.3mm.

While 9.3x74R barrels are more uniform than older 9.3s, many variations of action and materials exist. Use 35 Whelen loads as a guide to working up handloads. I find that 56 grains of 4064 works well with 285-gr. bullets in most good single barrels. Double rifles, of course, must be individually regulated for load. Start low, work up gradually. I like the 9.3x74R and would be most happy to see some American manufacturer chamber rifles for it.

Wide choice of bullet weight makes this cartridge ideal for use in single shots or double rifles for American game. FN over and unders, if still made and offered in the U.S., should find a ready market among sportsmen hunting elk, moose, or game of similar size. For years my favorite all-round rifle was an early Sauer M30 Luftwaffe drilling. Its two 12 gauge tubes and the 9.3x74R barrel made it a real "go anywhere, take anything" rig. The Luftwaffe case held cartridges, accessories, and gun. Airlines did not seem to be able to destroy the case so the gun traveled a lot and had more than its share of use.

The rimless 9.3 has considerable following the world over. It is found frequently in Canada, but most are used outside the Western Hemisphere.

The 9.3x57

A great many 9.3x57mms used to be made. During the 1920s fairly large quantities of 8x57 Mausers were rebarreled to 9.3x57 and dumped into commercial channels. Commercial Mausers and Mannlicher-Schoenauers were chambered for the cartridge. The 9.3x57mm, about the equivalent of the 358 Winchester, is useful for the same purposes. Norma offers 232- and 285-gr. loadings—the 232-gr. at 2329 fps and the heavy bullet at 2067. A number of American hunters display a fondness for the 9.3x57mm as a woods cartridge for black bear and boar. Reloading the 57mm cases is easy, and cast bullets give good accuracy with mild loads. Any 57mm cases may be necked up to 9.3 and any of the 9.3mm bullet weights may be used. Loads for Winchester's 358 may serve as a guide.

The 9.3x62

Among the 9.3mm family of cartridges, the most often found is the 9.3x62mm. In American publications the 9.3x62 is often compared to the wildcat 35 Whelen, which it does resemble in some ways. While case length is nearly identical to the Whelen, and both can be made from 30-06 brass, 9.3 loadings are more powerful than those recommended for the Whelen. 9.3x62mm ballistics duplicate or exceed those of the 9.3x 74R loadings in most cases, so this cartridge really performs more like the 338 than it does like the 35 Whelen.

Barnes' *Cartridges of the World* says that the 9.3x62 was introduced in 1905 by the firm of Otto Bock. It was intended to provide colonists in German Colonial Africa with a reliable cartridge in an inexpensive arm. Recently a large number of fine Mauser 9.3x62mm rifles turned up in the U.S. Most of these had seen African use, and could be had in quite good condition at very attractive prices. New guns in 9.3x62mm are currently made by nearly every European maker, including FN, FFV-Carl Gustaf, Brno, and H&H.

A thoroughly reliable load, the 9.3x 62mm has been for years the most widely distributed of the world's medium bore cartridges. Its fine ballistics make it ideally suited for any American game on which a 338 or a 375 would be considered OK.

My first 9.3x62mm was a 6¼-lb. Simson Model 98. The rifle had considerable stock drop, a steel buttplate, and a classic German stock with sharp comb. When the rifle went off, I always wondered if the game was hurt as badly as I was. Soon after this, a fine Husqvarna M1950 came my way, complete with scope, double set triggers, and barrel-mounted sling swivels. The 9.3x62 suddenly seemed remarkably civilized, and it became a favorite elk cartridge.

Most die makers offer 9.3x62mm tools. Mine are RCBS. Cases may be easily made from 30-06 brass. Often it is easier to use the 30-06 cases than to wait for 9.3x62mm brass. Dealers will order for you, but delivery is quite slow, particularly if orders go through jobbers or wholesalers. I usually write direct to the manufacturer or importer and have the cases and components shipped to a licensed dealer. Dealers appreciate reducing the paperwork and delivery is speeded up.

If 9.3x62mm reloading data is not available, it is possible to use 35 Whelen data and get fine results. Remember that heavy loads in some light rifles will split stocks. Try 35 Remington charges and light bullets in the 6 to 7 pound guns—not for safety, but certainly for your own comfort.

For elk and similar game, 53 grains of 3031 behind the 286-gr. soft point is a fine load. In my Husqvarna this gives about 2400 fps, is quite accurate, and expands well. With 257- and 297-gr. bullets, the 9.3x62 can be loaded to duplicate 338 performance in good rifles.

The 9.3x64

Most powerful of the 9.3mms is the 9.3x64mm Brenneke. Designed for African and Asian game, it exceeds the 375 H&H in every performance category. In a number of ways Brenneke was ahead of his time, for the 9.3x64 pre-dated the 375 Weatherby by 35 years. Standard DWM loading of this cartridge uses the superb 297-gr. TUG bullet at 2640 fps. Muzzle energy is 4550 ft. lbs., retaining 3000 at 300 meters.

Used rifles in 9.3x64mm are not uncommon in East Africa. They and the cartridge are almost unknown in the U.S. New rifles in this chambering are made or offered by Waffen-Frankonia, Mauser, and other Continental armsmakers.

9.3mm Ballistics

		Velocity/fps				Energy/ft. lbs.				Trajectory/drop†		
Cartridge	Bullet/grs.	M	100	200	300	M	100	200	300	100	200	300
9.3x72R	193DWM	1925	1600	1400	1245	1590	1090	835	666	.55	5.7	16.6
9.3x72R	200Norma	2230	1800	1445	1180	2215	1440	930	620	.6	5.0	15.2
9.3x74R	232Norma	2634	2304	2009	1742	3551	2735	2080	1564	.2	2.8	8.1
9.3x74R	*232Norma	2634	2350	2092	1855	3551	2846	2255	1773	.2	2.7	7.6
9.3x74R	258RWS	2620	2441	2255	1845	3910	3411	2914	2030	.3	3.0	7.5
9.3x74R	262DWM	2530	2345	2140	1860	3700	3196	2665	2200	.3	3.2	8.1
9.3x74R	285DWM	2330	1980	1760	1605	3440	2490	1970	1635	.5	4.0	11.1
9.3x74R	*285Norma	2362	2088	1837	1612	3544	2769	2144	1651	.4	3.5	9.8
9.3x74R	293DWM	2360	2160	1998	1870	3580	3000	2560	2250	.3	3.1	8.7
9.3x57	232Norma	2329	2032	1763	1527	2795	2127	1602	1202	.4	3.7	10.6
9.3x57	286Norma	2067	1818	1595	1404	2714	2099	1616	1252	.6	4.8	13.2
9.3x62	232Norma	2624	2304	2009	1742	3551	2735	2080	1564	.2	2.8	8.1
9.3x62	258RWS	2700	2490	2300	1850	4160	3537	3017	2190	.3	2.9	7.4
9.3x62	262DWM	2530	2345	2140	1860	3720	3196	2665	2200	.3	3.2	8.0
9.3x62	285DWM	2360	2010	1775	1605	3540	2570	2000	1620	.4	3.7	10.6
9.3x62	285RWS	2329	2017	1810	1670	3436	2582	2072	1764	.4	3.9	10.4
9.3x62	*285Norma	2362	2088	1873	1612	3544	2769	2144	1651	.4	3.5	9.8
9.3x62	293DWM	2515	2310	2150	2020	4110	3480	3010	2634	.36	2.8	7.5
9.3x64	285DWM	2750	2240	1930	1730	4790	3180	2365	1895	.3	3.0	8.8
9.3x64	293DWM	2640	2450	2290	2145	4550	3900	3410	3000	.29	2.4	6.7

*Solids †From line of bore, inches. Some of the DWM loads listed may not be available after 1972-73.

The 9.3x64mm is a bit over powerful for U.S. game, but it would make a good caliber for moose, grizzly and polar bear. Safari hunters would find the 9.3x64 a fine cartridge (in the 375 Weatherby class) for use on African plains game.

Loading components and tools for the 9.3x64mm are available in the U.S. Nonte's *Home Guide to Cartridge Conversions* explains the process of making cases from 300 H&H brass. I have never reloaded the 9.3x64mm, nor have I used it a great deal. What little experience there was with the cartridge was most satisfactory. A German friend, who uses a Merkel O&U double rifle in 9.3x64mm, prefers it to the 375 H&H.

Fate of the 9.3s

It is a bit of a mystery why the fine 9.3 family failed to achieve popularity in the U.S. Perhaps, as with the 6.5s and 8mms, the 9.3s were considered "too German" in the 1914-15 era. Possibly the introduction of the 35s and 375s during the 1920s and '30s played a part. Again, perhaps there wasn't a great enough performance difference to spark enthusiasm in European medium bores.

As a class the 9.3mm (.365") cartridges have a great many desirable features. Most chamberings offer versatility of loading and ballistic flexibility. Pressures tend toward the low side, yet with good performance levels. Sectional density and, therefore, retained velocity and energy are good.

Loaded cartridges are—or were—available from DWM, RWS, and Norma. Cases and bullets are usually available from distributors. Feeding any existing rifle in 9.3mm has been no major problem in recent years.

Custom 9.3mm rifles are not easily obtained in the U.S. While almost any action of reasonable strength will handle the 9.3 cartridges, barrels are almost unobtainable. Few, if any, U.S. barrelmakers produce 9.3 barrels, although some will rechamber existing 9.3s*. Flaig's does import barrels of this size on special order. Paul Jaeger, who has connections in Germany, can probably obtain 9.3 barrels in a reasonable time, to order.

As one of the world's largest and most widely distributed calibers, the 9.3mm clan deserves more attention than it has received from American sportsmen—though it won't get it! There seems to be a general reluctance to publish articles on European medium bore cartridges among U.S. gun magazine editors. They claim, with some justification, that there is no interest in them, and that "further medium bore rifle cartridges are not needed." I doubt that there will be any stampede to buy 9.3s, although those advertised in the *Shotgun News* seem to sell quickly enough. Nevertheless, sportsmen should be made aware that the 9.3mms—or some of them—are useful, available, and effective. No one need shy away from these not so odd "oddballs." Some may even want to try a custom 9.3mm.

Barreling a rolling block or other strong single shot action to 9.3x72R would be a fine choice for the timber deer hunter. A No. 1 Ruger in 9.3x74R could be a superb long range medium bore. Mauser, Winchester, or Remington bolt actions should produce a fine basis for 9.3x62 or 9.3x64 custom sporters.

I have used various 9.3mms over a span of nearly 20 years. This experience has been gained over a wide variety of terrain and climatic conditions, and on many varieties of large, thin-skinned game. That much experience seems to have produced several examples of disappointment with other cartridges by those who used them; I cannot remember even one with any 9.3mm. ●

*We queried several people on their ability and willingness to furnish 9.3mm barrels. The following firms can supply barrels in one or another of the various 9.3mm chamberings:

Firearms Center Inc. (113 Spokane, Victoria, Tex. 77901)—Dumoulin and Dschulnigg.

John E. Weir, Jr. (3304 Norton Ave., Independence, MO 64052)—Rheinmetall.

P.O. Ackley (2235 Arbor Lane, Salt Lake City, Utah 84117).

Sanders Custom Gun Service (2358 Tyler Lane, Louisville, KY 40205).

There are doubtless others who offer 9.3mm barrels, but the following men are *not* tooled for this caliber:

Ed Shilen.

Wm. H. Hobaugh.

Federal Firearms, Inc.

Smith & Wesson 35 Auto Pistols a history for collectors

This flawed, ill-starred pistol, though superbly fitted and finished, had a short and unhappy life.

by DONALD M. SIMMONS, JR.

JUST WHAT combination of ingredients go to make up a successful handgun design is a mystery. Were these skills too easily blended there would be no unsuccessful models, and every pistol would be as renowned as Carl Walther's PP, the Pedersen-designed Remington Model 51 or John M. Browning's 45 automatic, U. S. Model 1911. In the specific area of pocket automatic pistol design the alchemy and blending of these components have perennially eluded the first-line revolver manufacturing firm of Smith & Wesson. Their rare model 35 automatic is an example of what could have been both a revolutionary and successful pistol. Although this pistol gives evidence of ingenuity it was never accepted by the public. A failure in the market place 60 years ago, though, can still be a very interesting study for today. A detailed look into what made the revolutionary S&W 35 automatic a loser makes a fascinating study, and it may keep future designers from taking the same primrose path.

One of the fallacies so often perpetrated by a company's overzealous management is to assume that expertise in one branch of design leads to over-all knowledge in all branches. Since the American Civil War Smith & Wesson has made first class revolvers; in fact, during the post-war years, until 1869, they were the only U. S. manufacturers of rear-loading cartridge revolvers. This hammerhold on the revolver's development was theirs because they owned Rollin White's 1885 patent on a revolver with a cylinder bored straight through. Today, all cartridge revolvers still must have White's open rear cylinder for loading. The two titans of American handguns, Colt and S&W, were always in keen competition, each making a full line of excellent revolvers up to the opening of the 20th century. Then Colt, while continuing their revolver manufacture, began development and production of the then new fangled automatic pistol. Colt's management decided to produce John M. Browing's high powered, recoil-operated automatics. This choice proved to be a slow mover as a sales item, probably because of the American shooter's love of the large caliber, high powered revolver. The powers at S&W must have laughed at their main competitor's pioneering troubles. Colt's Models 1900, 1902, (Sporting and Military), and the 1903 pocket automatics, all in 38 ACP (Automatic Colt Pistol) caliber, piled up a rather unimpressive sales record. These early automatics in the 10 years between 1900 and 1910 had sold only a little over 32,000 pistols.

Colt must have asked their designing genius, John Browning, to come up with a different, more salable automatic as early as 1902, and he offered Colt his newly-designed pocket automatic of 1903 in 32 ACP. By the year 1910, sales of these little Colt pistols had reached over 100,000. Added to this impressive quantity were 5,000 similar automatics in the then new 380 ACP caliber, about three times the number of blowback automatics in a shorter period.

This amazing sale of a revolutionary design must have been viewed with envy by Smith & Wesson's top management. Sometime in 1909 they acquired the U. S. right to manufacture a pocket automatic pistol designed and owned by the Belgian firm of Charles Philibert Clement in Liege. Clement had made small automatics from 1903 and was a quality producer. The firm's metier was in what we would call the vest pocket automatic

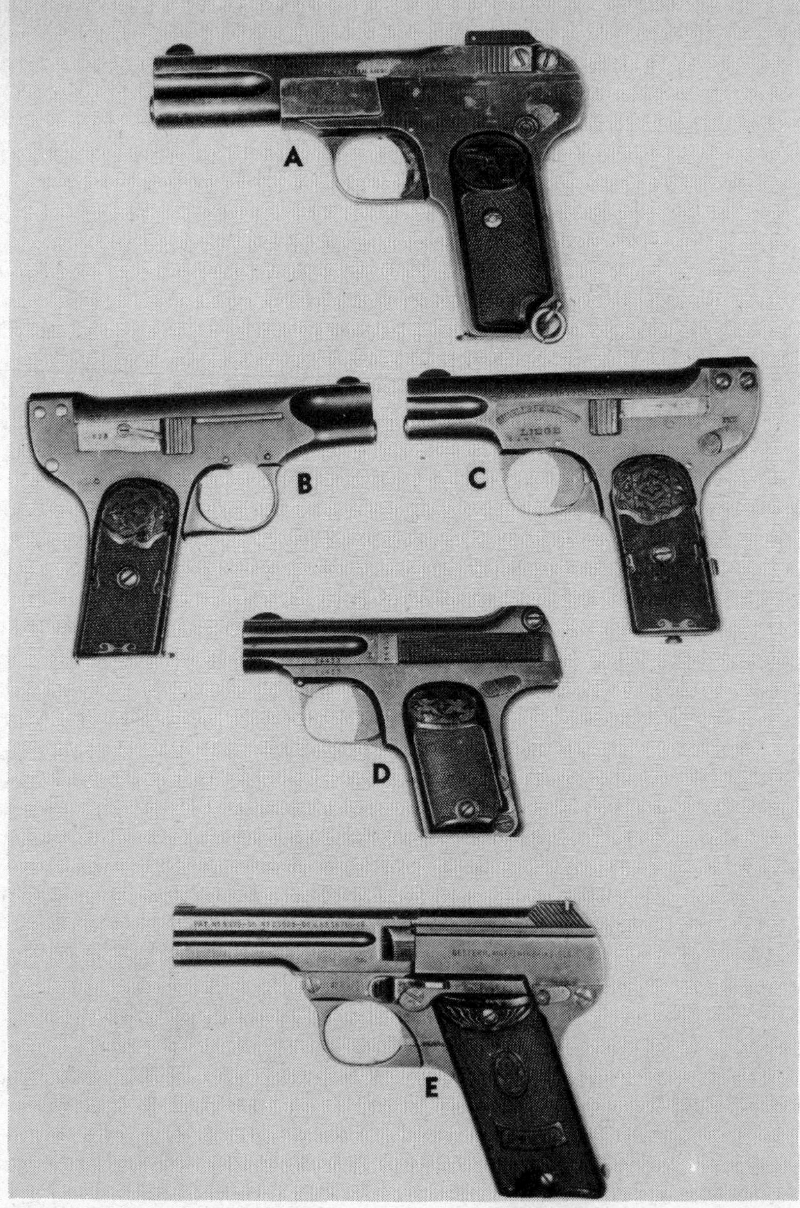

Lineage of the Model 35. **A**—Browning FN 7.65mm Model 1900, SN 5071. **B**—Very early Clement 5mm Model 1903, SN 975. **C**—Clement 5mm Model 1903, SN 9246. **D**—Clement 6.35mm Model 1909, SN 14453. **E**—Steyr 7.65mm Model 1909, SN 19368.

rather than in the larger, pocket automatics. The bulk of their production was in 5mm Clement and 6.35mm Browning (25 ACP), not in the 7.65mm Browning or 32 ACP. Smith & Wesson planned to use the larger version of the Clement, ignoring the smaller calibers.

At this point in our history we find that good revolver designers are not necessarily good self-loading (automatic) pistol designers. Smith & Wesson's R & D team was given a workable 6.35mm (25 ACP) 1909 Clement as a starter. In order to understand the later development of the S&W 35 pistol's design, it is helpful to follow the design of the Clement from its inception.

Clement Pistols

When John M. Browning introduced his first pocket automatic pistol in 1900 via the Belgian firm of Fabrique Nationale d'Armes de Guerre (FN), he started a whole new concept in automatic pistols. More than a million of Browning's Model 1900 in 32 ACP were sold in a very few years. Clement entered the automatic pistol field in 1903 with a 5mm baby pistol that looked like a small 1900 Browning. While the 1903 Clement never achieved anything like the Browning's popularity, it led Clement to design a line of well-made small automatic pistols in 5mm, 25 ACP and 32 ACP. The last type of Clement was the Model 1909, made from that year until the advent of World War I, which stopped the sales of such an unwarlike arm—its design was ingenious and, in some ways, unique. While all Clements owe a debt to Browning's 1900 pistol they never copied the Browning feature of having a slide that recoiled during firing. The Clement used a bolt only and, because they were made primarily for low pressure cartridges, they had no trouble with this design. Some of its features were:

1. A no-tool-releasing rear-pivoted barrel, which made cleaning easy.
2. A concealed hammer rather than a striker.
3. A no-tool-releasing back strap which allowed the entire firing mechanism to be cleaned. This unique feature has (to my knowledge) never been duplicated by any other maker.
4. A hammer-locking manual safety.
5. A side-button magazine release (like the Colt 1911 but located at the bottom rear of the grip).

All and all a very nice package, overlooking the low mass bolt. This was the package that Smith and Wesson's designers were given in 1909, and what they finally evolved 4 years later makes up the fascinating early history of the Smith & Wesson 35 automatic pistol.

Some misguided expert used the name "Model 1913" for the S&W 35. This is a completely non-factory, ambiguous, and redundant designation. There is only one Smith & Wesson 35 caliber automatic, and that is all the name necessary. The S&W automatic pistol which superseded the 35 is called correctly the Smith & Wesson 32 automatic pistol (not Model 1925).

The S&W 35 Cartridge

The revolver-oriented Smith & Wesson design team was horrified by the gilding metal jacket found on bullets for jam free use in self-loading arms. One of their first decisions was to design a new type of cartridge, one which would eliminate abrasive barrel wear in their new Clement pistol's redesign. The designers came up with a new concept called the half-mantled projectile—the new bullet had an exposed lead rear to engage the barrel's rifling but had a gilding metal front cap to facilitate feeding from the magazine. Thus the new Smith & Wesson automatic would have barrel life equivalent to that of an all-lead bullet shooting

Sketch A—see text for details

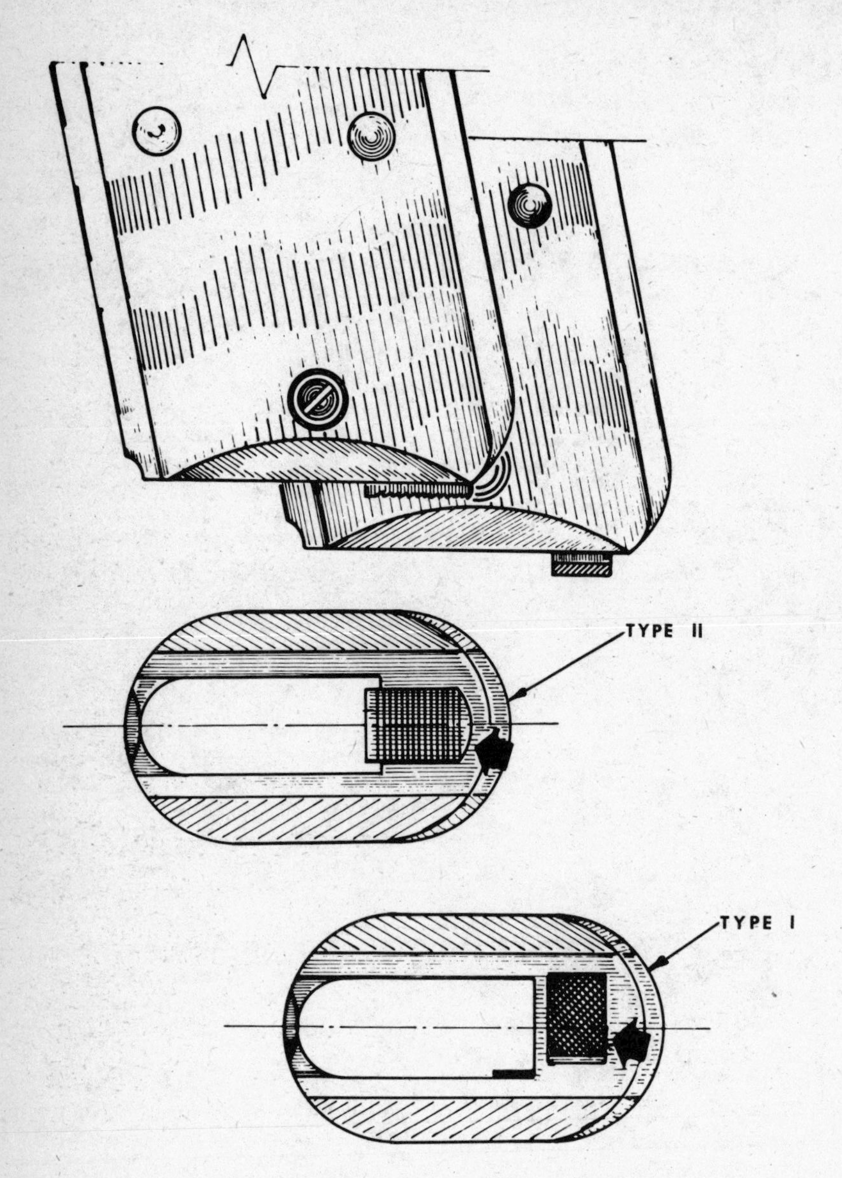

revolver. Up to this point, the "half-mantle" bullet was a good idea, albeit designed for a defensive type of pistol which would not usually fire more than a couple of hundred cartridges in its lifetime.

Next, two steps taken by Smith & Wesson nullified all the expected public acceptance of their new cartridge.

First, though very close to a 32 ACP in dimensions, they called it the 35 S&W, giving it an undeserved uniqueness which made the shooter fear that he might have a difficult time finding this special cartridge.

Second, because of the low mass bolt, the new S&W 35 cartridge had to be loaded to give even less breech pressure than the already impotent 32 ACP. The S&W round used a .320-inch diameter bullet weighing 76 grains, compared to the 32 ACP's .314-inch diameter and 73 grains. The S&W 35 developed a muzzle velocity of only 809 feet per second against the 32 ACP's 955, and the S&W 35 had a muzzle energy of only 110 foot pounds compared to the 32 ACP's 154. The ever-popular 45 ACP gives a muzzle velocity of only 855 feet per second yet developes a muzzle energy of 405 pounds—almost 4 times that of the ill-fated 35 Smith & Wesson.

The ammunition made by Remington, Winchester, and Peters was still offered by Stoeger in their 1938 catalog, but by 1939 they marked the 35 S&W ammunition as discontinued.

Good Features of the 35 S&W

What did the S&W 35 have going for it after 4 years of redesign?

1. The barrel can still be released without tools for cleaning. The pivot point of the barrel is ingeniously designed so that the screw which holds the barrel assembly to the frame takes no wear during rotation or operation of the pistol. The pistol could be fired with complete safety without the screw in place.
2. The bolt can be detached from the recoil spring to facilitate the loading of the first cartridge from the magazine to the barrel's chamber.
3. The bolt is completely trapped in the frame and barrel assembly so that under no circumstances can it be blown into the shooter's face. The bolt has no ribs or grooves to retain it to the frame. The whole bolt is trapped between the frame and the barrel.
4. As originally manufactured, the S&W 35 offered a very foolproof grip safety. Unlike most palm-operated grip safeties the S&W was deactivated by the natural placement of the second finger of the shooter's right hand. The finger motions, although unconscious, required that the safety be first pushed to the left and then depressed before a loaded pistol could be fired. Chances of an accidental discharge by an untrained person were effectively reduced by this type of safety.
5. The sights were mounted on a non-recoiling part, thus giving assurance to lifetime accuracy.
6. The bolt-mounted ejector does not protrude at the time when the bolt is picking up a cartridge from the magazine, avoiding jamming.
7. The grips were held in place by only one screw, but are secured on three sides by a dovetailed groove around the frame in the grip area. These grips are fancy walnut riveted to a steel mounting plate.
8. The S&W 35's hardened sear, uniquely pivoted from the hammer, has an engagement of over one-third of an inch, which is unusually long and makes for great positiveness.
9. The quality of the intricate machining has rarely been equalled in the world of firearms manufacture. The finish is superb as would be expected in a pre-World War II Smith & Wesson.

S&W 35 Variations

Considering the small number of S&W 35 pistols made, there is a wealth of variations. Serial number 1

Sketch B—see text for details

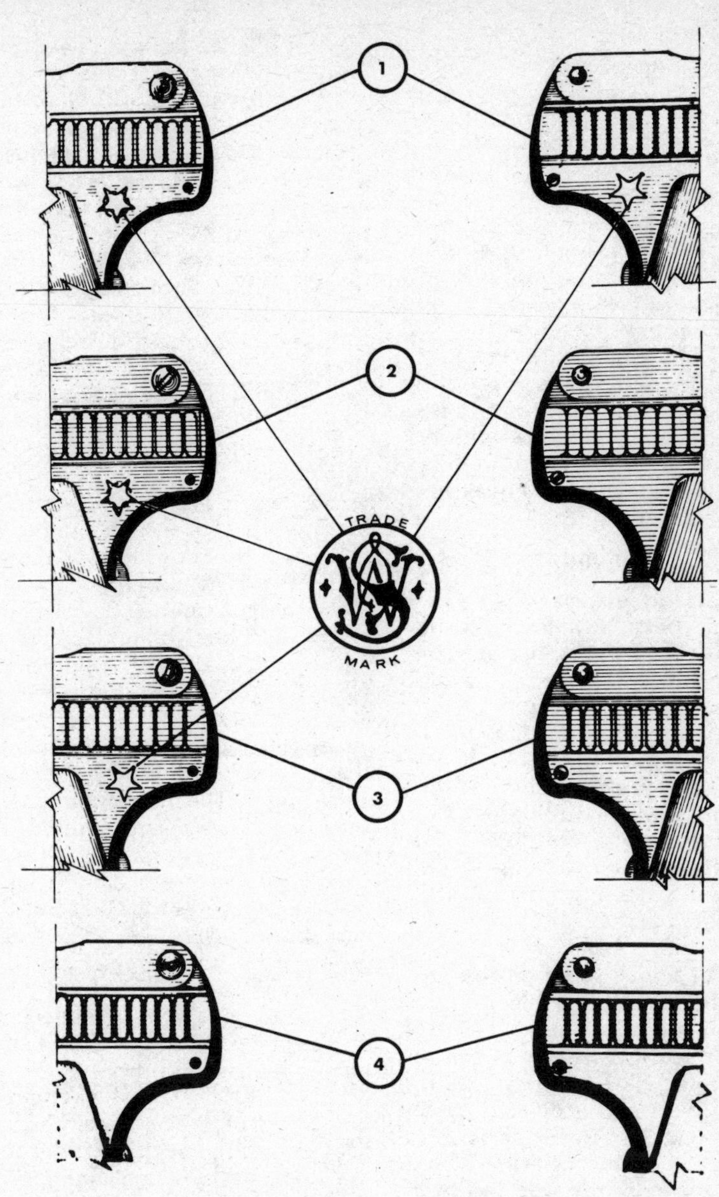

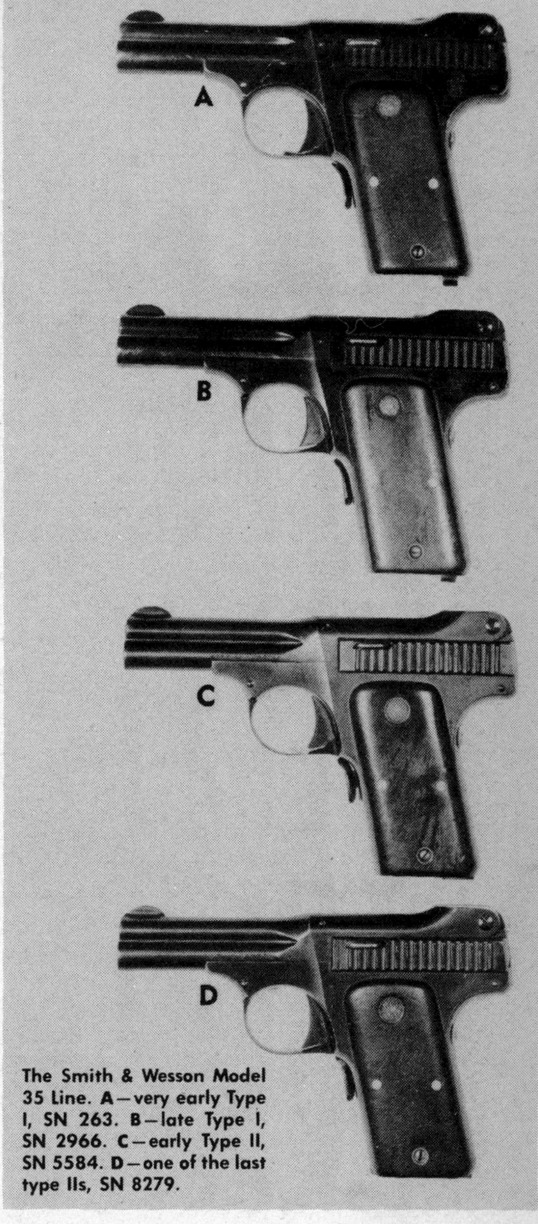

The Smith & Wesson Model 35 Line. A—very early Type I, SN 263. B—late Type I, SN 2966. C—early Type II, SN 5584. D—one of the last type IIs, SN 8279.

was shipped May 6, 1913; the last one, number 8350, was shipped Jan. 27, 1921, although S&W 35s were still sold by dealers in the mid 1920s. During the production period, there are over 30 known variations. The successful Colt 32 ACP Model of 1903 had only two minor variations by the time it reached serial number 8350. I have arranged the S&W 35 into two easily-recognized types. Type I has the early side-operating magazine latch, Type II has the more conventional rearward-moving latch (see Sketch A). Roy Jinks, Product Manager-Handguns (Historian) at S&W estimates that the change in magazine catches occurred around serial number 3125. There would therefore be about 3125 Type I pistols and 5225 of Type II. All the rest of the differences found have been called variations. I'll discuss each and give it a number which can be used as a reference to the Sketches. Many variations may have been incorporated into the same run of pistols, but unless all pistols were examined it would be impossible to state this as a fact.

The reasons for most of the changes in Smith & Wesson's 35 were caused by the light weight of the slide (bolt), or derived from field complaints and lack of public acceptance. (Part of the unacceptance stemmed from the special caliber but some came also from the price. In the 1920s a Colt 32/380 was $20.50, a Savage 32/380 was $19.00, a Remington 32/380 was $19.50, yet the Smith & Wesson 35 was a startling $35.00. Added to this was the cost of ammunition. The 32 ACP then cost $2.42 per 100 but the 35 S&W cost $2.74 per 100; not much in these days of inflation but a lot in the 1920s and 1930s.

Sketch B

The intertwined or monogram S&W logo located on the rear of the frame is the first variation encountered. As originally planned the emblem would have been on the right side of the pistol, because a safety lever was to have been on the opposite side. In fact, the frames had been pre-drilled for the safety, but it was never used in production. When, at the last minute, the unique palm manual safety was decided on, the hole for the normal

Clement safety was plugged and in order to conceal this plug, a second identical logo was stamped on the right side. This novel palm safety operated as follows:

With the hammer cocked the safety wheel was rolled upward with the right thumb. To deactivate this safety the palm of the shooter's hand could be rolled over the safety's wheel just as the pistol was being gripped for shooting. The safety also had a secondary function—it could only be applied when the arm was cocked, thereby serving as a cocking indicator.

These variation I pistols are rare with their characteristic double S&W logo. They run from serial number (SN) I through at least SN 297 and no further than SN 489. By SN 489, the logo on the right side was deleted, but the plugged hole on the left still was covered by the logo stamping. This type 2 variation lasted through SN 2029 and no further than SN 2966. Then the logo, though still being used on the left, no longer covers the plugged safety hole by SN 2966. The hole is no longer there. This fact is interesting because it shows that S&W made an initial run of 2000 to 3000 frames before the first pistol was ever sold. These non-plugged frames with the left side logo go at least as far as SN 6061 and no further than SN 7373, and are called variation 3. These are the most common of the frame stamping variation. The last variation starts by at least SN 7373 and terminates at SN 8350.

Sketch C—see text for details

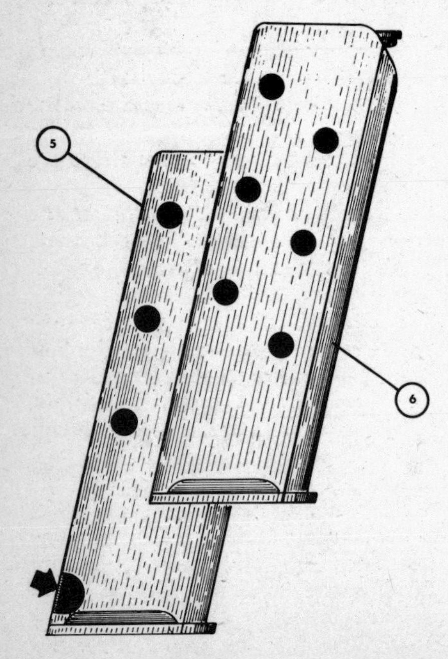

These variation number 4 pistols have no S&W logo on either side of the frame.

Sketch C

The next variation is directly related to the change from Type 1 to Type 2. With that change in the magazine catch, it was no longer necessary to have a locking hole in the wall of the magazine. Variation 5 magazines have the locking hole used in Type 1 pistols. These magazines are found in pistols numbered from 1 to 3125 and the non-locking hole magazines (variation 6), are found from SN 3125 to terminal SN 8350. It is well to note that a variation 5 magazine will work in both Type 1 and 2 pistols, but a variation 6 magazine can only be used in a Type 2 pistol.

Sketch D

The next three variations concern the finger safety. All of S&W's competitors—Colts, Remingtons, Harrington & Richardsons, and the Savages of 1915—have a grip safety. Each of these American pocket automatics used this simple, almost automatic, safety device. S&W elected to use a finger safety, which was moved by the second finger, and was located immediately below the trigger. This safety had to be first pushed to the left and then to the rear to deactivate the safety. This sequence of motions was unconscious to a right-handed shooter but look out if you were left handed. These double motion safeties are variation 7, and have been observed from SNs 1 through 2029 but no further than SN 2966. Probably due to complaints from left handers, the leftward unlocking was deleted. The old finger safety was used with the redundant rivet hold originally meant for the flat spring whose function was to resist left-hand motion. These interim safeties are variation 8 and have been seen mixed in with the variation 7 safeties. The lowest SN with an 8 safety seen is 1787 and the highest is SN 3845. The last finger safety is exactly like 8 except it has no rivet hole. These variation 9s started by at least SN 4128 and lasted until terminal SN 8350. One pistol in my collection, serial 1384, has had both the finger safety and its safety block removed by a professional or, more likely, the S&W factory.

Sketch E

The barrel assembly is one showing many changes, most of them readily visible externally. The barrel as-

Sketch D—see text for details

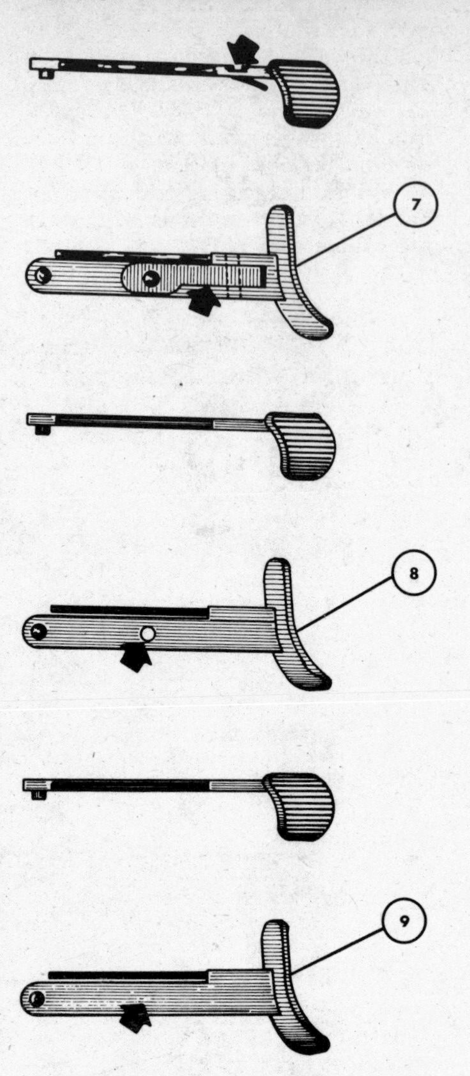

sembly is also interesting because it is the only part which need be moved for stripping a 35 S&W automatic. In order to field strip this pistol the magazine is removed and the chamber checked to make sure no round is in it. Now, the left forefinger is hooked over the muzzle while the left thumb is inserted through the trigger guard from left to right. Now grasp the frame in the right hand, moving the left thumb forward; this releases the trigger guard from the frame and allows the barrel assembly to be rotated upward and rearward. This is the full strip for cleaning, as it even allows the barrel to be cleaned from the chamber and to avoid wear on the important rifling at the muzzle.

The first series of barrel variations centers around the stampings on the barrel proper. Variation 10 has the words "35 S&W AUTO CTG" stamped on the right side of the barrel only. These pistols are found from SN 1 through at least SN 6061. Variation

11 has the words "SMITH & WESSON" on the right side and on the left the words "35 S&W AUTO CTG." This variant has been seen from SN 7373 to terminal SN 8350. One pistol is known which has a number beyond terminal (8358), and this pistol has no caliber designation stamp on the barrel. This is very unusual in that the caliber designation was stamped on the barrel while it was "in the white" and unpolished. I have a barrel bought when S&W was selling all the spare parts for the S&W 35 a few years back (see photo 4).

Variation 12 has to do with the position of the pin which holds the recoil-rod guide bushing in the barrel. In this variation the pin is below the axis of the recoil spring; such barrels have been seen from SN 1 to at least SN 3547. Variation 13 finds the pin moved up and slightly larger in diameter. The pin is now above the axis of the recoil spring. These high-pinned barrels have been seen from SN 3845 to terminal SN 8350.

The next series of variations has to do with the recoil-spring guide-rod's tunnel in the barrel. Variation 14 has a half-round tunnel with a top groove to key the rod, and has been seen from SN 1 through at least SN 4128. Variation 16 has a square milled cut to replace the half-round and requires no keyway. This type tunnel has been seen from SN 5133 to terminal SN 8350. Some of the variation 14 barrels were remachined to a square groove like number 16 but the non-functional keyway remained or offered the same cross sectional groove for either type guide rod. These variation 15 tunnels have been seen as low as SN 1384 (a factory reworked gun), and as high as SN 5584.

The rare nickel-blue Smith & Wesson Model 35s —from top, serial numbers 1787, 1897, 4128.

Sketch F

Variations in the slide or bolt of the S&W 35 were mostly traceable to increasing the weight of that part so as to reduce its velocity when recoiling. Variation 17 seems always to be found with variations 19 and 21, which can be described as follows:

Variation 17—has a half-round protuberance which follows the previously-discussed recoil-spring guide-rod groove in the barrel.

Variation 19—has a square bottom which rides directly in the frame.

Variation 21—the bolt release catch is narrow across the top of the bolt.

These variations have been seen on from SN 1 to at least SN 4128.

The second variations found on the bolt are:

Variation 18—no protuberance from the bolt's top surface.

Variation 20—the bottom of the bolt has small skirts, which hang down below the juncture of the bolt and the frame.

Variation 22—the bolt release catch is much larger across the bolt except in the area of engagement with the recoil-spring guide-rod assembly.

These late variations in the bolt have been seen from SN 5133 to terminal SN 8350 (again excepting SN 1384, which is of the late type). Also, at the bottom of Sketch F is the same bolt fitting into the same recess, but sized to the same weight that Smith & Wesson finally had to produce for their 32 automatic. One can readily

Sketch E—see text for details

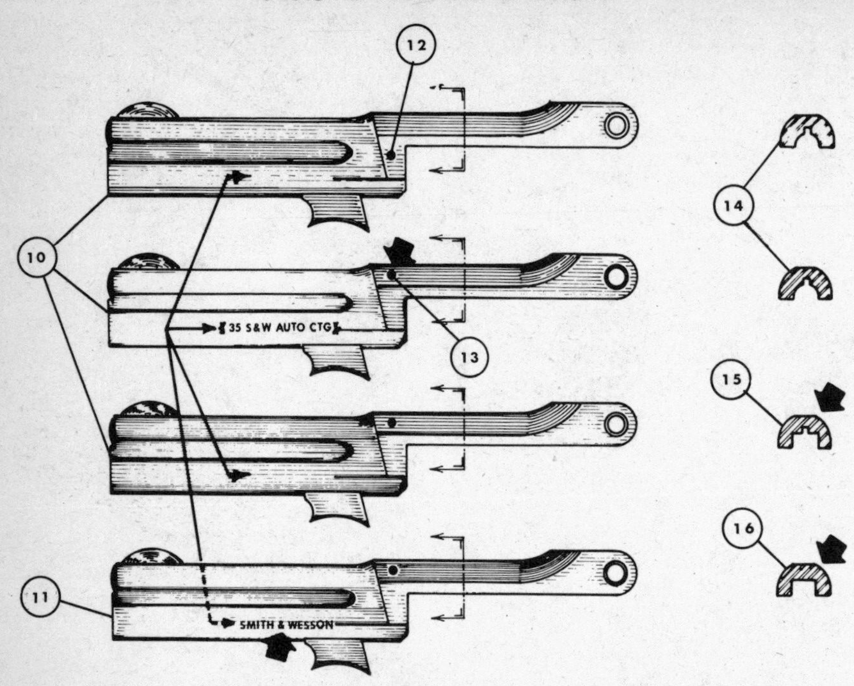

see how much metal would have had to be added to reduce the bolt's velocity and also what an awkward appearance this would have given the 35 Smith & Wesson. Little wonder they decided to completely redesign the S&W 32.

In a mistaken effort to reduce the rearward velocity of the low-mass bolt during recoil, a stronger recoil spring was used. The original spring was so stiff that no one with weak hands could pull the bolt to full recoil position without first depressing the bolt-release catch. These springs, called variation 23, used an average of 39 coils made from .044″ wire. They have been seen from SN 1 to at least SN 4128. Variation 24 used only a 31-coil spring but of .051″ diameter wire. These have been seen on SN 5133 to terminal SN 8350. These later springs made the action so stiff that no one could retract the bolt without using the release.

Sketch G

The recoil-spring guide rod had many modifications. The normal and most common rod (variation 25) had a front-mounted screwed-on nut, pinned to the rod through its smaller diameter. This meant that the entire assembly, including the rod's bushing, had to be driven out of the barrel to the rear for removal. This type of assembly has been seen from SN 1 through SN 297—a very small number. Superseding this came variation 27, which differs from 25 only in that the large-diameter section is deeper and now has the securing pin through it. This type has been seen from SN 1098 through at least SN 4128. Intermixed between variations 25 and 27 is variation 26, which has no securing pin or bushing. Its screw slot lets it be unscrewed from the muzzle of the pistol. These rare variation 26 nuts have been seen on pistols 110, 667 and 772. They may well have been the designer's original method of assembly, but because of the potential of the nut unscrewing during use were probably abandoned. They never appear on guns with SNs over 1000. Variation 28 is the final change in the recoil spring nut. The nut is by now a cylinder of only one diameter and is pinned, as were variations 25 and 27. This large nut type has been seen from SN 5133 to terminal SN 8350.

The next area of change in the recoil-spring guide assembly is in the presence of and pin location of the bushing. The early pistols, as noted under barrel assembly, had the bushing securing pin mounted low in the barrel. These (variation 29) have been observed from SN 1 to at least SN 3547. The next type of bushing has the securing-pin hole at the top, this form variation 31. These run from about SN 3845 to terminal SN 8350. Intermixed with the variation 29 bushing are those rare non-bushing specimens with screwdriver-slotted nut variation. These (variation 30) appear only on SNs 110, 667 and 772.

The last variation in the recoil-spring guide group is the shape of the rear end of the rod. If it is half-round with a spline on top, it is variation 32, and has been noted from SN 1 through at least SN 4128. The later

Sketch F—see text for details

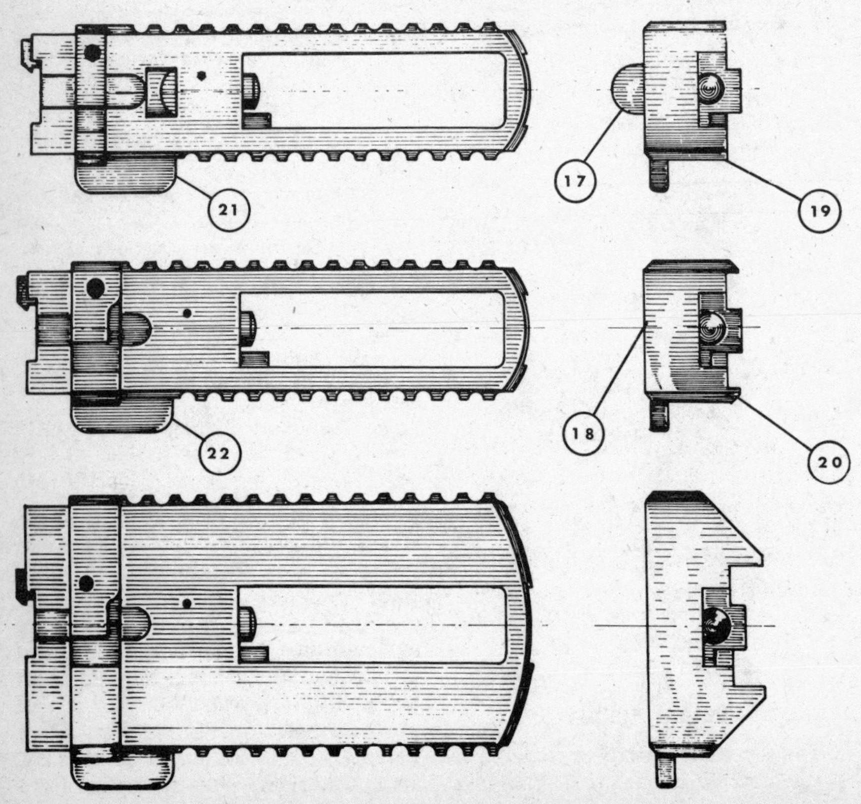

pistols had a rod with a square end only. This represents variation 33 and has been seen from SN 5133 to terminal SN 8350.

Sketch H

The hammer and sear assembly went through one change. Variation 34 has a notch cut on the flat of the left side of the hammer, the function of which was to act as a rest for the never-used manual safety discussed under Sketch B. Apparently many hammers had been machined before the palm type manual safety was decided on and, since this hammer with the notch would work just as well with the palm safety pistol, they were used for a while. These notched hammers (variation 34) have been seen from SN 1 to at least SN 3845, showing that many hammers appear to have been made before any pistols were sold. Variation 35, without the notch, starts at least by SN 4128 and goes to terminal SN 8350.

S&W 35 Numbering

Most American-made pocket automatics have only one frame-located serial number stamping, but the S&W 35 has 8 places where the serial is located! This proliferation of numbers has it more like a high class European pistol than an American one. The interest in these numbers to a collector is that the authenticity of a piece can easily be checked if all numbers match. The serial number on the frame (the legal number) is on the foregrip. The barrel number shows when it is swung into the open position. The slide (bolt) can be read by removing the barrel and turning the bolt bottom side up. Each grip assembly has the serial number on its backup plate, visible by removing the grip screws and sliding the grip assembly *down* and off the pistol. The trigger has the number on its lower-back rounded surface, while the trigger guard is stamped on the left flat at the pivot point. Finally, the hardened steel insert for sear engagement is stamped with the serial number.

There are two more numbers found on these S&Ws that can cause some confusion. When the back grip-insert was first fitted to the frame the pistol had not yet been serial numbered. In order that these two pieces could be mated for life they were each given the same match number, which is *not* the same as the serial number.

The match number on the frame is found on the right rear at the base of the barrel pivot point, and on the grip insert. It is on top and can be seen looking down on the frame with hammer forward and the barrel swung to the rear in the cleaning position. The match number is now visible through the clearance hole left by the hammer. It is not advisable for the amateur gunsmith to try to remove the grip insert from the frame.

Details of Clement and S&W 35s—from top, Clement 1909 open for cleaning, SN 14328. S&W 35 open for cleaning, SN 1384. Partially finished barrel for S&W Model 35 (all stamping is already present).

Patent History

The top of the barrel of each Smith & Wesson 35 carries this stamping:

Smith & Wesson Springfield Mass. USA
Pat'd September 15 1910 Dec. 13 1910
Feb. 28 1911, July 30 1912, Sept. 24 1912

The following section will deal in detail with each of these patents and explain their importance to the S&W 35.

The basic Clement patent assigned to Smith & Wesson was applied for in the U.S. on July 20, 1909 and issued on September 15, 1910 as patent number 970,307. Next, on November 19, 1909, Joseph H. Wesson applied for a

Sketch G—see text for details

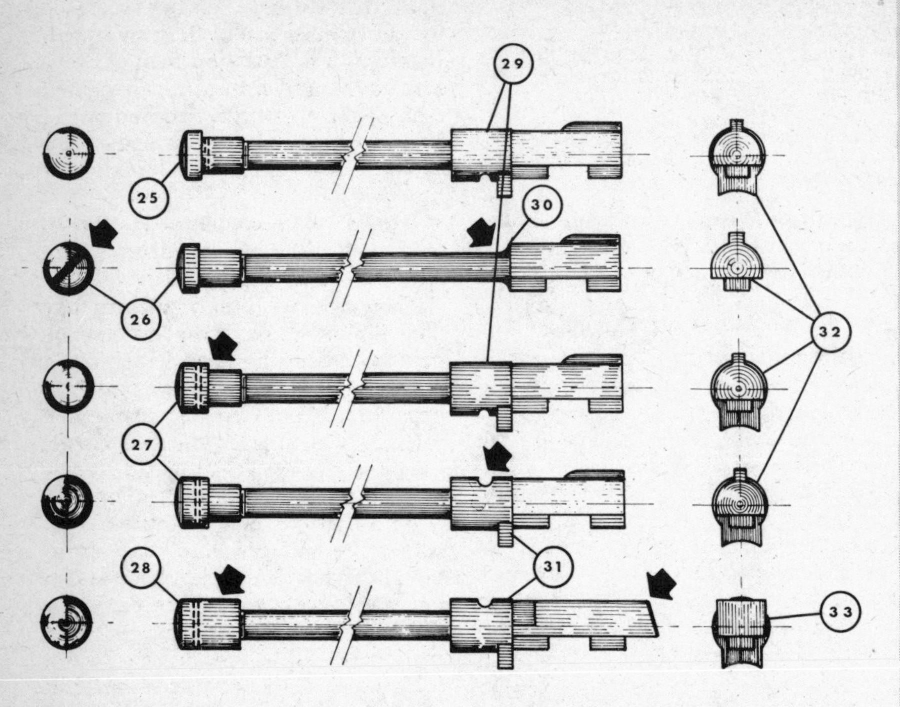

A Smith & Wesson Model 35 and others—from top, S&W Model 35, SN 263, S&W 32 ACP, SN 263 (a one in a million combination). A. Gavage 7.65mm Nazi-marked, SN 3440. S&W Model 61 Escort, 22 LR, SN B11145 (nickeled). Sterling Model P.P.L. 380 ACP, SN 003733.

patent on the finger safety in a much more complicated form than finally used. This patent was granted on December 13, 1910, number 978,415. On October 13, 1910, Joseph H. Wesson applied for a patent covering the hinged-to-hammer sear and its unusual disconnector; the patent was granted as number 985,482 on February 28, 1911.

In the Joseph H. Wesson patent number 1,033,971 granted July 30, 1912 (applied for in April of 1911), we find the first indication that S&W were having trouble with their lightweight bolt. This patent is on the recoil-spring release catch and, buried in the dry language of the patent, we find these prophetic words—"This (the catch) admits to the use of a much stronger spring (recoil) and improves the automatic action of the pistol." As noted earlier, the recoil spring was made so stiff—in the mistaken belief that the bolt's velocity could be so reduced—that cocking the arm without operating the release catch is impossible—even by a physical culturist.

The final patent date listed on the top of the pistol's barrel represents number 1,039,232, issued on September 24, 1912 and applied for in December of 1910. Also a Joseph Wesson patent, this concerns the improved ejector which is used in all 35s. This ejector is attached to the bolt, not the frame as is more usual. The ejector only protrudes from the breech face of the bolt when that part is in full recoil; this arrangement leaves no characteristic hole in the breech face to interfere with feeding.

Joseph H. Wesson also had applied for a patent in February of 1912. Number 1,041, 928, this was issued October 22, 1912. It again concerned the possible redesign of the 35 to give a heavier bolt. Again in patent number 1,181, 416 of May 2, 1916, applied for in November of 1914, Wesson had designed a much more conventional slide rather than a bolt. Here are his words from the patent admitting the mistakes made in the S&W 35:

"In automatic pistols as in said patent (1,033,971, the S&W 35) the reaction di(s) places backwardly only the breechblock (bolt). The weight of the breechblock by its inertia tends to steady the arm against the reaction of discharge. This steadying effect is sufficient in an arm of the usual small caliber and with a light projectile and small charge employed in the cartridge fired in such arms; but for a larger and heavier arm employing cartridges having heavier bullets and impelled by a larger charge, the reaction would not be adequately taken up by the weight of the breechblock alone unless this were made impracticably large and heavy."

Amen, Joe, Amen! After 5 years, from 1909 to 1914, the truth finally dawned. Only the superb workmanship and the large stop on the frame kept the S&W 35 from being a danger to the shooter.

To finish the patent history, Edward S. Pomeroy unveils the greatly improved Smith & Wesson 32 ACP automatic with patent number 1,382,317 of June 21, 1921, applied for in January of 1921. This has Joseph Wesson's full slide with a bolt which can be detached by the release catch as in the 35 for initial loading of the chamber. The 32 also had no awkward palm manual safety but did have a magazine safety preventing the firing of a chambered round if the magazine was

Model	Maker	Caliber	Bullet/Slide Weight
1903	Clement	5mm Clement	2.09 oz.
1909	Clement	6.35mm (25 ACP)	2.22 oz.
1909	Steyr	7.65mm (32 ACP)	2.61 oz.
35	S&W	35 S&W	2.79 oz. (bolt type 19)
35	S&W	35 S&W	3.35 oz. (bolt type 20)
N/A	Gavage	7.65mm (32 ACP)	3.45 oz.
PPL	Sterling Arms	380 ACP	5.41 oz.
32 ACP	S&W	32 ACP	8.00 oz. (normal slide design)
1900	Browning	7.65mm	9.11 oz. (where it all started)

removed from the gun. It also retained the finger safety.

There is a misleading statement in McHenry and Roper's excellent classic book* on Smith & Wesson's handguns. The authors say that many members of the Federal Bureau of Investigation carried Model 35s during World War I. The late Mr. J. Edgar Hoover said that this statement is misleading on two counts. One, before June 18, 1934, agents weren't authorized to make arrests or carry weapons. Two, the name of the organization during World War I was the Bureau of Investigation. It was not renamed the Federal Bureau of Investigation until July 1, 1935.

Conclusion

When the last pistol was shipped from the factory in January of 1921, Smith & Wesson closed the book on their ill-starred 35 automatic. One can understand their embarrassment with this mis-designed pistol but, though the S&W 35 was based on a misconception, it was not alone in that respect. Even more strange, it was not the last pistol to be designed under the same wrong ideas of light bolts backed by ultra heavy recoil springs. In 1971/72, the new firm of Sterling Arms Co. of Buffalo, N.Y., piggy backing off their successful 22 blow-back design, came out with their Model P.P.L. or 287 in 380 ACP caliber which, by all appearances, again plumps for light bolts in blow-back automatics. For whatever reasons, the pistol was quickly taken off the market, and apparently only a few were made. A letter to the firm questioning the design and the theory was never answered.

As recently as World War II, the Belgian firm of Armand Gavage produced another S&W type automatic in 32 ACP caliber. This one was used by the Nazis when they over-ran Belgium. The Austrian firm of Steyr also marketed a Belgian-designed auto pistol in 1909 which had one of the lightest bolts ever used in a 7.65mm (32 ACP) blow-back automatic pistol.

To give some comparative figures on this light bolt syndrome, the following table is presented:

However the design failure may have haunted Smith & Wesson, no firm need hide its head which could make such a beautiful piece of machining. The S&W 35 is made like a Swiss watch, with hardened steel parts wherever wear could by expected. These pistols were offered in three different metal finishes—the normal superb S&W blue, the conventional nickel (which is rare), and a combination of both, these having a nickel frame and barrel with all other parts blue. These last are very rare.

How much is a S&W 35 worth? Let me say, to preface my remarks on worth, that in our inflation-ridden era it is hard to put a fixed value on anything. Here are some recent (1973-75) prices seen in periodicals:

100% blue/nickel	$325
60% blue	$120
98% blue	$345
95% blue	$320
80% nickel*	$180
99% blue	$195

*may not be original nickel

One can see that there is a great deal of spread in these prices, and that condition makes a big difference. The collector can, by studying the variations mentioned here find small runs of rare features. As an example, take the variation shown in Sketch B, variation 1, the double logo stamped 35. These are rare-rare, but they bring little more today than a run of the mill variant. Tomorrow?

Smith & Wesson, with all their savvy and skill, couldn't make a perfect pistol, but it is or will be a great collectors' piece. ●

*Stackpole Co., Harrisburg, PA, 1958.

Sketch H—see text for details

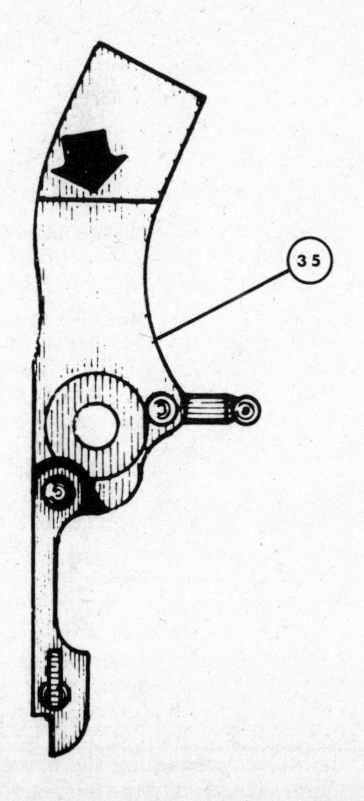

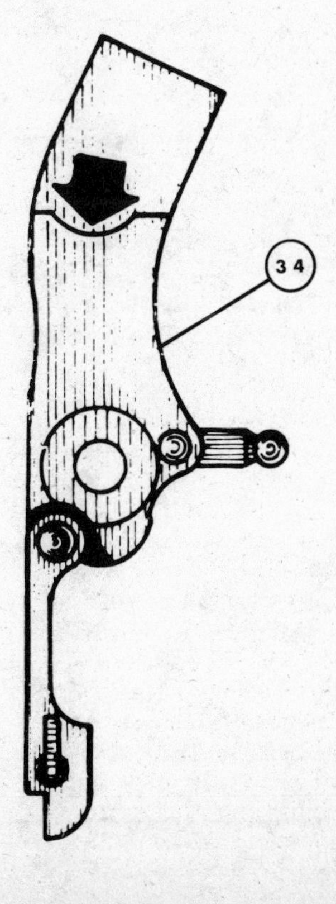

Acknowledgements

Fred H. Miller and Roy G. Jinks (Smith & Wesson). Sidney Aberman (special thanks). K. F. Hellyer, Frank Glaisner, James E. Keenan, David P. Sullivan, Bernardo L. Quinn, Patric L. Kunity, John Edgar Hoover, Wallace Grable, Thomas Kelleher, Ernest Lang, Robert L. Fernandes, Daniel Byrne, Richard Schaefer, Steve Matuch, Paul Hendel (photographer) and Mrs. Donald M. Simmons, Jr., editor and typist.

The Practical Light Sporter

A standard complaint about many of today's factory-built rifles among experienced big game hunters is that there is too much wood in the stocks, the barrels are too long and beefy and, in short, they're too damned heavy for mountain hunting. Here are the author's suggestions and solutions for some of the problems, his means of getting a light yet efficient rifle for the high places.

by JAMES R. OLT

The practical light sporter should be made in a caliber powerful enough for tough and heavy game. This 6-point elk was shot by Jim Olt with a 270 (handloaded with the 150-gr. Nosler bullet) in the Absarakas of Wyoming.

THE GENERAL TREND in the development of the modern sporting rifle has been toward more power. Magnum cartridges have appeared like spring flowers in a mountain meadow, but progress has come more slowly in the weight and handiness departments. The Model 70 Winchester or 721 Remington of 1950, in 270 or 30-06, weighed 9 to 10 lbs. with 4x scope, sling and cartridges.

The new M70 Winchester and 700 Remington weigh about 8¾ to 9½ lbs. with a 4x scope (probably with an alloy tube), sling and cartridges. An improvement, yes, but light as they could be without going off the deep end. A standard complaint about many of today's factory-built rifles among experienced big game hunters is that there is too much wood in the stocks, the barrels are too long and beefy and, in short, they're too damned heavy for mountain hunting.

The development of the lightweight rifle in this country has been curiously slow considering much of the best hunting country in North America is either in mountains or rugged foothills. For several decades our major firearms makers produced rather heavy bolt-action rifles. Twenty-four and even 26″ barrels were standard, and stocks were downright clubby. But heavy rifles were more stable and accurate, everybody knew that. Early custom jobs on Springfield and Enfield actions also ran to the hefty side. Then the widespread use of the scope after WW II added another pound.

However, certain gun writers, most notably Jack O'Connor, for years the stalwart Shooting Editor of *Outdoor Life,* continually ragged the major arms companies for lighter and handier big game rifles. O'Connor wrote often and enthusiastically of the joys of hunting with an 8-lb. 270. And it came to pass that large numbers of the shooting multitudes grew weary of staggering around under 10-lb. rifles.

Winchester saw the light and introduced the slick little M70 Featherweight with a 22" barrel in 1952. This was basically the standard 70 action lightened 3 ozs. by using an alloy trigger guard and magazine assembly, neither of which had traditionalists swooning with joy. The stock contained far more wood than it should have also. The advertised weight was 6¾ lbs., but I recently weighed a 70 Featherweight in 308 that ran closer to 7¼ lbs., bare and empty.

Gary Stafford glassing a slope in the Skeena Mountains of British Columbia. Backpack hunting in country like this is the best reason in the world for an 8-lbs.-complete rifle.

The 70 Featherweight Barrel

But, oh, the barrel on the 70 Featherweight! By eliminating all but a quarter-inch of the long and heavy shoulder and the rear sight boss on the standard 70 barrel; by shortening the barrel to 22" and tapering it to a trim .560" muzzle, Winchester came up with the sweetest barrel contour for a light sporter seen before or since. The 70 Featherweight, though not the Princess Petite of light rifles, was a step in the right direction, and it's been much mourned since it was discontinued in 1964.

At about this same time, the 1950s, some far out stuff was going on among custom gun builders. Barrels were chopped to 18½" and turned down to the contours of limp soda straws. Some found it necessary to leave nodes of metal to damp the wild vibrations. Toothpick stocks were whittled lighter and lighter until there was barely enough to hang onto. Lighter and lighter woods were experimented with; wild cherry was common, and I'm sure balsa wood was considered though I have no evidence it was actually used.

The results were 30-06 rifles, complete with scope and sling and fully loaded, weighing 6½ lbs. and less! Users of these ultra-light monstrosities were seen wobbling around rifle ranges glassy-eyed from recoil and temporarily deafened by the ferocious muzzle blast. Such fine cartridges as the 270 were ballistically emasculated by the too-short barrels, and the spindly tubes were highly sensitive to the slightest changes in bedding pressure. Many barrels would walk the group clear off the target as they heated up on the second and third shots. But they were light and handy all right.

Well, then how much should a light rifle weigh? When is a rifle needlessly heavy and when is it too light? The answer will depend much on what cartridge it is to be chambered for. Based on my own hunting for the mountain game of North America and the experiences of some other veteran hunters, I feel that the practical light rifle should be a bolt action for reliability, and weigh 8 lbs. when chambered for such all-round cartridges as the 270 Winchester, 280 Remington or 30-06—including scope and mounts, sling and cartridges. To get the most out of the flatter-shooting cartridges (usually loaded with slow-burning powders) the barrel should be 22", no shorter. Such rifles weighing much over 8 lbs. means you're carrying unnecessary steel and wood for hunting in rough country.

The 8-lb. Rifle

An 8-lb. 270 or 280 will have a bit of recoil, but it won't kill you. Matter of fact, an 8-lb. 270 with the 130-gr. bullet at 3140 fps produces 16.88 foot pounds of recoil. With its 22" barrel and a 4x scope mounted low it will slide beautifully in and out of a saddle scabbard. It will swing quickly in the alders and carry like a dream for hunting afoot in rough country. In a word—*handy.* A 7x57 Mauser might be scaled a half-pound lighter without objectionable recoil, but I wouldn't want a 7mm Magnum under 8½ lbs., and 9 lbs. would suit me better. I bruise easy.

But the 8-lbs.-complete goal means that the rifle—minus sight, sling and ammo—can't weigh much over 6½ lbs., 6¾ at most. This narrows the field considerably. At the present writing there is only one commonly available factory rifle I consider light enough for all-round use. It is the excellent little Ruger 77 in the standard calibers with a 22" barrel—and a lot of rifle for the money. For the mountain hunter who wants a factory-made light and handy rifle, this is it. I've weighed several Ruger 77s in 270 and 30-06 with 4x scopes, and all came close to the 8-lbs.-complete category.

The Ruger 77 action is a takeoff with minor modifications of the old reliable '98 Mauser. It utilizes the super reliable Mauser claw-type extractor. Bill Ruger enticed Lenard Brownell, the famed Wyarno, Wyoming stockmaker and gunbuilder, to come east and design the stocks for the 77 and No. 1 Single Shot rifles. The result is a classic-style stock that is handsomely shaped and nicely checkered with no excess wood to add unnecessary weight.

There are a few other factory-built rifles that almost qualify as lightweights. The Remington 700 and Savage 110 come close at 7 and 6¾ lbs. respectively. The medium action Sako Forester is cute and light but being chambered for such cartridges as the 243 and 308, it hardly qualifies for heavier game at long ranges.

But suppose you crave something extra? Maybe the 280 Remington or the 284 Winchester in a bolt action turn you on. Or maybe you yearn for a fine custom stock built to fit your long (or short) neck. Then, of course, a custom rifle is the only alternative.

But coming up with a truly light practical custom rifle is a good bit easier said than done. From my own experiences, I blush to confess, and from the experiences of hunting pals who fell into the same traps, many intended light custom rifles end up vastly heavier than hoped for. In other words, just ordering a custom rifle with a 22" barrel doesn't mean it will be light.

The Overweight Lightweight

Let's consider a hypothetical situation that the late Earle Stanley Gardner might have called, "The Case of the Overweight Lightweight." Friend Melvin has made a few bucks and intends to do some serious hunting in the future. He plans to go after elk in Wyoming and maybe Stone sheep in B.C., but old Mel isn't as lean and tough as he used to be. He has had his fill of deer hunting with a heavy rifle so he decides to get a real light sheep rifle built up. He found a good 2¾-lb. Springfield action and sent it off to be rebarreled in 30-06 with a 22" light sporter-contour tube weighing exactly 2¼ lbs. He then sent his 5-lb. barreled action to be custom stocked with a highly-figured piece of American walnut with Monte Carlo cheekpiece, rosewood fore-end tip and what have you. The stock weighed a bit over 2½ lbs. To the now over 7½ lb. rifle Melvin adds a popular 2-7x variable power scope in two-piece mounts that happen to weigh 18 ozs. together. Ol' Mel than hangs a 9-oz. 1" military sling to his already 8-lb., 10 oz. beauty. A magazine full of 180-gr. Core-Lokts adds another 5 ozs. Then poor Melvin puts the whole works on a scale and screams, "Damn! My little sheep rifle turned out to be a 9½-lb. clunker!" Get the picture?

The beginning of any custom rifle is the choice of the action, and here is where the lad who lusts after something light and handy has to be very careful. Because it is in selecting the right action and barrel that you're going to save real weight—perhaps a pound or more—that cannot be eliminated any other way. Certainly not by whittling down a stock a bit or by choosing one brand of scope over another.

For anyone wanting a practical light sporter built up I suggest he get a copy of *Bolt Action Rifles*, by Frank de Haas and published by Digest Books, Inc. Mr. de Haas lists weights and specifications of all bolt actions, military and commercial, as well as masterfully pointing out good, bad and indifferent features of design. It is a must for every serious rifle nut's reference library.

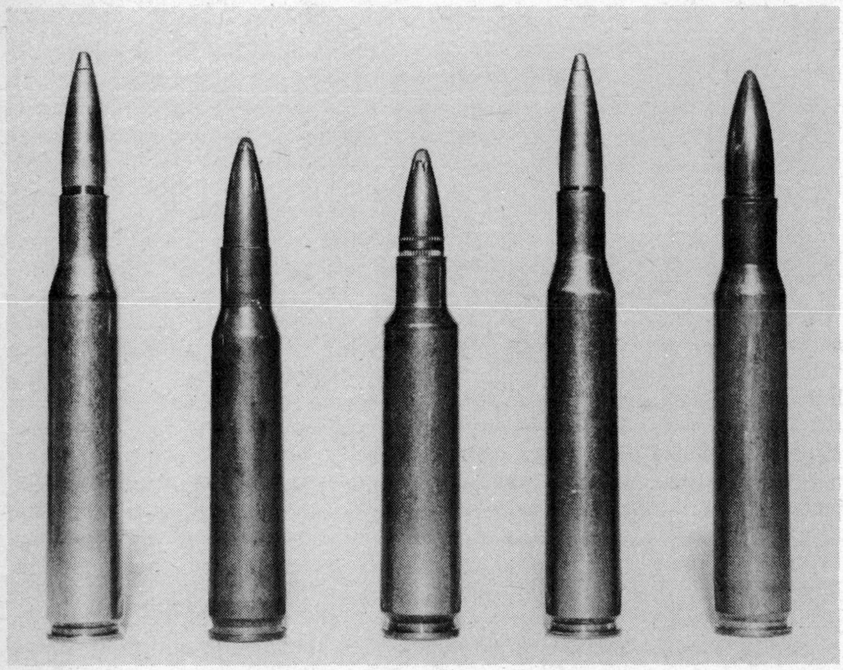

Good cartridges for the light mountain rifle. From left—270 Winchester, 7x57 Mauser, 284 Winchester, 280 Remington and 30-06 Springfield.

Choosing the Right Action

Certain actions are absolutely unsuitable for a lightweight rifle. The Enfield, for example, weighs 58 ozs., and there is no way to get it appreciably lighter. The fine Champlin action weights 52 ozs. The Weatherby Mark V and Texas Ranger Magnum actions are also heavyweights. These actions are excellent for big bore magnum cartridges, and in rifles of heavy recoil where 10 lbs. feels good, but they're too much steel for a light 270.

The pre-64 M70 Winchester has been used as the basis for some of the finest custom rifles ever gazed upon by mortal man. The action has some fine points; an excellent adjustable trigger, the Mauser-type claw extractor and a bolt handle that is the most beautifully shaped of anything seen yet. Alas, the M70 is not a particularly good choice for a lightweight rifle. It weighs 48 ozs. with a steel trigger guard and magazine.

The FN Mauser and Model 98 large-ring Mauser actions weigh 44 ozs., though it is possible to get a fairly lightweight rifle with an action this heavy. The Remington 700 long, though a shade heavy at 43 ozs., will also do. The excellent Sako L-61 Finnbear and the Springfield are both 44-oz. actions also.

My choice of all available bolt actions, commercial and military, for a

A head-on closeup of the two receiver rings—the G33/40 small ring Mauser at left, the F.N. large ring Mauser at right. SR Mausers are from 2 to 4 ounces lighter than F.N. or LR '98 Mauser actions.

practical light rifle is the small-ring (SR) Mauser—of which there are several versions. I recently weighed a '98 Erfurt SR action on an accurate postal scale—exactly 42 ozs. Not bad. But for my money the most desirable SR Mauser action of all is the G33/40, built by the Czechs for German ski troops and paratroops. All I've weighed go exactly 40 ozs. G33/40s are getting quite hard to find, I might add, and for good reason. Basically a very smooth SR '98 Mauser, it was further lightened by milling lightening cuts along the rails. Also, part of the forward receiver ring is milled away. The trigger guard, not so clumsy-looking as the standard '98 guard, can be so shaped and thinned as to be actually beautiful.

Among commercial rifle actions the older version of the Husqvarna is basically a SR Mauser; made from excellent Swedish steel. Weighing 40 ozs., it's an excellent choice for a light custom rifle. Being slightly conservative in my taste in rifles I can't work up much enthusiasm for the later HVA M-8000 action, but it is a 40-oz. action. Another good light action is the BSA and, of course, there wouldn't be a thing wrong with a custom job on the 42-oz. Ruger 77 long action.

You pays your money and you takes your pick. My first preference is the G33/40 SR '98 Mauser, my second the old style Husqvarna action, my third choice might be an FN Mauser, but I'd certainly pray for a light piece of wood. Somebody else may be hipped on the 700 Remington short action for a light custom 284 Winchester, or maybe you can't live without a pre-64 M70. Good luck, but will an 8¾-lb. rifle do?

Lightening Touches

Not much can be done to lighten an action—a common practice is to drill out the magazine walls with a series of holes, but that doesn't save much actual weight. Some gunsmiths hollow out the bolt knob, drill a few holes in the action rails and follower. But that's about all you can do short of an extensive milling project to cut down the outside dimensions of the receiver. Better to choose a light action at the start. Certain triggers are needlessly heavy, weighing 3-4 ozs., but an excellent adjustable trigger such as the Timney Sportsman weighs only 1½ ozs. Anodized aluminum alloy trigger guards are available for a number of actions, too, but on weighing one such for the FN/'98 Mausers it went exactly 1 oz. less than the excellent all-steel FN hinged floorplate guard. I much prefer a steel guard over an alloy job.

A 24″ barrel weighs at least 4 ozs. more than a 22″ barrel with a similar contour. With the 7x57, 270, 280 and 30-06 a 24″ barrel is unnecessary. All these cartridges perform right up to the full potential of their case capacity in a 22″ barrel, but going to a 20″ tube is a mistake; you'll lose 100-150 fps muzzle velocity and greatly increase muzzle blast. On the other hand the 264 and 7mm Magnums definitely need 24″ barrels to come close to their advertised muzzle velocities. A 7mm Magnum out of a 22″ barrel is actually doing no more than a handloaded 270 or 280, and the muzzle blast will burn the ears off a brass monkey.

I said before that the barrel contour on the M70 Featherweight rifle is the best I've seen for a practical lightweight rifle. Such tubes, exactly as described, are made by the G.R. Douglas Barrel Co. Such barrels may sound light and whippy, but in fact there is more beef and stiffness than you might think. I've owned several Douglas Featherweights and have seen many others shoot, and they are accurate and stable. Most put 3 shots consistently under an inch with the proper bullet and load. What more can you ask from a purely hunting rifle?

Other custom barrel makers don't catalog a barrel as light as the Douglas Featherweight at this writing. Apex Barrel's "00" 22″ barrel weighs 38 ozs. Shilen's No. 1 barrel, 20″ long, weighs 40 ozs. His 22″ barrel, the No. 2, goes 44 ozs. It might be possible to get a special contour or have a gunsmith turn another brand or a factory barrel to the M70 Featherweight contour, but I'll take the Douglas Featherweight—I know what they'll do.

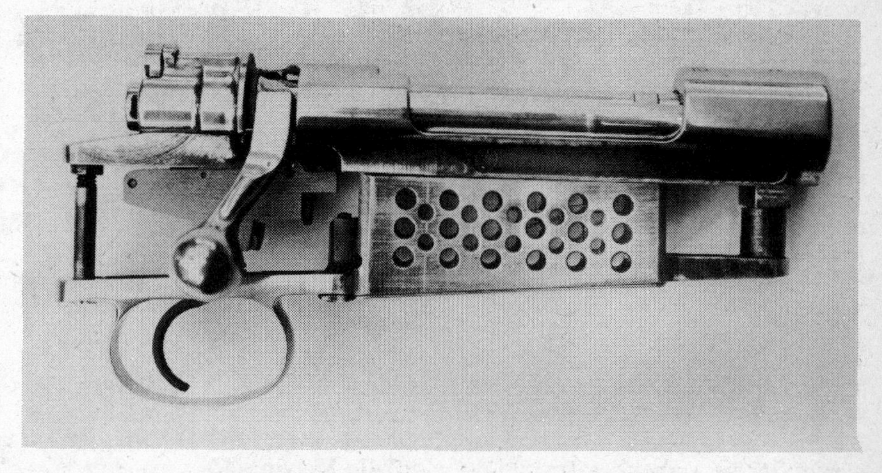

Probably the finest action available for a practical lightweight sporter is the G33/40 small ring Mauser. Note holes drilled in magazine to save additional weight.

Routing the fore-end, as illustrated, and drilling a series of ⅞ to 1" holes in the butt will shave 4 ounces from the average sporter stock.

muzzle velocity it is hot on the heels of the 7mm Magnums, but with considerably less recoil and muzzle blast. It has killing power and penetration aplenty for such heavy game as elk, moose and caribou, and it shoots flat enough for the longest shots at antelope. Ammo for the 270 is available in little out-of-the-way places all over North America in good 130-gr. factory loadings from at least half a dozen loading companies. Such is not the case, unfortunately, with the 280 Remington.

My No. 1 light 270 with the 22" Douglas barrel chronographs the 130-gr. Nosler and 62.0 grains of 4831 at 3219 fps muzzle velocity. Mildly loaded with the 130-gr. Speer and 60.0 grains of 4831, it chronographs at 3141 fps. This is my mule deer and antelope load. My heavy game 270 load is the 150-gr. Nosler and 58.0/H4831 for 3021 fps by actual chronograph test. By comparison my custom 7mm Remington Magnum with a 24" Apex barrel gives the 160-gr. Nosler, the 68.0/4831, some 3104 fps. If there is an appreciable difference in killing power and trajectory between the handloaded 270 and the 7mm Magnum I cannot tell it.

With a suitable light action and 22" featherweight barrel it is quite possible to have a barreled action weighing no more than 4½ lbs. The battle for a practical light rifle is half over, but you can still blow the project in the choice of the stock. Preferences in stock design, like women and automobiles, are purely a personal thing. My own taste runs to the classic style

Selecting the Cartridge

There are a bevy of fine cartridges suitable for the practical light mountain (or plains) rifle. The ancient but still excellent 7x57 Mauser, the old reliable 270 Winchester, the neglected 280 Remington and the versatile 30-06 are all good choices. The 284 Winchester might also be a possibility for a medium-length action, say the 700 Remington short. For game no heavier than mule deer the 243 Winchester, 6mm Remington and the versatile 257 Roberts are all excellent killers and flat shooting. Also, a 6mm or a 25 caliber can be built on a medium-length action for an ultra-light rifle that won't kick you out from under your hair.

The flat-shooting 25-06 and the excellent wildcat 6.5-06 need, unfortunately, a 24" barrel to get the velocity they're capable of producing. In my book this rules them out for a light and handy mountain rifle. The same holds true for the 264 Winchester, 7mm Remington and Weatherby Magnums. Also, these 7mm Magnums, while otherwise pet cartridges of mine, give a rather grim dose of recoil in a 8-lbs.-complete rifle.

I would personally prefer a 280 Remington over the little 7x57 for the simple reason that the 280 can produce about 200 fps more velocity, with bullets of the same weight, than the 7x57. The 280 is quite impressive handloaded with 160-gr. bullets and Norma 205 powder, and Hodgdon 4831 is also quite good. There is very little difference between the 280 handloaded and the factory 7mm Remington Magnum, and virtually no difference in muzzle velocity when both cartridges are chronographed from a 22" barrel. (It's been rumored that Remington might breath some new life into the otherwise dying 280 by bringing it out as the 7mm/06, loaded up to 54,000 psi pressure levels.) I'd also choose the 270 or the 280 over the 30-06 for a light mountain rifle because of flatter trajectory, a bit more punch at long range and less recoil.

But my favorite lightweight rifle cartridge is the 270. Handloaded with a good 150-gr. bullet at 3000 fps

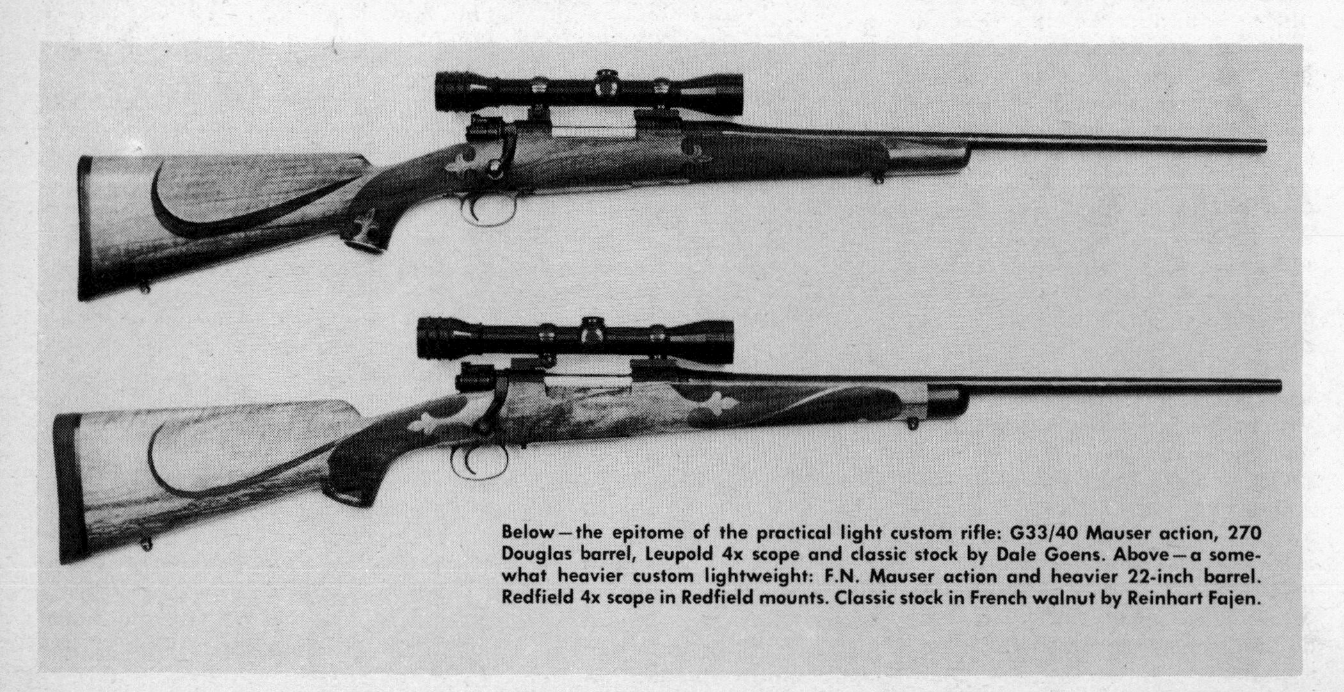

Below—the epitome of the practical light custom rifle: G33/40 Mauser action, 270 Douglas barrel, Leupold 4x scope and classic stock by Dale Goens. Above—a somewhat heavier custom lightweight: F.N. Mauser action and heavier 22-inch barrel. Redfield 4x scope in Redfield mounts. Classic stock in French walnut by Reinhart Fajen.

stock. Rollover cheekpieces, flaring fore-ends, rosewood grip caps and fore-end tips and flashy electric guitar finishes bring on acute attacks of nausea and, frankly, give me the creeps. But if this is what you need to be happy...

However, there is a good reason for choosing a classic stock on a lightweight rifle, even though it may appear rather mousey to lovers of the flamboyant. Stocks with "California Space Age" styling contain much excess wood in their humpbacked Monte Carlo combs, flared fore-ends and drooping pistol grips. Such creations are heavy, often weighing 3 lbs. or more with the fittings and, to my eyes, ugly enough to frighten a crocodile.

The Classic Stock

The classic stock, I am convinced, can be the lightest of all the various sporter stock designs. By eliminating the Monte Carlo and the rest of the unneeded lumber, a classic stock can be built to weigh only 2-2¼ lbs. with the fittings, and not feel spindly. By fittings I mean a rifle butt pad or checkered steel buttplate—take your pick, the weight is about the same—a checkered steel grip cap, ebony fore-end tip and quick detachable swivel studs.

French walnut, my favorite of all stock woods, weighs on the average about 2 lbs. less per cubic foot than American walnut. Consequently a stock in French walnut usually comes out weighing a few ounces less than the same stock in American walnut. I could go on and on about its elegant beauty; how it is stronger and harder than most other woods, hence it holds fine checkering better and takes a finish better without soaking up oil and turning black. All this is fact, but another sad fact is that French walnut is getting more expensive by the month, and the really choice stuff is becoming extremely difficult to find, no matter how much dough you can spend.

There are other good woods for a light stock. The best American walnut is quite good, but I recommend the straight-grain grades. Highly figured American walnut can weigh like lead. Myrtle, about the same weight as French walnut, can make excellent light stocks. Wild cherry, quite light and stable, lacks figure or distinctive coloration. Maple and Mesquite are always too heavy for use on a light rifle. Whatever wood is used, pick straight grain wood for a light stock—the stump figure and feather crotch bring extra and unwanted weight.

The stocks on many factory rifles, and also some so-called custom stocks, can only be described as "clubby". This can be caused by poor basic design, but more often it is due to a certain thickness throughout the stock. The grip is too thick, the fore-end is too long with too much wood, etc., and the stock just doesn't have that good feel. My favorite light rifle, stocked by the incomparable Dale Goens, has a pistol grip only 4½" in diameter. The fore-end is only 1½" wide at the center of the checkering pattern, and only extends 10¼" past the receiver ring. This may sound too thin, but though I have large hands and long fingers I can assure you the stock isn't too skinny. It feels better than any rifle I have handled thus far. Keeping the outside stock dimensions pared down can save a good bit of weight on the finished rifle.

About 4 ozs. can be removed from the typical sporter stock by drilling a series of deep ⅞" to 1" holes in the buttstock, and by routing out the fore-end. This is all out of sight, of course. A few more ounces could be saved by eliminating the cheekpiece, as on the Ruger 77 stock, but I'm unwilling to give up the feel and looks of a nicely-shaped cheekpiece. It may seem silly to worry about 4 ozs., but in the words of the candy bar makers, friend, this is a big quarter-pound. Again, practical light rifles don't just happen. Saving a few ounces here and there soon becomes a pound or more on the finished product.

Scopes and Mounts

After much planning and forethought, we now have a slim, trim little rifle that, we hope, weighs no more than 6½ lbs. without sights. More ounces can be saved or added by the choice of scope and mounts. Most 2-7x variable power scopes weigh 11-13 ozs. depending on the brand, while the popular 4x scopes average 9-10 ozs. I find a straight 4x scope with a medium crosswire reticle excellent for all-round use, and I confess that the 2-7x variable power scopes on some of my hunting rifles are usually set on 4 power. I do remember in British Columbia turning down to 2x for hunting grizzlies along small, twisting salmon streams, and I also vividly recall turning the power selector ring up to 7x to knock off a big bull Osborne caribou at 400 yards in a windswept basin high above timber-line. But I must also admit that I could have done the job quite as well with a straight 4x scope—as my hunting partner did.

For light weight and reliability under all conditions the 4x scope is impossible to beat, and it is what I use on my light mountain rifles. For comparison here are the weights of some popular 4x scopes: Leupold M8 9 ozs., Weaver K4 9½ ozs., Redfield Widefield 10 ozs., Bausch & Lomb Balfor 11 ozs., Bushnell Scopechief 10½ ozs., Lyman All American 10 ozs., Realist 9 ozs., Unertl Hawk 10½ ozs. and the Weatherby Imperial 10¼ ozs. I happen to prefer the Leupold M8 4x of all the now-available 4x scopes. It is as light as the lightest, exceptionally reliable and moisture-proof, and the optics are absolutely superb.

I strongly recommend 2-piece scope mounts over the one-piece type. The base alone for the Buehler or Redfield bridge mounts weighs 4 ozs. Two-piece mounts such as the Redfield SR weigh 5¼ ozs., Leupold M3, 4¼ ozs., Conetrol 5½ ozs., and Weaver detachable top mounts 4 ozs. Bridge mounts complete go 7 ozs. and more.

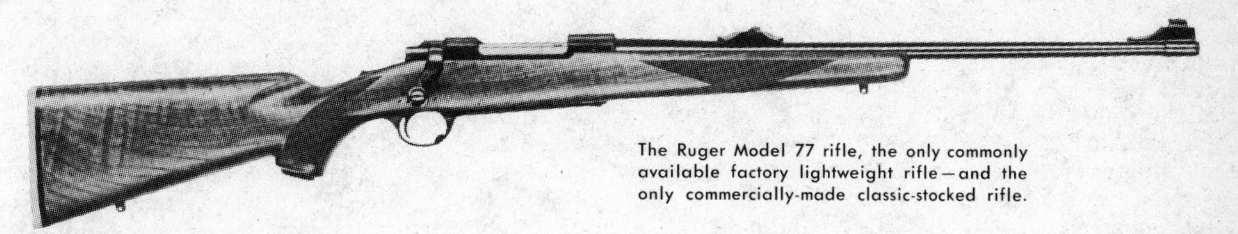

The Ruger Model 77 rifle, the only commonly available factory lightweight rifle—and the only commercially-made classic-stocked rifle.

The author with trophy double-shovel Osborne caribou. Hunting high country game like this can mean long hikes afoot. The ideal rifle is light yet powerful enough for the heavy stuff.

But no matter how you slice it, one of the lighter 4x scope and mount combinations is going to weigh about 14 ozs. So our darling little 6½ lb. rifle is now up to 7 lbs., 6 ozs. with sight. Such cartridges as the 270 or 30-06 with 150-gr. bullets weigh about an ounce apiece, so add 5 more ounces for a magazine full of elk killers, and that brings Little Betsy up to 7 lbs. 11 oz.

I weighed several of the 1″ military type slings so commonly used these days, and they averaged a rather shocking 9 ozs. That seems incredible —a sling weighing over half a pound! By comparison, a Hunter ⅞″ Whelen sling with QD swivels weighs only 5 oz. Need I say more? I much prefer the one-piece Whelen sling over the rather cumbersome military rig anyway. Once you get the loop of the Whelen sling adjusted for your build and tie it permanently with the leather lacing, it is quick and foolproof to get into for the sitting position or prone shooting.

My Dale Goens Special

So there it is, a rifle that weighs 8-lbs.-complete with 4x scope, ⅞″ Whelen sling and a full magazine. It is a delight to carry afoot in the roughest country, yet still has enough weight so as not to bend the bridgework when chambered for a cartridge of sufficient power and penetration for game of the 600-1200 lb. range. The 22″ barrel is quick and handy, yet not so short as to ruin ballistically a fine cartridge. The stock can be trim and handsome without feeling the slightest bit spindly.

My favorite light mountain rifle followed this pattern exactly. After a good bit of searching I found a smooth G33/40 Mauser action. With a Timney trigger it weighed exactly 2½ lbs. after it had been slicked up and the magazine swiss cheesed. I sent the action to Dale Goens, who fitted the 2-lb. Douglas Featherweight 22″ barrel chambered for the 270 Winchester, polished the action, engine turned the bolt, checkered the knob and gave the whole works a noglare satin finish blue job.

In my humble opinion, Dale Goens is as fine a custom stockmaker as anyone who has ever practiced the art. To say he is an artist in wood has been said, and it is an understatement. He stocked my light 270 barreled action with a beautiful, hard and light piece of French walnut. He kept the stock as slim and trim as a pretty maiden's ankle, and saved more precious weight by drilling the buttstock and routing out the fore-end. His oil-type finish is as smooth as a baby's cheek, the fleur-de-lis 24-line checkering with a ribbon is flawless. I'm sorry to say the photographs don't do justice to this superb piece of work —the stock has to be seen to be appreciated.

Handsome is as handsome does. With a 4x Leupold scope, the rifle fully loaded and slung, she weighs right on 8 lbs. This beautiful little mountain rifle shoots both the 130-gr. and 150-gr. Nosler bullets well under an inch for 3 shots. The 130-gr. Speer also shoots under an inch, and to the same point of impact as the Noslers. After several extreme changes of temperature and humidity there has been absolutely no discernible change in the point of impact. It is truly a practical light sporter. ●

Profile of an Engraver

ROBERT D. SWARTLEY

BECAUSE OF OUR relationship – I'm Bob's brother – I suppose I *am* prejudiced in his favor, but for all that it is nonetheless quite true that connoiseurs of gun engraving consider Robert Swartley one of the best firearm engravers on the American scene.

The story of Swartley's progress in engraving is, I think, about like that of other American gun engravers. There is no set procedure for becoming an accomplished master in this demanding art. There are no official schools for gun engravers, no standard textbooks, no formulated knowledge to learn, and no exams, the passing of which designates you to be a professional. You have to do it mostly on your own, with long, diligent practice, plus a true and dedicated love of the art itself.

Bob started his gun engraving apprenticeship early. By the time he had reached his teens he had already found two enduring passions – guns and art. Roaming the hills and valleys of California's Napa County, a 22 rifle in hand, he hunted a variety of small game. At the same time, however, his eye for the artistic often took over – he felt a particular satisfaction in viewing and sketching the natural character found in a gnarled old oak tree, for instance. As time went on he came to appreciate more and more the wild beauty of the game he hunted. He soon became accomplished at sketching, with nature's creatures his chief subjects.

During this period, Bob took up wood carving as well – with wood, he's said, he could feel the substance respond to his efforts, to grow in his hands, to take on the character he'd moulded into the wood.

By the time he'd graduated from high school, Bob had things pretty well figured out. If he was going to make a living at either of the two things he liked best, it would probably have to be firearms – wood carvers were, and still are, in low demand. That was why he enrolled in the gunsmithing school at the Colorado School of Trades in Denver. Working as a gunsmith would make a living, so he'd have the best of both worlds!

The Turning Point

But Swartley still had that eye for art. A short time after arriving at the gunsmithing school he happened across a magazine illustrating the work of the great Austrian-born gun engraver, Rudolph J. Kornbrath. That event proved to be the major turning

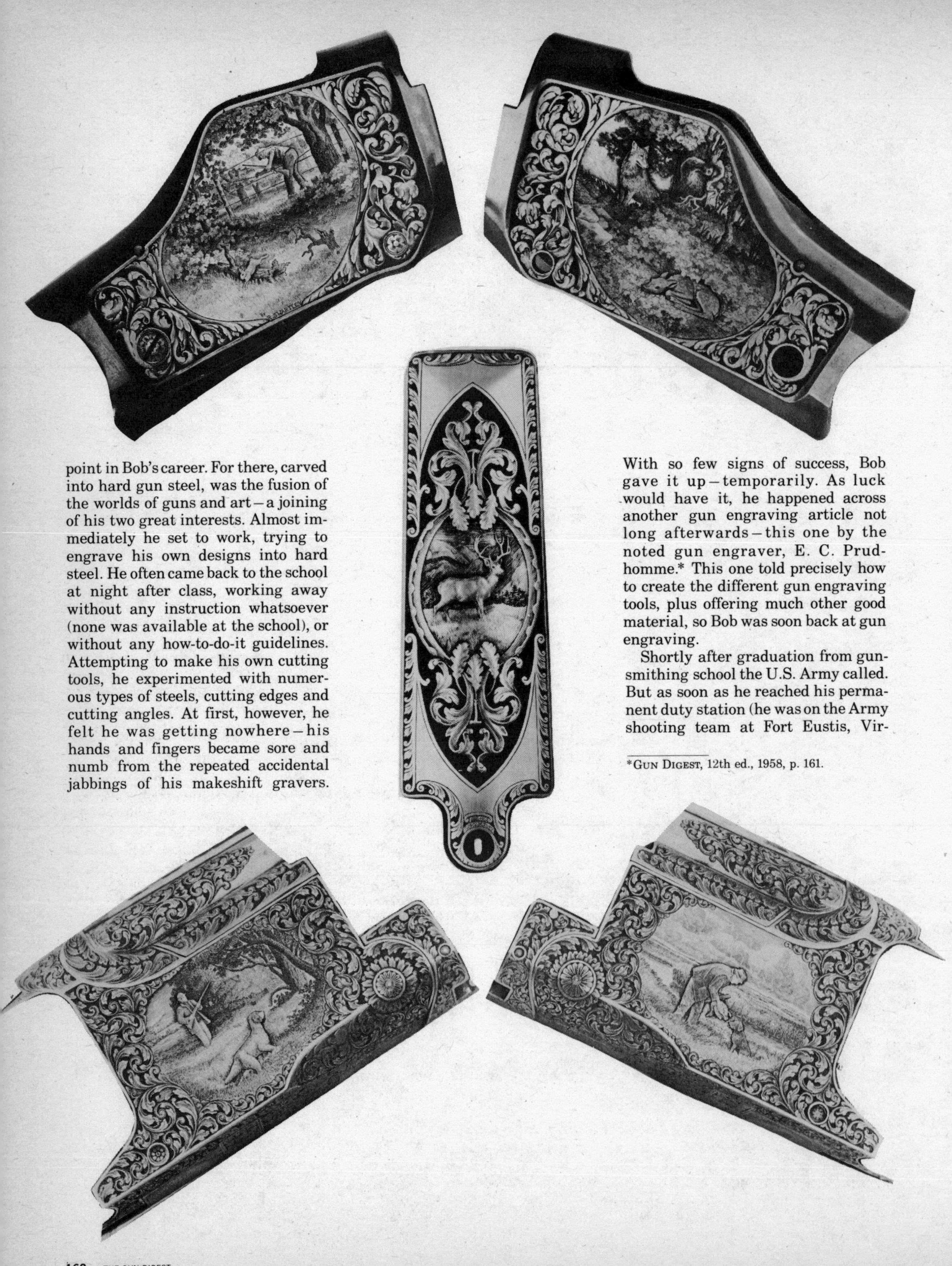

point in Bob's career. For there, carved into hard gun steel, was the fusion of the worlds of guns and art—a joining of his two great interests. Almost immediately he set to work, trying to engrave his own designs into hard steel. He often came back to the school at night after class, working away without any instruction whatsoever (none was available at the school), or without any how-to-do-it guidelines. Attempting to make his own cutting tools, he experimented with numerous types of steels, cutting edges and cutting angles. At first, however, he felt he was getting nowhere—his hands and fingers became sore and numb from the repeated accidental jabbings of his makeshift gravers.

With so few signs of success, Bob gave it up—temporarily. As luck would have it, he happened across another gun engraving article not long afterwards—this one by the noted gun engraver, E. C. Prudhomme.* This one told precisely how to create the different gun engraving tools, plus offering much other good material, so Bob was soon back at gun engraving.

Shortly after graduation from gunsmithing school the U.S. Army called. But as soon as he reached his permanent duty station (he was on the Army shooting team at Fort Eustis, Vir-

*GUN DIGEST, 12th ed., 1958, p. 161.

ginia) Bob sent for his engraving tools, which had been pre-packed and ready to go. From that time on, and for the next 15 years, he practiced the gun engraving art—part time at first, while working as a gunsmith—with little interruption. A major lucky break came when, on leaving the service, he went to work in Abercrombie and Fitch's New York gunshop, under the watchful and critical eye of yet another leading gun engraver, Joseph Fugger—one of the world's greatest, and himself a one-time protege of Rudolph Kornbrath. For the two years he was there he refined even further a talent which had already been well developed.

At the present time Bob lives with his wife and son in Napa, California. Working full time in his own shop, his clientele is today international. His jobs range from a simple scrollwork pattern for the casual gun enthusiast to the full and elaborate coverages for confirmed — and affluent — gun fanciers. As with virtually all top gun engravers, here and abroad, Bob has a waiting list now, jobs he can't get at for some time.

Whenever feasible Bob takes to the mountains and the meadows, where he sketches, photographs, and makes notes of scenes having a potential value for future engraving designs. Bob is also involved in the etching of engraved wildlife plates for use in printing.

Swartley's customers usually give him only a general idea of what they want, leaving the execution and ultimate design in his hands. That's as it should be, of course, for "The important thing is to please your own artistic sense. If you do that, the final result won't be far wrong," Bob has said.

Rarely is Swartley completely satisfied with his completed work. He's continually striving for greater perfection of idea and execution, which is exactly the kind of attitude necessary to produce work of the highest standard—a standard difficult to attain, but truly beautiful to behold in its ultimate realization. *Ronald Swartley.*

Europe in the Rain—

France, Italy, Austria and Spain

St. Etienne and Brescia revisited.
The gunmakers of Ferlach and red deer in the Steiermark.
Eibar and the guns made by the Basques.

by JOHN T. AMBER

MY VISIT TO THE Continent last year was, I think, one of the most instructive and successful trips I've made abroad in recent years. I don't say it was as enjoyable as some other treks I've made over there, for the weather just wouldn't cooperate. I don't think I saw three bright days out of the near-30—it was rain, rain, rain day and night with, during my few days in the Austrian hunting country, deep in an Alpine sector, some 10 inches of snow on the rugged terrain and more falling. When it wasn't raining it was cloudy and cold most days.

Nevertheless, I saw numerous interesting firearms and firearms factories, plus getting a chance to shoot some of the guns, and I learned a lot. In addition, and decidedly not least, I met many new people, some of whom I'd corresponded with, but all of them men doing a good job and full of enthusiasm—matter of fact, one factory I'll be getting to later has a woman as its managing director.

As arranged, Raymond Caranta—our Continental editor and contributor—met me at Marseille's Marignane airport and drove me to Aix and his guest house. Next morning, on 27 September, we made an early start for St. Etienne, some hundred or so miles to the north, and where we'd be spending several days.

St. Etienne has been the center of French gunmaking for centuries, literally, and I'd guess that over 90 per cent of all firearms made in France are produced in or around the ancient town.

Caranta and I had visited St. Etienne first in 1971 (see GUN DIGEST 27th ed., p. 50 for my account of that trip), but we'd spent only a few hours there on that occasion, and the only gunmaker we had called on was Darne—makers of the unusual if not unique sliding-breech side-by-side shotgun they've had in production for nearly 75 years.

This time, however, Raymond and I would be seeing several factories, most of their production shotguns, and meeting their management people.

Before Raymond and I began making our rounds, however, we attended a luncheon—a gourmet luncheon, *naturellement*—hosted by the President of the Chambre Syndicate des Fabricants d'Armes, Remy Chatain. Also there were several executives from various French gunmaking companies—Manufrance, Verney-Carron, Manu-Arm, Picard-Fayolle—and others. We talked about our plans and arranged a tight schedule.

We didn't, of course, keep to our schedule completely, losing an hour or so here, as much or more at another place. So some manufacturers were, regrettably, passed up, but we did visit the major organizations, including France's largest distributor of firearms and related products.

But before I put down the firms called on I'll have to make an admission that rather embarrasses me. During that previous visit we'd made to the Darne works, which included a lengthy tour of the factory, I'd been impressed with the excellent quality, the meticulous fitting and assembly of the Darne guns. A great deal of handwork was being lavished on these shotguns, even on the lesser grades.

These are the Manufrance clay bird over-unders. Top, the boxlock Falcor Skeet with ventilated rib, finger-ledged hand-filling fore-end and single trigger • The straight-gripped trap gun, a sidelock Falcor, offers the same fore-end and ventilated rib as their Skeet double, but is standard with two triggers • The Robust side-by-side double gun, here in ejector grade and with a "swamped" and very low top rib, is Manufrance's best selling shotgun.

Yet I must confess that I was surprised—agreeably and gratifying, of course—at the clear evidence of quality control I saw at virtually all of the factories Caranta and I went to, the constant inspection work, and the impressions of crisp, well-put-together guns I gained as I handled and examined the various models and types.

The Manufrance factory exemplifies, I think, what I've just written. Manufrance has been likened to Sears, Roebuck before this, and with some justification. This old firm, established circa 1874, publishes a thick annual catalog displaying a very broad array of consumer products, quite like Sears. The Manufrance catalog I'm looking at, an older one that runs to 680 pages, devotes the first 107 pages to firearms of all kinds and types along with the usual assortment of those things having to do with guns and shooting. Manufrance, however, manufactures at St. Etienne most, if not all, of the firearms it markets (plus many other products of no interest here, such as bicycles and the like), in contrast to Sears, which contracts for much, perhaps most, of the arms it offers.

As I've intimated the Manufrance factory was a bit of a surprise. I don't know exactly just what I'd expected, but it wasn't the vast, multi-storied plant I saw, and one that took us a couple of hours to go through. Full of modern machinery, many of the tools of the most sophisticated type—tape fed, automated monsters the equal of those anywhere—the factory was spotless, orderly and obviously well organized and managed.

The current *Manufacture Francaise d'Armes et Cycles de St. Etienne* (Manufrance for short) catalog shows firearms in big variety, these ranging from single barrel shotguns and rimfire rifles through shotguns in side-by-side or o-u, slide action and autoloading types. Their Fusil Robust, an excellent side-by-side double gun made in various grades, has sold well over 700,000 units, in France and abroad. Centerfire bolt rifles, on Mauser actions, are also available.

Cataloged also are some cartridges we don't see here—in addition to the common 12, 16, 20 and 410 guns, one model of the single barrel Simples can be had in 14 gauge. One of the less expensive O-U rifles is offered in a 9mm rimfire caliber.

Cane guns are cataloged (or were until recently), made for 12mm and 14mm shotshells. Recently cataloged was a bolt action rifle, its one barrel chambered for three 22 LR cartridges, all of them fired with one pull of the trigger! Rifled barrels can be had for some shotgun models. They are not intended for slug shooting, however, but to throw broad patterns at very short ranges. As you'll learn later, the Bretton over-under rather specializes in such rifled tubes.

Manufrance, as one might expect, does a very big mailorder business, but it also has stores in some 70 French cities, large and small.

Manufrance can't be charged with modesty—their best grade Fusil Ideal, a side-by-side double gun made in various grades, sells in France today for 5,600 francs, and they were once described in their catalog as "the most perfect and best shotgun in the world." Well, if you don't blow your own horn...

Made in Manufrance's custom shop, the Ideal is certainly a beautiful shotgun, beautifully built and a pleasure to handle. The Ideal can be had in boxlock or sidelock version.

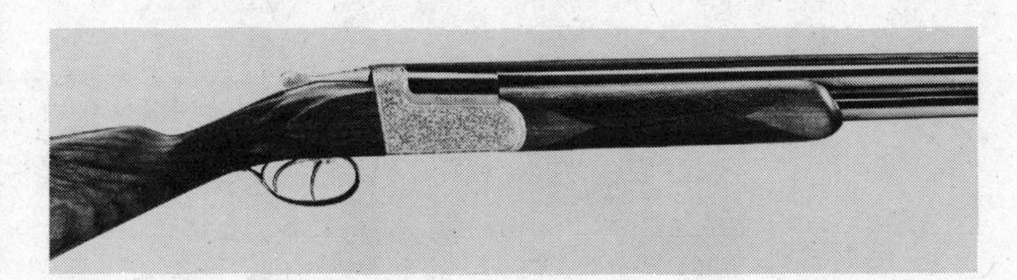

Left—Verney-Carron's Model 747 is the Sagittaire over-under at its best—full fancy wood, best quality engraving in a restrained elegant style.

Even in the most modern gun factories, barrel straightening remains a job for the trained and critical eyes of men.

Verney-Carron

In operation continuously since 1820, Verney-Carron is one of the oldest gunmaking organizations in the world, if not the oldest. Even today, members of the Verney-Carron family are very much active in the management of the company—which is also, I understand, the largest privately-held maker of fine shotguns in France. The factory and general offices are in St. Etienne, with branches in Paris, Lyon and Marseille.

Yet, in spite of Verney-Carron shotguns being well and favorably known throughout all of Europe, with a growing market in Great Britain over the past several years, I doubt that many of you reading this will recognize the name or know much about the firm. Until a few years ago, neither did I—my first Verney-Carron catalog arrived sometime in the mid-1960s.

The Verney-Carron factory, covering an immense area, is as well equipped as any I've seen, here or abroad—light and airy, the heavy machinery is ultra-modern and sophisticated, with automation evident everywhere to do the early-stage metal removal. Nevertheless, the various models—and there's a good variety, both in type and quality—are fully hand fitted and finished. Even on the less-expensive grades the joining of wood to metal is excellent, the metal polishing and bluing first class, the functioning of the lockwork smooth and crisp.

I was particularly impressed with a low-profile Verney-Carron over-under shotgun, made in 12 gauge only, called the Sagittaire—a gun exhibiting a variety of genuinely unique features, their total not found on any other double barreled gun anywhere.

One of the many modern machine tools in the Verney-Carron factory—this one a semi-automatic lathe.

1 The firing pins, for example, are 100% straight-line and coil-spring actuated, as our illustration shows. If the gun is put away in cocked condition, no problem—coil springs won't take a set or be weakened.

2 Twin tapered steel pins, especially heat treated, are housed in the standing breech face. On closing the gun these bolts move forward into mating recesses either side of the barrel breech, locking the gun solidly.

3 Because loading a shotshell into the lower barrel is a problem with many over-unders, the Sagittaire is locked when fully opened, making loading of either barrel easy.

4 The Sagittaire fore-end, because of its interior metal fittings, is readily adjustable in case any looseness should develop after long-sustained shooting—which lots of European guns get in a single season.

5 The fore-end of the ejector-type Sagittaires (the lowest-cost Model 728 has simple extractors) carries none of the ejector mechanism—all such components are housed alongside the barrels. A lost or damaged fore-end, then, can be replaced at less cost. Incidentally, Verney-Carron absolutely guarantees the ready interchangeability of buttstocks, fore-ends and action parts.

6 The powerful ejectors, actuated by the triggers, are struck forcibly by their hammers, not merely pushed. This different-ejector system also allows the barrels to be assembled to the breech whether the ejectors and/or firing pins are cocked or not—no fiddling of any kind required!

The Sagittaire is offered in 5 versions—3 with pistol grip stocks, two of these with ejectors, and two with straight-grip stocks, both ejectors. All have receivers finished in "old silver" and all have double triggers, the preferred system abroad. Otherwise, quality and extent of engraving, plus wood figure and checkering determine the price. The styling is true classic.

All Sagittaire models, even the cheapest, are guaranteed for 2 years against defects in material or workmanship. Unfortunately these excellent shotguns are not available in the U.S. Production of the Sagittaire models is only about enough to meet the strong European and British demand. Verney-Carron also makes a line of side-by-side double barreled shotguns and autoloading smoothbores, but I don't have space to cover these in detail here. The double guns are well made sidelocks, again classically fashioned, the auto a non-gas operated type.

Like so many gunmaking companies these days, the Verney-Carron line is much less extensive than it was years ago. Mr. Claude Verney-Carron, General Manager of the company, kindly gave me a copy of their 1899-1900 catalog, its 164 pages filled with a great variety of firearms and associated shooting-hunting goods. There's a profusion of shotguns shown, outside hammer types in the main, with actions of Lefaucheux, underlever, sidelever and top snap design. Double rifles and 3-barrel guns were offered, as were single rifles of many kinds. Numerous revolver types are pictured but, for whatever reason, no autoloading pistols.

Picard-Fayolle

This is the firm I mentioned earlier whose Managing Director is a woman, Mmle. Therese Ducat. Miss Ducat conducted Caranta and I through her factory and talked about the several versions of the Dactu over-under shotgun, which is the sole type manufactured. It was obvious that Miss Ducat knew her stuff, that she was highly knowledgeable about shotgun design and construction. We learned also that she is a first class claybirder and an ardent hunter—as, in fact, so many European women are.

The low-profile Dactu gun, first produced in 1954 by this old firm—it was established in 1894—also offers straight-line firing pins and is strongly locked up via twin side lugs. The Dactu is a well made and excellently finished shotgun, available in 12, 16 or 20 gauge, with or without ejectors, and the option of a semi-pistol grip or straight grip stock. A graceful and handsome gun, the Dactu has a lively, well balanced feel, the weight noticeably between the hands. Much hand craftsmanship goes into this otherwise machine-made double—wood to metal fit is very good, with polishing and finishing near faultless. Two triggers are standard, and the top tang safety also acts as a barrel selector. Three extractor grades and 5 ejector qualities are cataloged. Several action finishes can be had—

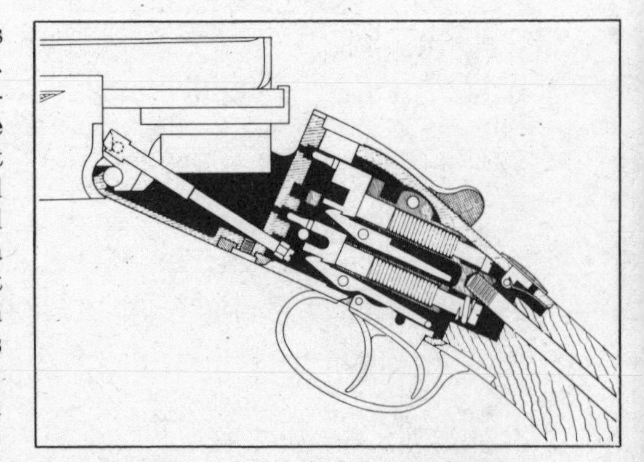

The world-patented Dactu firing mechanism uses straight-line, coil-spring actuated firing pins. Note also short, simple ejector-cocking arm.

blue, silver gray or color hardening. Barrels are given special attention at Picard-Fayolle—beautifully polished inside, they are delivered to the buyer perfectly straight. Regardless of grade, Dactu barrels carry a stamped "Guaranteed Yardage" figure, this based (I gathered) on pattern compatibility with range. Standard barrel length is 28 inches, standard chokes half and full, but other lengths/chokes can be special ordered. Average weight for the Dactu is 2.9 kg, or about 6.4 lbs. A light and attractive gun, the Dactu and, like the Verney-Carron Sagittaire, I'd like to have brought samples of each back home, but it wasn't convenient—I didn't want to lug a couple of long guns around for the rest of the trip.

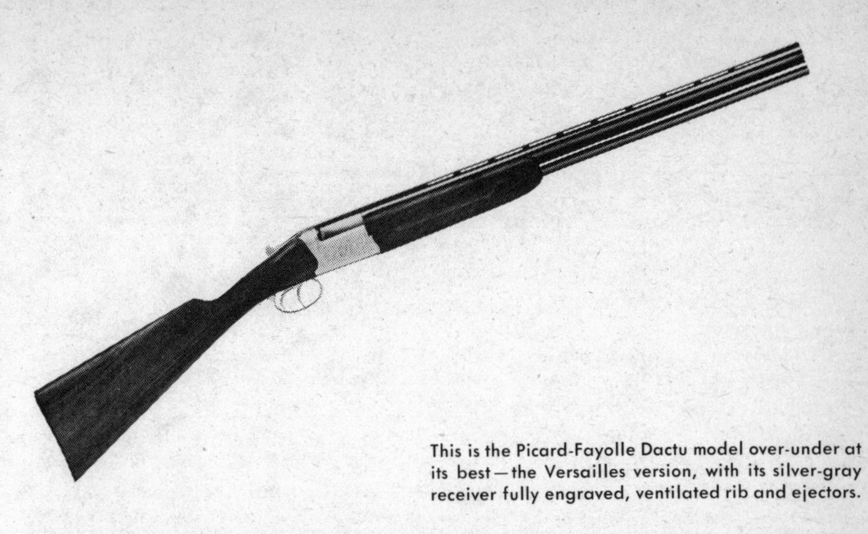

This is the Picard-Fayolle Dactu model over-under at its best—the Versailles version, with its silver-gray receiver fully engraved, ventilated rib and ejectors.

Baby Bretton

I'm not going to go into minute detail on this ultra-light weight (under 5-lbs.) over-under shotgun here. The unusual B.B. was reported on fully in these pages a while back by Roger Barlow, including the results of extensive field shooting with the gun (see GUN DIGEST, 19th ed., 1965).

Introduced in 1936, this virtually all-alloy gun is still selling very well, though of course the factory is a relatively small one and production limited to a degree. Still, as Caranta and I waited while Mr. Bretton answered his phone, Raymond said to me that Mr. Bretton had just told the caller that he couldn't promise delivery before 6 months! Now that's for an unusual gun, not traditional in form or function, not materially changed for the sake of newness since its inception, and not all that cheap. Base price in France last fall was 1625 francs, over $400.

For those who don't know the Baby Bretton, here are a few highlights—the two-piece receiver slides open or closed on a pair of sturdy guide rods, the unlocking-locking managed by a right-side lever. The aluminum alloy barrels may be unscrewed and replaced by others in a few minutes, literally—there are no side ribs. Four barrels are available—improved cylinder, half-choke and full, plus a rifled barrel for very short range shooting. The rifling acts to spread the load, of course; it is not intended for rifled-slug use.

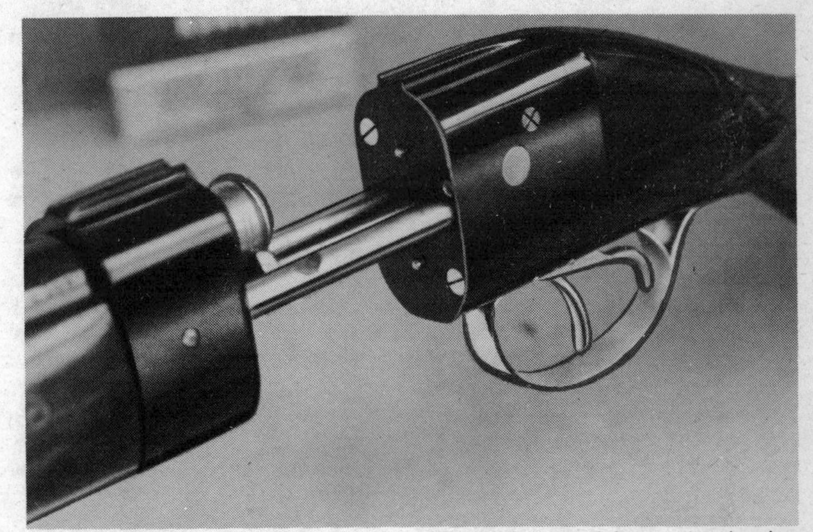

The Baby Bretton slides open or closed on the pair of sturdy rods seen here, these movements controlled by a right-side lever.

Made only in 12 or 16 gauge, the Baby Bretton is offered in 3 grades—the M65 Standard and the M70 Superior are alike except for chambering and official French proofing; 12,500 and 17,000 psi respectively. The De Luxe model, otherwise like the M70, carries scroll engraving on both sides of the matte-chromed receiver, has a select walnut stock and matching fore-end, and is generally better finished throughout.

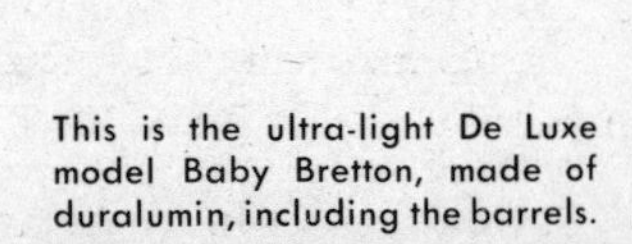

This is the ultra-light De Luxe model Baby Bretton, made of duralumin, including the barrels.

Manu-Arm

This firm, located at the St. Etienne suburb of Veauche, makes a variety of light and inexpensive long guns. Most of the rifles produced are 22 Long Rifle bolt actions in several modifications, but a bolt rifle and an over-under gun in 9mm rimfire are also made, as is an autoloader in 22 LR. Mr. Remy Chatain, owner-operator of Manu-Arm and a genial and entertaining guy—gave Caranta and I the full tour of his very big factory. I hope M. Chatain won't mind my saying here that his factory does not have ultra-modern machine tools we saw elsewhere in St. Etienne, no tape-fed automated monsters. But what real need, of course, for such costly equipment when only low-cost, popular priced rimfire firearms are being produced? Manu-Arm does very well without such sophisticated tooling—instead, there are so many large, if older, tools, that each of them remains jigged and fixtured *permanently*. Set up time is thereby reduced to near-zero, and the production rate reflects it—Manu-Arm produces over 1,000 firearms a day, yet delivery is 6 months or more delayed, or was at the time of our visit. Distribution, we were told, is not limited to France: Manu-Arm rifles are sold over much of the Continent. The stocks, by the way, are supplied by Sile, Inc., the world-wide manufacturers of stocks and blanks for guns of all types and many grades of quality. We saw hundreds of outsize cartons holding Sile finished stocks.

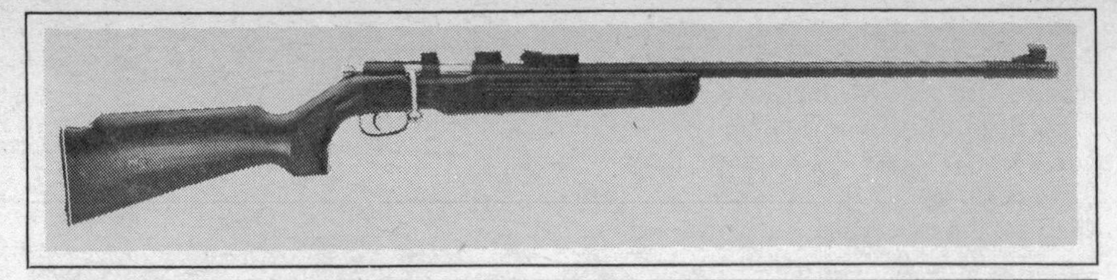

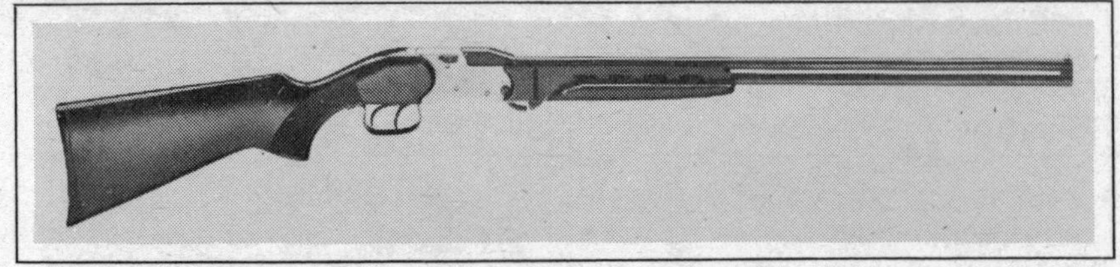

Top—The Manu-Arm Model 16, a 22 rimfire rifle, has provisions for mounting a scope sight • The lower Manu-Arm, called the Mini-Super, is a 9mm smoothbore over-under.

Georges Granger

I hope no one minds my saying that I've held the most exciting news I learned in St. Etienne for the last. I was prepared to meet a good gunmaker, for Caranta had told me that Mr. Granger was considered France's top custom shotgun builder. What I wasn't ready for was the discovery—after several hours of talk with Mr. Granger and a close examination of a fully finished pair of Fusil Aiglons (the shop name) and his action/lock-work—that Mr. Granger may well be the best damned gunmaker in the world. I know, awfully high praise, and comparisons are said to be odious, but—my opinion, of course—Mr. Granger's work is equal to if not superior to the best pre-war Purdeys, Holland & Hollands or Grant & Lang.

Mr. Granger's "best" gun is a detachable sidelock side-by-side double, the takedown lever mounted on the left-side plate. This is as superbly crafted a shotgun as I've seen, and in every respect. I went over one of these inside and out, using a magnifying glass, and I found no area that could be faulted in the least degree. Mr. Granger was oficially proclaimed, a few years back, as the "Best Workman in France," and there's no question in my mind that he more than deserves this significant award, a public recognition of his unmatched skills.

Skills it is, too, multiple ones, for Mr. Granger makes his creations from scratch, starting with a rectangle of solid steel and going from there. Mr. Granger has only one shop assistant, a young man who, he said, is "coming along nicely." Mr. Granger does all the stocking work as well—whether on the lever-detachable sidelock or two lesser grades, these last comprising a screw-demountable sidelock and boxlock gun. Both of these less costly doubles are also beautifully made. I could see no lessening of quality in either. Only the checkering and engraving are not done in the Fusil Aiglon shop—the checkering is entrusted to an outside specialist, another master craftsman. The floral-motif engraving, classic and elegant in its simplicity, is done by a graduate of the famed Beaux Arts school.

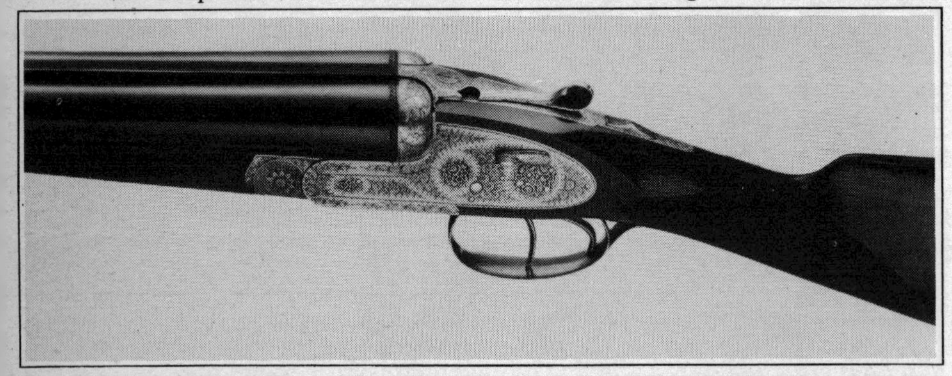

Above left—this is Georges Granger's "best" gun, a lever-detachable sidelock that exemplifies the finest quality gunmaking found anywhere • The Granger Boxlock, made in 12, 16 or 20 gauge, is a superbly-built and finished double gun.

All Granger barrels, regardless of grade, receive a special honing treatment inside, which assures optimum point of impact and superior patterns. Virtually every Granger double is made to the customer's order, and such clients, especially the grouse and partridge shooters, most often want a pair of guns. Such is Granger's ability that he guarantees to make his pairs "absolutely identical" in weight, form, dimensions and balance!

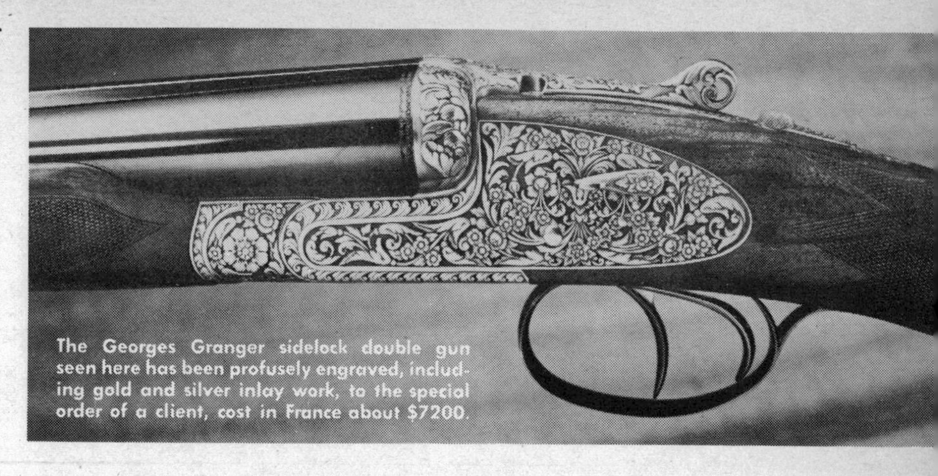

The Georges Granger sidelock double gun seen here has been profusely engraved, including gold and silver inlay work, to the special order of a client, cost in France about $7200.

Granger's production is, of course, quite small. When we were there he told us there was about a two-year wait for delivery. His No. 8 double, the boxlock, sells this year for 8,500 francs, or about $2,000, depending on the value of the dollar. No. 12, the screw-detachable sidelock, is 9,900 francs, and his "best" gun, the incomparable double with lever-release lockplates, is priced at 20,600 francs, say close to $5,000. No, that is not for a pair, that's the single gun cost. Expensive? Sure, but Granger's customers are, in effect, standing in a queque. Consider—a loaded Cadillac can run to ten grand these days, right? What will that big gas guzzler be worth a mere 5 years from now? What will George Granger's magnificent "best" gun bring at the same time? Correct again—inflation being what it is, maybe the same 10 big ones!

Brescia and the Armi Famars Castore 270

As I've said, the rains came down last fall. Caranta and I left Aix in a steady drizzle, bound for Milan, where Renato Gamba would meet us, and drive me to Brescia. The last couple of hours before reaching Milan found us driving in heavy rain, high winds and early darkness. I didn't envy Raymond his long drive back to Aix, but he made it without incident, and so did we to Brescia.

The stay in Brescia this time was a short one. I'd come by to pick up the outside hammer double gun I've ordered from Mario Abbiatico in 1973, the model 270 Castore (see GUN DIGEST 29, pp. 157-164), not the one shown in that issue on p. 161. Armi Famars offers three outside-hammer doubles, two others beside the Castore 270. I'd wanted to use the Castore on a partridge shoot in Spain (which will be commented on later), but the shotgun wasn't ready. There'd been an accident—Mario had, as I hoped he would, used a very fancy piece of French walnut for the buttstock, and it had broken at the grip, already fully checkered!

Apart from that minor tragedy, the rest of the 12 gauge gun was completed, and I marveled again at its superb quality. Mario had finished the 27½-inch barrels to a rich, deep brown, beautifully smooth, in keeping with the spirit of its outside hammers. Fine gold lines had been inlaid at breech and muzzle ends, giving a nice touch of contrast against the warm brown color. The sidelocks and hammers had been given a French gray treatment, as had the guard. The elaborate Armi Farmars monogram/crest, in gold, is inlaid into the bottom of the fore-end, plus my initials; the company's name—also in gold—is let into the rib. Two triggers are fitted, which I'd asked for, and opening the gun brings the hammers to full cock and ejects the fired cases. The hammers, of course, may be lowered fully down or to half-cock.

Because I won't be able to do a field report on the Castore 270 myself, I loaned the gun to Roger Barlow, a writer known to many of you via articles of his we've carried in past issues. Roger is a long-time devotee of the smoothbore and, if his report on the Armi Famars hammer gun arrives on time, you'll find the story elsewhere in this issue.

An unusual and highly interesting feature of the Castore hammergun are the polished oval fences. The crown in the top lever is gold, as are double lines at the barrel breeches and muzzles. *Roger Barlow photo.*

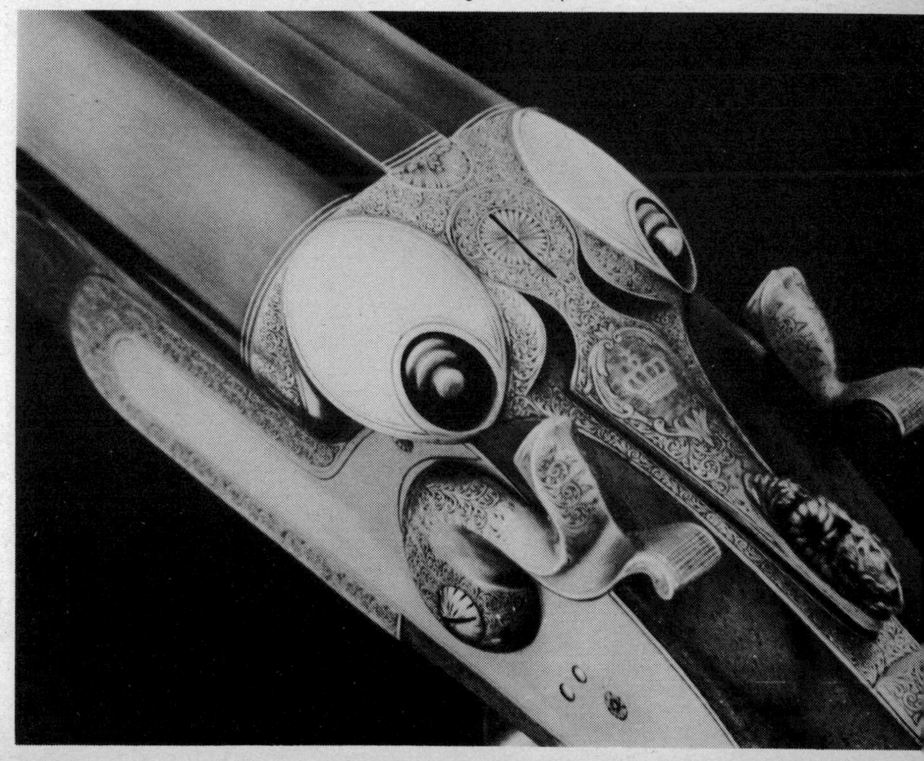

Armi Fabbri—Brescia

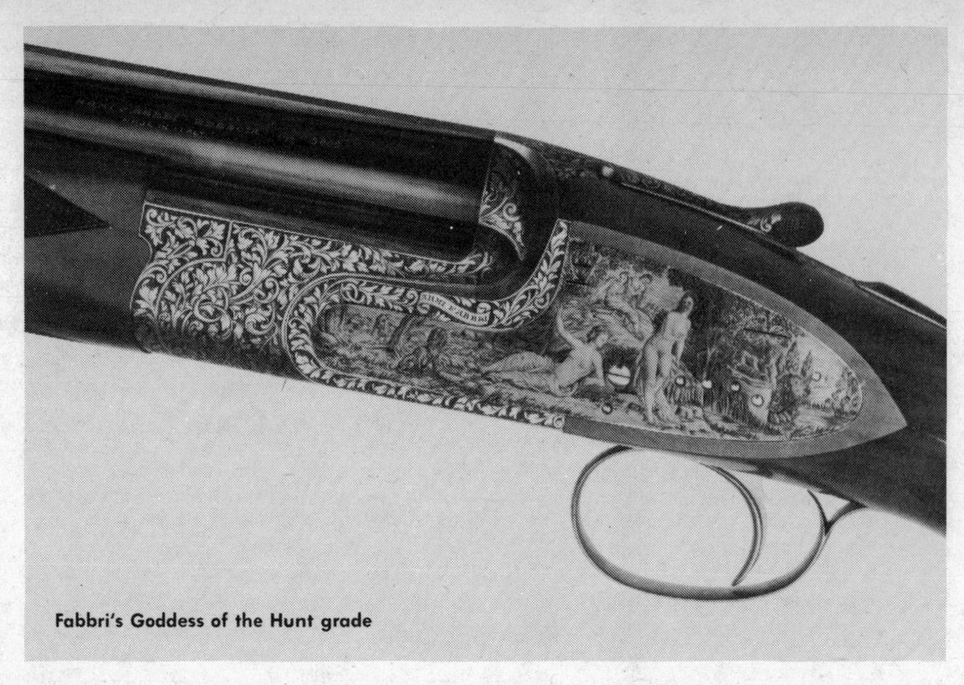
Fabbri's Goddess of the Hunt grade

As I write this, in March of 1975, the U.S. is in a serious recession. I needn't discuss that at length here; our general circulation publications are full of it. But are you aware that many, if not most, big-dollar products are selling as well or better than ever? Luxury autos, big boats, jewelry, posh estates, are being grabbed up at record rates.

So are firearms, particularly such famous-name shotguns as Purdeys, Holland & Hollands, Bosses, et al. A recent auction in London brought nearly $18,000 for a pair of Boss doubles—used ones! Armi Fabbri can be considered in the same class, never mind that the firm is relatively unknown compared to the gunmakers just mentioned—they're well known indeed to claybird shooters throughout the world, particularly the affluent ones.

In spite of prices that start at about $7,000, and quickly run to $12,000 or more, at the time of my visit their production was sold out for nearly two years. Most of these orders, virtually all for competition type guns, had been for the higher priced models. For what it's worth, Fabbri is not making one for me, but after spending several hours at the shop I can see a lot of justification for the high prices.

I was impressed more than I'm going to be able to convey after seeing how slowly the fabrication of a Fabbri went, the meticulous inspections made of every component part, the use of test and check techniques and tools not to be found elsewhere, all of them creations of Mr. Fabbri. Signor Fabbri is not a desk-bound executive—he works in the shop virtually full time, closely supervising the efforts of the workmen, making sure that the various machines function correctly, seeing that all operations go as they should, yet finding time to design machines and their tooling that would and do enhance production rates. One machine that I saw made—in a semi-automatic fashion—the intricate, convoluted cuts required on the vertical stem or shank actuated by the top snap lever—a considerable time-saver. Another Fabbri-designed development, amazing to watch, performed a hinge-pin operation on the Boss-type over-under Fabbri makes. In the original Boss action, a low-profile type, the short, stubby hinge pins, one at either side of the receiver, are made separately, then screw-fastened to the inner walls of the receiver. Mr. Fabbri demonstrated a machine he'd made that cut these short steel stubs *integral* with the U-shaped interior of the over-under receiver. Don't ask me exactly how, but I saw it work—roughly, a sort of rise-and-fall tool programmed to make the circular cuts required. I watched in awe!

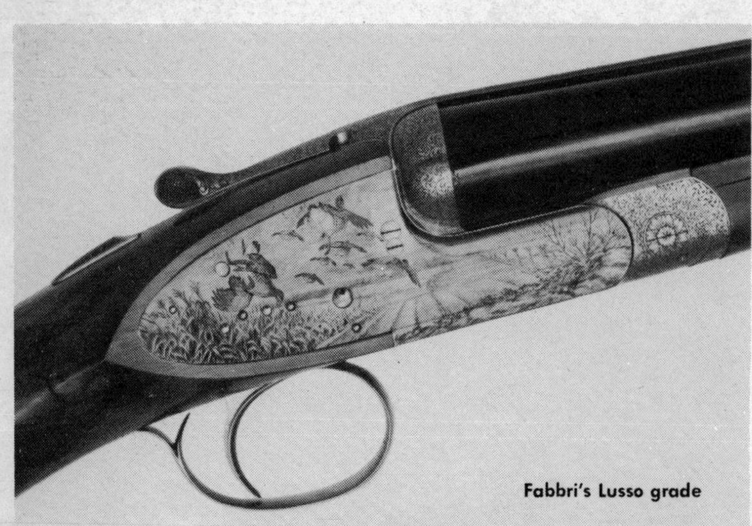
Fabbri's Lusso grade

Good barrels can be considred the ultimate requirement if the shotgun is to perform at its best—barrels that won't warp, stay straight after much shooting, and show bores and chokes perfectly finished, fully round and symmetrical inside and out, the barrel walls of uniform thickness at any point over their length.

That is the way Fabbri barrels are made. The individual barrels enter the Fabbri shop as undrilled rough-forged blanks of "chopper-lump" type—the breech area that will subsequently form the section that carries the bolting cuts. Then follows the usual turning and boring to bring the still-separate barrel to final dimensions and near-final finish. But it was the time-consuming, easy-does-it techniques used in the barrel making that make Fabbri barrels something else!

At an early stage in the barrel turning—when enough metal has been removed to permit the test—each barrel is placed in a Magnaflux fixture to detect incipient flaws, cracks or whatever. The slightest defect junks that barrel—a scrap can standing nearby held some 15-20 discarded barrels.

Another test device is used to detect the uniformity of barrel-wall dimensions during the several turning operations, and used not merely once. Leonard Puccinelli—VP for Fabbri, U.S. born and speaking better English than I—was my guide and translator during the visit, Signor Fabbri having little English. Leonard told me that barrels by Fabbri are held to *zero* wall thickness, and that each barrel makes some dozen trips through the barrel-straightening machine before it is paired with its mate. I saw some of that—I watched one barrel through several stages of processing and, during the relatively short time I was there, it was straightened 6 or 7 times.

Fabbri shotguns are generally conceded to be the best target guns in the world. After seeing how they're made, I can readily agree.

Renato Gamba and Mario Abbiatico were, as always, the most gracious of hosts. Renato took me for a drive to Lake Garda again, this time along its western shores, and the day for once was clear if not sunny. Mario took me home for dinner one night, after I'd gone to see his new house a building, where I met his charming wife and kids. The next night Mario and I went to a top-flight Brescian restaurant, high above the city, and enjoyed another good dinner. We had a long and interesting talk about gunmaking. I didn't get to bed until after one in the morning, and at 7:00 AM I'd be leaving Brescia for Klagenfurt and the visit to Ferlach and the hunting country north of it.

The Fabbri Credo

Because I couldn't begin to remember what Mr. Fabbri told me about his unique methods in gunmaking, Leonard Puccinelli set down some detailed notes for me, and here they are:

"Apart from the rough-forged barrel blanks, which are prepared to Fabbri specifications by Boehler of Austria, every Fabbri gun is built in its entirety in the factory as far as metal fabrication goes—engraving is done outside, as is usual in Italy and elsewhere, and the buttstock and fore-ends are also made away from the plant.

"Fabbri set out to perfect what he considers the two most important factors in a shotgun's performance—the barrels and the single trigger. *(next page, please)*

Here is the Armi Fabbri over-under in Majestic grade, and I wish it could be shown in color. The special engraving and relief chiseling is done in gold and silver, a striking display of artistry when viewed first hand.

"Fabbri's objective is to produce barrels which have perfect interior and exterior surfaces, uniform wall thickness with bore concentricity, straight bores, and concentric chokes with sharp entrance and exit angles. Only these characteristics will produce a barrel free of stress, with minimum vibration, uniform reaction during recoil, ballistic uniformity, consistent pellet impact centers and distribution, and maximum pellet penetration. If you build a barrel as perfectly as possible from the start in every operation, the performance is there when you finish – that is Fabbri's credo.

"In Fabbri's conception, a shotgun's single trigger should be as precise and quick as a match rifle's. To achieve precision there must be a minimum of movement, a minimum of weight and number of parts, and minimum surfaces under friction. The Fabbri single trigger has a total of 4 moving parts. They weigh 25 grams or 0.89 ozs., including trigger blade and inertia block, which pivots on a .05mm surface – virtually a pinpoint. The trigger has a total trigger-travel movement of .9mm, or less than 4/100-inch for *either* barrel. Within the sidelock mechanism the hammer falls a total of 16mm (6/10 inch). These figures are the lowest of any fine shotgun being built today.

"Another design advantage includes a *completely* milled fore-end iron for strength, quite a feat considering the complex surfaces and contours, again the *only* fine shotgun so built. Another plus is the lowest profile 12 gauge over-under action made: 2.38 inches measured from the crown of the standing breech to the bottom of the action floor."

Mr. Puccinelli then listed for me the hundreds of operations – machine and hand – that go into making a Fabbri shotgun. There are, unfortunately, far too many to list here, but I'll put down some highlights at least. The machines I'll mention were all designed by Mr. Fabbri to perform the special jobs required of them, tools *not* to be found otherwise. Most of these machines, too, were built by Mr. Fabbri, as were and are most of the small tools used with them.

First in importance among the Fabbri machines is one called the Rotary Reamer Bench. Here the rough barrels are fixed to a tracked sled, moved back and forth by hand, while the barrels are preliminarily drilled, reamed, honed, choked and polished internally before external turning is completed.

As I've noted, the barrels receive numerous straightenings during this barrel work, initially via a light-beam setup once the barrel is smooth enough inside, plus the manual eyeballing repeatedly done. Perhaps the most important task of all at this stage is obtaining the barrel concentricity and uniform wall thickness that Fabbri demands. The barrel goes at least twice to a Fabbri-designed vertical gauge fixture that determines concentricity-wall thickness to a tolerance of zero (0.000") to plus .02mm or .00078".

Another important Fabbri-designed tool – used in the final reaming – is a 3-dimensional reamer head that brings the cylinder bore, the choke and the front parallel section to full dimension (except for final honing) *simultaneously*.

Then (and this is Fabbri's second "top secret" design) a similar tri-dimensional tool, fully adjustable for any degree of choke, is used for the final honing, again of cylinder, choke and parallel. A glass-smooth finish results from the use of the carefully contoured stones and, most importantly, the crisp and sharp edges of the choke angles are *unaltered*. This unique system is considered a genuine milestone in shotgun barrel production.

Now comes the final polishing of the barrel tubes – both before and after their mating and brazing – and a bluing system designed and built by Fabbri. Some 15 coats of hot rust blue are applied, each coat followed by a hand carding or steelwooling. The barrels are placed in an automated heat cabinet, electric relays controlling temperature and humidity. The ringing of a bell signals a workman to start carding the barrels and to place them in a boiling water bath, after which the process resumes. An ingenious and well-planned system.

I've mentioned the very special machine that Fabbri designed and built to cut the short round stubs inside his over-under actions, but here's a better description of the machine – which does various other job as well – as put down by Leonard Puccinelli: "This tool, which we call our Action Frame Cutter Bench, is an upright 4-sided affair with an electric motor mounted centrally inside.

"This motor drives an oscillating arm by belt which, in turn, drives 4 separate cutting/slotting stations mounted externally to the 4 sides. Each of these cutter stations is an ingeniously designed fixture with jig and cutter for performing the following cutting/slotting operations on the over-under and side-by-side actions:

Sta. 1 – Barrel rear surface recess (o-u).
Barrel lug rear surface recess (o-u).
Barrel lug forward surface recess (o-u).
Lug recesses action (s-s).

Sta. 2 – Right/left trunnion pegs (o-u) cut simultaneously from *inside* the over-under action (a major feat considering the extremely limited work space). Missile-steel trunnion rings are later pressure-installed after heating.

Sta. 3 – Slot for bolt (missile-steel) (o-u).
Slots for cocking levers (s-s).

Sta. 4 – Stop surface for barrel full-open position (o-u).

The angles and contours of the above cuttings as well as the cutter speed, cutters and belt/arm tension and drag are all extremely critical and were developed after much experimentation. These are only 8 of the 130-odd machine/hand cutting, slotting, shaping and finishing operations done to produce a Fabbri action frame from a solid rectangular block of nickel-chrome steel." ●

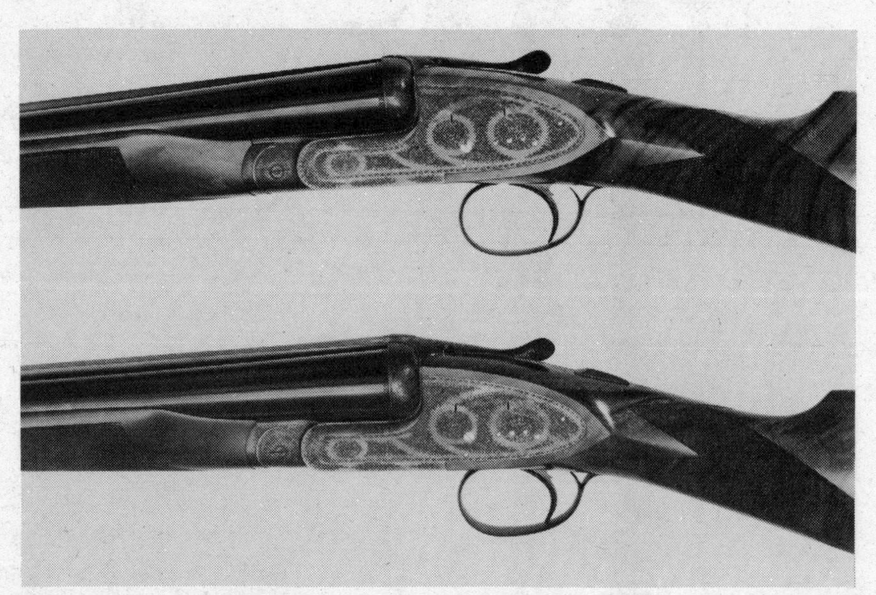

This matched pair of sidelock guns, rose and scroll engraved in the English pattern, is Fabbri's Super Pigeon grade, the locks case-hardened in color.

Austria

The train trip to Klagenfurt was an over-long day of frustration—the connecting train at Venice left an hour late and, as we rolled along in the rainy, wild and windy evening, it got later. I was in the dining car as we passed through Klagenfurt, the stop not announced—or if it was I didn't hear it! I spent the night at a small place called Bruck an dem Mur, reaching Klagenfurt the next day at noon.

Franz Marktl (one of our best engravers), back in Ferlach for a visit, wasn't at the station when I arrived, of course, for he'd met my train the night before, when I'd failed to alight. So I called John Fanzoi, one of Ferlach's best and best-known gunmakers, who drove in and picked me up. We spent the afternoon at his shop, where I examined closely one of the side-by-side double rifles he specializes in. The Ferlach gunmakers produce a great variety of rifle and shotgun types, but few such DB rifles—it is hardly a big market. Fanzoi had not long before sent a 458 DB rifle to the U.S., made for Lee Jurras, which I'd also seen, and I've now ordered a similar one. I don't know whether John talked me into it or if I did that myself.

Fanzoi showed me a new bullet, one he'd help develop and used in two calibers so far—7x57 and 7x64, rimmed or rimless, by Hirtenberger, the old Austrian ammunition company. Called the ABC bullet, it weighs 160 grains and looks much like a Nosler bullet in color, bronze rather than gilding metal. Controlled progressive upset or expansion is claimed for it, out to 300-400 yards. A small tip of lead appears at the nose, but not until I got home did I learn just how the ABC bullet is made. Fanzoi had given me a box of 10 rounds in 7x64, and I pulled a bullet from one to section. I got a surprise—the ABC bullet is a solid mass of brassy metal (Tombak) except for a very small and narrow tapered piece of lead that ends in the lead point mentioned before. This bit of lead is about ⅝-inch long, not over $^{3}/_{16}$-inch at its widest (nose), and tapers to $^{5}/_{64}$-inch at its bottom. The ABC bullet—1.35 inches over-all—appears to have been screw-machine turned, rather than drawn, judging by the circumferential tool marks found from top to bottom of the bullet.

The forepart is conical. At the bottom of this pencil-point section there are 8 half-moon areas, the rounded fronts very slightly raised, perhaps by .001-inch or so. These will, I was told, act as saw teeth on entering an animal, the rotational velocity of the bullet resulting in and enhance severe tissue damage. Raymond Caranta told me he planned to attend a European test of the ABC bullets, on which he'd send us a report. We'll try to carry his account, space and time permitting, elsewhere in this issue.

No chance to try these yet—I'm waiting for a Steyr rifle in 7x64 rimless, about which you'll hear later.

The next several days were hectic. Franz knows everyone in the area, and we spent the daylight hours visiting one gunmaker after another. Franz stays with his father in Treibach, some 20 miles from Ferlach, so I put up at a very nice hotel there, Franz picking me up each morning.

The Franz Sodia factory is the largest one in Ferlach, and several hours were spent there, watching the many models in production and examining in his showroom the sample guns there. Besides the usual side-by-side and over-under shotguns or rifle-shotgun over-unders, Sodia makes single-barrel, break-open rifles *(kipplauf)*, drillings in forms not usually seen (one shot barrel over a rifle barrel with another, smaller-caliber barrel to the right of the other two, these called *bock-drilling)*, outside hammer rifle-shotguns in over-under type, and various others. The current Franz Sodia catalog shows his many models clearly and carries detailed data on them, though all is German.

A type I'd like to have is an over-under double rifle called a *bergstutzen*—mountain rifle. The lower barrel may be had in game calibers—5.6x57R, 7x57R, 243 Win., 270 Win., and 30-06, plus some others. The top barrel is chambered for the 22 Magnum rimfire or 22 Hornet, 222 Rem. or the 5.6x50R. Such a rifle would be usable year round, a combined var-

This Fanzoi-made over-under 12 bore has the full de luxe treatment — raised gold figures on the sidelocks, best quality figured walnut showing carving at grip and fore-end.

A Fanzoi sidelock side-by-side double rifle, caliber 375 H&H, the demi-block (chopper bump) barrels of Antinit or rustproof steel. Ejectors, of course, and the standing breech has Purdey-style side clips.

minter and a big game rifle.

Another big factory in Ferlach is that of the *Genossenschaft* or Arms Association. This factory is jointly owned and operated by some 15 gunmakers in Ferlach. Much of the major work in producing a gun is done there, with the final finishing and engraving done in the several owners' individual shops. This appears to be a sound and satisfactory situation—the cost of buying big and expensive machine tools is shared by the group. By the nature of things, there appears to be less down-time for the big equipment—one of the group may want a run of this or that this week, another member will use a different set of tools or plan his operations for next week.

I was, again, impressed by the high quality in general of Ferlach-made guns—the excellent wood-to-metal jointing and finishing, the quality and good functioning of the locks, many of them so different.

I think this comment to me by John Fanzoi shows that these Austrian gunmakers know what they are doing—during my visit to his home-cum-shop, he told me he had, the day before, test-fired a 458 double he'd made—its first such firing—and found it printing left and right barrel shots into less than two inches at 60 meters! He frankly admitted that such good results didn't always happen, that sometimes he had to do further "regulating" of the twin barrels before he got that kind of performance. (In this section you'll find a report on a 375 H&H over-under rifle I have, made years ago by Anton Sodia of Ferlach.)

Marktl and I spent a most enjoyable couple of hours with Albin Obiltschnig, Austria's most famous gun engraver. Over the past several years the GUN DIGEST has carried many photographs of his superb work, so I don't need to dwell on its remarkable quality, the lifelike figures inlaid in gold, usually in high relief, the command he has of anatomy and modelling. What you may not know is that the senior Obiltschnig is 81 years old, and that much if not most of his great efforts have been done after he reached 70.

The old gentleman works at home, in recent years assisted by his talented son. Albin showed us three lockplates he was at work on, though these wouldn't be finished for several weeks—he couldn't, he said, put in the long hours he used to!

The Ferlach visit, ended all too soon, found Marktl, his father and I driving to Donnersbachwald, gateway to a very large game preserve of the same name deep in the Steiermark section of Austria. In spite of another cold and rainy day, with low clouds concealing the mountain tops, we enjoyed the ride through spectacular alpine country. I hadn't been expected until evening, but our arrival in mid-afternoon meant that I could fire my "qualifying" shot that day, not the next morning. A Steyr bolt rifle in 7x64 was waiting for me, along with a box of 175-gr. RWS cartridges. The small shooting hut held a chair and, across a sloped platform, a folded blanket. After Herr Helmut Kirner had fired a couple of shots to check the rifle's zero, I sat down and pointed the muzzle at the target, 200 meters away and some 25 degrees above. I got lucky—my first shot went in about a half-inch from center. Lucky indeed, I thought, for my first glance through the 4x scope worried me—the reticle was one of those beloved by many central European hunters, a very thick, sharply-pointed post with equally broad flat-ended posts reaching toward center from either side. A good type for shooting in near-darkness at ranges of a hundred meters, even a bit farther, maybe, but far from my idea of a long range style.

Because there was still an hour or so of shooting light left, though the skies were dark and a fresh snowfall threatened, Herr Kirner suggested we drive up to the house of the man

The late Albin Obiltschnig, one of the world's greatest engravers, stands outside his modest Ferlach home. He died April 18, 1975 at age 81.

The Bergstutzen offers two calibers—one for big game, the other a smaller rim- or centerline chambering. This is the F. Sodia Model 557 in De Luxe grade.

who'd be my chamois guide the next day or so. As we drove up the steep winding road, Kirner and his partner were scanning the opposite slope for red deer. It was now well after 5 and growing darker by the minute. Parking the car on a small flat area before the guide's house, both men raised their binoculars to glass the far hillside—and there moved a couple of stags, feeding slowly away from us at a quartering angle.

Kirner grabbed my rifle from the car, handed it to me and threw a blanket across the roof of the small car. He indicated with his fingers that the range was "over 300 meters," laid the rifle on the blanket and motioned me to shoot! Kirner had about as little English as I have German, otherwise I'd have protested—it was now almost 6 o'clock, quite dark, and the stags, even through the glass, appeared to be hardly more than gray blobs. The big pointed post covered up a good 60% of the deer, its point lost in the gloom. Now the deer were even farther off. I said to myself "To hell with it," brought the point of the post, what I could see of it, to the top of the deer's shoulder and pulled the trigger.

As I recovered from the recoil, I saw that the deer was down forward, but moving back toward the forest. I'd been lucky again, sort of. As I shot, Kirner told me, the stag had moved left a bit, my shot entering a little too far back, but he felt sure it wouldn't go far.

The next morning, after a brief but fruitless search the night before, one of Kirner's men located the stag—about a hundred meters from where he'd been hit—and had brought in the head. A smallish rack, far from top trophy quality, but of the size I'd been allowed to shoot—and I could not take another!.

That same afternoon my chamois guide, Willi Koeberl and I were driven up into the mountains in the 4-wheel drive Haflinger—a Steyr-made vehicle that handled the rough and rocky road very well. Our destination was one of the many cabins that dot the preserve, ours named *Ahornkoglhütte* and lying about 2,000 meters elevation. There had been several snowfalls, some couple of weeks earlier than normal and, as we ground up to the hut, we found ourselves in about 10 inches of it. A beautiful picture, the clean fresh snow covering everything, the Alps soaring skyward all round us, but if we'd even see a chamois we'd be fortunate—they'd all be holing up in the thick timber, out of the snow.

Willi soon had a fire going and the kettle on for tea—it was about 20 degrees F outside. Willi had no English at all, but we got along well, my feeble attempts at German breaking us up a few times. A good cook, too, he fixed us a nice dinner, including a bottle of wine. The fire would die down or out during the night, so I slept under four blankets—which weren't quite enough! Snow had started falling again as we went to bed, giving us another couple of inches, we could see on leaving the bunks at first light. A wan sun was out, but only just.

We hunted all that day, slogging through the snow, gradually getting higher as we moved up rugged, rocky gorges. Soon after mid-day we topped out onto a narrow but open flat, with a clear view across a valley to a thinly-treed slope opposite. We were now at about 2500 meters elevation, Willi said. We could see for several hundred yards to our left and right, and visibility was good. We had a bite to eat, then sat back and kept our glasses working—if any chamois appeared we should be able to see them. After an hour or so, with no movement of anything, Willy and I hiked down to the hut and the waiting Haflinger. We stopped several times to scan other mountain sides, but nothing moved. The chamois hunt was over, for the next day it snowed heavily.

Steyr-Daimler-Puch—and the P-18 Gas Pistol

I reached Steyr the next day, there to meet Dr. Constantin Breitenfeld and several other firearms people, among them Horst Wesp, the designer who had made a considerable contribution to the development of Steyr's new Model P-18 delayed-blowback gas pistol, of which more a bit later.

I had met Dr. Breitenfeld—Managing Director of Steyr-Daimler-Puch—at the NSGA show held in Chicago early in 1974. All of the many Steyr and Steyr-Mannlicher rifle models were on view at their booth, and I'd stopped by to look them over.

During our talks Dr. Breitenfeld suggested that I might be interested in visiting the S-D-P factory at Steyr and, perhaps, get in a few days hunting red deer and chamois—*hirsch* and *gams* in German. I said I just might like to do that.

I was given an extensive tour of the vast and busy factory, ultra modern big machines mingling with the usual array of older types—lathes, drill press, etc. I won't take up space here commenting on the several Steyr-Mannlicher rifles now in production—except for one. The various S-M rifles—sporting and match, half- and full-stocked—are shown in our catalog pages.

Our hunting cabin in the Austrian alps, Willi Koeberl in the doorway.

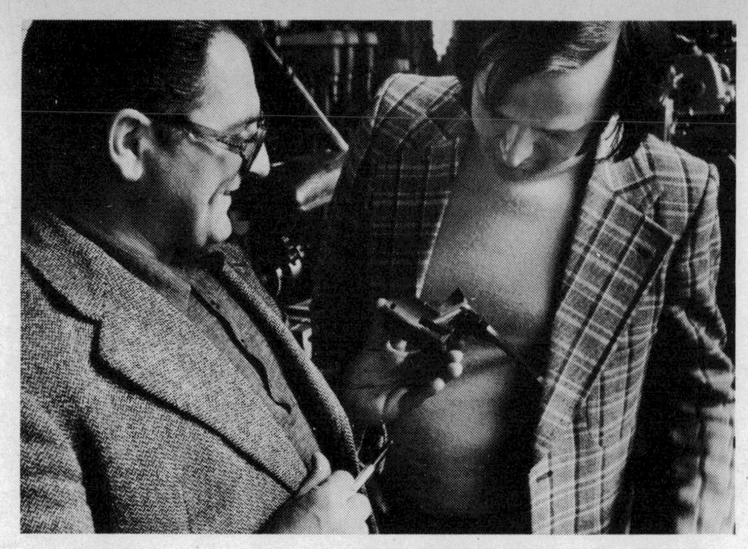

Franz Sodia (left) makes a fine point with Franz Marktl.

Left — H. Kirner and John Amber's small stag.

The exception is the Model SSG, a match-sniper model made only in caliber 308, and furnished with a walnut or synthetic (plastic) stock. I shot one of these, plastic-stocked, that had just been machine-rest fired to check grouping. As Dr. Breitenfeld and I entered the underground 200-meter range, we found some Austrian army officers observing the firing of a string of SSG rifles, part of a government contract. Interestingly, the Steyr-designed machine rest permitted the operator to adjust the scope-equipped rifles for each shot. Of the several rifles I saw tested none made worse than a 2.5-inch group, and this for 10 shots. Most of these groups were nearer to 2 inches! That's damn good for off-the-line rifles at 200 meters, and probably says something for the plastic stocks and the unique design of the SSG rifle. Unlike any other rifles I'm familiar with, the barrel of the SSG is held in an extension of the receiver ring (and integral with it), the length of the receiver-barrel section over *two inches* long. Obviously, this long threading — over twice the length of conventional rifles — results in a much greater stiffness and rigidity in the barrel-supporting area, thus reducing if not fully eliminating the tendency to droop that virtually all barrels exhibit.

The adjacent range, at 100 meters, had only a sandbag for resting the fore-end, the buttstock unsupported. Sitting down, I shouldered the rifle and looked through the scope — pointed post again, though this time not so broad, and the light on the target good. My 10 shots went into just over an inch, the rangemaster said — targets were being viewed on a captive TV — a grid-ruled TV screen. The trigger pull, for an army-contract rifle, was quite crisp and clean, without creep, letoff about 4 pounds. Again, an excellent performance, especially so in view of who did the shooting.

Soon afterward Mr. Wesp invited me to examine and fire the new Steyr "gas" pistol, the P-18. I've put it that way because this 9mm Parabellum autoloader is not gas-operated as that

Top notch engraving by a young man.

Right — An action filer in Ferlach.

term is usually understood – there is no gas piston or like device actuating the breechblock. Instead, the non-locked breech is, momentarily, retarded to allow the gas pressure to subside enough to avoid excessive impact and battering – a recoil buffer is also used. The barrel is rigidly fixed and segmentally (rounded-edge) rifled. The fixed barrel offers better accuracy, at least potentially. The polygonal rifling, it is said, is more efficient in handling cartridge energy – I'm not sure just what that means.

The big advantage of this new and novel design – I think you'll agree – lies in the use of the burning gases to *control and reduce recoil.* This is how it's managed – imagine a separate barrel bushing, its muzzle end carrying a hemispherical cap, locked to the slide by means of a couple of lugs.

Above – the new Steyr Model P-18 auto pistol, caliber 9mm Parabellum, uses the propellant gases to reduce recoil and retard the blowback breechblock's rearward movement. • Left – this bronze memorial in Steyr honors Josef Werndl, founder of Steyr-Daimler-Puch and the inventor of the Austrian military rifle bearing his name. • Below – Steyr's new P-18 auto pistol disassembled. Note that the barrel is fixed in position. Mushroom-like object at upper left is barrel bushing; when the gun is fired the burning gases exert pressure against the hollowed cap interior, markedly reducing recoil.

When a cartridge is fired the burning gases – in addition to delaying the breechblock – flow forward, striking the interior surface of the hemispherical cap, thus pushing the whole gun forward – and thereby reducing recoil.

I can testify that it works – I fired the P-18 at a target about 10 meters away, trying its regular double action system and in single action. I shot while standing, using both hands, and resting them on a lightly-padded board. Shooting with my normal glasses, I found both sights rather blurry, yet I managed – out of the first 10 rounds – to put 6 or 7 into a ragged hole of about an inch diameter. In the circumstances I felt that wasn't bad, but the thing that had impressed me immediately and forcefully was the level of recoil – quite soft and mild, the gun rising in my hands less than half the amount that would have occurred with, say, the S&W 9mm auto.

Designer Wesp had accompanied me to the range, had disassembled the new pistol and put it back together, and had handed me filled magazines during the firing. When I'd finished, he surprised me a lot further! The ammo I'd been shooting, all of it, had been hot *machine gun stuff*, not standard loads – cartridges producing some 30-40 per cent more gas pressure.

The Steyr P-18 pistol will function equally well with all types of 9mm Parabellum cartridges, I was told – those of higher pressure delay the breechblock's opening a little longer, I understand, thus reducing the residual pressure to acceptable levels.

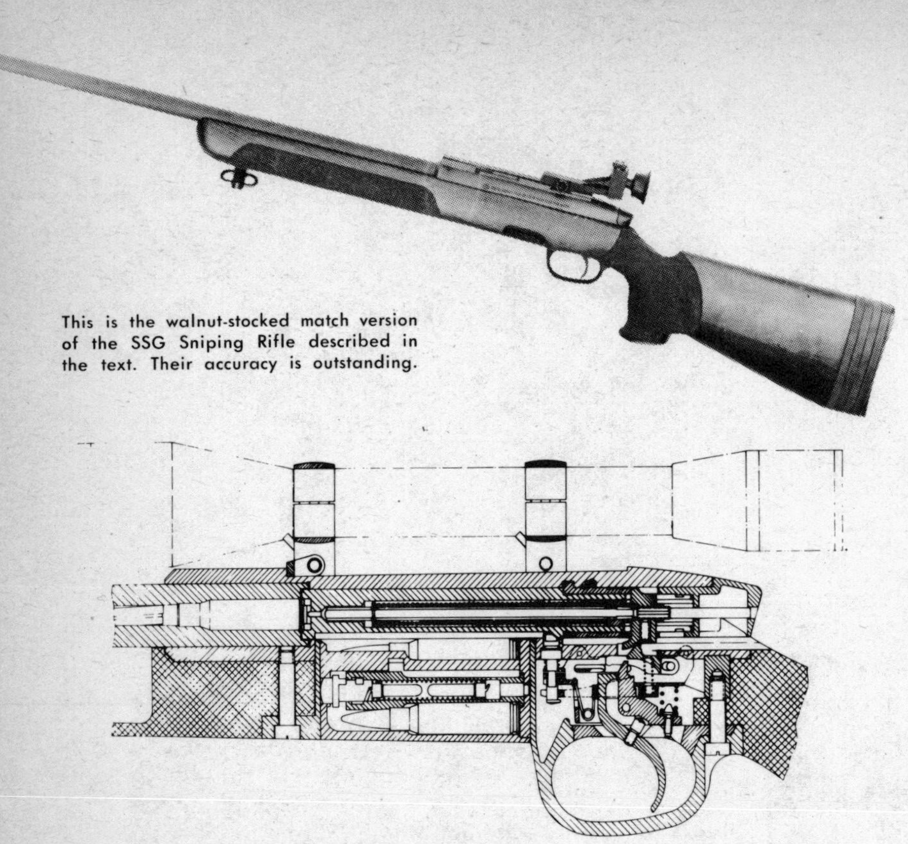

This is the walnut-stocked match version of the SSG Sniping Rifle described in the text. Their accuracy is outstanding.

Sectioned view of the Steyr Model sniper rifle, described in the text. Note the unusually long (57mm) support given the barrel by the integral receiver extension.

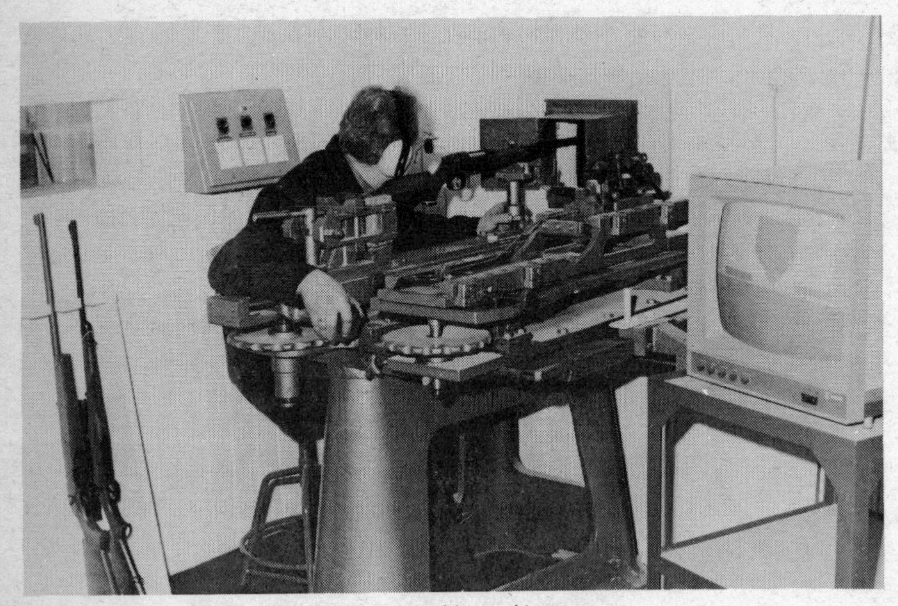

This is the recoil-absorbing, quickly-adjustable machine rest used by S-D-P to test accuracy, the range here 200 meters. Closed-circuit TV at right shows exact placement of bullet strikes.

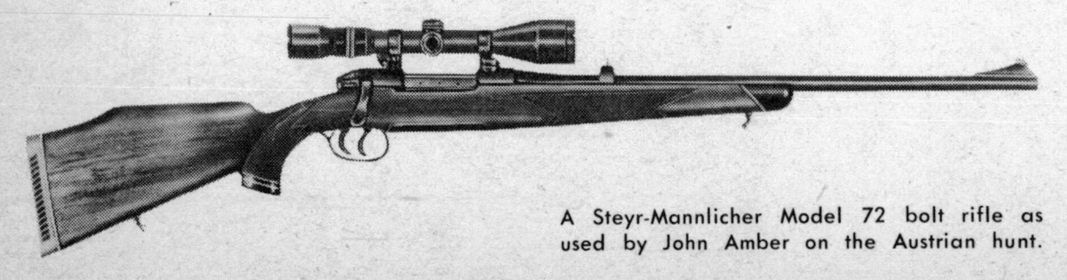

A Steyr-Mannlicher Model 72 bolt rifle as used by John Amber on the Austrian hunt.

Designed for police/military and civilian use, the P-18 will be supplied in full-auto fire or standard form, via different trigger-group systems, neither convertible to the other. The standard magazine, a staggered-feed type, holds 18 cartridges. A 36-round magazine will be available (at least with the full-auto pistol), as will a combination skeleton buttstock/holster—the latter will also hold cleaning gear and oversize magazine. A target version of the P18 may also be made, it's said, these with adjustable sights and match trigger.

L.E.S., the Skokie, Illinois-based importers of the Steyr rifle line, have contracted with Steyr-Daimler-Puch to manufacture and distribute the non-full automatic P-18 pistol in the U.S. Just when finished pistols will be on dealers' shelves I don't know, but I was told a while back that the target date was fall 1975. List price for the standard-version P18 has not been fully fixed, but $180 or so, perhaps, could be close. In a phone talk with the L.E.S. people I learned that some changes will be made in the P-18 Steyr pistol—instead of the receiver halves being made of two stampings welded together, the L.E.S. pistol receiver will be investment cast. In addition the L.E.S. P-18 autoloader will be made of stainless steel throughout.

During an excellent dinner Dr. Breitenfeld gave me one evening, our table overlooking the gleaming Steyr river, I told him about the early snows at Donnersbachwald and my failure to even see a chamois. I mentioned, too, that Mr. Kirner had commented on the weather hazards of an October hunt, suggesting that I return in late August or early September, when good weather would be assured. Dr. Breitenfeld agreed completely—"Come back next year," he said. Maybe I will!

My last night in Steyr was spent with Mr. Wesp, a well-informed gun nut and hunter in addition to his arms design skills. He will soon be, I believe, made chief of gun design for Steyr. We lingered too long over another good dinner, and I didn't get to sleep until after midnight. My flight to Frankfurt-Madrid would leave at 5.45 the next morning (October 18) from Linz, some 25 miles away. I'd have to sleep fast.

The plane left Linz over two hours late—SOP of course. Frankfurt lay under heavy fog. I made the Madrid flight with only minutes to spare, exhausted by the long, long walk from one gate to another. It *must* have been a mile, no less.

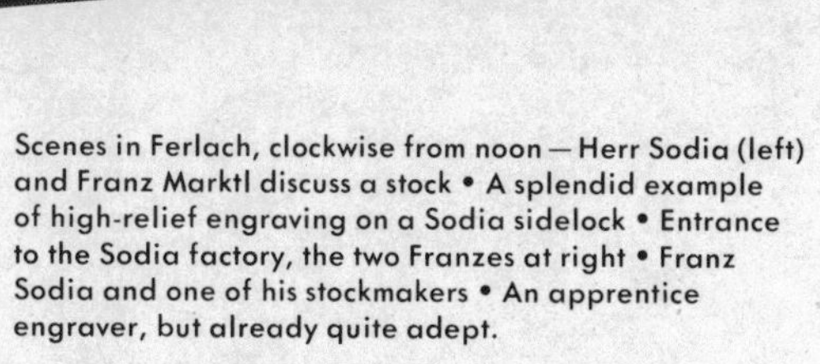

Scenes in Ferlach, clockwise from noon—Herr Sodia (left) and Franz Marktl discuss a stock • A splendid example of high-relief engraving on a Sodia sidelock • Entrance to the Sodia factory, the two Franzes at right • Franz Sodia and one of his stockmakers • An apprentice engraver, but already quite adept.

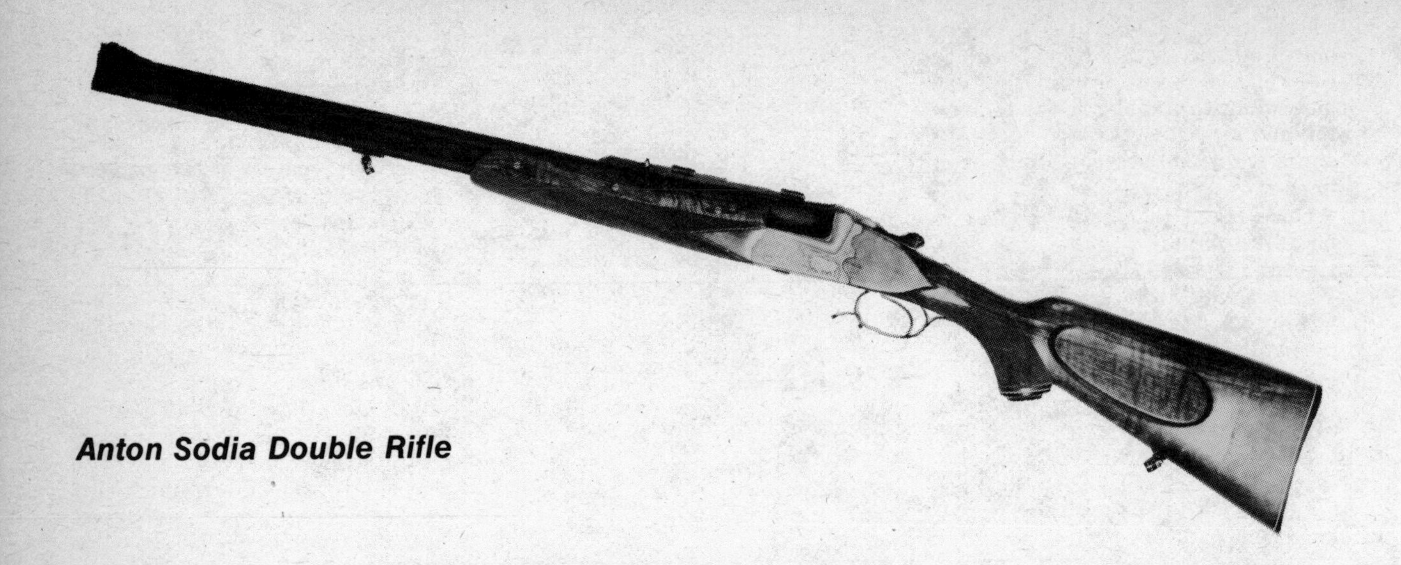

Anton Sodia Double Rifle

This rifle, an over-under in caliber 375 H&H belted magnum, was made by Anton Sodia of Ferlach some years ago—about 1955, as far as I can tell from the proofmarks. I bought it from a man who'd had it made for an African hunt—he'd spent several years in Europe—but he couldn't find the time to get away.

It had been fired, he said, only about two dozen times, and its general condition bears that out—the breech faces show no evidence of much shooting, and the bores seem to be about as new. The outside finish—wood and metal—appears quite fresh. Action lockup is very tight, and it still opens a bit stiffly. As noted in the table of specs, the rifle has a single trigger and ejectors, non-selective. I've had no trouble with the single trigger yet—knock wood—but then I've fired it less than 50 rounds thus far. The trigger is of mechanical type, which I much prefer, especially on a rifle that may see use on dangerous game.

The action is locked by double Kersten barrel lugs and two underlugs as well. The Kersten bolt fits tightly, with no sign of slop or play—more evidence of little use. I haven't yet checked the underlugs for fit, but there seems to be no shake or looseness anywhere.

The stock dimensions are about average for this type of rifle. Length of pull is 13⅞", drop at comb 1⁷⁄₁₆", at heel 2⁵⁄₁₆" from the open sights line. The comb could be a little higher, now that I've put a scope on it, though the drop at comb was OK with the original iron sights. The pull is short for me, too, especially in a shirt-sleeve rifle. I'll fit a slip-on rubber butt pad, as I usually have to do.

The front sight is a metal bead, nominally ¹⁄₁₆-inch diameter, I suppose. It mikes 0.655". The open rear sight has a matching, small U-notch. Both are too small, in my opinion, and the open leaf is not the style I prefer—which is a broad, shallow V-notch. On a rifle I'd use at short range or on dangerous game (with the quick-detachable scope removed), I want a front bead big and bold, one I can catch instantly. A ⅛-inch bead wouldn't be at all too big. At 50 yards, that ⅛-inch front sight subtends only 11¼ inches, with this rifle's 20-inch iron sight radius. That'd be no sighting handicap on big game animals—on the contrary, it would help. I can't understand why these tiny beads persist. Anyway, wanting the use of a scope, I talked about the problem of having a mount made with Richard Hodgson of Boulder, Colorado. Dick does really beautiful metalsmithing—and equally fine custom stocking. He thought he could make suitable mounts or adapt some two-piece German-made bases and rings I had on hand, so I sent him the barrels along with my bits and pieces.

Some time later I got the barrels back. I was prepared for something nice, inasmuch as Dick had told me he'd found my bases and rings not suitable for the job he wanted to do, but I was still surprised at the superb quality and execution I saw in these handsome mounts.

They're utterly simple, of course. Hodgson made transverse cuts in the rib, fitting a base into each cut. These bases, dovetailed in section, are radiussed on top to allow the use of the iron sights when the scope and rings are removed. Each base carries two integral lugs at the forward end, one

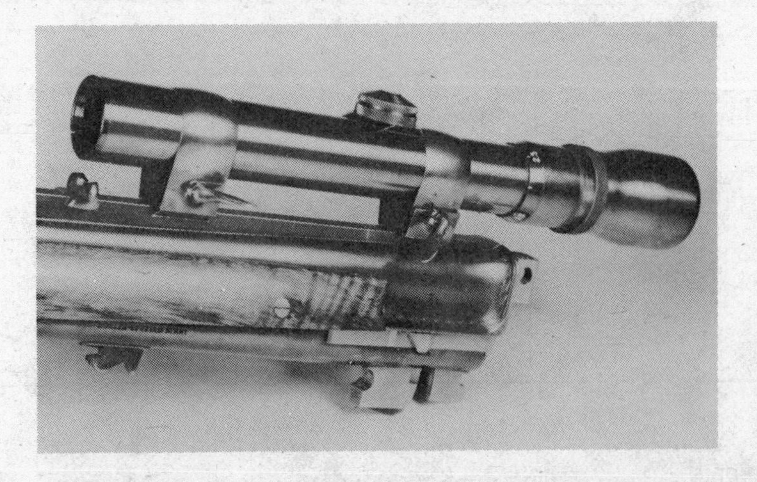

Richard Hodgson, a master metalsmith in Boulder, Colorado, created this handmade scope mount for the Sodia 375 H&H double rifle. Rear lever has been released slightly to show how the locking element moves outward. When levers are tightened (as at front) the joint lines are virtually undetectable.

on either side of the radius cut. When the rings are slid onto the bases, these paired lugs act as both locaters for the rings and as stops to prevent the scope moving forward under recoil. Removing and replacing the scope between shots shows no change in point of impact.

Once I had the scope mounted, I had little trouble getting the rifle sighted in. A few shots with 270-gr. Winchester cartridges gave me rather wide groups, bottom and top barrels alternately—these went into 6-7 inches at 75 yards. Winchester 300-gr. Silvertips halved those figures at the same range, with the 3 inches or so between shots being lateral, not vertical. I have a hunch this 375 was regulated with British cartridges, but I had none of these to try.

I then started working up a load for 300-gr. Nosler bullets, my first choice in hunting bullets. This was easily done, too—I loaded 78.0, 79.0 and 80.0 grains of 4350, and it was the 80-gr. charge that did the trick. Group spread for 6 shots, 3 from each barrel, was about identical at some 3 inches, and elevation was no more than a quarter-inch below the level reached with the 300-gr. Silvertips. Later on I was gratified to find that muzzle velocity figures for both Nosler and Silvertip loads were identical. The chronograph showed exactly the same foot seconds for both, with MV at 2609 fps.

Anton Sodia Double Rifle

Cal.: 375 Holland & Holland Belted.

Bbls.: 26", round, Böhler Antinit, over-under.

Action: Boxlock, double underlugs plus double Kersten locking bolts. Low relief engraved, showing American moose and bison, greyed finish. Top tang, lever and guard are also engraved.

Trigger: Single, non-selective, lower barrel fires first, mechanical, not inertial.

Stock: High-contrast, fiddle-back grained French walnut, pistol gripped, fine-line checkering fore and aft; fore-end is 2-piece type, a la Merkel, with center-lever release. Horn p.g. cap and buttplate, checkered. Dimensions from iron sight line—1⁷⁄₁₆"x 2⁵⁄₁₆"x13⅞".

Sights: Single broad-blade open rear, with U-notch, small bead front on ramp.

Weight: 8¼ lbs. with iron sights; 9 lbs. scant with 1½-4½x Weaver scope in R. Hodgson mount.

The French walnut stock and fore-end show good figure and contrast, with a nice bit of fiddleback grain; the color is a warm reddish-brown.

The pistol grip area and the fore-end are well covered with a multi-point diamond checkering pattern, about 24 lines per inch. The top of the diamonds are slightly flattened in the typical European tradition.

White line spacers at the grip cap and buttplate add a touch of something, though I hesitate to say just what in a family publication. They'll come off one day.

The top tang safety, I'm sorry to say, is an automatic one. I'll have to get that changed. On a rifle that may see action on dangerous game I want a manual safety. I don't intend to stand there bending the trigger and wondering why the gun doesn't fire!

The single trigger has functioned without a bobble so far. Non-selective, it fires the lower barrel first. As I've said, its action is mechanical, not inertial—the upper barrel fires whether the lower cartridge is touched off or not. That's good insurance in a tight spot.

The ejectors work well; fired cases are kicked forcibly rearward, landing some 6 feet or more behind the shooter.

Sling swivels are sited fore and aft, but they'll handle nothing wider than ⅝-inch straps. They're not of quick-detachable type. Happily, the tapered-end sling that came on the rifle is about 1⅛-inches wide at the center.

I took this rifle on the Kenya hunt in 1973, thinking I'd use it on buffalo or lion, but that wasn't to be. J.T.A.

Range Testing the Steyr Model 72 Rifle

If Sunday, May 4, proved a rainless, not-too-cold day, old friend Ron Wozny would come out to the Farm and shoot the Mannlicher-Schönauer 7x64mm rifle for me. It was and he did—because of some physical problems that hit me during early 1975, I won't be able to shoot a rifle for some months yet.

I'd put a Bushnell 4x scope on the M-S 72, using the 2-piece bases and rings sent with the rifle. The receiver ring and bridge are tapped for bases, but the hole separations are quite short, not accepting any U.S. bases I know about.

Sighting-in done, using the new Bushnell portable collimator, Ron ran four 3-shot groups over the 100-yd. distance, the ammo RWS stuff loaded with the 162-gr. Brenneke Torpedo-Ideal bullet (TIG). Average spread was 1.5 inches, with a low/high of 1.1" -1.72". All went into the same point-of-impact area, no shots "walking".

Ron also noticed the stiff working of the action, which eased a little as he shot, and he liked the double set trigger very much, that is, when used in the set mode. Pull unset is about 4 lbs., quite crisp, and about 4 ounces when set—and very clean.

I had only 9 rounds of the ABC ammo, and I'd wanted to use these in a penetration/expansion test if possible. We couldn't get this arranged in time, though, so 5 of these were shot for group. Maximum spread was a disappointing 3.4 inches, and Ron agreed that we'd both heard the same thing—a marked difference in muzzle-report level from shot to shot, and he'd felt a difference in recoil as well. Surprising, of course, so I'll pull the bullets from the rest of the ABC ammo and check out what I can.

Not knowing when and if factory 7x64mm ammo would reach me in time, I asked Fred Huntington to send me a trim-form die to convert U.S. brass (280, 30-06) to the metric caliber, and a set of loading dies, of course.

Using some Federal 30-06 cases, trimming wasn't needed, so 10 loads were easily readied—47 grains of old Hodgdon H-4831 and some equally old or older 175-gr. HP bullets. Three of these were fired and formed the brass OK, but went low (below the targets) with the hunting-ammo scope adjustment, so the others will be shot another time. J.T.A.

Partridge in Spain

Happily, one of the few nice days of the trip presented itself on October 20 – a brilliant Sunday, the sky clear and cloudless, a light wind blowing. This was the day of the big shoot for redlegs, my host the former head of sport and touring in Spain, Manuel Fraga Iribarne – now the Spanish ambassador to the United Kingdom. I had first met Don Manuel some years ago – he had been most helpful in my being granted a permit to shoot a Spanish ibex, not an easy ticket to obtain (see GUN DIGEST, 24th ed., 1970).

After a get-acquainted dinner the night before, our cavalcade of cars left for the shooting area about 40 miles from Madrid – beautiful rolling country that grows grapes and olives in profusion – the many-acred domain of Don Eduardo Barreiros. Our party, some 13 gunners, quickly left for the first beat of the day, our transportation a string of Land Rovers. As is the standard practice in Spain, each of us was assigned two *secretarios*, as they're called, one of whom does the gun loading.

I was using a pair of AYA sidelock double 12s I'd borrowed from Seymour Ziebert, an old friend and long-time resident in Madrid. Don Manuel had left London with a group of English shooters he'd invited over, and I'd noticed – as we were uncasing our guns – a pretty fair number of Purdeys and Holland & Hollands being put together by the Britons.

The shooting went well, the partridge coming over our blinds in good fashion generally and, after not having shot *perdiz* for several years, I didn't do very well on the first go-round. I'd forgotten how damned fast redlegs fly and their habit of skimming close to the ground until they sight the blinds. However, by swinging ahead of them by twice as far as I'd been doing – or farther – I started to connect.

The management of the shoot was exceptionally well organized. As soon as we finished one beat and the *secretarios* had collected the birds, off we went in the Land Rovers to the next venue, as the English say – no delay. Around 2 o'clock, when we'd finished our third stand, we returned to Don Barreiros' shooting lodge for a sumptuous lunch – I know there were four kinds of wine, at least, and an array of dishes that Escoffier would have praised.

The last two beats took us almost to dusk, with over 700 redlegs in the bag. I was, of course, a long way from being top gun, but it had been a great and greatly enjoyable day, and I'd put down about 50 birds – better than good for me!

A drive has just finished, and my other secretario is out looking for downed birds.

A lull during the partridge shoot. Our host, Don Manuel Fraga Iribarne, stands right of center.

The Gunmakers of Eibar

Two days later, the rain a heavy downpour, Ziebert and I left by air for the visit to Spain's centuries-old gunmaking center. As we approached Eibar we could see the flooded fields, the overflowing streams and hundreds of new waterfalls coursing down the hills. There are no canvas tunnels to shield the passengers at Eibar airport – Ziebert and I were about soaked as we reached the terminal doors.

Our first visit was to the AYA (Aguirre y Aranzabel) factory, and once more I was surprised at the immensity of the place, the vast floorspace and the several-story building. AYA sells shotguns the world over, and their production is big. The range of models is also big – 28 models are cataloged, many of these – especially those in the better grades – obtainable with a variety of extras, and made to the customer's specifications, if desired.

With one exception – an inexpensive single barrel – all AYA smoothbores are double-barreled, most of the better grades with genuine sidelocks, some of these lever-detachable. Almost as many boxlock guns are also made, usually with Anson & Deeley lockwork. Two over-under guns are available – the Super with detachable sidelocks, the Coral a boxlock. These two O-Us have double Kersten top bolting and ejectors. Apart from the inexpensive single barrel, the price range of AYA guns is very wide; there's a price to suit most anyone. The most expensive AYA is about 10 times the cost of the lowest.

Don Gregorio Garralda (left) and Seymour Ziebert discuss one of many AYA shotguns on view in their showroom.

Center—Jesus Barrenchea, head of Armas Garbi—makers of excellent Spanish shotguns—holds one of his best-quality sidelock doubles.

As I've said, I had borrowed a pair of AYA sidelock ejector guns for the redleg shoot, both closely matched in all respects and fitted with single selective triggers. So you can guess what happened—I ordered an AYA sidelock, their No. 1 grade, in 20 gauge and to be furnished with an extra set of barrels. This No. 1 grade is not, curiously, their best grade; it's a cut or two below. In general appearance it looks much like a Purdey, even to the scroll/floral engraving design. I'd hoped this straight-gripped gun would reach me in time for a shooting report on it, but it hasn't.

Another famed Spanish gunmaker is Ignacio Ugartechea, maker also of an extensive array of models—some dozen types altogether. Price range and quality is on a par with AYA; the sidelock ejector guns I examined were handsome, well-balanced guns, their finishing and execution excellent. On our visit to the Ugartechea plant, during which Ziebert and I had a lengthy talk with Don Ignacio, he showed us the one remaining specimen of a fine double rifle that had once been in production, but I couldn't induce him to make one for me!

(Ziebert, by the way, knows just about everybody in the firearms field in Spain. He's personally acquainted with most of the gunmakers, and I didn't know how I'd managed without his generous help. More importantly, maybe, he was cordially received wherever we went, and his command of Spanish—as well as the various dialects—is good indeed.)

Live pigeon shooting is a perfectly legal sport in Spain, and a highly popular one, too, at least for those who can afford it. The pigeon club near Madrid is a busy place most weekends, all three rings going strong. Armas Garbi, the next gunmaking firm we called on, makes guns for both hunting and target shooting, but it is his competition doubles that form the bulk of his business. They've won a reputation for performance and reliability in a demanding field—the dedicated target shooter fires thousands of cartridges annually.

Garbi's better grade doubles, all made in sidelock form, are fairly expensive, even by Spanish standards, but it's not hard to see why. They're beautifully put together, the joining of wood to metal faultless, the lockwork highly polished and carefully hand fitted. Garbi's best grade, the Model 200 Super, is a strikingly handsome gun—the profuse engraving on this model is a "specialty of the house," not applied to other Garbi models, and the walnut (at least on the several Model 200s I saw) was beautifully figured. Rough blanks of this quality would bring several hundred dollars in the U.S. All of the better grade Garbi guns can be ordered to the customer's dimensions and taste, without extra cost – and most of them are. Matched pairs are available as a matter of course – most Spanish shooters, as well as other Europeans, order guns in pairs because much of the shooting is at driven birds.

I didn't order a Garbi gun, much as I'd have liked to. As my wife often says –much too often– why do you need another gun?

A day or so later, landing in Chicago, it started to rain. ●

Ignacio Ugartechea (right), president of the gunmaking firm that bears his name, looks over a boxlock receiver awaiting further processing.

Pennsylvania Bicentennial Commission Commemorative Longrifle

We're prejudiced, of course, but in the face of the numerous and meretricious products being urged on us in the name of the bicentennial celebration, the project outlined here is a noteworthy one, and truly a limited issue.

The state that gave birth to the famous long rifle of American history has authorized its re-creation as a significant part of its bicentennial celebration. The Pennsylvania Bicentennial Commission is presenting a serially numbered, limited edition of 200 commemorative longrifles and correspondingly numbered powder horns for serious collectors of bicentennial memorabilia.

Gunmakers John Bivins of Winston-Salem, North Carolina and Thomas White of Worthington, Ohio will handcraft the rifles to a general pattern created by Mr. Bivins especially for the bicentennial. The rifles will not be a copy of any existing antique rifle, but will represent in *style* and *carving* the Lancaster school of gunsmithing during the Revolutionary War period. The Bicentennial Rifles will not be reproduced again, in their entirety, following production of the initial 200.

Each rifle will be marked with the Pennsylvania Bicentennial Commission seal and numbered—under the barrel, and on a plate permanently affixed to the interior of the patchbox. The accompanying powder horn will be designed and produced by Mr. White. Each horn will be scrimshawed in a pattern appropriate to Pennsylvania (names, areas, etc.).

Only the finest of components will be used for this project in order to complement the talents of the craftsmen involved. Special investment castings have been designed and produced to assure the authenticity of the metal parts used. Thousands of stock blanks are being carefully examined to obtain the best that are available.

Rifle barrels will be produced by Robert Paris & Son of Gettysburg, Pennsylvania. These barrels will be swamped (flared) in the manner of the quality rifles the period represented. They will be 50 caliber and 44 inches long. The well-known locks of C. E. "Bud" Siler of Asheville, North Carolina, will complete the handsome and authentic package.

It should be pointed out that these will be eminently usable commemorative rifle sets, should the owner so desire. Each rifle set will include a target showing the striking point of the bullet, a brochure including instructions on using and caring for the arm, and a five-year warranty on parts.

Throughout the planning stages of this project the emphasis has been placed on quality and accuracy of re-

From left—John Bivins, who will make a hundred of the longrifles; Bud Siler, supplier of the flint locks; Don Hartnett, director of the project, and Tom White, who is to make the other half of the rifles, and all of the powder horns.

Top of the Commemorative longrifle, showing raised carving and initial plate.

production. We believe that we have created a collectible commemorative rifle of unique beauty and lasting value.

Rifles may be ordered by sending a check to V. Donald Hartnett, (Project Director, Pennsylvania Bicentennial Commission, 202 Hystone Ave., Johnstone, PA 15905). The cost per set is $2250; Pennsylvania residents must add the 6% state sales tax ($135). Orders will be processed on a first-come, first-served basis. Total production will take about two and one-half years to complete because of the amount of handwork involved.

The customer, on sending his check, will receive a receipt bearing an assigned rifle set number and approximate delivery date.

The patchbox, made of brass, is correct for the Revolutionary War period, as are the guard and the flint lock.

This handsome and traditional powder horn, designed and executed by Tom White, will accompany each of the Bivins and White longrifles.

Note the PBC longrifle's cheekpiece form, the raised carvings and brass lockstrap, the traditional trigger.

The PBC Commemorative longrifle barrels, 50 caliber and 44 inches long, will be made by Robert Paris and Son. Elegant, strong, and fully functional, these superb rifles will be a joy to own and, if desired, to shoot.

Some of the 22 varmint cartridges that date from the Hornet of 1932 to the 22-250 Remington that appeared in commercial form in 1965. From left—22 Hornet, 218 Bee, 222 Remington, 222 Remington Magnum, 224 Weatherby, 225 Winchester, 22-250 Remington and 220 Swift.

The Great 22 Varminters

Some were greater than others, certainly, but there is no question that those of 22 caliber offer the best selection for the average varmint hunter, the individual who will be shooting a variety of species under average conditions. Here they are, reviewed and appraised.

by BOB HAGEL

THOUGH THIS TREATISE will deal almost exclusively with 22 centerfire cartridges—particularly those with magnum capacity cases for the .22" bore size—a few words about the 22 rimfires that, probably, led to the development of the first black powder centerfires, may be in order.

Apparently the rimfire 22 Short was not only the first U.S. 22 cartridge, but was also the first self-contained metallic cartridge. The little cartridge got its start as a revolver round chambered in the Smith & Wesson First Model in about 1857. It is still with us and going strong after nearly 120 years of use in every conceivable rifle and pistol. Considering the length of time it has been around, and its popularity, it is safe to say that more 22 Short ammunition has been fired than any other cartridge; probably more than several of any other cartridges combined.

It was followed by the more powerful 22 Long about 1871, the 22 Extra Long around 1880, and the 22 Long Rifle about 1887. The latter three were logical developments for more power following the 22 Short; it was also logical that someone would come up with the idea of a 22 centerfire to make use of the accuracy of this caliber and extend its range for small game shooting, pest control and target work.

Early History

Apparently the first successful attempt in this direction was the 22 Extra Long Maynard. This centerfire was not a great deal more powerful than the 22 LR of that day, and not as powerful as the high velocity 22 LR of today. It appeared about 1882 and was followed shortly by the 22 Winchester Centerfire in 1885. In its black powder loading the 22 WCF boosted a 45-gr. bullet along at a claimed 1540 feet per second (fps). It was, perhaps, the first step toward a 22 centerfire *varmint* cartridge.

Probably the last of the black powder 22 centerfires was the little known 22-15-60 Stevens, a rather long skinny cartridge that was said to drive a 60-gr. bullet at about 1150 fps. This cartridge did not appear until near the turn of the century, and would not appear to have been well adapted to smokeless powder; that likely contributed to the fact that it never became very popular. It would have been a good cartridge for taking small game for the pot with its 60-gr. bullet; it shot fairly flat at small game ranges, and it was a good killer without being overly destructive.

In fact, this is one place that these older centerfire 22s, and the modern 22 LR, have it all over the big 22 high velocity cartridges of today: you could kill small game and eat it, too. That's something you don't do with today's hotshots!

The 22 Hornet

The 22 Hornet, which first appeared as a wildcat based on the 22 WCF cartridge, as the brainchild of Townsend Whelen and Grosvenor Wotkyns, was the cartridge that certainly started the climb to the 22 varmint cartridges we've been using ever since. The Hornet was not much of a varmint cartridge by today's standards, but it was pretty hot stuff when it appeared in Griffin & Howe, Savage, Sedgley and Winchester rifles in the early '30s. The 45-gr. factory bullet now steps along at nearly 2700 fps, and it was and is a good cartridge on all varmints from ground squirrels to chucks out to 150 yards or so. On chucks and jackrabbits it is not too difficult to hit them at 200 yards, but lack of bullet blowup and the consequent lack of quick killing power make it less than desirable at that range.

Another thing about the Hornet is that handloading it doesn't improve velocity much over today's factory offering. This wasn't always the case —in 1932 the Winchester factory-loaded Hornet had an advertised muzzle velocity of 2350 fps. The powder charge was 10.4 grains of Du Pont's No. 1204.

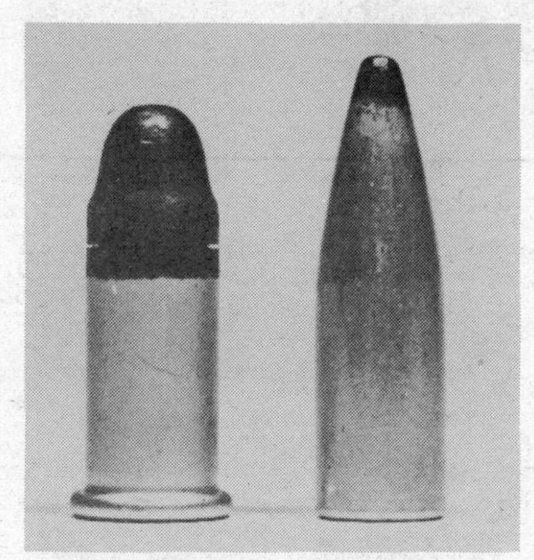

Though the 22 Short has no place in the 22 centerfire field, and can hardly be considered a varmint cartridge, it does hold several records no other cartridge can ever attain. It is not only the first 22 cartridge commercially loaded in America, but the oldest self-contained metallic cartridge. It dates back to 1857, and there's no question that more 22 Shorts have been fired than any other cartridge. Further, it is still going so strong that no other cartridge is ever likely to catch up in all-time sales. Here it is overshadowed by a 60-gr. Hornady bullet!

The 220 Swift

The echoes of the Hornet success had hardly died down when Winchester again stirred varmint hunters to shouts of joy with the introduction of the 220 Swift. The Swift was one of those rare cartridges that, while no one realized it at the time, was not to be surpassed by any other commercial cartridge in the next 40 years or so. Little wonder that it caused a great deal of comment and all kinds of unfounded speculation! Not only has there never been a factory 22 caliber cartridge that gave more velocity, there has never been one of any other caliber either. It remains *the* all-round varmint cartridge, it is still right there at the top of the heap where it started life. When Winchester saw fit to discontinue chambering it in the Model 70, then discontinue even loading ammo for it, they didn't make one of the most brilliant moves in company history. Sales were undoubtedly down, but sales of the 225 Winchester that "replaced" it didn't leave a blazing trail either.

218 Bee and 219 Zipper

Shortly after the advent of the Swift, Winchester also brought out a pair of rimmed cartridges in the form of the 218 Bee and 219 Zipper for lever action rifles. These were good cartridges which bracketed the later 222 Remington in the velocity department. The 218 Bee pushed a 46-gr. bullet along at nearly 2900 fps in factory loading, which advertised figure was probably a bit optimistic, and doing little if any better than that in handloads. The 219 had a bit more boiler room, being built on the 25-35 case, and factory 56-gr. bullets were said to travel along at just over 3100 fps. It was possible to boost the 55-gr. weight .224" bullet along at about 3500 fps with near-maximum charges of 4064, 4320 and 4895, and this figure could surely be equaled today with some of the newer W-W ball powders or Norma 203 in bolt action rifles.

Neither of these cartridges was ever to become highly popular. There were several reasons for this: For one thing, they seemed rather "plane Jane" compared to the Swift. For another, the lever actions they were chambered in left something to be desired in attaining real accuracy. True, these lever guns were certainly accurate enough for short-range pest shooting around the farm, and for small-game shooting, but small-game *cartridges* they were not, in spite of the fact that they have been listed as such. Being rimmed, they were not suited to bolt actions without magazine modifications. They were both ideal for single-shot actions and proved to be very accurate and good varmint cartridges in the single shooters. But this was during a period when few shooters looked backward with fits of nostalgia in an attempt to recapture something from the unhurried past, and there weren't many single shots rebarreled to the rimmed 22s.

Some of these same reasons, most likely, were responsible for the failure of the 22 Savage Hi-Power cartridge to gain more popularity when it appeared in 1912. Promoted and advertised as a big game cartridge, it never caught on as a varmint round.

The 222

After the flurry of new 22-caliber varmint cartridges appearing in the 1930s had subsided, little was done in the 22 line until Remington produced the "baby '06" in the form of the 222 Remington in 1950. The 222 was popular right from the start, and for

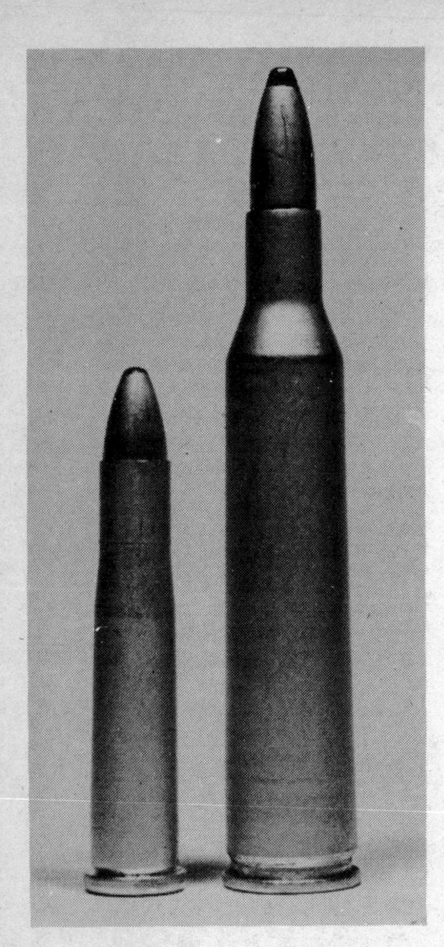

Call 'em Mutt & Jeff if you will, these two cartridges, of contrasting size and velocity, are the first two Winchester entries into the 22 caliber varmint cartridge field. Strangely, they appeared only about three years apart. The 22 Hornet at left was followed shortly by more powerful cartridges such as the 218 Bee, 219 Zipper and the later 222 Remington, but the 220 Swift still stands as velocity king. Not only of the 22 clan, but for all commercially-loaded cartridges.

good reasons. Like the Hornet, it was quite accurate usually with factory ammunition in factory rifles and, if you wanted to get serious with it and handload, it was then, and still is, the most consistently accurate 100-yard cartridge ever produced. There may be those who disagree with that statement, but if you doubt it just take a look at the records from any bench rest match. There are always a number of rifles in the top ten that are chambered for the plain 222 Remington.

Not only was the 222 one of the finest match grade cartridges ever produced, it is also one of the best varmint cartridges for the great bulk of varmint hunting. This is especially true in farm country because of its low noise level compared to cartridges like the Swift and 22-250. It is completely reliable out to around 200 yards with any good bullet of 50/55 grains on all varmints up to chucks and jackrabbits. While I don't consider it the best choice, I've killed bobcats and coyotes at that range with one.

Most of the 222 rifles I've used shot their tightest groups at velocities of around 3000 fps with 50/52-gr. bullets. However, many of the loads used by bench rest competitors are loaded hot as hell, probably over the 3200 fps listed as standard for the 50-gr. factory load. For whatever it is worth, I have yet to chronograph a factory 50-gr. 222 load in a standard 24" barrel that gave 3100 fps. A bit over 3000 fps is what most of them show on the clock.

The 222 Remington Magnum

The 222 Remington Magnum, which didn't appear until 1958, never became really popular. It is, however, a good cartridge, and will give higher velocity than the standard 222 in spite of what some loading manuals show. One of the popular manuals shows that it is possible to get 3400 fps with a 50-gr. bullet with both the 222 Remington and 222 Remington Magnum with *maximum* loads, both rifles having 26" barrels. When you consider that the magnum case holds 4 grains more of Ball-C2 than does the standard 222, and the great difference that even 1 grain of powder makes in velocity at this case capacity, it is obvious that something is amiss. Everything else being equal, pressures have got to be a lot higher in the standard case.

Actually, the 222 Remington Magnum has from 100-200 fps more muzzle speed than its standard predecessor, depending on bullet weight and powder used, if both are loaded to the same pressures. And it is just that much better as a varmint cartridge. It shoots that much flatter, expands the same bullets that much farther away and, therefore, kills that much better. I've killed many rockchucks at over 250 yards with it and it gave instant, violent kills in all cases.

The 223

The 223 Remington, which is the commercial version of the 5.56mm military round, has never achieved any great popularity. This might well be expected because it falls midway between the 222 and the larger 222 Magnum. It hasn't got too much on the 222 and is surpassed by the 222 Magnum. There was a flurry of interest, according to my mail, because some shooters felt it might well be a desirable cartridge because military brass seemed likely to become available in large quantities for free. I haven't heard much about this angle of late.

Weatherby's 224 Varmintmaster

When we consider all of the high velocity cartridges that Roy Weatherby has conceived and commercialized, it seems odd that it took him so long to bring out a high velocity 22 cartridge. Perhaps this isn't quite correct because there was a 220 Weatherby Rocket made on an improved 220 Swift case back in the days when Roy was first getting started, but it was never factory loaded. But it was not until 1963 that Weatherby unveiled a cute little belted case in the form of the 224 Weatherby Varmintmaster. Strangely, unlike the other Weatherby cartridges, the 224 was not a particularly high velocity number. Weatherby velocity figures indicate 3750fps for the 50-gr. bullet and 3650 for the 55-gr. Yet with the 24" barreled test rifle I had, factory 55-gr. ammo gave only 3525 on my chronograph, and handloads ran about the same. It is possible to boost the velocity of the 50-gr. bullet to around 3700 fps, and the 55-gr. to quoted factory ballistics, but my experience showed that loads of any powder at that velocity level were damn hot, and accuracy was pretty sour. The best loads I ever worked up for accuracy were with around 32 grains of Norma 203, 4064, 4320 and 4895 behind 52/55-gr. bullets. These loads never gave quite 3600 fps, running from 3450 to 3550, depending on bullet and powder. Accuracy was very good at this velocity-pressure level, with many bullets and loads down around the 1 minute of angle (MOA) point. According to some of the loading dope put out it is possible to get 22-250 velocities from the 224 Weatherby, but if you do pressures will be so high that very short case life is the result. In fact, if you want to push the 22-250 to the same pressures, velocity will be considerably higher because of the greater case capacity.

The 225 Winchester

The latest Winchester offering in the 22 varmint field never really got off the ground. There isn't a thing wrong with the 225 Winchester except that it is a rimmed cartridge, so it isn't ideal for bolt action rifles. Winchester overcame the feeding problems created by rimmed cartridges in staggered-column Mauser type magazines, by using the long Model 70 action and slanting fillers front and rear so that the first cartridge loaded has its rim to the rear of the next one on top. However, this setup wasn't

Varmint bullets in .224" diameter are almost unlimited today. These are only some of the most popular. From left, in the 5 groups, are: Hornady 45-gr.; Hornady, Speer, Sierra and Remington PL 50-gr.; 52-gr. Remington BR, Sierra 52-gr., Speer 52-gr., Sierra 53-gr. and Hornady 53-gr., all hollow points; Speer, Sierra, and Hornady 55-gr.; Sierra 63-gr., Hornady 60-gr. and Speer 70-gr. heavyweights; new Nosler 50-gr. SP, 52-gr. HP, 55-gr. SP, and older 55-gr. Zipedo.

very practical for custom riflemakers, so cartridge sales ran low and so did sales of Winchester rifles chambered for the 225. Another bad situation was created for the 225 Winchester, as well as the 224 Weatherby, when the wildcat 22-250, with its great popularity already built in, became a commercial number in Remington rifles. Also, the 225 didn't come up to the performance level of the 220 Swift it nominally replaced.

Matter of fact, the 225 is a very good varmint round. It is potentially a highly accurate cartridge (given a good barrel, as always) that falls between the 224 Weatherby and the 22-250 in case capacity and velocity. Its performance level is also between, right where you would expect it. In my work with it when it first appeared I found that, like the 224 Weatherby, if you tried to push it to 22-250 velocity you ran into pressure problems and accuracy fell off. With the heavy-barrel test rifle I had I found that 4064 gave the best accuracy with 52-gr. bullets and, in this instance, at maximum pressures.

The 22-250

No one will ever know why it took the big arms companies so long to realize that the 22-250 was such a good varmint cartridge. That it had great sales appeal is brought home by the fact that when Remington chambered it in their Model 700 rifle with no changes whatever from its wildcat form, Weatherby and Winchester soon followed suit. In fact, Winchester dropped chambering for the 225 entirely in favor of the 22-250.

It is pretty hard to say anything about the 22-250 that hasn't been said hundreds of times. One could put it briefly and say that it is one of the top varmint 22 caliber cartridges of all time, and certainly the most popular, both in wildcat and factory loadings. But there are also many things that have been claimed for the 22-250 that are a bit on the optimistic side, and some that are not quite correct.

It has been said often that it will do about anything the 220 Swift will do, and do it with less barrel wear and at lower pressures. Let's face the cold facts: The 22-250 is one hell of a good cartridge, but it has no built in magic or mystic powers. If you try to load it to 220 Swift velocity with the same bullets, pressures will be prohibitive, and if there is any difference in barrel wear, neither you no I will be able to see it. I've found that any time you step a 55-gr. bullet along at 3700 fps from a 24" barrel in a 22-250, pressures are about as high as permissible, and it is just as easy to get 3850 fps from a Swift with the same barrel length and the same bullet with the right powder—if not easier!

This isn't to say that the 22-250 isn't one of the great all-time cartridges, and it isn't to say that it is not probably the best choice of the high velocity 22s for all forms of varmint hunting. But it certainly will not outperform the Swift or some of the wildcats with slightly more powder capacity.

The Swift Today

As far as the Swift goes, it is one of those cartridges that gives extremely good accuracy at full throttle. It has always been loaded to full throttle in factory loading and you can't improve on factory velocity much with the same bullets by handloading. But you can improve on the bullets you use in handloads over the factory offering. Unfortunately, Winchester not only discontinued chambering for the Swift cartridge, they also quit loading ammunition for it. They do still make

Here the writer shoots a 22-250 in rockchuck country. An old wildcat that went commercial, the 22-250 is extremely versatile for all kinds of varmint shooting, from ground squirrels to coyotes.

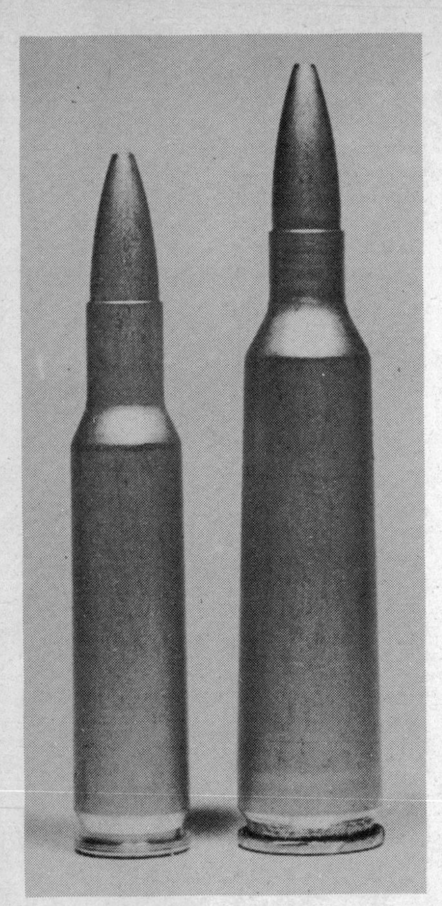

The 222 (left) and 22-250 Remingtons are probably the most popular varmint cartridges of all time, and sure two of the best.

unprimed cases. Norma is the only company that loads Swift ammo, and Norma products are hard to come by in this country. The only commercial rifles that have been chambered for the Swift in this country, since Winchester dropped it, was a limited number of Ruger bolt action 77s. Apart from those few thousand Ruger 77s, by the way, no other company ever produced Swift-chambered rifles except Winchester. I sometimes wonder whether, if the Swift were to be revived in a full production rifle,* it wouldn't turn out something like the 244-6mm Remington – maybe varmint hunters would realize what a hell of a good cartridge it is and sales would be good.

A Summation

In summing up the 22 varmint cartridges a few comments are in order. First, we haven't really come very far in cartridge development in the last 40 years. Maybe we've even slipped a cog or two when you consider the disappearance of the Swift, at least from the Winchester line. Second, one or another of the 22 varmint cartridges will take care of at least 95% of today's varmint shooting; only highly specialized varminting calls for anything of larger caliber. Third, if you want your 22 varminter to be at its effective best, use bullets that have proven highly explosive. Fourth, your 22 speedster is not a small game cartridge if you are thinking of the pot – unless you prefer chowder with a liberal helping of hair and hide. Last, don't let anyone con you into the idea that the heaviest bullets in 22 caliber, such as the 60/63-gr. types, will shoot flatter at the longest varmint ranges than will the well-shaped 52/53-gr. hollow points, or even the best shaped 50-gr. bullets. If you don't believe these lighter bullets, with their higher initial velocity, are still flatter out to 500 yards than the heavy bullets, take a look at the drop charts found in the Hornady and Sierra manuals. They also expand just as well or better at the longer ranges. Velocity of even the 50-gr. bullet is about the same at 500 yards as with the heavy bullet, and the only place the heavy bullet is of any advantage would be on something like coyotes because of the greater retained energy. Anyway, 500 yards is too far for varmint shooting with any 22 caliber cartridge.

There is no question that the 22 varmint cartridges are the best choice for the average varmint hunter, the individual who will be shooting all varmints under average conditions. ●

*Bill Ruger has told us that the 220 Swift chambering in the Model 77 rifle will be standard practice in 1974. If sales prove good, I imagine the Swift chambering will continue in subsequent years.

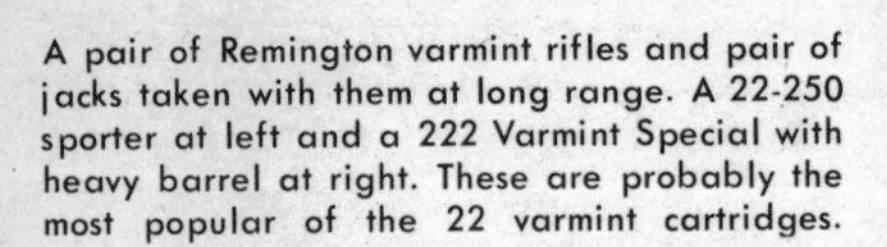

A pair of Remington varmint rifles and pair of jacks taken with them at long range. A 22-250 sporter at left and a 222 Varmint Special with heavy barrel at right. These are probably the most popular of the 22 varmint cartridges.

ALTHOUGH DECLARED obsolete by German Ordnance, and rarely are target matches of any class won with it, the Luger remains an object of intense interest. Mention the Luger and most men's eyes light up, and—"Do you have one? Do you want to sell it?" are typical questions. Disregarding the gun collector's market, concerned primarily with variations in models throughout the years and historical connotations, what is there about the Luger that continues to command the interest of shooters? Well, it is fine appearing, neither too big nor too small, of just the right weight, obviously well made with closely fitted parts, solid, precise and durable are words that come to mind. Neither are there shaky slide, loose springs or bucket-of-bolts rattles. It is chambered for a load (9mm Parabellum-Luger) that has world-wide popularity for military, police and sporting use, a load that is again neither too big nor too small but just right. Its splendid graceful, sloping grip makes it handle well (it points like "pointing your finger") and its general appearance is handsome and impressive. It is one of the most popular and talked about guns ever made.

So much for eye appeal, workmanship and generalities—what about performance? The first disappointment in shooting the Luger will be its lack of reliable functioning. All those precisely made parts cannot atone for a poor feed system, and a worse ejection system. Finally, its complex action of delicately balanced cams, springs and lever arms requires near perfect ammunition. These factors were reported on in greater detail in the 20th edition of the GUN DIGEST.

As for accuracy, again we have the strange anomaly of seeming precision design and manufacture but dubious performance on the target range. I had an

Fig. 1. The best of the Lugers—one of the last made by Mauser. A P-08 in 9mm caliber, 4" barrel, code marked "S42," date of manufacture 1941.

The Best of the Military Lugers

The author feels that the most desirable Luger-Parabellums were made between 1934 and 1942—with some exceptions. Here's how he rates them, what to look for when buying one and how to make one shoot better.

by ROBERT A. BURMEISTER

American Eagle 7.65mm caliber Luger that grouped well and recently I acquired an "S42" 9mm Luger that shoots 2" groups at 20 yards using an arm rest. On the other hand I've shot Lugers that were, some of them, good for only 4" at 20 yards.

There is no question but that the Luger is a basically accurate pistol and, under certain conditions, can produce excellent results. It has a well-designed, well-made, solidly mounted barrel and a solid, tight fitting breech—yet there are three big handicaps: the sights are poor and difficult to adjust; the trigger pull varies from bad to fair, and even new commercial ammunition is apparently not up to 38 Special or 45 ACP target ammunition standards. When I get an arm-rest 2" group at 20 yards with the Luger, I am doing so in spite of those three factors.

Carrying a Luger brings up another basic disadvantage—you need a second thumb to get the safety off. I can see why German Ordnance declared it obsolete. The Luger is much slower in getting off the first shot than its successor, the Walther P38 or the excellent Smith & Wesson M39-2.

Still, such negative comments rarely discourage the man who wants one. He'll likely say "I still want one. Which is the best? How do you tell a good Luger?

The problem of selecting a "good" Luger is not easy. New Lugers of original design—having the short-recoil toggle breech mechanism suitable for the 7.65mm Luger and 9mm Luger—were unobtainable until recently. Now the Mauser-made Luger (or Parabellum) of Swiss pattern is offered, but all other short-recoil type Lugers around are second hand. And it's been that way for a long time. My own experience with Lugers has involved several dozen, 7.65mm and 9mm, with barrel lengths of 3⅝", 4", 4¾", 6" and 8", yet none were new. I've never shot a new Luger.

How then to select one? As in all dealings for a used item the best rule is *caveat*

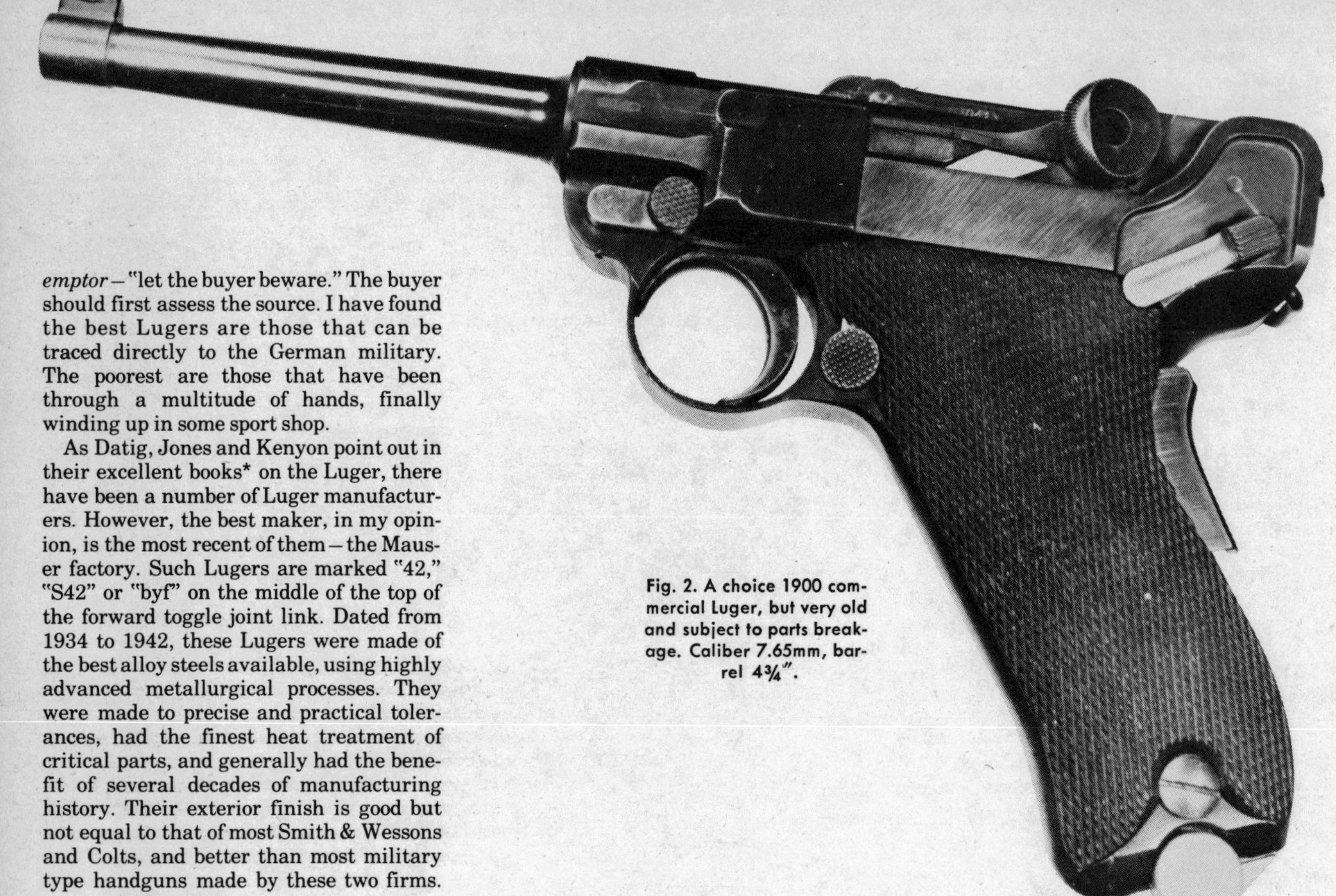

Fig. 2. A choice 1900 commercial Luger, but very old and subject to parts breakage. Caliber 7.65mm, barrel 4¾".

emptor—"let the buyer beware." The buyer should first assess the source. I have found the best Lugers are those that can be traced directly to the German military. The poorest are those that have been through a multitude of hands, finally winding up in some sport shop.

As Datig, Jones and Kenyon point out in their excellent books* on the Luger, there have been a number of Luger manufacturers. However, the best maker, in my opinion, is the most recent of them—the Mauser factory. Such Lugers are marked "42," "S42" or "byf" on the middle of the top of the forward toggle joint link. Dated from 1934 to 1942, these Lugers were made of the best alloy steels available, using highly advanced metallurgical processes. They were made to precise and practical tolerances, had the finest heat treatment of critical parts, and generally had the benefit of several decades of manufacturing history. Their exterior finish is good but not equal to that of most Smith & Wessons and Colts, and better than most military type handguns made by these two firms.

Mauser 42 Luger

Fig. 1 is a fine example of a "42" Luger made in 1941. A 9mm military issue, the frame under the left toggle is marked "PO8," the date abbreviated over the rear end of the barrel. On some Lugers the date is not abbreviated, but in any case the date digits should not be confused with the various parts numbers. The part numbers appear as follows: The serial number (9621) of the gun in fig. 1 is shown on the frame in front and on the left side of the receiver. The last two digits of the serial number (21) also appear on the locking bolt (ahead of the trigger), on the trigger plate (above the trigger), on the rear of the rear link of toggle joint, on the trigger under the trigger plate, on the trigger bar, on the rear of the forward toggle joint link, on top of the hold-open latch, on the connecting pin between rear link and receiver, on top of ejector, and on the forward part of the safety bar. Thus 12 parts are numbered. Lugers such as this one (if dated between 1934 and 1942) are the best available, I believe; they are the ultimate in Luger design, materials and workmanship.

A commercial issue pistol made in 1900 is shown in fig. 2. It has a 4¾" barrel and is in 7.65mm caliber. It differs from later military models in that its parts are not

**Luger Pistol,* by F. A. Datig, Alhambra, Ca., 1962 *Lugers at Random,* by Chas. Kenyon, Jr., Chicago, Ill., 1970 *Luger Variations,* by H. E. Jones, Torrance, Ca. 1967

Tips on Buying a Used Luger

Date: Best guns are dated 1934 through 1942. Usually only the last two digits of date appear on top of rear end of barrel.

Code name: Best guns are marked on top "42" or "S42" or "byf." Some excellent commercial guns were made in this WW II period but are quite rare.

Bluing: Must be original. Slight holster wear is a good sign. If the gun has been reblued there may be questions about its history—it may have been damaged through faulty assembly, parts worn and replaced improperly, etc.

Barrel: Clean with solvent before examining. Lands should be clean, sharp and free from pits.

Parts: Last two digits of serial number should appear on various parts (see text). If mixed numbers occur gun needs careful checking for it is a repaired gun. Disassemble and reassemble—all parts should fit snugly and yet can be inserted without force.

Firing pin and mainspring: Test by cocking pistol, then insert flat-ended wood pencil in bore, muzzle pointing up. Be sure pencil does not rest on extractor but is all the way home on breech. Pull trigger. Pencil should come flying out if firing pin and spring are OK.

Trigger pull: Should be at least 5.0 pounds. If less chances are someone worked on it. This in turn means that considerable checking is now needed because these trigger parts are easily damaged.

Functioning: Check functioning by loading magazine with 5 cartridges. Work through action by hand. Feed, extraction and ejection should be smartly executed. Repeat by test firing if possible.

Economics: If gun is in good shape except for pitted barrel it may be a good buy—depending on price! Same for faulty magazine. New barrels and magazines can be bought but damaged receivers, frames, links, trigger plates, etc., are hard to find, to replace, repair or adjust.

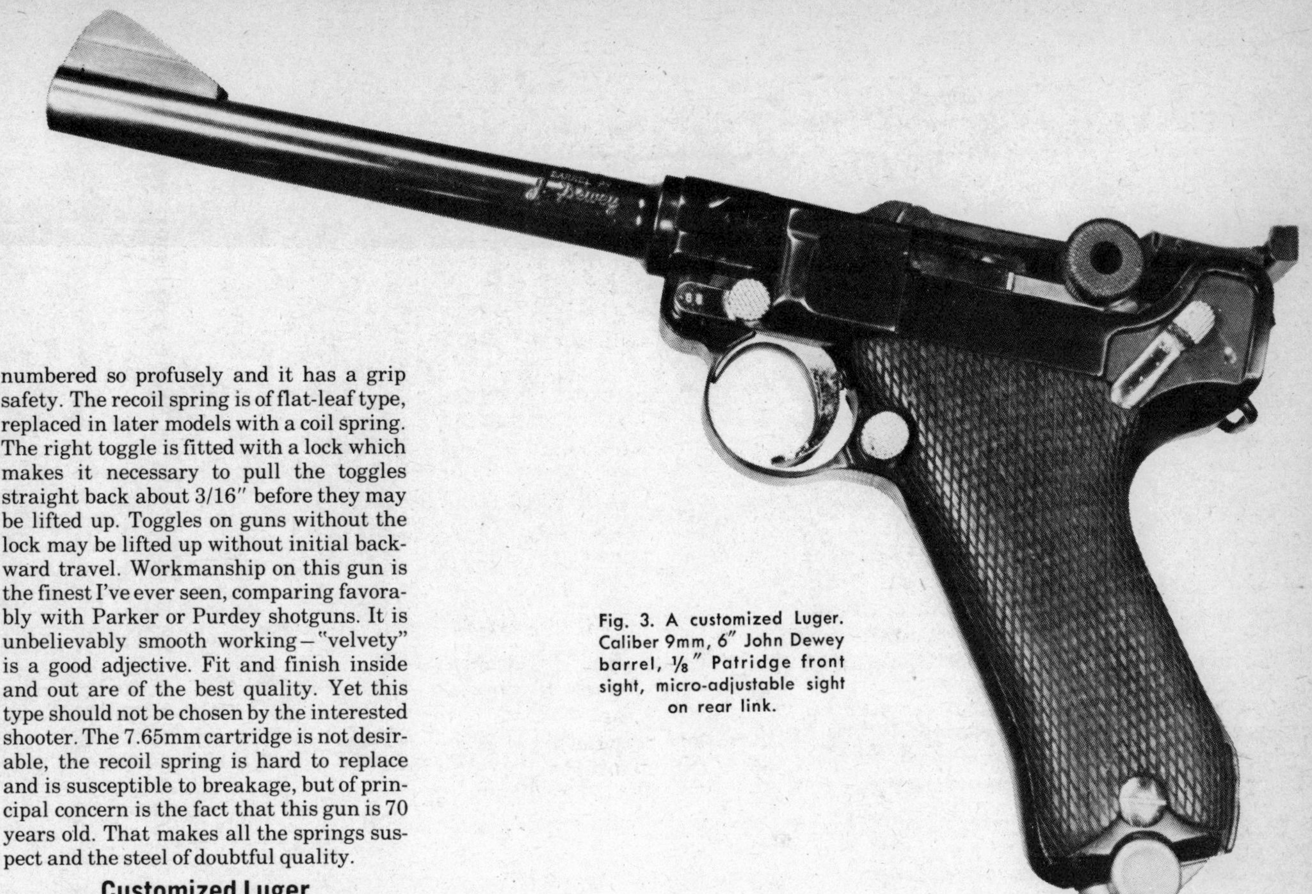

Fig. 3. A customized Luger. Caliber 9mm, 6″ John Dewey barrel, ⅛″ Patridge front sight, micro-adjustable sight on rear link.

numbered so profusely and it has a grip safety. The recoil spring is of flat-leaf type, replaced in later models with a coil spring. The right toggle is fitted with a lock which makes it necessary to pull the toggles straight back about 3/16″ before they may be lifted up. Toggles on guns without the lock may be lifted up without initial backward travel. Workmanship on this gun is the finest I've ever seen, comparing favorably with Parker or Purdey shotguns. It is unbelievably smooth working—"velvety" is a good adjective. Fit and finish inside and out are of the best quality. Yet this type should not be chosen by the interested shooter. The 7.65mm cartridge is not desirable, the recoil spring is hard to replace and is susceptible to breakage, but of principal concern is the fact that this gun is 70 years old. That makes all the springs suspect and the steel of doubtful quality.

Customized Luger

Fig. 3 shows what can be done to make a target pistol out of a mine-run military Luger. A custom built 6″ barrel has been installed by John Dewey . This barrel measures 0.579″ at the muzzle and 0.632″ one-half inch in front of receiver. The added weight improves the balance considerably. The front sight is a Patridge-type ⅛″ blade on a ramp silver soldered to a flat milled on the barrel. The rear sight is a ⅛″ Micro adjustable for windage and elevation. It is silver soldered to the rear link, the old rear sight ground away. Trigger pull has been reduced to 4.0 pounds. While this pull is a big improvement over the 7 to 9 pound trigger pulls usually found on Lugers, it is still somewhat spongy, doesn't compare to the crisp letoff of a Colt Gold Cup 45 or the Smith & Wesson M52 automatic. Table I shows how this rebarreled Luger compares to the standard military issue of fig. 1 and the 1900 commercial model of fig. 2.

In addition to custom built Luger barrels there are several sources of imported barrels. These are usually offered in 4″, 6″ and 8″ lengths. No front sights are furnished; the original front sight must be reinstalled on the new barrel (a dovetailed slot is provided for this purpose). The rear sight on the link can be opened up to a ⅛″ square notch and then used with the standard pyramidal front sight. This is better than the original front sight combination but not as good as when both front and rear are of the square post Patridge type. Neither Patridge nor bead sights are commercially available for the standard Luger front sight dovetailed slot; they have to be custom made.

Improvement of the Luger's trigger pull is a difficult job, even for a competent gunsmith, because of the many moving parts and engaging surfaces in the trigger assembly. If your Luger's trigger pull is tolerable, say between 5 and 7 pounds, I'd leave it alone.

Summarizing, then—the best Lugers, in the writer's opinion, are those of the most recent manufacture. Commercial models are often choice specimens but are apt to be very old, therefore of questionable metal quality. Customizing is a good way to improve a Luger, for a longer barrel can be installed, the trigger pull improved somewhat, and the inadequate military issue sights can be replaced with modern adjustable ⅛″ Patridge sights. ●

Table I
Comparison of Lugers

	"42" Luger Fig. 1	1900 Luger Fig. 2	Rebb'ld Luger Fig. 3
Caliber		7.65mm P	9mm P
Weight	1.99 lbs.	1.97 lbs.	2.16 lbs.
Barrel length	4″	4¾″	6″
Length over-all	8¾″	9¾″	10¾″
Front sight height above center line of bore	⅝″	⅝″	⅞″
Sight radius	7⅞″	8½″	10¼″
Trigger pull	7.0 lbs.	5.9 lbs.	4.0 lbs.

Now nearing its centennial celebration year, the famous old company looks forward with confidence to another century of service to shooters everywhere.

The Lyman Story

by MASON WILLIAMS

ABOUT 1876, a young man named William Lyman became dissatisfied with the coarse, open V-type sights commonly used in those days. An ardent sportsman and knowledgeable about firearms, he'd learned their shortcomings through personal hunting experience. The more he used them the more he became convinced that the V-sight was an unsatisfactory way of aiming a rifle, and that something considerably better was needed.

A few years earlier, Civil War Sharpshooters had used Vernier rear sights attached to the upper grip of their rifles, enabling them to shoot accurately at long distances. From that time on target shooters had turned almost exclusively to these Vernier sights for precision shooting, but Lyman knew that these high, delicate sights would not stand up under hunting abuse, nor did the tiny opening usually found in the sight disc permit enough light to come through for field use. In other words, they were impractical for hunting, and he decided to improve them. He wanted an adjustable, strong rear sight close to his eye, and he wanted to be able to throw the rifle up to his shoulder and instantly "get on-target." With this in mind, he made his way to the Metropolitan Washing Machine Company, one of the Lyman businesses located on the Lyman Farm in Middlefield, Conn.

There, at the age of 24, he founded the Lyman Gun Sight Company, for that same year he was granted a patent covering a tang peep or aperture sight. Before long, he took over a room in the plant to produce sights for sale to the public.

In those days, front sight beads were round-faced. The tiny gold or ivory bead, mounted near the muzzle was, under ideal light conditions, quite practical. However, on those days when sunlight streamed from the sky at all angles, glancing off the round bead to distort and alter the true sight picture, these rounds beads left a lot to be desired. William Lyman developed a front sight with a flat face that gave minimal light distortion, remaining sharp and clear under virtually all shooting conditions. He appreciated the advantages of gold and ivory and he kept them. This combination of a practical rear sight and a clearly distinguishable front sight was a revolutionary combination that had a terrific impact upon the shooting public, so much so that his correspondence was filled with testimonial letters. Today, it is difficult to appreciate the effect the new Lyman sights had on the shooting world of the 1890s, when shooting was a big time sport, comparable to today's baseball and football. These sights were enthusiastically accepted not only by the average American hunter, but by the professional shooters who put on demonstrations and entered contests where thousands of dollars could be won or lost in an afternoon.

This massive and heavy tool is an Ideal Armory Press, made about 1900 or so for military use essentially. Automatic primer feeding and ejection of the sized and recapped case are speed features.

Lyman's 48 Sight

At the turn of the century, the U.S. Army was searching for a rifle to replace the 30-40 Krag. The development and acceptance of the Model 1903 Springfield rifle opened up an entirely new field for the Lyman firm. Lyman had been making rear sights for various hunting rifles, the Model 47 with adjustable windage being in widespread use. The Model 47 was a modified Model 1A with fine windage adjustment built into the top of the sight stem. In addition, Lyman Nos. 21, 35 and 38 sights, while fully adjustable, were not strong enough nor were their adjustments positive enough for use on a high power, high velocity rifle like the Springfield. They had been more than adequate on the Winchester Model 86s and 95s, and on other comparable rifles, but they did not measure up to the requirements for the Springfield. After years of experimenting that included modifications based on voluminous correspondence with a young army lieutenant named Townsend Whelen, Lyman brought out the Model 48 receiver sight in 1910. This new sight was so well designed that it became highly popular overnight. In the July 6, 1911 issues of *Arms and the Man,* Lieutenant Whelen wrote a glowing report on the Lyman 48. Even today, it stands as the sight against which all others are measured. They are today, as then, hand-fitted and hand-assembled by a few old employees. Today, Lyman sights are so universally recognized and used that the company continues to be the leader in the field, producing more metallic sights than all other sight manufacturers combined.

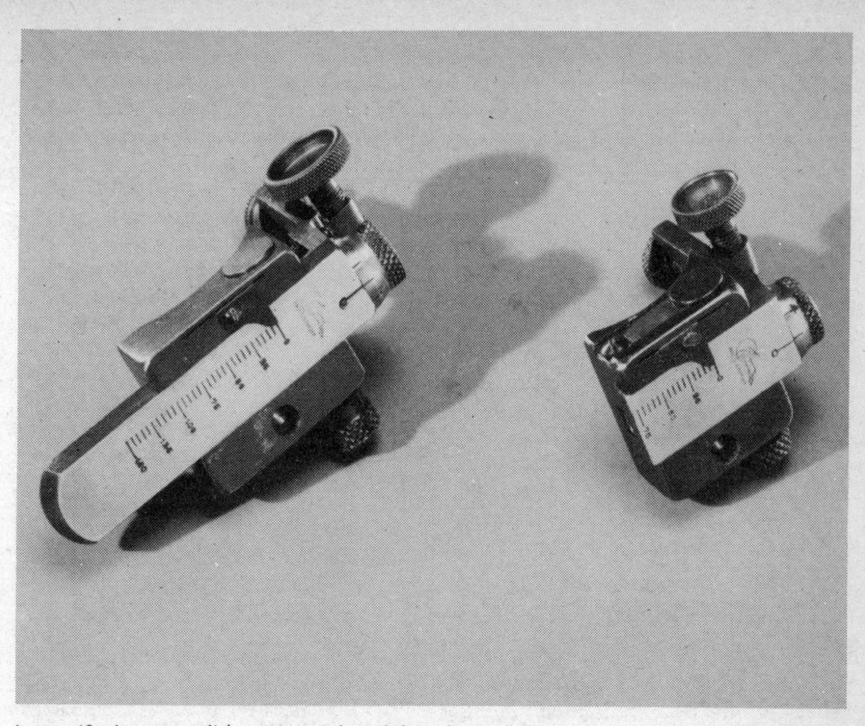

Lyman 48 micrometer-click receiver sight at left is of long-slide type for extreme long range shooting. The 48 Lyman at right is of later type, its short slide offering ample adjustment for usual ranges.

Early Tools

Back in the days when William Lyman was a young man, John Barlow, a hunter, outdoorsman, and a machinist, was conducting experiments in improving the crude tools then used for the reloading of metallic ammunition and shotshells. His simple, easy-to-use tools caught on rapidly and soon became well known to all shooters. He founded the Ideal Manufacturing Company in 1884 and, sometime in the next few years, he put together the first *Ideal Hand Book.* The exact publication date is not known but it carries testimonial letters dated 1891. The growth of the Ideal Company can be seen in the *No. 12 Hand Book,* which lists some 8 variations of the famous "tong tool." Models 1, 2, 4, 6 and 8 had moulds in the ends. These tools are so simple to use that a man can sit on a log in the wilderness and reload his fired cartridges—and many have done just that. Surprisingly enough, sales of this tool, in its modern form, have increased substantially in recent years. Gone is the old iron-and-steel frame, replaced by a lightweight alloy to reduce weight, but it's otherwise basically unchanged from the original 1884 Barlow design.

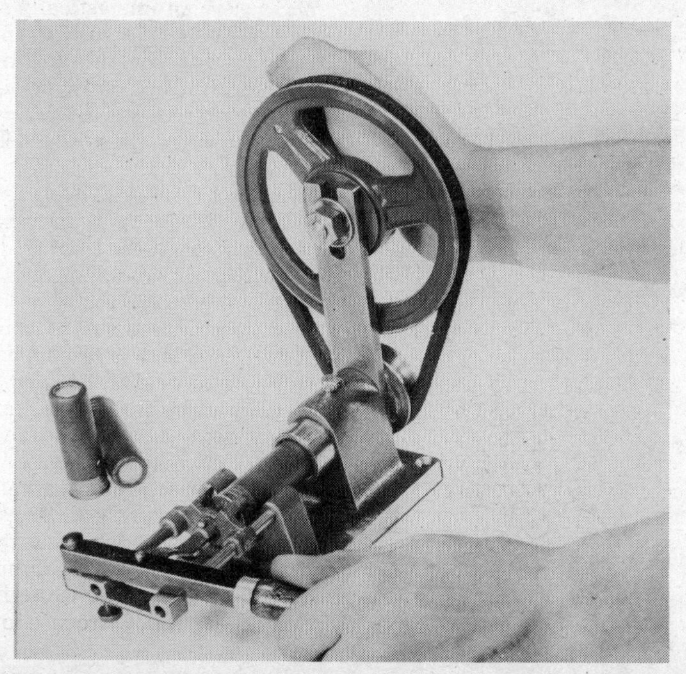

The Lyman Ideal Star Crimper combined the best features of their earlier Models I, II and V. It could be hand operated or motor driven.

Other items listed in the *No. 12 Hand Book,* which came out about 1900, are bullet resizers, shotshell crimpers, shotshell pocket loaders, case resizers, "Star" crimpers for shotshells, and the Universal Powder Measures Models 1, 2, 3 and 4. Ideal also offered the Model 1899 loading machine, which would reload shotshells in 10, 12, 14, 16 and 20 gauge.

The Ideal Perfection Mould, made for both grease-grooved and paper-patched bullet-casting, had an adjustable plug that allowed the shooter to alter bullet weight. The regular Ideal moulds were conventional, single-cavity types that covered just about every form, weight and caliber of bullet then in use.

Sometime around 1908 to 1910, Marlin Firearms bought out Ideal and the ensuing issues of the *Ideal Hand Book,* commencing with No. 20, carried the Marlin name at the bottom of the front cover. In 1924 Phinias Talcott bought the company from Marlin, but a few months later turned round and sold it to Lyman in October of 1925. Lyman has continued to publish the *Ideal Hand Books,* and has manufactured tools ever since.

Lyman Scopes

In 1928, Lyman bought the Winchester and Stevens lines of rifle

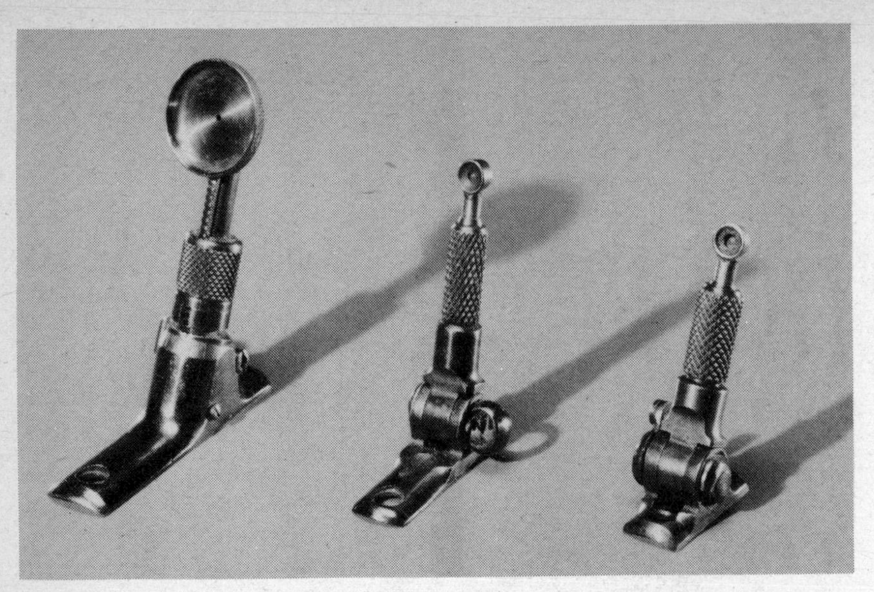

Lyman tang sights. At center is a standard No. 1 type; left, an early micrometer elevation style, and at right a lever-locking No. 1A.

scopes, thus giving Lyman another entirely new but related market and a greatly increased sales potential. However, Lyman never manufactured its own lenses, preferring to buy them, made to their specifications, from specialists in that field. The first Lyman scope offered was the 5-A (a duplicate of the Winchester 5-A) that made its debut on February 6, 1929. The 438 was Lyman's first design, appearing March 5, 1930. The Lyman 3x Stag big game scope went on the market May 18, 1933, but it was a complete flop. To offset this, the first Lyman Targetspot match rifle scope left the factory August 16, 1933 and, like the Model 48 micrometer sight, proceeded to make history—and it still is a top choice among target shooters. Then came a series of scopes for 22 rimfire rifles, and on April 1, 1937, Lyman introduced the Super-targetspot scope and, later in the same year, the Junior Targetspot. Then came the first really practical and modern big-game, high-power-rifle scope to appear on the American market—the Lyman Alaskan. This was followed, in 1948, by the Challenger, the Wolverine in 1953 and finally the original All American in 1954. On December 8, 1961, Lyman shipped the first Perma-Center All-American rifle scopes that remain leaders in the Lyman line today.

Cutts Comps

In the middle of the depression, in 1932, Charles Lyman had enough faith in America's recovery and in the growth of trap and Skeet shooting to buy rights to the Cutts Compensator, a recoil-absorbing, interchangeable choke tube device. This had been designed originally by Colonel Cutts for use on cannons and rifles. It proved to be one of Lyman's most profitable investments. It soon sold in large numbers, with Lyman also installing it on shotguns—as accredited gunsmiths later did also—and that installation department continues busy today.

Then, some years ago, economic and other problems arose to plague the Lymans, and a decision was made that a new approach to the changing times, plus the need for modern financing methods and better sales promotion was in order. The Lymans had always operated a close-knit family business, but despite an increasing flow of orders, new products and planning were needed if Lyman was to retain its share of business and gain new markets. No longer could the Lymans pitch in—as they did during depression years—and work for nothing to pull the company out of trouble. No longer could they continue to confine their thinking solely to Middlefield and the family organization.

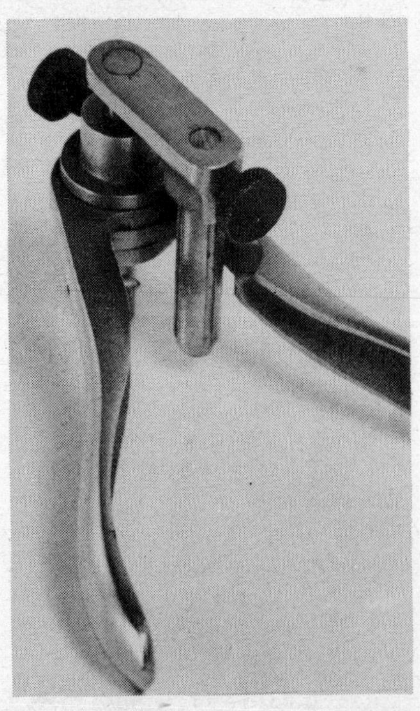

The tool shown here is a case indenter. The case is placed on the central spindle and the handles closed to let the small pin (at left) form a dimple or depression in the case neck or wall, at one or more of 4 places. Two thumbscrews allow vertical adjustment of the case.

Because of all this the Lymans ordered a survey of the entire organization—it took a year to complete—then brought in as president the man who ran the survey. Roland Van Name.

For 10 years Van Name guided Lyman through the intricacies of modern-day financial and business problems, bringing in several capable executives who aided in improving Lyman's public image, as the modern cant has it.

In September of 1969, Van Name retired and, at the same time, control and management of the Lyman company was turned over to the Leisure Group, an organization with headquarters in Los Angeles, California. This holding company controls many widely diversified businesses, among them lawn mower and camping trailer manufacturing. Lyman has been placed in a division that includes High Standard—gunmakers—and Sierra Bullets. Ken Wright, now Operations Manager for Lyman, is understandably reticent about future plans at this stage, but he did say that there will be much new product development in the immediate future. Plans are being redrawn for a new plant. Lyman's Research and Development section will be substantially expanded—more people, more chronographs, more pressure guns are planned. A new backstop has already been bulldozed for the R&D section.

There will be a few changes that may disconcert some old Lyman customers, at least. In the past Lyman stocked over 900 cast lead bullet mould styles, some for such oddball calibers as the 23, only a few of which were ever sold, yet the moulds remain in stock. Lyman plans to reduce stock moulds to around 600, these to be available through normal channels. The others will go into a special order group, available at a premium price directly from Lyman. In the meantime those in doubt about a mould's availability can write to Lyman at Middlefield, Conn. ●

Scopes and Mounts

Here's a detailed report—with current prices for most products—on what's been developed in scopes, mounts and related accessories over the past year.

by BOB BELL

A SCOPELESS rifle is a rarity in the hunting field anymore. An obvious necessity on a super-accurate varmint rifle chambered for one of today's hotshot cartridges, they're just as popular in the big game woods. During the past deer season in Pennsylvania, a state that annually fields almost one million whitetail hunters, I didn't see one iron-sighted rifle. Obviously, I observed only a minute number of the total hunters, but the situation is clear: scopes are popular. Deservedly so. They greatly increase the hunter's efficiency. Thus they sell well, which makes scope manufacturing a going business, which in turn leads to product proliferation and improvement. Which brings us to this year's models.

Redfield has had an extensive line of scopes for many years—in fact, what might be called several lines, for they offer Traditional (round eyepiece) models in most powers, both straight and variable, and Widefield scopes in a similar range, as well as a top quality target model, the 3200, and the 6400 benchrest scope. This company also has been a leader in developing useful innovations, such as the non-magnifying reticle in variable power scopes, the field-increasing ocular system which they call the Widefield, solid mounts and an internally-adjusted target scope, the Accu-Range reticle that takes much of the guesswork out of long-range shooting, and, a year or so ago, the Low Profile objective lens unit for hunting scopes. Doubtless there are other Redfield-developed features, but these prove my point that this is a progressive company.

This year they have extended their total line by 5 scopes. Three of these are the Traditional line, a 6x, an 8x and a 10x, while the Widefield additions are a 6x Low Profile glass and a 3-9x with special features for a challenging shooting game that is gaining many followers. Let's look at these individually.

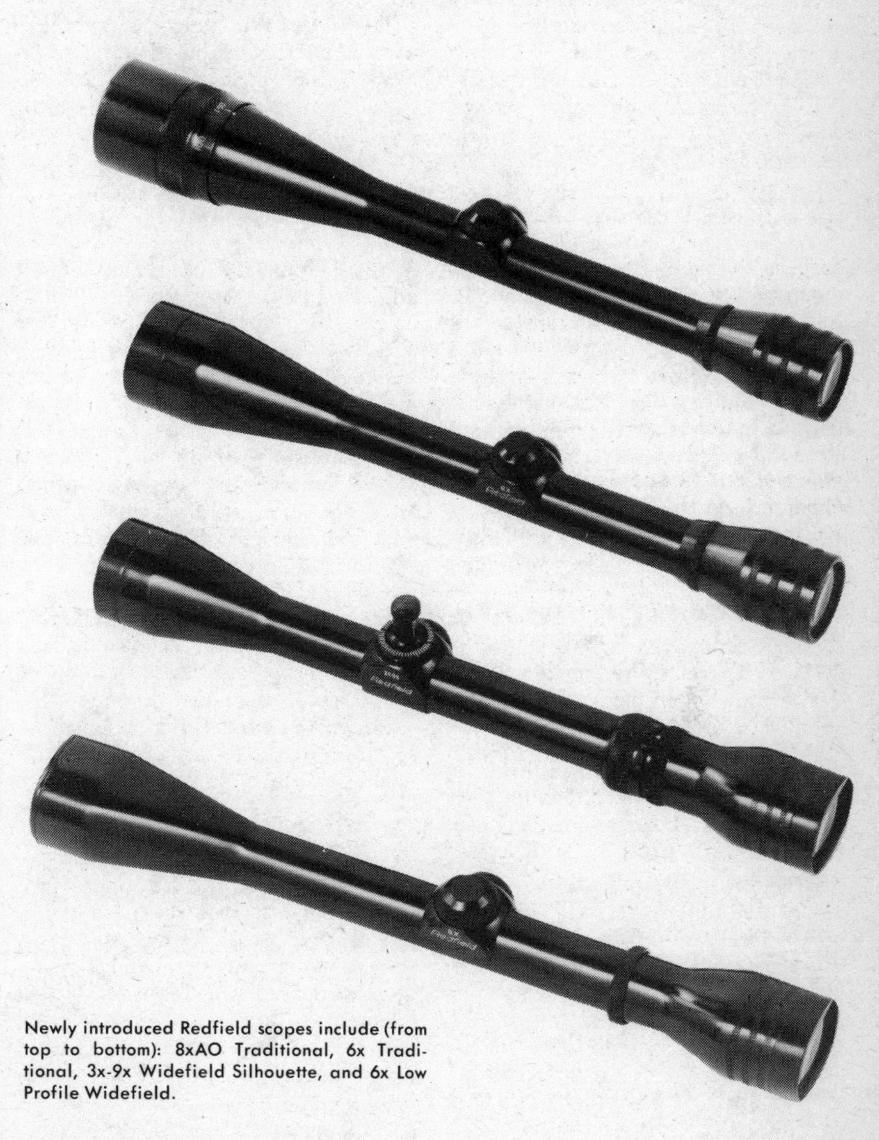

Newly introduced Redfield scopes include (from top to bottom): 8xAO Traditional, 6x Traditional, 3x-9x Widefield Silhouette, and 6x Low Profile Widefield.

The 6x Traditional is obviously intended for long-range big game hunting. As with all Redfields except one model used primarily on high quality 22 rimfires, this 6x is built on a 1″ tube, has about 3½″ eye relief, which makes it usable on magnum calibers, and a 19-foot field. This is 5 feet less than the Widefield of this power, but this is unimportant in a scope used for plains or mountain hunting. Field "grows" with range, and distant targets usually are taken while motionless or nearly so. This 6x has internal adjustments graduated in half-minutes, with a maximum movement of 60 moa—notably more than the 46 moa possible in the Widefield 6x. It has the 4-Plex reticle (crosswire w/4 posts), which could well be the best choice for big game hunting, the posts being conspicuous in any shooting light and the crosswire intersection making precise aim possible. Price, $81.

The 8x AO gets its name from its Adjustable Objective unit. This is an adjustment sleeve, with reference marks for ranges, on the scope's objective bell. As with a target scope, it lets you focus precisely for range (from 50 yards to infinity), thus removing all parallax and getting the best possible target image. Built-in stops prevent overturning the sleeve. It sticks in my mind that this is Redfield's first 8x scope, but I might be wrong. At any rate, it should be a fine choice for medium range varminting and extremely long range pronghorn or deer hunting. One reticle only, the 4-Plex. $99.80.

The 10x AO is a higher-power version of the 8x AO, being the same size and weight (see our catalog section for physical specs on all scopes), but of course losing some field as magnification goes up. It too has the 4-Plex reticle and price is $110. (I've often wondered why price should increase with magnification when there's no other apparent difference in two scopes—I can't believe it's more difficult or costly to build a 10x than an 8x—but it always does. Not only at Redfield, of course, but with all makers. Maybe it's a psychological necessity.)

New in the Widefield line is the 6x LP. As with last year's 4x Low Profile, this one also has the "flattened" objective unit which permits the lowest possible mounting of a scope of this magnification. This might seem a questionable characteristic, but anyone who's tried to get the optimum relationship between rifle barrel and scope knows it isn't. It's amazing how often a scope's objective unit just rubs the barrel, necessitating either a higher mount or moving the scope forward, as it's a bad practice to have any contact here. Moving the scope can foul up your eye relief too—another thing to be avoided if quick aim is ever a necessity. This 6x LP has a maximum internal adjustment of 46 moa, 24-foot field, the 4-Plex reticle, and sells for $115.70.

The 3-9x Widefield is Redfield's most popular variable. The new version of this unit is the 3-9x MS, the initials an abbreviation for "Metallic Silhouette." For those unfamiliar with the term, it's a hellishly tough shooting game that originated in Mexico and has worked its way northward. Competitors shoot offhand at metal silhouettes of various game animals (desert sheep, javalina, wild turkey, etc.) at ranges to 500 meters or so. The constant range-changing is hard on the scope's internal adjustments—which may well be my understatement for the year. Anyway, as an aid to the shooters who thrive on this game, this MS scope has a protruding vertical-adjustment knob which is marked off in meters from 200 to 500. Once zeroed in and set up, the shooter does not have to keep in mind his minute-of-angle changes between the various ranges; he just dials the proper meter mark and concentrates on aiming and squeezing.

This MS scope is available on special order with any of the reticles listed for the 3-9x Widefield, which makes it $150.30 with MCH, PCH, 4-Plex or 4-PCCH, $162.80 with 3″-1″ dot. It can also be ordered with Accu-Range.

We described the RM (Receiver Mounted) 6400 target scope in GD29. However, this short, solidly mounted, internally adjusted model was in scant supply during the past year. So scant that few shooters have yet seen it. However, it is expected to be available in reasonable numbers by the time this reaches print. In 16, 20 or 24 power, with fine or medium crosswires, ⅛″ or ¼″ dot, it lists at $229.

Redfield Jr. and FR scope mount rings now come with hex socket screws, a definite improvement over the old slotted style. I wish I had a nickel for every conventionally-slotted screwhead I buggered up with a screwdriver. I know the bit about grinding drivers to fit, being careful and all that jazz, but I still have problems. Hex sockets make a lot more sense for guys like me. Now if someone would only convince the gun people to drill and tap their actions for sturdier screws than the traditional 6/48s (which admittedly did a good job of attaching a Lyman 48 aperture sight), some more of our problems would be solved. It'd be even nicer if they made mounting blocks integral with the actions, a la the Sako and Ruger designs; but apparently there was shooter resistance to these—which shows how stupid we are—so there's no telling when Remington or Winchester might make the move. For a so-called rational species, we shooters sure have some odd mental blocks.

Browning continues to offer the 4 scopes mentioned last year, probably on the assumption—which is doubtless correct—that they cover the field well enough for a company whose primary business is not selling scopes. Called the Wide Angle models, the big game glasses live up to their billing. The 4x has a 37-foot field, the 2-7x variable 50-20 feet, and the 3-9x has 39-15 feet at 100 yds. These are with round eye-pieces, too, so the vertical dimension equals the horizontal, something that's pleasing to me at least. You don't get something for nothing in optics, so eye relief is a bit shorter in these glasses than many others of the powers quoted, but at 3″ or so it's enough if the scope is properly mounted. Browning also supplies a fine little 4x on a ¾″ tube for rimfire shooters.

Buehler, Inc., has for many years been producing mounts the equal of any in the world. Some would say they're superior to any, and it would be hard to prove them wrong, but we happen to have a number of fine mount manufacturers in this country so I won't go that far. I have used Buehler mounts on various guns for several decades, though, so know first-hand that they are top quality all the way.

Most any rifle and a number of handguns can be fitted with these mounts. As new guns come along, Buehler adapts to them, and this year has a special 2-piece base set for the Ruger No. 3 Single Shot Carbine, Code R3, to match holes now drilled and tapped at the factory. For the Ruger 10/22 users, Code R1 two-piece Buehler bases fit the factory holes. Buehler now also supplies 6x48 socket head cap screws in 4 lengths for mounting purposes.

Buehler's new mount for Ruger #3 Single Shot (Code R3) is a 2-piece base set that matches holes that are drilled and tapped at factory.

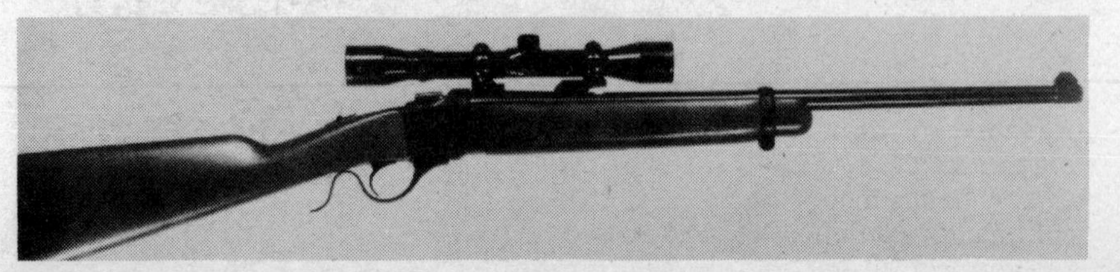

Bushnell has added a handful of new scopes to their already lengthy line, with some new and interesting features that should be popular with many hunters. Their Scopechief line is now up to the Series VI, with the introduction of a straight 4x and a 3-9x variable. At first view these seem conventional. Each has their Multi-X reticle (4 posts w/crosswires) and normal physical specs. The thing that makes them different is a "Rangemaster" adjustment of the reticle. This is a built-in compensator for bullet drop. The turret housing atop the tube contains a dial calibrated in yards. After zeroing in and setting the dial to agree with your zero distance, the dial is "locked in" to the elevation adjustment; from then on, after making an estimate of range you simply turn the Rangemaster dial to the desired yardage, hold right on, and shoot. A window in the rear of the turret shows the dial calibrations. The Rangemaster comes with three separate calibrated dials which have been computer calculated for factory loads and velocities, plus one blank dial for wildcat loads. Dials are calibrated to 500 yards. The 4x Scopechief VI is priced at $79.50, the 3-9x at $118.50.

Bushnell's Rangemaster compensates for bullet drop.

The Rangemaster unit also is offered in several Banner models—the 3-9x with 32mm objective, $79.95; 3-9x 38mm, $99.95; 3-9x 40mm, $89.95; 4x 32mm, $59.95 and 4x 40mm, $74.95.

In addition, three Banners are made with round-eyepiece Wide Angle lenses. These include two variables, the 3-9x 38mm and a 1.75x-4.5x, and the straight 4x 40mm scope. Where a typical 3-9x has a field of about 39-13 feet, the Wide Angle measures 43-14.6 feet. In the 4x, the WA field is 37+, notably greater than that of a standard 4x.

New in the mount line is a set of 1" split rings that fit Weaver-style bases. The mating surfaces of the rings are cut at an angle so that tightening the screws pulls the top half both down and around the scope tube. Allen-head screws are used throughout and a hardened steel crossbolt fits a cross slot in the bases, to prevent movement under recoil. Up to 10 MOA windage adjustment can be had by reversing the rings. $11.95 per set.

Another new unit from Bushnell is the pocket size TruScope—a small boresighter. Three adjustable arbors cover calibers from 22 through 45. Measuring 3½x2¾x1⅛ inches and weighing only 4 oz., this could be a handy item at any time and worth a great amount on a long, back-country hunting trip, as it permits easy verification of rifle zero without firing a shot. $24.95.

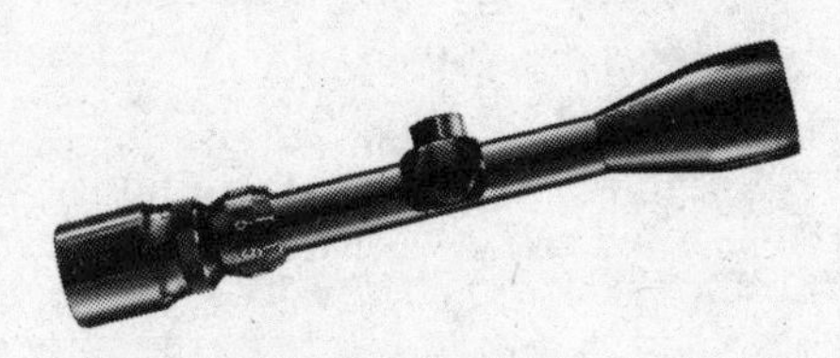

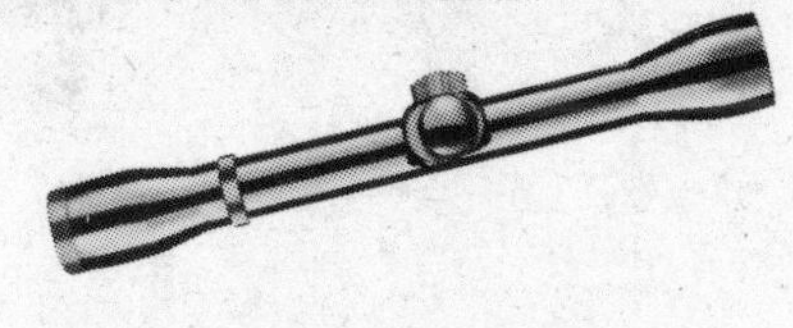
Banner Riflescopes with Rangemaster—above 3x-9x 38mm and below 4x 32mm.

Bushnell's TruScope boresighter.

Conetrol base and rings on Sako L-61R action.

Conetrol now has both bridge and 2-piece bases for the left hand M700 Remington action—in both long and short lengths—in its Custum line of mounts. Custum bases, either 1- or 2-piece, regularly list for $14.95, but George Miller advises that a 10% surcharge on these has been made necessary by the current economy. The Custum bases will take all three lines of Conetrol rings—Huntur, Gunnur and Custum.

Conetrol now has bases for the imported Steyr and Kleinguenther rifles also, and has newly-designed bases for the Thompson Contender handgun, accommodating all 4 screw holes in the new Contender barrels. Recoil of handguns, though mathematically less than that of rifles, applies a sort of discombombulating effect on mounts, which has led to the fourth hole in current TC barrels.

In an interesting aside, Miller writes that "...the honor of fitting more high-power rifles than anybody else in the mount business does not any longer belong to Weaver or Redfield, but to Conetrol. We have bases for all popular rifles *and* for the Steyr guns, the dovetailed-receiver guns (Sako, LSA-55, Brno, BSA, Savage 2400, etc.), the 660 Mauser and others. Not a bad accomplishment for a company as young as Conetrol." With that we gotta agree.

Davis Optical Co. continues to offer their Spot Shot target scopes and has held the line on prices—$89.50 for the 1½" objective (powers 10 through 30), $69.50 for the 1¼" (10 through 20). These are interesting for their method of focus adjusting—by sliding the objective unit rather than screwing it in or out.

Davis also makes booster units for objectives, raising the power of hunting scopes to 6x or 8x. They can fit the early Weavers, such as the 330, 440 and 29S, as well as newer models. Prices, $18-$29.50. Going the other way, long eye relief eyepieces cut the power of hunting models about in half and at the same time extend the eye relief to make practicable units for handguns. Price, $15.

E.C. Herkner Co., longtime maker of the Echo mount, has sold their equipment to Quaco Industries Ltd., St. Martins, St. John County, New Brunswick, Canada EOG 2ZO.

Hutson now offers their Handgunner scope in two magnifications, 1x and 1.7x, the former at $45 and the higher mag at $49.50. An adjustable mount, with rings, is offered for a number of popular handguns at $16.95, with a gun base adaptor at $9.95. It's usually necessary to drill and tap one 6x48 hole to fit the adaptor.

Kesselring "See-Em-Under" scope mounts have been discontinued in several models, but with additions for several rifles not previously fitted. They're made for the Remington 760, 740, Winchester 100, 88, Savage 99, Marlin 336, at $24. The 7mm Brno QD mount has been dropped, and the split ring dovetail model is now made for the 22 Brno, Steyr and Krico, as well as the Sako. $22.50. Rings come in various heights and for scope tubes of several diameters.

Leupold & Stevens, Inc., announced their Vari-X II and Vari-X III scopes in time for this review in last year's GD, but at that time we hadn't had a chance to try any in the field. That has been remedied, for in June 1974, at the Outdoor Writers conference in Quebec City, Joe St. Denis said he could scrounge up one of these in time for some fall hunting I had planned. Being a fan of the smaller variables for big game hunting, I asked to see one of the new 1½-5x Vari-X III glasses. It arrived shortly, was snugged into the Redfield Jr. mount atop my old 338 Magnum, and before long was involved in a quickie-type moose hunt on Alaska's Katmai Peninsula. "Quickie" because that really wasn't set up as a hunting trip. But who can go that far, no matter what the basic objective, without having a go at some kind of hunting?

As it turned out the only moose I saw were those from the bush plane and the remains of one which a friend had killed but couldn't get out of the alders before a brownie got to it. We did see—and got fairly close to—what was probably the same bear, but the season wasn't open at the time so I could do nothing but study him through that gin-clear Leupold, crosswires centered on a head that looked big as a bushel basket, and silently cuss myself for being there a few weeks too soon.

Altogether, I had but three days to hunt on that trip—wet days, as can be expected at that time and place, but the scope's innards stayed clear and dry throughout. This, along with the 64-foot field at bottom power, was mighty comforting, for we spent most of our time working through those alders and small patches of muskeg where visibility was closer to 20 feet than 20 yards, and if we happened to stumble onto a cantankerous brown bear I wanted to know I could get the crosswires on him right now. I sure didn't want to shoot one during a closed season, but I sorta preferred that to having one chew on me for any length of time. All in all, it gave me a funny feeling to be working through that thick stuff, knowing those big critters were in the area—much like the old WW II days when we prowled the bombed and shelled towns of northern Europe. Back then, I used to wish I had something bigger than the little 30-caliber carbine issued to me; here I at least had the 338 stuffed full of 250-gr. Nosler handloads—but there were moments when thoughts of a 458 went through my mind.

The Leupold got another workout in October, when I again tried for a moose, this time north of Blind River, Ontario. I flew into one of Air-Dale Ltd.'s bush camps and spent a week crisscrossing those sugarloaf hardwood ridges and beaver dam swamps. There were moose in there, but I couldn't put antlers on any of 'em (cows aren't very photogenic) and came home again without firing a shot. I've reached the conclusion that the wanderings of those big ugly critters and myself just aren't meant to coincide in time and space.

The toughest moment for the scope came when my footing collapsed as I was skirting a rock face and I tumbled down about 6 or 8 feet. I didn't drop the rifle but, in trying to catch myself, I swung it out from my body, holding it at the balance, scope down, and the scope smacked solidly against a downed tree when I came to a stop. I was concerned enough about this to fire a shot—something I hate to do when hunting, except at game. It was still in zero, which speaks well for both the scope and the mount.

At the current price of $131.50 Leupold isn't exactly giving this model away but, as with anything else, when you want top quality you have to pay a reasonable amount. I've been using variable power scopes for a lot of years now, and a lot of good ones are available, but if someone were to pin me down and twist my arm until I made a choice, this little Vari-X III Leupold is the one I'd go with. It belongs on a back-country huntin' rifle.

Vari-X IIIs are also made in 2½-8x and 3½-10x, the former an excellent choice for big game at any range, the latter a combination big game/varmint glass. The Vari-X IIs, somewhat lower in price, come in the 3 conventional sizes for large game, while the M8 straight powers begin at 2x and go to 24x.

Leupold Vari-X III scopes: (top to bottom) 1.5x, 2.5-8x and 3.5-10xAO.

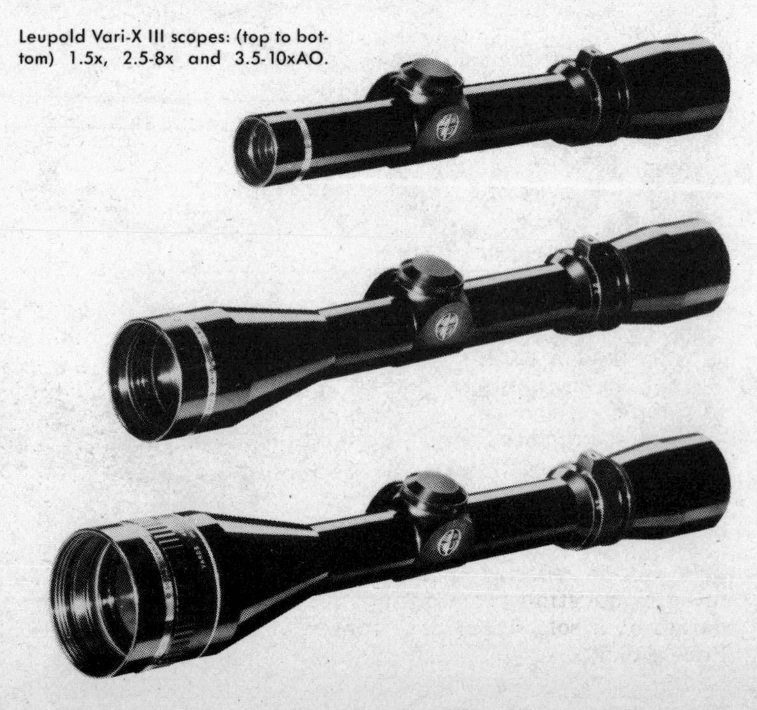

Lyman has no new scopes this year, their All-American straight powers in magnifications from 2½x to 10x covering the hunting and varmint shooting fields, while their 20x Lightweight Benchrest model has found a home on many stoolshooters' outfits. For the other paper punchers, the old reliable Super-Targetspot is still a great choice, and in the last year or two a pair of variables—3.9x and 1.75-5x—have gained followings. Both variables have enlarged objectives—somewhat unusual in the 1.75-5x size. This gives a larger-than-normal exit pupil at 5x, which makes for fast aiming as well as high light transmission.

I've been using the straight power Lymans, from 2½x to 10x, on a number of rifles for quite a few years, with excellent success. They've proved weatherproof when the weather was awful, and the adjustments, though of unusual value in some powers, have been accurate. I like 'em.

Saunders external adjustment knobs on Lyman AWBR.

Nydar Div., Swain Nelson Co., makes the Nydar shotgun sight. This is not a scope but an optical aiming device. I saw my first Nydar in the late '40s, but never having hunted or shot claybirds with one I can't comment from first hand knowledge. The Nydar consists of a reticle, a prism, and a reflector lens mounted on a metal unit. The reticle, a dot within a circle, is seen at a distance, apparently floating in space, in the same optical plane as the target.

The Nydar sight is $35, the mount $11.

W.H. Siebert has added a new optical device to his line. (Wally Siebert, for new readers who might not be familiar with his work, converts short, medium-power varmint scopes into short high-power benchrest scopes at a cost of $35 or so; his efforts have been largely responsible for the proliferation of this type among today's hot shooters.) Anyway, his latest gizmo is called the Mini-Borescope. It looks like a cleaning rod guide with a lens in it, and its purpose is to make it possible for a rifleman to examine the chamber, throat and the first few inches of the bore—areas of critical interest to precision-accuracy shooters. The unit has no integral light source, but normally enough light can be reflected onto the surfaces in question by pointing the barrel at a soft fluorescent tube. Price, $16.50.

S&K Mfg. Co. has added a new design to their Insta-Mount line, one of the best systems for attaching scopes to military rifles. The latest item is specifically designed for the M1, and follows the suggestions of competitive rifleman Hugh Palmer. Price with 1″ satin-finished steel rings is $42.

Saunders Gun & Machine Shop makes two items for benchrest shooters. One is a plastic sunshade (offered in several lengths) with a threaded adaptor that screws into the objective unit of a target scope. A stubby shade is made for the 20x Lyman AA, which permits the shooter to use a rolled up target if he likes, while leaving the focusing reference marks exposed.

Dick Saunders also offers External Adjustment Knobs for the Lyman LWBR scope. They are easily installed by removing the turret caps and screwing the knobs on in their place. A spring-loaded blade fits into the slot that's cut to take a coin. The knobs can be marked to show basic zeroes at various ranges (as for metallic silhouette shooting), or used essentially as external adjustments on target scopes. $15.50 delivered.

Thompson/Center Arms has replaced their Puma handgun scope with a new 1½x model called the Lobo. This scope, built on a ⅞″ aluminum tube, has internally adjustable, constantly-centered crosswires and 16-foot field. The T/C people say it will take the recoil of any calibers offered in the Contender, which includes the 44 Magnum, 25-35, 357 Herrett and similar hotshots. Price is $44.50, plus $7.50 for the mount. The Lobo mount is also available at the same price for several Rugers, various Smith & Wessons, and can be had for the Bushnell Phantom scope on the Contender model.

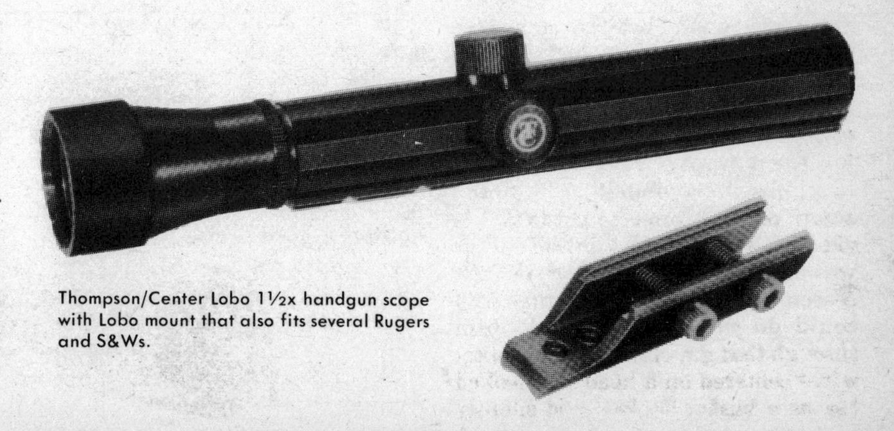
Thompson/Center Lobo 1½x handgun scope with Lobo mount that also fits several Rugers and S&Ws.

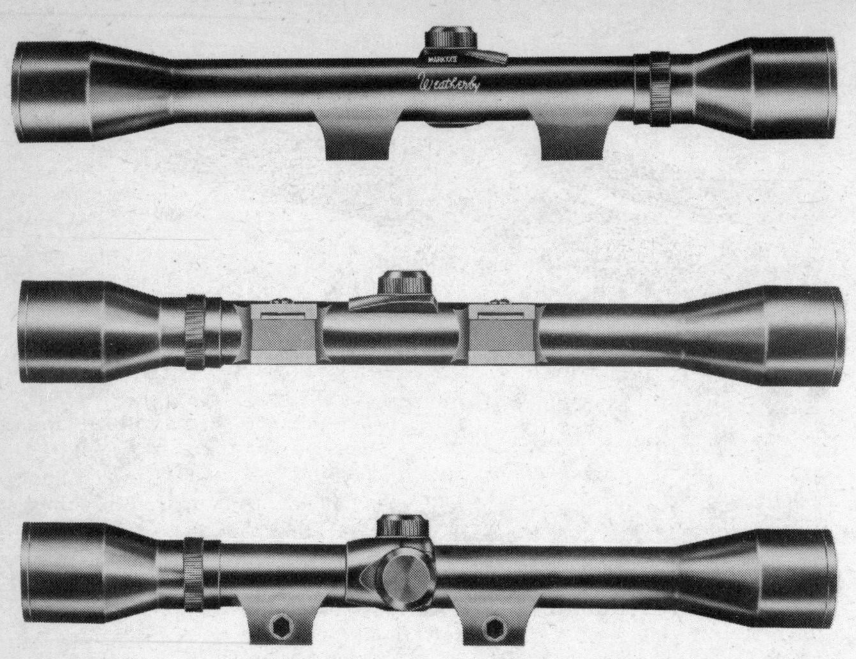

New Weatherby 4x scope with dovetail mounts for 22 rimfire rifles.

Weatherby 2¾x Premier has a 14.5mm exit pupil.

Weatherby's Imperial line of scopes has been around for quite a few years—and a fine bunch of scopes they are—but I get the feeling that they are pushing the slightly lower priced Premier line more. There isn't an awfully big difference in cost, and the guy who springs for a Weatherby rifle isn't too likely to quibble over another 10 or 20 bucks if he wants an Imperial.

Just as I was about to tell you something about the Imperial line, word has reached me that Weatherby is no longer cataloging the higher-priced Premier scopes. I imagine that a number of them can be found, however, in dealers' stocks, perhaps now at marked-down prices.

These Premiers are fine scopes, all built on 1" tubes, of course. Of more interest is the fact that all powers (2¾x, 4x and 3-9x) have the same 40mm objective lens. This gives an exit pupil of 4.4mm at 9x, which is about ideal for use under all light conditions the hunter will encounter. The lower powers have much larger exit pupils—14.5mm in the 2¾x, 10mm in the 4x—which provide more light than the human eye can accommodate. However, these large exit pupils make it easy to catch quick aim, as the eye does not have to be so precisely lined up as it does with a tiny pupil. This can be important when hunting deer or elk in thick cover, say, or for use on dangerous game. Whether this factor outweighs the increase in bulk and weight which come with the large objective, the buyer will have to decide for himself.

The Premiers also have binocular-type focusing, with reference marks that make it easy to return to previously determined settings. This makes it easier and faster to focus for the user's individual eyesight than turning the fine-threaded ocular unit found on most scopes. Scopes with this latter method are seldom precisely focused for the user's eyes, as the method is time consuming and the human eye's ability to adapt to a slightly out-of-focus condition keeps the shooter from ever knowing if the scope is perfectly adjusted.

Premiers also are available with the Lumi-Plex reticle, the popular 4 posts w/crosswires, but it differs in that the reticle reflects back to the shooter's eye light entering the ocular (rear) lens of the scope. This makes the reticle contrast well against a dark background, thus it's usable under poor shooting conditions. Crosswires, tapered post, and open dot reticles also are offered in the Premiers.

W.R. Weaver Co. has one or two new mounts this year, but no new scopes. However, in the works is a model intended for the silhouette ????. Guess that's understandable when you consider that the current Weaver line consists of 21 different models, ranging from the inexpensive D jobs, designed for rimfires, on up through the long-popular straight-power K models, the variables, and the Wider-View options on various Ks and Vs. Except in the target scope area, Weaver has the field well blanketed.

As an aside, Weaver avers that their K models, introduced just after WW II with the K2.5 and K4, are the world's most popular telescopic sight line. It's also claimed that the K4, which has been improved several times in the years since (as have all the other Ks), is the biggest selling hunting scope on the market. I don't doubt this for a moment. The K4 is to the scope field what the M94 Winchester is to the gun field. It's hard to find anyone who hasn't owned at least one of each sometime in his life.

One of my favorite Weavers, often mentioned in these pages, is the little

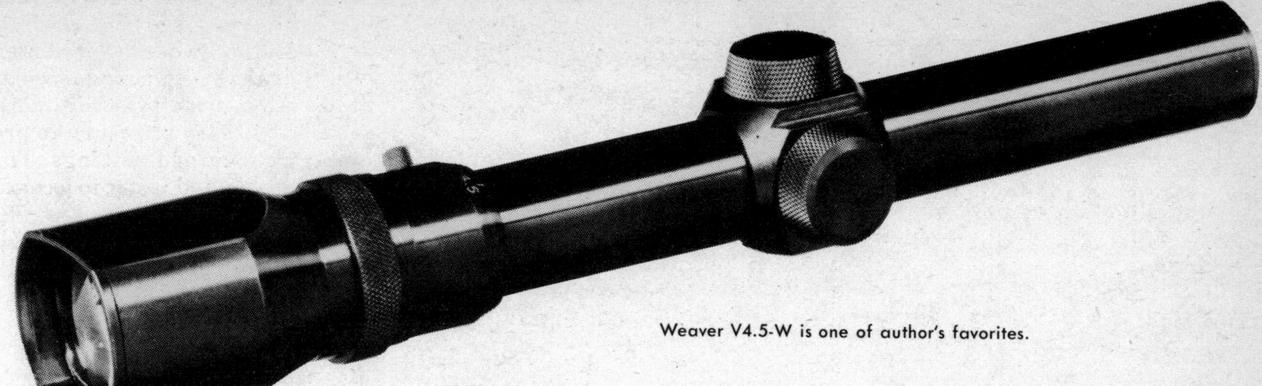

Weaver V4.5-W is one of author's favorites.

V4.5. It's mounted on my pet deer gun, a Mannlicher-stocked 284 Mauser, and again last December proved its worth. On my sixth day of hunting, most of this time in miserably wet and foggy weather, I had my chance at about 60 yards. The big Lee Dot settled on the spine close behind the shoulder and the 140-gr. Nosler gave an instant kill—as it should have, considering a clocked velocity of just a whisper under 3000 fps from the 57/4350 load. This is a great size and style of big game scope, small enough to look at home on a hunting rifle, yet providing the optics needed for all kinds of shooting.

But to get to the new Weaver mounts. The first is an all-steel (both rings and base) bridge mount, which reflects a notable change in thinking for this El Paso company. The rings are 1" split style, nicely machined, particularly the contouring of the bulge which accepts the allen-headed screws (one to a side). They come in regular and Hi-Style heights, the latter necessary for scopes having objective diameters greater than 1¾"; these also provide clearance for the bolt handle when using large-eyepiece scopes such as the Wider-View models. The Hi-Style also is made with an extension on one ring, which gives ¾" greater latitude in mounting scopes with non-standard eye relief, or perhaps one with an adjustment turret in an unusual position.

The mount base bridges the action opening, has an integral recoil lug to engage the rear face of the receiver ring, and is fastened to the action by three allen-headed screws. The top of the base is relieved transversely to a depth of about 1/32" to accept the flat portion of the bottom halves of the rings. Each of these is secured to the base by another allen-head screw inserted through a hole in the bottom of the ring.

When assembled, with all screws pulled up tightly, this seems to make a solid, sturdy unit. There's no doubt about the strength of the various pieces; however, I do question one aspect of the design. The machining in the top of the base which accepts the rings is about 20/32" (.625) wide, while the rings themselves are about 1/32" less (approximately .594). Before the joining screws are pulled up tightly, the rings can turn slightly before making contact with the shoulders on the relieved section of the base. Perhaps this is necessary to accommodate for minute inaccuracies in the scope tube or whatever. Nevertheless, the net effect is that these shoulders do not act as recoil abutments for the rings (unless or until the screws bend slightly under usage), and thus the scope's inertia must be absorbed strictly by the two connecting screws. If that was the intention, why bother making those two relieved sections at all? They serve no other purpose that I can see and increase production costs.

There is no windage adjustment in this mount, the apparent assumption being that the scope's internal adjustments can handle all normal zeroing.

Price of the steel top rings is $17 per pair ($21.50 for the extension style), $11 for the base.

Weaver also has a new "see through" mount in the works. Though not announced in their latest literature, samples have been shown to some writers. As with other makes, this design holds the scope high enough to permit the shooter to look under it and use his iron sights in an emergency. This Weaver is different, though, in that a strong sideways twist detaches the scope from the mount bases. There are times when this is desired by some hunters—in wet, thick brush country, when shipping the rifle as baggage on a plane, or whatever. The scope is remounted just as easily, and the maker says it locks back into zero.

Williams Gun Sight Co. has two fine scope lines, their Guide-Line and the Twilight models. These have been mentioned before, but it seems worthwhile to give a bit more detail on one particular scope, the 2-6x Guide-Line. This one is unusual because the clear diameter of its objective lens is 26mm. This is smaller than most scopes of this magnification range, and makes for a neat and handy hunting glass. Large objectives are necessary for high-power scopes, in order to get enough light transmission under typically gloomy hunting conditions. However, there's little point in going above a 5mm exit pupil in a scope, as that's all the human eye can normally admit. Size of the exit pupil is determined by dividing the diameter of the unobstructed objective lens in millimeters by the magnification. This scope, set at 6x, has an EP of 4.3mm, which is plenty large under all but the worst light conditions. However, if more light transmission is needed, it's a simple matter to reduce the magnification to 5x, which will enlarge the EP to better than 5mm, or to 4x, which will give an EP of almost 7mm—all the human eye can use even in near total darkness. So set, you have enough magnification for shooting big game at any reasonable distance, under any reasonable lighting conditions—and you have these advantages in a scope that's smaller than many straight 4x glasses. This is something that should be considered by more hunters. Too many of us work on the ridiculous theory that if a scope is bigger, or of higher magnification, it's got to be better. That's not so. In fact, on a true big game rifle the reverse is usually closer to the truth. •

The Pronghorn Rifle

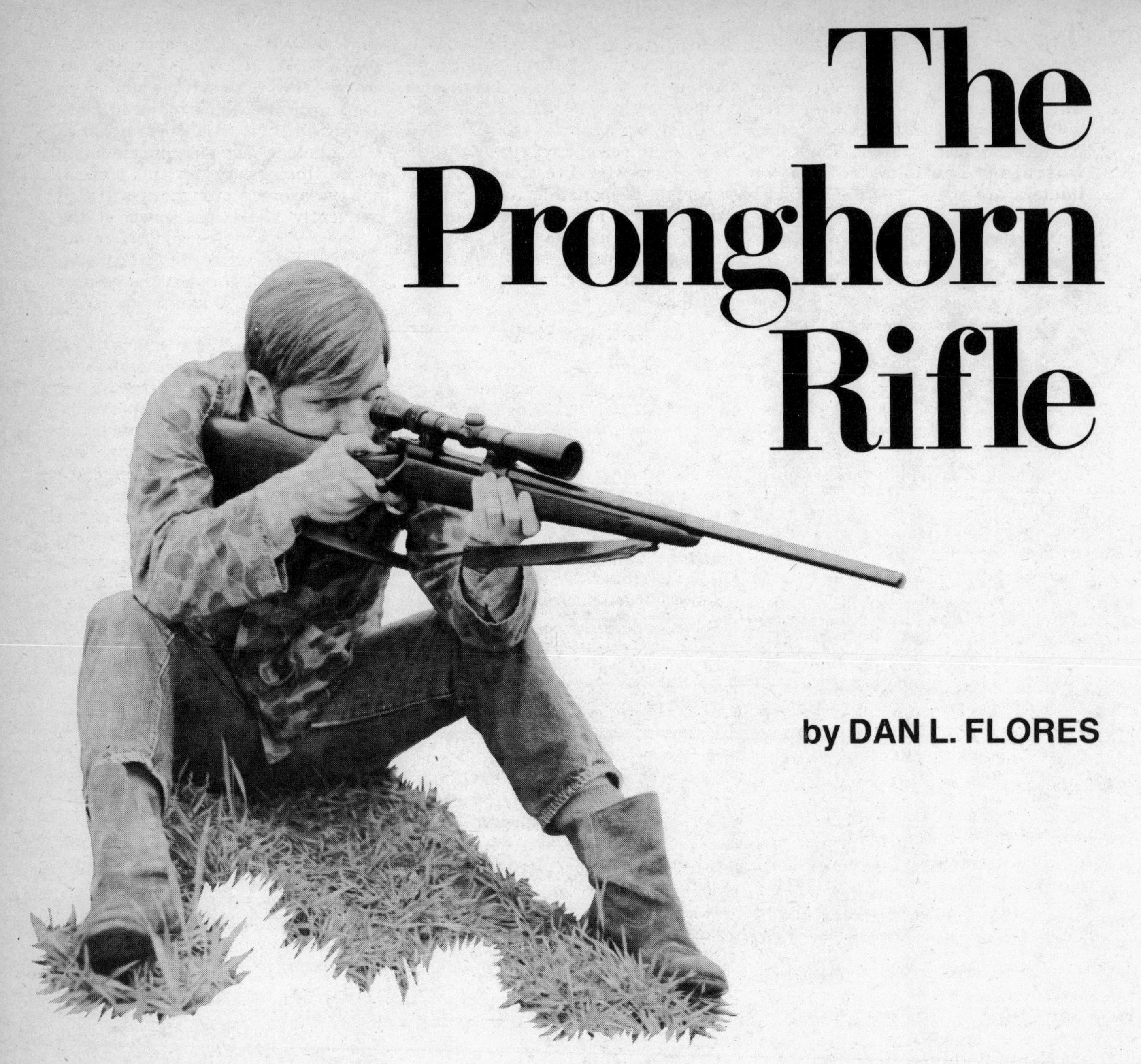

by DAN L. FLORES

In much antelope country a solid sitting position is the best bet, as it will get the muzzle up high enough to shoot over intervening sagebrush and greasewood. The pronghorn is a creature of the wide, windswept plains. Good bucks, like this one, usually require long stalks and pinpoint shooting over great distances.

Hunting the great open plains or stalking the ever alert antelope in broken foothill country can make a difference when choosing the optimum caliber—as can your shooting skill and experience. The author surveys the scene, lists the cartridges he finds suitable and effective, and offers an excellent table of proven handloads.

THE LOCATION is Wyoming, in the famous Red Desert. Two antelope hunters lie prone on a slight rise in the sagebrush. Far, far away, over 400 yards across the flat, a handsome pronghorn buck stands broadside, watching. The buck knows the hunters are there, but the distance is great and he's curious. The hunters discuss the range. Finally one of them rests his rifle over a springy bush. With held breath, while his companion watches through binoculars, the hunter carefully touches off the shot. The crack of the 270 laces across the vast, level plain, and the buck spins and pitches forward on its nose.

Now we switch locations—to West Texas. A rangy antelope buck with heavy, black horns is grazing in a valley nestled among rolling foothills. Suddenly it throws its head up and focuses its large eyes on an object—a hunter—crouching in the brush on the ridgecrest. Instantly the antelope is on the move, racing across the valley. The hunter quickly rolls to the sitting position, swings smoothly, and begins shooting at the running buck, the range about 150 yards. At the third shot the buck stumbles with the impact of the bullet, but covers another 30 yards before crashing to the ground in a swirling cloud of dust.

The two episodes just cited aren't a figment of anyone's imagination. They really happened, and I think they go a long way toward making a valid point about pronghorn hunting and pronghorn rifles—when pondering which piece of ordnance for antelope, at least two approaches can be taken, with the choice depending primarily on the type of terrain you'll be hunting over (plains or broken foothill country), and whether your preference (or skill) runs to long range sniping or close-in stalking. Certainly shooting skill and experience should play an important part in the selection. From what I've observed, antelope are responsible for a higher percentage of missed shots, than just about any other game animal—the bulk of the missing by pilgrims who overestimate their expertise on running antelope.

Antelope Habits

The pronghorn antelope offers, today, the only true plains hunting in North America. In fact, because pronghorns are basically found in plains and prairie environments, antelope hunting is usually considered the ultimate long range rifleman's game. There's a valid reason for this, because even in rough, rolling antelope range, pronghorns are shot, on the average, at greater distances than any other North American big game animal. No other hunting on the continent is quite like it, with the bagging of a buck pronghorn usually having about as much in common with whitetail deer hunting as paddleball has to tennis.

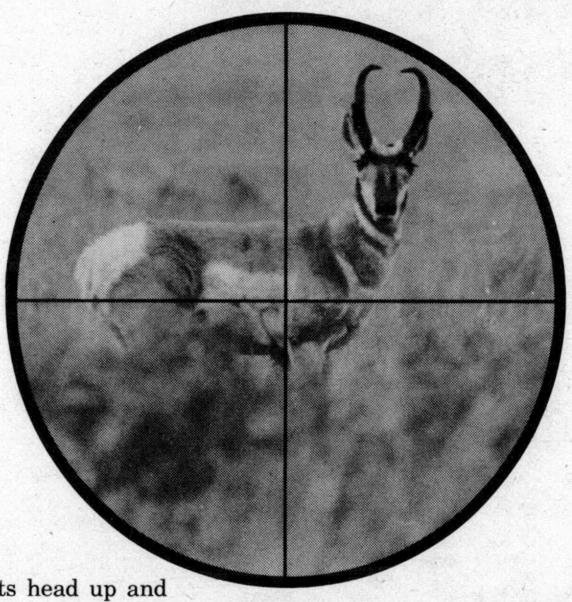

The pronghorn is a creature admirably adapted by evolution to survive and flourish in the Great Plains of our trans-Mississippi West. Great speed and almost phenomenal sight are the pronghorn's defenses in a vast land where, often enough, little if any cover exists. Unlike deer the antelope makes no attempt to hide or sulk in its habitat, for it feels secure in the knowledge that it can easily spot, and if necessary run away from, any possible threat. Thus the antelope is quite content in wide open country where it can be seen but rarely approached by hunters. If the pronghorn has a weakness, it lies in the animal's unfailing curiosity. Close brushes with hunters have enlightened many of the trophy bucks in this respect, but the average pronghorn will still frequently stand and gawk at the hunter for a few seconds before departing. The longer the distance between hunter and game, the greater this interval of recognition is likely to be.

The emphasis in this article, then, will be on the long range pronghorn rifle—the traditional rig. Though it is true that antelope range into some rough, broken country where stalks can be concluded at relatively close distances, the majority of antelope are hunted in areas where the liklihood of a close shot at a *standing* antelope is slim indeed. I'm not arguing with the close-in approach—every hunter owes it to himself and the game to approach it as closely as possible for a clean kill, but too often in antelope hunting a really close stalk means having to shoot at running animals. On an animal which can run 60 mph when it is serious about it, the chances of missing or wounding are great. I have greater faith in my ability to take a steady rest, with plenty of time, and nail a standing buck in the chest at 300 or 400 yards.

Such 'way off shots are far from unusual. In fact, on a typical antelope hunt a 150- or 200-yard shot can be considered pretty darned close. 250 yards is about average for a good shot, and in hard-hunted country there will be plenty of opportunities at 300-500 yards. As an example, on my first pronghorn hunt in Wyoming, our 4 bucks were taken at 300, 125, 450, and 335 yards! To me it makes good sense to use a rifle that will handle not only the short range opportunities, but also the long range ones which crop up with alarming regularity in pronghorn hunting.

Antelope Rifles

The antelope rifle then, more so than any other type of big game rifle, should be capable of shooting flat and hitting hard at great distances. Because of the ranges involved, plus the relatively small size of the quarry (with a broadside kill area of about 10x10 inches), the pronghorn rifle must also provide better than average accuracy. Ideally, a good antelope rifle should shoot groups of about 1½ inches or less at 100 yards, which in most rifles would mean a group size of about 8 inches at 400 yards—well within the vital area of a pronghorn

End result of a long stalk and a perfectly-placed shot.

buck, but that rifle had better be held steadily! The average 3 minute-of-angle (MOA) deer rifle might be OK for stalking antelope and laying down a barrage at them, but it lacks the necessary accuracy for long range shooting. Action type makes little difference here so long as the rifle is chambered for a suitable cartridge, and so long as it provides the accuracy desired. Traditionally, pronghorn rifles have been bolt guns (though many shooters now use such good, accurate single shots as the Ruger No. 1), but lately some of the lever actions and semi-autos have been closing the accuracy gap. I've seen a couple of M99 Savages that would really shoot, and from what I've heard the new Browning semi-autos turn in quite respectable groups. By and large, though, the man who hopes to secure a suitably accurate rifle for pronghorns has a better chance of getting one in a bolt action.

The physical dimensions of the antelope rifle aren't critical. Since most of the hunting will be over fairly level ground, some extra weight and barrel length can be accepted in the interest of higher accuracy and better performance. A 24- or 26-inch barrel is no handicap in pronghorn hunting. Nor, for that matter, is a barrel a bit on the heavy side. I know a gunsmith in Sheridan, Wyoming, who habitually uses a specially made, heavy-

These 4 cartridges represent the minimum pronghorn artillery; with good bullets all are excellent. From left—243, 244/6mm, 257 Roberts and 25-06.

barreled 264 for antelope, and he swears by it. Impractical? Maybe, but one can't argue much with *his* success. Conducive to accuracy, nearly as much so as a good barrel, is a good, crisp trigger pull of around 2½-3 lbs.

Caliber Choices

The pronghorn is neither a very large, nor a particularly hardy, critter. An exceptional buck may weigh 120-125 pounds on the hoof, but most will be considerably lighter, with the average mature buck going around 105 lbs. With chest hits antelope are not hard to put down—in my experience not nearly as difficult to drop as a whitetail deer. Most centerfire game cartridges will kill an antelope quite handily—the difficulty lies in *hitting* 'em. The criterion for a pronghorn cartridge, then, should center around hitting ease rather than great power. Flat trajectory and light recoil, along with accuracy, are what make a cartridge/rifle easy to hit with. Couple these with ample power and you have the makings of a pronghorn cartridge. The requirement for flat trajectory would automatically rule out numbers like the 30-30, 32 Special, 35 Remington, 25-35, 44 Magnum, *et al,* and common sense tells us that such calibers as the 338 and 375 are certainly out of place on a hundred-pound animal. We have left, though, numerous excellent cartridges between the two extremes. Here is a list of recommended pronghorn cartridges and bullet weights:

- 243 Winchester with 90/105 gr. spitzers
- 6mm Remington with 90/105-gr. spitzers
- 240 Weatherby with 90/105-gr. spitzers
- 250-3000 with 100-gr. spitzers (handloads)
- 257 Roberts with 100-gr. spitzers (handloads)
- 25-06 Rem. with 100/120-gr. spitzers
- 257 Weatherby with 100/120-gr. spitzers
- 6.5 Rem. Magnum with 120-gr. spitzers
- 264 Win. Magnum with 120/140-gr. spitzers
- 270 Win with 110/130-gr. spitzers
- 270 Weatherby with 130/150-gr. spitzers
- 7x57 with 125/140-gr. spitzers (handloads)
- 284 Win. with 125/140-gr. spitzers
- 280 Rem. with 125/140-gr. spitzers
- 7mm Magnum with 125/154-gr. spitzers
- 308 Win. with 150-gr. spitzers
- 30-06 Spgf. with 150-gr. spitzers
- 300 Magnums with 150/180-gr. spitzers

These, as I said, are recommended. Although I personally see no reason why the 22-250 or 220 Swift, loaded with either the 60-gr. Hornady HP or the 70-gr. Speer to maximum velocities could not be used with perfect satisfaction on antelope out to around

This heavy-horned buck was taken at nearly 400 yards by Jimmy Hall, his rifle a Ruger M77 in 243 with 6x Redfield. Although not usually recommended for such distant doings, the 243 is deadly in the hands of a good shot.

Six of the top cartridges for hunting trophy antelope, where shots are apt to be very long, are from left—25-06, 264, 270, 280, 284, 7mm Magnum.

250 yards, most western states prohibit their use. On the other end of the scale, the various 300 Magnums really have an excess of power for antelope, though they do have some application in ultra long range shooting.

The 6mms and 25s

Widespread popularity of a number of the above-listed rounds dictates that some special attention be given them here, and we'll start with the 243 and 6mm. With proper bullets these cartridges offer nearly perfect penetration and energy release for antelope. I've heard them called cripplers by some people, but anyone who has had fairly extensive experience on game with the 6mms is bound to come away with a different opinion. I've seen instant kills made on big buck antelope at over 300 yards with these cartridges—one while a guide was whispering into my partner's ear that the rifle would never do it. The best bullets in 243 or 6mm are the 95- and 100-gr. spitzers. With the newer powders much higher velocities are obtainable from the 6mms than were thought possible before. In my M70 Featherweight, for example, the 95-gr. Nosler can be driven to 3,282 fps with 47/4831, and the 100-gr. Sierra can be moved along at over 3,150 with 47/N205. These loads don't appear really hot in my 243, but duplicate them with caution. In the 6mm, a favorite load teams the 105-gr. Speer spitzer with 45.5/IMR-4831 for over 3,100. All the bullets listed here, by the way, are proven veterans on game.

In the same energy category as the 6mms are the old but still good 250 Savage and 257 Roberts. With 100-gr. spitzer bullets either cartridge is solidly adequate for antelope. The old 250 will dirve a 100-gr. bullet to 3,000 fps with either 41/4350 or 38/4320, and the 257 will do an easy 3,200 with 49/4831, or a grain less of the newer IMR-4831. Like the 6mms, these two 25s are all that anyone could ask for up to 300 yards or so, with genial recoil and superb accuracy (usually) making them, again like the 6s, ideal for the city hunter whose shooting skill isn't up to 400-yard shots, and who is adverse to the recoil of larger calibers.

The 25-06 is enjoying great popularity, and well it might. It is a truly superb pronghorn cartridge, maybe the best. My own tests indicate that the 100-gr. spitzer can be propelled to nearly 3,400 fps with 57 grains of N205, but despite the obvious excellence of the 100-gr., I prefer the 117/

120-gr. spitzers in this cartridge; they shoot flatter past 300 yards and buck crosswinds with considerably more authority. A favorite pronghorn load in my Remington M700 is the 117-gr. Sierra in front of 55/N205 for over 3,200. I've used this load extensively on both game and varmints, and it is outstanding. Another fine antelope load is 54/IMR-4831 teamed with the 120-gr. Hornady HP for 3,213.

270 and 30-06

Two classic cartridges for pronghorns, and indeed for all western game, are the 270 and the 30-06. For antelope the 130-gr. in the 270 is classic medicine. My longest shot on a pronghorn was a 450-yard hit on a good 14-inch buck with the 130-gr. Nosler and 55/4350 in the 270. This load produces about 3,100 in the 24-inch barrel of my M70 standard rifle. The 130-gr. can be pushed to 3,200 with 60/IMR-4831, or by 62 grains of N205 or H-4831. Though 150-gr. 270 loads are terrific for Mule deer and elk, most bullets in this weight are a mite hard jacketed for pronghorns, tending to "pencil through" at extended ranges. The 110-gr. Sierra is not a bad bet, though, and it can be driven to nearly 3,400 fps in a 270.

The spry, septuagenarian 30-06 is at its best on antelope with a 150-gr. spitzer at around 3,000 fps. My pet load is 60/4350 with the 150-gr. Hornady for 3,025 from a 22-inch barrel. The Hornady has an exceptionally good reputation as a killer on medium game, and it expands quite easily. Some 150-gr. 30 caliber bullets—notably the Silvertip and the Core-Lokt—don't upset well on thin-skinned antelope after velocity has fallen off.

Close stalks for pronghorns often result in shots like this, but with an animal capable of 60 miles an hour, a good case can be made for longer distance shooting at stationary targets!

Among magnum cartridges, the most popular with antelope hunters seem to be the 264 and 7mm Remington. The 240 and 257 Weatherby magnums are also terrific long range pronghorn cartridges, as is the 270 Weatherby, but the appeal of these cartridges is based as much on the Weatherby image as it is on their capabilities.

Winchester's 264 magnum seems to have been created with antelope hunting in mind. 100-gr. 264 loads are designed for blowup on varmints, though, and shouldn't be used on game. Two superb pronghorn loads for the 264 are the 120-gr. Sierra bullet rolling along at 3,533 with 68/N205, and the 125-gr. Nosler backed by 65/IMR-4831 for 3,400. These velocities are obtained in the 26-inch barrel of my M70 Westerner—my favorite pronghorn rifle. The 7mm Remington Magnum, which is today the most popular magnum cartridge around, will also knock antelope flat clear out to 400-500 yards. A top-performing load for pronghorns in the Big 7 is the 139-gr. Hornady in front of 69.5/IMR-4831 (or 71.5/H-4831) for nearly 3,375 fps. Both charges are quite hot, so work up to them slowly and carefully.

With any rifle to be used specifically for antelope, bullet selection is of vital import. Lead nose spitzers and spitzer boattails are basic, as is a high ballistic co-efficient (at least .320, and preferably in the .400s) for retaining velocity and bucking the stiff winds that prevail on the plains. Medium-weight game bullets are preferred in all calibers; heavier slugs won't open properly on an antelope's light frame at long range, and varmint bullets are simply too destructive.

Selected Pronghorn Loads

Cartridge	Bullet/grs.	Powder/grs.	MV/fps
243 Win.	95 Nosler	47 /IMR-4831	3,282*
243 Win.	100 Sierra	47 /N205	3,164*
6mm Rem.	95 Nosler	48 /IMR-4831	3,300
6mm Rem.	105 Speer	45.5/IMR-4831	3,100
250-3000	100 Hornady	41 /4350	3,000
257 Roberts	100 Hornady	49 /H-4831	3,200
25-06 Rem.	100 Sierra	57 /N205	3,347*
25-06 Rem.	117 Sierra	54.5/IMR-4831	3,262*
26-06 Rem.	117 Sierra	55 /N205	3,210*
25-06 Rem.	120 Hornady HP	54 /IMR-4831	3,213*
264 Win. Mag.	120 Sierra	68 /N205	3,533*
264 Win. Mag.	125 Nosler	65 /IMR-4831	3,400*
264 Win. Mag.	140 Hornady	63 /IMR-4831	3,147*
270 Win.	110 Sierra	51.5/4064	3,375
270 Win.	130 Nosler	55 /4350	3,103*
270 Win.	130 Sierra BT	62 /H-4831	3,200
7mm Rem. Mag.	139 Hornady	69.5/IMR-4831	3,375
7mm Rem. Mag.	154 Hornady	67 /N205	3,125
30-06 Spgr.	150 Hornady	60 /4350	3,023*

*Chronographed Velocities.
All loads are at or near maximum, and should be approached cautiously from below.

Long Range Zeros

Irrespective of bullet weight, the antelope rifle should be zeroed at the longest possible distance that will not cause overshooting at medium ranges. A peak midrange trajectory rise of 4 inches can be tolerated, meaning that we can zero the 6mm, 25-06, 270, *et al* at from 250 to 300 yards, the flatter magnums at about 325 or thereabouts. With the use of a ballistics chart, such as those found in the Hornady and Sierra loading manuals, drop figures for almost any cartridge/bullet/velocity can be easily determined. A hotly-loaded 270 with the 130-gr. Hornady at 3,200 fps muzzle velocity, for example, can be zeroed at 300 yards, with a rise of 4.1 inches at 200. At 400 yards the bullets will strike 9.9 inches below the point of aim, and at 500 yards 26.7 inches low. Any rifleman who is experienced enough to estimate range with some degree of accuracy should be pretty deadly with those figures (or those of his own rifle and load) committed to memory or pasted to the buttstock.

Proper glassware for antelope hunting is critical. Some specialists use 8x and 10x varmint scopes for antelope, but those hunters who use one rifle for several species usually select variables or straight 4x scopes. I prefer a straight 6x. I find that a 4x a tiny bit lacking in magnification, and I am coming more and more to dislike variables. I've never had any trouble with fixed-power scopes, but I've ex-

A pronghorn rifle *par excellence*—the M70 Westerner 264 with Weaver K6 and 140 gr. handloads accounted for this Wyoming buck.

perienced a number of breakdowns with variables. Further, those which have no provision for focusing and parallax adjustment quite often show a great deal of reticle movement at long range. A 3x-9x variable made by a highly-touted company is mounted on my 243. At 400 yards it has *13 inches* of lateral parallax (measured on a target). That's not exactly conducive to accurate shooting. Reticle choice is simple, as nothing beats a plain medium or thin crosshair. By the way, the pronghorn is one big game species that a rangefinder reticle can be successfully employed on.

An experienced rifleman shooting a high velocity, tight-grouping rifle should be pretty deadly on standing antelope to about 425-450 yards if he can estimate range/wind and learns to take advantage of whatever rest he can find. Doping wind* and estimated range come with experience, but using a rest is just common sense and takes no particular skill. The prone position is often easy to assume in pronghorn hunting, though in very flat country some shots will have to be taken from the sitting position. Shots at running antelope, also, are handled more efficiently from the sitting or kneeling. Because of the nature of antelope hunting, there is usually ample time to set up in a steady position, carefully estimate range, wind drift, etc., and then squeeze off the shot. If everything was done right, you'll have antelope steaks.

Antelope hunting is a long range rifleman's sport, and must be approached from that direction (I'm not talking about chasing animals down with 4-WDs and then throwing offhand covey shots at whole bands of animals—under those circumstances it doesn't make any difference what kind of rifle you use), more so than any other type of big game hunting in this country.

Close shots do happen, but they are not the norm. Those accounts of wide, windswept prairies, of patient glassing with a spotting scope while you lay on your belly in the sage, and of exciting stalks and tricky, long distance shots at black horned old bucks are more than just romance and fantasy. Those thing actually happen unless you go out of your way to avoid them.

In closing, one hard and bitter grain of truth emerges which I cannot surpress. It is this: most of the antelope missed are not hit because of any inadequacy on the part of the rifle/cartridge combo, but because of inadequacy on the part of the shooter. It shouldn't be much of a trick to learn how to compensate for a few inches of bullet drop, or how to touch off a shot at a game animal without jerking the trigger, but the fact remains that thousands of pronghorns *are* missed each fall for just those reasons. So, if you expect excellence on the part of your rifle, be prepared to produce in like manner. The best and most accurate antelope rifle in the world, firing the flattest shooting cartridge, is of precious little use unless it is pointed right! •

*Sierra Bullets' latest edition (1974) of their *Reloading Manual* contains extensive wind deflection tables, well worth studying.

Star's PD 45

Custom-made combat pistols have been around for years–at a hefty price. Now there's a production equivalent, made in Spain, at less than half the usual cost.

by GEORGE C. NONTE, JR.

MOST BIG-BORE fans of the autoloader considered it a major breakthrough when Colt introduced its aluminum-framed Commander variation of the Government Model in 1949. Much was made of its compactness and light weight, and equal accolades came when the steel-framed Combat Commander was introduced in 1972.

Women aren't usually enamored of 45 autos, but Jean Eades doesn't find the Star PD objectionable; Dick Eades seems concerned, though.

Here's the Star PD45, field stripped. Barrel and link remain in slide. Captive recoil spring has plastic buffer at rear (right) of spring.

a potent small package

Those were the *only* attempts by domestic makers to produce what we now call a "combat autoloader" for the ubiquitous 45 ACP cartridge. Otherwise it's been up to the foreigners, and thus far the Spanish firm, Star Bonifaccio Echeverria, has taken the lead. Its first effort was the light-alloy 9mm Parabellum (Luger) Starlight some years back—and now we have a similar development in the Model PD, this one in 45 auto caliber.

The Star PD is shorter, lighter, shallower, and thinner than the Commander—even more so than the full-size Colt Gold Medal, Llama, and Star Model P. The new PD is 7.25" long with its 3.88" barrel, and it weighs 23½ ounces empty. All this makes it roughly 10% smaller and lighter than the lightweight Commander, the only other 45 in its class.

But the above figures don't tell the entire story. The butt is nearly ½" shorter than other 45 autos, and its thinner grips, of checkered walnut, make it far more concealable than the big guns. When ensconced in a thin-leather, well-fitted, high-ride belt holster or tucked inside one's waistband, it seems to protrude little more than most 380 autos. This high degree of concealability was the major goal of Star and the Garcia Corp. (the sole importer and distributor) in this extensive development of the basic Star Model P. Their success is obvious.

In redesigning the Model P to produce the PD, the following steps were taken:

Model P Changes

The frame butt was shortened (from the bottom) about .480". The frame material was changed from steel to high-strength, aluminum alloy. The slide and barrel were shortened 1.22", from the muzzle, and one locking lug was eliminated from both. The slide was tapered at the top from front to rear and narrowed near the muzzle; a dummy rib was machined into the top of the slide.

The recoil spring was changed to a fully captive system with full-length guide and a plastic slide buffer; the barrel bushing was modified to be compatible.

The slide and manual safety were redesigned so that the latter functions as a dismounting latch. A new, fully-adjustable, low-profile rear sight of combat/target style was inletted into the upper rear of the slide.

In addition, various minor alterations were made to insure maximum compatibility of slide, barrel, and frame in the new shorter length. Particular attention was paid to the development of a feed ramp and associated parts that would give *in production guns* 100% feed reliability with high-performance cartridges of the Super Vel type—that make of ammo is no more, sad to say, but the HP varieties remain available.

Early development work was done with the basic Model P magazine shortened to 6-round capacity. However, a new 7-shot magazine will be supplied, it is said, with production guns—thus the full 8-round capability of all the big 45 autos is retained with a butt nearly a half-inch shorter.

The magazine is like those found in all big Star autos—a sheet-metal box holding a stamped follower, wire spring and detachable bottom plate. The magazine also has the "full-magazine indicator" of its bigger brothers—a lug or protrusion on the base of the follower is pushed through a hole at the rear of the floorplate when the magazine is fully loaded.

Shown here at full recoil in author's hands, the PD45 has no more apparent recoil than the standard Colt Commander. Note fired case in air above gun.

This is a helpful convenience—you know by feel if the magazine you grab is fully charged.

If the pin does not protrude, it may be that the magazine is partially loaded or empty. (Incidentally, it appears that merely installing the Model PD's follower in the old Model P's magazine would increase the latter's capacity one round. In this way one could have a 9-shot Model P if he chose.)

In spite of all these modifications nearly all PD lockwork parts remain interchangeable with the Model P; hammer, sear, trigger, disconnector, sear bar, safety, magazine catch, etc. The PD does not, however, have the magazine safety of the Model P—an abomination on a combat gun. Star has wisely deleted it from the PD to save the shooter the trouble of removing it and throwing it away. The long firing pin of earlier Star autos has finally given way to one of Browning inertia type. Unlike other Stars, the PD may be safely carried with the hammer fully down on a chambered cartridge; even then the firing pin cannot be forced against the primer. It is spring retracted and secured by a pin hidden under the rear sight.

In functioning the PD follows the other big Star pistols exactly. Barrel and slide recoil a short distance, locked together by ribs atop the barrel; then the pivoted barrel link pulls the barrel free of the slide; the barrel halts against the frame and the slide continues rearward to extract and eject the fired case while compressing the recoil spring and forcing the hammer to full cock. The sear holds the hammer while the slide runs forward to feed the chamber a cartridge and strike the barrel, causing the latter to rise and engage the locking surfaces.

Lockup in the PD differs from other Browning-type 45 autos only in this way—one locking lug has been removed to allow the barrel bushing to come back farther over the barrel, a move made necessary by the shorter slide. This leaves one free-standing lug and the raised portion over the chamber to take the locking load. This is quite adequate, and I foresee no problems at all in this area. Over 15 years ago I shot extensively Colt 45 autos that were short one locking lug and had no trouble at all.

Field stripping the PD is a bit different than with other Stars; here's the drill: with magazine out and chamber empty, draw the slide back until the safety may be pressed upward to engage the slide notch, thus holding the slide in dismount position; press the slide stop to the left (from right) and withdraw; turn the safety down and ease the slide/barrel unit forward off the frame; invert the slide and lift the recoil spring unit out; rotate the barrel bushing about 45 degrees counterclockwise and remove; draw the barrel out from the front of the slide. Turning out 4 screws allows removal of the grips for further cleaning.

Reassembly is, inevitably, the reverse of the above.

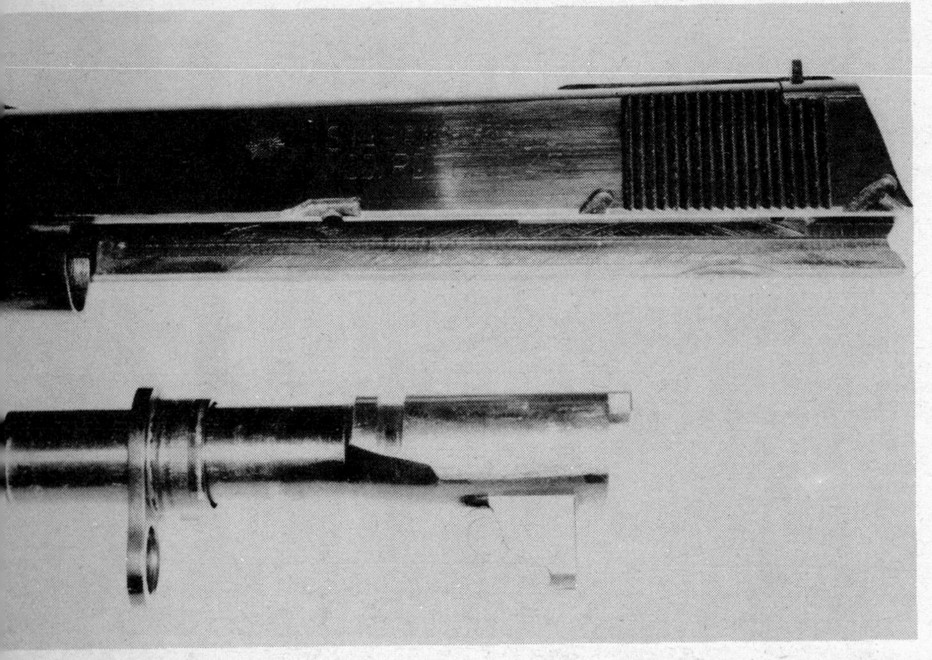

Star PD 45's short barrel and slide have only one locking rib and mating rib recess.

Rounded-edge "combat" rear sight, let into upper rear of slide, is adjustable for windage and elevation.

Handling and Shooting

The Star PD handles well. It has rather thin, checkered grips, and the front strap carries deep, lateral serrations to improve one's hold. It feels a bit muzzle-light, compared to the Commander, but seems to point a bit better. One might expect recoil to be rather sharp—and technically it probably is—but it *feels* no worse than the Commander. Recovery in rapid fire is just as quick as with the Commander, in spite of the lighter muzzle and its lighter weight.

Shooting the PD at 25 yards produced better accuracy than we expected; better than many GI 45s, and equal to most commercial Colt GMs. A too-high front sight on the sample made it necessary to run the rear sight 'way up in elevation to zero. A couple file strokes would have cured that, but we didn't want to cobble up a sample gun being sent on to other people for examination and tests. I'd do it in a minute on a production gun.

Pete Dickey, our good friend from Garcia and "father" of the PD, had promised us *perfect* feeding with any ball or high-performance, factory

Star PD 45 compared with standard M1911A1 45 auto, the latter a 1927 Argentine model.

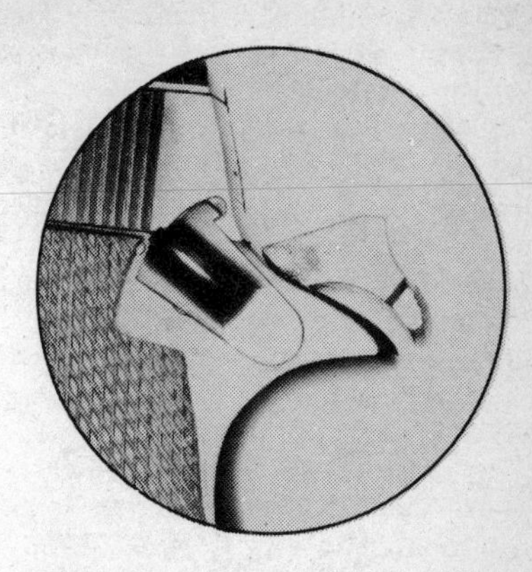

Basic Star safety cams hammer off sear. More positive than Colt or Browning design, it also acts as takedown latch.

loads—particularly the now-defunct Super Vel 190-gr. JHP. He was right—no malfunctions whatever occurred with any ammunition we could find. We did not, however, shoot any pipsqueak, semi-wadcutter target loads. They serve no real purpose in a gun of this type.

The case ejection pattern was good, empties being well clear of the shooter. A fired case in your face can be terribly distracting, especially during serious social intercourse.

By the time we finished, our sample gun had digested over 1000 rounds of assorted ball and high-performance ammunition. Careful inspection showed no visible wear, just broken-in bright spots that reduce friction and improve reliability. We'd not hesitate in the least to carry it, cocked and loaded, into a dangerous situation.

The Star PD isn't cheap at about $175 (no exact price is available), and it's offered only in blue finish. On the other hand, the PD has features that cannot be obtained in *any* other production gun, though they can be had in custom combat conversions at $400-$500. That makes it a pretty good buy in my book. It's the gun for you if you want the smallest, lightest, most concealable 45 auto around. ●

Dick Eades found he could shoot as well at 25 yards with our sample PD as with a 45 Colt Gold Cup.

The Rottweil OVER UNDER

The instantly detachable Rottweil trigger unit represents precision workmanship throughout. The hammers are driven by powerful coil springs that are totally enclosed. In this photo the near hammer is in its fired position and has rebounded slightly, which allows the spring-loaded firing pin to withdraw from the primer indent—an excellent feature.

GUN DIGEST EXCLUSIVE

This well-made Skeet shooters' smoothbore, new to America, reveals several unusual design differences—all useful and desirable, all excellently integrated. Rottweil's special shotshells add measurably to the gun's performance.

by WALLACE LABISKY

Like a great many other O/U guns the Olympia '72 is under-bolted, necessitating a rather deep frame (2⅝″) at the standing breech. In this action-open view the ejectors are at full "lift," and this is the amount (⅜″) that unfired shells are elevated for manual removal.

IN MUNICH, at the XX Olympiad in 1972, Konrad Wirnhier took the gold medal in the International Skeet event following a 25-bird, tie-breaking shoot-off with two other competitors. Wirnhier, representing West Germany, shot the winning 220x225 score using a Rottweil (Dynamit Nobel) over-under specially designed for this low-gun, fast-bird-style competition.

This same 12-ga. gun, now designated the Rottweil-Skeet Olympia '72, is currently being brought to these shores by Golden Shield Armourers, Inc., P.O. Box 45043, Exchange Park, Dallas, TX 75235*. As we go to press, the price for the standard Skeet model with selective single trigger runs $1,475. That's getting a bit rich for my peasant blood, but the really gung-ho Skeeter, whether he plays by domestic or international rules, probably won't mind the tariff.

With obvious careful engineering from muzzles to buttstock, the Olympia '72 hosts some highly interesting design concepts. Take the chokes, for example, which are going to make most shooters do a quick double-take. Eight-gauge muzzles?

That's right. And it's all because of a special recess-type choke that is designed to "improve shot stringing and to throw flawless and more effective patterns than conventional skeet chokes," in the words of Dynamit Nobel.

The choke section of each tube is about 3″ long, with a reverse cone at the rear leading into a 1⅜″ long recess that permits the shot charge to expand considerably over nominal bore diameter. The choking effect occurs at a point 1 1/16″ behind the muzzle where the forward cone swages the shot charge down to .747″ diameter. From this point forward, the bore I.D. gradually flares to .833″ at the muzzle.

To accommodate this special choke the Rottweil people had to substantially increase the outside diameter of the barrels at the muzzle end. This enlargement begins about 4¾″ back, but isn't readily discernible to the eye until the final 4″. At this point the barrel O.D. is .840″, with the "growth" continuing to .904″ at the muzzles.

G. W. Tharp, president of GSA, told me that this special choke allows the shot charge to physically separate from the wad, and that the wad will be traveling some 2″-3″ behind the payload on muzzle exit. This is said to result in a fast-opening pattern with balanced pellet distribution.

So what happened at the pattern board? Using Dynamit Nobel's Rottweil Skeet load (1⅛ ozs. No. 9 shot without protecting cup or sleeve), both barrels of the test gun delivered 25-yard patterns that ranged 42″ to 44″ wide. The under barrel placed 65.1% of the load (422 pellets) in a 30″ circle, while the over barrel averaged 63.8%

*Late in May of this year Dynamit Nobel (West Germany) notified us that the Olympia '72 is not an exclusive Rottweil import of the Golden Shield Co. See our report in Shooter's Showcase on the correct situation.

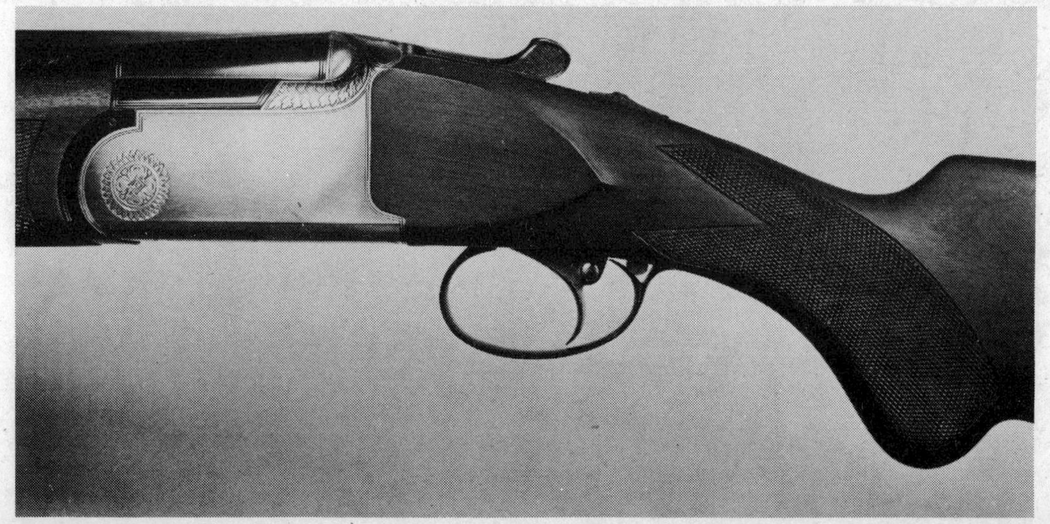

Despite its rather steep price tag, the Olympia '72 carries very little engraving, and the stock wood is on the plain side. The bright and smoothly polished frame receives a special chemical-process treatment to make it rust resistant. Reminiscent of early-1900 styling is the pistol grip with its rounded butt.

(413 pellets) for 5 shots. Pattern regularity was excellent and, in terms of pellet distribution within the 30″ circle, both tubes made a good showing with very few patches. So, as an alibi for lost targets one couldn't justifiably fault the performance of this choke/load combination.

Also at 25 yards, the Smith & Wesson Skeet load (Flite-Max shot-cup wad) printed a 65.0% average from the over barrel. However, regularity and pellet distribution weren't quite as good as with the Rottweil loading. There was markedly stronger center density and, in turn, a loss in annular coverage.

Given time to do so, I'm certain that a 1⅛ x 9 handload could be worked up to match the Rottweil offering but my somewhat hurried initial attempt fell flat. Using the Remington All-American hull with the WW209 primer and 22.0/Trap 100, I used a ½″ W-W fiber wad sandwiched between two .070″ card wads. Average efficiency from the Olympia's under barrel was 52.6% and the extreme density variation yo-yoed to 120 pellets. Poor, poor! Obviously, this wad column failed to provide a good gas seal. Some shot balling was also in evidence—another sign of powder gas blowing past the wads.

Olympia '72 Features

In terms of action type, the Olympia '72 is neither a boxlock nor a sidelock. Rather, it has a trigger action, meaning that—except for the retractable type firing pins—all of the fire-control system is incorporated with the trigger unit. This trigger unit is instantly detachable by simply depressing a spring-loaded release in the rear of the guard.

In addition to the selective single trigger (barrel selector is located in the trigger web), two other trigger units are available (or will be in the near future)—a non-selective single trigger and conventional double triggers.

Because the lower tang is held to highly precise dimensions during manufacture these trigger units will interchange without any need for fitting, and each unit is made with its own base plate and guard. Both of the single triggers mentioned are of the inertia type, which requires recoil to ready the mechanism for the second pull. Prices, when the units are purchased as additional equipment, were not available at press time.

Another interesting piece of design is seen in the ejector system, which does not depend on any fore-end parts but is contained entirely in the monoblock breech. On firing the coil-spring-powered ejectors are "armed" by the cocking slides, which move forward along the floor of the frame, causing a pair of vertical arms to rise and engage notches in the ejector legs. Primary extraction of fired shells prior to ejection is ⅛″, but the extraction of unfired shells for manual removal is a full ⅜″ for easy grasping. A cleverly engineered system!

Here the Rottweil selective single trigger unit is seen alongside its mortise in the lower tang. Note selection button in trigger web. Three interchangeable units are offered—selective single, non-selective single and conventional double triggers. None requires special fitting.

The 68cm (26¾″) Skeet tubes are hammer forged from special Böhler barrel steel and chamber cones are nearly a full inch in length. The 11mm-wide ventilated top rib tapers ever so slightly from .425″ at the breech to .405″ at the muzzles. This is a level rib with a flat surface that has a median groove about 1/10″ wide. The median is engraved with longitudinal lines, the slightly-elevated flanking areas crosscut with somewhat finer lines. As a result, the median shows up several shades lighter. So it serves not only as an extra visual aid in barrel/target alignment, but it also helps to confirm and "lock in" a precise eye/rib relationship. There is a sleeved white-bead front sight of ⅛″ diameter.

Since the Olympia '72 is an underbolted gun, a la Browning, the frame depth runs to 2⅝″. The barrels pivot within the frame on a trunnion arrangement as opposed to the usual full-width crosspin. Because of the trigger action, and because of the cocking arrangement (an arm fixed to the fore-end iron), the frame sides

The Olympia's selective ejector system is contained entirely in the monoblock breech. In this close-up photo the near ejector (for the over barrel) has reached the primary extraction position, and is held by a sliding vertical arm, the latter having been actuated by the cocking slide. As the action comes fully open the vertical arm will be cammed downward and the ejector will be released to continue its travel and throw the fired shell clear.

and bottom are solid—no "trapdoor" openings, and no transverse tumbler and sear pins. As the Dynamit Nobel people say, the frame is designed "to provide extraordinary reinforcement at all stress points."

As it should be on a claybird gun, the tang safety is nonautomatic. And something you don't often see nowadays is an extra-wide trigger face (5/16") that angles to the right rear—definitely a concession to the right-handed shooter. The trigger pulls for the test gun, by the way, are clean. They weigh 5¼ lbs. (under barrel) and 4½ lbs. (over barrel) regardless of the firing sequence.

Stock measurements for the test gun run 14⅝" for pull, with drops of 1⁷⁄₁₆" at the comb, 2" at the Monte Carlo, and 2⅝" at the heel. Considering that the Olympia is designed for low-gun skeet, the 14⅝" pull strikes me as a tad long for the average shooter. The buttplate is of black plastic. The non-fluted comb starts with about ¼" of width and broadens to about 1⅜" at the Monte Carlo break. Cast-off is listed as about 0.12" at the comb and 0.32" at the heel. And, unless my eyes are playing tricks, I'd say there is a bit more cast-off at the toe than at the heel.

Quality Rules

Moderately dark in color and straight-grained, the European walnut carries an oil finish, with the buttstock and fore-end well matched. The grip and fore-end are nicely checkered, this being 22-line work. However, because of the lack of figure and the type of finish, the wood has a "plainish" look.

The U-shaped fore-end is short (9⁷⁄₁₆" including the hardware), has no finger grooves, but is comfortable and functional just the same, as is the modified pistol grip with its rounded butt.

The craftsmanship is generally excellent. The metal work is superbly clean, inside and out, and the wood-to-metal unions are perfect. The frame, the tangs and the trigger are polished bright and smooth and are chemically finished with a special rust-resistant process, while all other exterior metal is deeply blued.

A large amount of engraving is one thing this gun doesn't have, but then I've never known lavish ornamentation to be of any help in smashing clays. Although used sparingly (on the frame and the fore-end release), the engraving is flawlessly executed and, in terms of styling, unmistakably Teutonic.

The test gun weighs 7 lbs., 14 ozs., and the point of balance occurs ¾" forward of the barrel hinge or about 6" ahead of the trigger. While the weight is centered mainly between one's hands, there is a slight weight-forward feeling—which is precisely what most Skeet buffs prefer.

According to a Dynamit Nobel brochure, interchangeable barrels of 70cm (27½") length are available for this Rottweil O-U. It is assumed that these longer tubes for field and trap use are conventionally choked, and the available combinations are ¼ and ¾, and ½ and Full. Rib width is the same for the Skeet barrels. But as of this writing, we have not been able to get the word on price, nor whether factory fitting will be required.

Late News

Rottweil's optional trigger units will cost about $250-$275; extra barrel sets with conventional choke system, $850; stocks will carry recoil pads and be of better walnut, with trap and live pigeon versions of the Olympia '72 due within months. A genuine sidelock '72 and a special single barrel trap gun will appear eventually, the latter a boxlock with 34" barrels.

In order to accommodate the special recess-type chokes, the outside diameter of the Olympia barrels is much larger than normal, with the increase starting about 4¾" behind the muzzles. Inside measurements at the muzzles are very close to those of an 8-gauge gun!

Rottweil Target Loads

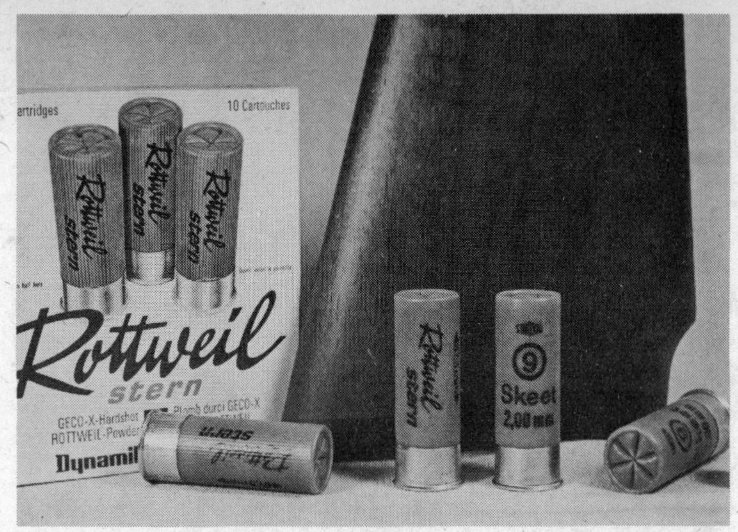

The Rottweil 12-ga. Skeet load and the Olympia '72 over-under are a matched team for top target-breaking performance. These plastic 6-point fold-crimp loads, using a hair-felt and cork wad column, carry 1⅛ ozs. No. 9 shot. The shells have a fired length of only 2⅝".

With the Olympia '72 Skeet gun when it arrived was a small quantity of Rottweil (Dynamit Nobel) shotshells—12-ga. Stern (Skeet), Supertrap 32 and Super Pichón (pigeon) loads. All are plastic-bodied shells with a 6-point fold crimp and are packaged in flat, 10-round boxes.

European shotshells are, in general a bit more colorful than their North American counterparts. This is primarily because of emphasis on attractive and contrasting tube markings that show both numerical shot size and pellet diameter in millimeters and the usual brand designations and logos. On the useful side, foreign shotshell manufacture has, for the most, kept pace with modern technology (especially the Rottweil operation). Ballistically the loads compare very favorably with what the U.S. ammo companies offer.

All of these Rottweil target loads use a case of built-up construction having a ribbed surface and a gas-tight head, formed in part by a securely anchored plastic basewad which forms a deep, semi-conical "powder chamber." The primers are a 209-size battery-cup type and rust free (Sinoxid mixture). The propellant charges consist of a flake-type Rottweil smokeless powder with a granule structure very similar in appearance to Alcan AL-8.

The Rottweil Stern load was the first to command my attention, as G.W. Tharp of GSA had informed me that this loading and the Olympia '72 Skeet gun are a specially matched team. The Stern shell has a fired length of 67.5mm, thus it can be used in chambers as short as 2⅝". The load is 1⅛ ozs. of Geco-X-Hardshot (chilled) in 2.00mm (.078+") size, hence pellet diameter and count are practically the same as for U.S. 9s (.080" nominal).

The wad column, in which I was particularly interested, consists of a 9/16" paper-covered hair-felt wad over the powder, plus a 3/16" cork wad of slightly less than 16-ga. diameter. The purpose of this sub-caliber wad (in addition to regulating crimp space) is apparently to produce a concavity at the base of the shot column and thereby help in producing a fast-opening pattern. Load velocity is not given on the box, but it is assumed to be a nominal 1,200 fps.

The Supertrap 32 loads, in pale blue tubes with silver markings, are a full 70mm (2¾") long. This is likewise a 1⅛-oz. loading, but with nickel-plated hardshot of No. 7 or 2.41mm (.094+") diameter, like U.S. No. 7½s (.095" nominal). Like most current U.S. trap shells, the Supertrap carries a one-piece plastic shot-cup wad. Again, velocity is presumably 1,200 fps.

With a black tube and gold markings, the Super Pichón load is assembled in a 2¾" shell holding 1¼ ozs. of nickel-plated hard shot. Velocity is probably about 1,220 fps. My samples were marked as containing size 8 or 2.25mm diameter pellets, virtually identical to our No. 8 shot. Again the wadding consists of a plastic shot-cup, of much the same design as that used in the Supertrap shell, except for a shorter cushioning section.

Shortly before this was written a number of Supertrap 32 and Super Pichón loads were burned on migrating crows, and I certainly cannot fault their performance in any way. The empty 70mm hulls were then taken to the handloading bench, where it was learned that the cup-type basewad will interfere with proper wad seating unless the powder chosen is bulky enough to slightly overflow the "powder chamber." Even then, if plastic wads are being used, the situation calls for one with a very shallow obturating cup in order to insure powder contact.

One such 1⅛-oz. "recipe" I found entirely satisfactory involves the Alcan 220 Max-Fire primer with 23.0/AL-120 and the Alcan Uni-Seal Type "D" shot-cup wad. The crimp space with a full-weight charge of 8s runs 7/16" and the 6-point closures were adequately recessed. This loading probably develops a MV slightly in excess of 1,200 fps. For certain, I know it was devastating on crows. ●

Both the Rottweil Supertrap 32 (1⅛ ozs.) and the Super Pichón (1¼ ozs.) are loaded with nickel-plated hard shot. These plastic-bodied 12-ga. shells are of 2¾" length and both loads employ a one-piece, plastic shot-cup wad. German No. 7 shot is the equivalent of U.S. No. 7½, while their 8s are the same as U.S. 8s.

The Ultimate 250-3000

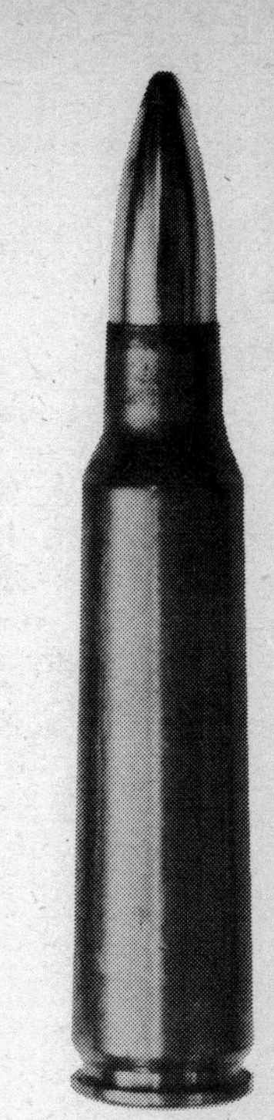

A variety of 250-3000 rifles have come and gone the past 60-odd years, and the author has owned some half-dozen of them. He argues strongly that the old 25 and his new rifle for it make an unbeatable combination—for varmints, small game and deer.

by VERNON E. MEGEE
(General, USMC Ret'd)

WHEN SAVAGE ARMS brought out their new 25-caliber cartridge in 1914, the catalog announcement stressed the sensational velocity of 3,000 fps, but failed to explain how this quantum step in ballistics was achieved. It took America's foremost small arms expert, the late Colonel Townsend Whelen, to ferret out the truth.

As reported by Whelen in his book, *The American Rifle,* 1917, the original 250-3000 cartridge, designed and developed for the Savage Model 99 lever action rifle, reached its advertised velocity (with the powders then available) only by loading it to a pressure approximating 50,000 foot pounds (fp). The rifle could withstand this high pressure, but the fired cases could be rechambered only by forcing; nor could they be readily resized with the hand-type loading tools available before World War I.

As more progressive-burning powers were developed, the ammunition makers were able to sustain the original 3,000 fps velocity given the 87-gr. bullet, and some 2,800 fps for the later 100-gr. projectile, with a reduced chamber pressure of no more than 44,000 fp. In more recent and current loadings the factory advertised velocities have been increased to 3,030 and 2,820 fps respectively. Hardly a significant improvement over a period of 60 years!

During this long period the 150-gr. loading of the 30-06, for instance, has been upped from the original 2,700 to 3,000 fps muzzle velocity, without appreciable increase in pressure. Other cartridges on the sporting list have been similarly improved. It would appear that the 250-3000 cartridge was being arbitrarily held down to mild pressure to insure smooth functioning in the Model 99 rifle—and perhaps to foster its well deserved reputation for superior hunting accuracy.

Since 1920 we have had several strong bolt action rifles chambered for the 250-3000 cartridge. The Model 1920 (later Model 20) Savage, so chambered, was based on the Mauser short-action design. This was, for its time, a handsome, lightweight hunting rifle, and a generally desirable arm.

Contemporary critics complained of its skimpy and ill-designed stock, its poor trigger, and the unreliability of the bolt-sleeve-mounted rear aperture sight. Despite its then modern design and excellent accuracy this bolt action rifle never became overly popular in the lever action era. It was discontinued by Savage in 1928.

The Savage Company replaced the Model 20 with the rear-locking, short-throw, bolt action Model 40, chambered for the 250-3000 cartridge, among others. Compared with the Model 99 and the discontinued Model 20, the new offering had no particular merit other than an excellent stock and a detachable magazine. The Model 40, in turn, was discontinued after a few years.

Early Custom 250s

Back in the early thirties, a Philadelphia custom gunsmith, named Sedgely, advertised a short-action 1903 Springfield bolt rifle with a 22″ barrel, chambered for the 250-3000 cartridge. This was a beautifully proportioned and well-balanced little rifle, selling at the time for something under $100—about twice the price of a contemporary factory-produced bolt action rifle, and well worth it.

Few could afford such a custom arm in Depression days; those who could treasured such a jewel very highly. I recall drooling over a friend's short-action Sedgely-Springfield, and listening to his account of its superior accuracy; however, I never quite managed one of these rifles for myself. If any remain today they would truly be prized as collector's items.

Contemporaneously with Sedgely's limited output, the better known custom gunmaking firm of Griffin and Howe, in New York City, began making very handsome—and quite expensive—custom built rifles based on the imported Mauser short action, chambered among other short cartridges for the 250-3000 Savage. These rifles were fitted with hand-checkered stocks of Circassian walnut, to the customer's specifications, with highly finished and sometimes engraved metal work. Thus they were superior in appearance to the Sedgely—if no more accurate and reliable. Since only the affluent sportsman could hope to be included among Griffin and Howe's clientele, not many of these masterpieces appeared in the field. I haven't seen one in years—not even in collections.

In the early thirties Winchester also chambered their Model 54—and later their Model 70—for the 250-3000 cartridge. Both of these offerings came in the standard long action—24″ medium-weight barrel category, exceptionally accurate but longer and heavier than need be for the small cartridge. Both rifles enjoyed a well-deserved reputation among Western varmint hunters.

Winchester dropped the 250-3000 chambering after World War II, about the time that the hot new 243 caliber made its debut. There are those of us still around who viewed this shift as a ballistic mistake, even though the change proved profitable enough for Winchester.

While owners of these various bolt action 250-3000 caliber rifles may well have experimented with loads heavier than factory standard, I do not recall reading of their efforts. During the past 40 years I have used the 250-3000 cartridge extensively, and have written about it from time to time, but my own observations have been based entirely on the performance possibilities of the Savage Model 99 with the original 1-14″ rifling twist. I had never owned or shot a bolt action rifle in this caliber.

Thus when Ruger announced a year or so ago that he would include the 250-3000 chambering in production runs of his new Model 77 shorter actioned rifle, I decided that I must have one. Only after several months wait was I able to obtain delivery.

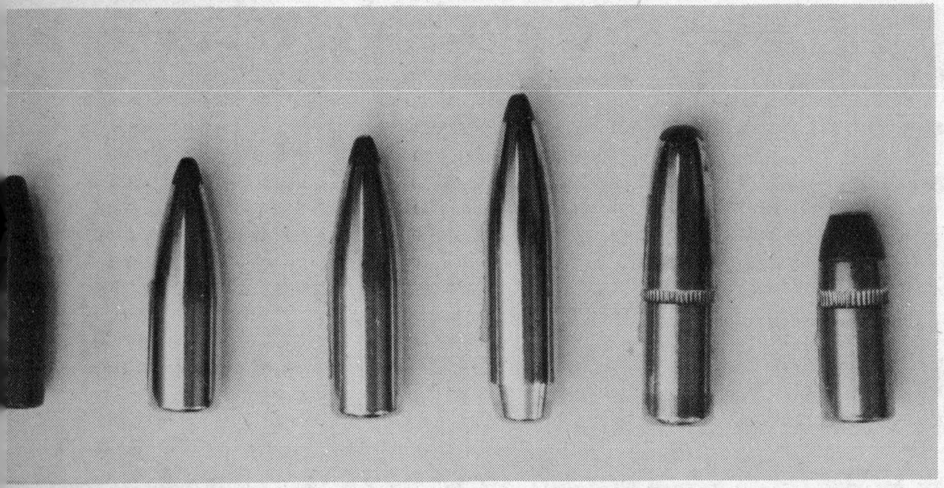

Bullets for the 250-3000. From left—Hornady 75-gr. Spire Point (varmint). Sierra 87-gr. Spitzer SP (varmint). Sierra 100-gr. Spitzer SP (deer). Sierra 117-gr. BTSP (LR deer). Hornady 117-gr. RNSP (deer-bear-brush). Winchester 86-gr. SP (small game).

The Ruger 77 Rifle

The latest 77 Ruger retains the excellent qualities and none of the faults of the above mentioned predecessors. It is light and handy as befits the cartridge for which it is chambered. The action is exceptionally strong, reliable, and smooth working. The genuine walnut stock is of classic design, well proportioned for use of a telescopic sight, hand checkered and oil finished. The 22″ lightweight tapered barrel is precision chambered and rifled, the rate of 1-10″ twist.

Detailed description of the mechanical features of the Ruger Model 77 rifle has been published in various journals and catalogs, so need not be repeated here. Two innovations in bolt action design, which contribute materially to the exceptional accuracy of the Ruger rifle, are worthy of mention, however. One is the slanted action screw up front, which holds the barrel lug snug against the recoil shoulder in the stock; the other is the integrally-machined scope bases on the receiver, which eliminate shifting zeros caused by loose scope mounts.

My test rifle had a rather stiff working bolt, compared with earlier samples from the production line, and a rather heavy 4½-lb. trigger pull (acceptable for field shooting, but rather heavy for bench rest testing). Both defects tended to disappear with use; the bolt wore in, and I became accustomed to the trigger pull.

Troubled mildly at first with horizontal fliers, I was able to improve accuracy by inserting a .004″ metal shim between barrel and forearm tip, thus free-floating the barrel between the chamber section and the shim bearing point.

Expansion of a fired factory case miked .0012″ at the base, .005″ at the shoulder and .007″ at the neck. These measurements indicate normal chamber clearance, with no pressure problems to be anticipated from that source. I was somewhat disappointed to find the chamber so closely throated for factory ammunition, with zero tolerance for longer-seated bullets. This meant that the longer spitzer bullets must encroach on the none too generous powder space when properly seated, thus limiting the use of the bulkier slow-burning powders. Since

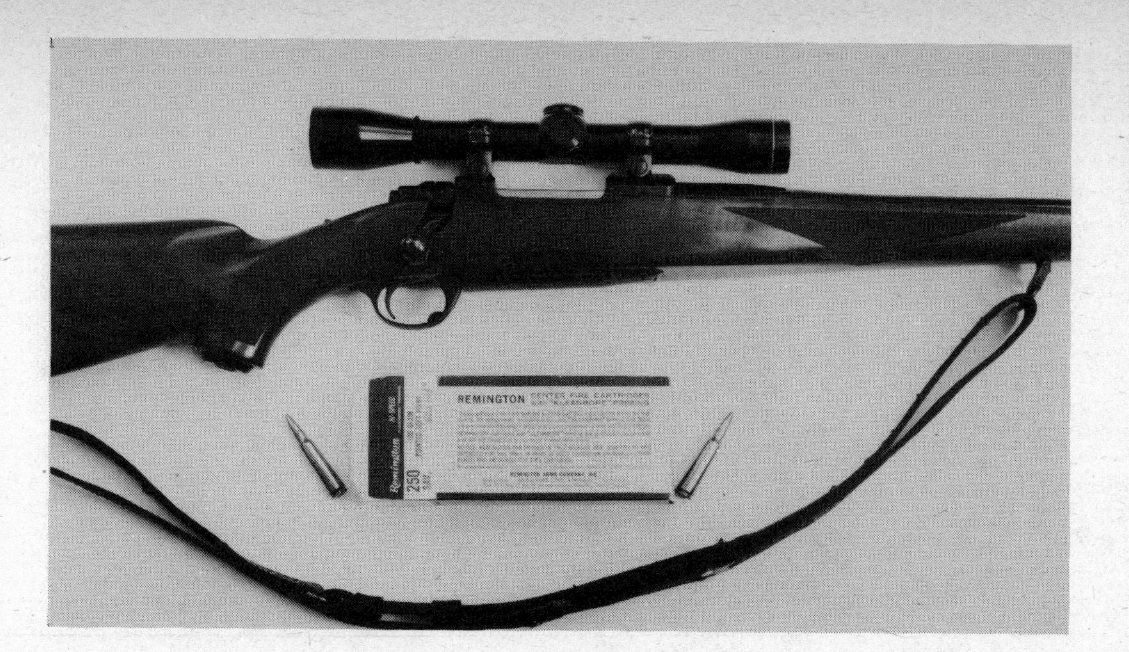

The shorter-action Ruger 77 in 250-3000 caliber is a handsome, lightweight hunting rifle, unexcelled as a combination small game, varmint, and deer rifle.

the magazine will accept cartridges considerably longer than standard, I had hoped to be able to gain powder room and reduce pressure by seating the longer spitzers no deeper than the base of the neck. This could well be accomplished by free-boring for .100" or so, but doing so might adversely affect the accuracy of factory ammunition. Naturally, the rifle manufacturer would not elect to chance this.

Test Trials

In outlining the tests I wanted to make, I gave thought to the 1-10" rifling twist as compared with the 1-14" twist previously standard for 250-3000 rifles. Based on my rather extensive experience in testing other Ruger rifles of different caliber having this faster twist, I discounted without trial the 60-gr. bullets, for other than reduced loads. I expected the 75-gr. bullet to be marginally accurate at speeds above 3,000 fps, but very fine for reduced loads below 2,300. So it proved in the actual tests. With full charges the 75-gr. bullet printed 1.5" groups at 100 yards, but sprayed all over a 7-inch circle at 200. The 87-gr., 90-gr., 100-gr., and 117-gr. bullets all checked out as MOA possibilities, many 3-shot groups under one inch being registered on the 100-yard targets. The 60-gr., 75-gr., and 86-gr. soft-nose bullets, ahead of selected loads of shotgun powders, all grouped 5 shots within a half-inch at 50 yards during the reduced-load tests, and would hold 1.5" at the 100-yard range.

In checking recommended load lists in the various handloaders manuals, I found that Speer publishes maximum loads which run in some cases two grains above the recommended powder charge given in other manuals. Speer tests were made with a Mauser rifle having a 24" barrel, which evidently handled pressures up to an estimated 49,000 fp without excessive case expansion. Velocities given are as much as 100 fps or more above factory standard.

I felt confident that the Ruger action, with new Remington brass, would handle Speer's maximum loads without difficulty, thus extending the range and power of the 250-3000 cartridge appreciably.

Since IMR 4320 appears to be the optimum powder for this small case, I selected this propellant with Hornady 117-gr. round-nose bullets for my pressure tests. Three cases each were loaded with 36, 37, 38, 38.5, 39, 39.5 and 40 grains of 4320 powder. Up to 38.5 grains (1.5 grains above Speer's maximum charge as listed for the 120-gr. bullet) there was no evidence whatever of excessive pressure. Beginning at 39 grains and up to 40 grains there were progressive symptoms; a slight increase of bolt lift effort, minor cratering of primers, and a measurable expansion of the case just ahead of the extractor groove (compared with that miked on a once-fired factory case). Cases required frequent trimming, but only one primer pocket out of the lot showed unusual expansion. Pressure of the 40-gr. load probably exceeded 52,000 fps, but the 250-3000 case withstood repeated firing at this level without apparent damage. Loading at this level of pressure is to be construed only as an indication of the margin of

Selected Loads for the Ruger 250-3000

Nos.	Powder grs.	Bullet grs.	Primer	Groups* ins.	Impact†
Small Game Loads—50 yards					
1.	4756/15	H60 SP	R 9½	0.48	−0.4
2.	4756/15	H75 OP	R 9½	0.30	−0.1
3.	X-700/9.1	H60 SP	R 9½	0.58	−0.8
4.	X-700/9.1	W86 SP	R 9½	0.59	−2.2
5.	X-700/10	H75 OP	CCI	0.35	+0.2
Mid-Range Loads—100 yards					
6.	4064/34	Si87 SP	R 9½	0.95	−0.4
7.	4064/35	H75 OP	CCI	1.20	+0.6
8.	4320/35	H75 OP	CCI	0.80	+0.2
Full Power Loads—100 yards					
9.	4064/37	Si87 SP	R 9½	0.48	+0.2
10.	4320/38.5	Si100 SP	R 9½	0.70	+0.3
11.	4320/36.7	H117 RN	R 9½	0.38	+0.65
12.	4350/40	H117 RN	R 9½	1.05	+0.50
13.	N-205/42.5	H117 RN	R 9½	0.72	+0.40

*3-shot groups, selected from among the best fired.
†Impact based on 200-yard zero, 100-gr. factory load.
H: Hornady. Si: Sierra. W: Winchester. R: Remington.

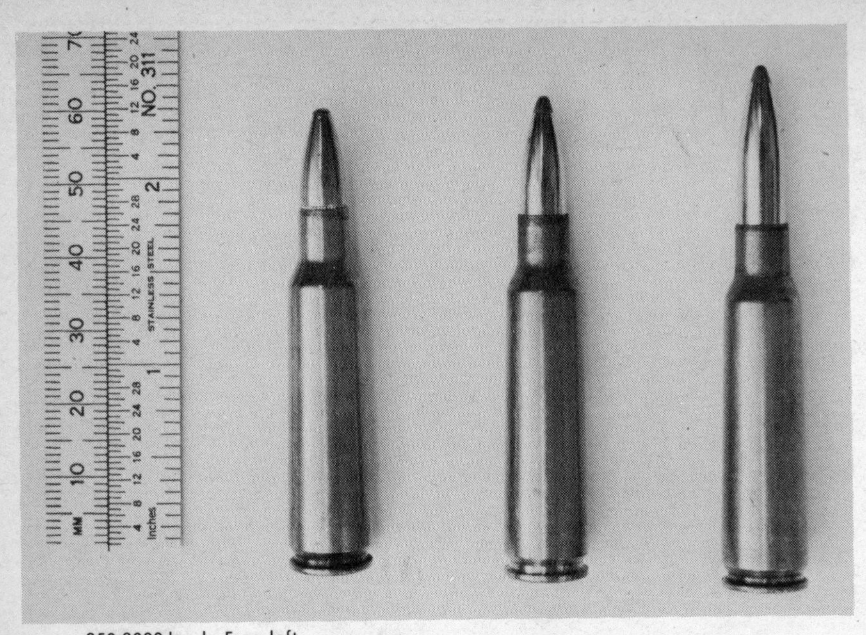

250-3000 loads. From left—
Remington factory load, 100-gr. PSP.
Handload, Sierra 117-gr. BT, seated to maximum length for Ruger chamber.
Handload, Sierra 117-gr. BT, bullet seated to base of neck. Optimum seating for heavy loads, but Ruger rifle would require some lengthening of throat.

safety available in a strong bolt action; it is *not* recommended as a steady diet. Dropping back to 38 grains of IMR 4320 cured all excessive pressure symptoms, and gave acceptable accuracy (within 1.5 MOA), indicating that the maximum loads listed by Speer could be used as a safe practicable guide for preparing heavy hunting loads. Better accuracy was usually obtained with a grain or two less powder, and was maintained with a considerably lesser charge.

A check of available bullets and their trajectory charts indicated that the Sierra 117-gr. boat-tail spitzer might be expected to give the highest remaining energy at 300 yards and beyond, with an adequately flat trajectory. When loaded to a muzzle velocity of 2,800 fps this bullet registers 1264 fp of energy delivered at 300 yards range; which compares favorably with 1235 fp shown at *200 yards* for the 100-gr. factory bullet leaving the muzzle at about the same velocity. This 117-gr. bullet is very accurate when fired from a 1-10" twist barrel; it does not shoot at all well from a barrel with the slower 1-14" twist.

Big Ranging Gain

Thus we gain 50% in effective range by increasing the chamber pressure to about 49,000 fp, a mild level for modern factory loads in other calibers, and by using a heavier, streamlined bullet. We also gain appreciably in reduction of wind drift at the longer ranges. This loading qualifies as a potent combination for mid-range work on game up to the size of large muledeer—and puts the venerable 250-3000 into an entirely different ball park.

By the same token the Ruger will give safely an honest 2950 fps velocity with the 100-gr. bullet, 3150 with the 87-grainer, and 3200 with the 75-gr. bullet, using Speer's maximum loads of suitable powders. Groups of 1.5 MOA may be expected with all these loads, except for the 75-gr. bullet at the longer ranges, as previously noted.

The 250-3000 cartridge has always been noted for its ability to shoot both 87-gr. and 100-gr. factory bullets into the same small impact zone not larger than 2 MOA, up to at least 200 yards. The new Ruger does this beautifully, showing less than an inch vertical difference between group centers for these two loads. In addition, my particular rifle groups with full loads *all* bullets from 75- to 117-gr. weight within two inches at 100 yards, and all spitzer bullets above 75 grains into a circle of comparative diameter at 200 yards, and even beyond.

Furthermore, loads of a given powder may vary as much as three grains without changing the point of impact more than an inch at 100 yards; the vertical deviation of groups with varying charges being no greater than might be incurred from shifting position at the shooting bench. I know of no other cartridge that will consistently do this, and attribute this versatility and lack of sensitivity in loading to the optimum design of the cartridge in relation to its caliber. It is these characteristics which make the 250-3000 cartridge superior to its rivals, endear it to its adherents, and which have kept it alive for 60 years.* Now we have in the new Ruger rifle a worthy companion for this superlative cartridge.

The small capacity and sharp shoulder of the 250-3000 cartridge facilitate working up mid-range and reduced loads. Performance is ex-

---

*Gen. Megee seems to view the 250-3000 cartridge as "superior to its rivals" in versatility, lack of sensitivity, etc. within reasonable case form limits. I don't think such magic qualities should be attributed to any particular case design in a given caliber. Assuming a good barrel/action/stock combination, virtually any case configuration can be made to shoot accurately. This is not meant to negate the fact that certain case forms are more versatile than others, have an ability to handle low, medium and high velocity loads about equally well, always assuming a first class barrel. There are no good rifle *models*—there are good individual, particular, specific rifles, and there are bad ones. J.T.A.

250-3000
50 and 100-Yard Groups

No.	Powder grs.	Bullet grs.	Groups, ins.	
1.	4756/15	H60 SP	0.25	50 yards
2.	X-700/9.1	W86 SP	0.35	
3.	X-700/9.1	H60 SP	0.51	
4.	X-700/9.1	W86 SP	0.68	
5.	X-700/10	H75 OP	0.35	
6.	4064/34	Si87 SP	0.55	100 yards
7.	4064/34	Si87 SP	0.90	
8.	4064/37	Si87 SP	0.48	
9.	4320/37	Si100 SP	0.95	
10.	N-205/42.5	H117 RN	0.72	

To convert 3-shot groups to 5-shot possibilities multiply by 1.23. The groups pictured are selected from the best obtained.
Groups shown were transposed from original targets for better reproduction.

250-3000
50 and 100-Yard Groups

No.	Powder, grs.	Bullet, grs.	Groups, ins.	
1	4756/15	H 60 SP	0.25	50 yards
2	X-700/9.1	W 86 SP	0.35	
3	X-700/9.1	H 60 SP	0.51	
4	X-700/9.1	W 86 SP	0.68	
5	X-700/10	H 75 OP	0.35	
6	4064/34	Si 87 SP	0.55	100 yards
7	4064/34	Si 87 SP	0.90	
8	4064/37	Si 87 SP	0.48	
9	4320/37	Si 100 SP	0.95	
10	N-205/42.5	H 117 RN	0.72	

To convert 3-shot groups to 5-shot possibilities multiply by 1.23. The groups pictured are slelected from the best obtained.

Groups shown were transposed from original targets for better reproduction.

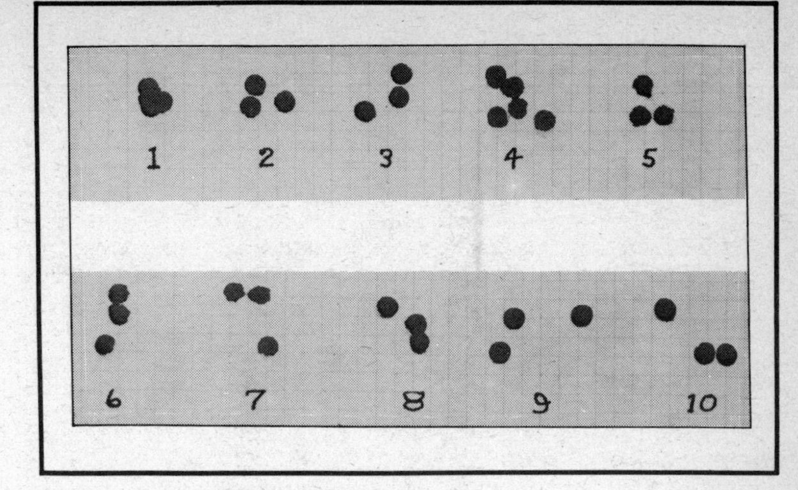

cellent with a wide range of components; groups measuring less than 0.5″ at 50 yards become commonplace. Of all the medium calibers the 250-3000 is best adapted to small game shooting. The 25 caliber has long been considered optimum for such hunting, and there is a wide variety of suitable bullets available. Loaded to 25-20 WCF velocities, with identical bullets, the 250-3000 cartridge is even more accurate than the best of the old repeating rifles chambered for the 25-20 WCF case.

When the Ruger 250-3000 is sighted-in for 200 yards with full loads, mid-range loads with 75-gr. bullets loaded to around 2200 fps print on point of aim at 50 and 100 yards (with telescopic sight), while squirrel loads at around 1500 fps print only an inch or so lower at the shorter range. I find this uncommon trait highly desirable in a hunting rifle; one is prepared for any game from squirrel to deer merely by shifting loads.

Powder and Bullets

The felicitous design of the 250-3000 cartridge permits also a considerable latitude in full-load development. As pointed out, the cartridge is not sensitive to small variations in the powder charge, and it will shoot well with any suitable powder. My particular rifle prefers 4320 and 4064 for the real tight groups, but does almost as well with 4895 and 4350. The case is too small to hold without tamping full charges of 4831, and even 4350 has to be coaxed into the alloted confines. Norma 205 is probably the best powder to use with the heavier bullets – if it can be found. I have used 3031, 4198, and Ball C2 with the lighter bullets quite successfully, but I find little merit in the other available ball powders – particularly when approaching maximum loads in the 250-3000 case. If I had to choose but one powder for this cartridge with all bullet weights, IMR 4320 would win hands down.

While the long 120-gr. spitzer bullets will fully stabilize and shoot accurately at 250-3000 velocities, they have heavier jackets which might not expand reliably at the longer ranges. For this reason I would relegate these bullets to larger cartridges of higher velocity. In the 250-3000 their ballistic performance is inferior to that of the 117-gr. boat-tail spitzer at ranges beyond 200 yards.

The Hornady 117-gr. round nose soft point bullet loaded to 2700-2800 fps is my choice in the 250-3000 for brush country deer hunting, of the type we have in central Texas. This would also be a good load for eastern and northern timber and swamp hunting for deer and the odd bear. It is very accurate and expands reliably, usually passing through the animal and leaving a good blood trail. Lighter bullets of higher velocity in the small calibers cannot be counted on to do this. Unless the animal is put down with a neck or spine shot it may, though fatally wounded, run for 100 yards or more through thick brush and over hard rocky ground, leaving not a single drop of blood to aid the trailer. The option of using the heavier soft nose bullet greatly extends the effectiveness of the 250-3000 for this kind of hunting.

While the new 250-3000 rifles with the 1-10″ rifling twist will not handle the lightest bullets at top velocity nearly so well as the older arms with the slower twist, they more than make up for it on the heavy bullet side. The 87- and 100-gr. bullets seem to shoot equally well with either twist. The new 250-3000 thus becomes a much more effective deer rifle, particularly at the longer ranges, and with the 87-gr. bullet an equally good varmint rifle – compared with its predecessors. When the 117-gr. boat-tail spitzer bullet is used we enter a different category of range and power, one in which the older 250-3000 rifles cannot compete.

In summary, I find that this new Ruger rifle in 250-3000 caliber, with both factory ammunition and the handloads listed, is at least as accurate and much more versatile than any of its rivals. It is also admittedly less powerful – but not appreciably so in the field. Recoil with the heaviest loads is negligible and the muzzle blast comparatively mild; both qualities conducive to accurate shooting. While the bolt action Ruger may be expected to shrink 100-yard groups no more than one inch over those fired in a Model 99 lever action Savage, its ability to better handle the more powerful loads makes it the better choice for the experimental shooter.

For a combination deer, antelope, varmint, turkey, and small game rifle, the new Model 77 Ruger in the 250-3000 chambering would be a most felicitous choice. As for me, after more than 40 years of experience with the cartridge, I have at last found the *ultimate* 250-3000. ●

NORMA is no new name to most of us in the shooting world, obviously. For many years shooters have turned to this company for cases and fixed ammunition not obtainable elsewhere. Such products are available in many sporting goods outlets.

But the company makes and markets an excellent line of loading components, particularly powders, and these are relatively little known and, apparently, little used. Recently I traveled from Idaho Falls to Boise, a distance of some 300 miles. En route I tried to buy Norma powders in most of the sporting goods outlets of four major cities and several small towns. I was able to locate one can of 204 in Idaho Falls and one can of 201 in Twin Falls. Either the demand is not there or the supply sources are not pushing the powders.

I've used these powders for years, in a wide variety of calibers, finding the line excellent and complete—a powder is offered for every purpose, housed in attractive red and black 400-gram cans. My first experience was with the slower-burning numbers in the nitrocellulose rifle series. Little or no loading data was available off local shelves and it was a matter of start way low and work up gradually. Some surprisingly accurate and apparently powerful loads were developed in this fashion in a variety of calibers. I later wrote to Norma and obtained their Loading Data booklet, and I also found reprints of Norma material in Ackley's Vol. II. These were valuable, largely as a check on my load weights and a confirmation on my powder choices for a given caliber. I did not always find that we agreed in the matter of optimum powder choice for a given case. Loading data is still difficult to locate; Speer lists some loads for 205 in some magnum calibers and Volume II of Ackley has a list of factory loadings using these powders, reprinted from a Norma publication. Most manuals* do not consider them, except to show them in an occasional burning-rate chart. Each Norma number seems to have a DuPont counterpart, but appearances are deceptive. All Normas are comparatively small-grained, and it was the ease and accuracy with which they fed through a powder measure that first attracted me to them. They are evidently heavily graphite-coated, and perhaps carry a special inhibitor or deterrent agent, to make possible the combination of slow-burning rates and small-grain size. I recently asked Norma-Precision, of South Lansing, New York, if this were the case. I was told that powder chemistry was not a matter they cared to discuss. So, as usual with Norma, we discover the answers as we go.

*Norma rifle powders are well represented in the new Hornady Handbook, Vol. II, but Norma handgun powders are not seen among the handgun powder charges listed.

Norma Powder Notes

During the past few months I conducted extensive experiments with the Norma line, burning it through rifle calibers ranging from the 45-70 to the 222 Remington. Any questions

THE NORMA POWDERS

...A Study in Red and Black

by ROBERT SHERWOOD

I had about Norma products are largely answered now. I'll comment on the rifle, pistol and shotgun propellants, in the order of their burning rates, giving as much information as I can about each. The accompanying tables may further illustrate the best potential of each number.

The magnum cases are well served by Norma propellant powders. From left—264, 300 H&H, 338, 375 H&H and 458.

Norma 200: Apparently one of the hardest of the Norma line to locate, at least in the Intermountain region, this is a fine-grained fast-burning nitrocellulose. It most closely resembles DuPont 4198 in burning rate and characteristics, but not in appearance. It is slightly faster-burning than 4198. It is especially useful in straight-cased cartridges of medium-to-large capacity, particularly with lead and lighter-jacketed bullets. I found it very useful in the 45-70, the 444 Marlin and the 32-40. It was also excellent in the 30-30 Winchester and 303 British with bullets of the 130-gr. weight class. Although I did not try it in them, it should be good in the 218 Bee and the 22 Hornet with bullets of 50 to 55 grains. It proved excellent in the 222 Remington with 50-gr. bullets.

Norma 201: This is another powder highly useful in straight-cased cartridges. Somewhat slower in burning rate than N-200, it is most closely like DuPont's veteran powder, 3031; it is just a whit slower burning. I

These are excellent powders, versatile and highly desirable in a great range of cartridges—rifle, handgun and shotshell. Their potential for accurate loadings is unexcelled. All too often, though, they are hard—or impossible—to find.

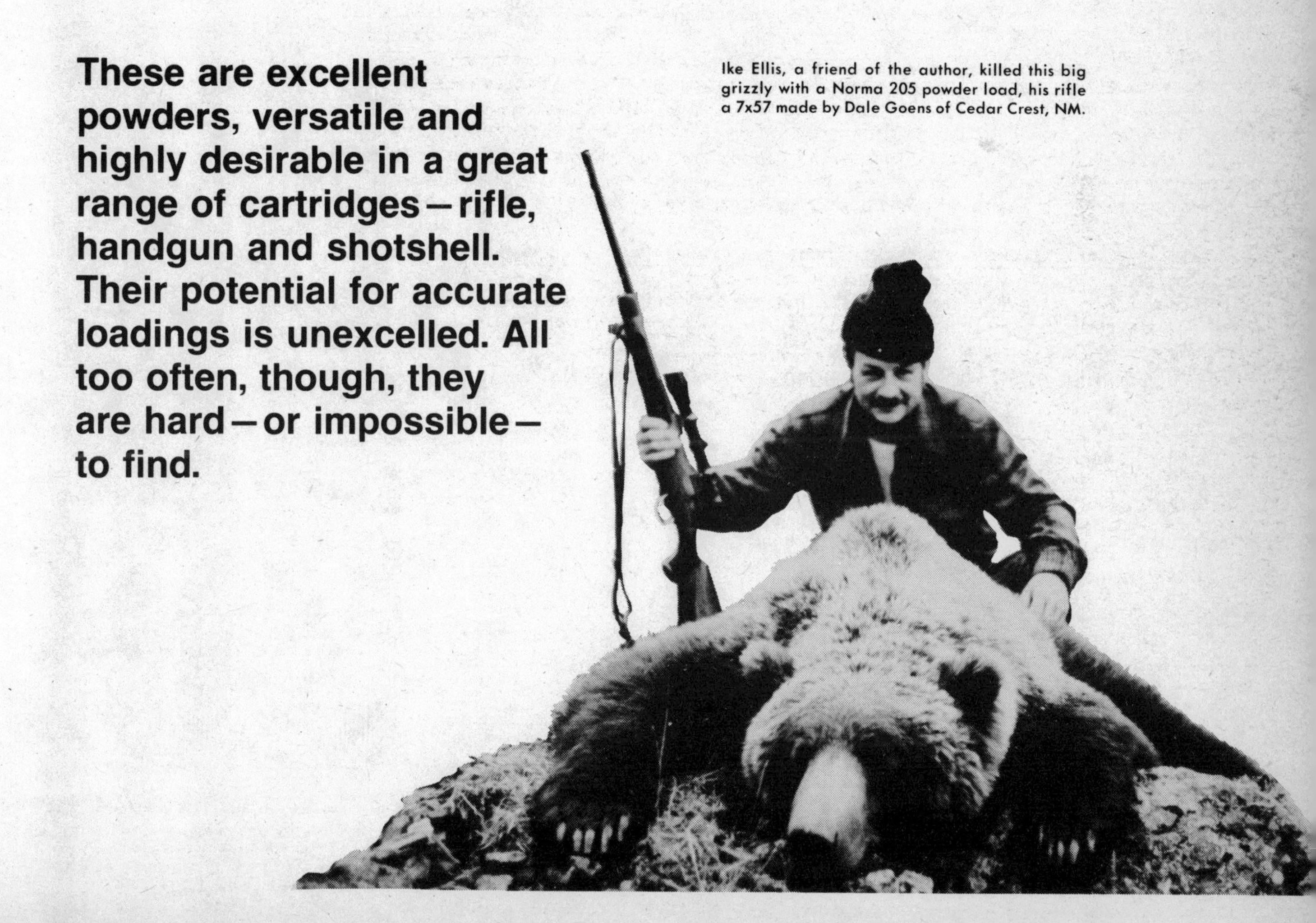

Ike Ellis, a friend of the author, killed this big grizzly with a Norma 205 powder load, his rifle a 7x57 made by Dale Goens of Cedar Crest, NM.

found it *the* best powder with the 45-70 and the 400-gr. Speer bullet, and one of the best for the 444 Magnum with the 265-gr. Hornady. Very good results were obtained with the 50- and 55-gr. weights in the 22-250 and with the 150-gr. Speer bullets in the 30-30 Winchester. It was also excellent with the lighter bullets in the 6.5x55, the 250-3000 Savage and the 7x57. Good results were obtained using 201 in the 30-06, particularly with the 150- and 165-gr. Speer bullets. It is probably the best of the Norma series with the heavier bullets in the 222 Remington. I found it could be loaded grain for grain with 3031, reaching maximum pressures within a half grain of that venerable DuPont.

For some odd reason there is no 202; at least none I ever heard of. Anyway, there is enough overlap without it.

Norma 203: This is Norma's intermediate rifle powder, nearly a duplicate of 4064 in burning characteristics and pressure levels per unit of weight. I've turned out more accurate loads, in a wider range of calibers, with this powder than any other I have used. It's the best powder in the Norma series for the 22-250 with bullets of 50-60 grains. I've shot groups using this powder and the Speer 52-gr. hollow point that I hesitate to talk about! Few would believe it. It proved an excellent choice for maximum loads in the medium-capacity militaries with the medium and heavy bullet weights. I found it one of the most useful powders of all brands in the 300 Savage, the 303 British, the 7.65 Mauser and the 8x57, using bullets in the 165-200-gr. class. Combining it with light- to medium-weight bullets in the 250-3000, the 7x57 and the 6.5x55 produced some extremely accurate loads of reasonable power. It is ideal for use in the 30-06 with the 150- and 165-gr. bullets. I also got some powerful loads of hunting accuracy in the 45-70 with it, but I didn't get the gilt-edged accuracy I'd got with N-201. I could, using the 400-gr. Speer bullet and 50 grains of 203, get loads that would go within 4 inches at 100 yards and, in the words of one onlooker, "shoot lengthwise through a railroad tie." They were aimed with a fixed open sight from a good rest. I did get as good a level of accuracy as one might get from the 30-30 when I combined 203 with the 170-gr. Speer flat-nose. It is a very versatile powder and one that can be stretched to function well in all but the very smallest and very largest centerfire cartridges. In repeated tests with 203 and 4064, I found that both flattened primers and tightened the bolt lift on identical weights, using the same Speer 170-gr. bullet.

Norma 204: This, a medium-slow powder, is close to 4350; if anything it is a bit slower burning. It is one of the best choices for use in the 22-250 with the Speer 70-gr. semi-spitzer. It proved excellent in the 250 Savage, the 6.5x55 and the 7x57, using the heaviest bullets available in those calibers. Some years ago I found good use for it, using the heavier bullets in the 6.5 Remington Magnum. It throws 180s, 200s and 220s at high velocity and with good accuracy from the 30-06. My first use of it was in the 308 Norma Magnum. It was one of the best powders usable in that cartridge with the 180- and 200-gr. Speer bullets. It should be an excellent choice for most magnums of this class,

TABLE III

30-06 Loads Using Norma Powders

Bullet/grs.	Powder/grs.	EMV
150	203/53.0	2970
165	204/58.0	2850
180	205/59.5	2700
200	205/58.0	2570

MAXIMUM LOADS—APPROACH WITH CAUTION
All loads above used Remington cases, Speer bullets, and CCI 200 primers.
EMV = estimated muzzle velocity.

TABLE I

Straight Case Rifle Loads Using Norma Powders

Cal.	Case	Bullet/grs.	Primer	Powder/grs.	Remarks
45-70	Rem.	400 Speer	CCI200	200/35.5	Accurate
45-70	Rem.	400 Speer	CCI200	201/45.0	Most acc.
45-70	Rem.	400 Speer	CCI200	203/50	Hunting acc.
45-70	Sup-X	350 Lead HP	CCI200	200/39.5	Accurate
45-70	Sup-X	385 Lead	CCI200	200/36.3	Accurate
45-70	Rem.	475 GC	CCI200	200/34.0	Most acc.
444	Rem.	240 Speer	CCI200	200/44.0	Good
444	Rem.	265 Horn.	CCI200	201/50.5	Good
32-40	Rem.	170 Rem.	Rem 9½	200/20.5	Most acc.
32-40	Rem.	170 Rem.	Rem 9½	201/28.2	Accurate

NOTE: The 45-70 rifle used in these tests was a Navy Arms replica of the Remington rolling block. These loads are all too heavy for such arms as the 1873 Springfield trapdoor and other old black powder types.

TABLE II

308 Norma Magnum Loads Using Norma Powders and Cases

Bullet/grs.	Primer	Powder/grs.	EMV*	Remarks
150 Speer	CCI250	204/71.5	3250	Very acc.
150 Speer	CCI250	205/80.5	3400	Accurate
165 Speer	CCI200	204/72.0	3170	Most acc.
165 Speer	CCI250	205/79.5	3300	Acc. powerhouse
180 Speer	CCI200	204/70.0	3100	Very acc.
180 Speer	CCI250	205/79.0	3250	Acc.—powerful

*EMV = estimated muzzle velocity.

Two like performers—the 270 Winchester (at left) and the 280 Remington. The latter round, sad to say, seems destined for the graveyard. Both perform excellently with Norma powders 203 and 204.

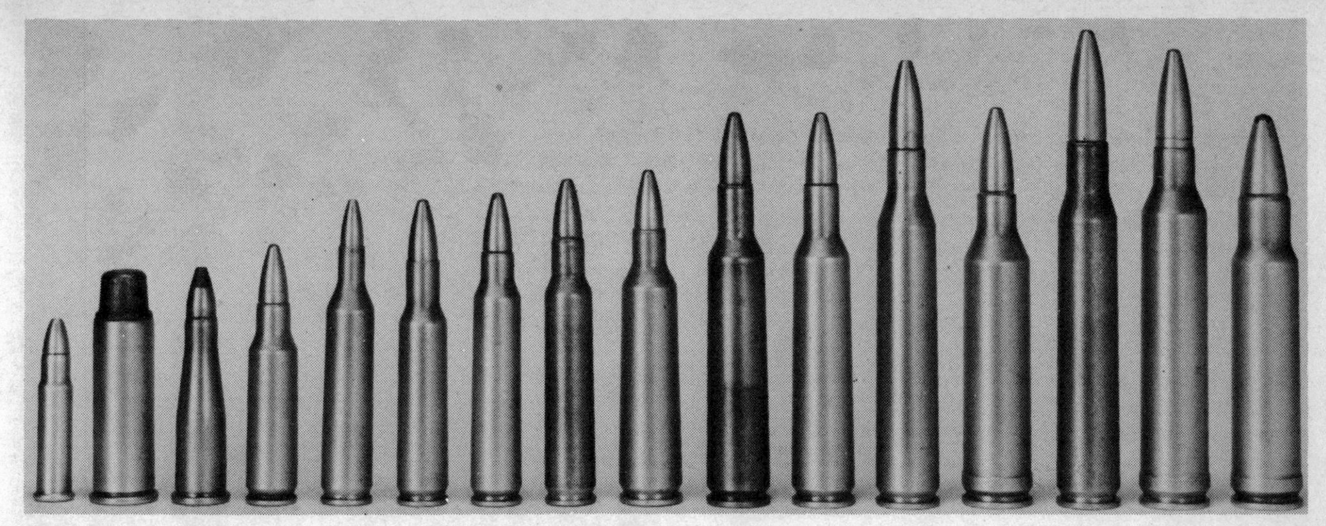

There's a Norma powder eminently suitable for any and all of these 15 cartridges—all introduced by Remington since 1950.

if my results with the 308 Norma were any indication. I have probably killed more animals with bullets driven by 204 than with any other powders of the Norma series; I think of it as a powder for hunting loads, although it does very accurate target work in many cases with the heavier bullet weights. Pressures are very low for the velocities obtained and case life is extremely long with all but the very max loadings with it.

Norma 205: This is the slowest of the series, much like Hodgdon's 4831; when I first started loading it in the 308 Norma Magnum I used 4831 data and got about the same results. It is a far more dense and much smaller-grained powder than 4831, and it's extremely versatile. I used it in the 6.5 Remington Magnum with the medium bullet weights as well as the heavies in that diameter, and got excellent results. It seems to really make magnums out of such cartridges as the 7x57, 6.5x55, 257 Roberts and the various 6mms, using the heaviest bullets available for those calibers. I used it in the 22-250 with the 70-gr. Speer semi-spitzer and found that the combination produced accuracy, good trajectory and all the killing power one could ask for from that case. Normally one cannot get enough 4831 in most cases to get excess pressure; this is not true of N-205 because of its comparatively small grain size. An equal weight of 205 occupies far less space than does 4831, and I have been able to stick a bolt a little too tightly several times when working up maximums.

My friend Ike Ellis, of Ike's Gun Shop in Idaho Falls, had a custom Mauser 7x57 built by Dale Goens. In this rifle he proceeded to load 140-gr. Noslers ahead of 56 grains of 205, using Super X cases and CCI Mag primers. He chronographed this concoction at 3126 feet per second (fps). I think his pressures were a shade high, even for a 98 Mauser action; he confided to me that he blew a primer with 57.5 grains. After shooting 10 shots into something much under an inch he dashed off to the Yukon and mashed a moose and a grizzly with one shot apiece from the Goens rifle. He doesn't expect to carry anything much bigger on his next safari, barring the required big calibers for use on dangerous game.

N-205 has received a bit more publicity than the other powders of the series, and it's much more in demand, particularly by the over-bore capacity lads. The *Speer Handbook*

TABLE IV

Medium-Military Loads Using Norma Powders

Cal.	Bullet/grs.	Case	Primer	Powder/grs.	EMV
7.65 Mau.	Speer 175	R-P	CCI200	203/47	2550
303 Br.	Speer 150	Norma	CCI200	203/44	2700
303 Br.	Speer 160	Norma	CCI200	203/41	2400
6.5x55	Speer 100	Norma	CCI200	203/46	3200*
6.5x55	Speer 100	Norma	CCI200	201/44	3120*
6.5x55	Speer 120	Norma	CCI200	203/44	2950*
6.5x55	Speer 140	Norma	CCI200	204/48	2800*
6.5x55	Norma 156	Norma	CCI200	205/50.5	2800*
7x57	Speer 145	DWM	CCI200	203/43.0	2750
7x57	Speer 160	DWM	CCI200	204/48.0	2700
7x57	Nosler 140	W-W	CCI200	205/55.5	3126†
300 Sav.	Speer 165	W-W	Fed.210	203/42.0	2600
308 WCF	Speer 165	W-W	CCI200	203/43.2	2650

*Fired from a 23.75" barrel.
EMV = estimated muzzle velocity.
† Actual chronograph figure.

TABLE V

250-3000 Savage Loads Using Norma Powders

Bullet/grs.	Case	Primer	Powder/grs.	EMV
60 Speer	Norma	CCI200	200/30.5	3220
87 Speer	Norma	CCI200	201/33.0	3000
100 Speer	W-W	CCI200	201/31.0	2800
100 Speer	W-W	CCI200	203/32.5	2800
120 Speer	Norma	CCI200	205/36.0	2570
120 Speer	Norma	CCI200	205/40.5	2610

EMV = estimated muzzle velocity.

(No. 8) lists N-205 loads for many calibers. N-205 is hard to get in this part of the country, and doesn't last long on the shelves. The velocity figures obtained with Speer's chronograph are impressive, to say the least; it seems to be able to get a couple of hundred feet per second over its competitors when used with maximum loadings. N-205 has been discovered, and it may be here to stay.

Handgun Powders

Norma supplies only two pistol powders, though Speer lists several handgun loads using Norma shotgun powders as well. My acquaintance with the pistol powders is recent, but I am impressed thus far.

Norma 1010: Every can of this I have been able to get has a little sticker that indicates it has been produced in Great Britain. When I queried Norma-Precision about this they were somewhat evasive about who and where in Great Britain. Guess I'll never know but it is good powder. It is quite fast burning, though a bit slower than Bullseye. I shot it extensively in the 357 magnum, using 146-gr. wadcutters, and had friends shoot it in their 38 Specials, using wadcutters and the lighter cast bullets. We used it much as one would use Bullseye—lighter bullets and small charges gave good accuracy. It is a fine powder for target work.

Norma 1020: This is a magnum pistol powder, measurably faster burning than 2400, but somewhere in that league. I got excellent results with this powder in the 357 and 44 magnums, using the good Speer jacketed-bullet series and maximum charges. The loads were accurate and with plenty of demolition capabilities. It is truly a magnum pistol powder and should give excellent results in 41 magnum and 45 Colt as well. Speer lists many loads using it and we found that most of them were good; those we worked up using the new jacketed Speer 357 diameter bullets were excellent. We also got fine results with the heavier hard-cast lead bullets.

The most recent Norma powders to hit our shores are two shotgun types; one can do about everything with them that any form of scattergunning calls for.

Norma 2010: This is a fast-burning propellant, designed for trap, Skeet and very light field loads. Speer lists some light target handgun loads with it as well.

Norma 2020: This is a relatively slow-burning shotgun powder, good for heavy and medium hunting loads. Speer lists some handgun loads for it also.

This, then, is the powder story of the red and black canisters that Norma offers. All-in-all, an excellent line of powders, covering every need of the American shooter.

Bruce Hodgdon will soon be marketing H-205 powder, newly made for him abroad, and ballistically identical to Norma 205. ●

TABLE VI
22-250 Loads Using Norma Powders

Bullet/grs.	Case	Primer	Powder/grs.	EMV
45	Rem.	Rem. 9½	201/34.0	3800
50	Rem.	CCI200	201/33.5	3700
50	Rem.	CCI200	203/36.0	3700
55	Rem.	CCI200	203/35.0	3500
55	Norma	CCI200	204/39.0	3500
70	Rem.	CCI200	204/35.5	3100
70	Rem.	CCI200	205/38.5	3200

All loads with Speer bullets.
EMV = estimated muzzle velocity.

TABLE VII
30-30 Loads Using Norma Powders

Bullet/grs.	Case	Primer	Powder/grs.	EMV
100	W-W	Fed. 210	200/31	2800
130	W-W	Fed. 210	200/30	2500
150	W-W	CCI200	201/33	2350
150	Rem.	Fed. 210	200/27	2300
170	Rem.	Rem. 9½	200/25	2100
170	W-W	CCI200	201/30	2100
170	W-W	CCI200	203/34	2200

All loads with Speer bullets.
EMV = estimated muzzle velocity.

TABLE VIII
Handgun Loads Using Norma Powders

Cal.	Bullet/grs.	Case	Primer	Powder/grs.	EMV
38 Spec.	148 WC	Rem.	CCI500	1010/3	800
38 Spec.	158 SWC	Rem.	CCI500	1020/10	1180
38 Spec.	110 JHP	Rem.	CCI500	1020/14	1370
38 Spec.	140 JHP	Rem.	CCI500	1020/12	1180
38 Spec.	158 JSP	Rem.	CCI500	1020/11	1140
357	110 JHP	Norma	CCI500	1020/17	1500
357	125 JHP	Norma	CCI500	1020/15	1450
357	140 JHP	Norma	CCI500	1020/14	1300
357	158 JSP	Norma	CCI500	1020/13	1200
44 Mag.	240 JSP	Rem.	CCI350	1020/17.5	1350

All loads with Speer bullets.
EMV = estimated muzzle velocity.

Norma Booklets Loads & Ballistics

Two excellent publications are available from the Norma Company. If your dealer does not have these, write to Norma Precision, South Lansing, NY 14882.

One is called *Norma Ballistics*, an oblong booklet of 44 pages. In addition to 500 yards for Norma factory rifle cartridges and detailed data on handgun rounds, each caliber entry (with only a few exceptions) also shows the type and quantity of Norma powder used in that cartridge as its factory load. Pressures in pounds per square inch (psi) are also shown for each load listed.

All of this material is repeated, in full, in metric terms and values. There is also a conversion-factor chart and a ballistic data guide in 6 languages. Obviously, given the factory powder charge, the handloader can easily drop his initial trial by 5%-10% and work his way up. Norma bullets are indicated, of course, but there are several such for many calibers, and a little balancing of bullets weights, where needed, is soon done.

The other booklet, of 12 oblong pages, is called *Norma Loading Data*. This publication contains all of the data described above except ballistics (MV and psi are included), plus considerably more handgun load data. In this volume shotshells are also well covered, the components listed being of U.S. make. Nearly 100 loads are listed.

Hämmerli's Newest and Finest

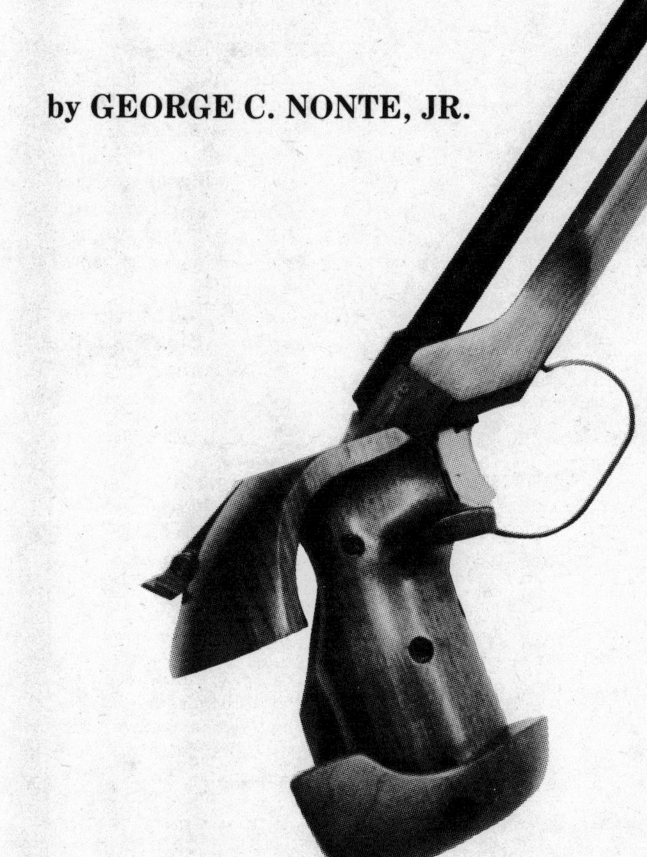

by GEORGE C. NONTE, JR.

the Model 150 Free Pistol

This new no-holds-barred match pistol won't win any beauty contests, but it lays 'em in there—at a price!

MENTION "Free Pistol" among the uninitiated and you're likely to get a blank stare—or else some wit will quip "Sure, I'll take one if it's free."

Unfortunately, the free pistol has been publicized little and understood less in this country. The rest of the world conducts most of its pistol matches under international rules, and therefore knows the free pistol well. Under U.S.A. rules slow-fire matches are fired with conventional autos or revolvers; the international shooter uses a highly specialized arm much more suited to the task.

The term "free" was most likely first applied to this type of gun because, under the rules, it is almost entirely free of restrictions. The gun must be mechanically safe, and optical sights and arm or wrist-supporting grips are prohibited. Beyond that, type, weight, sights, trigger pull, grips, etc., may be almost anything the designer or shooter wishes.

The Hämmerli M150 Free Pistol has introduced a new style, radically altering the traditional configuration. The widely-separated fore-end permits a fully free-floating barrel, the fore-end's width also preventing the slender barrel and front sight from touching the bench when the pistol is laid down.

Typically, the European-developed free pistol is a single shot, weighs about 2- to 2½ pounds, carries a tapered light barrel, has precisely adjustable sights, highly individualized grips, and a very sophisticated adjustable set trigger. Quality of workmanship is of the highest order, and assembly, testing, and finishing are hand operations performed by old-school gunmakers. Accuracy is of a degree seldom associated with handguns, for at 50 meters the free pistol must be capable of placing all its shots in the 25mm (about one inch) diameter X-ring of the international slow-fire target.

Because of these criteria, no successful free pistol has ever been made in this country. A decade or so back High Standard produced a few unique "electric trigger" guns for this purpose, but never put the model into series production.

The most recent and highly refined free pistol we've seen is the Hämmerli Model 150, caliber 22 Long Rifle, made in Switzerland. Hämmerli, once an independent company, is now a division of SIG (Swiss Industrial Company), well-known maker of SIG auto pistols and CETME-type roller-locked M510 series military assault rifles.

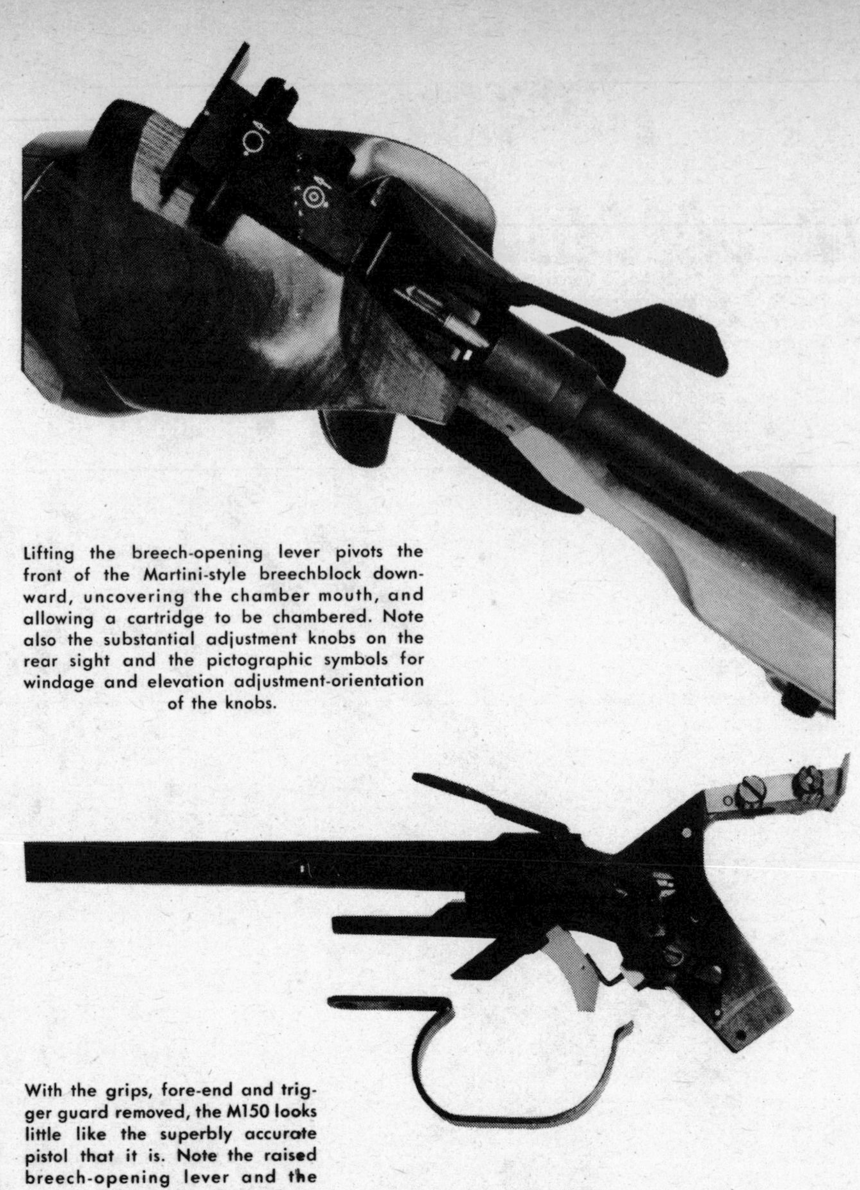

Lifting the breech-opening lever pivots the front of the Martini-style breechblock downward, uncovering the chamber mouth, and allowing a cartridge to be chambered. Note also the substantial adjustment knobs on the rear sight and the pictographic symbols for windage and elevation adjustment-orientation of the knobs.

With the grips, fore-end and trigger guard removed, the M150 looks little like the superbly accurate pistol that it is. Note the raised breech-opening lever and the shorter cocking lever beneath it.

The M150 has a Martini-type action operated by a long finger lever on the left side of the receiver. Raising this lever lowers the front of the rear-pivoted breechblock to expose the chamber and raise the twin extractors slightly, freeing the fired case. Further lever movement does not affect the breechblock, but moves the extractors about ⅜-inch to pull the case clear. When the lever is released, the extractors return to the loading position.

A cartridge is then inserted until it engages the extractors, after which depressing the lever closes the breech.

When the action is open, a hole through the breechblock aligns with the bore. This allows easy visual inspection of the chamber and bore, and also permits cleaning from the breech, thus avoiding rifling damage often produced by cleaning from the muzzle.

Closing the breech leaves the firing pin cocked, but before firing the fully-adjustable single-set trigger must be set. This is done by pressing downward the lower and shorter lever on the left of the receiver. The trigger design is such that there is no hazard in unlimited dry firing. However, the firing pin is not to be cocked for dry fire—*only* the trigger. The trigger is factory lubricated with dry molybdenum disulphide, so should *never* be oiled.

The barrel is slender, tapering from .630-inch ahead of the breech reinforce to .540-inch behind the front sight band. Barrel length is 11 inches, though it appears a bit more because the massive front sight band extends beyond the muzzle to protect it from danger.

The M150 possesses an unusual form of wood fore-end, its rear end attached to a bracket extending forward and downward from the receiver. The screws which secure the fore-end also hold the unusually large strip-

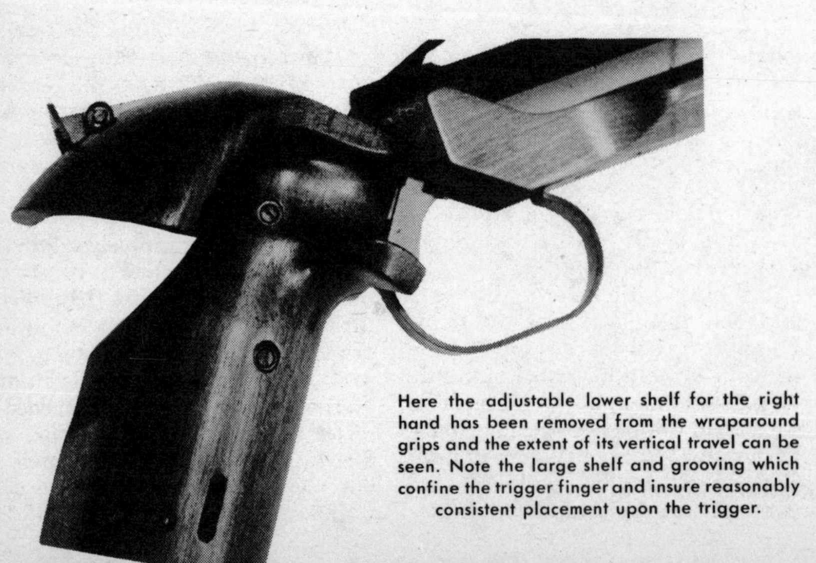

Here the adjustable lower shelf for the right hand has been removed from the wraparound grips and the extent of its vertical travel can be seen. Note the large shelf and grooving which confine the trigger finger and insure reasonably consistent placement upon the trigger.

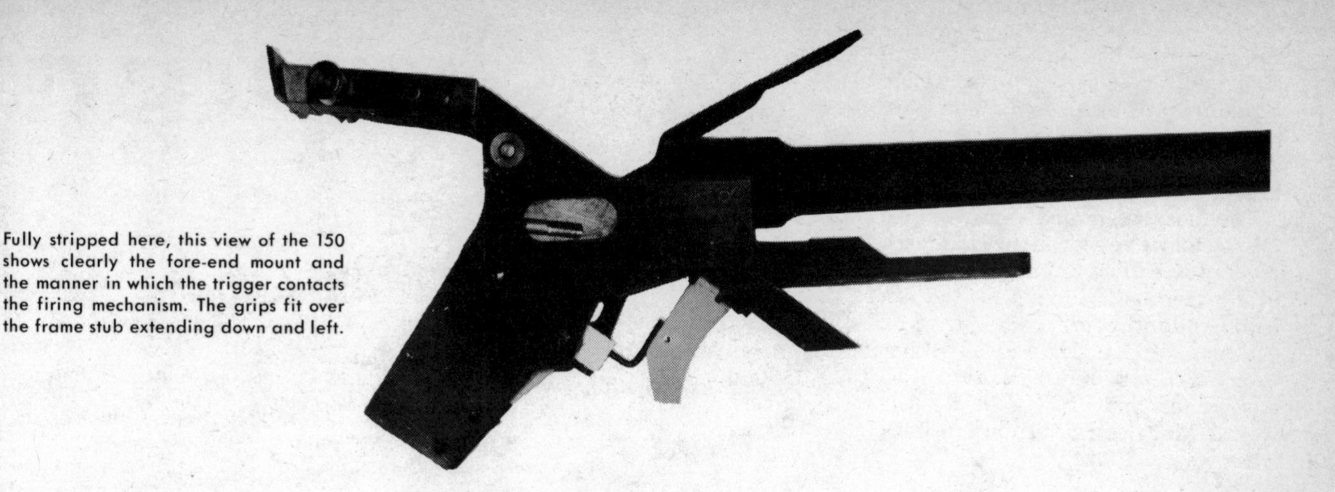

Fully stripped here, this view of the 150 shows clearly the fore-end mount and the manner in which the trigger contacts the firing mechanism. The grips fit over the frame stub extending down and left.

steel trigger guard.

The fore-end clears the barrel by about ½-inch except at the receiver. It is, simply a 1.875-inch wide, .825-inch thick guard which prevents the barrel from touching anything when the gun is rested on the shooting bench. So long as one does not deliberately place the M150 upside down, the barrel or sights cannot come in contact with any level surface the gun is placed on. The massive grips and fore-end form an effective barrier.

The sights are quite large and fully adjustable. Eight clicks per revolution of the adjusting knob are provided for both windage and elevation. Each click has a value of 10mm (.4″) at 50 meters. Both knobs are placed horizontally on the left side of the rear sight base and are clearly marked. The base is pinned to a tang on the receiver, but can be removed without difficulty for maintenance.

The front sight is unusual in that the undercut blade is carried in a massive split band made of aluminum alloy. The band is clamped to the barrel by a single socket-head screw, which also clamps the two halves of the longitudinal male dovetail over the bottom of the blade. The base is easily removed—and by loosening the screw, it may be rotated about the barrel. I'm not certain what purpose this serves, but perhaps it is to allow individual shooters to set the sight so that it *looks* vertical. Some free rifle shooters deliberately cant their rifles.

The wood grips are of typical free-pistol style. A fixed top shelf extends out over the hand, and a lower shelf is adjustable vertically for individual fit. There is a wide rest for the trigger finger, and another for the thumb, to provide maximum control of the gun. The grips are of plain dense wood, smooth finished and without checkering.

The cross-slotted screw shown here (partially hidden by the mainspring) serves to adjust sear-spring tension.

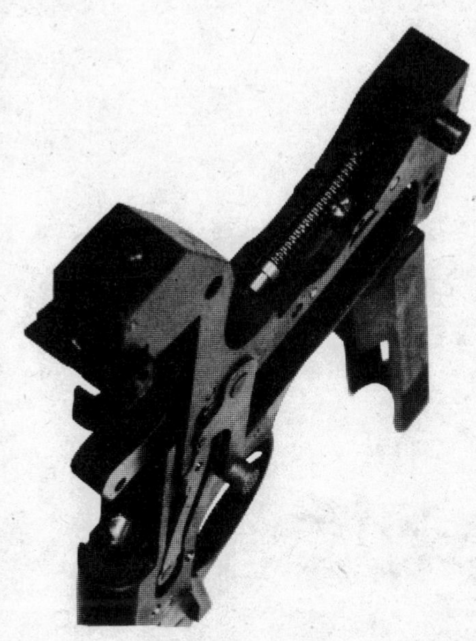

Over-all length is 17½ inches, height 6½ inches, width 4½ inches, weight 43 ounces.

Our sample Hämmerli M150 was obtained from Gil Hebard Guns (Knoxville, Illinois, 61448). It exhibited excellent workmanship throughout, though there has been no particular effort expended to make the gun shiny and pretty. For example, all parts except the breechblock and rear sight are finished matte black—and though smooth, are not highly polished. Yet in all areas where it is desirable, metal-to-metal fit is very precise. In short, it is purely a *functional* mechanism, with no money wasted on frills—which is a good thing. If they'd tried to make it fancy there is no telling how much more it would cost than the current $375 retail price. Even that may have increased by the time you read this.

This scribe simply isn't capable of checking the performance of this gun. No machine rest available will accept it, and I'm not half marksman enough to begin extracting its mechanical accuracy. It does handle as a free pistol should, and functioning is flawless. I've hit what I shot at with it, but that doesn't begin to tell the story. The best evidence we have of its accuracy potential is the test target furnished by the factory—which measures only .366-inch, center to center of widest shots. That is, in fact, a one-hole group. When a handgun shoots that close, it's performing better than many rifles.

The Hämmerli M150 comes in a rigid molded black case, complete with a comprehensive 32-page instruction booklet printed in four languages. A 10-piece tool kit is also supplied, sufficient for any operation that may be safely performed by the shooter.

Pistols such as this are offered in quite limited quantities, partly because there aren't all *that* many international slow-fire shooters, partly because of the price, and partly because production is limited by the skill and handwork needed to make them right. If you want the *finest* in slow-fire guns, this is it, but place your order and expect to wait—they are not plentiful. ●

Custom

WINSTON G. CHURCHILL
Stocked in full fancy New Zealand walnut for Dave Petzal of *Field & Stream* on a left-hand Weatherby action, the checkering on this classic-styled 300 Weatherby rifle is a fleur de lis pattern, 28-line.

JACK DEVER
This left-hand Mathieu action has a Shilen stainless barrel, cal. 7mm Rem. Mag., is stocked in French walnut and checkered 24-line in a diamond design. Buttplate and grip cap are Biesen's checkered steel.

DONALD E. FOLKS
A 7mm Rem. Mag. rifle stocked in a fancy grade of French walnut, the checkering a fleur de lis pattern, the action a Mauser 98, the scope a Redfield 4x on Redfield bases.

DALE GOENS
Unusually fancy-figured exhibition grade Circassian walnut, from Russia, graces this handsome 270 rifle made for Dr. Peter Fenchak. The action, a pre-64 M70, has Blackburn's guard; the ribboned fleur de lis checkering is 24-line.

EARL MILLIRON
Clean, crisp lines distinguish this custom stockwork, in French walnut, the action a 98-type Mauser, the caliber 257 Roberts. Special metalwork, by Tom Burgess, includes guard, grip cap, bolt handle, etc.

NORMAN H. SCHIFFMAN
Sharp-lined, graceful styling, the wood French walnut checkered 24-line without borders. Pre-64 M70 action, cal. 270, a Leupold scope carried in Conetrol mounts.

Guns

WINSTON G. CHURCHILL
Stocked in full fancy New Zealand walnut for Dave Petzal of *Field & Stream* on a left-hand Weatherby action, the checkering on this classic-styled 300 Weatherby rifle is a fleur de lis pattern, 28-line.

JACK DEVER
This left-hand Mathieu action has a Shilen stainless barrel, cal. 7mm Rem. Mag., is stocked in French walnut and checkered 24-line in a diamond design. Buttplate and grip cap are Biesen's checkered steel.

DONALD E. FOLKS
A 7mm Rem. Mag. rifle stocked in a fancy grade of French walnut, the checkering a fleur de lis pattern, the action a Mauser 98, the scope a Redfield 4x on Redfield bases.

DALE GOENS
Unusually fancy-figured exhibition grade Circassian walnut, from Russia, graces this handsome 270 rifle made for Dr. Peter Fenchak. The action, a pre-64 M70, has Blackburn's guard; the ribboned fleur de lis checkering is 24-line.

EARL MILLIRON
One of Milliron's finest works is this classic 280 on a square-bridge *Mauserwerke* action. Metalwork by Tom Burgess, owned by Alex Schimek of Toronto, Canada.

NORMAN H. SCHIFFMAN
Sharp-lined, graceful styling, the wood French walnut checkered 24-line without borders. Pre-64 M70 action, cal. 270, a Leupold scope carried in Conetrol mounts.

AL BIESEN
A pre-64 M70 Winchester was used for this 375 H&H Magnum. The wood is French walnut, all work done by Al Biesen. Built for Alex Schimek of Toronto, Canada.

JAMES K. CLOWARD
Select French walnut stocks this pre-64 M70-actioned rifle in classic style. The barrel is a Douglas in cal. 270 Winchester, the scope a Redfield.

FLYNN'S CUSTOM GUNSMITHING
A Remington M700 in 25-06 caliber, stocked in fiddleback Claro walnut with straightforward, simple lines. The scope is a Leupold.

H. L. GRISEL
A pre-64 M70 action, Shilen barreled in 7x57 and stocked in classic fashion with nicely figured French walnut. The steel grip cap and trapped buttplate are engraved.

CLAYTON NELSON
Made for Jim Carmichel on a pre-64 M70 and classic-stocked in fancy French walnut, checkering is an 8-point—fleur de lis combination. Barrel is a Douglas in 280 Remington. Nelson made new guard, trapped buttplate and skeleton grip cap.

SMITTY'S GUN SHOP
A 98 Mauser forms the basis for this custom sporter, the caliber Bob Smith's special "Twenty-Five." Stocked in select American walnut and finely checkered.

BOB WILLIAMS
Stocked in figured English walnut, this is a 270 on a pre-64 M70 action, the guard and hinged floorplate by Williams. Checkering is 24-line in a 2-panel pattern.

SHILEN RIFLES, INC.
Ed Shilen's own DGA action and barrel are used for this single-shot 22-250 varmint rifle, the walnut stock also by Shilen. A fully adjustable trigger is standard.

BOB WINTER
Stocked in California English walnut, this elegant 25-06 rifle has Douglas barrel, the action a pre-64 M70. Skeleton buttplate, grip cap and a Clayton Nelson guard.

HUBERT J. HECHT
Stocked to match the original lines and style, this is a Sempert & Krieghoff (Suhl) drilling, the wood French walnut checkered 22-line. The steel buttplate is trapped, the guard and grip cap of Indian horn.

CHARLES DE VETO
High contrast French walnut stocks this FN Mauser-actioned rifle in 375 H&H Magnum, the ribboned checkering 24-line to an old Leonard Mews pattern.

CARL ROTH, Jr.
A left-hand Savage 110 action, fitted with a pre-64 M70 guard and floorplate, carries a 308 Norma Magnum barrel, used without the headspace ring. The stock is well figured American black walnut, California styled.

DUANE WIEBE
Douglas-barreled 7mm Rem. Mag. on a pre-64 M70 action, the stock is of California English walnut, 33-line fleur de lis checkering. Blackburn-made guard, skeleton buttplate and grip cap.

RUSSELL ZEERYP
Stocked in Mannlicher (full length) style, this is a Sako-actioned 243, the wood fancy maple with an unusual checkering pattern.

JOHN E. MAXSON
This Featherweight pre-64 M70 rifle, cal. 243, is stocked in simple, attractive form, the wood fancy French walnut checkered 24-line in a fleur de lis pattern. Niedner-type checkered steel buttplate and grip cap are fitted.

TALMAGE ENTERPRISES
California stock styling, using fancy Mesquite wood on a left-hand Ranger Arms action, the Douglas barrel in cal. 308. The scope is a Leupold in Buehler mounts.

FRED M. BERGEN
Mauser-actioned 338 Magnum stocked in full fancy fiddleback maple, with Canjar trigger and quick-release hinged floorplate. Leupold scope in Redfield mount.

RALPH P. BONE
A 6mm Remington, the barrel by A&M (not now partners), the French walnut stock checkered 28-line in a ribboned fleur de lis pattern. Checkered bolt handle, ebony fore-end tip and Canjar trigger.

ABE and VAN HORN
Mauser 98/09 action, modified magazine holds 5 rounds. Select walnut stock with low Monte Carlo comb, special open sights.

STEPHEN L. BILLEB
Mark X Mauser-actioned in 7mm Rem. Mag., the American walnut stock is skip-checkered 20-line and oil finished, the stock fittings of zebrawood.

PACHMAYR GUN WORKS
English Circassian walnut, full fancy figured, was used to stock this clean-lined pre-64 M70 Winchester.

TREVALLION GUNSTOCKS
A Model 12 Winchester pump gun, gracefully stocked in dense, figured walnut; note schnabel fore-end style.

C. D. MILLER
DeHaas-Miller falling-block single shot, stocked in figured American walnut, the rifle a 222.

HAL HARTLEY
Mauser 98 action, the barrel a Douglas, classically stocked in Hal's favorite fancy fiddleback maple.

BILL McGUIRE
Ultra-fancy Circassian walnut stocks this pre-64 M70, a handsome example of the classic style.

Bill McGuire also makes best quality gun cases to special order, using only the finest leathers over hardwood frames, all hardware solid brass, linings top grade billiard felting.

The Plight of The Hornet

For a cartridge that was once strongly at the top among varmint hunters, its near-demise has been a strange thing. Will it make a comeback? The author's crystal ball is murky, but he's been shooting three new Hornet rifles. That says something. Load tables are included.

by DON LEWIS

Photos by Helen Lewis

WHEN I SAW MY farmer friend running across the barnyard waving for me to stop, I thought something dreadful was wrong. In an instant, my mind pictured an electric fire in the barn since Bill had told me earlier he was having the wiring repaired. I lost no time cutting into his driveway and sliding to a stop. When I hit the ground, I had a small fire extinguisher in my hand.

"You can't shoot chucks with an aerosol can," Bill flipped good naturedly. "What the devil are you up to?"

"Well, the way you were running and waving, I thought the barn was on fire."

"I'm glad you're wrong, but I guess I was stepping pretty lively. The problem is I'm having trouble with a new resident under the apple tree in the corner of the hayfield. That diggin' rascal isn't satisfied with all the holes left by his cousins and has started two more. I hope you have one of your long range outfits with you."

"Sounds to me like you have good soil," I ribbed.

"You can set up right here by the wagon shed and that'll give you a long 175-yard shot at that miniature bulldozer."

"That's fine with me. I'm anxious to see what my new Hornet will do, and this is the shot to find out."

"*Hornet,*" Bill nearly shouted. "Man, I thought that flyswatter was put to rest 10 years ago. Anyway, what do you mean, 'new Hornet'? I know for a fact they stopped making them."

"That *was* exactly right, but now there are three firms I know of chambering for the 22 Hornet, and I have a beautiful Walther KKJ Model to prove it."

Before we could continue our friendly debate, Bill motioned to me that the chuck's head was showing. One look through the binoculars sent me running for the new Walther. I could still hear Bill complaining that the Hornet wouldn't cover the distance, but I had no fears.

I knew from previous hunts that the old apple tree was 160 steps away. I had printed the Walther almost 2 inches high at 100 yards with a 45-gr. Sierra in front of 9.2 grains of 2400 ignited by a Remington 6½ primer. My chronograph showed this combination had an instrumental velocity at 15 feet of 2,497 fps. At 160 yards, I could freeze the Dual X reticle in the new all-steel Weaver 6x scope smack on the chuck's head.

Sliding into a prone position, I rested the new Hornet against a wood chopping block and set the rear trigger. When the crosshairs remained motionless for several seconds on the chuck's head, I touched the front trigger. The resounding thud of the bullet making contact was ample evidence that the Hornet had made short work of the pesky hole digger.

Brief History

In an era where the magnum cartridge reigns supreme and long range varmint shooting is in vogue, relating a mere 160-yard chuck shot with a cartridge that had been phased out could be bordering on heresy. Even Bill had referred to the little Hornet as a "flyswatter." Nonetheless, it had just proved it was capable of doing what it was originally designed for—adding another 100 yards on to the effective 75 yards of the 22 Long Rifle rimfire.

I don't see much point in delving into the Hornet's history except to point out the cartridge was on the market before any American arms factory chambered a rifle for it. Many gunsmiths in the early depression days chambered for the Hornet in barrels with the same internal dimensions as the conventional 22 rimfire. Since these dimensions were approximately a .217″ bore and a .223″ groove, the first Hornet bullets put out by Winchester in 1932 were .223″ diameter. Before the middle 1930s, Winchester offered the Hornet in their Model 54 bolt action, Savage chambered their 23D and Stevens brought out a single shot in their Walnut Hill action, both for the little centerfire.

The varmint hunters of that time finally had something more potent than the 22 rimfire or the 22 Winchester Center Fire, the latter a black powder job which sent a 45-gr. slug out the muzzle only a couple of hundred feet faster than the 22 Long Rifle shell. However, this was nothing compared to the 2,350 fps the new Hornet offered. Back then, Savage had their 22 Hi-Power and 250-3000 in the 99 lever action model, but neither caught the fancy of the varmint shooter. Custom gunsmiths turned out a maze of expensive .224″ caliber varmint outfits built on all

That's the Ruger No. 3 carbine Lewis is shooting here, the scope a Unertl 1" 6x.

types of actions, but money was scarce and the multitude of varmint busters welcomed the Winchester 54 Hornet with open arms.

Probably the Hornet's toughest competitor was the 218 Bee. Quite a controversy raged over the merits of each, but my tests always proved there was little or no difference between them—perhaps a slight nod went to the Bee. This argument might still have been going on if Remington's 222 hadn't made its debut, but from that moment on both the Hornet and Bee began to fade. The advent of the 222, though dooming the Hornet, also brought varmint hunting into a sharper focus for all hunters. By the end of 1950, the Hornet was all but forgotten, and the era of speed and long range shooting made its appearance.

Hornet Misunderstood

From my long association with the 22 Hornet, I see it as a misunderstood cartridge. First, although it was the first mass produced long range varmint cartridge, it is not long range in the vernacular of today's varmint hunter. That point must be clearly understood. Second, I have always thought the little cartridge was its own worst enemy. With a very limited case capacity and the fast-burning powders needed, handloading for the Hornet can be a touchy matter.

In the tiny Hornet case, a few tenths of a grain difference in the powder charge is important. I ran the gamut from 8.6 grains of 2400 to 11 grains, going up in two-tenths (0.20) of a grain jumps. I didn't expect dramatic results first off since two-tenths is difficult to work with. Interestingly, velocity did increase slightly with each increment for a mean average of about 35 fps. In all honesty, the readings were not consistent—the highest gain was 64 fps, the lowest just 13. The over-all gain in the 2.4 grains of powder increase was 370 fps. With the tiny Hornet case, that's significant.

For years writers have credited the original Hornet cartridge as having 2,600 fps muzzle velocity, but that doesn't jibe with the early factory figures. Valid or not, the contemporary advertised speed—initially—was 2350. It's my belief that Hornet velocity is very limited in this area. In fact, I'm against going all out for sheer velocity in any rifle, but especially one chambered for the Hornet. My own choice is 9.2 grains of 2400 behind the 45-gr. bullet, but not just because its velocity is under 2,500 fps, which I consider maximum. That load showed only a 13 fps extreme variation in my chronograph tests.

I'm sure some may think this degree of consistency in velocity indicates precise powder measurement, but I'm not totally sold on that idea. From my experience with thousands of rounds fired through the chronograph screens I have learned that some powder-weight/bullet-weight combinations give more consistent readings than others, and that with them super fussy powder weighing isn't a must. Along the bullet weight line, I favor the 40- and 45-gr. bullets in the Hornet simply because the 50-gr. and up bullets don't stabilize well in the Hornet's slow 1-turn-in-16-inches twist.

There's no point in trying to hide the fact that the Hornet case requires careful loading procedures. Its size alone indicates there is no room for guesswork. I believe today's Hornet cases are heavier, but I had several that retired early when velocity got beyond 2,600 fps. In reality, there's no sense in pushing the Hornet beyond 2,500 fps. At the very best, its maximum accurate range is less than 200 yards, and subtracting 25 yards from that figure will put the Hornet cartridge in a much truer classification. Case and barrel life will certainly be extended with the lower velocities, so why strive for extra speed that serves no purpose?

Hornet Potential

The main reason I have classed the Hornet as a 150-175 yard outfit is its accuracy potential. Unfortunately, the 22 Hornet rifle right off the assembly line never whipped up much enthusiasm at the benchrest. Firing the latest 3 rifle entries—a Ruger No. 3 single shot, the Savage/Anschutz 1432 and Walther's KKJ—gave only a few groups that fell under one inch at 100 yards. If I had to give a franker figger, I couldn't go below 1¼". This may raise the hackles of some true-blue Hornet fans, but that was my findings on the 100-yard range.

Even though the Hornet may not fall in the one-holer category, it's still a fine varmint cartridge—within its range. It's also a fact that finding the *right* powder charge and bullet/

primer combination could reduce my classification considerably. Years back, I had a Model 54 scoped with a 10x Fecker Target Scope that often cut inch groups and less. I had to be ultra consistent in every aspect of loading, but the end results were worth the extra effort.

Being a devoted Hornet fan, I was somewhat chagrined when the rifle companies quit chambering for it. Naturally, it was like a shot in the arm to learn the little cartridge was getting some attention again. The chuck hunter in me made me yearn for the Ruger No. 3 single shot. However, after I'd fired some very nice groups with the Savage/Anschutz and Walther's KKJ model, I realized that all 3 were darn good shooting outfits.

Three Hornets

Ruger's No. 3 is a short, compact outfit, only 38½" over-all, the wood genuine walnut. It has a 22" barrel with a 1-in-16" right-hand twist that comes close to being a lightweight target barrel. In fact, the rifle weighs 6 pounds without a scope, and that's fairly heavy for such a short rifle. The No. 3 looks much the same as Ruger's No. 1 rifle excepting that the stock is straight (no pistol grip), and the No. 3's lever is a simpler one.

The No. 3 single shot has a "snap action" ejector, which sends the empty case flying when the lever is activated. Since hunting empty cases under field conditions is no fun, the ejector spring unit can be altered (remove the fore-end and back off the ejector-strut adjustment screw with an allen head wrench), making the ejector function as an extractor only.

The author with his Savage/Anschutz 22 Hornet rifle, the scope a Redfield 6x Widefield.

The No. 3's trigger is adjustable for weight of pull only, and the barrel is drilled and tapped for target bases. I can't see much sense in putting these factory bases only just over 3 inches apart, center to center. To accept the long 1" 6x Unertl Target Scope, I installed a front base 7¼" from the rear base. This better supported the long scope and also gave a ¼" impact change for each click of the scope metering wheels at 100 yards.

Savage's Anschutz 1432 is almost an exact replica of their Model 54 22 rimfire sporter. The 1432 has a 24" barrel with a 1-in-16" RH twist. The rifle has a French walnut Monte Carlo stock and fore-end, the latter having a graceful schnabel design. The trigger is factory set, my test model scaling out at just 4 pounds. Over-all length is 43⅝", total weight 6¾ pounds. The receiver is grooved for the clamp-type 22 rimfire type scope mount, and it's also tapped. I used two Weaver number 11 bases to mount the 6x Redfield Widefield. I must admit I like the smoothness of the 1432's bolt, but the 5-shot clip protrudes enough to detract from the inherent beauty of the 1432's design.

Walther's KKJ rifle (Interarms,

Don Lewis and the three new Hornets. From left—the Savage-Anschutz, the Walther and the Ruger. The chuck was taken at 135 yards.

Ltd., Alexandria, Virginia) reflects a classic beauty common on some of the fine muzzleloaders of yesteryear. I can't say that the stock has a high comb, but it has a cheekpiece that serves the same purpose. Surprisingly, for a rifle measuring over 41" long, the Walther weighs just 5½ pounds. Barrel length is 22½" and clip capacity is 5. The KKJ is available with either single or double triggers.

My test model has the double set trigger option, which I believe is tops for the varmint or benchshooter. With this set up, the rear trigger is first "cocked" or "set," after which only a gentle touch against the front trigger fires the rifle. It's possible to fire this trigger assembly by simply pulling the front trigger, and I was surprised to find it took just under 4 pounds to release, but there was a great amount of fore and aft play.

The rear trigger should never be set until the shooter is ready to fire. In case the shot can't be taken, lift the bolt handle and pull slightly to the rear, then touch the front trigger. Best advice is to use care and caution with any type of adjustable or set trigger assembly.

22 Hornet Tests

Bullet/grs.	Powder/grs.		MV[1]	EV[2]	Ruger	Sav/Anschutz	Walther
Sierra 40	2400	9.8	2664[3]	57	1½	1¾	1
Sierra 40	2400	10.6	2813[3]	16	1¾	1⅞	1½
Sierra 45	2400	9.6	2530	51	1¼	1¼	1¼
Sierra 45	2400	10.4	2650[3]	28	1½	1¼	1¼
Sierra 45	2400	10.6	2684[3]	18	1¾	1½	1¼
Sierra 45	4227	10.5	2366	50	1⅛	1⅛	1
Sierra 50	4227	8	1783	131	1⅛	1¼	1⅛
Sierra 55	4227	9	1963	70	1⅛	1⅛	1¼
Sierra 55	4227	9.5	2009	32	1¼	1⅛	1⅛
Nosler 52	4227	11.5	2504	12	1	⅞	¾

The rifle used for chronographing was the Model 1432 Savage-Anschutz. The K-233 Avtron chronograph was the instrument employed. Remington cases and No. 6½ primers.

MV[1]=muzzle velocity, the average of 3 groups for each rifle.

EV[2]=extreme variation in foot seconds.

Superposed 3 indicates maximum or near-maximum loads. Approach from below by reducing charge shown at least 10%.

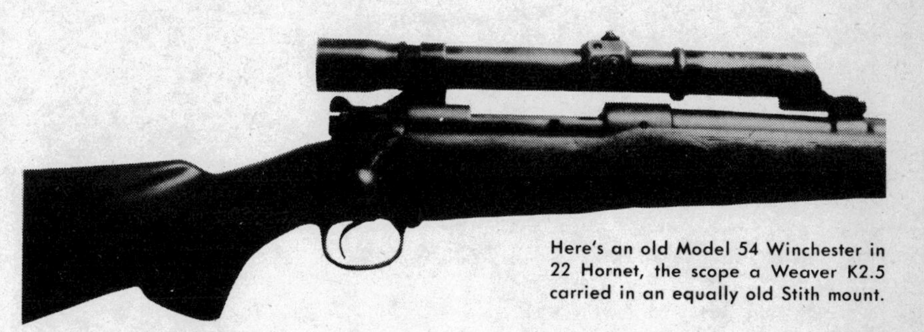

Here's an old Model 54 Winchester in 22 Hornet, the scope a Weaver K2.5 carried in an equally old Stith mount.

Summary

I made the transition from the 22 rimfire to the Hornet and, for me, it was a giant step. I can't forget the excitement that ran through my veins shortly after World War II when I bought a new Winchester Model 43 chambered for the Hornet. At that moment in my life, the 22 Hornet reigned supreme, and the Model 43 was meant to be a lifetime investment.

With what the little Hornet has to offer—or doesn't have, according to your likes—I may be a voice crying unheeded when I suggest to the modern varmint shooter that the 22 Hornet has a genuine place in today's hunting picture. I'm well aware that the demand for bigger and faster cartridges has somewhat overshadowed sound thinking. Yet, with the ever encroaching shadow of urbanization and the disappearance of farmlands, my plea for the short range Hornet and its low noise level is worthy of serious consideration.

Still, I don't entertain any high hopes the 22 Hornet will be a smash hit at the sales counter, but I do think it deserves proper recognition as a true varmint cartridge, applicable for many of today's conditions. It's somewhat of a paradox that the little Hornet centerfire—which lighted the way for the modern varmint cartridge—was relegated to the ranks of the unwanted. Back on centerstage again via the 3 fine rifles I've described, the Hornet is fighting to make a comeback. How well it does is entirely up to the varmint hunters across the nation. I can't speak for the rest of you, but this varmint hunter isn't going to overlook the potential of the Hornet cartridge. For a cartridge that was once number one, it seems strange it was nearly forgotten but, that's the plight of the Hornet. ●

The author holds the ancient 54 Winchester Hornet. The other two rifles (from left) are a Model 43 Winchester Hornet wearing a Weaver K4-60B scope in Stith mount, and a 23D Savage Hornet, its scope a Weaver 330 in 4x power in a Stith mount.

ALVIN WHITE

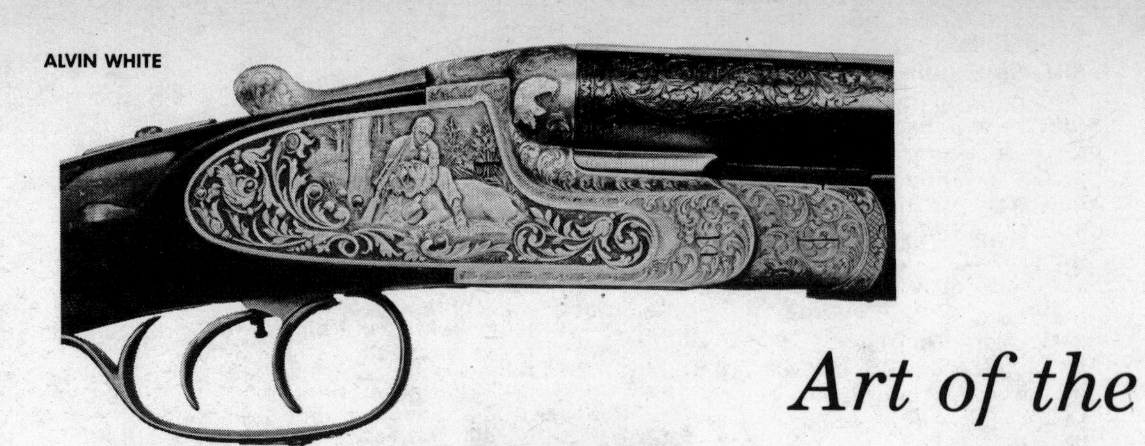

Art of the

JOHN E. WARREN

KENNY HUNT

Left—T.J. KAYE

Right—JOS. C. BAYER

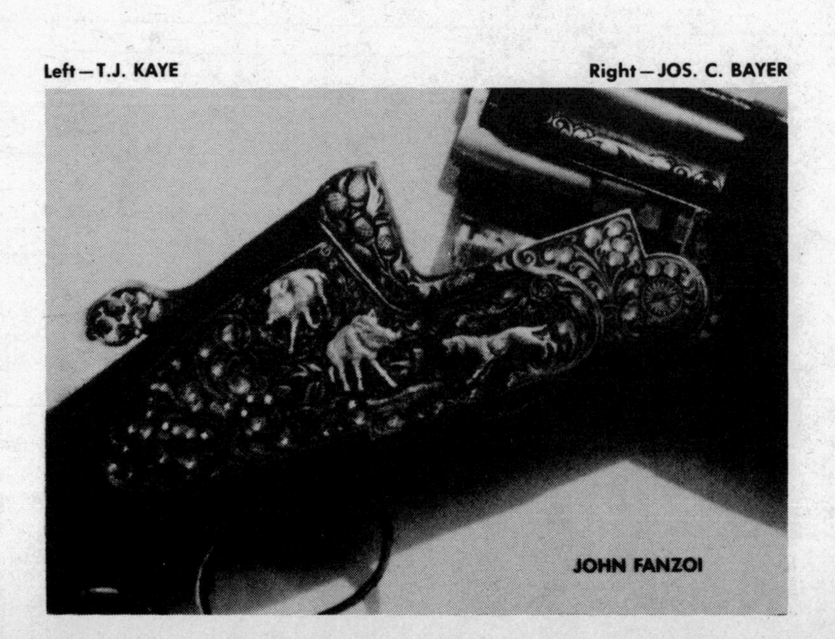

JOHN FANZOI

Engraver

KEN HURST

WM. H. MAINS

HOWARD V. GRANT

E.J. KOEVENIG

Left — F.E. HENDRICKS

Right — BILL DYER

ALVIN WHITE

RAY VIRAMONTEZ
SMITH & WESSON
RUSS SMITH
HANS PFEIFFER
SMITH & WESSON
B.J. GWINNELL
TOM OVERBEY
MILLER GUN WORKS

AMERICAN BULLETED CARTRIDGES

A detailed and comprehensive report on recently developed and introduced metallic cartridges and components—including a few potent bigbores.

by KENNETH L. WATERS

LATEST DEVELOPMENTS IN METALLIC CARTRIDGES

There's no doubt that the simultaneous occurrences of an economic squeeze and an energy crisis have had their effects on our cartridge and reloading components manufacturers. First it was copper, then brass and, most recently, powder which have been in tight—sometimes non-existent—supply, and at ever increasing prices. Powder, especially, has increased in cost at such frequent intervals and in such substantial leaps as to appear unjustifiable.

Naturally, all this has influenced not only the prices posted for factory ammo, but has also prompted policy decisions to reduce unnecessary expenditures and cut back on new developments. The annual appearance of new commercial metallic cartridges to which we became accustomed in the '50s and early '60s seems unlikely to be repeated, at least in the foreseeable future.

The picture is not all bleak, however. At least 4 of the big companies have programmed improvements of one sort or another, and a number of growing firms have announced plans to produce ammunition in previously discontinued calibers—a step that can easily prove more welcome to shooters than would the introduction of a totally new cartridge. Too, handloading has been boosted.

On balance therefore, we're not pessimistic. With some adjustments here and there in our outlook and personal choices, it's entirely possible we'll find ourselves enjoying shooting in 1976 even more than in previous years. That is, if we are successful in defeating the moves of the anti-gunners.

Winchester-Western

The emphasis at Winchester-Western this year is on serving handloaders, the market potential of ammunition components having been at last fully recognized. W-W's 16th Annual Seminar, held in December, 1974, at Belmont Plantation in South Carolina, included a forum during which the company's plans for 1975 were explained in detail to the assembled gun writers, including yours truly.

Bill Williams discussed the planning and criteria that had gone into their bullet designs, starting with those intended for downing big game where a heavy jacket with special internal configuration is combined with a lead core of carefully regulated hardness. This to provide controlled expansion, tailored insofar as possible to the remaining or striking velocities of the various bullets at most nearly predictable ranges. For example, 308 and 30-06 game slugs are designed to expand at 250-yards without disintegrating at closer ranges. Although accuracy is important, with these big-game bullets upset performance comes first.

With varmint bullets, on the other hand, accuracy is of primary importance, and here bullet fragmentation on impact is desirable. Jackets are made just strong enough to withstand the forces of acceleration and rotational torque. Winchester is confident that their new .224", 6mm and 30-caliber bullets will prove equal in accuracy to those of any other commercial manufacturer. Certainly, they have the facilities to produce such bullets.

Ed Matunas explained the advantages of the new W-W Ball powders, emphasizing their lowered rate of barrel erosion (due to lower flame temperature) and more even heating of barrels. Increased chemical stability of these powders is expected to insure a longer shelf life, and their high-density grain structure will appeal to handloaders, both for uniform flow through powder measures and because these small granules occupy less space within cartridge cases. You'll also be glad to know that the sooty fouling tendencies of the original line of "BR" powders, introduced in 1968, has been corrected in their new line. I found the older powders capable of fine accuracy, and we were assured that the new editions are even more so. Those tested to date have certainly performed very well indeed.

Biggest news in the powder line is W-W's announcement of a new slow-burning propellant to be known as 785, replacing the old 780BR. Uniformity of velocity and

New W-W bullets—5 new "superaccuracy bullets, designed to offer the bench rest and varmint shooter the best quality bullets available for handloading." Packed 100 to the box, the new match bullets come in white boxes carrying the big red W.

pressure, regardless of the type of primer used, has been the goal in developing this new powder. In fact, magnum primers are not needed, so they say!

This writer had found W-W 230 to be one of the very finest of powders for match accuracy loads in pistol and revolver cartridges, but because its flattened spheres had shown a tendency to "bridge" across the drop tubes of some powder measures, it is being replaced by a new version designated 231, alleged to be even better than 230. Since some ballistic changes have inevitably resulted from these doings, the new powders should *not* be loaded in the same charges as their predecessors.

Incidentally, W-W published reloading data averages about 95% of SAAMI maximums in centerfire rifle and handgun cartridges, but this *isn't* to say that charges may be exceeded with impunity. They're generally plenty warm as is. And a final component note: Winchester's bench-rest primer program has been temporarily discontinued.

As for factory-loaded cartridges, Winchester is introducing a new high accuracy 22 Long Rifle match cartridge, identified as the Super Match Gold, adapted for use in *both* rifles and pistols with a 40-gr. bullet at 1120 fps (the same as the Mark III)—premium ammo for the ultimate in accuracy, they say.

Another W-W 22 Long Rifle development—this one for small game and varmint hunters—is the new Dynapoint cartridge with a 40-gr. semi-hollow-point "dry lubricated" bullet, designed for maximum mushrooming effect. Already tested in Australia on the tough jackrabbits abounding there, W-W claims unequaled Long Rifle killing power for the new rimfire ammo.

Also added are a pair of loadings for the 6mm Remington with 80-gr. PSP and 100-gr. PP(SP) bullets, plus a single loading in 223 Remington caliber with a 55-gr. PSP bullet.

Also, to correct a mistake in last year's ABC column, the FMC-bullet loading for the 30 Carbine has *not* been discontinued, appearing along with the 110-gr. HSP loading in the W-W 1975 arms and ammunition catalog.

Norma

Having, as I write this, just received a shipment of Norma 205, 203 and 201 powders—the first available in more than two years—it appears that once again things are looking up for this valuable source of Swedish imports. We also learned that other Norma components, including bullets, primers and cases (pocketed for American Boxer-type primers, as usual) will also be arriving.

Of equal importance to this shooter of foreign calibers are Norma's plans to include such cases and/or cartridges as the 7x57R, 7x64, 9.3x57 and 9.3x62. Two boxes of the last named, with plastic spitzer tips instead of lead, have also been received, and I can't wait to try them as soon as the infernal stormy weather permits.

One word of caution: I'd advise against using too generous charges of the new lot of N205 powder until some experience with it has been acquired. Differences in previous lots have been noted by a number of experimenters and, at this point-in-time (hmm), we can't be sure where the new lot will locate in the comparative scale or order of burning rates.

Late in May it was learned, via a letter from Evan Sheldon (Norma's U.S. agent) that all Norma sporting powders have been discontinued. Taking their place, he said, would be a comprehensive line of new powders, coded MRP, but no further details are known at the moment.

Remington

In last year's column we announced the introduction of a new 185-gr. JHP hi-vel Remington loading for the 45 Auto pistol without having had an opportunity to test it. Since then it has been tried in a trio of pistols—a new Colt Commemorative, a Mark IV Series 70 Government model, and a Gold Cup Match pistol, firing 5-shot groups at 50 yards. The best the un-tuned Commemorative would do was 4¾", while the Mark IV went into 4", but the Gold Cup kept them in a neat 2½" (from rest, of course). Not bad accuracy for high velocity non-target ammo!

Expansion still isn't all I'd like to see for a hunting bullet. Possibly the jacket could stand a bit more thinning in the ogive area—I'm not sure. Regardless, I'll repeat what I said last year, it's still a far better bullet than the old standard 230-gr. FMJ. You'll find it a spunky load, even in the full-size Government pistol.

Federal

The No. 1 news item from Federal this year is the addition of a 165-gr. bullet loading in 30-06 caliber. What, you may ask, is so big about another 30-06 load? Well, for some years now we've known that 165 grains is the optimum bullet weight for the 30-06 cartridge, and handloaders have been using streamlined slugs of this weight to flatten trajectories, retain velocities and decrease wind drift. Yet for reasons unknown, until now, none of the big U.S.

ammo makers has seen fit to produce that weight.

Federal has wisely taken the 165-gr. Sierra boat-tail soft point bullet and loaded it to a M.V. of 2800 fps. claiming higher velocity and striking energy at 300 yards and beyond than any other 30-06 factory load, plus a significant reduction in wind drift over long ranges. What's more, the ballistic comparison they make with the 300 Winchester Magnum 150-gr. loading is nothing short of astounding; the 165-gr. 30-06 is shown as traveling 100 fps faster at the 500-yard mark, and delivering 240 foot pounds (fp) more kinetic energy with *one-third* less wind drift!

This is what Federal has officially claimed, and similar treatment would also benefit the 308 and 300 Savage. I haven't had an opportunity to check it out as yet, but they aren't given to making wild statements, so I suspect its right. Better try them before you disagree. The following is a copy of their published comparative ballistics table:

A further point worth noting has been brought out in a Federal release – with 38 Special ammunition being loaded to two quite different pressure and velocity levels – generally referred to as "standard" and "high velocity" – some manufacturers of revolvers with aluminum alloy frames have withdrawn their approval of the use of high velocity ammo in certain models.

Consequently, Federal as well as other member companies of the Sporting Arms and Ammunition Manufacturer's Institute, (SAAMI), including Winchester, Remington and Speer, have adopted a standard practice of adding "+P" to the case headstamp of such ammunition to positively identify it as being loaded to higher pressures. Additionally, a warning statement explaining this appears on the new boxes containing these higher velocity, higher pressure cartridges. Shooters are thus warned that this ammo is to be used *only* in firearms especially designed to handle it, as per manufacturer's recommendations.

		Velocity (fps)			Energy (ft/lbs)			Wind Drift
Caliber	Bullet Style and Weight	Muzzle	300 yds.	500 yds.	Muzzle	300 yds.	500 yds.	10 mph crosswind 500 yds.
30-06	165 B.T.S.P.	2800	2240	1910	2870	1840	1340	19.9"
30-06	150 S.P.	2910	2080	1620	2820	1450	875	31.2"
30-06	180 S.P.	2700	2040	1660	2910	1670	1110	27.1"
300 Win Magnum	150 S.P.	3290	2340	1810	3610	1830	1100	28.2"

Suggested retail price for a 20 round box is $8.20. Catalog No. 3006D.

Dynamit Nobel

Ever since DWM folded, American shooters of certain European metric rifle calibers have been wondering what they might have to do for ammo and components. Then last summer Dynamit Nobel, which includes the famous old German RWS organization, opened a Washington, D.C. office, and many, if not all DWM numbers, will be offered by RWS.

This group is now distributing fresh sporting ammo to selected wholesalers in the U.S., including a most comprehensive line-up of calibers. Empty brass cases and the excellent German controlled-expansion big-game bullets will also be available. If you've ever wanted to try (and who hasn't), the famous H-Mantle, D-Mantle, Brenneke-TIG and now the new Cone Point bullets, this is your chance.

Calibers offered are 5.6mm, 6.5, 7, 8 (both sizes), 9.3mm and 375 H&H, including rimmed cases as well as rimless. Listed are some of the hard-to-find numbers we're often asked about, such as the 9.3x74R, 9.3x72R, 9.3x64, 8x57JR and JRS, 7x65R, 7x57R, 6.5x57 and 5.6x57. They'll all be pocketed for American Boxer-type or "anvil" primers, making reloading ever so much easier and allowing us to use standard American primers! Not that there's anything wrong with RWS Boxer primers (long available here), a favorite among bench shooters.

Testing of representative calibers has already been started with the 7mm Cone Points, with results that make me wish it were hunting season. Brass is beautifully polished and annealed, and they shoot as accurately as they appear – 1¼" groups at 100 yards from an iron-sighted ex-Venezuelan Mauser military rifle. We'll have more to tell at a later date following a lot of upcoming test firing.

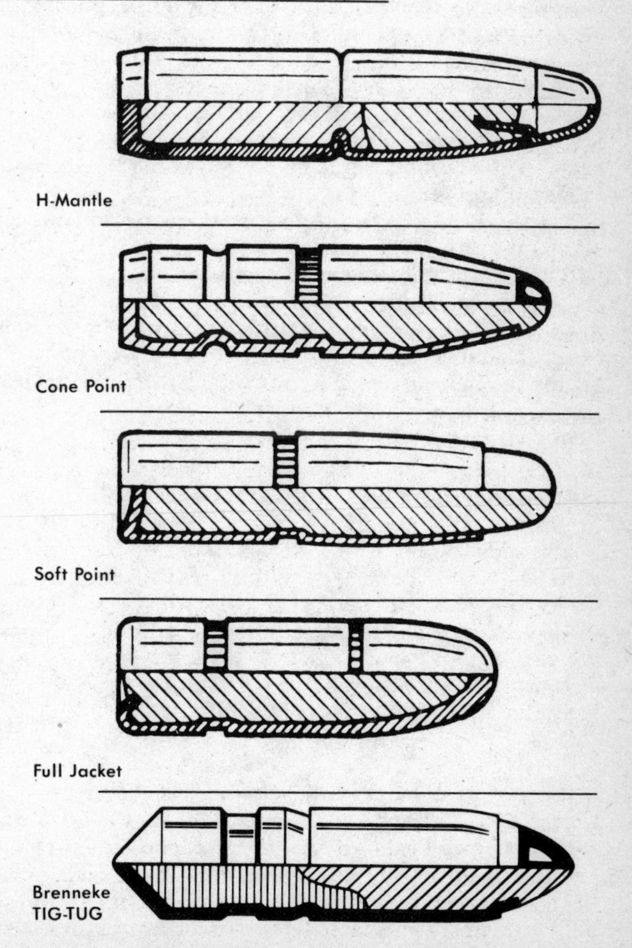

RCBS

By now just about everybody knows about Fred Huntington's import—the big RCBS 45 Basic rimmed case which can be used to form the famous Sharps 45-120-3¼" cartridge, or shortened and reformed to produce 27-plus other calibers. We made a preliminary announcement of that significant event in the last GUN DIGEST. What we didn't know then, however, was that Fred would produce a wildcat cartridge using that case, calling it the 458 RCBS.

Through the courtesy of Val Forgett of Navy Arms this writer has for some months worked with a big replica Rolling Block single-shot rifle chambered for this new cartridge—the 45 Basic case shortened to 2.75". Using a set of RCBS reloading dies, we've tried nearly all kinds and weights of 45-caliber rifle bullets, driven by some stiffish loads.

Space doesn't permit anything like a full report on the cartridge and rifle here, except to say that it's an amazingly strong and accurate combination, producing all the power you're ever apt to need this side of the Atlantic (and most of the other side as well). One quickly comes to appreciate the considerable weight of this big rifle for its recoil-taming properties. Ballistics approaching those of the famous English elephant cartridges are obtainable in rifles of sufficient action strength—I believe Fred used a Jeffery Farquharson as his test rifle—and it should prove a most excellent chambering in double rifles for big game. I predict you'll be hearing more about this one as time goes on.

Brass Extrusion Laboratories, Ltd.

Along with the widespread rebirth of interest in rifles of yester-year together with their modern replicas, has come a growing demand for cartridges in the old calibers. Not content just to collect them, today's enthusiast wants to shoot the old history makers. But those relatively few surviving original cartridges are now expensive collector's items themselves, often deteriorated from age, their caked powder charges seldom accurate, and the corroded cases unfit for reloading.

Hence, there is a market—not large by commercial standards, but vociferous, enthusiastic and apparently willing to back those demands with the green stuff. Still, no one seemed sufficiently interested in filling the void, at least to the extent of making the necessary investment of capital and hard work required.

This fascinating group—the British African cartridges—was dropped from production by Kynoch just as American shooters were acquiring the rifles for them in unprecedented numbers. As supplies dwindled, prices rose, often astronomically, with all the appearance of a standoff in which the large ammunition makers weren't interested in doing anything about it, and most small enterprises couldn't afford to.

Then, early in 1975, a new outfit called Brass Extrusion Laboratories, Ltd., of Bensenville, Illinois, announced that they had constructed plant facilities and acquired the necessary tooling to produce cylindrical cases of drawn brass in basic sizes from which the big British cases could be formed. This has to be one of the outstanding recent developments in the area of metallic cartridges! Good news, too, B.E.L. plans to make all their cases for American primers.

First, there will be a 500 Basic from which, in addition to the 500-3" Nitro, can be formed the 470 Nitro, 465 H&H (500/465), 476 Nitro, 500/450 Magnum Nitro, 500/450 No. 1 Express and 500/450 No. 2 Musket. I believe cases will also be offered in 3½" length, from which can be formed the impressive 475 No. 2 and 450 No. 2 Nitro.

Next will come brass for the big 50-90-2½" and 50-140-3¼" Sharps, then the mighty 577-3" and the once-popular 280 Ross. I'm hoping eventually also for the 404 Nitro (from which can be formed the 333 Jeffery), the 425 Westley Richards, 416 Rigby and 450-3¼" Straight (and its offspring, the 450/400 and 360 No. 2).

Jim Bell, B.E.L.'s proprietor, told us it is his intention to make all cases for which a run of 100,000 can be justified. Owners of the big British rifles, here and abroad, should be enormously cheered by this news!

East Surrey Firearms, Ltd.

Working along similar lines, an English firm named East Surrey Firearms, Ltd., headquartered in London, has gone into production on some of the British African cartridges including, to date, the 505 Gibbs for magazine rifles, and the 577-3" and 600-3" Nitro Express for double rifles. Scheduled to follow are 500, 470 and 465 ammo for doubles, plus the 416 and 404 for bolt action rifles.

Available as factory-loaded cartridges charged with Cordite powder, in addition to empty drawn-brass cases, they will also offer suitable bullets in both solid and soft point types. Unfortunately, so we're told, at least some of these cases are being pocketed for the big Berdan primers, but it may be this has been done (along with the use of Cordite powder) so that existing double rifles, regulated

Steps in the production of Brass Extrusion Laboratories, Ltd. cases: (left to right) bunted case head; with primer pocket and headstamp; a finished case with the flash hole drilled, and one of the first cases—the 500 Base.

East Surrey cartridges: From left—600 Nitro, 577 Nitro, 505 Gibbs, Kynoch 505 Gibbs for comparison, 500 Jeffrey and Kynoch 500/3¼".

for English components, will continue to group both barrels together. We'll just have to wait and see, but in any case, it's another happy event.

Amm-O-Mart

Good news from Canada has it that this aggressive Ontario-based concern is offering new cases for handloaders in several calibers uncommon on this side of the border, of which I predict two will prove especially interesting to U.S. shooters.

These are the 43 (or 11mm) Mauser, recently discontinued by C.I.L. and for which large numbers of military surplus 71/84 Mauser rifles have been sold in this country; and the 6.5x53R rimmed Mannlicher cartridge chambered in numerous British sporting rifles dating back to the turn of the century, as well as Dutch and Roumanian military Mannlicher-actioned rifles.

Interarms

Of course practically every shooter has heard of Interarms—the big importing group with American headquarters in Alexandria, Virginia. Their diverse line of foreign commercial and military surplus arms needs no introduction. But I wonder how many know that Interarms also imports a considerable variety of European metallic ammunition?

For example, in hard-ball FMJ military loadings, there are 6.5mm Mannlicher, 6.5 Dutch (6.5x53R), 7.35 Italian, 7.62mm Russian Rimmed, 7.65 Mauser, 8x56R Austrian, 7.62x39 and, naturally, 8x57 Mauser. In hunting ammo with expanding bullets, they list the 6.5 Swedish, 303 British, 7mm and 8mm Mausers, 7.65 Mauser and that hard-to-get number, the 9x57mm Mauser. Interarms pistol ammo includes the 9mm Steyr, 9mm Bergmann-Bayard, 9mm Browning Long and 30 Mauser.

However, one word of caution is in order here—these cartridges may have corrosive primers, so be *sure* to clean your rifles and pistols thoroughly immediately after use, either with hot water or one of the bore cleaning solvents approved for dissolving corrosive salts.

Dixie Gun Works

Sample 50-70 Government cases, sent to me by Ernest Tidwell of Dixie Gun Works, bear the headstamp initials "DGW", measure 1.75" in length, and are pocketed for standard American Large Rifle primers. Drawn from new brass, they're stronger and better than the old original 50-70 cases ever were, and are well worth the asking price of $10.00 per box of 20.

There seem to be a surprising number of old 50-70 caliber rifles still around, many of whose owners would like to fire them, and these new cases provide the best as well as the safest means of doing so.

With a little work, such as turning down rims and reforming, these cases (although a bit short) can also be made to serve as brass for 45-75 and 50-95 Winchesters. Thus, we have still another valuable contribution to the growing list of enterprises intended to reactivate the famous old rifles of yesteryear. As most of our readers already know, Dixie Gun Works is located in Union City, Tennessee (38261).

New Hodgdon Powders

Late in 1974, Hodgdon announced the addition of two new powders—H-322 and H-205—to his extensive line-up. At the time however, only H-322 was available for testing, and as this is written in 1975, H-205 has not yet been tested by the author.

H-322 is an extruded (stick-type) single-base powder with very small granules, intended to fill the gap in the scale of burning rates between H-4198 and BL-C(2), and provide fine accuracy along with reasonably high velocities in "standard" type (non-magnum) cartridges from the 222 Remington thru the 8mm Mauser.

In the 222, it gives only slightly less velocity than BL-C(2) with 50-gr. bullets, and a bit *higher* muzzle speeds with lighter bullets. It will also deliver higher velocities from the 8x57, but in more sharply bottle-necked cases, such as the 243 and 308, it falls below the slower burning BL-C(2). Also, it is not as well suited for use with the heavier bullets in most calibers. Its forte is fine accuracy, and early trials indicate the probability of highly successful performance in this regard.

H-205, likewise an extruded powder, is said to have the same (slow) burning rate as Norma's 205, but Bruce Hodgdon emphasizes that *only* Hodgdon's loading data is to be used with his powder, and his newest Manual No. 22 lists a very considerable amount of data with H-205.

According to that excellent hard-cover handbook, while H-205 "will give good results with most medium to large capacity cases," it is capable of outstanding performance in the big 30-caliber cartridges from 30-06 through the magnums. It will, for example, drive bullets of all weights from 110-gr. through 180-gr. in the 300 Winchester Magnum to higher velocities than any other Hodgdon powder type. I'm looking forward to giving this newest powder a thorough trial.

CCI

My guess is that the boys at CCI have really started something with their new pair of high accuracy primers—BR-2 for Large Rifle, and BR-4 for Small Rifle.

Basically, I'm told, these new caps are manufactured from the same materials as the regular CCI primers, but with utmost care exercised in their fabrication to insure maximum uniformity, the work being done by top hands working in an unhurried, spare-no-effort fashion.

While there's no reason these primers couldn't be used in loads for a 30-30 or other ordinary hunting musket,

they are intended to fire-off special accuracy loads such as those meant for benchrest and match target competitions. Having seen what they will do in a Shilen-barreled 223 Carl Gustaf actioned benchrest rifle I've been testing of late, I can report that the new primers measure up to their maker's claims.

When you think of it, this is a perfectly logical action CCI has taken inasmuch as the primer is the one component over which a handloader has no control. He can sort and neck-ream cases, spin bullets for concentricity, vary powder charges and employ all sorts of special procedures and loading techniques, but must accept his primers on faith. It is therefore reassuring to know that he can now obtain primers made with the same care and attention to details as all of his own operations.

Marlin's 35 Remington

I'm not sure this is the proper place to say it, but its something I feel needs saying, so here goes:

Every now and again some badly misinformed soul makes a sad announcement to the effect that "no rifles are being chambered for the 35 Remington cartridge," or that the 35 Remington "is dying." I recall one such dolt claiming that this cartridge was hard to come by, and another who declared that Marlin had dropped the caliber in their Model 336 lever gun.

So here and now I want to dispel all those silly notions. The 35 Remington cartridge is still a *very* popular deer round for timber and brush country. I wouldn't be amazed, in fact, to learn that more rifles in this caliber are in use today than ever before! Remington offers the cartridge in two different bullets weights (150-and 200-gr.), Winchester with two different types of bullets—both 200-gr.—and Federal also makes it in the standard 200-gr. loading.

Marlin's 1975 catalog shows their Model 336-A rifle and 336-C carbine as being available in 35 Remington caliber, and I'm told that a substantial percentage of orders specify this chambering. I can add my personal observation that a majority of the new Marlins I've seen hunters carrying over the last couple of seasons have been in 35 Remington caliber, which in my neck of the woods has a reputation for making more reliable kills than the 30-30.

Thus the 35 Rem. cartridge is very much alive and doing well in the handy and reliable Marlin 336, so you can disregard the next time one of these unfounded reports appears.

The Dollars and Cents of Wildlife

The importance of America's wildlife is typically measured in terms of intangible values, not dollars and cents. Yet, though it seems out of place to put a price tag on ducks or deer, their economic significance cannot be overlooked. Baldly stated, poetic visions of flora and fauna alone can never match the promises of economic bonanza from anxious real estate developers, for example.

But can our wildlife be seen as an income-producing commodity? Yes, if the economic importance of wildlife use is adequately recognized. When it is, the figures are staggering. The 1970 National Survey of Fishing and Hunting published by the Interior Department's Fish and Wildlife Service shows that some 128 million Americans, age 9 and over, participated in one or more outdoor recreational activities in 1970. A breakdown of this total according to type of activity reveals that some 97 million Americans enjoyed a form of outdoor recreation directly associated with wildlife use.

Besides hunters and fishermen (who together make up more than half of this total), this category includes wildlife and bird photographers, bird-watchers, and nature walkers. Together, these millions of Americans spent a total of 1.6 billion recreation days in the out-of-doors. Translating these figures into dollars and cents, hunters and fishermen, for example, pumped 7.1 billion dollars into the economy during the year.

The billions sportsmen spend each year for equipment, travel, and lodging represent, however, only one part of the economic picture. Millions of acres of state game lands, purchased with revenue from hunting license sales and an 11 per cent excise tax on sporting arms and ammunition, are open to sightseers, picnickers, hikers, and campers, as well as hunters. What's more, a recent study conducted by the U.S. Bureau of Sport Fisheries and Wildlife reveals that these areas are eleven times more heavily used by non-hunting outdoor recreationists than by hunters.

An analysis of the use data from the Bureau survey shows that, of the 86 activities listed, hunting, which makes all the rest possible, ranked far below several other popular uses. Sightseeing ranked first with 28.3%; followed by fishing, 19%; picnicking, 18%; camping, 15%; and hunting with 9%. Although picnicking and sightseeing aren't directly associated with wildlife use, without wildlife these state game lands might likely be so many shopping centers or industrial parks—and hunters pay for all of this.

Most Americans would agree that the true worth of our nation's wildlife lies in its aesthetic beauty. Hunters agree, but they can also point out that wildlife is a great, self-renewing resource paying to all annual dividends in the billions.

NDT

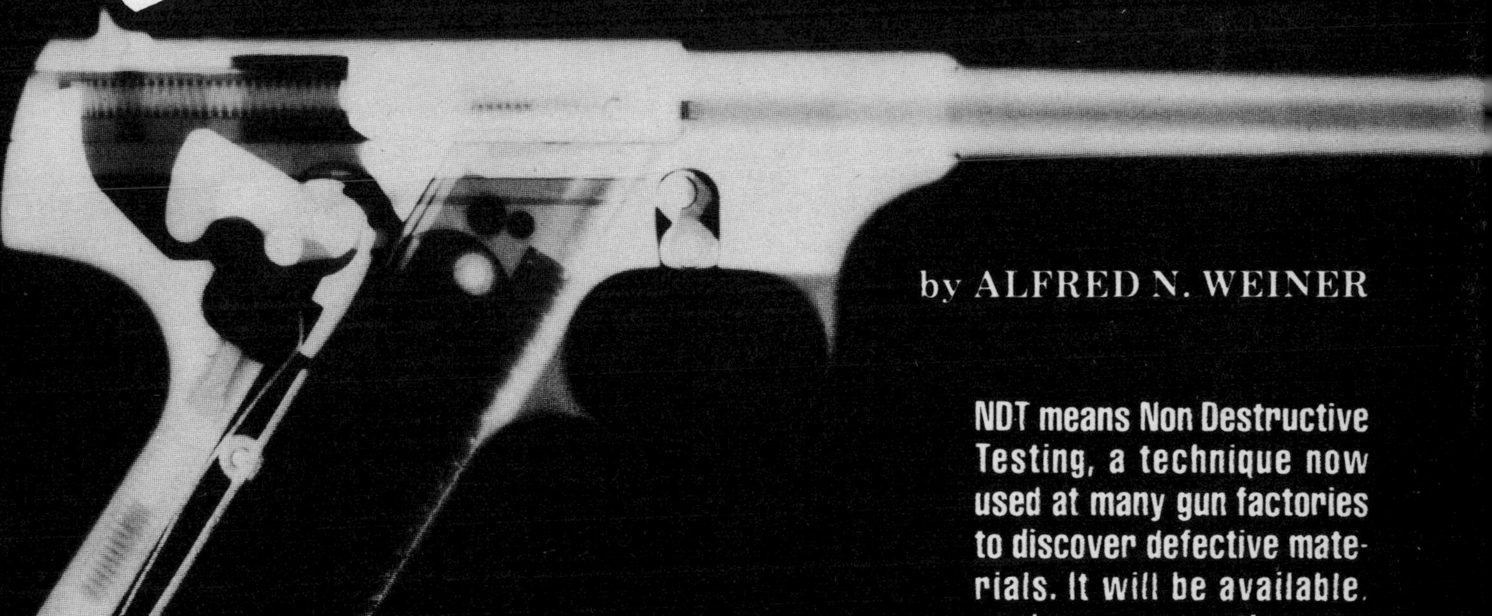

by ALFRED N. WEINER

NDT means Non Destructive Testing, a technique now used at many gun factories to discover defective materials. It will be available, perhaps sooner than you think, at local gunsmiths.

Fig. 1. X-ray exposure (positive print) of a 1925-30 Colt early model Woodsman 22 automatic pistol.

Fig. 2. Positive print of a neutron radiograph provides proof that the three cartridges are properly manufactured and ready to be fired.

A GOOD NEIGHBOR knocks at your front door, shows you an old GI 45 auto, and says, "I bought this, knowing it doesn't work; I thought it could be fixed, but I can't open it; will you take it apart and see what's wrong with it?"

You examine the gun but you can't take it apart either. You feel uncomfortable, for the gun isn't safe to handle or work on; there might well be a live cartridge in the chamber.

What would you do in this case? Normally—and it's usually good advice—you suggest that he handle the gun very carefully and take it to a qualified gunsmith.

But hold that sage suggestion—with a technique called Nondestructive Testing (NDT) the interior of the gun can be examined, loaded or unloaded, without disassembly, not changing the usefulness or material, and in complete safety.

An NDT examination of this 45 will show the cause of the jammed parts and any other conditions for potential malfunctions, such as internal flaws in the material.

Unfortunately, at this time, you can't use NDT in your basement workshop or in your friendly gunsmith's shop; you'll have to take the gun to a laboratory that has the equipment.

To understand why this equipment isn't available today, look at the characteristics of the NDT process and equipment. Think back to an X-ray that was taken of your teeth, a sprain, or a broken bone. One type of NDT provides the same black and white films as a medical or dental technician furnishes.

That fully loaded 45—or other firearm—can be examined by similar X-rays without any danger; the rays won't affect the live rounds.

The gun industry uses NDT to sort various types of metal that look alike, in production to detect faulty material before parts are made, to detect faulty parts before assembly, and to measure proper thickness of parts. Many NDT methods are related to your senses. X-rays, infrared rays, microwaves, and other radiation are similar to seeing light. Ultrasonic methods relate to hearing because of mechanical vibrations. Testing for surface quality and smoothness are like touching.

The mass-manufacture of the WW II German Luger and the U.S. M-1 Garand made use of NDT for the various parts; aircraft bomb designs, nuclear weapon/reactor technology, and space exploration have factors of time, hazards, and costs that made maximum reliability very important.

How it Works

For example, consider what happens to a single gun part using NDT. The rays, produced by an X-ray generator and partly absorbed as they pass through the test part, are recorded on X-ray film, the film type depending on the thickness of the test material. Some materials hold back X-rays more than others, as also do thicker materials. As with regular photographic film, the more X-rays that reach the film, the darker will be the image. Short-wavelength X-rays (and gamma rays) can pass through such relatively thick materials as billets of steel intended for gun barrels. Gamma rays usually have a nuclear origin based on a radioactive substance, a common source being radioactive Cobalt-60, obtainable in various sizes and radiation intensities.

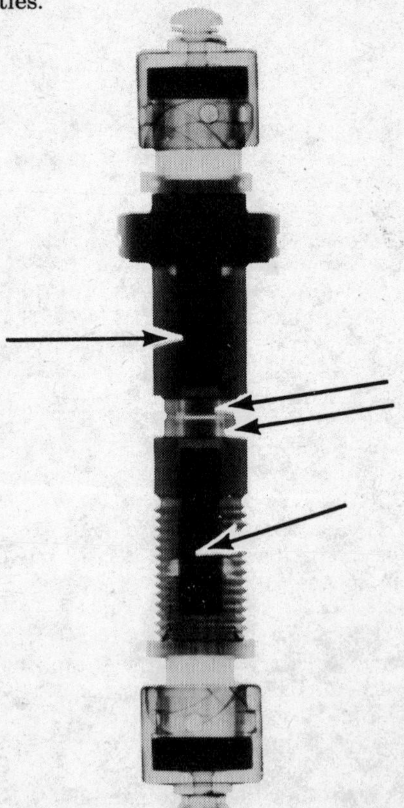

Fig. 3. Positive print of a neutron radiograph inspecting explosives inside a metal container, such as explosive bolts. Arrows point to the explosive material. The bolts are seen to be properly armed to do their job without flaws or separations in the containers.

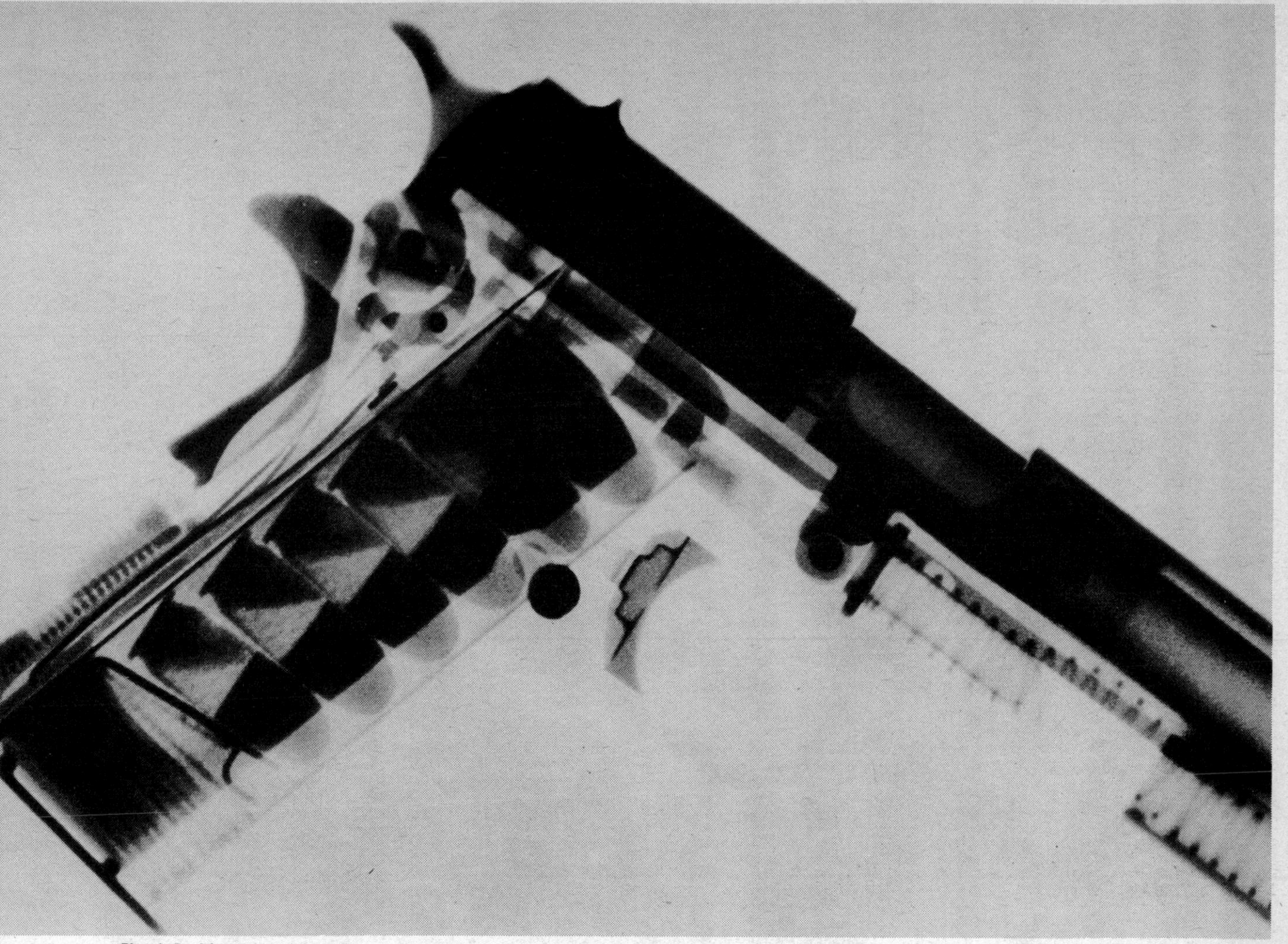

Fig. 4. Positive print of a neutron radiograph showing the inner mechanism of a fully loaded 45 automatic pistol.

X-ray machines come in a variety of sizes and shapes. The smaller ones, operating usually at less than 100,000 volts, are used to inspect the thin-metal stampings used in the cheaper, mass-produced guns. Typical industrial machines, up to 300,000 volts, are used to inspect steel as thick as 3 inches. Larger machines, gradually becoming more common, are useful on steel many inches thick, or other heavy materials.

X-rays also differentiate between less dense materials (steels, etc.) and such heavy metals as silver and the like.

Flaws in a gun part can be detected by X-rays if the thickness – in the path and direction taken by the X-ray beam – is about 2% of the specimen thickness in the same direction. For example, in a piece of steel 2 inches thick, a flaw that is thin and flat will be detected if it is at least 0.040″ thick. With less thick flaws, the darkening difference on the X-ray film would be too small to be easily seen.

Radiographic detection of cracks is not always possible. The crack must be quite wide or so-positioned that the X-rays pass along its length for some distance. This kind of defect is usually detected by other NDT methods, such as fluoroscopy. In this technique the film is replaced by a phosphor screen. The dark and light areas of the fluoroscope picture are reversed and not permanent. Fluoroscopy has two advantages; no waiting for a film to be developed, and the part being inspected can be rotated in many directions for various views.

Although some gunmakers use X-ray equipment for NDT operations, information on such usage or the equipment is not readily available. They consider their testing operations confidential, but most factory applications apply to gun parts and small subassemblies. In certain cases raw metal and finished barrels are being inspected.

For nonfactory repairs and testing the smallest NDT equipment is too expensive and too large for the average gunsmith. However, NDT service, to one degree or another, can be had from any one of 263 commercial and institutional laboratories, these in a few major cities in every state. For a complete list refer to the *Directory of Testing Laboratories-Commercial and Institutional,* No. STP333A, published by the American Society For Testing and Materials, 1916 Race St., Philadelphia, PA 19103. Your local public or university library may have a copy; or write ASTM.

For the future, improved designs, using new lightweight housings and shielding, will reduce the size and cost of the equipment. The average gunsmith will be able to afford a unit that is low in cost and small enough to let him include NDT operations in his services – and provide safer guns for your use. ●

Credits: Fig. 1 furnished by Thomas E. Peterson, Public Relations Dept. and Laboratory staff, Du-Pont Photo Products X-Ray Division. Figs. 2, 3 and 4 courtesy of the J. Walter Thompson agency for the American Society for Nondestructive Testing.

New Checkering Cradle—low, low cost and easy to make.

The cradle described here has other uses besides checkering—stock stripping or finishing, glass bedding, making detail photographs, you name it.

by V. P. KISNER

Cradle in use, holding rifle stock.

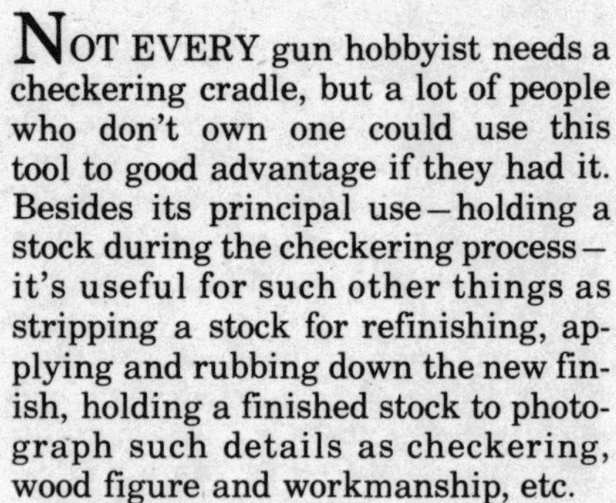

NOT EVERY gun hobbyist needs a checkering cradle, but a lot of people who don't own one could use this tool to good advantage if they had it. Besides its principal use—holding a stock during the checkering process—it's useful for such other things as stripping a stock for refinishing, applying and rubbing down the new finish, holding a finished stock to photograph such details as checkering, wood figure and workmanship, etc.

The cradle shown in the photos, which works very well, is easy to make and easy to use. It's quick-adjustable—just tilt the movable standard slightly forward and slide it to the desired position, swing the stock between centers in the holding fixtures, and tighten the pivot bolts. That strap-iron locking loop on the movable standard, which comes down and around the bar, levers up against the bottom of the bar, then the bottom of the movable standard is cammed

The pistol grip pattern above is one of many Stan de Treville's designs, this one inspired by famed stockmaker Leonard Mews.

Easy-Build Checkering Cradle

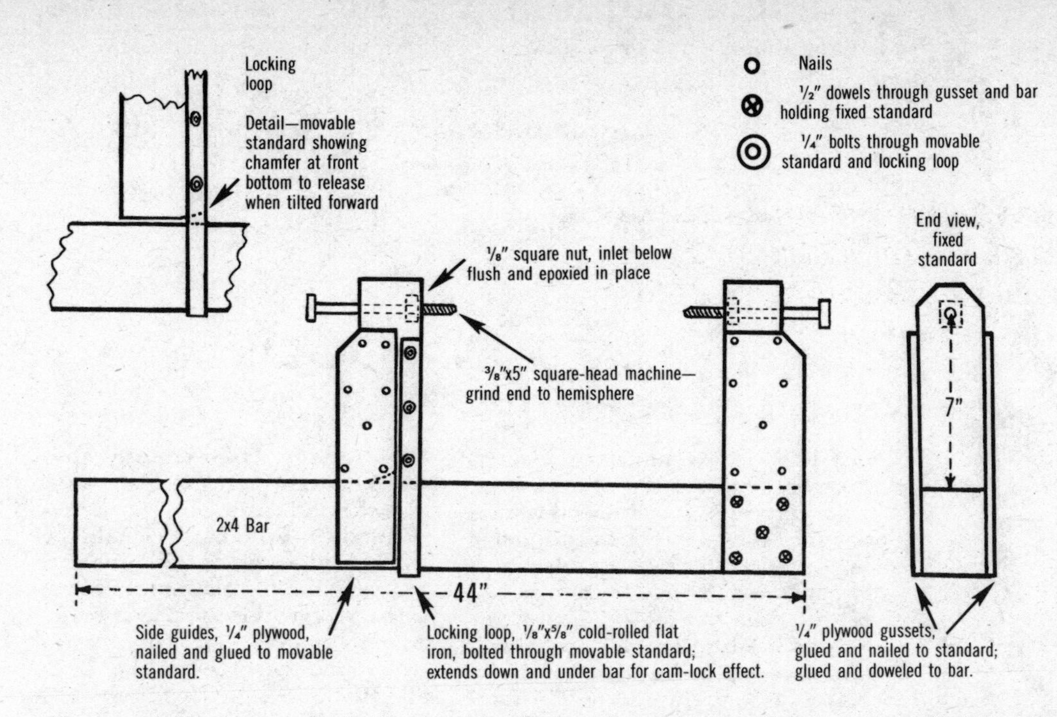

Dimensional drawing. 6" from top of bar to center of pivot bolts is ample except, possibly, for a full-length-stocked or heavy target style rifle. Chamfering (arrow) permits movable standard to tilt, to also move back and forth.

down against the top of the bar, holding everything in place by friction.

The bar is a length of 2x4 placed on edge—pick out a good straight one, free of knots.

The fixed standard at one end is also a 2x4, attached to the bar with ¼" plywood gussets on both sides, glued and nailed to the standard; glued and doweled to the bar.

The movable standard is another 2x4 with side-guides of ¼" plywood glued and nailed; the locking loop is attached with ¼" bolts.

The holes (through the tops of the standards) for the pivot bolts should be drilled to fit the bolts exactly so there will be no wobble. Nuts which fit the pivot bolts are inletted just below flush into the front faces of the standard and epoxied into place. Wing-headed pivot bolts, if available, would be a convenience.

Beyond these bare specs, the dimensional drawing and the photo captions pretty well tell the story; you should be able to make one in an evening without difficulty, and at a cost of $2-3 or so.

In use, this cradle is best held in a swivel-base bench vise; these permit rapid adjustment and swapping ends as necessary to expedite the job in hand. •

For those who can't or won't do it themselves, Bob Brownell of Montezuma, Iowa, has a rugged, all-wood cradle that costs $8.25. Ed.

Parts of cradle. Movable standard, (A) off bar to show construction. Round fixture (B), used to hold tip (left, below) was turned from a piece of broken baseball bat. Recess which accepts end of stock is cone-shaped and lined with heavy felt. Back side is drilled about ½" deep for pivot bolt. When bolts are adjusted so this fixture is in solid contact with face of standard, the stock will withstand fairly heavy pressure without rotating; it is not locked solidly; tip will slip in fixture before fixture will turn. But holder (C) was made from piece of 1" board; recessed rim was bent from galvanized sheet, attached with nails, lined with heavy felt. Make this slightly oversize; smaller butts can be wrapped with rags or tape for snug fit. In stripping or refinishing work, dispense with this fixture; remove buttplate and make small recess in end of stock for pivot bolt.

Trouble Shooting the Ruger Carbines

The 44 Magnum has an area or two that could become troublesome, but the 10/22 seems completely free of problems. Both function fully reliably in virtually all circumstances.

by J. B. WOOD

Ruger 44 Magnum Carbine

Ruger Autoloading Carbine, caliber 44 Remington.

IN 1955, when Smith & Wesson and Remington introduced the 44 Magnum cartridge, it became the most powerful commercial handgun round in the world. Personally, I feel that the only need for such a cannon-caliber in a sidearm might be as a back-up weapon in bear country. Its paper ballistics are impressive: Muzzle Velocity 1,470 feet-per-second, 1,275 foot-pounds of energy at the muzzle. Super Vel's 180-gr. load, in fact, offers 2005 fps and 1607 ft. lbs., both muzzle figures. Its capabilities are limited, however, by the relatively short barrel of a handgun.

The 44 Magnum really came into its own in 1961, when Ruger introduced a compact, beautifully engineered semi-automatic carbine chambered for the cartridge. In the Ruger Carbine's 18½-inch barrel, the 44 Remington round develops 1,720 fps, 1,580 ft. lbs. at the muzzle, demonstrating that a good deal of its power is wasted in a handgun.

As can be said for all Ruger arms, the Carbine is a mechanical masterpiece. The 44 Magnum cartridge, with its rimmed case and intense gas-sealing aspects, presented certain problems for a self-loading action, but Ruger design engineers solved them admirably. A short-stroke, gas-operated piston, a turning bolt, and an extra sturdy extractor took care of the heavy obturation. The rimmed case is efficiently handled by a 4-round tubular magazine, a foolproof cartridge stop, and an ingeniously contoured lifter.

Even the best designs, however, are susceptible to quirks which may occasionally require the attention of a gunsmith. The Ruger Carbine is no exception.

Magnum handgunners are familiar with the problem of action screws being loosened by powerful recoil. Nylon plugs set into the threads have lessened this effect, and a drop of Loctite often cures it completely. The latter remedy, however, can make later removal for cleaning or repair somewhat difficult.

The Ruger Carbine has similar occasional ailments, but in this case the recoil-affected elements are pins. In the trigger group, those which have a tendency to shift are the trigger-pivot pin (C-21), the lifter-cam pin (C-57), and the lifter-latch pivot pin (C-37). Loosening of these parts will not necessarily cause trouble, as the interior of the stock will prevent them from traveling far enough to free the parts.

In the bolt, however, there are two pins which can cause some difficulty when loosened. The extractor pivot pin (C-16) and, especially, the firing-pin retaining pin (C-13), will completely jam the action if they back out, with a possibility of damage to the internal mechanism. Since the bolt is subjected to repeated movement and impact, these two pins are also more apt to loosen than those in the trigger group.

Correcting the potential problem is so simple that I am surprised it isn't done during final assembly by the manufacturer. If your Carbine develops this ailment, just have a competent gunsmith "stake" the 5 pins by making a small punch-depression by the head of each to retain them. This will take care of things almost indefinitely.

The pin-loosening ailment is not a serious point for criticism of the Carbine, and in any event is simply and inexpensively corrected. In fact, the design of the gun is so neatly executed that I can find only one point which caused me some concern. The trigger group housing is an alloy casting, and with this use I have no quarrel. A machined-steel group would have made the Carbine prohibitively expensive.

There is one alloy part, however, which might cause trouble some day.

The trigger group, with arrows showing the lifter latch pivot pin (left) trigger pin (center), and lifter cam pin (upper right). All are subject to occasional loosening and, on the piece shown, these have been staked to keep them in place.

The bolt, with arrows showing the extractor pin (left) and firing pin retaining pin (right), are especially susceptible to recoil loosening. Note that on this bolt, the pins have been staked to prevent this.

The lifter latch (C-35), located at the rear of the loading port, releases the lifter for loading, and releases the bolt when it is locked open. More importantly, it is also a prime factor in the feed system. During the firing cycle, its narrowed upper arm is struck a healthy slap by the base of the cartridge driven rearward by the magazine spring. This pivots the latch, releasing the lifter to transport the round. It is possible that this repeated impact on a relatively narrow projection of an alloy part might cause deformation or breakage; in my opinion steel would be better in this application. To be fair, though, this is a purely hypothetical objection, as I have never heard of one which had broken.

There are several other fine points in the design of the Carbine. The bolt, when locked in position for firing, has 4 surfaces bearing against strong shoulders inside the receiver—one forward, three at the rear. The receiver, completely enclosed except for the ejection port and cocking handle slot, is made from a solid block of steel, a welcome surprise in today's ghastly trend to formed and welded sheet-steel. After viewing the machining inside the receiver, I am amazed that Ruger has kept the price for the basic model down to $117.

One final thought on repair or extensive cleaning. Takedown of the Ruger Carbine is a job I don't recommend for any but the most advanced amateur. Takedown should be done by a competent gunsmith, preferably one with much experience in self-loaders. The gun is not unnecessarily complicated, but there is an interdependence of certain parts which might prove difficult for those not thoroughly familiar with them. ●

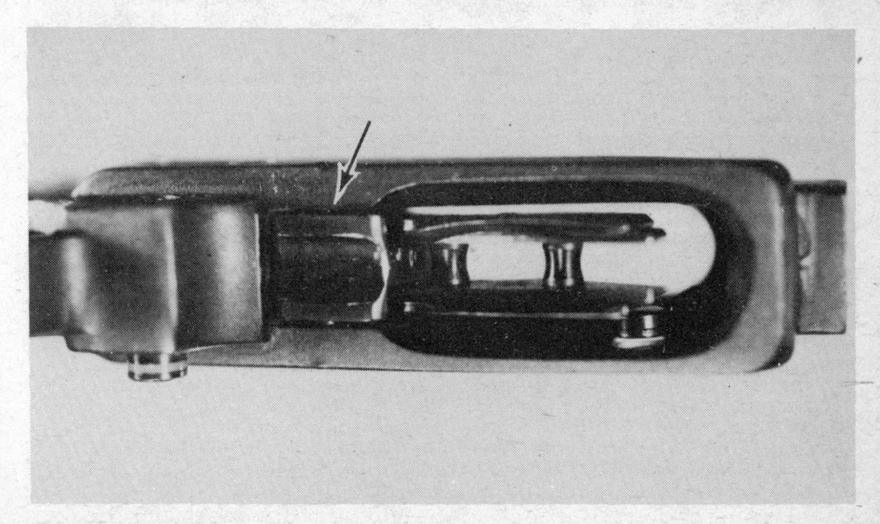

Underside of the trigger group, the laminated carrier visible in the loading port. The arrow points to the alloy lifter latch, a part which the writer suggests should have been made of steel.

(a) An earlier Ruger 10/22 Sporter, now discontinued, had sling swivels, no barrel band, and a specially contoured stock.

(b) The full Mannlicher-style stock and European type forward sling swivel made the Ruger International, no longer available, a beautiful carbine.

(c) The newest 10/22, the Deluxe Sporter, offers hand checkering on fore-end and pistol grip. Sling swivels. Barrel band is omitted.

Ruger 10/22 Carbine

IN 1964, Ruger introduced a small-caliber companion to the 44 Magnum Carbine. Designated the 10/22, it was and is chambered for the 22 Long Rifle cartridge; the first number refers to the capacity of its unique rotary box magazine. From the "trouble-shooting" standpoint, it is a nightmare. Nothing ever goes wrong with it!

Over the past 8 years I've seen only *one* which required the attention of a gunsmith. That one had a ruined sear, caused by the unwise experimentation of its owner. His amateur surgery was, by the way, unnecessary, as the 10/22 has a rather good trigger pull, considering its semi-automatic action.

Before beginning this article, I dismantled and re-examined my own 10/22, looking for any inherent weakness which might be a possible source of trouble in the future. Finally, in desperation, I asked the manufacturer for an honest answer to an embarrassing question: Were there any particular parts for which they received frequent orders? Here's what Steve Vogel of Ruger had to say:

"Very frankly, the only parts we sell in any quantity for the 10/22 are magazines, scope base adapters and stocks, in that order."

Since the first two items are usually ordered as extras, it would seem that the only thing that ever happens to a 10/22 is the occasional replacement of a busted or marred stock!

For the gunsmith, another disturbing thing about the 10/22 is the reliability of its cartridge feed system.

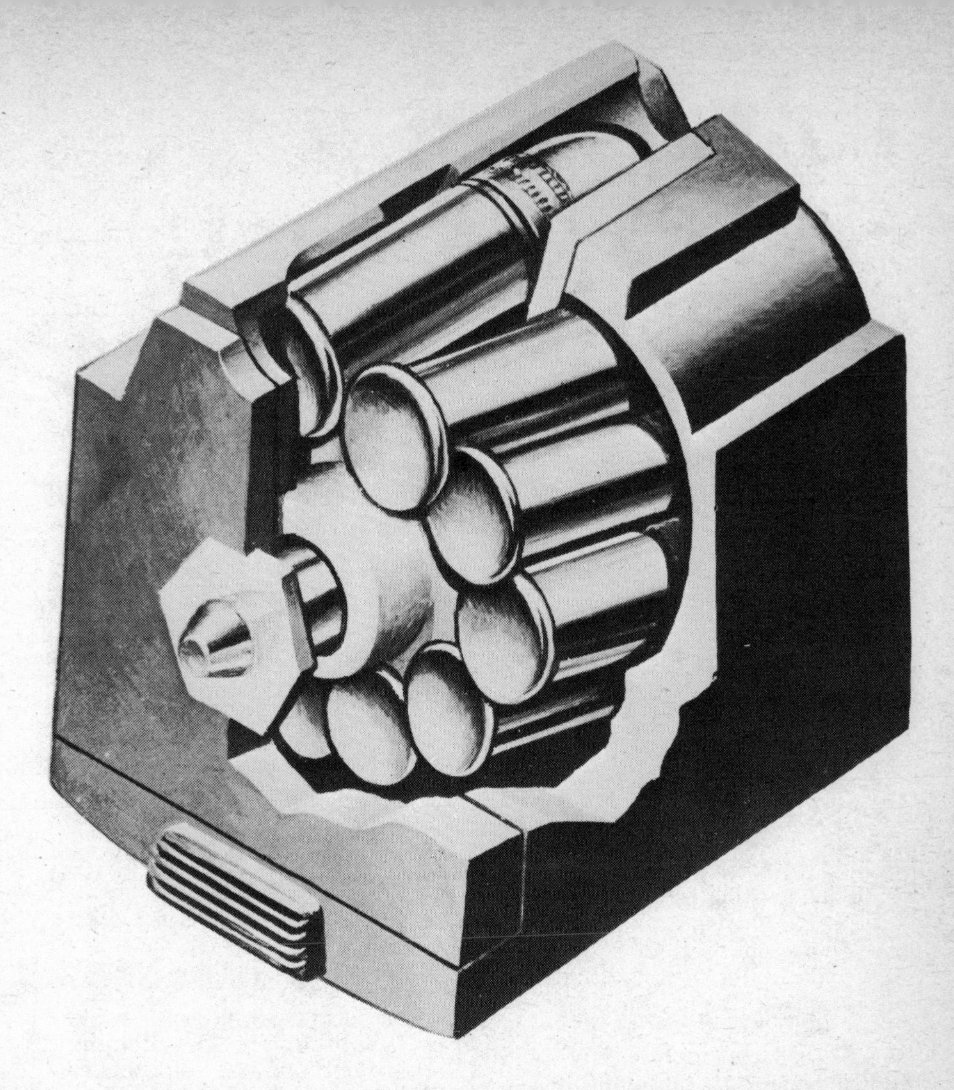

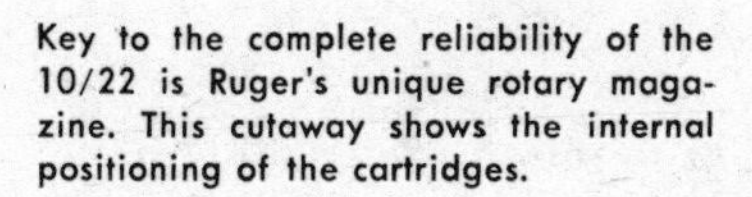

Key to the complete reliability of the 10/22 is Ruger's unique rotary magazine. This cutaway shows the internal positioning of the cartridges.

The detachable box magazine, with its nylon rotary impeller (Ruger calls it the "rotor") delivers cartridges to the steel feed throat regardless of the firing speed. In fact, the 10/22 with a damaged sear, mentioned earlier, was firing full automatic, and would empty the 10-round magazine in one rapid burst, without a single jam!

Gun purists may object to the magazine's non-metallic rotor and body, but I've concluded that its construction is even stronger than if it were made of sheet steel. I can remember, back when the 10/22 was first introduced, seeing a Ruger salesman demonstrate its strength by standing on it, with no harm to the magazine. Try that with a sheet-steel type! Then, too, the magazine "throat," where wear might be expected to occur, is of steel. These compact little magazines sell for only $4.50 each, making it convenient and economical to carry several, preloaded, when hunting or plinking.

The 10/22 has several other good design points: The trigger group contains the entire firing mechanism, except for the bolt and its spring, and includes a high-speed pivoting hammer for fast lock time. The cross-bolt pushbutton safety locks trigger and sear. The barrel is securely held to the receiver by two heavy bolts and a special dovetail block, a very strong and rigid system which aids accuracy. The bolt hold-open lock is designed to require slight retraction of the bolt for release, preventing accidental operation.

Externally, the 10/22 Carbine is almost identical to the 44 Magnum Carbine, weighing only 12 ounces less. Anyone owning the 44 Magnum would benefit from practice shooting with the 10/22, as their handling qualities are quite similar.

The 10/22 has been offered in 4 models, and is currently available in two of these. The basic differences are in style of stock and fittings. The standard carbine has a simple stock design with a barrel band, a curved metal buttplate, and a suggested retail list price of $56.50. The Sporter, now discontinued, had no barrel band, and the stock had a raised comb, full pistol grip, and sculptured finger grooves in the fore-end portion. Sling swivels were included. The International model was available from 1965 to 1969, and in my opinion was the most beautiful 10/22 ever offered. The graceful lines of its full Mannlicher-type stock, with European-style front sling swivel, are pleasing to the eye, and the shooter's forward hand has a choice of positions. It is no longer available, even on special order, and there are no plans to produce it again. The company has never officially revealed exactly how many of this model were made, but I have heard that the number was around 1500. A fairly small amount, as Ruger collectors will be quick to note.

The other currently offered 10/22, the newest in the line, is the Deluxe Sporter. The stock shape follows the same lines as the standard carbine, but lacks the barrel band, has sling swivels, and is supplied with fine hand-checkering on the fore-end and pistol grip. The price is $64.50.

Incidentally, the instruction folder supplied with each new 10/22 is the most complete, most clearly written and understandable information I have seen supplied with a new gun.

Perhaps, after another 8 or 9 years, the 10/22 may develop some quirk which would make it a good subject for *Trouble-Shooting,* but I doubt it. ●

HANDGUN Stopping Power

The ability of the handgun's bullet to act as an effective deterrent in combat or self-defense has been of intense interest for many years—and never more so than today. Here is a carefully researched exploration of various past stopping power formulas, correlated and critically compared.

by KENNETH L. WALTERS

Introduction

THE PROBLEM of calculating handgun stopping power has been of interest to sportsmen and military men for decades. As early as 1927, J.S. Hatcher was proposing an empirical formula for relative stopping power (RSP) based largely on handgun projectile kinetic energy.[1] By 1935 Hatcher had changed his method so that RSP was proportional to projectile momentum.[2] This formula, Hatcher's second, and variations thereof, have been in use to the present day.

Within the past few years several articles have appeared which contain variations of Hatcher's equation[3-5,7] Thus it seems appropriate to re-examine the RSP formula, compare the several implied alterations, and examine their results. Of the three variations discussed, all differ from Hatcher's second formula only in the number of terms sacrificed in the name of computational simplification.

Hatcher's RSP Calculation

For reasons no longer obvious, General Hatcher presented his second RSP calculation in prose only. Thus the first workable formula of which the author is aware appeared in 1972 in the excellent book by M.H. Josserand and J. A. Stevenson.[3] These authors postulated, Equa. (1):

$$RSP = WVAyH$$

where W = bullet weight in grains,
V = initial velocity in feet per second,
A = cross-sectional area in square inches,
y = an empirical bullet-shape factor discussed later,
and H = Hatcher's unit of bullet mass, i.e., Hatcher's Constant.

Hatcher's own work clearly indicates the formula to be that shown above but without the last term, the Hatcher Constant, and using bullet mass, M, instead of bullet grain weight. Unfortunately this equation (Equation 2 below) yields values inconsistent with Hatcher's own pub-

$$RSP = MVAy \quad \text{Equation (2)}$$

lished results. To quote Josserand: "those who endeavor to work a given cartridge through the Hatcher formula (Equation (2) and arrive at a figure for RSP which will correspond to those Hatcher gives in his tables are foredoomed to disappointment; the esteemed general used a unit of mass known only to himself, and did not leave the key to posterity."[3] Josserand, however, successfully back calculated and determined the missing constant to be 0.00000221.

Hatcher's Constant

As it seems difficult to believe General Hatcher deliberately obscured his own calculations, the author has examined Hatcher's constant in detail, and found a nearly four-decade old error. Consider the following steps necessary to convert bullet weight in grains to bullet mass as required by Formula 2. First, convert the bullet weight in grains to the corresponding weight in pounds. For a bullet weighing one grain this is:

1 grain = 1 grain/7000 grains per pound = 0.0001428 lbs. Second, convert the bullet weight in pounds to the corresponding bullet mass. Again, for a one-grain bullet this is:

Equation (3)

$$\text{mass} = \frac{\text{bullet weight in pounds}}{\text{acceleration of gravity}} = \frac{0.0001428 \text{ lbs.}}{32.16 \text{ ft/sec}^2} = 0.00000444 \text{ lbs-sec}^2\text{/ft}$$

This value for the mass of a one-grain bullet is clearly twice Hatcher's constant, and the factor of two comes directly from an error in Hatcher's formula for projectile momentum. Hatcher states: "Note—if the energy and velocity of a bullet are known, the momentum is obtained by dividing the energy by the velocity."[2] The correct expression is obtained, however, by dividing twice the energy by the projectile velocity.[6]

Oddly enough Hatcher's error has been repeated quite recently. Jeff Cooper, in his interesting article "Stopping Power Revisited," states: "General Hatcher's use of mass, measured in pounds divided by twice the constant of gravity...does give us a physically correct measure of momentum in pounds/feet."[4]

As the General may well have known, his error is of no real conse-

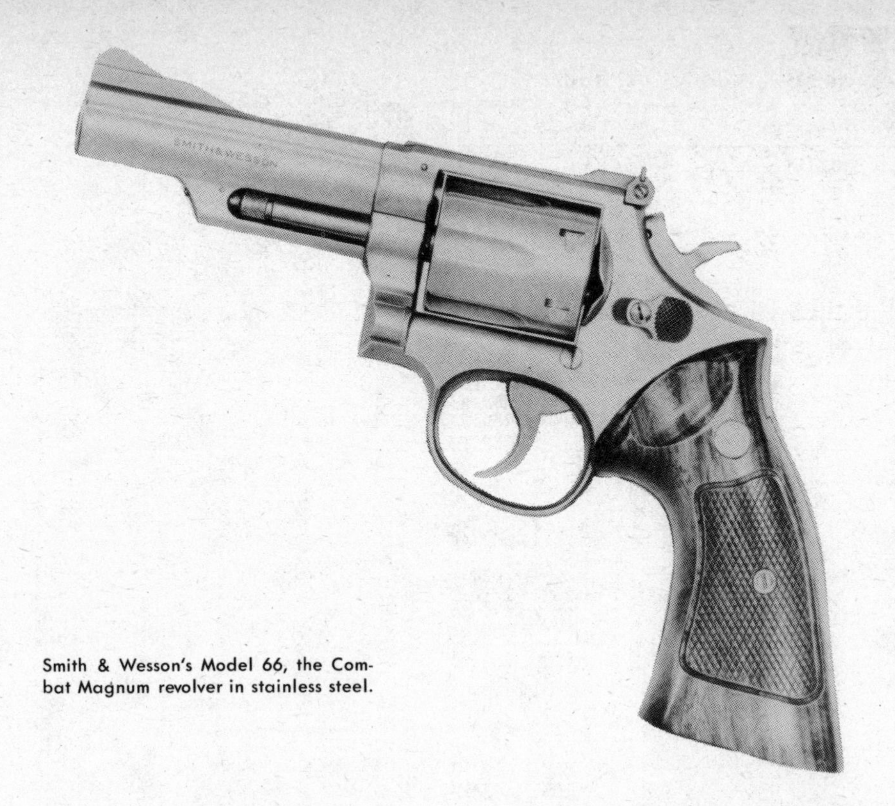

Smith & Wesson's Model 66, the Combat Magnum revolver in stainless steel.

quence. Its net effect is to simply halve an arbitrary multiplier used in his bullet shape factors.

Hatcher's formula as presented by Josserand (Equation (1) is essentially correct. Its only, minor fault is the use of a magical multiplier, H, determined by back calculation. To eliminate this difficulty and for ease in comparisons with the other equations to be discussed, Equation (1) can be rewritten as:

Equation (4)

$$RSP = \frac{1}{2(32.16)} \quad \frac{WV}{7000} \quad A \quad y$$

Alternate RSP Equations

Formulas 4 thru 7, as indicated below, represent the variations of Hatcher's equation, intentionally or otherwise, known to the author. Equations 6 and 7 have been obtained from secondary sources since the author's library does not contain the original works.

$$\text{Hatcher's RSP} = \frac{1}{2(32.16)} \quad \frac{WV}{7000} \quad \frac{A\,y}{} \qquad \text{Equa. (4)}$$

$$\text{Cooper's RSP} = \frac{WV}{10000} \quad \frac{A}{0.102} \qquad \text{Equa. (5)}$$

$$\text{Taylor's KO} = \frac{WV}{7000} \quad \text{Caliber}^{5} \qquad \text{Equa. (6)*}$$

$$\text{Keith's p/ft} \quad \frac{WV}{7000} \quad {}^{5} \qquad \text{Equa. (7)*}$$

*These equations were probably intended for use with rifle data, where the factors omitted from Hatcher's formula are considerably less critical.

Since it seems generally accepted that stopping efficiency of the normal round-nose jacketed 45ACP bullet is twice that of the standard round-nose lead 38 Special bullet, all 4 indicators of stopping power will be used on these two cartridges. The necessary data used are as indicated in the Table and marked by an asterisk. Considering the 38 Special first, Hatcher's method yields 30.10 vs 61.83 for a ratio of 1:2.05. Similarly Cooper's yields 13.35 vs 30.48 (1:2.28), Taylor's 6.79 vs 12.60 (1:1.86), and Keith's 19.07 vs 27.93 (1:1.46).

Effects of Approximations

The main differences between Formulas 4 thru 7 are the increasing number of terms either dropped or approximated. While the author has insufficient references to decide if this is an intentional approximation in Taylor's and Keith's work, it clearly is in Cooper's equation. Consider the following quotes.[4]

"General Hatcher's highly educated guess should be the standard. It was there first, it is as valid as anything we have, and it is everyone's property. ...To repeat, I do not advocate the replacement of the Hatcher Scale. I only suggest that you can do my 'short form' (Equation (5) in your head, while the General's calculations are too cumbersome for that."

To assist in this mental calculation, Cooper provides the A/0.102 ratio worked out for all real cases of interest. His table, however, lists the wrong A value for the 44-caliber case and the A ratio quoted, using either the value presented or the correct one, is also in error.

If the whole point of the various "short forms" of Hatcher's equation is simplification, there is obviously a way of greatly reducing the work in Hatcher's equation without sacrificing any of its inherent value. This can be done by just dropping all the physical conversion factors.

$$RSP = \frac{WVAy}{1,000,000} \qquad \text{Equation (8)}$$

The factor of 1,000,000 is used to more conveniently place the decimal point. This could be done before actual calculation by dividing the bullet-grain weight, bullet velocity, and y values all by 100 each. With this simple task done the formula becomes:

$$RSP = WVAy \qquad \text{Equation (9)}$$

For the two bullet comparisons previously discussed, this equation (or Equation 8), yields identical values of 13.62 vs 27.98 for a ratio of 1:2.05, exactly that predicted by Hatcher's second equation. Regardless of the formula used, the great majority, this author included, will need paper and pencil to do the calculations. Thus there seems to be no real reason for using any approximation technique (such as Equations 5 thru 7) since the price paid is a possible severe loss of accuracy. For these calculations, the reader is advised to use either Equations 1, 4 or 8. All yield the same *relative RSP values* and Equation 8 is particularly nice because no unnecessary conversions are made.

Note that the answer obtained from Equation 9 can be easily converted to those obtained from Equations 1 or 4 by simply multiplying the results by 2.21. Only Equations 1 and 4, however, will directly give RSP results exactly like Hatcher's results.

Expanding Bullets

M.H. Josserand and Jeff Cooper[3,4] have both realized the possible inability of the RSP method in handling expanding bullets. As such handgun projectiles were not even dreamed of in the 1930s, this is more than understandable. It is the author's contention, however, that Hatcher's calculation will work here also. Based largely on the excellent discussion of expanding bullets given by Cooper[4], there seem to be at least two ways to

Descriptive Ballistics Information[1]				Ballistics Information Necessary for Calculations[3]					Handgun Stopping Power[5]				
Cartridge	Barrel Length	Data Source	Bullet (grains)	Velocity (fps)	Area Col. 1	Shape Factor Col. 2	Caliber Col. 3	Product Col. 4[4]	Cooper's RSP	Keith's p/ft	Taylor's KO	Equation 8	Hatcher's RSP
22 LR	2⅛	17	40	860	0.039	1000	0.22	34400	1.32	4.91	1.08	1.34	2.96
	6	3	40	1060	0.039	1000	0.22	42400	1.62	6.06	1.33	1.65	3.65
22 LR H.V.[2]	2⅛	17	37	897	0.039	1350	0.22	33189	1.27	4.74	1.04	1.75	3.86
	6	3	40	1125	0.039	1350	0.22	45000	1.72	6.43	1.41	2.36	5.26
25 ACP	2	3	50	810	0.049	900	0.25	40500	1.95	5.79	1.45	1.79	3.95
32 ACP	4	3	77	900	0.076	900	0.31	69300	5.16	9.90	3.07	4.74	10.48
380 ACP	4⁷⁄₁₆	14	95	925	0.102	900	0.355	87875	8.79	12.55	4.46	8.07	17.83
380 ACP H.V.[2]	4⁷⁄₁₆	14	88	1104	0.102	1350	0.355	97152	9.72	13.88	4.93	13.38	29.57
	3⅞ (assumed)	18	88	1040	0.102	1350	0.355	91520	9.15	13.07	4.64	12.60	27.85
38 Super	5	3	130	1280	0.102	900	0.355	166400	16.64	23.77	8.44	15.28	33.76
9mm Luger	4	3	124	1120	0.102	900	0.355	138880	13.89	19.84	7.04	12.75	28.18
9mm Luger H.V.[2]	4 (assumed)	10	108	1280	0.100	1350	0.355	138240	13.55	19.75	7.01	18.66	41.24
38 Special	2	12	200	572	0.102	1000	0.356	114400	11.44	16.34	5.82	11.67	25.79
	4	15	158	845	0.102	1000	0.356	133510	13.35	19.07	6.79	13.62	30.10
	6	13	158	850	0.102	900	0.356	134300	13.43	19.19	6.83	12.33	27.25
38 Special H.V.[2]	2	11	110	1030	0.100	1350	0.3564	113300	11.11	16.19	5.77	15.30	33.80
	3½	11	110	1135	0.100	1350	0.3564	124850	12.24	17.84	6.36	16.85	37.25
	6	11	110	1295	0.100	1350	0.3564	142450	13.97	20.35	7.25	19.23	42.50
357 Magnum	2½	15	158	1128	0.102	900	0.3564	178224	17.82	25.46	9.09	16.36	36.16
	6	15	158	1298	0.102	900	0.3564	205084	20.51	29.30	10.46	18.83	41.61
	8⅜	3	158	1410	0.102	1100	0.3564	222780	22.28	31.83	11.36	25.00	55.24
357 Magnum H.V.[2]	3½	11	110	1300	0.100	1350	0.3564	143000	14.02	20.43	7.28	19.30	42.66
41 Magnum	6	16	210	972	0.132	1100	0.410	204120	26.42	29.16	11.96	29.64	65.50
	6	16	210	1386	0.132	1100	0.410	291060	37.67	41.58	17.05	42.26	93.40
44 Magnum	6½	3	240	1470	0.146	1250	0.429	352800	50.50	50.40	21.62	64.39	142.29
45 ACP	5	15	230	850	0.159	900	0.451	195500	30.48	27.93	12.60	27.98	61.83
44 Special	3	19	246	1000	0.146	900	0.429	246000	35.21	35.14	15.08	157.88	71.44
	3	19	158	1100	0.146	1250	0.429	173800	24.88	24.83	10.65	154.92	70.10
9mm Police	3.6	20	95	1050	0.102	900	0.355	99750	9.98	14.25	5.06	44.72	20.24
380 ACP	3.6	20	95	984	0.102	900	0.355	93480	9.35	13.35	4.74	41.91	18.97
32 ACP	3.6	20	77	984	0.076	900	0.31	75768	5.65	10.82	3.36	25.31	11.45
22 LR	3.6	20	40	968	0.039	1000	0.22	38720	1.48	5.53	1.22	7.38	3.34
45 ACP	4.4	20	230	804	0.159	900	0.451	184920	28.83	26.42	11.91	129.24	58.48
22 LR Conv. Unit	4.4	20	40	968	0.039	1000	0.22	38720	1.48	5.53	1.22	7.38	3.34

1—Barrel length and velocity measuring devices used affect reported velocity, hence, indirectly, all indices of handgun stopping power indicated.

2—Values reported for stopping power of high velocity expanding bullets should be considered as an absolute upper limit. It is assumed that these bullets arrive on target with sufficient velocity for proper expansion, and that the bullet expands correctly.

3—Cross-sectional bullet area in square inches is represented in equations 1, 2, 4, 5, 8, 9 and 10 by the symbol A and listed in Column 1.

The empirical bullet shape factor is represented in equations 1, 2, 4, 5, 8, 9 and 10 by the symbol y and listed in Column 2.

Bullet caliber as used in Equation 6 is listed in Column 3.

4—Bullet weight times bullet velocity is necessary in all the methods for calculating handgun stopping power. This intermediate result is provided in Col. 4.

5—Cooper's RSP is calculated by multiplying the entry in Column 4 by that in Column 1 and dividing the result by 1020.

Keith's p/ft is calculated by dividing the entry in Column 4 by 7,000. Note the ease in interconverting between Taylor's and Keith's indices.

Taylor's KO is calculated by multiplying the entry in Column 4 by that in Column 3 and dividing the result by 7,000.

Entries in Equation 8 are calculated by multiplying the entry in column 4 by the entries in both Column 1 and Column 2. This result is divided by 1,000,000. Note Equation 8 results are related to Hatcher's values by multiplying the former by 2.21.

Hatcher's RSP is calculated by multiplying the entry in Column 4 by the entries in both Column 1 and Column 2. This result is then divided by 452488.6877 or multiplied by 0.00000221—whichever is considered easier.

---

handle this difficulty.

High-speed expanding bullets depend on two factors in order to effect their increased stopping power. These are, obviously, their increased velocity upon target impact, and the large wound caused by their expansion. Mr. Cooper's contribution to the RSP calculation rests upon his apparent ability to gather data as to the reliability of these expanding bullets when they encounter a human target.

Given this type of data, which some have called "wound ballistics," the RSP equation, Equation 8, could be altered to include the probability of bullet expansion, p, and the expected area increase after contact, A′. This inclusion would modify the RSP equation to:

$$RSP = 2.21\ WVAy\,(1 + pA') \quad \text{Equa. 10}$$

$$\text{where } p = \frac{\text{number of successful bullet expansions}}{\text{total number of cases examined}}$$

$$A' = \frac{\text{total area after contact minus A}}{6A}$$

The factor of 6 in the A′ expression is to limit the size the pA′ term can multiply a given RSP calculation. For a 100% certain bullet expansion p=1.00, its maximum value. Thus if the total area after contact could be expected to be no larger than 2.5A, the 1+pA′ term would yield:

$$\begin{aligned} 1+pA' &= 1+1(2.5A-A)/6A \\ &= 1+A(2.5-1)/6A \\ &= 1+1.5/6 \\ &= 1.25 \end{aligned}$$

This factor of 1.25 coupled with a probably y factor of 1100 produces an Equation 4 type RSP value of 30.11 for the high speed 380 vs 29.57 predicted using y=1350. Thus Equation 10 could predict a RSP value for this cartridge ranging from 24.09 to 30.11, depending solely on the p and A′ values used.

The 2.5A value for total area after contact seems reasonable since this yields a value of 0.102(2.5) or 0.255 for a 38-caliber bullet. This implies that the 38 is approximately 0.57 caliber upon contact. Should this value be too conservative, the 6 could be replaced with something more reasonable.

Such p and A′ values would have to be determined by examination of large amounts of data and would have to be determined separately for each major type of bullet used, i.e., 9mm, 38 Spl., etc.

As an interim method, until accurate p and A′ values can be reliably determined, the author suggests that the RSP equation could be used in its current form, Equation 8 or alternately Equation 4, with the modification that y = 1350 for expanding bullets. With this empirical addition, a deliniation of the y values becomes:

y=900 for jacketed bullets with round nose,
1000 for jacketed bullets with flat points or lead bullets with rounded noses,
1050 for lead bullets with blunt rounded points or with small flat on point,
1100 for lead bullets with large flat on point,
1250 for lead bullets with square point or the equivalent, and
1350 for high-velocity, expanding bullets.

Since the use of this new y value is an attempt to expand Equation 8 to allow for high-speed expanding bullets, if p and A′ values are later determined, the new y = 1350 must be dropped to avoid duplicate correction.

It should be noted that Equation 10 is completely compatible with Equations 1 and 4 for normal, non-expanding bullets assuming the factor of 1,000,000 has been divided out as was done in Equation 9. In Equation 10 both the probability of bullet expansion, p, and the area increase A′ will be very nearly zero, and so the pA′ product will be even closer to zero. Thus the 1+pA′ term will approach unity, yielding an equation equivalent to Equation 4.

Sample Calculations

Since several different calculations are being compared, a tabular arrangement of the data is helpful. One such arrangement is indicated in the Table, which also provides a simplified calculational technique for all the methods discussed.

Hatcher's RSP is calculated by multiplying the entry in Column 4 by the entries in both Column 1 and Column 2. This result is then multiplied by 0.00000221 or divided by 452488.6877, whichever is preferred.

Equation 8 values are calculated by multiplying the entry in Column 4 by the entries in both Column 1 and Column 2. The resulting product is divided by 1,000,000. These values can be converted to Hatcher's RSP numbers by a multiplication by 2.21.

Keith's p/ft results are obtained by dividing the entry in Column 4 by 7,000. Taylor's KO is obtained by multiplying the result of the Keith calculation by the entry in Column 3.

Cooper's RSP is calculated by multiplying the entry in Column 4 by that in Column 1 and dividing the result by 1020.

For the specific case of the 45ACP cartridge discussed earlier and marked with an * in the Table, these computational schemes are worked out below. Note, with the recent revolution in inexpensive electronic calculators, including the Texas Instrument Model TI-3500 used by the author, no real effort is necessary

Equation 8 = Col. 4 (Col. 1) (Col. 2)/1,000,000
= 195,500 (0.159) (900)/1,000,000 = 27.98
Hatcher's RSP = Equation 8 Value (2.21)
= 27.98 (2.21) = 61.83
Keith's p/ft = Col. 4/7,000 = 195,500/7,000 = 27.93
Taylor's KO = Keith's Value (Col. 3) = 27.93 (0.451) = 12.60
Cooper's RSP = Col. 4 (Col. 1)/1020 = 195,500 (0.159)/1020 = 30.48

to obtain the results indicated. Since it is not now possible to accurately evaluate the p and A′ terms in Equation 10, no such results are included in the Table.

For the Sake of Completeness

In addition to the approaches to calculating RSP based on the Hatcher method, two other articles have appeared in recent years dealing with this problem but from an entirely different approach.[8,9] For those who may have seen these works, they are referenced but as yet do not appear to be workable theories from which RSP type calculations can be made.

Conclusions

The real proof of any theory is its ability to stand the test of time. Hatcher's relative stopping power theory has existed for nearly 40 years without ever being successfully challenged. Indeed, its only minor flaw, the non-inclusion of high speed expanding bullets, may be easily overcome by the methods contained herein. ●

References

1. Hatcher, J. S., *Pistols and Revolvers and Their Use,* 1927, Small-Arms Technical Publishing Co., Plantersville, SC.
2. Hatcher, J. S., *Textbook of Pistols and Revolvers,* Ch. 12, 1935, Small-Arms Technical Publishing Co. Plantersville, SC.
3. Josserand, M. H., and Stevenson, J. A., *Pistols, Revolvers, and Ammunition,* Ch. 6, 1972, Crown Publishers, Inc., New York, NY.
4. Cooper, J., "Stopping Power Revisited," 1973 *Guns & Ammo Annual,* pp. 24-29, 1972, Petersen Publishing Co., Los Angeles, CA.
5. Fowler, T., "Knock-Out Values," 1973 *Guns & Ammo Annual,* pp. 312-313, 1972, Petersen Publishing Co., Los Angeles, CA.
6. Resnick, R., and Halliday, D., *Physics for Students of Science and Engineering,* Vol. I, p. 122, Ch. 7, 1962, John Wiley & Sons, Inc., New York, NY.
7. Waters, K., "Ye Compleate Exterior Ballistics," 25th ed. GUN DIGEST, pp. 289-291, 1970, Digest Books, Inc., Northfield, IL.
8. Menck, T. W., "Estimating Bullet Punch," p. 88, *Guns & Ammo,* May 1972, Petersen Publishing Co., Los Angeles, CA.
9. Cooper, J., "Jeff Cooper on Handguns," pp. 56, 78, *Guns & Ammo,* May 1970, Petersen Publishing Co., Los Angeles, CA.
10. "Super-Vel Loading Manual," *Handloader's Digest,* 5th ed., p. 68, 1970, Digest Books, Inc., Northfield, IL.
11. Grennell, D. A., and Williams, M., *Handgun Digest,* p. 41, 1972, Digest Books, Inc., Northfield, IL.
12. Ibidem, p. 43.
13. Ibidem, p. 64.
14. Ibidem, p. 188.
15. Ibidem, p. 36.
16. Ibidem, p. 37.
17. Hargrove, Allen, "Rating 'Panic Pistol' Power," *Guns & Ammo,* November 1972, pp. 48-49, Petersen Publishing Co., Los Angeles, CA.
18. Terrel, Ron, "The .380 Auto Pistols," *Guns & Ammo,* February 1973, pp. 38-44, Petersen Publishing Co., Los Angeles, CA.
19. Hurwitz, Harvey G., "Charter Arms .44 Special Bulldog—The Not Quite Magnum," pp. 24-6, *Gun Sport,* March 1974, Pittsburgh, PA.
20. "SIG-Sauer Presents," an extensive factory pamphlet delineating their new line of double action automatics, available from SIG.

Lighten Those Loads

The rifle calibers in common use today—the 270, 308, 30-06, the several magnums—can't be boosted much by handloading. But all of them can be made more versatile, more pleasant to shoot, the rifle more long lived, through lower-velocity loading.

by H. V. STENT

HOW CAN handloading most help the big-game hunter?

By developing loads with the utmost velocity and power? Many articles emphasize this so much that they're strewn with such warnings as "Too strong for some rifles," and "Work up to with caution," while "Hot" and "Max" are tossed around like confetti at a wedding.

For the few slowpoke cartridges still manufactured, maximum handloads can indeed be rejuvenating. Factory loads with the 450-gr. bullet in the 45-70, for example, amble along at a leisurely 1320 fps; top handloads in strong rifles can jump that to over 1900 or more, safely.

But the most written about rifles in common use—the Magnums and such calibers as the 270, 308, 30-06, which we may call the Mediums—are already factory loaded to high speeds and pressures. You can't boost most of them much more. Trying to do so means more kick and muzzle blast, faster bore erosion and action setback, and risk of real trouble if you use somebody else's Red-Hot Max handload in a rifle that is tighter bored and chambered than the one in which the load was developed.

Admittedly, some lucky shooters seem quite impervious to recoil and muzzle blast, some luckier ones need not worry about how fast they wear a rifle out. No doubt there are also some who relish living dangerously: "Bill nearly blew his head off yesterday with an overload."

Most of us, however, are pretty fussy about safety limits. We use rifles whose factory loads are as potent as we want, and see little profit in striving for an extra 50 or 100 foot seconds of velocity in rifles that are already close to, or over, the 3000 fps mark, and with energy up to two tons.

Turn to *underloads,* however, instead of overloads, and handloading has much greater possibilities. You can make your favorite, or only rifle much more versatile, and shooting it much more fun.

Versatility-Variety

Versatility is important, because we have such a variety of big game in North America. Much the most hunted are deer—average weight, 150-200 pounds, range shot at, mostly under 100 yards, white tail or big ears. Occasional shots go over 100, very few over 200. For this size game at these ranges, the experience of millions of hunters indicates that 30-30 power is about right, and doesn't ruin eatin' meat.

Black bear can be classed right in with deer for size, range, and killing power required.

Antelope are smaller than deer, sheep a bit bigger, goats about the same size but maybe tougher. Ranges for all these are a bit longer, even though shots over 200 yards aren't as common as the inexperienced might think. A bit flatter trajectory and power farther out than the 30-30 offers might be advisable; something between it and the Mediums. Not that these aren't splendid rifles for such animals, but they do have a surplus of power for such game at ordinary ranges.

Addicts of bigger boomers may bristle at that "surplus of power" bit, but the 270 and 30-06 have been used with solid satisfaction on moose and elk for 48 and 67 years respectively. Newer members of the club, such as the 308, 280 Remington and 284 Winchester, as well as the oldest of them all, the 7x57, are in the same power class.

Now elk weigh up to 1000 pounds, moose go up to 1200 generally, and in Alaska up to nearly 1800. Any rifle powerful enough for them must have a surplus of power for deer-sized game. Conversely, if you demanded for moose the same power-weight ratio as the 30-30 has for deer, Roy Weatherby's biggest shoulder-buster would be barely enough! No wonder that, for animals of this size, including the big polar grizzly, and Alaskan brown bears, some hunters like to carry such Magnums as the 7mm Remington, the various 300s, the 338 Winchester, 350 Norma and 375.

To use Magnum power on deer, however, is about like jumping into a 3-ton truck to tool down to the neighborhood supermarket for a pound of hamburger; and that same hamburger will be a lot nicer meat than the black bloody mess you're apt to get if you shoot a little 150-pound deer at 50 yards with a cartridge powered to macerate a moose at 400!

Whether you use Magnum or Medium, it's logical to load *down* for deer. Down to around 30-30 levels should be okay; about 2400 fps for 140/150-gr. bullets, 2200 for 170/180-gr. Go higher if you wish, but not much or you'll start getting the black hamburger effect.

To get flatter trajectory and longer range for sheep, goat, or antelope shooting, somewhere around 2600-2800 fps with 130/150-gr. bullets, according to caliber should do well enough.

On the big stuff—elk, moose, large bear—many Magnum owners will want to use full factory power. So will many users of Mediums. Funny thing is, they have considerably less power than the Magnum men, yet are generally quite satisfied with it. With some reason, too. The 7x57 is about the lightest of the Mediums, yet its 175-gr. bullet at only 2300 fps or so has killed tens of thousands of Africa's biggest animals, including thousands of elephants. Did we say "big stuff?" As far as range is concerned, Jack O'Connor has killed elk at 600 yards with his beloved 270 and 130-gr. bullets.

Most of us haven't the skill to justify shooting at elk at more than half that range. On moose, most shots come at ordinary woods ranges—25 to 150 yards. We could load down both Magnums and Mediums to the old 7x57 level, and still be adequately gunned for the nearest to elephants we have in North America. Too, we could always carry in belt or pocket a few full-power loads for that rare but dreamed-of long shot across a lake, burn or canyon. Far-seen game does not usually hurry away, and there's time to both change cartridges and adjust your sights.

Why Light Loads?

Why use lighter loads? To be sporting. To have more challenge for one's hunting skill, like the lads who hunt with bows and arrows. More importantly, perhaps, to have more comfortable, more accurate shooting.

An awful lot of shooters are not comfortable with full power loads, even in Mediums. To expert shots in constant practice, that may seem hard to believe, but to the common casual hunter who fires his big game rifle only a few times a year, even the 16-odd pounds of back-push and moderate crack of the 270 are disturbing. The higher he goes up the scale, to 20 pounds for the 308 and 30-06, 24 for the 7mm Remington Magnum, 30-up for the 300s and 338, and 44 for the 375, the more objectionable recoil and muzzle blast become.

True, even a Magnum's hefty bump and boom may pass unnoticed in the excitement of shooting any big game animal. But when it comes to firing in cold blood at a target or other mark, for sighting in or practice, the ordinary hunter feels his shoulder punched, his cheekbone jarred, his ears assaulted—and he doesn't like it. He's apt to shy away from all further practice, or develop a flinch, or both.

Either way, he's going to shoot poorly, to miss or wound game he should have dropped. I've heard guides grumble about clients missing moose and deer at 50 yards with all the time in the world to aim. "Couldn't hit a bull's behind with a bagful of buckshot!" One hunter in southern Alberta messed up so many shots with his fine scoped 300 Magnum that his guide set up a target on a 2-foot square backboard and told him to try for the bull at 100 yards. He missed the whole board, and there are many more like him.

Most hunters just aren't good enough marksmen, chiefly through lack of practice, to shoot big game effectively at more than moderate ranges. They don't need far-reaching cartridges and, whether they admit it or not, they don't like kick and muzzle blast. I'm convinced that thousands of shooters would flinch less and practice more, be deadlier on game and enjoy shooting a great deal more if they used lighter loads.

Low Load Data Big Game

For specific low-load data consult any of the good reloading handbooks (Lyman, Speer, Hornady, et al), but if they don't go low enough for the deer loads mentioned, you can start off by buying a can of DuPont or Hodgdon 4895, and load 40 grains of it with the 130-gr. bullet in the 270, the 139-gr. in 280 or 284, the 150-gr. in the 308 or 30-06. If you want to use the 170-gr. 30-30 bullet in either of those last two, 40 grains will still be fine in the 30-06, but cut it down to 36 in the shorter 308.

For the 7mm Remington and 300 H&H Magnums, 44 grains of the same powder will push 139- and 150-gr. bullets, respectively, at around 2500, but the Winchester 300 Magnum needs 50 grains. The 170-gr. bullets could use 43 grains in the H&H, 47 in the Winchester.

Whatever load you select, try a few at the target first thing. If they don't suit you, increase or decrease the powder load by a grain or half-grain at a time until you get what you like.

For farther-reaching loads for antelope, geep and shoats—sorry, sheep and goats—dipping into the same bucket of 4895 for 42 grains will send the 130-gr. bullet of the 270 zipping along at 2700. In case you think that's not much of a zip, it'll carry out to about 350 yards before dropping to the approximately 1800 fps which killed Jack O'Connor's elk at 600 yards.

Forty-four grains for the 139-gr. bullet in 280 and 284, and 150 for the 308s, will give much the same speed. It takes 46 grains to boost a 150-gr. bullet to around 2700 fps. in the 30-06, 50 in the 300 H&H Magnum, 52 in the 300 Winchester, while the 7mm takes 48 behind its 139- or 140-gr. bullet.

When it comes to lighter-than-factory loads for moose, elk and big bears you'll probably use heavier bullets. If you want to keep using 4895, 42 grains will get you 2600 fps with a 150-gr. bullet in the 270, 41 will propel the 175-gr. at the old 7x57 speed of 2300 or a little better in the 280 or 284, and ditto the 180-gr. in the 30-06. In the 308, 39 grains will do the trick with the 180-gr. bullet. In the Magnums, try 43 for the 7mm, 47 for the 300 H&H, 49 for the 300 Winchester—these giving around 2400 with 175-gr. or 180-gr. missiles.

You don't have to use 4895, of course, if you can find equivalents in other powders; with the heavier bullets 4895 is not as good as some others, such as 4350. You'll probably find that the mildest loads in the handbooks come as low as you want with the heavy bullets, too; consult them, including Norma's. If you're using a 7x57, refer to a handbook for *all* loads, as its case hasn't the capacity of others mentioned.

Low Load Data Small Game-Varmints

So much for lighter loads in big game. But hold on, folks, don't go away. Two or more other whole fields lie open in the big, wide, wonderful world of handloading.

Varmint loads, for instance. Load light bullets to whatever speed suits your notions and shooting ability. Few need more speed and flatness than 3000 fps provides, and many will be happy with less. I've had fun on groundhogs with the 125-gr. Sierra bullet in 30 caliber at 2500 fps.

In all 30 calibers the 110-gr. bullets, too, are fine for varmints, likewise the short-coated 100-gr. Plinkers made by Speer and Hornady, probably the cheapest jacketed bullets you can buy. Speer quotes up to 3300 fps for them in a 300 Magnum, and I've used them as low as 1000 fps in the smaller 30s. You'll probably have to experiment a bit to find the best combination of speed and accuracy for you, but it's all good practice. Indeed, mild-recoiling light-bullet loads can turn target practice with a big rifle from a pain to a pleasure, and accuracy can be superb.

Plinkers are also for plinking: shooting at tin cans, bits of wood, and other casual marks, or at pests at moderate ranges. This is the sort of fun-shooting that makes 22 rimfires so popular, and high-powered rifles can be loaded down to 22 velocities for the same uses. First critter I ever shot with a big game rifle was a jack-rabbit with a plinking load in a 30-06, and the thrill of it is with me still.

Unfortunately, DuPont no longer makes 4759, a powder especially useful for very light rifle loads, though they are considering reviving it.* Hercules' Unique is still available, however, and in Mediums try 8-10 grains of it behind such light bullets as the 90- or 100-gr. in the 270, 120-gr. in the 28s, 100 or 110 in the 30s. Or heavier ones if they're handier. It'll give you around 1000-1600 fps velocity.

In the big Magnum cases such a tiny load would be as lost as a mouse dropped in the desert, so use another good Hercules powder, No. 2400. Twenty-four grains of it should give you somewhere around 1500 fps.

Warning. Unique and 2400 are fast-burning powders, types that build up pressure in a hurry. Never load the same weights of them as of rifle powders; make sure you never put a double portion in one case. The amounts mentioned are just starters, of course, but don't vary them more than a few grains without consulting a handbook. Put a full load of Unique into a rifle case and you could wind up minus a rifle—or your head!

Sight Settings-Accuracy

With any less-than-factory-power loads you will find that the bullets don't land on the target where factory loads do. Usually they hit several inches lower. That doesn't matter for group shooting, which is the best test of the accuracy of different loads, but when you settle on one, you'll probably want to set your sights so the load hits center. That means, as mentioned before, a sight adjustment in the hunting field if you want to switch from a low load to a full-power one.

There are tricks to this. By trying various combinations you may be able to work out, say, a rather light deer load and a pretty strong moose load that shoot fairly close to the same center; I've recently done this with a 284. Or a woods-range load that shoots close to the mark at 100 yards and a long-range load that centers at 300 with the same sight setting.

Scopes with two horizontal crosshairs, or crosshair with post(s) offer two different aiming points. Some iron aperture sights have a quick-release button that enables you to carry the sights raised for light loads and at a touch drop it to full-power setting. Also, I've used the bottom of the front sight when using a plinking load for grouse and the top or bead when shooting full-power loads.

If you have accuracy difficulties with the very light plinking loads, it could be lack of uniformity in measuring the powder, but it could also be because this little bit of powder is sliding around in the case like mercury on a tray. My own remedy for this is to take a 1-inch or so square of toilet paper, fold it to fit the case, and tamp it very lightly down on the powder to hold it close to the primer.

The lighter the loads you use, the longer your cartridge cases will last for reloads, and the only handicap to their cheapness is the cost of the bullets. But something can be done about that too. It may not be your particular bag, but a lot of handloaders have found that casting their own bullets is a whole fascinating hobby in itself. Instead of paying 4 to 10 cents each for jacketed bullets, you can cast your own for a couple of pennies apiece. If you can scrounge lead cheap and beg some old linotype plates from a printing office for hardening, you may get down below rimfire ammo costs.

Lyman's new handbook on cast bullets gives full details on bullet casting, and lists lots of loads. Some of them go up to 2200 fps with good weight bullets, so they're not just for plinking.

If you have reloading tools and haven't tried underloads, you may, as the actress said to the bishop, be missing half the fun. And if you haven't started reloading yet—good heavens, man, you're missing it all! ●

*Happily, 4759 is again available and a new DuPont booklet lists numerous loads for it, in a variety of calibers. DuPont-made 4831, introduced in 1973, is also covered.

Your Deer is Down, What Next?

A lot of money and hard work goes into bagging a deer, yet relatively few hunters know what to do when it comes to field dressing their kill and getting it to a freezer.

With venison carrying a high price tag on the retail market, every hunter should avoid the risk of spoilage by learning the proper dressing and handling procedures.

Clumsy knife work during gutting results in a punctured bladder or entrails. A dull knife can make a mess of the job. Delayed cooling of the carcass can affect the texture and taste of the meat.

Essential equipment includes a sharp knife, plastic bags for carrying out the heart and liver, and a rag for wiping the carcass clean once the job is finished.

A difference of opinion seems to exist on two phases of field dressing a deer—slitting the throat to facilitate bleeding and removing scent glands from the legs to prevent contamination of the meat.

According to some, both procedures are necessary. Anyone who has gutted a deer, however, knows that internal bleeding leaves little room for the throat-cutting ritual. As for the scent glands, if you don't touch them, you won't contaminate the meat when you attend to the field dressing. That's the only way scent can be transferred to the meat.

Basic eviscerating procedure begins with freeing the anus to slitting the abdomen full length and emptying the body cavity. Draining the cavity and wiping it clean completes the job, but not until the heart and liver are tucked away in plastic bags. These are delicacies, so don't discard them.

Two mistakes are common at this point. One calls for washing out the cavity with water, which only softens the flesh and encourages bacterial growth. The other involves transporting the carcass on the hood of the car, where proper cooling can be delayed by the hot engine. The car roof is better, and the trunk is best—as long as it's legal.

Immediate removal of the hide following arrival at your destination is recommended. Find a local butcher to cut up the carcass or at least instruct you as to how it should be done.

Don't be careless or indifferent with any phase of the operation, from the time the deer is down to the time it has been cut up and packaged for the freezer. It has cost you a sizable sum of money in the first place, and a sloppy job could turn an otherwise delicious meal into a disaster. ●

JOHN NELSON COOPER

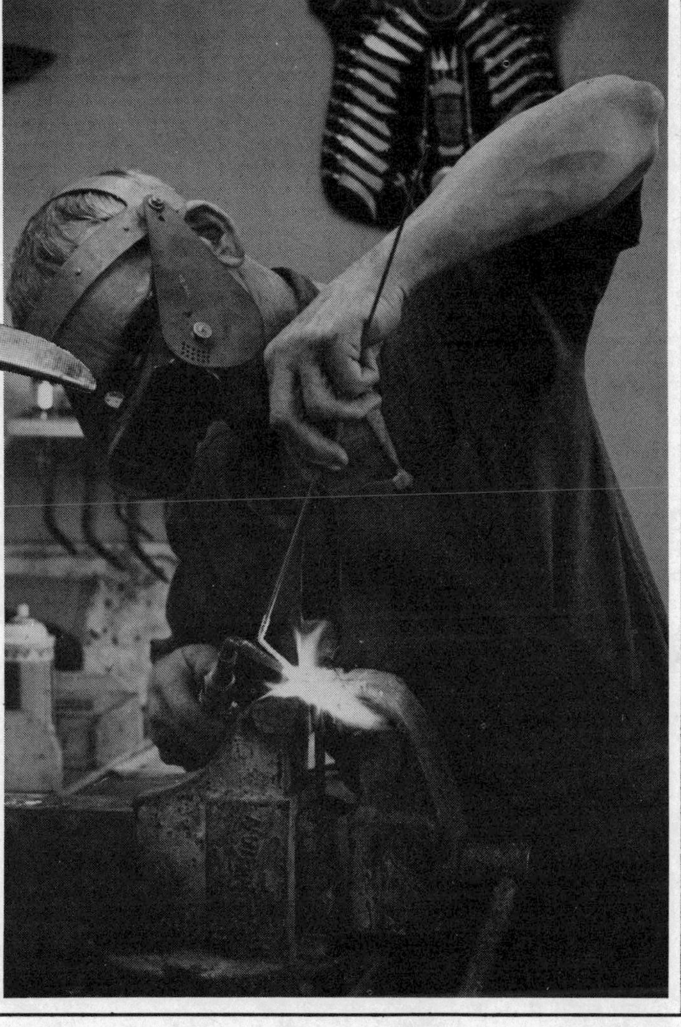

Heart of the Cooper knife is the bonding of blade, hilt and handle into one patented unit, a process developed by Cooper over 40 years ago. Here Cooper is brazing the cartridge brass hilt to the blade, the result a completely sealed hilt. No blood or acids can build up in that area.

-veteran knifemaker

Text and illustrations by Walter L. Rickell

Guaranteed for the life of the original buyer, Cooper blades are famous for their edge-holding quality. Here's how they're made, entirely by hand, under two U.S. patents.

A full custom blade, made by Cooper from a customer's wooden model. Note sawtooth spine and sweeping handle.

THE CUSTOM KNIFE, in the past few years, has really come of age. So many new makers have hit the scene that you can hardly count 'em. Many of them, of course, are merely jumping on the moneywagon, fellows who've been making knives for only a few months or so. Many of their blades look good, especially to the eye of the layman, but that old adage, "beauty is only skin deep" surely applies in numerous cases. One maker to whom this does not apply, a man who has been making knives since 1921, is John Nelson Cooper. His knives are not only good looking, but eminently serviceable and long lasting.

The Cooper knife is different, too, in its construction. Made under two U.S. patents (3,481,038 and 3,595,104) it is guaranteed for the lifetime of its owner as long as it is used for its de-

Shown here is the model used by Cooper to gain his two U.S. patents. Top is the bandsawed steel blade with the tang arc-welded into place and the rough shaped brass hilt. Next below, the hilt in place, with the brazing shown between blade and hilt. Also shown is the Micarta handle material and the brass butt cap. Third, the rough shaped knife. Next, the semi-finished knife with major shaping completed. Last, the finished, polished knife. The style shown is Cooper's Apache fighting knife • Some of Cooper's blades, all made via his patented methods. 1, boot; 2, special dagger, only 4½" over-all; 3, special Comanche with hollow-tube handle; 4, Siskiyou Papoose; 5, Mini-Bowie; 6, Siskiyou; 7, Osage; 8, California hunter; 9, Iron Mistress; 10, Attack/Survival with hollow handle for first aid or survival gear.

signed purpose. The Cooper method achieves a solid, 100% bonding of blade, hilt and handle; corrosive effects of blood and acid build-up around the hilt cannot weaken the tang. This commonly ruins the best of handmade and commercial blades, built by standard methods.

Cooper blades, all made by the stock-removal method, are of high carbon tool steel. They hold an edge far longer than many other well-known knives. No special secrets or gimmicks are used, just high quality materials and the knowledge and ability that has been his for almost 50 years.

The *only* handle material Cooper uses is Micarta, a phenolic-resin linen long used in the electrical industry. Introduced to it in 1942, while serving in the Army, he found it more stable and long lasting than wood, hard rubber, lucite, antler, bone or leather.

Here's how Cooper makes a knife: After bandsawing the blade to the design profile selected, a bolt of the same high quality steel is arc-welded to the blade, forming the tang. Then a cartridge brass hilt is fitted, brazed into place on the blade. Next, a temporary handle is attached and the basic grinding and shaping completed. Now the blade is heat treated to correct hardness, so it will hold that long-lasting Cooper edge, the Micarta handle is epoxied into place and the butt cap screwed home under very heavy pressure. (Only Micarta, Cooper feels, would hold up under such force.) Now the knife is carried through to a semi-finished or 90% state through a series of grinders, reaching its ultimate shape through sight, sound and rhythm. No jigs or guides are used, thus each knife is an individual piece, even though nominally the same model and design. After this come the final touches—shaping, polishing and sharpening, done on a series of abrasive belts.

John Nelson Cooper made his first real knife when he was 15. Before that he'd carved them from wood, his love of the art born in him. Those first blades were not the kind he makes today, to be sure. They were types familiar to a young Pennsylvania coalminer, such as kitchen, butchering and paring knives. It wasn't until 1929 that he made his first hunting blade, but from this small beginning he's developed the complete line available today, all bearing the Cooper eagle and all of the superb quality it stands for. •

John Nelson Cooper at the wheel on one of the many grinding operations used in making these handcrafted knives. The stock-removal method is used exclusively.

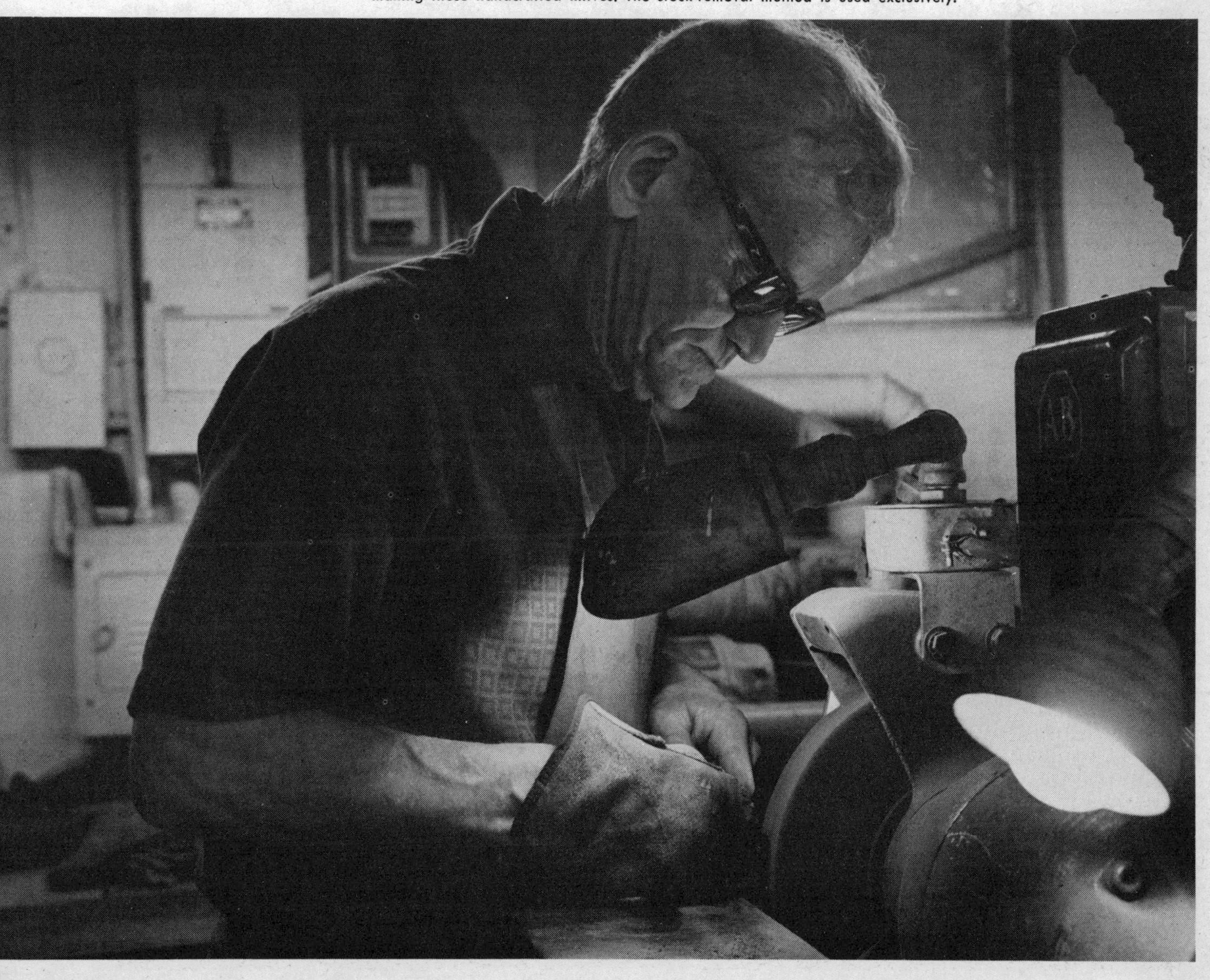

KNIVES

Nolen Knives

Jim Nolen and his brother started making knives about 1972, first as a part-time activity, then as a virtually full-time effort. Catering primarily to hunters wanting exceptionally handsome working knives, some of the 15-odd knives they make will surely appeal to collectors also. The knife I have is made from D-2 steel, a high-carbon, chrome-moly steel, which, though not a stainless steel, is highly rust resistant and tough. Nolen knives are completely handmade in their shop and to the customer's order. D-2 steel won't take a "show" polish, but it looks damn handsome to me. My handle is of tigertail maple, but they offer almost anything a man could ask for. The handsome finish comes from well-rubbed linseed oil.

The Nolens say they don't design their knives for beauty but for practical use—perhaps they look so good because that's often the result of good basic design. Jim Nolen also said that "a knife isn't really good unless it truly fits the user's hand." Well, mine fits my hand like a Purdey fits the shooter it was made for.

A four-color brochure is available for a stamped, large envelope, showing all types offered. Prices start at about $50 and go to $150 for the big Bowie blades. Write to Nolen Knives, Box 6216, Corpus Christi, TX 78411.

Roger Barlow

The Knife Collectors Club

A.G. Russell's organization has taken off—membership has grown greatly in just a few years, and the $9.50 fee lets your membership run indefinitely. Special bulletins—offering new models of all kinds, often at good discounts—are mailed 8-10 times a year. Other benefits accruing include a "full and prompt refund" policy, no questions asked. Write to the Club at 1705 Highway 71, North, Springdale, AR 72764 for complete information.

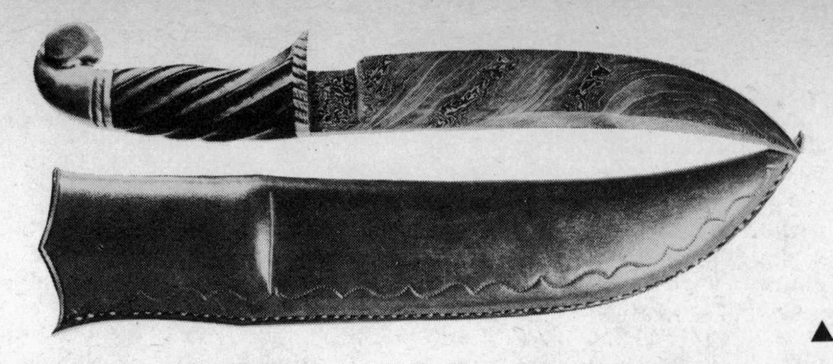

Heritage Custom Knives

Pictured here are the 8 well-made knives comprising the Heritage line today, the two engraved blades done by Bryson Gwinnell. From left, their Adirondack model in 4 forms—Standard, Deluxe, Custom and Presentation ($75 to $195); next, the 4 Sid Bell Skinners in grades as before, their prices $65 to $185. Numerous options are available, and all Heritage Knives are serialized, registered in the owner's name, and sold with a lifetime guarantee.

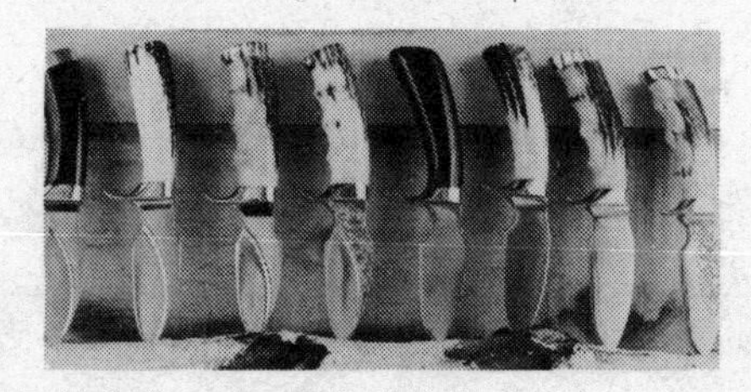

Clyde Fischer

The handsome knife shown here was made for your editor early in 1975—and it's a highly functional, excellently done specimen of Fischer's high skills. Just over 9" long, the $\frac{1}{8}$"-stock blade is 4$\frac{7}{8}$" long, the finger-grooved handle a fancy-figured piece of Texan mesquite. All trim is brass, including an oval name plate let into the top of the handle. The butt cap carries a well-carved head of the hunter's patron, Saint Hubertus.

Clyde is going to call this pre-production sample the Boar Hunter, or something like that.

Wm. F. Moran, Jr.

After much research, extensive experimentations and tireless efforts, Bill Moran has learned to recreate the famous Damascus steels of centuries ago. An over-simplified explanation would be to call these layered or laminated steels (which they are, in fact), but that begs the question of *how* they're made. Moran will send you a full page treatment on the process as he does it, but much is left unsaid, as he notes.

I'm looking at an 8x10 photo that reveals the delicate flow of the Damascus pattern, the wavy light and dark cloud-like tones to be seen, and I wish I could reproduce this picture in full size or larger. Still, I hope you can get some idea of what a blade made of 512 layers looks like. The knife pictured has a 9" blade, mounted in brass with a spirally-fluted rosewood handle inlaid with silver wire. The sheath is of wood, covered with 11-oz. leather.

As Moran says, his Damascus blade knives require a very long time to complete, so he can only make about ten a year. That—and the high risk of having to scrap a 99% completed blade—explains the high cost of such knives, about $1,200 and more.

Moran is a unique craftsman, working alone in unique ways to produce blades of a quality unsurpassed. His story is well worth writing for.

Naifeh Knives

A metalsmith for many years (gold, silver, etc.), Woody Naifeh started making his rather unusual pocket knives in 1969. At the start these all-handmade pocket knives had only brass handles, but he's now offering them with stainless steel or sterling silver handles, and with tool steel or SS blades and springs. These well-made knives, simple and elegant, cost $40 to $65. Write for Naifeh's leaflet and information on other models.

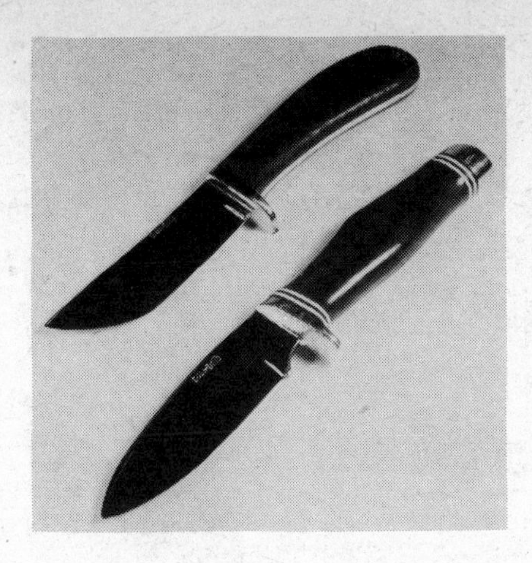

Dan-D Custom Knives

Made by Dan Dennehy—one of the most rugged of individuals and a founding member of the Knifemakers Guild—the knives pictured are his ProSkinner No. 2 (at top), the 4" blade of 3/16" stock and a full tang type with Micarta slab handles. The other is Dan's Drop Point No. 3-B, the tang concealed, with Micarta handles and a butt cap fitted. Dan's big 48-page catalog sells for $1, and it's well worth it.

Harvey McBurnette

This well-known blade maker, entirely self-taught, produces a variety of good looking, yet fully serviceable knives. Now he's developed another skill, also without instruction—the art of etching. The American Bicentennial Bowie-type pictured is 16 1/4" over-all, the D-2 steel stock 1/4" thick, and etched on it are the Battle of Bunker Hill on one side and the Liberty Bell on the other. Both scenes are very well done, and these limited-issue stickers will cost about $1,000.

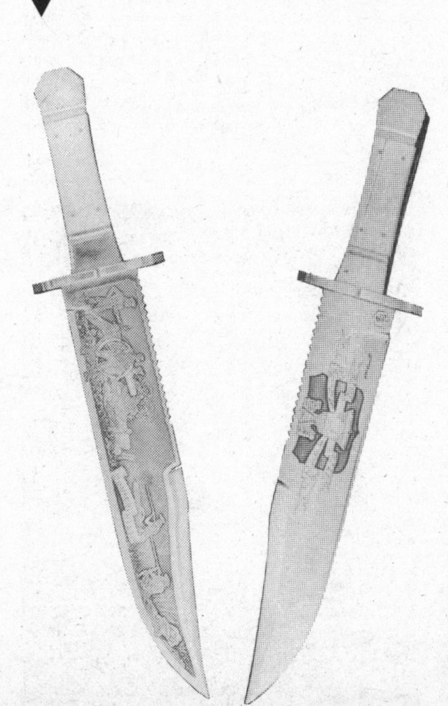

L. E. (Red) Brown

Red calls the top knife pictured his heavy-duty skinner, these about $45. The two blades at bottom are new with Brown—both miniatures, one is a skinner type, the other in Bowie form. Both are part of a 4-knife set, the others a standard type and a broad skinner, price for the set $100.

W.C. Wilber

I suggest you write for this custom knifemaker's literature, for reading it will show you what makes a dedicated craftsman, and how he got that way. A full-time cutler, he works unassisted, and every blade he sends out carries his no-time-limit guarantee. His knives are of full-tang type, tapered to 1/16" for lightness, and made of 440-C stainless steel. A broad range of scales are offered, including fancy woods, plus engraving (usually by Hans Pfeiffer), scrimshawing or etching. The knife shown is Wilber's Model SG, a small game type with its 4" blade hand-worked on the back, a $20 option over the $90 regular price.

John J. Schwarz

A long-time custom gunsmith, Schwarz has also been making knives for well over 30 years, all blades hand forged. He can make almost any knife required, up to short swords, and of best quality steels, standard or stainless. The folding knife shown is a heavy-duty locking type, now made with blades of 3 5/8", 4 1/2" or 5 1/8", these $50 each. Send 50¢ for Schwarz's brochure, showing his sheath type hunters and combat knives.

Heinrich H. Frank

There is no question at all that Frank makes the handsomest folding knives seen anywhere, and I can only hope that the photograph reproduced here lets you see just how brilliantly done they are. The blades pictured show his Large and Small Capers and Skinners, plus the pocket knives. Frank's price range runs from $225 to $500, and his delivery time is about two years. His well-illustrated catalog is $1.

Michael Collins

A specialist custom maker, Collins offers hand carved scrimshawed ivory handles on his blades—your design(s) or his—besides making conventional blades to customer order. Write for details and prices.

Zack Knives

Don Zaccagnino makes a big variety of custom knives, all excellent examples of high craftsmanship, and his photos are so good I wish I had space for several. However, 4 of his styles are shown, these being (from the top) the No. 23 Caper, No. 17 Lil Skinner, No. 21 Outdoorsman and No. 12, Eagle Custom. Zack has a new catalog ready, yours for $1, and I'd get one.

GRAVERMEISTER

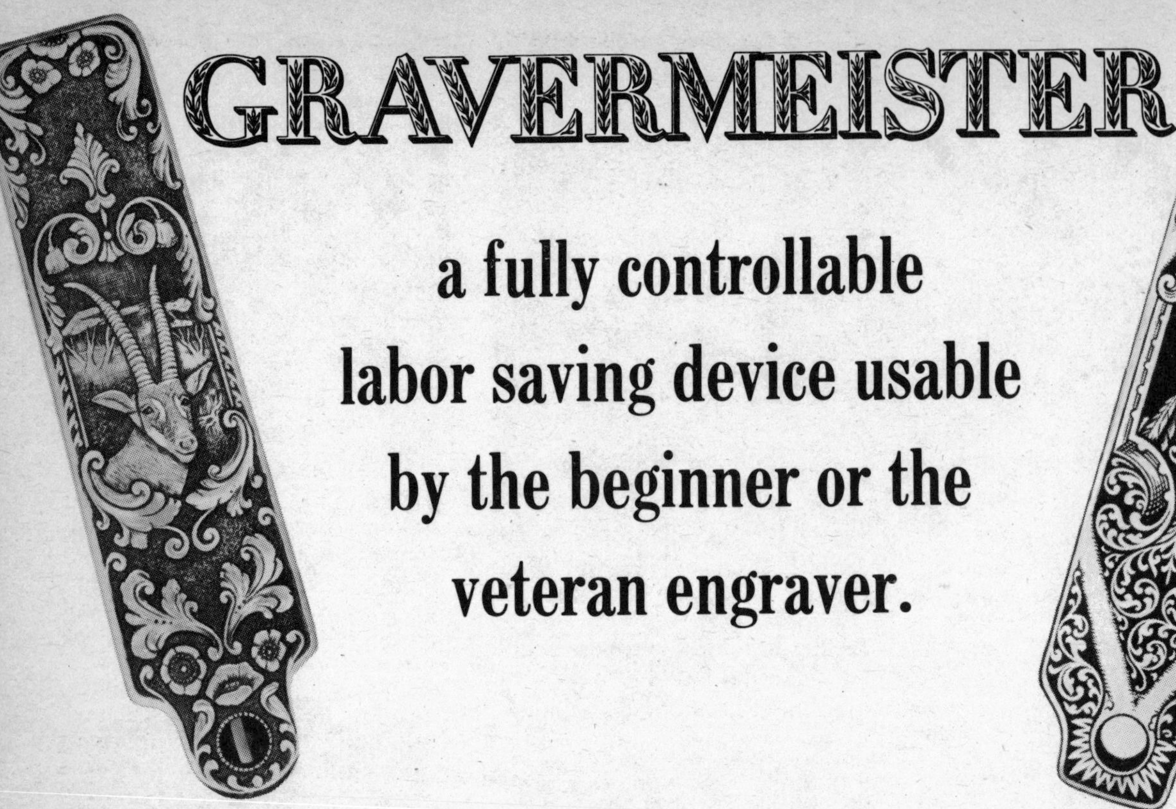

a fully controllable labor saving device usable by the beginner or the veteran engraver.

A Springfield floorplate done in high relief, an example shown in the book *The Art of Engraving* by James B. Meek.

A Springfield floorplate with the Indian done in high relief by James B. Meek. An example shown in his book *The Art of Engraving*.

by THOMAS H. RIKER

WHEN A GUN FANCIER thinks about the process of engraving, what does his mind conjure up? I've always pictured a craftsman diligently bent over a Colt revolver or Purdey shotgun transforming polished steel into masterpieces of scrolls and figures. He would be holding either a hand burin or a hammer and graver. Either method requires infinite control to carve the metal. This means that even before the artistic work begins, the beginning engraver must devote months and even years to learning to cut smooth, bright lines and curves. He may then progress to mastering the art of layout and anatomy. Many budding engravers never reach this point due to the arduous task of learning tool control. Unfortunately, this learning progression has existed since the first engraver laid chisel to steel.

Now there's a machine available that is revolutionizing the mechanics of engraving. Larry Wilson, head of A.A. White Engravers, once commented that the one tool available which could replace the traditional hammer and graver is the American-made Gravermeister. More and more U.S. engravers are using this useful machine, and they've been bought by several European and U.S. gunmakers. No question, the Gravermeister is a valuable addition to the craft.

I learned of this machine by accident. For years I'd been fascinated by examples of engraving found in books and on friends' cherished guns. I kept telling myself that one day I would try my hand at this magic art but I never got up enough nerve to take the plunge. Then, one day, while leafing through the big Bob Brownell catalog, wishing I had one of everything in it, I came across the Gravermeister. As described, this machine might be just what I was unconsciously waiting for. I called GRS in Boulder, Colorado, makers of the Gravermeister, and made an appointment with their John Rohner for a demonstration. That demonstration decided me—if I was ever going to engrave this was the way to go.

The Gravermeister is a brainchild of Rohner and his partner, Don Glaser—examples of their engraving have appeared in the GUN DIGEST over the years. Rohner began engraving as a hobby in 1953, using the standard tools of the trade.

After a few years and a few hundred pounds of scrap metal, Rohner could pretty much predict the results of his efforts. For the next 3 years he worked in much the same manner, except that now his results began to compare with some of the professionals. Then, in 1958, Rohner concluded that there had to be a better way.

Don Glaser is a mechanical engineer and machine designer who holds over 100 U.S. and foreign patents in the graphic arts industry. Many of them relate to such pneumatic systems as the one used in the Gravemeister. He designed the Gravermeister to reduce manual labor, to speed the work, and to make it possible for a beginner to start engraving without having to spend the long time required to learn precise hammer control.

Essentially the machine is an air-operated hammer capable of delivering controlled impacts at speeds of from 800 to 1200 strokes per minute. The speed of the stroke is varied by positioning a sliding arm. The impact force is controlled by depressing or releasing a foot pedal. Because of

The GRS Magnablock, a precision holding device with features found in no other engraving block.

The DG 3 sharpening fixture for use with the Gravermeister.

All precious metal inlaying may be performed, from cutting the back ground away to hammering the metal into place and sculpting the figures, if any. Although the Gravermeister was designed for metal engraving it may also be used for woodworking, ivory carving, bronze chasing, die cutting, print making, numerous jewelry operations, etc. The Gravermeister handpiece holds any kind of tool with a shank up to ¼″ in diameter. As you can see, this allows the machine to be used for hundreds of applications, many of which are still undiscovered.

All of the examples of fine engraving shown in this article were done exclusively with the Gravermeister, including the gold inlays.

There is some resistance to the Gravermeister—some engravers contend that the end result cannot be considered a "work of art" because a machine was used. I cannot agree with this. The planning, layout and execution of the work is the same. The Gravermeister simply eliminates most of the physical exertion needed to make the cuts. Given sufficient time, a technician can be trained to cut lines and arcs with the machine or with a graver and hammer—this doesn't make him an engraver. To quote James B. Meek in his book *The Art of Engraving*—published by F. Brownell & Son—"It is hard to imagine the extraordinarily gifted and inventive master-sculptor Michelangelo not using an air-powered chisel to speed up his work, if it had been available to him, for it would have saved him countless hours chipping away at those huge blocks of marble. After all, it's the master's hand guiding the tool

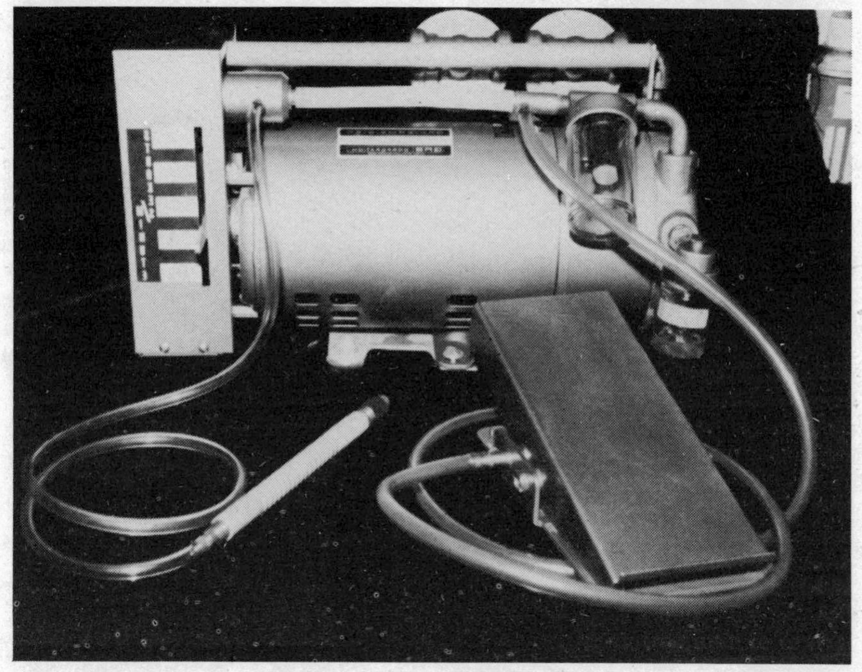

This is the Gravermeister complete, ready to go to work at $495.

the large range of adjustments available, and the precise control possible, delicate cuts can be combined with heavy material-removal for any desired effect.

Since the Gravermeister provides the muscle to push the graver through the metal, the engraver may now focus most of his attention on where he is cutting. Now he can create better cuts, faster and with much less fatigue. Such time-consuming jobs as background matting are done far faster than usual.

A S&W revolver engraved by James B. Meek. The grips were done by the engraver in ivory.

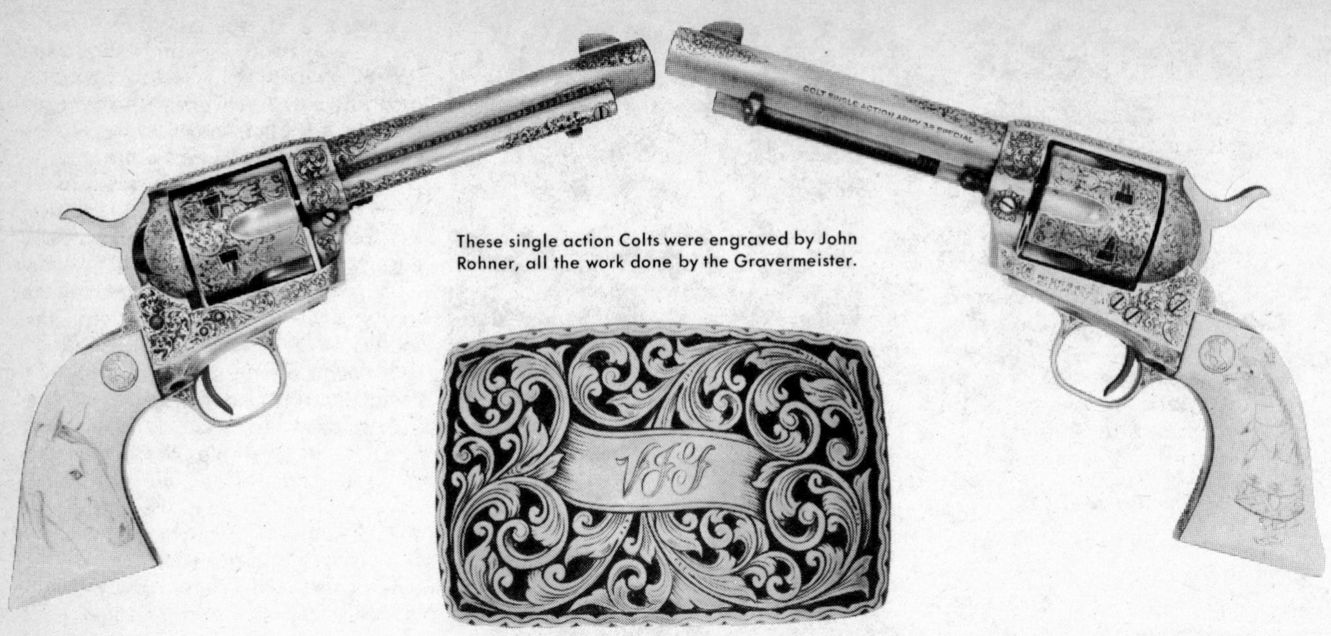

These single action Colts were engraved by John Rohner, all the work done by the Gravermeister.

Don Glaser engraved this plate using the Gravermeister.

—whether it be mechanically powered or hammer-powered—that controls the quality of the finished job, and in the end it is the finished job that will receive the critical appraisal, regardless of how the job was accomplished."

The work shown in this article was done by 4 engravers who realize the merits of the Gravermeister. John Rohner and Don Glaser have already been introduced.

James B. Meek of Newton, Iowa, has been engraving for some 37 years and is a recognized master. When he first learned about the Gravermeister, he was skeptical. About five years ago, he decided to try the machine. How he now feels is best stated by a quote from his new book *The Art of Engraving*. He says, "For my own use, I'd prefer giving up the chasers hammer and chisel to ever surrendering my Gravermeister."

Wayne Potts of Denver, Colorado, has been an artist for the best part of his life and has been engraving for better than 10 years. Like most engravers, he began work using the accepted tools of the trade. Five years ago Potts began using an adaptation of the Gravermeister. He used several of the components of the Gravermeister and improvised others. The results he obtained were pretty good, but a year ago he bought a complete unit from the GRS Corp. and has been progressing by leaps and bounds ever since.

The best way to end this article is to quote Larry Wilson, one of the leading authorities on engraving in America today.

He says—"Ulrich, Nimschke and Gustave Young would all have endorsed the Gravermeister." ●

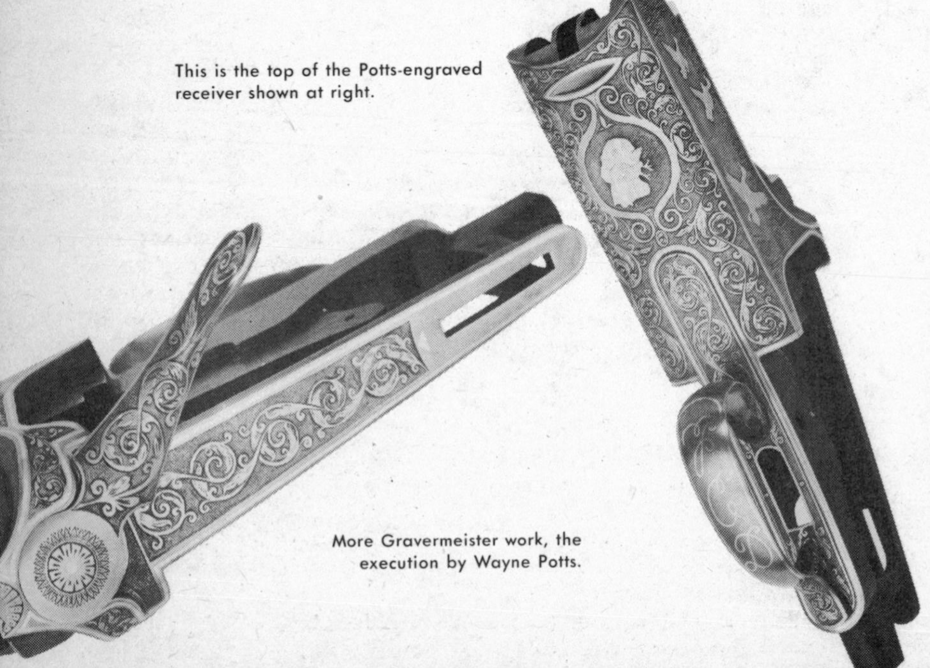

This is the top of the Potts-engraved receiver shown at right.

More Gravermeister work, the execution by Wayne Potts.

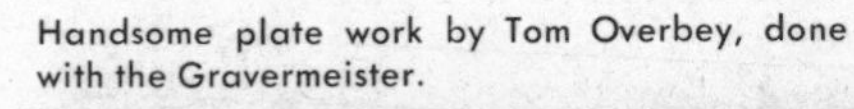

Handsome plate work by Tom Overbey, done with the Gravermeister.

Shooter's Showcase

Al Barney's Custom Grips

Al Barney, the man who made and marketed Fitz Grips for many long years, is now retired, but he still keeps his clever hands in by making custom grips—those shown are of walnut, fitted to a Stoeger Luger. They're very well made, and Al might—just might—make you a pair. His address is: P.O. Box 49393, Los Angeles, CA 90040.

Artistic Arms

I've described the Sharps-Borchardt replica action this firm makes at some length in previous issues, so I'll only note here that the latest version of the action shows great improvement—a crosspin safety is now available, as is a pistol-grip curved lever, this with an enlarged grasping section at the rear, and the general finishing is much better. Plane surfaces and radiused areas are cleanly done, and I like the matte or dull gray finish now used, at least on some versions. The bright-polished breechblock is engine-turned on its sides, and the trigger is color-hardened. I'm pleased to see, too, that the company name now appears—in small letters—underneath the action, leaving the broad areas of the sidewalls completely available to the engraver. J.T.A.

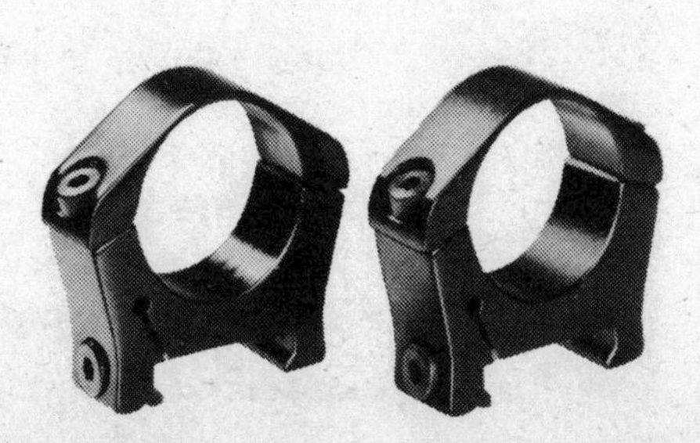

Gun Record Book

The times being what they are—break-ins and rip-offs ever on the increase—the gun owner should keep a detailed and complete record of his firearms. A new and valuable book, one with every entry form needed, is the "Gun Collections Record Book," these holding 25 double-page sheets in loose-leaf form, cost $4. Extra sheets (25) are $1, and the wise man will keep two sets of records, one at home, the other at his office or bank. Write to B.J. Co., 1917 St. Philip St., New Orleans, LA 70016. J.T.A.

Precision Snap Caps

Well-made dummy cartridges, needed in many firearms for safe snapping practice, haven't been easy to find, but Frank's Machine Shop (11529 Tecumseh-Clinton Rd., Clinton, MI 49236) makes them in a wide variety, and with other calibers to come, modern and old. I've examined some of these (9mm, 38 Spl., 45-70), and they're very nicely done—a perfect fit in the guns I tried 'em in.

Available now are 25, 380 and 45 auto, 41 and 44 Magnum, among others, these at $11.95 per set of 6, plus singles in 30-30, 30-06, 444 Marlin, 35 Auto Mag., etc., at $5 each. Ask for a quote on your caliber. No, not cheap, but these solid brass snap caps should last about forever. J.T.A.

New Bushnell "10-plus-10" Riflescope Mounts

Bushnell's latest innovation is a unique set of 1" scope rings with built-in *windage* adjustment. Up to 10 minutes of angle (MOA) in either direction eliminates the need for shimming when zeroing-in the rifle, or of using up the available windage adjustment of the riflescope. By reversing the front mount 10 MOA is obtained from right to left; reversing the rear ring gives 10 MOA from left to right.

Tops of the clamp rings pull down and around the scope via allen-head screws, providing shot-after-shot holding power under the heaviest of magnum rifle recoil. Mounts mate securely with standard-type (Weaver) bases without wobble or twist.

The precision-machined mounts, of high-strength aluminum, weigh only 1.8 ozs., sell for $11.95. J.T.A.

Robert G. West

West has been doing excellent general gunsmithing for many years, but he's a barrel specialist primarily—he fits highest quality barrels in calibers from 22 to 45, to the customers specifications, and reblues the furnished action, too, for $75. However, a big specialty of West's is his reboring of rifle barrels. He can handle calibers from 6mm (.243") to 58, any twist from 6-inch to 30", 36", 48" and 60", thus round ball rerifling can be managed, too. West has on hand some 60 chambering reamers, and he can also do gain-twist rerifling.

Last—and this can be important to some of our readers—West does some rifle barrel relining, cost about $35 and up. Write to him on this work. J.T.A.

Fortress Publications, Inc.

This over-the-border company (Box 241, Stoney Creek, Ontario, Canada L8G 3X9) offers a very wide selection of interesting titles—books and booklets covering virtually all phases of firearms literature and related subjects. Besides new books, Fortress publishes and/or distributes numerous catalogs in facsimile editions, using British, European and United States original sources.

Military, edged weapons, history and uniforms are among the subjects covered. Write for their listings.

Richland Arms

This Blissfield, Michigan firm (321 W. Adrian St.) offers a kit for constructing—with ordinary tools—a percussion or flintlock Pennsylvania pistol of Revolutionary War type. The one-piece stock is fully shaped and 95% inletted, the 45-caliber 10" barrel is octagon in form and all fittings are solid brass. Over-all length is 16", weight is 38 ozs. The caplock version is $49, the flinter $6 more. J.T.A.

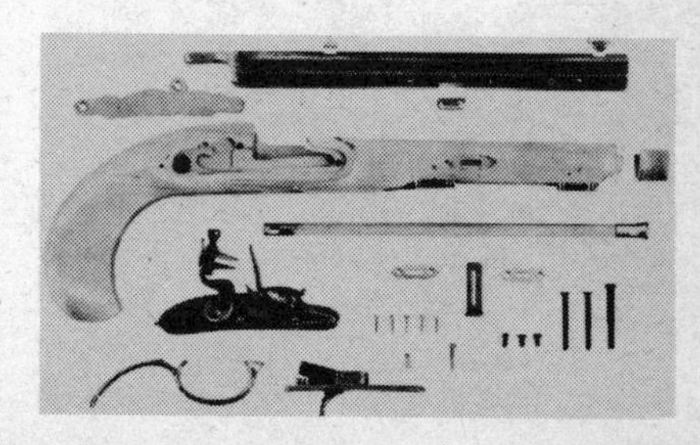

Know Your P38

That's the title of a new and valuable booklet, authored and offered by E.J. Hoffschmidt, famed gun illustrator (exploded views, notably), auto pistol authority and writer of numerous volumes in the gun field. This new book of 72 pages comprises a history of Walther P38 auto pistols, reveals among numerous photos and line drawings several P38s not heretofore seen, and sells for $2.95 postpaid.

The first book published by Blacksmith Corp. (Harpsichord Turnpike, Stamford, CT 06903) was *Know Your 45,* a quite similar treatment of the U.S. Gov't. 45 auto pistol, Models 1911 and 1911A1, same price. Other titles will soon follow and if they're like the two listed here, you'll want them. J.T.A.

The Accurate Rifle

A thorough reading of Warren Page's newest book will clearly benefit all who handload for the rifle—what rifleman, be he a reloader or not, isn't interested in accuracy? That, in fact, is the real name of the game, isn't it?

Warren Page covers the entire spectrum in detailing how to get and maintain an accurate rifle—for hunters as well as pure accuracy nuts. His chapters range from the selection, care and tuning of the rifle itself through a broad, well-reasoned discussion of calibers, bullets and loads, tool and die adjustments, shooting techniques, scopes and their choice, plus a lot more than I have room for.

The Accurate Rifle, published by Winchester Press, has 238 pages, is well-illustrated, and is priced at $8.95. Highly recommended. J.T.A.

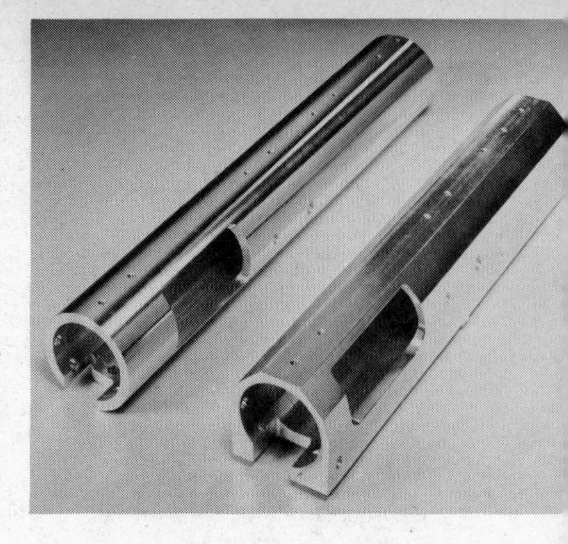

Alvin Davidson's high strength alloy sleeves, made for most Remington bolt action rifles.

New Synthetic Gun Oil

Birchwood Casey, long-time leader in developing, manufacturing and marketing of gun care products, introduced a new gun oil in mid-1974.

According to Birchwood Casey, this is a chemically pure, non-gumming lubricant with many advantages over petroleum-based oils—superior corrosion resistance, lower evaporation rate, and a higher viscosity that assures performance in extreme temperatures—from −55°F to +300°F. The new oil also has a natural solvency or cleaning action.

Our sample was tested for flow action after being stored at zero temperature (in my deep freeze) for 24 hours, and delivery from spout can or aerosol can was faultless.

The new Synthetic oil is now being sold at gunshops, hardware and sporting goods stores in a 4-oz. spout can and a 6-oz. aerosol. Want more dope? Write to A.W. Carlson, Birchwood Casey, 7900 Fuller Rd., Eden Prairie, MN 55343. J.T.A.

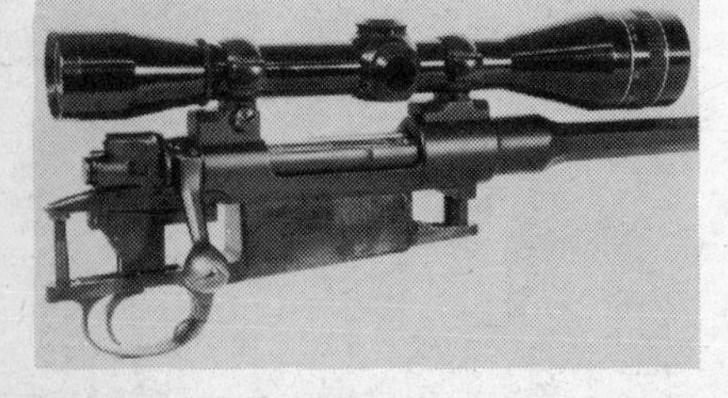

Mauser action, modified by Herman Waldron, carries half-octagon barrel, special safety, etc.

RWS-Geco-Rottweil

The entire Dynamit-Nobel line—which includes the above-named makers of ammunition and firearms (the Rottweil Olympia 72 is one such), including RWS primers, percussion caps, Brenneke shotgun slugs, etcetera—will now be imported and distributed exclusively by Eastern Sports Distributors, P.O. Box 28, Milford, New Hampshire 03055. Their phone number is AC603-673-4967.

Ample stocks of all Dynamit Nobel products will be kept on hand, I was told, insuring prompt delivery to U.S. dealers. I've used many of these German-made products over the last decade or so, and I've never been disappointed—the quality and performance is excellent.

Shotgun authority Wallace Labisky agrees—look for his Testfire Report on the Rottweil Olympia 72 over-under shotgun elsewhere in this issue. J.T.A.

Herman Waldron, Metalsmith

I'm sorry we don't have room to show more of Waldron's excellent work, or the time to get more material prepared, but at least the one picture shown reveals his high skills.

The Mauser action holds a half-octagon barrel, a bolt handle to match, custom scope bases (taking Redfield rings) a special safety and a new hinged floorplate and guard bow with release lever inside. Waldron does this and much more, all of it in first class, precision fashion. J.T.A.

Alvin Davidson Stool Shooter Tools

Several useful products are made and offered by Davidson, among them a lightweight barrel-clamp and action-wrench set for switch-barrel competitors. Made for most common barrel tapers, the aluminum split clamp is 2.75″ long, the action wrench fits all Remingtons except the Model 788, and cost is $40; additional barrel bushings (5 are available) are $6 each.

Davidson's specialty is action sleeves, round- or flat-bottomed, and made extra strong of 7075-T6 aluminum alloy. Supplied for most Remington bolt actions (except the M788) their maximum length is 11.5 inches and weight in that length is 19 ozs.—they can be readily shortened to reduce weight and both are pre-drilled and tapped for standard and extra guard screws.

The modified-octagon and flat-bottom sleeve sells for $50, the round one is $40.

Other Davidson tools are: loading ramps for Remington actions, $4 to $6; a mainspring changing tool ($5.25), also for Remington actions, and an ingenious bullet-seating depth checker that attaches to dial or vernier calipers. The seating depth of "best shooting" loads is quickly determined and, if recorded, can be duplicated with other bullets. Calibers offered are 22, 6mm and 30, price $12. Add calibers are $5.

Davidson will gladly furnish full information for a stamped large envelope. His address is 1215 Branson, Las Cruces, NM 88001. J.T.A.

CENTER RIFLE CARTRIDGES — BALLISTICS AND PRICES

Winchester-Western, Remington-Peters, Federal and Speer-DWM

Most of these centerfire loads are available from Winchester-Western and Remington-Peters. Loads available from only one source are marked by a letter, thus: Winchester (a); Western (b); Remington (c); Peters (d); Speer-DWM (f). Those fewer cartridges also available from Federal are marked (e). Contrary to previous practice, W-W and R-P prices are not necessarily uniform, hence prices are approximate.

Cartridge	Bullet Wt. Grs.	Bullet Type	Velocity (fps) Muzzle	Velocity 100 yds.	Velocity 200 yds.	Velocity 300 yds.	Energy (ft. lbs.) Muzzle	Energy 100 yds.	Energy 200 yds.	Energy 300 yds.	Mid-Range Trajectory 100 yds.	Mid-Range Trajectory 200 yds.	Mid-Range Trajectory 300 yds.	Price for 20*
17 Remington	25	HP, PL	4020	3290	2630	2060	900	600	380	230	—	1.5	7.3	$ 5.25
218 Bee*	46	HP	2860	2160	1610	1200	835	475	265	145	0.7	3.8	11.5	11.75
22 Hornet*	45	SP	2690	2030	1510	1150	720	410	230	130	0.8	4.3	13.0	10.25
22 Hornet* (c, d)	45	HP	2690	2030	1510	1150	720	410	230	130	0.8	4.3	13.0	9.85
22 Hornet*	46	HP	2690	2030	1510	1150	740	420	235	135	0.8	4.3	13.0	9.85
222 Remington (a, e)	50	PSP, MC, PL†	3200	2660	2170	1750	1140	785	520	340	0.5	2.5	7.0	4.50
222 Remington Magnum (c, d)	55	SP, PL†	3300	2800	2340	1930	1330	955	670	455	0.5	2.3	6.1	4.90
222 Remington Magnum (c, d)	55	HP, PL	3300	2830	2400	2010	1330	975	700	490	0.5	2.3	6.1	5.25
223 Remington (a, c, d, e)	55	SP, PL†, PSP	3300	2800	2340	1930	1330	955	670	455	0.5	2.1	5.4	4.90
22-250 Remington	55	PSP	3810	3270	2770	2320	1770	1300	935	655	0.3	1.6	4.4	5.25
22-250 Remington (c, d)	55	HP, PL	3810	3330	2890	2490	1770	1360	1020	760	0.4	1.7	4.3	5.25
225 Winchester (a, b)	55	PSP	3650	3140	2680	2270	1630	1200	875	630	0.4	1.8	4.8	5.05
243 Winchester (e)	80	PSP, PL†	3500	3080	2720	2410	2180	1690	1320	1030	0.4	1.8	4.7	6.25
243 Winchester (c, d)	80	HP, PL	3450	3050	2675	2330	2115	1650	1270	965	0.4	1.9	4.9	6.65
243 Winchester (e)	100	PP, CL, PSP	3070	2790	2540	2320	2090	1730	1430	1190	0.5	2.2	5.5	6.25
6mm Remington (a, c, d)	80	PSP, HP, PL†	3450	3130	2750	2400	2220	1740	1340	1018	0.4	1.8	4.7	6.25
6mm Remington (a, c, d)	100	PCL, PSP	3190	2920	2660	2420	2260	1890	1570	1300	0.5	2.1	5.1	6.25
244 Remington (c, d)	90	PSP	3200	2850	2530	2230	2050	1630	1280	995	0.5	2.1	5.5	5.70
25-06 Remington (c, d)	87	HP	3500	3070	2680	2310	2370	1820	1390	1030	0.4	2.0	5.1	6.80
25-06 Remington (c, d)	120	PSP, CL	3120	2850	2600	2360	2590	2160	1800	1480	0.5	2.2	5.6	6.80
25-20 Winchester*	86	L, Lu	1460	1180	1030	940	405	265	200	170	2.6	12.5	32.0	9.05
25-20 Winchester*	86	SP	1460	1180	1030	940	405	265	200	170	2.6	12.5	32.0	10.10
25-35 Winchester	117	SP, CL	2300	1910	1600	1340	1370	945	665	465	1.0	4.6	12.5	6.35
250 Savage (a, b)	87	PSP, SP	3030	2660	2330	2060	1770	1370	1050	820	0.6	2.5	6.4	5.85
250 Savage	100	ST, CL, PSP	2820	2460	2140	1870	1760	1340	1020	775	0.6	2.9	7.4	5.85
256 Winchester Magnum* (b)	60	OPE	2800	2070	1570	1220	1040	570	330	200	0.8	4.0	12.0	10.80
257 Roberts (a, b)	87	PSP	3200	2840	2500	2190	1980	1560	1210	925	0.5	2.2	5.7	6.40
257 Roberts (a, b)	100	ST, CL	2900	2540	2210	1920	1870	1430	1080	820	0.6	2.7	7.0	6.40
257 Roberts	117	PP, CL	2650	2280	1950	1690	1820	1350	985	740	0.7	3.4	8.8	6.40
6.5 Remington Magnum (c)	100	PSPCL	3450	3070	2690	2320	2640	2090	1610	1190	0.4	1.9	5.0	8.40
6.5mm Remington Magnum (c)	120	PSPCL	3030	2750	2480	2230	2450	2010	1640	1330	0.5	2.3	5.7	8.40
264 Winchester Magnum	100	PSP, CL	3700	3260	2880	2550	3040	2360	1840	1440	0.4	1.6	4.2	8.40
264 Winchester Magnum	140	PP, CL	3200	2490	2700	2480	3180	2690	2270	1910	0.5	2.0	4.9	8.40
270 Winchester	100	PSP	3480	3070	2690	2340	2690	2090	1600	1215	0.4	1.8	4.8	6.80
270 Winchester (e)	130	PP, PSP	3140	2880	2630	2400	2850	2390	2000	1660	0.5	2.1	5.3	6.50
270 Winchester	130	ST, CL, BP, PP	3140	2850	2580	2320	2840	2340	1920	1550	0.5	2.1	5.3	6.80
270 Winchester (c, d)	150	CL	2800	2440	2140	1870	2610	1980	1520	1160	0.6	2.9	7.6	6.80
270 Winchester (a, b, e)	150	PP	2900	2620	2380	2160	2800	2290	1890	1550	0.6	2.5	6.3	6.80
280 Remington (c, d)	150	PCL	2900	2670	2450	2220	2800	2370	2000	1640	0.6	2.5	6.1	6.80
280 Remington (c, d)	165	CL	2820	2510	2220	1970	2910	2310	1810	1420	0.6	2.8	7.2	6.80
284 Winchester (a, b)	125	PP	3200	2880	2590	2310	2840	2300	1860	1480	0.5	2.1	5.3	6.80
284 Winchester (a, b)	150	PP	2900	2630	2380	2160	2800	2300	1890	1550	0.6	2.5	6.3	6.80
7mm Mauser (e)	139	SP	2710	2440	2190	1960	2280	1850	1490	1190	0.7	3.0	7.8	6.80
7mm Mauser (e)	175	SP	2490	2170	1900	1680	2410	1830	1400	1100	0.8	3.7	9.5	6.80
7mm Remington Magnum	125	CL	3430	3080	2750	2450	3260	2630	2100	1660	0.6	1.8	4.7	8.40
7mm Remington Magnum (e)	150	PP, CL	3260	2970	2700	2450	3540	2940	2430	1990	0.4	2.0	4.9	8.40
7mm Remington Magnum (e)	175	PP	3070	2720	2400	2120	3660	2870	2240	1750	0.5	2.4	6.1	8.40
7mm Remington Magnum (c, d)	175	PCL	3070	2860	2660	2460	3660	3170	2740	2350	0.5	2.1	5.2	8.40
30 Carbine* (e)	110	HSP, SP	1980	1540	1230	1040	950	575	370	260	1.4	7.5	21.7	10.70
30-30 Winchester (c, d)	150	CL	2410	1960	1620	1360	1930	1280	875	616	0.9	4.5	12.5	5.30
30-30 Winchester (e)	150	HP	2410	2020	1700	1430	1930	1360	960	680	0.9	4.2	11.0	5.30
30-30 Winchester (a, b)	150	PP, ST, OPE	2410	2020	1700	1430	1930	1360	960	680	0.9	4.2	11.0	5.30
30-30 Winchester (e)	170	PP, HP, CL, ST, MC	2220	1890	1630	1410	1860	1350	1000	750	1.2	4.6	12.5	5.30
30 Remington	170	ST, CL	2120	1820	1560	1350	1700	1250	920	690	1.1	5.3	14.0	6.35
30-06 Springfield (a, b)	110	PSP	3370	2830	2350	1920	2770	1960	1350	900	0.5	2.2	6.0	6.80
30-06 Springfield	125	PSP	3200	2810	2480	2200	2840	2190	1710	1340	0.5	2.2	5.6	6.80
30-06 Springfield (c, d)	150	BP	2970	2710	2470	2240	2930	2440	2030	1670	0.5	2.4	6.0	6.80
30-06 Springfield (e)	150	PP	2970	2620	2300	2010	2930	2280	1760	1340	0.6	2.5	6.5	6.80
30-06 Springfield	150	ST, PCL, PSP	2970	2670	2400	2130	2930	2370	1920	1510	0.6	2.4	6.1	6.80
30-06 Springfield	180	PP, CL, PSP	2700	2330	2010	1740	2910	2170	1610	1210	0.7	3.1	8.3	6.80
30-06 Springfield (e)	180	ST, BP, PCL	2700	2470	2250	2040	2910	2440	2020	1660	0.7	2.9	7.0	6.80
30-06 Springfield	220	PP, CL	2410	2120	1870	1670	2830	2190	1710	1360	0.8	3.9	9.8	6.80
30-06 Springfield (a, b)	220	ST	2410	2180	1980	1790	2830	2320	1910	1560	0.8	3.7	9.2	6.80
30-40 Krag	180	PP, CL	2470	2120	1830	1590	2440	1790	1340	1010	0.8	3.8	9.9	6.90
30-40 Krag	180	ST, PCL	2470	2250	2040	1850	2440	2020	1660	1370	0.8	3.5	8.5	6.90
30-40 Krag (a, b)	220	ST	2200	1990	1800	1630	2360	1930	1580	1300	1.0	4.4	11.0	6.90
300 Winchester Magnum (a, c, e)	150	PP, PCL	3400	3050	2730	2430	3850	3100	2480	1970	0.4	1.9	4.8	8.70
300 Winchester Magnum (a, c, e)	180	PP, PCL	3070	2850	2640	2440	3770	3250	2790	2380	0.5	2.1	5.3	8.70
300 Winchester Mag (a, b)	220	ST	2720	2490	2270	2060	3620	3030	2520	2070	0.6	2.9	6.9	8.70
300 H&H Magnum (a, b)	150	ST	3190	2870	2580	2300	3390	2740	2220	1760	0.5	2.1	5.2	9.35
300 H&H Magnum	180	ST, PCL	2920	2670	2440	2220	3400	2850	2380	1970	0.6	2.4	5.8	8.70
300 H&H Magnum (a, b)	220	ST, CL	2620	2370	2150	1940	3350	2740	2260	1840	0.7	3.1	7.7	8.70
300 Savage (e)	150	PP	2670	2350	2060	1800	2370	1840	1410	1080	0.7	3.2	8.0	6.20
300 Savage	150	ST, PCL	2670	2390	2130	1890	2370	1900	1510	1190	0.7	3.0	7.6	6.60
300 Savage (c, d)	150	CL	2670	2270	1930	1660	2370	1710	1240	916	0.7	3.3	9.3	6.60
300 Savage (e)	180	PP, CL	2370	2040	1760	1520	2240	1660	1240	920	0.9	4.1	10.5	6.35
300 Savage	180	ST, PCL	2370	2160	1960	1770	2240	1860	1530	1250	0.9	3.7	9.2	6.60
303 Savage (c, d)	180	CL	2140	1810	1550	1340	1830	1310	960	715	1.1	5.4	14.0	7.00
303 Savage (a, b)	190	ST	1980	1680	1440	1250	1650	1190	875	660	1.3	6.2	15.5	6.75
303 British (e)	180	PP, CL	2540	2300	2090	1900	2580	2120	1750	1440	0.7	3.3	8.2	6.85
303 British (c, d)	215	SP	2180	1900	1660	1460	2270	1720	1310	1020	1.1	4.9	12.5	6.60
308 Winchester (a, b)	110	PSP	3340	2810	2340	1920	2730	1930	1340	900	0.5	2.2	6.0	6.80
308 Winchester (a, b)	125	PSP	3100	2740	2430	2160	2670	2080	1640	1300	0.5	2.3	5.9	6.80
308 Winchester (e)	150	PP	2860	2520	2210	1930	2730	2120	1630	1240	0.6	2.7	7.0	6.55
308 Winchester	150	ST, PCL	2860	2570	2300	2050	2730	2200	1760	1400	0.6	2.6	6.5	6.80
308 Winchester (e)	180	PP, CL	2610	2250	1940	1680	2720	2020	1500	1130	0.7	3.4	8.9	6.55
308 Winchester	180	ST, PCL	2610	2390	2170	1970	2720	2280	1870	1540	0.8	3.1	7.4	6.80
308 Winchester (a, b)	200	ST	2450	2210	1980	1770	2670	2170	1750	1400	0.8	3.6	9.0	6.80
32 Winchester Special (c, d, e)	170	HP, CL	2280	1920	1630	1410	1960	1390	1000	750	1.0	4.8	12.5	5.45
32 Winchester Special	170	PP, ST	2280	1870	1560	1330	1960	1320	920	665	1.0	4.8	13.0	5.30
32 Remington (c, d)	170	CL	2120	1800	1540	1340	1700	1220	895	680	1.0	4.9	13.0	6.60
32 Remington (a, b)	170	ST	2120	1760	1460	1220	1700	1170	805	560	1.1	5.3	14.5	6.60
32-20 Winchester*	100	SP	1290	1060	940	840	370	250	195	155	3.3	15.5	38.0	9.65
32-20 Winchester*	100	SP, L, Lu	1290	1060	940	840	370	250	195	155	3.3	15.5	38.0	7.75
8mm Mauser (e)	170	PP, CL	2570	2140	1790	1520	2490	1730	1210	870	0.8	3.9	10.5	6.80

CENTERFIRE RIFLE CARTRIDGES — BALLISTICS AND PRICES (continued)

Cartridge	Bullet Wt. Grs.	Bullet Type	Velocity (fps) Muzzle	Velocity 100 yds.	Velocity 200 yds.	Velocity 300 yds.	Energy (ft. lbs.) Muzzle	Energy 100 yds.	Energy 200 yds.	Energy 300 yds.	Mid-Range Trajectory 100 yds.	Mid-Range Trajectory 200 yds.	Mid-Range Trajectory 300 yds.	Price for 20*
338 Winchester Magnum (a, b)	200	PP	3000	2690	2410	2170	4000	3210	2580	2090	0.5	2.4	6.0	$9.10
338 Winchester Magnum (a, b)	250	ST	2700	2430	2180	1940	4050	3280	2640	2090	0.7	3.0	7.4	9.10
338 Winchester Magnum (a, b)	300	PP	2450	2160	1910	1690	4000	3110	2430	1900	0.8	3.7	9.5	9.10
348 Winchester (a)	200	ST	2530	2220	1940	1680	2840	2190	1670	1250	0.7	3.6	9.0	9.50
348 Winchester (c, d)	200	CL	2530	2140	1820	1570	2840	2030	1470	1090	0.3	3.8	10.3	9.50
35 Remington (c, d)	150	CL	2400	1960	1580	1280	1920	1280	835	545	0.9	4.6	13.0	6.15
35 Remington (e)	200	PP, ST, CL	2100	1710	1390	1160	1950	1300	860	605	1.2	6.0	16.5	6.15
350 Remington Magnum (c, d)	200	PCL	2710	2410	2130	1870	3260	2570	2000	1550	0.7	3.0	7.7	8.40
350 Remington Magnum (c, d)	250	PCL	2410	2190	1980	1790	3220	2660	2180	1780	0.8	3.7	9.2	8.40
351 Winchester Self-Loading*	180	SP	1850	1560	1310	1140	1370	975	685	520	1.5	7.8	21.5	13.45
358 Winchester (a, b)	200	ST	2530	2210	1910	1640	2840	2160	1610	1190	0.8	3.6	9.4	8.40
358 Winchester (a, b)	250	ST	2250	2010	1780	1570	2810	2230	1760	1370	1.0	4.4	11.0	8.40
375 H&H Magnum	270	PP, SP	2740	2460	2210	1990	4500	3620	2920	2370	0.7	2.9	7.1	10.80
375 H&H Magnum	300	ST	2550	2280	2040	1830	4330	3460	2770	2230	0.7	3.3	8.3	10.80
375 H&H Magnum	300	MC	2550	2180	1860	1590	4330	3160	2300	1680	0.7	3.6	9.3	10.80
38-40 Winchester*	180	SP	1330	1070	960	850	705	455	370	290	3.2	15.0	36.5	11.50
44 Magnum* (c, d)	240	SP	1750	1360	1110	980	1630	985	655	510	1.6	8.4	—	4.85
44 Magnum (b)	240	HSP	1750	1350	1090	950	1630	970	635	480	1.8	9.4	26.0	4.85
444 Marlin (c)	240	SP	2400	1845	1410	1125	3070	1815	1060	675	1.0	5.4	16.5	6.85
44-40 Winchester*	200	SP	1310	1050	940	830	760	490	390	305	3.3	15.0	36.5	13.80
45-70 Government	405	SP	1320	1160	1050	990	1570	1210	990	880	2.9	13.0	32.5	8.40
458 Winchester Magnum	500	MC	2130	1910	1700	1520	5040	4050	3210	2570	1.1	4.8	12.0	20.10
458 Winchester Magnum	510	SP	2130	1840	1600	1400	5140	3830	2900	2220	1.1	5.1	13.5	13.20

* Price for 50 HP—Hollow Point SP—Soft Point PSP—Pointed Soft Point PP—Power Point L—Lead Lu—Lubaloy ST—Silvertip HSP—Hollow Soft Point MC—Metal Case BT—Boat Tail MAT—Match BP—Bronze Point CL—Core Lokt PCL—Pointed Core Lokt OPE—Open Point Expanding †PL—Power-Lokt (slightly higher price) (1) Not safe in handguns or Win. M73.

WEATHERBY MAGNUM CARTRIDGES — BALLISTICS AND PRICES

Cartridge	Bullet Wt. Grs.	Bullet Type	Velocity (fps) Muzzle	Velocity 100 yds.	Velocity 200 yds.	Velocity 300 yds.	Energy (ft. lbs.) Muzzle	Energy 100 yds.	Energy 200 yds.	Energy 300 yds.	Mid-Range Trajectory 100 yds.	Mid-Range Trajectory 200 yds.	Mid-Range Trajectory 300 yds.	Price for 20
224 Weatherby Varmintmaster	50	PE	3750	3160	2625	2140	1562	1109	1670	1250	0.7	3.6	9.0	$6.95
224 Weatherby Varmintmaster	55	PE	3650	3150	2685	2270	1627	1212	881	629	0.4	1.7	4.5	6.95
240 Weatherby	70	PE	3850	3395	2975	2585	2304	1788	1376	1038	0.3	1.5	3.9	9.95
240 Weatherby	90	PE	3500	3135	2795	2475	2444	1960	1559	1222	0.4	1.8	4.5	9.95
240 Weatherby	100	PE	3395	3115	2850	2595	2554	2150	1804	1495	0.4	1.8	4.4	9.95
247 Weatherby	87	PE	3825	3290	2835	2450	2828	2087	1553	1160	0.3	1.6	4.4	9.95
247 Weatherby	100	PE	3555	3150	2815	2500	2802	2199	1760	1338	0.4	1.7	4.4	9.95
247 Weatherby	117	SPE	3300	2900	2550	2250	2824	2184	1689	1315	0.4	2.4	6.8	9.95
270 Weatherby	100	PE	3760	3625	2825	2435	3140	2363	1773	1317	0.4	1.6	4.3	9.95
270 Weatherby	130	PE	3375	3050	2750	2480	3283	2685	2183	1776	0.4	1.8	4.5	9.95
270 Weatherby	150	PE	3245	2955	2675	2430	3501	2909	2385	1967	0.5	2.0	5.0	9.95
7mm Weatherby	139	PE	3300	2995	2715	2465	3355	2770	2275	1877	0.4	1.9	4.9	9.95
7mm Weatherby	154	PE	3160	2885	2640	2415	3406	2874	2384	1994	0.5	2.0	5.0	9.95
300 Weatherby	150	PE	3545	3195	2890	2615	4179	3393	2783	2279	0.4	1.5	3.9	10.95
300 Weatherby	180	PE	3245	2960	2705	2475	4201	3501	2925	2448	0.4	1.9	5.2	10.95
300 Weatherby	220	SPE	2905	2610	2385	2150	4123	3329	2757	2257	0.6	2.5	6.7	10.95
340 Weatherby	200	PE	3210	2905	2615	2345	4566	3748	3038	2442	0.5	2.1	5.3	10.95
340 Weatherby	210	Nosler	3165	2910	2665	2435	4660	3948	3312	2766	0.5	2.1	5.0	10.95
340 Weatherby	250	SPE	2850	2580	2325	2090	4510	3695	3000	2425	0.6	2.7	6.7	10.95
378 Weatherby	270	SPE	3180	2850	2600	2315	6051	4871	4053	3210	0.5	2.0	5.2	12.95
378 Weatherby	300	SPE, FMJ	2925	2610	2380	2125	5700	4539	3774	3009	0.6	2.5	6.2	20.95
460 Weatherby	500	RN, FMJ	2700	2330	2005	1730	8095	6025	4465	3320	0.7	3.3	10.0	24.95

Trajectory is given from scope height. Velocities chronographed using 26″ bbls. Available with Nosler bullets; add $2.00 per box.
SPE—Semi-Pointed Expanding RN—Round Nose PE—Pointed Expanding FMJ—Full Metal Jacket

RIMFIRE CARTRIDGES — BALLISTICS AND PRICES

Remington-Peters, Winchester-Western, Federal & Cascade Cartridge, Inc.

All loads available from all manufacturers except as indicated: R-P (a); W-W (b); Fed. (c); CCI (d). All prices are approximate.

CARTRIDGE	BULLET WT. GRS.	BULLET TYPE	VELOCITY FT. PER SEC. MUZZLE	VELOCITY 100 YDS.	ENERGY FT. LBS. MUZZLE	ENERGY 100 YDS.	MID-RANGE TRAJECTORY 100 YDS.	HANDGUN BARREL LENGTH	BALLISTICS M.V. F.P.S.	BALLISTICS M.E. F.P.	PRICE FOR 50
22 Short T22 (a, b)	29	C, L*	1045	810	70	42	5.6	6″	865	48	$ .98
22 Short Hi-Vel.	29	C, L	1125	920	81	54	4.3	6″	1035	69	.98
22 Short HP Hi-Vel. (a, b, c)	27	C, L	1155	920	80	51	4.2	—	—	—	1.07
22 Short (a, b)	29	D	1045	—	70	—	—	—	—	(per 500)	9.00
22 Short (a, b)	15	D	1710	—	97	—	—	—	—	(per 500)	9.00
22 Long Hi-Vel.	29	C, L	1240	965	99	60	3.8	6″	1095	77	1.07
22 Long Rifle T22 (a, b)†-1	40	L*	1145	975	116	84	4.0	6″	950	80	1.12
22 Long Rifle (b)†-2	40	L*	1120	950	111	80	4.2	—	—	—	1.85
22 Long Rifle (b)†-3	40	L*	—	—	—	—	—	6¾″	1060	100	1.85
22 Long Rifle (d)†-4	40	C	1165	980	121	84	4.0	—	—	—	.99
22 Long Rifle Hi-Vel.	40	C, L	1285	1025	147	93	3.4	6″	1125	112	1.23
22 Long Rifle HP Hi-Vel. (b, d)	37	C, L	1315	1020	142	85	3.4	—	—	—	1.24
22 Long Rifle HP Hi-Vel. (a, c)	36	C	1365	1040	149	86	3.4	—	—	—	1.24
22 Long Rifle (b, c)	No.	12 Shot	—	—	—	—	—	—	—	—	2.32
22 WRF [Rem. Spl.] (a, b)	45	C, L	1450	1110	210	123	—	—	—	—	3.19
22 WRF Mag. (b)	40	JHP	2000	1390	355	170	1.6	6½″	1550	213	3.05
22 WRF Mag. (b)	40	MC	2000	1390	355	170	1.6	6½″	1550	213	3.05
22 Win. Auto Inside lub. (a, b)	45	C, L	1055	930	111	86	—	—	—	—	3.27
5mm Rem. RFM (a)	38	PLHP	2100	1605	372	217	Not Available				4.48

†—Target loads of these ballistics available in: (1) Rem. Match; (2) W-W LV EZXS, Super Match Mark III; (3) Super Match Mark IV and EZXS Pistol Match; (4) CCI Mini-Group. C—Copper plated L—Lead (Wax Coated) L*—Lead, lubricated D—Disintegrating MC—Metal Case HP—Hollow Point JHP—Jacket Hollow Point PLHP—Power-Lokt Hollow Point

NORMA C.F. RIFLE CARTRIDGES — BALLISTICS AND PRICES

Norma ammunition loaded to standard velocity and pressure is now available with Nosler bullets in the following loads: 270 Win., 130-, 150-gr.; Super 7x61 (S&H), 160-gr.; 308 Win., 180-gr.; 30-06, 150-, 180-gr., all at slightly higher prices. All ballistic figures are computed from a line of sight one inch above center of bore at muzzle. Write for their latest prices.

			Velocity, feet per sec.				Energy, foot pounds				Max. height of trajectory, inches			
Cartridge	Bullet Wt. Grs.	Type	V Muzzle	V 100 yds.	V 200 yds.	V 300 yds.	E Muzzle	E 100 yds.	E 200 yds.	E 300 yds.	Tr. 100 yds.	Tr. 200 yds.	Tr. 300 yds.	Price for 20
220 Swift	50	SP	4111	3611	3133	2681	1877	1448	1090	799	.2	.9	3.0	$7.05
222 Remington	50	SP	3200	2660	2170	1750	1137	786	523	340	.0	2.0	6.2	4.60
22-250	50	SP	3800	3300	2810	2350	1600	1209	885	613	Not Available			5.25
	55	SP	3650	3200	2780	2400	1637	1251	944	704	Not Available			5.25
243 Winchester	100	SP	3070	2790	2540	2320	2093	1729	1433	1195	.1	1.8	5.0	6.25
6mm Remington	100	SP	3190	2920	2660	2420	2260	1890	1570	1300	.4	2.1	5.3	6.25
250 Savage	87	SP	3032	2685	2357	2054	1776	1393	1074	815	.0	1.9	5.8	6.00
6.5 Carcano	156	SP	2000	1810	1640	1485	1386	1135	932	764	Not Available			8.50
6.5 Japanese	139	SPBT	2428	2280	2130	1990	1820	1605	1401	1223	.3	2.8	7.7	8.50
	156	SP	2067	1871	1692	1529	1481	1213	992	810	.6	4.4	11.9	8.50
6.5 x 55	139	SPBT	2789	2630	2470	2320	2402	2136	1883	1662	.1	2.0	5.6	8.50
	156	SP	2493	2271	2062	1867	2153	1787	1473	1208	.3	2.9	7.9	8.50
270 Winchester	110	SP	3248	2966	2694	2435	2578	2150	1773	1448	.1	1.4	4.3	6.80
	130	SPBT	3140	2884	2639	2404	2847	2401	2011	1669	.0	1.6	4.7	6.80
	150	SPBT	2802	2616	2436	2262	2616	2280	1977	1705	.1	2.0	5.7	6.80
7.5 x 55 Schmidt Rubin (7.5 Swiss)	180	SP	2650	2450	2260	2060	2792	2350	1990	1665	Not Available			8.70
7 x 57	110	SP	3068	2792	2528	2277	2300	1904	1561	1267	.0	1.6	5.0	6.95
	150	SPBT	2756	2539	2331	2133	2530	2148	1810	1516	.1	2.2	6.2	6.95
7mm Remington Magnum	150	SP	3260	2970	2700	2450	3540	2945	2435	1990	.4	2.0	4.9	8.40
7 x 61 S & H (26 in.)	160	SPBT	3100	2927	2757	2595	3415	3045	2701	2393	.0	1.5	4.3	9.45
30 U.S. Carbine	110	SPRN	1970	1595	1300	1090	948	622	413	290	.8	6.4	19.0	4.40
308 Winchester	130	SPBT	2900	2590	2300	2030	2428	1937	1527	1190	.1	2.1	6.2	6.80
	150	SPBT	2860	2570	2300	2050	2725	2200	1762	1400	.1	2.0	5.9	6.80
	180	SPBT	2610	2400	2210	2020	2725	2303	1952	1631	.2	2.5	6.6	6.80
	180	SP	2610	2400	2210	2020	2725	2303	1952	1631	.7	3.4	8.9	7.50
7.62 Russian	180	PSPBT	2624	2415	2222	2030	2749	2326	1970	1644	.2	2.5	6.6	8.50
308 Norma Magnum	180	DC	3100	2881	2668	2464	3842	3318	2846	2427	.0	1.6	4.6	10.98
30-06	130	PSPBT	3281	2951	2636	2338	3108	2514	2006	1578	.1	1.5	4.6	6.80
	150	PS	2972	2680	2402	2141	2943	2393	1922	1527	.0	1.9	5.7	6.80
	180	PSPBT, SPDC	2700	2494	2296	2109	2914	2487	2107	1778	.1	2.3	6.4	6.80
	180	SPDC	2700	2494	2296	2109	2914	2487	2107	1778	Not Available			7.50
7.65 Argentine	150	SP	2920	2630	2355	2105	2841	2304	1848	1476	.1	2.0	5.8	8.50
303 British	130	SP	2789	2483	2195	1929	2246	1780	1391	1075	.1	2.3	6.7	7.00
	150	SP	2720	2440	2170	1930	2465	1983	1569	1241	.1	2.2	6.5	7.00
	180	SPBT	2540	2340	2147	1965	2579	2189	1843	1544	.2	2.7	7.3	7.00
7.7 Japanese	130	SP	2950	2635	2340	2065	2513	2004	1581	1231	.1	2.0	5.9	8.50
	180	SPBT	2493	2292	2101	1922	2484	2100	1765	1477	.3	2.8	7.7	8.50
8mm Mauser (.323 in.)	123	SP	2888	2515	2170	1857	2277	1728	1286	942	Not Available			7.00
	196	SP	2526	2195	1894	1627	2778	2097	1562	1152	Not Available			7.00
358 Winchester	250	SP	2250	2010	1780	1570	2811	2243	1759	1369	Not Available			8.85
358 Norma Magnum	250	SP	2790	2493	2231	2001	4322	3451	2764	2223	.2	2.4	6.6	11.05

P—Pointed SP—Soft Point HP—Hollow Point FP—Flat Point RN—Round Nose BT—Boat Tail MC—Metal Case
DC—Dual Core SPS—Soft Point Semi-Pointed NA—Not announced *Price for 50

CENTERFIRE HANDGUN CARTRIDGES — BALLISTICS AND PRICES

Winchester-Western, Remington-Peters, Norma and Federal

Most loads are available from W-W and R-P. All available Norma loads are listed. Federal cartridges are marked with an asterisk. Other loads supplied by only one source are indicated by a letter, thus: Norma (a); R-P (b); W-W (c). Prices are approximate.

Cartridge	Bullet Gr.	Bullet Style	Muzzle Velocity	Muzzle Energy	Barrel Inches	Price Per 50
22 Jet (b)	40	SP	2100	390	8⅜	$9.65
221 Fireball (b)	50	SP	2650	780	10½	4.45
25 (6.35mm) Auto*	50	MC	810	73	2	6.15
256 Winchester Magnum (c)	60	HP	2350	735	8½	10.10
30 (7.65mm) Luger Auto	93	MC	1220	307	4½	9.75
32 S&W Blank (b, c)	No bullet		—	—	—	4.35
32 S&W Blank, BP (c)	No bullet		—	—	—	4.35
32 Short Colt	80	Lead	745	100	4	5.35
32 Long Colt, IL (c)	82	Lub.	755	104	4	5.60
32 Colt New Police	100	Lead	680	100	4	6.50
32 (7.65mm) Auto*	71	MC	960	145	4	7.00
32 (7.65mm) Auto Pistol (a)	77	MC	900	162	4	6.50
32 S&W	88	Lead	680	90	3	5.35
32 S&W Long	98	Lead	705	115	4	5.60
32-20 Winchester	100	Lead	1030	271	6	7.75
32-20 Winchester	100	SP	1030	271	6	9.20
357 Magnum (b)*	158	SP	1550	845	8⅜	9.20
357 Magnum	158	MP	1410	695	8⅜	9.20
357 Magnum	158	Lead	1410	696	8⅜	7.80
357 Magnum (a)	158	JHP	1450	735	8⅜	9.20
9mm Luger (a)	116	MC	1165	349	4	8.30
9mm Luger Auto*	124	MC	1120	345	4	8.70
38 S&W Blank	No bullet		—	—	—	4.75
38 Smith & Wesson	146	Lead	685	150	4	6.55
38 S&W (a)	146	Lead	730	172	4	6.15
38 Special Blank	No bullet		—	—	—	7.00
3b Special, IL (c)	150	Lub.	1060	375	6	6.75
38 Special, IL (c)	150	MP	1060	375	6	8.20
38 Special	158	Lead	855	256	6	6.60
38 Special	200	Lead	730	236	6	6.90
38 Special	158	MP	855	256	6	8.20
38 Special (b)	125	SJHP	Not available			8.20
38 Special (b)	158	SJHP	Not available			8.20
38 Special WC (b)	148	Lead	770	195	6	6.75
38 Special Match, IL (c)	148	Lead	770	195	6	6.75
38 Special Match, IL (b, c)	158	Lead	855	256	6	6.75
38 Special Hi-Speed*	158	Lead	1090	425	6	7.10
38 Special (a)	158	RN	900	320	6	6.75
38 Short Colt	125	Lead	730	150	6	6.00
38 Short Colt, Greased (c)	130	Lub.	730	155	6	6.00
38 Long Colt	150	Lead	730	175	6	6.60
38 Super Auto (b)	130	MC	1280	475	5	7.40
38 Auto, for Colt 38 Super (c)	130	MC	1280	475	5	7.40
38 Auto	130	MC	1040	312	4½	7.40
380 Auto*	95	MC	955	192	3¾	7.15
38-40 Winchester	180	SP	975	380	5	11.50
41 Remington Magnum (b)	210	Lead	1050	515	8¾	10.15
41 Remington Magnum (b)	210	SP	1500	1050	8¾	11.60
44 S&W Special	246	Lead	755	311	6½	9.00
44 Remington Magnum	240	SP	1470	1150	6½	11.75
44 Remington Magnum	240	Lead	1470	1150	6½	11.75
44-40 Winchester	200	SP	975	420	7½	13.80
45 Colt	250	Lead	860	410	5½	9.05
45 Colt, IL (c)	255	Lub., L	860	410	5½	9.05
45 Auto	230	MC	850	369	5	9.40
45 ACP (a)	230	JHP	850	370	5	9.95
45 Auto WC*	185	MC	775	245	5	9.95
45 Auto MC (a, b)	230	MC	850	369	5	9.95
45 Auto Match (c)	185	MC	775	247	5	9.90
45 Auto Match, IL (c)	210	Lead	710	235	5	9.95
45 Auto Match*	230	MC	850	370	5	9.90
45 Auto Rim (b)	230	Lead	810	335	5½	9.85

IL—Inside Lub. JSP—Jacketed Soft Point WC—Wad Cutter
RN—Round Nose HP—Hollow Point Lub—Lubricated
MC—Metal Case SP—Soft Point MP—Metal Point
LGC—Lead, Gas Check JHP—Jacketed Hollow Point

SHOTSHELL LOADS AND PRICES

Winchester-Western, Remington-Peters, Federal & Eley

In certain loadings one manufacturer may offer fewer or more shot sizes than another, but in general all makers offer equivalent loadings. Sources are indicated by letters, thus: W-W (a); R-P (b); Fed. (c); Eley (d). Prices are approximate.

GAUGE	Length Shell Ins.	Powder Equiv. Drams	Shot Ozs.	Shot Size	PRICE FOR 25
MAGNUM LOADS					
10 (a[1], b)	3½	5	2	2	$11.05
12 (a, b, c)	3	4½	1⅞	BB, 2, 4	6.15
12 (a[1], b)	3	4¼	1⅝	2, 4, 6	6.15
12 (a)	3	Max	1⅜	2, 4, 6	6.15
12 (a[1], b, c, d)	2¾	4	1½	2, 4, 5, 6	6.15
16 (a, b, c, d)	2¾	3½	1¼	2, 4, 6	5.35
20 (a, b, c)	3	3¼	1¼	4, 6, 7½	5.45
20 (a[1])	3	Max	1 3/16	4	5.45
20 (a[1], b, c, d)	2¾	3	1⅛	2, 4, 6, 7½	4.85
LONG RANGE LOADS					
10 (a, b)	2⅞	4¾	1⅝	4	6.55
12 (a[1], b, c, d)	2¾	3¾	1¼	BB, 2, 4, 5, 6, 7½, 9	4.85
16 (a, b, c, d)	2¾	3¼	1⅛	4, 5, 6, 7½, 9	4.45
20 (a[1], b, c, d)	2¾	2¾	1	4, 5, 6, 7½, 9	4.20
28 (a, b)	2¾	2¼	¾	6, 7½, 9	4.20
28 (c)	2¾	2¼	⅞	4, 6, 7½, 9	4.05
410 (b)	2½	max.	½	4, 6, 7½, 9	3.40
410 (b)	3	max.	11/16	4, 5, 6, 7½, 9	3.95
FIELD LOADS					
12 (a, b, c)	2¾	3¼	1¼	7½, 8	4.30
12 (a, b, c, d)	2¾	3¼	1⅛	4, 5, 6, 7½, 8, 9	4.15
12 (a, b, c, d)	2¾	3	1	4, 5, 6, 8	3.80
16 (a, b, c, d)	2¾	2¾	1⅛	4, 5, 6, 7½, 8, 9	3.80
16 (a, b, c)	2¾	2½	1	6, 8	3.65
20 (a, b, c, d)	2¾	2½	1	4, 5, 6, 7½, 8, 9	3.70
20 (a, b, c)	2¾	2¼	⅞	6, 8	3.40
SCATTER LOADS					
12 (a, b)	2¾	3	1⅛	8	4.35
TARGET LOADS					
12 (a, b, c)	2¾	3	1⅛	7½, 8	4.05
12 (a, b, c)	2¾	2¾	1⅛	7½, 8	4.05
16 (a, b, c)	2¾	2½	1	9	3.85
20 (a, b, c)	2¾	2¼	⅞	9	3.40
28 (a, c)	2¾	2¼	¾	9	4.20
410 (a, b, c, d)	3	Max	¾	9	4.20
410 (a, b, c)	2½	Max	½	9	3.35
SKEET & TRAP					
12 (a, b, c, d)	2¾	3	1⅛	7½, 8, 9	4.05
12 (a, b, c, d)	2¾	2¾	1⅛	7½, 8, 9	4.05
16 (a, b, c, d)	2¾	2½	1	9	3.80
16 (c)	2¾	1⅛	1⅛	8, 9	3.80
20 (a, b, c)	2¾	2¼	⅞	9	3.40
BUCKSHOT					
12 (a, b, c)	3 Mag.	4½	—	00 Buck—15 pellets	8.50
12 (a, b, c)	3 Mag.	4½	—	4 Buck—41 pellets	8.50
12 (b)	2¾ Mag.	4	—	1 Buck—20 pellets	7.35
12 (a, b, c)	2¾ Mag.	4	—	00 Buck—12 pellets	7.35
12 (a, b, c)	2¾	3¾	—	00 Buck— 9 pellets	6.60
12 (a, b, c)	2¾	3¾	—	0 Buck—12 pellets	6.60
12 (a, b, c)	2¾	3¾	—	1 Buck—16 pellets	6.60
12 (a, b, c)	2¾	3¾	—	4 Buck—27 pellets	6.60
16 (a, b, c)	2¾	3	—	1 Buck—12 pellets	6.50
20 (a, b, c)	2¾	2¾	—	3 Buck—20 pellets	6.50
RIFLED SLUGS					
12 (a, b, c, d)	2¾	3¾	1	Slug	7.60
16 (a, b, c)	2¾	3	⅞	Slug	7.25
20 (a, b, c)	2¾	2¾	⅝	Slug	7.00
410 (a, b, c)	2½	Max	⅕	Slug	6.60

W-W 410, 28- and 10-ga. Magnum shells available in paper cases only, as are their scatter and target loads; their skeet and trap loads come in both plastic and paper.

RP shells are all of plastic with Power Piston wads except: 12 ga. scatter loads have Post Wad: all 10 ga., 410-3" and rifled slug loads have standard wad columns.

Federal magnum, range, buckshot, slug and all 410 loads are made in plastic only. Field loads are available in both paper and plastic.

Eley shotshells are of plastic-coated paper.

[1]—These loads available from W-W with Lubaloy shot at higher price.

Left—Federal has reintroduced a favorite, old-style shotshell target load, the 12 gauge, 1⅛ ounce load which has no shot sleeve or shot protector. Called the "Special", it is a 3 dram equivalent load with paper case and 1⅛ ounces of extra hard shot in sizes 7½, 8 and 9. Suggested retail price is about 10 cents per box higher than that of Federal's paper tube Champion shell.

BERETTA MODEL 76 AUTO PISTOL
Caliber: 22 LR, 10-shot magazine.
Barrel: 6″.
Weight: 35 oz. **Length:** 9½″.
Stocks: Checkered plastic wrap-around.
Sights: Interchangeable blade front, adj. rear.
Features: Competition-type, non-glare ribbed heavy bbl., external hammer.
Price: **$175.00**

COLT GOLD CUP NAT'L MATCH MK IV Series 70
Caliber: 45 ACP, 7-shot magazine.
Barrel: 5″, with new design bushing.
Length: 8⅜″. **Weight:** 38½ oz.
Stocks: Checkered walnut, gold plated medallion.
Sights: Ramp-style front, Colt-Elliason rear adj. for w. and e., sight radius 6¾″.
Features: Arched or flat housing; wide, grooved trigger with adj. stop; ribbed-top slide, hand fitted, with improved ejection port.
Price: Colt Royal Blue **$256.00**

COLT WOODSMAN MATCH TARGET AUTO PISTOL
Caliber: 22 LR, 10-shot magazine.
Barrel: 4½″ or 6″.
Length: 10½″ (4½″ bbl.). **Weight:** 39 oz. (6″ bbl.), 34½ oz. (4½″ bbl.).
Stocks: Walnut with thumbrest; checkered.
Sights: Ramp front with removable undercut blade; ⅛″ standard, 1/10″ on special order; Colt-Elliason adjustable rear.
Features: Wide trigger, automatic slide stop.
Price: Colt Blue only **$164.95**

COLT WOODSMAN SPORT AND TARGET MODEL
Caliber: 22 LR, 10-shot magazine.
Barrel: 4″ (Sport), 6″ (Target).
Length: 9″ (4″ bbl.). **Weight:** 30 oz. (4″ bbl.) 32 oz. (6″ bbl.).
Stocks: Walnut with thumbrest; checkered.
Sights: Ramp front, adjustable rear for w. and e.
Features: Wide trigger, automatic slide stop.
Price: Colt Blue only **$147.50**

Colt Targetsman
Same as Woodsman S&T model except: 6″ bbl. only; fixed blade front sight, economy adj. rear; without auto. slide stop **$99.50**

HAMMERLI STANDARD, MODELS 208 & 211
Caliber: 22 LR.
Barrel: 5.9″, 6-groove.
Weight: 37.6 oz. (45 oz. with extra heavy barrel weight). **Length:** 10″.
Stocks: Walnut. Adj. palm rest (208), 211 has thumbrest grip.
Sights: Match sights, fully adj. for w. and e. (click adj.). Interchangeable front and rear blades.
Features: Semi-automatic, recoil operated. 8-shot clip. Slide stop. Fully adj. trigger (2¼ lbs. and 3 lbs.). Extra barrel weight available. Gil Hebard, importer.
Price: Model 208, approx. **$470.00** Model 211 approx. **$440.00**

HAMMERLI MODEL 230 RAPID FIRE PISTOL
Caliber: 22 S.
Barrel: 6.3″, 6-groove.
Weight: 43.8 oz. **Length:** 11.6″.
Stocks: Walnut. Standard grip w/o thumbrest (230-1), 230-2 has adj. grip.
Sights: Match type sights. Sight radius 9.9″. Micro rear, click adj. Interchangeable front sight blade.
Features: Semi-automatic. Recoil-operated, 6-shot clip. Gas escape in front of chamber to eliminate muzzle jump. Fully adj. trigger from 5¼ oz. to 10½ oz. with three different lengths available. Designed for International 25 meter Silhouette Program. Gil Hebard, importer.
Price: Model 230-1 .... **$455.00**
Price: Model 230-2 .... **$485.00**

HANDGUNS—TARGET AUTOLOADERS

HI-STANDARD SUPERMATIC STANDARD CITATION

Caliber: 22 LR, 10-shot magazine.
Barrel: 5½″ bull weight.
Length: 10″ (5½″ bbl.). **Weight:** 42 oz. (5½″ bbl.).
Stocks: Checkered walnut with or w/o thumbrest, right or left.
Features: Adjustable trigger pull; over-travel trigger adjustment; double acting safety; rebounding firing pin.
Sights: Undercut ramp front; click adjustable square notch rear.
Price: 5½″ bull barrel **$169.50**

HI-STANDARD SUPERMATIC TROPHY MILITARY

Caliber: 22 LR, 10-shot magazine.
Barrel: 5½″ heavy, 7¼″ fluted.
Length: 9¾″ (5½″ bbl.). **Weight:** 44½ oz.
Stocks: Checkered walnut with or w/o thumbrest, right or left.
Features: Grip duplicates feel of military 45; positive action mag. latch; front- and backstraps stippled. Trigger adj. for pull, over-travel.
Sights: Undercut ramp front; frame mounted rear, click adj.
Price: Either bbl. length **$175.00**

HI-STANDARD (*ISU) OLYMPIC AUTO PISTOL

Caliber: 22 Short, 10-shot magazine.
Barrel: 6¾″ round tapered, with stabilizer.
Length: 11¼″. **Weight:** 40 oz.
Stocks: Checkered walnut w or w/o thumbrest, right or left.
Sights: Undercut ramp front; click adj., square notch rear.
Features: Integral stabilizer with two removable weights. Trigger adj. for pull and over-travel; Citation grade finish.
Price: Blued **$204.00**
*Complies with all International Shooting Union regulations.
Olympic model with frame-mounted rear sight **$204.00**

HI-STANDARD S'MATIC CITATION MILITARY

Caliber: 22 LR, 10-shot magazine.
Barrel: 5½″ bull, 7¼″ fluted.
Length: 9¾″ (5½″ bbl.). **Weight:** 46 oz.
Stocks: Checkered walnut with or w/o thumbrest, right or left.
Sights: Undercut ramp front; frame mounted rear, click adj.
Features: Same as regular Citation plus military style grip, stippled front- and backstraps, positive magazine latch.
Price: Either bbl. length **$169.50**

HI-STANDARD VICTOR

Caliber: 22 LR, 10-shot magazine.
Barrel: 4½″, 5½″.
Length: 8¾″ (4½″ bbl.). **Weight:** 43½ oz. (4½″ bbl., vent. rib), 43¾ oz. (solid rib), 46 oz. (5½″ bbl., vent. rib), 46¼ oz. (solid rib).
Stocks: Checkered walnut.
Sights: Undercut ramp front, rib mounted click adj. rear.
Features: Vent. rib, interchangeable barrel, 2 - 2¼ lb. trigger pull, blue finish, back and front straps stippled. Also available with aluminum solid rib.
Price: Either bbl. length **$209.00**
Price: Solid rib, either bbl. length **$198.00**

RUGER Mark 1 TARGET MODEL AUTO PISTOL

Caliber: 22 LR only, 9-shot magazine.
Barrel: 6⅞″ or 5½″ bull barrel (6-groove, 14″ twist).
Length: 10⅞″ (6⅞″ bbl.). **Weight:** 42 oz. with 6⅞″ bbl.
Stocks: Checkered hard rubber.
Features: Rear sight mounted on receiver, does not move with slide; wide, grooved trigger.
Sights: ⅛″ blade front, micro click rear, adjustable for w. and e. Sight radius 9⅜″ (with 6⅞″ bbl.).
Price: Blued, either barrel length **$86.50**

SIG/HAMMERLI P240 TARGET PISTOL

Caliber: 38 Special Wadcutter, 5-shot.
Barrel: 6″.
Weight: 4¼ oz. **Length:** 10″ over-all.
Stocks: Walnut, target style, unfinished.
Sights: Match sights; ⅛″ undercut front, ⅛″ notch micro rear click adj. for w. and e.
Features: Semi-automatic, recoil operated; meets I.S.U. and N.R.A. specs for Center Fire Pistol competition; double pull trigger adj. from 2 lbs., 15 ozs.; to 3 lbs., 9 ozs.; trigger stop. Comes with extra magazine, cleaning rod, special screwdriver, carrying case, From Gil Hebard.
Price: **$650.00**
Price: 22 cal. conversion unit (avail. late 1975) **$255.00**

SMITH & WESSON 22 MATCH HEAVY BARREL M-41

Caliber: 22 LR, 10-shot clip.
Barrel: 5½″ heavy, without muzzle brake. Sight radius, 8″.
Length: 9″. **Weight:** 44½ oz.
Stocks: Checkered walnut with modified thumbrest, usable with either hand.
Features: ⅜″ wide, grooved trigger; adj. trigger stop.
Sights: ⅛″ Patridge on ramp base. S&W micro click rear, adj. for w. and e.
Price: S&W Bright Blue, satin matted top area **$172.00**

Smith & Wesson Conversion Kit

Converts Models 41 from 22 Short to 22 LR and vice versa. Consists of barrel, slide, magazine, slide stop and recoil spring.
Price, parts only **$75.00**
Price, factory installed and tested **$85.00**
Price, 5½″ heavy bbl. only with sights for M41 .... **$43.00**

SMITH & WESSON 38 MASTER Model 52 AUTO

Caliber: 38 Special (for Mid-range W.C. with flush-seated bullet only). 5-shot magazine.
Barrel: 5″.
Length: 8⅝″. **Weight:** 41 oz. with empty magazine.
Stocks: Checkered walnut.
Sights: ⅛″ Patridge front, S&W micro click rear adj. for w. and e.
Features: Top sighting surfaces matte finished. Locked breech, moving barrel system; checked for 10-ring groups at 50 yards. Coin-adj. sight screws. Dry firing permissible if manual safety on.
Price: S&W Bright Blue **$267.50**

CVA/UNIQUE D.E.S. 69 TARGET PISTOL

Caliber: 22 LR.
Barrel: 5.91″.
Weight: Approx. 35 oz. **Length:** 10.63″ over-all.
Stocks: French walnut target style with thumbrest and adjustable shelf; hand checkered panels.
Sights: Ramp front, micro. adj. rear mounted on frame; 8.66″ sight radius.
Features: Meets U.I.T. standards. Comes in a fitted hard case with spare magazine, barrel weight, cleaning rod, tools, proof certificate, test target and two year guarantee. Fully adjustable trigger; dry firing safety device. Imported from France by Connecticut Valley Arms.
Price: Right-hand **$375.00**
Price: Left-hand **$395.00**

SMITH & WESSON 22 AUTO PISTOL Model 41

Caliber: 22 LR or 22 S, 10-shot clip.
Barrel: 7⅜″, sight radius 9 5/16″ (7⅜″ bbl.).
Length: 12″, incl. detachable muzzle brake, (7⅜″ bbl. only).
Weight: 43½ oz. (7⅜″ bbl.).
Stocks: Checkered walnut with thumbrest, usable with either hand.
Features: ⅜″ wide, grooved trigger with adj. stop; wgts. available to make pistol up to 59 oz.
Sights: Front, ⅛″ Patridge undercut; micro click rear adj. for w. and e.
Price: S&W Bright Blue, satin matted bbl., either caliber **$172.00**

WALTHER GSP MATCH PISTOL

Caliber: 22 LR, 32 S&W wadcutter (GSP-C), 5-shot.
Barrel: 4½″.
Weight: 44.8 oz. (22 LR), 49.4 oz. (32). **Length:** 11.8″ over-all.
Stocks: Walnut, special hand-fitting design.
Sights: Fixed front, rear adj. for w. & e.
Features: Available with either 2.2 lb. (1000 gm) or 3 lb. (1360 gm) trigger. Spare mag., bbl. weight, tools supplied in Match Pistol Kit. Imported from Germany by Interarms.
Price: GSP **$429.00**
Price: GSP-C **$499.00**
Price: 22 cal. conversion unit for GSP-C **$279.00**
Price: Optional carrying case for GSP-OSP **$22.00**

WALTHER OSP RAPID-FIRE PISTOL

Similar to Model GSP except 22 Short only, stock had adj. free-style hand rest.
Price: **$429.00**

COLT DIAMONDBACK REVOLVER
Caliber: 22 S, L or LR, or 38 Special, 6 shot.
Barrel: 2½″ or 4″, with ventilated rib.
Length: 9″ (4″ bbl.). **Weight:** 24 oz. (2½″ bbl.), 28½ oz. (4″ bbl.).
Stocks: Checkered walnut, target type, square butt.
Features: Ventilated rib; grooved, crisp trigger; swing-out cylinder; wide hammer spur.
Sights: Ramp front, adj. notch rear.
Price: Colt Blue **$176.00**
Price: Nickel finish (38 Spl. only) **$188.00**

COLT PYTHON REVOLVER
Caliber: 357 Magnum (handles all 38 Spec.), 6 shot.
Barrel: 2½″, 4″ or 6″, with ventilated rib.
Length: 9¼″ (4″ bbl.). **Weight:** 38 oz. (4″ bbl.).
Stocks: Checkered walnut, target type, square butt.
Features: Ventilated rib; grooved, crisp trigger; swing-out cylinder; target hammer.
Sights: ⅛″ ramp front, adj. notch rear.
Price: Colt Blue .... **$253.00** Nickeled **$282.00**

SMITH & WESSON COMBAT MASTERPIECE
Caliber: 38 Special (M15) or 22 LR (M18), 6 shot.
Barrel: 2″ (M15) 4″ (M18)
Length: 9⅛″ (4″ bbl.). **Weight:** Loaded, 22 36½ oz, 38 30 oz.
Stocks: Checkered walnut, Magna. Grooved tangs and trigger.
Sights: Front, ⅛″ Baugham Quick Draw on ramp, micro click rear, adjustable for w. and e.
Price: Blued, M-15 and M-18 .... **$135.00**
Price: Nickel M-15 .... **$145.00**
Price: M-18, blued **$135.00**

SMITH & WESSON MASTERPIECE TARGET MODELS

Model: K-22 (M17).	K-22 (M48).
Caliber: 22 LR, 6 shot.	22 RF Magnum, 6 shot.
Barrel: 6″, 8⅜″.	4″, 6″ or 8⅜″
Length: 11⅛″ (6″ bbl.).	11⅛″ (6″ bbl.).
Weight: 38½ oz. (6″ bbl.).	39 oz.(6″ bbl.).
Model: K-32 (M16). (Illus.)	K-38 (M14).
Caliber: 32 S&W Long, 6 shot.	38 S&W Special, 6 shot.
Barrel: 6 inches.	6″, 8⅜″.
Length: 11⅛ inches.	11⅛ inches. (6″ bbl.)
Weight: 38½ oz. (Loaded).	38½ oz. (6″, loaded).

Features: All Masterpiece models have: checkered walnut, Magna stocks; grooved tang and trigger; ⅛″ Patridge front sight, micro. adj. rear sights. Swing out cylinder revolver. For 8⅜″ barrel add **$6.50**
Price: Blued, all calibers M-17, 6″ bbl. **$135.00**
Price: Blued, all calibers M-48, 6″ bbl. **140.00**

SMITH & WESSON 1955 Model 25, 45 TARGET
Caliber: 45 ACP and 45 AR, 6 shot.
Barrel: 6½″ (heavy target type).
Length: 11⅞ inches. **Weight:** 45 oz.
Stocks: Checkered walnut target.
Sights: ⅛″ Patridge front, micro click rear, adjustable for w. and e.
Features: Tangs and trigger grooved; target trigger and hammer standard, checkered target hammer. Swing-out cylinder revolver. Price includes presentation case.
Price: Blued **$215.00**

Smith & Wesson Accessories
Target hammers with low, broad, deeply-checkered spur, and wide-swaged, grooved target trigger. For all frame sizes, **$5.75** (target hammers not available for small frames). Target stocks: for large-frame guns, **$14.25** to **$16.00**; for med.-frame guns, **$12.00** to **$14.50**; for small-frame guns, **$10.75** to **$14.00**. These prices applicable only when specified on original order.

As separately-ordered parts: target hammers and triggers, **$9.25**; stocks, **$13.75-$24.00**.

TAURUS MODEL 86 TARGET MASTER REVOLVER
Caliber: 38 Spec., 6-shot.
Barrel: 6″ only.
Weight: 41 oz. **Length:** 11¼″ over-all.
Stocks: Over size target-type, checkered Brazilian walnut.
Sights: Patridge front, micro. click rear adj. for w. and e.
Features: Blue finish with non-reflective finish on barrel. Imported from Brazil by International Distributors.
Price: **$115.50**
Price: Model 96 Scout Master, same except in 22 cal **$115.50**

ASTRA CONSTABLE AUTO PISTOL

Caliber: 22 LR, 10-shot; 32 ACP, 8-shot; and 380 ACP, 7-shot.
Barrel: 3½".
Weight: 26 oz.
Stocks: Moulded plastic.
Sights: Adj. rear.
Features: Double action, quick no-tool takedown, non-glare rib on slide. 380 available in blue or chrome finish. Imported from Spain by Garcia.
Price: Blue **$150.00**
Price: Chrome **$165.00**

AUTO MAG AUTO. PISTOL

Caliber: 44 Auto Mag or 357 Auto Mag, 7-shot.
Barrel: 6½".
Weight: 57 oz. (44), 54 oz. (357). **Length:** 11½" over-all.
Stocks: Checkered polyurethane.
Sights: Target-type ramp front, fully adj. rear.
Features: Short recoil, rotary bolt system. Made of stainless steel. Conversion unit available to change caliber using same frame. Comes in plastic carrying case with extra magazine, wrenches, lubricant and manual. From High Standard and Lee E. Jurras & Assoc.
Price: 44 AMP, 357 AMP or 41 JMP (Jurras only) **$500.00**
Price: Conversion unit (6½" or 8½") **$195.00**

BAUER 25 AUTOMATIC PISTOL

Caliber: 25 ACP, 6-shot.
Barrel: 2⅛".
Weight: 10 oz. **Length:** 4".
Stocks: Plastic pearl or checkered walnut.
Sights: Recessed, fixed.
Features: Stainless steel construction, positive manual safety, magazine safety. With padded zipper case.
Price: Satin stainless steel **$94.95**

BERETTA MODEL 951 AUTO PISTOL

Caliber: 9mm Para., 8-shot magazine.
Barrel: 4½".
Weight: 31 oz. **Length:** 8".
Stocks: Moulded plastic.
Sights: Fixed.
Features: Crossbolt safety, external hammer, slide stays open after last shot.
Price: **$260.00**

BERETTA MODEL 70S AUTO PISTOL

Caliber: 380 ACP, 7-shot magazine.
Barrel: 3⅝".
Weight: 23¼ oz. **Length:** 6¼".
Stocks: Checkered plastic wrap-around.
Sights: Fixed front and rear.
Features: External hammer.
Price: **$145.00**

BERETTA DA AUTO PISTOL

Caliber: 380 ACP, 13-shot magazine.
Barrel: 3¾".
Weight: 23 oz. **Length:** 6½" over-all.
Stocks: Smooth walnut.
Sights: Blade front, rear drift adj. for w.
Features: Double-action, 14 shot capacity; right hand/left hand safety; reversible magazine release; free-falling magazine; round spur non-snagging hammer; inertia firing pin; non-tool takedown.
Price: .... To be announced.

BERNARDELLI MODEL 60 AUTO PISTOL
Caliber: 22 LR, 10-shot; 32 ACP, 8-shot; and 380, 7-shot.
Barrel: 3½".
Weight: 26 oz. **Length:** 6⅓".
Stocks: Checkered plastic.
Sights: Post front, click adj. rear.
Features: Manual and magazine safeties. Optional thumb rest grips, $10.00. Imported from Italy by Kleinguenther's, Liberty.
Price: **$90.00**

BERNARDELLI MODEL 80 AUTO PISTOL
Caliber: 22 LR (10-shot); 32 ACP (8-shot); 380 ACP (7-shot).
Barrel: 3½".
Weight: 26½ oz.
Stocks: Checkered plastic with thumbrest.
Sights: Ramp front, white outline rear adj. for w. & e.
Features: Hammer block slide safety; loaded chamber indicator; dual recoil springs; serrated trigger; inertia type firing pin. Imported from Italy by Interarms.
Price: Model 80 .... **$149.00**
Price: Model 90 (as above except 6" bbl.) **$169.00**

Bernardelli Model 100 Target Pistol
Similar to Model 80 except has 5.9" barrel and barrel weight; checkered walnut thumbrest grips; 22 LR only (10-shot). **$249.00**

BUDISCHOWSKY TP-70 AUTO PISTOL
Caliber: 25 ACP or 22 LR, 6-shot.
Barrel: 2.6".
Length: 4⅔". **Weight:** 12⅓ oz.
Stocks: Checkered ABS plastic.
Sights: Fixed. Full length serrated rib.
Features: Double action, exposed hammer, manual and magazine safeties. Slide stop, action hold-open after last shot. All stainless steel construction. Norton Armament Corp., manufacturer.
Price: 25 ACP **$125.00**
Price: 22 LR **$135.00**

COLT COMMANDER AUTO PISTOL
Caliber: 45 ACP, 7 shot; 38 Super Auto, 9 shot; 9mm Luger, 9 shot.
Barrel: 4¼".
Length: 8". **Weight:** 27 oz.
Stocks: Sandblasted walnut.
Features: Grooved trigger and hammer spur; arched housing; grip and thumb safeties.
Sights: Fixed, glare-proofed blade front, square notch rear.
Price: Blued **$175.50**

Colt Combat Commander
Same as Commander except steel frame, wood panel grips, weight 36½ oz. (9mm and 38 Super).
Price: Blue or satin nickel **$175.50**

COLT GOV'T MODEL MK IV/SERIES 70
Caliber: 9mm, 38 Super, 45 ACP, 7-shot.
Barrel: 5".
Weight: 40 oz. **Length:** 8⅜" over-all.
Stocks: Sandblasted walnut panels.
Sights: Ramp front, fixed square notch rear.
Features: Grip and thumb safeties, grooved trigger. Accurizor barrel and bushing. Blue finish or nickel in 45 only.
Price: Blue **$175.50**
Price: Nickel **$192.00**

BROWNING HI-POWER 9mm AUTOMATIC PISTOL
Caliber: 9mm Parabellum (Luger), 13-shot magazine.
Barrel: $4^{21}/_{32}$ inches.
Length: 7¾" over-all. **Weight:** 32 oz.
Stocks: Walnut, hand checkered.
Sights: Fixed front; rear adj. for w.
Features: External hammer with half-cock safety, thumb and magazine safeties. A blow on the hammer cannot discharge a cartridge; cannot be fired with magazine removed. Fixed rear sight model available.
Price: Fixed sight model **$254.50**
Price: 9mm with rear sight adj. for w. and e. **$274.50**

Browning Renaissance Hi-Power 9mm Auto
Same as Browning Hi-Power 9mm Auto except: fully engraved, chrome plated, polyester pearl grips **$800.00**

Colt Conversion Unit
Permits the 45 and 38 Super Automatic pistols to use the economical 22 LR cartridge. No tools needed. Adjustable rear sight; 10-shot magazine. Designed to give recoil effect of the larger calibers. Not adaptable to Commander models. Blue finish **$94.00**

COLT HUNTSMAN AUTO PISTOL

Caliber: 22 LR, 10-shot magazine.
Barrel: 4″, 6″.
Length: 8⅝″ (4″ bbl.). **Weight:** 29½ oz. (4″ bbl.), 31 oz. (6″ bbl.).
Stocks: Checkered walnut. Wide trigger.
Sights: Fixed ramp front, square notch rear, non-adjustable.
Price: Colt Blue **$109.50**

F.I. MODEL D AUTO PISTOL

Caliber: 380 ACP, 6-shot.
Barrel: 3⅛″.
Weight: 20 oz. **Length:** 6⅛″ over-all.
Stocks: Checkered walnut.
Sights: Blade front, rear adj. for w.
Features: Loaded chamber indicator, all steel construction. Thumb safety locks hammer. No magazine safety. Lanyard ring. Made by Firearms International Industries. From Garcia/F.I.
Price: Approx. **$150.00**

F.I.E. E27 TITAN PISTOL

Caliber: 25 ACP, 6-shot magazine
Barrel: $2\frac{7}{16}$″.
Length: 4⅝″ over-all. **Weight:** 12 oz.
Stocks: Checkered plastic.
Sights: Fixed.
Features: External hammer; fast simple takedown. Made in U.S.A.
Price: Blued .... **$42.80** Chromed: **$45.70**

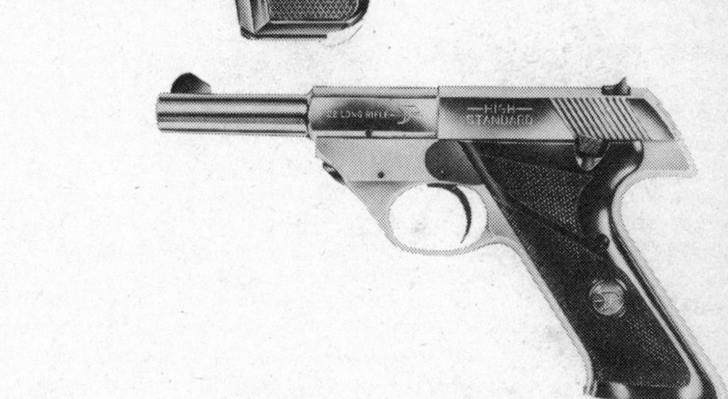

HIGH STANDARD SPORT-KING AUTO PISTOL

Caliber: 22 LR, 9-shot.
Barrel: 4½″ or 6¾″.
Weight: 39 oz. (4½″ bbl.). **Length:** 9″ over-all (4½″ bbl.).
Stocks: Black checkered plastic.
Sights: Blade front, fixed rear.
Features: Takedown barrel. Blue or nickel finish.
Price: Either bbl. length, blue finish **$99.95**
Price: Nickel finish **$109.95**

INDIAN ARMS STAINLESS DOUBLE ACTION AUTO

Caliber: 380 ACP, 6-shot magazine.
Barrel: 3¼″.
Weight: 20 oz. **Length:** $6\frac{1}{16}$″.
Stocks: Checkered walnut.
Sights: Fixed blade front, drift-adj. rear.
Features: All stainless steel, natural or blued finish. Double action, stays open after last shot. Optional lock with key to lock safety is integral with slide. From Indian Arms.
Price: With or without safety lock, either finish **$185.00**

LLAMA MODELS VIII, IXA AUTO PISTOLS

Caliber: Super 38 (M. VIII), 45 ACP (M. IXA).
Barrel: 5″.
Weight: 30 oz. **Length:** 8½″.
Stocks: Checkered walnut.
Sights: Fixed.
Features: Grip and manual safeties, ventilated rib. Engraved, chrome engraved or gold damascened finish available at extra cost. Imported from Spain by Stoeger Industries.
Price: **$159.95**

Consult our Directory pages for the location of firms mentioned.

HI-STANDARD SHARPSHOOTER AUTO PISTOL

Caliber: 22 LR, 9-shot magazine.
Barrel: 5½″.
Length: 9″ over-all. **Weight:** 45 oz.
Stocks: Checkered laminated plastic.
Sights: Fixed, ramp front, square notch rear adj. for w. & e.
Features: Wide, scored trigger; new hammer-sear design. Slide lock, push-button take down.
Price: Blued **$130.00**

LLAMA XI AUTO PISTOL

Caliber: 9mm Para.
Barrel: 5″.
Weight: 38 oz. **Length:** 8½″.
Stocks: Moulded plastic.
Sights: Fixed front, adj. rear.
Features: Also available with engraved, chrome engraved or gold damascened finish at extra cost. Imported from Spain by Stoeger Industries.
Price: **$159.95**

LLAMA MODELS XV, XA, IIIA AUTO PISTOLS

Caliber: 22 LR, 32 ACP and 380.
Barrel: 3 11/16″.
Weight: 23 oz. **Length:** 6½″.
Stocks: Checkered plastic, thumb rest.
Sights: Fixed front, adj. notch rear.
Features: Ventilated rib, manual and grip safeties. Model XV is 22 LR, Model XA is 32 ACP, and Model IIIA is 380. Models XA and IIIA have loaded indicator; IIIA is locked breech. Imported from Spain by Stoeger Industries.
Price: **$124.95**

MKE MODEL TPK AUTO PISTOL

Caliber: 32 ACP, 8-shot; 380, 7-shot.
Barrel: 4″.
Weight: 23 oz. **Length:** 6½″.
Stocks: Checkered black plastic.
Sights: Fixed front, adj. notch rear.
Features: Double action with exposed hammer; safety blocks firing pin and drops hammer. Chamber loaded indicator pin. Imported from Turkey by Firearms Center.
Price: **$154.00**
Price: With Armaloy finish **$184.00**

MAUSER HSc AUTO PISTOL

Caliber: 32 ACP, 380 ACP, 7-shot.
Barrel: 3⅜″.
Weight: 23 oz. **Length:** 6.05″.
Stocks: Checkered walnut.
Sights: Fixed.
Features: Double action, manual and magazine safeties. Imported from Germany by Interarms.
Price: .... **$199.00** Nickel plated **$219.00**

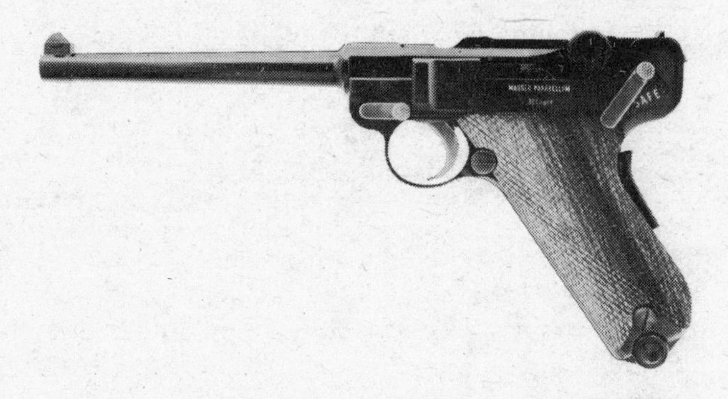

MAUSER PARABELLUM AUTO PISTOL

Caliber: 30 Luger, 9mm Para., 8-shot.
Barrel: 4″ (9mm), 4″ and 6″ (30 Luger).
Weight: 32 oz. **Length:** 8⅔″ (4″ bbl.).
Stocks: Checkered walnut.
Sights: Fixed.
Features: Manual and grip safeties, American eagle over chamber. Imported from Germany by Interarms.
Price: **$299.00**

MAUSER PARABELLUM P-08

Caliber: 30 Luger, 9mm Parabellum, 8-shot clip.
Barrel: 6″ in 30 Luger, 4″ and 6″ in 9mm Parabellum
Weight: 32 oz. **Length:** 4″ bbl—8.66″; 6″ bbl—10.63″.
Stocks: Checkered Walnut.
Sights: Fixed.
Features: Differs from current '06 with classic '08 details, including different take-down lever, trigger, safety and curved front strap. Limited production marked with American eagle over chamber and Mauser banner on the toggle. Imported by Interarms.
Price: **$399.00**

PLAINFIELD MODEL 71

Caliber: 22 LR (10-shot) and 25 ACP (8-shot).
Barrel: 1″.
Length: 5⅛″ over-all. **Weight:** 25 oz.
Stocks: Checkered walnut.
Sights: Fixed.
Features: Easily converts from 22 cal. to 25 cal. by changing bolt, bbl. and magazine. Stainless steel frame and slide.
Price: With conversion kit. . **$87.00** M71 in 22 cal. only **$66.00**
Price: M71 in 25 cal. only **$66.00**

Plainfield Model 72

Same as Model 71 except: has 3½″ bbl. and aluminum slide.
Price: Model 72 & conversion kit **$95.95**
Price: 22 cal. only **$75.95**
Price: 25 cal. only **$75.95**

RUGER STANDARD MODEL AUTO PISTOL
Caliber: 22 LR, 9-shot magazine.
Barrel: 4¾" or 6".
Length: 8¾" (4¾" bbl.). **Weight:** 36 oz. (4¾" bbl.).
Stocks: Checkered hard rubber.
Sights: Fixed, wide blade front, square notch rear.
Price: Blued **$69.00**

SMITH & WESSON 9mm MODEL 39 AUTO PISTOL
Caliber: 9mm Luger, 8-shot clip.
Barrel: 4".
Length: 7⁷⁄₁₆". **Weight:** 26½ oz., without magazine.
Stocks: Checkered walnut.
Sights: ⅛" serrated ramp front, adjustable rear.
Features: Magazine disconnector, positive firing pin lock and hammer-release safety; alloy frame with lanyard loop; locked-breech, short-recoil double action; slide locks open on last shot.
Price: Blued .... **$148.50** Nickeled **$164.00**

L-E-S P-18 AUTO PISTOL
Caliber: 9mm Para.
Barrel: 5.5", stationary; polygonal rifling.
Weight: Approx. 36 oz.
Stocks: Checkered resin.
Sights: Post front, V-notch rear drift adj. for w.
Features: Gas operated, double action; stainless steel; inertia firing pin; hammer drop safety; 18-shot magazine. Completely manufactured in U.S.A. From L-E-S.
Price: **$175.00**

SMITH & WESSON MODEL 59 DOUBLE ACTION
Caliber: 9mm Luger, 14-shot clip.
Barrel: 4".
Length: 7⁷⁄₁₆" over-all. **Weight:** 27½ oz., without clip.
Stocks: Checkered high impact moulded nylon.
Sights: ⅛" serrated ramp front, square notch rear adj. for w.
Features: Double action automatic. Furnished with two magazines. Blue finish.
Price: Blued **$178.50**
Price: Nickel **$194.50**

STAR BKS STARLIGHT AUTO PISTOL
Caliber: 9mm Para., 8-shot magazine.
Barrel: 4¼".
Weight: 25 oz.
Stocks: Checkered plastic.
Sights: Fixed.
Features: Blue or chrome finish. Magazine and manual safeties, external hammer. Imported from Spain by Garcia.
Price: Blue **$160.00**
Price: Chrome **$170.00**

STAR SUPER SM
Caliber: 380 ACP, 10-shot.
Barrel: 4".
Weight: 22 oz. **Length:** 6⅝" over-all.
Stocks: Plastic, checkered.
Sights: Blade front, adj. rear.
Features: Blue or chrome finish. Loaded chamber indicator, thumb safety. Imported from Spain by Garcia.
Price: Blue **$145.00**
Price: Chrome **$155.00**

STAR FRS AUTO PISTOL
Caliber: 22 LR, 10-shot magazine.
Barrel: 6".
Weight: 30 oz.
Stocks: Checkered plastic.
Sights: Fixed front, adj. rear.
Features: External hammer, manual safety. Available in blue or chrome (Model FRS-C). Alloy frame. Imported from Spain by Garcia.
Price: Blue **$120.00**
Price: Chrome **$130.00**

STAR MODEL AS AUTO PISTOL

Caliber: 38 Super, 9-shot.
Barrel: 5″.
Weight: 37½ oz. **Length:** 8½″.
Stocks: Checkered walnut.
Sights: Fixed.
Features: Blue or chrome finish. Magazine and manual safeties, wide-spur hammer. Imported from Spain by Garcia.
Price: Blue **$160.00**
Price: Chrome **$170.00**

STAR MODEL FM AUTO PISTOL

Caliber: 22 LR, 10-shot magazine
Barrel: 4¼″.
Weight: 30 oz.
Stocks: Checkered plastic.
Sights: Fixed front, adj. rear.
Features: Blue or chrome finish. External hammer, manual safety. Imported from Spain by Garcia.
Price: Blue **$120.00**
Price: Chrome **$130.00**

STAR MODEL PD AUTO PISTOL

Caliber: 45 ACP, 7-shot magazine.
Barrel: 3.8″.
Weight: 25 oz. **Length:** 7″ over-all.
Stocks: Checkered walnut.
Sights: Ramp front, fully adjustable rear.
Features: Rear sight milled into slide; thumb safety; grooved non-slip front strap; nylon recoil buffer; inertia firing pin; no grip or magazine safeties. From Garcia.
Price: Blue **$210.00**
Price: Chrome **$220.00**

STERLING MODEL 300

Caliber: 25 ACP, 6-shot.
Barrel: 2½″.
Length: 4½″ over-all. **Weight:** 13 oz.
Stocks: Cycolac, black or white.
Sights: Fixed.
Features: All steel construction.
Price: Blued .... **$69.95** Satin nickel **$74.95**

STERLING MODEL 302

Caliber: 22 LR, 6-shot.
Barrel: 2½″.
Length: 4½″ over-all. **Weight:** 13 oz.
Stocks: Cycolac, black or white.
Sights: Fixed.
Features: All steel construction.
Price: Blue **$69.95**
Price: Satin nickel **$74.95**

STERLING MODEL 400 DOUBLE ACTION

Caliber: 380 ACP, 7-shot.
Barrel: 3¾″.
Length: 6½″ over-all. **Weight:** 24 oz.
Stocks: Simulated checkered walnut.
Features: All steel construction. Double action.
Price: Blued .... **$129.95** Satin nickel **$134.95**

STOEGER LUGER 22 AUTO PISTOL

Caliber: 22 LR, 12-shot (11 in magazine, 1 in chamber).
Barrel: 4½" or 5½".
Weight: 30 oz.
Stocks: Checkered wood, identical to P-08.
Features: Action remains open after last shot and as magazine is removed. Grip and balance identical to P-08.
Price: Either bbl. length **$99.95**
Price: Kit includes extra clip, charger, holster **$109.95**
Price: Adj. sight model **$109.95**

WALTHER PP AUTO PISTOL

Caliber: 22 LR, 32 ACP, 8-shot; 380 ACP, 7-shot.
Barrel: 3.86".
Weight: 23½ oz. **Length:** 6.7".
Stocks: Checkered plastic.
Sights: Fixed, white markings.
Features: Double action, manual safety blocks firing pin and drops hammer, chamber loaded indicator on 32 and 380, finger rest extra magazine provided. Imported from Germany by Interarms.
Price: (22 LR) **$212.00**
Price: (32 and 380) **$199.00**
Price: Engraved models start at **$600.00**

Walther PPK/S Auto Pistol

Same as PP except bbl. 3.27", length 6.1" o.a.
Price: 32 or 380 ACP **$199.00**
Price: 22 LR **$212.00**
Price: Engraved models start at **$600.00**

WALTHER P-38 AUTO PISTOL

Caliber: 22 LR, 30 Luger or 9mm Luger, 8-shot.
Barrel: 4 15/16" (9mm and 30), 5 1/16" (22 LR).
Weight: 28 oz. **Length:** 8½".
Stocks: Checkered plastic.
Sights: Fixed.
Features: Double action, safety blocks firing pin and drops hammer, chamber loaded indicator. Matte finish standard, polished blue, engraving and/or plating available. Imported from Germany by Interarms.
Price: 22 LR **$285.00**
Price: 9mm or 30 Luger **$255.00**
Price: Engraved models start at **$700.00**

HANDGUNS—REVOLVERS, SERVICE & SPORT

ARMINIUS REVOLVERS

Caliber: 38 Special, 32 S&W Long (6-shot); 22 Magnum, 22 LR (8-shot).
Barrel: 4" (38 Spec., 32 S&W, 22 LR); 6" (38 Spec., 22 LR 22 Mag.).
Weight: 35 oz. (6" bbl.). **Length:** 11" (6" bbl. 38).
Stocks: Checkered plastic.
Sights: Ramp front, fixed rear on standard models, w. & e. adj. on target models.
Features: Ventilated rib, solid frame, swing-out cylinder. Interchangeable 22 Mag. cylinder available with 22 cal versions. Imported from West Germany by Firearms Import & Export.
Price: .... **$70.50** to **$99.95**

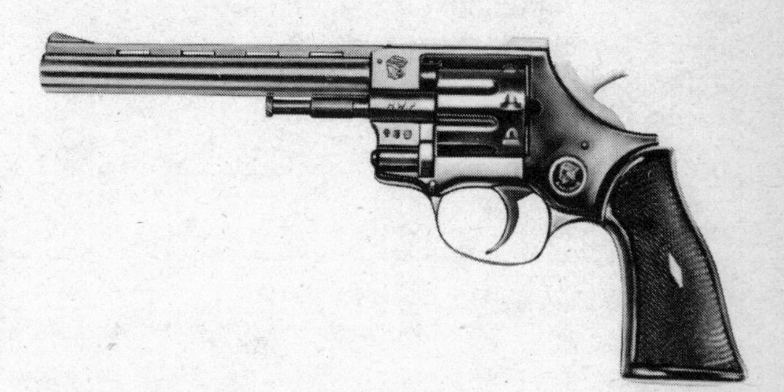

ASTRA 357 MAGNUM REVOLVER

Caliber: 357 Magnum, 6-shot.
Barrel: 3", 4", 6".
Weight: 40 oz. (6" bbl.). **Length:** 11¼" (6" bbl.).
Stocks: Checkered walnut. Magna-style on 3", target-type on 4" and 6".
Sights: Fixed front, rear adj. for w. and e.
Features: Swing-out cylinder with countersunk chambers, floating firing pin. Imported from Spain by Garcia
Price: 3", 4", or 6" **$185.00**

APACHE REVOLVERS

Caliber: 22 LR, 8 shot; 32 S&W, 7 shot; 38 Special, 6 shot.
Barrel: 4", 3" (available in 38 Special only).
Stocks: Checkered plastic.
Sights: Fixed front, rear adj. for w. & e.
Features: Ventilated rib on bbl. Imported from Germany by Jana.
Price: **$86.00**

CHARTER ARMS BULLDOG
Caliber: 44 Special, 5-shot.
Barrel: 3″.
Weight: 19 oz.
Stocks: Checkered plastic.
Sights: Patridge type 9/64″ front, square notch rear.
Features: Wide trigger and hammer, chrome-moly steel frame, unbreakable firing pin, transfer bar ignition.
Price: **$138.00**

CHARTER ARMS POLICE BULLDOG
Caliber: 38 Special, 6-shot.
Barrel: 4″.
Weight: 20 oz. **Length:** 7¼″ over-all.
Stocks: Hand checkered American walnut.
Sights: Full length ramp front; fully adj. combat rear.
Features: Accepts both regular and high velocity ammunition; enclosed ejector rod; full length ejection of fired cases.
Price: Blue only, approx. **$135.00**

CHARTER ARMS "UNDERCOVER" REVOLVER
Caliber: 38 Special, 5 shot.
Barrel: 2″ or 3.
Length: 6¼″ (round butt). **Weight:** 16 oz.
Stocks: Smooth walnut.
Sights: Fixed; matted ramp front, ⅛″ wide blade.
Features: Wide trigger and hammer spur
Price: Polished Blue .... **$104.00** Nickel **$115.00**
Price: With checkered, finger-rest Bulldog grips (blue) **$111.00**

Charter Arms Undercoverette
Like the Undercover, but a 6-shot 32 S&W Long revolver available with 2″ barrel only, and weighing 16½ oz.
Price: Polished blue **$105.00**
Price: With checkered finger-rest Bulldog grips **$112.00**

Charter Arms Pathfinder
Same as Undercover but in 22 LR caliber, and has 3″ bbl. Fitted with adjustable rear sight, ramp front. Weight 18½ oz.
Price: Blued **$114.60**
Price: With checkered, finger-rest Bulldog grips **$121.00**

COLT AGENT REVOLVER
Caliber: 38 Special, 6 shot.
Barrel: 2″ (Twist, 1-16).
Length: 6⅝″ over-all. **Weight:** 16 oz.
Stocks: Checkered walnut, round butt. Grooved trigger.
Sights: Fixed, glare-proofed ramp front, square notch rear.
Price: Blued .... **$141.00** With a hammer shroud installed .. **$146.00**

COLT COBRA REVOLVER
Caliber: 38 Special, 6 shot.
Barrel: 2″.
Length: 6⅝″ over-all. **Weight:** 16½ oz.
Stocks: Checkered walnut, round butt. Grooved trigger.
Sights: Fixed, glare-proofed ramp front, square notch rear.
Price: Blued .... **$143.00** Nickeled **$162.00**

COLT DETECTIVE SPECIAL
Caliber: 38 Special, 6-shot.
Barrel: 2″.
Length: 6⅝″ over-all. **Weight:** 22 oz.
Stocks: Full, checkered walnut, round butt.
Sights: Fixed, ramp front, square notch rear.
Features: Glare-proofed sights, smooth trigger. Nickel finish, hammer shroud available as options.
Price: Blue **$140.00**
Price: Nickel **$149.50**

Colt Hammer Shroud
Facilitates quick draw from holster or pocket. Hammer spur projects just enough to allow for cocking for single action firing. Fits only Colt Detective Special, Cobra and Agent revolvers. Factory installed on new guns, **$5,** or as a kit for installation. Blued only **$6.00**
Factory installed on your gun (listed above). Blued only **$7.50**

Consult our Directory pages for the location of firms mentioned.

COLT OFFICIAL POLICE Mk III REVOLVER
Caliber: 38 Special, 6 shot.
Barrel: 4".
Weight: 33 oz.
Length: 9⅜".
Stocks: Checkered walnut, service style.
Sights: Fixed, glare-proofed ramp front, square notch rear.
Price: Blued **$147.00**

Colt Lawman Mk III Revolver
Same as Official Police MK III but with 2" or 4" heavy barrel. Weight 35 oz. (4" bbl.). 357 only.
Price: Blued .... **$149.50** Nickeled **$158.50**

COLT TROOPER MK III REVOLVER
Caliber: 357 Magnum, 6-shot.
Barrel: 4" 6".
Length: 9½" (4" bbl.). **Weight:** 39 oz. (4" bbl.), 42 oz, (6" bbl.).
Stocks: Checkered walnut, square butt. Grooved trigger.
Sights: Fixed ramp front with ⅛" blade, adj. notch rear.
Price: Blued with target hammer and target stocks **$188.00**
Price: Nickeled **$200.00**

F.I.E. ARMINIUS MODEL F38 REVOLVER
Caliber: 38 Special.
Barrel: 2" or 4".
Length: 6¼" over-all. (2" bbl.). **Weight:** 27 oz.
Stocks: Checkered plastic, Bulldog style.
Sights: Fixed.
Features: Swing-out cylinder. Made in U.S.A.
Price: Blued 2" .... **$67.95** 4" bbl. **$67.95**

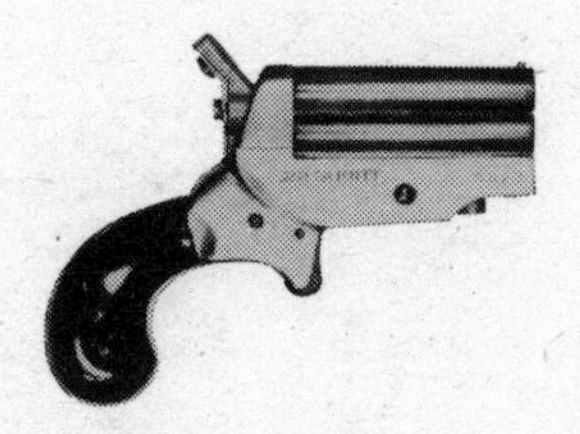

4 ACE DERRINGER MODEL 200
Caliber: 22 Short, 4-shot.
Barrel: 1 11/16"
Weight: 5 oz. **Length:** 3⅜" over-all.
Stocks: High impact black plastic; round butt.
Sights: Post front.
Features: Spur trigger, barrel selector on hammer. Manganese bronze frame. Rifled, blued steel barrels. Cased presentation sets in Gold or Nickel and fully engraved available. From 4 Ace Mfg. Co.
Price: Model 200 .... **$52.95**
Price: Model 202 (as above except 22 LR) **$56.95**
Price: Model 200A (225 in walnut presentation box) **$71.50**
Price: Model 200B (cased pair as above, consec. numbers) **$124.95**
Price: Model 200, Gold or Nickel finish **$69.95**
Price: Model 202, Gold or Nickel finish **$72.95**

HARRINGTON & RICHARDSON Model 622 REVOLVER
Caliber: 22 S, L or LR, 6 shot.
Barrel: 2½", 4", round bbl.
Weight: 22 oz. (2½" bbl.).
Stocks: Checkered black Cycolac.
Sights: Fixed, blade front, square notch rear.
Features: Solid steel, Bantamweight frame; snap-out safety rim cylinder; non-glare finish on frame; coil springs.
Price: Blued, 2½", 4", bbl. **$51.50**
Price: Model 632 (32 cal.) **$54.50**

HARRINGTON & RICHARDSON Model 732 Guardsman
Caliber: 32 S&W or 32 S&W Long, 6 shot.
Barrel: 2½" or 4" round barrel.
Weight: 23½ oz. (2½" bbl.), 26 oz. (4" bbl.).
Stocks: Checkered, black Cycolac.
Sights: Blade front; adjustable rear on 4" model.
Features: Swing-out cylinder with auto. extractor return. Pat. safety rim cylinder. Grooved trigger.
Price: Blued .... **$62.50** Nickel (Model 733) 2½" bbl. only **$69.50**

H&R SPORTSMAN Model 999 REVOLVER
Caliber: 22 S, L or LR, 9 shot.
Barrel: 6" top-break (16" twist), integral vent. rib.
Length: 10½". **Weight:** 30 oz.
Stocks: Checkered walnut, semi-thumbrest.
Sights: Front adjustable for elevation, rear for windage.
Features: Wide hammer spur; rest for second finger.
Price: Blued **$89.50**

HARRINGTON & RICHARDSON M-949 FORTY-NINER
Caliber: 22 S, L or LR, 9 shot.
Barrel: 5½″ round with ejector rod.
Weight: 31 oz.
Stocks: One-piece smooth walnut frontier style.
Sights: Round blade front, adj. rear.
Features: Contoured loading gate; wide hammer spur; single and double action. Western type ejector-housing.
Price: H&R Crown-Luster Blue **$59.50**
Price: Nickel (Model 950) **$69.50**

H&R Model 940 Ultra "Side-Kick" REVOLVER
Caliber: 22 S, L or LR, 9 shot.
Barrel: 6″ target weight with ventilated rib.
Weight: 33 oz.
Stocks: Checkered walnut with thumbrest.
Sights: Ramp front; rear adjustable for w. and e.
Features: Swing-out, safety rim cylinder; safety lock and key.
Price: H&R Crown-Luster Blue **$79.50**

H&R Model 939 Ultra "Side-Kick" Revolver
Like the Model 940 but with a flat-sided barrel.
Price: H&R Crown-Luster Blue **$82.50**

HARRINGTON & RICHARDSON Model 926 REVOLVER
Caliber: 22 S, L, or LR, 9-shot, 38 S&W 5-shot.
Barrel: 4″. **Weight:** 31 oz.
Stocks: Checkered walnut.
Sights: Fixed front, read adj. for w.
Features: Top-break, double or single action
Price: Blued **$84.50**

HARRINGTON & RICHARDSON Model 929 "Side-Kick"
Caliber: 22 S, L or LR, 9 shot.
Barrel: 2½″, 4″ or 6″.
Weight: 26 oz. (4″ bbl.).
Stocks: Checkered, black Cycolac.
Sights: Blade front; adjustable rear on 4″ and 6″ models.
Features: Swing-out cylinder with auto. extractor return. Pat. safety rim cylinder. Grooved trigger. Round-grip frame.
Price: Blued, 2½″, 4″ or 6″ bbl. **$62.50**
Price: Nickel (Model 930), 4″ bbl. **$69.50**

HARRINGTON & RICHARDSON Model 925 "Defender"
Caliber: 38 S&W 5 shot.
Barrel: 2½″.
Length: 7½″ over-all. **Weight:** 22 oz.
Stocks: Smooth walnut, birds-head style, one piece wrap-round.
Sights: Rear with windage adj.
Features: Top-break double action, push pin extractor.
Price: H&R Crown Luster Blue **$79.50**

HIGH STANDARD HIGH SIERRA DOUBLE ACTION
Caliber: 22 LR and 22 LR/22 Mag., 9-shot.
Barrel: 7″ octagonal.
Weight: 36 oz. **Length:** 12½″ over-all.
Stocks: Smooth walnut.
Sights: Blade front, fixed or adj. rear.
Features: Gold plated backstrap and trigger guard.
Price: Fixed sights, dual cyl. **$122.00**
Price: Adj. sights, dual cyl. **$127.95**

HIGH STANDARD DOUBLE-NINE CONVERTIBLE
Caliber: 22 S, L or LR, 9-shot (22 WRM with extra cylinder).
Barrel: 5½″, dummy ejector rod fitted.
Length: 11″ over-all. **Weight:** 32 oz.
Stocks: Smooth walnut, frontier style with medallion
Sights: Fixed blade front, notched rear.
Features: Western styling; rebounding hammer with auto safety block; spring-loaded ejection.
Price: Blued .... **$112.00** Nickeled **$122.00**

High Standard Long Horn Convertible
Same as the Double-Nine convertible but with a 9½″ bbl., fixed sights, blued only, Weight: 40 oz.
Price: With dual cyl. **$122.00**

HI-STANDARD SENTINEL MKII, MKIII

Caliber: 357 or 38 Spec.
Barrel: 2½", 4", 6".
Weight: 38 oz. (4" bbl.). **Length:** 9" over-all (4" bbl.).
Stocks: Walnut, service type or combat.
Sights: Fixed on MKII. MKIII has fully adj. rear.
Features: Cylinder latch located in front of cylinder. Fast lock time. Blue finish only.
Price: MKII **$120.00**
Price: MKIII **$154.95**

HI-STANDARD SENTINEL MK I AND MK IV

Caliber: 22 LR (MK I), 22 Mag. (MK IV), 9-shot.
Barrel: 2", 3" or 4".
Weight: 21½ oz. (2"). **Length:** 6⅞" over-all (2" bbl.).
Stocks: Smooth walnut.
Sights: Ramp front, fixed or adj. rear.
Features: Blue or nickel finish (add $10 for nickel).
Price: Fixed sights, blue finish, 22 LR **$109.00**
Price: Adj. sights, blue finish, 22 LR **$119.00**
Price: Magnum, 2" bbl., fixed sights **$109.00**
Price: Magnum, 3" bbl., adj. sights **$119.00**

IVER JOHNSON TARGET MODEL T-526 REVOLVER

Caliber: 22 S or LR, 8 shot, double action.
Barrel: 4½", 6".
Length: 10¾" (6" bbl.). **Weight:** 30½ oz. (6" bbl.).
Stocks: Checkered thumbrest, Tenite.
Sights: Adjustable Patridge type.
Features: Flash Control cylinder, adj. mainspring.
Price: Blue **$57.75**

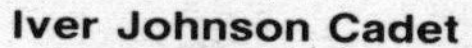

Iver Johnson Cadet

Same as Model 55 except with 2½" barrel only, rounded tenite grips; weight 24 oz. Price, blued **$52.00**
Also available in 38 S&W caliber, 5 shot **$59.75**
Price: 22 Mag. **$52.00**

IVER JOHNSON SPORTSMAN REVOLVER

Same as Model 57A except without adjustable sights. Price **$53.75**

IVER JOHNSON SIDEWINDER REVOLVER

Caliber: 22 S, L, LR, 8 shot.
Barrel: 6".
Length: 11¼". **Weight:** 31 oz.
Stocks: Plastic Stag Horn.
Sights: Fixed, blade front.
Features: Wide spur hammer, half-cock safety, scored trigger, Flash Control cylinder, recessed shell head, push rod ejector.
Price: Blued **$56.60**
Price: Model 50-B with dual cyl. (22 LR/22 Mag.) **$60.35**
Price: Model 50-SD, dual cyl., adj. sights **$73.00**

KASSNAR/SQUIRES BINGHAM M-100D REVOLVER

Caliber: 22 LR/22 Mag.; 38 Spec.
Barrel: 3", 4" or 6".
Weight: 44 to 48 oz.
Stocks: Checkered hardwood, target style.
Sights: Ramp front, open rear adj. for e.
Features: Double action; vent rib barrel. Imported by Kassnar.
Price: **$99.95**

LIBERTY KODIAK REVOLVER

Caliber: 22 LR, 22 MWR (8-shot), 32 S&W, 38 Spec. (6-shot).
Barrel: 24", 4".
Weight: 27 oz. (2" bbl.). **Length:** 6¾" (2" bbl.).
Stocks: Smooth wood.
Sights: Fixed.
Features: Swing-out cylinder. Blue finish (22 and 32 cals.), blue or chrome (38 cal.). Imported by Liberty.
Price: 22 cal. **$39.95**
Price: 32 cal. **$44.95**
Price: 38 cal. **$49.95**

LLAMA "MARTIAL" REVOLVERS
Caliber: 22 LR, 22 RFM, 38 Special.
Barrel: 6″, 4″ (except 22 LR).
Weight: 22 LR 24 oz., 38 Special 31 oz. **Length:** 9¼″ (4″ bbl.).
Stocks: Checkered walnut.
Sights: Fixed blade front, rear adj. for w. & e.
Features: Ventilated rib, wide spur hammer. Chrome plating, engraved finishes available. Imported from Spain by Stoeger Industries.
Price: **$139.95**
Price: Commanche 357 Mag. **$169.95**

NORTH AMERICAN ARMS MINI REVOLVER
Caliber: 22 short, 5-shot.
Barrel: 1″.
Length: 3¼″ over-all.
Stocks: Polished walnut.
Features: Finished in hard chrome. Spur trigger.
Price: **$80.00**

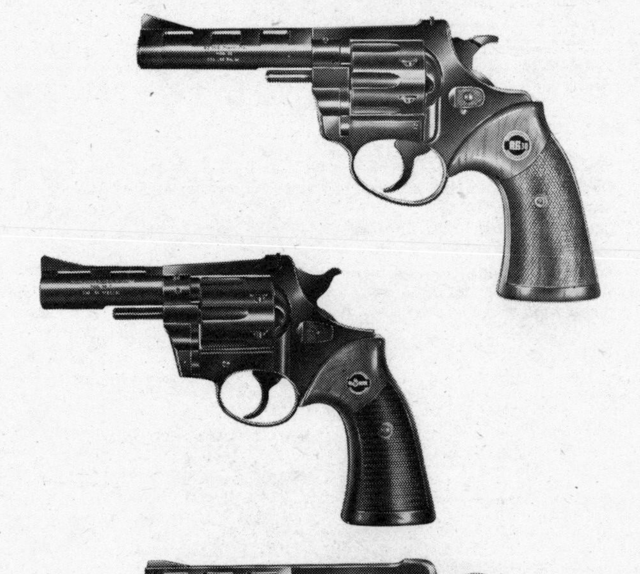

RG30 REVOLVER
Caliber: 22 LR and 32, 6-shot.
Barrel: 4″.
Weight: 30 oz. **Length:** 9″.
Stocks: Checkered plastic.
Sights: Fixed front, rear adj. for w.
Features: Swing-out cylinder, choice of blue or nickel ($8.00 additional) finish. Imported from Germany by R. G. Industries.
Price: (22) .... **$59.95** (32) **$59.95**

RG 38S REVOLVER
Caliber: 38 Special, 6-shot.
Barrel: 3″ and 4″.
Weight: 3″, 31 oz.; 4″, 34 oz. **Length:** 3″, 8½″; 4″, 9¼″.
Stocks: Checkered plastic.
Sights: Fixed front, rear adj. for w.
Features: Swing out cylinder with spring ejector, choice of blue or nickel finish. Imported from Germany by R. G. Industries.
Price: Blue **$69.95**
Price: Nickel **$83.95**

RG 57 REVOLVER
Caliber: 357 Magnum.
Barrel: 4″.
Weight: 44 oz. **Length:** 9½″.
Stocks: Checkered plastic.
Sights: Fixed rear.
Features: Swing out cylinder, spring ejector, steel frame. Imported from Germany by R. G. Industries.
Price: **$124.95**

RG MODEL 88 REVOLVER
Caliber: 38 Spec., 357 Mag.
Barrel: 4″.
Weight: 33 oz. **Length:** 9″ over-all.
Stocks: Checkered walnut.
Sights: Fixed.
Features: Swing out cylinder, spring ejector. Wide spur hammer and trigger. Imported by RG Industries.
Price: **$139.95**

RG63 WESTERN STYLE REVOLVER
Caliber: 22 LR, 8-shot; 38 Spec., 6-shot.
Barrel: 5″.
Weight: 34-36 ozs. **Length:** 10¼″.
Stocks: Checkered plastic.
Sights: Fixed.
Features: Slide ejector rod, choice of blue or nickel. Imported from Germany by R. G. Industries.
Price: Blue (22) **$52.95**
Price: Blue, 38 Spec. **$61.95**
Price: Nickel, 38 Spec. **$74.95**

RUGER POLICE SERVICE-SIX Models 107 and 108
Caliber: 357 (Model 107), 38 Spec. (Model 108), 6-shot.
Barrel: 2¾″ or 4″.
Weight: 33½ oz (4″ bbl.). **Length:** 9¼″ (4 bbl.) over-all.
Stocks: Checkered American walnut, semi-target style.
Sights: Patridge-type front, square notch rear.
Features: Solid frame with barrel, rib and ejector rod housing combined in one unit. All steel construction. Field strips without tools.
Price: Model 107 (357) **$130.00**
Price: Model 108 (38) **$112.00**
Price: Mod. 707 (357), Stainless, 4″ **$149.00**
Price: Mod. 708 (38), Stainless, 4″ **$135.00**

RUGER SECURITY-SIX Model 117
Caliber: 357 Mag. (also fires 38 Spec.), 6-shot.
Barrel: 2¾″, 4″ or 6″.
Weight: 35 oz. (4″ bbl.). **Length:** 9¼″ (4″ bbl.) over-all.
Stocks: Hand checkered American walnut, semi-target style.
Sights: Patridge-type front on ramp, rear adj. for w. and e.
Features: Music wire coil springs throughout. Hardened steel construction. Integral ejector rod shroud and sighting rib. Can be disassembled using only a coin.
Price: **$143.50**

RUGER STAINLESS SECURITY-SIX Model 717
Caliber: 357 Mag. (also fires 38 Spec.), 6-shot.
Barrel: 2¾″, 4″ or 6″.
Weight: 35 oz. (4 bbl.). **Length:** 9¼″ (4″ bbl.) over-all.
Stocks: Hand checkered American walnut.
Sights: Patridge-type front, fully adj. rear.
Features: All metal parts except sights made of stainless steel. Sights are black alloy for maximum visibility. Same mechanism and features found in regular Security-Six.
Price: **$167.50**

RUGER SPEED-SIX Models 207 and 208
Caliber: Model 207—357 Mag. (also fires 38 Spec.); Model 208—38 Spec. only, 6-shot.
Barrel: 2¾″ or 4″.
Weight: 31½ oz. **Length:** 7½″ over-all.
Stocks: Round butt design, diamond pattern checkered American walnut.
Sights: Patridge-type front, square-notch rear.
Features: Same basic mechanism as Security-Six. Hammer without spur available on special order. All steel construction. Music wire coil springs used throughout.
Price: Model 207 (357 Mag.) **$130.00**
Price: Model 208 (38 Spec. only) **$112.00**
Price: Mod. 737 (357), Stainless **$149.00**
Price: Mod. 738 (38), Stainless **$135.00**

ROSSI REVOLVERS
Caliber: 22 LR, 22 Mag., 32 S&W Long (6-shot), 38 Spec. (5-shot).
Barrel: 3″, 6″ (22 Mag. only).
Weight: 22 oz.
Stocks: Smooth wood.
Sights: Ramp front, adj. rear.
Features: Full length barrel rib. Blue or nickel finish. Imported by Garcia.
Price: 3″ bbl., blue **$85.00**
Price: 3″ bbl., nickel **$92.00**
Price: 6″ bbl., blue **$92.00**

SMITH & WESSON M&P Model 10 REVOLVER
Caliber: 38 Special, 6 shot.
Barrel: 2″, 4″, 5″ or 6″
Length: 9¼″ (4″ bbl.). **Weight:** 30½ oz. (4″ bbl.).
Stocks: Checkered walnut, Magna. Round or square butt.
Sights: Fixed, ⅛″ ramp front, square notch rear.
Price: Blued .... **$109.00** Nickeled **$119.00**

Smith & Wesson 38 M&P Heavy Barrel Model 10
Same as regular M&P except: 4″ ribbed bbl. with ⅛″ ramp front sight, square rear, square butt, wgt. 34 oz.
Price: Blued .... **$109.00** Nickeled **$119.00**

SMITH & WESSON Model 13 H.B. M&P
Caliber: 357 and 38 Special, 6 shot.
Barrel: 4″.
Weight: 34 oz. **Length:** 9¼″ over-all.
Stocks: Checkered walnut, service.
Sights: ⅛″ serrated ramp front, fixed square notch rear.
Features: Heavy barrel, K-frame, square butt.
Price: Blue only, M-13 .... **$120.00**
Price: Model 65, as above in stainless steel **$145.50**

SMITH & WESSON Model 14 K-38 MASTERPIECE
Caliber: 38 Spec., 6-shot.
Barrel: 6″, 8⅜″.
Weight: 38½ oz. (6″ bbl.). **Length:** 11⅛″ over-all (6″ bbl.)
Stocks: Checkered walnut, service.
Sights: ⅛″ Patridge front, micro click rear adj. for w. and e.
Price: 6″ bbl. **$135.00**
Price: 8⅜″ bbl. **$141.50**

SMITH & WESSON 357 COMBAT MAGNUM Model 19
Caliber: 357 Magnum and 38 Special, 6 shot.
Barrel: 2½″, 4″, 6″.
Length: 9½″ (4″ bbl.). **Weight:** 35 oz.
Stocks: Checkered Goncala Alves, target. Grooved tangs and trigger.
Sights: Front, ⅛″ Baughman Quick Draw on 2½″ or 4″ bbl., Patridge on 6″ bbl., micro click rear adjustable for w. and e.
Price: S&W Bright Blue or Nickel **$167.50**

SMITH & WESSON 44 MAGNUM Model 29 REVOLVER
Caliber: 44 Magnum, 44 Special or 44 Russian, 6 shot.
Barrel: 4″, 6½″, 8⅜″.
Length: 11⅞″ (6½″ bbl.). **Weight:** 47 oz. (6½″ bbl.), 43 oz. (4″ bbl.).
Stocks: Oversize target type, checkered Goncala Alves. Tangs and target trigger grooved, checkered target hammer.
Sights: ⅛″ red ramp-front, micro. click rear, adjustable for w. and e.
Features: Includes presentation case.
Price: S&W Bright Blue or Nickel 4″, 6½″ **$235.00**
Price: 8⅜″ bbl. **$241.50**

SMITH & WESSON HIGHWAY PATROLMAN Model 28
Caliber: 357 Magnum and 38 Special, 6 shot.
Barrel: 4″, 6″.
Length: 11¼″ (6″ bbl.). **Weight:** 44 oz. (6″ bbl.).
Stocks: Checkered walnut, Magna. Grooved tangs and trigger.
Sights: Front, ⅛″ Baughman Quick Draw, on plain ramp. micro click rear, adjustable for w. and e.
Price: S&W Satin Blue, sandblasted frame edging and barrel top . **$140.00**
Price: With target stocks **$147.50**

SMITH & WESSON 32 REGULATION POLICE
Caliber: 32 S&W Long (M31), 6 shot.
Barrel: 2″, 3″, 4″.
Length: 8½″ (4″ bbl.). **Weight:** 18¾ oz. (4″ bbl.).
Stocks: Checkered walnut, Magna.
Sights: Fixed, 1/10″ serrated ramp front, square notch rear.
Price: Blued .... **$107.00** Nickeled **$117.00**

SMITH & WESSON 38 CHIEFS SPECIAL & AIRWEIGHT
Caliber: 38 Special, 5 shot.
Barrel: 2″, 3″.
Length: 6½″ (2″ bbl. and round butt). **Weight:** 19 oz. (2″ bbl.; 14 oz. AIRWEIGHT).
Stocks: Checkered walnut, Magna. Round or square butt.
Sights: Fixed, 1/10″ serrated ramp front, square notch rear.
Price: Blued std. M-36 ... **$111.00** Standard weight Nickel ... **$121.00**
Price: Blued AIR'W M-37 . **$115.00** AIRWEIGHT Nickel **$130.00**

SMITH & WESSON 38 M&P AIRWEIGHT Model 12
Caliber: 38 Special, 6 shot.
Barrel: 2 or 4 inches.
Length: 6⅞″ over-all. **Weight:** 18 oz. (2″ bbl.)
Stocks: Checkered walnut, Magna. Round or square butt.
Sights: Fixed, ⅛″ serrated ramp front, square notch rear.
Price: Blued .... **$114.00** Nickeled **$129.00**

SMITH & WESSON 357 MAGNUM M-27 REVOLVER
Caliber: 357 Magnum and 38 Special, 6 shot.
Barrel: 3½″, 5″, 6″, 8⅜″.
Length: 11¼″ (6″ bbl.). **Weight:** 44 oz. (6″ bbl.).
Stocks: Checkered walnut, Magna. Grooved tangs and trigger.
Sights: Any S&W target front, micro click rear, adjustable for w. and e.
Price: S&W Bright Blue or Nickel, 3½″, 5″, 6″ **$195.00**
Price: 8⅜″ bbl. **$201.50**

SMITH & WESSON 32 HAND EJECTOR Model 30
Caliber: 32 S&W Long, 6 shot.
Barrel: 2″, 3″, 4″.
Length: 8 inches (4″ bbl.). **Weight:** 18 oz. (4″ bbl.).
Stocks: Checkered walnut, Magna.
Sights: Fixed, 1/10″ serrated ramp front, square notch rear.
Price: Blued .... **$107.00** Nickeled **$117.00**

Smith & Wesson 60 Chiefs Special Stainless
Same as Model 36 except: 2″ bbl. and round butt only.
Price: Stainless steel **$135.00**

SMITH & WESSON 1953 Model 34, 22/32 KIT GUN
Caliber: 22 LR, 6 shot.
Barrel: 2″, 4″.
Length: 8″ (4″ bbl. and round butt). **Weight:** 22½ oz. (4″ bbl.).
Stocks: Checkered walnut, round or square butt.
Sights: Front, ¹⁄₁₀″ serrated ramp, micro. click rear, adjustable for w. & e.
Price: Blued .... **$120.00** Nickeled **$130.00**

Smith & Wesson Bodyguard Model 38 Revolver
Caliber: 38 Special; 5 shot, double action revolver.
Barrel: 2″.
Length: 6⅜″. **Weight:** 14½ oz.
Features: Alloy frame; integral hammer shroud.
Stocks: Checkered walnut, Magna.
Sights: Fixed ¹⁄₁₀″ serrated ramp front, square notch rear.
Price: Blued .... **$115.00** Nickeled **$130.00**

Smith & Wesson Bodyguard Model 49 Revolver
Same as Model 38 except steel construction. Weight 20½ oz.
Price: Blued .... **$113.00** Nickeled **$123.00**

SMITH & WESSON 41 MAGNUM Model 57 REVOLVER
Caliber: 41 Magnum, 6 shot.
Barrel: 4″, 6″ or 8⅜″.
Length: 11⅜″ (6″ bbl.). **Weight:** 48 oz. (6″ bbl.).
Stocks: Oversize target type checkered Goncala Alves wood and target hammer. Tang and target trigger grooved.
Sights: ⅛″ red ramp front, micro. click rear, adj. for w. and e.
Price: S&W Bright Blue or Nickel 4″, 6″ **$235.00**
Price: 8⅜″ bbl. **$241.50**

SMITH & WESSON 41 M&P Model 58 REVOLVER
Caliber: 41 Magnum, 6 shot.
Barrel: 4″.
Length: 9¼″ over-all. **Weight:** 41 oz.
Stocks: Checkered walnut, Magna.
Sights: Fixed, ⅛″ serrated ramp front, square notch rear.
Price: Blued .... **$130.00** Nickeled **$140.00**

SMITH & WESSON MODEL 64 STAINLESS M&P
Caliber: 38 Special, 6-shot.
Barrel: 4″.
Length: 9½″ over-all. **Weight:** 30½ oz.
Stocks: Checkered walnut, service style.
Sights: Fixed, ⅛″ serrated ramp front, square notch rear.
Features: Satin finished stainless steel, square butt.
Price: **$135.00**

SMITH & WESSON MODEL 66 STAINLESS COMBAT MAGNUM
Caliber: 357 Magnum and 38 Special, 6-shot.
Barrel: 4″.
Length: 9½″ over-all. **Weight:** 35 oz.
Stocks: Checkered Goncala Alves target.
Sights: Front, ⅛″ Baughman Quick Draw on plain ramp, micro click rear adj. for w. and e.
Features: Satin finish stainless steel, grooved trigger with adj. stop.
Price: **$185.00**

SMITH & WESSON MODEL 67 K-38 STAINLESS COMBAT MASTERPIECE
Caliber: 38 special, 6-shot.
Barrel: 4″.
Length: 9⅛″ over-all. **Weight:** 34 oz. (loaded).
Stocks: Checkered walnut, service style.
Sights: Front, ⅛″ Baughman Quick Draw on ramp, micro click rear adj. for w. and e.
Features: Stainless steel. Square butt frame with grooved tangs, grooved trigger with adj. stop.
Price: **$152.00**

DAN WESSON MODEL 8-2 & MODEL 14-2

Caliber: 38 Special (Model 8-2); 357 (Model 14-2), both 6 shot.
Barrel: 2½", 4", 6", 8". "Quickshift" interchangeable barrels.
Weight: 34 oz. (4" bbl.) **Length:** 9¼" over-all (4" bbl.).
Stocks: "Quickshift" Powerwood Traditional, checkered, walnut grain. Interchangeable with three other styles.
Sights: ⅛" serrated ramp front, rear fixed.
Features: Interchangeable barrels; 4 interchangeable grips; few moving parts, easy disassembly.
Price: Satin Blue, 2½", 4" or 6" bbl. either model **$130.00**
Price: Satin Blue, 8" bbl. **$143.00**

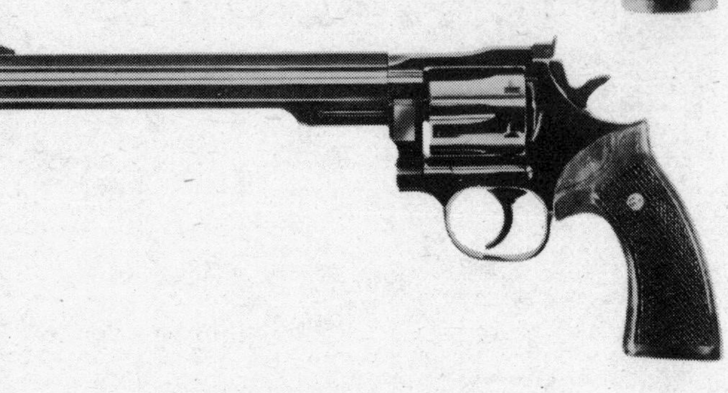

DAN WESSON MODEL 9-2 & MODEL 15-2

Caliber: 38 Special (Model 9-2); 357 (Model 15-2), both 6 shot.
Barrel: 2½", 4", 6", 8". "Quickshift" interchangeable barrels.
Weight: 36 oz. (4" bbl.). **Length:** 9¼" over-all (4" bbl.).
Stocks: "Quickshift" Powerwood Target, checkered, walnut grain. Interchangeable with three other styles.
Sights: ⅛" serrated blade front, rear adj. for w. & e.
Features: Interchangeable barrels; four interchangeable grips; few moving parts, easy disassembly; Bright Blue finish only.
Price: Models 9-2H, 15-2H (bull barrel shroud, 2½", 4", 6" **$168.00**
Price: As above, 8" barrel **$205.00**
Price: Models 9-2V, 15-2V (vent. rib bbl. shroud) 2½", 4", 6" **$188.00**
Price: As above, 8" bbl. **$205.00**
Price: Models 9-2VH, 15-2VH (vent. rib, bull bbl. shroud) 2½", 4", 6" **$188.00**
Price: As above, 8" bbl. **$225.00**

TAURUS MODEL 74 SPORT REVOLVER

Caliber: 32 S&W Long, 6-shot.
Barrel: 3".
Weight: 22 oz. **Length:** 8¼" over-all.
Stocks: Oversize target-type, checkered Brazilian walnut.
Sights: Serrated ramp front, rear adj. for w. and e.
Features: Imported from Brazil by International Distributers.
Price: Blue **$77.00**
Price: Nickel **$79.20**

TAURUS MODEL 80 STANDARD REVOLVER

Caliber: 38 Spec., 6-shot.
Barrel: 3" or 4".
Weight: 31 oz. (4" bbl.). **Length:** 9¼" over-all (4" bbl.).
Stocks: Checkered Brazilian walnut.
Sights: Serrated ramp front, square notch rear.
Features: Imported from Brazil by International Distributors.
Price: Blue **$69.30**
Price: Nickel **$71.50**

TAURUS MODEL 82 HEAVY BARREL REVOLVER

Caliber: 38 Spec., 6-shot.
Barrel: 3" or 4", heavy.
Weight: 33 oz. (4" bbl.). **Length:** 9¼" over-all (4" bbl.).
Stocks: Checkered Brazilian walnut.
Sights: Serrated ramp front, square notch rear.
Features: Imported from Brazil by International Distributors.
Price: Blue **$71.50**
Price: Nickel **$74.80**

TAURUS MODEL 84 SPORT REVOLVER

Caliber: 38 Spec., 6-shot.
Barrel: 4".
Weight: 30 oz. **Length:** 9¼" over-all.
Stocks: Checkered Brazilian walnut.
Sights: Serrated ramp front, rear adj. for w. and e.
Features: Imported from Brazil by International Distributors.
Price: Blue **$77.00**
Price: Nickel **$79.20**

TAURUS MODEL 94 SPORT REVOLVER

Caliber: 22, 6-shot.
Barrel: 4".
Weight: 23 oz. **Length:** 9¼" over-all.
Stocks: Oversize target-type, checkered Brazilian walnut.
Sights: Serrated ramp front, rear adj. for w. and e.
Features: Imported from Brazil by International Distributors.
Price: Blue **$77.00**
Price: Nickel **$79.20**

BISON SINGLE ACTION REVOLVER
Caliber: 22 LR.
Barrel: 4¾".
Weight: 20 oz.
Stocks: Imitation stag.
Sights: Fixed front, adj. rear.
Features: 22 WRM cylinder also available ($5.00 additional). Imported from Germany by Jana.
Price: **$48.00**

COLT SINGLE ACTION ARMY REVOLVER
Caliber: 357 Magnum or 45 Colt, 6 shot.
Barrel: 4¾", 5½" or 7½".
Length: 10⅞" (5½" bbl.). **Weight:** 37 oz. (5½" bbl.).
Stocks: Black composite rubber with eagle and shield crest.
Sights: Fixed. Grooved top strap, blade front.
Price: Blued and case hardened 4¾", 5½" bbl. **$246.50**
Price: Nickel with walnut stocks **$294.00**
Price: Buntline Spec. .... **Special order only.**
Price: With 7½" bbl. **$253.00**

Colt Single Action Army—New Frontier
Same specifications as standard Single Action Army except: flat-top frame; high polished finish, blue and case colored; ramp front sight and target rear adj. for windage and elevation; smooth walnut stocks with silver medallion.

Price: **$294.00**

COLT PEACEMAKER 22
Caliber: 22 LR/22 Magnum.
Barrel: 4⅜", 6" or 7½" (Buntline).
Length: 9⅝" (11¼" in 6", 12¾" for Buntline). **Weight:** 29½ oz. (31 oz. in 6", 33 oz. for Buntline).
Stocks: Black composite rubber with eagle and shield crest.
Sights: Fixed. Grooved top strap, blade front.
Features: Color case hardened frame, all steel construction, smooth trigger, knurled hammer spur.
Price: Blued, dual cyl. **$96.50**
Price: Buntline, dual cyl. **$102.50**

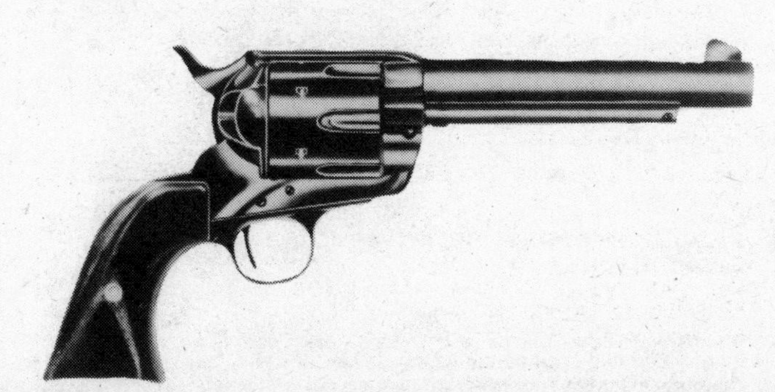

COLT NEW FRONTIER 22
Caliber: 22 LR/22 Magnum.
Barrel: 4⅜", 6" or 7½" (Buntline).
Length: 9⅝", (11¼" w/6" bbl., 12¾" for Buntline). **Weight:** 28 oz. (30½ oz. w/6" bbl., 32 oz. for Buntline).
Stocks: Black composite rubber with eagle and shield crest.
Sights: Ramp front, adjustable rear.
Features: Blue finish, smooth trigger, knurled hammer spur.
Price: Dual cyl. **$108.00**
Price: Buntline Dual cyl. **$113.50**

F.I.E. "SHERIFF" SINGLE ACTION REVOLVER
Caliber: 22 LR/22 Mag., 357 Mag., 44 Mag., 6-shot.
Barrel: 5½".
Weight: 42 oz. (357).
Stocks: Smooth walnut.
Sights: Fixed.
Features: Positive hammer block system. Brass backstrap and trigger guard. Case hardened steel frame. Comes in wood box. Imported from Argentina by Firearms Import & Export.
Price: **$94.95**

F.I.E. E15 BUFFALO SCOUT REVOLVER
Caliber: 22 LR, 22 Mag., 6-shot.
Barrel: 4¾.
Length: 10" over-all. **Weight:** 30 oz.
Stocks: Black plastic.
Features: Slide spring ejector.
Sights: Fixed.
Price: Blued **$34.95**
Price: Model E15MB with extra interchangeable 22 WMR Mag. cylinder, blue finish **$42.95**
Price: Chrome, single cyl. **$41.95**
Price: Chrome, dual cyl. **$47.95**

HAWES SILVER CITY MARSHAL REVOLVER
Caliber: 22 LR, 22 LR/22 WRM, 357, 44 Mag., 45 L.C.
Barrel: 6″ (357, 44, 45), 5½″ (22 cal.).
Weight: 44 oz. **Length:** 11¾″ over-all.
Stocks: White Pearlite.
Sights: Fixed.
Features: Nickel plated frame, brass backstrap and trigger guard, blue barrel and cylinder. Imported by Hawes Firearms.
Price: .... **$116.60** to **$258.95**

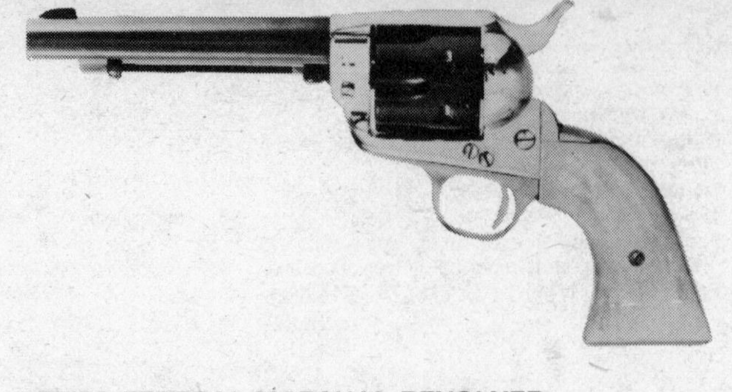

HAWES SAUER WESTERN MARSHAL REVOLVERS
Caliber: 357 Magnum, 44 Magnum, 45 Long Colt, 22 Magnum, 22 LR, 6-shot.
Barrel: 6″ (357 Mag., 44 Mag., 45) and 5½″ (22 Mag., 22 LR).
Weight: 44 oz. (big bore), 40 oz. (small bore). **Length:** 11¾″ and 11¼″.
Stocks: Rosewood (big bore), moulded stag (small bore).
Sight: Blade front.
Features: Single action. Interchangeable cyclinders available for 357/9mm Para., 45 LC/45 ACP (**$211.60**); 44 Mag./44-40 (**$220.20**). Imported from West Germany by Hawes.
Price: 357 Mag., 44 Mag., 45 LC **$171.60**
Price: 44 Mag. **$180.20**
Price: 22 LR **$89.95**
Price: 22 LR with 22 Mag. cylinder **$114.95**

HAWES FEDERAL MARSHAL REVOLVER
Caliber: 357, 44 Mag., 45 L.C.
Barrel: 6″.
Weight: 44 oz. **Length:** 11¾″ over-all.
Stocks: Smooth walnut.
Sights: Blade front, fixed rear.
Features: Color case hardened frame, brass backstrap and trigger guard. Combo cylinder models avail. same cals. as Western Marshal (**$249.95, $260.45** resp.). Imported by Hawes Firearms.
Price: .... **$209.95** to **$220.45**

HAWES DEPUTY MARSHAL REVOLVER
Caliber: 22 LR, 22 LR/22 WRM.
Barrel: 5½″.
Weight: 34 oz. **Length:** 11″ over-all.
Stocks: Black, white or wood.
Sights: Fixed.
Features: Available in std. blue finish with black grips, with brass backstrap and trigger guard and wood grips, with completely chromed finish and white grips, or with chrome frame, brass backstrap and trigger guard, blue cylinder and barrel and white grips. Imported by Hawes Firearms.
Price: .... **$59.95** to **$85.95**

Hawes Montana Marshal Revolver
Same as Western Marshal except with solid brass backstrap and trigger guard.
Price: .... **$109.95** to **$245.70**

Hawes Texas Marshal Revolver
Same as Western Marshal except full nickel finish and white Pearlite grips.
Price: .... **$116.60** to **$259.90**

HAWES CHIEF MARSHAL REVOLVER
Caliber: 357 Magnum, 44 Magnum, 45 Long Colt; 6-shot.
Barrel: 6″.
Weight: 48 oz. **Length:** 11¾″.
Stocks: Extra large smooth rosewood.
Sights: Ramp target front, rear adj. for w. & e.
Features: Single action. Combo cylinder models avail., same cals. as Western Marshal (**$249.95, $260.45** resp.). Extra heavy frame. Imported from West Germany by Hawes.
Price: .... **$207.25** to **$217.60**

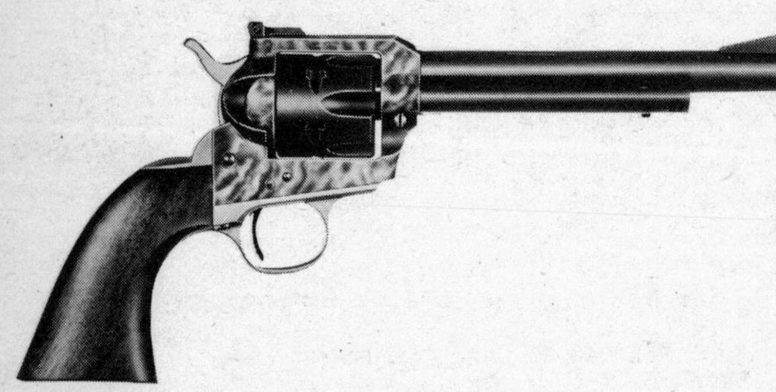

IVER JOHNSON CATTLEMAN TRAILBLAZER
Caliber: 22 S, L, LR, 22 Mag.
Barrel: 5½″ or 6½″.
Weight: 2½ lbs.
Stocks: Smooth walnut.
Sights: Ramp front, rear adj. for w. and e.
Features: Comes with interchangeable magnum cylinder. Single action. Case-hardened frame, brass backstrap and trigger guard. Imported by Iver Johnson.
Price: **$132.00**

I. J. CATTLEMAN BUCKHORN MAGNUM
Caliber: 357, 38 Spec., 44 Mag., 45 LC.
Barrel: 6½″, 7½″ (44 Mag.), 5¾″ or 7½″ (357, 38, 45).
Weight: 2¾ lbs.
Stocks: Smooth walnut.
Sights: Ramp front, rear adj. for w. and e.
Features: Single action. Blued barrel, case-hardened frame, brass backstrap and trigger guard. Imported by Iver Johnson.
Price: 357, 45 LC **$166.95**
Price: 44 Mag. **$191.25**

IVER JOHNSON CATTLEMAN BUNTLINE BUCKHORN MAGNUM
Caliber: 357, 38 Spec., 44 Mag., 45 LC, 6-shot.
Barrel: 18″.
Weight: 3½ lbs.
Stocks: Smooth walnut.
Sights: Ramp front, rear adj. for w. and e.
Features: Single action. Blued barrel, case-hardened frame, brass trigger guard and backstrap. Comes with detachable shoulder stock. Imported by L.A. Distributors.
Price: 357, 45 LC .... **$316.20** 44 Mag. **$333.95**

IVER JOHNSON CATTLEMAN MAGNUM

Caliber: 357, 44 Mag., 45 LC, 6-shot.
Barrel: 4¾", 5½" or 7¼". 44 Mag. avail. with 6", 6¼" or 7¼".
Weight: 2½ lbs.
Stocks: Smooth walnut.
Sights: Fixed.
Features: Case-hardened frame, single action, blued barrel, brass backstrap and trigger guard. Imported by Iver Johnson.
Price: 357, 45 LC .... **$151.75** 44 Mag. **$175.95**

KASSNAR/JAGER SINGLE ACTION REVOLVER

Caliber: 22 LR/22 Mag.; 357; 45 Colt; 44-40.
Barrel: 5½" or 6½".
Weight: 46 oz.
Stocks: Smooth European walnut.
Sights: Fixed or adjustable.
Features: Case hardened frame; solid brass backstrap and trigger guard. Imported by Kassnar.
Price: **$119.95**

LIBERTY MUSTANG

Caliber: 22 LR, 22 Mag. or combination, 8-shot.
Barrel: 5".
Weight: 34 oz. **Length:** 10¼" over-all.
Stocks: Smooth rosewood.
Sights: Blade front, adj. rear.
Features: Single action, slide ejector rod. Imported by Liberty.
Price: With one cylinder **$36.95**
Price: With two cylinders **$44.95**

RG 66 SUPER SINGLE ACTION REVOLVER

Caliber: 22 LR, 22 Mag., 6-shot.
Barrel: 4¾".
Weight: 32 oz. **Length:** 10".
Stocks: Checkered plastic.
Sights: Fixed front, rear adj.
Features: Slide ejector rod, choice of blue or nickel finish. Model 66M is combo set with both 22 LR and 22 mag. cylinders. Imported from Germany by R. G. Industries.
Price: Blue .... **$50.95**; (Model 66M) **$57.95**
Price: Nickel .... **$55.95**; (Model 66M) **$68.95**
Price: Blue (6") .... **$53.95**; Magnum **$61.95**
Price: Blue (9") .... **$54.95**; Magnum **$64.95**

RUGER NEW MODEL SUPER SINGLE-SIX CONVERTIBLE

Caliber: 22 S, L, LR, 6-shot. 22 WMR in extra cylinder.
Barrel: 4⅝", 5½", 6½" or 9½" (6-groove).
Weight: 32 oz. (6½" bbl.) **Length:** 11⅞" over-all (6½" bbl.).
Stocks: Smooth American walnut.
Sights: Improved patridge front on ramp, fully adj. rear protected by integral frame ribs.
Features: New Ruger "interlocked" mechanism, transfer bar ignition, gate-controlled loading, hardened chrome-moly steel frame, wide trigger, music wire springs throughout, independent firing pin.
Price: 4⅝", 5½", 6½" barrel **$92.25**
Price: 9½" barrel **$105.45**
Price: 4⅝", 5½", 6½" bbl., stainless steel **$141.75**
Price: As above with single cyl., 4⅝", 5½", 6½" **$87.50**
Price: 9½" bbl. **$100.50**
Price: 5½", 6½", stainless steel **$123.00**

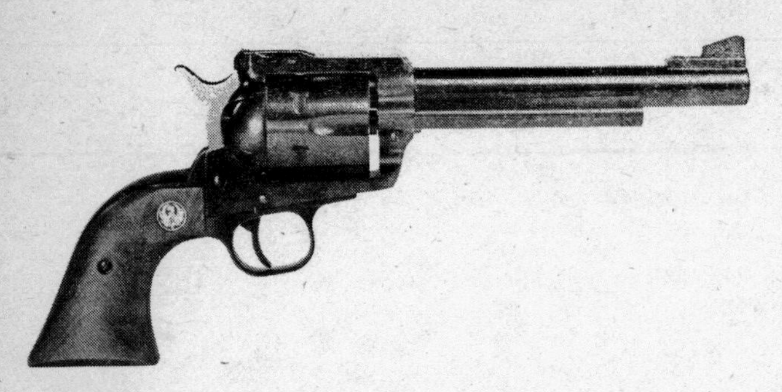

RUGER NEW MODEL BLACKHAWK REVOLVER
Caliber: 357 or 41 Mag., 6-shot.
Barrel: 4⅝" or 6½", either caliber.
Weight: 40 oz. (6½" bbl.). **Length:** 12¼" over-all (6½" bbl.).
Stocks: American walnut.
Sights: ⅛" ramp front, micro click rear adj. for w. and e.
Features: New Ruger interlocked mechanism, independent firing pin, hardened chrome-moly steel frame, music wire springs throughout.
Price: Blued **$119.75**
Price: Stainless steel (357) **$149.75**

Ruger New Model 357/9mm Blackhawk
Same as the 357 Magnum except furnished with interchangeable cylinders for 9mm Parabellum and 357 Magnum cartridges **$142.80**
9mm cylinder, fitted to your 357 Blackhawk **$16.00**

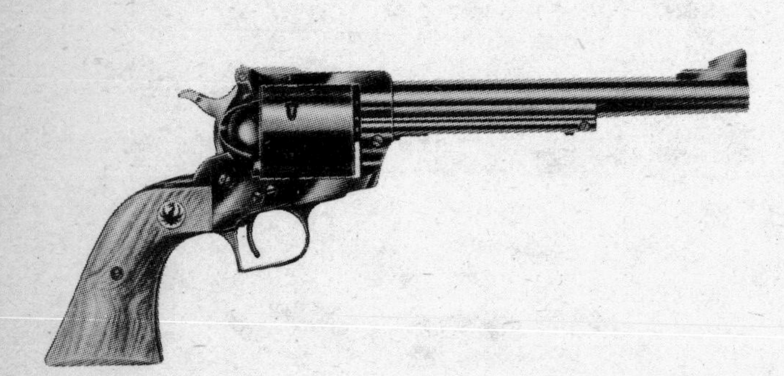

RUGER NEW MODEL SUPER BLACKHAWK
Caliber: 44 Magnum, 6-shot. Also fires 44 Spec.
Barrel: 7½" (6-groove, 20" twist).
Weight: 48 oz. **Length:** 13⅜" over-all.
Stocks: Genuine American walnut.
Sights: ⅛" ramp front, micro click rear adj. for w. and e.
Features: New Ruger interlocked mechanism, non-fluted cylinder, steel grip and cylinder frame, square back trigger guard, wide serrated trigger and wide spur hammer. Deep Ruger blue.
Price: **$157.50**

Ruger New Model 30 Carbine Blackhawk
Specifications similar to 45 Blackhawk. Fluted cylinder, round-back trigger guard. Weight 44 oz., length 13⅛" over-all, 7½" barrel only.
Price: **$119.75**

RUGER NEW MODEL CONVERTIBLE BLACKHAWK
Caliber: 45 Colt or 45 Colt/45 ACP (extra cylinder).
Barrel: 4⅝" or 7½" (6-groove, 16" twist).
Weight: 40 oz. (7½" bbl.). **Length:** 13⅛" (7½" bbl.).
Stocks: Smooth American walnut.
Sights: ⅛" ramp front, micro click rear adj. for w. and e.
Features: Similar to Super Blackhawk, Ruger interlocked mechanism. Convertible furnished with interchangeable cylinder for 45 ACP.
Price: Blued, 45 Colt **$119.75**
Price: Convertible **$142.80**

SMITH & WESSON K-38 S.A. M-14
Caliber: 38 Spec., 6-shot.
Barrel: 6", 8⅜".
Length: 11⅛" over-all (6" bbl.). **Weight:** 38½ oz. (6" bbl.).
Stocks: Checkered walnut, service type.
Sights: ⅛" Patridge front, micro click rear adj. for w. and e.
Features: Same as Model 14 except single action only, target hammer and trigger.
Price: 6" bbl. **$155.00**
Price: 8⅜" bbl. **$161.50**

THE VIRGINIAN SINGLE ACTION REVOLVER
Caliber: 357 Mag., 45 Colt, 6-shot.
Barrel: 4⅝", 5½", 7½".
Weight: 2½ lbs. (357 w/5½" bbl.). **Length:** 11" over-all (5½" bbl.).
Stocks: One-piece walnut.
Sights: Blade front, fixed notch rear.
Features: Chromed trigger guard and backstrap, blue barrel, color case-hardened frame, unique safety system. Made by Hammerli. Imported by Interarms.
Price: **$220.00**

HAMMERLI MODEL 120 TARGET PISTOL

Caliber: 22 LR.
Barrel: 10″, 6-groove.
Weight: 44.1 oz. **Length:** 14.8″.
Stocks: Walnut. Standard grip with thumb rest (120-1), adjustable grip on 120-2.
Sights: Fully adj. micro click rear (match type), sight radius is 9.9″ or 14.6″. Interchangeable front sight blade.
Features: Single shot with new action operated by lateral lever. Bolt fully encloses cartridge rim. Target trigger adj. from 1.8 oz. to 12 oz. Trigger position adj. Gil Hebard, importer.
Price: Model 120-1 .... **$210.00**
Price: Model 120-2 .... **$240.00**
Price: Model 120-2 Heavy Barrel (5.7″, 41 oz.) **$240.00**

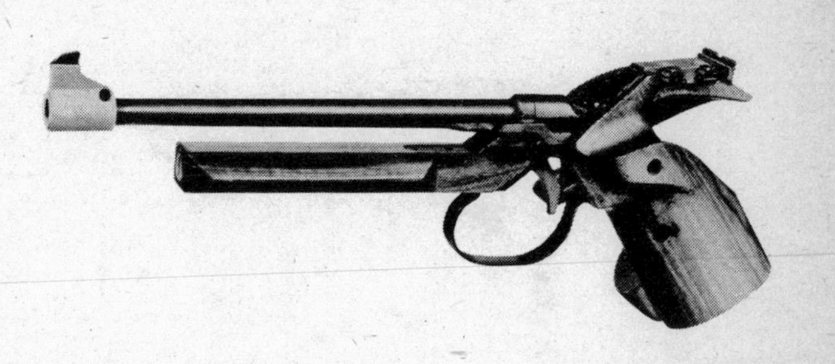

HAMMERLI MODEL 150 FREE PISTOL

Caliber: 22 LR.
Barrel: 11.4″, 6-groove. Free floating.
Weight: 42.4 oz. Up to 49.4 oz. with weights. **Length:** 15.4″.
Stocks: Walnut. Special anatomical design with adj. palm shelf.
Sights: Match sights. Sight radius 14.6″. Micro-click rear with interchangeable blade.
Features: Single shot Martini-type action operated by a lateral lever. Straight line hammerless ignition is vibration-free with an ignition time of 0.0016 sec. New set-trigger design fully adj. Low barrel and sight line. Extra weights availabe. Gil Hebard, importer.
Price: Including fitted case **$620.00**

HI-STANDARD D-100 AND DM-101 DERRINGER

Caliber: 22 S, L or LR: 22 Rimfire Magnum. 2 shot.
Barrel: 3½″, over and under, rifled.
Length: 5″ over-all. **Weight:** 11 oz.
Stocks: Smooth plastic.
Features: Hammerless, integral safety hammerblock, all steel unit is encased in a black, anodized alloy housing. Recessed chamber. Dual extraction. Top break, double action.
Sights: Fixed, open.
Price: Blued .... **$74.00** Nickel **$87.00**
Price: 22 WMR, Blued .... **$74.00** Nickel **$87.00**

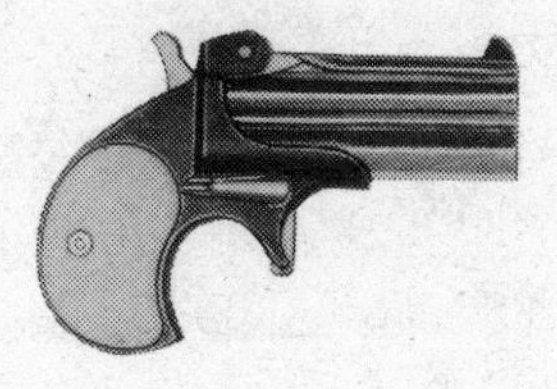

HAWES FAVORITE SINGLE SHOT PISTOL

Caliber: 22 S, L, LR.
Barrel: 8″.
Weight: 20 oz. **Length:** 12″.
Stocks: Laminated wood or plastic.
Sights: Fixed front, adj. rear.
Features: Tilt up action, blued bbl., chromed frame. Imported by Hawes Firearms. Copy of an early Stevens Favorite tip-up pistol.
Price: With plastic grips **$72.95**
Price: With Rosewood grips **$79.95**

F.I.E. MODEL D-38 DERRINGER

Caliber: 38 Special.
Barrel: 3″.
Weight: 14 oz.
Stocks: Checkered white plastic.
Sights: Fixed.
Features: Blue frame, chrome barrels. Spur trigger. Made in U.S.A.
Price: **$43.95**

MERRILL SPORTSMAN'S SINGLE SHOT

Caliber: 22 S, L, LR, 22WMR, 22WRF, 22 Rem. Jet, 22 Hornet, K-Hornet, 357, 38 Spl., 256 Win. Mag., 45 Colt/410 (3″).
Barrel: 9″ hinged type break-open. Semi-octagon.
Length: 10½″. **Weight:** 54 oz.
Stocks: Smooth walnut with thumb & heel rest.
Sights: Front 125″ blade, square notch rear adj. for w. & e.
Features: .355″ rib on top, grooved for scope mounts, auto. safety, cocking indicator, hammerless.
Price: **$225.00**
Price: Extra bbls. .... **$49.50** Wrist rest attachment **$15.50**

ROLLING BLOCK SINGLE SHOT PISTOL
Caliber: 22 LR, 22 WRM, 5mm Rem. Mag., 357 mag.
Barrel: 8″.
Weight: 2 lbs. **Length:** 12″.
Stocks: Walnut.
Sights: Front adj. for w., buckhorn adj. for e.
Features: Polished brass trigger guard. Supplied with wooden display box. Imported by Navy Arms.
Price: **$125.00**

REMINGTON MODEL XP-100 Bolt Action Pistol
Caliber: 221 Fireball, single shot.
Barrel: 10½ inches, ventilated rib.
Length: 16¾ inches. **Weight:** 60 oz.
Stocks: Brown nylon one-piece, checkered grip with white spacers.
Features: Fits left or right hand, is shaped to fit fingers and heel of hand. Grooved trigger. Rotating thumb safety, cavity in fore-end permits insertion of up to five 38 cal., 130-gr. metal jacketed bullets to adjust weight and balance. Included is a black vinyl, zippered case.
Sights: Fixed front, rear adj. for w. and e. Tapped for scope mount.
Price: Including case **$144.95**

THOMPSON-CENTER ARMS CONTENDER
Caliber: 218 Bee, 221 Rem., 25-35 Win., 30-30 Win., 22 S, L, LR, 22 WMR, 22 Rem. Jet, 22 Hornet, 22 K Hornet, 256 Win., 9mm Parabellum, 38 Super, 357/44 B & D, 38 Spl., 357 Mag., also 222 Rem., 30 M1, 45 ACP, 44 Mag., 5mm Rem., 45 Long Colt.
Barrel: 8¾″, 10″, tapered octagon. Single shot.
Length: 13¼″ (10″ bbl.). **Weight:** 43 oz. (10″ bbl.).
Stocks: Select checkered walnut grip and fore-end, with thumb rest. Right or left hand.
Sights: Under cut blade ramp front, rear adj. for w. & e.
Features: Break open action with auto-safety. Single action only. Interchangeable bbls., both caliber (rim & center fire), and length. Drilled and tapped for scope. Engraved frame.
Price: Blued (rimfire cals.) **$155.00**
Price: Blued (centerfire cals.) **$155.00**
Price: Extra bbls. **$57.00**
Price: 30 Herrett and 357 Herrett bull bbl. with fore-end, less sights **$62.00**
Price: As above except with sights **$67.00**
Price: Bushnell Phantom scope base **$7.50**
Price: Fitted walnut case **$39.50**
Price: 357 and 44 Mag. vent. rib, internal choke bbl. **$62.00**

UNIVERSAL ENFORCER MODEL 3000 AUTO CARBINE
Caliber: 30 M1 Carbine, 30-shot magazine.
Barrel: 10¼″ with 12-groove rifling.
Length: 17¾″. **Weight:** 4½ lbs.
Stocks: American walnut with handguard.
Features: Uses surplus 5- or 15-shot magazine. 4½-6 lb. trigger pull.
Sights: Gold bead ramp front. Peep rear adj. for w. and e. 14″ sight radius.
Price: Blue finish **$168.00**
Price: Nickel plated finish **$194.95**
Price: Gold plated finish **$212.95**

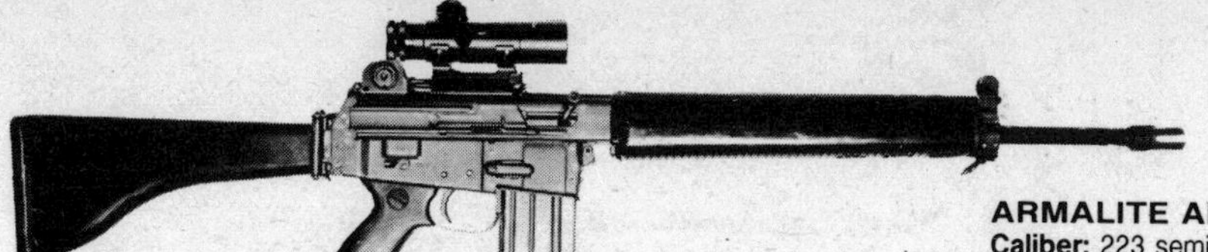

ARMALITE AR-180 SPORTER CARBINE

Caliber: 223 semi-automatic, gas operated carbine.
Barrel: 18¼″ (12″ twist).
Weight: 6½ lbs. **Length:** 38″ over-all
Stock: Nylon folding stock, phenolic fiber-glass heat dissipating fore-end.
Sight: Flip-up "L" type sight adj. for w., post front adj. for e.
Features: Safety lever accessible from both sides. Flash hider slotted to prevent muzzle climb.
Price: **$294.30**
3x (2.75 x 20mm) scope with detachable side-mount. **$88.49**
Extra 5-round magazine **$5.75**

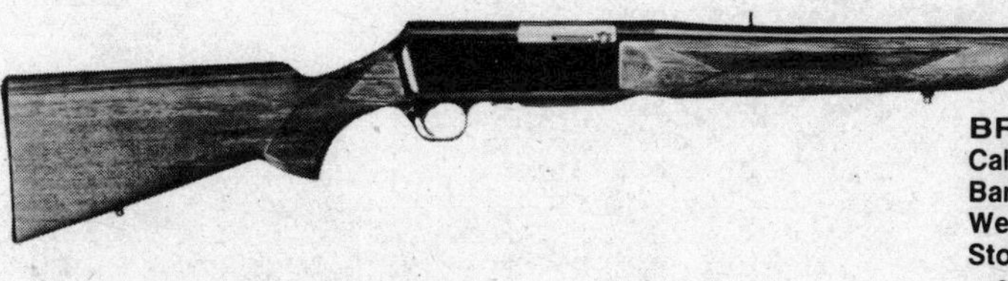

BROWNING HIGH-POWER AUTO RIFLE

Caliber: 243, 270, 30-06, 308.
Barrel: 22″ round tapered.
Weight: 7⅜ lbs. **Length:** 43½″ over-all.
Stock: French walnut p.g. stock (13⅝″x2″x1⅝″) and fore-end, hand checkered.
Sights: Adj. folding-leaf rear, gold bead on hooded ramp front.
Features: Detachable 4-round magazine. Receiver tapped for scope mounts. Trigger pull 4 lbs.
Price: Grade I **$439.50**
Price: Grade IV **$990.00**

Browning Magnum Auto Rifle

Same as the standard caliber model, except weighs 8½ lbs., 45¼″ over-all 24″ bbl., 3-round mag., Cals. 7mm Mag., 300 Win. Mag. and 338 Mag.
Grade I .... **$479.50** Grade IV **$1,030.00**
Other Grades and prices to **$1,200.00**

COLT AR-15 SPORTER

Caliber: 223 Rem.
Barrel: 20″.
Weight: 7¼ lbs. **Length:** 38⅜″ over-all.
Stock: Reinforced polycarbonate with buttstock stowage compartment.
Sights: Post front, rear adj. for w. and e.
Features: 5-round detachable box magazine recoil pad, flash suppressor, sling swivels.
Price: **$297.50**

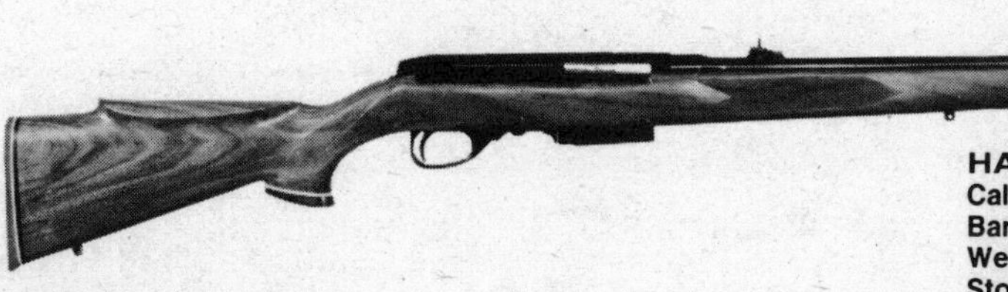

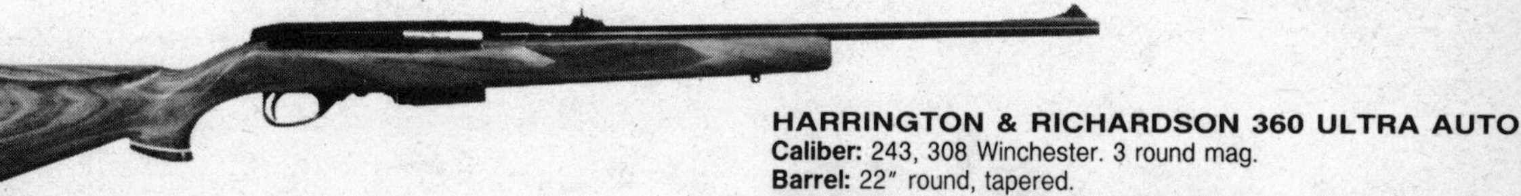

HARRINGTON & RICHARDSON 360 ULTRA AUTO

Caliber: 243, 308 Winchester. 3 round mag.
Barrel: 22″ round, tapered.
Weight: 7½ lbs. **Length:** 43½″ over-all.
Stock: One-piece American walnut Monte Carlo p.g. stock, roll-over cheekpiece.
Sights: Open adj. rear sight, gold bead ramp front.
Features: Sliding trigger guard safety. Manually operated bolt stop. Receiver tapped for scope mount.
Price: **$225.00**

M-1 TANKER GARAND

Caliber: 7.62 NATO (308), 8-shot clip.
Barrel: 17½″.
Weight: 8½ lbs.
Stock: Birch, walnut finish.
Sights: Blade front, peep rear adj. for w. & e.
Features: Gas-operated semi-automatic. Shortened version of M-1 Garand rifle. From National Ordnance.
Price: **$249.00**

NATIONAL ORDNANCE M-1 CARBINE

Caliber: 30 Carbine, 15-shot magazine.
Barrel: 18″.
Weight: 5½ lbs. **Length:** 35½″ over-all.
Stock: Walnut.
Sights: Blade front, rear adj. for w. and e.
Features: Gas operated, cross lock safety, hammerless, military style.
Price: **$109.00**
With scope base mounted **$119.00**
With folding "paratrooper" stock and 30-shot magazine **$139.00**
With scope base mounted **$149.00**

PJK M-68 CARBINE
Caliber: 9mm Luger, 30-shot magazine.
Barrel: 16 3/16".
Weight: 7 lbs. **Length:** 29¾".
Stock: Metal.
Sights: Blade front, aperature rear.
Features: Straight blowback operation, cross-bolt safety, removeable flash hider. Semi-automatic only.
Price: **$189.00**
Price: Scope Model has full length scope base on receiver top and cocking handle is on left side **$209.95**

PLAINFIELD MACHINE CO. CARBINE
Caliber: 30 U.S. Carbine or 223 (5.7mm)
Barrel: 18" six-groove.
Weight: 6 lbs. **Length:** 35½" over-all.
Stock: Glossy finished hard wood.
Sights: Click adj. open rear, gold bead ramp front.
Features: Gas operated semi-auto carbine. 15-shot detachable magazine.
Price: **$114.00**
Paratrooper. With telescoping wire stock, front vertical hand grip **$135.00**
Plainfielder. With walnut Monte Carlo sporting p.g. stock **$150.00**

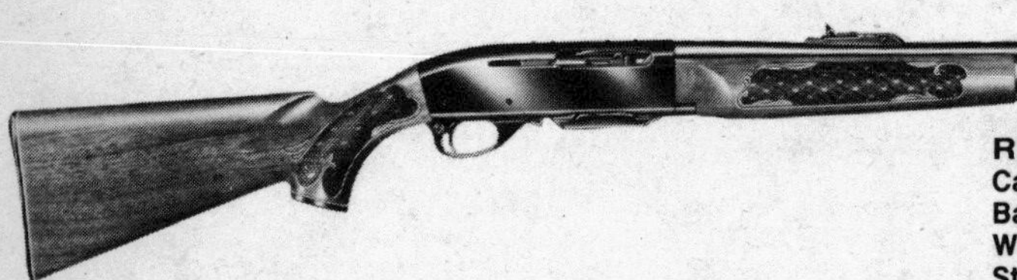

REMINGTON 742 WOODMASTER AUTO RIFLE
Caliber: 243 Win., 6mm Rem., 280 Rem., 308 Win. and 30-06.
Barrel: 22" round tapered.
Weight: 7½ lbs. **Length:** 42" over-all
Stock: Walnut (13¼"x1⅝"x2¼") deluxe checkered p.g. and fore-end.
Sights: Gold bead front sight on ramp; step rear sight with windage adj.
Features: Positive cross-bolt safety. Receiver tapped for scope mount. 4-shot clip mag.
Price: **$214.95**
Extra 4-shot clip magazine **$6.00**
Sling strap and swivels (installed) **$10.50**
Peerless (D) and Premier (F) grades .... **$800.00** and **$1,550.00**
Premier with gold inlays **$2,400.00**

Remington 742 Carbine
Same as M742 except: 18½" bbl., 38½" over-all, wgt. 6¾ lbs. Cals: 30-06, 308 Win. **$214.95**

Remington 742 BDL Woodsmaster
Same as 742 except: "stepped" receiver, Monte Carlo with cheekpiece (right or left), whiteline spacers, basket-weave checkering on p.g. and fore-end, black fore-end tip, RKW finish (13 5/16"x1⅝"x1 13/16"x2½"). Cals. 30-06, 308 .... **$234.95**

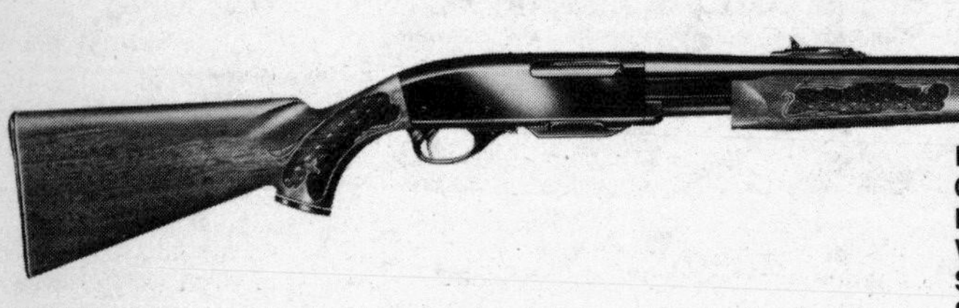

REMINGTON 760 GAMEMASTER SLIDE ACTION
Caliber: 6mm Rem., 243, 270, 308 Win., 30-06.
Barrel: 22" round tapered.
Weight: 7½ lbs. **Length:** 42" over-all.
Stock: Checkered walnut p.g. and fore-end (13¼"x1⅝"x2⅛") RKW finish
Sights: Gold bead front sight on matted ramp, open step adj. sporting rear.
Features: Detachable 4-shot clip. Cross-bolt safety. Receiver tapped for scope mount.
Price: **$184.95**
Sling strap and swivels (installed) **$10.50**
Extra 4-shot clip **$5.25**

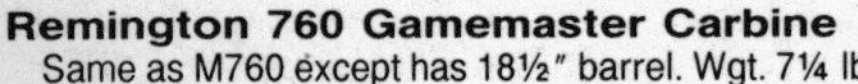

Remington 760 Gamemaster Carbine
Same as M760 except has 18½" barrel. Wgt. 7¼ lbs., 38½" over-all. Cals: 308 Win. and 30-60 .... **$184.95**

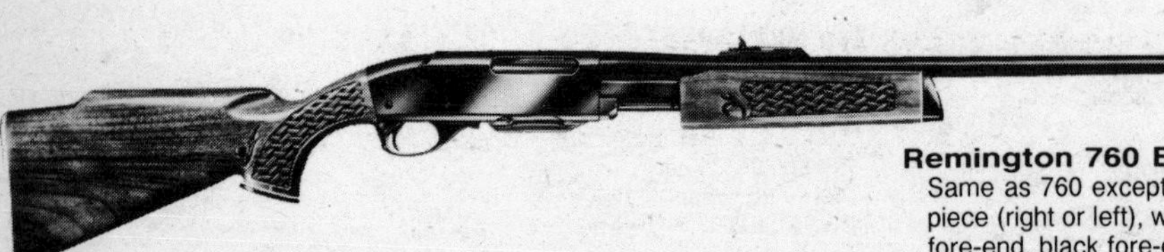

Remington 760 BDL Gamemaster
Same as 760 except: "stepped receiver," Monte Carlo stock with cheek-piece (right or left), whiteline spacer, basket-weave checkering on p.g. and fore-end, black fore-end tip, RKW finish. (13 5/16"x1⅝"x1 13/16"x2½"). Cals. 270, 30-06, 308 .... **$204.95**
Also in Peerless (D) and Premier (F) grades .... **$800.00** and **$1,550.00**
(F), with gold inlay **$2,400.00**

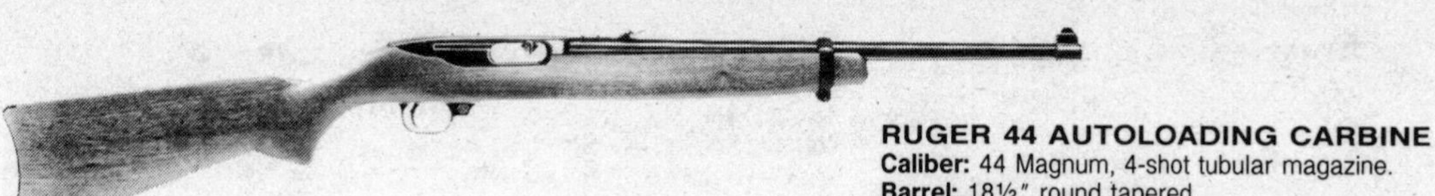

RUGER 44 AUTOLOADING CARBINE
Caliber: 44 Magnum, 4-shot tubular magazine.
Barrel: 18½" round tapered.
Weight: 5¾ lbs. **Length:** 36¾" over-all
Stock: One-piece walnut p.g. stock (13⅜"x1⅝"x2¼")
Sights: 1/16" front, folding leaf rear sights.
Features: Wide, curved trigger. Sliding cross-bolt safety. Receiver tapped for scope mount, unloading button.
Price: **$154.50**

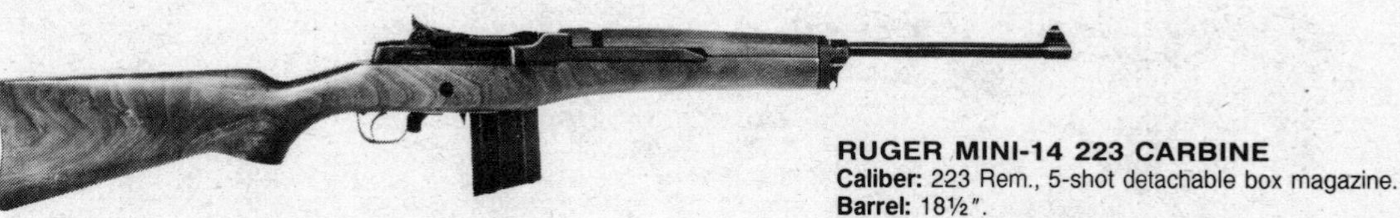

RUGER MINI-14 223 CARBINE
Caliber: 223 Rem., 5-shot detachable box magazine.
Barrel: 18½".
Weight: 6½ lbs. **Length:** 37¼" over-all.
Stock: Walnut, steel reinforced.
Sights: Gold bead front, fully adj. rear.
Features: Fixed piston gas-operated, positive primary extraction. 20-shot magazine available only to police departments. **Factory accepting police orders only for balance of 1975.**
Price: **$200.00**

RUGER 44 AUTOLOADING DELUXE CARBINE
Caliber: 44 Magnum, 4-shot tubular magazine.
Barrel: 18½" round tapered.
Weight: 5¾ lbs. **Length:** 36¾" over-all.
Stock: One piece American walnut with sling swivels.
Sights: Gold bead front, Ruger adj. peep rear.
Features: Automatic bolt hold-open after last shot, magazine unloading button. Drilled and tapped for scope mount.
Price: **$159.00**

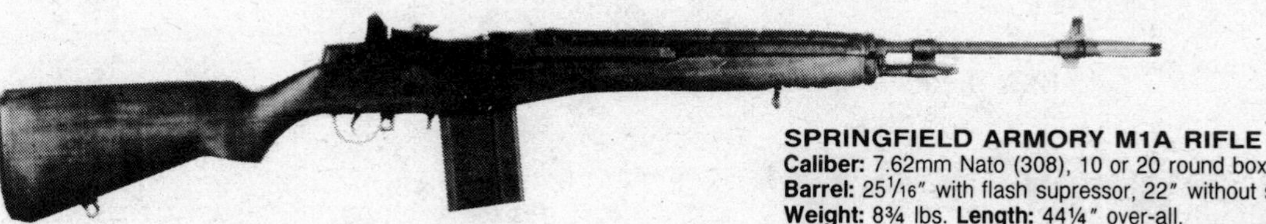

SPRINGFIELD ARMORY M1A RIFLE
Caliber: 7.62mm Nato (308), 10 or 20 round box magazine.
Barrel: 25 1/16" with flash supressor, 22" without supressor.
Weight: 8¾ lbs. **Length:** 44¼" over-all.
Stock: American walnut with walnut colored heat-resistant fiberglass handguard.
Sights: Military, square blade front, full click-adjustable aperture rear.
Features: Commercial equivalent of the U.S. M-14 service rifle with no provision for automatic firing. From Springfield Armory. Military accessories available including 4X or 6X ART scope and mount.
Price: Standard M1A Rifle (approx.) **$375.00**
Price: Match Grade (approx.) **$495.00**
Price: Barreled receiver with Match Grade Barrel (approx.) **$250.00**

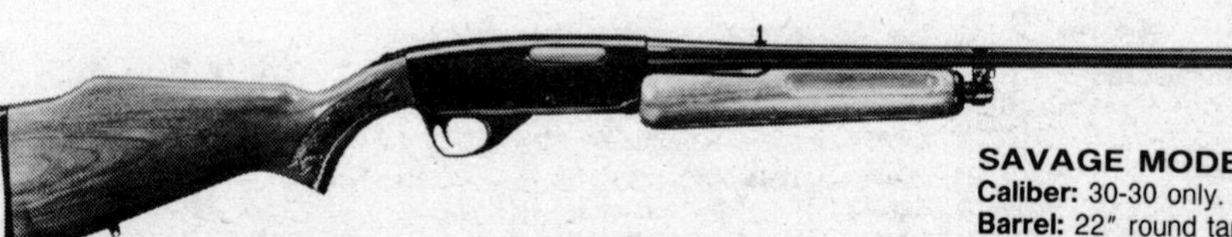

SAVAGE MODEL 170 SLIDE ACTION
Caliber: 30-30 only. 3-shot mag.
Barrel: 22" round tapered.
Weight: 6¾ lbs. **Length:** 41½" over-all.
Stock: Walnut (14"x1½"x2½"), with checkered p.g. Hard rubber buttplate.
Sights: Gold bead ramp front, folding-leaf rear.
Features: Hammerless, solid frame tapped for scope mount. Top tang safety.
Price: **$119.95**

Savage Model 170-C Slide Action Rifle
Same as Model 170 except has 18½" barrel, no Monte Carlo on stock. Silent-Lok feature eliminates slide handle rattle. **$119.95**

CENTERFIRE RIFLES—AUTOLOADING & SLIDE ACTION

UNIVERSAL 1003 AUTOLOADING CARBINE

Caliber: 30 M1, 5-shot magazine.
Barrel: 18″
Weight: 5½ lbs: **Length:** 35½″ over-all
Stock: Walnut stock inletted for "issue" sling and oiler, blued metal handguard.
Sights: Blade front aperture rear. With protective wings, adj.
Features: Gas operated, hammerless. Cross lock safety. Receiver tapped for scope mounts.
Price: **$118.95**
Price: Model 1011 nickel plated **$131.95**
Price: Model 1016 gold plated **$194.95**

Universal Model 1002 Carbine
Same as Model 1000 except: Military type with metal handguard. Blue
Price: **$122.95**

VALMET M-62/S RIFLE

Caliber: 7.62x39mm, 15- and 30-shot detachable box magazines.
Barrel: 16⅝″.
Weight: 8¾ lbs. **Length:** 36⅝″ over-all.
Stock: Fixed metal tube. Walnut optional.
Sights: Hooded post front adj. for w., tangent peep rear adj. for e.
Features: Finnish semi-automatic version of the AK-47. Basic Kalashnikov design (gas piston operating a rotating bolt assy.). Imported by Interarms.
Price: Metal stock version **$329.00**
Price: Wood stock version **$339.00**

VALMET M-72S

Caliber: 223, 15- and 30-shot detachable magazines.
Barrel: 16⅝″.
Weight: 8¾ lbs. **Length:** 36⅝″ over-all.
Stock: Wood or reinforced resin (ABS).
Sights: Open tangent rear sight adjustable for elevation. Post front sight with protectors, adjustable for windage.
Features: Finnish semi-automatic version of AK-47. Imported by Interarms.
Price: Resin Stock **$349.00**
Price: Wood Stock **$359.00**

CENTERFIRE RIFLES—LEVER ACTION

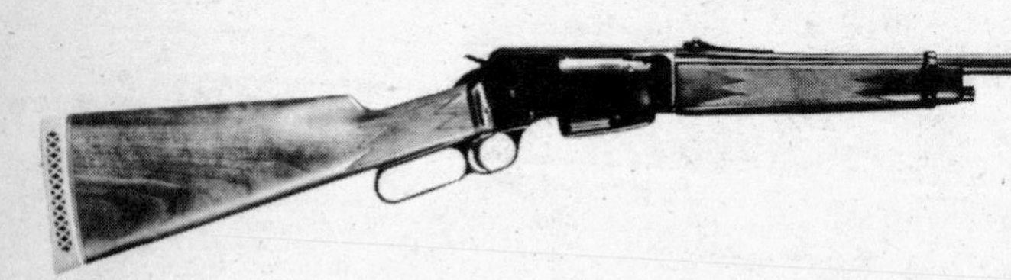

BROWNING BLR LEVER ACTION RIFLE

Caliber: 243 or 308 Win. 4-shot detachable mag.
Barrel: 20″ round tapered.
Weight: 6 lbs. 15 oz. **Length:** 39¾″ over-all.
Stock: Checkered straight grip and fore-end, oil finished walnut (13¾″x1¾″x2⅜″).
Sights: Square notch adj. rear, gold bead on hooded ramp front.
Features: Wide, grooved trigger; half-cock hammer safety. Receiver tapped for scope mount. Recoil pad installed.
Price: **$234.50**

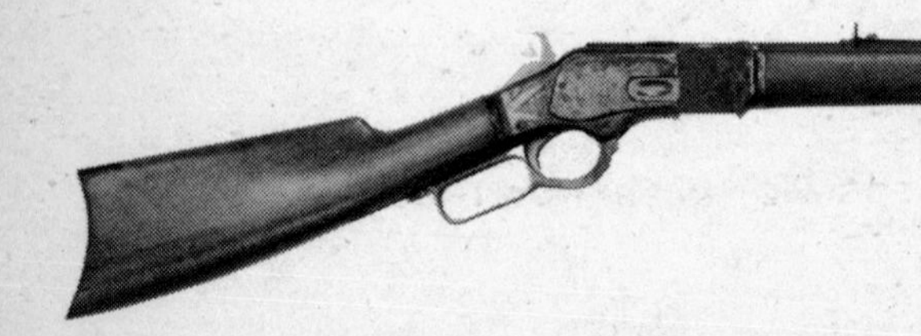

DIXIE ENGRAVED MODEL 1873 RIFLE

Caliber: 44-40.
Barrel: 23½″, octagon.
Weight: 7¾ lbs. **Length:** 43″ over-all.
Stock: Walnut.
Sights: Blade front, adj. rear.
Features: Engraved and case hardened frame. Duplicate of Winchester 1874. Made in Italy. From Dixie Gun Works.
Price: **$295.00**

MARLIN 336C LEVER ACTION CARBINE
Caliber: 30-30 or 35 Rem., 6-shot tubular magazine
Barrel: 20″ Micro-Groove.
Weight: 7 lbs. **Length:** 38½″
Stock: Select American black walnut, capped p.g. with white line spacers.
Sights: Ramp front with Wide-Scanhood, semi-buckhorn folding rear adj. for w. & e.
Features: Gold plated trigger, receiver tapped for scope mount, offset hammer spur, top of receiver sand blasted to prevent glare.
Price: **$126.95**

Marlin 336A
Same action as the 336C with 24″ round barrel, ½-magazine tube with 5-shot capacity. Blued fore-end cap and sling swivels. Available in 30-30 Win. only **$132.95**

Marlin 336T Lever Action Carbine
Same as the 336C except: straight stock; cal. 30-30 only. Squared finger lever. .... **$126.95.**

Marlin Glenfield 30A Lever Action Carbine
Same as the Marlin 336C except: checkered walnut finished hardwood p.g. stock, 30-30 only, 6-shot. **$118.95**

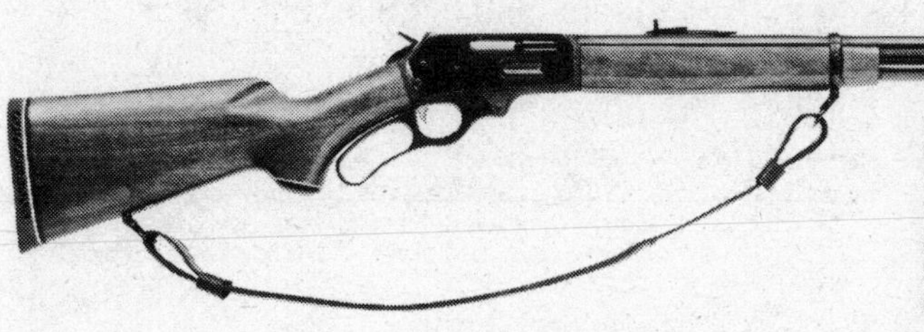

MARLIN 444 LEVER ACTION SPORTER
Caliber: 444 Marlin, 4-shot tubular magazine
Barrel: 22″ Micro-Groove.
Weight: 7½ lbs. **Length:** 40½″
Stock: American black walnut, capped p.g. with white line spacers, recoil pad.
Sights: Hooded ramp front, folding semi-buckhorn rear adj. for w. & e.
Features: Gold plated trigger, receiver tapped for scope mount, offset hammer spur, leather sling with detachable swivels.
Price: **$145.00**

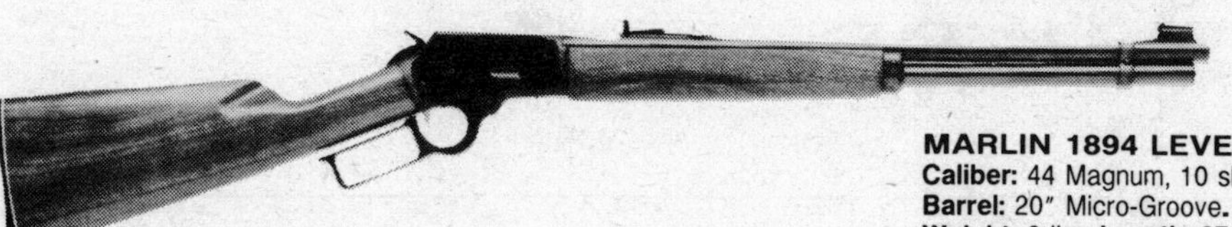

MARLIN 1894 LEVER ACTION CARBINE
Caliber: 44 Magnum, 10 shot tubular magazine
Barrel: 20″ Micro-Groove.
Weight: 6 lbs. **Length:** 37½″
Stock: American black walnut, straight grip and fore-end.
Sights: Hooded ramp front, semi-buckhorn folding rear adj. for w. & e.
Features: Gold plated trigger, receiver tapped for scope mount, offset hammer spur, solid top receiver sand blasted to prevent glare.
Price: **$126.95**

MARLIN 1895 LEVER ACTION RIFLE
Caliber: 45-70, 4-shot tubular magazine.
Barrel: 22″ round.
Weight: 7 lbs. **Length:** 40½″.
Stock: American black walnut, straight grip.
Sights: Bead front, semi-buckhorn folding rear adj. for w. and e.
Features: Solid receiver tapped for scope mounts or receiver sights, offset hammer spur.
Price: **$185.00**

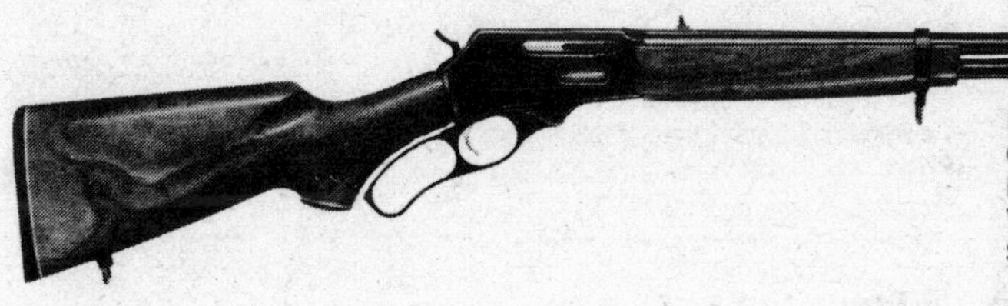

MOSSBERG MODEL 472 LEVER ACTION
Caliber: 30-30, 6-shot magazine. PCA
Barrel: 20″.
Weight: 7½ lbs. **Length:** 38½″ over-all.
Stock: Walnut, fluted comb, p.g., rubber buttplate, white line spacers at p.g. cap and butt.
Sights: Ramp front, rear adj. for e.
Features: Trigger moves with lever on opening, hammer-block safety. Solid top receiver with side ejection. Also available with straight grip stock, either cal., same price
Price: **$143.21**
Price: "Brush Gun". 18″ bbl., straight stock, 30-30 only **$143.21**
Price: 472 PRA (24″ bbl., hooded ramp front sight, ½ magazine tube)**$147.23**

MOSSBERG 472 "ONE IN FIVE THOUSAND" CARBINE
Caliber 30-30
Barrel: 18″
Stock: Straight grip walnut.
Sights: Ramp front, rear adj. fore.
Features: Collector's series edition. Brass buttplate, brass saddle ring and barrel bands, gold trigger. Indian scenes etched on both sides of receiver.
Price: **$164.80**

NAVY ARMS "1873" MODEL RIFLE
Caliber: 357 Mag., 44-40.
Barrel: 24″ (rifle, octagon); 20″ (carbine, round), 16½″ (trapper).
Weight: 9 lbs. (rifle); 7½ lbs. (carbine).
Stock: Walnut.
Sights: Blade front, step adj. rear.
Features: Available in blue, case-hardened or nickel (44-40 only) finish. Sliding dust cover, lever latch. Imported by Navy/Replica.
Price: Rifle **$210.00**
Price: Carbine **$210.00**
Price: Trapper **$210.00**
Price: Model 1001 .... **$1,000.00**

NAVY ARMS MODEL 66 LEVER ACTION RIFLE
Caliber: 22 LR, 38 Special, 44-40.
Barrel: 16½″, 19″, 24″.
Weight: 9¼ lbs. **Length:** 39½″.
Stock: Walnut.
Sights: Fixed front, folding rear.
Features: Replica of Winchester Model 1866 "Yellowboy." Available with three grades of engraving, selected stock and fore-end at additional cost. 22 LR also available with 16½″ bbl. (Trapper's Model). Imported by Navy Arms.
Price: Trapper & Carbine **$195.00**
Price: 24″ octagon bbl. (illus.) **$225.00**

PEDERSEN 4700 CUSTOM DELUXE LEVER RIFLE
Caliber: 30-30 Win., 35 Rem.
Barrel: 24″.
Weight: 7½ lbs. **Length:** 42½″ over-all.
Stock: Hand finished American black walnut; beavertail fore-end.
Sights: Hooded ramp front, open adjustable Guide rear.
Features: Receiver drilled and tapped for scope mounts; custom cheekpiece contoured for scope sights; hammer block manual safety with rebounding hammer.
Price: **$200.00**

SAVAGE 99E LEVER ACTION RIFLE
Caliber: 300 Savage, 243 or 308 Win., 5-shot rotary magazine.
Barrel: 20″ Chrome-moly steel.
Weight: 7 lbs. **Length:** 39¾″ over-all.
Stock: Walnut finished with checkered p.g. and fore-end (13½x1½x2½).
Sights: Ramp front with step adj. sporting rear. Tapped for scope mounts.
Features: Grooved trigger, slide safety locks trigger and lever.
Price: **$168.50**

Savage 99A Lever Action Rifle
Similar to the 99E except: straight-grip walnut stock with schnabel fore-end, top tang safety, no magazine window. Folding leaf rear sight. Available in 250-3000 (250 Savage), 243 or 308 Win. **$194.50**

Savage 99C Lever Action Clip Rifle
Similar to M99A except: Detachable staggered clip magazine with push-button ejection. Wgt. about 6¾ lbs., 41¾″ over-all with 22″ bbl. cals. 243, 308 .... **$199.50**

CENTERFIRE RIFLES—LEVER ACTION

Savage 99 CD Lever Action Rifle
Similar to Model 99C except: removable bead ramp front; removable adjustable rear sight; white line recoil pad and p.g. cap; weight 7 lbs., Monte Carlo stock and grooved fore-end; hand checkered; q.d. sling with swivels. Comes in 250-3000 or 308.
Price: **$219.95**

WESTERN FIELD 72 LEVER ACTION CARBINE
Caliber: 30-30, 6-shot magazine.
Barrel: 18″, 20″.
Weight: 7½ lbs. **Length:** 38½″ over-all; 36½″ (Carbine model).
Stock: Walnut, fluted comb, p.g., rubber buttplate and p.g. cap with white spacers.
Sights: Ramp front, rear adj. for e.
Features: Trigger moves with lever on opening, hammer-block safety. Gold plated trigger. Solid top receiver with side ejection.
Price: Standard Model **$129.95**
Price: 18″ bbl., straight stock, steel buttplate **$109.95**

Winchester 94 Antique Carbine
Same as M94 except: color case-hardened and scroll-engraved receiver, brass-plated loading gate and saddle ring. 30-30 only **$132.50**

WINCHESTER 94 LEVER ACTION CARBINE
Caliber: 30-30, (12″ twist). 6-shot tubular mag.
Barrel: 20″
Weight: 6½ lbs. **Length:** 37¾″ over-all
Stock: Walnut straight grip stock and fore-end (13″x1¾″x2½″).
Sights: Bead front sight on ramp with removable cover; open rear. Tapped for receiver sights.
Features: Solid frame, top ejection, half-cock hammer safety.
Price: **$122.50**

CENTERFIRE RIFLES—BOLT ACTION

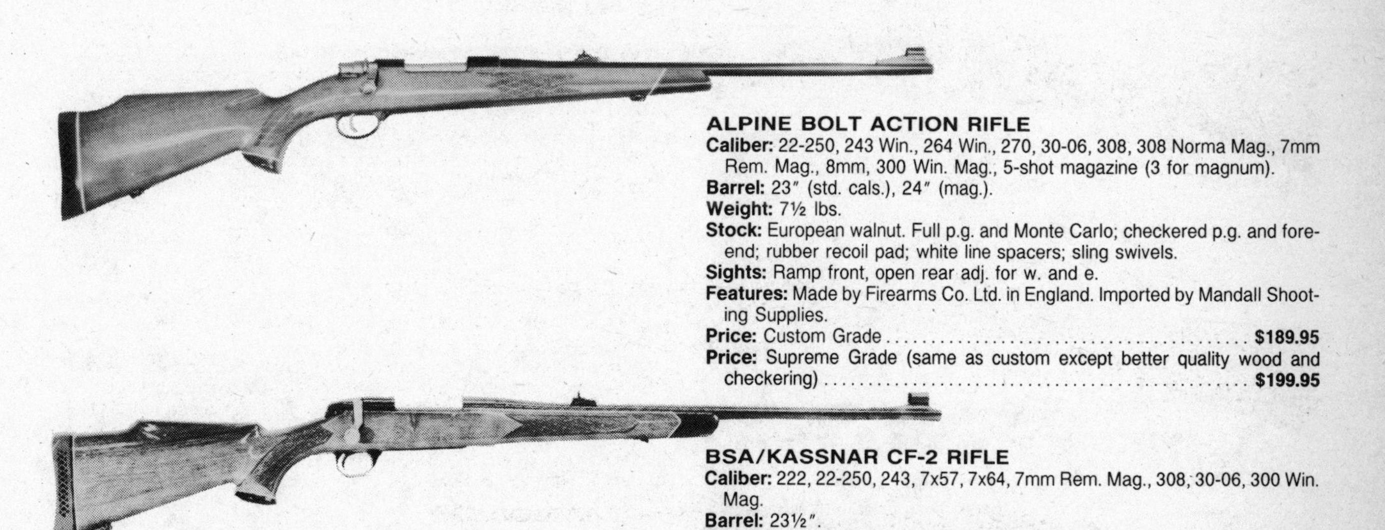

ALPINE BOLT ACTION RIFLE
Caliber: 22-250, 243 Win., 264 Win., 270, 30-06, 308, 308 Norma Mag., 7mm Rem. Mag., 8mm, 300 Win. Mag., 5-shot magazine (3 for magnum).
Barrel: 23″ (std. cals.), 24″ (mag.).
Weight: 7½ lbs.
Stock: European walnut. Full p.g. and Monte Carlo; checkered p.g. and fore-end; rubber recoil pad; white line spacers; sling swivels.
Sights: Ramp front, open rear adj. for w. and e.
Features: Made by Firearms Co. Ltd. in England. Imported by Mandall Shooting Supplies.
Price: Custom Grade **$189.95**
Price: Supreme Grade (same as custom except better quality wood and checkering) **$199.95**

BSA/KASSNAR CF-2 RIFLE
Caliber: 222, 22-250, 243, 7x57, 7x64, 7mm Rem. Mag., 308, 30-06, 300 Win. Mag.
Barrel: 23½″.
Weight: 7¼ lbs.
Stock: Hand checkered walnut. Roll over Monte Carlo cheekpiece. Rosewood fore-end tip and p.g. cap. Rubber recoil pad.
Sights: Williams hooded front, rear adj. for w. and e.
Features: Adjustable trigger, side safety. Enclosed bolt face. Drilled and tapped for scope mounts. Hinged floorplate. Imported by Kassnar Imports.
Price: **$269.95**

CHAMPLIN RIFLE

Caliber: All std. chamberings, including 458 Win. and 460 Wea. Many wildcats on request.
Barrel: Any length up to 26″ for octagon. Choice of round, straight taper octagon, or octagon with integral quarter rib, front sight ramp and sling swivel stud.
Length: 45″ over-all. **Weight:** About 8 lbs.
Stock: Hand inletted, shaped and finished. Checkered to customer specs. Select French, Circassin or claro walnut. Steel p.g. cap, trap buttplate or recoil pad.
Sights: Bead on ramp front, 3-leaf folding rear.
Features: Right or left hand Champlin action, tang safety or optional shroud safety, Canjar adj. trigger, hinged floorplate.
Price: From **$1,280.00**

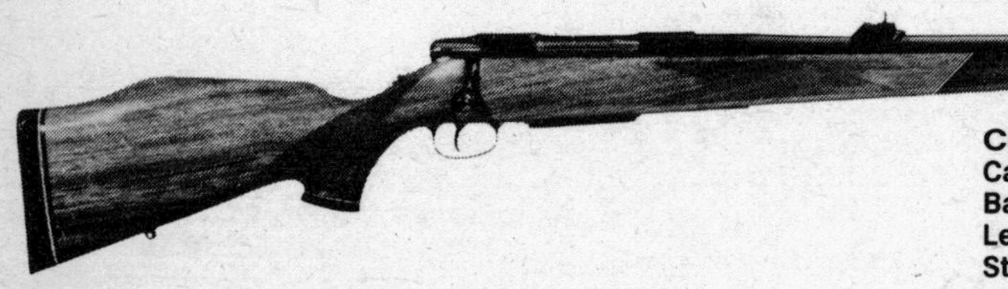

CHURCHILL "ONE OF ONE THOUSAND"

Caliber: 270, 308, 30-06, 7mm Rem. Mag., 300 Win. Mag., 375 H&H, 458 Win.
Barrel: 24″ (average).
Weight: 8 lbs. (30-06). **Length:** 44″ (24″ bbl.).
Stock: Select European walnut.
Sights: Hooded gold bead ramp front, 3-leaf folding rear.
Features: Commercial Mauser action, adj. trigger, hinged floorplate swivel-mounted rubber recoil pad with cartridge trap, p.g. cap recess holds extra front sight, bbl. mounted sling swivel. Lifetime guarantee. Only 1,000 rifles being produced. Fitted leather case available. By Churchill (Gunmakers) Ltd., imported by Interarms.
Price: **$1,000.00**

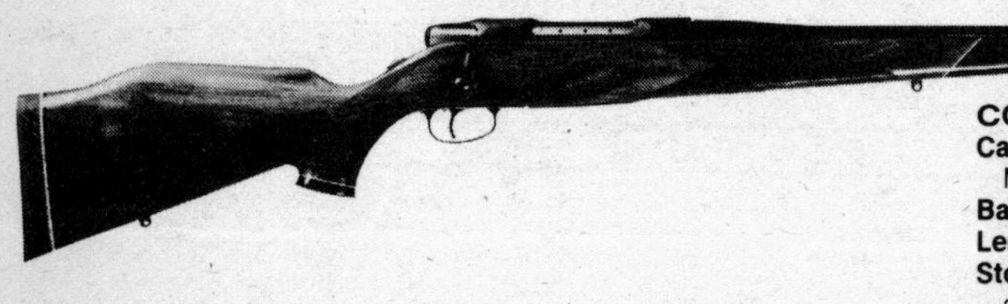

Colt Sauer Short Action Rifle

Same as standard rifle except chambered for 22-250, 243 and 308 Win. 24″ bbl., 43″ over-all. Weighs 7½ lbs. 3-shot magazine. **$498.50**

COLT SAUER GRAND AFRICAN

Caliber: 458 Win. Mag.
Barrel: 24″, round tapered.
Length: 44½″ over-all. **Weight:** 10½ lbs.
Stock: Solid African bubinga wood, cast-off M.C. with cheekpiece, contrasting rosewood fore-end and p.g. caps with white spacers. Checkered fore-end and p.g.
Sights: Ivory bead hooded ramp front, adj. sliding rear.
Price: **$549.00**

COLT SAUER RIFLE

Caliber: 25-06, 270, 30-06, (std.), 7mm Rem. Mag., 300 Wea. Mag., 300 Win. Mag. (Magnum).
Barrel: 24″, round tapered.
Length: 43¾″ over-all. **Weight:** 8 lbs. (std.).
Stock: American walnut, cast-off M.C. design with cheekpiece. Fore-end tip and p.g. cap rosewood with white spacers. Hand checkering.
Sights: None furnished. Specially designed scope mounts for any popular make scope furnished.
Features: Unique barrel/receiver union, non-rotating bolt with cam-actuated locking lugs, tang-type safety locks sear. Detachable 3- and 4-shot magazines.
Price: Standard cals. ...... **$498.50** Magnum cals. **$498.50**

DUMOULIN BOLT ACTION RIFLE

Caliber: All commercial calibers.
Barrel: 25″.
Weight: 7 lbs. **Length:** 43″.
Stock: French walnut with rosewood p.g. cap and fore-end tip, standard or skip line checkering, recoil pad.
Sights: Optional, available at extra cost.
Features: Made to customer requirements using Sako or FN action, with or without engraving (3 grades available). Imported from Belgium by Firearms Center.
Price: .... from **$575.00**

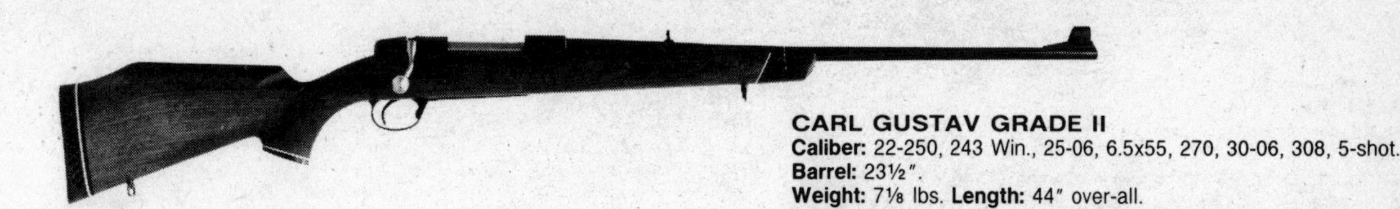

CARL GUSTAV GRADE II
Caliber: 22-250, 243 Win., 25-06, 6.5x55, 270, 30-06, 308, 5-shot.
Barrel: 23½″.
Weight: 7⅛ lbs. **Length:** 44″ over-all.
Stock: European walnut, hand checkered.
Sights: Hooded ramp front, folding leaf rear.
Fatures: Externally adj. trigger, silent safety, 80° bolt lift, enclosed bolt face, hinged floor plate. Also available in left hand version. Imported from Sweden by Stoeger Industries.
Price: **$399.95**
Price: Left-hand version as above except 6.5×55 .... **$329.95**

Carl Gustav Grade II Magnum
Same as Grade II except: has rubber recoil pad. Available in 7mm Rem., 300 Win.
Price: **$414.95**

CARL GUSTAV GRADE III
Caliber: 22-250, 243 Win., 25-06, 6.5x55, 270, 30-06, 308, 5-shot.
Barrel: 23½″.
Weight: 7⅛ lbs. **Length:** 44″ over-all.
Stock: French walnut, hand checkered.
Sights: None furnished.
Features: Engraved floor plate, detachable swivels, jeweled bolt. Imported from Sweden by Stoeger Industries.
Price: **$499.95**

Carl Gustav Grade III Magnum
Same as Grade III except: has recoil pad and internal modifications to handle magnum calibers.
Price: **$519.95**

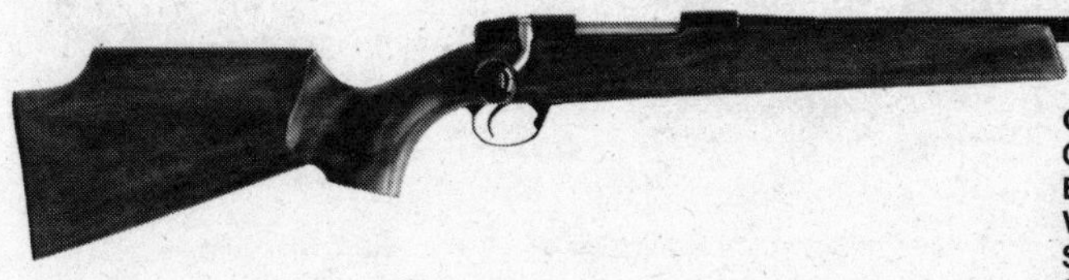

CARL GUSTAV V-T
Caliber: 222 Rem., 22-250, 243, 6.5x55.
Barrel: 27″. Bbl. diameter .850″.
Weight: 9½ lbs. **Length:** 47½″ over-all.
Stock: European walnut.
Sights: None furnished. Drilled and tapped for scope mounts.
Features: Wundhammer p.g., full-floating barrel, externally adj. trigger, large bolt handle. Imported from Sweden by Stoeger Industries.
Price: **$449.95**

HARRINGTON & RICHARDSON 300 BOLT ACTION
Caliber: 22-250, 243, 270, 308, 30-06 (5-shot), 7mm Rem. Mag., 300 Win. Mag. (3-shot)
Barrel: 22″ round, tapered.
Weight: 7¾ lbs. **Length:** 42½″ over-all.
Stock: American walnut, hand checkered p.g. and fore-end, Monte Carlo, roll-over cheekpiece.
Sights: Adjustable rear, gold bead ramp front.
Features: Hinged floorplate; sliding side safety; sling swivels, recoil pad. Receiver tapped for scope mount. Sako action.
Price: **$279.50**

HARRINGTON & RICHARDSON 301 ULTRA CARBINE
Similar to M300, except: Mannlicher style stock (no roll-over cheek-piece) metal fore-end tip. 18″ bbl., 39″ over all, wgt. 7¼ lbs., not available in 22-250. .... **$299.50**

HARRINGTON & RICHARDSON 317 ULTRA WILDCAT
Caliber: 17 Rem., 222, 223 or 17/223 (handload) 6-shot magazine.
Barrel: 20″ round, tapered.
Weight: 5¼ lbs. **Length:** 38½″ over-all.
Stock: Walnut, hand polished, hand checkered capped p.g. and fore-end, with Monte Carlo.
Sights: None. Receiver dovetailed for integral scope mounts.
Features: Sliding side safety, adj. trigger. included. Sliding side safety, adj. trigger.
Price: **$285.00**
Model 317P has better wood, basketweave checkering **$500.00**

HERTER'S MARK J9 RIFLE
Caliber: 22-250, 25-06, 243, 6mm, 270, 308, 30-06, 264, 7mm mag., 300 Win. Mag.
Barrel: 23½″.
Weight: 8 lbs. **Length:** 42½″.
Stock: Black walnut, rollover cheek piece, ebonite p.g. cap and butt plate.
Sights: Ramp front, rear adj. for w. and e.
Features: Also available w/o sights, with Mannlicher or beavertail style stocks. Three grades (Hunter's, Supreme, Presentation) differ stock finish, style. Also available as actions or barreled actions. Imported from Yugoslavia by Herter's.
Price: Hunter's Grade **$114.00**
Price: Supreme Grade **$117.75**
Price: Presentation Grade **$132.70**

Consult our Directory pages for the location of firms mentioned.

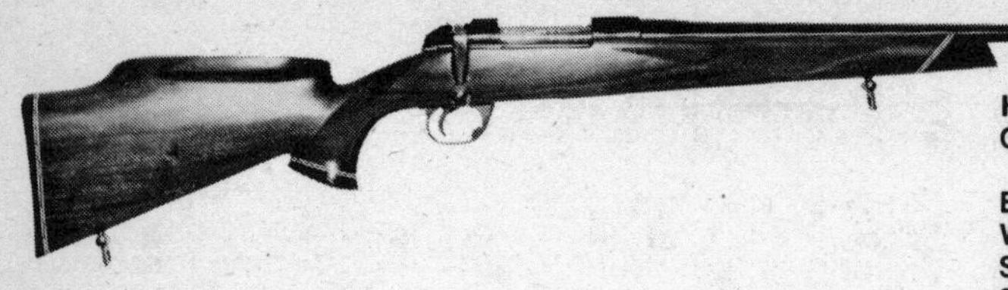

HERTER'S MARK U9 RIFLE

Caliber: 222, 222 mag., 223, 22-250, 25-06, 243, 6mm, 284, 308, 270, 30-06, 264, 7mm mag., 300 Win.
Barrel: 23½".
Weight: 6¼ lbs. **Length:** 42½".
Stock: American walnut, Monte Carlo, p.g.
Sights: Ramp front, rear adj. for w. and e.
Features: Also available less sights, with Mannlicher style stock, Douglas barrels (338 and 458 mag. plus above cals.). Three grades (Hunter's, Supreme, Presentation) differ in stock finish, style. Also available as actions or bbld. actions, bench rest, target or varmint versions. Imported from England by Herter's.
Price: Hunter's Grade **$129.95**
Price: Supreme Grade **$140.95**
Price: Presentation Grade **$148.75**

Ithaca LSA-65 Bolt Action Rifle
Same as the LSA-55 except in 25-06, 270 or 30-06 caliber (4-shot clip only).
Price: **$249.95**
Price: LSA-65 Deluxe **$279.95**

ITHACA LSA-55 BOLT ACTION RIFLE

Caliber: 243, 308, 22-250, 6mm Rem. 270 and 30-06.
Barrel: 23" round tapered, full-floating.
Weight: About 6½ lbs. **Length:** 41½" over-all
Stock: Hand checkered walnut, Monte Carlo with built-in swell on p.g.
Sights: Removable rear adj. for w. & e. ramp front.
Features: Detachable 3-shot magazine, adj. trigger, top tang safety. Receiver tapped for scope mounts.
Price: 243, 308, 22-250, 6mm & 222 .... **$249.95**
Price: 270, 30-06 & 25-06 .... **$249.95**
Price: 222 heavy bbl. **$329.95**
Price: Heavy Bbl., 22-250 .... **$329.95**
Price: Deluxe (except heavy bbl. models) **$279.95**

Ithaca LSA-55 Deluxe Bolt Action
Same as the std. except rollover cheekpiece, fore-end tip and pistol grip cap of rosewood with white spacers. Scope mount rings supplied. Sling swivels installed.
Price: 243, 308, 22-250 & 6mm **$279.95**
Price: 25-06, 270 & 30-06 .... **$279.95**
Price: 222 cal. **$279.95**

KLEINGUENTHER K-14 INSTA-FIRE RIFLE

Caliber: 243, 25-06, 270, 7x57, 7mm Rem. Mag., 30-06, 300 Win. Mag., 308 Win., 308 Norma, 375 H&H.
Barrel: 24", 26".
Weight: 7⅜ lbs. **Length:** 43½" over-all.
Stock: Available in light, medium or dark walnut. Monte Carlo, hand checkered, cheekpiece, rosewood fore-end tip, rosewood p.g. cap with diamond inlay.
Sights: None furnished. Drilled and tapped for scope mounts.
Features: Ultra fast lock/ignition time. Rubber recoil pad, hidden clip, external trigger adj., recessed bolt face, 60° bolt lift. Imported from Germany by Kleinguenther's.
Price: Std. cals. .... **$448.00** Mag. cals. **$448.00**

MARK X RIFLE

Caliber: 22-250; 243, 270, 308 Win.; 30-06; 25-06; 7×57; 7 mm Rem. Mag; 300 Win. Mag.
Barrel: 24".
Weight: 7½ lbs. **Length:** 44".
Stock: Hand checkered walnut, Monte Carlo, white line spacers on p.g. cap, buttplate and fore-end tip.
Sights: Ramp front with removable hood, open rear adj. for w. and e.
Features: Sliding safety, quick detachable sling swivels, hinged floorplate. Also available as actions or bbld. actions. Imported from Europe by Interarms.
Price: From .... **$213.00** With adj. trigger from **$223.00**

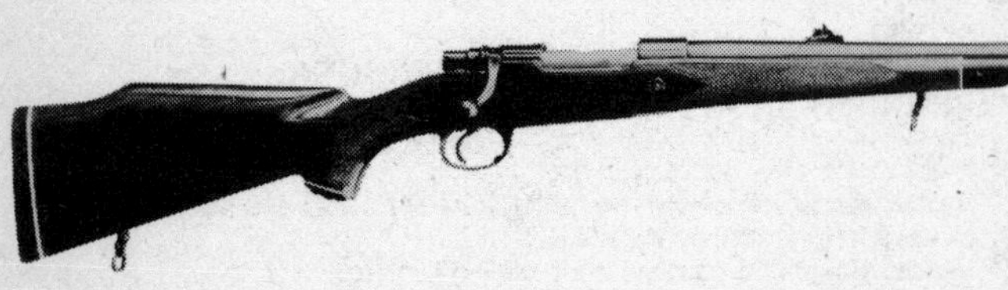

MARK X ALASKAN MAGNUM RIFLE

Caliber: 375 H&H, 458 Win. Mag.; 3-shot magazine.
Barrel: 24".
Weight: 8¼ lbs. **Length:** 32" over-all.
Stock: Select walnut with crossbolt; hand checkered p.g. and fore-end; Monte Carlo; sling swivels.
Sights: Hooded ramp front; open rear adj. for w. & e.
Features: Hinged floorplate; right-hand thumb (tang) safety; adj. trigger. From Interarms.
Price: **$295.00**

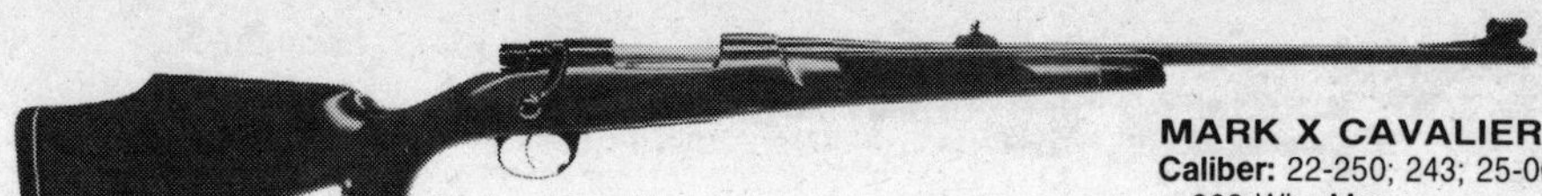

MARK X CAVALIER RIFLE

Caliber: 22-250; 243; 25-06; 270; 7×57; 7mm Rem. Mag.; 308 Win.; 30-06; 300 Win. Mag.
Barrel: 24″.
Weight: 7½ lbs. **Length:** 44″.
Stock: Checkered Walnut with Rosewood fore-end tip and pistol grip cap, Monte Carlo cheek piece and recoil pad.
Sights: Ramp front with removable hood, open rear adjustable for windage and elevation.
Features: Contemporary-styled stock with sculptured accents; roll over cheek piece and flat bottom fore-end. Adjustable trigger and quick detachable sling swivels, standard. Receiver drilled and tapped for receiver sights and scope mounts. Also available without sights. Imported by Interarms.
Price: From **$277.00**

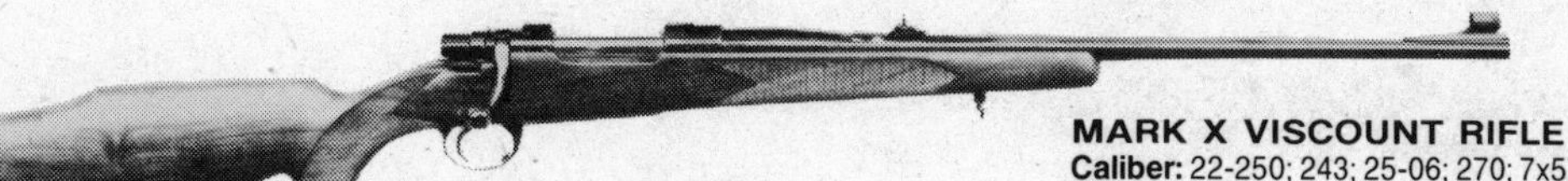

MARK X VISCOUNT RIFLE

Caliber: 22-250; 243; 25-06; 270; 7x57; 7mm Rem. Mag.; 308 Win.; 30-06; 300 Win. Mag.
Barrel: 24″.
Weight: 7½ lbs. **Length:** 44″.
Stock: Genuine Walnut stock, hand checkered with 1″ sling swivels.
Sights: Ramp front with removable hood, open rear sight ajustable for windage and elevation.
Features: One piece trigger guard with hinged floor plate, drilled and tapped for scope mounts and receiver sight, hammer-forged chrome vanadium steel barrel. Avail. with adj. trigger. Imported by Interarms.
Price: From **$199.00**

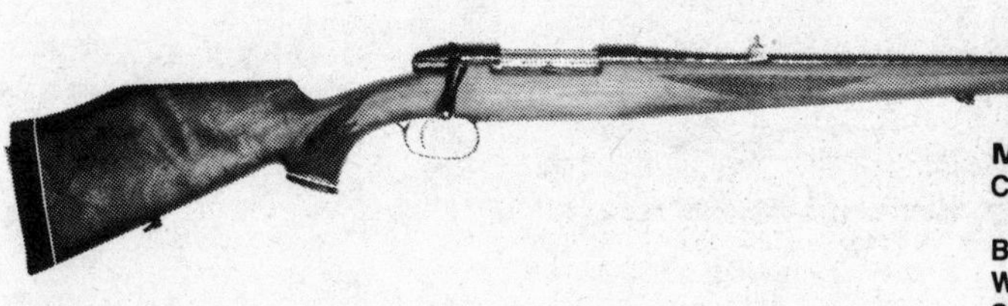

MANNLICHER-SCHOENAUER M-72 MODEL L/M

Caliber: 22-250, 5.6x57, 6mm Rem. 243, 6.5x57, 270, 7x57, 7x64, 30-06, 308 Win.
Barrel: 20″ (full stock), 23½″ (half stock).
Weight: 7¼ lbs. (full stock). **Length:** 40″ over-all (full stock).
Stock: Full Mannlicher or standard half stock, oil or varnish finish. Rubber recoil pad, hand checkered walnut, Monte Carlo cheekpiece.
Sights: Ramp front, open U-notch rear.
Features: 6 forward locking lugs. 60° bolt throw, wing-type safety. Choice of interchangeable single or double set triggers. Drilled and tapped for scope mounting. Imported by L.E.S.
Price: **$650.00**

MANNLICHER-SCHOENAUER M-72 MODEL T

Same as Model S except weighs 9¼ lbs., available in 9.3x64, 375 H&H Mag., and 458 Win. Mag. only **$800.00**

MANNLICHER-SCHOENAUER M-72 MODEL S

Caliber: 6.5x68, 7mm Rem. Mag., 8x68S, 9.3x64, 375 H&H Mag.
Barrel: 25½″.
Weight: 8½ lbs. **Length:** 46″ over-all.
Stock: Walnut half-stock style, varnished or oil finish. Rubber recoil pad, hand checkered. Monte Carlo cheekpiece.
Sights: Hooded ramp front, U-notch open rear.
Features: 6 forward locking lugs. 60° bolt throw. Wing-type safety. Choice of interchangeable single or double set triggers. Drilled and tapped for scope mounts. Custom engraving and stock carving avail. Imported by L.E.S.
Price: **$750.00**

MOSSBERG 800 SERIES BOLT ACTION RIFLE

Caliber: 22-250, 243 and 308. 4-shot magazine.
Barrel: 22″ AC-KRO-GRUV round tapered.
Weight: 6½ lbs. **Length:** 42″ over-all.
Stock: Walnut, Monte Carlo, checkered p.g. and fore-end.
Sights: Gold bead ramp front, adj. folding-leaf rear.
Features: Top tang safety, hinged floorplate, 1″ sling swivels installed. Receiver tapped for scope mounts.
Price: **$165.98**

Mossberg 800 V/T Varmint Target Rifle

Model 800 with heavy 24″ bbl, target scope bases, no iron sights. Cals. 243 and 22-250 only. 44″ overall, wgt. about 9½ lbs. **$178.87**

Mossberg 800SM Scoped Rifle

Same as M800 except has Mossberg M84 4x scope, but no iron sights. Wgt. 7½ lbs. **$195.57**

MOSSBERG 810A BOLT ACTION RIFLE

Caliber: 30-06, 270, 4-shot magazine, 338, 3-shot.
Barrel: 22″ AC-KRO-GRUV, straight taper.
Weight: 7½ to 8 lbs. **Length:** 42″ over-all.
Stock: Walnut Monte Carlo with checkered fore-end and capped p.g. recoil pad and sling swivels installed.
Sights: Gold bead on ramp front, folding-leaf rear.
Features: Receiver tapped for metallic sight or scope mounts. Top tang safety. Detachable box magazine.
Price: **$177.44**
Price: With 4x scope as 810 ASM **$211.06**

Mossberg 810C Bolt Action Rifle

Same as 810A except in 270 Win. **$165.98**
With 4x scope as 810 CSM **$195.57**

OMEGA III BOLT ACTION RIFLE
Caliber: 25-06, 270, 30-06, 7mm. Rem. Mag., 300 Win. Mag., 338 Win. Mag.
Barrel: 22″ or 24″.
Weight: 7¼ lbs. **Length:** 42″ over-all (24″ bbl.).
Stock: Choice of two styles: Monte Carlo or Cassic. In either Claro walnut or laminated walnut and maple.
Sights: None furnished.
Features: Octagonal bolt, square locking system with enclosed bolt face gives 50 degree lift. Rotary magazine holds five standard or four magnum cartridges; cross bolt safety; fully adj. trigger; interchangeable stock and fore-end. Hi-Shear Corp./Ordnance Division.
Price: **$399.50**
Extra set of stocks **$99.50**

PARKER-HALE SUPER 1200 BOLT ACTION RIFLE
Caliber: 22-250, 243 Win., 6mm Rem., 25-06, 270 Win., 30-06, 308 Win., 7mm Rem. Mag., 300 Win. Mag.
Barrel: 24″.
Weight: 7¼ lbs. **Length:** 45″.
Stock: 13.5″ x 1.8″ x 2.3″. Hand checkered walnut, rosewood p.g. and fore-end caps, fitted rubber recoil pad with white line spacers.
Sights: Bead front, folding adj. rear. Receiver tapped for scope mounts.
Features: 3-way side safety, single-stage adj. trigger, hinged mag. floorplate. Model 1200P has scroll engraved action, trigger guard and mag. floorplate, detachable swivels, no sights; avail. only in 243, 30-06. Varmint Model (1200V) has glass-bedded action, free-floating bbl., avail. in 22-250, 6mm Rem., 25-06, 243 Win., without sights. Imported from England by Jana.
Price: .... **$219.95** (**$234.95**, mag. cals.)
Price: 1200P .... **$279.95** 1200V **$234.95**

PEDERSEN 3000 BOLT ACTION RIFLE
Caliber: 270, 30-06, 7mm Rem. Mag., 338 Win. Mag., 3-shot magazine.
Barrel: 22″ (270, 30-06), 24″ (7mm Rem. Mag., 338 Win. Mag.).
Weight: 7 lbs. **Length:** 42″ over-all.
Stock: Walnut, roll-over cheekpiece, M.C., wrap-around checkering at p.g. and fore-end.
Sights: Drilled and tapped for scope mounts. Iron sight model available.
Features: Adjustable trigger, sling swivels, medium weight barrel, bull barrel on 338. Grades differ in extent of engraving and stock figure. Mossberg M800 action.
Price: Grade I **$880.00**
Price: Grade II **$715.00**

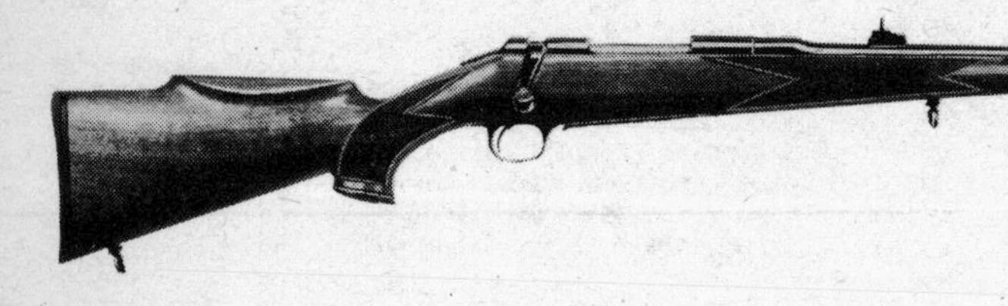

PEDERSEN 3500 BOLT ACTION RIFLE
Caliber: 270, 30-06, 7mm Rem. Mag., 3-shot magazine.
Barrel: 22″ (270, 30-06), 24″ (7mm Rem. Mag.).
Weight: 7 lbs. **Length:** 42″ over-all.
Stock: American black walnut; 20 l.p.i. hand checkered in high and low comb; Monte Carlo roll-over cheekpiece; rosewood p.g. cap and fore-end tip.
Sights: None. Drilled and tapped for scope mounts.
Features: Damascened bolt with four in-line locking lugs; hinged steel floorplate; trigger adjustable for sear let-off and weight of pull.
Price: **$284.50**

REMINGTON 700 ADL BOLT ACTION RIFLE
Caliber: 222, 22-250, 6mm Rem., 243, 25-06, 270, 7mm Rem. Mag., 308 and 30-06.
Barrel: 22″ or 24″ round tapered.
Weight: 7 lbs. **Length:** 41½″ to 43½″
Stock: Walnut, RKW finished p.g. stock with impressed checkering, Monte Carlo (13⅜″x1⅝″x2⅜″).
Sights: Gold bead ramp front; removable, step-adj. rear with windage screw.
Features: Side safety, receiver tapped for scope mounts.
Price: (except 7mm Rem. Mag.) **$189.95**
Price: 7mm Rem. Mag. **$204.95**

Remington 700 BDL Bolt Action Rifle
Same as 700-ADL, except: fleur-de-lis checkering; black fore-end tip and p.g. cap, white line spacers. Matted receiver top, quick release floorplate. Hooded ramp front sight. Q.D. swivels and 1″ sling **Price:** **$219.95**
Available also in 17 Rem., 6.5 Rem. Mag., 350 Rem. Mag., 7mm Rem. Mag., 264 and 300 Win. Mag., caliber. 44½″ over-all, weight 7½ lbs. . **$234.95**
Peerless Grade .... **$725.00** Premier Grade **$1,425.00**

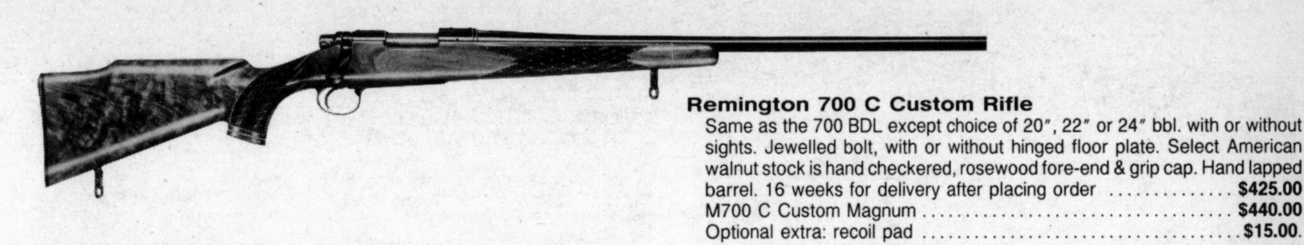

Remington 700 C Custom Rifle
Same as the 700 BDL except choice of 20″, 22″ or 24″ bbl. with or without sights. Jewelled bolt, with or without hinged floor plate. Select American walnut stock is hand checkered, rosewood fore-end & grip cap. Hand lapped barrel. 16 weeks for delivery after placing order **$425.00**
M700 C Custom Magnum **$440.00**
Optional extra: recoil pad .... **$15.00.**

Remington 700 Safari
Same as the 700 BDL except 375 H&H or 458 Win. Magnum calibers only. Hand checkered, oil finished stock with recoil pad installed. Delivery time is about five months. **$410.00**

Remington 700 BDL Varmint
Same as 700 BDL, except: 24″ heavy bbl., 43½″ over-all, wgt. 9 lbs. Cals. 222, 223, 22-250, 6mm Rem., 243 and 25-06. No sights........ **$234.95**

Remington 700BDL Left Hand
Same as 700 BDL except: mirror-image left-hand action, stock. 270, 30-06 **$224.95;** 7mm Rem. Mag. **$239.95**

REMINGTON 788 BOLT ACTION RIFLE
Caliber: 222 (5-shot), 22-250, 223 Rem., 6mm Rem., 243, and 308 (4-shot).
Barrel: 22″ round tapered (24″ in 222, 223 and 22-250).
Weight: 7-7½ lbs. **Length:** 41⅝″ over-all.
Stock: Walnut finished hardwood with Monte Carlo and p.g. (13⅝″x1⅞″x2⅝″).
Sights: Blade ramp front, open rear adj. for w. & e.
Features: Detachable box magazine, thumb safety, receiver tapped for scope mounts.
Price: **$124.95**
Sling strap and swivels, installed **$6.25**
Model 788 with Universal Model UE 4x scope, mounts and rings in cals. 6mm Rem., 243 Win., 308 and 22-250 .... **$149.95**

Remington 788 Left Hand Bolt Action
Same as 788 except cals. 6mm & 308 only and left hand stock and action.
Price: **$129.95**

RUGER 77 BOLT ACTION RIFLE
Caliber: 22-250, 243, 6mm. 250-3000, (5-shot).
Barrel: 22″ round tapered.
Weight: 6¾ lbs. **Length:** 42″ over-all.
Stock: Hand checkered American walnut (13¾″x1⅝″x2⅛″), p.g. cap, sling swivel studs and recoil pad.
Sights: Optional gold bead ramp front, folding leaf adj. rear, or scope rings.
Features: Integral scope mount bases, diagonal bedding system, hinged floor-plate, adj. trigger, tang safety. Scope optional.
Price: With Ruger steel scope rings **$215.00**
Price: With rings and open sights **$230.00**

Ruger Model 77 Magnum Rifle
Similar to Ruger 77 except: magnum-size action. Calibers 25-06, 270, 7x57, 30-06 (5-shot), 7mm Rem. Mag., 300 Win. Mag., 338 Win. Mag., 458 Win. Mag. (3-shot). 270 and 30-06 have 22″ bbl., all others have 24″. Weight and length vary with caliber.
Price: With rings only, 338 Win. Mag. **$230.00**
Price: With rings only, all cals. except 458 .... **$215.00**
Price: With rings and sights, 338 .... **$298.00**
Price: With rings and sights, 458 .... **$298.00**
Price: With rings and sights, other cals. **$230.00**

RUGER MODEL 77 VARMINT
Caliber: 22-250, 220 Swift, 243, 6mm, 25-06.
Barrel: 24″ heavy straight tapered, 26″ in 220 Swift.
Weight: Approx. 9 lbs. **Length:** Approx. 44″ over-all.
Stock: American walnut, similar in style to Magnum Rifle.
Sights: Barrel drilled and tapped for target scope blocks. Integral scope mount bases in receiver.
Features: Ruger diagonal bedding system, Ruger steel 1″ scope rings supplied. Fully adj. trigger. Barreled actions available in any of the standard calibers and barrel lengths.
Price: **$215.00**
Price: Barreled action only all cals. except 338 .... **$167.50**
Price: Bbld. action, 338 and 458 .... **$232.50**

Ruger Model 77 Magnum Round Top
Same as Model 77 except: round top receiver, drilled and tapped for standard scope mounts. Open sights are standard equipment. Calibers 25-06, 270, 30-06, 7mm Rem. Mag., 300 Win. Mag., 338 Win. Mag.
Price: All cals. except 338 .... **$215.00**
Price: 338 .... **$230.00**

SAKO MODEL 74 SUPER SPORTER

Caliber: 222, 223, (short action); 243, (medium action); 270, 30-06, 7mm Mag., 300 Mag., 338 Mag., 375 H&H Mag. (long action).
Barrel: 23″ (222, 223, 243), 24″ (other cals.).
Weight: 6¾ lbs. (short); 6¾ lbs. (med.); 8 lbs. (long).
Stock: Hand-checkered European walnut.
Sights: None furnished.
Features: Adj. trigger, hinged floorplate. 222 and 223 have short action, 243 has medium action, others are long action. Imported from Finland by Garcia.
Price: Short action **$325.00**
Price: Medium action **$325.00**
Price: Long action **$325.00**
Price: Magnum cals. **$325.00**

Sako Model 74 Deluxe Sporter

Same action as M-74 except has select wood, Rosewood p.g. cap and fore-end tip. Fine checkering on top surfaces of integral dovetail bases, bolt sleeve, bolt handle root and bolt knob. Vent. recoil pad, skip-line checkering, mirror finish bluing.
Price: 222 or 223 cals. **$470.00**
Price: 22-250, 243 .... **$470.00**
Price: 270, 30-06 .... **$470.00**
Price: 7mm Rem. Mag. 375 H&H **$470.00**

Sako Heavy Barrel

Same as std. Super Sporter except has beavertail fore-end; available in 222, 223 (short action), 22-250, 243, (medium action). Weight from 8¼ to 8½ lbs. 5-shot magazine capacity.
Price: 222, 223 (short action) **$325.00**
Price: 22-250, 243 (medium action) **$325.00**

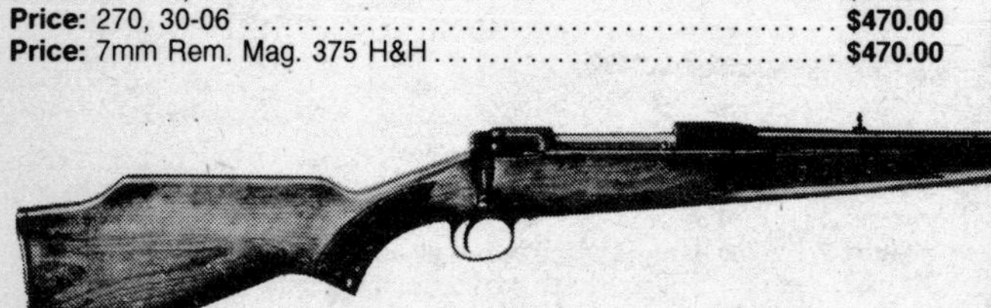

SAVAGE 110E BOLT ACTION RIFLE

Caliber: 30-06, 4-shot. Also 7mm Rem. Mag., 3-shot.
Barrel: 22″ round tapered (7mm 24″).
Weight: 6¾ lbs. (7mm-7¾ lbs.) **Length:** 40½″ (20″ bbl.)
Stock: Walnut finished hardwood with Monte Carlo, checkered p.g. and fore-end, hard rubber buttplate.
Sights: Gold bead removable ramp front, step adj. rear.
Features: Top tang safety, receiver, tapped for peep or scope sights. Right or left hand models available.
Price: Std. cals. **$145.00**
Price: Magnum **$159.85**

Savage 110D Bolt Action Rifle

Same as 110E except: 22″ bbl. (24″ on Mag.); walnut stock, cheekpiece; recoil pad on mag.; folding-leaf rear sight; weight 6¾-8 lbs. Cals. 243, 270 and 30-06. Also available in 7mm Rem.
Price: Right hand std. cals. . **$180.50** Left hand std. cals. **$185.75**
Price: Right hand, magnum . **$195.00** Left hand, magnum **$199.50**

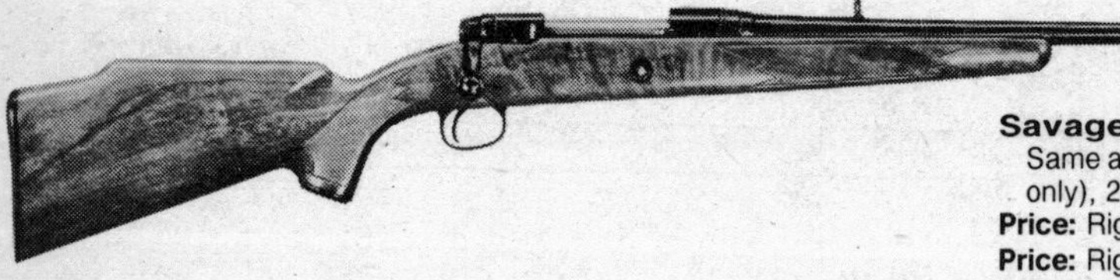

Savage 110C Bolt Action Rifle

Same as the 110D except: Detachable box magazine. Cals. 243 (right-hand only), 270 and 30-06 (4-shot). Also in 7mm Rem. (3-shot) at $15 extra.
Price: Right hand std. cals. **$180.50** Left hand (110 CL) std. cals. **$185.75**
Price: Right hand, magnum . **$195.00** Left hand, magnum **$199.50**

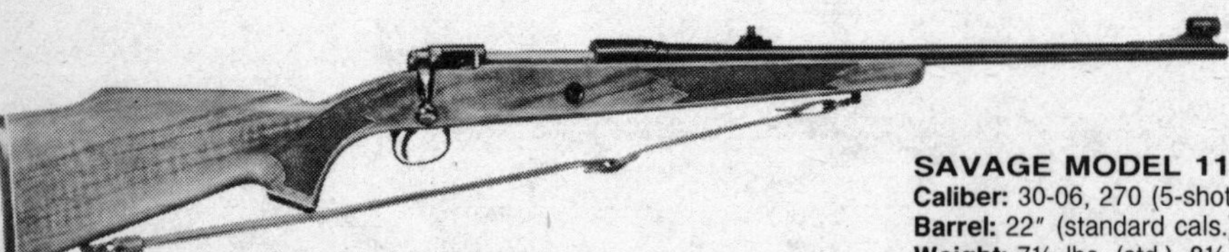

SAVAGE MODEL 111 CHIEFTAIN BOLT ACTION RIFLE

Caliber: 30-06, 270 (5-shot), 7mm Rem. Mag. (4-shot).
Barrel: 22″ (standard cals.), 24″ (mag. cals.). Free floating.
Weight: 7½ lbs. (std.), 8¼ (mag.) **Length:** 43″ over-all.
Stock: Walnut, Monte Carlo, hand checkered fore-end and p.g., p.g. cap, white spacers.
Sights: Removeable hooded ramp front, open rear adj. for w. and e.
Features: Top tang safety, ejector clip magazine, teardrop design bolt handle. Stainless steel barrel in magnum calibers. Drilled and tapped for scope mounts.
Price: Standard calibers **$212.00**
Price: Magnum calibers **$222.00**

SAVAGE 340 CLIP REPEATER

Caliber: 22 Hornet, 222 Rem. (4-shot) and 30-30 (3-shot).
Barrel: 24″ and 22″ respectively.
Weight: About 6½ lbs. **Length:** 40″-42″
Stock: Walnut, Monte Carlo, checkered p.g. and fore-end white line spacers.
Sights: Gold bead ramp front, folding-leaf rear.
Features: Detachable clip magazine, sliding thumb safety, receiver tapped for scope mounts.
Price: **$111.65**

SPRINGFIELD MODEL 1903-A3
Caliber: 30-06, 5-shot magazine.
Barrel: 24″.
Length: 43¼″ over-all. **Weight:** 8½ lbs.
Stock: American walnut.
Sights: Military ramp front, peep rear adj. for w. & e.
Features: Bolt action. All parts, including receiver, are new manufacture. From National Ordnance.
Price: **$99.00**

SAVAGE 112-V BOLT ACTION RIFLE
Caliber: 222, 22-250, 220 Swift, 25-06, 243, single shot.
Barrel: 26″ tapered, 13/16″ at muzzle.
Weight: 9¼ lbs. **Length:** 47″ over-all.
Stock: Walnut. Free floating varmint stock with high, deeply fluted comb, Wundhammer swell at p.g., Hand checkered (20 l.p.i.). White spacer at recoil pad, 1¼″ q.d. swivels.
Sights: None. Drilled and tapped for scope mounting.
Features: Designed expressly for varmint shooting. Recessed bolt face; 3 gas ports; top tang safety; chrome moly steel barrel. Stock measures 13½″, drop at comb and heel 9/16″ (measured from barrel centerline).
Price: **$219.00**

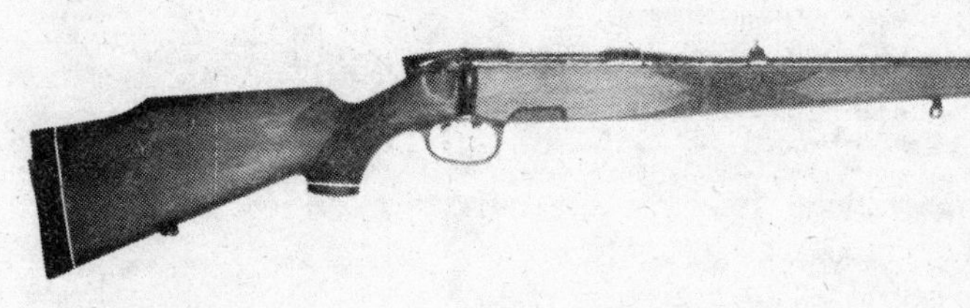

STEYR-MANNLICHER MODEL M
Caliber: 6.5x55, 270, 7x57, 7x64, 30-06, 8x57JS, 9.3x62, 5-shot.
Barrel: 20″ (full stock).
Weight: 6½ lbs. (full stock). **Length:** 39″ over-all (full stock).
Stock: Full Mannlicher or standard half stock. Rubber recoil pad, hand checkered walnut. Monte Carlo cheekpiece.
Sights: Ramp front, open U-notch rear.
Features: Extra magazine included. Choice of interchangeable double set or single trigger. Detachable 5-shot rotary magazine. 6 rear locking lugs. Drilled and tapped for scope mounting. Imported by L.E.S.
Price: **$495.00**

Steyr-Mannlicher Model L
Same as Model M except available only in 22-250, 5.6x57, 6mm Rem., 243, 308 Win. Custom hand engraving and stock carving as well as heavy barrel varmint version available **$445.00**

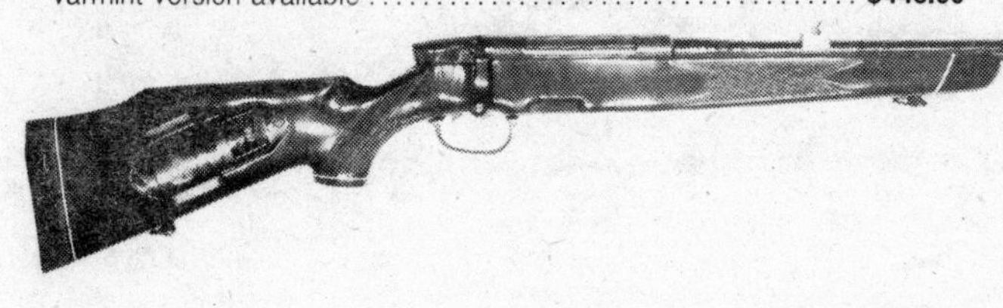

Steyr-Mannlicher Model S/T
Same as Model S except available only in 9.3x64, 375 H&H, 458 Win. Mag., has 23½″ barrel (458 has 23½″). Choice of interchangeable single or double set triggers. Detachable 4-shot Makrolon rotary magazine. Extra magazine (included) fits in recess in buttstock **$585.00**

STEYR-MANNLICHER MODEL SL
Caliber: 222, 222 Rem. Mag., 223, 5.6x50 Mag.
Barrel: 20″ (full stock), 23½″ (half stock).
Weight: 5½ lbs. **Length:** 38¼″ over-all (20″ bbl.).
Stock: Hand checkered walnut with Monte Carlo cheekpiece. Either full Mannlicher or half stock.
Sights: Ramp front, open U-notch rear.
Features: Choice of interchangeable single or double set triggers. Extra magazine included. Detachable "Makrolon" rotary magazine. 6 rear locking lugs. Drilled and tapped for scope mounts. Custom hand engraving and stock carving avail. Imported by L.E.S.
Price: **$415.00**

Steyr-Mannlicher Model S
Same as Model SL except available in 6.5x68, 257 Weatherby Mag., 264 Win. Mag., 7mm Rem. Mag., 300 H&H, 308 Norma Mag., 8x68S, 338 Win. Mag., 9.3x64, 375 H&H Mag. Avail. only with half-stock. Extra magazine fits in buttstock recess **$565.00**

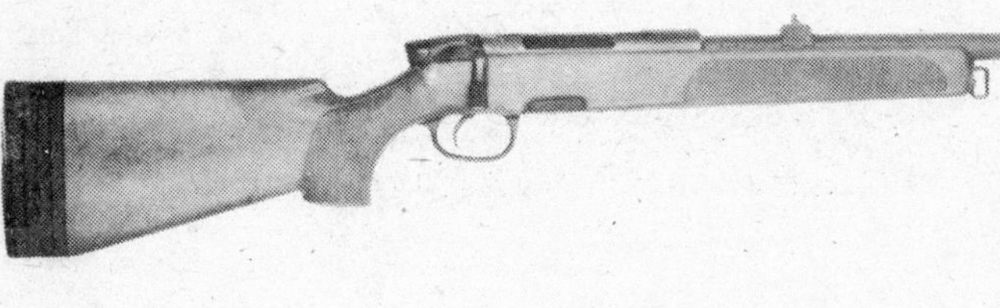

STEYR-MANNLICHER MODEL SSG
Caliber: 308 Win.
Barrel: 25½″.
Weight: 8½ lbs. **Length:** 44½″ over-all.
Stock: Walnut or synthetic.
Sights: Hooded blade front, folding leaf rear or Walther diopter match sight.
Features: Extra magazine included with rifle. 6 rear locking lugs, 60° bolt throw. Adj. trigger. Optional 10-shot magazine available. Imported by L.E.S.
Price: Synthetic stock **$475.00**
Price: Walnut **$525.00**

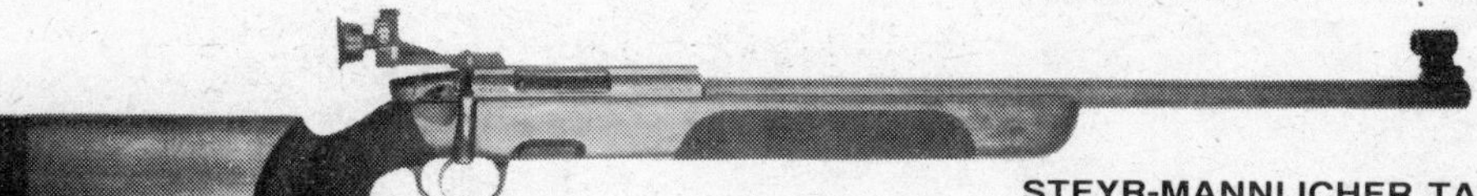

STEYR-MANNLICHER TARGET RIFLE—MODEL MATCH
Caliber: 308 Win.
Barrel: 25½″.
Weight: 9½ lbs. **Length:** 44½″ over-all.
Stock: Walnut or synthetic.
Sights: Hooded blade front, folding leaf rear or Walther diopter match sight.
Features: Extra magazine included with rifle. 6 rear locking lugs, 60° bolt throw. Adj. trigger. Optional 10-shot magazine available. Imported by L.E.S.
Price: Synthetic stock **$625.00**
Price: Walnut stock **$645.00**

TRADEWINDS HUSKY MODEL 5000 BOLT RIFLE

Caliber: 270, 30-06, 308, 243, 22-250.
Barrel: 23¾".
Weight: 6 lbs. 11 oz.
Stock: Hand checkered European walnut, Monte Carlo, white line spacers on p.g. cap, fore-end tip and butt plate.
Sights: Fixed hooded front, adj. rear.
Features: Removeable mag., fully recessed bolt head, adj. trigger. Imported by Tradewinds.
Price: **$295.00**

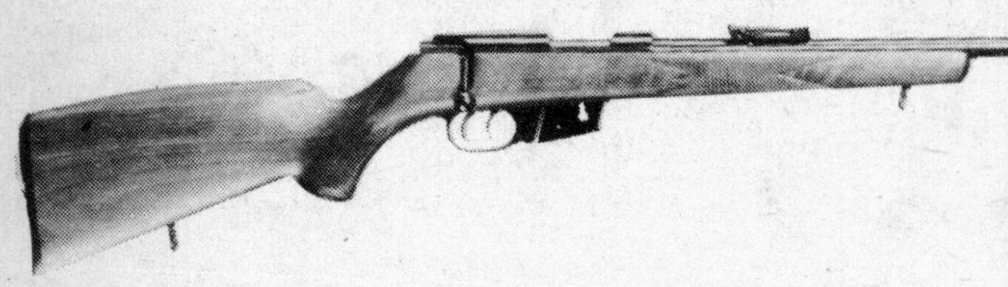

WALTHER KKJ SPORTSMAN RIFLE

Caliber: 22 Hornet; 5-shot.
Barrel: 22½".
Weight: 5½ lbs. **Length** 41½" over-all.
Stock: Hand checkered walnut with cheekpiece.
Sights: Hooded ramp front; adj. rear for w. & e. Dovetailed for scope mounting.
Features: Double set triggers avail.; left-hand stock avail. on special order ($20 extra). From Interarms.
Price: With standard trigger **$339.00**
Price: With double set trigger **$359.00**

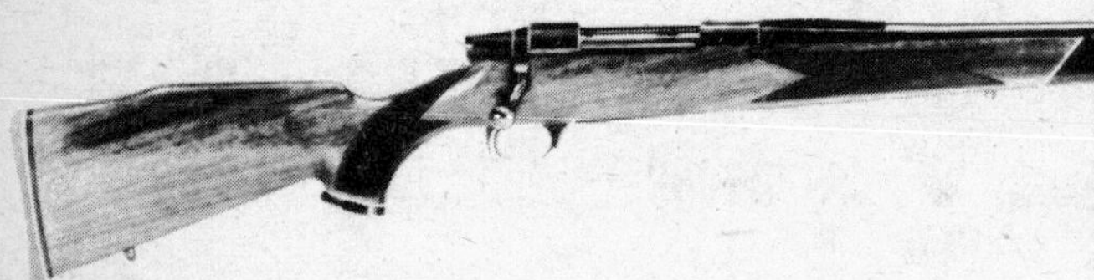

WEATHERBY VANGUARD BOLT ACTION RIFLE

Caliber: 25-06, 243, 270, 30-06 and 308 (5-shot), 7mm Rem. and 300 Win. Mag. (3-shot).
Barrel: 24" hammer forged.
Weight: 7⅞ lbs. **Length:** 44½" over-all.
Stock: American walnut, p.g. cap and fore-end tip, hand inletted and checkered, 13½" pull.
Sights: Optional, available at extra cost.
Features: Side safety, adj. trigger, hinged floorplate, receiver tapped for scope mounts.
Price: **$269.50**

WEATHERBY MARK V BOLT ACTION RIFLE

Caliber: All Weatherby Cals., 22-250 and 30-06.
Barrel: 24" or 26" round tapered.
Weight: 6½-10½ lbs. **Length:** 43¼"-46½"
Stock: Walnut, Monte Carlo with cheekpiece, high luster finish, checkered p.g. and fore-end, recoil pad.
Sights: Optional (extra).
Features: Cocking indicator, adj. trigger, hinged floorplate, thumb safety, quick detachable sling swivels.
Price: Cals. 224 and 22-250, std. bbl. **$429.50**
With 26" semi-target bbl. **$439.50**
Cals. 240, 257, 270, 7mm, 30-06 and 300 (24" bbl.) **$449.50**
With 26" No. 2 contour bbl. **$459.50**
Cal. 340 (26" bbl.) **$459.50**
Cal. 378 (26" bbl.) **$549.50**
Cal. 460 (26" bbl.) **$649.50**

Weatherby Mark V Rifle Left Hand

Available in all Weatherby calibers except 224 and 22-250 (and 26" No. 2 contour 300WM). Complete left handed action; stock with cheekpiece on right side. Prices are $10 higher than right hand models except the 378 and 460WM are unchanged.

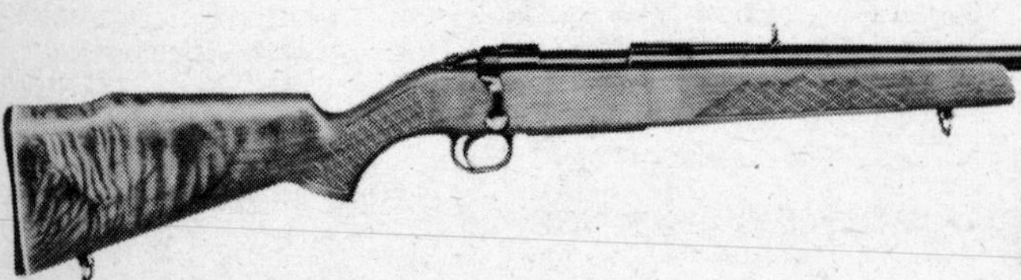

WESTERN FIELD MODEL 732 BOLT ACTION RIFLE

Caliber: 7mm (4-shot), 30-06 (5-shot).
Barrel: 22".
Weight: 8½ lbs. (30-06). **Length:** 43½" over-all.
Stock: Walnut. Monte Carlo cheekpiece, checkered p.g. and fore-end.
Sights: Gold bead front, adj. folding leaf rear.
Features: Adjustable trigger. Rubber recoil pad, p.g. cap. Receiver drilled and tapped for scope mounts. 1" sling swivels. Top receiver safety.
Price: 7mm **$183.00**
Price: 30-06 .... **$170.00**

WESTERN FIELD 780 BOLT ACTION RIFLE

Caliber: 243, 308, 5-shot mag.
Barrel: 22" round tapered.
Weight: 6½ lbs. **Length:** 42" over-all.
Stock: Walnut, Monte Carlo, checkered p.g. and fore-end.
Sights: Ramp, gold bead front; rear adj. for e.
Features: Recessed bolt head, top tang safety, hinged magazine floorplate, Receiver tapped for scope mount.
Price: **$157.00**

WHITWORTH EXPRESS RIFLE

Caliber: 7mm Rem. Mag., 300 Win. Mag., 375 H&H; 458 Win. Mag.
Barrel: 24".
Weight: 7½-8 lbs. **Length:** 44".
Stock: Classic English Express rifle design of hand checkered, select European Walnut.
Sights: Three leaf open sight calibrated for 100, 200, 300 yards, ramp front with removable hood.
Features: Solid rubber recoil pad, barrel mounted sling swivel, adjustable trigger, hinged floor plate, solid steel recoil cross bolt. Imported by Interarms.
Price: **$425.00**

WINCHESTER 70A BOLT ACTION RIFLE

Caliber: 222, 22-250, 243, 25-06, 270, 30-06, 308.
Barrel: 22" (25-06, has 24").
Weight: 7⅛ to 7½ lbs. **Length:** 42½" (22" bbl.).
Stock: Monte Carlo, checkering at p.g. and fore-end.
Sights: Removeable hooded ramp front, adj. open rear.
Features: Sling swivels installed, three position safety, deep cut checkering.
Price: **$200.00**

Winchester 70A Magnum Rifle

Same as 70A except with black recoil pad and in these cals.: 264, 7mm Rem., 300 Win., 3-round mag. capacity. Wgt. 7¼ lbs. 24" bbl., 44" over-all. R. H. twist: 9" in 264, 9½" in 7mm Rem. 10" in 300 Win. **$215.00**

Winchester Model 70A Police

Same as Model 70A except: 30-06 or 308 only, stock is tung oil finished.
Special order only **$194.00**

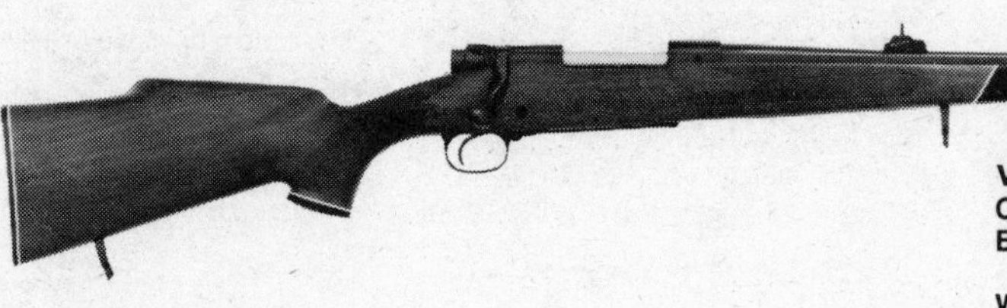

WINCHESTER 70 STANDARD RIFLE

Caliber: 222, 22-250, 25-06, 243, 270, 308 and 30-06, 5-shot.
Barrel: 22" swaged, floating. 10" twist (222 & 22-250 have 14" twist, 308 is 12").
Weight: 7½ lbs. **Length:** 42½" over-all.
Stock: Walnut, Monte Carlo, (13½"x1¾"x1½"x2⅛") checkered p.g. and fore-end.
Sights: Removable hooded bead ramp front, adj. open rear.
Features: Sling swivels installed, steel p.g. cap, hinged floorplate, receiver tapped for scope mounts.
Price: **$235.00**

Winchester 70 Target Rifle

Same as M70 except: heavy 24" barrel, contoured aluminum handstop that fits left and right hand shooter, high comb target stock. Tapped for micrometer sights, clip slot in receiver, cals. 308 and 30-66. **Special order only—prices to dealers on request.**

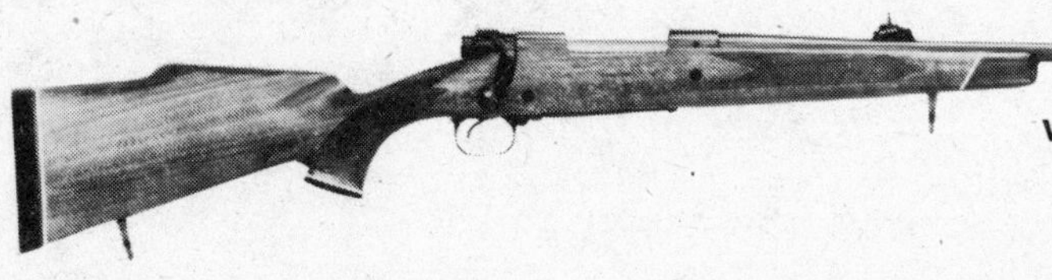

Winchester 70 Magnum Rifle

Same as M70 Standard except with recoil pad and in these magnum cals.: 7 Rem., 264, 300, 338 Win., 375 H&H, 3-round mag. capacity. Wgt. 7¾ lbs. (8½ lbs. in 375), 24" bbl., 44½" over-all. R.H. twist: 9" in 264, 9½" in 7mm, 10" in 300, 338. .... **$250.00**
Cal. 375 H&H **$350.00**

Winchester 70 African

Same as M70 Standard except: 458 Win. Mag. only, 3-shot. 22" non-floating heavy bbl. 14" twist. Stock measures 13½"x1⅜"x1¾"x2⅜", has ebony fore-end tip and grip cap; wgt. 8½ lbs., recoil pad and special rear sight.
Price: **$415.00**

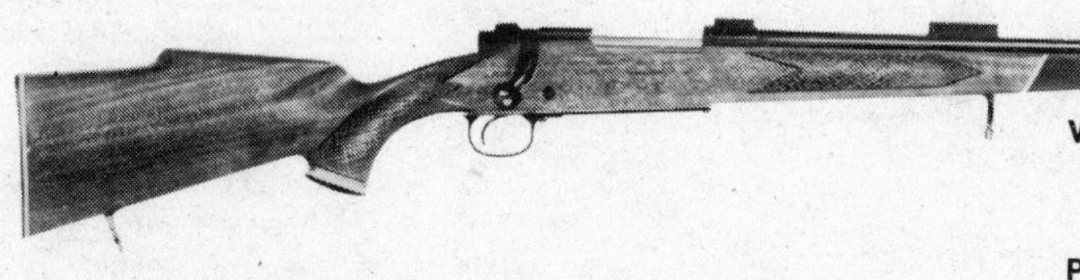

Winchester 70 Varmint Rifle

Same as M70 Standard except: 222, 22-250, and 243 only, target scope blocks, no sights, 24" heavy bbl., 14" twist in 22-250, 10" twist in 243. 44½" over-all, 9¾ lbs. Stock measures 13½"x9/16"x15/16"x3/8" from bore line.
Price: **$250.00**

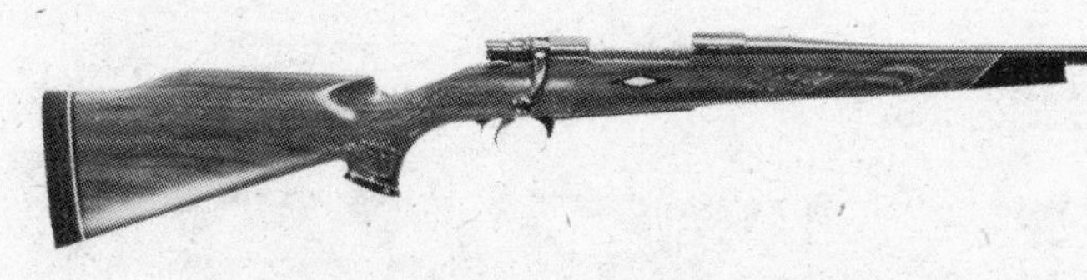

WINSLOW BOLT ACTION RIFLE

Caliber: All standard cartridges (magnum add $10).
Barrel: 24" Douglas premium. (Magnums 26")
Weight: 7-7½ lbs. **Length:** 43" over-all.
Stock: Hand rubbed black walnut, choice of two styles
Sights: None. Metallics available at extra cost.
Features: Receivers tapped for scope mounts, QD swivels and recoil pad installed. 4-shot blind mag.
Price: Regal Grade **$488.00**
Regent, Regimental, Crown, Emperor and Imperial grades in ascending order of carving, engraving and inlaying, to **$4,375.00**
Regal grade Varmint in 17/222 (std or Mag.) or 17/223.
Price: From **$540.00**

Consult our Directory pages for the location of firms mentioned.

CENTERFIRE RIFLES—SINGLE SHOT

BSA MARTINI ISU MATCH RIFLE

Caliber: 22 LR, single shot.
Barrel: 28″.
Weight: 10¾ lbs. **Length:** 43-44″ over-all.
Stock: Match type French walnut butt and fore-end; flat cheekpiece, full p.g.; spacers are fitted to allow length adjustment to suit each shooting position; adj. buttplate.
Sights: Modified PH-1 Parker-Hale tunnel front, PH-25 aperture rear with aperture variations from .080″ to .030″.
Features: Fastest lock time of any commercial target rifle; designed to meet I.S.U. specs. for the Standard Rifle. Fully adjustable trigger (less than ½ lb. to 3½ lbs.). Mark V has heavier barrel, weighs 12¼ lbs. From Freelands Scope Stands.
Price: I.S.U., Standard weight **$400.00**
Price: Mark V heavy bbl. **$415.00**

Consult our Directory pages for the location of firms mentioned.

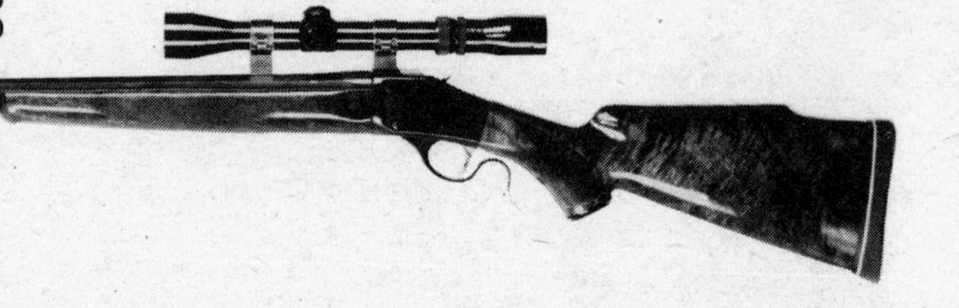

BROWNING MODEL '78 SINGLE-SHOT RIFLE

Caliber: 30-06, 25-06, 6mm Rem. 22-250.
Barrel: 26″, tapered octagon or heavy round.
Length: 42″ over-all. **Weight:** Oct. bbl. 7¾ lbs. Heavy round bbl. 8½ lbs.
Stock: Select walnut, hand rubbed finish, hand checkered (13⅝″x1⅛″*x8/32″*). Rubber recoil pad. *Bore measurement.
Sights: None. Furnished with scope mount and rings.
Features: Closely resembles M1885 High Wall rifle. Falling block action with exposed hammer, auto. ejector. Adj. trigger (3½ to 4½ lbs.) Half-cock safety.
Price: **$314.50**

GREYHAWK MODEL 74 ROLLING BLOCK RIFLE

Caliber: 22 Hornet, 222, 223, 44-40 Win., 44 Mag., 38 Spcl., 357 Mag., single shot.
Barrel: 24″ full octagon; .75″ O.D. (22 cals.), .85″ O.D. (other cals.).
Weight: 6¼ to 7 lbs. **Length:** 40″ over-all.
Stock: American walnut; straight grip; hand-rubbed oil finish with polished blue steel buttplate and fore-end band.
Sights: Square blade ramp front, adjustable folding leaf rear.
Features: Extracts rimmed and rimmless cartridges. Available with receiver-mounted fully adjustable peep sight **($7.50)**, scope mounts attached for most 1″ scopes with eye relief of 2″ to 12″ (no iron sights) **($16.00)**; fixed 1″ swivels **($5.25)** or q.d. swivels **($7.00)**; 1″ embossed Whelen type sling **($8.58)**, adjustable trigger, 1 to 6 lbs. **($7.50)**. From Greyhawk Arms.
Price: Standard rifle **$129.00**

Harrington & Richardson Model 155 "Shikari"

Caliber: 44 Rem. Mag. or 45-70, single-shot.
Barrel: 24″ or 28″ 45-70, 24″ (44 Mag.).
Weight: 7-7½ lbs. **Length:** 39″ over-all (24″ bbl.).
Stock: Walnut finished hardwood.
Sights: Blade front, adj. folding leaf rear.
Features: Blue-black finish with color case hardened frame. Exposed hammer. Solid brass cleaning rod with hardwood handle included.
Price: Either caliber **$79.50**

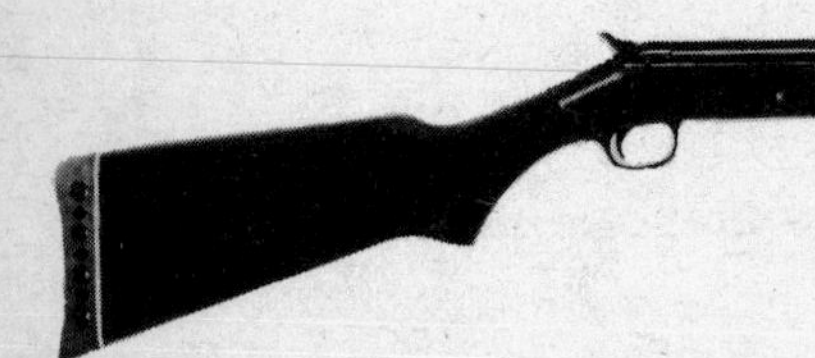

HARRINGTON AND RICHARDSON 158 TOPPER RIFLE

Caliber: 30-30 and 22 Hornet.
Barrel: 22″ round tapered.
Weight: 5¼ lbs. **Length:** 37½″
Stock: Walnut finished stock and fore-end; recoil pad.
Sights: Lyman folding adj. rear and ramp front sights.
Features: Side lever break-open action with visible hammer. Easy takedown. Converts to 20 ga. Shotgun with accessory bbl. ($20 extra).
Price: 22 Hornet or 30-30 .... **$62.50**
Price: Rifle/shotgun combo **$79.50**

CENTERFIRE RIFLES—SINGLE SHOT

HYPER-SINGLE RIFLE

Caliber: All calibers, standard and wildcat.
Barrel: Choice of maker, weight, length (std. twist and contours).
Length: To customer specs. **Weight:** To customer specs.
Stock: To customer specs. AA fancy American black walnut is standard.
Sights: None furnished. Drilled and tapped for scope mounts.
Features: Falling block action. Striker rotates on bronze bearing and is powered by dual coil springs. Trigger adj. for weight, pull and travel. Tang safety. Octagon receiver on special order (same price).
Price: Complete Rifle .....**$1,200.00** Barreled action **$775.00**
Price: Action only (blank extractor) **$600.00**
Price: Stainless steel barrel (extra) **$60.00**
Price: Fluted or octagon barrel (extra) **$75.00**

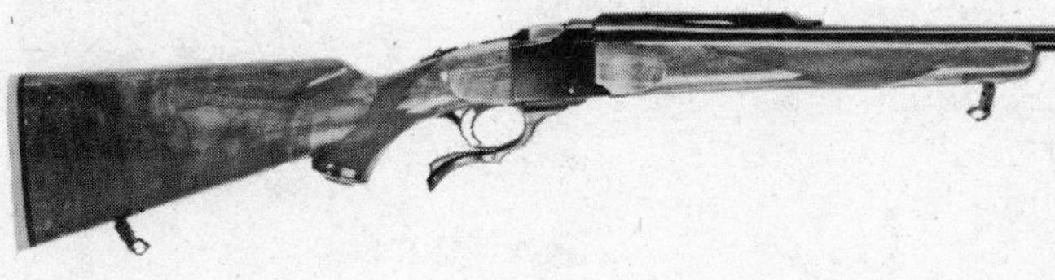

RUGER NUMBER ONE SINGLE SHOT

Caliber: 22-250, 243, 6mm Rem., 25-06, 270, 30-06, 7mm Rem. Mag., 300 Win., 45-70, 458 Win. Mag., 375 H&H Mag.
Barrel: 26″ round tapered with quarter-rib (also 22″ and 24″, depending upon model).
Weight: 8 lbs. **Length:** 42″ over-all.
Stock: Walnut, two-piece, checkered p.g. and fore-end (either semi-beavertail or Henry style).
Sights: None, 1″ scope rings supplied for integral mounts. 3 models have open sights.
Features: Under lever, hammerless falling block design has auto ejector, top tang safety. Standard Rifle 1B illus.
Price: **$265.00**
Available also as Light Sporter, Medium Sporter, Special Varminter or Tropical Rifle **$265.00**
Price: Barreled action, blued only **$140.00**

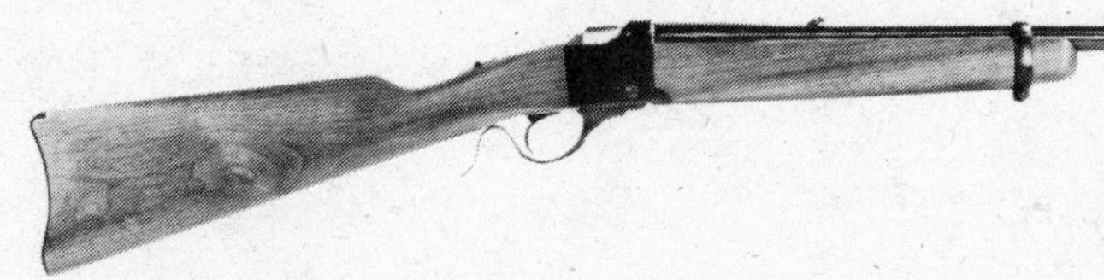

RUGER NO. 3 CARBINE SINGLE SHOT

Caliber: 22 Hornet, 30-40 Krag, 45-70.
Barrel: 22″ round.
Weight: 6 lbs. **Length:** 38½″.
Stock: American walnut, carbine-type.
Sights: Gold bead front, adj. folding leaf rear.
Features: Same action as No. 1 Rifle except different lever. Has auto ejector, top tang safety, adj. trigger.
Price: **$165.00**

CENTERFIRE RIFLES—REPLICAS

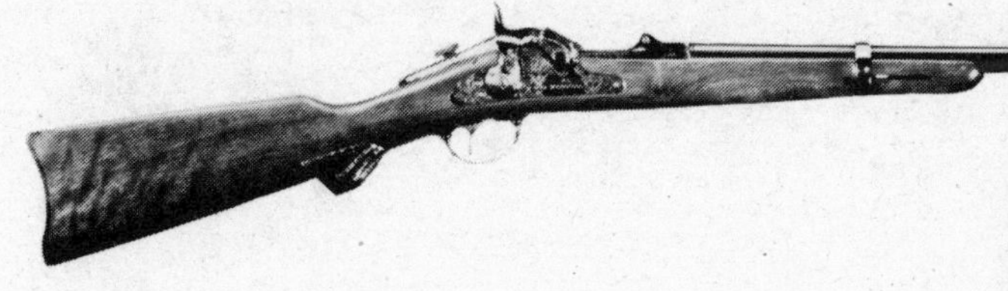

HARRINGTON & RICHARDSON L.B.H. Commemorative Carbine

Caliber: 45-70, single shot.
Barrel: 22″.
Weight: 7 lbs., 4 oz. **Length:** 41″.
Stock: American walnut with metal grip adapter.
Sights: Blade front, tang mounted aperature rear adj. for w. and e.
Features: Replica of the 1871 Springfield carbine. Engraved breech block, side lock and hammer. Action color case hardened. Each comes with book entitled "In the Valley of the Little Big Horn".
Price: **$225.00**

H & R 1873 SPRINGFIELD RIFLE

Caliber: 45-70, single shot.
Barrel: 32″.
Weight: 8¾ lbs. **Length:** 52″ over-all.
Stock: Full length American walnut.
Sights: Blade front, leaf rear adj. for e.
Features: Authentic replica of the 1873 "Trapdoor" rifle. Color case hardened breech block and buttplate, remainder blue-black. Serialized limited production of 1000 rifles. Contact factory regarding availability.
Price: **$280.00**

HARRINGTON & RICHARDSON Officers Model 1873

Caliber: 45-70, single shot
Barrel: 26″ round.
Weight: About 8 lbs. **Length:** 44″ over-all
Stock: Oil finished walnut, checkered at wrist and fore-end white metal tipped.
Sights: Blade front, vernier tang rear adj. for w. & e.
Features: Replica of the 1873 Springfield has engraved breech block, side lock and hammer. comes with commemorative plaque.
Price: **$262.50**

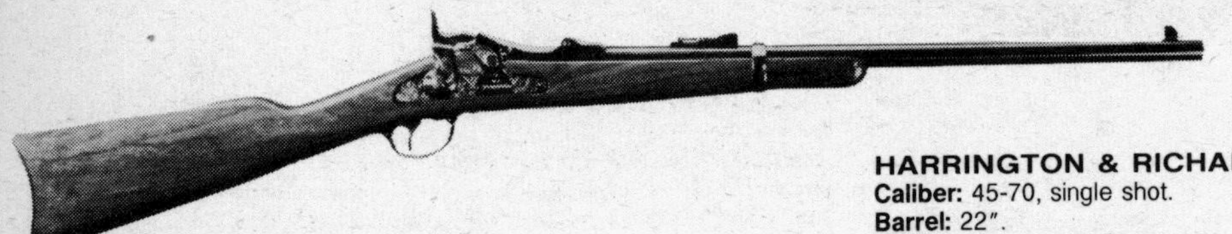

HARRINGTON & RICHARDSON Cavalry Model Carbine
Caliber: 45-70, single shot.
Barrel: 22".
Weight: 7 lbs. **Length:** 41".
Stock: American walnut with saddle ring and bridle.
Sights: Blade front, barrel mounted leaf rear adj. for e.
Features: Replica of the 1871 Springfield Carbine. Blue-black finish.
Price: **$169.50**
Deluxe version shown has engraved breech block, side lock & hammer.
Price: **$225.00**
Springfield Armory Museum silver plated carbine **$1,100.00**

NAVY ARMS ROLLING BLOCK RIFLE
Caliber: 45-70, 444 Marlin.
Barrels: 26½".
Stock: Walnut finished.
Sights: Fixed front, adj. rear.
Features: Reproduction of classic rolling block action. Available in Buffalo Rifle (octagonal bbl.) and Creedmore (half round, half octagonal bbl.) models. Imported by Navy Arms.
Price: **$165.00**
Price: Creedmore Model **$185.00**

ROLLING BLOCK BABY CARBINE
Caliber: 22 LR, 22 Hornet, 357 Mag.
Barrel: 20", octagon.
Weight: 4¾ lbs. **Length:** Approx. 35" over-all.
Stock: Walnut.
Sights: Blade front, rear adj. for e.
Features: Small rolling block action is color case hardened with blue barrel. Trigger guard and buttplate polished brass. Imported by Navy/Marietta Replica Arms.
Price: **$135.00**

NAVY ARMS MODEL 1875 REVOLVING RIFLE
Caliber: 357 Mag., 45 L.C.
Barrel: 20".
Weight: 5 lbs. **Length:** 38".
Stock: Walnut, brass butt plate.
Sights: Front blade adj. for w., buckhorn rear adj. for e.
Features: Action resembles Remington Model 1875 revolver. Polished brass trigger guard. Imported by Navy/Replica.
Price: **$195.00**

STAR ROLLING BLOCK CARBINE
Caliber: 30-30, 357 Mag., 44 Mag.
Barrel: 20".
Weight: 6 lbs. **Length:** 35" over-all.
Stock: Walnut, straight grip.
Sights: Square bead ramp front, folding leaf rear.
Features: Color case-hardened receiver, crescent buttplate. Forged steel receiver. Imported by Garcia.
Price: Approx. **$160.00**

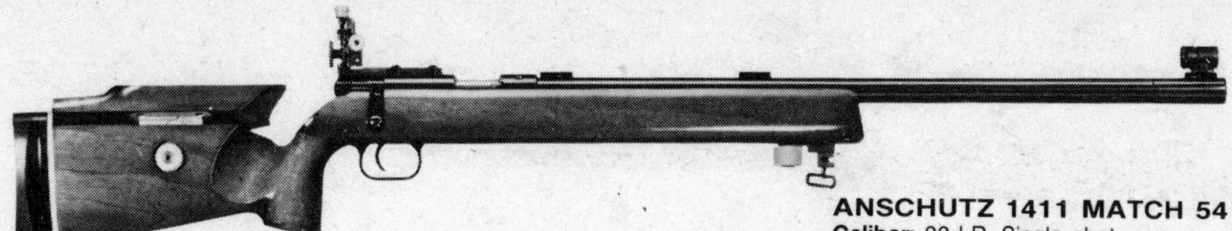

ANSCHUTZ 1411 MATCH 54 RIFLE

Caliber: 22 LR. Single shot.
Barrel: 27½ round (15/16″ dia.)
Weight: 11 lbs. **Length:** 46″ over-all.
Stock: French walnut, American prone style with Monte Carlo, cast-off cheekpiece, checkered p.g., beavertail fore-end with swivel rail and adj. swivel, adj. rubber buttplate.
Sights: None. Receiver grooved for Anshutz sights (extra). Scope blocks.
Features: Single stage adj. trigger, wing safety, short firing pin travel. Available from Savage Arms.
Price: **$370.00**
Price: Left hand stocked rifle, no sights **$389.50**

Anschutz 1407 Match 54 Rifle

Same as the model 1411 except: 26″ bbl. (⅞″ dia.), weight 10 lbs., 44½″ over-all to conform to ISU requirements and also suitable for NRA matches. Available from Savage Arms.
Price: **$340.00**
Price: Left hand stocked rifle, no sights **$357.50**

Anschutz 1413 Super Match Rifle

Same as the model 1411 except: International type stock with adj. cheekpiece, adj. aluminum hook buttplate, weight 15½ lbs., 50″ over-all. Available from Savage Arms.
Price: **$585.00**
Price: Left hand stocked rifle, no sights **$605.00**

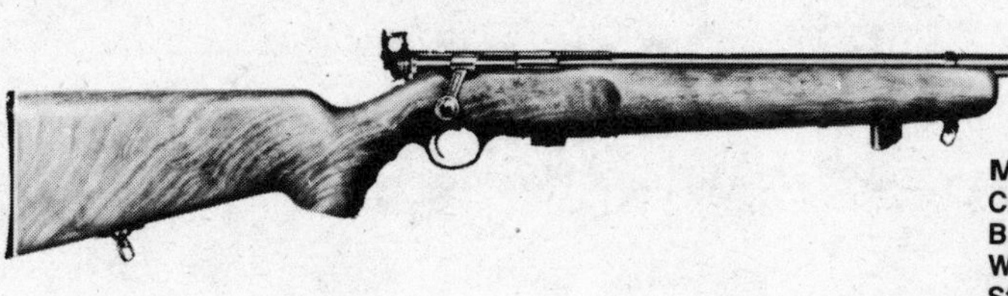

MOSSBERG MODEL 144 TARGET RIFLE

Caliber: 22 LR only. 7-shot clip.
Barrel: 26″ round (15/16″ dia.)
Weight: About 8 lbs. **Length:** 43″ over-all.
Stock: Walnut with high thick comb, cheekpiece, p.g., beavertail fore-end, adj. handstop and sling swivels.
Sights: Lyman 17A hooded front with inserts, Mossberg S331 receiver peep with ¼-minute clicks.
Features: Wide grooved trigger adj. for wgt. of pull, thumb safety, receiver grooved for scope mounting.
Price: **$100.28**

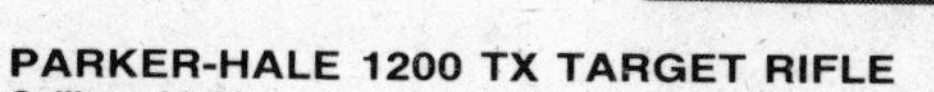

PARKER-HALE 1200 TX TARGET RIFLE

Caliber: 30-06.
Barrel: 26″.
Weight: 10½ lbs. **Length:** 46¾″.
Stock: 13 3/16″ x 1 11/16″ x 1 15/16″. Oil finish, full beavertail, p.g., vent. rubber butt pad.
Sights: Micro adj. ¼″ click rear, interchangeable element tubular front.
Features: Full floating bbl., epoxy bedded action, fully adj. trigger, selected bbl. Imported from England by Jana.
Price: **$279.95**

REMINGTON 40-XB RANGEMASTER TARGET Centerfire

Caliber: 222 Rem., 222 Rem. Mag., 223 Rem., 22-250, 6mm x 47, 6mm Int., 6mm Rem., 243, 25-06, 7mm Rem. Mag., 30-338 (30-7mm Rem. Mag.), 300 Win. Mag., 7.62 NATO (308 Win.), 30-06. Single shot.
Barrel: 27¼″ round (Stand. dia.-¾″, Hvy. dia.-⅞″)
Weight: Std.—9¼ lbs., Hvy.—11¼ **Length:** 47″
Stock: American walnut with high comb and beavertail fore-end stop. Rubber non-slip buttplate.
Sights: None. Scope blocks installed.
Features: Adjustable trigger pull. Receiver drilled and tapped for sights.
Price: Standard ss., stainless steel **$325.00**
Price: Repeating model **$350.00**
Price: Extra for 2 oz. trigger **$45.00**

REMINGTON 40-XC NAT'L MATCH COURSE RIFLE

Caliber: 7.62 NATO, 5-shot.
Barrel: 23¼″, stainless steel.
Weight: 10 lbs. without sights. **Length:** 42½″ over-all.
Stock: Walnut, position-style, with palm swell.
Sights: None furnished.
Features: Designed to meet the needs of competitive shooters firing the national match courses. Position-style stock, top loading clip slot magazine, anti-bind bolt and receiver, bright stainless steel barrel. Meets all I.S.U. Army Rifle specifications. Adjustable buttplate, adjustable trigger.
Price: **$415.00**

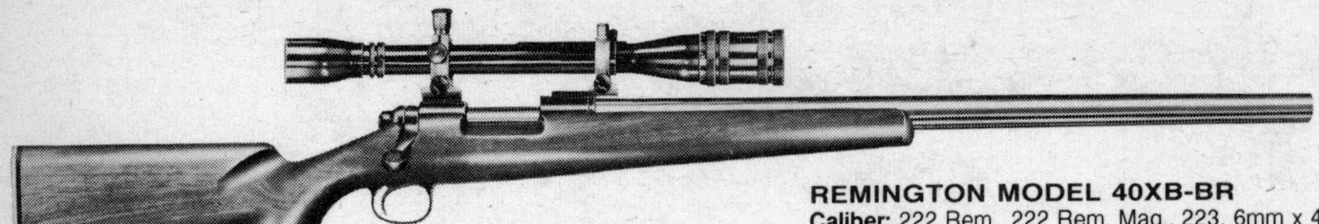

REMINGTON MODEL 40XB-BR
Caliber: 222 Rem., 222 Rem. Mag., 223, 6mm x 47, 7.62 NATO (308 Win.).
Barrel: 20″ (light varmint class), 26″ (heavy varmint class).
Length: 38″ (20″ bbl.), 44″ (26″ bbl.). **Weight:** Light varmint class, 7¼ lbs., Heavy varmint class, 12 lbs.
Stock: Select walnut.
Sights: None. Supplied with scope blocks.
Features: Unblued stainless steel barrel, trigger adj. from 1½ lbs. to 3½ lbs. Special 2 oz. trigger at extra cost. Scope and mounts extra.
Price: **$299.95**

REMINGTON 40-XR RIMFIRE POSITION RIFLE
Caliber: 22 LR, single-shot.
Barrel: 24″, heavy target.
Weight: 10 lbs. **Length:** 43″ over-all.
Stock: Position-style with front swivel block on fore-end guide rail.
Sights: Drilled and tapped. Furnished with scope blocks.
Features: Meets all I.S.U. specifications. Deep fore-end, buttplate vertically adjustable, wide adjustable trigger. Redfield Olympic front and rear sights available with 10 inserts for $55.25.
Price: **$250.00**

REMINGTON 540-XR RIMFIRE POSITION RIFLE
Caliber: 22 LR, single-shot.
Barrel: 26″ medium weight target. Countersunk at muzzle.
Weight: 8 lbs., 13 oz. **Length:** Adj. from 43½″ to 46¾″.
Stock: Position-style with Monte Carlo, cheekpiece and thumb groove. 5-way adj. buttplate and full length guide rail.
Sights: None furnished. Drilled and tapped for target scope blocks. Fitted with front sight base.
Features: Extra-fast lock time. Specially designed p.g. to eliminate wrist twisting. Adj. match trigger. Match-style sling with adj. swivel block ($8.00) and sight set ($34.50) available.
Price: **$134.95**

Remington 540-XRJR Junior Rimfire Position Rifle
Same as 540-XR except fitted with 1¾″ shorter stock to fit the junior shooter, Over-all length adjustable from 41¾″ to 45″. Length of pull adjustable from 11″ to 14¼″.
Price: **$134.95**

SAVAGE/ANSCHUTZ 64 MATCH RIFLE
Caliber: 22 LR only. Single shot.
Barrel: 26″ round (11/16″ dia.)
Weight: 7¾ lbs. **Length:** 44″ over-all.
Stock: Walnut finished hardwood, cheekpiece, checkered p.g., beavertail fore-end, adj. buttplate.
Sights: None (extra). Scope blocks.
Features: Sliding side safety, adj. single stage trigger, receiver grooved for Anschutz sights.
Price: .... **$158.50** 64L (Left hand) **$173.50**
As above but with Anschutz 6723 Match Sight Set.
Price: Model 64S (Right hand) **$203.50**
Price: 64SL (Left hand) **$218.50**

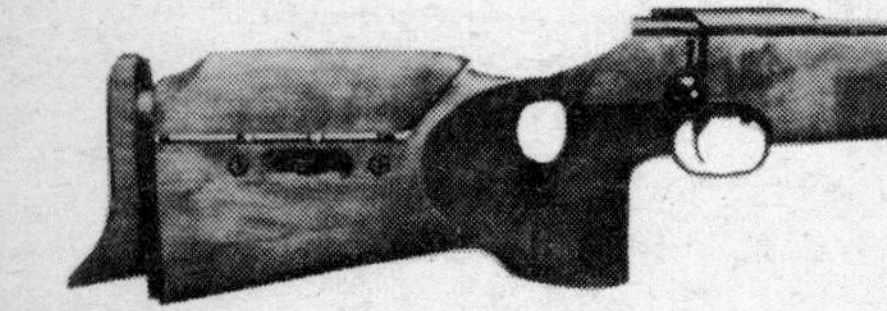

WALTHER MOVING TARGET MATCH RIFLE
Caliber: 22 LR.
Barrel: 23.6″.
Weight: 8 lbs. 5 oz. **Length:** 42″ over-all.
Stock: Walnut thumb-hole type. Fore-end and p.g. stippled.
Sights: Globe front, micro adj. rear.
Features: Especially designed for running boar competition. Receiver grooved to accept dovetail scope mounts. Adjustable cheekpiece and butt plate. 1.1 lb. trigger pull. Imported by Interarms.
Price: **$379.00**
Price: Left-hand model **$407.00**

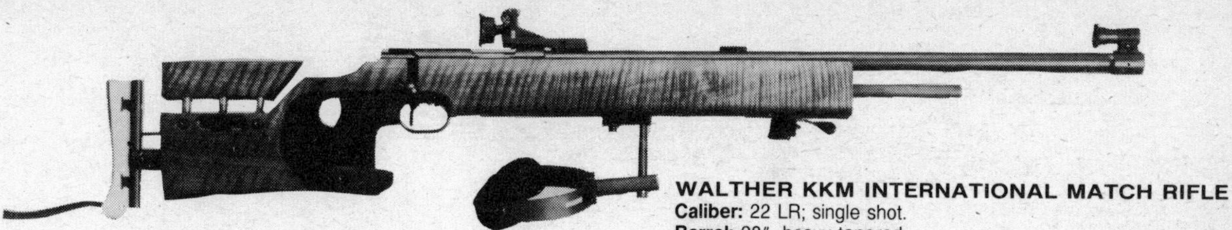

WALTHER KKM INTERNATIONAL MATCH RIFLE

Caliber: 22 LR; single shot.
Barrel: 28", heavy tapered.
Weight: 15½ lbs. **Length:** 46" over-all.
Stock: Heavy walnut with thumbhole; adj. hook buttplate, hand shelf, palm rest and adj. cheek-rest. Left hand stock avail.
Sights: Olympic type front with interchangeable post and aperture inserts; precision aperture rear with micro click adjustments for w. & e.
Features: Fully adjustable match trigger; many match accessories available. From Interarms.
Price: **$549.00**
Price: Left hand model **$584.00**

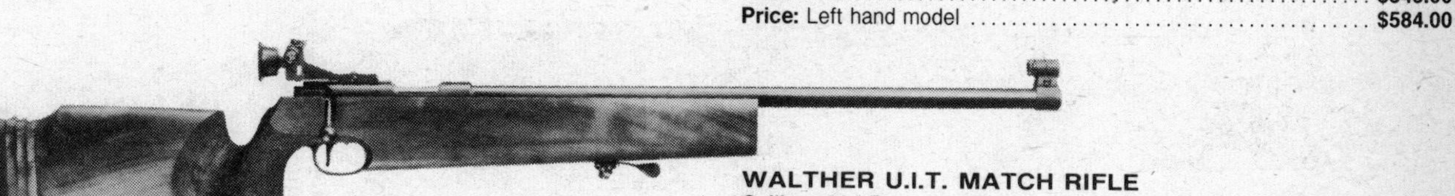

Walther "Prone 400" Match Rifle

Especially designed for prone shooting with split stock to allow cheekpiece adjustment. Caliber 22 LR with scope blocks.
Price: **$429.00**
Price: Left-hand model **$457.00**

WALTHER U.I.T. MATCH RIFLE

Caliber: 22 LR.
Barrel: 25½".
Weight: 10 lbs., 3 oz. **Length:** 44¾".
Stock: Walnut, adj. for length and drop; fore-end guide rail for sling or palm rest.
Sights: Interchangeable post or aperture front, micro adj. rear.
Features: Conforms to both NRA and U.I.T. requirements. Fully adj. trigger. Left hand stock available on special order. Imported from Germany by Interarms.
Price: **$389.00**
Price: Left-hand model **$417.00**

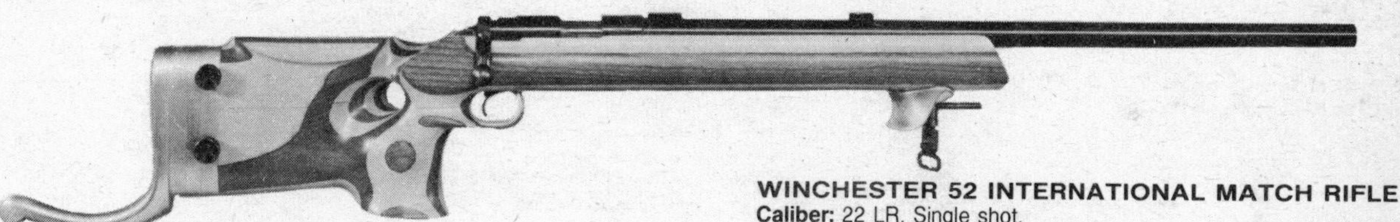

WINCHESTER 52 INTERNATIONAL MATCH RIFLE

Caliber: 22 LR. Single shot.
Barrel: 28" heavy bbl.
Weight: 13½ lbs. **Length:** 44½"
Stock: Laminated International-style, aluminum fore-end assembly, adj. palm rest.
Sights: Receiver tapped for sights and scope bases; scope blocks are included.
Features: Non-drag trigger. Lead-lapped barrel with Winchester muzzle counterbore. Options include Kenyon or ISU triggers.
Price: .... **Special Order Only.**

WINCHESTER 52 INTERNATIONAL PRONE RIFLE

Caliber: 22 LR, single shot.
Barrel: 28".
Weight: 11½ lbs. **Length:** 46" over-all.
Stock: Oil finished walnut. Designed for international prone position target shooting. Removable full roll-over cheekpiece for easy bore cleaning.
Sights: None. Receiver drilled and tapped for sights or scope.
Features: Same features as Model 52 International Match rifle except as noted above. **Special order only.**
Price: .... **Price on request.**

WINCHESTER 52D BOLT ACTION TARGET RIFLE

Caliber: 22 LR only. Single shot.
Barrel: 28", standard or heavy weight.
Weight: 9¾ lbs. Std. 11 lbs. Hvy. **Length:** 46"
Stock: Marksman stock of choice walnut with full length accessory channel and adj. bedding device and non-slip butt pad.
Sights: None. Barrel tapped for front sight bases.
Features: Adjustable trigger.
Price: .... **Special Order Only.**

WINCHESTER 70 INT'L ARMY MATCH RIFLE

Caliber: 308 (7.62mm NATO) 5-shot.
Barrel: 24" heavy-contour.
Weight: 11 lbs. **Length:** 43¼" over-all.
Stock: Oil finished walnut, (12" x 1¼" x 1¼") meets ISU requirements.
Sights: None. Receiver tapped for M70 sights (available at extra cost).
Features: Fore-end rail takes most std. accessories, vertically adj. buttplate, externally adj. trigger, glass bedded action.
Price: Match and Ultra Match .... **Special Order Only.**

DRILLINGS, COMBINATION GUNS, DOUBLE RIFLES

COLT SAUER DRILLING

Caliber: 12 ga., over 30-06, 12 ga. over 243.
Action: Top lever, cross bolt, box lock.
Barrel: 25″ (Mod. & Full).
Weight: 8 lbs. **Length:** 41¾″ over-all.
Stock: American walnut, oil finish. Checkered p.g. and fore-end. Black p.g., cap, recoil pad. 14¼″x2″x1½″.
Sights: Blade front with brass bead, folding leaf rear.
Features: Cocking indicators, tang barrel selector, automatic sight positioner, set rifle trigger, side safety. Blue finish with bright receiver engraved with animal motifs and European-style scrollwork. Imported by Colt.
Price: **$1,650.00**

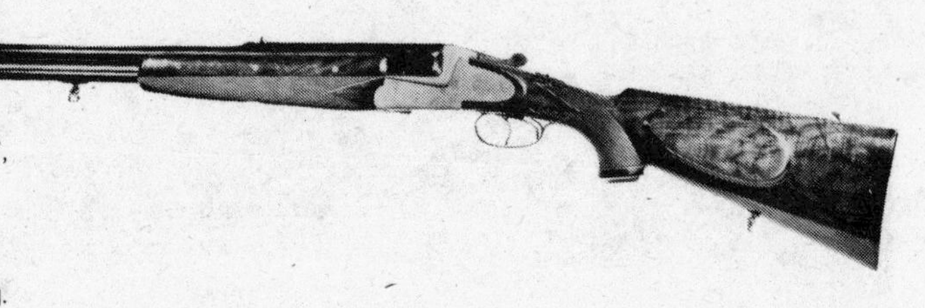

FERLACH O/U TURKEY RIFLE/SHOTGUN

Gauge: 12, 16, 20, and 22 Hornet, 222 Rem., 243, 257, 6.5x55, 270, 7x57, 30-06.
Action: Anson & Deeley boxlock.
Barrel: 22″ or 24″.
Weight: 6½ lbs.
Stock: Circassian walnut, hand checkered at p.g. and split fore-end, horn p.g. cap and buttplate.
Features: Double triggers, auto safety, engraved action. With or without cheekpiece, recoil pad. Imported from Austria by Flaig's.
Price: **$950.00**

GARCIA BRONCO COMBINATION O/U

Caliber: 22/410, 3″ chamber.
Barrel:: 18½″.
Weight: 3½ lbs. **Length:** 32″ over-all.
Stock: Skeletonized crackle finish alloy casting.
Sights: Post front, open rear.
Features: Cross-bolt safety; swing-out chamber; push button safety; instant takedown. From Garcia.
Price: **$69.00**

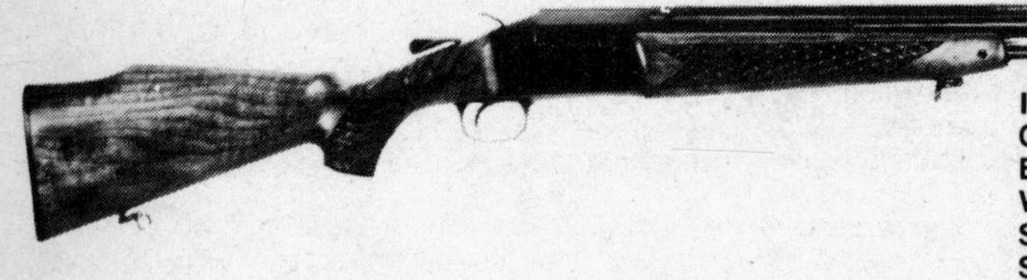

ITHACA TURKEYGUN

Caliber: 12 ga./222.
Barrel: 24½″ (Full).
Weight: 7½ lbs.
Stock: 14″x1⅝″x1⅞″x2¼″, walnut.
Sights: Ramp front, folding leaf rear.
Features: Detachable choke tubes (Full choke supplied, Mod., Imp. Cyl. available), rifle barrel, sling swivels, grooved for scope mounts. Imported by Ithaca.
Price: **$329.95**

KRIEGHOFF "TECK" DOUBLE RIFLE

Caliber: Most standard rimless and rimmed American and metric calibers, including 375 H & H and 458 Win. Mag.
Action: Kersten double cross bolt, double under-lug locking system.
Barrel: 25″.
Weight: From 8 lbs. **Length:** 42½″ over-all.
Stock: 14¼″x1¼″x2¼″, European walnut.
Sights: Sourdough front, express rear.
Features: Imported by Creighton & Warren.
Price: Teck, std. stock dimensions, 375, 458 .... **$2,800.00**
Price: Std. rifle with Lyman scope, German claw mounts **$2,750.00**
Special order rifles made to customer specs:
Price: Std. cals. **$2,464.00**
Price: Belted magnum cals. **$2,816.00**
Price: Model Ulm (sidelocks) **$3,695.00**
Price: Model Ulm (engraved, hand-detachable sidelocks) illus. ... **$4,495.00**
Price: Interchangeable o/u shotgun barrel **$695.00**
Price: Interchangeable o/u rifle barrel std. cals. **$1,450.00**
Price: Interchangeable o/u rifle barrel, magnum **$1,760.00**

Consult our Directory pages for the location of firms mentioned.

DRILLINGS, COMBINATION GUNS, DOUBLE RIFLES

KRIEGHOFF DRILLINGS

Caliber: 12 and 12 ga. (2¾″) and 30-06, 20 and 20 (3″) and 243 Win.
Action: Sidelock—Neptun; Boxlock—Trumpf.
Barrel: 25″, solid rib.
Weight: 7½ lbs. **Length:** 42″ over-all.
Stock: 14¼″x1¼″x2¼″, European walnut.
Sights: Sourdough front, express rear.
Features: Shot barrel locks cock on opening, rifle barrel cocked and rear sight raises by action of tang mounted slide. Split extractors. Free-floating rifle barrel avail. American scope can be mounted at factory with claw mounts **$250.00**. Imported by Creighton & Warren.
Price: Std. Trumpf with free-floating rifle bbl. **$2,500.00**
Price: Std. Trumpf with American Scope, claw mounts **$2,750.00**
Special order drillings made to customer specs.
Price: Boxlock action with optional engraving coverage and special stock features **$2,290.00**
Price: Sidelock version (Neptun) **$3,815.00**
Price: Deluxe Neptun (engraved) with hand-detachable locks, base **$4,840.00**

KRIEGHOFF RIFLE-SHOTGUN COMBO

Caliber: Top-12, 16, 20 (2¾″), 20 ga. 3″; lower-all popular U.S. and metric cartridges, rimless and rimmed.
Action: Sidelock—Ulm; Boxlock—Teck.
Barrel: 25″, solid rib.
Weight: 6¼ lbs. **Length:** 41″ over-all.
Stock: 14¼″x1¼″x2¼″, European walnut.
Sights: Sourdough front, express rear.
Features: Interchangeable rifle barrels in 22 Hornet, 222 Rem., 222 Rem. Mag. priced at $250.00. Scope optional. Imported by Creighton & Warren.
Price: 12 ga./30-06 or 222 Rem.—Teck **$2,115.00**
Price: Sidelock Ulm model **$3,170.00**
Price: Ulm Primus (deluxe) **$4,135.00**

SAVAGE MODEL 2400 O/U

Caliber: Top barrel 12 ga. (2¾″), bottom barrel 222 or 308.
Barrel: 23½″ separated barrels (Imp. Mod). Solid matted rib.
Weight: 7½ lbs. **Length:** 40½″ over-all.
Stock: Walnut, cut checkered p.g. and semi-beavertail fore-end (14″x1½″x1¾″x2½″).
Sights: Blade front, folding leaf rear.
Features: Action similar to Savage Models 333 and 330. White line rubber recoil pad, single selective trigger, sling swivels, Hand fitted action.
Price: **$399.50**

RIMFIRE RIFLES—AUTOLOADING & SLIDE ACTION

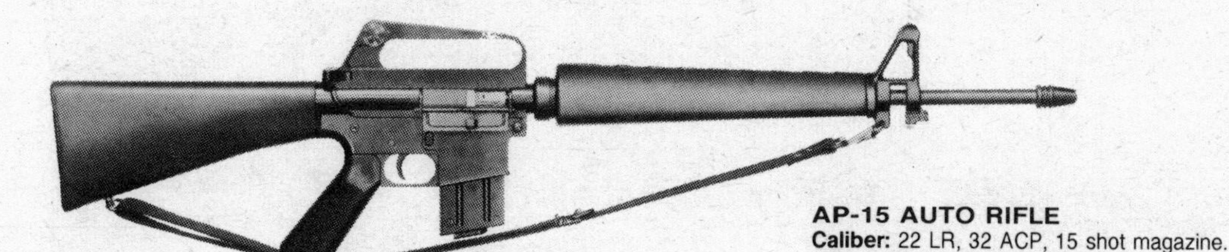

AP-15 AUTO RIFLE

Caliber: 22 LR, 32 ACP, 15 shot magazine.
Barrel: 20″ including flash reducer.
Weight: 6½ lbs. **Length:** 38½″ over-all.
Stock: Black plastic.
Sights: Ramp front, adj. peep rear.
Features: Pivotal take-down, easy disassembly. AR-15 look-alike. Sling and sling swivels included. Imported by Kassnar Imports.
Price: **$114.95**

Consult our Directory pages for the location of firms mentioned.

AMERICAN 180 AUTO CARBINE
Caliber: 22 LR, 177-round magazine.
Barrel: 16½″.
Weight: 5¾ lbs. (empty), 10 lbs. (loaded). **Length:** 36″ over-all.
Stock: High impact plastic stock and fore-end.
Sights: Blade front, peep rear adj. for w. and e.
Features: Available in selective fire version for law enforcement or semi-auto only for civilians. Laser-Lok laser beam sight available at extra cost. Imported from Austria by American International.
Price: **$340.00**
Price: Laser-Lok sight system **$455.00**
Price: Extra magazine and winding mechanism **$90.00**

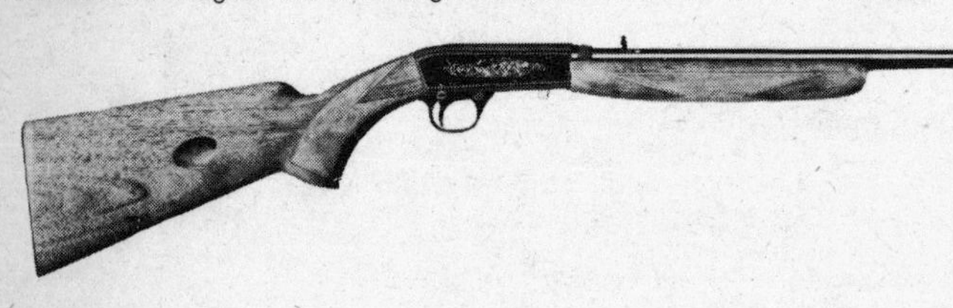

BROWNING AUTOLOADING RIFLE
Caliber: 22 LR,11-shot.
Barrel: 19¼ lbs.
Weight: 4¾ lbs. **Length:** 37″ over-all.
Stock: Checkered select walnut (13¾″x1[13]/16″x2⅝″) with p.g. and semi-beavertail fore-end.
Sights: Gold bead front, folding leaf rear.
Features: Engraved receiver is grooved for tip-off scope mount; cross-bolt safety; tubular magazine in buttstock; easy take down for carrying or storage.
Price: Grade I .... **$142.50** Grade II .... **$214.50** Grade III **$444.50**
Also available in Grade I, 22 S (16-shot) **$146.50**

CHARTER AR-7 EXPLORER CARBINE
Caliber: 22 LR, 8-shot autoloading.
Barrel: 16″ alloy (steel-lined).
Weight: 2¾ lbs. **Length:** 34½″/16½″ stowed.
Stock: Moulded grey Cycloac, snap-on rubber butt pad.
Features: Take-down design stores bbl. and action in hollow stock. Light enough to float.
Price: **$75.00**

COLT COURIER AUTOLOADING RIFLE
Caliber: 22LR, 15-shot tubular mag.
Barrel: 19⅜″.
Weight: 4¾ lbs. **Length:** 37″ over-all
Stock: Black walnut stock (13¾″x1⅝″x2¼″); tapered fore-end.
Sights: Hooded gold bead front sight with notched rear adj. for w. and e.
Features: Full length magazine tube; Cross-bolt Safety. Receiver grooved for tip-off scope mount.
Price: **$76.00**

Colt Stagecoach Autoloading Carbine
Similar to Courier except: 16″ bbl., 33⅝″ over-all. Scroll engraved receiver, with saddle ring. 22 LR only.
Price: **$87.50**

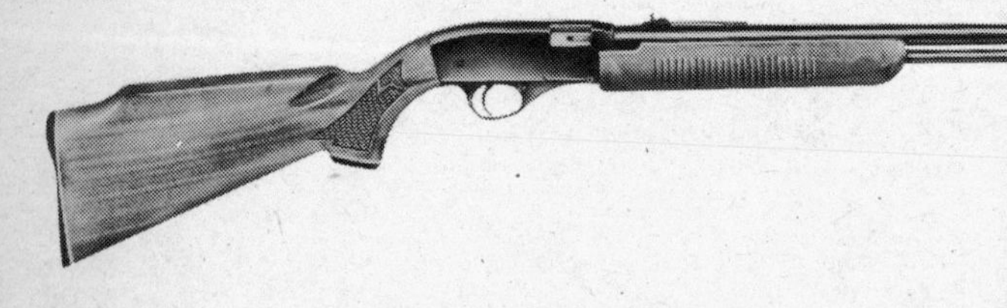

HIGH STANDARD FLITE-KING PUMP RIFLE
Caliber: 22 S (24), L (19), LR (17). Tubular magazine.
Barrel: 24″.
Weight: 5½ lbs. **Length:** 41¾″ over-all.
Stock: Walnut. Monte Carlo cheekpiece, semi-beavertail fore-end.
Sights: Post front, "Rocky Mountain" rear adj. for e.
Features: Checkered p.g., grooved slide handle, p.g. cap and buttplate with white line spacers. Side ejection. Receiver grooved for scope mount.
Price: **$99.95**

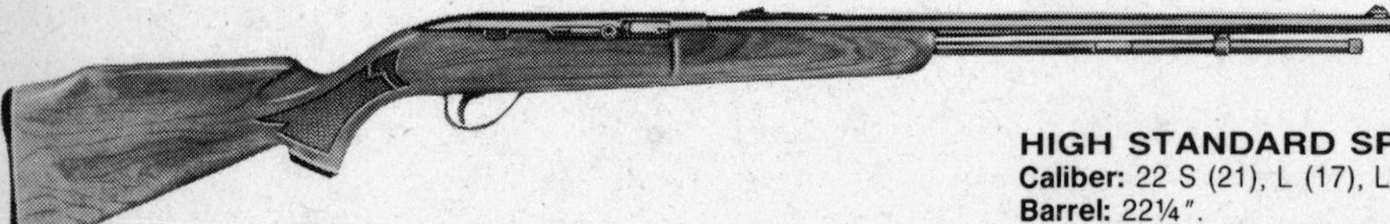

HIGH STANDARD SPORT KING AUTO RIFLE
Caliber: 22 S (21), L (17), LR (15). Tubular magazine.
Barrel: 22¼″.
Weight: 5½ lbs. **Length:** 42¾″ over-all.
Stock: Walnut. Monte Carlo cheekpiece, semi-beavertail fore-end.
Sights: Post front, "Rocky Mountain" rear adj. for e.
Features: Right-side thumb safety, side loading magazine. Checkered p.g. with cap. Receiver dove-tailed for scope mounting.
Price: **$99.95**

MARLIN 49DL AUTOLOADING RIFLE
Caliber: 22 LR, 18-shot tubular magazine
Barrel: 22″ Micro-Groove.
Weight: 5½ lbs. **Length:** 40½″
Stock: American black walnut, Monte Carlo capped p.g., checkered fore-end and p.g.,
Sights: Blade ramp front, step rear adj. for w. & e.
Features: Gold plated trigger, bolt hold-open for safety and cleaning, scroll-engraved receiver grooved for tip-off scope mounts.
Price: **$69.95**

Marlin 99C Autoloading Rifle
Same as the Marlin 49DL except: one piece American black walnut stock with checkered p.g. and fore-end.
Price: **$62.95**

MARLIN GLENFIELD 60 AUTOLOADER
Caliber: 22 LR, 18-shot tubular mag.
Barrel: 22″ round tapered.
Weight: About 5½ lbs. **Length:** 41″ Over-all.
Stock: Walnut finished Monte Carlo, checkered p.g. and fore-end.
Sights: Blade ramp front, step adj. rear.
Features: Chrome plated trigger, matted receiver is grooved for tip-off mounts.
Price: **$53.95**

MARLIN 99 M1 AUTOLOADING CARBINE
Caliber: 22 LR, 9-shot tubular magazine
Barrel: 18″ Micro-Groove
Weight: 4½ lbs. **Length:** 37″
Stock: Monte Carlo American black walnut with p.g. and handguard. White buttplate spacer.
Sights: Blade on band type ramp front, removable flat-top mid-sight adj. for w. & e.
Features: Gold plated trigger, bolt hold-open, serrated receiver top is grooved for tip-off scope mount, sling swivels attached.
Price: **$62.95**

Marlin 989 M2 Autoloading Carbine
Same as the Marlin 99 M1 carbine except 7-shot detachable clip magazine.
Price: **$62.95**

MOSSBERG MODEL 353 RIFLE
Caliber: 22 LR, 7-shot clip.
Barrel: 18″ "AC-KRO-GRUV".
Weight: 5 lbs. **Length:** 38″ over-all.
Stock: Walnut, checkered at p.g. and fore-end. Black Tenite two-positions.
Sights: Open step adj. U-notch rear, bead front on ramp.
Features: Sling swivels and web strap on left of stock, extension fore-end folds down for steady firing from prone position. Receiver grooved for scope mounting.
Price: **$73.55**

REMINGTON NYLON 66MB AUTO RIFLE
Caliber: 22 LR, 14-shot tubular mag.
Barrel: 19⅝″ round tapered.
Weight: 4 lbs. **Length:** 38½″ over-all.
Stock: Moulded Mohawk Brown Nylon, checkered p.g. and fore-end.
Sights: Blade ramp front, adj. open rear.
Features: Top tang safety, double extractors, receiver grooved for tip-off mounts.
Price: **$74.95**
Price: Model 66GS (22 Short only) **$84.95**
Price: With Universal UA 4x scope **$79.95**

Remington Nylon 66AB Auto Rifle
Same as the Model 66MB except: Apache Black Nylon stock, chrome plated receiver.
Price: **$79.95**

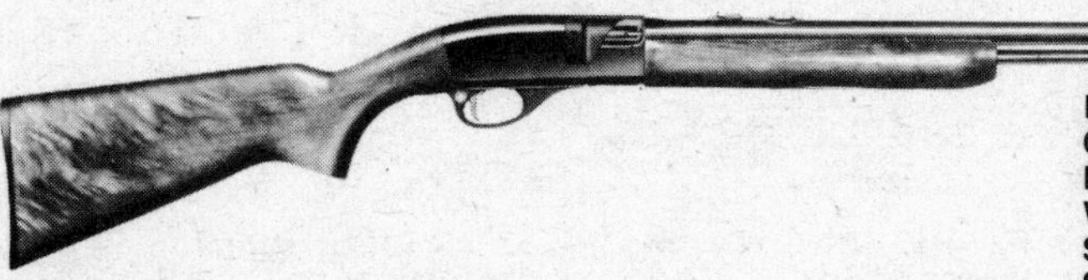

REMINGTON 552A AUTOLOADING RIFLE
Caliber: 22 S (20), L (17) or LR (15) tubular mag.
Barrel: 23″ round tapered.
Weight: about 5¾ lbs. **Length:** 42″ over-all.
Stock: Full-size, walnut with p.g.
Sights: Bead front, step adj. open rear.
Features: Positive cross-bolt safety, receiver grooved for tip-off mount.
Price: **$89.95**
Price: M552GS (22 Short only) **$101.95**

Remington Model 552BDL Auto Rifle
Same as Model 552A except: Du Pont RKW finished checkered fore-end and capped p.g. stock. Blade ramp front and fully adj. rear sights.
Price: **$99.95**

Remington 552C Autoloading Carbine
Same as the Model 552A rifle except: 21″ bbl., weight 5½ lbs., 40″ over-all.
Price: **$84.95**

RIMFIRE RIFLES—AUTOLOADING & SLIDE ACTION

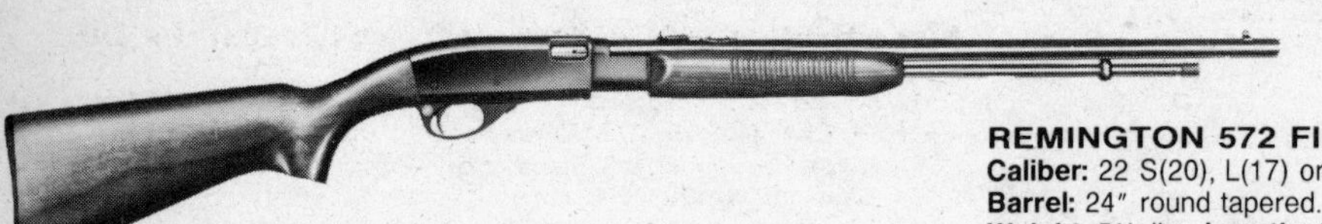

REMINGTON 572 FIELDMASTER PUMP RIFLE
Caliber: 22 S(20), L(17) or LR(14). Tubular mag.
Barrel: 24″ round tapered.
Weight: 5½ lbs. **Length:** 42″ over-all.
Stock: Genuine walnut with p.g. and grooved slide handle.
Sights: Bead post front, step adj. open rear.
Features: Cross-bolt safety, removing inner mag. tube converts rifle to single shot, receiver grooved for tip-off scope mount.
Price: **$94.95**
Price: Sling and swivels installed **$8.75**

Remington Model 572 BDL Deluxe
Same as the 572 except: p.g. cap, RKW finish, checkered grip and fore-end, ramp front and fully adj. rear sights.
Price: **$104.95**
Price: Sling and swivels installed **$8.75**

Remington Model 572 SB
Similar to the 572, but has smoothbore bbl. choked for 22 LR shot cartridges.
Price: Sling and swivels installed. **$8.75**
Price: **$104.95**

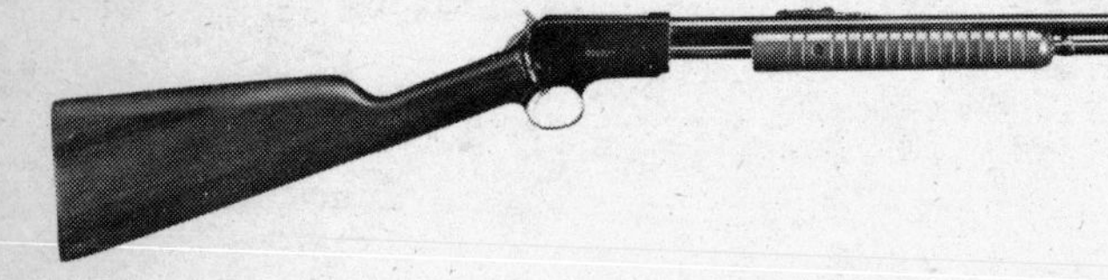

ROSSI GALLERY PUMP RIFLE
Caliber: 22 S, L or LR (Standard), 22 RFM (Magnum).
Barrel: 22½″.
Weight: 5¾ lbs.
Stock: Walnut, straight grip, grooved fore-end.
Sights: Fixed front, adj. rear.
Features: Capacity 20 Short, 16 Long or 14 Long Rifle. Quick takedown. Imported from Brazil by Garcia.
Price: Standard **$115.00**
Price: Magnum **$125.00**

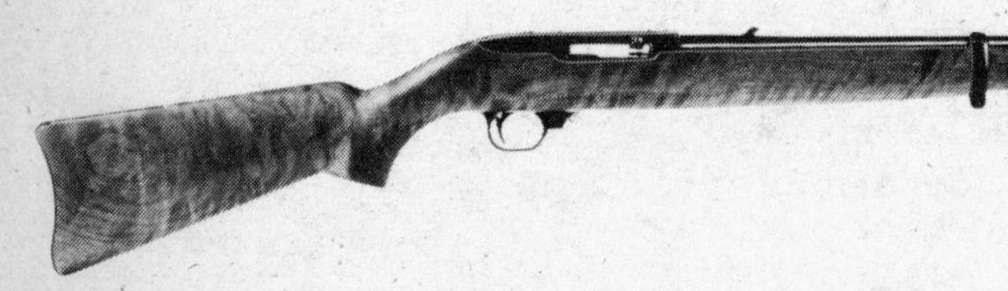

RUGER 10/22 AUTOLOADING CARBINE
Caliber: 22 LR, 10-shot rotary mag.
Barrel: 18½″ round tapered.
Weight: 5 lbs. **Length:** 37″ over-all.
Stock: American walnut with p.g. and bbl. band.
Sights: Gold bead front, fully adj. folding leaf rear.
Features: Detachable rotary magazine fits flush into stock, cross-bolt safety, receiver tapped and grooved for scope blocks or tip-off mount. Scope base adapter furnished with each rifle.
Price: **$73.50**

Ruger 10/22 Auto Sporter
Same as 10/22 Carbine except: Hand checkered p.g. and fore-end with straight buttplate, no bbl., bands, sling swivels.
Price: **$86.50**

SQUIRES BINGHAM M16 SEMI AUTO RIFLE
Caliber: 22 LR, 15-shot clip.
Barrel: 16½″.
Weight: 6 lbs. **Length:** 38½″ over-all.
Stock: Black painted mahogany.
Sights: Post front, rear adj. for e.
Features: Box magazine, muzzle brake/flash suppressor. Imported by American Import.
Price: **$99.95**

SQUIRES BINGHAM M20D SEMI AUTO RIFLE
Caliber: 22 LR, 15-shot clip.
Barrel: 19½″.
Weight: 6 lbs. **Length:** 40½″ over-all.
Stock: Pulong Dalaga wood with contrasting fore-end tip.
Sights: Blade front, V-notch rear adj. for e.
Features: Positive sliding thumb safety. Receiver grooved for tip-off scope mount. Flash suppressor/muzzle brake. Imported by American Import.
Price: **$72.95**

TRADEWINDS MODEL 260-A AUTO RIFLE
Caliber: 22 LR, 5-shot (10-shot mag. avail.).
Barrel: 22½″.
Weight: 5¾ lbs. **Length:! 41½″.**
Stock: Walnut, with hand checkered p.g. and fore-end.
Sights: Ramp front with hood, 3-leaf folding rear, receiver grooved for scope mt.
Features: Double extractors, sliding safety. Imported by Tradewinds.
Price: **$165.00**

RIMFIRE RIFLES—AUTOLOADING & SLIDE ACTION

WEATHERBY MARK XXII AUTO RIFLE, CLIP MODEL
Caliber: 22 LR only, 5- or 10-shot clip loaded
Barrel: 24″ round contoured.
Weight: 6 lbs. **Length:** 42¼″ over-all.
Stock: Walnut, Monte Carlo comb and cheekpiece, rosewood p.g. cap and fore-end tip. Skip-line checkering.
Sights: Gold bead ramp front, 3-leaf folding rear.
Features: Thumb operated side safety also acts as single shot selector. Receiver grooved for tip-off scope mount. Single pin release for quick takedown.
Price: **$159.50**
Extra 5-shot clip .... **$4.25** Extra 10-shot clip **$4.95**

Weatherby Mark XXII Tubular Model
Same as Mark XXII Clip Model except: 15-shot tubular magazine. **$159.50**

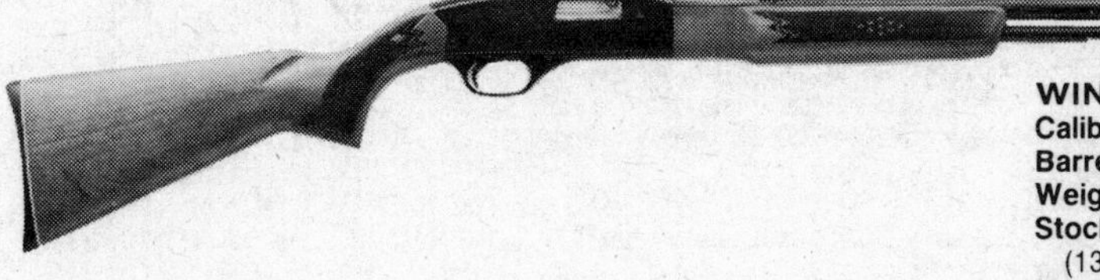

WINCHESTER 290 AUTOLOADING RIFLE
Caliber: 22 L (17) or LR (15), tubular mag.
Barrel: 20½″ round tapered (16″ twist).
Weight: 5 lbs. **Length:** 39″ over-all.
Stock: 2-piece walnut finished hardwood. checkered p.g. and fore-end, (13⅝″x1¾″x2¾″).
Sights: Bead post front, step adj. rear.
Features: Cross-bolt safety, composition buttplate with white line spacer, receiver grooved for tip-off scope mount.
Price: **$80.95**

WINCHESTER MODEL 490 AUTO RIFLE
Caliber: 22 LR only, detachable 5-shot clip.
Barrel: 22″.
Weight: 6 lbs. **Length:** 42″ over-all.
Stock: Walnut, checkered p.g. and fore-end, p.g. cap.
Sights: Folding leaf rear, hooded ramp front.
Features: Receiver grooved for scope mounting, hold-open lock, cross bolt safety. Ten-shot clip available at $5.95, 15-shot $6.95.
Price: **$110.00**

Winchester 190 Auto Rifle
Same as M290 except: No checkering, pistol grip cap or buttplate spacer.
Price: **$67.95**

RIMFIRE RIFLES—LEVER ACTION

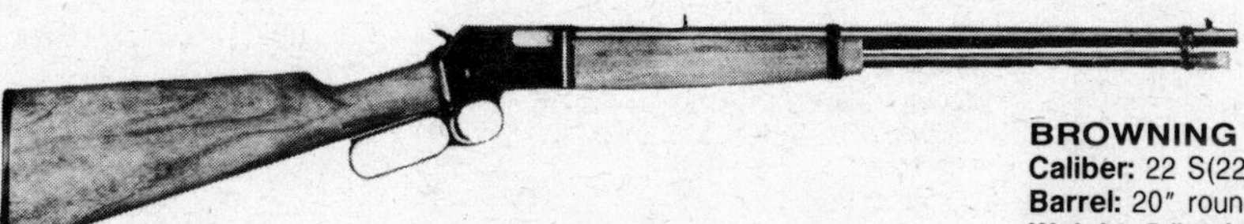

BROWNING BL-22 LEVER ACTION RIFLE
Caliber: 22 S(22), L(17) or LR(15). Tubular mag.
Barrel: 20″ round tapered.
Weight: 5 lbs. **Length:** 36¾″ over-all.
Stock: Walnut, 2-piece straight grip western style.
Sights: Bead post front, folding-leaf rear.
Features: Short throw lever, ½-cock safety, receiver grooved for tip-off scope mounts.
Price: Grade I **$114.50**
Price: Grade II, engraved receiver, checkered grip and fore-end .. **$129.50**

ITHACA MODEL 72 SADDLEGUN
Caliber: 22 LR, 15-shot magazine tube.
Barrel: 18½″.
Weight: 5 lbs.
Stock: American walnut.
Sights: Hooded front, step-adj. rear.
Features: Half-cock safety, steel receiver grooved for scope mounts.
Price: **$114.95**
Price: Model 72 with 4x scope **$129.95**
Price: 22 WMR, std. grade **$134.95**

Ithaca Model 72 De Luxe
Same as standard Model 72 except has octagon barrel, engraved silver-finish frame, "semi-fancy" European walnut stock, steel buttplate **$159.95**

RIMFIRE RIFLES—LEVER ACTION

MARLIN GOLDEN 39A LEVER ACTION RIFLE
Caliber: 22 S(26), L(21), LR(19), tubular magazine.
Barrel: 24″ Micro-Groove.
Weight: 6¾ lbs. **Length:** 40″.
Stock: American black walnut with white line spacers at p.g. cap and buttplate.
Sights: Bead ramp front with detachable "Wide-Scan" hood, folding rear semi-buckhorn adj. for w. and e.
Features: Take-down action, receiver tapped for scope mount (supplied), gold plated trigger, sling swivels, offset hammer spur.
Price: **$120.95**

NAVY ARMS MODEL 66 LEVER ACTION RIFLE
Caliber: 22 LR, 38 Special, 44-40.
Barrel: 16½″, 19″, 24″.
Weight: 9¼ lbs. **Length:** 39½″.
Stock: Walnut.
Sights: Fixed front, folding rear.
Features: Replica of Winchester Model 1866 "Yellowboy." Available with three grades of engraving, selected stock and fore-end at additional cost. 22 LR also available with 16½″ bbl. (Trapper's Model). Imported by Navy Arms.
Price: Trapper & Carbine **$195.00**
Price: 24″ octagon bbl. **$225.00**

MARLIN GOLDEN 39M CARBINE
Caliber: 22 S(21), L(16), LR(15), tubular magazine.
Barrel: 20″ Micro-Grove.
Weight: 6 lbs. **Length:** 36″.
Stock: American black walnut, straight grip, white line buttplate spacer.
Sights: "Wide-Scan" bead ramp front with hood, folding rear semi-buckhorn adj. for w. and e.
Features: Squared finger lever. Receiver tapped for scope mount (supplied) or receiver sight, gold plated trigger, offset hammer spur, sling swivels, take-down action.
Price: **$120.95**

WINCHESTER 9422 LEVER ACTION RIFLE
Caliber: 22 S(21), L(17), LR(15). Tubular mag.
Barrel: 20½″ (16″ twist).
Length: 37⅛″ over-all. **Weight:** 6½ lbs.
Stock: American walnut, 2-piece, straight grip (no p.g.).
Sights: Hooded ramp ront, adj. semi-byckhorn rear.
Features: Side ejection, receiver grooved for scope mounting, takedown action.
Price: **$149.95**

Winchester 9422M Lever Action Rifle
Same as the 9422 except chambered for 22 WMR cartridge, has 11-round mag. capacity **$154.95**

RIMFIRE RIFLES—BOLT ACTION

HARRINGTON & RICHARDSON 865 PLAINSMAN RIFLE
Caliber: 22 S, L or LR. 5-shot clip mag.
Barrel: 22″ round tapered.
Weight: 5 lbs. **Length:** 39″ over-all.
Stock: Walnut finished hardwood with Monte Carlo and p.g.
Sights: Blade front, step adj. open rear.
Features: Cocking indicator, sliding side safety, receiver grooved for tip-off scope mounts.
Price: **$59.50**

MARLIN 780 BOLT ACTION RIFLE
Caliber: 22 S, L, or LR; 7-shot clip magazine.
Barrel: 22″ Micro-Groove
Weight: 5½ lbs. **Length:** 41″
Stock: Monte Carlo American black walnut with checkered p.g. White line spacer at buttplate.
Sights: "Wide-Scan" ramp front, folding semi-buckhorn rear adj. for w. & e.
Features: Gold plated trigger receiver anti-glare serrated and grooved for tip-off scope mount.
Price: **$57.95**

Marlin 781 Bolt Action Rifle
Same as the Marlin 780 except: tubular magazine holds 25 Shorts, 19 Longs or 17 Long Rifle cartridges. Weight 6 lbs. **$59.95**

Marlin 782 Bolt Action Rifle
Same as the Marlin 780 except: 22 Rimfire Magnum cal. only, weight about 6 lbs. Sling and swivels attached. **$64.95**

Marlin 783 Bolt Action Rifle
Same as Marlin 782 except: Tubular magazine holds 13 rounds of 22 Rimfire Magnum ammunition. **$66.95**

Marlin Glenfield 20 Bolt Action Repeater
Similar to Marlin 780, except: Walnut finished checkered p.g. stock, without Monte Carlo, conventional rifling. **$47.95**

MOSSBERG MODEL 340B RIFLE
Caliber: 22 S, L, LR, 7-shot clip.
Barrel: 24″ "AC-KRO-GRUV".
Weight: 6 lbs. **Length:** 43½″ over-all.
Stock: Walnut finish with p.g., Monte Carlo and cheek piece, sling swivels.
Sights: Mossberg S331 receiver peep with ¼-minute adjustments for w. and e. S320 Mossberg hooded ramp front.
Features: Front sight offers choice of post or aperture elements. "Magic 3-Way" clip adjusts for Short, Long or Long Rifle cartridges. Receiver grooved for scope mount.
Price: **$69.84**

MOSSBERG MODEL 321K
Caliber: 22 S, L, LR, single shot.
Barrel: 24″.
Length: 43½″ over-all. **Weight:** 6½ lbs.
Stock: Walnut finish, cheekpiece, checkered p.g. and fore-end.
Sights: Ramp front, adj. rear.
Features: Hammerless bolt action with drop-in loading platform and automatic safety, black buttplate. Model 321B has S330 peep sight with ¼-minute click adjustments.
Price: **$56.84**

MOSSBERG MODEL 341 RIFLE
Caliber: 22 S, L, LR, 7-shot clip.
Barrel: 24″ "AG-KRO-GRUV"
Weight: 6½ lbs. **Length:** 43½″ over-all.
Stock: Walnut, checkered p.g. and fore-end, Monte Carlo and cheek piece. Buttplate with white line spacer.
Sights: Open, U-notch rear adj. for w. and e.
Features: Sliding side safety, 8 groove rifling, "Magic 3-way" clip adjusts to Short, Long or Long Rifle cartridges.
Price: **$64.58**

MOSSBERG MODEL 640K CHUCKSTER
Caliber: 22 WMR. 5-shot clip mag.
Barrel: 24″ AC-KRO-GRUV.
Weight: 6 lbs. **Length:** 44¾″ over-all.
Stock: Walnut, checkered p.g. and fore-end, Monte Carlo comb and cheek-piece.
Sights: Ramp front with bead, fully adj. leaf rear.
Features: Grooved trigger, sliding side safety, double extractors, receiver grooved for tip-off scope mounts and tapped for aperture rear sight.
Price: **$74.12**

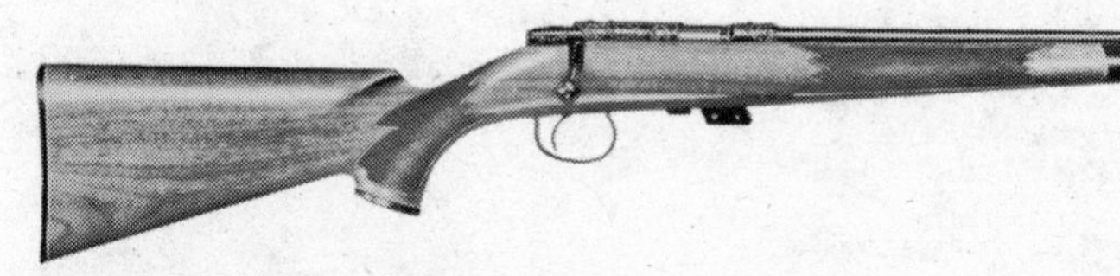

Remington Model 582 Rifle
Same as M581 except: tubular magazine under bbl. holds 20 S, 15 L or 14 LR cartridges. Wgt. 5½ lbs.
Price: **$79.95**

REMINGTON MODEL 541-S
Barrel: 24″
Weight: 5½ lbs. **Length:** 42⅝″.
Stock: Walnut, checkered p.g. and fore end.
Sights: None. Drilled and tapped for scope mounts or receiver sights.
Features: Clip repeater. Thumb safety. Receiver and trigger guard scroll engraved.
Price: **$159.95**
Price: Extra 10-shot clip **$4.00**

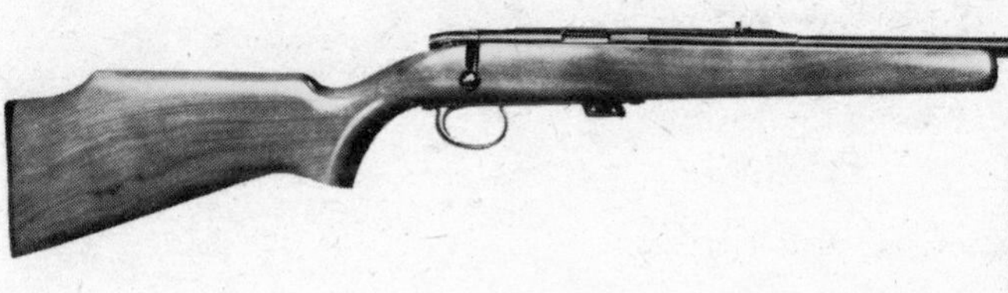

REMINGTON MODEL 581 RIFLE
Caliber: 22 S, L or LR. 5-shot clip mag.
Barrel: 24″ round.
Weight: 4¾ lbs. **Length:** 42⅜″ over-all.
Stock: Walnut finished Monte Carlo with p.g.
Sights: Bead post front, screw adj. open rear.
Features: Sliding side safety, wide trigger, receiver grooved for tip-off scope mounts.
Price: **$69.95**
Price: Left hand action and stock **$74.95**

SAVAGE/ANSCHUTZ MODEL 54 SPORTER
Caliber: 22 LR. 5-shot clip mag.
Barrel: 23″ round tapered.
Weight: 6¾ lbs. **Length:** 42″ over-all.
Stock: French walnut, checkered p.g. and fore-end. Monte Carlo roll-over comb, schnabel fore-end tip.
Sights: Hooded ramp gold bead front, folding-leaf rear.
Features: Adj. single stage trigger, wing safety, receiver grooved for tip-off mount, tapped for scope blocks.
Price: **$330.00**
Price: Model 54M (22 WRM) **$345.00**

Savage/Anschutz Model 1432 Sporter
Same as Model 54 except chambered for 22 Hornet, 24″ barrel, 5-shot capacity, over-all length 43⅝″ **$360.00**

RIMFIRE RIFLES—BOLT ACTION

SAVAGE/ANSCHUTZ 164 BOLT ACTION RIFLE

Caliber: 22 LR. 5-shot clip mag.
Barrel: 24″ round tapered.
Weight: 6 lbs. **Length:** 40¾″ over-all
Stock: Walnut, hand checkered p.g. and fore-end, Monte Carlo comb and cheekpiece, schnabel fore-end.
Sights: Hooded ramp gold bead front, folding-leaf rear.
Features: Fully adj. single stage trigger, sliding side safety, receiver grooved for tip-off mount.
Price: **$189.50**
Price: Model 164M in 22 WRM (4-shot) **$204.50**

SAVAGE MODEL 65-M RIFLE

Caliber: 22 WRM, 5-shot.
Barrel: 20″ lightweight, free floating.
Weight: 5 lbs. **Length:** 39″ over-all.
Stock: Walnut, Monte Carlo comb. checkered p.g. and fore-end.
Sights: Gold bead ramp front, step adj. open rear.
Features: Sliding side safety, double extractors, receiver grooved for tip-off scope mount.
Price: **$62.90**

Savage/Stevens Model 34 Rifle

Same as the Model 65-M except: 22 LR, walnut finished hardwood stock, bead post front sight.
Price: **$51.00**

TRADEWINDS MODEL 311-A BOLT ACTION RIFLE

Caliber: 22 LR, 5-shot (10-shot mag. avail.).
Barrel: 22½″.
Weight: 6 lbs. **Length:** 41¼″.
Stock: Walnut, Monte Carlo with hand checkered p.g. and fore-end.
Sights: Ramp front with hood, folding leaf rear, receiver grooved for scope mt.
Features: Sliding safety locks trigger and bolt handle. Imported by Tradewinds.
Price: **$150.00**

SQUIRES BINGHAM M14D BOLT ACTION RIFLE

Caliber: 22 S, L, LR, 5-shot clip.
Barrel: 19½″.
Weight: 6 lbs. **Length:** 41″ over-all.
Stock: Pulong Dalaga wood with contrasting fore-end tip. Monte Carlo cheekpiece.
Sights: Hooded ramp front, V-notch rear adjustable for e.
Features: Positive sliding thumb safety, receiver grooved for tip-off scope mount. Also available in 22 mag. as model 15. Imported by American Import.
Price: Model 14D **$69.95**
Price: Model 15 .... **$109.95**

WALTHER KKJ RIMFIRE SPORTSMAN

Caliber: 22 LR, 22 WRM; 5-shot.
Barrel: 22½″.
Weight: 5½ lbs. **Length: 41½″ over-all.**
Stock: Hand checkered walnut; p.g.; cheekpiece.
Sights: Hooded ramp front, open rear adj. for w. & e. Dovetailed for scope mounting.
Features: Double set triggers avail.; left-hand stock avail. on special order ($20 extra). From Interarms.
Price: 22 LR, std. trigger **$319.00**
Price: 22 LR, double set trigger **$339.00**
Price: 22 WRM, std. trigger **$339.00**
Price: 22 WRM, double set trigger **$359.00**

WESTERN FIELD 832 BOLT ACTION RIFLE

Caliber: 22 S, L, LR; 7-shot clip.
Barrel: 24″ round tapered.
Length: 43″ over-all. **Weight:** 6½ lbs.
Stock: Walnut p.g. and fore-end, checkered p.g.
Sights: Ramp front, rear adj. for e.
Features: Thumb operated safety, sling swivels.
Price: **$62.00**
Price: Model 822 in 22 WRM (illus.) **$69.99**

RIMFIRE RIFLES—SINGLE SHOT

GARCIA BRONCO 22 RIFLE

Caliber: 22 S, L or LR. Single-shot.
Barrel: 16½″ round.
Weight: 3 lbs. **Length:** 32″ over-all.
Stock: Skeletonized crackle finished alloy casting.
Sights: Protected blade front, adj. rear.
Features: Cross-bolt safety, swing-out chamber, ultra lightweight for easy portability, instant takedown.
Price: **$39.00**

HARRINGTON & RICHARDSON MODEL 750 PIONEER

Caliber: 22 S, L or LR. Single-shot.
Barrel: 22″ round tapered.
Weight: 5 lbs. **Length:** 39″ over-all.
Stock: Walnut finished hardwood with Monte Carlo comb and p.g.
Sights: Blade front, step adj. open rear.
Features: Double extractors, feed platform, cocking indicator. sliding side safety, receiver grooved for tip-off scope mount, tapped for aperture sight.
Price: **$49.50**

ITHACA MODEL 49 SADDLEGUN

Caliber: 22 S, L or LR. Single-shot.
Barrel: 18″ round.
Weight: About 5½ lbs. **Length:** 34½″ over-all
Stock: Two-piece walnut, checkered straight grip, fore-end has bbl. band.
Sights: Bead post front, step adj. open rear.
Features: Rebounding hammer safety, Martini-type lever action. Rifle can be ordered with shorter (youth) stock at no extra cost.
Price: **$49.95**
Price: Chambered for 22 WRM only **$59.95**

MARLIN 101 SINGLE SHOT RIFLE

Caliber: 22 S, L or LR; Single shot.
Barrel: 22″ Micro-Groove.
Weight: 4½ lbs. **Length:** 40″
Stock: Monte Carlo American black walnut with p.g. and white line spacer at buttplate.
Sights: Ramp front with "Wide-Scan"™ hood, folding semi-buckhorn rear adj. for w. & e.
Features: Gold plated trigger, T-shaped cocking knob, non-jamming feed throat, receiver grooved for tip-off scope mount. Manual cocking action.
Price: **$41.95**

REMINGTON MODEL 580 SINGLE SHOT RIFLE

Caliber: 22 S, L or LR. Single-shot.
Barrel: 24″ round tapered.
Weight: 4¾ lbs. **Length:** 42⅜″ over-all.
Stock: Walnut finished hardwood, Monte Carlo comb and p.g., black composition buttplate.
Sights: Bead post front, screw-lock adj. rear.
Features: Single screw take-down, integral loading platform, sliding side safety, receiver grooved for tip-off mount, can be had with 1″ shorter (youth) stock.
Price: **$59.95**
Price: M580 SB (smooth bore) **$64.95**

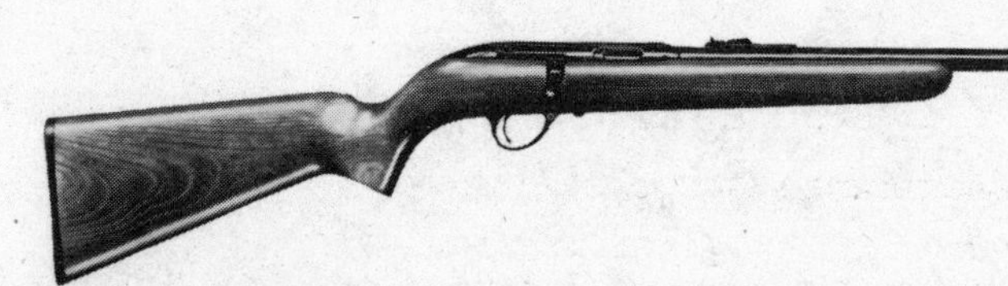

SAVAGE STEVENS MODEL 73 SINGLE SHOT RIFLE

Caliber: 22 S, L or LR. Single-shot.
Barrel: 20″ round tapered.
Weight: 4¾ lbs. **Length:** 38½″ over-all.
Stock: Walnut finished hardwood.
Sights: Bead post front, step adj. open rear.
Features: Cocks on opening, automatic safety, key locks trigger against unauthorized use, may be had with 12½″ pull stock (youth model) at same cost.
Price: **$36.50**

SAVAGE STEVENS MODEL 72 CRACKSHOT

Caliber: 22 S, L, LR.
Barrel: 22″ octagonal.
Weight: 4½ lbs. **Length:** 37″.
Stock: Walnut, straight grip and fore-end.
Sights: Blade front, step adj. rear.
Features: Deluxe version of Model 74, color case hardened frame.
Price: **$66.50**

SHOTGUNS—AUTOLOADING

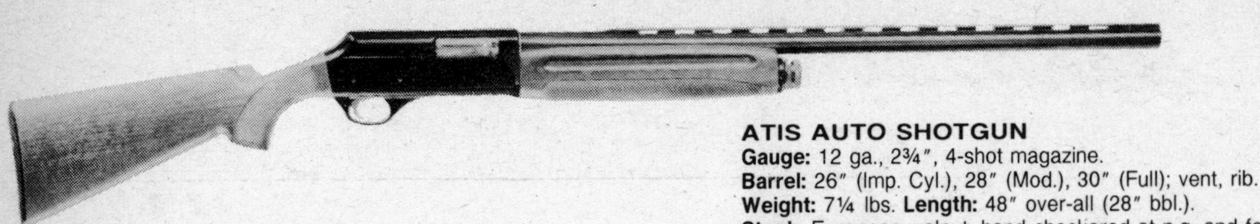

ATIS AUTO SHOTGUN

Gauge: 12 ga., 2¾", 4-shot magazine.
Barrel: 26" (Imp. Cyl.), 28" (Mod.), 30" (Full); vent, rib.
Weight: 7¼ lbs. **Length:** 48" over-all (28" bbl.).
Stock: European walnut, hand checkered at p.g. and fore-end.
Features: Lightweight aluminum receiver; chrome plated bolt and lock assembly. Imported by Interarms.
Price: Right-hand **$239.00**
Price: Left-hand **$289.00**

BENELLI AUTOLOADING SHOTGUN

Gauge: 12 and 20 ga. (5-shot, 3-shot plug furnished).
Barrel: 26" (Skeet, Imp. Cyl., Mod.); 28" (Spec., Full, Imp. Mod., Mod.). Vent. rib.
Weight: 6¾ lbs.
Stock: European walnut. 14"x1½"x2½". Hand checkered p.g. and fore-end.
Sights: Metal bead front.
Features: Quick interchangeable barrels within gauge. Cross-bolt safety. Hand engraved on higher grades. Imported from Italy by Diana Import Co.
Price: Standard model **$436.75**
Price: Engraved **$545.25**

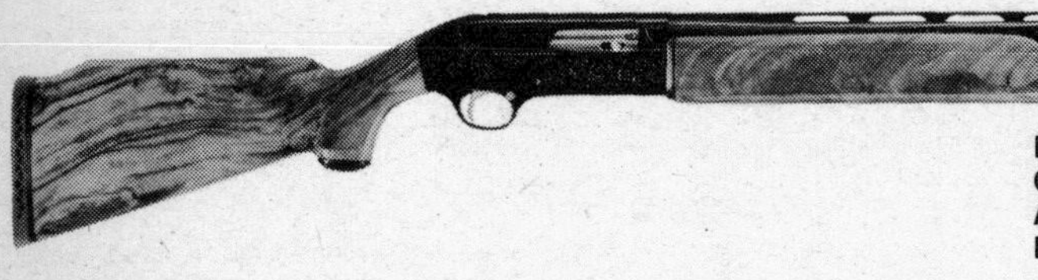

BERETTA AL-3 AUTO SHOTGUNS

Gauge: 12 or 20 (4-shot, 3-shot plug furnished). 2¾" or 3" chambers.
Action: Gas-operated autoloader.
Barrel: 12 ga., 30l or 28" (Full), 28" (Mod.), 26" (Imp. Cyl.); 20 ga., 28" (Full or Mod.), 26" (Imp. Cyl.); 12 ga. Trap, 30" (Full); 12 or 20 ga. Skeet, 26" (Skeet); 12 ga., 3" mag. 30" (Full), 28" (Mod.).
Weight: 12 ga. 7 lbs., 20 ga. 6½ lbs., Trap 7½ lbs.
Stock: Hand checkered European walnut, p.g. Monte Carlo on trap models.
Features: AL-3 has hand-engraved receiver and ventilated rib. Crossbolt safety.
Price: AL-3 .... **$310.00**
Price: AL-3 Trap or Skeet **$360.00**
Price: AL-3 3" Magnum **$345.00**

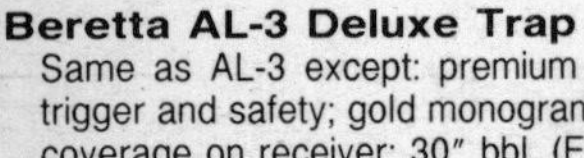

Beretta AL-3 Deluxe Trap

Same as AL-3 except: premium grade stock and fore-end; gold plated trigger and safety; gold monogram escutcheon inlaid in butt; full engraving coverage on receiver; 30" bbl. (Full or Imp. Mod.) **$575.00**

BREDA AUTOLOADING SHOTGUN

Gauge: 12 only (5-shot, 3-shot plug furnished), 2¾" chamber.
Action: Recoil operated.
Barrel: 26" (Imp. Cyl., Mod., Full), vent, rib; interchangeable choke tubes.
Weight: 7 lbs.
Stock: Walnut finished hardwood; p.g. and fore-end checkered.
Features: Receiver made of lightweight aluminum alloy. Also available for 3" shells (29" vent. rib barrel). Imported by Diana Imports Co.
Price: Standard Model **$289.95**
Price: Magnum **$434.50**
Price: Interchangeable choke tubes **$19.60**

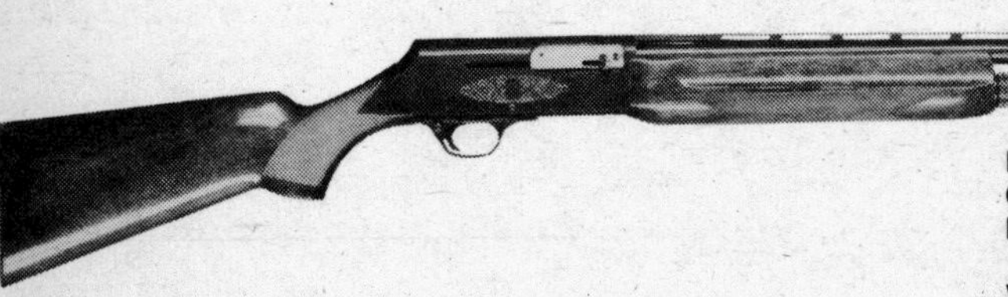

BROWNING B/2000 GAS OPERATED AUTO SHOTGUN

Gauge: 12 ga.; 5-shot, 4-shot in Magnum.
Barrel: 26", 28" or 30" in 2¾" Field Models, plain or vent. rib; 28", 30" or 32" in 3" Magnum models, vent. rib only.
Weight: 7½ lbs. (26" vent. rib) **Length:** 45⅜" (26" bbl.).
Stock: French walnut, hand checkered, full pistol grip, no recoil pad 14¼"x1⅝"x2½".
Sights: Medium raised bead, German nickel silver.
Features: Internal self-cleaning gas system, soft recoil, speed loading/unloading, extra bbls. interchangeable without factory fitting. No adjustment necessary to gas system for varying loads.
Price: Vent. rib **$309.50**
Price: Plain bbl. **$289.50**
Price: Vent. rib, 3" Mag. **$309.50**
Price: Buck Special **$309.50**
Price: Trap and/or Skeet Models .... **To be announced**

Browning B-2000 20 Gauge

Same as 12 ga. B-2000 except: vent. rib barrel only; front and center ivory sight beads on Skeet barrel only; 24" Buck Special barrel 26" (Full, Mod., Imp. Cyl., Cyl., Skeet); 28" (Full or Mod.); extra barrels available, 2¾" or 3" chambers (3" not available in 26" Cyl. bore, 26" Skeet or 24" Buck Special). Weight is about 6¾ lbs, length with 26" barrel is 46½". Vent. rib barrel only **$309.50**

SHOTGUNS—AUTOLOADING

Browning Auto-5 Magnum 12

Same as Std. Auto-5 except: chambered for 3″ magnum shells (also handles 2¾″ magnum and 2¾″ HV loads). 28″ Mod., Full; 30″ and 32″ (Full) bbls. 14″x1⅝″x2½″ stock. Recoil pad. Wgt. 8¾ lbs.

Price: Vent. rib only **$434.50**

Browning Auto-5 Magnum 20

Same as Magnum 12 except barrels 28″ Full or Mod., or 26″ Full, Mod. or Imp. Cyl. With ventilated rib, 7½ lbs. **$434.50**

Browning Auto-5 Light Skeet

Same as Light Standard except: 12 and 20 ga. only, 26″ or 28″ bbl. (Skeet). With vent. rib. Wgt. 6⅜-7½ lbs. **$434.50**

BROWNING AUTO-5 LIGHT 12, 20 and SWEET 16

Gauge: 12, 20, 16; 5-shot; 3-shot plug furnished; 2¾″ chamber.
Action: Recoil operated autoloader; takedown.
Barrel: 26″ (Skeet boring in 12 & 20 ga., Cyl., Imp. Cyl., Mod. in 16 & 20 ga.); 28″ (Skeet in 12 ga., Full in 16 ga., Mod., Full); 30″ (Full in 12 ga.).
Weight: 12 ga. 7¼ lbs., 16 ga. 6¾ lbs., 20 ga. 6⅜ lbs.
Stock: French walnut, hand checkered half-p.g. and fore-end. 14¼″ x 1⅝″ x 2½″.
Features: Receiver hand engraved with scroll designs and border. Double extractors, extra bbls. interchangeable without factory fitting; mag. cut-off; cross-bolt safety.
Price: Vent. rib only **$434.50**

Browning Auto-5 Light 12, 16, 20, or 12 Buck Special

Same as A-5 Light model except: 24″ bbl. choked for slugs, gold bead front sight on contoured ramp, rear sight adj. for w.&e. Wgt. 12 ga., 7 lbs.; 16 ga., 6⅜ lbs.; 20 ga., 6 lbs. 2 oz.; 3″ Mag. 12, 8¼ lbs. Illus.

Price: **$434.50**

All Buck Specials are available with carrying sling, detachable swivels and swivel attachments for $13.00 extra.

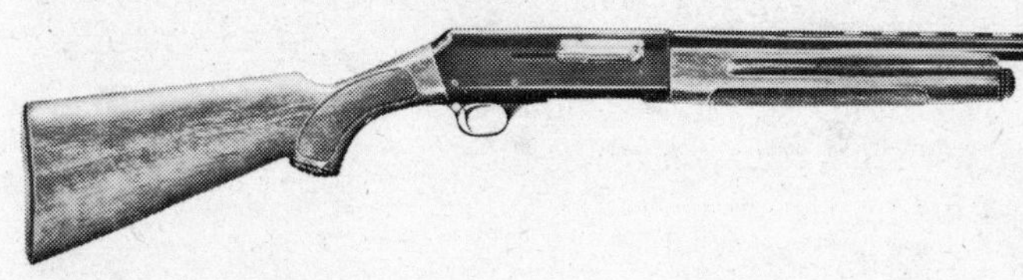

Franchi Slug Gun

Same as Standard automatic except 22″ cylinder bored bbl., adj. rear sight, sling swivels.

Price: **$329.95**

FRANCHI MAGNUM AUTO SHOTGUN

Gauge: 12 or 20, 3-inch shells.
Action: Recoil-operated automatic.
Barrel: 32″, 12 ga.; 28″, 20 ga., both Full.
Weight: 12 ga. 8¼ lbs., 20 ga. 6 lbs.
Stock: Epoxy-finished walnut with recoil pad.
Features: Chrome-lined bbl., easy takedown. Available with ventilated rib barrel. Imported from Italy by Stoeger Industries.
Price: **$329.95**
Price: Vent. rib **$349.95**

FRANCHI STANDARD AUTO SHOTGUN

Gauge: 12, 20 or 28, 5-shot. 2¾″ or 3″ chamber.
Action: Recoil-operated automatic.
Barrel: 24″ (Imp. Cyl. or Cyl.); 26″ (Imp. Cyl. or Mod.); 28″ (Skeet, Mod. or Full); 30″, 32″. (Full).
Weight: 12 ga. 6¼ lbs., 20 ga. 5 lbs. 2 oz.
Stock: Epoxy-finished walnut.
Features: Chrome-lined bbl., easy takedown, 3-round plug provided. Available with plain round or ventilated rib barrel. Imported from Italy by Stoeger Industries.
Price: Plain bbl. 12 or 20 ga. **$284.95**
Price: Vent. rib 12 or 20 ga. **$299.95**
Price: Hunter model (engraved, 12 or 20) **$349.95**
Price: "EL Dorado" Model **$429.95**

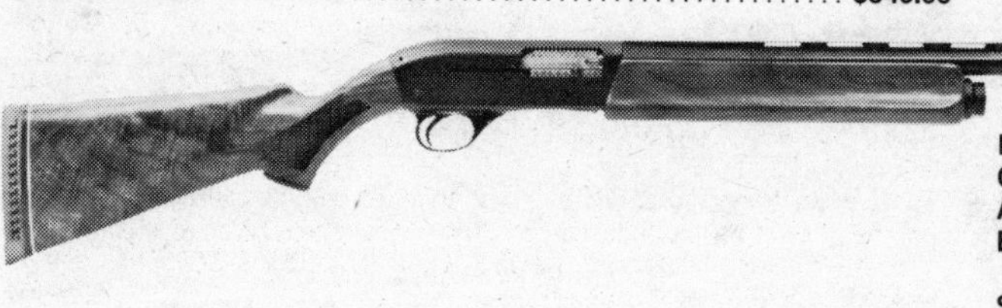

HI-STANDARD SUPERMATIC DELUXE AUTOS

Gauge: 12 ga. (5-shot; 3-shot plug furnished). 20 ga. (3 shots only).
Action: Gas operated autoloader (12 ga. 2¾″, 20 ga. 3″ chambers).
Barrel: 12 gauge, 30″ (Full), 26″ (Imp. Cyl.), 12 and 20 gauge, 28″ (Mod. or Full). Plain Barrel.
Stock: 14″x1½″x2½″. Walnut, checkered p.g. and semi-beavertail fore-end. Recoil pad. 20 ga. guns have longer fore-end with sloped front.
Weight: 7½ lbs. (12 ga.) 47¾″ over-all (12, 28″).
Features: 12 ga. uses all 2¾″ shells, 20 ga. all 2¾″ or 3″ shells, including rifled slugs, manual adjustment, engraved receiver.
Price: Field, plain bbl., no rib **$203.50**
Price: Deluxe vent. rib, checkered stock, w/o adj. choke **$225.50**
Price: Checkered stock, vent.-rib, adj. choke **$230.95**
Price: Duck, 3″ Magnum, 12 ga., 30″ full, recoil pad, with vent. rib bbl. **$225.50**

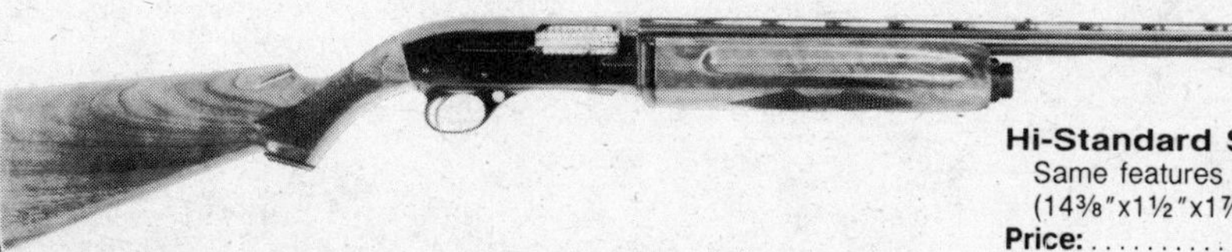

Hi-Standard Supermatic Trap

Same features as Supermatic Skeet except: 30″ full choke barrel; stock (14⅜″x1½″x1⅞″); recoil pad. Wgt. 8 lbs. 12 ga. only.

Price: **$236.50**

Hi-Standard Supermatic Skeet

Same as Supermatic DeLuxe except: 26″ Skeet choke bbl.; all external parts high polished; internal parts super finished; better grade American walnut stock (no recoil pad) and fore-end with cabinet finish. weight about 7½ lbs. **$230.95**

HIGH STANDARD SHADOW AUTO SHOTGUN

Gauge: 12 or 20 (2¾" and 3" chambers).
Action: Gas operated
Barrel: 26" (Imp., Skeet), 28" (Imp. Mod., Mod., Full), 30" (Full, Trap). Full airflow rib.
Weight: 7 lbs.
Stock: American walnut. Hand checkered p.g. and wide fore-end.
Sights: Metal bead front.
Features: Self-cleaning gas system. Highly polished octagonal bolt. Take-down, interchangeable barrels, p.g. cap on all models, recoil pad available on 3" mag. models. Crossbolt safety. Imported by High Standard.
Price: **$269.00**

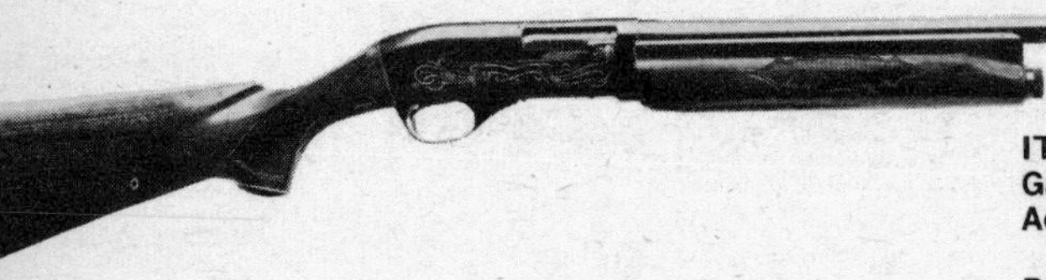

ITHACA MODEL 51 FEATHERLIGHT AUTOMATIC

Gauge: 12 ga. 2¾" chamber.
Action: Gas-operated, rotary bolt has three locking lugs. Takedown. Self-compensating for high or low base loads.
Barrel: Roto-Forged, 30" (Full), 28" (Full, Mod., or Skeet), 26" (Imp. Cyl. or Skeet). Extra barrels available. Raybar front sight. Vent. rib $25.00 extra.
Stock: 14"x1⅝"x2½". Hand checkered walnut, white spacers on p.g. and under recoil pad.
Weight: About 7½ lbs.
Features: Hand fitted, engraved receiver, 3 shot capacity, safety is reversible for left hand shooter.
Price: Standard **$239.95**
Price: Deluxe with vent. rib **$269.95**

Ithaca Model 51 Magnum

Same as Standard Model 51 except has 3" chambers.
Price: Magnum Standard **$264.95**
Price: Magnum vent. rib **$294.95**

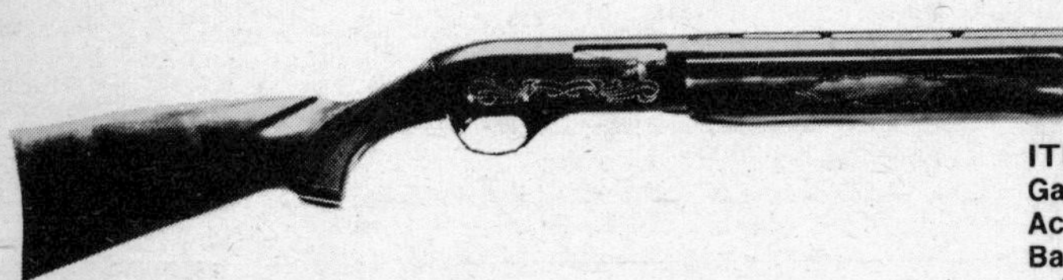

ITHACA MODEL 51 20 GAUGE

Gauge: 20 only, 2¾" or 3" chamber.
Action: Gas-operated rotary bolt.
Barrel: Standard Grade, 26" (Imp. Cyl.), 28" (Full, Mod.), Target Grade, 26" (Skeet).
Weight: 7½ to 8½ lbs.
Stock: 14"x1½"x2¼", American walnut.
Sights: Raybar front sight.
Features: Quick take-down, reversible safety, interchangeable barrels. Easily field stripped without tools.
Price: Standard model **$239.95**
Price: Standard model with vent. rib **$269.95**
Price: Standard magnum **$264.95**
Price: Vent. magnum **$294.95**
Price: Deluxe Skeet **$299.95**

Ithaca Model 51 Featherlight Deluxe Trap

Same gun as Model 51 Trap with fancy American walnut stock, 30" (Full or Imp. Cyl.) or 28" (Full or Imp. Mod.) barrel.
Price: .... **$339.95** With Monte Carlo stock **$354.95**

Ithaca Model 51 Featherlight Deluxe Skeet

Same gun as Model 51 Skeet with fancy American walnut stock, 28" or 29" (Skeet) barrel.
Price: **$299.95**

ITHACA MODEL 51 DEERSLAYER

Gauge: 12 or 20 ga., 2¾" chamber.
Action: Gas-operated, semi-automatic.
Barrel: 24", special bore.
Weight: 7½ lbs. (12 ga.), 7¼ lbs. (20 ga.).
Stocks: 14"x1½"x2¼", American walnut. Checkered p.g. and fore-end.
Sights: Raybar front, open rear adj. for w. and e.
Features: Sight base grooved for scope mounts. Easy takedown, reversible safety.
Price: **$264.95**

ITHACA MODEL XL 900

Gauge: 12 (2¾"), 20 (2¾", 3" chamber); 5 shot capacity.
Action: Gas-operated autoloader.
Barrel: 12 ga., Field Grade - 30" (Full), 28" (Full or Mod.), 26" (Imp. Cyl.); 20 ga., 28" (Full or Mod.,) 26" (Imp. Cyl,), Trap - 30" (Full or Imp. Mod.), Skeet - 26" (Skeet).
Weight: 6¾ lbs. **Length:** 48" overall.
Stock: 1½"x2½"x14" (Field Grade). Walnut finish.
Sights: Ventilated rib with Raybar front sight on field grades; Bradley-type on target grades.
Features: Self-compensating gas system, reversible safety, action release button.
Price: Ventilated rib .... **$244.95** Trap grade (12 ga. only) **$269.95**
Price: Skeet grade .... **$269.95** Slug gun **$239.95**
Price: Trap Monte Carlo **$269.95**

ITHACA MODEL XL 300

Gauge: 12 (2¾"), 20 (2¾" or 3" chamber).
Action: Gas-operated autoloader.
Barrel: 12 ga. Field Grade - 30" (Full), 28" (Full or Mod.), 26" (Imp. Cyl.). 20 ga. Field Grade - 28" (Full or Mod.) 26" (Imp. Cyl.). Trap Grade - 30" (Full or Mod.); Skeet-26" (Skeet).
Weight: 7½ lbs. **Length:** 48" over-all.
Stock: 1½"x2½"x14" (Field Grade). Walnut.
Sights: Raybar front sight on ventilated rib.
Features: Self-compensating gas system, reversible safety.
Price: Standard .... **$219.95** Ventilated rib **$234.95**

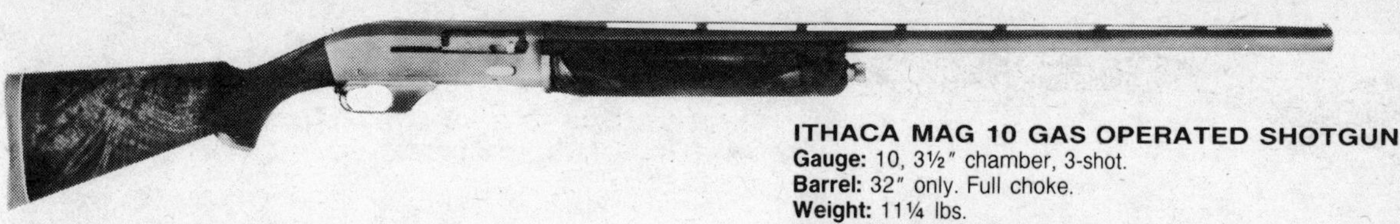

LJUTIC BI MATIC AUTO SHOTGUN

Gauge: 12 ga. only.
Barrel: 30" (standard), 26" to 32"; choked to customer specs.
Weight: Approx. 10 lbs.
Stock: To customer specs. Oil finish, hand checkered.
Features: Two-shot, low recoil auto designed for trap and Skeet. One-piece actuating rod; pull or release trigger. Available with right- or left-hand ejector. From Ljutic Industries.
Price: **$1,500.00**
Price: Extra Barrel **$500.00**

ITHACA MAG 10 GAS OPERATED SHOTGUN

Gauge: 10, 3½" chamber, 3-shot.
Barrel: 32" only. Full choke.
Weight: 11¼ lbs.
Stock: American walnut, checkered p.g. and fore-end (14⅛"x2⅜"x1½"), p.g. cap, rubber recoil pad.
Sights: White Bradley.
Features: "Counterecoil gas system. Piston, cylinder, bolt, charging lever, action release and carrier made of stainless steel. ⅜" vent. rib. Reversible cross-bolt safety. Low recoil force.
Price: **$499.95**

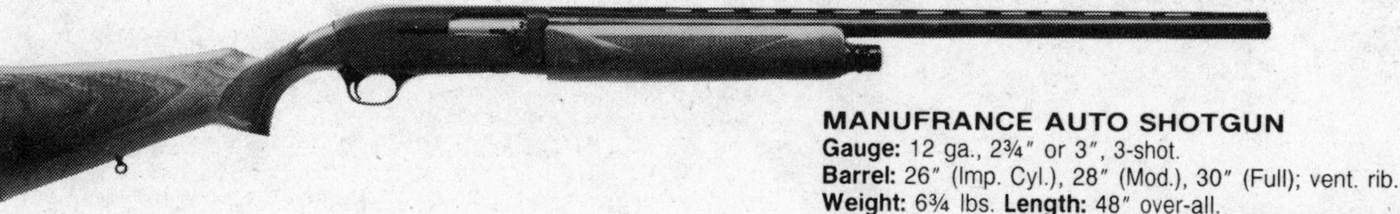

MANUFRANCE AUTO SHOTGUN

Gauge: 12 ga., 2¾" or 3", 3-shot.
Barrel: 26" (Imp. Cyl.), 28" (Mod.), 30" (Full); vent. rib.
Weight: 6¾ lbs. **Length:** 48" over-all.
Stock: French walnut, hand checkered p.g. and fore-end.
Features: Magazine selector; black matte finish receiver; quick take-down; interchangeable barrels available. Imported by Interarms.
Price: **$315.00**

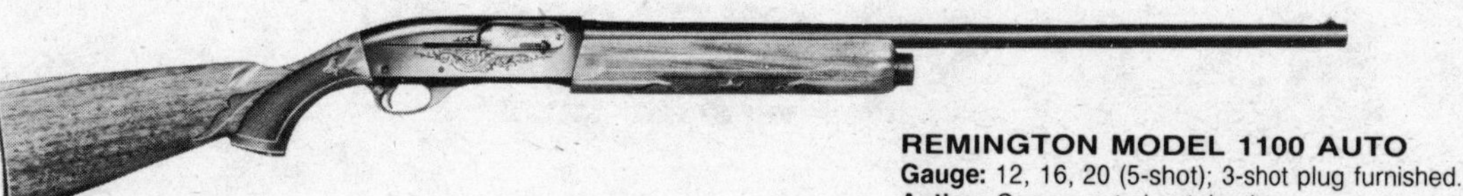

Remington 1100 Magnum

Same as 1100 except: chambered for 3" magnum loads. Available in 12 ga. (30") or 20 ga. (28") Mod. or Full, 14"x1½"x2½" stock with recoil pad, Wgt. 7¾ lbs. **$239.95**
Price: With vent. rib **$264.95**
Price: Left hand model with vent. rib **$269.95**

REMINGTON MODEL 1100 AUTO

Gauge: 12, 16, 20 (5-shot); 3-shot plug furnished.
Action: Gas-operated autoloader.
Barrel: 26" (Imp. Cyl.), 28" (Mod., Full), 30" Full in 12 ga. only.
Stock: 14"x1½"x2½" American Walnut, checkered p.g. and fore-end.
Weight: 12 ga. 7½ lbs., 16 ga. 7⅜ lbs., 20 ga. 7¼ lbs.; 48" over-all (28" bbl.).
Features: Quickly interchangeable barrels within gauge. Matted receiver top with scroll work on both sides of receiver. Crossbolt safety.
Price: .... **$219.95** With vent. rib **$244.95**
Price: Left hand model with vent. rib **$249.95**

Remington 1100D Tournament Auto

Same as 1100 Standard except: vent. rib, better wood, more extensive engraving **$800.00**

Remington 1100F Premier Auto

Same as 1100D except: select wood, better engraving **$1,550.00**
With gold inlay **$2,400.00**

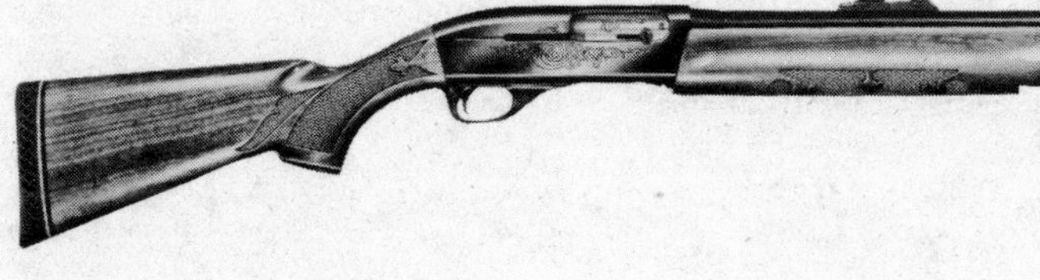

Remington 1100 Deer Gun

Same as 1100 except: 12 ga. only, 22" bbl. (Imp. Cyl.), rifle sights adjustable for w. and e.; recoil pad with white spacer. Weight 7¼ lbs. **$239.95**

Remington 1100 SA Skeet

Same as the 1100 except: 26" bbl., special skeet boring, vent. rib, ivory bead front and metal bead middle sights. 14"x1½"x2½" stock. 20 and 12 ga. Wgt. 7½ lbs.
Price: **$254.95**
Price: 1100 SB (better grade walnut) **$279.95**
For Cutts Comp add **$25.00**
Left hand model with vent. rib **$259.95**
28 & 410 ga., 25" bbl. **$264.95**

Remington 1100 20 ga. Lightweight

Basically the same design as Model 1100, but with special weight-saving features that retain strength and dependability of the standard Model 1100.
Barrel: 28" (Full, Mod.), 26" (Imp. Cyl.).
Weight: 6½ lbs.
Price: .... **$229.95** With vent. rib **$254.95**
Price: 20 ga. Lightweight magnum (28" Full) **$249.95**
Price: With vent. rib **$279.95**

Remington 1100 Small Gauge

Same as 1100 except: 28 ga. 2¾" (5-shot) or 410, 3" (except Skeet, 2½" 4-shot). 45½" over-all. Available in 25" bbl. (Full, Mod., or Imp. Cyl.) only.
Price: Plain bbl. .... **$229.95** With vent. rib **$254.95**

Remington 1100 TB Trap

Same as the 1100 except: better grade wood, recoil pad. 14⅜"x1⅜"x1¾" stock. Wgt. 8¼ lbs. 12 ga. only. 30" (Mod., Full) vent. rib bbl. Ivory bead front and white metal middle sight.
Price: .... **$289.95** With Monte Carlo stock **$299.95**
Price: 1100TB Trap, left hand **$294.95**
Price: With Monte Carlo stock **$304.95**

Remington 1100 Extra bbls.: Plain **$54.95** (20, 28 & 410, **$57.95**). Vent. rib **$79.95** (20, 28 & 410, **$82.95**). Vent. rib Skeet **$84.95.** Vent. rib Trap **$84.95** Deer bbl. **$65.95,** Skeet, with cutts comp. **$109.95.** Available in the same gauges and chokes as shown on guns.

SMITH & WESSON MODEL 1000 AUTO

Gauge: 12 only, 2¾" chamber, 4-shot.
Action: Gas-operated autoloader.
Barrel: 26" (Skeet, Imp. Cyl.), 28" (Imp. Mod., Mod., Full), 30" (Full).
Length: 48" over-all (28" bbl.). **Weight:** 7½ lbs. (28" bbl.).
Stock: 14"x1½"x2⅜", American walnut.
Features: Interchangeable crossbolt safety, vent. rib with front and middle beads, engraved alloy receiver, pressure compensator and floating piston for light recoil.
Price: **$249.95**
Price: Extra barrels (as listed above) **$84.95**

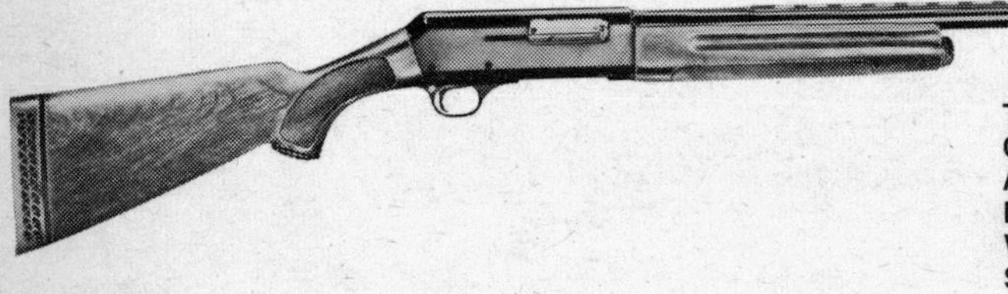

TRADEWINDS H-170 AUTO SHOTGUN

Gauge: 12 only, 2¾" chamber.
Action: Recoil-operated automatic.
Barrel: 26", 28" (Mod.) and 28" (Full), chrome lined.
Weight: 7 lbs.
Stock: Select European walnut stock, p.g. and fore-end hand checkered.
Features: Light alloy receiver, 5-shot tubular magazine, ventilated rib. Imported by Tradewinds.
Price: **$259.50**

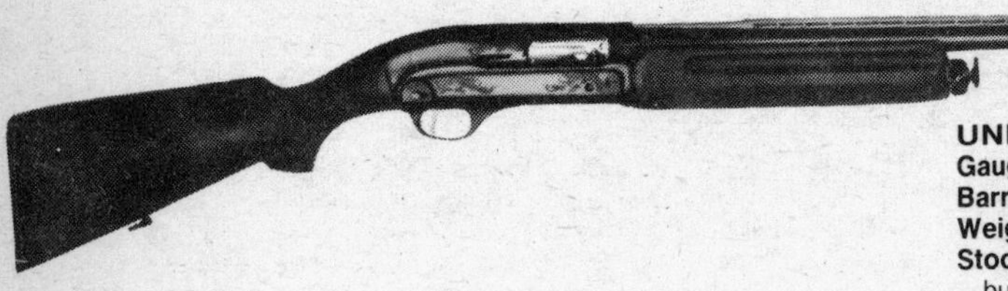

UNIVERSAL BAIKAL MC-21 AUTO SHOTGUN

Gauge: 12 ga., 2¾" chamber. 5-shot.
Barrel: 26" (Imp. Cyl.), 28" (Mod.), 30" (Full). Vent. rib.
Weight: 7½ lbs.
Stock: Hand checkered walnut with cheekpiece. White spacers at p.g. and buttplate. Hand rubbed finish.
Features: Chrome barrel and chamber. Reversible safety. Instant take-down including trigger housing. Interchangeable barrels. Target grade trigger. Magazine cut-off. Imported by Universal Sporting Goods.
Price: **$262.00**

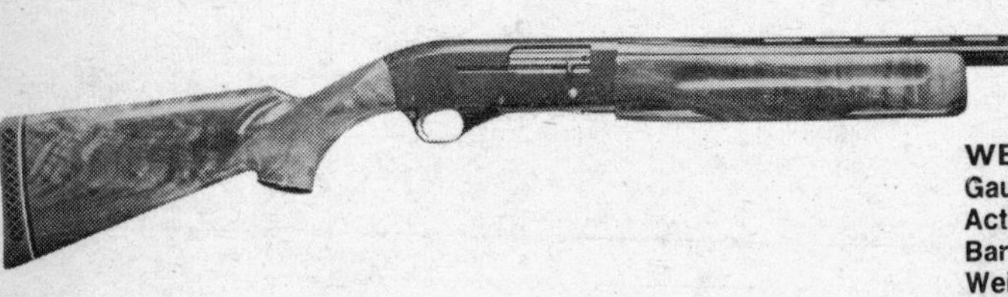

WEATHERBY CENTURION AUTO

Gauge: 12 only, 2¾" chamber.
Action: Gas operated autoloader with "Floating Piston."
Barrel: 26" (Mod., Imp. Cyl, Skeet), 28" (Full, Mod.), 30" (Full), Vent. Rib.
Weight: About 7½ lbs. **Length:** 48¼ (28").
Stock: Walnut, hand checkered p.g. and fore-end, rubber recoil pad with white line spacer.
Features: Cross bolt safety, fluted bolt, gold plated trigger. Extra interchangeable bbls. **$99.95**
Price: Field or Skeet grade . **$289.50** Trap grade **$319.50**

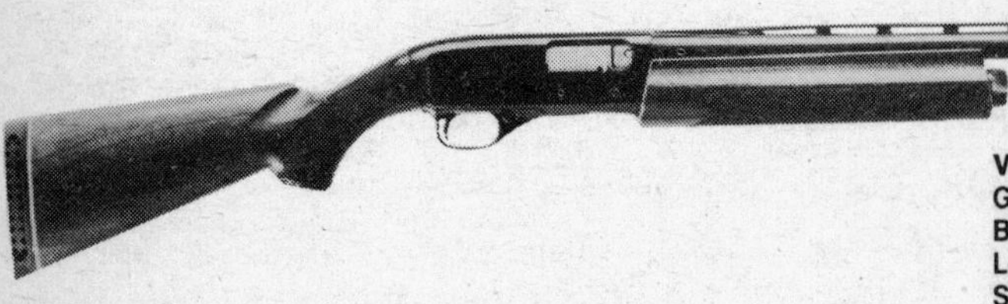

WINCHESTER SUPER-X MODEL 1 AUTO SHOTGUN

Gauge: 12, 4-shot.
Barrel: 26" (Imp. Cyl.), 28" (Mod., Full), 30" (Full).
Length: 46" over-all (26" bbl.)
Stock: American walnut with cut-checkered p.g. and fore-end, 14"x1½"x2½" (Field).
Sights: Metal bead front.
Features: Receiver and all metal parts made of machined steel. Straight-line, 3-piece bolt, short-stroke gas system, all steel trigger assembly, steel shell carrier.
Price: Vent. rib **$330.00**
Extra Barrels:
Price: Field, plain, 26", 28", 30" (Full, Mod., Imp. Cyl.) **$62.95**
Price: Field, vent. rib, 26", 28", 30" (Full, Mod., Imp. Cyl.) **$92.95**
Price: Trapor Skeet, 26", 30", (Full, Skeet) **$94.95**

Winchester Super-X Model 1 Trap and Skeet Models

Same as Field model except: Trap has 30" bbl., vent. rib (Full) and regular or Monte Carlo stock. Engraved receiver, red bead front sight, black rubber recoil pad with white spacer—**$385.00.** for regular stock, **$395.00** for Monte Carlo. Skeet model has 26" vent. rib barrel (Skeet), otherwise same as trap gun—**$385.00.**

SHOTGUNS—AUTOLOADING

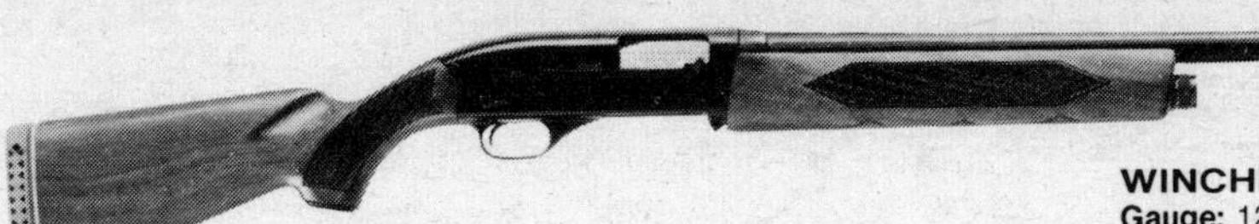

WINCHESTER 1400 AUTOMATIC MARK II

Gauge: 12, and 20 (3-shot).
Action: Gas operated autoloader. Front-locking 4-lug rotating bolt locks in bbl. Alloy receiver. Push button action release.
Barrel: Winchoke 28″, Full, Mod. and Imp. Cyl. tubes only. Metal bead front sight.
Stock: 14″x1½″x2⅜″. American walnut, new-design checkered p.g. and fore-end; fluted comb, p.g. cap, recoil pad.
Weight: With 26″ bbl., 20 ga. 6½ lbs., 16, 12 ga. 6¾ lbs.; 46⅝″ over-all.
Features: Self-compensating valve adjusts for std. or magnum loads. Bbls. interchangeable without fitting. Crossbolt safety in front of trigger guard.
Price: .... **$194.95** With vent. rib **$214.95**

SHOTGUNS—SLIDE ACTION

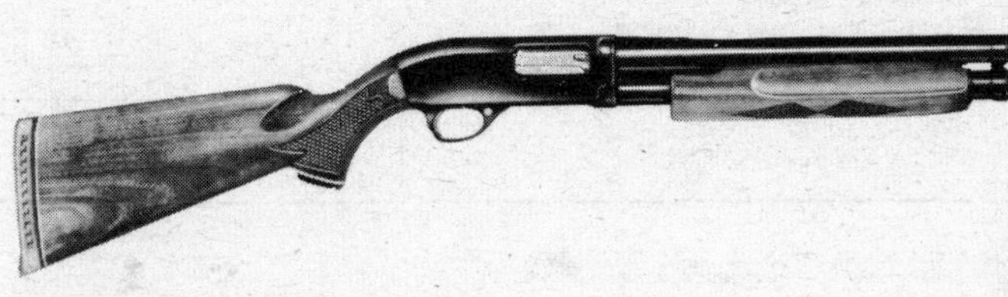

HI-STANDARD FLITE-KING DELUXE PUMP GUNS

Gauge: 12, 20, 28, and 410 (6 shots; 3-shot plug furnished).
Action: "Free-falling" slide action.
Barrel: 12 ga., 30″ (Full); 12, 20 ga., 28″ (Mod. or Full), 26″ (Imp. Cyl.); 410, 26″ (Full). 12 ga. barrels interchangeable.
Stock: 14″x1½″x2½″. Walnut, checkered p.g. and fore-end. Recoil pad except: 410 & Skeet guns.
Weight: 12 ga. 7¾ lbs., 20, 410 ga. 6½ lbs.
Features: Side ejection.
Price: Field **$148.50**
Price: 12 ga., with adj. choke, 27″ bbl **$154.00**
Price: De Luxe Rib, with vent. rib, w/o adj. choke **$170.00**
Price: 12 and 20 ga., as above with adj. choke **$175.95**
Price: Brush, 12 ga. only with 20″ cyl. bbl., grooved fore-end, adj. rifle sights. Stock (14¼″x1½″x1⅞″) 39¾″ over-all **$170.50**

Hi-Standard Flite-King Trap

Same features as Flite-King Skeet except: 30″ full choke; Monte Carlo stock with recoil pad. About 8¼ lbs. 12 ga. only **$198.00**

Hi-Standard Flite-King Skeet

Same as Flite-King DeLuxe except: Vent. rib, no recoil pad; 26″ Skeet choke bbl.; all external parts high polished; internal parts super finished; better grade American walnut stock (14″x1½″x2½″) and fore-end with cabinet finish. Wgt. 12 ga. 7½ lbs., 20, 6¼ lbs., 28 and 410 ga. 6¼ lbs. **$186.95**

ITHACA MODEL 37 FEATHERLIGHT

Gauge: 12, 16, 20 (5-shot; 3-shot plug furnished).
Action: Slide; takedown; bottom ejection.
Barrel: 26″, 28″, 30″ in 12 ga. 26″ or 28″ in 16 or 20 ga. (Full, Mod. or Imp. Cyl.).
Stock: 14″x1⅝″x2⅝″. Checkered walnut capped p.g. stock and fore-end.
Weight: 12 ga. 6½ lbs., 16 ga. 6 lbs., 20 ga. 5¾ lbs.
Features: Ithaca Raybar front sight; decorated receiver; crossbolt safety; action release for removing shells.
Price: **$169.95**
Price: With vent. rib stock (14″x1½″x2½″) **$194.95**

Ithaca Model 37 Deerslayer

Same as Model 37 except: 26″ or 20″ bbl. designed for rifled slugs; sporting rear sight, Raybar front sight; rear sight ramp grooved for Redfield long eye relief scope mount. 12, 16, or 20 gauge. With checkered stock, beavertail fore-end and recoil pad.
Price: **$189.95**
Price: As above with special select walnut stock **$209.95**

Ithaca Model 37 De Luxe Featherlight

Same as Model 37 except: checkered stock with p.g. cap; beavertail fore-end; recoil pad. Wgt. 12 ga. 6¾ lbs.
Price: .... **$174.95** With vent. rib **$199.95**

Ithaca Model 37 Supreme

Same as Model 37 except: hand checkered beavertail fore-end and p.g. stock, Ithaca recoil pad and vent. rib **$319.95**
37 Supreme also with Skeet (14″x1½″x2½″) or Trap (14½″x1½″x1⅞″) stocks at no extra charge. Other options available at extra charge.

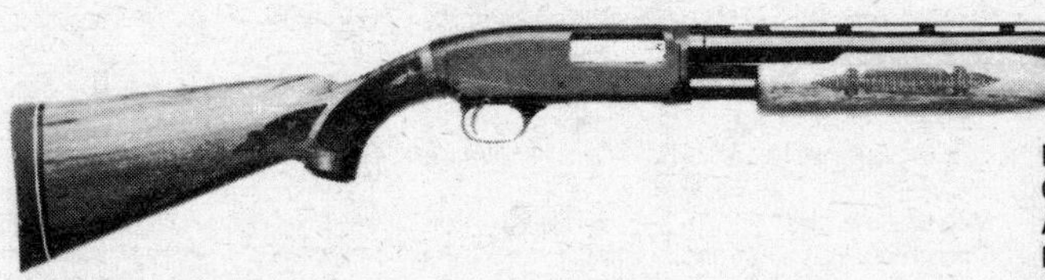

MARLIN 120 MAGNUM PUMP GUN

Gauge: 12 ga. (2¾″ or 3″ chamber) 5-shot; 3-shot plug furnished.
Action: Hammerless, side ejecting, slide action.
Barrel: 26″ (Imp. Cyl.), 28″ (Mod.), 30″ (Full), with vent. rib. or 40″ MXR plain.
Stock: 14″x1½″x2⅜″. Checkered walnut, capped p.g., semi-beavertail checkered fore-end.
Length: 50½″ over-all (30″ bbl.). **Weight:** About 7¾ lbs.
Features: Interchangeable bbls., slide lock release; large button cross-bolt safety.
Price: **$169.95**
Price: Extra barrels **$55.00**

Marlin 120 Trap Gun

Same as 120 Magnum except: Monte Carlo stock and full fore-end with hand-cut checkering. Stock dimensions are 14¼″x1¼″x1¾″. Available with 30″ Full choke barrel with vent. rib. **$234.95**

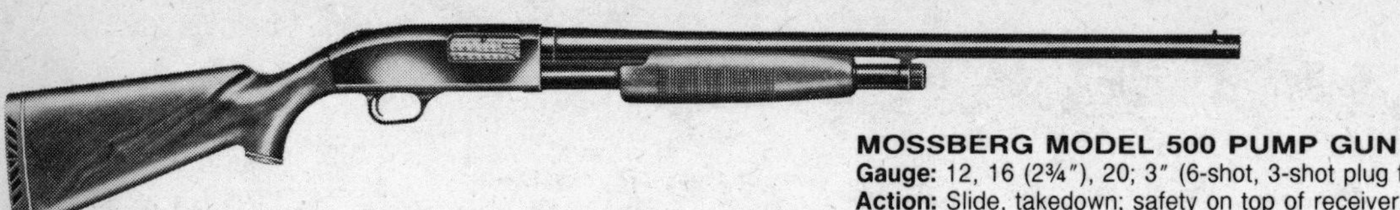

MOSSBERG MODEL 500 PUMP GUN

Gauge: 12, 16 (2¾″), 20; 3″ (6-shot, 3-shot plug furnished).
Action: Slide, takedown; safety on top of receiver.
Barrel: 26″ (Imp. Cyl.) 28″ (Full or Mod.), 30″ (Full), 12 ga. only. Also 12 ga. 18½″ cylinder, for police only).
Stock: 14″x1½″x2½″. Walnut p.g., extension fore-end. Recoil pad. 13 oz. steel plug furnished for use with Magnum barrel.
Weight: 12 ga. 6¾ lbs., 45¼″ over-all (26″ bbl.).
Features: Easy interchangeability of barrels; side ejection; disconnecting trigger makes doubles impossible; straight-line feed.
Price: Standard barrel **$137.06**
Price: With C-Lect Choke, 3″ Mag., or 24″ Slugster bbls. **$142.71**
Price: Extra barrel, 2¾″ chamber **$40.90**
Price: Extra Magnum, C-Lect Choke or Slug, bbl. **$40.90**

Mossberg Model 500A Super Grade

Similar to the Model 500 except: vent. rib bbls. in 12 ga. (2¾″) or 20 ga. (3″); 26″ (Skeet), 28″ (Mod., Full), and 30″ Full (12 ga. only) 2¾″ or 3″ mag. Checkered p.g. and fore-end stock with fluted comb and recoil pad (14″x1½″x2½″).
Price: 12 or 20 ga. **$153.28**
Price: 12 ga. 3″ Magnum or C-Lect Choke 12 and 20 ga. **$161.79**

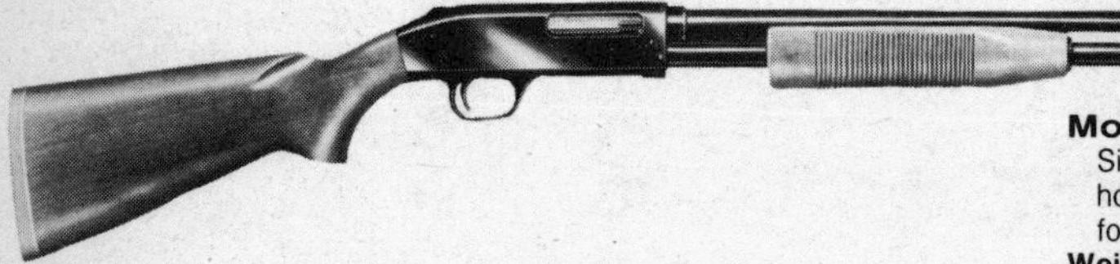

Mossberg Model 500E

Similar to Model 500 except: 410 bore only, 26″ bbl. (Full, Mod. or Imp. Cyl.); holds six 2¾″ or five 3″ shells. Walnut stock with smooth p.g. and grooved fore-end, fluted comb and recoil pad (14″x1¼″x2½″).
Weight: About 5¾ lbs., length over-all 46″.
Price: Standard barrels **$137.06**
Price: Pigeon Grade, 26″, Mod., or Skeet bbl., vent. rib **$192.44**

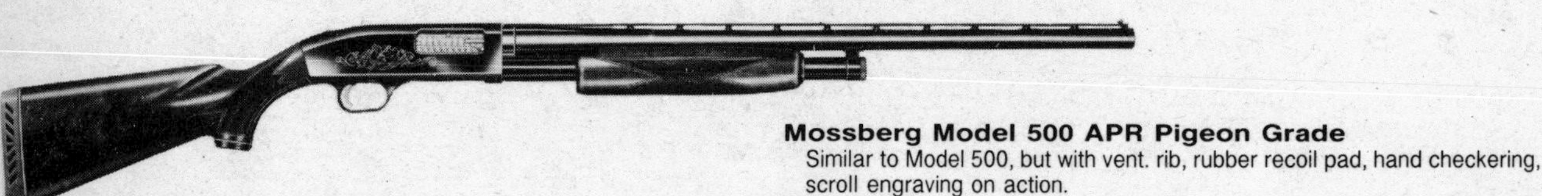

Mossberg Model 500 APR Pigeon Grade

Similar to Model 500, but with vent. rib, rubber recoil pad, hand checkering, scroll engraving on action.
Price: **$192.44**
Price: 500 APTR trap gun 30″ full choke barrel, M.C. stock, 14½″x1½″x2″, additional barrels available. **$199.98**

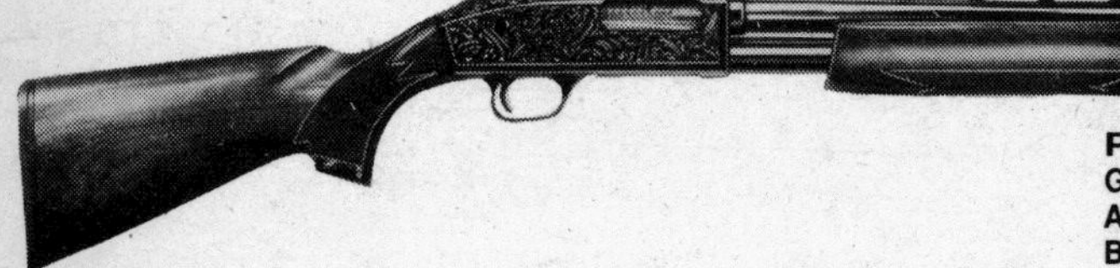

PEDERSEN 4000/4500 DELUXE PUMP SHOTGUN

Gauge: 12, 20 410 (2¾″ chamber).
Action Slide, takedown.
Barrel: 26″, 28″, 30″ (Full, Mod., Imp., Cyl., Skeet Trap). "Slugster" 12 ga. bbl. interchangeable.
Weight: 6¾ lbs. **Length:** 45¼″ over-all (26″ bbl.).
Stock: 14″x1½″x2½″. Select hand checkered American walnut with recoil pad.
Features: Ornately engraved receiver; deep lustre blue; rosewood p.g. cap.
Price: Deluxe Model 4000 Hunting and Skeet (full coverage floral engraved receiver) **$275.00**
Price: M4000 Trap **$283.00**
Price: M4500 Hunting and Skeet (scroll engraved receiver) **$225.00**
Price: M4500 Trap **$233.00**

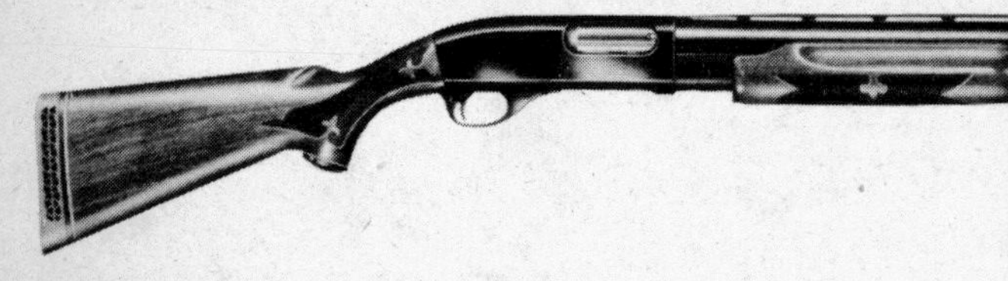

REMINGTON 870 WINGMASTER PUMP GUN

Gauge: 12, 16, 20, (5-shot; 3-shot wood plug).
Action: Takedown, slide action.
Barrel: 12, 16, 20, ga., 26″ (Imp. Cyl.); 28″ (Mod. or Full); 12 ga., 30″ (Full).
Stock: 14″x1⅝″x2½″. Checkered walnut, p.g.; fluted extension fore-end; fitted rubber recoil pad.
Weight: 7 lbs., 12 ga. (7¾ lbs. with Vari-Weight plug); 6¾ lbs., 16 ga.; 6½ lbs., 20 ga. 48½″ over-all (28″ bbl.).
Features: Double action bars, crossbolt safety. Receiver machined from solid steel. Hand fitted action.
Price: Plain bbl. .... **$159.95** Vent. rib **$184.95**
Price: Riot gun, 18″ or 20″ Riot bore, (12 ga. only) **$144.95**
Price: Riot gun, 20″ Imp. Cyl., rifle sights **$154.95**
Price: Left hand, vent. rib., 12 and 20 ga. **$189.95**

Remington 870 Small Gauges

Exact copies of the large ga. Model 870, except that guns are offered in 20, 28 and 410 ga. 25″ barrel (Full, Mod., Imp. Cyl.).
Plain barrel **$169.95**
D and F grade prices same as large ga. M870 prices.
Price: With vent. rib barrel **$194.95**
Price: Lightweight Magnum, 20 ga. plain bbl. (5¾ lbs.) **$189.95**
Price: Lightweight Magnum, 20 ga., vent. rib bbl. **$214.95**

Remington 870D Tournament

Same as 870 except: better walnut, hand checkering, Engraved receiver & bbl. Vent.-rib. Stock dimensions to order **$800.00**

Remington 870F Premier

Same as M870D, except select walnut, better engraving **$1,550.00**

SHOTGUNS—SLIDE ACTION

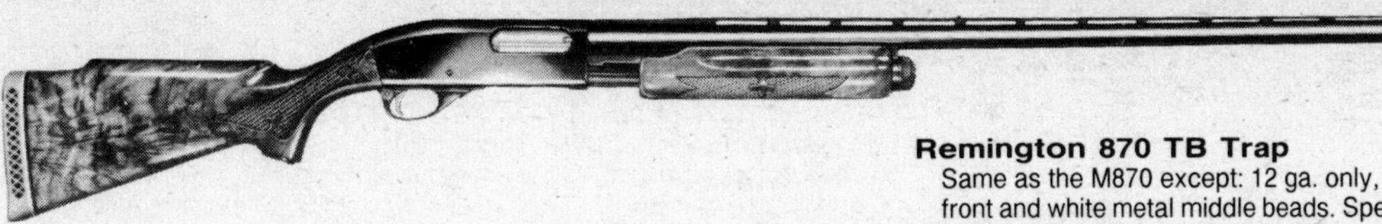

Remington 870 Extra Barrels
Plain **$44.95.** Vent. rib **$69.95.** Vent. rib Skeet **$77.95.** Vent. rib Trap **$74.95.** 34″ Trap **$84.95.** With rifle sights **$55.95.** Available in the same gauges and chokes as shown on guns.

Remington 870 Magnum
Same as the M870 except 3″ chamber, 12 ga. 30″ bbl. (Mod. or Full), 20 ga. 28″ bbl. (Mod. or Full). Recoil pad installed. Wgt., 12 ga. 8 lbs., 20 ga. 7½ lbs.
Price: Plain bbl. .... **$179.95** Vent. rib bbl. **$204.95**
Price: Left hand model, vent rib. bbl. **$229.95**

Remington Model 870 Brushmaster Deluxe
Carbine version of the M870 with 20″ bbl. (Imp. Cyl.) for rifled slugs. 40½″ over-all, wgt. 6½ lbs. Recoil pad. Adj. rear, ramp front sights. 12 or 20 ga. Deluxe **$179.95**

Remington 870 TB Trap
Same as the M870 except: 12 ga. only, 30″ (Mod., Full) vent. rib. bbl., ivory front and white metal middle beads. Special sear, hammer and trigger assy. 14⅜″x1½″x1⅞″ stock with recoil pad. Hand fitted action and parts. Wgt. 8 lbs. **$224.95**
Price: With Monte Carlo stock **$234.95**
Price: Add **$5.00** for left hand model

REMINGTON 870 ALL AMERICAN
Gauge: 12 only.
Barrel: 30″ full choke.
Weight: 7 lbs.
Stock: Select walnut, fluted extension fore end, cut checkered.
Features: Receiver, trigger quard and breech fully engraved. Special "All American" shield fitted to left side of receiver. RK-W finished wood. Pistol grip cap has gold plate for initials. Supplied with luggage type, foam lined case.
Price: Standard or Monte Carlo stock **$575.00**

Remington 870 SA Skeet
Same as the M870 except: 26″ bbl. Skeet bored. Vent. rib with ivory front and white metal middle beads. 14″x1⅝″x2½″ stock with rubber recoil pad, 12 or ga. only **$189.95**
Price: Add for Cutts comp. **$25.00**
Price: 28 and 410 ga., 25″ bbl., no recoil pad **$199.95**

Savage Model 30-D Combination
Same as standard Model 30-D except: comes with an interchangeable 22″ slug barrel for deer. 12 gauge only **$183.95**

Savage Model 30 Field Grade
Same as Model 30 except plain bbl. and receiver, hard rubber buttplate.
Price: **$127.50**

SAVAGE MODEL 30-D PUMP GUN
Gauge: 12, 20, and 410, 5-shot (410, 4-shot) 3-shot plug furnished. All gauges chambered for 3″ Magnum shells.
Action: Slide, hammerless, take-down; side ejection; top tang safety.
Barrel: Vent. rib. 12, 20 ga. 26″ (Imp. Cyl.); 28″ (Mod. or Full); 12 ga., 30″ (Full); 410, 26″ (Full).
Stock: 14″x1½″x2½″. Walnut, checkered p.g., grooved extension fore-end, recoil pad.
Weight: 7 lbs. (410, 6¼ lbs.). Over-all 49½″ (30″ bbl.).
Features: Decorated steel receiver; plated trigger.
Price: **$148.50**

Savage Model 30 Slug Gun
Same as the Model 30 Field Grade but with 22″ bbl., 12 or 20 ga. only, with rifle sights **$131.75**

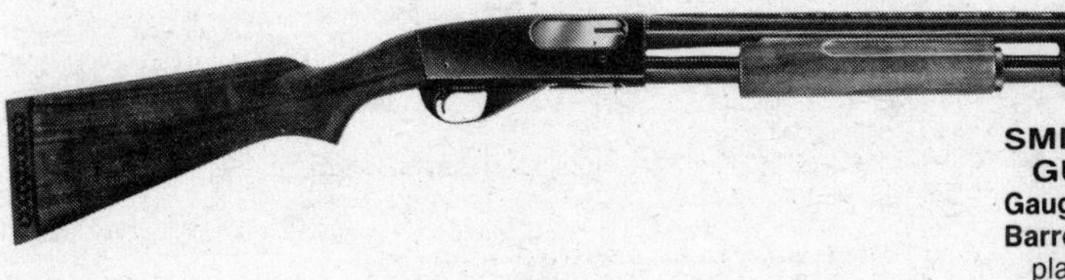

SMITH & WESSON MODEL 916 EASTFIELD PUMP GUN
Gauge: 12, 20 (3″), 16 (2¾″), 6-shot (3-shot plug urnished).
Barrel: 20″ (Cyl.), 26″ (Imp. Cyl.), 28″ (Mod., Full or adj. choke) 30″ (Full), plain. Vent. rib 26″, 28″, 30″.
Weight: 7¼ lbs. (28″ plain bbl.).
Stock: 14″x2½″x1⅝″, American walnut, fluted comb, finger-grooved fore-end.
Features: Vent. rib, vent. recoil pad, adj. choke available as options. Satin finish steel receiver with non-glare top.
Price: Plain bbl., no recoil pad **$110.50**
Price: Plain bbl. with recoil pad **$115.00**
Price: Vent. rib and recoil pad (illus.) **$131.75**

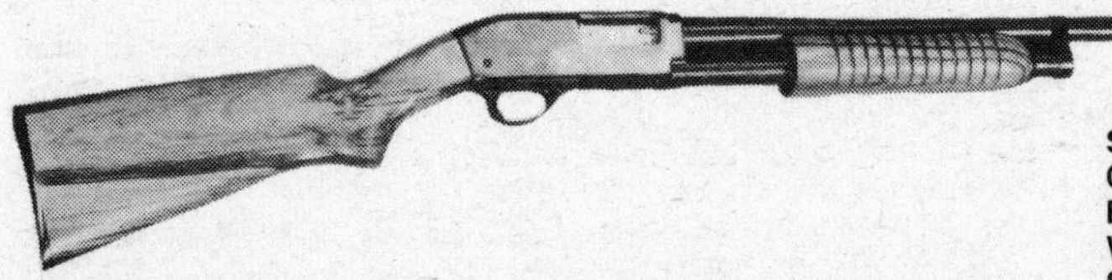

SQUIRES BINGHAM M30/28 PUMP SHOTGUN
Gauge: 12 ga. (2¾″ chamber), 5-shot.
Barrel: 20″ (Cyl.), 28″ (Mod.), 30″ (Full).
Weight: 7 lbs. **Length:** 49¾″ over-all.
Stock: Pulong Dalaga wood.
Sights: Brass bead front.
Features: Blued frame and barrel. Cross-bolt safety. Damascene bolt. 5-shot capacity, plugged for 3. Imported from the Philippines by American Import.
Price: **$109.95**

SHOTGUNS—SLIDE ACTION

WEATHERBY PATRICIAN PUMP

Gauge: 12 only, 2¾" chamber.
Action: Short stroke slide action.
Barrel: 26" (Mod. Imp. Cyl, Skeet), 28" (Full, Mod.), 30" (Full) Vent. Rib.
Weight: About 7½ lbs. **Length:** 48⅛ (28" bbl.)
Stock: Walnut hand checkered p.g. and fore-end, white line spacers at p.g. cap and recoil pad.
Features: Short stroke action, hidden magazine cap, crossbolt safety. Extra interchangeable bbls. **$89.95**
Price: Field or Skeet grade **$249.50** Trap grade **$279.50**

WESTERN FIELD 550 PUMP SHOTGUN

Gauge: 12 and 20.
Action: Slide action, takedown; top tang safety.
Barrel: 12 ga. 26" (Variable); 28" (Mod.); 30" (Full); 20 ga. 26" (Variable); 28" (Mod., Full).
Stock: Walnut finished p.g. stock, molded buttplate, serrated fore-end.
Weight: 8½ lbs.
Features: Straight-line feed, interchangeable bbls., trigger disconnector prevents doubling.
Price: **$97.00**
As above, but with variable choke in 12 or 20 ga. **$120.00**
Slug gun with 24 bbl. without choke **$135.00**
Magnum 12 ga., 30" bbl. (Full Choke) **$97.00**
Deluxe Vent. rib models available, fixed or variable choke **$155.00**

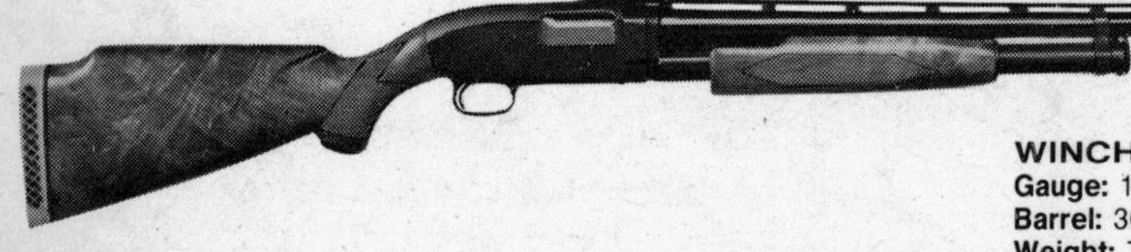

WINCHESTER MODEL 12 TRAP

Gauge: 12 only, 2¾"; 6-shot (3-shot plug).
Barrel: 30" (Full); vent. rib.
Weight: 7¾ lbs. **Length:** 49¾" over-all.
Stock: Select walnut (14⅜"x1⅜"x1⅞"); Monte Carlo measures 14⅜"x1½"x2⅛".
Features: Vent. rib; hand checkered stock; engine turned bolt.
Price: **$460.00**
Price: Monte Carlo stock **$470.00**

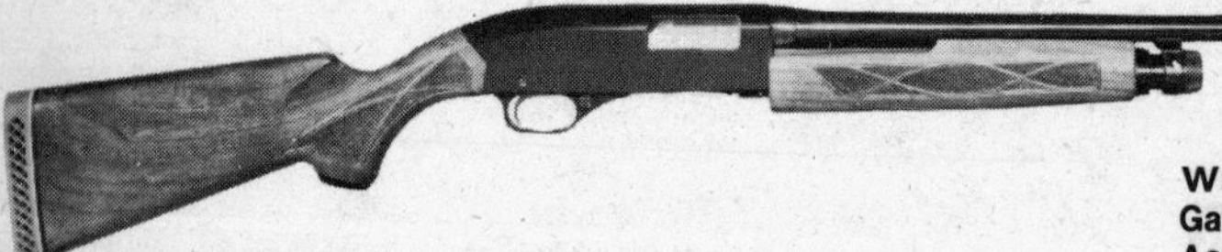

WINCHESTER 1200 FIELD PUMP GUN

Gauge: 12 and 20 (5-shot; 3-shot plug installed).
Action: Slide; front locking 4-lug rotating bolt locks into bbl. Alloy receiver, cross-bolt safety in front of trigger guard. Take-down.
Barrel: 26" (Imp. Cyl.), 28" (Mod., Full) and 30" Full (12 ga. only). Metal bead front sight.
Stock: 14"x1⅜"x2⅜". American walnut with new-design checkered p.g. and fore-end; fluted comb, recoil pad. Steel p.g. cap.
Weight: 12 ga. 6½ lbs. with 26" bbl. 46⅝" over-all.
Price: . . . . **$149.95** With vent. rib **$169.95**

Consult our Directory pages for the location of firms mentioned.

Winchester 1200 Field 3" Magnum

Same as 1200 except: 12 and 20 ga. only, 2¾" or 3" shells, 28" and 30" full choke bbls., 3 lbs. with 38" bbl., 48⅝" over-all.
Price: . . . . **$159.95** With vent. rib **$179.95**

Winchester 1200 Extra Barrels: Field w/o sights, 12, 20 ga. **$47.95.** Field with vent. rib, 12, 20 ga. **$67.95**

Winchester 1200 with interchangeable choke tubes which are screwed into the barrel and tightened with supplied wrench. Available in 12, 16, and 20 ga. (28") Mod. tube. Price: Field **$154.95** vent. rib **$174.95.** Extra tubes in Full, Mod. or Imp. Cyl. **$5.95.** Wrench **$1.50.**

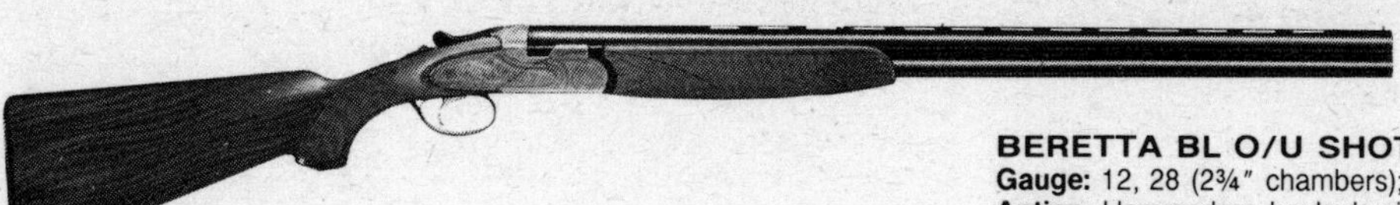

BERETTA BL O/U SHOTGUNS

Gauge: 12, 28 (2¾″ chambers); 12 mag., 20 (3″ chambers).
Action: Hammerless boxlock with gold-plated single-selective trigger. BL-6 has sideplates.
Barrel: 12 ga., 30″ or 28″ (Mod., Full), 26″ (Imp. Cyl., Mod.); 20 ga., 28″ (Mod., Full), 26″ (Mod., Full); 28 ga., 28″ (Mod., Full), 26″ (Imp. Cyl, Mod.); 12 ga. Trap, 30″ (Imp. Mod., Full); 12 or 20 ga. Skeet, 26″ (Skeet, Skeet).
Weight: 7¼ lbs. (12 ga.), 6 lbs (20 and 28 ga.), 7½ lbs (Trap and 12 ga. Mag.).
Stock: 14⅛″x1½″x2½″ (Standard), 14⅜″x1⅜″x1¾″ (Trap), hand-checkered European walnut, p.g.
Features: Hand-engraved receivers, ventilated rib. BL-4 has more engraving and checkering than BL-3, is available with two sets of barrels. BL-6 has additional hand-engraved sideplates, specially selected wood.
Price: From .... **$475.00** (BL-3) to **$875.00** (BL-6 Trap or Skeet)

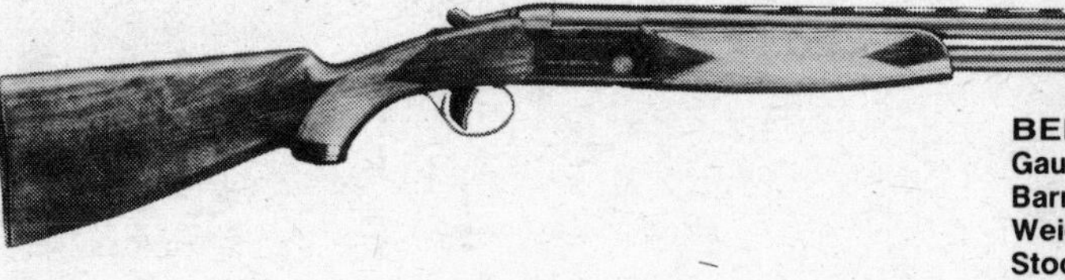

BERETTA BL-2/S O/U SHOTGUN

Gauge: 12 ga., 3″ chambers on magnum model.
Barrel: 26″ (I.C. & Mod.); 28″ (Mod. & Full); 30″ mag. (Mod. & Full). Vent. rib.
Weight: 7 to 7¼ lbs.
Stock: 14⅛″x1½″x2½″. Hand checkered, walnut finish.
Sights: Metal bead front.
Features: Selective "Speed-Trigger"—pull top part of trigger for more open-choked (lower) barrel, bottom part for upper (tighter-choked) barrel, or reverse order.
Price: 3″ Mag. **$395.00**
Price: Field, 28″ bbl. **$380.00**
Price: Field, 26″ bbl. **$380.00**

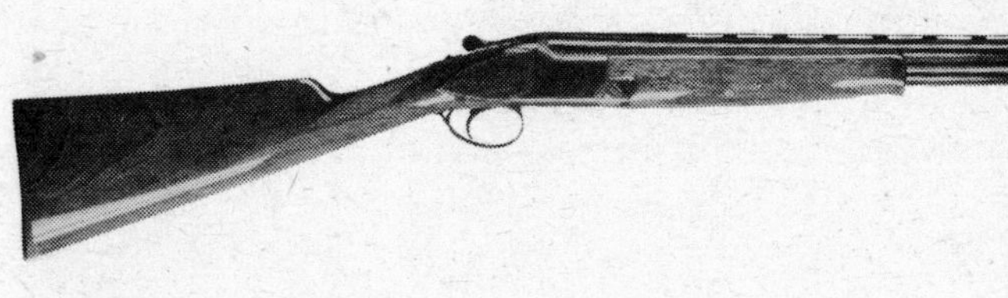

BROWNING SUPERPOSED SUPER-LIGHT

Gauge: 12, & 20 2¾″ chamber.
Action: Boxlock, top lever, single selective trigger. Bbl. selector combined with manual tang safety.
Barrels: 26½″ (Mod. & Full, or Imp. Cyl. & Mod.)
Stock: Straight grip (14¼″ x 1⅝″ x 2½″) hand checkered (fore-end and grip) select walnut.
Weight: 6⅜ lbs., average.
Features: Slender, tapered vent. rib. Hand rubbed finish, engraved receiver.
Price: Grade 1 .... **$1,170.00**
Diana **$2,000.00**
Midas **$2,700.00**

Browning Superposed Lightning Trap 12

Same as Browning Lightning Superposed except: semi-beavertail fore-end and ivory sights; stock, 14⅜″x1 7/16″x1⅝″. 7¾ lbs. 30″ (Full & Full, Full & Imp. Mod. or Full and Mod.) Grade 1 **$1,120.00,** Diana **$1,970.00,** Midas **$2,670.00.**

Superposed Broadway Trap 12

Same as Browning Lightning Superposed except: ⅝″ wide vent. rib; stock, 14⅜″x1 7/16″x1⅝″. 30″ or 32″ (Imp. Mod, Full; Mod., Full; Full, Full). 8 lbs. with 32″ bbls. Grade 1 **$1,160.00,** Diana **$2,010.00,** Midas **$2,720.00.**

Browning Superposed Lightning Skeet

Same as Standard Skeet except: 12 and 20 ga. only. Wgt. 6½-7¾ lbs. Grade 1 **$1,200.00,** Diana **$1,970.00,** Midas **$2,670.00.**

Browning Superposed Combinations

Standard and Lightning models are available with these factory fitted extra barrels: 12 and 20 ga., same gauge bbls.; 12 ga., 20 ga. bbls.; 20 ga., extra sets 28 and/or 410 gauge; 28 ga., extra 410 bbls. Extra barrels may be had in Lightning weights with Standard models and vice versa. Prices range from **$1,675.00** (12, 20 ga., one set extra bbls. same gauge) for the Grade 1 Standard to about **$6,500.00** for the Midas grade in a 4-barrel matched set (12, 20, 28 and 410 gauges).

Browning Superposed Magnum 12

Browning Superposed 3″ chambers; 30″ (Full and Full or Full and Mod.) barrels, Stock, 14¼″x1⅝″x2½″ with factory fitted recoil pad. Weight 8 lbs. Grade 1, **$1,100.00,** Diana **$1,950.00,** Midas **$2,650.00.**

Browning Superposed Lightning

7-7¼ lbs. in 12 ga. 6-6¼ lbs. in 20 ga. Grade 1 **$1,100.00,** Diana **$1,950.00,** Midas **$2,650.00.**

Browning Superposed All-Gauge Skeet Set

Consists of four matched sets of barrels in 12, 20, 28 and 410 ga. Available in either 26½″ or 28″ length. Each bbl. set has a ¼″ wide vent. rib with two ivory sight beads. Grade 1 receiver is hand engraved and stock and fore-end are checkered. Weight 7 lbs., 10 oz. (26½″ bbls.), 7 lbs., 12 oz. (28″ bbls.). Grade 1 **$3,400.00,** Diana **$4,800.00,** Midas **$6,500.00.**

SHOTGUNS—OVER-UNDER

BROWNING CITORI O/U SHOTGUN

Gauge: 12 and 20 ga.
Barrel: 26", 28" (Mod. & Full, Imp. Cyl. & Mod.), 30" (Mod. & Full, Full & Full) in 12 ga., 26" or 28" in 20 ga., same chokes.
Weight: 7½ lbs. (26", 12 ga.) 6¾ lbs. (26", 20 ga.)
Length: 43" over-all (26" bbl.).
Stock: Dense walnut, hand checkered, full pistol grip. Beavertail fore-end. Recoil pad on 12 ga. field guns and Trap and skeet models.
Sights: Medium raised sights, German nickel silver.
Features: Barrel selector integral with safety, auto. ejectors, three-piece takedown.
Price: Field Model (12 or 20 ga.) **$395.00**
Price: Trap Model, 12 ga. only (30" bbl. only) **$415.00**
Price: Skeet Model, 12 or 20 ga. (26" & 28" bbls.) **$405.00**

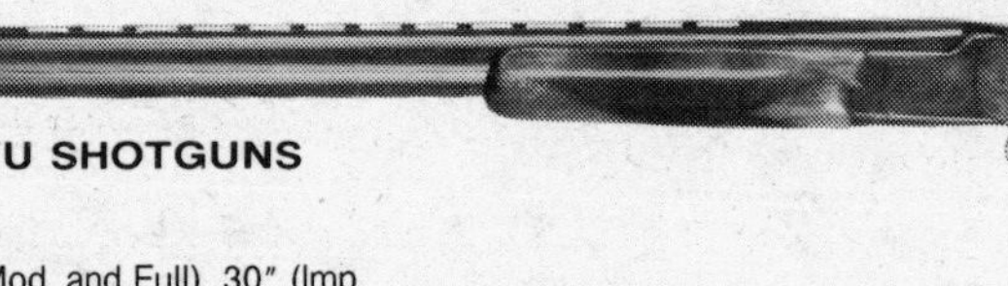

CHARLES DALY VENTURE GRADE O/U SHOTGUNS

Gauge: 12 (2¾" chambers), 20 (3" chambers).
Action: Boxlock, single selective inertia trigger.
Barrel: 26" (I.C. and Mod., Skeet and Skeet), 28" (Mod. and Full), 30" (Imp. Mod. and Full) 12 only.
Weight: 12 ga., 7 lbs.; 20 ga., 6 lbs. 5 oz.
Stock: 14"x1½"x2½" checkered walnut, p.g.
Features: Ventilated rib, manual safety, auto ejectors. Imported from Japan by Sloan's.
Price: **$399.00**
Price: 30", Monte Carlo Venture Trap **$425.00**
Price: Venture Skeet **$415.00**

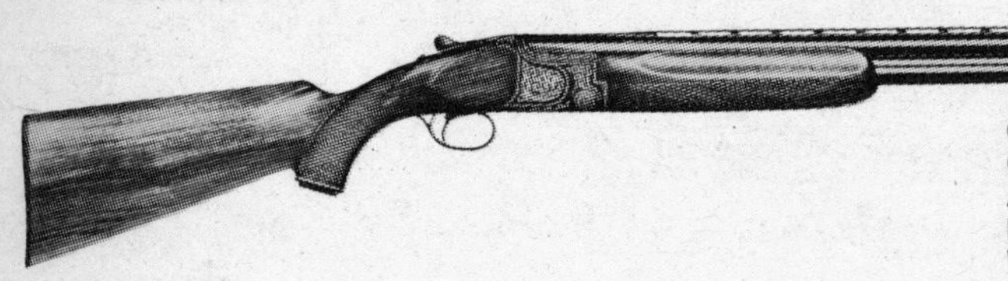

CHARLES DALY SUPERIOR GRADE O/U SHOTGUN

Gauge: 12, 20 (2¾" chambers except 20. Field models, 3")
Action: Boxlock, single selective inertia trigger.
Barrel: Same as Field Grade plus 28" 12, 20 (Skeet & Skeet).
Weight: 12 ga., 7¼ lbs.; others, 6 lbs. 10 oz.
Stock: 14"x1½"x2½" checkered walnut, p.g., beavertail fore-end.
Features: Ventilated rib. "Selexor" (Diamond Grade only) permits shooter to select auto ejection or merely extraction. Imported from Japan by Sloan's.
Price: Superior Grade **$450.00**
Price: Superior Grade Trap **$450.00**
Price: Diamond Grade, Field, Skeet, Trap **$550.00**
Price: Diamond Grade Flattop Trap **$595.00**

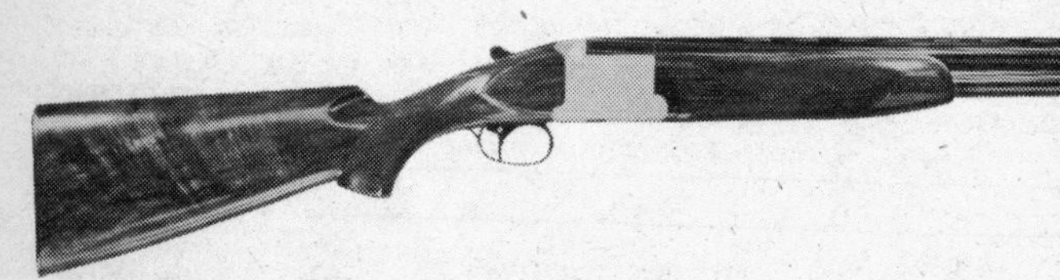

FRANCHI FALCONET O/U SHOTGUN

Gauge: 12 or 20 ga.
Action: Hammerless with overhead-sear trigger and auto. safety.
Barrel: 24", 12 or 20 ga. (Cyl. & Imp. Cyl.); 26", all except 410 (Imp. Cyl. & Mod.), 410 (Mod. & Full); 28", all (Mod. & Full); 30", 12 ga. (Mod. & Full); 26", all except 16 ga. (Skeet 1-Skeet 2); 30" 12 ga. Trap (Mod. & Full).
Weight: 6 lbs. (approx.) except Skeet 7½ lbs. and Trap 8¼ lbs.
Stock: Epoxy finished walnut.
Features: Chrome-lined barrels, selective single trigger, auto ejectors. Available with "Buckskin" or "Ebony" (Blue) colored Frames. Skeet and Trap models have 10mm rib, middle sight, non-auto safety. Imported from Italy by Stoeger Industries.
Price: Ebony 12 & 20 ga. **$499.95**
Price: Buckskin **$499.95**
Price: Silver **$599.95**
Price: Model 3003 Trap or Skeet **$3,000.00**
Price: Peregrine 400 .... **$695.00**
Price: Peregrine 451 .... **$595.00**

GARCIA BRONCO COMBINATION O/U

Caliber: 22/410, 3" chamber.
Barrel: 18½".
Weight: 3½ lbs. **Length:** 32" over-all.
Stock: Skeletonized crackle finish alloy casting.
Sights: Post front, open rear.
Features: Cross-bolt safety; wing-out chamber; push button safety; instant takedown.
Price: **$69.00**

HIGH STANDARD SHADOW SEVEN O/U SHOTGUN

Gauge: 12 (2¾" chambers).
Action: Boxlock.
Barrel: 27½" (Skeet & Skeet, Mod. & Imp., Full & Mod.); 29¾" (Full & Full, Imp. Mod. & Full).
Weight: 8 lbs. (29¾" bbl.)
Stock: American walnut. Hand checkered p.g. and fore-end. Field & Skeet: 14"x1⅜"1⅞"; Trap: 14⅜"x1⅜"x1⅞".
Sights: Metal bead front.
Features: Solid frame. Single selective gold-plated trigger, automatic selective ejectors. Manual safety. Vent. rib. Imported by High Standard.
Price: **$499.95**

Consult our Directory pages for the location of firms mentioned.

HIGH STANDARD SHADOW INDY O/U SHOTGUN
Gauge: 12 (2¾" chambers).
Action: Boxlock with 4 locks.
Barrel: 27½" (Skeet & Skeet), 29¾" (Full & Full, Imp. Mod. & Full).
Weight: 8 lbs., 2 oz. (29¾" bbl.).
Stock: American walnut. Skip-line checkered p.g. and fore-end. Air ducting fore-end. Vent. rubber recoil pad. Field & Skeet: 14"x1½"x2½"; Trap: 14⅜"x1⅜"x1⅞".
Sights: Metal bead center and front.
Features: Wide aluminum airflow rib. Hand engraved frame. Single selective trigger, selective auto. ejectors. White spacers at p.g. and recoil pad. Chrome plated bores. Highly polished and damascened action. Imported by High Standard.
Price: **$595.00**

Ithaca-SKB Model 680 English O/U
Gauge: 12 or 20 ga.
Action: Boxlock.
Barrel: 26" or 28" (Full & Mod., Mod. & I.C.).
Weight: 7 lbs.
Stock: 14"x1½"x2⅝", straight grip, walnut, wrap-around checkering.
Features: Auto. selective ejectors, Bradley-type sights on target grades. Single selective trigger, chrome lined barrels with black chrome exteriors.
Price: **$509.95**

ITHACA PERAZZI MT-6 O/U
Gauge: 12 only (2¾" chambers).
Barrel: 30", 32". Five screw-in choke tubes are supplied. (Extra Full, Full, Imp. Mod., Mod., Imp. Cyl.) Vent. rib barrel.
Weight: 8¼ lbs.
Stock: European walnut, checkered p,.g. and fore-end (24 l.p.i.) Dimensions to customer specs.
Features: Unique striped receiver design; wide target-style single selective trigger; wide target-style rib with self-aligning sighting ramp; special lacquer finished stock and fore-end; new fore-end latching system compensates for normal wood shrinkage and expansion. Barrels can be adjusted for point of impact. Comes with fitted hard case. Imported from Italy by Ithaca.
Price: **$2,495.00**

Ithaca SKB 600 Trap Grade O/U
Same as 500 Field Grade except 30" bbl. (Imp. Mod., Full, or Full, Full), fine scroll engraved receiver; bead middle sight; Monte Carlo stock (14½"x1½"x1½"x2"), p.g. white line spacer and recoil pad.
Price: **$499.95**
Field Grade 600, on recoil pad or Monte Carlo **$499.95**
Trap Grade 700, features select walnut oil finished stock and band engraved receiver **$599.95**

ITHACA SKB 500 FIELD GRADE O/U
Gauge: 12 (2¾" or 3" chambers), 20 (3").
Action: Top lever, hammerless, boxlock; gold-plated single selective trigger; automatic ejectors, non-auto safety.
Barrel: 26" vent. rib (Imp. Cyl., Mod.); 28" (Imp. Cyl., Mod. or Mod., Full); 30" (Mod., Full); 12 ga., 2¾" chambers. 26" (Imp. Cyl., Mod.); 28" (Mod., Full); 20 ga., 3" chambers.
Stock: 14"x1½"x2⅝". Walnut, checkered p.g. and fore-end, p.g. cap, fluted comb.
Weight: 7½ lbs. (12); 6½ lbs. (20).
Features: Border scroll engraved receiver. Chrome lined bbls. and action. Raybar front sight.
Price: **$399.95**
Price: Magnum model **$419.95**

ITHACA MIRAGE O/U
Gauge: 12 only (2¾" chambers).
Action: Boxlock type, interchangeable hammer-trigger group. Single selective trigger, specify choice of firing order.
Barrel: 28", 30", or 32" (Skeet and Skeet or Extra-Full and Mod.). Vent. rib.
Weight: 8¼ lbs. **Length:** 44" over-all.
Stock: Walnut, hand checkered with schnabel fore-end, (14"x1½"x2⅜"). Rubber recoil pad.
Price: Trap model **$1,995.00**
Price: Skeet model **$1,995.00**
Price: Live Bird Model **$1,995.00**

ITHACA-SKB TRAP DOUBLES MODEL 600, 700 O/U
Gauge: 12 ga. (2¾" chambers).
Barrel: 30" or 32", special bore.
Weight: 8 lbs.
Stocks: 14"x1½"x1⅞", American walnut, hand fitted, hand checkered, curved trap pad. Available with M.C. stock.
Sights: Bradley-type.
Features: Double locking lugs, non-automatic safety. Built expressly for shooting doubles and Continental/International style trap. Model 700 has select wood, extra-wide rib, more detailed scroll work on frame.
Price: Model 600 .... **$499.95**
Price: Model 700 (deluxe version of 600) **$599.95**

Ithaca SKB 600 Skeet Grade O/U
Same as 600 Trap except: 12 or 20 ga., 26" or 28" bbls. (Skeet, Skeet), stock (14"x1½"x2⅝"), standard buttplate and whiteline spacer. Weight 7½ lbs.
Price: **$499.95**
Skeet Grade 700, select walnut oil finished stock and band engraved receiver **$599.95**

Ithaca-SKB Model 600 Small Bore Skeet
Same as Model 600 Trap except: comes in 20, 28 (2¾") and 410 (2½") as a set (three barrels, one frame), choked Skeet & Skeet, 28". Weight 7¼ lbs.
Price: **$509.95**

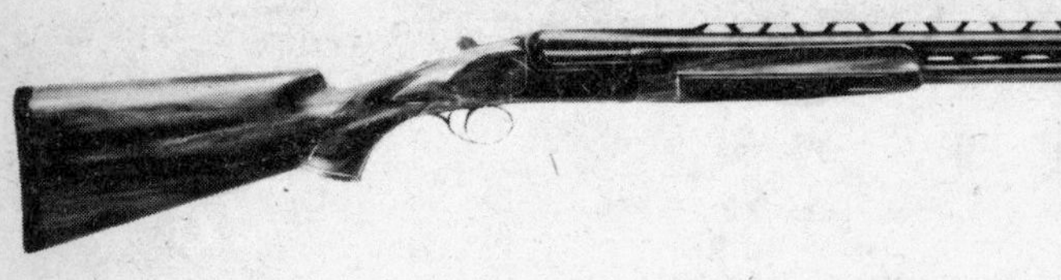

Ithaca MX-8 Combination

Same as MX-8 Trap Gun except comes with interchangeable single barrel (32″ or 34″).

Price: **$2,995.00**

ITHACA/PERAZZI COMPETITION I TRAP O/U

Gauge: 12 only (2¾″ chambers).

Action: Boxlock type, interchangeable hammer-trigger group. Single non-selective trigger, specify choice of firing order.

Barrel: 30″ or 32″ (upper Full, lower, Imp. Mod.), vent rib has concave surface with deep cuts.

Stock: Interchangeable, 6 standard (1³⁄₁₆″ to 1½″ at comb x1⅜″ to 1⅞″ at heel) and 3 Monte Carlo (1⅜″ to 1⁹⁄₁₆″x1⅜″ to 1⁹⁄₁₆″) of walnut; all have 14½″ pull. Fore-end has slight taper and finger groove for firm grip.

Weight: About 7¾ lbs.

Features: Extra trigger-hammer groups are available to change firing sequence and/or trigger pull. Custom stocks also available.

Price: **$1,295.00**
Extra trigger-hammer group **$150.00**
Extra stock **$150.00**

KASSNAR/FIAS SK-1 O/U SHOTGUN

Gauge: 12 or 20 ga. (3″ chambers).

Action: Top lever break open, boxlock, Greener cross bolt.

Barrel: 26″ (Imp. Cyl. & Mod.), 28″ (Mod. & Full), 30″ (Mod. & Full), 32″ (Full & Full).

Weight: 6-6½ lbs.

Stock: Select European walnut. 14″x2¼″x1¼″.

Features: Double triggers and non-automatic extractors. Checkered p.g. and fore-end. Imported by Kassnar Imports.

Price: **$279.95**

Kassnar/Fias SK-4 O/U Shotgun

Same as SK-3 except has selective automatic ejectors, select wood, beavertail fore-end. Trap model (SK-4T) has wide tapered rib **$369.95**

Kassnar/Fias SK-3 O/U Shotgun

Same as SK-1 except has single selective trigger **$299.95**

KLEINGUENTHER'S CONDOR O/U SHOTGUN

Gauge: 12, 20 (2¾″ or 3″ chambers).

Action: Purdey type double lock.

Barrel: 26″ (I.C. & Mod., Skeet & Skeet); 28″ (Full & Mod., I.M.& Mod.); 30″ (Full & Full, Full & Mod.) 12 mag. only.

Weight: 6½ lbs. (26″20) to 7 lbs.3oz. (30″12).

Stock: 14″x1½″x2½″ handcheckered walnut, p.g. and fore-end, recoil pad.

Features: Single selective trigger, auto ejectors, manual tang safety, vent. rib. Skeet Grade has extra wide rib. Imported from Italy by Kleingunther.

Price: Field grade **$395.00**
Price: Skeet **$448.00**

ITHACA MX-8 TRAP GUN

Gauge: 12 only (2¾″ chambers).

Action: Boxlock type, single non-selective trigger; interchangeable trigger-hammer group offers choice of firing order.

Barrel: 30″ or 32″, especially bored for international clay target shooting. High concave vent rib has 5″ ramp.

Stock: Custom, finely checkered (oiled or lacquer finish) European walnut, interchangeable with other models, 9 available including Monte Carlo.

Weight: About 8 lbs.

Features: Ventilated middle rib has additional vent ports for maximum heat dissipation, better balance and smoother swing.

Price: **$2,995.00**
Extra trigger-hammer group **$150.00**
Extra stock **$150.00**

ITHACA-SKB MODEL 880 CROWN GRADE O/U

Gauge: 12 or 20.

Action: Boxlock with sideplates.

Barrel: Trap 30″ or 32″ (Full & Imp. Mod.), Skeet 26″ (Skeet & Skeet), 20 ga. Skeet 28″ (Skeet & Skeet).

Weight: 7 lbs. (Skeet), 8 lbs. (Trap).

Stock: 14½″x2″x1½″x1½″ Trap with M.C., 14″x2½″x1½″ Skeet. Full fancy French walnut.

Sights: Bradley-type.

Features: Hand-honed action, extensive engraving and checkering. Gold-inlaid "crown" on bottom of frame.

Price: **$1,134.95**

IVER JOHNSON SILVER SHADOW O/U SHOTGUN

Gauge: 12 ga. only.

Barrel: 28″ (Mod. & Full). Vent. rib.

Weight: 8¼ lbs.

Stock: Walnut. Checkered p.g. and fore-end.

Sights: Metal bead front.

Features: Single or double trigger. Imported from Italy by Iver Johnson.

Price: Single trigger **$272.25**
Price: Double trigger **$259.95**

Kassnar/Fias SK-4D O/U Shotgun

Same as SK-4 except has deluxe receiver engraving, sideplates, better wood **$410.00**

Kleinguenther's Condor Trap O/U Shotgun

Same as Field Grade except wide rib, Monte Carlo stock, 12 ga. only, 28″ (Full & Mod.); 30″ or 32″ (I.M.& Full, Full & Full), weight 7 lbs.7oz.

Price: **$448.00**

KRIEGHOFF "TECK" O/U SHOTGUN
Gauge: 12, 16, 20 (2¾"), 20 (3").
Action: Boxlock.
Barrel: 28½", vent. rib, choked to customer specs.
Weight: 7 lbs. **Length:** 44" over-all.
Stock: 14¼"x1¼"x2¼", European walnut.
Features: Kersten double crossbolt system. Interchangeable barrels. Imported from Germany by Creighton & Warren.
Price: With ejectors **$2,115.00**
Price: Interchangeable double rifle barrels up to 7mm Rem. Mag. **$1,450.00**
Price: Double rifle barrels, 7mm, 375, 458 Win. Mag. **$1,760.00**
Price: Interchangeable shotgun-rifle barrel combination **$965.00**
Price: Model Ulm with sidelocks **$3,170.00**
Price: Model Ulm with hand-detachable engraved sidelocks **$4,135.00**

KRIEGHOFF MODEL 32 O/U SHOTGUN
Gauge: 12, 20, 28 & 410.
Action: Boxlock.
Barrel: 28", 30", 32", 34".
Stock: Hand checkered walnut, p.g., beavertail fore-end.
Features: Three-way safety (manual, auto or inoperative). Selective single trigger, ejectors and ventilated rib. Other barrel lengths, chokes to order. Available with fancier walnut and relief engraving and silver and gold inlays. Extra barrels available. Imported from Germany by Krieghoff Gun Co.
Price: .... **$1,295.00** to **$11,000.00**

KRIEGHOFF VANDALIA TRAP MODEL
Gauge: 12 only.
Action: Boxlock.
Barrel: 30", 32", 34". Available as either single or over/under.
Stock: Hand checkered walnut, p.g., beavertail fore-end.
Weight: About 9 lbs.
Features: Three-way safety (manual, auto or inoperative). Selective single trigger, ejectors and full length vent. rib. Other bbl. lengths, chokes to order. Available with fancier walnut and relief engraving and silver and gold inlays. Extra bbls. available. Imported from Germany by Krieghoff Gun Co.
Price: .... **$1,695.00** to **$6,995.00**

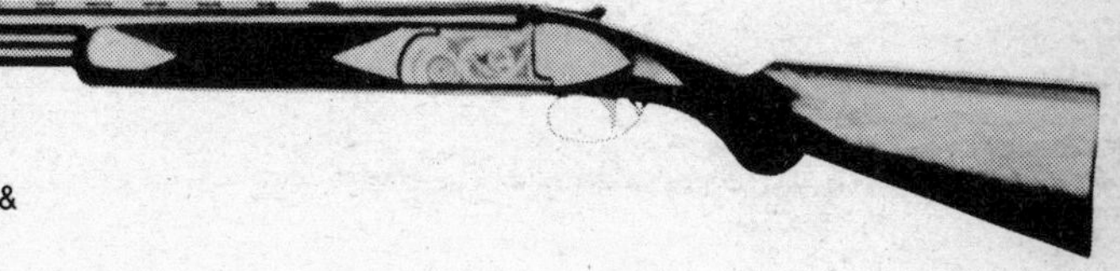

LAMES FIELD MODEL O/U
Gauge: 12 only (3" chambers).
Barrel: 26" (Imp. Cyl. & Mod.), 28" (Mod. & Full), 30" (Mod. & Full or Full & Full).
Weight: 8½ lbs.
Stock: Walnut, checkered p.g. and fore-end, rubber recoil pad.
Features: Vent. rib with front bead, engraved receiver, auto. ejectors, single selective trigger. Imported from Italy by Jana.
Price: **$369.95**

Lames Skeet Model
Same as Field Model except: semi-beavertail fore-end with wrap-around checkering, stock with Skeet dimensions, double vent. ribs, 2¾" chambers, 26" (Skeet & Skeet).
Price: **$455.00**

Lames Std. Trap "Monte Carlo"
Same as Field Model except: M.C. type stock, checkered semi-beavertail fore-end, wide vent. rib, front and center bead sights. 2¾" chambers. 30" (Full & Full or Imp. Mod. & Full), 32" (Imp. Mod. & Full).
Price: .... **$480.00** With standard stock design **$455.00**

Lames California Trap
Same as Standard Trap except: double vent. ribs, M.C. stock, luminous front and center sights.
Price: **$650.00**

Lames Double Vent. Rib Model
Same as Field Model except: has conventional top vent. rib plus ventilated separation between barrels. Imported from Italy by Jana.
Price: **$440.00**

LAURONA MODEL 71-G O/U SHOTGUN
Gauge: 12 (3" chambers).
Action: Hammerless, gold-plated double selectable triggers, auto. safety.
Barrel: 26" (Imp. Cyl. & Mod.); 28" (Full & Mod.); 30" (Full & Full), 30" (Full & Mod.), vent. rib.
Stock: Hand-checkered walnut, p.g., vent. rubber recoil pad.
Feature: Chromed bores, vent. rib. Imported from Spain by Jana.
Price: **$250.00**

LJUTIC BI GUN O/U SHOTGUN
Gauge: 12 ga only.
Barrel: 28" or 33", choked to customer specs.
Weight: To customer specs.
Stock: To customer specs. Oil finish, hand checkered.
Features: Hollow-milled rib; choice of pull or release trigger; pushbutton opener in front of trigger guard. From Ljutic Industries
Price: **$3,500.00**
Price: Matched set of barrels .... **$750.00** to **$1,000.00**

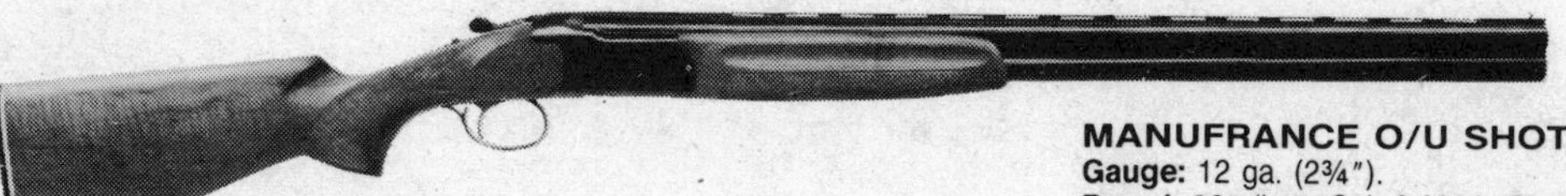

MANUFRANCE O/U SHOTGUN
Gauge: 12 ga. (2¾").
Barrel: 26" (Imp. Cyl. & Mod., Skeet), 28" (Mod. & Full); vent. rib.
Weight: 7¾ lbs. **Length:** 48" over-all.
Stock: Hand checkered walnut; white spacer at butt.
Features: Single selective trigger; automatic ejectors; chrome lined barrels. Imported by Interarms.
Price: **$615.00**

GEBRUDER MERKEL 201E O/U

Gauge: 12, 16, 20, 28, 3″ chambers on request.
Action: Kersten double crossbolt.
Barrel: 26″ (Mod. & Imp. Cyl., Cyl. & Imp. Cyl).
Weight: 6¾ lbs.
Stock: Walnut with p.g. or English style. 14¼″x1½″x2¼″.
Features: Double, single or single selective trigger, cocking indicators. Fine hunting scene engraving. Imported by Champlin Firearms.
Price: With single selective trigger **$1,900.00**

Gebruder Merkel 200E O/U

Similar to 201E except: English arabesque engraving and color case-hardening.
Price: With single non-selective trigger **$1,500.00**

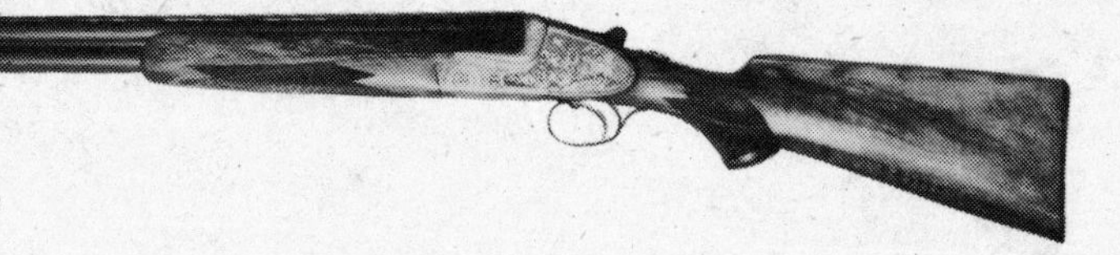

GEBRUDER MERKEL MODEL 203E O/U

Gauge: 12, 16, 20, 28, 3″ chambers on request.
Action: Merkel H&H hand-detachable side locks with double sears. Double crossbolt breech.
Barrel: 26″ (Mod. & Imp. Cyl.).
Weight: 7 lbs.
Stock: Deluxe walnut with p.g. or English style. 14¼″x1½″x2¼″.
Features: Double, single or single selective trigger. Cocking indicators. Choice of arabesque or fine hunting scene engraving. Imported by Champlin Firearms.
Price: With single selective trigger **$3,400.00**

Gebruder Merkel Model 303E O/U

Similar to Model 203E except: double hook-bolting in conjunction with double crossbolt breech. Finer quality.
Price: **$4,200.00**

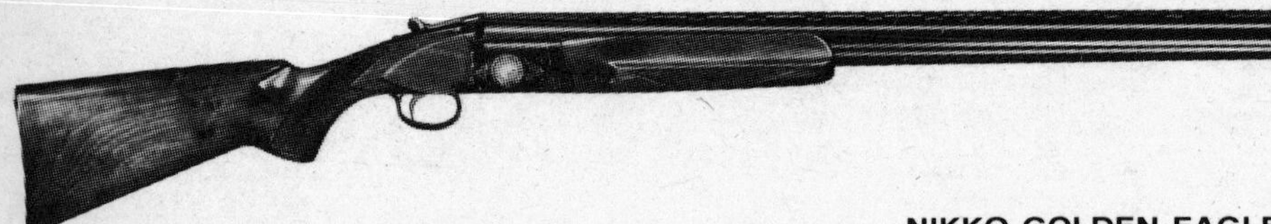

Nikko Golden Eagle Grade II O/U

Similar to Grade I except: Field only has mechanical trigger, others have inertia type; finer engraving and checkering; Trap model has wider rib; Field has brass beads, Skeet and Trap have ivory.
Price: Grade II Field **$725.50**
Price: Grade II Trap **$899.50**
Price: Grade II Skeet **$799.50**

Nikko Golden Eagle Grade III Grandee O/U

Similar to Grade I except: 12 ga. only, 26″ (Skeet & Skeet) or 30″ (Full & Imp. Mod.); finer checkering and nearly full coverage receiver engraving; silver finish receiver.
Price: Grade III Grandee Trap **$2,299.50**
Price: Grade III Grandee Skeet **$2,299.50**

NIKKO GOLDEN EAGLE GRADE I O/U

Gauge: 12 ga. (2¾″ or 3″) or 20 ga. (2¾″).
Action: Boxlock.
Barrel: 26″ (Mod. & Imp. Cyl., Skeet & Skeet), 28″ (Mod. & Imp. Cyl., Full & Mod., Skeet & Skeet), 30″ (Full & Full, Full & Mod., Full & Imp. Mod.), 32″ (Full & Full, Full & Imp. Mod., Full & Mod.).
Weight: 7¼-8 lbs.
Stock: 14″x1½″x2½″x⅛″ cast-off (Field); 14⅜″x1⅜″x1⅞″x¼″ cast-off (Trap): select walnut.
Features: Single selective gold plated mechanical trigger; vent. top and side ribs; selective ejectors; non-automatic tang safety/barrel selector; rubber recoil pad. Lifetime warranty to original owner. Imported by Nikko Sporting Firearms.
Price: Grade I Field **$699.50**
Price: Grade I Trap **$823.50**
Price: Grade I Skeet **$751.50**

Pedersen 1000 Series O/U, Grade II

Same as Grade I except: standard stock dimensions (14″x2½″x1½″x2″), less fancy wood, different receiver engraving.
Price: Hunting **$1,540.00**
Price: Trap model (with trap dimensions) Monte Carlo **$1,570.00**
Price: Skeet & Hunting (3″ Mag.) **$1,555.00**

PEDERSEN 1000 SERIES CUSTOM O/U GRADE I

Gauge: 12 or 20 ga.
Action: Boxlock.
Barrel: To customer specs.
Weight: To customer specs. **Length:** To customer specs.
Stock: Dimensions to customer specs. American walnut, hand checkered p.g. and fore-end, rubber recoil pad.
Features: Vent. rib, single selective trigger, automatic ejectors, gold filled, hand engraved receiver, gun made entirely to customer specifications.
Price: Hunting, Skeet or Trap **$1,980.00**

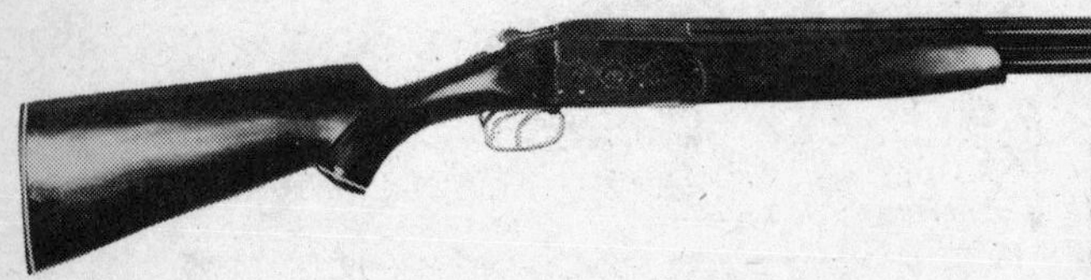

PRIDE OF BRAZIL O/U SHOTGUN

Gauge: 12 only, 2¾″.
Barrel: 28″ (Mod. & Full); vent. top and middle ribs.
Weight: 7¾ lbs.
Stock: Hand checkered hardwood.
Features: Auto. safety; auto. ejectors; double triggers; engraved receiver. Imported from Brazil by Firearms Import & Export.
Price: **$189.95**

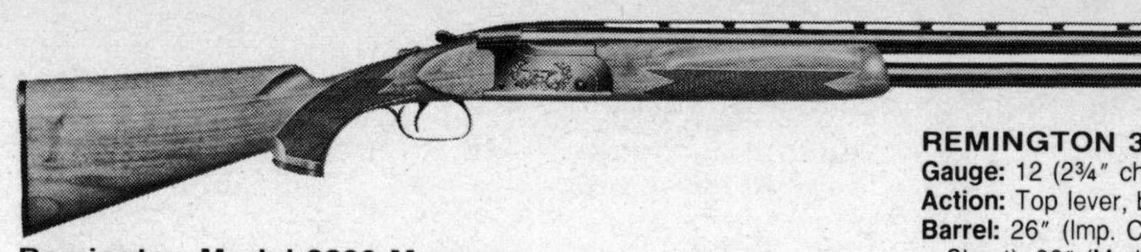

REMINGTON 3200 O/U

Gauge: 12 (2¾" chambers).
Action: Top lever, break open. Single selective trigger.
Barrel: 26" (Imp. Cyl. & Mod., Skeet & Skeet), 28" (Mod. & Full, Skeet & Skeet), 30" (Mod. & Full, Full & Full, Imp. Mod. & Full). Vent. rib.
Weight: 7¾ lbs. (26" bbl.).
Stock: 14"x1½"x2⅛", American walnut. Checkered p.g. and fore-end. Modified beavertail fore-end on field model, full on trap and Skeet.
Features: Super-fast lock time, separated barrels, engraved receiver, unbreakable firing pins, combination barrel selector/safety, wide trigger, shield-covered breech.
Price: Field (illus.) .... **$595.00** Skeet **$650.00**

Remington Model 3200 Magnum

Same as standard 3200 Field except: 3" chambers, barrels 30" (Full & Full, Mod. & Full) **$620.00**
Price: Special Trap **$740.00**

Remington 3200 Trap

Same as 3200 Field except barrels are 30" (Full & Full, Imp. Mod. & Full). Stock measures 14⅜"x13¼"x1½" **$675.00**

Savage Model 24-D O/U

Caliber: Top bbl. 22 S, L, LR or 22 Mag.; bottom bbl. 20 or 410 gauge.
Action: Two-way top lever opening, low rebounding visible hammer, single trigger, barrel selector spur on hammer, separate extractors, color case-hardened frame.
Barrel: 24", separated barrels.
Weight: 6¾ lbs. **Length:** 40".
Stock: Walnut, checkered p.g. and fore-end (14"x1½"x2½").
Sights: Ramp front, rear open adj. for e.
Features: Receiver grooved for scope mounting.
Price: **$97.65**

SAVAGE MODEL 24-F.G. O/U

Same as Model 24-D except: color case hardened frame, stock is walnut finished hardwood, no checkering or M.C.
Price: **$82.50**

Savage Model 24-V

Similar to Model 24-DL except: 222 Rem. or 30-30 and 20 ga. only; stronger receiver; color case-hardened frame; barrel; band; folding leaf rear sight; receiver tapped for scope **$119.50**

SAVAGE MODEL 330 O/U

Gauge: 12 (2¾" chambers), 20 ga. (3" chambers).
Action: Top lever, break open. Selective single trigger, auto top tang safety locks trigger, coil springs.
Barrel: 26" (Mod. & Imp. Cyl.), 28" or 30" (Mod. & Full).
Stock: 14"x1½"x2½"). Walnut, checkered p.g. and fore-end, hard rubber plate.
Weight: About 7 lbs., 46½" (30" bbl.) over-all.
Features: Monoblock locking rails are engaged by locking shield that snaps forward as gun is closed. This shield overlaps the breech for added strength.
Price: **$299.95**

Savage Model 330 O/U Set

Identical to the Model 330 but with two sets of barrels, one in 12 ga. the other in 20 (Mod. & Full). Same fore-end fits both sets of bbls. Comes with padded case with pocket for extra bbl.
Price: Factory fitted **$415.00**

SAVAGE MODEL 24-C O/U

Caliber: Top bbl. 22 S, L, LR; bottom bbl. 20 gauge cyl. bore.
Action: Take-down, low rebounding visible hammer. Single trigger, barrel selector spur on hammer.
Barrel: 20" separate barrels.
Weight: 5¾ lbs. **Length:** 35" (taken down 20").
Stock: Walnut finished hardwood, straight grip.
Sight: Ramp front, rear open adj. for e.
Features: Trap door butt holds two shotshells and ten 22 cartridges, comes with special carrying case. Measures 5"x22" when in case.
Price: **$92.60**

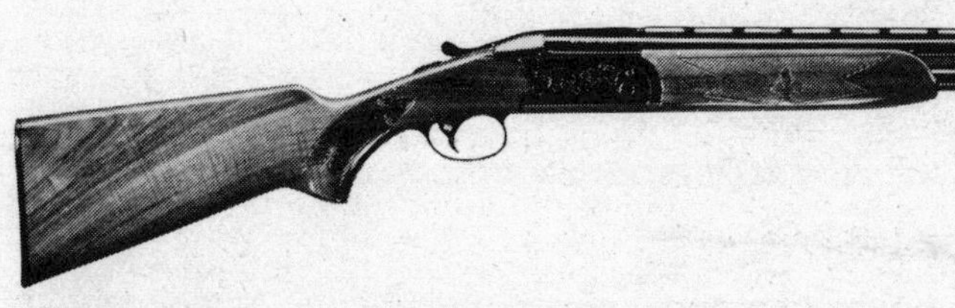

SAVAGE 333 O/U

Gauge: 12 (2¾"), 20 (2¾" & 3" chambers).
Action: Top lever, break open.
Barrel: 26" (Skeet & Skeet or Imp. Cyl. & Mod.), 28" (Mod. & Full), 30" (Mod. & Full, 12 ga. only).
Weight: 6¼ to 7¼ lbs.
Stock: 14"x1½"x2½", French walnut. Fleur-de-lis checkering.
Features: Single selective trigger, auto. safety, ejectors, cocking indicators. Engraved steel receiver.
Price: **$381.50**

SAVAGE 333-T

Same specifications as Model 330 except has trap specifications and features: 30" bbl. choked Imp. Mod. and Full, manually operated top tang safety (disconnects trigger from sears), stock measures 14½"x1½"x1½" at Monte Carlo, 2½" heel. Over-all length 47", taken down 30", weight 7¾ lbs. Has extra-wide ventilated rib, extractors, recoil pad.
Price: **$381.50**

UNIVERSAL OVER WING O/U SHOTGUN

Gauge: 12, 20 (3″ chambers).
Action: Top lever, hammerless, boxlock, double triggers.
Barrel: 26″ vent. rib (Imp. Cyl., & Mod.); 28″ or 30″ (Mod. & Full). Front & middle sights.
Stock: 14″x1½″x2⅝″. Walnut, checkered p.g. and fore-end. Recoil Pad.
Weight: 7½ lbs. (12); 6½ lbs. (20).
Price: **$289.95**

UNIVERSAL BAIKAL MC-5 O/U

Gauge: 20 ga. (2¾″ chambers).
Barrel: 26″ (Imp. Cyl. & Mod., Skeet & Skeet).
Weight: 5¾ lbs.
Stock: Fancy hand checkered walnut. Choice of p.g. or straight stock, with or without cheekpiece. Fore-end permanently attached to barrels.
Features: Fully engraved receiver. Double triggers, extractors. Chrome barrels, chambers and internal parts. Hand-fitted solid rib. Hammer interceptors. Imported by Universal Sporting Goods.
Price: MC-5 .... **$682.50**
Price: MC-6 (as Skeet gun, single non-selective trigger, raised rib, weighs 7½ lbs.) **$825.00**

UNIVERSAL BAIKAL MC-7 O/U

Gauge: 12 or 20 ga. (2¾″ chambers).
Barrel: 12 ga. 28″ (Mod. & Full), 20 ga. 26″ (Imp. Cyl. & Mod.).
Weight: 7 lbs. (12 ga.), 6¾ lbs. (20 ga.)
Stock: Walnut. Hand checkered with or without p.g. and cheekpiece. Beavertail fore-end.
Features: Fully chiseled and engraved receiver. Chrome barrels, chambers and internal parts. Double trigger, selective ejectors. Solid raised rib. Single selective trigger available. Imported by Universal Sporting Goods.
Price: **$1,982.50**

UNIVERSAL BAIKAL MC-8 O/U

Gauge: 12 ga. (2¾″ chambers).
Barrel: 26″ special parabolic Skeet, 28″ (Mod. & Full). Available in 2 bbl. sets.
Weight: 7¾ lbs.
Stock: Fancy walnut. Beavertail fore-end permanently attached to barrels. Hand checkered p.g. and fore-end. Monte Carlo.
Features: Handmade competition shotgun. Blued, engraved receiver. Double triggers, extractors. Chrome barrels, chambers and internal parts. Hand fitted vent. rib. Available with single selective trigger and selective ejectors at customer's request. Imported by Universal Sporting Goods.
Price: **$845.00**

UNIVERSAL BAIKAL IJ-27 O/U

Gauge: 12 ga. (2¾″ chambers).
Barrel: 26″ (Skeet & Skeet), 28″ (Mod. & Full), 30″ (Imp. Mod. & Full).
Weight: 7¾-8¼ lbs.
Stock: Hand checkered walnut, rubber recoil pad. Ventilated fore-end. White spacers at p.g. and recoil pad.
Features: Double triggers. Chrome barrels, chambers and internal parts. Hand-fitted vent. rib. Hand engraved and silver inlayed receiver, trigger guard and fore-end latch. Imported by Universal Sporting Goods.
Price: **$235.94**
Price: With selective ejectors **$265.25**

UNIVERSAL BAIKAL MC-9-01 O/U

Gauge: 12 ga. (2¾″ chambers).
Barrel: 28″ (Mod. & Full), 30″ (Imp. Mod. & Full). Special parabolic chokes.
Weight: 8 lbs.
Stock: Fancy walnut. Hand checkered p.g. with cheekpiece. Rubber recoil pad with white spacers. Monte Carlo. Ventilated fore-end.
Features: Handmade sidelock competition shotgun. Removable sideplates. Chrome barrels, chambers and internal parts. Single selective target trigger, selective ejectors, cocking indicators. Hand engraved receiver and trigger guard. Hand fitted vent. rib. Imported by Universal Sporting Goods.
Price: Special order only **$1,508.00**

UNIVERSAL BAIKAL MC-109 O/U

Gauge: 12 ga. (2¾″ chambers).
Barrel: To customer's specifications. Choice of chokes.
Weight: 7¼ lbs.
Stock: Fancy walnut. Choice of p.g. or straight stock, with or without cheekpiece. Beavertail fore-end. Hand carved and checkered to customer's specs.
Features: Handmade sidelock shotgun. Removable sideplates. Chrome barrels, chambers and internal parts. Single selective trigger, selective ejectors, cocking indicators, hammer interceptors. Hand chiseled scenes on receiver to customer specs. Gold inlays to customer specs. Imported by Universal Sporting Goods.
Price: Special order only **$3,055.00**

WEATHERBY REGENCY O/U SHOTGUN

Gauge: 12 ga. (2¾″ chambers), 20 ga. (3″ chambers).
Action: Boxlock (simulated side-lock) top lever break-open. Selective auto ejectors, single selective trigger (selector inside trigger guard).
Barrel: 28″ with vent rib and bead front sight, Full & Mod., Mod. & Imp. Cyl. or Skeet & Skeet.
Stock: American walnut, checkered p.g. and fore-end (14¼″x1½″x2½″).
Weight: 12 ga. 7⅜ lbs., 20 ga. 6⅞ lbs.
Features: Mechanically operated trigger. Top tang safety, Greener cross-bolt, fully engraved receiver, recoil pad installed.
Price: 12 or 20 ga. Field and Skeet **$699.50**
Price: 12 ga. Trap Model **$749.50**

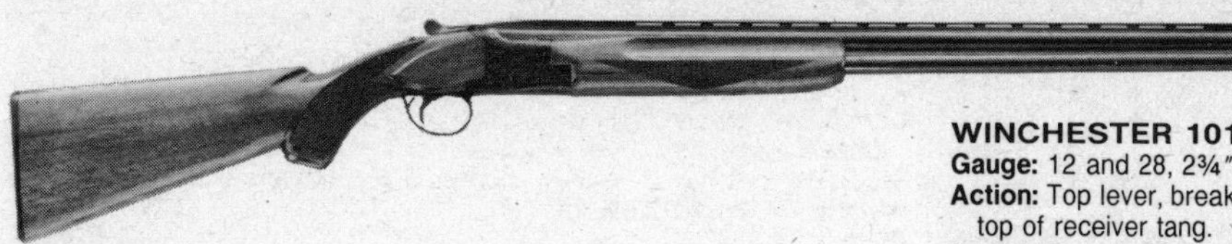

WINCHESTER 101 OVER/UNDER Field Gun
Gauge: 12 and 28, 2¾"; 20 and 410, 3".
Action: Top lever, break open. Manual safety combined with bbl. selector at top of receiver tang.
Barrel: Vent. rib 26" 12, 26½", 20 and 410 (Imp. Cyl., Mod.), 28" (Mod & Full), 30" 12 only (Mod. & Full). Metal bead front sight. Chrome plated chambers and bores.
Stock: 14"x1½"x2½". Checkered walnut p.g. and fore-end; fluted comb.
Weight: 12 ga. 7¾ lbs. Others 6¼ lbs. **Length:** 44¾" over-all (28" bbls.).
Features: Single selective trigger, auto ejectors. Hand engraved receiver.
Price: 12 or 20 ga. **$580.00**
Price: 28 or 410 ga. **$610.00**

Winchester 101 Magnum Field Gun
Same as 101 Field Gun except: chambers 3" Magnum shells; 12 ga. only 30" (Full & Full or Mod. & Full); hand-engraved receiver, select French walnut stock with fluted comb, hand-checkered pistol grip and beavertail fore-end with recoil pad **$590.00**

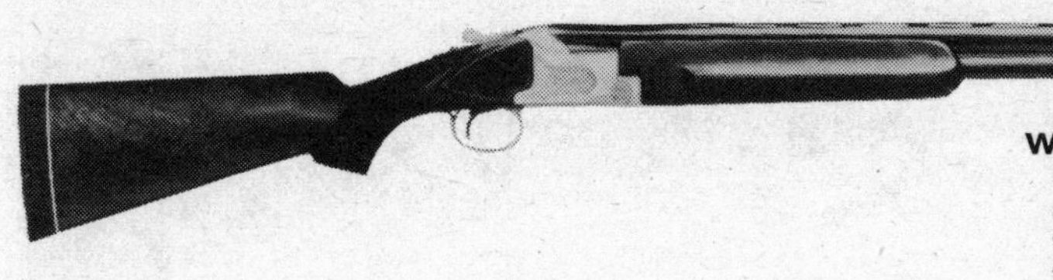

Winchester Model 101 Pigeon Grade Trap Gun
Same as Model 101 Field except has new-design vent. rib with bead front and middle sights, hand-engraved satin finish receiver, knurled, non-slip trigger. Stock and fore-end of fancy French walnut, hand checkered p.g. and fore-end. 12 ga. only, 2¾" chambers, 30" or 32" (I.M. & Full). Stock measures 14⅜"x1⅜"x1⅞". Weighs 8¼ lbs.
Price: Standard trap stock **$695.00**
Price: Monte Carlo stock **$700.00**

Winchester 101 Skeet
Same as M-101 except: 12 ga., 26" bbls., 20, 26½", 28 & 410, 28". Bored Skeet and Skeet only, 12 or 20 ga. **$620.00**
M101 in 28 or 410 .... **$650.00**

Winchester 101 Combination Skeet Set
Same as 101 20 ga. Skeet except: Includes Skeet bbls. in 410 & 28 ga. Vent. ribs match 20 ga. frame. With fitted trunk case **$1,300.00**

A. ZOLI DELFINO S.P. O/U
Gauge: 12 or 20 (3" chamber).
Barrel: 28" (Mod. & Full); vent. rib.
Weight: 5½ lbs.
Stock: Walnut. Hand checkered p.g. and fore-end; cheekpiece.
Features: Color case hardened receiver with light engraving; chrome lined barrels; automatic sliding safety; double triggers; ejectors. From Mandall Shooting Supplies.
Price: **$290.00**

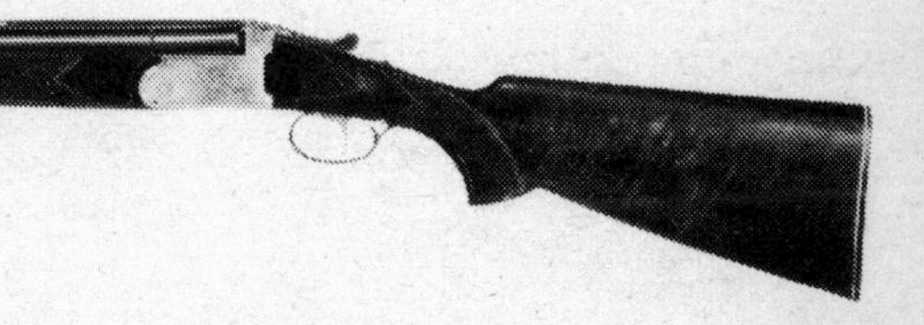

ZOLI SILVER SNIPE O/U SHOTGUN
Gauge: 12, 20 (3" chambers).
Action: Purdey type double boxlock, crossbolt.
Barrels: 26" (I.C.& Mod.), 28" (Mod.&Full), 30", 12 only (Mod.& Full); 26" Skeet (Skeet & Skeet), 30" Trap (Full & Full).
Weight: 6½ lbs. (12 ga.).
Stock: Hand checkered European walnut, p.g. and fore-end.
Features: Auto safety (exc. Trap and Skeet), vent rib, single trigger, chrome bores. Imported from Italy by Galef.
Price: Field grade **$369.50**

Zoli Golden Snipe O/U Shotgun
Same as Silver Snipe except selective auto ejectors.
Price: Field Grade **$435.00**

ZOLI GRAY EAGLE O/U SHOTGUN
Gauge: 12 (Model 300) or 20 (Model 302), 3" chambers.
Action: Hammerless, with auto safety and top lever release.
Barrel: 28" (Mod. and Full), 26" (Imp. Cyl. and Mod.).
Weight: 6 lbs. 13 oz. (12); 6¼ lbs. (20).
Stock: Hand checkered selected walnut, p.g., ebonite butt plate with white spacer.
Features: Ventilated rib, chrome plated bore. Imported from Italy American Import.
Price: **$421.25**

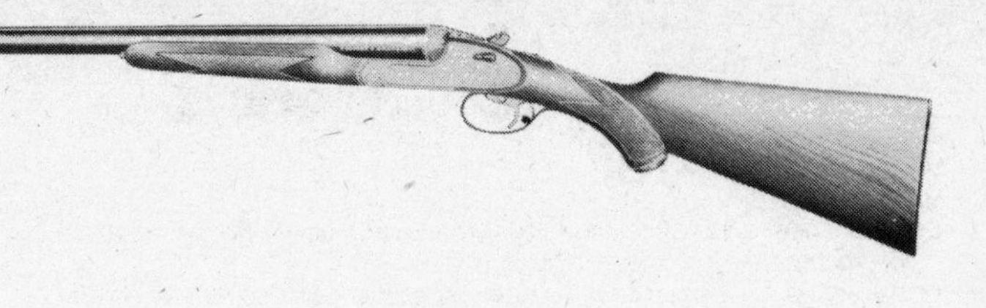

AYA MODELS 56 & 53E DOUBLE BARREL SHOTGUNS

Gauge: 12, 20 (2¾" chambers standard, 3" on request).
Action: Heavy competition sidelock frame, triple bolting.
Barrel Up to 30" (length and choke customer specified).
Stock: Made to customer specifications.
Features: Auto safety and ejectors, loading indicators, matted rib, gas escape valves, folding front trigger, engraved frame. Made to customer requirements, 12-18 month delivery. Model 53-E same except has hand detachable locks, concave rib. Imported from Spain by JBL Arms.
Price: 56 .... **$1,200.00**
Price: 53E **$900.00**

Aya XXV/SL Double Barrel Shotgun Churchill Copy

12 & 20 ga., 2¾" chamber only, narrow top rib, 25" bbl.
Price: **$860.00**

Aya No. 1 Double Barrel Shotgun

Same as 56 except lightweight frame, concave rib, double bolting, 2¾" chambers only.
No. 2 similar to No. 1 except without loading indicators or folding front trigger.
Price: No. 1 .... **$1,200.00**
Price: No. 2 .... **$730.00**

BERETTA GR DOUBLE BARREL SHOTGUNS

Gauge: 12 (2¾" chambers), 20 (3" chambers).
Action: Improved Greener action.
Barrel: 12 ga. 30" or 28" (Mod., Full), 26" (Imp. Cyl., Mod.) 20 ga. 28" (Mod., Full), 26" (Imp. Cyl., Mod.)
Weight: 12 ga. 7 lbs., 20 ga. 6½ lbs., 12 ga. Mag. 8 lbs.
Stock: 14" x 1½" x 2½" hand checkered European walnut stock and semi-beavertail fore-end.
Features: Ventilated rib. Model GR-2 has double triggers; GR-3 has single selective trigger; GR-4 has single selective trigger, auto ejectors, engraved action and select wood.
Price: .... **$475.00**(GR-2) to **$650.00**(GR-4)

BROWNING B-SS

Gauge: 12 (2¾"), 20 (3").
Action: Top lever break-open action, top tang safety, single trigger.
Barrel: 26" (Mod. and Full or Imp. Cyl. and Mod.), 28" (Mod. and Full), 30" (Full & Full or Mod & Full).
Weight: 6¾ lbs. (26" bbl.); 7 lbs. (28" bbl.); 7¼ lbs. (30" bbl.).
Stock: 14¾"x1⅝"x2½". Walnut, hand checkered. Full p.g., full beavertail fore-end.
Features: Automatic safety, automatic ejectors. Hand engraved receiver, mechanical trigger.
Price: **$319.50**

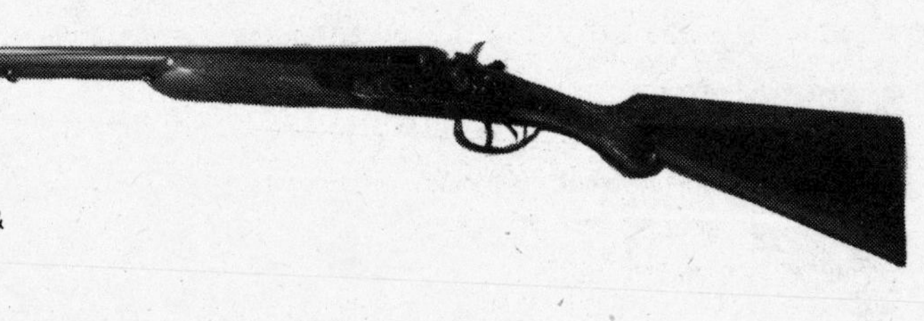

CRUCELEGUI HERMANOS MODEL 150 DOUBLE

Gauge: 12 or 20 (2¾" chambers).
Action: Greener triple crossbolt.
Barrel: 20", 26", 28", 30", 32" (Cyl. & Cyl., Full & Full, Mod. & Full, Mod. & Imp. Cyl., Imp. Cyl. & Full, Mod. & Mod.).
Weight: 5 to 7¼ lbs.
Stock: Hand checkered walnut, beavertail fore-end.
Features: Exposed hammers; double triggers; color casehardened receiver; sling swivels; chrome lined bores. From Mandall Shooting Supplies.
Price: **$179.95**

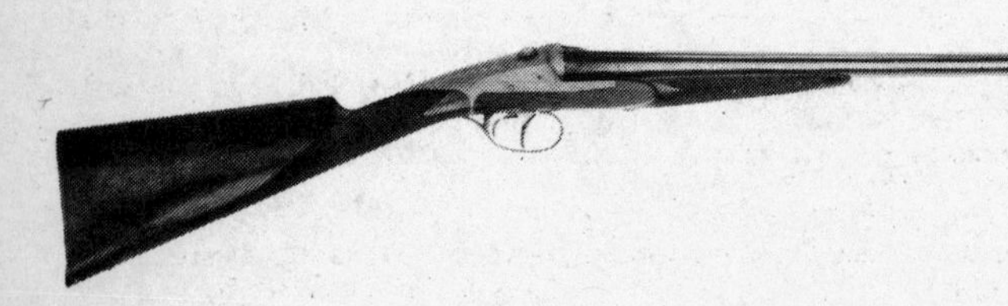

DARNE SLIDING BREECH DOUBLE

Gauge: 12, 16, 20 or 28.
Action: Sliding breech.
Barrel: 25½" to 27½", choice of choking.
Weight: 5½ to 6½ lbs.
Stock: European walnut, hand checkered p.g., and fore-end. English style or semi-p.g.
Features: Double triggers, selective ejectors, plume or raised rib, case-hardened or engraved receiver. Available in 8 grades, stock or custom made. Imported from France by Firearms Center, Inc.
Price: from **$475.00**

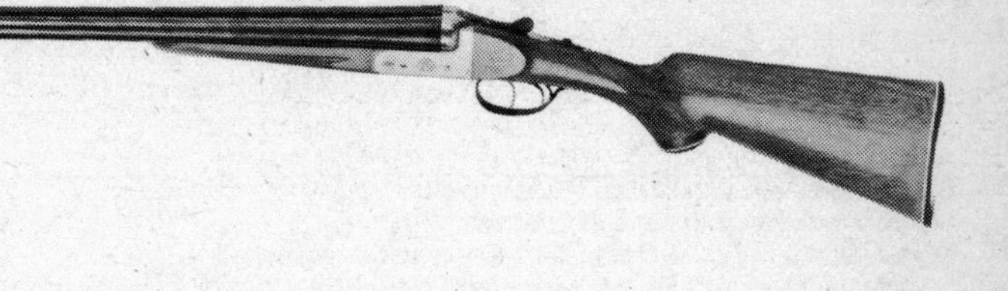

DAVIDSON 63B MAGNUM DOUBLE SHOTGUN
Gauge: 10 (3½" chambers).
Barrel: 32" 10 (Full & Full).
Weight: 10 lbs. 10 oz.
Stock: Hand finished checkered European walnut, beavertail fore-end, white line spacers on p.g. cap and recoil pad.
Features: Auto safety, manual extractors, gold-plated double triggers (front hinged), engraved nickel-plated action. Imported from Europe by Davidson.
Price: 10 ga. **$209.95**

DAVIDSON MODEL 73 "STAGECOACH" SHOTGUN
Gauge: 12 or 20 Mag. (3" chambers).
Barrel: 12 ga. 20" (Imp. Cyl. & Mod.), 20 ga. 20" (Mod. & Full).
Weight: Approx. 7 lbs.
Stock: Select European walnut stock and fore-end, checkered p.g. and fore-end with saddle stitched border. Full p.g. with white spacers and at butt.
Features: Exposed hammers; solid matted rib ⅜" wide at breech; brass bead front sight; double locking lugs with Greener crossbolt; engraved receiver; manual ejectors. Imported by Davidson Firearms.
Price: **$169.95**

DAVIDSON MODEL 63B DOUBLE BARREL SHOTGUN
Gauge: 12, 16, 20 (2¾" chambers); 410 (3" chambers).
Action: Anson & Deeley with crossbolt (no crossbolt on 410).
Barrel: 30" 12 (Mod. & Full); 26" (I.C. & Mod.) and 28" (Mod. & Full) all except 410; 410, 25" (Full & Full) only.
Weight: 12 ga., 7 lbs.; 16, 20, 6½ lbs.; 410 ga., 5 lbs. 11 oz.
Stock: Hand finished checkered European walnut, white line spacers on p.g. cap and butt plate.
Features: Auto safety, manual extractors, gold-plated double triggers, engraved nickel-plated frame. Imported by Davidson.
Price: **$169.95**

F.I.E. DOUBLE BARREL SHOTGUN
Gauge: 12, 20, (2¾"), 410 (3").
Action: Boxlock.
Barrel: 12 and 20 ga. 28" (Mod. & Full); 410 ga. 26" (Mod. & Full).
Stock: Hand checkered walnut, beavertail fore-end, white line spacers on p.g. cap and butt plate.
Features: Raised matted rib, double triggers, engraved receiver. Auto. safety. Imported from Brazil by Firearms Import & Export.
Price: **$139.95**

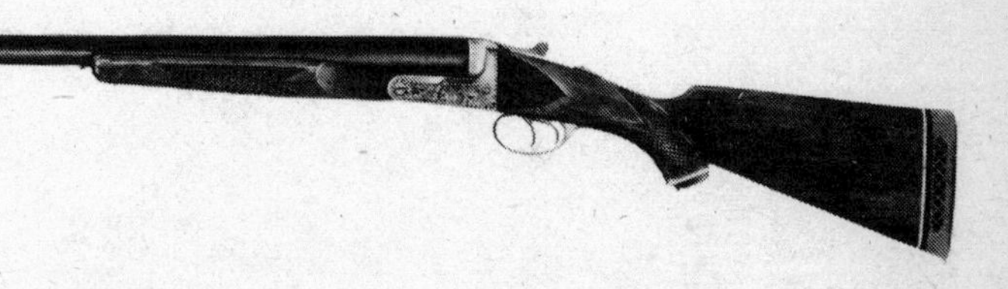

FALCON GOOSE DOUBLE BARREL SHOTGUN
Gauge: 10 (3½-inch chambers).
Action: Anson & Deeley with Holland type extractors, double triggers.
Barrel: 32" (Full and Full).
Weight: 11 lbs.
Stock: Hand checkered walnut, plastic p.g. cap and rubber recoil pad with white spacers.
Features: Auto safety, rubber recoil pad, engraved action. Imported from Spain by American Import.
Price: **$336.00**

ITHACA SKB 280 ENGLISH DOUBLE
Gauge: 12 ga. (2¾"), 20 ga. (3").
Barrel: 25", 26" (Mod. & I.C.), 28" (Full & Mod.).
Weight: 6½ to 7⅛ lbs.
Stock: English style straight grip. 14"x1½"x2⅝".
Features: Wrap-around checkering, semi-beavertail fore-end. Receiver hand engraved with quail and English scroll. Simulated oil finish stock.
Price: **$439.95**

GALEF'S DOUBLE BARREL SHOTGUN
Gauge: 10 (3½"); 12, 20, 410 (3"); 16, 20 (2¾").
Action: Modified Anson & Deeley boxlock, case hardened.
Barrels: 32" 10, 12 only (Full & Full); 30" 12 only (Mod.& Full); 28" all exc. 410 (Mod.& Full); 26" 12, 20, 28 (I.C.&Mod.); 26" 410 only (Mod.& Full); 22" 12 only (I.C.& I.C.).
Weight: 10½ lbs.(10), 7¾ lbs.(12) to 6 lbs.(410).
Stock: Hand checkered European walnut, p.g., beavertail fore-end, rubber recoil pad. Dimensions vary with gauge.
Features: Auto safety, plain extractors. Imported from Spain by Galef.
Price: 10 ga. .... **$278.20** 12 - 410 .... **$209.95**

Ithaca SKB 200E Field Grade Double
Same as 100 Field Grade except: automatic selective ejectors, bead middle sight and scroll engraving on receiver, beavertail fore-end. White line spacers. Gold plated trigger and nameplate **$424.95**

Ithaca SKB 200E Skeet Grade
Same as 200E Deluxe Field Grade except: recoil pad, non-auto. safety. Bbls. 26" 12 ga. or 25" 20 ga. (Skeet, Skeet). Wgt. 7¼ and 6¼ lbs.
Price: **$439.95**

ITHACA SKB 100 FIELD GRADE DOUBLE
Gauge: 12 (2¾" chambers) and 20 (3").
Action: Top lever, hammerless, boxlock, automatic safety, single selective trigger, non-automatic extractor.
Barrel: 12 ga. 26" (Imp. Cyl., Mod.). 28⅛ or 30" (Mod., Full). 20 ga. 28" (Mod., Full). 25" (Imp. Cyl., Mod.).
Stock: 14"x1½"x2⅝". Walnut, hand checkered p.g. and fore-end, p.g. cap, fluted comb.
Weight: 7 lbs. (12 ga.); 6 lbs. (20 ga.).
Features: Automatic safety. Chrome lined action and barrels, hand engraved receiver.
Price: **$299.95**

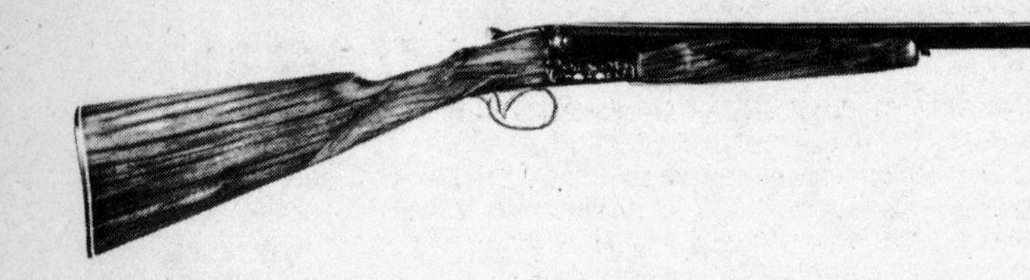

ITHACA-SKB MODEL 280 QUAIL DOUBLE

Gauge: 20 only (3″ chambers).
Barrel: 25″ (I.C. & I.C.).
Weight: 6½ lbs.
Stock: 14″x1½″x2⅝″, English style.
Features: Designed for quail and upland game shooting. Straight stock, wrap-around checkering, scroll game scene on frame, semi-beavertail fore-end. Auto. selective ejectors, single trigger.
Price: **$439.95**

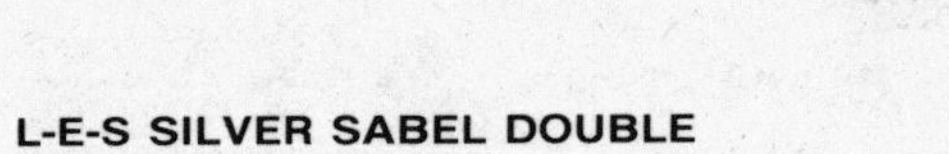

KLEINGUENTHER'S BRESCIA SHOTGUN

Gauge: 12, 20 (2¾″ chambers).
Action: Anson & Deeley.
Barrel: 28″ (Full & Mod. or I.C. & Mod.), chrome lined.
Weight: 6½ lbs.
Stock: Hand checkered walnut, p.g. or straight, recoil pad.
Features: Double triggers, engraved action. Imported from Italy by Kleinguenther.
Price: **$234.00**

L-E-S SILVER SABEL DOUBLE

Gauge: 12 (2¾″ or 3″) or 16.
Action: Sidelock system with Purdey bolt; double safety sears.
Barrel: 26″ or 28″ (Full & Imp. Mod.); solid high rib.
Weight: 7½-8½ lbs.
Stock: Monte Carlo stock with semi-beavertail fore-end; hand checkered European walnut.
Features: Automatic selective ejectors; auto. safety; double triggers. Engraved models available. Imported by L-E-S.
Price: **$435.00**

L-E-S SABEL DOUBLE BARREL

Gauge: 12 (2¾″ or 3″) or 16.
Action: Anson & Deeley with Purdey bolt.
Barrel: 26″ or 28″ (Full & Imp. Mod.), Solid concave rib.
Weight: 7-8 lbs.
Stock: European walnut; straight English style grip; hand checkered.
Features: Double triggers; auto safety; Holland extractors; no recoil pad or butt plate. Imported by L-E-S.
Price: **$235.00**

LOYOLA MAGNUM DOUBLE BARREL SHOTGUN

Gauge: 10 (3½ chambers); 12, 20 and 410 (all 3″ chambers).
Action: Hammerless, double trigger, auto. safety.
Barrel: 12, 20 ga. 26″ (Imp. Cyl., Mod.), 28″ (Full, Mod.); 10, 12 ga. 30″ (Full, Mod.); 10 ga. 32″, 12 ga. 30″ and 410 ga. 26″ (Full, Full).
Stock: Checkered walnut, p.g., fitted rubber recoil pad.
Features: Available with solid or vent. rib. ($20.00 additional). Imported from Spain by Jana.
Price: .... **$160.00** (12, 20, 410 ga.), **$195.00** (10 ga.)

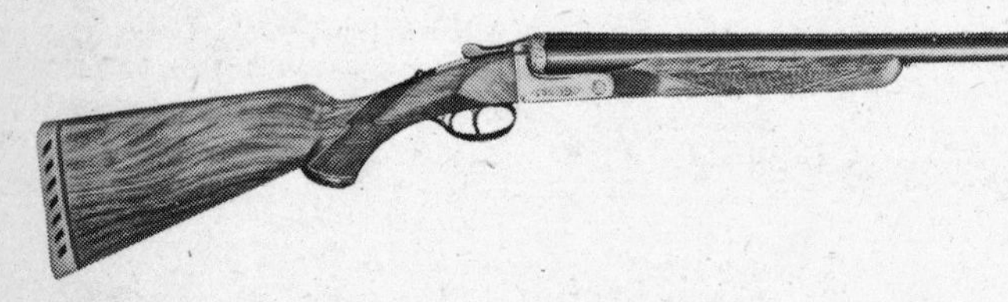

MERCURY MAGNUM DOUBLE BARREL SHOTGUN

Gauge: 10 (3½″), 12 or 20 (3″) magnums.
Action: Triple-lock Anson & Deeley type.
Barrel: 28″ (Full & Mod.), 12 and 20 ga.; 32″ (Full & Full), 10 ga.
Weight: 7¼ lbs. (12 ga.); 6½ lbs. (20 ga.); 10⅛ lbs. (10 ga.). **Length:** 45″ (28″ bbls.).
Stock: 14″ x 1⅝″ x 2¼″ walnut, checkered p.g. stock and beavertail fore-end, recoil pad.
Features: Double triggers, front hinged, auto safety, extractors; safety gas ports, engraved frame. Imported from Spain by Tradewinds.
Price: .... **$198.50** (12, 20 ga.)
Price: .... **$249.50** (10 ga.)

GEBRUDER MERKEL 147S SIDE-BY-SIDE

Gauge: 12, 16, 20 ga. with 3″ chambers on request.
Action: Sidelock with double hook bolting and Greener breech. Trigger catch bar.
Barrel: 26″ (Mod. & Imp. Cyl., Cyl. & Imp. Cyl.).
Weight: 6½ to 6¾ lbs.
Stock: Walnut finish. English style or p.g., 14¼″x1½″x2¼″.
Features: 30% faster trigger than conventional lock design. Hunting scene engraving. Highest grade side-by-side Merkel. Double, single or single selective trigger. Imported by Champlin Firearms.
Price: With double trigger **$1,700.00**

GEBRUDER MERKEL 47S SIDE-BY-SIDE

Gauge: 12, 16, 20, 3″ chambers on request.
Action: Sidelock with double hook bolting and Greener breech.
Barrel: 26″ (Mod. & Imp. Cyl.).
Weight: 6¼ to 6¾ lbs.
Stock: Walnut with p.g. or English style. 14¼″x11½″x2¼″.
Features: Double, single or single selective trigger. Cocking indicators. English arabesque engraving. Imported by Champlin Firearms.
Price: With double trigger **$1,200.00**

GEBRUDER MERKEL 147E SIDE-BY-SIDE

Gauge: 12, 16, 20, 3″ chambers on request.
Action: Anson-Deeley with double hook bolting and Greener breech.
Barrel: 26″ (Mod. & Imp. Cyl., Cyl. & Imp. Cyl.).
Weight: 6¼ to 6½ lbs.
Stock: Walnut. English style or p.g., 14¼″x1½″x2¼″.
Features: Hunting scene engraving. Double, single or single selective trigger. Imported by Champlin Firearms.
Price: With double triggers **$850.00**

PREMIER AMBASSADOR DOUBLE BARREL SHOTGUN
Gauge: 12, 16 (2¾"); 20, 410 (3").
Action: Triple Greener crossbolt, Purdey avail. on 410; side locks.
Barrels: 22" exc. 410; 26" all (Mod. & Full).
Weight: 7¼ lbs. (12) to 6¼ lbs. (410). **Length:** 44½".
Stock: 14" x 1⅝" x 2½" checkered walnut, p.g., beavertail fore-end.
Features: Cocking indicators, double triggers, auto safety. Imported from Europe by Premier.
Price: **$209.40**

Premier Continental Double Hammer Shotgun
Same as Ambassador except outside hammers, not avail. in 410.
Price: **$190.40**

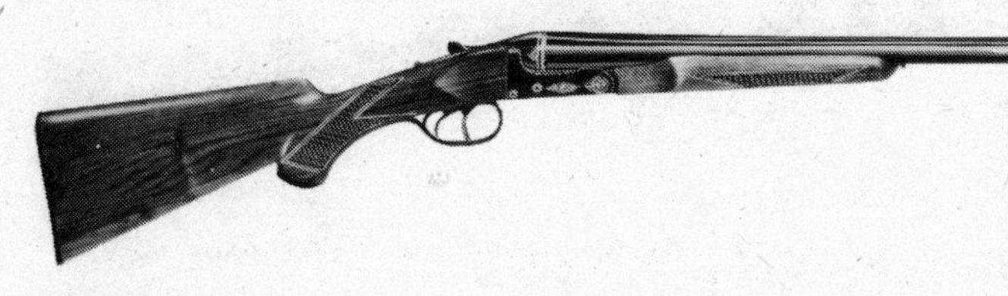

PREMIER REGENT DOUBLE BARREL SHOTGUN
Gauge: 12, 16, 28 (2¾" chambers); 20, 410 (3" chambers).
Action: Triple Greener crossbolt; Purdey optional on 28, 410.
Barrels: 26" (I.C. & Mod.) exc. 28 and 410 only (Mod. & Full); 28" (Mod. & Full); 30" 12 only (Mod. & Full).
Weight: 7¼ lbs. (12) to 6⅛ lbs. (410). **Length:** 42½" (26" bbls.).
Stock: 14" x 1⅝" x 2½" checkered walnut, p.g. and fore-end.
Features: Matted tapered rib, double triggers, auto safety. Extra bbl. sets avail. Imported from Europe by Premier.
Price: **$154.50**

Premier Brush King Double Barrel Shotgun
Same as Regent except 12 and 20 ga. only, 22" bbls. (I.C. & Mod.), weight 6¼ lbs. (12), 5¾ lbs. (20).
Price: **$165.75**

Premier Magnum Double Barrel Shotgun
Similar to Regent except 10 ga. (3½" chambers) 32" or 12 ga. (3" chambers) 30", both Full & Full. Recoil pad, beavertail fore-end.
Price: 12 ga. **$173.60**
Price: 10 ga. **198.00**

ROSSI OVERLAND DOUBLE BARREL SHOTGUN
Gauge: 12, 20 (3" chambers).
Action: Sidelock with external hammers; Greener crossbolt.
Barrel: 12 ga., 20" (Imp. Cyl., Mod.) 20 ga., 20" (Mod., Full).
Weight: 6½ to 7 lbs.
Stock: Walnut p.g. with beavertail fore-end.
Features: Solid raised matted rib. Imported from Brazil by Garcia.
Price: **$175.00**

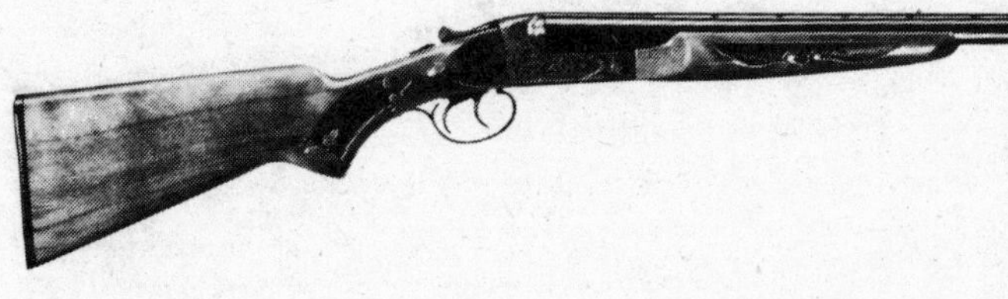

SAVAGE/FOX B 24" LIGHTWEIGHT
Gauge: 12, 20 (2¾" & 3" chambers).
Action: Hammerless, top lever, double triggers.
Barrel: 24", 12 & 20 ga. (Imp. Cyl. & Mod.), 26" (Imp. Cyl. & Mod.), 28" (Mod. & Full), 30" (Mod. & Full, 12 ga. only), 26", 410 ga. (Full & Full).
Weight: 7 to 8 lbs.
Stocks: 14"x1½"x2½", select walnut. Checkered p.g. and fore-end.
Features: Color case-hardened frame, beavertail fore-end, vent. rib.
Price: **$174.50**

SAVAGE FOX MODEL B-SE Double
Gauge: 12, 20, 410 (20, 2¾" and 3"; 410, 2½" and 3" shells).
Action: Hammerless, takedown; non-selective single trigger; auto. safety. Automatic ejectors.
Barrel: 12, 20 ga. 26" (Imp. Cyl., Mod.); 12 ga. (Mod., Full); 410, 26" (Full, Full). Vent. rib on all.
Stock: 14"x1½"x2½". Walnut, checkered p.g. and beavertail fore-end.
Weight: 12 ga. 7 lbs., 16 ga. 6¾ lbs., 20 ga. 6½ lbs., 410 ga. 6¼ lbs.
Features: Decorated, case-hardened frame; white bead front and middle sights.
Price: **$199.50**
Also available with double triggers, case hardened frame, without white line spacers and auto. ejectors as Model B **$174.50**

SAVAGE-STEVENS MODEL 311 DOUBLE
Gauge: 12, 16, 20, 410 (12, 20 and 410, 3" chambers).
Action: Top lever, hammerless; double triggers, auto top tang safety.
Barrel: 12, 16, 20 ga. 36" (Imp. Cyl., Mod.); 12 ga. 28" (Mod., Full); 12 ga. 30" (Mod., Full); 410 ga. 26" (Full, Full).
Length: 45¾" over-all. **Weight:** 7-8 lbs. (30" bbl.).
Stock: 14"x1½"x2½". Walnut finish, p.g., fluted comb.
Features: Box type frame, case-hardened finish.
Price: **$137.50**

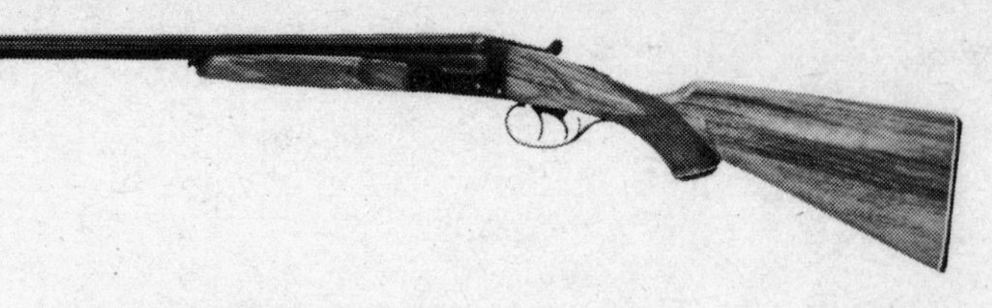

SLOAN'S P-O-S DOUBLE BARREL SHOTGUN

Gauge: 10, 12, 20 or 410 (3" chambers except 10, 3½"; 28, 2¾").
Action: Hammerless, double triggers.
Barrel: 32" 10, 30" 12 (Full & Full); 30" 12, 28" 12 or 20, 26" 28 or 410 (Mod. & Full); 26" 12 or 20 (I.C. & Mod.).
Stock: Checkered walnut, p.g. cap and buttplate with white line spacers.
Features: Imported from Spain by Charles Daly.
Price: 12, 20 .... **$150.00**
Price: 10 ga. **$199.00**

Sloan's P-O-S Coach Gun
Similar to standard P-O-S except has exposed hammers, 12 or 20 ga. only with 20" barrels **$160.00**

STAR GAUGE DOUBLE BARREL SHOTGUN

Gauge: 12 ga. (2¾"); 20 ga., 410 (3").
Barrel: 26" (Imp. Cyl. & Mod., Full & Full, Mod. & Full), 28" (Mod. & Full; solid rib.
Weight: 7¼ lbs. (12 ga.). **Length:** 45¼" (with 28" bbl.).
Stock: European walnut (14"x1⅛"x1¾"); checkered p.g. and fore-end; rubber recoil pad.
Features: Color case hardened receiver; auto ejectors; double triggers. Imported by Interarms.
Price: **$249.00**

UGARTECHEA DOUBLE BARREL SHOTGUN

Gauge: 12 (Model 1302), 20 (Model 1303), 28 (Model 1304), 410 (Model 1305). All 3-inch chambers except 28 ga.
Action: Anson & Deeley, gold plated double triggers.
Barrel: 30" (Mod. and Full) 12 ga., 28" (Mod. and Full) 12 and 20 ga., 26" (Imp. Cyl. and Mod.) 12 and 20 ga., (Mod. and Full) 28 ga., (Full and Full) 410 ga.
Stock: Hand checkered walnut, ebonite p.g. cap and butt plate with white spacers, beavertail fore-end.
Features: Scroll engraving. Imported from Spain by American Import.
Price: **$295.00**

UNIVERSAL BAIKAL MC-10 SIDE-BY-SIDE

Gauge: 12 or 20 ga. (2¾" chambers).
Barrel: 12 ga. 28" (Mod. & Full), 20 ga. 26" (Imp. Cyl. & Mod.).
Weight: 6 lbs. (20 ga.), 6¾ lbs. (12 ga.).
Stock: Fancy walnut. Hand checkered p.g. and fore-end. Choice of full p.g. or straight stock. Semi-beavertail fore-end.
Features: Fully engraved receiver with animal and bird scenes. Engraved trigger guard and tang. Double trigger. Chrome barrels, chambers and internal parts. Raised solid rib. Extractors or selective ejectors. Auto. safety, sling swivels. Imported by Universal Sporting Goods.
Price: **$910.00**

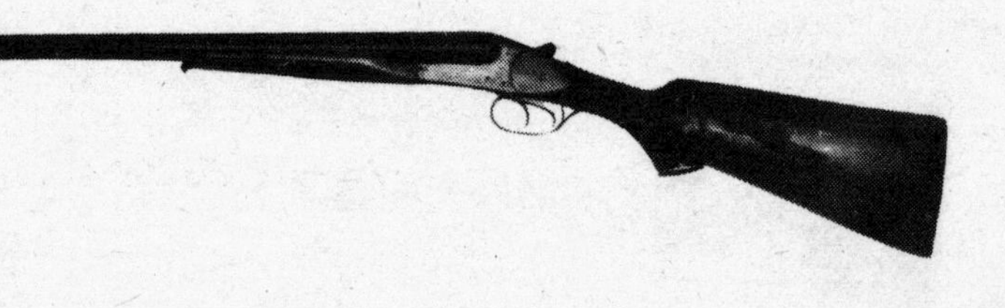

UNIVERSAL BAIKAL IJ-58M SIDE-BY-SIDE

Gauge: 12 ga. (2¾" chambers).
Barrel: 26" (Imp. Cyl. & Mod.), 28" (Mod. & Full).
Weight: 6¾ lbs.
Stock: Walnut. Hand checkered p.g. and beavertail fore-end. Rubber recoil pad. White spacers at p.g. and butt.
Features: Hinged front double trigger. Chrome barrels and chambers. Fore-end center latch. Hand engraved receiver. Extractors. Imported by Universal Sporting Goods.
Price: **$151.85**

UNIVERSAL BAIKAL TOZ-66 SIDE-BY-SIDE

Gauge: 12 ga. (2¾" chambers).
Barrel: 20" (Imp. Cyl. & Mod.), 28" (Mod. & Full).
Weight: 6¼-6½ lbs.
Stock: Walnut. Hand checkered p.g. and beavertail fore-end. Rubber recoil pad with white spacers at p.g. and butt.
Features: Exposed hammers. Chrome barrels and chambers. Fore-end center latch. Hand engraved receiver. Extractors. Imported by Universal Sporting Goods.
Price: **$145.63**

UNIVERSAL BAIKAL MC-111 SIDE-BY-SIDE

Gauge: 12 ga. (2¾" chambers).
Barrel: To customer's specifications, choice of chokes.
Weight: 7 lbs.
Stock: Fancy walnut. Choice of p.g. or straight stock. Gold and silver inlays in butt. Semi-beavertail fore-end. Monte Carlo. To customer's specifications.
Features: Handmade sidelock shotgun. Removable sideplates. Chrome barrels, chambers and internal parts. Selective ejectors, single selective trigger, hammer interceptors, cocking indicators. Hand chiseled scenes on receiver to customer specs. Gold inlays as requested. Sling swivels on barrel and butt. Imported by Universal Sporting Goods.
Price: Special order only **$2,340.00**

SHOTGUNS—DOUBLE BARREL

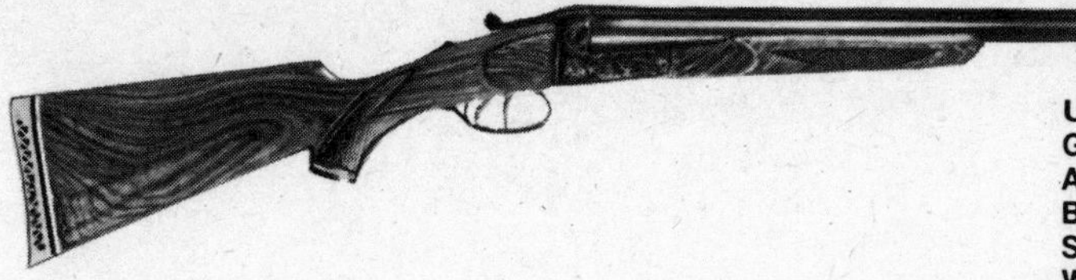

UNIVERSAL DOUBLE WING DOUBLE

Gauge: 12, 20 and 410 (3″ chambers).
Action: Top break, boxlock.
Barrel: 26″ (Imp. Cyl., Mod.); 28″ or 30″ (Mod., Full; Imp., Mod.; Full & Full).
Stock: Walnut p.g. and fore-end, checkered.
Weight: About 7 lbs.
Features: Double triggers; Recoil pad. Beavertail style fore-end.
Price: **$189.95**
Price: 10 ga. 3½″ chamber 32″ Full and Full (M2030) **$230.00**
Price: 410 ga. **$205.00**

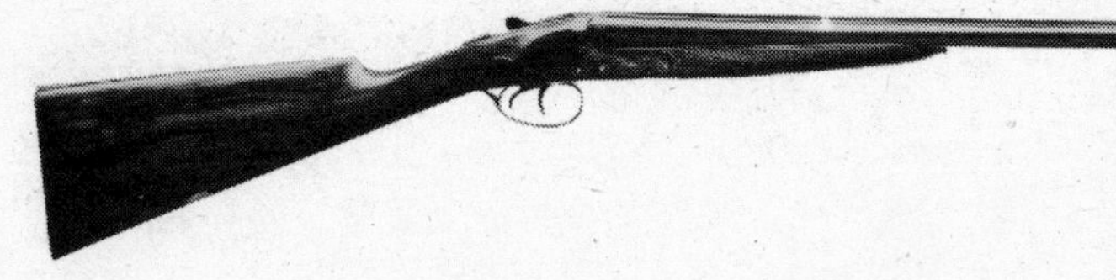

WEBLEY & SCOTT SIDE-BY-SIDE SHOTGUNS

Gauge: 20 ga. (3″ chambers), 28 ga. (2¾″ chambers).
Action: Boxlock.
Barrel: 26″ (Imp. & Imp. Mod.), 28 ga., 25″ (Imp. & Imp. Mod.).
Weight: 6 lbs. (20 ga.), 5½ lbs. (28 ga.).
Stock: Walnut, straight grip. 14⅝″x1½″x2¼″.
Features: Engine-turned flat rib. Engraved action. Checkered p.g. and fore-end. Comes with fitted leather case, snap caps, complete cleaning equipment. Imported by Harrington & Richardson.
Price: Model 720 (20 ga.) **$1,950.00**
Price: Model 728 (28 ga.) **$1,950.00**

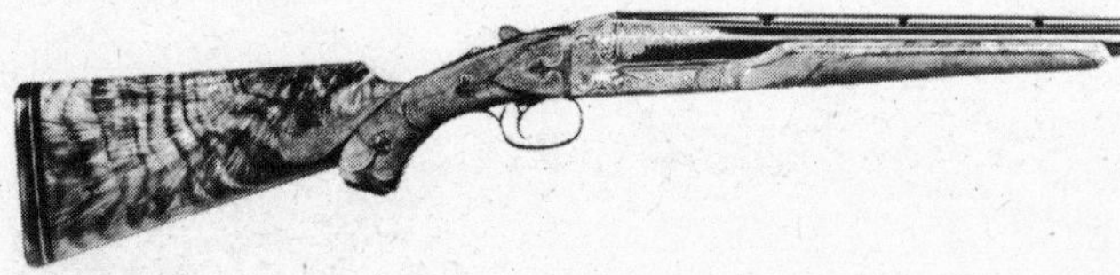

WINCHESTER 21 CUSTOM DOUBLE GUN

12, 16 or 20 ga. Almost any choke or bbl. length combination. Matted rib, 2¾″ chambers, rounded frame, stock of AA-grade full fancy American walnut to customer's dimensions; straight or p.g., cheekpiece, Monte Carlo and/or offset; field. Skeet or trap fore-end.
Full fancy checkering, engine-turned receiver parts, gold plated trigger and gold oval name plate (optional) with three initials .....**Price on request.**

Winchester 21 Grand American

Same as Custom and Pigeon grades except: style "B" stock carving, with style "6" engraving, all figures gold inlaid; extra pair of bbls. with beavertail fore-end, engraved and carved to match rest of gun; full leather trunk case or all, with canvas cover ....**Price on request.**

Winchester 21 Pigeon grade

Same as Custom grade except: 3″ chambers, available in 12 and 20 ga.; matted or vent. rib, leather covered pad (optional); style "A" stock carving and style "6" engraving (see Win. catalog); gold inlaid p.g. cap, gold name-plate or 3 gold initials in guard ....**Price on request.**

SHOTGUNS—BOLT ACTION

MARLIN GOOSE GUN BOLT ACTION

Gauge: 12 only, 2-shot (3″ mag. or 2¾″).
Action: Bolt action, thumb safety, detachable clip.
Barrel: 36″, Full choke.
Stock: Walnut, p.g., recoil pad, leather strap & swivels.
Weight: 7¼ lbs., 57″ over-all.
Features: Tapped for receiver sights. Swivels and leather carrying strap. Gold-plated trigger.
Price: **$74.95**

Marlin 55S Slug Gun

Same as Goose Gun except: 24″ barrel, iron sights (rear adj.), drilled and tapped for scope mounting. Comes with carrying strap and swivels. Weight is 7 lbs., over-all length 45″. **$79.95**

MOSSBERG MODEL 395K BOLT ACTION

Gauge: 12, 3-shot (3″ chamber).
Action: Bolt; takedown; detachable clip.
Barrel: 28″ with C-Lect-Choke.
Stock: Walnut finish, p.g. Monte Carlo comb; recoil pad.
Weight: 6¾ lbs. **Length:** 47½″ over-all.
Features: Streamlined action; top safety; grooved rear sight.
Price: **$80.70**
Also available in 20 ga. 3″ chamber 28″ bbl. 6¼ lbs., as M385K **$74.88**

MOSSBERG MODEL 183K BOLT ACTION

Gauge: 410, 3-shot (3″ chamber).
Action: Bolt; top-loading mag.; thumb safety.
Barrel: 25″ with C-Lect-Choke.
Stock: Walnut finish, p.g., Monte Carlo comb., rubber recoil pad w/spacer.
Weight: 6¾ lbs. **Length:** 43½″ over-all.
Features: Moulded trigger guard with finger grooves, gold bead front sight.
Price: **$69.40**
Price: As 183T without choke **$64.78**

Mossberg Model 395S Bolt Action

Same as Model 395K except 24″ barrel with adjustable folding leaf rear sight and ramp front, for use with slugs. Sling supplied **$82.17**

SHOTGUNS—BOLT ACTION

SAVAGE-STEVENS 58 BOLT ACTION SHOTGUN

Gauge: 410 ga. (2½″ or 3″ chamber), 3-shot clip.
Action: Self-cocking bolt; double extractors; thumb safety.
Barrel: 24″, Full choke.
Stock: Walnut finish, checkered fore-end and p.g., recoil pad.
Weight: 5½ lbs. **Length:** 43″ over-all.
Features: Crisp trigger pull, Electro-Cote stock finish.
Price: **$59.95**

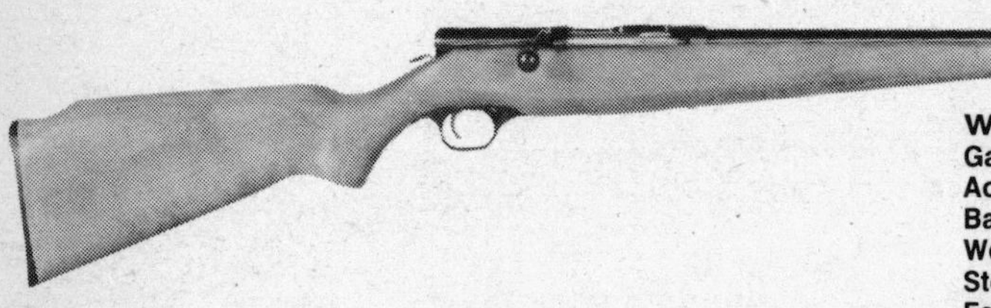

WESTERN FIELD 150C BOLT ACTION SHOTGUN

Gauge: 410 (3″ chamber).
Action: Self cocking, bolt action. Thumb safety. 3-shot magazine.
Barrel: 24″, full choke.
Weight: 5½ lbs. **Length:** 44½″ over-all.
Stock: Hardwood, Monte Carlo design.
Features: Top loading.
Price: **$62.00**

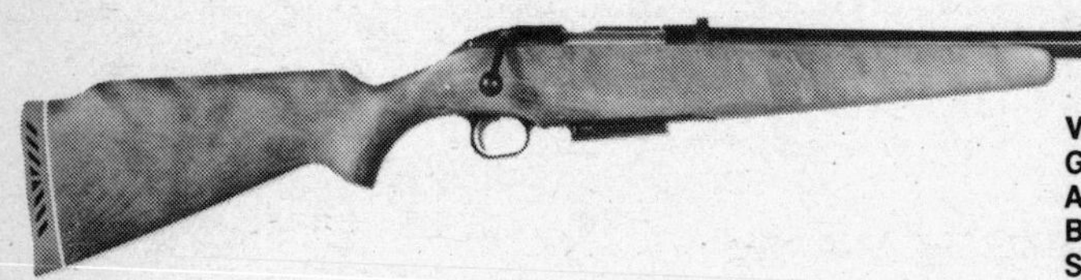

WESTERN FIELD 172 BOLT ACTION SHOTGUN

Gauge: 12 (3″ chamber).
Action: Self-cocking bolt. Thumb safety, double locking lugs, detachable clip.
Barrel: 28″ adj. choke, shoots rifled slugs.
Stock: Walnut, Monte Carlo design, p.g., recoil pad.
Features: Quick removable bolt with double extractors, grooved rear sight.
Price: **$76.00**
M175 Similar to above except 20 ga., 26″ barrel **$74.00**
M170 Similar to 172 except has patridge front sight, folding-leaf adj. rear, comes with sling and swivels **$84.00**

SHOTGUNS—SINGLE BARREL

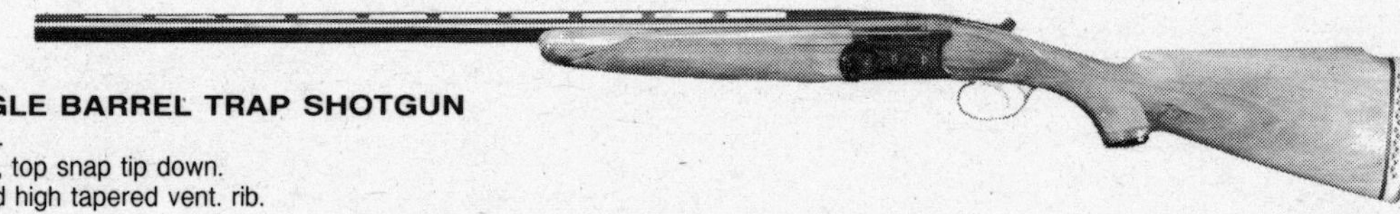

BERETTA MARK II SINGLE BARREL TRAP SHOTGUN

Gauge: 12 only; (2¾″ chamber).
Action: BL type, full width hinge, top snap tip down.
Barrel: 32″ or 34″, (Full), matted high tapered vent. rib.
Weight: 8¼ lbs.
Stock: 14⅜″ x 1⅜″ x 1¾″. Hand checkered European walnut, p.g.; rubber recoil pad, beavertail fore-end, Monte Carlo.
Features: Hand engraved receiver.
Price: **$410.00**

BROWNING BT-99 SINGLE BARREL TRAP

Gauge: 12 guage only (2¾″).
Action: Top lever break-open hammerless, engraved.
Barrel: 32″ or 34″ (Mod., Imp. Mod. or Full) with 11/32″ wide, high post floating vent rib.
Stock: French walnut, hand checkered full p.g. and beavertail fore-end, factory fitted recoil pad (14⅜″x1 7/16″x1⅝″).
Weight: 8 lbs. (32″ bbl.), 8⅛ lbs. (34″ bbl.).
Features: Automatic ejector, gold plated trigger has about 3½ lb. pull, no safety.
Price: **$399.50**

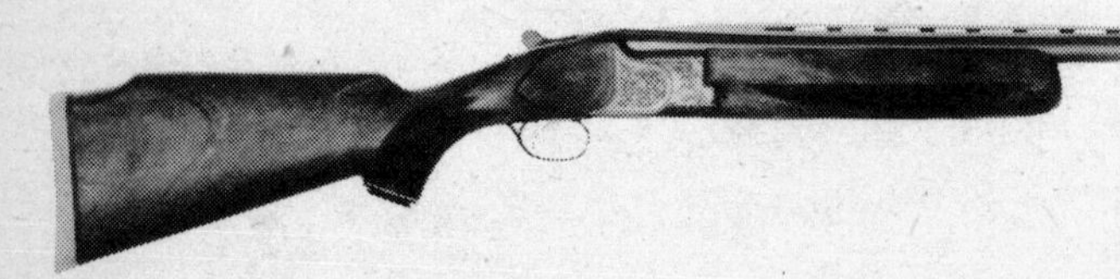

CHARLES DALY SUPERIOR GRADE SINGLE BARREL TRAP

Gauge: 12 only (2¾″ chamber).
Barrel: 32″ (Full), 34″ (Full).
Weight: About 6¼ lbs.
Stock: Monte Carlo, walnut, checkered p.g. and fore-end. 14⅜″x1½″x2½″x1½″.
Features: Special nickel-finish receiver, scroll engraving.
Price: **$295.00**

F.I.E. SINGLE BARREL SHOTGUN

Gauge: 12, 20 (2¾"), 410 (3").
Barrel: 12 & 20 ga. 28" (Full); 410 ga. (Full).
Weight: 6½ lbs.
Stock: Walnut stained hardwood, beavertail fore-end.
Sights: Metal bead front.
Features: Trigger guard is pulled to open action. Exposed hammer. Imported from Brazil by Firearms Import & Export.
Price: **$42.50**

GALEF COMPANION SINGLE BARREL SHOTGUN

Gauge: 12, 20, 410 (3"); 16, 28 (2¾").
Action: Folding boxlock.
Barrel: 28" exc. 12 (30") and 410 (26"), all Full.
Weight: 5½ lbs. (12) to 4½ lbs. (410).
Stock: 14"x1½"x2⅝" hand checkered walnut, p.g.
Features: Non-auto safety, folds. Vent. rib $5.00 additional. Imported from Italy by Galef.
Price: Plain bbl. .... **$71.00** Vent. rib **$78.50**

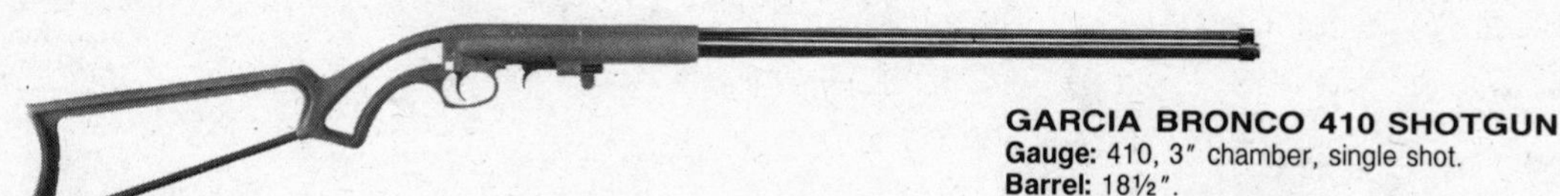

GARCIA BRONCO 410 SHOTGUN

Gauge: 410, 3" chamber, single shot.
Barrel: 18½".
Weight: 3½ lbs. **Length:** 32" over-all.
Stock: Skeletonized crackle finish alloy casting.
Features: Swing-out chamber; p.g. stock; push-button safety; instant take-down. From Garcia.
Price: **$49.00**

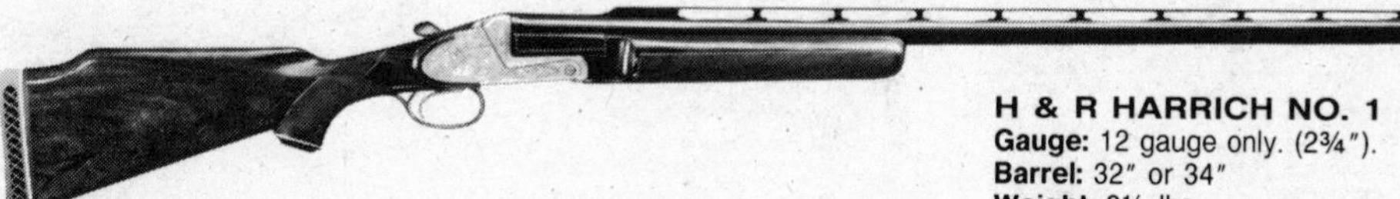

H & R HARRICH NO. 1

Gauge: 12 gauge only. (2¾").
Barrel: 32" or 34"
Weight: 8½ lbs.
Stock: Select walnut, checkered p.g. and beavertail fore-end 14¾"x1¼"x1¼"x2".
Features: Anson & Deeley type locking system with Kersten top locks and double under-locking lugs. Full length high line vent. rib. Hand engraved side locks.
Price: **$1,850.00**

H & R TOPPER MODELS 58 and 98

Gauge: 12, 20 and 410. (2¾" or 3" chamber), 16 (2¾" only).
Action: Takedown. Side lever opening. External hammer, auto ejection. Case hardened frame.
Barrel: 12 ga., 28", 30", 32", 36"; 20 and 410 ga., 28". (Full choke). 12, 16, 20 ga. available 28" (Mod.).
Stock: Walnut finished hardwood; p.g., (14"x1¾"x2½").
Weight: 5 to 6½ lbs., according to gauge and bbl. length.
Features: Self-adj. bbl. lock; coil springs throughout; auto. rebound hammer.
Price: M58 .... **$49.99**
Model 98, Topper Deluxe Chrome frame, ebony finished stock. 20 ga. and 410, 28" bbl. **$57.50**

H & R Topper Jr. Model 490

Like M158 except ideally proportioned stock for the smaller shooter. Can be cheaply changed to full size. 20 ga. (Mod.) or 410 (Full) 26" bbl. Weight 5 lbs., 40½" over-all **$52.50**

H & R Topper Buck Model 162

Same as M158 except 12 ga. 24" cyl. bored bbl., adj. Lyman peep rear sight, blade front, 5½ lbs.; over-all 40". Cross bolt safety: push-button action release **$62.50**

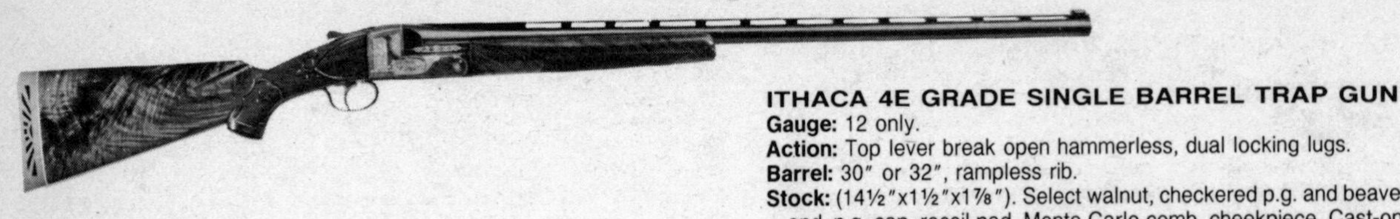

ITHACA 4E GRADE SINGLE BARREL TRAP GUN

Gauge: 12 only.
Action: Top lever break open hammerless, dual locking lugs.
Barrel: 30″ or 32″, rampless rib.
Stock: (14½″x1½″x1⅞″). Select walnut, checkered p.g. and beavertail fore-end, p.g. cap, recoil pad, Monte Carlo comb, cheekpiece, Cast-on, cast-off or extreme deviation from standard stock dimensions $100 extra. Reasonable deviation allowed without extra charge.
Features: Frame, top lever and trigger guard engraved. Gold name plate in stock.
Price: Custom made: **$2,500.00**

Ithaca 5E Grade Single Barrel Trap
Same as 4E except: Vent. rib bbl., better wood, more extensive engraving, and gold inlaid figures. Custom made: **$3,500.00**

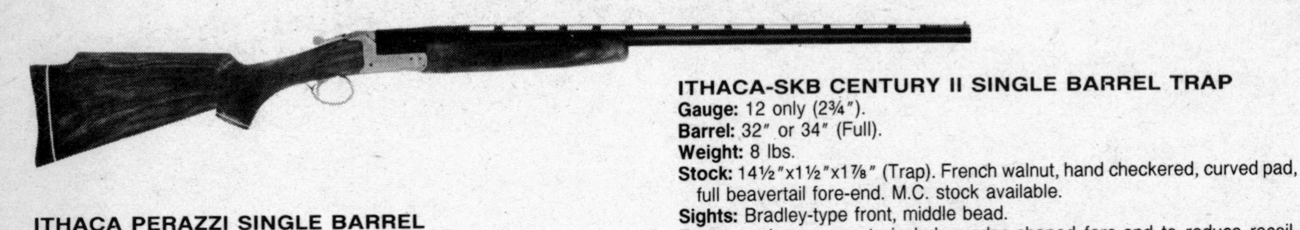

ITHACA-SKB CENTURY II SINGLE BARREL TRAP

Gauge: 12 only (2¾″).
Barrel: 32″ or 34″ (Full).
Weight: 8 lbs.
Stock: 14½″x1½″x1⅞″ (Trap). French walnut, hand checkered, curved pad, full beavertail fore-end. M.C. stock available.
Sights: Bradley-type front, middle bead.
Features: Improvements include wedge-shaped fore-end to reduce recoil, extra strength one-piece extractor, longer fore-end iron and latching system for tighter lock-up and easier removal. Stock dimension ⅛″ higher, new firing pin retention system.
Price: **$599.95**
Price: Monte Carlo stock **$599.95**

ITHACA PERAZZI SINGLE BARREL

Gauge: 12 (2¾″ chamber)
Action: Top lever, break open, top tang safety.
Barrel: 32″ or 34″; custom choking; ventilated rib.
Stock: Custom fitted European walnut in lacquered or oil finish.
Weight: About 8½ lbs.
Features: Hand-engraved receiver; interchangeable stocks available with some fitting.
Price: **$1,295.00**

ITHACA MODEL 66 SUPERSINGLE

Gauge: 20 or 410 (3″ chamber).
Action: Non-takedown; under lever opening.
Barrel: 12, 20 ga. 28″ (Mod., Full); 12 ga., 30″ (Full), 410, 26″ (Full).
Stock: Straight grip walnut-finish stock and fore-end.
Weight: About 7 lbs.
Features: Rebounding hammer independent of the lever.
Price: Standard **$59.95**

Ithaca Model 66 Supersingle Youth
Same as the 66 Standard except: 20 (26″ Bbl., Mod.) and 410 ga. (26″ Bbl., Full) shorter stock with recoil pad **$65.95**

IVER JOHNSON CHAMPION

Gauge: 12, 20 or 410 (3″ chamber).
Barrel: 12 gauge, 28″ or 30″; 20 gauge, 28″; 410, 26″; full choke.
Stock: Walnut finish, trap style fore-end.
Features: Takedown action, automatic ejection.
Price: Either gauge **$44.95**

KRIEGHOFF SINGLE BARREL TRAP SHOTGUN

Gauge: 12.
Action: Boxlock, short hammer fall.
Barrel: 32″ or 34″ (Full).
Weight: About 8½ lbs.
Stock: Monte Carlo with checkered p.g. and grooved beavertail fore-end.
Features: Thumb safety, vent. rib. Extra bbls. available **$445.00.** Available with various grades of decoration, wood. Imported from Germany by Krieghoff Gun Co.
Price: Standard **$1,295.00**
Monte Carlo Grade **$5,295.00**
Super Crown Grade **$6,695.00**
San Remo **$2,695.00**
Crown **$5,695.00**

LJUTIC DYN-A-TRAP SINGLE BARREL

Gauge: 12 ga. only.
Barrel: 33″ (Full).
Weight: Approx. 9 lbs.
Stock: Standard trap dimensions. Custom stock optional ($200.00).
Features: Regular pull trigger, release trigger optional ($75.00); extractor only; only 5 moving parts in action; Ljutic pushbutton opener. From Ljutic Industries.
Price: **$995.00**
Price: Release trigger **$75.00**
Price: Custom stock **$200.00**

LJUTIC MONO GUN SINGLE BARREL

Gauge: 12 ga. only.
Barrel: 34″, choked to customer specs; hollow-milled rib, 35½″ sight plane.
Weight: Approx. 9 lbs.
Stock: To customer specs. Oil finish, hand checkered.
Features: Pull or release trigger; removeable trigger guard contains trigger and hammer mechanism; Ljutic pushbutton opener on front of trigger guard. From Ljutic Industries.
Price: **$1,995.00**
Price: Extra barrel **$500.00**
Price: Release trigger **$75.00**

MONTE CARLO SINGLE BARREL SHOTGUN

Gauge: 12 (2¾″ chamber).
Action: Monte Carlo, bottom release.
Barrel: 32″ (Trap).
Weight: 8¼ lbs.
Stock: 14½″x1⅛″x1⅝″ hand checkered walnut, p.g., beavertail fore-end, recoil pad.
Features: Auto ejector, slide safety, gold plated trigger. Imported from Italy by Galef.
Price: **$195.00**

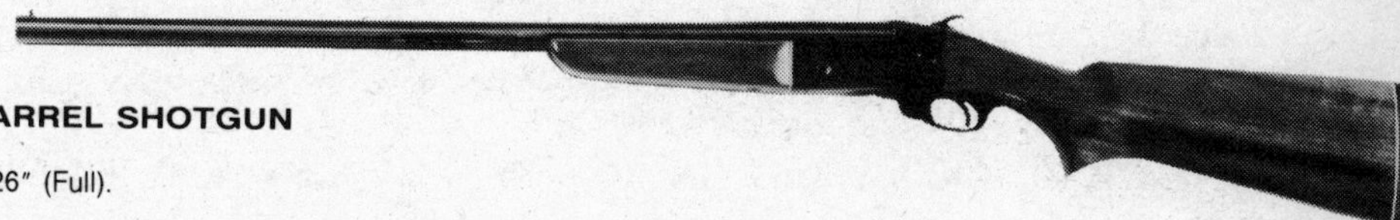

PRIDE OF BRAZIL SINGLE BARREL SHOTGUN

Gauge: 12, 20 (2¾″), 410 (3″).
Barrel: 12 & 20 ga. 28″ (Full); 410 ga. 26″ (Full).
Weight: 6½ lbs.
Stock: Walnut stained hardwood.
Sights: Metal bead front.
Features: Button on front of trigger guard opens action. Exposed hammer. Automatic extractor. Imported from Brazil by Firearms Import & Export.
Price: **$49.95**

SAVAGE-STEVENS MODEL 94-C Single Barrel Gun

Gauge: 12, 16, 20, 410 (12, 20 and 410, 3″ chambers).
Action: Top lever break open; hammer; auto. ejector.
Barrel: 12 ga. 28″, 30″, 32″, 36″; 16, 20 ga. 28″; 410 ga. 26″. Full choke only.
Stock: 14″x1½″x2½″. Walnut finish, checkered p.g. and fore-end.
Weight: About 6 lbs. **Length:** 42″ over-all (26″ bbl.).
Features: Color case-hardened frame, low rebounding hammer.
Price: 26″ to 32″ bbls. .... **$49.90** 36″ bbl. **$52.50**

Stevens M94-Y Youth's Gun

Same as Model 94-C except: 26″ bbl., 20 ga. Mod. or 410 Full, 12½″ stock with recoil pad. Wgt. about 5½ lbs. 40½″ over-all. **$52.50**

UNIVERSAL BAIKAL IJ-18 SINGLE BARREL

Gauge: 12 or 20 ga., 2¾″ chambers.
Barrel: 12 ga. 28″ (Mod.), 30″ (Full), 20 ga. 26″ (Mod.).
Weight: 5¾ lbs.
Stock: Walnut. Hand checkered p.g. and fore-end. White spacers at p.g. and plastice buttplate.
Features: Chrome barrel and chamber. Cross-bolt safety in trigger guard. Cocking indicator. Extractor. Imported by Universal Sporting Goods.
Price: **$53.15**

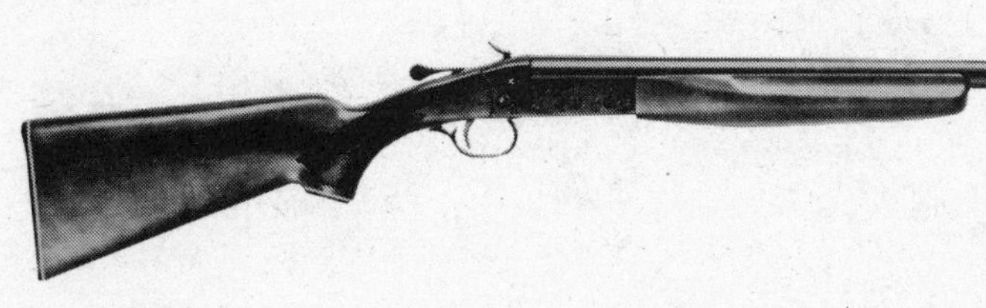

WINCHESTER 37A SINGLE SHOT

Gauge: 12, 20, 410 (3″ chamber), 16, 28 (2¾″ chamber).
Action: Top lever break-open, exposed hammer.
Barrel: 26″, 410 ga. (Full), 28″, 20 & 28 ga. (Full), 30″, 16 ga. (Full), 30″, 32″ 36″, 12 ga. (Full).
Length: 42¼″ over-all (26″ bbl.). **Weight:** 5½ to 6¼ lbs.
Stock: 14″x1⅜″x2⅜″, walnut finish.
Sights: Metal bead front.
Features: Checkered p.g. and fore-end bottom, gold plated trigger, engraved receiver, concave hammer spur. Grip cap and buttplate have white spacers. Auto. ejector. Top lever opens right or left.
Price: Standard Model, 12 ga. 26″-32″ bbl. **$59.95**
Price: 16, 20, 28 410 ga. **$59.95**
Price: 12 ga., 36″ bbl. **$64.95**

Winchester 37A Youth Model

Same as std. 37A except: shorter 26″ bbl., youth-size stock (12½″ pull), 40¾″ over-all length. Rubber recoil pad. Available only in 20 ga. (Imp. Mod.) or 410 (Full). **$64.95**

The following pages catalog the black powder arms currently available to U.S. shooters. These range from quite precise replicas of historically significant arms to totally new designs created expressly to give the black powder shooter the benefits of modern technology.

Most of the replicas are imported, and many are available from more than one source. Thus examples of a given model such as the 1860 Army revolver or Zouave rifle purchased from different importers may vary in price, finish and fitting. Most of them bear proof marks, indicating that they have been test fired in the proof house of their country of origin.

A list of the importers and the retail price range are included with the description for each model. Many local dealers handle more than one importer's products, giving the prospective buyer an opportunity to make his own judgment in selecting a black powder gun. Most importers have catalogs available free or at nominal cost, and some are well worth having for the useful information on black powder shooting they provide in addition to their detailed descriptions and specifications of the guns.

A number of special accessories are also available for the black powder shooter. These include replica powder flasks, bullet moulds, cappers and tools, as well as more modern devices to facilitate black powder cleaning and maintenance. Ornate presentation cases and even detachable shoulder stocks are also available for some black powder pistols from their importers. Again, dealers or the importers will have catalogs.

The black powder guns are arranged in four sections: Single Shot Pistols, Revolvers, Muskets & Rifles, and Shotguns. The guns within each section are arranged by date of the original, with the oldest first. Thus the 1847 Walker replica leads off the revolver section, and flintlocks precede precussion arms in the other sections.

BLACK POWDER SINGLE SHOT PISTOLS—FLINT & PERCUSSION

DIXIE WHEELOCK COURIER PISTOL
Caliber: 36.
Barrel: 4″, half octagon, half round; flared muzzle.
Weight: 1¼ lbs. **Length:** 7″ over-all.
Stock: Metal.
Sights: None.
Features: Replica of 1580 Courier Pistol. Frame and hammer of brass, engraved. Steel barrel. Comes complete with spanner. Imported from England by Dixie Gun Works.
Price: **$175.00**

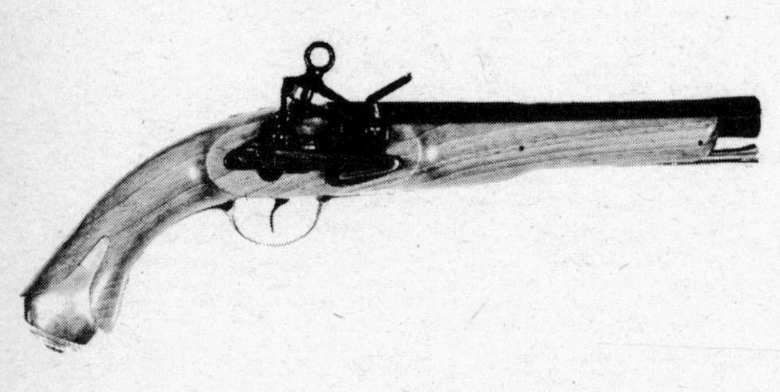

RIPOLL BELT PISTOL
Caliber: 61.
Barrel: 8¾″ rifled.
Length: 15″. **Weight:** 40 oz.
Stock: Walnut.
Features: Miquelet lock, cold-forged barrel, proof tested. Imported by CVA.
Price: **$84.95**

RIPOLL BOOT PISTOL
Caliber: 45.
Barrel: 4″, rifled.
Length: 8¼″ over-all. **Weight:** 17 oz.
Stock: Walnut.
Features: Miquelet lock, cold-forged barrel, proof tested. Imported by CVA.
Price: **$79.95**

TOWER FLINTLOCK PISTOL
Caliber: 45, 69.
Barrel: 8¼″.
Weight: 40 oz. **Length:** 14″ over-all.
Stock: Walnut.
Sights: Fixed.
Features: Engraved lock, brass furniture. Specifications, including caliber, weight and length may vary with importers. Available as flint or percussion. Imported by The Armoury, F.I.E., Hawes, C.V.A., Centennial, Dixie, Navy/Replica.
Price: . . . . **$23.00** to **$57.95.**

HARPER'S FERRY 1806 PISTOL
Caliber: 54.
Barrel: 10″.
Weight: 40 oz. **Length:** 16″ over-all.
Stock: Walnut.
Sights: Fixed.
Features: Case hardened lock, brass mounted browned bbl. Replica of the first U.S. Gov't.-made flintlock pistol. Imported by Navy/Replica.
Price: **$95.00**

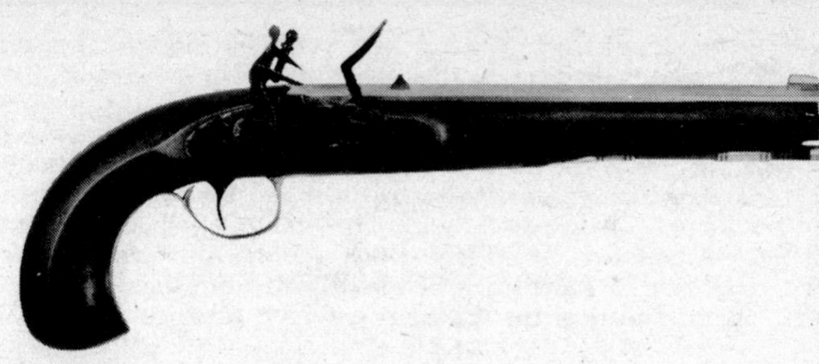

KENTUCKY FLINTLOCK PISTOL
Caliber: 44, 45.
Barrel: 10⅛″.
Weight: 32 oz. **Length:** 15½″ over-all.
Stock: Walnut.
Sights: Fixed.
Features: Case hardened lock, blued bbl.; available also as brass bbl. flint Model 1821 ($95.00, Navy). Imported by Navy/Replica, The Armoury, Century, Centennial, F.I.E., Jana, Dixie, C.V.A, Hawes, Kassnar, Markwell.
Price: .... **$40.95** to **$89.95**
Price: In kit form, from **$24.95**

KENTUCKY PERCUSSION PISTOL
Similar to above but percussion lock. Imported by Centennial, The Armoury, Navy/Replica, F.I.E., Hawes, Jana, C.V.A., Dixie, Century.
Price: .... **$26.95** to **$85.00**
Price: In kit form .... **$35.95** to **$54.95**

ENGLISH BELT PISTOL
Caliber: 44 (.451″ bore).
Barrel: 7″, octagonal, rifled.
Length: 12″ over-all.
Stock: Walnut.
Features: Case-hardened lock, brass furniture, fixed sights. Available in either flint or percussion. Imported by CVA.
Price: Percussion **$36.95**
Price: Flint **$40.95**
Also available in kit form, either flint or percussion. Stock 90% inletted.
Price: .... **$24.95** to **$30.95**

KENTUCKY BELT PERCUSSION PISTOL
Caliber: 45.
Barrel: 7″, rifled.
Weight: 29 oz. **Length:** 12″ over-all.
Stock: Walnut.
Sights: Fixed.
Features: Engraved lock, brass furniture, steel ramrod. Available as flint or percussion. Imported by The Armoury, C.V.A., Markwell Arms.
Price: .... **$22.95** to **$55.49.**
Price: Kit form, from **$30.80**

HARPER'S FERRY MODEL 1855 PERCUSSION PISTOL
Caliber: 58.
Barrel: 11¾″, rifled.
Weight: 56 oz. **Length:** 18″ over-all.
Stock: Walnut.
Sights: Fixed.
Features: Case hardened lock and hammer; brass furniture; blued bbl. Shoulder stock available, priced at $35.00. Imported by Navy/Replica.
Price: **$95.00**
Price: With detachable shoulder stock **$125.00**

DIXIE OVERCOAT PISTOL
Caliber: 39.
Barrel: 4″, smoothbore.
Weight: 13 oz. **Length:** 8″ over-all.
Stock: Walnut-finish hardwood. Checkered p.g.
Sights: Fixed.
Features: Shoots .380″ balls. Breech plug and engraved lock are burnished steel finish; barrel and trigger guard blued.
Price: Plain model **$26.95**
Price: Engraved model **$34.50**

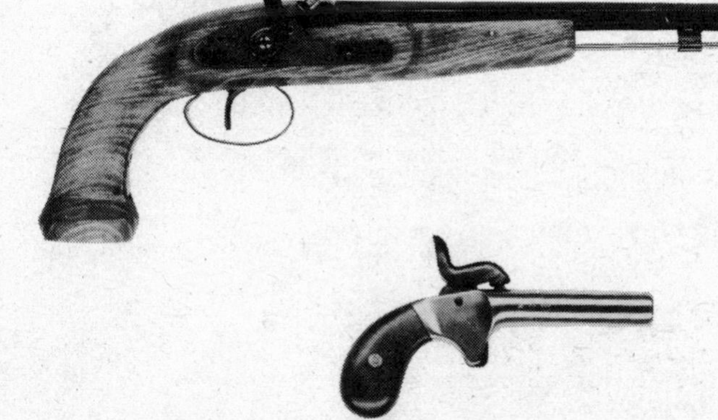

DIXIE DUELING PISTOL
Caliber: 44 to 50 cal. (varies with each gun).
Barrel: 9″, smoothbore, octagon.
Weight: 1¼ lbs. **Length:** 15¼″ over-all.
Stock: Maple, checkered.
Sights: Fixed.
Features: Shoots round ball or shot.
Price: **$79.95**

DIXIE BRASS FRAME DERRINGER
Caliber: 41.
Barrel: 2½″.
Weight: 7 oz. **Length:** 5½″ over-all.
Stock: Walnut.
Features: Brass frame, color case hardened hammer and trigger. Shoots .395″ round ball. Engraved model available. From Dixie Gun Works.
Price: Plain model **$27.95**
Price: Engraved model **$34.95**

BLACK POWDER SINGLE SHOT PISTOLS—FLINT & PERCUSSION

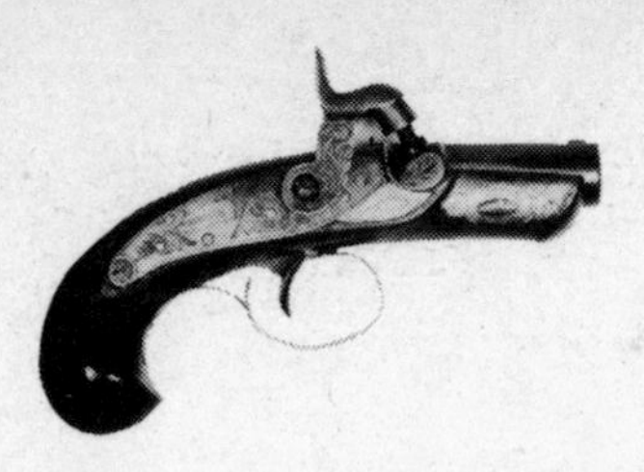

DIXIE LINCOLN DERRINGER
Caliber: 41.
Barrel: 2", 8 lands, 8 grooves.
Weight: 7 oz. **Length:** 5½" over-all.
Stock: Walnut finish, checkered.
Sights: Fixed.
Features: Authentic copy of the "Lincoln Derringer." Shoots .400" patched ball. German silver furniture includes trigger guard with pineapple finial, wedge plates, nose, wrist, side and teardrop inlays. All furniture, lockplate, hammer, and breechplug engraved. Imported from Italy by Dixie Gun Works.
Price: **$99.50**
Price: Kit (Not engraved) **$49.95**

PHILADELPHIA DERRINGER PERCUSSION PISTOL
Caliber: 41.
Barrel: 3⅛".
Weight: 14 oz. **Length:** 7" over-all.
Stock: Walnut, checkered grip.
Sights: Fixed.
Features: Engraved wedge holder and bbl. Also available in flintlock version (Armoury, $29.95). Imported by C.V.A., Markwell Arms, The Armoury,
Price: .... **$18.37** to **$39.95**
Price: Kit form **$25.25**

DIXIE PHILADELPHIA DERRINGER
Caliber: 41.
Barrel: 3½", octagon.
Weight: 8 oz. **Length:** 5½" over-all.
Stock: Walnut, checkered p.g.
Sights: Fixed.
Features: Barrel and lock are blued; brass furniture. From Dixie Gun Works.
Price: **$34.95**

BUCCANEER DOUBLE BARREL PISTOL
Caliber: 36 or 44 cal.
Barrel: 9½".
Weight: 40 oz. **Length:** 15½" over-all.
Stock: Walnut, one piece.
Sights: Fixed.
Features: Case hardened and engraved lockplate, solid brass fittings. Percussion or flintlock. Imported by Hawes Firearms, The Armoury.
Price: .... **$82.95** to **$91.60**

SINGLE SHOT PERCUSSION TARGET PISTOL
Caliber: 44.
Barrel: 9" octagonal.
Weight: 42 oz.
Stocks: Walnut.
Sights: Bead front, rear adj. for w. and e.
Features: Engraved scenes on frame sides; brass backstrap and trigger guard; case hardened frame and hammer. Imported by Navy/Replica.
Price: .... **$64.95** to **$70.00**
Price: Engraved model **$90.00**

DIXIE TROPHY WINNER 44
Similar to standard target pistol except has 10" barrel. Interchangeable shotgun barrel available.
Price: **$69.95**
Price: 28 ga. shotgun barrel **$12.95**

THOMPSON/CENTER PATRIOT PERCUSSION PISTOL
Caliber: 45.
Barrel: 9¼".
Weight: 36 oz. **Length:** 16" over-all.
Stock: Walnut.
Sights: Patridge-type. Rear adj. for w. and e.
Features: Hook breech system; ebony ramrod; double set triggers; coil mainspring. From Thompson/Center Arms.
Price: **$125.00**
With accessory pack (bullet mould T/C patches, adj. powder measure, short starter, extra nipple and nipple wrench).
Price: **$152.50**

TINGLE BLACK POWDER M1960 PISTOL
Caliber: 40, single shot, percussion.
Barrel: 8", 9", 10", or 12" octagon.
Length: 11¾ inches. **Weight:** 33 oz. (8" bbl.).
Stocks: Walnut, one piece.
Sights: Fixed blade front, w. adj. rear.
Features: 6-groove bbl., easily removable for cleaning; 1-in-30 twist.
Price: **$74.95**

WALKER 1847 PERCUSSION REVOLVER

Caliber: 44, 6-shot.
Barrel: 9″.
Weight: 72 oz. **Length:** 15½″ over-all.
Stocks: Walnut.
Sights: Fixed.
Features: Case hardened frame, loading lever and hammer; iron backstrap; brass trigger guard; engraved cylinder. Imported by Navy/Replica, Jana.
Price: .... **$100.00** to **$130.00**

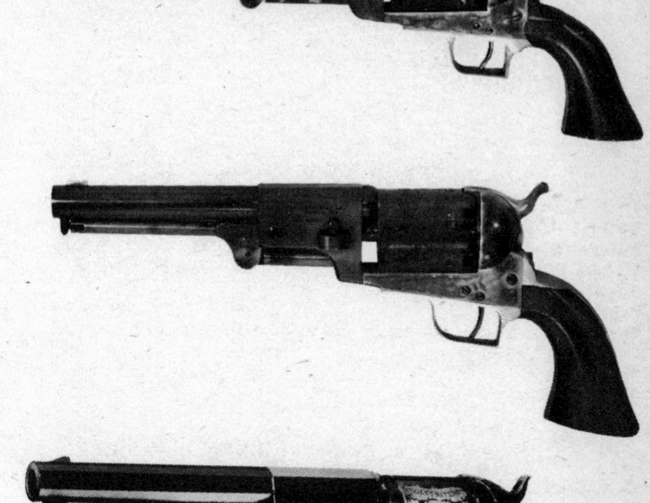

SECOND MODEL DRAGOON 1848 REVOLVER

Caliber: 44, 6-shot.
Barrel: 7½″.
Weight: 64 oz. **Length:** 14″ over-all.
Stocks: One piece walnut.
Sights: Fixed.
Features: Case hardened frame, loading lever and hammer; engraved cylinder scene; safety notches on hammer, safety pin in cylinder. Imported by Navy/Replica. First and Third Models also available.
Price: **$125.00**

COLT 3RD MODEL DRAGOON REVOLVER

Caliber: 44 (for .457″ round ball), 6-shot.
Barrel: 7½″.
Weight: 4 lbs., 2 oz. **Length:** 14″ over-all.
Stock: Oiled walnut, one piece.
Sights: Blade front, fixed V-notch rear.
Features: Brass backstrap and trigger guard. Color case hardened frame, hammer and loading lever. Blue barrel and cylinder engraved with original Ranger and Indian scene. Serial numbers resume at 20,901 where manufacture stopped in 1860. From Colt.
Price: **$204.95**

BABY DRAGOON 1848 PERCUSSION REVOLVER

Caliber: 31, 5-shot.
Barrel: 4″, 5″, 6″.
Weight: 24 oz. (6″ bbl.). **Length:** 10½″ (6″ bbl.).
Stocks: Walnut.
Sights: Fixed.
Features: Case hardened frame; safety notches on hammer and safety pin in cylinder; engraved cylinder scene; octagonal bbl. Imported by Navy/Replica, F.I.E., Jana.
Price: .... **$38.15** to **$95.00**

POCKET MODEL 1849 PERCUSSION REVOLVER

Caliber: 31, 5-shot.
Barrel: 4″, 6″.
Weight: 26 oz.
Stocks: Walnut finish.
Sights: Fixed.
Features: Round trigger guard; Colt stagecoach hold-up scene on cylinder. Imported by Navy/Replica.
Price: **$95.00**

1849 WELLS FARGO PERCUSSION REVOLVER

Caliber: 31, 5-shot.
Barrel: 3″, 4″, 5″, 6″.
Weight: 22 oz.
Stocks: Walnut.
Sights: Fixed.
Features: No loading lever; square-back trigger guard; case hardened frame and hammer; engraved cylinder; brass trigger guard and back-strap. Imported by Navy/Replica, Jana. Bbl. lengths may vary with importer.
Price: .... **$60.00** to **$95.00**

COLT 1851 NAVY PERCUSSION REVOLVER

Caliber: 36, 6-shot.
Barrel: 7½″.
Weight: 40½ oz. **Length:** 13″ over-all.
Stocks: Black walnut.
Sights: Fixed.
Features: Color case hardened frame; barrel and cylinder blued. Silver plated trigger guard and backstrap. Naval Scene engraving by W. L. Ormsby on cylinder. From Colt.
Price: **$136.00**

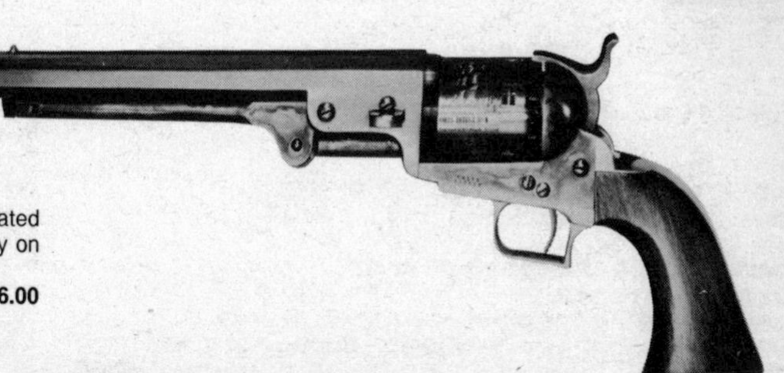

NAVY MODEL 1851 PERCUSSION REVOLVER

Caliber: 36 or 44, 6-shot.
Barrel: 7½".
Weight: 42 oz. **Length:** 13" over-all.
Stocks: Walnut finish.
Sights: Fixed.
Features: Brass backstrap and trigger guard; engraved cylinder with navy battle scene; case hardened frame, hammer, loading lever. Imported by Centennial, The Armoury, Navy/Replica, Hawes, Valor, Century, F.I.E., American Import, Jana, Dixie (illus.), Richland.
Price: Brass frame .... **$31.50** to **$66.60**
Price: Steel frame .... **$40.95** to **$100.00**
Price: Kit form (Centennial) **$30.95**

1851 NAVY-SHERIFF

Same as 1851 Sheriff model except: 4" barrel, fluted cylinder, belt ring in butt. Imported by American Import, Replica/Navy, Hawes, Richland, Armoury.
Price: .... **$50.00** to **$100.00**

LYMAN 1851 NAVY

Same as standard model except 36 cal. only, has square-back trigger guard, nickel plated backstrap, color case hardened frame ..... **$119.95.** Gun and kit (includes .357" single cavity round ball mould with handles, six spare nipples with wrench, Hodgdon's "Spit Ball" and Lyman's "Black Powder Basics" manual). **$124.95**

1851 SHERIFF MODEL PERCUSSION REVOLVER

Caliber: 36, 44, 6-shot.
Barrel: 5"
Weight: 40 oz. **Length:** 10½" over-all.
Stocks: Walnut.
Sights: Fixed.
Features: Brass back strap and trigger guard; engraved navy scene; case hardened frame, hammer, loading lever. Available with brass frame from some importers at slightly lower prices. Imported by The Armoury, Navy/Replica, Hawes, Markwell Arms.
Price: Steel frame .... **$41.95** to **$100.65**
Price: Brass frame .... **$34.95** to **$54.95**

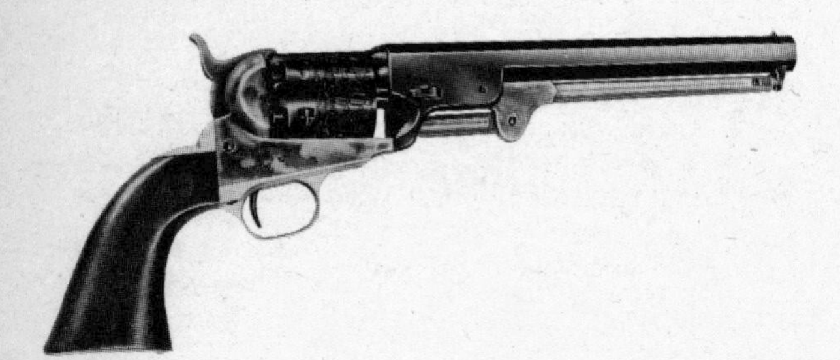

ARMY 1851 PERCUSSION REVOLVER

Caliber: 44, 6-shot.
Barrel: 7½".
Weight: 45 oz. **Length:** 13" over-all.
Stocks: Walnut finish.
Sights: Fixed.
Features: 44 caliber version of the 1851 Navy. Imported by Valor, The Armoury, Jana, Richland.
Price: .... **$33.50** to **$65.00**

NEW MODEL 1858 ARMY PERCUSSION REVOLVER

Caliber: 36 or 44, 6-shot.
Barrel: 6½" or 8".
Weight: 40 oz. **Length:** 13½" over-all.
Stocks: Walnut.
Sights: Fixed.
Features: Replica of Remington Model 1858. Also available from some importers as Army Model Belt Revolver in 36 cal., shortened and lightened version of the 44. Target Model (Centennial, Hawes, Navy/Replica) has fully adj. target rear sight, target front, 36 or 44 ($74.95-$152.45). Imported by Navy/Replica, Century, F.I.E., Hawes, C.V.A., Valor, American Import, Jana, The Armoury, Centennial, Markwell, Richland.
Price: .... **$49.95** to **$128.25**
Price: Kit form **$46.95**

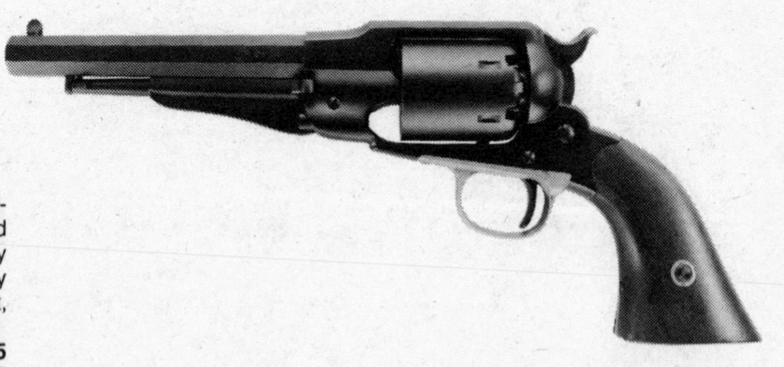

LYMAN 44 NEW MODEL ARMY REVOLVER

Caliber: 44, 6-shot.
Barrel: 8".
Weight: 40 oz. **Length:** 13½" over-all.
Stock: Walnut.
Sights: Fixed.
Features: Replica of 1858 Remington. Brass trigger guard and backstrap, case hardened hammer and trigger. Solid frame with top strap. Heavy duty nipples. Includes .451" single cavity mould block. From Lyman Gunsight Corp.
Price: **$115.95**

LYMAN 36 NEW MODEL NAVY REVOLVER

Caliber: 36, 6-shot.
Barrel: 6½".
Weight: 42 oz. **Length:** 12¼" over-all.
Stock: Walnut.
Sights: Fixed.
Features: Replica of 1860 Remington. Brass trigger guard and backstrap, case hardened trigger and hammer. Solid frame with top strap. Heavy duty nipples. Includes .375" single cavity mould blocks. From Lyman Gunsight Corp.
Price: **$115.95**

1860 ARMY PERCUSSION REVOLVER

Caliber: 44, 6-shot.
Barrel: 8".
Weight: 40 oz. **Length:** 13⅝" over-all.
Stocks: Walnut.
Sights: Fixed.
Features: Engraved navy scene on cylinder; brass trigger guard; case hardened frame, loading lever and hammer. Some importers supply pistol cut for detachable shoulder stock, have accessory stock available. Imported by Navy/Replica, Centennial, The Armoury, Hawes, Jana, Dixie, Lyman.
Price: .... **$44.95** to **$119.95**
1861 Navy: Same as Army except 36 cal., 7½" bbl., wt. 41 oz., cut for stock; round cylinder (fluted avail.), from Navy/Replica **$100.00**
Lyman 1860 Army gun and kit (includes single cavity round ball mould with handles, six spare nipples, nipple wrench, Hodgdon's "Spit Ball" and Lyman's "Black Powder Basics" manual). **$129.95**

1861 NAVY MODEL REVOLVER

Caliber: 36, 6-shot.
Barrel: 7½".
Weight: 2½ lbs. **Length:** 13" over-all.
Stocks: One piece smooth walnut.
Sights: Fixed.
Features: Shoots .380" ball. Case-hardened frame, loading lever and hammer. Cut for shoulder stock. Non-fluted cylinder. From Navy/Replica Arms.
Price: **$95.00**
Price: With full fluted cyl. **$95.00**

1862 POLICE MODEL PERCUSSION REVOLVER

Caliber: 36, 5-shot.
Barrel: 4½", 5½", 6½".
Weight: 26 oz. **Length:** 12" (6½" bbl.).
Stocks: Walnut.
Sights: Fixed.
Features: Half-fluted and rebated cylinder; case hardened frame, loading lever and hammer; brass trigger guard and back strap. Imported by Navy/Replica, Armoury.
Price: **$95.00**
Price: Cased with accessories **$125.00**

1862 POCKET NAVY MODEL REVOLVER

Caliber: 36, 6-shot.
Barrel: 4½", 5½", 6½".
Weight: 26 oz. **Length:** 12" over-all (6½" bbl.).
Stocks: Smooth walnut.
Sights: Fixed.
Features: Shortened version of std. Navy model. Case hardened frame, hammer and loading lever; brass backstrap and trigger guard. Imported by Navy/Replica Arms, Armoury.
Price: **$95.00**

GRISWOLD & GUNNISON PERCUSSION REVOLVER

Caliber: 36, 44, 6-shot.
Barrel: 7½".
Weight: 44 oz. (36 cal.). **Length:** 13" over-all.
Stocks: Walnut.
Sights: Fixed.
Features: Replica of famous Confederate pistol. Brass frame, backstrap and trigger guard; case hardened loading lever; rebated cylinder (44 cal. only). Imported by Navy/Replica, Markwell Arms.
Price: .... **$60.00** to **$72.03**
Price: Kit form (Markwell) **$57.57**

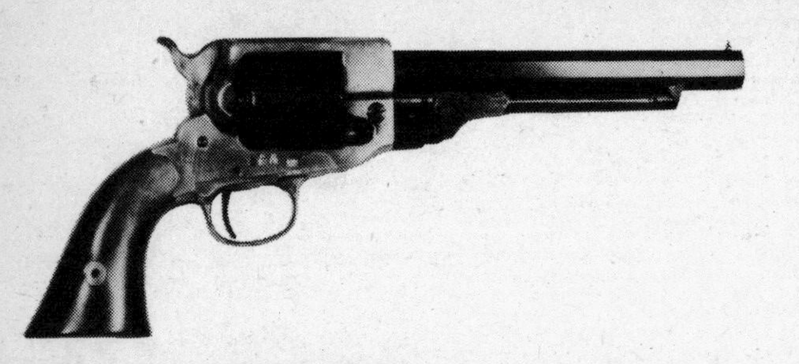

SPILLER & BURR REVOLVER
Caliber: 36.
Barrel: 7″, octagon.
Weight: 2½ lbs. **Length:** 12½″ over-all.
Stock: Two-piece walnut.
Sights: Fixed.
Features: Reproduction of the C.S.A. revolver. Brass frame and trigger guard. Also available as a kit. From Dixie, Navy/Replica.
Price: .... **$69.95** to **$75.00**
Price: Kit form **$39.95**

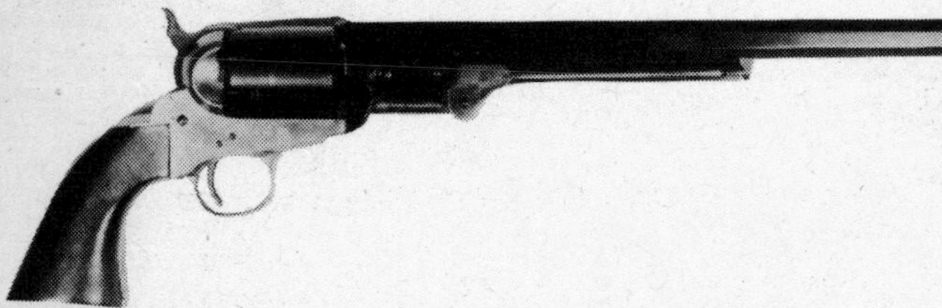

DIXIE "WYATT EARP" REVOLVER
Caliber: 44.
Barrel: 12″ octagon.
Weight: 46 oz. **Length:** 18″ over-all.
Stock: Two piece walnut.
Sights: Fixed.
Features: Highly polished brass frame, backstrap and trigger guard; blued barrel and cylinder; case hardened hammer, trigger and loading lever. Navy-size shoulder stock ($40.00) will fit with minor fitting. From Dixie Gun Works.
Price: **$62.50**

HIGH STANDARD LEECH & RIGDON REVOLVER
Caliber: 36, 6-shot.
Barrel: 7½″.
Weight: Approx. 40 oz. **Length:** 13¼″ over-all.
Stocks: Smooth walnut.
Sights: Fixed.
Features: Steel frame with satin nickel finish. Brass trigger guard and backstrap. Comes with deluxe walnut presentation case and reproduction Civil War belt buckle.
Price: **$145.00**

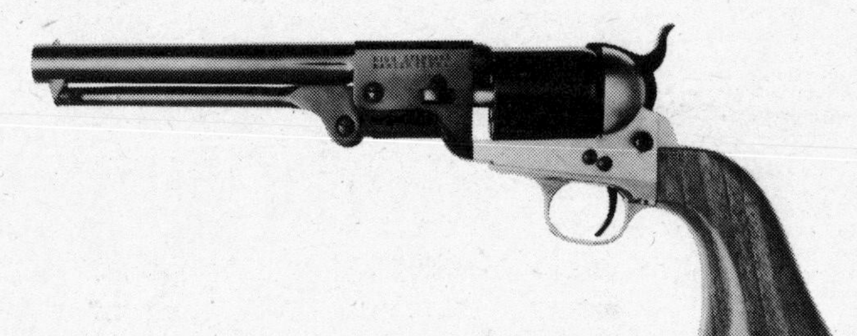

RICHLAND 44 BALLISTER REVOLVER
Caliber: 44, 6 shot.
Barrel: 12″.
Weight: 2¾ lbs.
Stock: Two-piece walnut.
Sights: Fixed.
Features: Barrel and cylinder blued, frame and trigger guard are brass; hammer and loading lever are color case hardened. From Richland Arms.
Price: **$76.00**

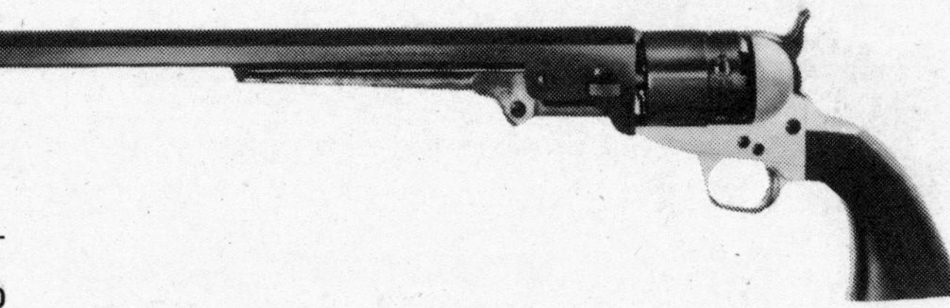

HI-STANDARD GRISWOLD & GUNNISON REVOLVER
Caliber: 36, 6-shot.
Barrel: 7½″.
Weight: Approx. 40 oz. **Length:** 13¼″ over-all.
Stocks: Smooth walnut.
Sights: Fixed.
Features: Brass frame and trigger guard, rest blued. Reproduction of Confederate versions of Colt 1851 Navy. Comes with Georgia White Pine presentation case and brass plate depicting Georgia state seal.
Price: **$145.00**

RUGER 44 OLD ARMY PERCUSSION REVOLVER
Caliber: 44, 6-shot. Uses .457″ dia. lead bullets.
Barrel: 7½″ (6-groove, 16″ twist).
Weight: 46 oz. **Length:** 13½″ over-all.
Stock: Smooth walnut.
Sights: Ramp front, rear adj. for w. and e.
Features: Stainless steel standard size nipples, chrome-moly steel cylinder and frame, same lockwork as in original Super Blackhawk. Also available in stainless steel in very limited quantities. Made in USA. From Sturm, Ruger & Co.
Price: Blued **$125.00**
Price: With brass Dragoon-style grip frame and wide trigger **$140.00**
Price: Stainless steel **$167.50**

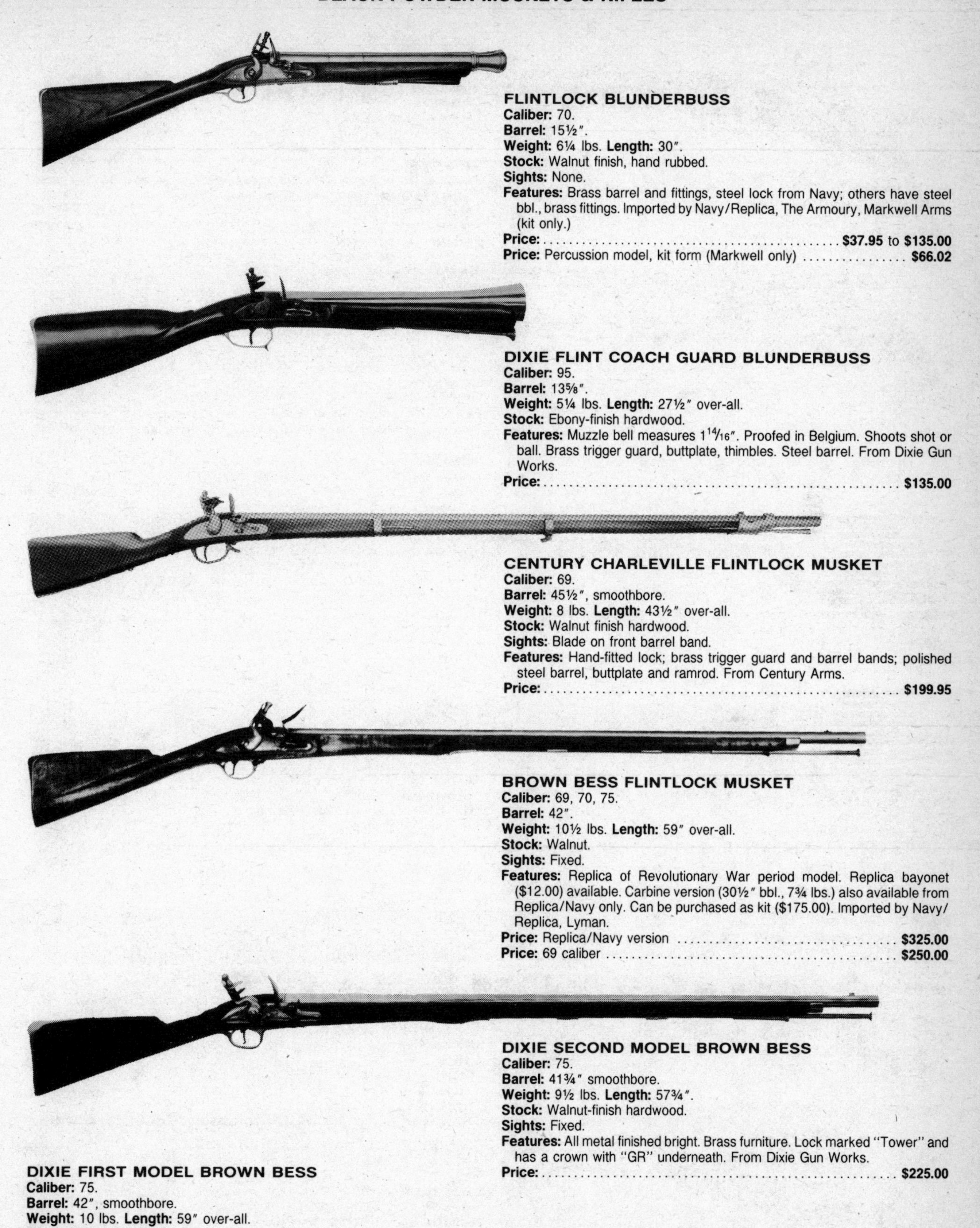

FLINTLOCK BLUNDERBUSS
Caliber: 70.
Barrel: 15½″.
Weight: 6¼ lbs. **Length:** 30″.
Stock: Walnut finish, hand rubbed.
Sights: None.
Features: Brass barrel and fittings, steel lock from Navy; others have steel bbl., brass fittings. Imported by Navy/Replica, The Armoury, Markwell Arms (kit only.)
Price: .... **$37.95** to **$135.00**
Price: Percussion model, kit form (Markwell only) **$66.02**

DIXIE FLINT COACH GUARD BLUNDERBUSS
Caliber: 95.
Barrel: 13⅝″.
Weight: 5¼ lbs. **Length:** 27½″ over-all.
Stock: Ebony-finish hardwood.
Features: Muzzle bell measures 1¹⁴⁄₁₆″. Proofed in Belgium. Shoots shot or ball. Brass trigger guard, buttplate, thimbles. Steel barrel. From Dixie Gun Works.
Price: **$135.00**

CENTURY CHARLEVILLE FLINTLOCK MUSKET
Caliber: 69.
Barrel: 45½″, smoothbore.
Weight: 8 lbs. **Length:** 43½″ over-all.
Stock: Walnut finish hardwood.
Sights: Blade on front barrel band.
Features: Hand-fitted lock; brass trigger guard and barrel bands; polished steel barrel, buttplate and ramrod. From Century Arms.
Price: **$199.95**

BROWN BESS FLINTLOCK MUSKET
Caliber: 69, 70, 75.
Barrel: 42″.
Weight: 10½ lbs. **Length:** 59″ over-all.
Stock: Walnut.
Sights: Fixed.
Features: Replica of Revolutionary War period model. Replica bayonet ($12.00) available. Carbine version (30½″ bbl., 7¾ lbs.) also available from Replica/Navy only. Can be purchased as kit ($175.00). Imported by Navy/Replica, Lyman.
Price: Replica/Navy version **$325.00**
Price: 69 caliber **$250.00**

DIXIE SECOND MODEL BROWN BESS
Caliber: 75.
Barrel: 41¾″ smoothbore.
Weight: 9½ lbs. **Length:** 57¾″.
Stock: Walnut-finish hardwood.
Sights: Fixed.
Features: All metal finished bright. Brass furniture. Lock marked "Tower" and has a crown with "GR" underneath. From Dixie Gun Works.
Price: **$225.00**

DIXIE FIRST MODEL BROWN BESS
Caliber: 75.
Barrel: 42″, smoothbore.
Weight: 10 lbs. **Length:** 59″ over-all.
Stock: Walnut finished.
Sights: Fixed.
Features: Brass furniture with bright barrel, lock and ramrod. Lock marked "Grice 1762" with crown and "GR" underneath. Original Brown Bess bayonets $25.00. Imported from England by Dixie Gun Works.
Price: **$425.00**

Lyman "Brown Bess" Musket
Musket with Shooting Accessory Kit (includes .715″ round ball single cavity mould with handles, 6 strips .015″ round ball patching, 8 oz. squeeze tube of Lyman patch and ball lubricant and "Black Powder Basics" manual **$275.00**

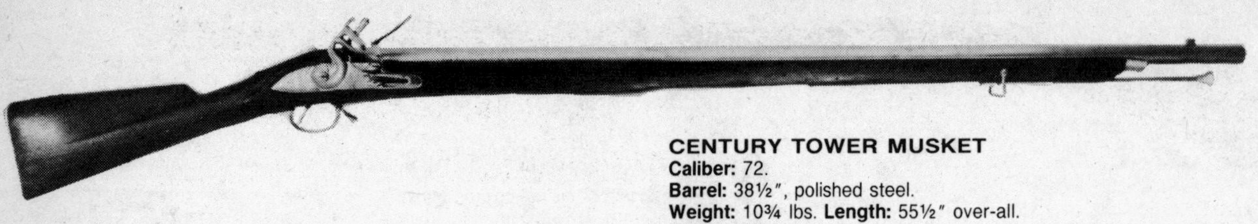

CENTURY TOWER MUSKET
Caliber: 72.
Barrel: 38½", polished steel.
Weight: 10¾ lbs. **Length:** 55½" over-all.
Stock: Walnut.
Sights: Fixed.
Features: Brass buttplate, trigger guard and thimbles; baynot lug; lock plate stamped with British crown. From Century Arms.
Price: **$199.95**

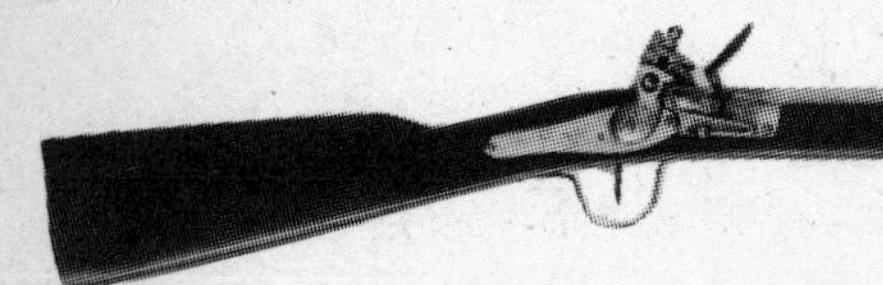

CENTURY LONG TOM MUSKET
Caliber: 56.
Barrel: 51".
Weight: 7¾ lbs. **Length:** 67¾" over-all.
Stock: Walnut finish hardwood.
Sights: Bead front only.
Features: Polished steel barrel and ramrod; 2-piece lock; buttplate, trigger guard and barrel brass plated. American eagle seal on lockplate.
Price: **$119.50**

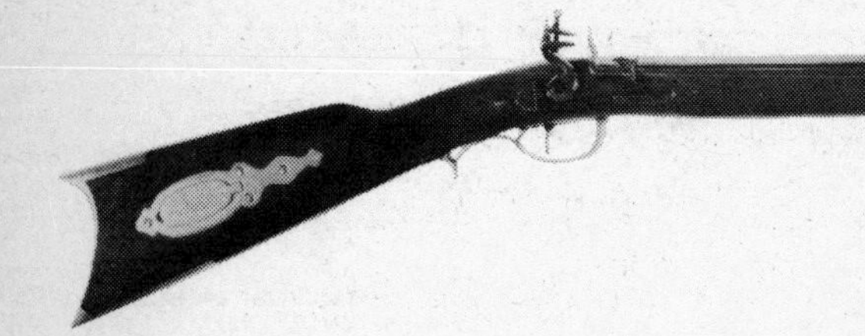

CENTURY "KENTUCKY" DELUXE RIFLES
Caliber: 45 (.453" bore).
Barrel: 36" octagon.
Weight: 6½ lbs. **Length:** 50" over-all.
Stock: Walnut finish.
Sights: Fixed.
Features: Brass nose cap, thimbles, buttplate and patch box. Case-hardened lock and hammer. Imported by Century Arms.
Price: Flintlock **$149.50**
Price: Percussion **$149.50**
Price: Matched pair (one of each) **$285.00**

PENNSYLVANIA LONG RIFLE
Caliber: 36 or 45.
Barrel: 39" octagonal.
Weight: 10½ lbs. **Length:** 55" over-all.
Stock: Full-length tiger striped maple, traditional Pennsylvania form.
Sights: Brass blade front, open notch rear.
Features: Solid brass engraved furniture (crescent buttplate, patch box, fore-end cap, etc.) From The Armoury.
Price: Flint or percussion form **$179.95**

CVA KENTUCKY RIFLE
Caliber: 44 (.451" bore).
Barrel: 34½", rifled, octagon (⅞" flats).
Length: 50" over-all.
Stock: Dark polished walnut.
Sights: Brass Kentucky blade type front. dovetail open rear.
Features: Available in either flint or percussion. Nipple wrench included. Imported by CVA.
Price: Percussion **$104.95**
Price: Flint **$107.95**

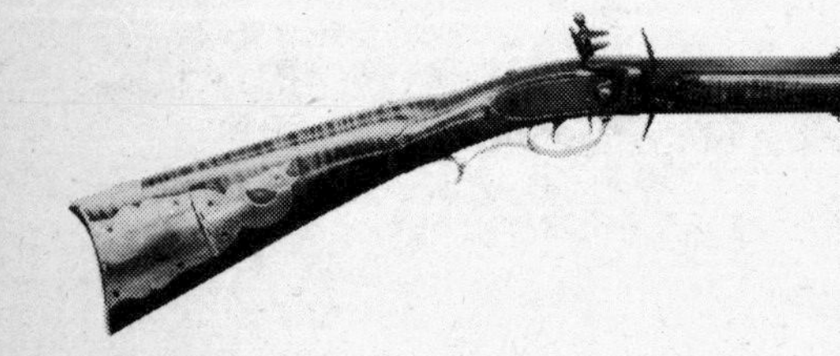

DIXIE FLINT SWIVEL BREECH RIFLE
Caliber: 45.
Barrel: 32", octagon.
Weigth: 11½ lbs. **Length:** 48½" over-all.
Stock: Curly maple.
Sights: Fixed.
Features: Wood panelled barrels rotate for second shot. Single trigger. Brass furniture. From Dixie Gun Works.
Price: Flintlock **$450.00**
Price: Percussion **$325.00**

KENTUCKY FLINTLOCK RIFLE
Caliber: 44 or 45.
Barrel: 35".
Weight: 7 lbs. **Length:** 50" over-all.
Stock: Walnut stained, brass fittings.
Sights: Fixed.
Features: Available in Carbine model also, 28" bbl. Some variations in detail, finish. Kits also available from some importers. Imported by Navy/Replica, Centennial, The Armoury, Century, Dixie and Challenger, F.I.E., Hawes, Kassnar.
Price: .... **$59.95** to **$165.00**

Kentucky Percussion Rifle
Similar to above except percussion lock. Finish and features vary with importer. Imported by Jana, Centennial, Navy/Replica, Firearms Import & Export, The Armoury, Century, Challenger, Dixie, Connecticut Valley, Valor, Hawes, Kassnar, Markwell Arms.
Price: .... **$54.95** to **$229.95**
Price: Kit form **$77.78**

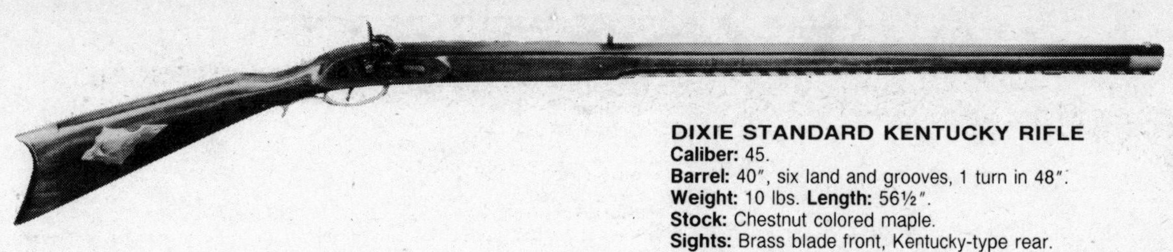

DIXIE STANDARD KENTUCKY RIFLE
Caliber: 45.
Barrel: 40″, six land and grooves, 1 turn in 48″.
Weight: 10 lbs. **Length:** 56½″.
Stock: Chestnut colored maple.
Sights: Brass blade front, Kentucky-type rear.
Features: Trigger guard, buttplate, patchbox and thimbles are brass. Double set triggers available ($8.50 extra). Color case hardened lock. From Dixie Gun Works.
Price: Percussion **$179.95**
Price: Flintlock **$189.95**

DIXIE PENNSYLVANIA PERCUSSION RIFLE
Caliber: 45.
Barrel: 40″, octagon.
Weight: 10 lbs. **Length:** 55″.
Stock: Maple, Roman nose comb.
Sights: Fixed, Kentucky open-type.
Features: Brass patchbox, wide buttplate, color case hardened lock, blue barrel. From Dixie Gun Works.
Price: Flint or percussion **$275.00**
Price: Engraved model, flint or percussion **$299.95**

KENTUCKIAN RIFLE & CARBINE
Caliber: 44.
Barrel: 35″ (Rifle), 27½″ (Carbine).
Weight: 7 lbs. (Rifle), 5½ lbs. (Carbine). **Length:** 51″ (Rifle) over-all, carbine 43″.
Stock: Walnut stain.
Sights: Brass blade front, steel V-Ramp rear.
Features: Octagon bbl., case-hardened and engraved lock plate. Brass furniture. Imported by Dixie.
Price: Rifle (illus.) or carbine, flint or percussion ...... **$135.00** to **$145.00**

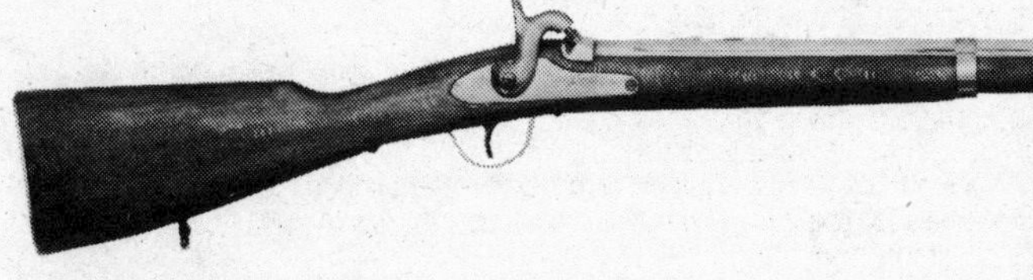

DIXIE PERCUSSION MUSKET
Caliber: 66.
Barrel: 37″, smoothbore.
Weight: 8 lbs. **Length:** 54″ over-all.
Stock: Walnut-finish hardwood.
Sights: Fixed.
Features: Made from old original parts but with new Belgian-proofed barrels. Shoots shot or .650″ ball. Also available as flintlock.
Price: Percussion **$93.00**
Price: Flintlock **$96.50**

CENTURY PERCUSSION MUSKET
Caliber: 69.
Barrel: 37″, part octagon, part round.
Weight: 7½ lbs. **Length:** 54″ over-all.
Stock: Walnut finish hardwood.
Sights: Bead front.
Features: Polished steel barrel, lock plate, hammer, barrel bands ramrod and trigger. From Century Arms.
Price: **$114.50**

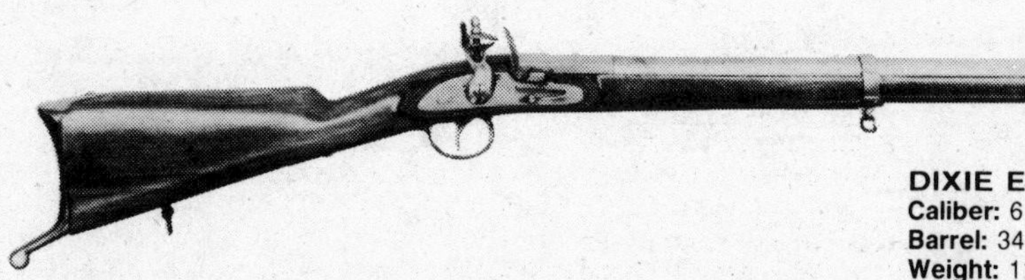

DIXIE ELEPHANT GUN
Caliber: 6 gauge.
Barrel: 34″, smoothbore.
Weight: 11 lbs. **Length:** 52″ over-all.
Stock: Walnut stained birch.
Sights: Fixed.
Features: Takes up to 225 grains of black powder. Sling swivels, hooked buttplate.
Price: **$113.00**

BLACK POWDER MUSKETS & RIFLES

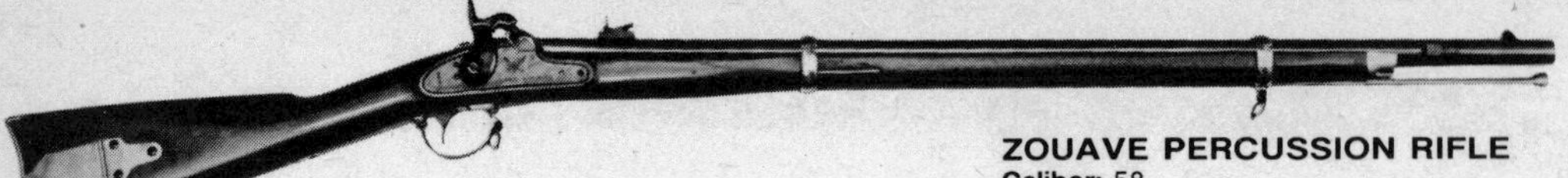

ZOUAVE PERCUSSION RIFLE
Caliber: 58.
Barrel: 32½".
Weight: 9½ lbs. **Length:** 48½" over-all.
Stock: Walnut finish, brass patch box and butt plate.
Sights: Fixed front, rear adj. for e.
Features: Some small details may vary with importers. Also available from Navy Arms as carbine, with 22" bbl. Extra 20 ga. shotgun bbl. $45.00. Imported by Navy/Replica, Centennial, The Armoury, Lyman, F.I.E., Dixie, Hawes, Richland, Kassnar.
Price: .... **$88.95** to **$168.00**
Lyman rifle and kit (includes 58 minie ball mould and handles, spare nipple and wrench, Lyman's Mini Lube and Lyman's "Black Powder Basics" book.
Price: **$190.00**
Price: From Lyman, without kit **$175.00**

MISSISSIPPI MODEL 1841 PERCUSSION RIFLE
Similar to Zouave Rifle but patterned after U.S. Model 1841. Imported by Navy/Replica.
Price: **$160.00**

NAVY 1861 SPRINGFIELD RIFLE
Caliber: 58.
Barrel: 40", rifled.
Weight: 8½ lbs. **Length:** 54¾" over-all.
Stock: American walnut.
Sights: Blade front, open step adj. rear.
Features: Full-size three-band musket reproduction. Imported by Navy/Replica.
Price: **$200.00**

ENFIELD PATTERN 1858 NAVAL RIFLE
Caliber: .577".
Barrel: 33".
Weight: 8½ lbs. **Length:** 48½" over-all.
Stock: European walnut.
Sights: Blade front, step adj. rear.
Features: Two-band Enfield percussion rifle with heavy barrel. 5-groove progressive depth rifling, solid brass furniture. All parts made exactly to original patterns. Imported from England by Jana.
Price: **$225.00**

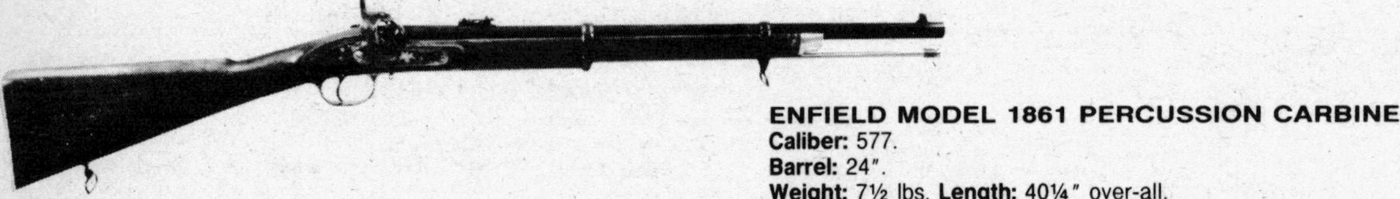

ENFIELD MODEL 1861 PERCUSSION CARBINE
Caliber: 577.
Barrel: 24".
Weight: 7½ lbs. **Length:** 40¼" over-all.
Stock: Walnut.
Sights: Fixed front, adj. rear.
Features: Percussion muzzle loader, made to original 1861 English patterns. Imported from England by Jana.
Price: **$225.00**

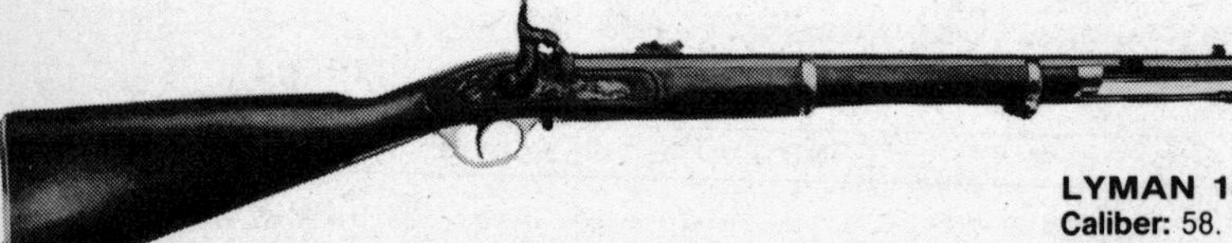

LYMAN 1861 ENFIELD "MUSKETOON" CARBINE
Caliber: 58.
Barrel: 24".
Weight: 7 lbs. **Length:** 40½" over-all.
Stock: Smooth walnut.
Sights: Fixed front, rear adj. for e.
Features: Case hardened lock, hammer and trigger, blued barrel and swivels; polished brass trigger guard, buttplate and barrel bands; steel ramrod.
Price: **$225.00**
Price: With Lyman Enfield Shooting Accessory Kit (includes 58 Minie ball single cavity mould with handles, Lyman's Minie Lube, spare nipple, wrench and "Black Powder Basics" manual **$240.00**

DIXIE ENFIELD MUSKETOON
Caliber: 58 (.577").
Barrel: 24", 6 lands, 6 grooves.
Weight: 7 lbs. **Length:** 41" over-all.
Stock: Walnut with brass fittings.
Sights: Original style fixed front, adjustable rear.
Features: Uses standard .575" Minie ball or .570" round ball. Made in Italy. From Dixie Gun Works and the Armoury.
Price: .... **$179.95** to **$186.00**

MORSE/NAVY RIFLE
Caliber: 45, 50 or 58.
Barrel: 26".
Weight: 6 lbs. (45 cal.). **Length:** 41½" over-all.
Stock: American walnut, full p.g.
Sights: Blade front, open fixed rear.
Features: Brass action, trigger guard, ramrod pipes. From Navy/Replica.
Price: **$80.00**
Price: 45 or 50 caliber, straight stock **$80.00**

ARMOURY R140 HAWKIN RIFLE

Caliber: 45 or 50.
Barrel: 29″.
Weight: 8¾″ to 9 lbs. **Length:** 45¾″ over-all.
Stock: Walnut, with cheekpiece.
Sights: Dovetail front, fully adjustable rear.
Features: Octagon barrel measures ⅜″ across flats; removable breech plug; double set triggers; blued barrel, brass stock fittings, color case-hardened percussion lock. Imported by The Armoury.
Price: **$179.00**

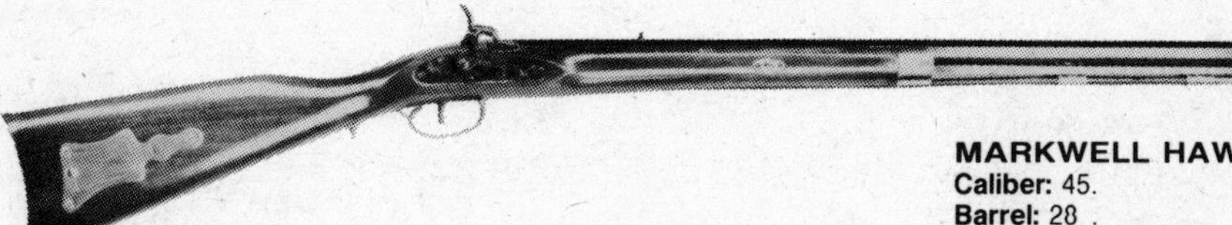

MARKWELL HAWKEN RIFLE

Caliber: 45.
Barrel: 28 .
Weight: 7 lbs. **Length:** 43½″ over-all.
Stock: Dark polished walnut.
Sights: Blade front, open read adj. for w.
Features: Brass patchbox, trigger guard, buttplate and furniture; color case hardened lock, rest blued. From Markwell Arms.
Price: **$119.95**
Price: Kit form **$89.75**

HAWKEN HURRICANE

Caliber: 45 or 50.
Barrel: 28″, octagon.
Weight: 6 lbs. **Length:** 44¾″ over-all.
Stock: American walnut.
Sights: Blade front, open fixed rear.
Features: American made. Curved buttplate, brass stock furniture. From Navy/Replica.
Price: **$195.00**
Price: Hawken Hunter (58 cal.) **$195.00**

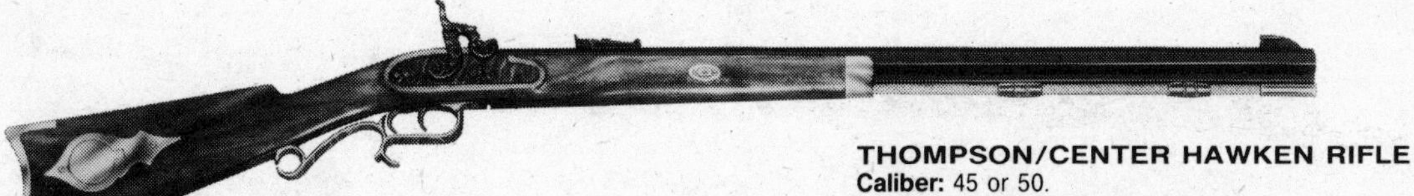

THOMPSON/CENTER HAWKEN RIFLE

Caliber: 45 or 50.
Barrel: 28″ octagon, hooked breech.
Stock: American walnut.
Sights: Blade front, rear adj. for w. & e.
Features: Solid brass furniture, double set triggers, button rifled barrel, coil-type main spring. From Thompson/Center Arms.
Price: Percussion Model .. **$205.00** Flintlock Model **$215.00**

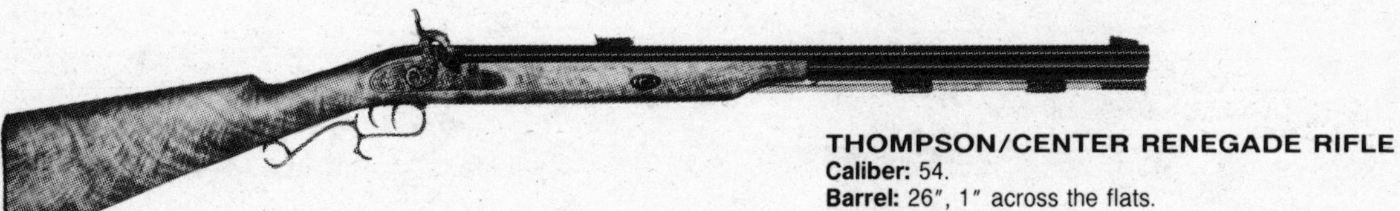

THOMPSON/CENTER RENEGADE RIFLE

Caliber: 54.
Barrel: 26″, 1″ across the flats.
Weight: 8 lbs.
Stock: American walnut.
Sights: Open hunting (partridge) style, fully adjustable for w. and e.
Features: Coil spring lock, double set triggers, blued steel trim.
Price: **$165.00**
Price: With accessory pack (includes 20 maxi-balls, maxi-lube, adjustable powder measure, bullet starter, nipple and nipple wrench) **$177.35**

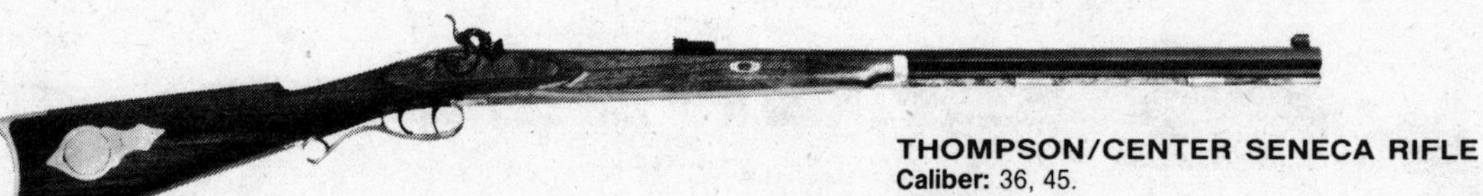

THOMPSON/CENTER SENECA RIFLE

Caliber: 36, 45.
Barrel: 27″.
Weight: 6½ lbs.
Stock: American walnut.
Sights: Open hunting style, square notch rear fully adj. for w. and e.
Features: Coil spring lock, octagon bbl. measures 13/16″ across flats, brass stock furniture.
Price: Rifle **$205.00**
Price: Rifle with accessory kit (includes bullet mould, patches, powder measure, short starter, extra nipple & nipple wrench) **$232.50**

H & R SPRINGFIELD STALKER
Caliber: 45 or 58.
Barrel: 28″ round.
Weight: 8 lbs. (45 cal.), 7½ lbs. (58 cal.). **Length:** 43″ over-all.
Stock: American walnut.
Sights: Blade front, rear open adj. for w. and e.
Features: Action similar to Civil War Springfield. Supplied with solid brass ramrod with hardwood handle and nipple wrench. Blue-black finish.
Price: **$185.00**

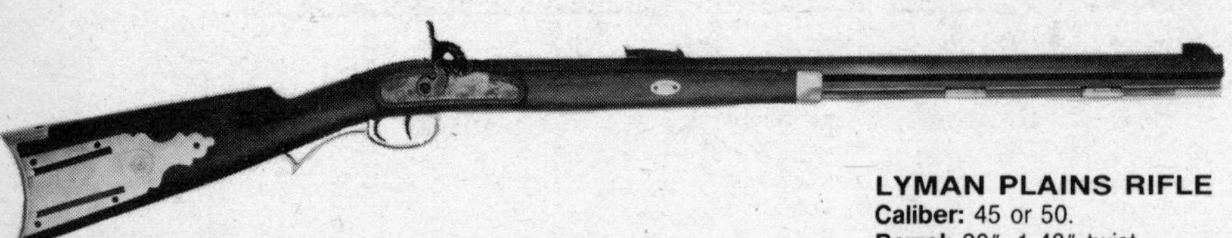

DIXIE PLAINSMAN RIFLE
Caliber: 45 or 50.
Barrel: 32″, octagon.
Weight: 8 lbs. **Length:** 47½″.
Stock: Cherry wood.
Sights: Brass blade front, buckhorn rear.
Features: Bolster-type breech plug with blow-out screw, brass stock furniture.
Price: 45 or 50 caliber **$175.00**

LYMAN PLAINS RIFLE
Caliber: 45 or 50.
Barrel: 28″, 1-48″ twist.
Weight: 8¾ lbs. **Length:** 45″ over-all.
Stock: European walnut.
Sights: Blade front, fully adj. rear.
Features: Double set trigger, hooked breech system, brass stock furniture, patch box. Imported from Italy by Lyman.
Price: Rifle only **$225.00**
Price: Rifle and kit (includes single cavity .440″ dia. round ball mould, handles, nipple wrench, ball starter, Lyman's patch lube, patches and Lyman's "Black Powder Basics" book) **$240.00**
Price: Lyman Accessory Shooting Kit **$26.00**

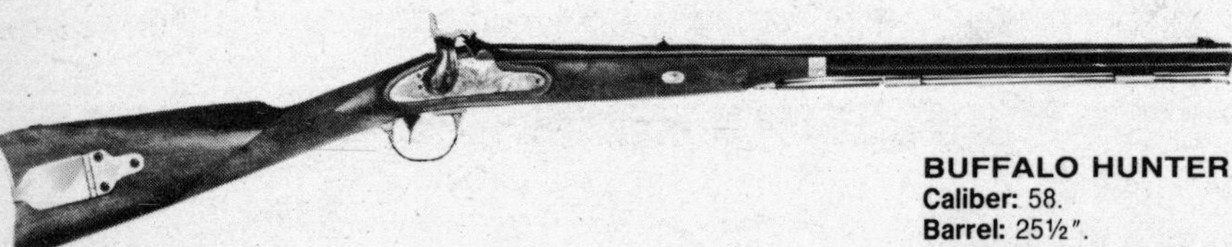

DICKSON BUFFALO HUNTER RIFLE/SHOTGUN
Similar to standard Buffalo Hunter except: over-all length 42″, no checkering, 26″ bbl, 58 caliber, imported by American Import.
Price: **$165.50**

BUFFALO HUNTER PERCUSSION RIFLE
Caliber: 58.
Barrel: 25½″.
Weight: 8 lbs. **Length:** 41½″ over-all.
Stock: Walnut finished, hand checkered, brass furniture.
Sights: Fixed.
Features: Designed for primitive weapons hunting. 20 ga. shotgun bbl. also available **$45.00**. Imported by Navy/Replica.
Price: **$160.00**

REVOLVING PERCUSSION CARBINE
Caliber: 44, 6-shot.
Barrel: 18″, 20″.
Weight: 5 lbs. **Length:** 38″ over-all.
Stock: Walnut, brass butt plate.
Sights: Blade front adj. for w., buckhorn rear adj. for e.
Features: Action based on 1858 Remington revolver. Brass trigger guard. Imported by Navy/Replica.
Price: **$165.00**

RICHLAND YORKSHIRE RIFLE
Caliber: 45.
Barrel: 36″, rifled, ⅞″ octagon.
Weight: 7½ lbs. **Length:** 51¾″ over-all.
Stock: Select maple.
Sights: Blade front, open U-notch rear.
Features: Adj. double set triggers. Brass front and rear sights, trigger guard, patch box, buttplate and fore-end. Case hardened lock plate.
Price: Percussion **$144.00**
Price: Flintlock **$153.00**

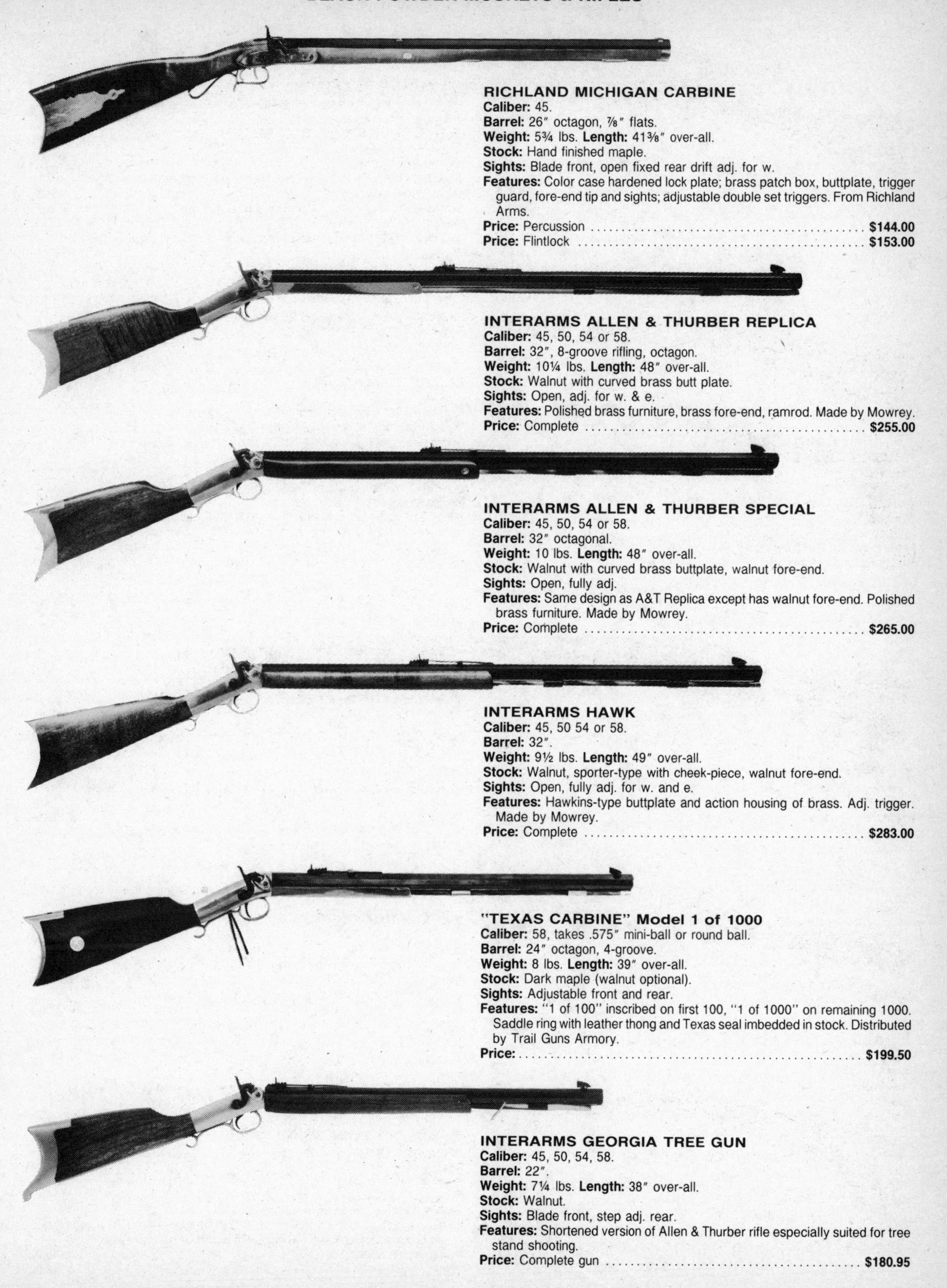

RICHLAND MICHIGAN CARBINE
Caliber: 45.
Barrel: 26″ octagon, ⅞″ flats.
Weight: 5¾ lbs. **Length:** 41⅜″ over-all.
Stock: Hand finished maple.
Sights: Blade front, open fixed rear drift adj. for w.
Features: Color case hardened lock plate; brass patch box, buttplate, trigger guard, fore-end tip and sights; adjustable double set triggers. From Richland Arms.
Price: Percussion **$144.00**
Price: Flintlock **$153.00**

INTERARMS ALLEN & THURBER REPLICA
Caliber: 45, 50, 54 or 58.
Barrel: 32″, 8-groove rifling, octagon.
Weight: 10¼ lbs. **Length:** 48″ over-all.
Stock: Walnut with curved brass butt plate.
Sights: Open, adj. for w. & e.
Features: Polished brass furniture, brass fore-end, ramrod. Made by Mowrey.
Price: Complete **$255.00**

INTERARMS ALLEN & THURBER SPECIAL
Caliber: 45, 50, 54 or 58.
Barrel: 32″ octagonal.
Weight: 10 lbs. **Length:** 48″ over-all.
Stock: Walnut with curved brass buttplate, walnut fore-end.
Sights: Open, fully adj.
Features: Same design as A&T Replica except has walnut fore-end. Polished brass furniture. Made by Mowrey.
Price: Complete **$265.00**

INTERARMS HAWK
Caliber: 45, 50 54 or 58.
Barrel: 32″.
Weight: 9½ lbs. **Length:** 49″ over-all.
Stock: Walnut, sporter-type with cheek-piece, walnut fore-end.
Sights: Open, fully adj. for w. and e.
Features: Hawkins-type buttplate and action housing of brass. Adj. trigger. Made by Mowrey.
Price: Complete **$283.00**

"TEXAS CARBINE" Model 1 of 1000
Caliber: 58, takes .575″ mini-ball or round ball.
Barrel: 24″ octagon, 4-groove.
Weight: 8 lbs. **Length:** 39″ over-all.
Stock: Dark maple (walnut optional).
Sights: Adjustable front and rear.
Features: "1 of 100" inscribed on first 100, "1 of 1000" on remaining 1000. Saddle ring with leather thong and Texas seal imbedded in stock. Distributed by Trail Guns Armory.
Price:........ **$199.50**

INTERARMS GEORGIA TREE GUN
Caliber: 45, 50, 54, 58.
Barrel: 22″.
Weight: 7¼ lbs. **Length:** 38″ over-all.
Stock: Walnut.
Sights: Blade front, step adj. rear.
Features: Shortened version of Allen & Thurber rifle especially suited for tree stand shooting.
Price: Complete gun **$180.95**

BLACK POWDER MUSKETS & RIFLES

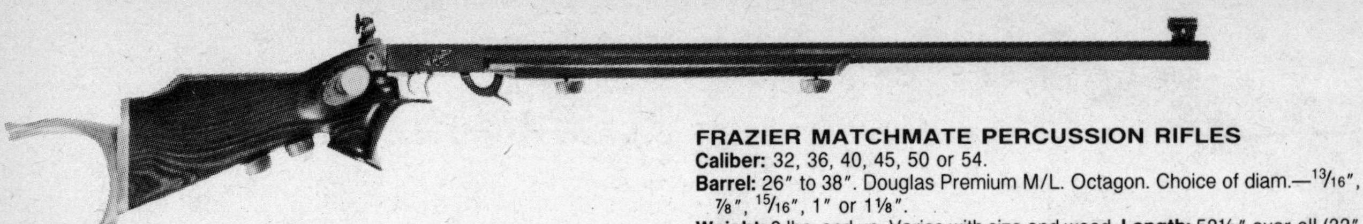

FRAZIER MATCHMATE PERCUSSION RIFLES

Caliber: 32, 36, 40, 45, 50 or 54.
Barrel: 26″ to 38″. Douglas Premium M/L. Octagon. Choice of diam.—13/16″, 7/8″, 15/16″, 1″ or 1⅛″.
Weight: 8 lbs. and up. Varies with size and wood. **Length:** 52½″ over-all (32″ bbl.).
Stock: Laminated of 5 layers of imported exotic high figure hardwoods. Thumbhole p.g., cheekpiece in line with bore. Satin finish. Adj. hooked butt-plate.
Sights: Globe front on detachable base (insert set included), Redfield #75 micro peep rear.
Features: A unique rifle designed for competition shooting. Underhammer action with Anschutz-Mauser set triggers. Comes with set of 8 weights to control balance, Lyman mould, short starter and rod. Adj. coil mainspring; stainless steel flashguard around nipple. Action housed in breech but removes easily for cleaning. Write for full specifics. From Clark K. Frazier.
Price: Standard Offhand Rifle, from **$600.00**
Price: Custom Offhand Rifle, from **$700.00**
Price: "National Unlimited" bench rest rifle, from **$700.00**

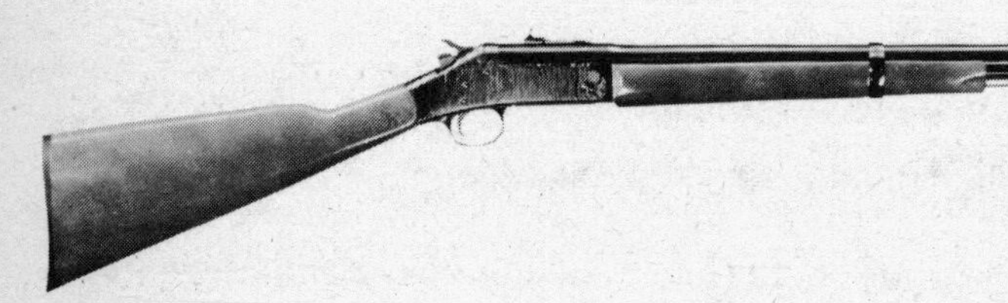

H & R HUNTSMAN PERCUSSION RIFLE

Caliber: 45, 58, 12 gauge, single shot.
Barrel: 28″, 30″, 32″ (58 cal.).
Weight: 6¼ lbs. (12 ga.), 7¼ lbs. (58 cal.), 8 lbs. (45 cal.). **Length:** 43″.
Stock: Walnut finished hardwood.
Sights: Open, rear adj. for w. and e., blade front.
Features: Action similar to Model 158 Topper. Enclosed nipple (#11 size). Supplied with rifle are brass ramrod with wood handle and nipple wrench. Blue-black finish with color case hardened frame. From Harrington & Richardson.
Price: 12 ga. **$79.50**
Price: 45 and 58 cals. **$88.50**
Price: 58 cal. 32″ bbl. **$97.50**

TINGLE M1962 MUZZLE LOADING RIFLE

Caliber: 36, 44 or 50.
Barrel: 32″ octagon, hook breech, 52″ twist.
Weight: 10 lbs. **Length:** 48″ over-all.
Stock: One-piece walnut with concave cheekpiece.
Sights: Blade front, step adj. V-notch rear.
Features: Solid brass furniture, double-set trigger with adj. pull, percussion lock.
Price: **$159.95**

BLACK POWDER SHOTGUNS

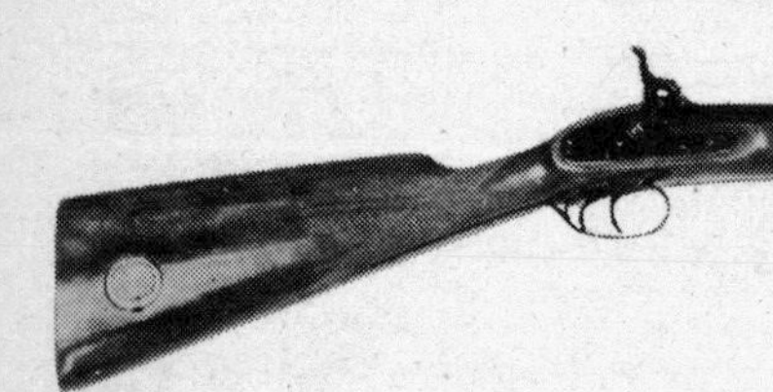

SINGLE BARREL FLINTLOCK SHOTGUN

Gauge: 28.
Barrel: 28″.
Weight: 4½ lbs. **Length:** 43″ over-all.
Stock: Walnut finish, choice of half or full stock. Imported by The Armoury.
Price: **$37.95**

FRONTIER PERCUSSION SHOTGUN

Gauge: 12 ga.
Barrels: 30″. (Mod. & Imp. Cyl.). Patent breech with threaded breech plugs.
Length: 46½″ over-all.
Stock: Walnut. Length of pull 14″.
Features: Patent breech for easy cleaning & disassembly. Front bead sight. Engraving on hardware. Brass patch box. Imported by CVA.
Price: **$139.95**

CVA 20 GA. PERCUSSION SHOTGUN

Gauge: 20 ga.
Barrel: 28″.
Weight: 5¾ lbs. **Length:** 43½″ over-all.
Stock: Oiled walnut. Checkered p.g.
Features: Blued barrels and locks. Brass tipped, hardwood ramrod. Double triggers. Imported by Connecticut Valley Arms.
Price: **$89.95**

DOUBLE BARREL PERCUSSION SHOTGUN

Gauge: 12.
Barrel: 30″ (I.C.& Mod.).
Weight: 6¼ lbs. **Length:** 45″ over-all.
Stock: Hand checkered walnut, 14″ pull.
Features: Double triggers, light hand engraving. Details vary with importer. Imported by Navy/Replica, The Armoury, Dixie.
Price: .... **$125.00** to **$175.00**

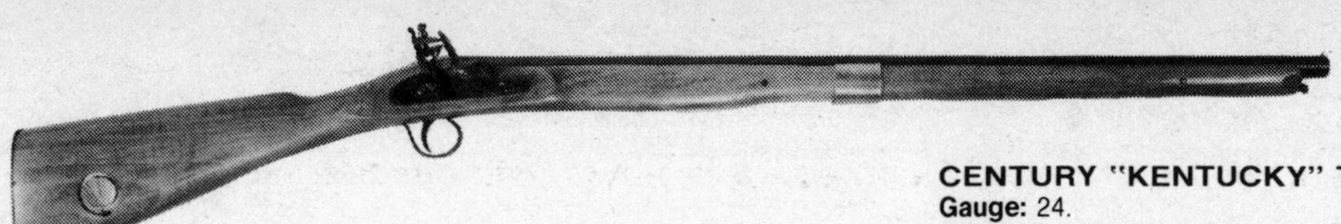

DIXIE FLINT FOWLING PIECE

Gauge: 14 ga.
Barrel: 37″.
Weight: 5½ lbs. **Length:** 52½″ over-all.
Stock: Walnut stained birch.
Sights: Fixed.
Features: Uses basic Harpers Ferry Pistol flintlock lock. Sling swivels. Bright-finished metal. From Dixie Gun Works.
Price: **$96.50**

CENTURY "KENTUCKY" TYPE SHOTGUN

Gauge: 24.
Barrel: 29″ (Cyl.).
Weight: 4¼ lbs. **Length:** 44″ over-all.
Stock: European walnut, checkered at wrist.
Sights: Bead front only.
Features: English style stock, inletted patch box; percussion or flintlock; steel ramrod. From Century Arms.
Price: Percussion, full stock **$44.50**
Price: Flintlock, full stock **$49.50**
Price: Percussion, sporter **$42.95**
Price: Flintlock, sporter **$47.95**

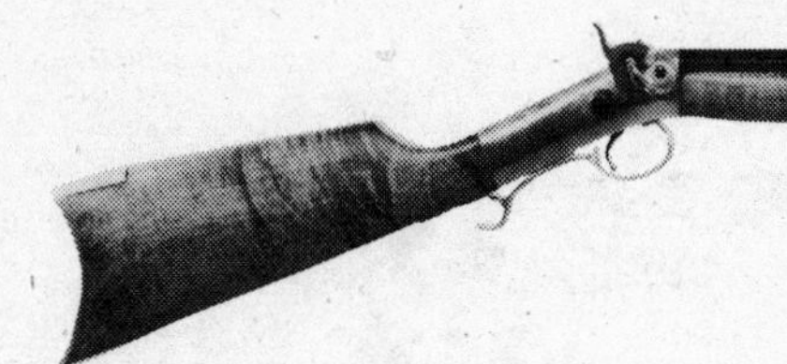

INTERARMS A. & T. 12 GAUGE SHOTGUN

Gauge: 12 ga. only.
Barrel: 32″, half octagon, half round.
Weight: 7½ lbs. **Length:** 48″ over-all.
Stock: Maple, oil finish, brass furniture.
Sights: Bead front.
Features: Available in percussion only. Uses standard 12 ga. wadding. Made by Mowrey.
Price: Complete **$240.00**

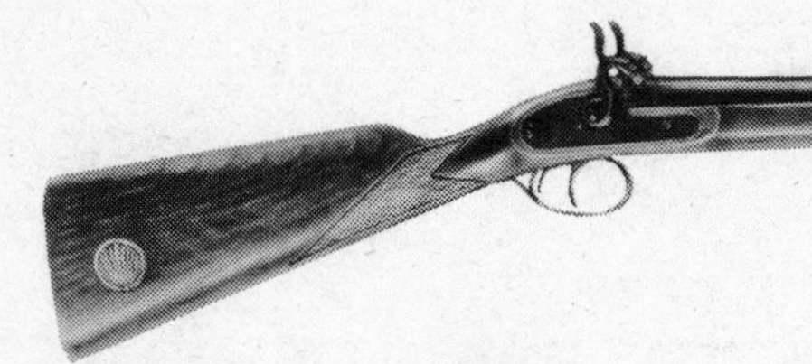

CENTURY DOUBLE BARREL SHOTGUN

Gauge: 20.
Barrel: 28″ (Cyl. & Cyl.).
Weight: 5¾ lbs. **Length:** 43½″ over-all.
Stock: One piece, walnut finish hardwood; checkered at wrist.
Sights: Bead.
Features: Inletted brass patch box; back lock action; blued barrels, lock and trigger guard; wooden ramrod; matted raised rib. From Century Arms.
Price: **$79.95**

MORSE/NAVY SINGLE BARREL SHOTGUN

Gauge: 12 ga.
Barrel: 26″.
Weight: 5 lbs. **Length:** 41½″ over-all.
Stock: American walnut, full p.g.
Sights: Front bead.
Features: Brass receiver, black buttplate. From Navy/Replica.
Price: **$80.00**

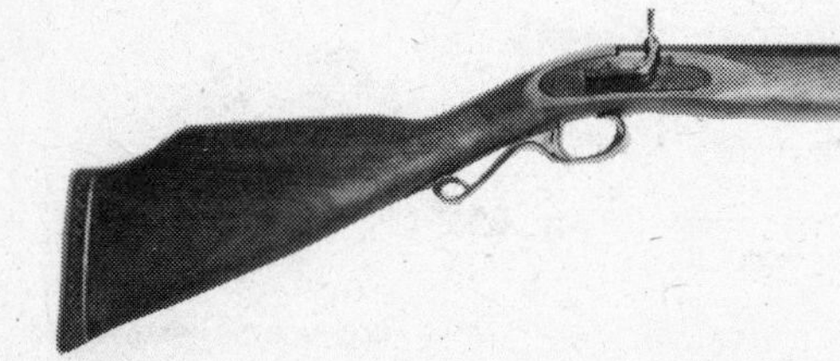

TINGLE PERCUSSION SINGLE BARREL SHOTGUN

Gauge: 12 only.
Barrel: 30″ cylinder bore.
Weight: 5 lbs.
Stock: Lacquered walnut.
Features: Mule ear side hammer lock, iron trigger guard, rubber recoil pad.
Price: Blued **$114.95**

CENTURY SINGLE BARREL PERCUSSION SHOTGUN

Gauge: 28.
Barrel: 31″ (Cyl.), part octagon.
Weight: 4¼ lbs. **Length:** 48½″ over-all.
Stock: Walnut finish hardwood; checkered at small of butt.
Sights: Bead front only.
Features: Suitable for ball or shot; blue barrel; lock, buttplate, trigger guard, breech and patch box are case hardened; steel ramrod. From Century Arms.
Price: **$59.50**

SINGLE BARREL PERCUSSION SHOTGUN

Gauge: 12, 20, 28.
Barrel: 28″.
Weight: 4½ lbs. **Length:** 43″ over-all.
Stock: Walnut finish, choice of half or full stock.
Features: Finish and features vary with importer. Imported by The Armoury, Dixie.
Price: .... **$32.95** to **$44.95**

AIR GUNS—HANDGUNS

Guns in this section are powered by: A) disposable CO^2 cylinders, B) hand-pumped compressed air released by trigger action, C) air compressed by a spring-powered piston released by trigger action. Calibers are generally 177 (BB or pellet) and 22 (ball or pellet); a few guns are made in 20 or 25 caliber. Pellet guns are usually rifled, those made for BB's only are smoothbore.

BEEMAN'S "ORIGINAL" 6 TARGET PISTOL

Caliber: 177, single shot.
Barrel: 7", rifled steel.
Weight: 3.2 lbs. **Length:** 16" over-all.
Power: Spring, barrel cocking.
Sights: Hooded front with interchangeable inserts, micro click rear with 4 rotating notches.
Features: Velocity 420 fps MV. Advanced recoilless action; precision adj. trigger. Imported by Beeman's.
Price: **$99.95**

BEEMAN'S "ORIGINAL" 10 MATCH PISTOL

Caliber: 177, single shot.
Weight: 3.3 lbs. **Length:** 16" over-all.
Power: Barrel cocking spring.
Stocks: Walnut with adjustable palm rest and sliding support plate.
Sights: Adj. post front from 2.5mm to 4.0mm width; adj. rear with interchangeable notches.
Features: Recoilless action; trigger adj. for length of pull, area of contact, travel length, pre-travel weight, pressure point and weight; auto. cocking safety trigger stop; eccentric sleeve rotates around rear of receiver to adj. rest for the back of the hand. Imported by Beeman's.
Price: **$299.50**

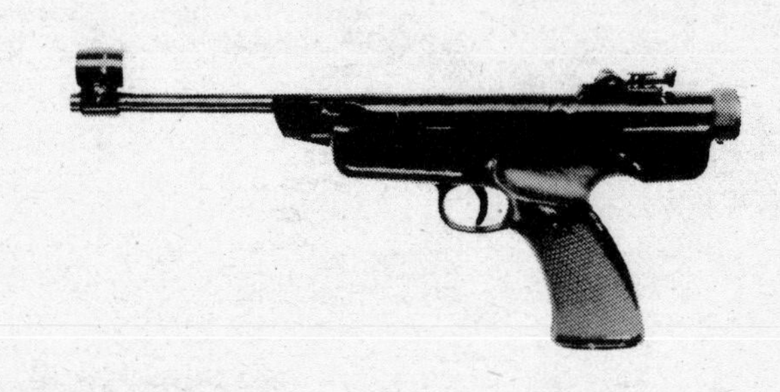

BEEMAN'S "ORIGINAL" 5 TARGET PISTOL

Caliber: 177 or 22, single shot.
Barrel: 7", rifled steel.
Length: 16" over-all. **Weight:** 3.1 lbs.
Power: Spring, barrel cocking.
Stocks: Checkered plastic thumbrest.
Sights: Hooded fixed front, micro-click rear with 4 rotating notches.
Features: Adjustable double-pull trigger. Velocity 420 fps MV. Imported by Beeman's.
Price: **$69.95**

BENJAMIN SUPER S. S. TARGET PISTOL SERIES 130

Caliber: BB, 22 and 177; single shot.
Barrel: 8"; BB smoothbore; 22 and 177, rifled.
Length: 11". **Weight:** 2 lbs.
Power: Hand pumped.
Features: Bolt action; fingertip safety; adj. power.
Price: M130, BB **$48.05**
Price: M132, 22 .... **$48.05** M137, 177 .... **$48.05**

CROSMAN MODEL "1300" MEDALIST II

Caliber: 22, single shot.
Barrel: 8", button rifled.
Length: 11¾". **Weight:** 37 oz.
Power: Hand pumped.
Features: Moulded plastic grip, hand size pump forearm. Cross bolt safety, self-cocking.
Price: **$40.51**

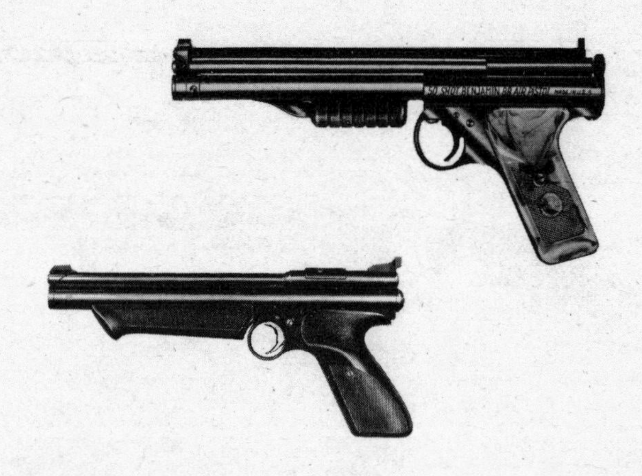

CROSMAN FRONTIER "36"

Caliber: BB, 18-shot.
Barrel: 4¾", smoothbore.
Length: 10⅜". **Weight:** 34 oz.
Power: Crosman CO^2 Powerlet
Features: Single-action, steel barrel, revolving cylinder. Walnut finish grips.
Price: **$29.95**

CROSMAN 454 BB PISTOL

Caliber: BB, 16-shot.
Length: 11" over-all. **Weight:** 30 oz.
Power: Standard CO^2.
Stocks: Contoured with thumb-rest.
Sights: Patridge-type front, fully adj. rear.
Features: Gives about 80 shots per powerlet, slide-action safety, steel barrel, die-cast receiver.
Price: **$34.91**

CROSMAN PEACEMAKER "44"

Caliber: 22, 6 shot.
Barrel: 4¾", button rifled.
Length: 10⅜". **Weight:** 34 oz.
Power: Crosman CO^2 Powerlet
Features: Revolving cylinder, walnut finished grips. Simulated gold hammer and trigger, positive valve design. Single-action.
Price: **$29.95**

CROSMAN MARK I TARGET PISTOL
Caliber: 22, single shot.
Barrel: 7¼", button rifled.
Length: 11". **Weight:** 42 oz.
Power: Crosman Powerlet CO^2 cylinder.
Features: New system provides same shot-to-shot velocity, adj. from 300- to 400 fps. Checkered thumbrest grips, right or left. Patridge front sight, rear adj. for w. & e. Adj. trigger.
Price: 22 or 177 .... **$39.28**

Crosman Mark II Target Pistol
Same as Mark I except 177 cal. **$39.28**

CROSMAN 38 TARGET REVOLVER M9
Caliber: 22, 6-shot.
Barrel: 6", rifled.
Length: 11 inches. **Weight:** 43 oz.
Power: CO^2 Powerlet cylinder.
Features: Double action, revolving cylinder. Adj. rear sight.
Price: **48.91**

Crosman 38 Combat Revolver
Same as 38 Target except 3½" BBL., 38 oz. **$48.91**

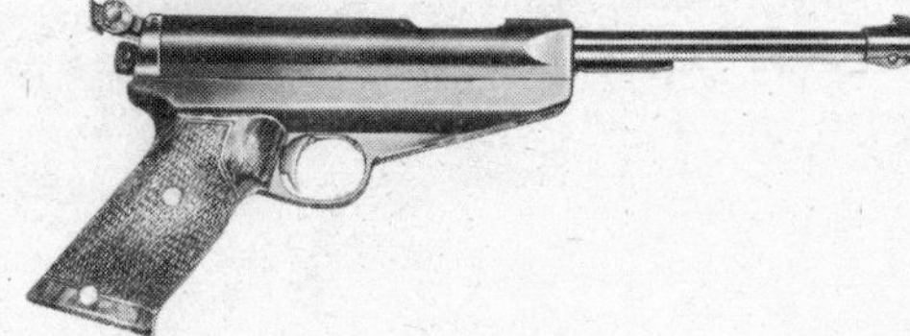

FEINWERKBAU F-65 AIR PISTOL
Caliber: 177.
Barrel: 7½".
Length: 14½" over-all. **Weight:** 42 oz.
Power: Spring, sidelever cocking.
Stocks: Walnut, stippled thumb-rest.
Sights: Front, interchangeable post element system, open rear, click adj. for w. & e. and for sighting notch width.
Features: Cocking effort 9 lbs. 2-stage trigger, 4 adjustments. Programs instantly for recoil or recoiless operation. Permanently lubricated. Special switch converts trigger from 17.6 oz. pull to 42 oz. let-off. Imported by Air Rifle Hdq., Beeman's
Price: .... **$269.50** to **$286.50**

Feinwerkbau Model 65 International Match Pistol
Same as FWB 65 pistol except: new adj. wood grips to meet international regulations, optional 3 oz. barrel sleeve weight. Imported by A.R.H., Beeman's.
Price: .... **$265.00** to **$299.50**

DAISY 179 SIX GUN
Caliber: BB, 12-shot.
Barrel: Steel lined, smoothbore.
Length: 11½". **Weight:** NA
Power: Spring.
Features: Forced feed from under-barrel magazine. Single action, molded wood grained grips.
Price: **$13.95**

DAISY 177 BB PISTOL
Caliber: BB, 150-shot.
Barrel: Formed steel, smoothbore.
Length: 11¼". **Weight:** NA.
Power: Spring.
Features: Gravity feed, adjustable rear sight, molded plastic thumbrest grips.
Price: **$13.95**

DAISY/FWB 65 TARGET PISTOL
Caliber: 177, single shot.
Barrel: 7½", rifled, fixed to receiver.
Length: 15½". **Weight:** 42 oz.
Power: Spring, cocked by left-side lever.
Features: Recoiless operation, may be set to give recoil; Micro. rear sight, 14" radius. Adj. trigger; normal 17.6 oz. pull can be raised to 48 oz. for training. Checkered, thumbrest target grips. Air Rifle Hdqtrs. or Daisy, importer.
Price: **$250.00**

HAMMERLI "MASTER" CO^2 TARGET PISTOL
Caliber: .177 waisted pellets.
Barrel: 6.4", 12-groove.
Length: 16". **Weight:** 38.4 oz.
Stocks: Plastic with thumbrest and checkering.
Sights: Ramp front, micro rear, click adj. Adj. sight radius from 11.1" to 13.0".
Features: Single shot, manual loading. Residual gas vented automatically. 5-way adj. trigger. Imported by HY-SCORE, Beeman's.
Price:.. **$79.95** to **$89.95**

HAMMERLI "SINGLE" CO^2 TARGET PISTOL
Caliber: .177 waisted pellets.
Barrel: 4.5", 12-groove.
Length: 12". **Weight:** 33 oz.
Stocks: Plastic with thumb rest and checkering.
Sights: Ramp front, micro-click rear. Adj. sight radius from 11.1" to 13.0".
Features: Single shot, easy manual loading, 4-way adj. trigger. Imported by HY-SCORE, Gil Hebard, Beeman's.
Price:.. **$69.95** to **$74.95**

HEALTHWAYS SHARPSHOOTER
Caliber: 175 (BB), 50-shot.
Barrel: 6¼".
Weight: 28 oz.
Power: Spring (barrel cocking).
Features: Easy cocking action. Loading pocket speeds and simplifies loading. Spring mechanism housed in grip.
Price:.. **$19.95**

HEALTHWAYS ML 175 CO^2 AUTOMATIC PISTOL
Caliber: BB, 100-shot repeater.
Barrel: 5¾", smooth.
Length: 9½". **Weight:** 28 oz.
Power: Standard CO^2 cylinder.
Features: 3 position power switch. Auto. ammunition feed. Positive safety.
Price:.. **$31.00**

HY-SCORE 816M TARGET PISTOL
Caliber: 177, single shot.
Barrel: 7" precision rifled.
Length: 16". **Weight:** 50 oz.
Power: Spring, bbl. cocking.
Features: Recoil-less firing, adj. trigger. Hooded front sight with 3 apertures, click adj. rear with 4 apertures. Plastic thumbrest target grips.
Price: In plastic case **$79.95**

HY-SCORE 815 Target Pistol
Same as Hy-Score M816 except: without recoil-less system; is slightly lighter; has fixed aperture front sight. In plastic case. Also in 22 cal. **$49.95**

MARKSMAN REPEATER PISTOL
Caliber: 177, 20-shot repeater.
Barrel: 2½", smoothbore.
Length: 8¼". **Weight:** 24 oz.
Power: Spring.
Features: Thumb safety. Uses BBs, darts or pellets. Repeats with BBs only.
Price: Black finish **$12.95**

HY-SCORE 814 JUNIOR PISTOL
Caliber: 177 darts BBs, single shot.
Barrel: Smoothbore.
Length: About 10". **Weight:** NA.
Power: Spring, compressed by screwing in breech plug.
Features: Checkered wooden grips.
Price: Blued **$7.95**

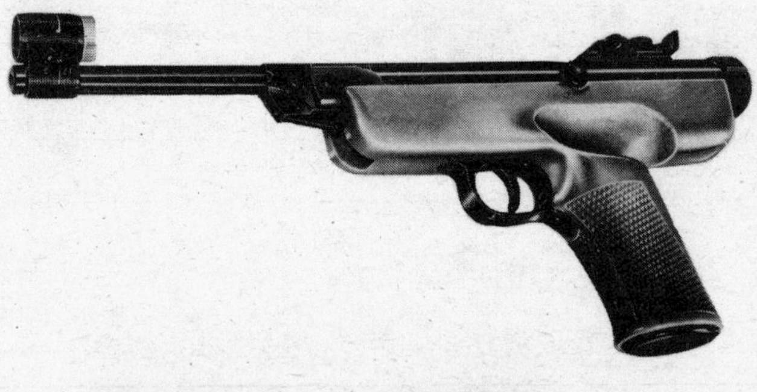

POWER LINE MODEL 62 TARGET AIR PISTOL
Caliber: 177 pellet, single shot.
Barrel: 7.2", rifled steel.
Length: 14⅞" over-all. **Weight:** 46 oz.
Power: Spring air.
Stock: Selected hardwood; contoured, articulated and adjustable to any shooting position.
Sights: Hooded ramp front, micro. adj. open rear.
Features: Crafted by Daisy. Long underlever for easy cocking.
Price:.. **$59.95**

POWERLINE CO^2 200 SEMI-AUTO PISTOL
Caliber: BB, 175-shot semi-auto.
Barrel: 7½", steel-lined, smoothbore.
Length: 11⅞", sight radius 9". **Weight:** 24 oz.
Power: Daisy CO^2 cylinders, 8½ grams (100 shots) or 12 grams (160 shots).
Features: Crafted by Daisy. 175-shot magazine; constant full power; valve system eliminates gas leakage; checkered thumbrest stocks; undercut ramp front sight and adjustable rear.
Price: **$39.00**

PRECISE/RO-72 BULLSEYE AIR PISTOL
Caliber: 177, single shot.
Barrel: 7¼", rifled.
Weight: 35 oz.
Power: Spring air, barrel cocking.
Stock: Molded plastic with thumb rest.
Sights: Hooded front, micro. adj. open rear for w. and e.
Features: Four interchangeable front sights—triangle, bead, narrow post, wide post. Rear sight rotates to give four distinct sight pictures.
Price: **$35.00**

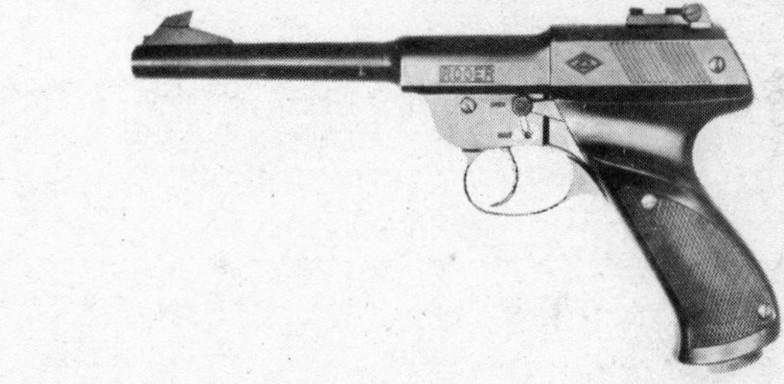

PRECISE/ROGER CO^2 BB PISTOL
Caliber: BB, 100-shot.
Barrel: 4¼", smooth.
Length: 10¼" over-all. **Weight:** 22 oz. **Sights:** Blade front, adj. rear.
Power: Standard CO^2 cartridge.
Features: Semi-automatic. Checkered plastic thumbrest target grips. Precise Imports, importer.
Price: **$30.00**

SMITH & WESSON MODELS 78G & 79G
Caliber: 22 cal. pellet (78G), 177 cal. pellet (79G), single-shot.
Barrel: 8½", rifled steel.
Weight: 42 oz.
Power: 12.5 gram CO^2 cartridge.
Stocks: Simulated walnut, checkered. Thumb rest. Left or right hand.
Sights: Patridge front, fully adj. rear with micro. click windage adjustment.
Features: Pull-bolt action, crossbolt safety, double sear trigger with adj. engagement. High-low power adjustment. Gun blue finish.
Price: **$41.00**

WALTHER MODEL LP-3
Caliber: 177, single shot.
Barrel: 9⅜", rifled.
Length: 13 3/16". **Weight:** 45½ oz.
Power: Compressedair, lever cocking.
Features: Recoiless operation, cocking in grip frame. Micro-click rear sight, adj. for w. & e., 4-way adj. trigger. Plastic thumbrest grips. Imported by Interarms.
Price: **$175.00**

Walther Model LP-3 Match Pistol
Same specifications as LP-3 except for grips, frame shape and weight. Has adjustable walnut grips to meet international shooting regulations. Imported by Interarms.
Price: **$210.00**

AIR GUNS—HANDGUNS

WALTHER MODEL LP-53 PISTOL

Caliber: 177, single shot.
Barrel: 9⅜".
Length: 12⅜" over-all. **Weight:** 40.5 oz.
Power: Spring air.
Features: Micrometer rear sight. Interchangeable rear sight blades. Target grips. Bbl. weight available at extra cost. Interarms, Alexandria, Va.
Price: **$105.00**

WEBLEY AIR PISTOLS

Model:	**Junior**	**Premier**
Caliber:	177	177 or 22
Barrel:	6⅛"	6½"
Weight:	23¼ oz.	37 oz.
Power:	Spring, barrel cocking	Same
Sights:	Adj. for w.	Adj. for w.&e.
Trigger:	Fixed	Adj.
Price:	**$49.50**	**$53.00** to **$76.00**

Features: Single stroke cocking, heavy steel construction, blued. Imported by A.R.H., Beeman's, Fanta.

WEIHRAUCH HW-70 AIR PISTOL

Caliber: 177, single shot.
Barrel: 6¼", rifled.
Length: 12¾" over-all. **Weight:** 38 oz.
Sights: Hooded post front, square notch rear adj. for w. and e.
Power: Spring, barrel cocking.
Features: Adj. trigger. 24-lb. cocking effort, 365 f.p.s. M.V.; automatic safety. Air Rifle HQ, Beeman's, importers.
Price: .... **$48.00** to **$53.00**

WISCHO CUSTOM MATCH PISTOL

Caliber: 177, single shot.
Barrel: 7" rifled.
Length: 15.8" over-all. **Weight:** 45 oz.
Stocks: Walnut with thumbrest.
Sights: Hooded read front, rear adj. for w. and e.
Power: Spring, barrel cocking.
Features: Cocking effort of 17 lbs.; M.V. 450 f.p.s.; adj. trigger. Optional scope and mount available. (**$56.50** installed). Air Rifle HQ, Beeman's importers.
Price: .... **$79.95** to **$87.50**

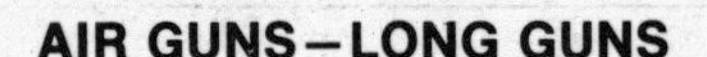

AIR GUNS—LONG GUNS

A.R.H. CUSTOM 120-X RIFLE

Caliber: 177 only.
Barrel: 18⅝".
Length: 44" over-all.
Power: Spring air, single stroke, barrel cocking.
Stock: Select American walnut with roll-over cheekpiece, Rosewood p.g. cap, white spacers, rubber buttplate, high gloss finish, detachable swivels.
Sights: Tunnel front with interchangeable inserts included, open rear. Match aperture or scope optional.
Features: Velocity 818 fps; cocking effort 16 lbs.; automatic safety; adjustable trigger. Accurized and recoil dampened. Custom trigger guard and trigger shoe. Imported and built by Air Rifle Headquarters.
Price: **$348.50**

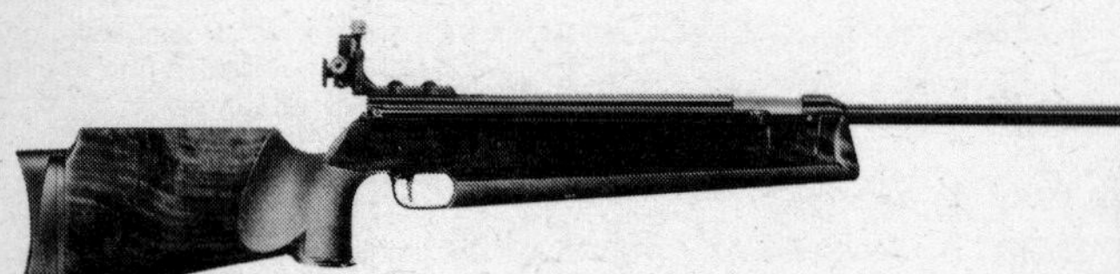

ANSCHUTZ 250 TARGET RIFLE

Caliber: 177, single shot.
Barrel: 18½", rifled, one piece with receiver.
Length: 45". **Weight:** 11 lbs. with sights.
Power: Spring, side-lever cocking, 17 lb. pull.
Features: Recoil-less operation. Two-stage adj. trigger. Checkered walnut p.g. stock with Monte Carlo comb & cheekpiece; adj. buttplate; accessory rail. Imported by Beeman's.
Price: Without sights **$374.00**
With #6723 match sight set **$399.00**

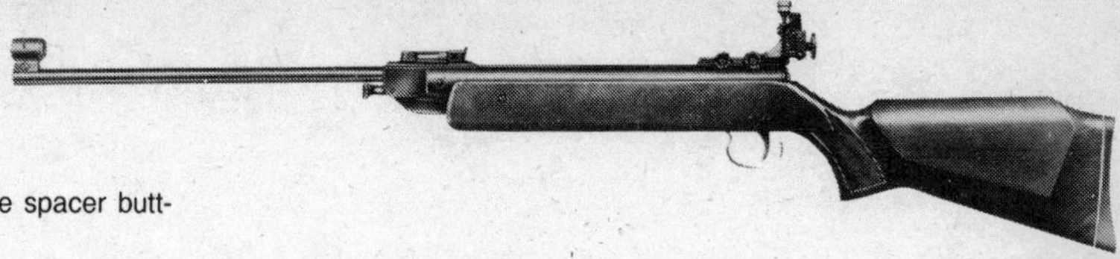

ANSCHUTZ 335 RIFLE
Caliber: 177, single-shot.
Barrel: 18½", 12-groove, rifled.
Length: 43" over-all. **Weight:** 7 lbs.
Power: Spring, barrel-cocking.
Stock: Checkered M.C. Stock with cheekpiece and white line spacer buttplate.
Sights: Tunnel front with blade, open rear adj. for w. & e.
Features: Special safety latch to prevent barrel backlash when breech is open. Imported by Beeman's.
Price: With open sight **$139.95**
Price: With #6706 match aperture sight **$169.95**

BEEMAN'S "ORIGINAL" 23 TARGET RIFLE
Caliber: 177, single shot.
Length: 36" over-all. **Weight:** 4 lbs.
Power: Spring, barrel cocking.
Sights: Blade front on dovetail; open rear with elevation slider.
Features: Velocity 480 fps MV. All steel, blued sights and body. Imported by Beeman's.
Price: **$49.95**

BEEMAN'S "ORIGINAL" 27 TARGET RIFLE
Caliber: 177, single shot.
Barrel: 18.7", rifled.
Length: 42" over-all. **Weight:** 6 lbs.
Power: Spring, barrel cocking.
Sights: Hooded front, 4-notch rotating rear micro. adj. for w. & e.
Features: Velocity 660 fps MV. Grooved for scope of peep sights; 17 lbs. single stroke cocking force; adjustable trigger. Imported by Beeman's.
Price: **$79.95**

ANSCHUTZ 275 REPEATER AIR RIFLE
Caliber: 173 (4.4 mm) lead balls, 6-shot clip.
Length: 41.3" over-all. **Weight:** 5.7 lbs.
Stock: Walnut finished hardwood.
Power: Spring air; piston cocked by bolt like Haenel or Mauser trainers.
Sights: Open, fixed.
Features: Approx. 450 fps. Rigid barrel/receiver unit. Imported by Beeman's.
Price: **$137.50**

BEEMAN'S "ORIGINAL" 35 SPORTER RIFLE
Caliber: 177, single shot.
Barrel: 19", rifled steel.
Length: 44.3" over-all. **Weight:** 7.1 lbs.
Power: Spring, barrel cocking.
Stock: Adult-size walnut finished, soft rubber buttplate.
Sights: Hooded front with removeable insert, steel rear adj. for w. & e.
Features: Scope and aperature sight ramp; adj. 2-stage trigger. Imported by Beeman's.
Price: **$99.95**

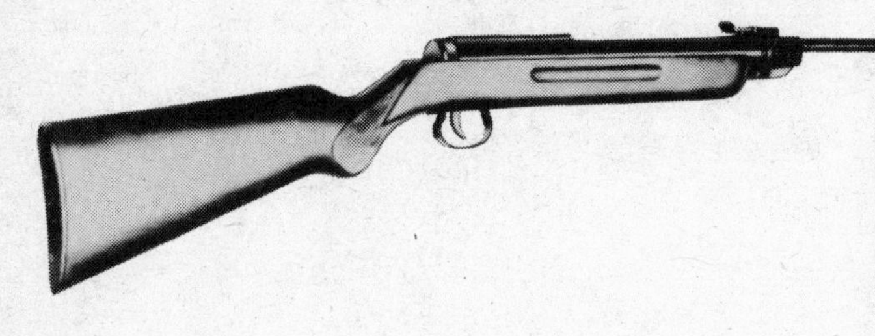

BSF 55, S-60, S-70 RIFLES

Model:	Bavaria 55	S-60 (illus.)	S-70
Caliber:	177 or 22	177 or 22	177
Barrel:	16"	19"	19"
Rifled:	Yes	Yes	Yes
Length:	40½"	43½"	43¾"
Weight:	6¼ lbs.	6½ lbs.	6½ lbs.
MV:	763, 580	763, 580	763
Sights:	Elev. only	w. & e.	w. & e.
Price:	**$93.00** to **$109.50**	**$109.00** to **$135.00**	**$124.00** to **$158.00**

Features: Spring powered, barrel cocking. Blued metal. Adj. 2-stage triggers. Beech stocks on B-55 and S-60, walnut stocks (optional) have checkered p.g. S-70 mechanically identical to S-60, Beech, checkered p.g. and fore-end. Raised cheek pad, curved rubber buttplate. Imported by Beeman's and Fanta.

BSF S-54 AIR RIFLES

Model:	S-54 Std.	S-54 Bayern	S-54 Match
Caliber:	177	177	177
Barrel:	19⅜"	19⅜"	19⅜"
Rifled:	Yes	Yes	Yes
Weight:	7¾ lbs.	8 lbs.	8¾ lbs.
MV:	669	669	669
Sights:	Adj.	Adj.	Adj.
Price:	**$110.00** to **$160.00**	**$120.00** to **$240.00**	**$130.00** to **$180.00**

Features: Spring powered, under lever cocking. Adj. 2-stage triggers. All three models are mechanically identical. Bayern and Match have select walnut stocks with checkered p.g. and fore-end. Match has polished, semi-curved aluminum buttplate. Standard has polished beech stock. Walnut optional at $4.00 extra. Imported by Beeman's and Fanta.

BSF AIR RIFLES

Model:	Bavaria 30	Junior	Media 45
Caliber:	177	177	177 or 22
Barrel:	13½"	15¼"	16"
Rifled:	Yes	Yes	Yes
Length:	34½"	38⅛"	39½"
Weight:	3½ lbs.	4½ lbs.	5¾ lbs.
MV:	465 fps.	561 fps.	682, 560 fps.
Sights:	Adj.	Adj.	Adj.
Price:	**$44.00** to **$65.00**	**$56.00** to **$75.00**	**$73.50** to **$85.00**

Features: Spring powered, barrel cocking. Polished beech stocks. Adj. triggers. Blued metal parts. Bavaria 30, Junior, Media 45 available from Fanta. Beeman's imports only the Model 45. Fanta imports all three.

BENJAMIN 3030 CO^2 REPEATER
Caliber: Steel BBs only.
Barrel: 25½", smoothbore, takedown.
Length: 36". **Weight:** 4 lbs.
Power: Standard CO^2 cylinder.
Features: Hammer lock safety. 30-shot repeater with permanent-magnet, shot-holder ammo feed.
Price: **$31.75**

BENJAMIN SERIES 340 AIR RIFLE
Caliber: 22 and 177 pellets or BB; single shot.
Barrel: 23″, rifled and smoothbore.
Length: 35″. **Weight:** 6 lbs.
Power: Hand pumped.
Features: Bolt action, walnut Monte Carlo stock and pump handle. Ramp-type front sight, adj. stepped leaf type rear. Push-pull safety.
Price: M340, BB **$54.80**
Price: M342, 22 .... **$54.80** M347, 177 .... **$54.80**

BENJAMIN SERIES 3100 SUPER REPEATER RIFLES
Caliber: BB, 100-shot; 22, 85-shot.
Barrel: 23″, rifled or smoothbore.
Length: 35″. **Weight:** 6¼ lbs.
Power: Hand pumped.
Features: Bolt action. Piggy back full view magazine. Bar V adj. rear sight. Walnut stock and pump handle.
Price: M3100, BB .... **$56.00** M3120, 22 rifled **$56.00**

CROSMAN 622 PELL-CLIP REPEATER
Caliber: 22, 6-shot rotating, clip
Barrel: 23″
Length: 40″. **Weight:** 6½ lbs.
Power: Crosman CO^2 Powerlet, pump action
Features: Removable 6-shot pell clip. Adjustable rear sight. Scope and mount extra.
Price: **$48.91**

CROSMAN MODEL 760 POWERMASTER
Caliber: BB, 180 shot.
Barrel: 19½″, smoothbore steel.
Length: 35″. **Weight:** 4⅛ lbs.
Power: High compression spring.
Features: Short stroke, power determined by number of strokes. Walnut finished checkered stock and forearm. Post front sight and adjustable rear sight. Cross-bolt safety. Scope and mount optional.
Price: **$36.66**

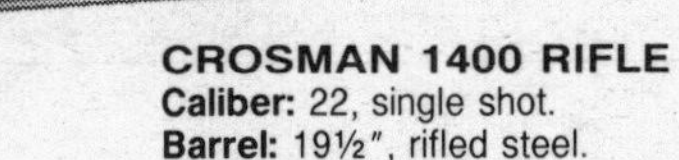

CROSMAN 1400 RIFLE
Caliber: 22, single shot.
Barrel: 19½″, rifled steel.
Length: 35½″. **Weight:** About 6 lbs.
Power: Hand pumped.
Features: Bolt action. Air-Trol valve prevents air lock from over-pumping. Adj. trigger, left or right hand safety. Scope and mount optional.
Price: **$55.91**

CROSMAN M-1 CARBINE
Caliber: BB, 270-shot.
Barrel: Smoothbore, steel.
Length: 35⅝″. **Weight:** 4½ lbs.
Power: Spring.
Features: Patterned after U.S. M1 carbine, uses slide action cocking, military type adj. sights. Hardwood stock.
Price: **$21.95**

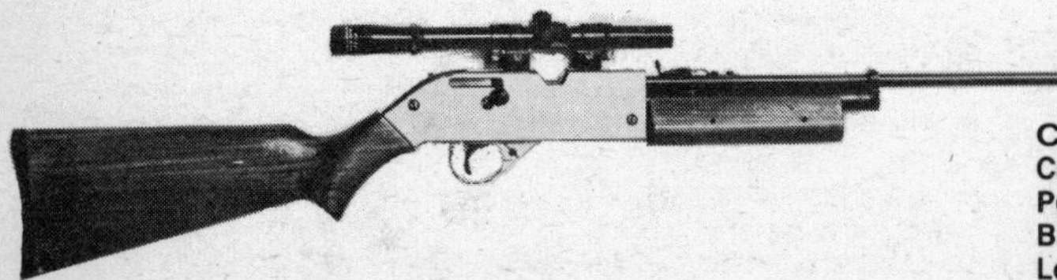

CROSMAN POWERMATIC "500"
Caliber: BB, 50-shot semiautomatic.
Barrel: 18″, smoothbore steel.
Length: 37¾″. **Weight:** 4½ lbs.
Power: Crosman CO^2 Powerlet.
Features: Positive safety, over 100 shots from one Powerlet. Walnut finished stock, grooved receiver for optional scope or peep sight. Rear sight is adjustable for windage and elevation.
Price: **$26.95**

CROSMAN 761XL PUMP RIFLE
Caliber: BB, 180-shot or 177 cal. pellet (single-shot).
Power: Hand pumped.
Barrel: 19″, button rifled.
Length: 36″ over-all. **Weight:** 4¾ lbs.
Stock: Full-size, walnut.
Sights: Hooded front, step adj. rear for w. & e.
Features: Receiver grooved for scope mounting, gold-colored receiver, cross-bolt safety.
Price: **$45.41**

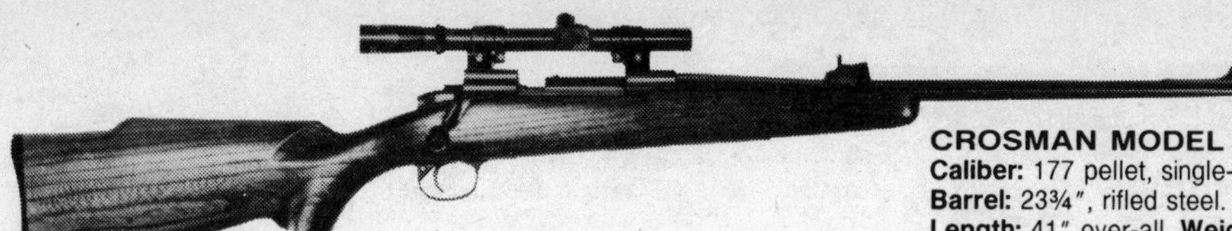

CROSMAN MODEL 70 CO^2 BOLT ACTION RIFLE

Caliber: 177 pellet, single-shot.
Barrel: 23¾″, rifled steel.
Length: 41″ over-all. **Weight:** 5¾ lbs.
Stock: Full-size hardwood, walnut finish, Monte Carlo-style.
Sights: Blade front, rear adjustable for w. and e.
Features: Average velocity 650 fps. Full sized gun. Cross bolt safety. Each powerlet (12.5 grams) gives an average of 40 shots. Crosman 4X Superscope and mounts available separately ($13.00).
Price: **$44.95**
Price: With scope and mounts **$57.95**

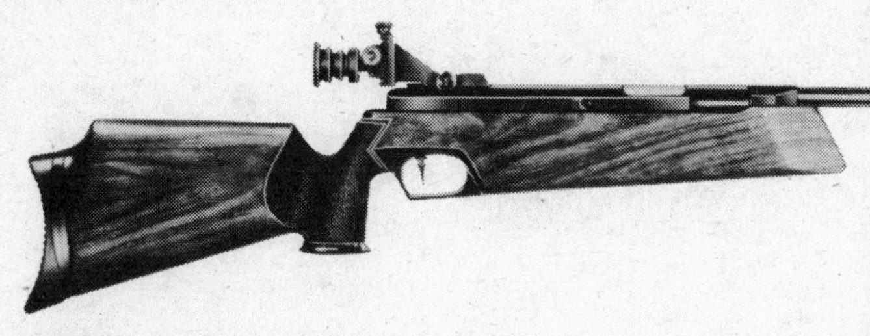

DAISY/FWB 4301

Caliber: 177, single shot.
Barrel: 29¼″, rifled.
Length: 45″. **Weight:** 11 lbs.
Stock: Walnut, Monte Carlo cheekpiece, checkered palmswell p.g.
Sights: Globe front with inserts, micro. adj. peep rear.
Power: Spring, barrel cocking.
Features: Adj. trigger, adj. buttplate.
Price: **$350.00**

DAISY MODEL 7404 PELLET RIFLE

Caliber: 177.
Barrel: Smooth bore.
Length: 35½″ over-all. **Weight:** 4¼ lbs.
Power: Spring air.
Stock: Stained hardwood with Monte Carlo cheekpiece.
Sights: Post ramp front, step adj. rear for e.
Features: X 5-shot repeater with removeable "Rota-Clip" pellet cylinder. Auto. trigger block safety. Model 7454 has rifled barrel.
Price: Model 7454 .... **$34.95**
Price: Model 7404 .... **$23.00**

DAISY RIFLES

Model:	**95**	**102**	**104**	**111**
Caliber:	BB	BB	BB	BB
Barrel:	18″	13½″	13½″	18″
Length:	35″	30¼″	30½″	35″
Power:	Spring	Spring	Spring	Spring
Capacity:	700	350	350	700
Price:	**$19.95**	**$13.85**	**$16.00**	**$18.95**

Features: 95 stock is wood, fore-end plastic; 111 and 104 have plastic stocks; 102 has wood stock; 104 has sighting tube w/aperture and is gold finished.

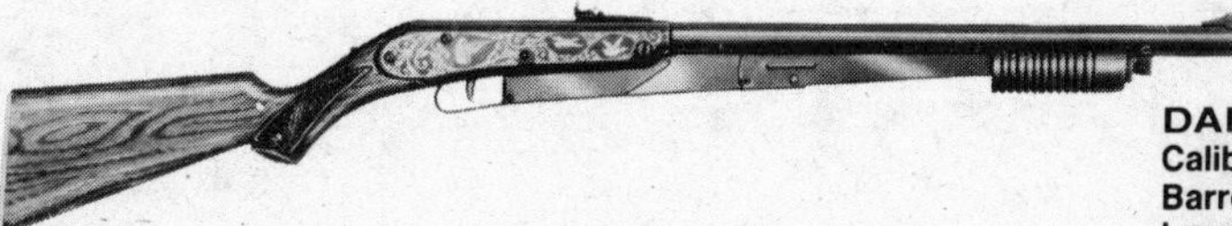

DAISY 25 PUMP GUN

Caliber: BB, 50-shot.
Barrel: 18″, smoothbore.
Length: 37¼″. **Weight:** NA.
Power: Pump cocking spring.
Features: Ramp front and adj. rear sights. BBs are spring-force fed.
Price: **$25.95**

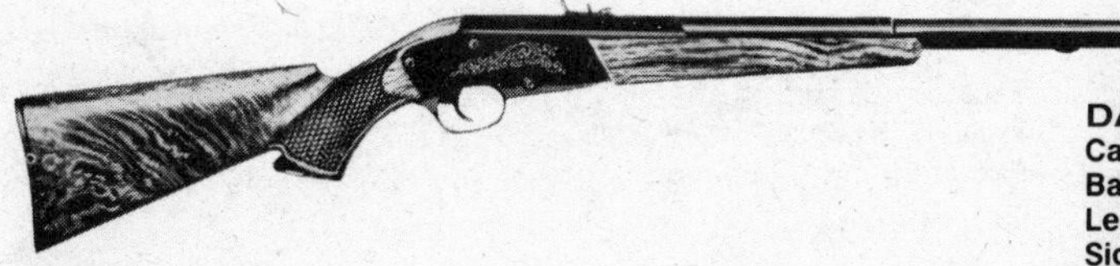

DAISY MODEL 86/70 SAFARI MK. I

Caliber: BB, 240-shot.
Barrel: 11″ smooth.
Length: 34¼″. **Weight:** 2 lbs.
Sights: Ramp front, V-notch rear.
Features: Plastic stock and fore-end, force-feed magazine. Trigger-guard cocking action with cross-bolt safety.
Price: **$19.95**

DAISY MODEL 5994 WELLS FARGO COMMEMORATIVE

Caliber: BB only.
Barrel: Smooth bore.
Length: 38⅜″ over-all. **Weight:** 3 lbs.
Power: Spring air.
Stock: Wood grain moulded plastic with replica Wells Fargo agent's star.
Sights: Post ramp front, step adj. rear for e.
Features: Antiqued gun metal receiver with Wells Fargo design. Side loading port. 40-shot magazine.
Price: **$34.00**

DAISY MODEL 98 MONTE CARLO BB RIFLE

Caliber: BB only.
Barrel: Smooth bore.
Length: 36″ over-all. **Weight:** 4 lbs.
Power: Spring air.
Stock: Wood grain moulded plastic with Monte Carlo cheekpiece.
Sights: Post ramp front, open rear adj. for e.
Features: Lever cocking, gravity feed. 700-shot magazine. Auto. trigger block safety.
Price: Approximately **$25.00**

DAISY 7938 RED RYDER COMMEMORATIVE BB CARBINE

Caliber: BB, 700-shot repeating action.
Barrel: Sturdy steel, under-barrel loading port.
Length: 35″ over-all. **Weight:** 3½ lbs.
Stock: Wood stock burned with Red Ryder lariat signature.
Sights: Post front, adjustable V-slot rear.
Features: Wood fore-end. Saddle ring with leather thong. Lever cocking. Gravity feed. Controlled velocity. Commemorates one of Daisy's most popular guns, the Red Ryder of the 1940s and 1950s.
Price: **$24.95**

DAISY 99 CHAMPION

Caliber: BB, 50-shot.
Barrel: 18″, smoothbore.
Length: 36¼″.
Power: Spring.
Features: Wood stock, beavertail fore-end; sling; hooded front sight with four insert apertures, adj. aperture rear, stock medallion.
Price: **$30.95**

DAISY 1894 SPITTIN' IMAGE CARBINE

Caliber: BB, 40-shot.
Barrel: 17½″, smoothbore.
Length: 38⅜″.
Power: Spring.
Features: Cocks halfway on forward stroke of lever, halfway on return.
Price: **$30.00**

FEINWERKBAU 300-S TYROLEAN MATCH RIFLE

Caliber: 177, single shot.
Barrel: 19.9″.
Length: 42.8″ over-all. **Weight:** 9.5 lbs.
Power: Spring air, sidelever.
Stock: Walnut. High Tyrolean cheekpiece, medium weight fore-end.
Sights: Globe front with inserts, micro. adj. rear aperture.
Features: Barrel and receiver recoil together to eliminate felt recoil. 4-way adj. trigger. Muzzle velocity 640 fps. Optional 12 oz. bbl. sleeve. Imported by A.R.H. and Beeman's.
Price: **$388.00**

FEINWERKBAU 300-S SERIES MATCH RIFLES

Caliber: 177.
Barrel: 19.9″, fixed solid with receiver.
Length: 42.8″ over-all. **Weight:** Approx. 10 lbs. with optional bbl. sleeve.
Power: Single stroke sidelever, spring piston.
Stock: Match model—walnut, deep fore-end, adj. buttplate. Std. model—walnut finish, lighter weight, regular fore-end, lacks p.g. cap.
Sights: Globe front with interchangeable inserts. Click micro. adj. match aperture rear.
Features: Recoilless, vibration free. Grooved for scope mounts. Permanent lubrication and seals. cocking effort 9 lbs. Optional 10 oz. bbl. sleeve. A.R.H. imports only Match; Beeman's imports both.
Price: Standard .... **$258.50** to **$325.00**
Price: 300-S Match .... **$345.00** to **$378.50**

FEINWERKBAU 124 SPORTER

Caliber: 177, 22.
Barrel: 18.3″.
Length: 43.5″ over-all. **Weight:** 6.3 lbs.
Power: Spring air; single stroke barrel cocking.
Stock: Walnut finished hardwood.
Sights: Tunnel front, fully adj. open rear.
Features: Velocity over 800 fps. Cocking effort 19 lbs. Automatic safety, adj. trigger. Standard model has no checkering or cheekpiece. Deluxe has checkered p.g. and fore-end, high comb cheekpiece, sling swivels and buttplate with white line spacer. A.R.H. has 177 cal. only, Beeman's both. Optional high power spring available from Beeman's. Imported by A.R.H. and Beeman's.
Price: Standard model **$139.50**
Price: Deluxe model .... **$164.50** to **$178.50**
Price: Deluxe left-hand .... **$159.50** to **$174.50**

Feinwerkbau 124 Custom Sporter
Same as Standard 124 except assembled in U.S. with select American walnut stock with rollover cheekpiece, rosewood p.g. cap, white line spacers, rubber buttplate, choice of super gloss or semi-gloss finish. Velocity approx. 820 fps, cocking effort 18 lbs. Special thumbhole stock. Accurized version of 124. Imported and assembled by Beeman's **$294.50**

HY-SCORE 810M OLYMPIC INTERNATIONAL RIFLE
Caliber: 177, single shot.
Barrel: 19¼" 12-groove rifled.
Length: 44". **Weight:** 9½ lbs.
Power: Spring (barrel cocking).
Features: Full cheekpiece, Monte Carlo stock, hand checkered; grooved fore-end, curved rubber buttplate. Adj. target receiver sight (includes 4 apertures), hooded front sight (includes 4 inserts).
Price: **$199.95**

M810SM Super Match
As above but with weight increased to 14 lbs., bbl. locking device, adj. stock, replaceable mainspring, MV 580 fps, accuracy tested: ¼" spread at 33'
Price: **$224.95**

HY-SCORE 809M TARGET RIFLE
Caliber: 22, single shot.
Barrel: 19" rifled.
Length: 44". **Weight:** 7 pounds.
Power: Spring, bbl. cocking.
Features: Adj. target receiver sight, aperture front with 4 inserts, in addition to open adj. middle sight also with 4 apertures.
Price: **$99.95**

ITHACA BSA METEOR & MECURY RIFLES
Caliber: 177 or 22.
Barrel: 18½" rifled.
Length: 42" over-all. **Weight:** 6 lbs. (Meteor), 7 lbs. (Mercury)
Stock: European hardwood. Mercury has Monte Carlo.
Sights: Blade front, micro. adj. rear (Meteor). Mecury has hooded front.
Features: Meteor—barrel cocking action. Adjustable single stage trigger, 3-5 lb. pull. Receiver dovetailed for standard scope mounts. 650 fps (177 cal.); 500 fps (22 cal.). Mercury—700 fps (177), 550 fps (22), comes with pellets, target, target holder and lubricant. Imported by Ithaca.
Price: Meteor **$49.95**
Price: Mercury **$89.95**

HY-SCORE RIFLES

Model:	**801**	**806**	**807**	**808**	**813**
Caliber:	22	177	22	177	22
Barrel:	15¾"	14½"	17⅜"	12"	14¼"
Rifled:	Yes	Yes	Yes	No	Yes
Length:	38½"	36½"	41¾"	33"	36½"
Weight:	5 lbs.	3¾ lbs.	5 lbs. 14 oz.	3 lbs.	4 lbs.
Power:	Spring	Spring	Spring	Spring	Spring
Price:	**$69.95**	**$34.95**	**$69.95**	**$17.95**	**$39.95**

Features: All are barrel cocking. All have adj. sights and regular triggers except 807, which has an adj. trigger. Staeble 2.2X scope and mt. available for all but 808, **$14.95.**
M813 and scope available at a combination price of **$33.40**
M801 available as 801M with click adj. receiver sight **$49.95**

MARKSMAN 740 AIR RIFLE
Caliber: 177, 400-shot.
Barrel: 15-½", smoothbore.
Length: 36-½". **Weight:** 4 lbs., 2 oz.
Power: Spring, barrel cocking.
Sights: Ramp front, open rear adj. for e.
Features: Automatic safety; fixed front, adj. rear sights; shoots 177 cal. BB's pellets and darts.
Price: **$24.95**

MARKSMAN MODEL 746 RIFLE
Caliber: 177 or 22, single-shot.
Barrel: 17⅜", rifled.
Length: 42" over-all. **Weight:** 6½ lbs.
Stock: Beech. Monte Carlo cheekpiece, checkered p.g.
Sights: Hooded ramp front, micro rear adj. for w. and e. **Power:** Spring, barrel cocking.
Features: Velocity of 580 fps; 3½ lbs. trigger pull; cocking effort of 22 lbs. Metal parts blued. Receiver grooved for scope mounting.
Price: Approx. **$75.00**

PIC CO^2 BOBCAT BOLT ACTION RIFLE
Caliber: 177, 22, single-shot.
Barrel: 19¼"
Length: 35" over-all. **Weight:** 4¾ lbs.
Power: Standard CO^2 cartridges.
Features: Walnut finish stock; receiver grooved for scope mounting. Precise Imports, importer.
Price: **$40.00**

PRECISE/SLAVIA MODEL 624
Caliber: 177, single-shot.
Barrel: 16", rifled.
Length: 38" over-all. **Weight:** 3¾ lbs.
Stock: Walnut finish hardwood, p.g., no buttplate or p.g. cap.
Sights: Hooded front, open leaf rear.
Features: Muzzle velocity 371 fps, barrel-cocking action. Imported by Precise Imports.
Price: **$36.00**

Precise/El Gamo Single Shot Rifle

Same as repeater version except: available in either 177 or 22 cal.; over-all length 41", weight 5¼ lbs.
Price: $70.00

PRECISE/EL GAMO TOURNAMENT AIR RIFLE

Caliber: 177, 22, single shot.
Barrel: 18". 12-groove rifling.
Length: 43" over-all. **Weight:** 6¾ lbs.
Power: Spring, barrel cocking.
Features: Micro. adj. rear sight, hooded front. Walnut finish stock; Monte Carlo comb with cheek piece, recoil pad. Receiver grooved for scope mounting. Precise Imports, importer.
Price: $80.00

PRECISE/EL GAMO REPEATER AIR RIFLE

Caliber: 177, 25-shot.
Barrel: 17½", 12 groove rifling.
Length: 37½". **Weight:** 6½ lbs.
Power: Spring, barrel cocking.
Features: M.V. 675 fps. Micro, adj. target sights, adj. trigger; target type recoil pad, M.C. comb and cheekpiece. Precise Imports, importer.
Price: $95.00

Precise/El Gamo Carbine Air Rifle

Same as Tournament model except has plain stock without Monte Carlo comb, cheekpiece $50.00

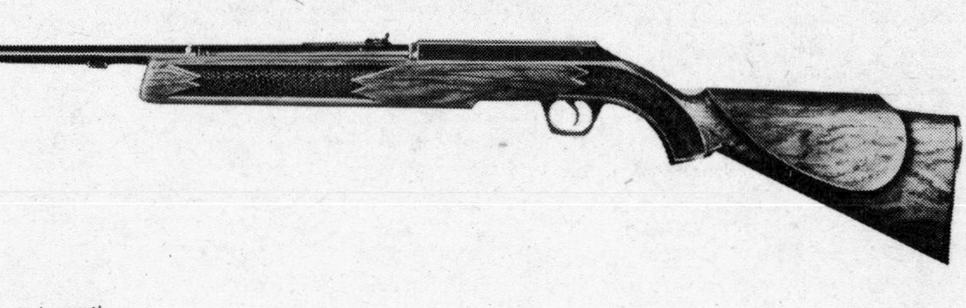

POWER LINE MODEL 770

Caliber: BB only, 200-shot magazine
Barrel: 18$^{13}/_{16}$", smoothbore.
Length: 39⅛ over-all. **Weight:** 4 lbs.
Power: Spring, lever cocking.
Stock: Fully contoured wood grain plastic with Monte Carlo.
Sights: Hooded ramp front, fully adj. open rear.
Features: Crafted by Daisy. Single stroke cocking system with automatic safety. With optional Model 808 4X scope as Model 1770 **(56.95)**.
Price: $34.95

POWER LINE MODEL 882

Caliber: 177, pellets or BB.
Barrel: 20½, decagon rifled.
Length: 37¾ over-all. **Weight:** 4½ lbs.
Power: Spring air.
Stock: Wood grain molded plastic with Monte Carlo cheekpiece.
Sights: Hooded front with 4 inserts, Williams receiver rear sight with micrometer adjustments.
Features: Crafted by Daisy. Official gun of the Daisy National Air Gun program
Price: $69.95

POWER-LINE 880 PUMP-UP AIR GUN

Caliber: 177 pellets, BB.
Barrel: Smooth bore, steel.
Length: 37¾" over-all. **Weight:** 6 lbs.
Power: Spring air.
Stock: Wood grain moulded plastic.
Sights: Ramp front, open rear adj. for e.
Features: Crafted by Daisy. Variable power (velocity and range) increase with pump strokes. 10 strokes for maximum power. 100-shot BB magazine. Cross-bolt trigger safety. Positive cocking valve.
Price: $43.95

POWER-LINE 881 PUMP-UP AIR GUN

Caliber: 177 pellets, BB.
Barrel: Decagon rifled.
Length: 37¾" over-all. **Weight:** 6 lbs.
Power: Spring air.
Stock: Wood grain moulded plastic with Monte Carlo cheekpiece.
Sights: Ramp front, step-adj. rear for e.
Features: Crafted by Daisy. Accurized version of Model 880. Checkered fore-end and p.g.
Price: $51.95

POWER LINE CO_2 300

Caliber: BB only, 5-shot magazine, semi-automatic.
Barrel: 19¾, smoothbore, steel.
Weight: 3 lbs.
Length: 37¼ over-all.
Power: Daisy cylinders, 12 grams (150 shots).
Stock: Molded plastic with wood grain and checkering.
Sights: Undercut ramp front, adj. rear.
Features: Crafted by Daisy. 200-shot magazine reservoir; constant full power. Also available with Model 808 4x detachable scope as Model 3300 ($67.95).
Price: $49.95

SHERIDAN BLUE AND SILVER STREAK RIFLES

Caliber: 5mm (20 cal.), single shot.
Barrel: 18½", rifled.
Length: 37". **Weight:** 5 lbs.
Power: Hand pumped (swinging fore-end).
Features: Rustproof barrel and piston tube. Takedown. Thumb safety. Mannlicher type walnut stock. Left-hand models same price.
Price: Blue Streak .... **$59.75** Silver Streak **$62.75**
Sheridan accessories: Intermount, a base for ⅜" Tip-Off scope mounts, **$7.75**; Sheridan-Williams 5DSH receiver sight, **$7.75** Sheridan Pelletrap, **$17.50**; Model 222 Targetrap **$49.50**; Model 333 Targetrap **$26.00**; Sheridan 5mm pellets, **$3.00** for 500. Weaver 4 x scope and Intermount installed **$21.70 (extra).**

SMITH & WESSON MODEL 77A

Caliber: 22, single shot.
Barrel: 22", rifled.
Length: 40" over-all. **Weight:** 6½ lbs.
Power: Hand pumped, swinging fore-end.
Stock: Hardwood, p.g., M.C., walnut finish.
Sights: Blade front, adj. notch rear.
Features: Automatic safety, receiver grooved for scope mounting.
Price.. **$46.50**

SMITH & WESSON MODEL 80 AUTO BB RIFLE

Caliber: BB, 50-shot tube magazine.
Barrel: 22".
Length: 39" over-all. **Weight:** 3¼ lbs.
Power: Standard CO^2 cylinder.
Stock: Walnut color, checkered, wood grain finish.
Sights: Ramp front, fully adj. rear.
Features: Top tang safety, receiver grooved for scope mounting, gas cut-off, fast CO^2 cartridge loading.
Price:.. **$37.50**

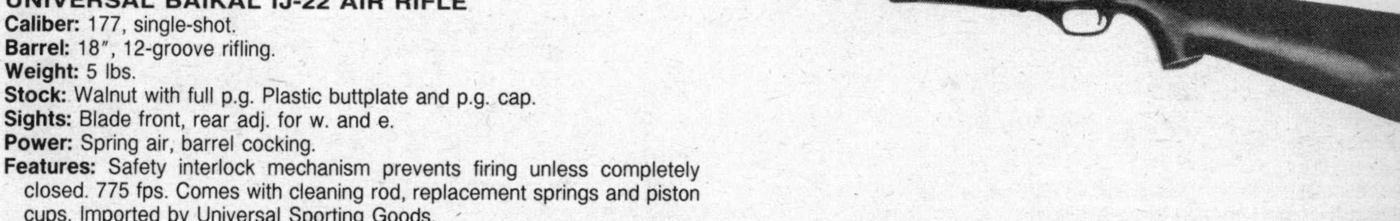

UNIVERSAL BAIKAL IJ-22 AIR RIFLE

Caliber: 177, single-shot.
Barrel: 18", 12-groove rifling.
Weight: 5 lbs.
Stock: Walnut with full p.g. Plastic buttplate and p.g. cap.
Sights: Blade front, rear adj. for w. and e.
Power: Spring air, barrel cocking.
Features: Safety interlock mechanism prevents firing unless completely closed. 775 fps. Comes with cleaning rod, replacement springs and piston cups. Imported by Universal Sporting Goods.
Price:.. **$29.95**

WALTHER LGV SPECIAL

Caliber: 177, single shot.
Barrel: 16", rifled.
Length: 41⅜". **Weight:** 11¼ lbs.
Power: Spring air (barrel cocking).
Features: Micro. click adj. aperture receiver sight; Adj. trigger. Walnut match stock, adj. buttplate. Double piston provides vibration-free shooting. Easily operated bbl. latch. Removable heavy bbl. sleeve. 5-way adj. trigger. Imported by Interarms.
Price:.. **$255.00**

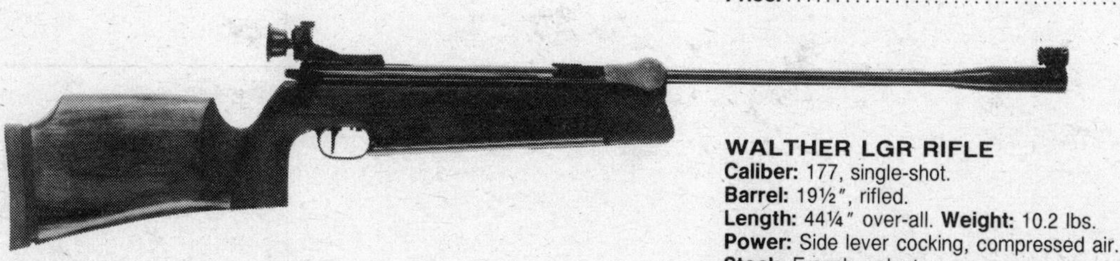

WALTHER LGR RIFLE

Caliber: 177, single-shot.
Barrel: 19½", rifled.
Length: 44¼" over-all. **Weight:** 10.2 lbs.
Power: Side lever cocking, compressed air.
Stock: French walnut.
Sights: Replaceable insert hooded front, Walther micro. adjustable rear.
Features: Recoilless operation. Trigger adj. for weight, pull and position. High comb stock with broad stippled fore-end and p.s. Imported by Interarms.
Price:.. **$315.00**

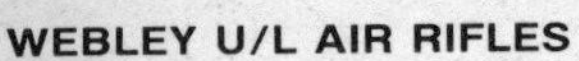

WEBLEY U/L AIR RIFLES

Model:	Mark III	Mark III Supertarget
Caliber:	177 or 22	177
Barrel:	18½"	18½" heavy
Rifled:	Yes	Yes
Sights:	Open, adj.	Parker Hale peep
Weight:	7¼ lbs.	8¼ lbs.
Power:	Spring air	Spring air
Price:	**$140.00** to **$150.00**	**$185.00** to **$195.00**

Features: High luster blue finish. Adjustable triggers. Supertarget has six hole aperture sight and stock holds interchangeable front sight elements. Imported by Beeman's, Fanta Air Rifles Universal Sporting Goods.

WEBLEY HAWK MK II AIR RIFLE

Caliber: 177 (650 fps), 22 (550 fps).
Barrel: 17⅞", rifled steel.
Length: 42¼" over-all. **Weight:** 6½ lbs.
Power: Spring air, barrel cocking.
Stock: Walnut, full p.g., Monte Carlo, rubber buttplate.
Sights: Hooded post front, fully adj. micro. rear.
Features: Consistent velocity. Adj. trigger, auto. safety. Comes with 2 interchangeable barrels. Imported by Beeman's, Fanta Air Rifles, Universal Sporting Goods.
Price: Approx. **$105.00**

WEIHRAUCH 35 SPORTER RIFLES

Model:	35/S	35L	35EB
Caliber:	177	177	177 or 22
Barrel:	19½"	19½"	19½"
Length:	45½"	43½"	45½"
Wgt. lbs.:	7.9	8	8
Rear sight:	open	open	Open
Front sight:	All with globe and 4 interchangeable inserts.		
Power:	All with spring (barrel cocking).		
Price:	**$118.50**	**$115.00** to **$129.95**	**$149.50**

Features: Trigger fully adj. and removable. Open rear sight slick adj. for w. and e. P.g. high comb stock with beavertail fore-end, walnut finish, except 35E have checkered walnut with standard cheekpiece. 35L has Tyrolean cheekpiece stock. Model 35EB available from Beeman's only. Air Rifle Hdqtrs., Beeman's, Fanta importers.

WEIHRAUCH 55 TARGET RIFLES

Model:	55SM	55MM	55T
Caliber:	177	177	177
Barrel:	18½"	18½"	18½"
Length:	43½"	43½"	43½"
Wgt. lbs.:	8	8	8
Rear sight:	aperture	aperture	aperture
Front sight:	All with globe and 4 interchangeable inserts.		
Power:	All with spring (bbl. cocking) .600 fps		
Price:	**$169.50**	**$189.50** to **$193.00**	**$188.00** to **$209.50**

Features: Trigger fully adj. and removable. Micrometer rear sight adj. for w. and e. on all. P.g. high comb stock with beavertail fore-end, walnut finish stock on 55SM. Walnut stock on 55MM, (illus.) Tyrolean stock on 55T. Model 55SM available only from Beeman's ($169.50). Air Rifle Hdqtrs., Beeman's, Fanta importers.

WEIHRAUCH 30 & 50 SERIES RIFLES

Model:	30 M-II	30S	50S	50E
Caliber:	177	177	177	177
Barrel:	16⅞"	16⅞"	18½"	18½"
Trigger:	fixed	fixed	adj.	adj.
Length:	40"	40"	43½"	43½"
Wgt., lbs.:	5½	5½	7	7¼
Price:	**$69.95**	**$72.00** to **$79.00**	**$81.00** to **$107.00**	**$118.00** to **$124.50**

Features: All are rifled and spring-operated by single stroke cocking. Post and ramp front sights (except 50S and 50E have globe fronts with 4 inserts). Open click rear sights, adj. for w. & e., except 30 Mk-11 has lock-screw windage. Walnut finished stocks. 50E has cheek-piece, checkering, ¾" sling swivels. MV of all 660-67 fps. Air Rifle Hdqtrs., Beeman's, Fanta importers.

WISCHO 70 SPORTING RIFLE

Caliber: 177 or 22, single shot.
Barrel: 16¼", rifled.
Length: 41". **Weight:** 6¼ lbs.
Power: Spring (barrel cocking).
Features: High velocity (750 fps in 177) and accuracy combined with rapid loading, can be reloaded in 5 seconds. Stock is walnut finished with checkered p.g. and buttplate. Open rear, bead front sights; receiver grooved for scope mounting. Trigger is adjustable. Air Rifle Headquarters, Beeman's, importers.
Price: .... **$104.50** to **$158.50**

WISCHO/BSF S54 RIFLE

Caliber: 177, single shot.
Length: 45½" over-all. **Weight:** 8¼ lbs.
Stock: Walnut finish on std. model. Walnut with checkering and cheepiece on Bayern.
Power: Spring air, underlever.
Sights: Open, adj. on std. and Bayern, aperture on Match model.
Features: Velocity 630 fps, rotating loading tap. Available in three grades. Match model has walnut stock with checkering and Swiss-type cheekpiece. Imported by Beeman's.
Price: Standard model **$160.00**
Price: Bayern model **$180.00**
Price: Match model **$240.00**

YEWHA TRIPLE B "DYNAMITE" SHOTGUN/RIFLE

Caliber: 25, single-shot.
Barrel: 23", smoothbore.
Length: 41" over-all. **Weight:** 6¾ lbs.
Power: Hand pumped, plunger.
Stock: Hardwood.
Sights: Post front, open rear.
Features: Use as rifle to fire lead balls or pellets (up to 950 fps. MV) or as unusually powerfull air shotgun with refillable plastic cartridges containing from 4 buckshot to 100 #9 birdshot. Patterns about 12" at 50 feet with #8 shot. Imported by Beeman's Precision Airguns.
Price: With accessory kit **$58.95**

Consult our Directory pages for the location of firms mentioned.

Contra-Jet Muzzle Brake

The steel tube on body of the C-J device has 48 intersecting slots that dissipate energy via the mutual interference of the emerging gases. Recoil energy is reduced nearly 38% (in cal. 308), accuracy is enhanced through lessened muzzle jump and flinching, yet no increase in muzzle blast occurs. Readily fitted by a competent gunsmith, the 3" long, 3½ oz. Contra-Jet is available in 25, 28, 30, 35, 37 and 45 calibers. Cost is from $32.50 to $40.00. Installation is not included but is available from the maker.

Cutts Compensator

The Cutts Compensator is one of the oldest variable choke devices available. Manufactured by Lyman Gunsight Corporation, it is available with either a steel or aluminum body. A series of vents allows gas to escape upward and downward, reducing recoil without directing muzzle blast toward nearby shooters. For the 12-ga. Comp body, six fixed-choke tubes are available: the Spreader—popular with Skeet shooters; Improved Cylinder; Modified; Full; Superfull, and Magnum Full. Full, Modified and Spreader tubes are available for 12, or 20, and an Adjustable Tube, giving Full through Improved Cylinder chokes, is offered in 12 or 20 gauges. Barrel adaptors in various internal diameters are available at $3.00 to permit exact fitting of Cutts Expansion Chambers. Cutts Compensator, complete with wrench and any single tube $27.50. All single choke tubes $7.50 each; adjustable tubes $18.00. No factory installation is available and stock is limited on gauges.

Dahl Muzzle Blast Controller

Only 1⅞" long by ¾" in diameter, this device is claimed to reduce recoil up to 30%. An outer sleeve, threaded onto the gun muzzle, is threaded on the inside to accept a machined plug which is bored through for bullet passage. Gas behind the bullet is bled off through slots in the plug, swirled through a number of tiny passages while contained by the sleeve, and then vented upward, this final action somewhat offsetting muzzle jump. Price is $27.50, installed.

Emsco Choke

E. M. Schacht of Waseca, Minn., offers the Emsco, a small diameter choke which features a precision curve rather than a taper behind the 1½" choking area. 9 settings are available in this 5 oz. attachment. Its removable recoil sleeve can be furnished in dural if desired. Choice of three sight heights. For 12, 16 or 20 gauge. Price installed, $22.95. Not installed, $17.50.

Herter's Rifle Recoil Eliminator

The Recoil Eliminator is a metal tube—1 15/16" long and ⅞" diam. in the standard model, same length and 1⅛" diam. in target type—which is screwed to the muzzle. Angled ports direct escaping gas upward and rearward, reducing recoil and muzzle jump. The target model has a shield to prevent muzzle blast from annoying nearby shooters. Weights are 2 oz. and 3 oz. respectively. Made for calibers 25 to 32. Price for standard, $3.00, $6.50 installed. Target, $4.50 and $8.00.

Vari-Choke

Herter's, Inc., supplies the Vari-Choke, which features a ball-bearing micro-click adjustment of the pattern sleeve, rather than the spring system used by others. This model has 8 choke settings, from Full to Improved Cylinder. With Recoil Eliminator, price is $18.97 installed; without Eliminator, $14.47.

Jet-Away Choke

Arms Ingenuity Corp., makers of the Jet-Away, say that this device controls patterns through partial venting of the powder gases which normally enlarge patterns. The Jet-Away has a series of three slots in the top of the tube and a sliding control sleeve. When the sleeve is in its rearward position, all slots are uncovered, the maximum of gas is vented and patterns are densest. To obtain more open patterns, the sleeve is moved to cover one or more slots. In 12, 16 or 20 gauge only, the Jet-Away is made of aluminum, weighs 3 ozs. $27.95 installed.

Lyman CHOKE

The Lyman CHOKE is similar to the Cutts Comp in that it comes with fixed-choke tubes or an adjustable tube, with or without recoil chamber. The adjustable tube version sells for $22.75 with recoil chamber, $19.00 without,

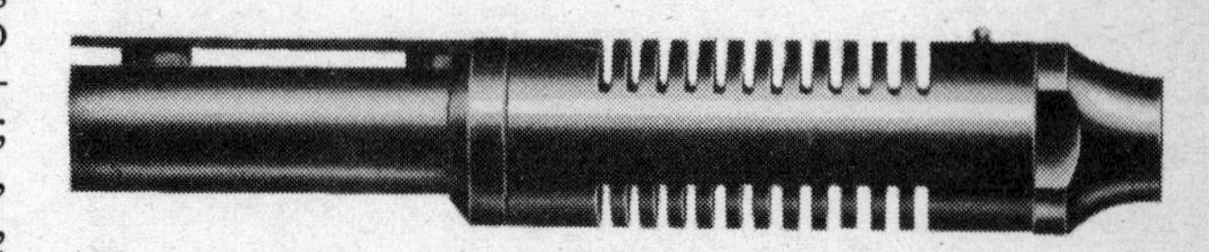

in 12 or 20 gauge. Lyman also offers a Single-Choke Adaptor at $3.00. This device may be used with or without a recoil-reduction chamber; cost of the latter is $3.75 extra. Available in 12 or 20 gauge only, no factory installation offered.

Mag-Na-Port

EDM is the process to "install" this muzzle brake on any firearm except those having shrouded barrels. EDM is a metal-erosion technique using carbon electrodes that control the area to be processed. The Mag-Na-Port brake utilizes small trapezoidal openings that go into and through the barrel that direct powder gases upward and outward to reduce recoil.

The resultant opening made by the EDM process is smoothly and cleanly made, with no burring in or out. No effect is had on bluing or nickeling outside the Mag-Na-Port area so no refinishing is needed. Cost for the Mag-Na-Port treatment is $29.50, plus transportation both ways.

Single barrel shotguns can be ported with four ports on both sides of the barrel for $39.50. Over-under shotguns are ported on both barrels, cost is $75.00.

Pendleton Dekicker

This Dekicker is unusual in that it is not a separate tube added onto a rifle muzzle but is machined into the barrel itself. Obviously, it cannot be installed by the customer. It must be sent to J. F. Mutter's Pendleton Gunshop, where a section of the bore a short distance behind the muzzle is relieved into an expansion chamber. Exit holes drilled at precise locations vent gas to lower apparent kick. Because metal is removed instead of being added, there is a small decrease in gun weight. Installation, including barrel polishing, is $50.00 for all calibers.

Poly-Choke

Poly-Choke Co., Inc., now is offering the Delux Signature Poly-Choke. It provides 9 choke settings to cover the complete pattern range as well as handle rifled slugs. It comes in two versions, the standard at $27.95, and the ventilated model at $29.95 installed. Fits 12, 16, 20 or 28 gauge. The Poly-Choke has been on the market for more than 40 years and is still gaining popularity.

Micrometer Receiver Sight

Receiver Sights

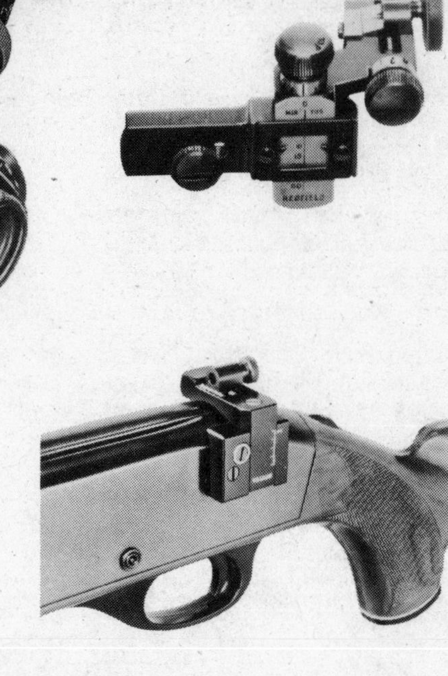

LYMAN No. 57
¼-min. clicks. Target or Stayset knobs. Quick release slide, adjustable zero scales. Made for almost all modern rifles. Price **$21.00**

LYMAN No. 66
Fits close to the rear of flat-sided receivers, furnished with target or Stayset knobs. Quick release slide, ¼-min. adj. For most lever or slide action or flat-sided automatic rifles. Price **$21.00**

REDFIELD No. 75
For Junior Target rifles. ¼-min. clicks for w. and e. Quick detachable extension, adj. to two positions. Available in two heights, scope or standard. For 75HW—Win. 75: 75HG and SG—Sav. 19; 75HV and SV—Stev. 416, Sears Ranger; 75HM and SM—Mossberg, master actions; 75HB and SB—Ballard; 75HR and SR—Win. SS, High Wall action only; Walnut Hill and 417; 75RT—Rem. 513T; 75RS—Rem. 513S; 75RX—Rem. 521. Price . **$21.00**

REDFIELD INTERNATIONAL MATCH
Spring loaded windage and elevation adjustments eliminate lost motion or backlash. Large adjusting screws. ¼-min. click values. Base and ⅞" disc. Fits same base as Olympic. Price **$42.60**
With base and "Sure-X" disc (see Sight Attachments). Price .. **$58.60**

REDFIELD INTERNATIONAL MARK 8
⅛-min. click adj. for windage and elevation distinguishes the Mark 8 which has all of the refinements of Redfield's International Match. Equipped with standard base and ⅞" disc. Price **$49.80**
With base and Sure-X disc (see Sight Attachments). Price **$65.80**

REDFIELD OLYMPIC
Elevation, windage, and extension adjustments. New elevation compensation. ¼-min. click. Base and ⅞" disc. Made for practically all target rifles. Price **$32.60**
Extra bases. Price **$6.00**
With base and Sure-X disc (see Sight Attachments). Price **$48.60**

WILLIAMS "FOOLPROOF"
Internal click adjustments. Positive locks. For virtually all rifles, plus Win., Rem. and Ithaca shotguns. Price **$16.25**
Add .50 for Twilight aperture. Extra shotgun aperture **$2.30**

B-SQUARE SMLE (LEE-ENFIELD)
For No. 4 and Jungle carbine. No drilling or tapping required. 3/32" disc furnished. Price **$4.95**

BUEHLER
"Little Blue Peep" auxiliary sight used with Buehler scope mounts. Price **$3.35**
Mark IV front sight for above .... **.95**

FREELAND TUBE SIGHT
Uses Unertl 1" micrometer mounts. Complete with bases for 22-cal. target rifles, inc. 52 Win., 37, 40X Rem. and BSA Martini. Price **$74.50**

LYMAN No. 53
Shotgun receiver sight, mounts compactly near rear of receiver. For most Win., Rem., Sav., Marlin, Mossberg, J. C. Higgins and Ithaca shotguns. Limited quantities and selection. Price **$7.00**

WILLIAMS 5-D SIGHT
Low cost sight for shotguns, 22's and the more popular big game rifles. Adjustment for w. and e. Fits most guns without drilling or tapping. Also for Br. SMLE. Price **$9.00**

WILLIAMS GUIDE
Receiver sight for .30 M1 Car., M1903A3 Springfield, Savage 24's, Savage-Anschutz rifles and Wby. XXII. Utilizes military dovetail; no drilling. Double-dovetail W. adj., sliding dovetail adj. for E. Price **$8.65**

Sporting Leaf and Tang Sights

BURRIS FOLDING LEAF
Two-way leaf rear sight with dovetail. Hefty spring holds sight in upright position. 2 heights—.450" to .575" (Model FLH), .350" to .475" (Model FLL. Price **$4.95**

BURRIS LEAF BASE
Screw-attaches with two screws into barrel. From bottom of dovetail to top of barrel measures .080". Use where there is no dovetail in barrel. Model FLBA has .562" hole span, FLBB has .625" span. Price **$2.98**

BURRIS SPORTING REAR SIGHT
Made of spring steel, supplied with multi-step elevator for coarse adjustments and notch plate with lock screw for finer adjustments. Price .. **$4.95**

HOPKINS & ALLEN NUMRICH MUSKET SIGHT
Three-way rear leaf sight designed for 58 cal. muzzle loading military rifles. Fixed V-notch for 50-yard range, flip-up aperture for 100 yards and V-notch for 200 yards. Particularly suited to Springfield and Zouave rifles. Price **$4.95**

LYMAN No. 16
Middle sight for barrel dovetail slot mounting. Folds flat when scope or peep sight is used. Sight notch plate adjustable for e. White triangle for quick aiming. 3 heights; A—.400" to .500", B—.345" to .445", C—.500" to .600". Price **$4.00**

MARBLE FALSE BASE
New screw-on base for most rifles replaces factory base. ⅜" dovetail slot permits installation of any Marble rear sight. Can be had in sweat-on models also. Price **$2.50**

MARBLE FOLDING LEAF
Flat-top or semi-buckhorn style. Folds down when scope or peep sights are used. Reversible plate gives choice of "U" or "V" notch. Adjustable for elevation. Price .... **$5.40—$6.00**
Also available with both w. and e. adjustment **$6.00**

MARBLE SPORTING REAR
With white enamel diamond, gives choice of two "U" and two "V" notches of different sizes. Adjustment in height by means of double step elevator and sliding notch piece. For all rifles; screw or dovetail installation. Price **$5.20—$6.60**

MARBLE SPORTING REAR
Single step elevator. "U" notch with white triangle aiming aid. Lower priced version of double step model. Price **$2.80**

NUMRICH KENTUCKY STYLE SIGHT
Standard dovetail, traditional notched rear sight. ¼" high. For Kentucky and Hawken type rifles. Price **$2.75**

NUMRICH LONG RANGE REAR TARGET SIGHT
Adjustable for w. and e. with 3-size aperture target sight disc. Particularly suited for H&A Underhammer rifles. Price **$5.95**

WILLIAMS DOVETAIL OPEN SIGHT
Open rear sight with s. and e. adjustment. Furnished with "U" notch or choice of blades. Slips into dovetail and locks with gib lock. Heights from .281" to .531". Price with blade **$5.00**

WILLIAMS GUIDE
Open rear sight with w. and e. adjustment. Bases to fit most military and commercial barrels. Choice of square "U" or "V" notch blade, 3/16", ¼", 5/16", or ⅜" high **$5.50**
Extra blades, each **$1.75**

Globe Target Front Sights

FREELAND SUPERIOR
Furnished with six 1" plastic apertures. Available in 4½"-6½" lengths. Made for any target rifle. Price with base **$19.00**
Price with 6 metal insert apertures **$22.00**

FREELAND JR
Same as above except standard dovetail mounting, various heights.
Price with base and 6 plastic apertures **$17.00**
Price with 6 metal insert apertures **$20.00**

FREELAND TWIN SET
Two Freeland Superior or Junior Globe Front Sights, long or short, allow switching from 50 yd. to 100 yd. ranges and back again without changing rear sight adjustment. Sight adjustment compensation is built into the set; just interchange and you're "on" at either range. Set includes base and 6 plastic apertures. Twin set (long or short) **$33.00**
Price with 6 metal apertures **$37.00**
Price, Junior Twin Set (long or short) plastic apertures **$30.00**
Price, Junior Twin Set (long or short) metal apertures **$35.00**

FREELAND MILITARY
Short model for use with high-powered rifles where sight must not extend beyond muzzle. Screw-on base; six plastic apertures. Price **$19.00**
Price with 6 metal apertures **$22.00**

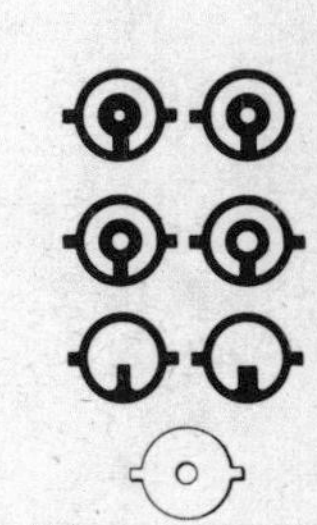

LYMAN No. 17A
7 interchangeable inserts which include 4 apertures, one transparent amber and two posts .50" and .100" in width. Price **$7.50**

REDFIELD Nos. 63 and 64
For rifles specially stocked for scopes where metallic sights must be same height as scopes. Instantly detachable to permit use of scope. Two styles and heights of bases. Interchangeable inserts. No. 64 is ¼" higher. With base, Price **$11.00**

REDFIELD No. 65
1" long, ⅝" diameter. Standard dovetail base with 7 aperture or post inserts which are not reversible. For any rifle having standard barrel slot. 13/32" height from bottom of base to center of aperture. No. 65NB same as above with narrow base for Win. 64 N.R.A., 70, and Savage 40, 45, and 99 with ramp front sight base. Price **$8.40**

REDFIELD No. 66
Replaces entire removable front sight stud, locked in place by screw in front of barrel band. ¾" from bottom of base to center of aperture. For Spgfld. 1903. Price **$8.40**

REDFIELD No. 68
For Win. 52, heavy barrel, Sav. 19 and 33, and other rifles requiring high front sight. 17/32" from bottom of base to center of aperture. Standard dovetail size only. Price **$8.40**

REDFIELD OLYMPIC
Detachable. 10 inserts—5 steel, sizes .090", .110", .120", .140", .150"; one post insert, size .100"; four celluloid, sizes .090", .110", .120", .140". Celluloid inserts in clear, green, or amber, with or without cross hairs. For practically all rifles and with any type rear sight. Fits all standard Redfield, Lyman, or Fecker scope blocks. With base, Price **$17.00**

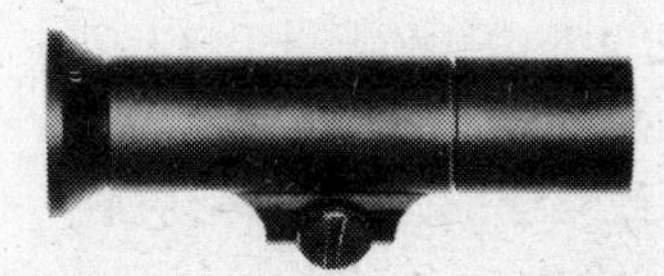

REDFIELD INTERNATIONAL SMALLBORE FRONT (Illustrated)
Similar to Olympic. Drop-in insertion of eared inserts. Outer sleeve prevents light leakage. Comes complete with 6 clear inserts and 6 skeleton inserts **$24.60**

REDFIELD INTERNATIONAL MILITARY BIG BORE
Same as International Match except tube only 2¼" long. For 30 cal. use Price **$24.60**

Ramp Sights

Williams Streamlined Ramp

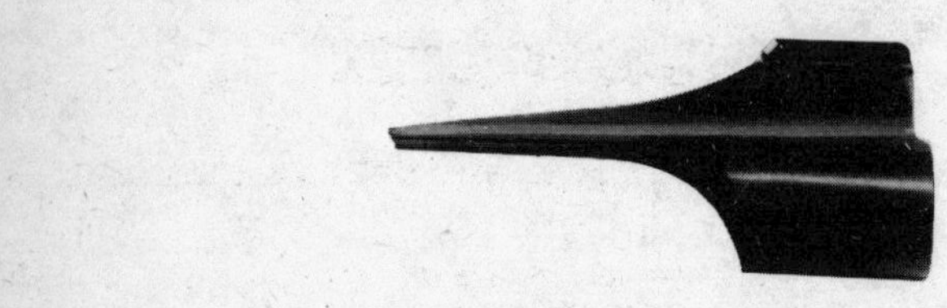

Burris Ramps.

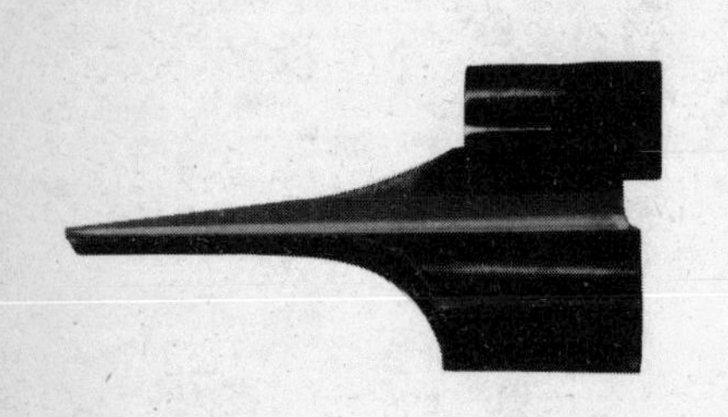

Lyman Screw-On ramps.

Front Sights

Lyman hunting front sights.

Burris Patridge.

Burris Gold Bead.

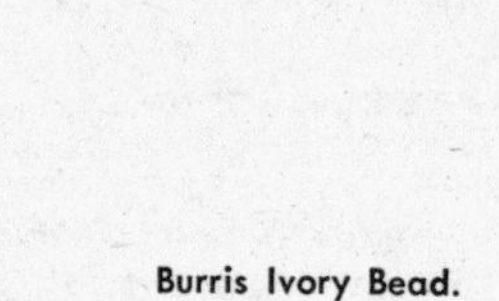

Burris Ivory Bead.

BURRIS
Top ramps, screw- and sweat-on ramps with ⅜" dovetail. Accepts .250" width (N) front sight. 8 heights available from .200" to .500". Price **$3.95**
Hoods for above ramps .... **.95**

BURRIS BAND RAMPS
Tapered to slip over the barrel and be driven on until snug. Set screw locks ramp in place. 7 heights available, 7 barrel diameters. Price **$9.95**
Hoods for above ramps .... **.95**

LYMAN SCREW-ON RAMP AND SIGHT
Used with 8-40 screws but may also be brazed on. Heights from .10" to .350". Price with sight ..... **$9.50 Price:** Ramp without sight **$5.50**

MARBLE CONTOUR RAMP
For late model Rem. 725, 740, 760, 742. 9⁄16" between mounting screws. Price **$6.00**

MARBLE RAMPS
Available in either screw-on or sweat-on style. 5 heights; 3⁄16", 5⁄16", ⅜", 7⁄16", 9⁄16". Standard ⅜" dovetail slot. Price **$5.00**
Hoods for above ramps **$1.40**

WILLIAMS SHORTY RAMP
Companion to "Streamlined" ramp, about ½" shorter. Screw-on or sweat-on. It is furnished in ⅛", 3⁄16", 9⁄32", and ⅜" heights without hood only. Price **$4.40**

WILLIAMS STREAMLINED RAMP
Hooded style in screw-on or sweat-on models. Furnished in 9⁄16", 7⁄16", ⅜", 5⁄16", 3⁄16" heights. Price with hood **$6.95**
Price without hood **$5.75**

WILLIAMS SHOTGUN RAMP
Designed to elevate the front bead for slug shooting or for guns that shoot high. Diameters to fit most 12, 16, 20 ga. guns. Fastens by screw-clamp, no drilling required. Price, with Williams gold bead **$4.40**
Price, without bead **$3.15**

BURRIS FRONT SIGHTS
Three styles: Patridge, gold or ivory bead. Widths are .250", .340", .500" and Mauser .310"............................... from **$2.95** to **$3.75**

LYMAN BLADE & DOVETAIL SIGHTS
Made with gold, silver or red beads 1⁄16" to 3⁄32" wide and in varying heights for most military and commercial rifles. Price **$4.00**

MARBLE STANDARD
Ivory, red, or gold bead. For all American made rifles. $w1/16" wide bead with semi-flat face which does not reflect light. Specify type of rifle when ordering **$2.70**

MARBLE-SHEARD "GOLD"
Show up well even in darkest timber. Shows same color on different colored objects; sturdily built. Medium bead. Various models for different makes of rifles so specify type of rifle when ordering. Also made for 30 or 9 mm Lugers, Colt's Single Action Army, Bisley Model, with plain sight or any other Colt's or S & W revolver with stationary front sight. Price **$3.80**

MARBLE CONTOURED
Same contour and shape as Marble-Sheard but uses standard 1⁄16" or 3⁄32" bead, ivory, red or gold. Specify rifle type **$2.90**

NUMRICH MUSKET FRONT SIGHT
Traditional 58 cal. front sight. Can be used for 58 caliber Springfield or Zouave replacement barrels., or '41 Mississippi barrel. Price **$1.95**

NUMRICH SILVER BLADE FRONT SIGHT
Same sight as used on H&A "Minuteman" rifle and Rolling Block "Buffalo Rifle." Suited for most ML and black powder cartridge guns. Price .. **$3.45**

WILLIAMS GUIDE BEAD SIGHT
Fits all shotguns. ⅛" ivory, red or gold bead. Screws into existing sight hole. Various thread sizes and shank lengths **$2.00**
Cultured Pearl Guide Bead **$5.00**

Handgun Sights

Bo-Mar Deluxe sight.

Micro handgun sight.

F.D.L Wondersight.

BO-MAR DE LUXE
Gives ⅜" w. and e. adjustment at 50 yards on Colt Gov't 45, sight radius under 7". For Colt, Hi-Standard, Ruger and S&W autos. Uses existing dovetail slot. Has shield-type rear blade. Write for current price.

BO-MAR HIGH STANDARD RIB
Full length, 8¾" sight radius, for all bull barrels and military. Slide alteration required. Write for current price.

BO-MAR LOW PROFILE RIB
Streamlined rib with front and rear sights; 7⅛" sight radius. Brings sight line closer to the bore than standard or extended sight and ramp. Weighs 4 oz. Made for Colt Gov't 45, Super 38, and Gold Cup 45 and 38. Write for current price.
With extended sight and ramp, 8⅛" radius, 5¾ oz. Write for current price.
Rib & tuner—inserted in Low Profile Rib—accuracy tuner. Adjustable for barrel positioning. Write for current price.

BO-MAR FRONT SIGHTS
⅛" tapered post, made for Colt, Hi-Standard, Ruger and S&W autos. Write for current price.

BO-MAR COMBAT RIB
For S&W Model 19 revolver with 4" barrel. Sight radius 5¾"; weight 5½ oz. Write for current price.

BO-MAR MINI RIB
Shortened version of the full-length rib with barrel positioner. Weight 2½ oz. For Colt Gov't 45 and Super 38. Write for current price.
Undercut ramp front sight. Write for current price.

BO-MAR FAST DRAW RIB
Streamlined full length rib with integral Bo-Mar micrometer sight and serrated fast draw sight. For Borwning 9mm, S&W 39, Colt Commander 45, Super Auto and 9mm. Write for current price.

F.D.L. WONDERSIGHT
Micrometer rear sight for Colt and S&W revolvers. 1-min. clicks for windage. Sideplate screw controls elevation **$9.95**

MICRO
Click adjustable w. and e. rear with plain or undercut front sight in ¹⁄₁₀", ⅛", or ⁵⁄₃₂" widths. Standard model available for 45, Super 38 or Commander autos. Low model for above pistols plus Colt Service Ace. Also for Ruger with 4¾" or 6" barrel. Price for sets **$20.00**
Price with ramp front sight **$23.50**
Adjustable rear sight only **$17.00**
Front ramp only, with blade **$9.00**

MMC COMBAT DESIGN
Available specifically for Colt M1911 and descendants, High Standard autos, Ruger standard autos. Adaptable to other pistols. Some gunsmithing required.
Price, less leaf **$13.00**
Plain leaf **$3.75**
White outline leaf **$5.60**

MMC NO. 5
Fully adjustable and replaces the factory sight for S&W M39 and M59. Supplied assembled, no gunsmithing required. ⅛" wide notch, white outline or plain.
Complete, plain **$33.70**
White outline **$35.65**
Extra for nickel **$4.45**

SLUG SITE
A combination V-notch rear and bead front sight made of adhesive-backed formed metal approx. 7" over-all. May be mounted, removed and re-mounted as necessary, using new adhesive from the pack supplied **$5.00**

Sight Attachments

FREELAND LENS ADAPTER
Fits 1⅛" O.D. prescription ground lens to all standard tube and receiver sights for shooting without glasses. Price without lens **$29.50**
Price: clear lens ground to prescription **$15.50**
Price: yellow or green prescription lens **$17.50**

MERIT ADAPTER FOR GLOBE FRONT SIGHTS
An Iris Shutter Disc with a special adapter for mounting in Lyman or Redfield globe front sights. Price **$15.00**

MERIT IRIS SHUTTER DISC
Eleven clicks gives 12 different apertures. No. 3 and Master, primarily target types, .022" to .125"; No. 4, ½" dia. hunting type, .025" to .155". Available for all popular sights. The Master Disc, with flexible rubber light shield, is particularly adapted to extension, scope height, and tang sights. All Merit Deluxe models have internal click springs; are hand fitted to minimum tolerance. Price .... **$14.00—$17.00**
Master .... **$17.00** Master Deluxe **$21.00**

Merit Master Target Disc

Merit Hunting Disc #4

Merit Deluxe Lens Disc

MERIT LENS DISC
Similar to Merit Iris Shutter (Model 3 or Master) but incorporates provision for mounting prescription lens integrally. Lens may be obtained locally, or prescription sent to Merit. Sight disc is ⁷⁄₁₆" wide (Mod. 3), or ¾" wide (Master). Lens, ground to prescription,**$9.60** Standard tints, **$11.10.** Model 3 Deluxe **$21.00**
Master Deluxe **$25.00**

REDFIELD SURE-X SIGHTING DISC
Eight hole selective aperture. Fits any Redfield target sight. Each click changes aperture .004". Price **$10.00**

REDFIELD SIGHTING DISCS
Fit all Redfield receiver sights. .046" to .093" aperture. ⅜", ½" and ⅞" O.D. Price, each **$2.20**

WILLIAMS APERTURES
Standard thread, fits most sights. Regular series ⅜" to ⅝" O.D., .050" to .125" hole. "Twilight" series has white reflector ring. .093" to .125" inner hole. Price, regular series ... **$1.20.** Twilight series **$1.70**
New wide open ⁵⁄₁₆" aperture for shotguns fits 5-D and Foolproof sights. Price **$2.30**

Shotgun Sights

FOR DOUBLE BARREL SHOTGUNS (PRESS FIT)
Marble 214—Ivory front bead, ¹¹⁄₆₄" ... **$1.80; 215**—same with .080" rear bead and reamers ... **$4.00. Marble 220**—Bi-color (gold and ivory) front bead, ¹¹⁄₆₄" and .080 rear bead, with reamers ... **$4.90; Marble 221**—front bead only ... **$3.00. Marble 223**—Ivory rear .080 ... **$1.60. marble 224**—Front sight reamer for 214-221 beads ... **$1.20; Marble 226**—Rear sight reamer for 223 .... **$1.60**

FOR SINGLE OR DB SHOTGUNS (SCREW-ON FIT)
Marble 217—Ivory front bead ¹¹⁄₆₄" ... **$2.00; Marble 216$3.60 Marble 218**—Bi-color front, ¹¹⁄₆₄" ... **$2.90; Marble 219 ... $4.00 Marble 223T**—Ivory rear .080 ... **$2.80**; with tap and wrench **$2.50**
Marble Bradley type sights 223BT—⅛", ⁵⁄₆₄" and ¹¹⁄₆₄" long. Gold, Ivory or Red bead **$2.20**

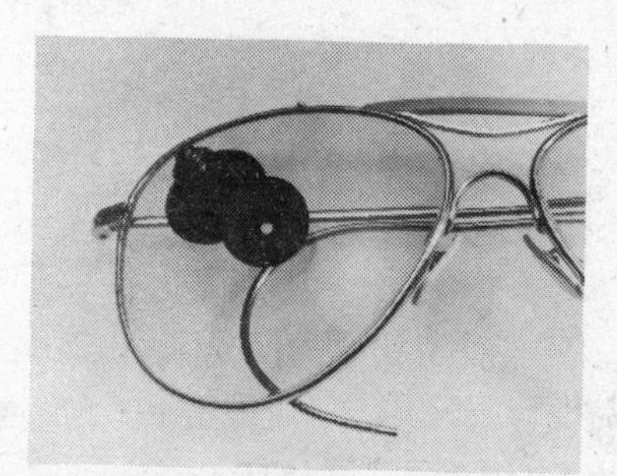

MERIT OPTICAL ATTACHMENT
For revolver and pistol shooters. Instantly attached by rubber suction cup to regular or shooting glasses. Any aperture .020" to .156". Price, **$14.00.** Deluxe (swings aside) **$16.00**

SCOPES & MOUNTS

HUNTING, TARGET♦ AND VARMINT♦ SCOPES

Maker and Model	Magn.	Field at 100 Yds. (feet)	Relative Bright-ness	Eye Relief (in.)	Length (in.)	Tube Diam. (in.)	W&E Adjust-ments	Weight (ozs.)	Other Data	Price
American Import Co.										
Dickson R218	2½	32	158	3	11.7	1	Int.	9.6		$43.25
Dickson R220	4	28.5	64	3	11.7	1	Int.	9.6	Standard reticle 4 post fully coated lenses. Anodized finish.	43.25
Dickson R226	6	18.5	43.5	3	12	1	Int.	10		48.75
Dickson R228	4	41	64	3	12	1	Int.	9.6	Wide angle.	65.50
Dickson R230	4	41	100	3	12	1	Int.	10.5	Wide angle.	70.25
Dickson R240	3-9	31.6-12.3	112-13	3	13.6	1	Int.	11.5		62.50
Dickson R242	3-9	31.6-12.3	177 19	3	13.3	1	Int.	12.2		67.25
Bausch & Lomb									Trophy models have internal ½ MOA adj. Straight powers have CH. Balfor B has CH; tapered CH, dualine, Balvar 8B has CH; post, tapered CH, RF, dualine.	
Trophy Baltur B	2½	42	164	3	12⅛	1	Int.	11		68.50
Trophy Balfor B	4	30	64	3	11⅞	1	Int.	11		79.50
Trophy Balvar 8B	2½-8	40-12½	207-20	3½	11⅞	1	Int.	12½		118.50
Browning										
22 Scope	4	24½	25	3	9½	.75	Int.	6	W/mt. $43.45 - $46.45.	31.95
Wide Angle	4	37	49	3¼	11½	1	Int.	12		84.95
Wide Angle	2-7	50-20	81-23	3¼	11¾	1	Int.	14½	Dot reticle $10 extra.	114.95
Wide Angle	3-9	39-15	72-17	3¼	16½	1	Int.	15		124.95
Burris										
4x Fullfield	3.8	37	49	3¼	11¼	1	Int.	11	3" dot $10.00 extra.	87.95
2x-7x Fullfield	2.5-6.8	50-19	81-22	3¼	11⅞	1	Int.	14	1"-3" dot $10.00 extra.	126.95
3x-9x Fullfield	3.3-8.6	40-15	72-17.6	3¼	12¾	1	Int.	15	1"-3" dot $10.00 extra.	129.95
									Dot, plex, crosshair and post crosshair reticles available.	
Bushnell									Scopchief VI models have Rangemaster feature. Automatic bullet drop compensation that eliminates hold-over.	
Scopechief VI	4	30	96	3½	11⅝	1	Int.	9¾		
Scopechief VI	3-9	39-13	265-29	3-3¾	11½	1	Int.	14		
Scopechief IV	2¾	43	87	4	10	1	Int.	9	Scopechief IV models have Command Post reticle with Magnetic Control Ring.	64.50
Scopechief IV	4	32	96	3¾	11¾	1	Int.	10¾		75.50
Scopechief IV	1½-4½	78-26	284-33	4¼-3¼	9¼	1	Int.	7¾		96.50
Scopechief IV	2½-8	44-15	226-24	4-3¼	11	1	Int.	11		99.50
Scopechief IV	3-9	39-13	241-27	3¾-3¼	11½	1	Int.	12		114.50
Scopechief II 22	3-8	30-12	55-6	2½-3	10¼	⅞	Int.	7½	Mount rail. Similar 4x at $29.95.	39.95
Scopechief V	4	30	96	3½	12¼	1	Int.	10¾	Battery powered Lite-Site reticles in Scopechief V models.	75.50
Scopechief V	1½-4	76-27½	213-27	4¼-3¼	10¾	1	Int.	12		96.50
Scopechief V	3-9	34-12½	169-27	3¾-3	12⅞	1	Int.	14		114.50
Custom 22	3-7	29-13	28-5	2¼-2½	10	⅞	Int.	6½	Similar 4x at $19.95.	24.95
Banner	2½	45	144	3½	11	1	Int.	8	Rangemasterd feature available in 4x and 3x-9x Banner models.	43.95
Banner RM	4	29	144	3½	12	1	Int.	10		54.95
Banner	4	37¼	150	3	12¼	1	Int.	12	Wide angle.	69.95
Banner	6	19½	42	3	13½	1	Int.	10½		64.95
Banner	10	12	24	3	14½	1	Int.	14½	Obj. focuses for range.	79.95
Banner	1½-4	63-28	294-38	3½	10½	1	Int.	10¼		67.95
Banner	1¾-4½	71-27	216-33	3	10¼	1	Int.	11½	Wide angle.	
Banner	3-9	39-13	172-19	3½	11½	1	Int.	11	With 40mm obj. $84.95.	74.95
Banner	3-9	43-14	242-27	3	12	1	Int.	14	Wide angle.	94.95
Banner	4-12	29-10	150-16	3¼	13½	1	Int.	15½	Obj. focuses for range.	94.95
Phantom	1⅓	24	441	6-17	7⅝	⅞	Int.	5	Phantoms intended for handgun use.	39.50
Phantom	2½	10	100	7-16	9¼	⅞	Int.	5½		49.50
Davis Optical										
Spot Shot 1½"	10, 12, 15, 20, 25, 30	10-4	—	2	25	.75	Ext.	—	Focus by moving non-rotating obj. lens unit. Ext. mounts included. Recoil spring $3.50 extra.	89.50
Spot Shot 1¼"	10, 12 15, 20,	10-6	—	2	25	.75	Ext.	—		69.50
Herter's										
Mark IV	4	30	64	3½	11½	1	Int.	9½	A variety of Panoramic reticles including dots and rangefinders available in different scopes at small price increase. Hudson Bay rimfire 4x, $19.95.	32.95
Mark XI	1½-4½	52-27	177-25	3½	9¼	1	Int.	—		33.95
Mark IA	3-9	14-41	157-18	3½	12½	1	Int.	14½		69.87
Mark XXI	4-12	11½-34	100-14	3½	13¼	1	Int.	12½		61.97
Hutson										
◆ Handgunner	1	9	—	25	5¼	—	Ext.	5	CH. ⅞" obj. lens. Adj. in mount, $16.95.	45.00
	1.7	4.5	—	25	5½	—	Ext.	5		49.50
Hy-Score										
Gold Dot 471UV	2½	42	96	3¾	11	1	Int.	7¾		39.95
Gold Dot 475UV	4	27	96	3½	12	1	Int.	9½	Alloy tubes, rubber eyebrow guards, nitrogen filled. CH, dual CH or post and CH.	44.95
Gold Dot 473UV	6	19½	50	3	13¼	1	Int.	10		49.95
Gold Dot 477UV	3-9	36-12	166-19	3	11½	1	Int.	11		64.95
Gold Dot 476UV	3-9	33-12	265-29	3¼	12½	1	Int.	13¼		74.95
Red Dot 489UV	4	30	96	3¾	11½	1	Int.	10½		74.95
Red Dot 487UV	3-9	39-13	241-27	3½	12¼	1	Int.	12¼		109.95

SCOPES & MOUNTS

Maker and Model	Magn.	Field at 100 Yds. (feet)	Relative Brightness	Eye Relief (in.)	Length (in.)	Tube Diam. (in.)	W&E Adjustments	Weight (ozs.)	Other Data	Price
Jana										
Jana 4x	4	29	—	3½	12	1	Int.	9	Deluxe model offers choice of dot or Dual-X reticle. Zoom offers choice of crosshair or Dual-X. Others have constantly centered reticles.	27.50
Economy 4x	4	29	—	3½	12	1	Int.	9		24.95
Deluxe	4	32	—	3½	12	1	Int.	9		32.50
Super	4	32	—	3½	12	1	Int.	—		34.50
JA-2	2½	32	—	—	12	1	Int.	9⅛		24.95
JA-6	6	17½	—	3⅛	12	1	Int.	9		28.95
Zoom	3-9	35-12	—	—	12½	1	Int.	13½		47.95
JA-420	4	15½	—	—	11	¾	Int.	5¼		10.95
JA-37	3-7	23-10	—	2½-3	11⅓	⅞	Int.	9½		19.95
Jason										
860	4	27¼	64	3½	12	1	Int.	9	Constantly centered reticles, ballbearing click stops, nitrogen filled tubes, coated lenses.	39.95
861	3-9	31½-12	112-12	3	13¼	1	Int.	13¾		59.95
865	3-9	31½-12	177-19	3	13½	1	Int.	15¼		64.95
Leupoid										
M8	2	25	100	8.18	8.45	1	Int.	7.25		58.50
M8	3	43	45	3.85	10.13	1	Int.	8.25	Constantly centered reticles; in addition to the crosshair reticle the post, tapered (CPC), post and duplex, and duplex reticles are optional at no extra cost. Dot reticle $12.00 extra. 2x suitable for handgun and Win. 94.	75.50
M8	4	30	50	3.85	11.50	1	Int.	9.00		81.50
M8	6	18	—	3.85	11.7	1	Int.	10.3		94.50
M8 AO	7½	14	32	3.60	12.60	1	Int.	12.75		112.50
M8 AO	10	10	16	3½	13	1	Int.	13¾		114.50
M8 AO	12	9	11	3½	14½	1	Int.	14		118.50
M8 AO	24	4½	—	3½	15¼	1	Int.	15½	Mounts solidly on action. ¼ MOA clicks. Crosshair or dot.	169.50
Vari-X II	1-4	70-28	—	4¼-3½	9½	1	Int.	9½		104.50
Vari-X II	2-7	42-18	144-17	3.7-4.12	11.00	1	Int.	10.75		112.50
Vari-X II	3-9	30.5-13	208-23	3.5-4.12	12.60	1	Int.	13.75	With adj. obj.—$136.50.	124.50
Vari-X III	1½-5	64-23	—	4½-3½	9¾	1	Int.	9¾		131.50
Vari-X III	2½-8	36-12½	—	4¼-3½	11¾	1	Int.	11½		142.50
Vari-X III	3½-10	29½-10½	—	4-3½	12¾	1	Int.	12¾		153.50
Lyman										
All-Americann	2½	43	—	3¼	10½	1	Int.	8¾	2, 3, or 4 minute dot reticle $12.50 extra. Choice or standard CH, tapered post, or tapered post and CH reticles. All-weather reticle caps. All Lyman scopes have new Perma-Center reticle which remains in optical center regardless of changes in W. & E.	74.95
All-American	3	35	—	3¼	11	1	Int.	9		74.95
All-American	4	30	—	3¼	12	1	Int.	10		74.95
All-American	6	20	—	3¼	13⅞	1	Int.	12¼		89.95
All-American 6x-P	6	20	—	3¼	14	1	Int.	14		109.95
◆ All-American	8	14	—	3¼	14⅜	1	Int.	13		114.95
◆ All-American	10	12	—	3¼	15½	1	Int.	13½	Adj. for parallax.	114.95
All-American	1¾-5	47-18	—	3	12¼	1	Int.	12¼		109.95
◆ L.W.B.R.	20	5.5	—	2¼	17⅛	1	Int.	15¼	⅛ or ¼ MOA clicks.	174.95
◆ All-American	3-9	39-13	—	3¾-3¼	10½	1	Int.	14		114.95
◆ Super Targetspot	10, 12, 15, 20, 25, 30	12, 9.3, 8.9, 5.6, 4.3, 4	86	2-1⅞	24-24⅜	.75	Ext.	24¼-25	Non-rotating objective lens focusing. ¼ MOA click adjustments. Sunshade, $4.95 extra. Wood case, $29.95 extra. 5 different dot reticles, $12.50 extra.	194.95
Marble										
A-2.5	2¾	43	164	3½	11¾	1	Int.	10¾	Duralumin tubes, nitrogen filled. Post, CH, dot or 3-post reticle. Variable have ½ MOA adj.	44.95
A-4.0	4	30	64	3½	11¾	1	Int.	10¾		49.95
VL-3.9	3-9	38½-12½	177-19	3¼	13½	1	Int.	15½		74.95
VS-3.9	3-9	37-10½	114-12	3¼	13½	1	Int.	13½		74.95
Marlin										
300	4	23	25	1½	11¾	⅞	Int.	9	Coated lenses, non-magnifying reticles. Tri-Post reticle.	19.95
500	3-7	24-10	49-16	1¾	12	⅞	Int.	9½		21.95
425	4	28	64	3½	—	1	Int.	—		35.95
825	3-9	34-11	—	3	—	1	Int.	—	A 4x Glenfield M200, suitable for 22 rifles, and with ½-minute adj., is $11.95.	49.95
Glenfield 400	4	28	64	3½	12	1	Int.	9		24.95
Nickel										
Supralyt	2½	42	64	3½	11½	1.024	Int.	7½		130.00
Supralyt	4	33	25	3½	11½	1.024	Int.	8		130.00
Supra	4	32	81	3½	11¼	1.024	Int.	9		145.00
Supra	6	21	36	3½	12½	1.024	Int.	9	¼ MOA click adjustments. Steel or alloy tubes. Weatherproof reticle caps. Crosshair, post and c.h. or post and crosshair reticles are standard. New "Diflex" coated lenses. Continental Arms Co.	145.00
◆ Supra Varminter	6	24	49	3¼-5	12¼	1.024	Int.	11½		160.00
Supra Vari-Power	1-4	66.5-27.3	153-28	3½	10½	1.024	Int.	13.1		180.00
Supra Vari-Power	1½-6	60-21.6	176-36	3½	12	1.181	Int.	14.8		225.00
Supra Vari-Power	2½-7	38-21	125-36	3½	11¾	1.024	Int.	11		190.00
Supra Vari-Power	2½-9	42-15.6	—	3½	14½	1.181	Int.	17.3		250.00
Supra Vari-Power	3-10	30-12	100-18.5	3½	12½	1.024	Int.	12½		225.00
Precise										
20241	4	23	14	2	11	.75	Int.	6¾		13.00
20254	4	29	64	3.6	12	1	Int.	9.1	Tapered Luma-Glo Crosshair.	39.00
20257	3-7	23-13	43-8	3	11½	.75	Int.	7½	Price with mount.	32.00
20262	4	29	64	3.6	12	1	Int.	9.1	Duplex Luma-Glo Crosshair.	38.00
20263	3-9	35.8-12.7	176.9-19.4	3.1-2.9	12.8	1	Int.	15.2	Duplex Luma-Glo Crosshair.	61.00
20244	4	29	64	3½	12	1	Int.	9	All scopes have constantly centered reticle.	35.00
20249	3-9	36-13	177-19	3	13⅓	1	Int.	15		58.00
20260	10	12.2	16	3	12½	1	Int.	10½		42.00
20382	4	37	64	3.3	11.8	1	Int.	10.5	Wideview, Dup. Amber-Glo.	51.00
Leatherwood Bros.										
Auto/Range	6	20	38	3-5	14⅝	1	Int.	18	Supplied with special mounts and range cams for most popular rifles and calibers.	119.50
Auto/Range	4	31	73	3-5	11	1	Int.	17		119.50
Auto/Range	1½-4½	65-26	225-49	3-5	12¼	1	Int.	17		129.50
Auto/Range	3-9	34-12	144-16	3-5	12¾	1	Int.	17		129.50

SCOPES & MOUNTS

Maker and Model	Magn.	Field at 100 Yds. (feet)	Relative Brightness	Eye Relief (in.)	Length (in.)	Tube Diam. (in.)	W&E Adjustments	Weight (ozs.)	Other Data	Price
Redfield										
Traditional	4	24½	27	3½	9⅜	.75	Int.	—	Traditionals have round lenses. 4-Plex reticle is standard.	36.50
Traditional	2½	43	64	3½	10¼	1	Int.	8½		59.70
Traditional	4	28½	56	3½	11⅜	1	Int.	9¾		70.40
Traditional	6	19	—	3½	12½	1	Int.	11½		81.00
Traditional 8xAO	8	15	—	3½	14⅛	1	Int.	13		99.80
Traditional AO	10	11½	18	3½	14⅛	1	Int.	13	Accu-Range reticle available on most variables at extra cost.	111.00
Traditional	2-7	42-14	207-23	3½	11¼	1	Int.	12		95.30
Traditional	3-9	34-11	163-18	3½	12½	1	Int.	13		111.30
Traditional	4-12	26-9	112-14	3½	13⅞	1	Int.	14	Also AO—$150.50.	138.00
Traditional	6-18	18-6	50-6	3½	13-15/16	1	Int.	18	Also AO—$162.00.	149.60
Widefield	2-¾	55½	69	3½	10½	1	Int.	8	Dot about $12 extra in Widefields.	78.40
Widefield	3.6	37½	84	3½	11½	1	Int.	10		89.00
Widefield	3.6	37½	84	3½	11½	1	Int.	10		103.30
Low Profile Widefield	5.5	24	54	3½	12¾	1	Int.	11		99.70
Widefield 6xLP	5.5	24	—	3½	12¾	1	Int.	11		115.70
Widefield	1¾-5	70-27	136-21	3½	10¾	1	Int.	11½		106.50
Widefield	2-7	49-19	144-21	3½	11¾	1	Int.	13		123.60
Widefield	3-9	39-15	112-18	3½	12½	1	Int.	14	MS feature $12.50 extra.	137.80
3200 Target	12,16, 20, 24	6½, 5¼, 4, 3¾	9, 6, 3¼, 2¼	2½	23¼	1	Int.	21	Mounts solidly.	199.00
6400 Target	16, 20, 24	6½, 5 4½	5¾, 3½, 2½	3	17	1	Int.	18	Mounts on receiver. CH or dot.	229.00
Sanders										
Bisley 2½x20	2½	42	64	3	10¾	1	Int.	8¼	Alum. alloy tubes, ¼" adj., coated lenses.	38.50
Bisley 4x33	4	28	64	3	12	1	Int.	9	Two other scopes are also offered: a 3-9x at $56.50, and a 6x45 at $42. rubber lens covers (clear plastic) are $2.50.	44.50
Bisley 6x40	6	19	45	3	12½	1	Int.	9½		46.50
Bisley 8x40	8	18	25	3¼	12½	1	Int.	9½		48.50
Bisley 10x40	10	12½	16	2½	12½	1	Int.	10¼		50.50
Bisley 5-13x40	5-13	29-10	64-9	3	14	1	Int.	14	Choice of reticles in CH, PCH, 3-post.	66.50
Southern Precision										
562	2½	40	144	3½	12	1	Int.	9¼	Centered reticles, CH or post. All elements sealed.	33.95
564	4	30	64	3½	12	1	Int.	9¼		33.95
567D	6	21	28	3¼	12	1	Int.	9¼		47.25
Swift										
Mark I 4x15	4	23	—	2	11	.75	Int.	6¾	All swift Mark I scopes, with the exception of the 4x15, have Quadraplex reticles and are fog-proof and waterproof. The 4x15 has cross-hair reticle and is non-waterproof.	12.50
Mark I 4x32	4	29	—	3½	12	1	Int.	9		45.00
Mark I 4x32 WA	4	37	—	3½	11¾	1	Int.	10½		49.00
Mark I 4x40 WA	4	35½	—	3¾	12¼	1	Int.	12		55.00
Mark I 3-9x32	3-9	35¾-12¾	—	3	12¾	1	Int.	13¾		55.00
Mark I 3-9x40 WA	3-9	42½-13½	—	2¾	12¾	1	Int.	14		65.00
Mark I 6x40	6	18	—	3¾	13	1	Int.	10		54.00
Mark I 1½-4½x32	1½-4½	55-22	—	3½	12	1	Int.	13		58.00
Tasco										
620W	3-9	35-14	177-19	3	12⅛	1	Int.	13	Lens covers furnished. Constantly centered reticles. Write the importer, Tasco, for data on complete line.	95.95
611W	2-5	58-19	100-16	3	11¼	1	Int.	10		79.95
627W	3-9	35-14	177-19	3½	12⅜	1	Int.	14		95.95
628V	3-9	42.15	177-19	3	12⅛	1	Int.	12¼		139.95
Tops										
4X	4	28½	64	3	11½	1	Int.	9½	Hard-coated lenses, nitrogen filled, shock-proof tested. Write Ed Paul, importer, for data on complete line.	23.95
8X	8	14½	16	3	13	1	Int.	10		29.95
3X-9X	3-9	33-15	175-19	3	12¾	1	Int.	14		39.95

Burris Co. has introduced a line of scopes giving "full circle view" in a true wide angle scope. Shown at left, they are the 4x, 2x-7x and a 3x-9x with black anodized tubes and round objective lenses. Burris also makes a wide line of scope mounts and metallic sights.

SCOPES & MOUNTS

Maker and Model	Magn.	Field at 100 Yds. (feet)	Relative Brightness	Eye Relief (in.)	Length (in.)	Tube Diam. (in.)	W&E Adjustments	Weight (ozs.)	Other Data	Price
United										
Golden Hawk	4	30	64		11⅞	—	Int.	9½		44.50
Golden Grizzly	6	18½	44		11⅞	1	Int.	11	Anodized tubes, nitrogen filled. Write United for data on complete line.	55.00
Golden Falcon	4-9	29½-14	100-20		13½	1	Int.	12¾		89.50
Golden Plainsman	3-12	33-12½	169-11		13½	1	Int.	12¾		110.00
Unertl										
Falcon	2¾	40	75.5	4	11	1	Int.(1′)	10	Black dural tube in hunting models. (2 oz. more with steel tube.)	61.00
Hawk	4	34	64	4	11¾	1	Int.(1′)	10.5		66.00
Condor	6	17	40	3-4	13½	1	Int.(1′)	12		83.00
◆ 1″ Target	6, 8, 10	16-10	17.6-6.25	2	21½	.75	Ext.	21		89.00
◆ 1¼″ Target	8,10,12, 14	12-6	15.2-5	2	25	.75	Ext.	25	Dural ¼ MOA click mounts.Hard coated lenses. Non-rotating objective lens focusing.	120.00
◆ 1½″ Target	8,10,12, 14,16,18, 20,24	11.5-3.2	—	2¼	25½	.75	Ext.	31		140.00
◆ 2″ Target	8,10,12, 14,16,18, 24,30,36	—	22.6-2.5	2¼	26¼	1	Ext.	44		188.00
◆ Varmint, 1¼″	6,8,10,12	14.1-7	28.7-1	2½	19½	.875	Ext.	26	¼ MOA dehorned mounts.	118.00
									With target mounts.	122.00
◆ Ultra Varmint, 2″	8,10 12,15	12.6-7	39.7-11	2½	24	1	Ext.	34	With dehorned mount.	153.00
									With calibrated head.	170.00
◆ Small Game	4,6	25-17	19.4-8.4	2¼	18	.75	Ext.	16	Same as 1″ Target but without objective lens focusing.	66.00
◆ Vulture	8 10	11.2 10.9	29 18½	3-4	15⅝ 16⅛	1	E or I	15½	Price with internal adj.	108.00
									Price with ¼ MOA click mounts.	133.00
◆ Programer 200	8,10,12, 14,16,18 20,24,30,36	11.3-4	39-1.9		26½	1	Ext.	45	With new Posa mounts.	234.00
◆ BV-20	20	8	4.4	4.4	17⅞	1	Ext.	21¼	Range focus unit near rear of tube. Price is with Posa mounts. Magnum clamp. With standard mounts and clamp ring. $156.00.	166.00
Universal										
Deluxe UC	2½	32	172	3½	12	1	Int.	9¼	Aluminum alloy tubes, centered reticles, coated lenses. Similar Standard series available at lower cost.	34.95
Deluxe UE	4	29	64	3½	12	1	Int.	9		35.95
Deluxe UL	3-9	34-12	177-18	3	12¾	1	Int.	15¼		57.95
Weatherby										
Mark XXII	4	25	50	2½-3½	11¾	⅞	Int.	9¼	Focuses in top turret.	44.50
Premier Standard	2¾	45	212	3½	11¾	1	Int.	12¼		89.50
Premier Standard	4	31	100	3½	12¾	1	Int.	12¼	Centered, non-magnifying reticles. Binocular focusing. Lumi-Plex or Open Dot, $5 extra.	99.50
Premier Standard	3-9	43½-14½	177-19	3	12	1	Int.	14¾		109.50
Premier Wide Angle	4	35¾	100	3	11¾	1	Int.	14		119.50
Premier Wide Angle	3-9	43½-14¾	177-19	3	12	1	Int.	14¾		129.50
Weaver										
K1.5	1½	56	—	3-5	9¾	1	Int.	7		34.95
K2.5	2½	43	—	3-6	10⅜	1	Int.	8½		44.95
K3	3	37	—	3-6	10⅜	1	Int.	8½		49.95
K4	4	31	—	3-5½	11¼	1	Int.	9½		59.95
K6	6	20	—	3-5	13⅝	1	Int.	11		69.95
K8	8	15	—	3-5	15⅜	1	Int.	12¼	Crosswires, post, rangefinder or Dual X reticle optional on all K and V scopes (except no RF in K1½, post in K8, 10, 12, or RF in V22). Dot $7.50 extra in K and V models only. Objective lens on K8, K10, K12, V9, V12 and V9-W focuses for range.	79.95
K10	10	12	—	3-5	15½	1	Int.	12½		84.95
K12	12	10	—	3-5	15¾	1	Int.	12½		94.95
K3-W	3	55	—	3¾	10¾	1	Int.	12½		64.95
K4-W	4	37½	—	3¾	12	1	Int.	13¼		74.95
K6-W	6	25	—	3¾	13¾	1	Int.	14¼		84.95
V4.5-W	1½-4½	70-26	—	4	10¾	1	Int.	14		84.95
V7-W	2½-7	53-20	—	3¾	12½	1	Int.	16		94.95
V9-W	3-9	41-16	—	3¾	13¾	1	Int.	19¾		104.95
V4.5	1½-4½	54-21	—	3-5	10	1	Int.	8½		69.95
V7	2½-7	40-15	—	3-5	11⅝	1	Int.	10½		79.95
V9	3-9	33-12	—	3-5	13	1	Int.	13		89.95
V12	4-12	24-9	—	4	13	—	Int.	13		99.95
V22	3-6	30-16	—	2	12½	.875	Int.	4½	$1 extra for Dual X reticle.	17.95
D4	4	28	—	2	11⅝	.875	Int.	4	D model prices include N or Tip-Off mount.	12.95
D6	6	18	—	2	12	.875	Int.	4		14.95
Qwik-Point	1	—	—	6	—	—	Int.	8	For rifles and shotguns. Projects red dot aiming point.	44.95
Williams										
Guide Line	4	29½	64	3¾	11¾	1	Int.	9½	Coated lenses, nitrogen filled tubes, ½ MOA adj. CH, dot, TNT or Guide reticle. Dot covers 3 MOA at 4x in all models.	93.25
Guide Line	1½-4½	78-26	196-22	4⅓-3¼	9½	1	Int.	7¾		124.75
Guide Line	2-6	60-20	169-18	3¼	10¼	1	Int.	10		124.75
Guide Line	3-9	39-13	161-18	3¾-3¼	12	1	Int.	14½		130.00
Twilight	2½	32	64	3¾	11¼	1	Int.	8½	$6.50 more for TNT reticle.	47.00
Twilight	4	29	64	3½	11¾	1	Int.	9½		52.50
Twilight	2-6	45-17	256-28	3	11½	1	Int.	11½		73.50
Twilight	3-9	36-13	161-18	3	12¾	1	Int.	13½		81.75
Wide Guide	4	35	64	3¼	12¼	1	Int.	14	CH, TNT or Guide reticle.	93.25

◆Signifies target and/or varmint scope.

Hunting scopes in general are furnished with a choice of reticle—cross hairs, post with crosshairs, tapered or blunt post, or dot crosshairs, etc.
The great majority of target and varmint scopes have medium or fine crosshairs but post or dot reticles may be ordered.

W—Windage E—Elevation MOA—Minute of angle or 1″ (approx.) at 100 yards, etc.

SCOPES & MOUNTS
TELESCOPE MOUNTS

Maker, Model, Type	Adjust.	Scopes	Suitable for	Price
Browning				
One Piece (T)	W only	1″ split rings	Browning, Winchester, Remington, Savage, Marlin.	**24.45**
One Piece (T)	No	¾″ split rings	Browning 22 semi-auto.	**6.50**
One Piece Barrel Mount Base	No	Groove mount	22 rifles with grooved receiver.	**9.50**
B-Square Co.				
M-1 Mono-Mount	No	1″ long eye relief Leupold M8-2X (mounts ahead of action).	30 M-1 carbine.	**9.95**
M94 Mono-Mount	No	1″ long eye relief Leupold M8-2ax (mounts ahead of action).	M94 Winchester.	**11.95**
M94 Side Mount	W&E	1″ Scopes.	All Winchester Model 94s (no drilling or tapping).	**14.95**
"Rib" Mount Rings and Bases	No	1″ Split Rings.	All popular rifles including those with grooved top receivers.	**Pr. Rings—11.95** **Pr. Bases— 1.50**
Dual Adjust	Yes Both W&E	All 1″ Scopes (has both W. and E. adjustment).	All popular rifles.	**Pr. Rings—17.95** **One-Piece Base— 5.95**
T-C Pistol Base	No	1″ Weaver Tip-Off or B-Square Rib mount rings. 1″ long eye relief Leupold M8-2X pistol scope.	For the Thompson-Center Contender, model pistols.	**B-Square Rings** **Pr.—11.95** **Pr. Bases— 5.95**
AR-15	No	Use any 1″ Weaver type top mount ring.	Colt AR-15 rifle.	**14.95**
Buehler				
One Piece (T)	W only	¾″ or 1″ solid rings; ⅞″, 1″ or 26mm split rings. 4″ or 5″ spacing.		**Mount complete Solid rings—26.50** **Mount complete Split rings—32.50**
One Piece "Micro-Dial" Universal	Yes	Same. 4″ ring spacing only.	Most popular models.	**Solid—34.25 Split—40.25**
Two Piece (T)	W only	Same. Rings for 26.5—27 mm adjust to size by shims.	All popular models.	**Solid—26.50** **Split—32.50**
One Piece Pistol Base	W only	Uses any Buehler rings.	S&W K. Colt, Ruger, Thompson	**Bases only—13.75**
One Piece (T)	W only	Same.	Rem. XP100 pistol.	**Base only—13.75**
Burris			Most Popular Rifles.	**Rings—17.95**
Supreme One Piece (T)	W only	1″ split rings, 3 heights		**1 piece base—10.95**
Trophy Two Piece (T)	W only	1″ split rings, 3 heights		**2 piece base— 9.95**
Bushnell			Most popular rifles.	**Rings—11.95**
Detachable (T)	W only	1″ split rings, uses Weaver bases.	Includes windage adj.	
Pivot (T)	No	1″ only.	Most popular rifles.	**11.45**
All Purpose	No	Phantom	V-block bottoms lock to chrom-moly studs seated into two 6-48 holes.	**9.50**
Rigid	No	Phantom	Heavy loads in Colt, S&W, Ruger revolvers, Rem. XP100, Ruger Hawkeye.	**9.50**
94 Win.	No	Phantom	M94 Win., end of bbl. clamp or center dovetail.	**9.50**
Clearview	No	1″	Most popular rifles. Uses Weaver bases.	**13.50**
Conetrol				
One Piece (T)	W only	1″ solid or split rings.	All popular rifles, including metric drilled foreign rifles.	**Huntur 17.85-22.85** **Gunnur 21.85-27.85** **Custum 27.85-34.85**
Two Piece (T)	W only	Same.		
Griffin & Howe				
Standard Double Lever (S)	No	1″ or 26mm split rings.	All popular models. (Garand $57.50; Win. 94 $55.00). High rings $27.50.	**52.50**
Holden				
Ironsighter (T)	No	1″ split rings.	Many popular rifles. rings have oval holes to permit use of iron sights. For 22 rimfire grooved receivers, ¾, ⅞ or 1 inch tubes, $6.95. For long eye relief scopes on M94, $19.95.	**14.95**
International Guns Inc. handles the complete line of Parker-Hale (British) Roll-Over and other scope mounts.				
Jaeger				
QD, with windage (S)	W only	1″, 26mm; 3 heights.	All popular models.	**45.00**
Jaguar				
QD Dovetail (T)	No	1″, 26mm and 26½mm rings.	For BSA Monarch rifle (Galef, importer).	**16.95**
Kesselring				
Standard QD (T)	W only	¾″, ⅞″, 1″, 26mm split rings.	All popular rifles, one or two piece bases.	**22.50**
See-Em-Under (T)	W only	Same.	Rem. 760, 740, Win. 100, 88, Marlin 336	**24.00**
Dovetail (T)	W only	1″, 26mm.	Steyr 22, Sako, Brno, Krico	**22.50**
Kris Mounts				
Two Piece (T)	No	1″, 26mm split rings.	Most popular rifles and Ruger	**5.98**
One Piece (T)	No	1″, 26mm split rings	Blackhawk revolver. Mounts have oval hole to permit use of iron sights.	**8.98**
Kwik-site (T)	No	1″ split rings	Wider-View, $15.75. Mounts scope high to permit iron sight use. Offset base for 94 Win.	**14.75** **19.95**

SCOPES & MOUNTS

Maker, Model, Type	Adjust.	Scopes	Suitable for	Price
Leupold				
STD (T)	W only	1" only, 3 heights.interchange with Redfield Jr. and Sr. components.	Most popular rifles.	**Rings—16.70** **Base—10.50**
Lyman All-American				
Tru-lock (T)	No	¾", ⅞", 1", 26mm, split rings.	All popular post-war rifles, plus savage 99, 98 Mauser. One or two piece bases.	**Base— 2.50** **Mounts—12.50**
Marble				
Game Getter (T)	No	1" only.	Many popular rifles. Has see-through base to permit use of iron sights.	**16.88**
Game Getter (S)	No	1" only.	Win. 64. Win. 94 side mount $17.80.	
Marlin				
One Piece QD (T)	No	1" split rings.	Most Marlin and Glenfield lever actions.	**7.95**
Numrich				
Side Mount	No	1" split rings.	M-1 carbine.	**7.95**
Pachmayr				
Lo-Swing (S)	Yes	¾", ⅞", 1", 26mm solid or split loops.	All popular rifles. Scope swings aside for instant use of iron sights.	**30.00**
Lo-Swing (T)	Yes	¾", ⅞", 1", 26mm split rings.	Adjustable base. Win. 70, 88; Rem. 721, 722, 725, 740, 760; Mar. 336; Sav. 99.	**35.00**
Parker-Hale				
Roll-Off	No	1" and 26mm.	Most popular rifles.	**13.95**
Precise Imports				
40421 (rings only)	No	1" tube; not over 32mm obj.	Fit Weaver bases.	**4.95**
40422 (rings only)	No	1" tube; 40mm obj. scopes.		**4.95**
Leatherwood Bros.				
V lock QD (T)	No	1" split rings.	Most popular rifles.	**13.00**
Redfield				
JR-SR (T)	W only	¾", 1", 26mm.	Low, med.& high, split rings. Reversible extension front rings for 1". 2-piece bases for Mannlicher-Schoenauer and Sako.	**29.20-53.00**
			Colt Sauer bases $33.00.	**20.00**
Swing-Over (T) base only	No	1". (Not for variables.)	Standard height split rings. Also for shotguns.	**17.80**
Ring (T)	No	¾" and 1".	Split rings for grooved 22's.	**9.80-12.00**
FR (T) bases	No	Takes ¾" or 1" rings.	See-thru bases $6.80; shotgun model $6.80 Rings $15.00.	**3.40**
S&K				
Insta-Mount (T) base only	No	Most take S&K or Weaver rings.	M1903, A3, M1 Carbine, Lee Enfield #3, #4, #5, P14, M1917, M98 Mauser, FN Auto, AR-15,	**11.00—20.00**
			AR-180, M-14, M-1. Bases—M94, 64.	**10.00**
Conventional rings and bases	No	1" split rings.	Most popular rifles. For "see through underneath" risers, add $4.15.	**24.20**
Sako				
QD Dovetail	W only	1" or 26mm split rings.	Sako, or any rifle using Sako action. 3 heights and extension rings available. Garcia, importer.	**33.00**
Savage				
No. 40 (S)	No	1"	For Savage 340.	**3.25**
No. 70	No	1"	For Savage 170, 170-C rifles.	**4.00**
Tasco				
710 and 712 series	Yes	1" split rings, regular or high.	Many popular rifles.	**5.95**
M722	No	Split rings.	For 22s with grooved receivers.	**5.95**
Unertl				
Posa (T)	Yes	¾", ⅞", 1" scopes	Unertl target or varmint scope.	**30.00-35.00**
¼ Click (T)	Yes	¾", 1" target scopes	Any with regular dovetail scope basis.	**27.00-32.00**
Dehorned Varmint (T)	Yes	¾", ⅞", 1" scopes	Add $3 for Posa.	**29.00-32.00**
Weaver				
Detachable Mount (T & S)	No	¾", ⅞", 1", 26mm.	Nearby all modern rifles. Extension rings, 1" $11.95.	**9.95**
Type N (S)	No	⅞" scopes only.	Same. High or low style mounts.	**2.00**
Pivot Mount (T)	No	¾", 1".	Most modern big bore rifles.	**14.95**
Tip-Off (T)	No	¾", ⅞".	22s with grooved receivers.	**3.95**
Tip-Off (T)	No	1", two-piece.	Same. Adapter for Lee Enfield—$2.00.	**9.95**
All Steel Rings	No	1" split rings.	Extension rings $21.50	**17.00**
All Steel Bases	No	Take 1" split rings.	Fits all Weaver top mount	**17.00**
See-Thru Mount	No	1" split rings.	bases. Snaps on, snaps off.	**15.95**
Williams				
Offset (S)	No	¾", ⅞", 1", 26mm solid, split or extension rings.	Most rifles (with over-bore rings, $23.30). Br. S.M.L.E. (round rec.) $6.60 extra.	**20.25**
OC (T)	No	Same.	Same. Add $9.80 for micro. windage ring.	**20.25**
QC (S)	No	Same.	Most rifles.	**20.25**
Sight-Thru	No	1", ⅞", sleeves $1.	Many modern rifles.	**17.00**

(S)—Side Mount **(T)—Top Mount** 22mm=.866" 25.4mm=1" 26mm=1.024" 26.5mm=1.045" 30mm=1.181"

Weaver's new See-Thru Mountfits all weaver Top-Mount bases. Allows the use of iron sights when necessary or preferred. It removes instantly with a quick twisting motion and replacement is just as easy with exact zero alignment. Made with split rings for 1" scopes.

SPOTTING SCOPES

BAUSCH & LOMB BALSCOPE Sr.—60mm objective, 20X. Field at 100 yds. 13 ft. Relative brightness, 9. Wgt., 48 oz. Length closed, 16 7/16". Rapid prismatic focusing **$189.50**
Also 15X, 20X, 25X, 40X, 60X eyepieces, each **$29.50**
20X wide angle eyepiece **$39.50**

BAUSCH & LOMB BALSCOPE ZOOM—15X to 60X variable power. 60mm objective. Field at 1000 yds. 150 ft. (15X) to 37½ feet (60X). Relative brightness 16 (15X) to 1 (60X). Wgt., 48 oz., 16 11/16" overall. Integral tripod lug. Straight eyepiece **$224.50**
With 45° eyepiece **$269.50**

BAUSCH & LOMB BALSCOPE 20—40mm objective. 20X. Field at 100 yds., 7.5 ft. 15⅝" overall, Wgt., 22 oz. **$45.50**

BAUSCH & LOMB BALSCOPE 10—30mm objective. 10X. Field at 100 yds. 7.5 ft. 10¼" overall, weight, 9 oz. **$19.95**

Bushnell Sentry II

BUSHNESS SPACEMASTER II—60mm objective, 25X. Field at 100 yds., 10.5 ft. Relative brightness, 5.76. Wgt., 39 oz. Length closed, 15¼". Prism focusing **$154.50**
15X, 20X, 25X, 40X and 60X eyepieces, each **$29.50**
20X wide angle eyepiece **$39.50**

BUSHNELL SPACEMASTER 45°—Same as above except: Wgt., 43 oz., length closed 16¼". Eyepiece at 45°, sliding sunshade **$189.50**

BUSHNELL SPACEMASTER II—20X-45X zoom. 60mm objective. Field at 100 yards 12-7.2 ft. Relative brightness 9-1.7. Wgt. 36 oz., length 11⅝". Price **$184.50**

BUSHNELL SENTRY II—20X. 50mm objective. Field at 100 yards 12 ft. Relative brightness 6.25 .... **$98.50**
Also 32X and 48X eyepieces, each **$27.00**

BUSHNELL ZOOM SPOTTER—40mm objective. 9X-30X variable power Price **$52.50**

BUSHNELL—10x30mm hand telescope. Field 183 ft. at 1000 yards. Weight 11 ozs.; 10" long. Tripod mount **$19.95**

HUTSON CHROMATAR 60—63.4mm objective. 22.5X eyepiece at 45D. Wgt. 24oz. 8" overall. 10½" foot field at 100 yards **$119.00**
15X or 45X eyepieces, each **$22.00**

HY-SCORE MODEL 460—60mm objective. 15X, 20X, 25X, 40X and 60X eyepieces included. Field at 100 yds. 15.8 to 3.2 ft. Length closed 11". Wgt., 35 oz. With case **$142.95**
Zoom—20X to 40X **$165.95**

PRECISE 21285—60mm objective, 15X to 30X zoom scope. About 15" long, weighs approximately 6 lbs. with adj. tripod **$100.00**

PRECISE 21287—60mm objective, interchangeable eyepieces of 15X, 20X, 30X, 40X, 60X. Sliding sunshade. Weighs about 6 lbs. with adj tripod. Price **$132.00**

Swift Model 841

REDFIELD FIFTEEN-SIXTY—15X-60X zoom. 60mm objective. Field at 100 yards 15.6-3.7 ft. Relative brightness 16-1. Wgt. 48 oz., length 16¾", **$229.00**
Tripod stand **$36.20**
Bipod stand **$36.20**
Carrying case **$47.20**
Window mount **$8.00**

REDFIELD FIFTEEN-FORTY-FIVE—Similar to above but power range is 15X-45X **$179.00**

SOUTHERN PRECISION MODEL 549—60mm objective and 5 eyepieces from 15X to 60X; extensible sunshade and folding tripod. Closed, 14¾", Wgt., 4¼ lbs. **$86.50**

SOUTHERN PRECISION ZOOM MODEL 547—60mm objective, 25X to 50X; ext. sunshade folding tripod. Closed, 18", wgt. 4½ lbs. with tripod (included) **$103.00**

SOUTHERN PRECISION MODEL 546—50mm objective, 25X. Folding tripod, leather case included. Closed, 13", wgt. 3 lbs. **$48.00**

SWIFT TELEMASTER M841—60mm objective. 15X to 60X variable power. Field at 1000 yards 160 feet (15X) to 40 feet (60X). Wgt. 3.4 lbs. 17.6" overall **$224.95**
Tripod for above **$58.50**
Photo adapter **$14.95**
Case for above **$42.50**

SWIFT MODEL 821—60mm objective. 15X, 20X, 30X, 40X and 60X eyepieces included. Field at 100 yds., 158 to 32 ft. Length 13½" (without sunshade). 6 lbs. **$199.95**

TASCO 18T ZOOM—60mm objective. 20X to 60X variable power. Field at 1000 yds., 158 ft. (16X) to 40 ft. (50X). Wgt. 4½ lbs. 18" overall **$119.95**

TASCO 28T ANGLEVIEW—60mm objective. 25X, resolves to 2 sec. at 100 yds. Rapid focus knob. Table top tripod with adj. elevation leg. Camera tripod adapter, extending sun shade. Wgt., 6 lbs., length 16½". Complete with lens covers **$199.95**

TASCO 8T SPOTTING 60—60mm objective, 4 par-focal, variable power eye-lenses 15X, 30X, 40X and 60X. Resolves 2.8 sec. at 100 yds. Wgt., 4 lbs., length 16½" **$199.95**

UNERTL RIGHT ANGLE—63.5mm objective. 24X. Field at 100 yds., 7 ft. Relative brightness, 6.96. Eye relief, ½". Wgt., 41 oz. Length closed, 19". Push-pull and screw-focus eyepiece. 16X and 32X eyepieces $18 each. Price **$139.00**

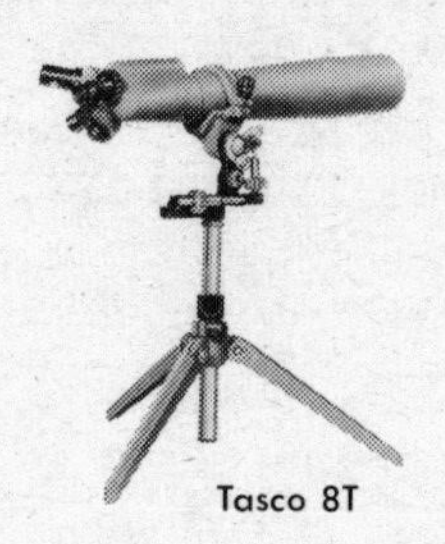
Tasco 8T

UNERTL STRAIGHT PRISMATIC—Same as Unertl Right Angle except: straight eyepiece and Wgt. of 40 oz. **$119.00**

UNERTL 20X STRAIGHT PRISMATIC—54mm objective. 20X. Field at 100 yds., 8.5 ft. Relative brightness, 6.1. Eye relief, ½". Wgt., 36 oz. Length closed, 13½". Complete with lens covers **$99.00**

UNERTL TEAM SCOPE—100mm objective. 15X, 24X. 32X eyepieces. Field at 100 yds. 13 to 7.5 ft. Relative brightness, 39.06 to 9.79. Eye relief, 2" to 1½". Weight, 13 lbs. 29⅞" overall. Metal tripod, yoke and wood carrying case furnished (total weight, 80 lbs.) **$485.00**

WEATHERBY—60mm objective, 20X-45X zoom **$175.00**
Tripod for above **$39.50**

SCOPE ATTACHMENTS

DAVIS TARGETEER—Objective lens/tube units that attach to front of low power scopes, increase magnification to 8X. 1¼" lens, **$25**, 1½" lens, **$29.50**

HERMANN DUST CAPS—Connected leather straps, hand made, natural color. For all popular scopes **$4.00**

LEE TACKHOLE DOTS—Various size dots for all scopes. **$12.50-$17.50**

PGS SCOPE SHIELDS—Flexible rubber, usable at front and rear, protect scopes from snow or rain. Made for all scopes **$3.95**

PREMIER RETICLES—Various size dots for all scopes, also special reticles to order. Price—**$7.00** to **$18.50.** **PREMIER WEATHER CAPS**—transparent, high light transmission. For all popular scopes. Price **$3.50** Special sizes **$5.00**

W. H. SIEBERT—Converts Lyman, Leupold and Weaver K model varmint scopes to 15X-24X, from **$30.00**

STORM KING LENS CAP—A hinged glass-and-rubber protector set (2), made in various sizes for all scopes. May be unhinged or sighted through. Anderson Gun Shop. Per pair **$3.95**

SUPREME LENS COVERS—Hinged protectors for most scope models, front and rear lenses shielded. Butler Creek Corp. Per pair, postpaid. **$7.50**

SPOTTING SCOPE STANDS

DAVIDSON MARK 245—Bipod adjustable for elevation, 9½"-14½". Side mount with two straps. Black crinkle finish. Length folded 16½". Price **$23.95**

FREELAND ALL ANGLE—Tripod adjustable for elevation. Left or right side mount with worm drive clamp. Folding legs. Clamps available for any scope tube size. Black, gray, or green crinkle finish. Price **$29.50**
Also 12", 18", 24" extensions available .... **$4.50-$7.50**

FREELAND OLYMPIC—Bipod adjustable for elevation. All angle mount with padded worm drive clamp. Folding legs. Clamps available for any scope tube size. Grey or green crinkle finish. Price **$31.50**
Also 12", 18", 24" extensions available .... **$4.50-$7.50**
Zoom head for tripod or bipod **$14.75**

FREELAND REGAL BIPOD—Choice of saddle or zoom head. All adjustment knobs are oversize for easy adjusting. Large "ball" carrying knob. Gray or green finish **$33.25**
Above with stability weight **$48.75**
Extension 12"-24" .... **$4.50-$7.50**

FREELAND GALLERY SPECIAL BIPOD—For all shooting positions. Zoom or saddle head. Adjustable for elevation. Comes with bipod base, gallery special head assembly and 12" extension. Gray or green finish, saddle head **$33.00**
As above with 18" extension **$33.60**
Gallery Tripod (includes base, saddle head assembly, and 12" extension **$29.85**
Zoom Gallery Bipod **$33.00**
Zoom Gallery Tripod **$29.85**

The Arms Library for

COLLECTOR • HUNTER • SHOOTER • OUTDOORSMAN

A selection of books—old, new and forthcoming—for everyone in the arms field, with a brief description by . . . JOE RILING

The ABC's of Reloading, by Dean A. Grennell, Digest Books, Inc., Northfield, IL. 1974. 8½"X11", 320 pp. Profusely illus. Paper bound. $6.95.
Written primarily for the novice, this book will also teach the pro a thing or two. A large amount of information on powder, primers, bullets, cases and shotshells.

Ballistics & the Muzzle Loading Rifle, by Wm. C. Herring, Nat'l. Muzzle Loading Rifle Assn., Friendship, IN, 1974. 111 pp., illus. Paper covers. $5.95.
A manual of black powder reloading and ballistic data.

Ballistics in the Seventeenth Century, by A. R. Hall. 1st J. & J. Harper ed. 1969 [from the Cambridge University Press ed. of 1952]. 186 pp., illus., with tables and diagrams. $13.50.
A profound work for advanced scholars, this is a study in the relations of science and war, with reference principally to England.

Cartridges of the World, by Frank C. Barnes, John T. Amber ed., Digest Books, Inc., Northfield, IL, 1972. 8½"x11", 384 pp. Profusely illus. Paperbound. $7.95.
The third edition of a comprehensive reference for hunters, collectors, handloaders and ballisticians. Covering over 1000 cartridges, loads, components, etc., from all over the world.

Centerfire American Rifle Cartridges, 1892-1963, by Ray Bearse, A. S. Barnes & Co., S. Brunswick, NJ, 1966. 198 pp., illus. $10.00.
Identification manual covering caliber, introduction date, origin, case type, etc. Self-indexed and cross-referenced. Headstamps and line drawings are included.

Centerfire Pistol and Revolver Cartridges, by H. P. White, B. D. Munhall and Ray Bearse. A. S. Barnes, NY, 1967, 85 pp. plus 170 pp., illus. $10.00.
A new and revised edition covering the original Volume I, Centerfire Metric Pistol and Revolver Cartridges and Volume II, Centerfire American and British Pistol and Revolver Cartridges, by White and Munhall, formerly known as Cartridge Identification.

Exterior Ballistics, by Edward J. McShane, John L. Kelley and Franklin V. Reno. The University of Denver Press, Denver, CO, 1953. 834 pp., illus. $20.00.
Theoretical and practical text on ballistics problems, based on extensive research of the W.W.II period. An exclusive with Ray Riling Arms Books Co.

Firearms Identification, by Dr. J. H. Mathews, Charles C. Thomas, Springfield, IL, 1973 3 vol. set. A massive, carefully researched, authoritative work published as:
Vol. I. **The Laboratory Examination of Small Arms.** . . . 400 pp., illus. $44.75.
Vol. II. **Original Photographs and Other Illustrations of Handguns.** 492 pp., illus. $44.75.
Vol. III. **Data on Rifling Characteristics of Handguns and Rifles.** 730 pp., illus. $69.50.

Handbook for Shooters and Reloaders, by P. O. Ackley, Salt Lake City, UT, 1970. *Vol. 1,* 567 pp., illus. $9.00. *Vol. II,* a new printing with specific new material. 495 pp., illus. $9.00. Both volumes. $19.50.

Handloader's Digest, 7th Ed., edited by John T. Amber, Digest Books, Inc., Northfield, IL, 1975. 288 pp., very well illus., stiff paper covers. $7.95.
This completely new edition contains the latest data on ballistics, maximum loads, new tools, equipment, etc., plus a fully illus. catalog section, current prices and specifications.

Hazards and Problems of Handloading, by Fred Tucker, Fred Tucker, Moore, OK, 1963. 70 pp., illus., paper covers. $2.50.
Covers features of handloading which are not always mentioned in standard manuals.

Hodgdon's Reloading Data Manual No. 22, Hodgdon Powder Co., Shawnee Mission, KS, 1974. 192 pp., illus. $2.95.
A concise guide of reloading data for Hodgdon powders.

Hornady Handbook of Cartridge Reloading, Rifle-Pistol, Vol. 2, by J. W. Hornady, Hornady Mfg. Co., Inc., Grand Island, NB, 1973. 512 pp., illus. $4.95.
A comprehensive guide to handloading and shooting; nearly 100 rifle/pistol cartridge combinations. Thousands of loads.

The Ideal Hand Book No. 27, a facsimile by Frontier Press, Arvada, CO, 1974. 127 pp., illus. Paper covers. $3.00.
A facsimile of the 1926 *Ideal Hand Book,* the first issued after the acquisition of the firm by Lyman Gun Sight Corp.

The Identification of Firearms and Forensic Ballistics, by Major Sir Gerald Burrard, A. S. Barnes & Co., NY, 1964. $15.00.
The fundamentals of forensic ballistics in easy to understand language.

Interior Ballistics, How a Gun Converts Chemical Energy to Projectile Motion, by E. D. Lowry. Doubleday and Co., NY, 1968. 168 pp., including index and bibliography., illus. with 4 halftones and 17 line drawings. $4.50.
An introduction to the history of small arms and weapons relative to the science of internal ballistics, especially for the layman and student.

Lee Reloading Handbook, by R. Lee, Lee Custom Engineering, Hartford, WI. 98 pp., illus. Paper, 98¢.
Manual on reloading ammunition of various types.

Lyman Black Powder Handbook, ed. by C. Kenneth Ramage, Lyman Products for Shooters, Middlefield, CT, 1975. 239 pp., illus. Paper covers. $5.95.
The most comprehensive load information ever published for the modern black powder shooter.

Lyman Cast Bullet Handbook. Lyman Gunsight Corp., Middlefield, CT, 1973. 260 pp., illus. Paper covers. $4.95.
A long-awaited and fine reference for handloaders.

Lyman Handbook No. 45. Lyman Gunsight Corp., Middlefield, CT, 1967. $4.95.
Latest edition of a favorite reference for ammunition handloaders, whether novice or veteran.

Make Muzzle Loader Accessories, by R. H. McCrory, R. H. McCory, Publ., 1971, 46 pp. Paper $2.25.
A revised 2nd ed. covering over 20 items from powderhorns to useful tools. Well illus.

Modern Handloading, by Maj. Geo. C. Nonte. Winchester Press, NY, 1972. 416 pp., illus. $10.00.
Covers all aspects of metallic and shotshell ammunition loading, plus more loads than any book in print; state and Federal laws, reloading tools, glossary.

The NRA Handloader's Guide. Ashley Halsey, Jr., ed. Nat'l Rifle Assn., Washington, DC, 1969, 312 pp., illus., paperbound. $5.00.
Revised edition of a reloading handbook, based on material published in *The American Rifleman.*

Pocket Manual for Shooters and Reloaders, by P. O. Ackley. publ. by author, Salt Lake City, UT, 1964. 176 pp., illus., spiral bound. $3.50.
Good coverage on standard and wildcat cartridges and related firearms in popular calibers.

Principles and Practice of Loading Ammunition, by Lt. Col. Earl Naramore. Stackpole Books, Harrisburg, PA, 1954. 915 text pages, 240 illustrations. $17.50.
Actually two volumes in one. The first part (565 pp.) deals with ballistics and the principles of cartridge making—and the chemistry, metallurgy, and physics involved. The second part (350 pp.) is a thorough discussion of the mechanics of loading cartridges. 1967 printing.

Professional Loading of Rifle, Pistol and Shotgun Cartridges . . ., by G. L. Herter, Mitchell, SD, 1970. 430 pp., illus., paper covers. $4.50.
Technical load data on small arms ammunition, with related articles on firearms and their use.

Shooter's Bible Black Powder Guide, by George Nonte, Shooter's Bible, Inc., S. Hackensack, NJ, 1969. 214 pp., well illus. $5.95.
Information on black powder weapons, ammunition, shooting, etc.

SAS Bullet Swage Manual, by Ted Smith, North Bend, OR, 1973. 68 pp., illus., spiral bound paper covers. $2.00.
Step by step instructions on bullet swaging for the beginner and expert alike.

Shooter's Bible Reloader's Guide, 3rd Ed., by R. A. Steindler, Shooter's Bible, Inc., S. Hackensack, NJ, 1975. 256 pp., illus. Paper covers. $5.95.
A revised and up-dated ed. of the standard guide on the subject of reloading.

Shotshell Handbook, by Lyman Handbook Staff. Lyman Gunsight Corp., Middlefield, CT, 1969. 160 pp., illus., stiff paper spiral-binding. $3.00.
The first book devoted exclusively to shotshell reloading. Considers: gauge, shell length, brand, case, loads, buckshot, etc., plus excellent reference section. Some color illus.

Shotshell Reloading Manual, rev. ed., 1972. Pacific Tool Co., Grand Island, NB, 1972. 96 pp., illus. Paper covers. $3.50.
Complete data for more than 300 modern shotshell loads, with detailed sequential drawings.

Sierra Bullets Reloading Manual, by Robert Hayden. Sierra Bullets, Santa Fe Springs, CA, 1971. 350 pp., illus. In loose-leaf binder. $4.85.
Reference manual on cartridge reloading, including ballistics and ammunition data on rifles and pistols.

Small Arms Ammunition Identification Guide. Normount Tech. Pub., Wickenburg, AZ, 1971. 151 pp., illus. Paper, $3.00.
A reprint of the guide originally published as FSTC-CW-07-02-66, revised.

Small Arms Ammunition Identification Guide, An Army Intelligence Document, Paladin Press. Boulder, CO, 1972. 254 pp., illus. Paper, $3.00.
An exact reprint of FSTC-CW-7068, 1969 updated. An identification guide for most countries.

Speer Manual for Reloading Ammunition No. 9, Speer, Inc., Lewiston, ID, 1974. 464 pp., illus. $5.50.
A popular manual on handloading, with authoritative articles on loading, ballistics, and related subjects. Revised and updated.

The .30-'06, by W. L. Godfrey, Elk Mountain Shooters Supply, Inc., Pasco, WA, 1975. 425 pp., illus. Spiral bound. $8.95.
A valuable source book for the advanced handloader.

Why Not Load Your Own? by Col. T. Whelen. A. S. Barnes, New York, 1957, 4th ed., rev. 237 pp., illus, $5.95.
A basic reference on handloading, describing each step, materials and equipment. Loads for popular cartridges are given.

The Winchester-Western Ammunition Handbook. Thomas Nelson & Sons, NYC, 1964. 185 pp., illus. $2.95.
Called the world's handiest handbook on ammunition for all types of shotguns, rifles and handguns. Full of facts, photographs, ballistics and statistics.

The Robert Abels Collection of Bowie Type Knives of American Interest, by Robert Abels, R. Abels, Inc., Hopewell Jct., NY, 1974. 20 pp., illus. Paper covers. $1.50.
A selection of American Bowie type knives from the collection of Robert Abels.

About Cannon in 1862, by Robert F. Hudson, American Archives Publ. Co., Topsfield, MA, 1971. 44 pp., illus. Paper, $4.00.
Reprint of an 18th century monograph on artillery pieces, with historical notes.
Accoutrement Plates, North and South, 1861-1865, by Wm. G. Gavin. Geo. Shumway, York, PA, 1975. 236 pp., 220 illus.
The 1st detailed study of Civil War belt buckles and cartridge box insignia. Dimensions, materials, details of manufacture, relative and dollar values given.
The Age of Firearms, by Robert Held. Digest Books, Inc., Northfield, IL, 1970. New, fully rev. and corrected ed., paper covers. 192 pp., fully illus. $4.95.
A popular review of firearms since 1475 with accent on their effects on social conditions, and the craft of making functional/artistic arms.
Air Guns, by Eldon G. Wolff. Milwaukee Public Museum, Milwaukee, WI, 1958. 198 pp., illus. Paper, $6.00.
A scholarly and comprehensive treatise, excellent for student and collectors' use, of air gun history. Every form of arm is described, and a list of 350 makers is included.
Air Guns and Air Pistols, by L. Wesley. A. S. Barnes Co., NY, 1964. 210 pp., illus. $5.00.
Latest, enlarged ed. of a standard work.
American Axes, by H. J. Kauffman. Stephen Greene Press, Brattleboro, VT, 1972. 151 pp., illus. $12.50.
A history of American axes and their makers.
American Breech-loading Small Arms: A Description of Late Inventions Including the Gatling Gun and a Chapter on Cartridges, by Bvt. Brig.-Gen. Charles B. Norton, U.S.V., Frontier Press, Arvada, CO, 1974, a facsimile edition. 308 pp., illus., paper covers. $12.50.
A survey of early inventions in the field of breech-loaders, with discussions of the principal systems.
American, British & Continental Pepperbox Firearms, by Jack Dunlap. H. J. Dunlap, Los Altos, CA, 1964. 279 pp., 665 illus. $15.00.
Comprehensive history of production pepperpots from early 18th cent. through the cartridge pepperbox. Variations are covered, with much data of value to the collector.
The American Cartridge, by Charles R. Suydam, Borden Publ. Co., Alhambra, CA, rev. ed., 1973. 184 pp., illus. $8.50.
An illus. study of the rimfire cartridge in the U.S.
American Engraved Powder Horns, by Stephen V. Grancsay. Originally published by The Metropolitan Museum of Art, at NYC, 1945. The 1st reprint publ. by Ray Riling Arms Books Co., Phila., PA, 1965. 96 pp. plus 47 full-page plates. $20.00.
A study based on the J. H. Grenville Gilbert collection of historic, rare and beautiful powder horns. A scholarly work by an eminent authority. Long out of print and offered now in a limited edition of 1000 copies.
American Knives, the First History and Collectors' Guide, by Harold L. Peterson. Scribner's, N.Y.C., 1958. 178 pp., well illus. $6.95.
A timely book to whet the appetite of the ever-growing group of knife collectors.
The American Percussion Revolver, by F. M. Sellers and Sam E. Smith. Museum Restoration Service, Ottawa, Canada, 1970. 200 pp., illus. $15.00.
All inclusive from 1826 to 1870. Over 200 illus., with profuse coverage on lesser-known arms.
American Polearms, 1526-1865, by R. H. Brown. N. Flayderman Co., New Milford, Conn., 1967. 198 pp., 150 plates. $14.50.
Concise history of pikes, spears, and similar weapons used in American military forces through the Civil War.
American Small Arms Research in W.W.II, Vol. I: Hand & Shoulder Weapons, Helmets & Body Armor, ed. by D. B. McLean, Normount Technical Publ., Wickenburg, AZ, 1975. 181 pp., illus. Paper covers. $8.95.
Describes and pictures nearly 300 experimental and developmental rifles, carbines, submachine guns, knives, helmets and armor.
American Socket Bayonets, 1717-1873, by D. B. Webster, Jr. Museum Rest. Service, Ottawa, Can. 1964. 48 pp., 60 illus. paperbound. $1.50.
Concise account of major types, with nomenclature, characteristics, and dimensions. Line drawings.
The American Sword 1775-1945, by H. L. Peterson. Ray Riling Arms Books Co., Phila., PA, 1973. 286 pp. plus 60 pp. of illus. $16.50.
1973 reprint of a survey of swords worn by U.S. uniformed forces, plus the rare "American Silver Mounted Swords." (1700-1815).
Antique Arms Annual, ed. by R. L. Wilson, S. P. Stevens, Texas Gun Coll. Assn., Waco, Texas. 1971. 262 pp., profusely illus. $15.00.
A magnificent work showing hundreds of fine color photographs of rare firearms. Decorated paper covers.
Antique European and American Firearms in the Hermitage Museum, by L. Tarassuk. Arco Pub. Co., NY, 1972. 224 pp., 130 pp. of illus., 54 pp. in full color. $20.00.
Selected from the museum's 2500 firearms dating from the 15th to 19th centuries, including the magnificently decorated Colt rifle and pistols presented by Samuel Colt to Tzars Nicholas 1st and Alexander II.
Antique Pistols, by S. G. Alexander, illus. by Ronald Paton. Arco Publ. Co., New York, 1963. 56 pp., 12 color plates. $15.00.
The large 8-color plates show 14 examples of the pistol-maker's art in England and U.S.A., 1690-1900. Commentary on each by a knowledgeable English collector.
Antique Weapons, A-Z, by Douglas J. Fryer. A & W Books, NY, 1974. 114 pp. illus. $3.98.
A concise survey of collectors' arms, including firearms, edged weapons, polearms, etc., of European and Oriental design, classified by types.
Antique Weapons for Pleasure and Investment, by R. Akehurst. Arco Pub. Co., N.Y., 1969. 174 pp., illus. $5.95.
Reprint of an English book covering an extensive variety of arms, including Japanese and Hindu edged weapons and firearms.
Les Armes Americaines 1870-1871 de las Defense Nationale, by P. Lorain and J. Boudriot. Librarie Pierre Petitot, Paris, France, 1970. French text, 96 pp., illus. $14.50.
Covers all U.S. weapons bought by the French government a century ago.
Armes Blanches Militaires Francaises, by Christian Aries. P. Petitot, Paris, 1968. Unpaginated, paperbound, 11 volumes. $9.50 per vol., $95.00 complete.
Pictorial survey of French military swords, in French text and line drawings in exact detail. The classifications in the various volumes are the author's own and do not follow any specific sequence. The work must be used as a complete set for maximum benefit.
Armour & Weapons, by Charles ffoulkes, Museum Rest. Serv., Ottawa, Ont., Can., 1975. 112 pp., illus. $8.50.
A facsimile of the 1909 London ed. written by one of the leading scholars of arms and armor of his day.
The Armourer and his Craft, by Charles ffoulkes. Frederick Ungar Publ. Co., N.Y., 1967. 199 pp., illus. $18.50.
Standard British reference on body armor, 11th-16th cent.; covering notable makers, construction, decoration, and use. 1st ed. 1912, now reprinted.
Armourers Marks, by D. S. H. Gyngell. Thorsons, Ltd., England, 1959. 131 pp., illus. $13.50.
Some of the marks of armourers, swordsmiths and gunsmiths of almost every foreign country.
Arms Archives, by H. B. Lockhoven, International Small Arms Publ., Cologne, W. Germany, 1969. Unpaginated but coded. Illus. English and German text, loose-leaf format. Available in 4 series; "A" Handguns, "B" Automatic Weapons, "C" Longarms, "D" Antique Arms. Each series in 4 installments at $10 per installment. Binders for each series $5.50.
A major breakthrough in arms literature. Scaled photographs of guns and their cartridges, fully described. Only 1st installment now available in series "D".
Arms and Armor Annual, Volume I, edited by Robert Held, Digest Books, Inc., Northfield, IL, 1973. 320 pp., illus., paper covers. $9.95; cloth $19.95.
Thirty outstanding articles by the leading arms and armor historians of the world.
Arms and Armor, by Vesey Norman. Putnam's N.Y.C., 1964. 128 pp., 129 illus. $3.98.
Authoritative, compact coverage of European armor and weapons prior to the age of firearms. Excellent illus., many in color.
Arms & Armor from the Atelier of Ernst Schmidt, Munich, by E. Andrew Mowbray, compiler. Mowbray Co., Providence, R.I., 1967. 168 pp., well illus. $11.95.
Principally a compilation of plates from the extremely rare Schmidt catalog displaying the famous replicas of medieval armor and weapons made in his shop from about 1870 to 1930. Limited edition.
Arms and Armor in Colonial America, 1526-1783, by H. L. Peterson. Crown, New York, reprint ed., 1964. 350 pp., illus. $4.98.
Well-organized account of arms and equipment used in America's colonization and exploration, through the Revolutionary period.
Arms and Armour, by Frederick Wilkinson, A. & C. Black Ltd., London. Reprint of 1969, 63 pp., well illus. $2.95.
A concise work for young readers describing edged weapons, polearms, armor, etc., mainly of European origin.
Arms and Armour, 9th to 17th Century, by Paul Martin, C. E. Tuttle Co., Rutland, Vt., 1968. 298 pp., well illus. $15.00.
Beautiful illustrations and authoritative text on armor and accessories from the time of Charlemagne to the firearms era.
Arms Collection of Colonel Colt, by R. L. Wilson. Herb Glass, Bullville, N.Y., 1964. 132 pp., 73 illus. Lim. deluxe ed., $16.50; trade ed., $6.50.
Samuel Colt's personal collection is well-described and photographed, plus new technical data on Colt's arms and life. 51 Colt guns and other revolving U.S. and European arms are included.
Arms and Equipment of the Civil War, by Jack Coggins, Doubleday & Co., Inc, NY, 1962. 160 pp., $5.95.
Tools of war of the blue and the grey. Infantry, cavalry, artillery, and navy: guide to equipment, clothing, organization, and weapons. Over 500 illus.
Arms Makers of Maryland, by Daniel D. Hartzler, George Shumway, York, PA, 1975. 200 pp., illus. $27.50.
A thorough study of the gunsmiths of Maryland who worked during the late 18th and early 19th centuries.
Arms Making In the Connecticut Valley, by F. J. Deyrup. George Shumway Publ., York, Pa., 1970. Reprint of the noted work originally publ. in 1948 by Smith College. 290 pp., line maps, $10.00.
A scholarly regional study of the economic development of the small arms industry 1798-1870. With statistical appendices, notes, bibliography.
Arms of the World—1911, ed. by Joseph J. Schroeder, Jr., Digest Books, Inc., Northfield, IL, 1972, 420 pp., profusely illus. $5.95.
Reprint of the Adolph Frank ALFA 21 catalog of 1911 in 4 languages—English, German, French, Spanish.
Artillery and Ammunition of the Civil War, by Warren Ripley. Van Nostrand Reinhold Co., New York, N.Y., 1st ed., 1970. 384 pp., well illus. with 662 black and white photos and line drawings. $22.50.
A fine survey covering both Union and Confederate cannon and projectiles, as well as those imported.
Artillery of the United States Land Service. Vol. I, Field Artillery 1848-1865, comp. by D. E. Lutz, Antique Ordnance Artificers, Jackson, MI, 1970. 64 pp. Paper, $5.00.
First of series containing drawings of artillery used during the Civil War. Limited ed., each copy numbered.
Artillery Through the Ages, by A. Manucy, Normount Armament Co., Wickenburg, AZ, 1971. 92 pp., illus. Paper, $2.50
A short history of cannon, emphasizing types used in America.
Arts of the Japanese Swords, by B. W. Robinson. Chas. E. Tuttle Co., Rutland, Vt., 1961. 110 pp. of descriptive text with illus., plus 100 full page plates, some in full color. $17.50.
An authoritative work, divided into 2 parts—the first on blades, tracing their history to the present day; the second on mounts and fittings. It includes forging processes; accounts of the important schools of swordsmiths; techniques employed, plus a useful appendix on care and cleaning.
Badges & Emblems of the British Forces 1940, Arms and Armour Press, London, 1968. 64 pp. Paper, $3.00.
Reprint of a comprehensive guide to badges and emblems worn by all British forces in 1940, including Welfare, Aux. Services, Nursing Units, etc. Over 350 illus.
Ballard Rifles in the H. J. Nunnemacher Coll., by Eldon G. Wolff. Milwaukee Public Museum, Milwaukee, Wisc., 2nd ed. 1961. Paper, 77 p. plus 4 pp. of charts and 27 plates. $3.50.
A thoroughly authoritative work on all phases of the famous rifles, their parts, patent and manufacturing history.
The Bannerman Catalogue 1903, Francis Bannerman Sons, New York, N.Y. Reprint released in 1960. 116 pp., well illus., $3.50.
A reprint in facsimile of this dealer's catalog of military goods of all descriptions, including weapons and equipment.
The Bannerman Catalog 1965, Francis Bannerman Sons, Blue Point, N.Y. The 100th anniversary ed., 1966. 264 pp., well illus. $5.00.
Latest dealer catalog of nostalgic interest on military and collector's items of all sorts.
Basic Documents on U.S. Marital Arms, commentary by Col. B. R. Lewis, reissue by Ray Riling, Phila., Pa., 1956 and 1960.
Rifle Musket Model 1855. The first issue rifle of musket caliber, a muzzle loader equipped with the Maynard Primer, 32 pp. $2.50.
Rifle Musket Model 1863. The Typical Union muzzle-loader of the Civil War, 26 pp. $1.75.

Breech-Loading Rifle Musket Model 1866. The first of our 50 caliber breechloading rifles, 12 pp. $1.75.

Remington Navy Rifle Model 1870. A commercial type breech-loader made at Springfield, 16 pp. $1.75.

Lee Straight Pull Navy Rifle Model 1895. A magazine cartridge arm of 6mm caliber. 23 pp. $3.00.

Breech-Loading Rifle Musket Model 1868. The first 50-70 designed as such. 20 pp. $1.75.

Peabody Breech-Loading Arms (five models)—27 pp. $2.75.

Ward-Burton Rifle Musket 1871—16 pp. $2.50.

Springfield Rifle, Carbine & Army Revolvers (cal. 45) model 1873 including Colt and Smith & Wesson hand arms. 52 pp. $3.00.

U.S. Magazine Rifle and Carbine (cal. 30) Model 1892 (the Krag Rifle) 36 pp. $2.50.

Bayonets Illustrated, by Bert Walsh, Bashall Eaves, Ireland, 1970. 49 pp., illus. $5.00.

162 detailed line drawings of bayonets from many countries and periods.

Bayonet Markings: A Guide for Collectors, by I. D. Davidson, I. D. Davidson, Brighton, England, 1973. 21 pp., illus., paper covers. $5.00.

A listing of nearly 150 sets of marks found on bayonets of various countries.

The Bedford County Rifle and its Makers, by Calvin Hetrick, George Shumway, York, PA, 1973. 39 pp., illus., paper covers. $4.00.

Reprint of Hetrick's study of the graceful and distinctive muzzle-loading rifles made in Bedford County. PA.

Blades and Barrels, by H. Gordon Frost. Walloon Press, El Paso, TX, 1972. 298 pp., illus. $16.95.

The first full-scale study about man's attempts to combine an edged weapon with a firearm.

Blunderbusses, by D. R. Baxter. Stackpole Books, Harrisburg, Pa., 1970. 80 pp., 60 illus. $4.95.

Traces blunderbuss development from the 16th century, covering basic designs, firing systems, the double blunderbuss and revolving pepperbox design.

The Book of Colt Engraving, by R. L. Wilson, Wallace Beinfeld Publ., Inc., Studio City, CA, 1974. 422 pp., illus. $29.95.

A precise and accurate history of Colt engraving. Presents photos of more than 700 guns, many in full color.

The Book of Colt Firearms, by R. Q. Sutherland and R. L. Wilson, Privately printed, Kansas City, Mo., 1971. 604 pp. 9x12", profusely illus. $50.00.

This exhaustive large work, highly informative and scholarly, contains 40 color plates showing 420 Colt firearms, plus 1258 black and white photographs.

The Book of the Continental Soldier, by Harold L. Peterson. Stackpole Books, Harrisburg, Pa, 1968. 287 pp., of large format profusely illus. with halftone, line, and including art work by H. Charles McBarron, Jr., Clyde A. Risley and Peter Copeland, $12.95.

A thorough and commendable work in every pertinent aspect. Covers in satisfying detail every facet of the soldier's existence.

The Book of Winchester Engraving, by R. L. Wilson, Wallace Beinfeld Publ., Inc. Studio City, CA, 1975. Over 400 pp., illus. $39.95.

Over 700 photos (many in full color) of the great engraved Winchesters in the world.

Bowie Knives, by R. Abels. Pub. by the author, NYC, 1960. 48 pp. profusely illus. Paper covers. $2.00.

A booklet showing knives, tomahawks, related trade cards and advertisements.

Bowie Knives From the Collections of Robert Abels and the Ohio Historical Society, by Wm. G. Keener and D. A. Hutslar. The Ohio Historical Society, 1962. 124 pp., profusely illus. Paper covers. $4.50.

Limited ed. of an original Museum Catalog of a special exhibit by the Ohio Historical Society.

Brass Spikes & Horsehair Plumes: A Study of U.S. Army Dress Helmets, 1872-1903, by Gordon Chappell, Arizona Pioneers Hist. Soc., Tucson, Ariz. 1966. 50 pp., illus. Paper covers. $3.00.

Historical monograph on military headgear of the period.

The Breech-Loader in the Service, 1816-1917, by Claud E. Fuller, N. Flayderman, New Milford, Conn., 1965. 381 pp., illus. $14.50.

Revised ed. of a 1933 historical reference on U.S. standard and experimental military shoulder arms. Much patent data, drawings, and photographs of the arms.

A voluminous work that covers handloading—and other things—in great detail. Replete with data for all cartridge forms.

British and American Flintlocks, by Fred. Wilkinson. Country Life Books, London, 1971. 64 pp., illus. $2.95.

Historical and technical aspects of flintlock firearms, in military and civilian use.

British and American Infantry Weapons of World War II, by A. J. Barker. 1st ed., 1969, Arco Publishing Co., New York, N.Y. 76 pp., illus., $3.50.

A British officer's survey that includes numerous specialized weapons, all are illustrated and described.

British Cut and Thrust Weapons, by John Wilkinson-Latham. Charles E. Tuttle Co., VT, 1971. 112 pp., illus. $7.50.

Well-illustrated study tracing the development of edged weapons and their adoption by the British armed forces. Describes in detail swords of cavalry and mounted troops, infantry, general officers, yeomanry, militia, the navy and air force.

British Military Bayonets from 1700 to 1945, by R. J. W. Latham. Arco Publ. Co., N.Y.C., 1969. 94 pp., ilus. $8.50.

History and identification catalog of British bayonets, with fine illustrations, marks, dimensions, and equipment of various British army units.

British Military Firearms 1650-1850, by H. L. Blackmore. Arco Publ. Co. Inc., New York, 1962. 296 pp. and 83 plates of photographs, line drawings, appendices and index. $10.00.

This excellent work admirably and authoritatively covers the subject in every detail. Highly recommended.

British Military Longarms 1715-1815, by D. W. Bailey, Stackpole Books, Harrisburg, PA, 1971. 80 pp., $4.95.

The Regulation service longarms of the British Army and Navy during a century of conflict in Europe, America and India, are fully described and illus.

British Military Longarms 1815-1865, by D. W. Bailey. Stackpole Books, Harrisburg, PA, 1972. 79 pp., illus. $4.95.

Concise account, covering muskets, carbines, rifles and their markings.

British Military Swords, From 1800 to the Present Day, by J. W. Latham, Crown Publishers, NY, 1967, 91 pp., illus. $3.95.

Survey of British swords used by various branches of the Army, with data on their manufacture, specifications, and procurement.

British Pistols and Guns, 1640-1940, by Ian Glendenning. Arco Publ. Co., NY, 1967. 194 pp., photos and drawings. $7.50.

Historical review of British firearms, with much data and illustration of furniture and decoration of fine weapons.

British Smooth-Bore Artillery, by Maj.-Gen. B. P. Hughes. Stackpole Books, Harrisburg, PA, 1969. 144 pp., illus. $14.95.

On the muzzle-loading artillery of the 18th and 19th centuries, covering dimensions, ammunition, and application.

The British Soldier's Firearm, 1850-1864, by C. H. Roads. Herbert Jenkins, London, 1964. 332 pp., illus. $14.50.

Detailed account of development of British military arms at the acme of the muzzle-loading period. All models in use are covered, as well as ammunition.

The Canadian Bayonet, by R. B. Manarey, Century Press, Alberta, Can. 1970. 51 pp. $5.00.

Illustrated history of the Canadian bayonet.

The Canadian Gunsmiths 1608-1900, by S. James Gooding. Museum Restoration Service, Canada, 1962. 322 pp., illus. $17.50.

Comprehensive survey of the gunmakers of Canada and the products of their skill, from early settlement to the age of the breech-loader.

Cartridge Headstamp Guide, by H. P. White and B. D. Munhall. H. P. White Laboratory, Bel Air, MD, 1963. 263 pp., illus. $10.00.

An important reference on headstamping of small arms ammo, by manufacturers in many countries. Clear illus. of 1936 headstamps of every type.

Cartridges for Collectors, by Fred A. Datig. Borden Publishing Co., Alhambra, Calif, Vol. I (Centerfire), 1958; Vol. II (Rimfire and Misc.) Types, 1963; Vol. III (Additional Rimfire, Centerfire, and Plastic,) 1967. Each of the three volumes 176 pp., well illus. and each priced at $7.50.

Vol. III supplements the first two books and presents 300 additional specimens. All illus. are shown in full-scale line drawings.

Cast Iron Toy Pistols 1870-1940, by Charles W. Best, Rocky Mountain Arms & Antiques, Englewood, CO, 1973. 217 pp., illus. $15.00.

Provides photographs and descriptions of most of the iron toy pistols made, plus values and rarity guides.

Cavalry Equipment 1874, reprint of *U.S. Ordnance Memoranda No. 18* by Francis Bannerman Sons, Blue Point, NY, 1969. 119 pp., 12 plates. $6.50.

An officers' report on details of equipment issued to U.S. cavalry units.

Civil War Carbines, by A. F. Lustyik. World Wide Gun Report, Inc., Aledo, ILL, 1962. 63 pp., illus. paper covers, $2.00.

Accurate, interesting summary of most carbines of the Civil War period, in booklet form, with numerous good illus.

Classic Bowie Knives, by Robert Abels. R. Abels, Inc., NY, 1967. 97 pp., illus. with numerous fine examples of the subject. $7.50.

A nostalgic story of the famous blades, with trade advertisements on them, and photos of users.

The Collecting of Guns, ed. by Jas. E. Serven. Stackpole Books, Harrisburg, PA, 1964. 272 pp., illus. $5.95.

A new and massive compendium of gun lore for serious collectors by recognized experts. Separate chapters cover major categories and aspects of collecting. Over 600 firearms illus. Handsomely designed, deluxe binding in slip case.

Collector's Guide to Luger Values 1972-73 Edition, by Michael Reese. Pelican Pub. Co., Gretna, LA, 1972. 10 pp., paper covers. $1.00.

Collector's guide to top prices.

The Collector's Handbook of U.S. Cartridge Revolvers, 1856 to 1899, by W. Barlow Fors, Adams Press, Chicago, IL, 1973. 96 pp., illus. $6.00.

Concise coverage of brand names, patent listings, makers' history, and essentials of collecting.

Collector's Illustrated Encyclopedia of the American Revolution, by Geo. C. Neumann and Frank J. Kravic, Stackpole Books, Harrisburg, PA, 1975. 288 pp., illus. $17.95.

Over 1,000 illus. show over 2,300 artifacts of the revolutionary period—from accoutrements to writing implements—with explanatory text for each.

A Collector's Pictorial Book of Bayonets, by F. J. Stephens, Stackpole Books, Harrisburg, PA, 1971. 127 pp., illus. $5.95.

Instant identification of bayonet types, plus their history and use.

Colt Commemorative Firearms, by R. L. Wilson, Robert E. P. Cherry, Geneseo, IL, 2nd ed., revised, 1973. 126 pp., illus. Deluxe edition $10.00. Paper covers $5.00.

A valuable guide to the collector of Colt commemorative firearms. Lists all models to date.

Colt Firearms Catalog July, 1932, a reprint in facsimile, by Frontier Press, Arvada, CO, 1973. 40 pp., illus., paper covers. $1.75.

All of the then current revolvers and automatic pistols.

Colt Firearms from 1836, by James E. Serven. New 7th ed. Foundation Press, La Habra, CA, 1973. 398 pp., illus. $19.95.

Excellent survey of the Colt company and its products. Updated with new SAA production chart and commemorative list.

Colt Tips, by E. Dixon Larson. Pioneer Press, Union City, TN, 1972. 140 pp., illus. Paper covers. $3.95.

Comprehensive, discriminating facts about Colt models from 1836 to 1898.

Colt's Variations of the Old Model Pocket Pistol, 1848 to 1872, by P. L. Shumaker. Borden Publishing Co., Alhambra, CA 1966, a reprint of the 1957 edition. 150 pp., illus. $6.00.

A useful tool for the Colt specialist and a welcome return of a popular source of information that had been long out-of-print.

Confederate Handguns, by Wm. A. Albaugh III. Hugh Benet Jr., and Edw. N. Simmons. Geo. Shumway, York, PA, 1963. 272 pp., 125 illus. $9.00.

Every known true Confederate pistol and revolver is described and illus., with the story of its maker and procurement by the C.S.A. Much new information includes listing of C. W. makers and dealers, information on replicas and fakes. Indispensable to the collector and student of these arms and their period.

Custer Battle Guns, by John S. du Mont, The Old Army Press, Ft. Collins, CO, 1974. 113 pp., illus. $8.95.

Complete story of the guns at the Little Big Horn.

The Custom Knife . . . II, by John D. Bates, Jr. and James H. Schippers, Jr., The Custom Knife Press, Memphis, TN, 1974. 112 pp., illus. $12.00.

The book of pocket knives and folding hunters. A guide to the 20th century makers' art.

Deanes' Manual of the History and Science of Fire-arms, by J. Deane. Standard Publications, Huntington, WV, 1946 facsimile reprint of the rare English original of 1858. 291 pp., three folding plates. $6.00.

A history of firearms, plus design and manufacture of military and sporting arms.

Decoy Collector's Guide 1963-1964-1965, ed. by H. D. Sorenson, Burlington, IA, 1971. Irregular pagination, illus., $15.00.

This volume includes all of the 12 booklets originally published as quarterlies.

Decoy Collector's Guide 1966-67 Annual, ed. by H. D. Sorenson, Burlington, IA, 1966. 125 pp., illus. $5.00.

Well-illustrated articles on American decoys.

Decoy Collector's Guide, 1968, ed. by H. D. Sorenson, 1967, Burlington, IA 128 pp, 75 photos. Spiral bound. $5.00.

History, decoy patents, carving, collecting, etc.

Digest of Patents Relating to Breech-Loading and Magazine Small Arms (1836-1873), by V. D. Stockbridge, WA, 1874. Reprinted 1963 by E. N. Flayderman, Greenwich, Conn. 180 pp., 880 illus. $12.50.
An exhaustive compendium of patent documents on firearms, indexed and classified by breech mechanism types, valuable reference for students and collectors.

Dutch Muskets & Pistols, by J. B. Kist, J. P. Puype, and W. Van Der Mark, George Shumway, York, PA, 1974. 176 pp., illus. $20.00.
An illus. history of 17th Century gunmaking in the Low Countries.

Early Firearms of Great Britain and Ireland from the Collection of Clay P. Bedford. The Metropolitan Museum of Art, NY, 1971. 187 pp., illus. $17.50.
Authoritative account of an exceptional body of historic firearms, and a detailed survey of three centuries of gunmaking.

Early Indian Trade Guns—1625 to 1775, by T. M. Hamilton. Museum of the Great Plains, Lawton, Okla. 1969. 34 pp., well illus., paper covers. $3.50.
Detailed descriptions of subject arms, compiled from early records and from the study of remnants found in Indian country.

Early Japanese Sword Guards, by Masayuki Sasano. Japan Pub. Trading Co., San Francisco, CA, 1972. 256 pp., illus. $12.50.
220 of the finest open-work sword guards, dating from early periods and representing most of the major schools.

Early Loading Tools and Bullet Molds, by R. H. Chamberlain. The Farm Tribune, Porterville, GA, 1971. 75 pp., illus. Paper covers, $3.00.
An excellent aid to collectors.

Early Percussion Firearms, by Lewis Winant, Wm. Morrow & Co., Inc., N.Y.C., 1959. 292 pp., illus. $2.98.
A history of early percussion firearms ignition—from Forsyth to Winchester 44-40, from flintlocks of the 18th century to centerfires. Over 230 illus. of firearms, parts, patents, and cartridges—from some of the finest collections here and abroad.

Edged Weaponry of the Third Reich, by Maj. John R. Angolia, R. James Bender Publ. Co., Mountain View, CA, 1974. 256 pp., illus. $12.95.
A concise guide to all the edged weapons of Hitler's Germany.

Edged Weapons of the Third Reich 1933-1945, by Frederick J. Stephens, Almark Publishing Co., London, England, 1972. 128 pp., illus., paper covers. $6.50.
A highly detailed and profusely illustrated guide for collectors of Nazi period edged weapons.

The Encyclopedia of Military History, by R. Ernest and Trevor N. Dupuy. Harper & Row, New York, NY, 1970. 1st ed., 1406 pp., well illus., in line and halftone. $20.00.
This massive single volume covers the subject from 3500 B.C. to the present time. A complete reference guide to the world's military history; narration of war and combat, tactics, strategy and weaponry. Over 250 maps, illus. of weapons, fortifications, etc.

English, Irish and Scottish Firearms, by A. Merwyn Carey. Arco Publishing Co., Inc., NY, 1967. A reprint. 121 pp., illus. in line and halftone. $6.50.
Out-of-print since 1954, this work covers the subject from the middle of the 16th century to the end of the 19th.

English Pistols & Revolvers, by J. N. George. Arco Publ. Co., Inc., N.Y.C., 1962, 256 pp., 28 plates, $12.00.
The 2nd reprinting of a notable work first publ. in 1938. Treats of the historical development and design of English hand firearms from the 17th cent. to the present. A much better book than the former reprint, particularly as to clarity of the tipped-in plates.

English Sporting Guns and Accessories, by Macdonald Hastings. Ward Lock & Co., London. 1st ed., 1969. 96 pp., well illus. $4.00.
A delightful monograph on shotguns and accessory equipment for hunting from 1800 to the advent of the breech loader, including historic arms and ammunition.

Ethan Allen, Gunmaker, by Harold R. Mouillesseaux, Museum Rest. Serv., Ottawa, Ont., Can., 1973. 170 pp., illus. $19.95.
A complete history of Ethan Allen, his arms and his companies.

European & American Arms, by Claude Blair, Batsford, London, and Crown Publ., N.Y.C., 1962, 192 pp., 9"x12". Profusely and magnificently illus. $6.95.
A complete visual encyclopedia on all sorts of arms of Europe and America with over 600 photographs of pieces from nearly all the major collections of Western Europe, America, and Russia, from about 1100 to 1850. A splendid text describes historical and technical developments.

European Armour in the Tower of London, by A. R. Dufty. H. M. Stationery Office, London, England, 1968. 17 pp. text, 164 plates, $12.60.
Pictorial record of almost 400 pieces of armor, helmets, and accouterments in the famous Tower of London collection.

European Arms & Armour, by Chas. H. Ashdown, Brussel & Brussel, NY, 1967. A reprint, 384 pp., illus. with 42 plates and 450 drawings. $5.95.
Historical survey of body armor up to the era of gunpowder, with some coverage on weapons and early firearms,

European Edged Weapons, by Terence Wise, Almark Publ. Co., Ltd, London, England, 1974. 96 pp., illus. Paper covers. $4.94. Hardbound. $7.25.
The development of swords, axes, bayonets, and other edged weapons in Europe.

Famous Guns from the Smithsonian Collection, by H. W. Bowman. Arco. Publ. Co., Inc., NY, 1967. 112 pp., illus. $3.50.
The finest of the "Famous Guns" series.

Famous Guns from the Winchester Collection, by H. W. Bowman. Arco Publ. Co., NYC, 1958 and later. 144 pp., illus. $3.50.
The gems of the hand and shoulder arms in the great collection at New Haven, CT.

Field Artillery Projectiles of the Civil War, 1861-1865, by S. C. Kerksis & T. S. Dickey, Phoenix Press, Kennesaw, GA, 4th printing, 1973. 307 pp., illus. $22.50.
Photographs, dimensions, and descriptions of 207 types of projectiles, plus other pertinent data.

'51 Colt Navies, by N. L. Swayze. Gun Hill Publ. Co., Yazoo City, MS, 1967. 243 pp., well illus. $15.00.
The first major effort devoting its entire space to the 1851 Colt Navy revolver. There are 198 photos of models, sub-models, variations, parts, markings, documentary material, etc. Fully indexed.

Firearms Curiosa, by Lewis Winant, Ray Riling, Philadelphia, PA, 2nd and deluxe reissue 1961, 281 pp., well illus. $5.00.
Reissue publ. by Bonanza Books, N.Y.C., 1965. $2.98.
An important work for those with an interest in odd, distinctive and unusual forms and firing.

The Firearms Dictionary, by R. A. Steindler. Stackpole Books, Harrisburg, PA, 1970. 256 pp., nearly 200 illus. $7.95.
A super single-source reference to more than 1800 English and Foreign gun-related words, phrases and nomenclature, etc. Highly useful to all armsmen—collectors, shooters, hunters, etc.

Firearms Past & Present, by Jaroslav Lugs, Grenville Publ. Co., Ltd., London, England, 1973. In two volumes, Vol. 1, text, 716 pp.; Vol. 2, plates, 429 pp. In slipcase. $50.00.
The English ed. of this extremely important work on firearm systems and their histories.

Flintlock Guns and Rifles, by F. Wilkinson, Stackpole Books, Harrisburg, PA, 1971. 80 pp., $4.95.
Illus. reference guide for 1650-1850 period showing makers, mechanisms and users.

The Flintlock, Its Origin and Development, by Torsten Lenk; J. T. Hayward, Editor, Holland Press, London, 1964. 192 pp., 134 illus. $30.00.
First English-text version of the 1939 Swedish work termed "the most important book on the subject." Original illus. are reproduced, and a new index and bibliography complete this valuable book.

Flintlock Pistols, by F. Wilkinson. Stackpole Books, Harrisburg, PA, 1968. 75 pp., illus. $4.95.
Illustrated reference guide by a British authority, covering 17th-19th century flintlock pistols.

Forsyth & Co.—Patent Gunmakers, by W. Keith Neal and D. H. L. Back. G. Bell & Sons, London, 1st ed., 1969, 280 pp., well illus. $12.95.
An excellent study of the invention and development of the percussion system by the Rev. Alexander Forsyth in the early 19th century. All Forsyth types are covered, plus a diary of events from 1768 to 1852.

.45-70 Rifles, by J. Behn, Rutgers Book Center, Highland Park, NJ, 1972. New ed., 150 pp., illus. $5.95.
Covers the official U.S. Army small arms cartridge and the weapons for its use.

The French Army in America, by E. P. Hamilton. Museum Restoration Service, Ottawa, 1967. 108 pp., illus. $3.00.
Concise historical coverage, illus. with contemporary documents and manual-of-arms plates. Text in English and French. Paper wrappers.

French Pistols and Sporting Guns, by A. N. Kennard. Transatlantic Arts, Inc., Levittown, NY, 1972. 63 pp., illus. $2.95.
Traces the technical evolution of French pistols and sporting guns from matchlock to breechloader.

French Military Weapons, 1717-1938, by James E. Hicks. N. Flayderman & Co., New Milford, CT, 1964. 281 pp., profusely illus. $9.50.
A valuable reference work, first publ. 1938 as *Notes on French Ordnance,* this rev. ed. covers hand, shoulder, and edged weapons, ammunition and artillery, with history of various systems.

The Fuller Collection of American Firearms, by H. L. Peterson. Eastern National Park & Monument Assn., 1967. 63 pp., illus. $2.50.
Illustrated catalog of principal military shoulder arms in the collection. Decorated paper wrappers.

The Gatling Gun, by Paul Wahl & D. R. Toppel. Arco Publ., N.Y.C., 1971. 168 pp., illus. $5.95.
History of the famed rapid-fire weapon used by many of the world's armies and navies from 1861.

German Belt Buckles 1919-1945, by Thomas Reid, The Montross Press, Houston, TX, 1974. 81 pp., illus., paper covers. $6.95.
Describes and pictures 170 buckles. Lists names of makers.

German Mauser Rifle—Model of 1898, by J. E. Coombes and J. L. Aney. A reprint in paper covers by Francis Bannerman Sons, New York, NY, of their 1921 publication. 20 pp., well illus. $1.50.
Data on the subject weapon and its W. W. I development. Bayonets and ammunition are also described and illus.

German 7.9mm Military Ammunition, 1888-1945, by Daniel Kent, Ann Arbor, MI, 1973. 158 pp., illus. $12.50.
An absorbing narrative about a single rifle and machine gun cartridge, its military and political history.

A Glossary of the Construction, Decoration and Use of Arms and Armor in all Countries and in all Times, by Geo. C. Stone, Jack Brussel, NY, 2nd reprint, 1966, 694 pp., illus. $10.98.
The outstanding work on its subject, authoritative and accurate in detail. The major portion is on oriental arms.

The Great Guns, by H. L. Peterson and Robt. Elman. Grosset & Dunlap, NY, 1972. $14.95.
Basic and general history with 70 full color illustrations and 140 photos of some of the finest guns from American collections. A well written text.

Great Weapons of World War I, by Com. G. Dooly, Walker & Co., NY, 1969, 340 pp., illus. $14.50.
Describes all the important weapons and system developments used during WWI.

The Gun and its Development, by W. W. Greener. Bonanza Books, NY, 1967. A reprint. 804 pp., profusely illus. $6.95.
A facsimile of the famous 9th edition of 1910. Covers history and development of arms in general with emphasis on shotguns.

Gun Collector's Digest, edited by Jos. J. Schroeder, Jr. Digest Books, Inc., Northfield, IL, 1974. 320 pp., illus. Paper covers. $6.95.
Articles on guns as an investment; rating gun condition; display and security; gun collecting and the law; building a collector's library; plus features on all sorts of collectors guns.

The Gun Collector's Fact Book, by Louis W. Steinwedel, Arco Publ. Co., NY, 1975. 256 pp., illus. Paper covers, $4.95. Cloth, $7.95.
An illus. introduction to "the gentle art of gun collecting"—where and how to buy antique guns, points that affect their value, and hints on restoration.

The Gun Collector's Handbook of Values 1975-1976, by C. E. Chapel, Coward, McCann & Geoghegan, Inc., NY, 1975. 462 pp., illus. $17.50.
Eleventh rev. ed. of the best-known price reference for collectors. Includes new chapters on Winchester and Smith & Wesson guns.

The Gun Digest Book of Knives, by B. R. Hughes and Jack Lewis. Digest Books, Inc. Northfield, IL, 1973. 288 pp., illus. Paper covers. $6.95.
Authoritative, in-depth study. How to collect, buy and care for knives. Illus. catalog section describes best blades from custom cutlers and knife factories.

Gun Digest Book of Modern Gun Values, by Dean A. Grennell & Jack Lewis, DBI Books, Inc., Northfield, IL, 1975. 288 pp., illus. $7.95.
Invaluable guide for buying, selling, trading or identifying guns—handguns, rifles and shotguns are covered in separate sections. Feature articles relate to collecting and values.

Gunmakers of Indiana, by A. W. Lindert. Publ. by the author, Homewood. IL, 1968, 3rd ed. 284 pp., illus. Large format. $15.00.
An extensive and historical treatment, illus. with old photographs and drawings.

Guns & Ammo Guidebook to Knives & Edged Weapons, ed. by Jim Woods, Petersen Publ. Co., Los Angeles, CA, 1974. 192 pp., illus. Paper covers. $4.95.
A review of custom cutlers, new knifemakers and old masters. Collecting of swords, bayonets, primitive and unusual edged weapons.

Guns and Gun Collecting, by De Witt Bailey; et al. Octopus Books, London, Eng., 1972. 128 pp., illus. $5.95.
A new look at the world of firearms, including not only the historical aspects but hunting and sporting guns and 19th and 20th century weapons of war. Nearly 180 photos, 78 in full color.

Guns Through the Ages, by Geoffrey Boothroyd. Sterling Publ. Co., N.Y.C., 1962, 192 pp., illus. $1.69.
A detailed illustrated history of small arms from the invention of gunpowder to today. Covers ignition methods, proof marks, fakes, ammo, etc. Bibliography.

The Gunsmiths of Canada, by S. James Gooding, Museum Rest. Serv., Ottawa, Ont., Can., 1974. 32 pp., illus. Paper covers. $2.00.
Names, dates and locations for over 800 gunsmiths, plus bibliography.

Gunsmiths of Ohio—18th & 19th Centuries: Vol. I, Biographical Data, by Donald A. Hutslar, George Shumway, York, PA, 1973. 444 pp., illus. $29.50.
An important source book, full of information about the old-time gunsmiths of Ohio.

Hall System Military Firearms and Conversions in the Museum Collection. Veteran Association of the First Corps of Cadets Museum, Boston, MA, 1973. 20 pp., illus. Paper covers. $1.50
Illustrates and describes various models, including several Confederate conversions.

Hall's Breechloaders, by R. T. Huntington, Geo. Shumway, Publ. 1972. 369 pp., illus. $15.00. Paper, $12.00.
Definitive treatise on John H. Hall and his inspectors. Shows all known models of the Hall rifle, appurtenances and pistol.

Handbook of Identification Marks on Canadian Arms, by R. Barrie Manarey, Century Press, Alberta, Can., 1973. 82 pp., illus. Paper covers. $6.00.
Lists over 1000 translations of codes and initials which appear on Canadian arms.

Handbuch Der Waffenkunde, by Wendelin Boeheim. Akademische D. U. V., Graz, Austria, 1966, 694 pp., illus. $14.00.
One of the famous works of 1890—long out-of-print. Now in a new printing, German text. Historical weapons and armor from the Middle Ages through the 18th century.

Handfeuerwaffen, by J. Lugs, Deutscher Militarverlag, Berlin, 1956. 2 Vol., 315 pp., illus. German text, $40.00.
Noted reference on small arms and their development in many nations. All types of weapons are listed described, and illustrated, with data on manufacturers.

Die Handfeuerwaffen, by Rudolf Schmidt, Vienna, Austria, 1968, Vol. I, text 225 pp., Vol. II, 76 plates. $20.00.
Reprint of an important 1875 German reference work on military small arms, much prized by knowledgeable collectors. The fine color plates in Vol. II show detailed and exploded views of many longarms and handguns.

Handfeuerwaffen System Vetterli, by Hugo Schneider; et al. Stocker-Schmid, A. G. Dietikon-Zurich, Switzerland, 1972. 143 pp., illus. $26.00.
Describes and illustrates the many models of Vetterli rifles and carbines, the bayonets and ammunition used with them. Many large clear illustrations. German text.

Heavy Artillery Projectiles of the Civil War 1861-1865, by S. C. Kerksis & T. S. Dickey. Phoenix Press, Kennesaw, GA, 1972. 277 pp., illus. $19.50. Privately pub., limited ed.
Covers use of the projectiles used by both combatants.

Hints to Riflemen, by H. W. S. Cleveland. Distributor, Robert Halter, New Hope, PA, 286 pp., illustrated. $10.00.
A reprint of the original 1864 edition, to which *Practical Directions for the use of the Rifle* has been added.

History and Collecting Case Pocket Knives, by D. P. Ferguson. D. P. Ferguson, Fairborn, OH, 1970. 24 pp., illus., paper, $1.00.
Handbook on knives made by W. R. Case & Sons Cutlery Co.

A History of Body Armor, by H. L. Peterson, Charles Scribner's Sons, NY, 1968. 64 pp., illus. $4.95.
From the fur and leather armor of primitive man to the nylon body armor and steel helmet of today.

A History of Firearms, by W. Y. Carman. Routledge & Kegan Paul Ltd., London, England, 1955. 207 pp., illus. $4.50.
A concise coverage, from earliest times to 1914, with emphasis on artillery.

A History of Firearms, by H. L. Peterson. Chas. Scribner's Sons, N.Y.C., 1961. 57 pp., profusely illus. $5.95.
From the origin of firearms through each ignition form and improvement to the M-14. Drawings by Daniel D. Feaser.

A History of Spanish Firearms, by James D. Lavin. Arco Co., NY, 1965. 304 pp., illus. $9.95.
This history, beginning with the recorded appearance of gunpowder in Spain, traces the development of hand firearms through their golden age—the eighteenth century—to the death in 1825 of Isidro Soler. Copious reproductions of short and long arms, list of gun makers and their "marks" a glossary, bibliography and index are included.

The History of Winchester Firearms 1866-1966, ed. by T. E. Hall and P. Kuhlhoff, Winchester-Western Press, New Haven, CT, 1966. 159 pp., illus. $10.00.
Called the collector's item of the century, this 3rd ed. of Geo. R. Watrous' work rises to new glory in its scope and illustrations, beautifully produced, with a slip case showing old hunting scenes by A. B. Frost and Frederic Remington. Limited ed.

Home Service Helmet 1878-1914 With Regimental Plates, The Collectors Series, London, n.d., 32 pp., illus. Paper, $4.00.
Taken from the Wilkinson-Latham collection.

Hopkins & Allen Gun Guide and Catalog (ca. 1913). Wagle Publ., Lake Wales, FA, 1972. 32 pp., illus. Paper covers. $3.75.
Facsimile of the original catalog. Shows the firms rifles, shotguns and pistols, and includes prices. Full color cover painting by Dan Smith.

The Identification and Analysis of Luger Proof Marks, by Robt. B. Marvin. R. B. Marvin, Jasper, FA, 1972. 88 pp., illus. Paper covers. $7.50.
Shows Luger pistol markings and their use in identifying the type of pistol. Complete cross index.

Identifying Old U.S. Muskets, Rifles and Carbines, by Arcadi Gluckman, Bonanza Books, NY, 1973. 489 pp., illus. $2.49.
A revision of Colonel Gluckman's *U.S. Muskets, Rifles and Carbines.*

I*XL Means I Excel, by Wm. R. Williamson, Robert E. P. Cherry, Geneseo, IL, 1974. 33 pp., illus. Paper covers $3.95.
Covers the entire line of Bowie type knives made by the famed old English firm of Wostenholm.

Identifying Old U.S. Muskets, Rifles & Carbines, by Col. A. Gluckman. Stackpole Books, Harrisburg, PA, 1973. 487 pp., illus. $2.98.
Collector's guide to U.S. long arms, first publ. 1959. Numerous models of each type are described and shown, with histories of their makers.

Illustrated British Firearms Patents 1714-1853, comp. and ed. by Stephen V. Grancsay and Merrill Lindsay. Winchester Press. NY, 1969. Unpaginated. $15.00.
Facsimile of patent documents with a bibliography. Limited, numbered ed. of 1000, bound in ¾ leather and marbled boards.

Insignia, Decorations and Badges of the Third Reich and Occupied Countries, by R. Kahl, Military Collectors Service, Kedichem, Holland, 1970. 135 pp., $14.00.
Handbook of regalia with descriptive text and over 800 line illus.

An introduction to British Artillery in North America, by S. J. Gooding. Museum Rest. Serv., Ottawa, 1965. 54 pp., illus., Paperbound. $2.00.
Concise account of such equipment used in America 1750-1850.

Italian Fascist Daggers, by Fred. J. Stephens. Militaria Pub. Ltd., London, England, 1972. 25 pp., illus., some in color. Paper covers. $5.
First publ. devoted to collecting the daggers of Fascist Italy.

Japanese Armour, by L. J. Anderson. Stackpole Books, Harrisburg, PA, 1968. 84 pp., illus. $4.95.
British reference on museum quality armor made by the Myochin and Saotome families between the 15th and 20th centuries.

Japanese Polearms, by R. M. Knutsen. Holland Press, London, 1963. 271 pp., well-illus. Line drawings and photos. $18.00.
Each category of Japanese spear is described and illus. in this hist. treatment, including schools of spear and sword fencing. Lists leading makers and glossary.

Japanese Sword Blades, by Alfred Dobree, George Shumway, York, PA, 1967. 39 pp., illus., in paper wrapers. $4.50.
A two-part monograph, reprinted from a notable work.

Japanese Sword Fittings: The Naunton Collection, by Henri L. Joly. W. M. Hawley, Hollywood, CA, 1973. 434 pp., illus. $50.
Reprint of the finest work ever done in English on the subject. 88 plates show 1300 fittings full size.

Kentucky Knife-Traders Manual, compiled by R. B. Ritchie. R. B. Ritchie, Hindman, KY, 1971. 66 pp., illus. Paper covers. $6.50.
Lists some 2000 pocket knives and their values by brands, pattern and condition, plus a listing of about 400 collectible razors.

The Kentucky Rifle, by J. G. W. Dillin. Geo. Shumway, York, PA, 1975. 6th Ed. 202 pp., illus. $20.00
A respected work on the long rifles developed in colonial days and carried by pioneers and soldiers. Much information of value to collectors and historians. Limited ed.

The Kentucky Rifle: A True American Heritage in Picture, compiled by Philip Cowan, et al. The Kentucky Rifle Assn. Wash., D.C., 1967. 110 pp., illus. $20.00.
Presents an outstanding group of Kentucky Rifles, most of them never before pictured.

The Kentucky Rifle, by Merrill Lindsay. Arma Press, NY/The Historical Society of York County, York, PA, 1972. 100 pp., 81 large colored illustrations. $15.
Presents in precise detail and exact color 77 of the finest Kentucky rifles ever assembled in one place. Also describes the conditions which led to the development of this uniquely American arm.

Kentucky Rifle Patchboxes & Barrel Marks, by Roy F. Chandler, Valley View Offset, Duncannon, PA, 1971. 400 pp., $20.00.
Reference work illustrating hundreds of patchboxes, together with the mark or signature of the maker.

Robert Klaas Sword and Dagger Catalog, Robt. Klaas, Solingen-Ohligs, W. Germany 1938. 32 pp., illus. Paper, $5.00.
Reprint of the original 1938 catalog. A rare reference work. 16 pp. of swords and daggers with original prices.

The Leather Jacket Soldier, by O. B. Faulk. Socio-Technical Pub., Pasadena, CA, 1971, 80 pp., illus. $10.00.
History of such Spanish military equipment of the late 18th century as lances, horse accoutrements, guns, uniforms, etc.

Light But Efficient, by A. N. Hardin and R. W. Hedden, A. N. Hardin, Pennsauken, NJ, 1973. 104 pp., illus. $7.95.
A study of the M1880 hunting and M1890 intrenching knives and scabbards. A must for the 45-70 era collector.

Longrifles of North Carolina, by John Bivins, Jr. Geo. Shumway, York, PA, 1968, 200 pp., profusely illus. $24.00.
Historical survey of North Carolina gunmakers and their production during the 18th and 19th centuries. Over 400 gunsmiths are included. Fine photographs.

Longrifles of Note, by Geo. Shumway, Geo. Shumway, York, PA, 1967. 90 pp., illus. Paper covers, $3.95.
A review of 35 fine American long rifles, with detailed illustrations showing their art work, plus descriptive material.

The Lure of Antique Arms, by Merrill Lindsay, David McKay, Co., NY, 1975. Illus. with more than 50 photos. $9.95.
A beginning collectors book. Everything a novice needs to know to take up the exciting (and profitable) hobby of collecting antique arms.

Maine Made Guns and Their Makers, by Dwight B. Demeritt, Main State Museum, Hallowell, ME, 1973. 209 pp., illus. $22.00.
A fine reference work on Maine gunsmiths.

Manhattan Firearms, by Waldo E. Nutter, Stackpole Books, Harrisburg, PA, 1958. 250 pp., illus., in halftone. $7.95.
Complete history of the Manhattan Firearms Mfg. Co., and its products. Excellent specialized reference.

Manual of Rifling and Rifle Sights, by Lt.-Col. Viscount Bury, M.P., Ray Riling Arms Books Co., Phila., PA, 1971. 47 pp., Paper, $3.50.
Reprint of 1864 London edition done for the British National Rifle Ass'n. 141 illus., plus 3 folding plates.

The Manufacture of Armour and Helmets in 16th Century Japan, by Sakakibara Kozan. Holland Press, London, 1963. 156 pp., 32 pp. of illus. $20.00.
Important reference on styles and steps of making Japanese armor, first publ. Tokyo, 1800. Eng. trans., revised by H. R. Robinson of Tower of London Armouries.

Mauser-Gewehre & Mauser-Patente, by R. H. Korn. Akademische Druck Graz, Austria, 1971. 440 pp. German text, most completely illustrated with copious line drawings, charts, many of them folding plates. $35.00.
Fine reprint of the extremely-rare original. Truly a must for every Mauser buff, it has never been surpassed.

Metal Uniform Insignia of the US Army in the Southwest, 1846-1902, by S. B. Brinckerhoff, Arizona Pioneers Hist. Soc., Tucson, Ariz., 1972, 28 pp., illus. Paper covers. $2.50.
Monograph on buttons, badges, buckles, and other uniform insignia.

Metallic Cartridges, T. J. Treadwell, compiler. The Armoury, NYC, 1959. Unpaginated. 68 plates. Paper, $2.95. Cloth, $5.95.
A reduced-size reproduction of U.S. Ordnance Memoranda No. 14, originally publ. in 1873, on regulation and experimental cartridges manufactured and tested at Frankford Arsenal, Philadelphia, Pa.

Militaria, by Frederick Wilkinson. Hawthorn Books, New York, NY, 1969. 1st U.S. ed. 256 pp., well illus. in halftone. $5.95.
Introduction to military items of interest to collectors, including prints, medals, uniforms, military miniatures, weapons, badges etc.

Military Arms of Canada, by Upper Canada Hist. Arms Soc. Museum Restoration Serv., West Hill, Ont., 1963. 43 pp., illus. $1.50.
Booklet cont. 6 authoritative articles on the principal models of Canadian mil. small arms. Gives characteristics of each, makers, quantities produced.

Military Breech-Loading Rifles, by V. D. Majendie and C. O. Browne, Fortress Publ., Inc., Stoney Creek, Ontario, Can., 1973. 129 pp. plus index, illus. $8.50.
An new ed. of the 1870 work dealing with the Snider, the Martini-Henry and Boxer ammunition.

Military Edged Weapons of the World, 1880-1965, by H. A. Mauerer, College Pt., NY, 1967. 151 pp., illus. $4.50.
Various swords, blades, etc., in a private collection are dimensioned, described, and photographed. A guide for collectors. Paper wrappers.

Military Sharps Rifles and Carbines, by R. E. Hopkins. Hopkins, Campbell, Calif., 1967. 141 pp., illus. $12.50.
A guide to the principal types, with photographs, patent data, technical details, etc.

Military Small Arms of the 20th Century, by Ian V. Hogg and John S. Weeks. Digest Books, Inc., Northfield, IL, 1973. 288 pp. Paper covers. $7.95.
Weapons from the world over are meticulously examined in this comprehensive encyclopedia of these military small arms issued since 1900. Over 600 illus.

Miniature Arms, by Merrill Lindsay. Winchester Press, New York, NY, 1970. 111 pp., illus. $5.95.
A concise study of small-scale replicas of firearms and other weapons of collector interest. Fine color photographs.

Monographie der K. K. Osterr.-Ung: Blanken und Handfeuer-Waffen, by Anton Dolleczek. Akademische Druck, Graz, Austria, 1970. 197 pp., illus. $10.00.
Facsimile reprint of a standard 1896 German work on military weapons. In German text, illus. with line drawings and color plate of regimental colors.

The NRA Collector's Series, Digest Books, Inc., Northfield, IL, 1971, 84 pp. paper covers $2.95.
Reprint of the three predecessors of *American Rifleman* magazine and the first edition of *American Rifleman.*

The NRA Gun Collectors Guide, by staff members of NRA. National Rifle Assn., Washington, D.C., 1972. 256 pp., well illus. $4.50.
A wealth of information on collecting and collectors arms, with 64 major and 41 short articles, selected from the last 18 years of in "The American Rifleman."

Louis Napoleon on Artillery: The Development of Artillery from the 14th to the 17th Century, by W. Y. Carman, Arms and Armour Press, Middlesex, England, 1967. 24 pp., illus. Paper covers. $2.75.
A reprinting of rare original material—10 finely engraved plates, with 70 drawings, on the development of artillery, plus brief text.

Native American Bows, by T. M. Hamilton. George Shumway, York, PA, 1972. 148 pp., illus. $12.
Summary of the history and development of bows native to America, from early times to the present.

The New Highland Military Discipline, by Geo. Grant. Museum Restoration Service, Ottawa, 1967. 32 pp., illus. $1.50.
Reprint of a Scottish drill manual, regimental history, with illus. contemporary and modern. Paper wrappers.

The 9-pdr. Muzzle Loading Rifle, by J. D. Chown. Museum Restoration Service, Ottawa, 1967. 32 pp., illus. $1.50.
Reprint of an early Canadian artillery manual, with historical notes. Paper wrappers.

Simeon North: First Official Pistol Maker of the United States, by S. North and R. North, Rutgers Book Center, Highland Park, NJ, 1972. 207 pp., illus. $7.95.
Exact reprint of the original. Includes chapters on New England pioneer manufacturers and on various arms.

The Northwest Gun, by Chas. E. Hanson Jr. Nebraska State Historical Society, Lincoln, NB, 1970. 85 pp., illus. Paper covers. $4.50.
The corner-stone of collecting Indian trade guns.

Notes on U.S. Ordnance, vol. II, 1776-1941, by James E. Hicks. Modern Books & Crafts, Greens Farms, Conn., 1971. 252 pp., illus. $8.00.
Updated version of a standard work on development of military weapons used by U.S. forces, from handguns to coast artillery and aerial bombs. This is not to be confused with Hicks 1940 United States Ordnance, referring mainly to Ordnance correspondence as Vol. II.

Oriental Armour, by W. R. Robinson. Reprint by Outlet Book Co., New York, NY, 1970. 256 pp., well illus. $4.95.
Traces the subject material from earliest times until it was finally discarded.

O.S.S. Special Weapons, Devices and Equipment, ed. by D. B. McLean, Normount Technical Publ. Co., Wickenburg, AZ, 1975. 114 pp., illus. Paper covers. $5.95.
Reproduction of the most fascinating materiel catalog ever issued, showing spy weapons of the legendary OSS.

An Outline of the History and Development of Hand Firearms, from the Earliest Period to About the End of the Fifteenth Century, by R. C. Clephan [Original ed., 1906]. A reprint in 1946 by Standard Publications, Inc., Huntington, W.Va. 60 pp., illus. $4.00.
A worthy facsimile of a very scarce, concise and scholarly work.

The Pennsylvania-Kentucky Rifle, by Henry J. Kauffman. Bonanza Books, NY, 1968. A reprint. 374 pp., illus. $4.95.
A classic work first publ. in 1960 on early long rifles. Makers descriptions, and manufacturing methods are covered.

Percussion Guns & Rifles, by D. W. Bailey. Stackpole Books, Harrisburg, PA, 1972. 79 pp., illus. $5.95.
A guide to the muzzle-loading percussion guns and rifles of the 19th century.

Pictorial History of Swords & Bayonets, by R. J. Wilkinson-Latham, Ian Allan, London, 1973. 299 pp., illus. $9.50.
Traces the evolution of swords, bayonets, dirks and daggers from their beginning until 1918.

Plates & Buckles of the American Military 1795-1874, by Sydney C. Kerksis, The Gilgal Press, Kenesaw, GA, 1974. 567 pp., illus. $25.00.
Covers some 448 different belt and accoutrement plates from the post-revolution period to the "Hagner" plate of 1874.

The Pleasure of Guns, by Jos. G. Rosa and Robin May, Octopus Books, Ltd., London, 1974. 96 pp., illus. with 135 full color photographs. $4.98.
The intricate and beautiful work of famous gunsmiths.

The Powder Flask Book, by Ray Riling. Bonanza Books, NY 1968. A reprint. 520 pp., large format, profusely illus. First re-issue of the 1953 original ed. $15.00. A limited number of the originals are available for inscription and autograph at $35.00.
Covers the literature on flasks, their makers, and users—hunters, shooters and the military—as well as showing the arms, cased or not, short and long. A relative price listing for collector advantage is included.

A Price Guide to Antique Guns & Pistols, by Peter Hawkins, Director of Antique Arms Sales at Christie's, London, Antique Collector's Club, Suffolk (England), 1973. 380 pp., with over 1000 illustrations. $25.00.
A realistic valuation guide for over 1,000 antique long guns and pistols, foreign and American.

Price List of the U.S. Cartridge Company's Ammunition, A 1969 reprint of the 1891 original, publ. by J. C. Tillinghast, Marlow, N.H. 29 pp., illus., paper covers. $2.50.
Displays many of the now hard-to-find cartridges.

A Primer of Military Knives: European & American Combat, Trench & Utility Knives, Part I, by Gordon Hughes and Barry Jenkins, publ. by the authors, Brighton (England), 1973. 24 pp., illus., paper covers. $5.00.
A primer on the knives used in the First and Second World Wars, with many line drawings.

A Primer of World Bayonets. G. Hughes, London, 1969. Unpaginated, illus. Paper, $5.00.
A comprehensive (2 vol.) manual on the bayonet.

Quellen zur Geschichte de Feuerwaffen, by A. Essenwein (ed./compiler) Akademische Druck, Graz, Austria, 1969. One volume of text (German) plus another of fascinating plates. 178 pp., text and 197 plates. $50.00.
A fine facsimile of a rare and most interesting German source book on the "History of Firearms," taken from original drawings of 1390-1700. A treasury for the serious scholar and/or artillery buff.

The Rampant Colt, by R. L. Wilson. Thomas Haas, Spencer, Ind., 1969. 107 pp., well illus. $10.00.
Study of Samuel Colt's coat-of-arms and the rampant colt figure used on Colt firearms and in advertising.

Rapiers, by Eric Valentine. Stackpole Books, Harrisburg, Pa., 1968. 76 pp., 58 photos., 3 drawings. $4.95.
A desirable monograph, first on its subject, to be publ. in English. Covers methods of authentication, renovation, cleaning and preservation.

Red Coat and Brown Bess, by Anthony D. Darling. Museum Restoration Service, Ottawa, Ontario, Can., 1970. Paper covers, 63 pp., very well illus., in line and halftone. $3.00.
An unusually excellent treatise on the British Army in 1774-1775. Includes detailed text and illus. of various models of the "Brown Bess," plus "Records of the Battles, Sieges and Skirmishes of the American Revolution."

Regulation Military Swords, by J. Wilkinson-Latham, Star Products, London, 1970. 32 pp., illus. Paper, $4.00.
Survey of military swords of U.S., England, France and Germany.

Remington Arms in American History, by A. Hatch, Rinehart & Co., NY, 1956. 359 pp., illus. $6.50.
Collector's guide with appendix of all Remington arms, ballistics tables, etc.

Remington Catalog (Price List) of 1885, a reprint in facsimile, by The Rocky Mountain Investment and Antique Co., Cheyenne, WY, 1969. 48 pp., well illus., paper covers. $2.50.
All rifles, handguns, cane gun, sights, cartridges, shotguns, accessories etc. A priced catalog.

Remington Firearms and Ammunition Catalog No. 107, 1923, a facsimile reprint, by Frontier Press, Arvada, CO, 1973. 192 pp., well illus., paper covers. $3.75.
All rifles, sights, ammunition, knives, etc., then current. A priced catalog.

The Remington Historical Treasury of American Guns, by Harold L. Peterson. Thomas Nelson & Sons, N.Y.C., 1966. 199 pp., illus. $2.95.
A historical saga woven into first-rate Americana through the facts and details of the Remington firm and their products.

Remington UMC 1915-16 Firearms & Ammunition Catalog, a facsimile by Collector Books, Paducah, KY, 1975. 80 pp., illus. Paper covers. $3.50.
All arms and ammunition fully illus. and priced.

The Revolver, Its Description, Management, and Use, by P. E. Dove. Arms and Armour Press, London, 1968. 57 pp., 6 engravings, stiff paper wrappers. $3.75.
A facsimile reprint of a rare classic, dealing principally with the Adams revolver compared to the qualities of the Colt.

Revolving Arms, by A. W. F. Taylerson, Walker and Co., New York, 1967. 123 pp., illus. $2.98.
A detailed history of mechanically-rotated cylinder firearms in Europe and the U.S. Primarily on handguns, but other types of revolving guns are included.

Rifled Infantry Arms, by J. Schon; trans. by Capt. J. Gorgas, USA. Dresden, 1855; facsimile reprint by W. E. Meuse, Schuylersville, NY, 1965. 54 pp., illus. $2.50.
Reprint of classic essay on European military small arms of the mid-19th century. Paper covers.

Romance of Knife Collecting, by Dewey P. Ferguson, Dewey P. Ferguson, Fairborn, OH, 3rd ed., 1972. 119 pp., illus. Paper covers, spiral bound. $5.00.
From stone to steel knives, care, patterns, counterfeiting, history of knife companies, etc.
Price Guide to above title, by D. P. Ferguson, same place, 1975. 88 pp., illus. Paper covers. $5.00.

Royal Sporting Guns at Windsor, by H. L. Blackmore. H. M. Stationery Office, London, England, 1968. 60 pp. text, 52 plates. $9.54.
Catalog of the most decorative and interesting guns in the Royal Armoury collection at Windsor Castle.

Russian Military Swords, 1801-1917, by E. Mollo. Historical Research Unit, London, Eng., 1969. 56 pp., illus. $7.50.
First book in English to examine and classify the various swords used by the Russian Army from Alexander I to the Revolution. 42 photos, 27 line drawings, 10 in color.

Samuel Colt's New Model Pocket Pistols; The Story of the 1855 Root Model Revolver, by S. Gerald Keogh, S. G. Keogh, Ogden, UT, 1974. 31 pp., illus., paper covers. $3.50; hardbound $8.50.
Collector's reference on various types of the titled arms, with descriptions, illustrations, and historical data.

The Samurai Swords, by J. M. Yumoto. Tuttle Co., Rutland, Vt., 1958. 191 pp., illus. $7.25.
Detailed information on evaluation of specimens, including origin and development of the Japanese blade.

Savage Automatic Pistols, by James R. Carr. Publ. by the author, St. Charles, Ill., 1967. A reprint. 129 pp., illus. with numerous photos. $6.50.
Collector's guide to Savage pistols, models 1907-1922, with features, production data, and pictures of each. A reprint of the circa 1912 Savage promotional and instructive booklet titled *It Banishes Fear* is recommended to accompany the above. Paper wrappers, 32 pp. $1.50.

Schuyler, Hartley & Graham Catalog, publ. by Norm Flayderman, Greenwich, Conn., 1961. 176 pp., illus. $9.50.
A reprint of a rare 1864 catalog of firearms, military goods, uniforms, etc. An extensive source of information for Civil War collectors.

Scottish Swords and Dirks, by John Wallace. Stackpole Books, Harrisburg, Pa., 1970. 80 pp., illus, $4.95.
An illustrated reference guide to Scottish edged weapons.

Scottish Swords from the Battlefield at Culloden, by Lord Archibald Campbell, Mowbray Co., Providence, RI, 1971. 63 pp., illus. $5.00.
Modern reprint of an exceedingly rare 1894 limited private ed.

Sears, Roebuck & Co. Catalogue No. 117, J. J. Schroeder, ed. A reprint of the 1908 work. Digest Books, Inc., Northfield, Ill., 1969, profusely illus., paper covers. $6.95.

This reprint of a famous catalog brings to all arms collectors a treasured replica of the collectibles and prices of yesteryear.

Shooter's Bible Gun Trader's Guide, 7th Ed., by Paul Wahl, Follett Publ. Co., Chicago, IL, 1975. 256 pp., illus. Paper covers. $5.95.

A standard reference work for the identification and evaluation of all types of sporting arms found in todays markets.

Shosankenshu, by H. L. Joly. Holland Press, London, 1963. Unpaginated. $13.50.

List of Japanese artists' names and kakihan found on sword furniture by the late European authority. Completed in 1919, previously unpubl., this is a facsimile of Joly's MS. and line drawings. Lists nearly 3,000 names.

Shotgun Shells: Identification, Manufacturers and Checklist for Collectors, by F. H. Steward. B. and P. Associates, St. Louis, Mo., 1969. 101 pp., illus., paper covers. $5.95.

Historical data for the collector.

Single-Shot Rifles, by James J. Grant. Wm. Morrow & Co., NYC, 4th printing 1964. 385 pp., illus. $10.00.

A detailed study of these rifles by a noted collector.

Small Arms, by Frederick Wilkinson, Hawthorne Books, Inc., New York, 1966. 256 pp., illus. $4.95.

A history of small firearms, techniques of the gunsmith, equipment used by combatants, sportsmen and hunters.

Small Arms and Ammunition in the United States Service, 1776-1865, by B. R. Lewis. Smithsonian Inst., Washington, D.C., 1968. 338 pp. plus 52 plates. $12.50.

2nd printing of a distinguished work for historians and collectors. A limited number of deluxe, signed and numbered copies (1st reprinting 1960) are available in full leather and gilt top at $25.

Small Arms of the Sea Services, by Robt. H. Rankin. N. Flayderman & Co., New Milford, CT, 1972. 227 pp., illus. $14.50.

Encyclopedic reference to small arms of the U.S. Navy, Marines and Coast Guard. Covers edged weapons, handguns, long arms and others, from the beginnings.

Smith and Wesson 1857-1945, by Robert J. Neal and Roy J. Jenks. A. S. Barnes and Co., Inc., NYC, 1975. 500 pp., illus. with over 300 photos and 90 radiographs. $25.00.

A long-needed book, especially for knowledgeable enthusiasts and collectors. Covers an investigation of the series of handguns produced by the Smith and Wesson Company.

The Soldier's Manual, by J. H. Nesmith. (First publ. in Philadelphia in 1824.) Geo. Shumway, York, Pa., 1963. 108 pp., frontis, and 11 color plates. $10.00.

Facsimile reproduction of an important early American militia drill manual, covering exercises with musket, pistol, sword, and artillery. The color plates depict accurately the picturesque uniforms and accoutrements of elite militia corps of Phila. and vicinity. Intro. by Anne S. K. Brown traces the origin of the text matter and the early engravers.

Southern Derringers of the Mississippi Valley, by Turner Kirkland. Pioneer Press, Tenn., 1971. 80 pp., illus., paper covers. $2.00.

A guide for the collector, and a much-needed study.

Spanish Military Weapons in Colonial America, 1700-1821, by S. B. Brinckerhoff & P. A. Chamberlain. Stackpole Books, Harrisburg, PA, 1972. 160 pp., illus. $14.95.

Spanish arms and armaments described and illustrated in 274 photographic plates. Includes firearms, accoutrements, swords, polearms and cannon.

Sporting Guns, by Richard Akehurst. G. P. Putnam's Sons, New York, NY, 1968. 120 pp., excellently illus. and with 24 pp. in full color. $5.95.

One of the noted Pleasures and Treasures series. A nostalgic tracing of the history of shooting, and of the guns and rifles used by the sportsman.

Springfield Armory, Pointless Sacrifice, by C. L. Dvarecka. Prolitho Pub., Ludlow, Mass., 1968. 177 pp., illus. Paper covers. $1.00.

Story of the armory's closing; contains names, particulars and the quantities made of Springfield arms.

Springfield Muzzle-Loading Shoulder Arms, by C. E. Fuller, F. Bannerman Sons, NYC, reprinted 1968. 176 pp., illus. $12.50.

Long-awaited reprint of an important 1930 reference work on weapons produced at Springfield Armory, 1795-1865, including ordnance reports, tables, etc., on flintlock and percussion models.

Stahlhelm; Evolution of the German Steel Helmet, by F. R. Tubbs, F. R. Tubbs, 1971. 104 pp., illus. Paper, $5.50.

Helmets used by the German Army from 1916 to date. Shields, frontal plates, liners, detailed drawings, camouflage, etc.

J. Stevens Arms & Tool Co. Catalog No. 51, facsimile by Frontier Press, Inc., Arvada, CO, 1974. 137 pp., illus. Paper covers. $4.00.

Facsimile of the 1904 catalog covering rifles, pocket rifles, pistols and shotguns etc.

Stevens Pistols and Pocket Rifles, by K. L. Cope, Museum Restoration Service, Ottawa, Can., 1971. 104 pp. $8.50.

All are shown, identified, detailed, variations, listings of dates, etc.

A Study of the Colt Single Action Army Revolver, by R. Graham, J. A. Kopec, and C. K. Moore, publ. by the authors, La Puente, CA, 1975. Over 500 pp., illus. $34.95.

A definitive work on the famous Colt Single Action revolver. Contains many new facts never before published.

Sword, Lance and Bayonet, by Charles ffoulkes and E. C. Hopkinson. Arco Publishing Co., NY, 1967. 145 pp., well illus. in line and halftone. $7.50.

A facsimile reprint of the first attempt at a consecutive account of the arms, both general and official use, since the discarding of armor.

The Sword and Same, by H. L. Joly and I. Hogitaro, Holland Press Ltd., London, 1971. 241 pp. plates and line drawings. $21.00.

New printing of Arai Hakuseki, "The Sword Book in Honcho Gunkiko" and "The Book of Same Ko Hi Sei Gi of Inaba Tsurio."

Swords & Blades of the American Revolution, by Geo. C. Neumann. Stackpole Books, Harrisburg, PA, 1973. 288 pp. well illus. $14.95.

An encyclopedia of 1,600 bladed weapons—swords, bayonets, spontoons, halberds, pikes, knives, daggers, and axes—used by both sides, on land and sea, in America's struggle for independence.

Swords for Sea Service, by Commander W. E. May, R. N. & P. G. W. Annis, H.M. S.O., London, 1970. 398 pp. in 2 volumes, $30.00.

Study based on the swords, dirks and cutlasses in the National Maritime Museum in Greenwich, plus many other outside weapons, and information on the British sword trade, industry, makers and retailers. 140 black and white plates, 3 color plates and many other illus.

The 36 Calibers of the Colt Single Action Army, by David M. Brown. Publ. by the author at Albuquerque, NM, new reprint 1971. 222 pp., well-illus. $15.00.

Edited by Bev Mann of *Guns Magazine*. This is an unusual approach to the many details of the Colt S.A. Army revolver. Halftone and line drawings of the same models make this of especial interest.

Thoughts on the American Flintlock Pistol, by Samuel E. Dyke, George Shumway, York, PA, 1974. 61 pp., illus. Paper covers. $5.00.

Reprint of the "Kentucky Pistol" section from Dillin's book "The Kentucky Rifle."

Thoughts on the Kentucky Rifle in its Golden Age, by Joe Kindig, Jr. George Shumway, York, PA, 1975. A facsimile reprint of the 1960 original. 561 pp., replete with fine arms and data on many makers. $29.95.

Covers mainly the arms and their makers in the Lancaster area of Pennsylvania. An authoritative work.

Toxophilus, by Roger Ascham. S. R. Pub. Ltd., Yorkshire, Eng., 1968. 230 pp., illus. $7.00

A facsimile reprint of the 1788 ed. still regarded as the classic text on archery.

Tsubas in Southern California, compiled by W. M. Hawley in cooperation with Japanese Sword Club of So. Calif., W. M. Hawley, Hollywood, CA, 1973. 302 pp., illus. $30.00.

A pictorial record of especially fine Japanese sword guards in the collections of members of the Nanka Token Kai. 1419 tsubas illus.

200 Years of American Firearms, by James E. Serven, DBI Books, Inc., Northfield, IL, 1975. 224 pp., illus. Paper covers. $7.95.

Covers the evolution of firearms in America from those carried by Spanish explorers to the M-16 rifle.

Underhammer Guns, by H. C. Logan. Stackpole Books, Harrisburg, PA, 1964. 250 pp., illus. $4.98.

A full account of an unusual form of firearm dating back to flintlock days. Both American and foreign specimens are included.

Uniforms and Badges of the Third Reich, by Rudolph Kahl, Military Collectors Service, Kedichem, Holland, 1970.

Volume I; NSDAP. 76 pp., 260 illus. $9.95.
Volume II: SA, NSKK, and SS. 120 pp., 523 illus. $9.95.
Volume III: HJ, NSFK, and RAD. 100 pp., 452 illus. $9.95.

Uniforms of the American, British, French, and German Armies in the War of the American Revolution, 1775-1783, by Lt. Charles M. Lefferts, We Inc., Old Greenwich, CT, 1970. 292 pp., illus. $8.00.

Reprint of the original 1926 ed. and the only book on its subject today.

U.S. Army Weapons 1784-1791, by Wm. H. Guthman, The American Soc. of Arms Coll., 1975. 94 pp., illus. Paper covers. $6.50.

A detailed study of the surplus weapons and accoutrements stored in Federal arsenals after the Revolutionary War.

U.S. Cartridge Co. Collection of Firearms, We, Inc., Old Greenwich, CT., 1970. 142 pp., illus. $6.00.

Describes each arm in detail as to manufacture, action, period of use, function, markings, patents, makers, etc.

U.S. Firearms: The First Century, 1776-1875, by D. F. Butler. Winchester Press, NY, 1971. 320 pp., illus. $15.00.

A rich mine of carefully researched information and data on American firearms of this period. Illustrated with photos, schematics and historical documents.

U.S. Martial and Collectors Arms, by D. Verlag. Military Arms Research Service, San Jose, CA, 1971. 83 pp. Paper covers. $2.50.

Complete listing of U.S. arms inspectors: names, initials used, types of guns inspected circa 1790s through 1964. Detailed tabulations of guns bought by U.S.; quantities; serial number ranges; contractors.

United States Martial Pistols and Revolvers, by Arcadi Gluckman, Bonanza Books, NY, 1973. 249 pp. plus 29 plates. $2.98.

Covers all martial short arms made in the U.S. by the government or private makers from 1799 to 1917.

U.S. Martial and Semi-Martial Single-Shot Pistols, by C. E. Chapel, Coward-McCann Inc., NYC, 1962. 352 pp., over 150 illus. $7.50.

Describes in detail all single shot martial pistols used by the US armed forces and by military units of the states. A definitive guide.

U.S. Military Firearms, 1776-1956, by Maj. Jas. E. Hicks. J. E. Hicks & Son. La Canada, Calif., 216 pp., incl. 88 pages of fine plates. $12.50.

Covering 180 years of America's hand and shoulder weapons. The most authoritative book on this subject. Packed with official data.

U.S. Military Small Arms 1816-1865, by R. M. Reilly. The Eagle Press, Inc., Baton Rouge, La., 1970. 275 pp., illus. $22.50.

Describes and superbly illustrates every known type of primary and secondary martial firearm of the period 1816-1865. Limited, numbered ed.

U.S. Ordnance Manual 1862, compiled by T. T. S. Laidley, Bvt. Major, Capt. of Ordnance. Ordnance Park Corp., Lyons, CO, 1970. 559 pp., illus., 33 plates. A limited numbered ed. $15.40.

Facsimile of the 3rd ed. of the 1862 *Ordnance Manual for the Use of the Officers of the United States Army.*

U.S. Sword Bayonets, 1847-1865, by R. V. Davis, Jr. Priv. prt., Pittsburgh, PA, 1963. 36 pp., 17 pl., paper. $6.00

Histories, production data, and good photos of U.S. military sword bayonets of Civil War era.

A Universal Military Dictionary, by Captain George Smith. The rare original book was published at London in 1779. This facsimile reprint was released in 1969 by Museum Restoration Service, Ottawa, Ontario, Can. 336 pp., 16 fold-out plates. $27.50.

A most useful reference for mean of arms interest. Offered only in a numbered, limited issue of 700 copies.

The Virginia Manufactory of Arms, by Giles Cromwell, University Press of Virginia, Charlottesville, VA, 1975. 205 pp., illus. $20.00.

The only complete history of the Virginia Manufactory of Arms which produced muskets, pistols, swords, and cannon for the state's militia from 1802 through 1821.

Waffen: Beitrag zur Historischen Waffenkunde, by J. H. Hefner-Alteneck. Akademische Druck, Graz, Austria, 1969. 58 pp., German text plus 100 plates. $30.00.

A descriptive text complements the fine illustrations depicting armor and weapons used in Europe from the middle ages through the 17th century.

Weapons of the British Soldier, by Col. H. C. B. Rogers. Seeley Service & Co., London, 1960. 259 pp., illus. in line and halftone plus full color frontis. $14.50.

The story of weapons used by the British soldier throughout the ages and the many developments in personal arms during the course of history.

The Webley Story, by Wm. C. Dowell, Skyrac Press, Leeds, Eng. 337 pp., profusely illus. $24.50.

Detailed study of Webley pistols and revolvers, covering over 250 specimens. This important reference also gives detailed listing of English small arms cartridge patents through 1880.

The Whitney Firearms, by Claud Fuller. Standard Publications, Huntington, W. Va., 1946. 334 pp., many plates and drawings. $20.00.

An authoritative history of all Whitney arms and their maker. Highly recommended. An exclusive with Ray Riling Arms Books Co.

The William M. Locke Collection, compiled by Robert B. Berryman, et al, The Antique Armory, Inc., East Point, GA, 1973. 541 pp., illus. $30.00.

A magnificently produced book illustrated with hundreds of photographs of guns from one of the finest collection of American firearms ever assembled.

Winchester Catalog of 1891, a facsimile reprint by the Rocky Mountain Investment and Antique Co., Cheyenne, WY, 1973. 84 pp., well illus., paper covers. $2.50.
All rifles, shotguns, reloading tools and ammunition of the time. A priced catalog.
Winchester Catalog No. 79, 1914, a facsimile reprint by Collector's Books, Paducah, KY, 1975. 128 pp., illus. Paper covers. $3.50.
Catalog and price list of rifles, carbines, muskets, shotguns, ammo., etc.
Winchester Catalog No. 80, 1916—50th Anniversary, a facsimile by Frontier Press, Arvada, CO, 1974. 224 pp., illus. Paper covers. $4.50.
50th Anniversary catalog and price list of rifles, carbines, shotguns, ammo, etc.
Winchester—The Gun That Won the West, by H. F. Williamson. Combat Forces Press, Washington, D.C., 1952. Later eds. by Barnes, NY 494 pp., profusely illus. $5.95.
A scholarly and essential economic history of an honored arms company, but the early and modern arms introduced will satisfy all but the exacting collector.
The Winchester Book, by Geo. Madis. Art & Reference House, Lancaster, Texas, 1971. 542 pp., illus. $25.00.
First release of 1,000 autographed deluxe copies at this special price. After these are sold only a standard ed. will be available, the price the same. $20.00.
The World of Guns, by Richard Akehurst. Crown Publ., NY, 1972. 127 pp., illus. $3.95.
Many full color plates tell the story of guns from the first simple handguns: guns in warfare, sporting guns, rifles, the American West, duelling pistols, etc.

GENERAL

A.B.C. of Snap Shooting, by Horace Fletcher, Americana Archives Publ. Co., Topsfield, MA., 1971. 48 pp., illus. Paper, $3.00.
Authentic reproduction of a rare 1881 original.
African Antelope, paintings by Peter Skirka, intro. and text by Wendell Swank. Winchester Press, NY, 1972. 144 pp., slipcased. $27.50.
Superbly illus. study, with full-color paintings of all 34 principal African antelope. The text describes the range, life cycle and characteristics of each animal.
Air Gun Batteries, by E. G. Wolff. Public Museum, Milwaukee, Wisc., 1964. 28 pp., illus., paperbound. 75¢.
Study of discharge mechanisms on reservoir air guns.
The Album of Gunfighters, by J. Marvin Hunter and Noah H. Rose, Warren Hunter, Helotes, Texas, 1965. 4th printing. 236 pp., wonderfully illus., with spectacular oldtime photos. $19.50.
For the serious gunfighter fan there is nothing to equal this factual record of the men-behind-the-star and the human targets that they faced.
To All Sportsmen; and Particularly to Farmers and Gamekeepers, by Col. Geo. Hanger, Richmond Publ. Co., Richmond, England, 1971. 226 pp. $12.50.
Reprint of an 1814 work on hunting, guns, horses, veterinary techniques, etc.
The American B.B. Gun, by A. T. Dunathan, A. S. Barnes, S. Brunswick, NJ, 1971. 154 pp., illus. $10.00.
Identification reference and a price guide for B.B. guns, plus a brief history and advertising plates.
American Bird Decoys, by W. J. Mackey Jr. Bonanza Books, NY, 1972. 256 pp., illus. $3.95.
The history and fine points of decoys for all gamebird species, with much data for collectors and hunters.
American Game Birds of Field and Forest, by F. C. Edminster, Book Sales, NY, 1972 490 pp. 99 plates. $6.95.
18 species; their origin, history, range, food, diseases, etc.
American Handmade Knives of Today, by B. R. Hughes. Pioneer Press, Union City, TN, 1972. 56 pp., illus. Paper covers. $2.95.
A primer for those developing an interest in handmade blades. Knowledgeable.
American Indian Tomahawks, by H. L. Peterson, Museum of the American Indian Heye Foundation, 1971. 142 pp., $10.00.
Brief description of various types and their makers. 314 illustrations, and many line drawings.
Americans and their Guns, compiled by Jas. B. Trefethen, ed. by Jas. E. Serven, Stackpole Books, Harrisburg, Pa., 1967. 320 pp., illus. $9.95.
The National Rifle Association of America story through nearly a century of service to the nation. More than a history—a chronical of help to novice and expert in the safe and proper use of firearms for defense and recreation, as well as a guide for the collector of arms.
America's Camping Book, by Paul Cardwell, Jr. C. Scribner's Sons, New York, NY 1st ed., 1969. 591 pp., well illus., in line and halftone. $10.00.
A fine illustrated guide to camping and woodcraft, with data on equipment, techniques, emergencies and nature study.
Archery: Its Theory and Practice, by H. A. Ford. Geo. Shumway, York, PA, 1971. 128 pp., illus. $6.00.
Reprint of the scarce 1856 ed.
Archery, by C. J. Longman and H. Walrond. Frederick Ungar Co., NY, 1967. 534 pp., illus. in line and halftone. $5.95.
Reproduction of a standard, important British reference work, first publ. in 1894, on the history, uses and techniques of archery.
Arco Gun Book, ed. by Larry Koller. Arco Publ. Co. Inc., NYC, 1962 397 pp., illus. $7.50.
A concise encyclopedia for arms collectors, shooters and hunters.
Arming the Union, by Carl L. Davis, National Univ. Publ., Kennikat Press, Port Washington, NY, 1973. 207 pp., illus. $12.50.
The fascinating story of how the Union armed itself during the Civil War and moved into a new era of warfare.
Armoured Fighting Vehicles, by Malcolm McGregor, Walker & Co., New York, 1967. 56 pp., illus. $15.00.
Describes 12 tanks and armored cars, representative of those used in the two World Wars. The illustrations in full-color are true scale drawn from actual models.
Armoured Forces, by R. M. Ogorkiewicz. Arco Pub. Co., NY, 1970. 475 pp., illus. $7.95.
A history of the armored forces and their vehicles.
Arms for Texas, by Michael J. Koury. The Old Army Press, Fort Collins, CO, 1973. 94 pp., illus. $7.50.
A study of the Republic of Texas guns.
Arms of the World: The 1911 Alfa Catalogue. Edited by Joseph J. Schroeder, Jr. Digest Books, Northfield, IL., 420 pp., Paper, $5.95.
Reprint in 4 languages of thousands of guns, cartridges, swords, helmets, tools, etc. Profusely illus., and priced the 1911 way.

The Art of Archerie, by Gervase Markham. A reprint of the 1634 original, publ. in London. Geo. Shumway, York, PA, 1968. 172 pp. $12.00.
This classic treatise, written to keep alive the art of archery in warfare, treats with the making of longbows and their use. A scholarly introduction to the new issue by S. V. Grancsay adds an enlightening historical perception.
Art for Conservation; The Federal Duck Stamps, by Jene C. Gilmore, with introd. by Robt. Hines, Barre Publ., Barre, MA, 1971. 94 pp., illus. $14.95.
Contains all the duck stamp illustrations from 1934 to 1972 with pertinent biographical, historical and philatelic data.

The Art and Science of Taking to the Woods, by C. B. Colby and B. Angier, Stackpole Books, Harrisburg, Pa. 1970, 288 pp. illus. $7.95. Also in paper covers. $3.95.
Illustrated camper's manual covering all types of outdoor living and transportation, for novice and expert alike.
The Art of Survival, by C. Troebst. Doubleday & Co., Garden City, NY. 1965. 312 pp. illus. $5.95.
Narratives of devices of survival in difficult terrain or circumstances and evaluation of rescue and life-saving procedures.

The Art of the Decoy: American Bird Carvings, by Adele Earnest. Clarkson N. Potter, Inc., NYC, 1966. $4.95.
The origin of a lost art explained, plus some data on the most famous carvers. Over 106 black-and-white photos, 35 line drawings and an 8-page insert in full color.
Artillery of the World, by Christopher F. Foss, Ian Allan, London, 1974. 192 pp., illus. $7.95.
Covers all types of artillery from anti-tank guns to recoiless weapons.
Asian Fighting Arts, by D. F. Draeger and R. W. Smith. Kodansha International Ltd., Tokyo, Japan. 2nd printing, 1969. 207 pp., well illus., in line and halftone. $12.50.
A work of monumental research, interesting to all involved in the science of fighting techniques. Covers eleven Asian skills, ranging from Chinese T'ai-chi and Burmese Bando to Japanese Jujitsu and the lethal Pentjak-silak of Indonesia.

The Atlantic Flyway, by Robt. Elman and Walter Osborne. Winchester Press, NY, 1972. 288 pp., illus. $15.
Fascinating word and picture study of one of the world's great migratory corridors. Past history, present problems and future prospects of wildfowling in this area. Over 250 magnificent color and black-and-white photos.
Author and Subject Index to the American Rifleman 1940-1950; 1951-1960; 1961-1970, by W. R. Burrell, Galesburg, MI, 1973. 64 pp., paper covers. Each index $6.50.
Alphabetical listing by author, title and subject.

Bayonet Fighting, by the Dept. of the Army, Normount Armament Co., Wickenburg, AZ, 1972. 76 pp., illus. Paper, $1.50.
Reprint of FM 23-25. Its principles, purpose, use, positions, training, etc.
Baron von Steuben and his Regulations, by Joseph R. Riling, Ray Riling Arms Books Co., Philadelphia, Penna., 1966. 207 pp., illus. $15.00.
A documented book on this great American Major General and the creation by him of the first official "Regulations." Includes the complete facsimile of these regulations.
Basic Nazi Swords & Daggers, by Peter Stahl. Die Wehrmacht Military Publ., Stanford, CA, 1972. 30 pp., illus. Paper covers. $2.
Pictures and identifies Nazi swords and daggers.
Battle Ships of World War I, by Anthony Preston. Stackpole Books, Harrisburg, PA, 1972. 259 pp. $9.98.
Illus. encyclopedia of the battlewagons of all nations, 1914-1918.
Being Your Own Wilderness Doctor, by Dr. E. Russel Kodet and Bradford Angier. Stackpole Books, Harrisburg, Pa., 1968. 127 pp., illus. In line drawings. $3.95.
Called the "outdoorsman's emergency manual" It offers security of knowing what to do best—in case of the worst.
The Best of Guns & Ammo, 1958-1962, ed. by Garry James, Petersen Publ. Co., Los Angeles, CA, 1975. 256 pp., illus. Paper covers. $4.95.
A gold star selection of timeless articles and features from 1958-1962 issues.
A Bibliography of Military Books up to 1642, by Maurice J. D. Cockle. A new reprint of the Holland Press, London, 1965. 320 pp., illus. $15.00.
Describes the important military books from the invention of gunpowder to subject date. A standard reference.
Birds in Our Lives, ed. by A. Stefferud and A. L. Nelson. Gov't. Prtg. Office, Washington, D.C. 20402, 1966, 576 pp., 80 drawings, 372 photos. $9.00.
61 authors have contributed to this great book, the illus. by Bob Hines. A successful effort to bring any and all readers an appreciation of—and an interest in—the part birds play in their lives.
Black Powder Gun Digest, edited by T. Bridges. Digest Books, Inc., Northfield, IL, 1972. 288 pp., illus. Paper covers. $6.95.
Comprehensive, authoritative book on black powder rifles, handguns, scatterguns and accessories. With a where-to-buy it directory.
Black Powder Guide, by Geo. Nonte, Jr. Shooter's Bible Publ., S. Hackensack, NJ, 1969. 214 pp., fully illus., $5.95.
A complete guide to muzzle-loading firearms of all types, their loading, repair and maintenance.
Black Powder Snapshots, by Herb Sherlock. Standard Publications. Huntington, W. VA, 50 pp., illus. $10.00.
Deluxe large volume containing 23 major Sherlock drawings and 95 punchy, marginal sketches.
The Book of the American West, ed. by Jay Monaghan. Julian Messner, New York, 1963. 608 pp., 200 illus. (many in color). $9.95.
A special chapter on frontier firearms is a feature of this massive work. 10 experts on Western hist. in as many fields of study contributed to the book. Illus. includ. works by the best contemporary artists.
The Book of the American Woodcock, by Wm. G. Sheldon, Ph.D. University of Mass. Press, Amherst, 1967. 227 pp., bibliography, appendices and index. $8.50.
Bow & Arrow Archer's Digest, ed. by Jack Lewis. Digest Books, Inc., Northfield, Ill., 1971. 320 pp., profusely illus. $5.95.
Comprehensive treatment of the art and science of archery.
Bowhunter's Digest, by C. R. Learn, DBI Books, Inc., Northfield, IL, 1974. 288 pp., illus. $6.95.
Covers large and small game bowhunting throughout the world. Many tips on camouflage, equipment and techniques to use.
The Boy's Book of Backyard Camping, by A. A. Macfarlan. Stackpole Books, Harrisburg, Pa. 1st ed. 1968. 160 pp., illus. in line. $4.50.
"How to use at-home space for the development of camping skills." Chapters on tents, equipment, cooking—all for out-of-doors enjoyment.
Boys in the Revolution, by Jack Coggins, Stackpole Books, Harrisburg, Pa., 1967. 96 pp., illus. $4.50.
Young Americans tell their part in the war for independence—what they did, what they wore, the gear they carried, the weapons they used, the ships they sailed on, the campaigns in which they fought.

Brassey's Infantry Weapons of the World, 1975, ed. by J. I. H. Owen, Brassey's, London, 1975. 323 pp., illus. $49.50.
Infantry weapons and combat aids in current use by the regular and reserve forces of all nations.
British and American Tanks of WW II, by P. Chamberlain and C. Ellis. Arco Pub. Co., New York., 1969 222 pp., illus. $9.95.
Complete, illus. history of American, British and Commonwealth tanks, 1939-1945. Photos, and precise specifications of each.
British Artillery Weapons & Ammunition 1914-1918, by I. V. Hogg & L. F. Thuston, Ian Allan, London, 1972. 255 pp., illus. $17.50.
A detailed description including types designed for use in 1919.
The British Code of Duel, Richmond Publ. Co., Richmond, England, 1971. 144 pp. Reprint of the 1824 ed. Reference on the laws of honour and the character of gentlemen. Together with **The Art of Duelling**, same publ., 1971. 70 pp. Reprint of the 1836 London ed. Both books $11.50.
Information useful to young Continental tourists.
The Cabinet of Natural History and American Rural Sports. Imprint Society, Barre Publ., Barre, MA, 1973. Unpaginated. $40.
Edited facsimile version of the extremely scarce sporting magazine published in America, 1830-31. Illus. with 56 lithographs, 12 in color, the remainder in one tint. The originals were the first colored sporting plates actually done in America.
Camper's Digest, 2nd ed. by Erwin and Peggy Bauer. Digest Books, Inc., Northfield, Ill. 60093, 1974. 288 pp., paper covers, $5.95.
Everything needed to be known about camping. Trails, tools, clothes, cooking. Articles by leading outdoor writers and campers.
Campground Cooking, edited by Charles and Kathleen Farmer, Digest Books Inc., Northfield, IL, 1974. 8½"X11", 288 pp. Profusely illustrated. Paperbound. $6.95.
Covers cooking for campers, hunters, backpackers, boaters, etc. with tips for game preparation, survival foods, favorite recipes.
The Camping Manual, compiled by Fred Sturges, Stackpole Books, Harrisburg, PA, 1967. 160 pp., illus. $3.95.
An excellent refresher on the fundamentals, with a digest of the newest methods and latest advice for those who want to enjoy camping more.
Carbine Handbook, by Paul Wahl. Arco Publ. Co., N.Y.C., 1964. 80 pp., illus. $6.00. Paperbound, $4.95.
A manual and guide to the U.S. Carbine, cal. .30, M1, with data on its history, operation, repair, ammunition, and shooting.
The Chi-Com Series, by Granville Rideout, Yankee Publ. Co., Ashburnham, MA, 1971. 246 pp., illus. $12.95
New definitive reference work on Chinese Communist weapons in Southeast Asia. Limited and numbered ed.
Chinese Weapons, by E.T.C. Werner, Ohara Publications, Inc., Los Angeles, CA, a facsimile ed., 1972. 128 pp., illus., paper covers. $4.50.
A general account of China's tools of war, including very early Chinese arms.
C.I.A. Special Weapons Supply Catalog, a facsimile reproduction by Paladin Press, Boulder, CO, 1975. 77 pp., illus. Paper covers. $5.95.
A catalog listing over 1000 items available for use by various governmental organizations.
Classic African Animals: The Big Five, text by Anthony Dyer, painting by Bob Kuhn. Winchester Press, NY, 1973. 128 pp., illus. $10.00.
The famed "Big Five" of Africa—lion, leopard, rhino, buffalo and elephant. A story of the animals themselves, magnificently illus. with 6 pages of color plus black-and-white drawings from Kuhn's African sketchbook. A deluxe limited, signed ed. $100.
The Classic Decoy Series, Ed Zern, text; M. C. Weiller, illustrator. Winchester Press, New York, NY 1969. A beautiful work picturing 24 American duck decoys in full color, printed on special paper and loose for framing. Decorated covers in slip case. Anecdotal text on each species shown. $100.00.
This deluxe collectors' work is offered in a strictly limited issue of 1000 copies, each signed by the artist and numbered.
Clubs to Cannon, by Brigadier O. F. G. Hogg, Gerald Duckworth & Co. Ltd., London, (England), 1968. 264 pp., illus. $10.50.
Warfare and weapons before the introduction of gunpowder.
The Code of Honor; or Rules for the Government of Principals and Seconds in Duelling, by John Lyde Wilson, Ray Riling Arms Books Co., Phila., PA, 1971. 48 pp. Paper, $3.50.
Reprint of the rare 1858 edition.
A Collection of U.S. Military Knives, Book II, by M. H. Cole, M. H. Cole, Birmingham, AL. Limited, numbered ed., 1973. 92 pp., illus. $10.00.
Profusely illustrated with line drawings of military knives. Lists makers and shows their trade marks.
The Complete Book of the Air Gun, by G. C. Nonte Jr. Stackpole Books, Harrisburg, PA, 1970. 288 pp., illus. $7.95.
From Plinking to Olympic competition, from BB guns to deluxe rifles, pistols, the air shotgun.
The Complete Book of Game Conservation, by Chas. Coles, Barrie & Jenkins, London, 1971. 394 pp., $18.50.
Definitive work on the subject. 181 illustrations including color reproductions of rare prints and original paintings.
Complete Book of Rifles and Shotguns, by Jack O'Connor, Harper & Bros., N.Y.C., 1961, 477 pp., illus. $8.95.
A splendid two-part book of encyclopedic coverage on every detail of rifle and shotgun.
Complete Book of Shooting, by Jack O'Connor et al. Outdoor Life—Harper & Row, N.Y.C., 1965. 385 pp., illus. $5.95.
Fundamentals of shooting with rifle, shotgun, and handgun in the hunting field and on target ranges.
The Complete Book of Trick and Fancy Shooting, by Ernie Lind, Winchester Press, NY, 1972. 159 pp., illus. $5.95.
Step-by-step instructions for acquiring the whole range of shooting skills with rifle, pistol and shotgun; includes practical hints on developing your own shooting act.
The Complete Cannoneer, compiled by M. C. Switlik. Antique Ordnance Artificers, Jackson, MI, 1971. 106 pp., illus., paper covers. $4.50.
A must for the modern cannoneer. Compiled in two sections. Part first contains "School of the Piece" as orginally published in Artillery Drill by George S. Patton, in 1861. Part second contains current observations on the safe use of cannon.
Conquering the Frontiers, by James E. Serven, The Foundation Press, Tucson, AZ, 1974. 256 pp., illus. $19.95.
Stories of American pioneers and the guns which helped them establish a new life.
Coping with Camp Cooking, by M. W. Stephens and G. S. Wells. Stackpole Books, Harrisburg, PA 1966. 94 pp., illus., decorated boards. $2.95.
Hints and recipes selected from the editors' writings appearing in *Camping Guide Magazine.*
Crossbows, by Frank Bilson, Hippocrene Books, Edison, NJ, 1975. 148 pp., illus. $8.95.
The first book to be written on crossbows since the beginning of the century. Describes construction, design, etc.
The Crossbow, by Sir Ralph Payne-Gallwey, Holland Press Ltd., London, 1971. 375 pp., illus. $25.00.
New printing of the only work devoted to the crossbow and such related weapons as the siege engine, balistas, catapults, Turkish bows and the Chinese repeating crossbow.
Crusade for Wildlife, by J. B. Trefethen. Stackpole Books, Harrisburg, PA, 1961. 377 pp., illus. $7.50.
History of the Boone and Crockett Club and its efforts to preserve wildlife in America, with accounts of the plight of threatened species.
Current American War Medals and Decorations, 1963-69, by E. E. Kerrigan. Medallic Publishing Co., Noroton Heights, CT 1st ed. 1969. Paper covers, 23 pp., illus. $3.00.
This supplement updates the author's *American War Medals and Decorations*, listing recently created awards and recipients.
Daggers, Bayonets & Fighting Knives of Hitler's Germany, by John R. Angolia. James Bender Pub. Co., Mountain View, CA. 1st ed. 1971. 334 pp., profusely illus. $14.95.
An exceptionally fine, useful compilation for collector, historian and student.
The Daggers and Edged Weapons of Hitler's Germany, by Maj. J. P. Atwood, Publ. privately for the author in Berlin, Germany, 1965. 240 pp. illus. New edition, 1967. $16.50.
Lavishly illus. with many plates in full color, this is an outstanding production, easily the best information (for the collector) on the subject.

Daggers and Fighting Knives of the Western World: From the Stone Age Unitl 1900, by Harold L. Peterson, Walker and Co., New York, 1967. 256 pp., illus. $2.98.
The only full-scale historical and analytical work on this subject, from flint knives of the stone age to British and American naval dirks.
Dead Aim, by Lee Echols, Acme Printing Co., San Diego, CA, a reprint, 1972. 116 pp., illus. $5.00.
Nostalgic antics of hell-raising pistol shooters of the 1930s.
Decoys of the Atlantic Flyway, by Geo. R. Starr, Jr., M.D., Winchester Press, NY, 1974. 308 pp., illus. with photographs by Geo. Dow. $17.95.
The art and history of decoy carving. Over 300 decoys illus. in color and b/w.
Decoys and Decoy Carvers of Illinois, by P. W. Parmalee and F. D. Loomis. Northern Illinois University Press, DeKalb, IL. 1st ed., 1969, 506 pp., illus. $17.50.
A comprehensive and handsome survey, replete with photographs—many in color. The work of the makers is analyzed, with comments on Illinois duck shooting over the past century.
Decoys Simplified, by Paul W. Casson, Freshet Press, Rockville Centre, NY, 1972. 95 pp. plus 20 plans. $14.95.
How to make inexpensive cork decoys with only a small amount of equipment.
Deer of the World, by G. Kenneth Whitehead. The Viking Press, NY, 1972. 194 pp., illus. $14.95.
Important reference. Covers all 40 species of deer and many sub-species. Describes appearances, habits, status and distribution.
Description of U.S. Military Rifle Sights, by Edw. A. Tolosky, E. A. Tolosky, Publ., 1971. 117 pp. Paper, $8.50.
Covers period from 1861 to 1940. New and excellent work for collectors and fans of the U.S. Military. Definitive text, full-size line drawings.

The Details of the Rocket System, by Col. Wm. Congreve. Museum Restoration Service, Ottawa, Canada, 1970. 85 pp., illus. $10.00.
Reprint of the 1814 1st ed. with details, photos and plates of rockets and their launchers. Edition limited and numbered.
The Diary of Colonel Peter Hawker, by Col. P. Hawker, Richmond Publ. Co., Richmond, England. 1971. 759 pp., illus. $18.95.
Reprint of the 1893 ed. covers shooting in every way and how to outwit your opponent!
Dictionary of Weapons & Military Terms, by John Quick, McGraw-Hill, NY, 1973. 515 pp., illus. $25.00.
Describes the principal weapons and weapon systems from ancient times to present day.
Die Handwaffen, by Werner Eckardt and Otto Morawietz. H. G. Schulz, Hamburg, 1957. 265 pp., 15 plates, 175 illus. $10.00.
An important work (in German) on German Service arms from their beginnings through World War II. A symposium on the subject—ancient, obsolete, semi-modern and modern.
The Double-Armed Man, by Wm. Neade, Geo. Shumway, Publ., York, PA, 1971. 51 pp., 7 woodcuts. $8.00.
Facsimile ed. of a little book published in London in 1625. Describes use of the longbow in combination with the pike. Limited to 400 numbered copies.
Eat the Weeds, by B. C. Harris. Barre Publ., Barre, MA, 1968. 223 pp., illus., paper covers $3.95.
Practical directions for collecting and drying herbs, for using edible plants and fruits as food and for medical purposes or as substitutes for cultivated vegetables.
Encyclopedia of Continental Army Units; Battalions, Regiments and Independent Corps, by Fred A. Berg, Stackpole Books, Harrisburg, PA, 1972. 160 pp. $6.95.
The official and unofficial designations, organizational history, commanding officers and ethnic composition for every unit of the Continental Army for which these facts are known.
Encyclopedia of British, Provincial, and German Army Units 1775-1783, by P. R. Katcher. Stackpole Books, Harrisburg, PA, 1973. 160 pp., illus. $6.95.
Definitive study of America's opposing forces, meant for historians, buffs, and students; covers units, placement, commanders, arms, etc.
Encyclopedia of Firearms, ed. by H. L. Peterson. E. P. Dutton, N.Y.C., 1964. 367 pp., 100 pp. of illus. incl. color. $14.95.
Fine reference work on firearms, with articles by 45 top authorities covering classes of guns, manufacturers, ammunition, nomenclature, and related topics.
Encyclopedia of Modern Firearms, Vol. 1, compiled and publ. by Bob Brownell, Montezuma, IA, 1959. 1057 pp. plus index, illus. $22.50. Dist. by Bob Brownell, Montezuma, IA 50171.
Massive accumulation of basic information of nearly all modern arms pertaining to "parts and assembly." Replete with arms photographs, exploded drawings, manufacturers' lists of parts, etc.
Engines of War, by Henry Wilkinson, The Richmond Publishing Co., Surrey (England), a facsimile ed., 1973. 268 pp., illus. $10.95.
The history of projectile weapons together with metallurgical observations and gunpowder manufacture.
The English Bowman, by T. Roberts. George Shumway, York, PA, 1973. 347 pp. $6.
Facsimile of the original work of 1801, with a new intro. by E. G. Heath. The art and practice of archery, the techniques of shooting and the elements of toxophily are examined, with comments on an earlier and similar work by Roger Ascham, called *Toxophilus.*

The Exercise of Arms, by Jacob de Gehyn, McGraw-Hill Book Co., NY, 1971. 250 pp. plus separate commentary by J. B. Kist, Dutch historian. $14.98.
Exact facsimile of original 1807 ed. now in Dutch archives, and based on concepts of troop organization and training developed by Prince Johann II. 117 copper engravings.
The Experts Book of the Shooting Sports, ed. by D. E. Petzal. Simon and Schuster, NY, 1972. 320 pp., illus. $9.95.
America's foremost shooting and hunting experts disclose the secrets of their specialties.
Explosives and Bomb Disposal Guide, by Robt. R. Lenz. Chas. C. Thomas, Springfield, IL, 1971. 303 pp., illus. $14.00.
Course of instruction on handling clandestine and sabotage devices; now being taught to all military bomb disposal technicians.
Explosives and Demolitions, U.S. Field Manual 5-25, Normount Armament Co., Forest Grove, OR. 215 pp., illus., paperbound. $4.95.
A reprint of the Army FM dated 14 May 1959.
Explosives and Homemade Bombs, by Jos. Stoffel. Chas. C. Thomas, Springfield, IL, 1972. 304 pp., illus. $14.00.
Elementary text on design and manufacture of explosive devices, for use as a text in training bomb disposal personnel.
Falconry, by Gilbert Blaine, Neville Spearman, London, 1970. 253 pp., illus. $7.50.
Reprint of a 1936 classic on training, handling, types, furniture, etc., of hawks, plus a glossary and list.
Die Faustfeuerwaffen von 1850 dis zur Gegenwart, by Eugene Heer, Akademische D.-u. V., Graz, Austria, 1972. 234 pp. of German texts, 215 pp. of illus. $30.00.
First volume in a series which will cover the history of Swiss firearms from 1800. The handguns issued between 1850 and 1950 are described and illustrated in considerable detail.
Feasting Free on Wild Edibles, by Bradford Angier. Stackpole Books, Harrisburg, PA, 1972. 285 pp., illus. $7.95.
More than 500 ways to banquet on nature's bounty. A one-vol. issue combining Angier's *Free for the Eating* and *More Free for the Eating Wild Foods.*
A Field Guide for Civil War Explosive Ordnance 1861-1865, by John D. Bartleson, G.P.O., Supt. of Documents, Washington, DC, 1974. 193 pp., illus. Paper covers. $5.00.
Illus. and describes almost 200 projectiles and includes radiograph photos of many projectile interiors.
Fighting Vehicles, by C. Ellis & P. Chamberlain. Hamlyn Publ., London, Eng., 1972. 96 pp. $3.95.
Illus. story of the tank, going back centuries. Covers mobile fortresses through Patton and W.W. II tanks to today's varied types.
Firearms, by Walter Buehr. Crowell Co., N.Y.C., 1967. 186 pp., illus. $5.95.
From gunpowder to guided missile, an illustrated history of firearms for military and sporting uses.
Firearms Control, by Colin Greenwood, Routledge & Kegan Paul, London (England), 1972. 274 pp. $11.75.
A study of armed crime and firearms control in England and Wales.
Firearms Dictionary, by R. A. "Bob" Steindler. Stackpole Books, Harrisburg, PA, 288 pp., illus. $7.95.
Firearms Encyclopedia, by Geo. C. Nonte, Jr., Outdoor Life-Harper & Row, NY, 1973. 341 pp., illus. $11.95.
A through Z coverage of gun and shooting terms.
Firearm Silencers, by D. B. McLean. Normount Armament Co., Wickenburg, AZ, 1968. 123 pp., illus., paperbound. $4.00.
The history, design, and development of silencers for U.S. military firearms.
Firearms, Traps & Tools of the Mountain Men, by Carl P. Russell. A. A. Knopf, NY, 1967. 448 pp., illus. in line drawings. $15.00.
Detailed survey of fur traders' equipment in the early days of the west.

The Fireside Book of Guns, by Larry Koller. Simon & Schuster, N.Y.C., 1959. 284 pp., illus. in artistic photography and full-color plates. $12.95
On all counts the most beautiful and colorful production of any arms book of our time, this work adequately tells the story of firearms in America—from the first explorers to today's sportsmen.
Four Studies on the History of Arms, by Arne Hoff, et al. Tjhusmuseet, Copenhagen, 1964. 145 pp., illus., paperbound. $6.75.
A Danish museum publication containing in English text scholarly monographs on arms topics of historic interest.
The A. B. Frost Book, by Henry M. Reed. Charles E. Tuttle Co., Rutland, VT, 1967. 149 pp., of large format with over 70 plates, 44 in color, and many line drawings. $20.00.
A collection of the sketches, drawings and paintings by a famous outdoor artist (1851-1928). Includes his noted sporting and shooting masterpieces.
Game Animals, by Leonard Lee Rue III. Harper & Row, NY, 1968. 655 pp., incl. appendix and index. Illus. with maps and photos. $6.50.
A concise guide to and field book of North American species.
Game and Bird Calling, by A. C. Becker, Jr., A. S. Barnes and Co., NY, 1972. 147 pp., illus. $7.95.
Discusses various types of calls and techniques used by hunters—tyros and professionals.
Game Bird Carving, by Bruce Burk. Winchester Press, NY, 1972. 256 pp. $12.50.
The first step-by-step book on bird carving techniques. Over 700 photographs and line drawings by the author.
Game Birds of North America, by Leonard Lee Rue and Douglas Allen, Jr., Outdoor Life-Harper & Row, NY, 1973. 490 pp., illus. $12.50.
Complete details on 75 species of American game birds. Profusely illustrated in color.
Game and Fish Cookbook, by H. and J. Barnett. Grossman Publ., New York, NY 1968, 162 pp., illus. $7.95.
Special culinary attention to fish and game, with interesting and different touches.
Game in the Kitchen, by B. Flood and W. C. Roux (eds.). Barre Publ., Barre, MA 1st ed., 1968, 234 pp., illus. $7.50.
A fish and game cookbook, with menus and information on preservation, cooking and serving.
Gas, Air and Spring Guns of the World, by W. H. B. Smith. Stackpole Books, Harrisburg, PA, 1957. 279 pp., well illus. $5.98.
A detailed, well-documented history of the air and gas gun industry throughout the world. It includes ancient and modern arms, and it devotes a chapter to accurate velocity tests of modern arms.
German Army Uniforms and Insignia 1933-1945, by B. L. Davis. World Publ. Co., NY, 1972. 224 pp. $12.
Every aspect of the uniforms, insignias, and accoutrements of the Third Reich Army are covered in detail. Many illus. in full color.

German Infantry Weapons, ed. by D. B. McLean. Normount Armament Co., Wickenburg, AZ, 1966. 191 pp., illus., paperbound. $3.50.
World War II German weapons described and illustrated, from military intelligence research.
German Infantry Weapons of World War II, by A. J. Barker. Arco Publ. Co., New York, NY 1969, 76 pp., illus. $3.50.
Historical and statistical data on all types of the subject weapons, ammunition, etc.
German Secret Weapons of World War II, by I. V. Hogg. Arco Pub. Co., NY, 1970. 80 pp., illus. $3.50.
Compact, comprehensive account of Germany's secret weapons, eccentric and brilliant. Includes plans and technical details.
German Tanks of World War II, by F. M. von Senger und Etterlin. Stackpole Books, Harrisburg, PA, 1969. 176 pp., nearly 300 photos and drawings. Large format. $11.95.
A fully illustrated and definitive history of German armoured fighting vehicles, 1926-1945. Written in English.
German Weapons-Uniforms-Insignia 1841-1918, by Maj. J. E. Hicks. J. E. Hicks & Son, La Canada, CA, 1958. 158 pp., illus. $6.00.
Originally published in 1937 as *Notes on German Ordnance 1841-1918,* this new edition offers the collector a wealth of information gathered from many authentic sources.
Gourmet Cooking for Free, by Bradford Angier. Stackpole Books. Harrisburg, PA 1970. 190 pp. illus. $4.95.
Cookery of large and small game, seafood and wild plants.
Great American Guns and Frontier Fighters, by Will Bryant, Grosset & Dunlap, NY, 1961. 160 pp., illus. $3.95.
Popular account of firearms in U.S. history and of the events in which they played a part.
The Great American Shooting Prints, selections and text by Robt. Elman. A. A. Knopf, NY, 1972. Large format. 72 full color plates. $25.
The hunting life in America as portrayed in paintings and lithographs from the 1820s to the present.
The Great Art of Artillery, by Casimir Simienowicz, with a new foreword by Brig. O. F. G. Hogg. S. R. Publi., Ltd., London, Eng., 1971. $15.00.
Facsimile of the original 1729 ed. Red-hot shot, chain shot and other incendiary "globes" are described in detail, and rockets are covered most extensively. Basically a work on fireworks—military and civil.

Grundriss der Waffenlehre, ed. by J. Schott, Akademische D. U. V., Graz, Austria, 1971. 395 pp. of German text, plus a 24 pp. Atlas. $22.50
Facsimile reprint of the 1876 ed. written by Edw. Zernin and publ. in Darmstadt and Leipzig.
Guide to the Soviet Navy, by Siegfried Breyer, U.S. Naval Institute, Annapolis, MD, 1971. 353 pp. $10.00.
Compact, comprehensive, up-to-date view of organization, construction, weapons, equipment, forces, bases and ports. Over 100 photos, plans, tables and maps, specifications and profiles.
Guide to United States Machine Guns, by K. F. Schreier, Jr., Normount Armament Co., Wickenburg, AZ, 1971. 178 pp., illus. Paper, $4.95.
All machine guns procured by the U.S. Armed Forces and some of an experimental nature.
Gun Carriages: An Aide Memoire to the Military Sciences, 1846, by R. J. Nelson. Museum Restoration Service, Ottawa, Canada, 1972. 64 pp. Paper covers. $3.00.
Originally prepared in 1846 as a manual for the officers of the British Army. Illus. with detailed scaled drawings, plus tables of dimensions and weights.
Gun Control, by Robert J. Kukla, Stackpole Books, Harrisburg, PA, 1973. 448 pp., illus. $8.95.
A written record of the efforts to eliminate the private possession of firearms in America.
Gun Digest, 30th ed., ed. by John T. Amber, DBI Books, Inc., Northfield, IL, 1975. 480 pp., illus. Paper covers. $8.95.
Known as the world's greatest gun book because of its factual, informative data for shooters, hunters, collectors, reloaders and other enthusiasts.

Gun Digest Book of Modern Gun Values, by Dean A. Grennell & Jack Lewis, DBI Books, Inc., Northfield, IL, 1975. 288 pp., illus. $7.95.
Invaluable guide for buying, selling, trading or identifying guns—handguns, rifles and shotguns are covered in separate sections. Feature articles relate to collecting and values.
The Gun Digest Book of Exploded Firearms Drawings, edited by H. A. Murtz, Digest Books, Inc., Northfield, IL, 1974. 288 pp., illus., paper covers. $5.95.
275 isometric views of modern and collectors' handguns and long guns.

Gun Digest Treasury, ed. by J. T. Amber, 4th ed., 1972. Digest Books, Inc. Northfield, IL. 352 pp. illus. Paper, $5.95.
The best from 25 years of the Gun Digest, selected from the annual editions.
The Gun, 1834, by Wm. Greener, with intro. by D. B. McLean. Normount Technical Publ., Wickenburg, AZ, 1971. 240 pp., illus. Paper, $4.95.
Reprint of the 1835 British ed. on various small firearms.
Gundogs, Their Care and Training, by M. Brander. A. & C. Black, London, Eng., 1969. 97 pp., illus. $4.95.
A British manual on hunting dogs.
Gun Fun with Safety, by G. E. Damon. Standard Publications, Huntington, W. VA, 1947. 206 pp., well illus. $6.00.
A long out-of-print work that is still much sought. A fine general coverage of arms and ammunition, old and new, with chapters on shooting, targets, etc., with safety always upper-most.
Gun Talk, edited by Dave Moreton. Winchester Press, NY, 1973. 256 pp., illus. $7.95.
A treasury of original writing by the top gun writers and editors in America. Practical advice about every aspect of the shooting sports.
The Gunfighter, Man or Myth? by Joseph G. Rosa, Oklahoma Press, Norman, OK, 1969. 229 pp., illus., (including weapons). $5.95.
A well-documented work on gunfights and gunfighters of the West and elsewhere. Great treat for all gunfighter buffs.
The Gunfighters, by Dale T. Schoenberger, The Caxton Printers, Ltd., Caldwell, ID, 1971. 207 pp., illus. $12.95.
Startling expose of our foremost Western folk heroes.
The Gun-Founders of England, by Charles ffoulkes, Geo. Shumway, York, PA, 1969. 133 pp., illus. $15.00.
Detailed study of cannon, casting. Describes preparation of moulds, castings, mfg. of powder and shot, etc.
The Gunner's Bible, by Bill Riviere. Doubleday, N.Y.C., 1965. 192 pp., illus. Paperbound. $1.95.
General Guide to modern sporting firearms and their accessories, for all shooters.
Gunology, by P. M. Doane. Winchester-Western, N.Y.C., 1968. 64 pp., illus., paperbound. $2.95.
A comprehensive course for professional sporting arms salesmen. Of great help to the arms man are the hundreds of questions on arms and hunting.
Guns, by Dudley Pope. Delacorte Press, N.Y.C., 1965. 256 pp., illus. $9.98.
Concise history of firearms, stressing early museum-quality weapons. Includes small arms as well as artillery, naval, and airborne types. Fine photographs, many in color.

Guns, by F. Wilkinson, Grosset & Dunlap, NY, 1971. 168 pp., $3.95.
From the discovery of gunpowder to the complex weapons of today. Over 100 photos in color.

Guns & Ammo 1975 Annual, Guns & Ammo magazine, Petersen Publ. Co., Los Angeles, CA, 1974. 368 pp., illus., paper covers. $4.95.
Annual catalog of sporting firearms and accessories, with numerous articles for gun enthusiasts.

Guns & Ammo Guide to Guns for Home Defense, by Elmer Keith, et al, Petersen Publ. Co., Los Angeles, CA, 1975. 176 pp., illus. Paper covers. $3.95.
How to select a gun for home defense, and learning how to use it.

Guns Illustrated 1976, 8th ed., edited by Harold A. Murtz, DBI Books, Inc., Northfield, IL, 1975. 288 pp., illus. Paper covers. $6.95.
The 1976 ed. combines all new feature articles for the shooter, collector and hunter with a complete catalog section of all available firearms.

Guns; An Illustrated History of Artillery, ed. by Jos. Jobe, New York Graphic Society, Greenwich, CT, 1971. 216 pp., illus. $17.98.
Traces the history and technology of artillery from its beginnings in the 14th century to its 20th century demise in the face of aerial bombs and guided missiles.

Guns and Shooting, by Maj. Sir Gerald Burrard. Barnes & Co., N.Y.C., 1962. 147 pp. $1.95.
Expanded from the author's earlier *In the Gunroom*, this contains 153 often-asked questions on shotguns and rifles, with authoritative answers covering guns, ammunition, ballistics, etc.

The Guns of Harpers Ferry, by S. E. Brown Jr. Virginia Book Co., Berryville, VA, 1968. 157 pp., illus. $12.50.
Catalog of all known firearms produced at the U.S. armory at Harpers Ferry, 1798-1861, with descriptions, illustrations and a history of the operations there.

Guns of the Wild West, by Elsie Hanauer. A. S. Barnes & Co., NY, 1973. 112 pp. $12.
History and development of the gun, the early frontiersmen who needed firearms to survive, and the early outlaws who used guns as part of their trade. Nearly 100 pages of full-color illus.

Guns of the World, edited by Hans Tanner, Petersen Publishing Co., Los Angeles, CA, 1972. 400 pp., illus., paper covers. $6.95.
A complete collectors and traders guide, with chapters by noted experts on various categories of rifles and handguns.

The Gunsmith in Colonial Virginia, by Harold B. Gill, Jr., University Press of Virginia, Charlottesville, VA, 1975. 200 pp., illus. Paper covers, $3.00; Cloth, $5.00.
The role of the gunsmith in colonial Virginia from the first landing at Jamestown through the Revolution is examined, with special attention to those who lived and worked in Williamsburg.

The Hall Carbine Affair; An Essay in Historiography, by R. Gordon Wasson, Privately Printed, Danbury, CT, 1971. 250 pp., illus. Deluxe slip-cased ed. of 250 copies. $75.00.
Based on the original work (limited to 100 copies) of 1941 and a 1948 revised ed. of only 750 copies. This issue, enlarged and re-researched, relates to sales and purchases of Hall carbines in the Civil War, in which J. Pierpont Morgan was involved.

Handbook for Hythe, by H. Busk, Richmond Pub. Co., Richmond, England, 1971. 194 pp., illus. $8.50.
Reprint of the 1860 ed. explaining laws of projectiles with an introduction to the system of musketry.

Handbook of Self-Defense for Law Enforcement Officers, by John Martone. Arco Publ. Co., New York, NY, 1968. 1st ed., 4th printing, 111 pp., $4.00.
A clearly-illustrated manual on offensive and defensive techniques recommended for the use of policemen.

Hatcher's Notebook, by Maj. Gen. J. S. Hatcher. Stackpole Books, Harrisburg, Pa., 1952. 2nd ed. with four new chapters, 1957. 629 pp., illus. $11.95.
A dependable source of information for gunsmiths, ballisticians, historians, hunters, and collectors.

Hibbard, Spencer, Bartlett & Co. Catalog. American Reprints, St. Louis, MO, 1969. 92 pp., illus. Paper, $5.00.
Reprint of 1884 catalog on guns, rifles, revolvers, ammo, powder flasks, etc. Descriptions and contemporary prices.

History of the British Army, by P. Young and J. P. Lawford. G. P. Putnam's Sons, NY, 1970. 304 pp., profusely illus., much in color. $15.00.
Traces history of the British Army from the early 17th century to the present.

A History of the Dress of the British Soldier, by Lt. Col. John Luard, Frederick Muller Ltd., London, 1971. 171 pp., illus. 50 plates. $15.00.
Reprint of the 1852 ed., limited to 400 numbered copies.

A History of Firearms, by Major Hugh B. C. Pollard, Burt Franklin, NY, a facsimile ed. with a new introduction by Joseph R. Riling, 1973. 320 pp., illus. $22.50.
An excellent survey of the development of hand firearms. Lists over 2,000 American and foreign gunmakers.

A History of Knives, by Harold L. Peterson. Charles Scripner's Sons, N.Y.C., 1966. 64 pp., illus. $5.95.
The fine drawings of Daniel D. Feaser combine with the author's commendable text to produce an important work. From the earliest knives of prehistoric man through the evolution of the metal knife.

A History of War and Weapons, 449 to 1660, by A. V. B. Norman and D. Pottinger. Thomas Y. Crowell Co., NY, 1966. 224 pp., well illus. with sketches. $6.95.
An excellent work for the scholar on the evolution of war and weapons in England. Many sketches of arms and weapons of all sorts add importance.

The Hitler Albums, Vol. I, by Roger J. Bender, R. J. Bender Publ. Co., Mountain View, CA, 1970. 144 pp., $10.95.
Complete photographic study of Mussolini's state visit to Germany in September, 1937. 175 photos and illus..

Home Book of Taxidermy and Tanning, by G. J. Grantz, Stackpole Books, Harrisburg, PA, 1969, 160 pp., illus. $7.95.
Amateur's primer on mounting fish, birds, animals, and trophies.

Home Guide to Muzzle Loaders, by Geo. C. Nonte, Jr., Stackpole Books, Harrisburg, PA, 1974. 219 pp., illus. $6.95.
From the basics of muzzle loading, its ammo, to the differences between the modern and replica muzzle loader, plus how-to-make one.

Home in Your Pack, by Bradford Angier, Stackpole Books, Harrisburg, PA, 1965. 192 pp., illus. $4.50.
An outdoorsman's handbook on equipment, woodcraft, and camping techniques.

Horse Equipments and Cavalry Accoutrements 1891. a reprint of U.S. Ordnance Memoranda No. 29 by Francis Bannerman Sons, Blue Point, NY, 1969, 23 pp., plus 20 plates. $3.50.
U.S. army cavalry equipment described and illustrated in line.

How to Build Your Home in the Woods, by Bradford Angier, Stackpole Books, Harrisburg, PA, 1967, 310 pp., illus. $7.00.
Detailed instructions on building cabins, shelters, etc., with natural materials. How to obtain food from nature, and how to live in the wilderness in comfort.

How to Cook His Goose (and other wild game), by Karen Green and Betty Black, Winchester Press, NY, 1973. 198 pp. $6.95.
An informative and delightful guide to preparing and cooking game of all types.

How to Defend Yourself, your Family, and your Home, by Geo. Hunter. David McKay, N.Y.C., 1967, 307 pp., illus. $6.95.
The only book available for the public at large that advocates their ownership of firearms—including handguns. Covers laws of self-defense, setting up home protection, and much else.

How to Live in the Woods on Pennies a Day, by Bradford Angier, Stackpole Books, Harrisburg, PA, 1971. 192 pp., illus. $6.95.
New reprint on modern-day wilderness living in America, plus cooking and recipes.

The Identification and Registration of Firearms, by Vaclav "Jack" Krcma, C. C. Thomas, Springfield, IL, 1971. 173 pp., illus. $17.50.
Analysis of problems and improved techniques of recording firearms data accurately.

Improvised Modified Firearms, Vol. I, by John Minnery and J. David Truby, Paladin Press, Boulder, CO, 1975. 130 pp., illus. $9.95.
Identifies types of improvised modified weapons as well as providing details of specific improvisations.

Indian and Oriental Armour, by Lord Egerton of Tatton. Stackpole Books, Harrisburg, PA, 1968. 178 pp., well illus., some in color. $14.95.
New edition of a rare work which has been a key reference for students of the subject, plus a creditable source on Oriental history.

Infantry Equipment 1875. A reprint of U.S. Ordnance Memoranda No. 19 by Francis Bannerman Sons, Blue Point, NY, 1969. 62 pp., plus 9 plates. $6.50.
A report covering materials, supplies, etc., to outfit troops in field and garrison.

Instructions for Use & Care of Gatling Guns, compiled by Commander J. D. Marvin, Fortress Publ., Stoney Creek, Ontario, Can., 1974. 43 pp. plus 5 folding plates, paper covers. $3.95.
A facsimile of the original 1875 manual on Naval Gatling Guns.

Instructions to Young Sportsmen: Guns and Shooting, by Col. P. Hawker, Richmond Publ. Co., Richmond, England, 1971. 507 pp., illus. $17.50. Deluxe ed., $35.00.
Reprint of the 1833 British work on guns, shooting and killing game.

Introduction to Muzzle Loading, by R. O. Ackerman. Publ. by the author, Albuquerque, NM, 1966. 20 pp., illus. with author's sketches. $1.50.
This booklet, in paper wrappers, will be Book No. 1 of a projected series. Contains a glossary of muzzle loading terms, and is aimed at the novice.

An Introduction to Tool Marks, Firearms and the Striagraph, by J. E. Davis. Chas. C. Thomas, Springfield, IL, 1st ed., 1958. 282 pp. $8.50.
Textbook on micro-contour analysis in criminalistics, with emphasis upon the striagraph in analysis of evidence.

Ironmaker To The Confederacy, by C. B. Dew. Yale Univ. Press, New Haven, 1966. 345 pp., illus. $10.00.
History of Joseph R. Anderson's Tredegar Iron works in Richmond, VA, which produced weapons and military equipment essential to the Confederacy's armed forces.

Jane's Infantry Weapons 1974-1975, ed. by F. W. A. Hobart, Jane's USA, NY, 1975. 843 pp., illus. with over 1500 photographs and diagrams. $65.00.
Deals with all weapons known to be in service throughout the world.

Jane's Weapons Systems: 1973-74, by R. T. Pretty and D. H. R. Archer, Editors. Jane's Yearbooks, London, 1973. 606 pp. illus. $65.00.
Catalog of military hardware of the major nations.

Japanese Infantry Weapons, ed. by D. B. McLean. Normount Armament Co., Wickenburg, AZ, 1966. 241 pp., well illus., paperbound. $4.95.
Survey of World War II Japanese weapons, based on military intelligence research.

The Japanese Sword and Its Fittings, by members of the Japanese Sword Society of New York. Cooper Union Museum, N.Y.C., 1966. Paper covers. 26 pp. of text plus many illus. $3.50.
The authoritative text in the form of a catalog describing the illus. of items in the possession of members of the society.

John Groth's World of Sport, by J. Groth. Winchester Press. NY, 1970. 160 pp., illus. $6.95.
Exotic and exciting sports recorded by a man whose vital drawings convey the essence of the action. 40 color paintings.

Johnson Rifles and Light Machine Guns, ed. by D. B. McLean. Normount Armament Co., Wickenburg, AZ, 1968. 55 pp., illus., paperbound. $2.50.
Manual on the only recoil-operated auto-loading rifle issued to U.S. forces.

Keith; An Autobiography, by Elmer Keith, Winchester Press, NY, 1974. 381 pp., illus. $10.00.
Memoirs of the bronc rider who became a world-famous big-game guide and the dean of American firearms authorities.

Knife Digest, ed. by Wm. L. Cassidy, Knife Digest Publ. Co., Berkeley, CA, 1974. 285 pp., illus. Paper covers. $5.95.
The first annual publ. for the cutlery enthusiast, collector and maker.

Knife Throwing: A Practical Guide, by H. K. McEvoy. C. E. Tuttle Co., VT, 1973. 112 pp., illus. Paper covers. $3.25.
For the amateur sportsman and experienced thrower as well. Building targets, buying information, etc. How to use knives and tomahawks in hunting game.

Knights in Armor, by S. Glubok, Harper & Row, NY, 1969. 48 pp., illus. $5.50.
Story of European body armor told for young readers.

Knives and Knifemakers, Sid Latham, Winchester Press, NY, 1973. 152 pp., illus. $15.00.
Lists makers and suppliers of knife making materials and equipment.

Kuhlhoff on Guns, by Pete Kuhlhoff, Winchester Press, NY, 1970. 180 pp., illus. $5.95.
A selection of firearms articles by the late Gun Editor of *Argosy* Magazine.

Lewis Automatic Machine Gun, publ. originally by Savage Arms Co., Utica, NY. A reprint by L. A. Funk, Puyallup, WA, 1969. 47 pp., illus., paper covers. $1.50.
This facsimile covers the Model 1916 gun, explaining all features of operation, action, nomenclature, stripping and assembly.

The Long African Day, by Norman Myers. The Macmillan Co., Riverside, NJ, 1973. 400 pp. $25.
300 magnificent photos and a perceptive text explore East Africa, an area whose wildlife and countryside may be the most beautiful, fascinating, and varied in the world.

The Machine Gun, Vol., II, Part VII, by Lt. Col. G. M. Chinn. Paladin Press, Boulder, Col., n.d. 215 pp., illus. $15.00.
Reprint of a 1952 Navy publication of Soviet WW II rapid fire weapons.

Machine Guns, by Peter Chamberlain and Terry Gander, Arco Publ. Co., NY, 1974. 64 pp., illus. Paper covers. $5.95.
Covers arms used by the principle countries taking part in WW II. Each machine gun is described and illus.

Manual of the Automatic Rifle (Chauchat), a facsimile by Frontier Press, Arvada, CO, 1974. 96 pp., illus. Paper covers. $2.65.
Facsimile of A.E.F. Manual 266 originally publ. in Nancy, France.

Marksmanship: Secrets of High Scoring from a World Champ, by Gary L. Anderson. Simon & Schuster, NY, 1972. 79 pp. $4.95.
Illus. step-by-step guide to target shooting. Covers equipment, ammunition, breath control, arm position, etc.

Marlin Catalog of 1897. A reprint in facsimile by the Rocky Mountain Investment and Antique Co.; Cheyenne, WY, 1969. 192 pp. Well illus., paper covers, $3.50.
All models are covered, cartridges, sights, engraving, accessories, reloading tools, etc.

Marlin Catalog, 1905, Rocky Mountain Investment and Antique Co.; Cheyenne, WY, 1971. 128 pp. Paper, $4.00.
Reprint. Rifles, shotguns, pistols, tools, cartridge information, factory engraving and carving illustrated and described.

Mexican Military Arms, The Cartridge Period, by James B. Hughes, Jr. Deep River Armory, Inc., Houston, TX, 1967. 135 pp., photos and line drawings. $4.50.
An interesting and useful work, in imprinted wrappers, covering the period from 1866 to 1967.

Military Modelling, by Donald Featherstone, A. S. Barnes and Co., NY, 1971. 159 pp., illus. $6.95.
Describes the art of moulding and casting, soldering, glueing, painting and construction of small figures.

Military Small Arms of the 20th Century, by Ian V. Hogg & John S. Weeks. Digest Books, Inc., Northfield, IL, 1973. 288 pp. Paper covers. $7.95.
Weapons from the world over are meticulously examined in this comprehensive encyclopedia of those military small arms issued since 1900. Over 600 illus.

Military Uniforms, 1686-1918, by Rene North. Grosset & Dunlap, NY, 1970. 159 pp., illus. $3.95.
Concise survey of European and U.S. military dress and its history during the principal wars. Profusely illus., with some colored drawings.

Modern ABC's of Bow and Arrow, by G. H. Gillelan. Stackpole Books, Harrisburg, PA, 1967. 160 pp., illus. $4.95.
Survey of techniques for beginners and experts in target archery as well as bowhunting.

Modern ABC's of Guns, by R. A. Steindler. Stackpole Books, Harrisburg, PA, 1965. 191 pp., illus. $4.95.
Concise lexicon of today's sporting firearms, their components, ammunition, accessory equipment and use.

NRA Firearms & Ammunition Fact Book. National Rifle Assn., Wash., D.C., 1970. 352 pp., illus. Paper covers. $2.
Articles, questions and answers, definitions, charts and tables. A wealth of accurate, sound information on everything connected with shooting.

New England Militia Uniforms and Accoutrements, by J. O. Curtis and Wm. H. Guthman. Old Sturbridge Inc., Sturbridge, MA, 1971. 102 pp. Paper covers. $4.
An identification guide which illustrates uniforms, epaulettes, helmets, helmet plates, belt buckles and cartridge pouches.

New Principles of Gunnery, by Benjamin Robins. Richmond Publ. Co., London, 1972. 190 pp. $11.75.
Facsimile of the rare 1742 ed. For anyone, including libraries, interested in gunnery, military history and technology.

The New Way of the Wilderness, By Calvin Rutstrum. Macmillan Co., New York, NY 1st ed., 1966 [4th printing]. 276 pp., illus. in line. $4.95.
An outdoorsman's manual on traveling and living in the open, with chapters on transportation, equipment, food, hunting and fishing for food.

L. D. Nimschke, Firearms Engraver, by R. L. Wilson. John J. Malloy, publisher, Teaneck, NJ, 1965. Quarto, 107 pp., profusely illus. $17.50.
Showing a wide variety of designs, initials and monograms and ever-somany portions of collectors' arms. A thoroughly interesting work for the collector and an inspiration to the engraver.

No Second Place Winner, by Wm. H. Jordan, publ. by the author, Shreveport, LA (Box 4072), 1962. 114 pp., illus. $6.50.
Guns and gear of the peace officer, ably discussed by a U.S. Border Patrolman for over 30 years, and a first-class shooter with handgun, rifle, etc.

The Order of the Death's Head, by Heinz Hohne, Coward-McCann, Inc., NY, 1970. 690 pp., illus. $12.50.
The Story of Hitler's S.S., the most horrifying organization ever invented by the Germans. Based on Himmler's personal staff files, the Nuremberg trials and the Reich Security Office.

O.S.S. Special Weapons Catalog, a facsimile reproduction by Paladin Press, Boulder, CO, 1975. 100 pp., illus. Paper covers, $5.95.
Catalog of special weapons devices and equipment.

The Other Mr. Churchill, by Macdonald Hastings. Dodd Mead, N.Y.C., 1965. 336 pp., illus. $1.98.
Important biography of a great London gunmaker and forensic ballistics expert, who contributed much to the color and excellence of British firearms tradition.

Outdoor Life Gun Data Book, by F. Philip Rice, Harper & Row Publ., Inc., NY, 1975. 480 pp., illus. $10.00.
Packed with formulas, data, and tips essential to the modern hunter, target shooter, gun collector, and all others interested in guns.

Outdoor Photographer's Digest, ed. by Erwin & Peggy Bauer, DBI Books, Inc., Northfield, IL, 1975. 288 pp., illus. $7.95.
Excellent guide to selection of equipment and techniques to use for the best in outdoor photography.

Outdoor Tips, by L. W. Johnson, Robt. Elman & Jerry Gibbs. Benjamin Co., NY, 1972. 190 pp., illus. Paper covers. $2.95.
Authoritative chapters on American hunting, fishing, camping, other outdoor activities.

Pageant of the Gun, by Harold L. Peterson. Doubleday & Co., Inc., Garden City, NY, 1967. 352 pp., profusely illus. $3.95.
A storehouse of stories on firearms, their romance and lore, their development and use through 10 centuries. A most satisfying history of firearms chronologically presented.

Paradise Below Zero, by Calvin Rutstrum. Macmillan Co., New York, NY 1st ed., 1968. 244 pp., illus. in line and halftone. $5.95.
On the rewards and methods of camping and travel in Eskimo country, including check lists of provisions, tools, equipment, clothing and ways of getting about.

Pictorial History of Tanks of the World 1915-45, by P. Chamberlain & C. Ellis. Stackpole Books, Harrisburg, PA, 1972. 256 pp., illus. $9.98.
All tanks produced for military service are pictured, including many rarely seen experimental models and prototypes.

Pictorial History of the Machine Gun, by F. W. A. Hobart. Drake Publ., Inc., NY, 1972. 256 pp. $9.95.
Text is enhanced by over 240 photos and diagrams and a table of machine gun data giving essential details on a large number of guns—some of which never got beyond the prototype stage.

Picture Book of the Continental Soldier, by C. K. Wilbur. Stackpole Books, Harrisburg, PA, 1969. 96 pp., well illus. $5.95.
A wealth of detailed material in text and fine drawings, depicting Revolutionary War weapons, accouterments, field equipment, and the routine of the solder's life. Included are artillery, edged weapons, muskets, rifles, powder horns, etc.

Picture Book of the Revolution's Privateers, by C. Keith Wilbur. Stackpole Books, Harrisburg, PA, 1973. 96 pp. $5.95.
Hundreds of drawn illus., plus explanatory text, show the privateersmen, their ships, gear, weapons, tactics, etc.

Pocket Guide to Archery, by H. T. Sigler. Stackpole Co., Harrisburg, PA, 1960. 96 pp., illus. $2.95.
Useful introduction to the subject, covering equipment, shooting techniques, and bow hunting of small game and deer.

A Pocket History of Artillery: Light Field Guns, by Franz Kosar, Ian Allan, London, 1974. 248 pp., illus. $7.25.
Covers guns of the European countries and the non-European major powers, from the beginning of this century to the present.

Practical Wildlife Management, by Geo. V. Burger. Winchester Press, NY, 1973. 224 pp., illus. $8.95.
Anyone interested in wildlife will find this an invaluable reference as well as entertaining, informative reading.

Presenting America's Aristocracy of Fine Cutlery, Grawolf Trading Co., Milwaukee, WI, 1971. Vol. 2 of a limited, numbered ed. Paper, $3.50.
Unpaginated with hundreds of illus. and explanations.

E. C. Prudhomme, Master Gun Engraver, A Retrospective Exhibition: 1946-1973, intro. by John T. Amber, The R. W. Norton Art Gallery, Shreveport, LA, 1973. 32 pp., illus., paper covers. $3.00.
Examples of master gun engraving by Jack Prudhomme.

Reading the Woods, by Vinson Brown. Stackpole Books, Harrisburg, PA, 1969. 160 pp. illus. $5.95.
Clues to the past, present and future development of wooded areas by observation of signs of change, decay, influences of water and wildlife, and the impact of man's presence.

The Records and Badges of Every Regiment and Corps in the British Army, by H. M. Chichester and Geo. Burges-Short. Fred. Muller, Ltd., London, 1970. A reprint of the 2nd ed. of 1900. 240 illus., in the text and 24 color plates $27.50.
A magnificent facsimile with gilt top giving the history, uniforms, colors and insignia in satisfying detail of much-wanted data on subject.

Records of the Scottish Volunteer Force 1859-1908, by Lt. Gen. Sir James Moncrieff Grierson. Frederich Muller, Ltd., London, 1972. 372 pp. $29.50.
Limited reprint of the rare classic on the history and uniforms of the Scottish Volunteers before the re-organization of 1908. 47 full-color plates show 239 different uniforms.

The Redbook of Used Gun Values, rev. 1975 ed., Publishers Dev. Corp., Skokie, IL, 1975. 130 pp. Paper covers. $2.50.
Today's values for commercial firearms, listed by manufacturers with a bonus listing of antique gun values.

Remington Arms Revised Price-List, 1902. Arthur McKee, Northport, NY, n.d. 64 pp. Paper covers. $3.50.
Reprint, fully illustrated.

Remington Firearms, 1906 Catalog, Arthur McKee, Northport, NY, n.d., 48 pp., illus. Paper covers. $3.50.
Reprint. Guns, parts, ammo., prices, etc.

Riot Control—Materiel and Techniques, by Rex Applegate. Stackpole Books, Harrisburg, PA 1969. 320 pp., illus. $9.95.
Originally released as *Kill or Get Killed*, later as *Crowd and Riot Control*. Designed for law officer training, plus deployment of personnel, chemicals and special equipment for best results.

Round Shot and Rammers, by H. L. Peterson. Stackpole Books, Harrisburg, PA, 1969. 128 pp., illus. $3.98.
Artillery in America Through the Civil War years, with much detail on manufacture, history, accessory equipment, and use of all types of cannon. Fine line drawings show the guns, their equipment, and the men who used them.

Russian Infantry Weapons of World War II, by A. J. Barker and John Walter, Arco Publ. Co., NY, 1971. 80 pp., $3.50.
History and development of World War II infantry weapons used by the Red Army. Each weapon is fully described and illus..

Sam Colt: Genius, by Robt. F. Hudson, American Archives Publ. Co., Topsfield, MA, 1971. 160 pp., illus. Plastic spiral bound. $6.50.
Historical review of Colt's inventions, including facsimiles of patent papers and other Colt information.

Scloppetaria, by Capt. H. Beaufroy, Richmond Publ. Co., Richmond, England, 1971. 251 pp. $14.00.
Reprint of the 1808 edition written under the pseudonym "A Corporal of Riflemen". Covers rifles and rifle shooting, the first such work in English.

The Search for the Well-Dressed Soldier 1865-1890, by Gordon Chappell. Arizona Hist. Society, Tucson, AR, 1972. 51 pp., illus. Paper covers. $2.50.
Developments and innovations in U.S. Army uniforms on the western frontier.

Secret Fighting Arts of the World, by J. F. Gilbey. Tuttle, Rutland, VT 1963. 150 pp., illus. $6.50.
20 chapters on advanced techniques of unarmed combat, described in anecdotal form.

Secret Weapons of the Third Reich, by L. E. Simon, We, Inc., Old Greenwich, CT, 1971. 248 pp., illus. $8.95.
Review of German World War II military research and its products.

Shooter's Bible, No. 66, ed. by Robert Koumjian, Shooter's Bible, So. Hackensack, NJ, 1975. 574 pp., illus. Paper covers. $6.95.
An annually-publ. guide to firearms, ammunition, and accessories.

Shooter's Bible Game Cook Book, by Geraldine Steindler. Follett Publ. Co., Chicago IL 1965. 224 pp., illus., cloth, $6.95; paper, $4.95.
Full information on preparing game for the table, including recipes and methods of field-dressing.

The Shooter's Guide: or Complete Sportsman's Companion, by B. Thomas, Richmond Publ. Co., Richmond, England, 1971. 264 pp., illus. $12.00.
Reprint of an 1816 British handbook on hunting small game, game laws, dogs, guns and ammunition.

Shooting, by M. Turner and St. Tucker, Cogswell & Harrison, London, 1970. 176 pp., illus. $2.95.
Instruction manual for novices and the young in sports.

Shooting the Muzzle-Loaders, ed. by R. A. Steindler, J. Philip O'Hara, Inc., Chicago, IL, 1975. 224 pp., illus. Paper covers. $6.95.
A complete treatise on the muzzle-loader written by experts. Covers rifle, shotgun and pistol.

The Shorebirds of North America, by Peter Matthiesen, ed. by Gordon Stout, with species accounts by R. S. Palmer. Viking Press, N.Y.C., 1967, 288 pp., 32 6-color plates, 10"x14", $22.50.
A magnificent book, probably the outstanding work on the shorebirds of the northern western world. 32 chapters cover 59 species. The illustrations are superb.

Silencers. Paladin Press, Boulder, CO, 1971 205 pp., illus. $9.95; paper covers. $5.95.
Reprint of Frankford Arsenal Report R-1896. The functional and physical details on foreign and domestic silencers, including patent drawings, engineering data, manufacture, etc..

Silencers, Snipers & Assassins, by J. David Truby, Paladin Press, Boulder, CO, 1972. 209 pp., illus. $15.95.
Traces development of silencers from their invention by Hiram Maxim in 1908 to American snipers' use during the Korean conflict.

Six-guns and Saddle Leather, by Ramon F. Adams. University of Oklahoma Press, Norman, OK, 1969, 801 pp., $25.00.
A bibliography of books and pamphlets on western outlaws and gunmen. A brand new revised and enlarged edition.

Sketch Book 76: The American Soldier 1775-1781, by R. Klinger and R. A. Wilder, Pioneer Press Books, Union City, TN, 1967. 53 pp., illus. Paper covers. $2.75.
Sketches, notes, and patterns compiled from a study of clothing and equipment used by the American foot soldier in the Revolutionary War.

Skills for Taming the Wilds, by Bradford Angier, Stackpole Books, Harrisburg, PA, 1967. 320 pp., illus. $6.95.
A handbook of woodcraft wisdom, by a foremost authority, showing how to obtain maximum comfort from nature.

Small Arms Identification and Operation Guide—Eurasian Communist Countries, by Harold E. Johnson, Inco., 1972. 218 pp., illus. Paper covers. $4.00.
Reprint of 1970 U.S. Army manual FSTC-CW-07-03-70.

Small Arms Lexicon and Concise Encyclopedia, by Chester Mueller and John Olson. Stoeger Arms, So. Hackensack, NJ, 1968. 312 pp., 500 illus. $14.95; paper covers $5.95.
Definitions, explanations, and references on antiques, optics, ballistics, etc., from A to Z. Over 3,000 entries plus appendix.

Small Arms of the World, by W. H. B. Smith and J. E. Smith. 10th ed., 1973. Stackpole Books, Harrisburg, PA. 786 pp., profusely illus. $9.98.
A most popular firearms classic for easy reference. Covers the small arms of 42 countries, clearly showing operational principles. A timeless volume of proven worth.

The Sportsman's Eye, by James Gregg, Winchester Press, NY, 1971. 210 pp., illus. $6.95.
How to make better use of your eyes in the outdoors.

Stoeger Mail Order and Gun Parts Catalog, 2nd ed. Stoeger Arms, So. Hackensack, NJ, 1972. 416 pp., illus. Paper covers. $3.95.
Lists over 1000 parts for handguns, rifles and shotguns, domestic and foreign. Includes gunsmith tools and accessories.

Stories of the Old Duck Hunters and Other Drivel, by Gordon MacQuarrie and compiled by Zack Taylor. Stackpole Books, Harrisburg, PA, 1967. 223 pp., illus. $6.95.
An off-beat relaxing and enjoyable group of 19 best-remembered outdoor stories, previously publ. in magazines.

The Story of the Guns, by Emerson Tennent. Richmond Publ. Co., Surrey, Eng., 1972. 364 pp. $11.50.
Reprint of the original 1864 London ed. Part I—The Rifled Musket, Part 2—Rifled Ordnance, Part 3—The Iron Navy.

Submachine Guns Caliber .45, M3 and M3A1, U.S. FM23-41 and TM 9-1217. Normount Armament Co., Wickenburg, AZ, 1967. 141 pp., illus., paperbound. $3.95.
Reprint of two U.S. Army manuals on submachine guns.

The Survival Handbook, by W. K. Merrill. Winchester Press, NY, 1972. 320 pp., illus. $5.95.
How to stay out of trouble in all kinds of terrain and weather. Detailed advice on shelter, food and first aid for those caught unexpectedly in disaster situations.

The Sword and the Centuries . . ., by Alfred Hutton, Charles E. Tuttle Co., Rutland, VT, 1973. 367 pp., illus. $8.50.
A facsimile of the scarce 1901 ed. Describes the various swords used in civilized Europe during the last 5 centuries.

Swords & Daggers, by Frederick Wilkinson. Hawthorn Books, NY, 1968. 256 pp., well illus. $5.95.
Good general survey of edged weapons and polearms of collector interest, with 150 pp. of illustrations and descriptions of arms from Europe, Africa and the Orient.

Tank Data 3, by H. E. Johnson. We Inc., Old Greenwich, CT, 1972. 208 pp., illus. $10.
Proving Ground Series. A collection of photos and data on tanks of all nations.

Tanks; An Illustrated History of Fighting Vehicles, by Armin Halle & Carlo Demand, New York Graphic Society, Greenwich, CT, 1971. 175 pp., illus. $16.98.
Comprehensively traces the development and technology of one of man's most complex and ingenious weapons.

Tanks and Other AFV's of the Blitzkrieg Era, 1939-1941, by B. T. White. The Macmillan Co., Riverside, NJ, 1973. 180 pp. $4.95.
Comprehensive, carefully illus. encyclopedia of the most important armored fighting vehicles developed by the principal countries at war.

Teaching Kids to Shoot, by Henry M. Stebbins. Stackpole Books, Harrisburg, PA 1966. 96 pp. illus. $2.95.
Designed for parents and leaders who want to develop safety conscious firearms-users.

Tear Gas Munitions. by T. F. Swearengen, Charles C. Thomas, Springfield, IL, 1966. 569 pp., illus. $34.50.
An analysis of commercial (riot) gas guns, tear gas projectiles, grenades, small arms ammunition, and related tear gas devices.

Technical Dictionary for Weapon Enthusiasts, Shooters and Hunters, by Gustav Sybertz. Publ. by J. Neumann-Neudamm, 3508 Melsungen, W. Germany, 1969, 164 pp., semi-soft covers. $7.50.
A German-English and English-German dictionary for the sportsman. An excellent handy work.

Tenting on the Plains, by Elizabeth Bacon Custer, Univ. of Oklahoma Press, Norman, OK, 1971. 706 pp. in 3 volumes, plus a 30-page intro. by Jane R. Stewart. Slip-cased. $8.85.
Deals with period after the Civil War when General Custer was stationed in Texas and Kansas.

The Thompson Gun, publ. by Numrich Arms, West Hurley, NY, 1967, 27 pp., illus., paper covers. $1.95.
A facsimile reprint, excellently done, of a 1923 catalog of Thompson sub-machine guns.

Thompson-Submachine Guns, compiled from original manuals by the publ. Normount Armament Co., Wickenburg, AZ, 1968. Over 230 pp., well illus., many exploded views. Paper wrappers. Cloth $7.00, Paper Covers $4.95.
Five reprints in one book: Basic Field Manual, Cal. 45, M1928AI (U.S. Army); Cal. 45, Model 1928, (for British); Cal., 45 (U.S. Ordnance); Model M1, Cal., 45 (U.S. Ordnance) and Ultra Modern Automatic Arms (Auto-Ordnance Corp.).

The Tournament, its periods and phases, by R. C. Clephan. Frederick Ungar Co., NY, 1967. A reprint. 195 pp., illus. with contemporary pictures plus half-tones of armor and weapons used by contestants, $16.50.
A rare and eagerly-sought work, long out-of-print. A scholarly, historical and descriptive account of jousting.

Training Your Own Bird Dog, by Henry P. Davis, G. P. Putnam's Sons, New York, NY. New rev. ed., 1969, 168 pp., plus 10 pp. of field trial records. Illus. with photographs. $5.95.
The reappearance of a popular and practical book for the beginner starting his first bird dog—by an internationally recognized authority.

Treasure Hunter's Digest, by Jack Lewis, DBI Books, Inc., Northfield, IL, 1975. 288 pp., illus. $7.95.
Tells where to go, how to find it, etc. with articles on techniques, legendary treasures and laws.

A Treatise on Ancient Armour and Weapons, by Francis Grose. Benchmark Pub. Co., Glendale, NY, 1970. Irregular pagination. $12.50.
Reprint of a 1786 British monograph showing numerous items from the Tower of London and other sites.

Treatise on Military Small Arms and Ammunition 1888, compiled by Col. J. Bond, R. A. Arms and Armour Press, London, Eng., 1971. 142 pp., illus. $8.75.
Facsimile of the original compiled in 1888 at the School of Musketry, Hythe, and accepted by the British Army as a definitive textbook.

Triggernometry, by Eugene Cunningham. Caxton Printers Lt., Caldwell, ID, 1970. 441 pp., illus. $7.95.
A classic study of famous outlaws and lawmen of the West—their stature as human beings, their exploits and skills in handling firearms. A reprint.

The True Book About Firearms, by R. H. Walton, Frederick Muller, Ltd., London, 1965. 143 pp., illus. $4.00.
How modern weapons work, are used and their effect on history.

Unconventional Warfare Devices and Techniques, a reprint of Army TM 31-200-1 234 pp., illus., paper covers. $10.00.
Published primarily for U.S. Army Special Forces. Deals with destructive techniques and their applications to targets in guerrilla warfare.

Uniforms, Organization and History of the Waffen SS, by R. J. Bender and H. P. Taylor. Borden Publ. Co., Alhambra, CA, 1969-1973. Various pagination. $9.95 each volume.
A projected 4-vol. set, of which 3 books are now ready. Detailed and intriguing study of Hitler's elite supermen.

United States Military Medals & Ribbons, by Philip K. Robles, Charles E. Tuttle Co., Rutland, VT, 1971. 187 pp., $12.50.
A definitive work; 139 plates in full color.

Use and Maintenance of the Browning "Hi-Power" Pistol, (No. 2 MK 1 and Commercial Models), by D. B. McLean. Normount Armament Co., Wickenburg, AZ, 1966. 48 pp., illus., paperbound. $2.00.
Covers the use, maintenance, and repair of various Browning 9mm parabellum pistols.

Warriors and Weapons of Early Times, by Niels M. Saxtorph. The Macmillan Co., Riverside, NJ, 1973. 244 pp. $4.95.
128 pages of superb color illus. of uniforms and military accoutrements from 300 B.C. to 1700, from all over the Old World.

Warriors' Weapons, by Walter Buehr. Crowell Co., NYC, 1963. 186 pp., illus. $5.95.
Illustrated history of pre-gunpower arms, from stone ax to crossbow and catapult.

Weapons of the American Revolution, and Accoutrements, by Warren Moore. A & W Books, NY, 1974. 225 pp., fine illus. $6.98.
Revolutionary era shoulder arms, pistols, edged weapons, and equipment are described and shown in fine drawings and photographs, some in color.

Weapons and Fighting Arts of the Indonesian Archipelago, by Donn F. Draeger. Chas. E. Tuttle Co., VT, 1972. 254 pp., illus. $12.50.
The varied combative forms of the islands, from empty-hand techniques to the use of spears, knives, the kris, etc.

The Weapons Merchants, by Bernt Engelmann, Crown Publ., Inc., NY, 1968. 224 pp., illus. $4.95.
A true account of illegal traffic in death-dealing arms by individuals and governments.

Weapons and Tactics, Hastings to Berlin, by Jac Weller, St. Martin's Press, New York, 1966. 238 pp., illus. $6.00.
Primarily on the infantry weapons of today, with basic data on those of the past.

Weapons of War, by P. E. Cleator. Crowell Co., NYC, 1968. 224 pp., illus. $6.95.
A British survey of warfare from earliest times, as influenced by the weapons available for combat.

A. A. White Engravers, Inc. A catalog, unpaginated, n.d. Paper covers. $2.00.
Current prices and illus. for the engraving of arms.

Whitewings: The White-winged Dove, ed. by C. Cottam & J. B. Trefethen. D. Van Nostrand Co., Princeton, NJ, 1968. 348 pp. $7.50.
Compendium of research publications on an important game bird of Texas and Arizona, the Southwest, including Mexico. Excellent photographs.

Wild Game Cookbook, by L. E. Johnson. Benjamin Co., NYC, 1968. 160 pp. $2.95.
Recipes, sauces, and cooking hints for preparation of all types of game birds and animals.

Wild Sanctuaries . . ., by Robert Murphy. E. P. Dutton & Co., Inc., New York, N.Y, 1968, 288 pp., over 250 photographs in color and monochrome, plus 32 maps, including those of the flyways. $12.95.
Concerns America's national wildlife refuges. An all-encompassing treatise on its subject with fascinating pertinent text.

Wilderness Cookery, by Bradford Angier. Stackpole Books, Harrisburg, PA, 1969. 256 pp., illus. $4.95.
An excellent work, one that will be of big interest to hunters, fishermen, campers, et al.

Wilderness Gear You Can Make Yourself, by Bradford Angier. Stackpole Books, Harrisburg, PA, 1973. 192 pp., illus. $6.95.
Detailed, illus. guide to let you make your own outdoor necessities.

The Wilderness Route Finder, by C. Rutstrum, Macmillan Co., NY, 1970. 214 pp. $4.95.
Complete guide to finding your way in the wilderness.

The Wildfowler's World, by Hanson Carroll and Nelson Bryant, Winchester Press, NY, 1973. 160 pp., illus. $12.95.
More than 100 breathtaking photographs, many in color, are included.

Wildlife Illustrated, by Ray Ovington, Digest Books, Inc., Northfield, IL. 1974. 8½"x11", 288 pp. Profusely illus. paperbound. $6.95.
Over 200 descriptions and sketches of North American game birds, animals and fishes. Covers lowland and upland game birds, small and large game animals, fresh- and saltwater fish with descriptions, habitat, and traits.

Wildwood Wisdom, by Ellsworth Jaeger. The Macmillan Company, New York, NY, 1964. 491 pp. well-illus. by author. $6.95.
An authoritative work, through many editions; about all there is to know about every detail for the outdoorsman.
Williams Blue Book of Gun Dealing, 1974-75, Williams Gun Sight Co., Davison, MI, 1975. 100 pp., illus. Paper covers. $3.50.
Enlarged ed. of the modern guide to gun values.
The World of the Moose, by Joe Van Wormer. J. B. Lippincott Co., Phila., PA, 1972. 160 pp., illus. $5.95.
A record of the life style of these animals in their wild and remote habitats.
The World of the Ruffed Grouse, by Leonard Lee Rue, III. J. B. Lippincott, Phila., PA, 1973. 160 pp., illus. $5.95.
A year-round survey of the ruffed grouse and its environment, habitat, enemies, and relation to man.
The World of the White-Tailed Deer, by L. L. Rue III. J. B. Lippincott Co., Phila., 1967. A reprint. 137 pp., fine photos. $5.95.
An eminent naturalist-writer's account of the year-round activities of the white-tailed deer.
The World of the Wild Turkey, by J. C. Lewis. J. B. Lippincott Co., Phila., PA, 1973. 158 pp., illus. $5.95.
The author takes the reader into the wilderness world of the turkey's 6 surviving subspecies.
The World's Submachine Guns (and Machine Pistols), by T. B. Nelson and H. B. Lockhoven. T. B. N. Enterprises, Alexandria, VA, 1962. 739 pp., profusely illus. $21.50.
The 2nd printing (1964) of the first work with descriptive data on all significant SMGs to date, arranged by national origin. A glossary in 22 languages is included. *Assault Rifles* by Musgrave and Nelson.
You and Your Retriever, by R. W. Coykendall, Jr. Doubleday & Co., Garden City, NY, 1963. 155 pp., illus. $4.95.
A text on early, intermediate and advanced training of retrievers, with full information for handlers.

The Art of Engraving, by James B. Meek, F. Brownell & Son, Montezuma, IA, 1973. 196 pp., illus. $19.95.
A complete, authoritative, imaginative and detailed study in training for gun engraving. The first book of its kind—and a great one.
Artistry in Arms. The R. W. Norton Gallery, Shreveport, LA., 1970. 42 pp., illus. Paper, $2.50.
The art of gunsmithing and engraving.
Building the Kentucky Pistol, by James R. Johnston, Golden Age Arms Co., Worthington, OH, 1974. 36 pp., illus. Paper covers. $4.00.
A step-by-step guide for building the Kentucky pistol. Illus. with full page line drawings.
Building the Kentucky Rifle, by J. R. Johnston. Golden Age Arms Co., Worthington, OH, 1972. 44 pp., illus. Paper covers. $5.
How to go about it, with text and drawings.
Checkering and Carving of Gun Stocks, by Monte Kennedy. Stackpole Books, Harrisburg, PA, 1962. 175 pp., illus. $12.95.
Rev., enlarged clothbound ed. of a much sought-after, dependable work.
Complete Guide to Gunsmithing, by C. E. Chapel. Barnes & Co., NYC, 1962. 479 pp., illus. $7.95
2nd rev. edition, known earlier as *Gun Care and Repair,* of a comprehensive book on all details of gunsmithing for the hobbyist and professional.
The Complete Rehabilitation of the Flintlock Rifle and Other Works, by T. B. Tryon. Limbo Library, Taos, NM, 1972. 112 pp., illus. Paper covers. $6.95.
A series of articles which first appeared in various issues of the *American Rifleman* in the 1930s.
Firearms Blueing and Browning, by R. H. Angier. Stackpole Books, Harrisburg, PA, 151 pp., illus. $6.95.
A useful, concise text on chemical coloring methods for the gunsmith and mechanic.
Gun Owner's Book of Care, Repair & Improvement, by Roy Dunlap, Outdoor Life-Harper & Row, NY, 1974. 336 pp., illus. $9.95.
A basic guide to repair and maintenance of guns, written for the average firearms owner.
Gunsmith Kinks, by F. R. [Bob] Brownell. F. Brownell & Son., Montezuma, I. 1st ed., 1969. 496 pp., well illus. $9.95.
A widely useful accumulation of shop kinks, short cuts, techniques and pertinent comments by practicing gunsmiths from all over the world.
The Gunsmith's Manual, by J. Stelle and W. Harrison, Rutgers Book Center, Highland Park, NJ, 1972. 376 pp., illus. $9.95.
Exact reprint of the original. For the American gunsmith in all branches of the trade.
Gunsmithing, by Roy F. Dunlap. Stackpole Books, Harrisburg, PA, 714 pp., illus. $12.95.
Comprehensive work on conventional techniques, incl. recent advances in the field. Valuable to rifle owners, shooters, and practicing gunsmiths.
Gunsmithing Simplified, by H. E. MacFarland. Washington, DC, 1950, A. S. Barnes, NYC, 1959. 303 pp., illus. $8.95.
A thorough dependable concise work with many helpful short-cuts.
Gunstock Finishing and Care, by A. D. Newell. Stackpole Books, Harrisburg, PA. A new printing, 1966. 473 pp. illus. $11.95.
Amateur's and professional's handbook on the selection, use and application of protective and decorative coatings on gun stocks.
Hobby Gunsmithing, by Ralph Walker, Digest Books, Inc., Northfield, IL, 1972, 320 pp., illus. Paper, $5.95.
Kitchen table gunsmithing for the budding hobbyist.
Home Gun Care & Repair, by P. O. Ackley. Stackpole Books, Harrisburg, PA, 1969. 191 pp., illus. $5.95.
Basic reference for safe tinkering, fixing, and converting rifles, shotguns, handguns.
Home Gunsmithing Digest, by Tommy Bish. Digest Books, Inc., Northfield, IL, 1970, 320 pp., very well illus. within stiff decorated paper covers. $5.95.
An unusually beneficial assist for gun owners doing their own repairs, maintenance, etc. 45 chapters on tools, techniques and theories.
HOW ... by L. Cowher, W. Hunley, and L. Johnston. NMLR Assn., IN, 1961. 107 pp., illus. Paper covers. $2.95.
This 1961 rev. ed., enlarged by 3 chapters and additional illustrations, covers the building of a muzzle-loading rifle, target pistol, and powder horn, and tells how to make gunflints.
Introduction to Modern Gunsmithing, by H. E. MacFarland. Stackpole Books, Harrisburg, PA, 1965. 320 pp., illus. $7.45.
Up-to-date reference for all gunsmiths on care, repair, and modification of firearms, sights, and related topics.

Lock, Stock and Barrel, by R. H. McCrory. Publ. by author at Bellmore, NY, 1966. Paper covers, 122 pp., illus. $4.00.
A handy and useful work for the collector or the professional with many helpful procedures shown and described on antique gun repair.
Master French Gunsmith's Designs of the 17th-18th Centuries, compiled by S. V. Grancsay. Winchester Press, New York, NY, 1970. A brand new work of 208 pp., beautifully illus. in facsimile. Numbered, limited issue of 1000 copies. $29.95.
Magnificient ornamentation of weapons taken from a superb collection of design books, gathered by a world authority. An inspiration and a must for the gunsmith-engraver.
The Modern Gunsmith, by James V. Howe. Funk & Wagnalls. NYC, 1970 reprint ed. (2 vols.). 910 pp., illus. $25.00.
Guide for amateur and professional gunsmiths on firearms design, construction, repair, etc.
The Modern Kentucky Rifle, How to Build Your Own, by R. H. McCrory. McCrory, Wantagh, NY, 1961. 68 pp., illus., paper bound. $3.50.
A workshop manual on how to fabricate a flintlock rifle. Also some information on pistols and percussion locks.
The NRA Firearms Assembly Guidebook to Shoulder Arms. National Rifle Assn., Wash., D.C., 1973. 203 pp. Paper covers. $4.
Text and illus. explaining the takedown of 96 rifles and shotguns, domestic and foreign.
The NRA Firearms Assembly Guidebook to Handguns. National Rifle Assn., Wash., D.C., 1973, 206 pp. Paper covers. $4.
Illus. articles on the takedown of 101 pistol and revolver models.
The NRA Gunsmithing Guide, National Rifle Association, Wash., DC, 1971. 336 pp., illus. Paper. $5.50.
Information of the past 15 years from the "American Rifleman," ranging from 03A3 Springfields to Model 92 Winchesters.
Pistolsmithing, by George C. Nonte, Jr., Stackpole Books, Harrisburg, PA, 1974. 560 pp., illus. $14.95.
A single source reference to handgun maintenance, repair, and modification at home, unequaled in value.
Professional Gunsmithing, by W. J. Howe, Stackpole Books, Harrisburg, PA, 1968 reprinting. 526 pp., illus. $12.95.
Textbook on repair and alteration of firearms, with detailed notes on equipment and commercial gunshop operation.
Recreating the American Rifle, by Wm. Buchel & Geo. Shumway, George Shumway, York, PA, 1973. 194 pp. illus. Paper $6.50.
A new edition with additional illustrations showing the workmanship of today's skilled rifle-makers.
Rifle Making in the Great Smoky Mountains, comp. by Gene Fries. Buffalo Bull Press, Cedar Rapids, IA, 1972. 40 pp., illus. Paper covers. $2.50.
Reprint of National Park Service Popular Study Series No. 13 by Dr. Arthur Kendall, publ. in 1941. Describes making the rifle, tools and operations involved, plus other short articles of interest to the muzzleloader.

Automatic Firearm Pistols, by Elmer Swanson, Wesmore Book Co., Weehawken, NJ. 1st (and only) ed. 1955, 210 pp., well illus. $15.00.
A veritable catalog exclusively on automatic handguns for collectors, with many line drawings and descriptions, plus then-market market values of each.
Book of Pistols & Revolvers, by W. H. B. Smith. Stackpole Books, Harrisburg, PA, 1968. 758 pp., profusely illus. $7.98.
Rev. and enlarged, this encyclopedic reference, first publ. in 1946, continues to be the best on its subject.
Browning Hi-Power Pistols. Normount Armament Co., Wickenburg, AZ, 1968. 48 pp., illus., paperbound. $2.00.
A handbook on all models of Browning Hi-Power Pistols, covering their use, maintenance and repair.
Colt Automatic Pistols, by Donald B. Bady, Borden Publ. Co., Alhambra, CA, 1974. 368 pp., illus. $12.50.
The rev. and enlarged ed. of a key work on a fascinating subject. Complete information on every automatic marked with Colt's name.
Combat Shooting for Police, by Paul B. Weston. Charles C. Thomas, Springfield, IL, 1967. A reprint. 194 pp., illus. $10.00.
First publ. in 1960 this popular self-teaching manual gives basic concepts of defensive fire in every position.
Cooper on Handguns, by Jeff Cooper, Petersen Publ. Co., Los Angeles, CA 1974. 256 pp., illus. Paper covers. $4.95.
The selection, use and care of handguns plus test results, specifications and opinions on almost every cartridge handgun made in the U.S.
The Encyclopedia of the Third Reich, Book 1, by R. B. Marvin. Universal Research, Inc., Fort Lauderdale, Fla., 1969, from offset typewritten copy. 37 pp., very clear and sharp illustrations, paper covers. $4.00
This volume considers only handguns, but is a concise collector's guide to the main types of W.W. II German pistols and revolvers.
Die Faustfeuerwaffen von 1850 bis zur Gegenwart, by Eugen Heer. Graz, Austria, 1971. 457 pp., illus. $30.
Historical treatment of pistols and revolvers for military use in the last half of the 19th century. German text.
Georgian Pistols; The Art and Craft of the Flintlock Pistol, 1715-1840, by Norman Dixon, Geo. Shumway, York, PA, 1971. 184 pp., illus. $14.00.
The art of the Georgian gunmaker, describing the evolution of the holster pistol and the duelling pistol, with the parallel changes in style of the turn-off pistol.
German Pistols and Revolvers 1871-1945, by Ian V. Hogg, Stackpole Books, Harrisburg, PA, 1971. 160 pp. $12.95.
Over 160 photos and drawings showing each weapon, plus exploded views of parts, including markings, firms, patents, mfg. codes, etc.
Guns Annual Book of Handguns, ed. by Jerome Rakusan, Publishers' Dev. Corp., Skokie, IL, 1974. 98 pp., illus., paper covers. $2.00.
Complete catalog listing all latest models and articles dealing with handguns.
The Handbook of Handgunning, by Paul B. Weston. Crown Publ., NYC, 1968. 138 pp., illus. with photos $4.95.
"New concepts in pistol and revolver shooting," by a noted firearms instructor and writer.
A Handbook on the Primary Identification of Revolvers & Semi-automatic Pistols, by John T. Millard, Charles C. Thomas, Springfield, IL, 1974. 156 pp., illus. $12.50.
A practical outline on the simple, basic phases of primary firearm identification with particular reference to revolvers and semi-automatic pistols.

Handbuch der Faustfeuerwaffen, by Gerhard Bock and W. Weigel. J. Neumann-Neudamm, Melsungen, Germany, 1968. 4th and latest ed., 724 pp., including index. Profusely illus. $21.00.
A truly encyclopedic work in German text on every aspect of handguns. Highly recommended for those who read German.
The Handgun, by Geoffrey Boothroyd. Crown Publishers, Inc., New York, NY, 1970. 564 pp., profusely illus., plus copious index. $10.95.
A massive and impressive work, excellently covering the subject from matchlocks to present-day automatics. Many anecdotes, much comment and pertinent data, including ammunition, etc.
Handguns Americana, by De Witt Sell. Borden Publ. Co., Alhambra, CA, 1972. 160 pp., illus. $8.50.
The pageantry of American enterprise in providing handguns suitable for both civilian needs and military purposes.
Home Gunsmithing the Colt Single Action Revolvers, by Loren W. Smith, Ray Riling Arms Books Co., Phila., PA, 1971. 119 pp., illus. $7.95.
Detailed, information on the operation and servicing of this famous and historic handgun.
The Inglis-Browing Hi-Power Pistol, by R. Blake Stevens, Museum Rest. Serv., Ottawa, Can., 1974. 28 pp., illus. Paper covers. $2.00.
The history of this scarce gun and its variations.
Japanese Hand Guns, by F. E. Leithe, Borden Publ. Co., Alhambra, CA, 1968. Unpaginated, well illus. $8.50.
Identification guide, covering models produced since the late 19th century. Brief text material gives history, descriptions, and markings.
John Olson's Handgun's Unlimited, by John Olson, J. Philip O'Hara, Inc., Chicago, IL, 1975. 192 pp., illus. Paper covers. $7.95.
An annual for the handgunner, devoted to his special interest.
Know Your 45 Auto Pistols—Models 1911 & A1, by E. J. Hoffschmidt, Blacksmith Corp., Stamford, CT, 1974. 58 pp., illus. Paper covers. $3.50.
A concise history of the gun with a wide variety of types and copies illus.
Know Your Walther P.38 Pistols, by E. J. Hoffschmidt, Blacksmith Corp., Stamford, CT, 1974. 77 pp., illus. Paper covers. $3.50.
Covers the Walther models, Armee, M.P., H.P., P-38—history and variations.
Law Enforcement Handgun Digest, by Dean Grennell and Mason Williams. Digest Books, Inc., Northfield, IL, 1972. 320 pp., illus. Paper covers. $5.95.
Written especially for law enforcement officers and handgun-enthusiasts. From selection of weapon to grips, ammo, training, etc.
The Luger Pistol (Pistole Parabellum), by F. A. Datig. Borden Publ. Co., Alhambra, CA, 1962. 328 pp., well illus. $8.50.
An enlarged, rev. ed. of an important reference on the arm, its history and development from 1893 to 1945.
Luger Variations, by Harry E. Jones, Harry E. Jones, Torrance, CA, 1975. 328 pp., 160 full page illus., many in color. $17.50.
A rev. ed. of the book known as "The Luger Collector's Bible."
Lugers at Random, by Charles Kenyon, Jr. Handgun Press, Chicago, IL. 1st ed., 1970. 416 pp., profusely illus. $15.00.
An impressive large side-opening book carrying throughout alternate facing-pages of descriptive text and clear photographs. A new boon to the Luger collector and/or shooter.
Lugers Unlimited, by F. G. Tilton, World-Wide Gun Reports, Inc., Aledo, IL, 1965. 49 pp., illus. Paper covers $2.00.
An excellent monograph about one of the most controversial pistols since the invention of hand firearms.
Mauser Pocket Pistols 1910-1946, by Roy G. Pender, Collectors Press, Houston, TX, 1971. 307 pp., $14.50.
Comprehensive work covering over 100 variations, including factory boxes and manuals. Over 300 photos. Limited, numbered ed.
The Mauser Self-Loading Pistol, by Belford & Dunlap. Borden Publ. Co., Alhambra, CA. Over 200 pp., 300 illus., large format. $12.50.
The long-awaited book on the "Broom Handles," covering their inception in 1894 to the end of production. Complete and in detail: pocket pistols, Chinese and Spanish copies, etc.
Mauser, Walther & Mannlicher Firearms, by W.H.B. Smith, with a intro. by John T. Amber. Stackpole Books, Harrisburg, PA, 1971. 673 pp., illus. $14.95.
W.H.B. Smith's three classics, now in one convenient volume.
Ed McGiverns' Book of Fast & Fancy Revolver Shooting, by Ed McGivern, Anniversary ed., Follett Publ. Co., Chicago, IL, 1975. 484 pp., illus. $10.00.
A facsimile of the much-sought-after classic by the dean of revolver shooters.
The Military Four, by Claude V. Holland. C. V. Holland, Bonita Springs, FL, 1972. 64 pp., illus. Paper covers. $3.50.
Technical data, photographs and history of the Luger, Colt, P-38 and Mauser broomhandle pistols.
Military Pistols and Revolvers, by I. V. Hogg. Arco Pub. Co., NY, 1970. 80 pp., illus. $3.50.
The handguns of the two World Wars shown in halftone illus., with brief historical and descriptive text.
The Modern Handgun, by Robert Hertzberg, A&W Books, NY, 1974. 112 pp., well illus. $1.49.
Pistols and revolvers of all types are traced from their beginnings. Data on modern marksmanship included.
Modern Pistol Shooting, by P. C. Freeman, Faber & Faber, London, England, rev. ed., 1973. 176 pp., illus. $7.50.
A guide for the competitive shooter.
The Official U.S. Army Pistol Marksmanship Guide, first authorized repro. of original U.S. Army work. J&A Publ., NY, 1972. 144 pp., illus. Paper covers. $4.95.
Every detail from sight alignment to International Pistol programs—technical and fundamental for championship shooting in easy-to-read illus. form.
The Original Mauser Automatic Pistol, Model 1930, a reprint by Harold C. Bruffett, Croswell, MI, 1973. 32 pp., illus., paper covers. $2.50.
Facsimile of the 1931 English-text export catalog on the "Broom Handle Mauser."
The "Parabellum" Automatic Pistol, the English version of the official DWM handbook on Luger pistols. Normount Armament Co., Wickenburg, AZ, 1968. 42 pp., illus. Paper wrappers. $1.50.
A user's handbook, a reference work for collectors. A reprint of the original detailed instructions on use, disassembly and maintenance. Includes three folding plates.
Pistol & Revolver Guide, 3rd Ed., by George C. Nonte, Follett Publ. Co., Chicago, IL, 1975. 224 pp., illus. Paper covers. $5.95.
A new and up-dated ed. of the standard reference work on military and sporting handguns.
The Pistol Shooter's Treasury, by Gil Hebard; et al. Gil Hebard Guns, Knoxville, IL, 1972. 128 pp., illus. Paper covers. $2.95.
Articles by noted handgun experts on all phases of selecting and shooting handguns.
Pistolen Atlas, by Karl R. Pawlas, Nuremberg, Germany, 1970. Arranged alphabetically by maker and model in loose-leaf binding. Each vol. $15.00.
Carefully planned and researched for the "automatic arms buff," shooter and collector, depicts hundreds of auto. pistols of all nations and of all calibers with excellent illus. and descriptive text in English, French, German and Spanish. 13 volumes projected, of which vols. 1, 2, 3, 5, 6, 7 and 8 are now ready.
Pistols, Revolvers, and Ammunition, by M. H. Josserand and J. Stevenson, Crown Publ. Co., NY, 1972. 341 pp., illus. $7.50.
Basic information classifying the pistol, revolver, ammunition, ballistics and rules of safety.
Report of Board on Tests of Revolvers and Automatic Pistols. From The *Annual Report* of the Chief of Ordnance, 1907. Reprinted by J. C. Tillinghast, Marlow, NH, 1969. 34 pp., 7 plates, paper covers. $3.00.
A comparison of handguns, including Luger, Savage, Colt, Webley-Fosbery and other makes.
The Revolver, 1818-1865, by A.W.F. Taylerson, Andrews & Frith, Crown Publ., NYC, 1968. 360 pp., illus. $7.50.
Noted British work on early revolving arms and the principle makers, giving production data and serial numbers on many models.
The Revolver 1889-1914, by A. W. F. Taylerson. Crown Pub. NY, 1971. 324 pp., illus. $7.50.
The concluding volume of this definitive work deals with Continental arms, American rimfire and centerfire, British centerfire, and obsolescent arms in use.
Saga of the Colt Six-Shooter, and the famous men who used it, by G. E. Virgines. Frederick Fell Co., New York, NY, 1969. 220 pp., well illus. $7.95.
History of the Colt Single action army revolver since 1873, with much information of interest to collectors and shooters.
Shooting to Live with the One-Hand Gun, by Wm. E. Fairbairn and Eric A. Sykes, Paladin Press, Boulder, CO, 1974. 96 pp., illus. $5.95.
Facsimile of the 1942 instruction manual on the use of the pistol for defense in police work.
Sixguns by Keith, by Elmer Keith, Bonanza Books, NY, 1974. (reprint of the 1961 ed.) 335 pp., illus. $4.95.
Long a popular reference on handguns, this work covers all aspects, whether for the shooter, collector or other enthusiasts.
Smith and Wesson Catalog of 1901, a reprint facsimile by The Wyoming Armory, Inc., Cheyenne, WY, 1969. 72 pp., well illus., paper covers. $2.25.
All models, engraving, parts and break-down lists, etc.
The Story of Colt's Revolver, by Wm. B. Edwards, Castle Books, NY, 1971. 470 pp. $9.98.
Biography of Samuel Colt and his invention. Hundreds of photos, diagrams, patents and appendix of original advertisements.
System Mauser, a Pictorial History of the Model 1896 Self-Loading Pistol, by J. W. Breathed, Jr., and J. J. Schroeder, Jr. Handgun Press, Chicago, IL, 1967. 273 pp., well illus. 1st limited ed. hardbound. $12.50.
10 Shots Quick, by Daniel K. Stern. Globe Printing Co., San Jose, CA, 1967. 153 pp., photos. $8.50.
History of Savage-made automatic pistols, models of 1903-1917, with descriptive data for shooters and collectors.
Textbook of Automatic Pistols, by R. K. Wilson and Ian V. Hogg, Stackpole Books, Harrisburg, PA, 1975. 416 pp., illus. $17.95.
Complete history of automatic hand-held weaponry, from the origins in the 19th century to now.
U.S. Pistols and Revolvers Vol. 1, D. B. McLean, compiler. Normount Armament Co., Wickenburg, AZ, 1968. 2nd printing, 198 pp., well illus., paper covers. $3.95.
A useful and reliable work from authoritative sources on M1911/M1911A1 Colt Pistols; M1917 S & W revolvers; M1917 and Detective Special Colt revolvers. Excellent for their use, maintenance and repair.
United States Single Shot Martial Pistols, by C. W. Sawyer, WE, Inc., Old Greenwich, CT, 1971. 101 pp., illus. $5.00.
History of pistols used by the U.S. Armed Services 1776-1871.
U.S. Test Trials 1900 Luger, by Michael Reese II. Coventry Publ. Co., Gretna, LA, 1970, illus. $15.00.
For the Luger Pistol collector.
Walther Models PP and PPK, 1929-1945, by James L. Rankin, assisted by Gary Green, James L. Rankin, Coral Gables, FL, 1974. 142 pp., illus. $15.00.
Complete coverage of the subject as to finish, proof marks and Nazi Party inscriptions.
The Walther P-38 Pistol, by Maj. Geo. C. Nonte, Paladin Press, Boulder, CO, 1975. 90 pp., illus. Paper covers. $3.95.
Covers all facets of the gun—development, history, variations, technical data, practical use, rebuilding, repair and conversion.
The Webley-Fosbery Automatic Revolver. A reprint of the original undated booklet pupl. by the British makers. Deep River Armory, Houston, TX, 1968. 16 pp., illus., paper. $3.00.
An instruction manual, parts list and sales brochure on this scarce military handgun.

African Hunting, by Wm. C. Baldwin. Abercrombie & Fitch Library, NY, 1967. 451 pp., illus. $15.00.
Limited printing of a much-desired book giving vivid accounts of big game hunting exploits in Africa. First publ. in 1863.
American Partridge & Pheasant Shooting, by Frank Schley. Abercrombie & Fitch Library, NYC, 1968. 238 pp., illus. $7.95.
Facsimile of an American sporting classic work, including detailed engravings of game birds.
The American Sportsman, by Elisha J. Lewis. Abercrombie & Fitch Library, NY, 1967, 510 pp., illus. $10.95.
Limited issue of a scarce classic American work on the hunting field, first publ. in 1851.
Art of Small Game Hunting, by Francis Sell. Stackpole Books, Harrisburg, PA, 1973. 192 pp., illus. $3.95.
An invaluable primer and skill sharpener for any hunter.
Art of Successful Deer Hunting, by F. E. Sell, Stackpole Books, Harrisburg, PA, 1971. 192 pp., paper, $3.95.
Illus. re-issue of "The Deer Hunter's Guide." Western hunting lore for rifle and bow-hunter.

Asian Jungle, African Bush, by Charles Askins. Stackpole Books, Harrisburg, PA, 1959. 258 pp., illus. $10.00.
A where-to-go and how-to-do guide for game-rich Indo-China. The African section deals with game, the use of various arms and ammo on specific species.
Bell of Africa, by W. D. M. Bell, with foreword and introduction by Wally Taber and Col. T. Whelen. N. Spearman and Holland Press, London, 1960. 236 pp., illus. $10.00.
On elephants and the hunter extracted from Bell's own papers, it includes an appendix on rifles and rifle shooting.
The Best of Nash Buckingham, by Nash Buckingham, selected, edited and annotated by George Bird Evans. Winchester Press, NY, 1973. 320 pp. $10.
Thirty pieces that represent the very cream of Nash's output on his whole range of outdoor interests—upland shooting, duck hunting, even fishing.
Big Game Hunting in the West, by Mike Cramond. Mitchell Press, Vancouver, B.C., Can., 1965. 164 pp., illus. $5.95.
Accounts of hunting many species of big game and predators are given plus a section on rifles, equipment, and useful tips for the field.
Big Game Hunting Around the World, by B. Klineburger and V. Hurst, Exposition Press, NY, 1969. 376 pp., illus. $15.00.
From hunting tigers in India to polar bears in the Arctic.
Big Game Hunting in New Zealand, by Gary Joll. Whitcombe & Tombs, Christchurch, NZ, 1971. 214 pp., illus. $8.50.
An experienced hunter's advice on various species of New Zealand game, guns, equipment, and other aspects of hunting.
Bird Hunting Know-How, by D. M. Duffey. Van Nostrand, Princeton, NJ, 1968. 192 pp., illus. $5.95.
Game-getting techniques and sound advice on all aspects of upland bird hunting, plus data on guns and loads.
The Black Panther of Sivanipalli, by Kenneth Anderson, George Allen & Unwin, Ltd., London, 257 pp., illus. $6.50.
The thrilling story of hunting a man-eating panther in the jungles of India.
Bobwhite Quail Hunting, by Charley Dickey, printed for Stoeger Publ. Co., So. Hackensack, NJ, 1974. 112 pp., illus., paper covers. $2.95.
Habits and habitats, techniques, gear, guns and dogs.
The Bobwhite Quail, its Life and Management, by Walter Rosene. Rutgers University Press, New Brunswick, NJ. 1st ed., 1969. 418 pp., photographs, maps and color plates. $20.00.
An exhaustive study of an important species which has diminished under the impact of changing agricultural and forestry practices.
The Book of Saint Albans, by Dame Juliana Berners, Abercrombie & Fitch, NY, 1966. Illus. $18.00.
Reprint of the rare 1810 Haselwood ed. on hawking, hunting, fishing etc. The first English sporting book.
Bow & Arrow Archer's Digest, by J. Lewis, Digest Books, Northfield, IL, 1971. 320 pp., illus. Paper, $5.95.
The encyclopedia for all archers, from picking a bow to varmint calling.
Bowhunter's Digest, by C. R. Learn, ed. by Jack Lewis, Digest Books, Inc., Northfield, IL. 1974. 8½"x11", 288 pp. Profusely illus. Paperbound. $6.95.
Large and small game bowhunting with much information on equipment, techniques and training.
Bowhunting, by M. R. James, The John Olson Co., Paramus, NJ, 1975. 224 pp., illus. $6.95.
Everything from bowhunting basics to advanced hunting techniques.
Bowhunting for Deer, by H. R. Wambold. Stackpole Books, Harrisburg, PA, 1964. 160 pp., illus. $5.95.
Useful tips on deer, their habits, anatomy, and how-when-where of hunting, plus selection and use of tackle.
A Boy and His Gun, by Edward C. Janes. A. S. Barnes & Co., New York, NY. 207 pp., illus., $5.00.
Introduction to rifles, shooting and hunting techniques for young shooters with practical hints on game shooting with rifle or shotgun.
The Call of the Maneater, by Kenneth Anderson, George Allen & Unwin, Ltd., London, 1962. 274 pp., illus. $5.00.
True tales of tiger hunting in the jungles of India.
Calling All Game, by Bert Popowski. Stackpole Books, Harrisburg, PA, 1952, 306 pp. Illus. $7.50.
Practical methods of attracting game, from quail to moose, using artificial decoys and calls.
Camp-Fires in the Canadian Rockies, by William T. Hornaday, The Abercrombie & Fitch Lib., NYC, 1967. 353 pp., illus. $13.95.
A facsimile of the 1906 classic book on big-game hunting in the wild terrain of Br. Columbia.
Camp-Fires on Desert & Lava, by William T. Hornaday, the Abercrombie & Fitch Lib., NYC, 1967. 366 pp., illus. $13.95.
A facsimile of the classic work on exploring the unknown Pinacate region of north-western Mexico in 1908.
Charles Morgan on Retrievers, ed. by Ann Fowler and D. L. Walters. Abercrombie & Fitch, NYC, 1968, 168 pp., illus. $12.50.
Based on years of success in schooling hunting dogs, this work gives full details of an expert's proven methods to guide experienced trainers.
Complete Book of Bow and Arrow, by G. H. Gillelan, Stackpole Books, Harrisburg, PA, 1971. 320 pp., illus. $9.95.
Encyclopedic reference on archery, gear, rules, skill, etc.
The Complete Book of Deer Hunting, by Byron W. Dalrymple, Winchester Press, NY, 1973. 247 pp., illus. $8.95.
Practical "how-to" information. Covers the 20 odd North-American subspecies of deer.
Complete Book of Hunting, by Clyde Ormond. Harper & Bros., NYC, 1962. 467 pp., well-illus. $6.95.
Part I is on game animals, Part II is on birds. Guns and ammunition, game, habitats, clothing, equipment, etc. hunters' tips are discussed.
Complete Guide to Hunting Across North America, by Byron Dalrymple. Outdoor Life, Harper & Row, NY, 1970. 848 pp., illus. with photos and 50 maps. $10.00.
A large reference work on hunting conditions, locating game, clothing, techniques, transportation, equipment for every region, etc.
Crow Shooting Secrets, by Dick Mermon. Winchester Press, New York, 1970. 149 pp., illus. $5.95.
An expert shares his secrets and touches all the bases.
Decoying Waterfowl, by A. C. Becker Jr. A. S. Barnes and Co., NY, 1973. 256 pp., illus. $12.
An in-depth study of decoy shape, paint finishes, and formations on the water, etc. Over 100 photos and drawings.
Deer Hunting; Tactics and Guns for Hunting All North American Game, by Norman Sprung, J. B. Lippincott Co., Phila., PA, 1973. 237 pp., illus. $7.95.
A comprehensive guide to deer hunting, focusing on whitetailed and mule deer.
The Dove Shooter's Handbook, by Dan M. Russell, Winchester Press, NY, 1974. 256 pp., illus. $6.95.
A complete guide to America's top game bird—natural history, hunting methods, equipment, conservation and future prospects.
The Duck Hunter's Handbook, by Bob Hinman, Winchester Press, NY, 1974. 252 pp., illus. $8.95.
Down-to-earth, practical advice on bagging ducks and geese.
Ducks of the Mississippi Flyway, ed. by John McKane. North Star Press, St. Cloud, MN, 1969. 54 pp., illus. $4.95.
A duck hunter's reference. Full color paintings of some 30 species, plus descriptive text.
The Education of a Bear Hunter, by Ralph Flowers, Winchester Press, NY, 1975. 288 pp., illus. $10.00.
Anyone who hunts bear will want this book for its wealth of hunting lore and woodcraft.
The Education of a Turkey Hunter, by Wm. F. Hanenkrat, Winchester Press, NY, 1974. 216 pp., illus. $8.95.
A complete course on how to hunt turkeys.
Elephant, by D. E. Blunt, Neville Spearman, London, 1971. 260 pp., illus. $12.50.
Reprint of a rare book, a hunter's account of the ways of an elephant.
Game Animals in New Zealand, by Gordon Roberts. A. H. & A. W. Reed, Sydney, Australia, 1968. 112 pp., illus. $8.25.
Pictures of wild, live animals in their natural and often remote habitats.
Game Bird Hunting in the West, by Mike Cramond. Mitchell Press, Vancouver, B.C., Can., 1967. 246 pp., illus. $5.95.
Identification and hunting methods for each species of waterfowl and upland game birds, plus a section on shotgun types, equipment, and related subjects for the hunter.
Game and the Gunner, by Pierre Pulling, Winchester Press, NY, 1973. 233 pp., illus. $8.95.
Observations on same conservation and sport hunting.
Good Hunting, by Jas L. Clark, Univ. of Oklahoma Press, Norman, Okla., 1966. 242 pp., illus. $7.95.
Fifty years of collecting and preparing habitat groups for the American Museum.
A Good Keen Man, by Barry Crump. A. H. & A. W. Reed, Sydney, Australia, 1969. 192 pp., illus. $6.50.
A popular tale of deer hunting in the New Zealand back-country.
The Great Arc of the Wild Sheep, by J. L. Clark, Univ. of Oklahoma Press, Norman, Okla., 1964. 247 pp., illus. $8.95.
Every classified variety of wild sheep is discussed, as found in North America, Asia & Europe. Numerous hunting stories by experts are included.
Great Game Animals of the World, by Russell B. Aitken. Winchester Press, NY, 1969. 192 pp. profusely ills. in monochrome and color. $22.50.
Accounts of man's pursuit of big game in all parts of the world, told in many fine pictures.
Green Hills of Africa, by Ernest Hemingway. Charles Scribner's Sons, NY, 1963. 285 pp. illus. $6.95.
A famous narrative of African big-game hunting, first published in 1935.
The Grizzly Bear, edited by B. D. and E. Haynes, Univ. of Oklahoma Press, Norman, Okla., 1966. 386 pp., illus. $7.95.
Collected stories about various encounters with the grizzly by mountain men, settlers, naturalists, scouts and others.
Grizzly Country, by Andy Russell. A. A. Knopf, NYC, 1973, 302 pp., illus. $7.95.
Many-sided view of the grizzly bear and his world, by a noted guide, hunter and naturalist.
Grouse Feathers, by Burton L. Spiller. Crown Publ., NY, 1972. 207 pp., illus. $7.50.
Facsimile of the original Derrydale Press issue of 1935. How to hunt the ruffed grouse, with stories of the author's experiences with dogs and guns from boyhood. Illus. by Lynn Bogue Hunt.
Grouse and Grouse Hunting, by Frank Woolner. Crown Pub., Co., NY, 1970. 192 pp., illus. $7.50.
The history, habits, habitat and methods of hunting one of America's great game birds.
Gun Dog, by Richard A. Wolters, E. P. Dutton, New York, NY, 1969. 1st ed., 11th Printing. 150 pp., well illus. $5.95.
A popular manual for upland bird shooters who want to train their dogs to perfection in minimum time.
Highland Stage of Otago, by D. Bruce Banwell. A. H. & A. W. Reed, Sydney, Australia, 1968. 169 pp., illus. $9.75.
The romantic history of Otago's red deer. Trophy statistics, fully checked for accuracy, are given. An invaluable reference work.
Horns in the High Country, by Andy Russell, Alfred A. Knopf, NY, 1973. 259 pp., illus. $6.95.
A many-sided view of wild sheep and the natural world in which they live.
How to Hunt American Game, by R. B. Vale. Stackpole Books, Harrisburg, PA. 5th printing, 1954. 199 pp., illus. $4.00.
Wildlife habits, conservation and the encouragement of hunting. Including the author's experiences in hunting game throughout America.
How to Hunt Small American Game, by L. A. Anderson. Funk and Wagnalls, New York, NY, 1969. 167 pp., well illus. $5.95.
A new basic guide for the small game hunter, similar to the author's 1959 *How to Hunt Deer and Small Game.* Written for beginner and expert, covers game, guns, equipment and game habits.
How to Hunt Whitetail Deer, L. A. Anderson. Funk & Wagnalls, NYC, 1968. 116 pp., illus. $5.95.
Useful reference for deer hunters, both novice and experienced, giving basic information and valuable pointers.
Hunt the Far Mountain, by Keith Severinsen. A. H. & A. W. Reed, Wellington, N.Z., 1970. 182 pp., illus. $9.00.
An introduction to every hunting trophy New Zealand offers.
Hunter's Digest, edited by Erwin A. Bauer. Digest Books, Inc., Northfield, IL, 1973. 320 pp., illus. Paper covers. $6.95.
The best ways, times and places to hunt the most popular species of large and small game animals in North America.
The Hunter's Field Guide to Game Birds & Animals of North America, by Robt. Elman, Alfred A. Knopf, NY, 1974. 655 pp. Over 357 illus., including 116 in full color. $12.50.
A comprehensive book on strategy and facts on over 100 game animals, upland birds and waterfowl in North America.
A Hunter's Fireside Book, by Gene Hill Winchester Press, NY, 1972. 192 pp., illus. $7.95
An outdoor book that will appeal to every person who spends time in the field—or who wishes he could.
A Hunter's Wanderings in Africa, by Frederick C. Selous, Books of Rhodesia, Bulawayo, So. Africa, 1970. 455 pp., illus. $22.50.
A facsimile reproduction of the rare 1881 ed. A narrative of nine years spent among the game of the far interior of So. Africa.
The Hunter's World, by C. F. Waterman. Random House, NY, 1970. 250 pp., illus. $15.00.
A book for those who welcome an expert's guidance, one who understands the terrain, feed, cover, etc., of the game they hunt. Profusely illus. in color.

Hunting the American Wild Turkey, by Dave Harbour, Stackpole Books, Harrisburg, PA, 1975. 256 pp., illus. $8.95.
The techniques and tactics of hunting North America's largest, and most popular, woodland game bird.

Hunting with a Camera; A World Guide to Wildlife Photography, by Erwin A. Bauer, Winchester Press, NY, 1974. 324 pp., illus. $12.95.
A practical book which will help every amateur photographer to take better wildlife photos.

Hunting Dog Know-How, by D. M. Duffey, Van Nostrand, Princeton, NJ, 1965. 177 pp., illus. $5.95.
Covers selection, breeds, and training of hunting dogs, problems in hunting and field trials.

Hunting Hounds: How to Choose, Train and Handle America's Trail and Tree Hounds, by David Michael Duffey. Winchester Press, NY, 1972. 192 pp., illus. $5.95.
Origin, development, selection, care and usage of every breed and strain, with entertaining anecdotes and practical training tips.

Hunting Moments of Truth, by Eric Peper and Jim Rikhoff, Winchester Press, NY, 1973. 208 pp., illus. $8.95.
The world's most experienced hunters recount 22 most memorable occasions.

Hunting the Ruffed Grouse, by Nick Sisley. Copyright, Nick Sisley, 1970. 136 pp., illus. $4.95.
A must for hunting this great game bird. The author, a grouse expert, is vice president of the Ruffed Grouse Society of America.

Hunting with Bow and Arrow, by George Laycock and Erwin Bauer. Arco Publ. Co., Inc., NYC, 1966. $3.95.
A practical guide to archery as a present-day sport. Mentions equipment needed and how to select it. Illus. instructions on how to shoot with ease and accuracy.

Hunting Upland Birds, by Chas. F. Waterman. Winchester Press, NY, 1972. 320 pp., illus. $8.95.
Excellent treatment of game habits and habitat, hunting methods, and management techniques for each of the 18 major North American gamebird species.

Hunting Weapons, by Howard L. Blackmore. Walker & Co., NY, 1971. 401 pp., illus. $17.50.
Covers sporting arms from the Middle Ages to the present, by a prominent British expert on historical weapons.

Hunting in Westland, by Lew Sutherland. A. H. & A. W. Reed, Sydney, Australia, 1970. 95 pp., illus. Paper covers. $5.75.
Intended to assist parties of experienced hunters in planning an expedition.

The Imperial Collection of Audubon Animals, original text by John James Audubon and Rev. John Bachman, illus. by John James and John Woodhouse Audubon. A magnificent quarto reproduction of the rare original by Hammond, Inc., Maplewood, NJ, 1967. 307 pp., 150 animals pictured in full color. $6.95.
Each illus. accompanied by engaging text, as in the 1st ed. of 1848, including accounts of Audubon's exploring trips. A most useful work for hunters who want to know their game.

Inside Safari Hunting, by D. Holman. G. P. Putnam's Sons, NY, 1970. 296 pp., illus. $6.95.
The work of the white hunter in Africa, based on the experiences of a second-generation professional.

Jaybirds Go to Hell on Friday & Other Stories, by Havilah Babcock, Holt, Rinehart & Winston, NY, 1972. 149 pp. $4.95.
A sparkling collection of stories about hunting and fishing by the nation's number one quail hunter.

Key to North American Waterfowl, by S. R. Wylie and S. S. Furlong. Livingston Publ. Co., Wynwood, PA, 1972. 32 pp., color illus. Plastic covers. $3.95.
Designed to help the hunter identify all species of ducks, geese and swans in winter plumage. Illustrated with color plates. Printed on waterproof, greaseproof, washable plastic.

Krider's Sporting Anecdotes, edited by Milnor H. Klapp. Abercrombie & Fitch Library, NY, 1966. 292 pp., illus. $8.00.
Limited issue of the much-wanted work on Philadelphia's renowned gunsmith, John Krider, publ. first in 1853. A rich fund of knowledge on upland shooting, dogs and match shooting, etc.

Living Off the Country, by B. Angier. Stackpole Books, Harrisburg, PA, 1959. 241 pp., illus. $6.95.
In a simple and entertaining manner the author explains how to live off nature when emergency arises and how to stay alive in the woods.

Man-Eaters & Jungle Killers, by Kenneth Anderson, George Allen & Unwin Ltd., London, 1970. 199 pp., illus. $8.50.
The author's methods and precautions in hunting the man-eaters of India.

Modern ABC's of Bird Hunting, by Dave Harbour, Stackpole Books, Harrisburg, PA, 1966. 192 pp., illus. $4.95.
From city's edge to wilderness this gives the occasional hunter the quickest way on how to increase his bag. Covers all game birds of the U.S. and Canada.

Modern Hunting with Indian Secrets, by Allan A. Macfarlan. Stackpole Books, Harrisburg, PA, 1971. 222 pp., $6.50.
How to acquire the new-old skills of the Redman, how to apply them to modern hunting.

Modern Turkey Hunting, by James F. Brady, Crown Publ., N.Y.C., NY, 1973. 160 pp., illus. $6.95.
A thorough guide to the habits, habitat, and methods of hunting America's largest game bird.

More Grouse Feathers, by Burton L. Spiller. Crown Publ., NY, 1972. 238 pp., illus. $7.50.
Facsimile of the original Derrydale Press issue of 1938. Guns and dogs, the habits and shooting of grouse, woodcook, ducks, etc. Illus. by Lynn Bogue Hunt.

Moss, Mallards & Mules and other Hunting and Fishing Stories, by Robert Brister, Winchester Press, NY, 1973. 216 pp., illus. $8.95.
A collection of 27 short stories on hunting and fishing.

Mostly Tailfeathers, by Gene Hill, Winchester Press, NY, 1975. 192 pp., illus. $8.95.
An interesting, general book about bird hunting with some stories on fishing.

My Health is Better in November, by Havilah Babcock, Holt, Rinehart & Winston, NY, 1970. 284 pp., illus. $5.95.
A classic collection of 35 stories from an author just as versatile with pen as with rod and gun.

NRA Hunting Annual, 1975. National Rifle Assn., Washington, DC, 1974. 176 pp., illus., paper covers. $2.50.
A directory of North American hunting, with features on guides, outfitters, etc.

The New Hunter's Encyclopedia, edited by Leonard Miracle and James B. Trefethen, plus specialized articles by over 60 outstanding contributors. Stackpole Books, Harrisburg, PA, 1972. 1054 pp., with 2047 photos, diagrams, drawings and full-color plates. $24.95.
A massive work covering every detail of every sort of hunting in the U.S., Canada and Mexico.

Nine Centuries of Hunting Weapons, by L. G. Boccia, Editrice Edam, Firenze, Italy, 1967. 181 pp., illus. with many fine photos of superb museum quality in full color. $15.00.
In Italian text, a historical survey of hunting weapons of Italian origin and their makers.

Nine Man-Eaters & One Rogue, by Kenneth Anderson, George Allen & Unwin Ltd., London, 1968. 251 pp., illus. $6.00.
Hunting the man-eating tigers and rogue elephants of the Indian jungles.

North American Big Game 1971 Edition, ed. by Robt. C. Alberts, Boone and Crockett Club, Pittsburgh, PA, 1971. 403 pp., illus. $15.00.
Tabulations of outstanding trophies compiled by the B & C Club.

North American Big Game Hunting, by Byron W. Dalrymple, Winchester Press, NY, 1974. 383 pp., illus. $10.00.
A comprehensive, practical guide, with individual chapters devoted to all native species.

The North American Waterfowler, by Paul S. Bernsen. Superior Publ. Co., Seattle, WA, 1972. 206 pp. $14.95.
The complete inside and outside story of duck and goose shooting. Big and colorful, illus. by Les Kouba. Contains an 8-minute 45 RPM duck calling record in back.

On Your Own in the Wilderness, by Col. T. Whelen and B. Angier. Stackpole Books, Harrisburg, PA, 1958. 324 pp., illus. $5.00.
Two eminent authorities give complete, accurate, and useful data on all phases of camping and travel in primitive areas.

One Man's Wilderness, by Warren Page, Holt, Rinehart and Winston, NY, 1973. 256 pp., illus. $8.95.
A world-known writer and veteran sportsman recounts the joys of a lifetime of global hunting.

Outdoor Life's Deer Hunting Book, by Jack O'Connor, et al, Harper & Row Publ., Inc., NY, 1975. 224 pp., illus. $7.95.
A major new work on deer hunting. Covers every aspect of the sport.

The Outlaw Gunner, by Harry M. Walsh, Tidewater Publishers, Cambridge, MD, 1973. 178 pp., illus. $8.50.
A colorful story of market gunning in both its legal and illegal phases.

Pack and Rifle, by Philip Holden. A. H. & A. W. Reed, Sydney, Australia, 1971. 194 pp., illus. $9.75.
The hunting days of a New Zealand Forest Service professional shooter. Hunts after red deer, sika, rusa, and sambar.

The Part I Remember, by Chas. F. Waterman, Winchester Press, NY, 1974. 199 pp., illus. $8.95.
Stories—mostly funny, all true—of the outdoor life, by a master outdoorsman and incomparable storyteller.

Paw Prints; How to Identify Rare and Common Mammals by Their Tracks. O. C. Lempfert, NY, 1972. 71 pp., illus. with actual size prints. $7.50.
An authoritive manual for hunters and outdoorsmen.

Petersen's Hunting Annual, 1975, by Jack O'Connor, et al., Petersen Publ. Co., Los Angeles, CA, 1975. 256 pp., illus. Paper covers. $4.95.
Written by well-known authors who are the best in their fields. From squirrels to safaris, this annual covers it all.

Pocket Guide to Animal Tracks, by L. M. Henderson, Stackpole Books, Harrisburg, PA, 1968. 57 pp., profusely illus., and bound in paper boards. $2.95.
Delightful text plus Henderson's most accurate line drawings show many signatures—paw and hoof prints, habits and characteristics, of 44 North American Small and big game.

The Practical Hunter's Dog Book, by John R. Falk, Winchester Press, NY, 1971. 314 pp., illus. $8.95.
Helps to choose, train and enjoy your gun dog.

Prehistoric Animals and Their Hunters, by I. W. Cornwall. F. A. Praeger, NY, 1968. 214 pp., illus. $7.50.
Describes animal species and hunting methods used in this period, plus uses made of the kills.

The Puma, Mysterious American Cat, by S. P. Young and E. A. Goldman, Dover Publ., NY, 1964, 358 pp., illus. Paper covers $3.50.
A two-part work: the first on the history, economic status and control: the second on classifications of the races of the puma.

Ranch Life and the Hunting Trail, by Theodore Roosevelt, 1894. A fine reprint by the Winchester Press, New York, NY, 1969, with introduction by Kermit Roosevelt. 168 pp., and includes the Frederic Remington illustrations from the original and those added from the 1908 edition. $6.98.
The far west of the 1880's of hunting and bags, of men and manners.

The Recollections of an Elephant Hunter, 1864-1875, by Wm. Finaughty, Books of Rhodesia, Bulawayo, So. Africa, 1973. 244 pp., illus. $22.50.
Facsimile reproduction of the rare 1916 ed. with additional illus. and new foreword and notes.

The Red Stags of the Rakaia, by D. Bruce Banwell. A. H. & A. W. Reed, Sydney, Australia, 1972. 165 pp., illus. $9.75.
An invaluable standard reference, and a lively, readable saga of a herd whose trophies have become world-famous.

The Rifle and Hound in Ceylon, by Samuel White Baker. Abercrombie & Fitch Library, NY, 1967. 422 pp., well illus. $15.00.
Limited printing of a classic description of elephant-hunting, deer-coursing and elk-hunting in the East. First published in the 1850s.

Rowland Ward's Records of Big Game, 15th ed., comp. by G. A. Best, Rowland Ward Pub., Ltd., 1971. 438 pp., illus. $45.00.
New edition of the authoritive record of big game kills in Africa, by species.

Safari, by Elmer Keith. Safari Publ., La Jolla, CA, 1968. 166 pp., illus. $7.95.
Guide to big game hunting in Africa, with anecdote and expert advice on hunting many species of game. Information on guns, ammunition, equipment, and planning the safari is included. Fine photographs.

Safari by Jet, through Africa and Asia, by Sister Maria del Rey, Charles Scribner's Sons, New York, NY, 1962. 308 pp., profusely illus., with photos, and line. $5.95.
Off-beat reading about an African-Asian grand tour, with tales of the land and the people of Tanganyika, Ceylon, the Philippines, Hong Kong, Taiwan, et al.

Safe Hunting, by Dick Pryce, Winchester Press, NY, 1974. 178 pp., illus. $7.95.
An introduction to hunting, guns, and gun safety.

Selected American Game Birds, by David Hagerbaumer and Sam Lehman, The Caxton Printers, Ltd., Caldwell, ID, 1972. The entire text of this book is executed in decorated calligraphy. $30.00.
Twenty-six of David Hagerbaumer's exquisite original watercolors, representing 29 bird species. A must for every book collector and art lover.

The Sharp Shooter, by Matt & Bruce Grant. A. H. & A. W. Reed, Sydney, Australia, 1972. 270 pp., illus. $10.50.
How to get the best out of rifles and ammunition. Covers hunting rifles, sights, stalking, ballistics, etc.

Sheep & Sheep Hunting, by Jack O'Connor, Winchester Press, NY, 1974. 308 pp., illus. $10.00.
Authentic detail about all varieties of wild sheep and how to hunt for them.

Shooting, A Complete Guide for Beginners, by John Marchington. Faber & Faber, London, Eng., 1972. 158 pp., illus. $9.75.
Guide to all aspects of shooting in the British manner, for all types of game.

Shooting for the Skipper, by Jack McNair. A. H. & A. W. Reed, Sydney, Australia, 1971. 153 pp., illus. $10.00.
Memories of a veteran New Zealand deer hunter.

Shooting Pictures, by A. B. Frost, with 24 pp. of text by Chas. D. Lanier. Winchester Press, NY, 1972. 12 color plates. Enclosed in a board portfolio. Ed. limited to 750 numbered copies. $50.
Frost's twelve superb 12" by 16" pictures have often been called the finest sporting prints published in the U.S. A facsimile of the 1895-6 edition printed on fine paper with superb color fidelity.

Shots at Mule Deer, by Rollo S. Robinson. Winchester Press, NY, 1972. 256 pp., illus. $8.95.
Describes the mule deer itself, its life cycle and its ways. There is a complete run-down of all appropriate deer rifles and cartridges, plus advice on their selection and proper field use.

Shots at Whitetails, by Larry Koller. A. A. Knopf, NY, 1970. 359 pp., illus. $7.95.
A new reprint, with all information on guns, loads, scopes, etc., brought up to date.

Small Game Hunting, by Clyde Ormond. Outdoor Life Books, NY, 1969. 126 pp., illus. $4.50.
Field-tested advice for increasing your take of chucks, squirrels, rabbits, crows, hawks, etc. Good information on guns, loads, field tips, etc.

A Sporting Chance . . ., by D. P. Mannix. E. P. Dutton & Co., NY, 1967. 248 pp., illus. with 50 photos. $1.98.
Unusual methods of hunting the exotic species from hounds to falcons. Inspiring reading for those desiring to get away from the commonplace.

Sporting Guns, by Richard Akehurst. G. P. Putnam's Sons, NYC, 1968. 120 pp., illus. $5.95.
History of shooting and of the guns and rifles developed to meet the hunter's needs, with anecdotes of the hunting field.

The Sportsman's Companion, by Lee Wulff. Harper & Row, N.Y.C., 1968. 413 pp., illus. $11.95.
Compendium of writings by various experts on hunting and fishing for American game. A useful reference for the outdoorsman.

Sportman's Guide to Game Animals, by Leonard Lee Rue III. Harper & Row [Outdoor Life Books], New York, NY, 1st ed., 2nd printing, 1969. 635 pp., illus. with photographs and maps. $6.50.
Exhaustive and capable coverage of the behavior and habits of all North American game animals.

Squirrels and Squirrel Hunting, by Bob Gooch. Tidewater Publ., Cambridge, MD, 1973. 148 pp., illus. $6.
A complete book for the squirrel hunter, beginner or old hand. Details methods of hunting, squirrel habitat, management, proper clothing, care of the kill, cleaning and cooking.

The Standard Book of Hunting and Shooting, R. B. Stringfellow, ed. 1st ed., in 1950 by the Greystone Press, New York, NY, 564 pp., very well illus. $10.00.
An excellent anthology on hunting in America, giving meaningful information on all major species and on all types of guns, sights, ammunition, etc. An abridgement of the larger *Hunters Encyclopedia.*

Successful Waterfowling, by Zack Taylor, Crown Publ., NY, 1974. 276 pp., illus. $8.95.
The definitive guide to new ways of hunting ducks and geese.

Tales from the Indian Jungle, by Kenneth Anderson, George Allen & Unwin Ltd., London, 1970. 204 pp., illus. $9.95.
Adventures in the pursuit of man-eating tigers and leopards.

Three Years' Hunting & Trapping America and the Great Northwest, by J. Turner-Turner Abercrombie & Fitch Library, N.Y.C., 1967. 182 pp., illus. $10.95.
Reprint of an 1888 account of a determined quest for valuable furs in one of the world's least hospitable regions.

Tiger in Sight, by Astrid Bergman Sucksdorff, Delacorte Press, NY, 1970. 110 pp., illus. $7.50.
Stalking tigers in the jungles of India.

Timberdoodle, by Frank Woolner, Crown Publ., Inc., NY, 1974. 168 pp., illus. $7.95.
A thorough, practical guide to the American woodcock and to woodcock hunting.

Topflight; A Speed Index to Waterfowl, by J. A. Ruthven & Wm. Zimmerman, Moebius Prtg. Co., Milwaukee, WI, 1968. 112 pp. $5.95.
Rapid reference for specie identification. Marginal color band of book directs reader to proper section. 263 full color illustrations of body and feather configurations.

Tracks of an Intruder, by Gordon Young. Winchester Press, NY, 1970. 191 pp., illus. $5.95.
Fascinating, first hand account of how an American naturalist gained recognition as a master hunter from the Montagnard Lahu tribesmen of Southeast Asia.

Travel & Adventure in Southeast Africa, by F. C. Selous. A & F Press, N.Y.C., 1967. 522 pp., illus. $15.00.
New edition of a famous African hunting book, first published in 1893.

A Treasury of African Hunting, ed. by Peter Barrett. Winchester Press, NY, 1970. 251 pp., illus. $9.95.
Outstanding accounts by noted writers and experts on African hunting, covering big game and small in many sections of the continent.

The Treasury of Hunting, by Larry Koller, Odyssey Press, N.Y.C., 1965. 251 pp., illus. $7.95.
Concise accounts of all types of hunting in the U.S. Excellent illustrations, many color photographs taken in various hunting fields.

Trophy Hunter in Asia, by E. T. Gates, Winchester Press, NY, 1971. 272 pp., illus. $12.50.
Hunting the rarest of game animals.

The Truth About Hunting in Today's Africa and how to go on a safari for $690.00, by G. L. Herter, Herter's, Inc., Waseca, Minn., 1970. 314 pp., well illus. $3.95.
Tells how to arrange safari costs, plus new data on weights, rifles and bullets derived from actual field tests.

The Unnatural Enemy, by Vance Bourjaily. The Dial Press, 1963. 182 pp., illus. $2.49.
Beautifully written episodes of bird-hunting.

The Upland Game Hunter's Bible, by Dan Holland. Doubleday, N.Y.C., 1961. 192 pp., illus. paper covers. $1.95.
Hunter's manual on the principal species of American upland game birds and how to hunt them.

The Upland Shooting Life, by George Bird Evans. A. A. Knopf, NY, 1971. 301 pp., illus. $10.
A basic shooting book by a writer-hunter. His experience in the fields, the pines, the birches, the alder swamps and the bushy borders in pursuit of upland game.

Water Dog. by R. A. Wolters, E. P. Dutton & Co., NY, 1964. 179 pp., illus. $5.95.
Rapid training manual for working retrievers.

Waterfowl in the Marshes, by A. C. Becker Jr. A. S. Barnes and Co., New York, NY, 1969. 155 pp., photographs. $7.50.
A highly informative and practical guide to waterfowl hunting in America.

Whitetail, by George Mattis. World Publ. Co., New York, NY, 1969. 273 pp., including index. Illus. $6.95.
Fundamentals and fine points of compelling interest for the deer hunter.

Wild Fowl Decoys, by Joel Barber. Dover Publ., N.Y.C., 1954. 156 pp., 134 illus., paperbound. $4.00.
A fine work on making, painting, care and use of decoys in hunting, recently reprinted. Full data on design and construction.

Wildfowling, by James Andrews, et al. Seeley, Service & Co., London, n.d. 352 pp., illus. $7.50.
Articles by British sportsmen on shooting wildfowl, guns, punting, and conditions in various areas. Vol. 29 of the Lonsdale Library.

RIFLES

The Accurate Rifle, by Warren Page. Winchester Press, NY, 1973. 256 pp., illus. $8.95.
A masterly discussion. A must for the competitive shooter hoping to win, and highly useful to the practical hunter.

The Blake Rifle, 1898, a facsimile by Frontier Press, Arvada, CO, [1974]. 87 pp., illus. Paper covers. $4.50.
A reprint of the original manual. Contains a complete description of the gun plus a section "Historical remarks on the Development of Arms."

Bolt Action Rifles, by Frank de Haas, ed. by John T. Amber, Editor of Gun Digest. Digest Books, Inc., Northfield, IL, 1971. 320 pp., illus. Paper, $7.95.
The definitive work, covering every major design since the Mauser of 1871.

The Book of Rifles, by W. H. B. Smith. Stackpole Books, Harrisburg, PA, 1963 (3rd ed.). 656 pp., profusely illus. $6.98.
An encyclopedic reference work on shoulder arms, recently up-dated. Includes rifles of all types, arranged by country of origin.

The Boy's Book of Rifles, by C. E. Chapel. Coward-McCann, N.Y.C., 1948, rev. ed., 1960. 274 pp., illus. $3.95.
For all young men of Boy Scout age at every phase of small-caliber marksmanship and safe gun handling. It tells how to qualify for NRA medals and Scout Merit Badges for Marksmanship.

Boy's Single-Shot Rifles, by Jas. J. Grant, William Morrow & Co., Inc., NY, 1967. 608 pp., illus. $10.00.
A wealth of important new material on an ever-popular subject, authoritatively presented. By the author of *Single Shot Rifles* and *More Single Shot Rifles.*

Browning Automatic Rifles, Normount Armament Co., Wickenburg, AZ, 81 pp., illus. Paper, $2.50.
Reprint of Ordnance Manual TM 9-1211, on all types of caliber 30's.

Carbines Cal. .30 M1, M1A1, M2 and M3, by D. B. McLean. Normount Armament Co., Wickenburg, AZ, 1964. 221 pp., well illus., paperbound. $3.95.
U.S. field manual reprints on these weapons, edited and reorganized.

Description and Instructions for the Management of the Gallery-Practice Rifle Caliber .22—Model of 1903. Inco., 1972. 12 pp., 1 plate. Paper, $1.00.
Reprint of 1907 War Dept. pamphlet No. 1925.

Description of Telescopic Musket Sights, Inco, 1972. 10 pp., 4 plates. Paper, $1.00.
Reprint of 1917 War Dept. pamphlet No. 1957, first publ. in 1908.

The First Winchester, by John E. Parsons. Winchester Press, New York, NY, 1969. 207 pp., well illus., $8.95.
This new printing of *The Story of the 1866 Repeating Rifle* (1st publ. 1955) is revised, and additional illustrations included.

Garand Rifles M1, M1C, M1D, by Donald B. McLean. Normount Armament Co., Wickenburg, AZ, 1968. Over 160 pp., 175 illus., paper wrappers. $3.95.
Covers all facets of the arm: battlefield use, disassembly and maintenance, all details to complete lock-stock-and-barrel repair, plus variations, grenades, ammo., and accessories; plus a section on 7.62mm NATO conventions.

Guns Annual Book of Rifles, ed. by Jerome Rakusan, Publishers Development Corp., Skokie, IL, 1974. 102 pp., illus., paper covers. $2.00.
Complete catalog listing plus feature articles on benchrest rifles, reloading, etc.

How to Select and Use Your Big Game Rifle, by Henry M. Stebbins, Combat Forces Press, Washington, 1952. 237 pp., illus. $6.50.
Concise valuable data on rifles, old and new—slide action, lever, semi automatic, and single shot models are covered.

The Hunting Rifle, by Jack O'Connor. Winchester Press, NY, 1970. 352 pp., illus. $8.95.
An analysis, with wit and wisdom, of contemporary rifles, cartridges, accessories and hunting techniques.

John Olson's Book of the Rifle, by John Olson, J. Philip O'Hara, Inc., Chicago, IL, 1974. 256 pp., illus. Paper covers. $5.95.
Rifle data "A to Z"—barrels, actions, stock, calibers, cartridges, ballistics, scopes, mounts, metallic sights, handloading, gunsmithing, muzzle-loading.

Johnson Semi-Automatic Rifle, Rotary Feed Model, 1941 Instruction Manual, by the Johnson Arms Co. Design Publ., Hyattsville, Md., 1969. 72 pp. illus., paper covers. $4.00.
A reprint of the original instruction manual.

Know Your M1 Garand, by E. J. Hoffschmidt, Blacksmith Corp., Stamford, CT, 1975. 84 pp., illus. Paper Covers. $3.50.
Facts about America's most famous infantry weapon. Covers test and experimental models, Japanese and Italian copies, National Match models.

Lee Arms Co. Catalogue of Patent Magazine Arms & Ammunition, a facsimile by Frontier Press, Arvada, CO, 1974. 15 pp., illus. Paper covers. $3.50.
A facsimile of the original 1879 Lee Arms Co. catalog.

Major Ned H. Roberts and the Schuetzen Rifle, by Gerald O. Kelver, G. O. Kelver, Publ., Mentone, IN, 1972. 99 pp., illus. $5.00.
Selected writings on old single shot rifles, sights, loads, etc.

Maynard Catalog of 1880, a reprint in facsimile by the Rocky Mountain Investment and Antique Co.; Cheyenne, WY, 1969. 32 pp., illus., paper covers. $2.25.
All models, sights, cartridges, targets etc.

Modern Breech-Loaders, Sporting and Military, by W. W. Greener, with intro. by D. B. McLean. Normount Tech. Publ., Wickenburg, AZ, 1971. 256 pp., illus. Paper covers. $5.95.
Reprint of the 1870 ed. Covers rifles, carbines, and the "new" breech-loading pistols.
Same title, this is a reprint of the 1871 ed. Lujac Publ., Pueblo, CO, 1972. 275 pp., illus. $5.95.
The Pennsylvania Rifle, by Samuel E. Dyke, Sutter House, Lititz, PA, 1975. 61 pp., illus. Paper covers. $3.00.
History and development, from the hunting rifle of the Germans who settled the area. Contains a full listing of all known Lancaster, PA gunsmiths from 1729 through 1815.
Pictorial History of the Rifle, By G. W. P. Swenson. Ian Allan Ltd., Shepperton, Surrey, England, 1971. 184 pp., illus. $9.50.
Essentially a picture book, with over 200 rifle illustrations. The text furnishes a concise history of the rifle and its development.
Position Rifle Shooting, by Bill Pullum and F. T. Hanenkrat. Winchester Press, NY, 1973. 256 pp., illus. $10.00.
The single most complete statement of rifle shooting principles and techniques, and the means of learning, teaching and using them, ever to appear in print.
The Rifle: and How to Use it, by H. Busk, Richmond Publ. Co., Richmond, England, 1971. 225 pp., illus. $9.00.
Reprint of the 1859 ed. Covers mid-19th century military rifles.
The Rifle Book, by Jack O'Connor. Random House (Knopf), N.Y.C., 1948. 3rd ed., 1964. 338 pp., illus. $10.00.
A definitive work, out-of-print until recently, which covers actions, design, ammunition, sights and accessories.
Rifles AR15, M16, and M16A1, 5.56 mm, by D. B. McLean. Normount Armament Co., Wickenburg, AZ, 1968. Unpaginated, illus., paper covers. $3.95.
Descriptions, specifications and operation of subject models are set forth in text and picture.
Ross Rifle Handbook 1907 (Reprint, 1917), a facsimile by Frontier Press, Arvada, CO, [1974] . 17 pp., 5 plates. Paper covers. $3.00.
A facsimile of the official manual on the Ross Rifle.
Schuetzen Rifles, History and Loading, by Gerald O. Kelver, Gerald O. Kelver, Publisher, Brighton, CO, 1972. Illus. $5.00.
Reference work on these rifles, their bullets, loading, telescopic sights, accuracy, etc. A limited, numbered ed.
Sharps Firearms, *v. 3, Pt. 3, Model 1874 Rifles*, by Frank M. Sellers and Dewitt Bailey II. Frank M. Sellers, Denver, Colo., 1969. 20 pp., illus., paper covers. $7.50.
A separately printed section of a continuing comprehensive collector's reference. This current work shows and describes the known M1874 variations.
Shooter's Bible Gunsight Guide, by George Nonte. Shooter's Bible, Inc., So. Hackensack, NJ, 1968. 224 pp., illus. $4.95.
Catalog data, descriptions and comment, plus articles on all types of modern gun sights.
Shooting the Percussion Rifle, by R. O. Ackerman. Publ. by the author, Albuquerque, N.M., 1966. 19 pp., illus. in line by the author. Paper wrappers, $1.50.
This well prepared work is Book No. 2 of a projected series. This one gives basic information on the use of the muzzle-loading rifle.
Sir Charles Ross and His Rifle, by Robt. Phillips and J. J. Knap, Museum Restoration Service, Ottawa, Canada., 1969. 32 pp., illus. Paper covers. $2.00.
The story of the man who invented the "Ross Model 1897 Magazine Sporting Rifle," the 1900 under the name of Bennett, and many others.
Small Bore Target Shooting, by H. G. B. Fuller. Herbert Jenkins, London, 1964. 264 pp., well illus. $8.50.
Authoritative English work, covering rifle types, buying hints, ammunition, accessories, and range technique.
Sniper Rifles of Two World Wars, by W. H. Tantum IV. Museum Restoration Service, Ottawa, Can., 1967. 32 pp., illus. $1.50.
Monograph on high-accuracy rifles used by troops in world wars I and II and in Korea. Paper wrappers.
Springfield Rifles, M1903, M1903A1, M1903A4, compiled by the publ. Normount Armament Co., Wickenburg, AZ, 1968. Over 115 pp., illus., paper wrappers. $2.95.
Routine disassembly and maintenance to complete ordnance inspection and repair; bore sighting, trigger adjustment, accessories, etc.
The '03 Springfields, by Clark S. Campbell, Ray Riling Arms Books Co., Phila, PA, 1971. 320 pp., illus. $16.50.
New, completely revised, enlarged and updated ed. based on the 1957 issue.
Target Rifle Shooting, by E. G. B. Reynolds & Robin Fulton. Barrie & Jenkins, London, Eng., 1972. 200 pp., illus. $9.50.
For the novice and intermediate shooter who wants to learn the basics needed to become a rifle marksman.
The .22 Rifle, by Dave Petzal. Winchester Press, NY, 1972. 244 pp., illus. $5.95.
All about the mechanics of the .22 rifle. How to choose the right one, how to choose a place to shoot, what makes a good shot, the basics of small-game hunting.
United States Rifle, Cal. .30, Model of 1917, a reprint of an official government booklet by Normount Publ. Co., Wickenburg, AZ, 1969. 80 pp., line illus., paper covers. $2.00.
A training manual issued by the War Department in 1918. A much-wanted and useful booklet.
United States Rifle 7.62 mm, M14 and M14E2, a reprint of an official government booklet by Normount Armament Co., Wickenburg, AZ, 1968. 50 pp., illus., paper covers. $2.50.
U.S. Army Field Manual 23-8, first published in 1965.
Westley Richards Modern Sporting Rifles and Cartridges. A reprint of an original undated catalog of the British makers. Safari Outfitters, Richfield, Conn., 1968. 60 pp. illus., paper. $4.95.
Facsimile of issue, covers big game rifles and ammunition.
The Winchester 1873 Handbook, by George W. Stone, Frontier Press, Arvada, CO, 1973. 137 pp., illus., a limited numbered ed. $18.95.
A definitive study of the Model 1873 Winchester. Covers the technical, mechanical and historical aspects of the gun.
Winchester '73 & '76, the First Repeating Center-Fire Rifles, by D. F. Butler. Winchester Press, New York, NY, 1st ed., 1970. 95 pp., well and tastefully illus. in line, halftones and photos. Color frontispiece. $7.95.
A complete history of the subject arms and their then-new ammunition, plus details of their use on America's western frontiers.
Wonderful World of the .22, by John Lachuk, et al, Peterson Publ. Co., Los Angeles, CA, 1972. 192 pp., illus., paper covers. $2.95.
Complete cataloging of .22 rifles and handguns—prices, specifications.

shotguns

American Partridge and Pheasant Shooting, Frank Schley. Abercrombie & Fitch Library, NY, 1967. 222 pp., illus. with detailed engravings of game birds. $7.95.
Limited printing of the rare sporting classic of 1877, considered for years the most important book available on the use of the scattergun.
The American Shotgun, by David F. Butler. Winchester Press, NY, 1973. 256 pp. $15.
Authoritive and profusely illus. Traces the entire evolution of the American shotgun and modern American shotshells.
Book of Shotgun Sports, by Sports Illustrated eds. J. B. Lippincott Co., Phila, PA, 1967. 88 pp., illus., $3.50.
Introduction to target shooting, game shooting, and gunmanship.
Clay Pigeon Marksmanship, by Percy Stanbury and G. L. Carlisle. Herbert Jenkins, London, 1964. 216 pp., illus. $7.50.
Handbook on learning the skills, with data on guns & equipment and competition shooting at all types of clay targets; by two eminent British writers.
Field, Skeet and Trapshooting, by C. E. Chapel. Revised ed. Barnes & Co., NYC, 1962. 291 pp., illus. $7.95.
A useful work on shotgun shooting, including gun types, ammo, accessories, marksmanship, etc.
The Fowler in Ireland. by Sir Ralph Payne-Gallwey, Richmond Publ. Co., Richmond, England, 1971. 503 pp., illus. $17.50.
Reprint of the 1882 work on wildfowling and wildlife in Ireland.
The Game Shot's Vade Mecum, by Michael Brander, A. & C. Black, London, 1st ed., 1965. 242 pp., illus. $7.50.
A British guide on the use of the shotgun in the hunting field, covers selection, marksmanship, game behavior and hunt management.
The Golden Age of Shotgunning, by Bob Hinman, Winchester Press, NY, 1971. 175 pp., illus. $8.95.
The story of American shotgun and wingshooting from 1870 to 1900.
Gough Thomas's Gun Book, by G. T. Garwood. A. & C. Black, London, England, 1969. 160 pp., illus. $8.95.
Excerpts of articles on the shotgun published in *Shooting Times*, by a noted British authority. Wide-ranging survey of every aspect on the shotgun, its use, behavior, care, and lore.
Gough Thomas's Second Gun Book, by G. T. Garwood, A. & C. Black, London, 1971. 227 pp., illus. $8.95.
More—and excellent—shotgun lore for the sportsman.
Guns Annual Book of Shotguns, ed. by Jerome Rakusan, Publishers Development Corp., Skokie, IL, 1974. 98 pp., illus., Paper covers. $2.95.
Contains complete catalog listing of 1975 models. Feature articles on sights, loads, guns, etc.
High Pheasants, by Sir Ralph Payne-Gallwey, Richmond Publ. Co., Richmond, England, 1970. 79 pp. $9.90.
The first and last word on its subject.
How to Shoot Straight, by Macdonald Hastings. A. S. Barnes and Co., New York, NY, 1970. 133 pp., illus., index ed. $5.95.
A companion volume to the author's *Churchill on Game Shooting*, and designed as a standard work on the modern game gun—a "teach-yourself" book.
How to be a Winner Shooting Skeet & Trap, by Tom Morton, Tom Morton, Knoxville, MD, 1974. 144 pp., illus. Paper covers. $8.95.
The author explains why championship shooting is more than a physical process.
John Olson's Book of the Shotgun, by John Olson, J. Philip O'Hara, Inc., Chicago, IL, 1975. 256 pp., illus. Paper covers. $6.95.
Covers all phases, from design and manufacture to field use and performance.
New England Grouse Shooting, by W. H. Foster, Chas. Scribner's, NY, 193 pp., illus. $12.50.
Many interesting and helpful points on how to hunt grouse.
The New Wildfowler in the 1970's by N. M. Sedgwick, et al. Barrie & Jenkins, London, Eng., 1970. 375 pp., illus. $11.50.
A compendium of articles on wildfowling, hunting practices and conservation. An updated reprint.
Parker, America's Finest Shotgun, by P. H. Johnson. Outlet Book Co., Inc., NY, 1968. 260 pp., illus. $2.95.
An account of a great sporting arm—from post Civil War until 1947, when it was sold to Remington. Values, models, etc.
Parker Brother Gun Catalog, 1869. B. Palmer, Tyler, TX, 1972. 14 pp., illus. Paper covers. $4.
Facsimile of Charles Parker's first issued catalog on "Parker Breech-Loading Shot Guns."
Parker Guns Catalog 1930, a reprint, by Guns Unlimited, Salt Lake City, UT, 1973. 32 pp., illus., paper covers. $4.95.
Facsimile reprint showing all models, including the Parker single barrel trap gun.
The Parker Gun An Immortal American Classic, by Larry L. Baer, published by the author, Visalia, CA, 1974. 94 pp., illus. $12.95.
Describes all Parker guns manufactured, with detailed facts and specifications.
Pigeon Shooting, by Richard Arnold. Faber & Faber, London, Eng., 1966. 162 pp., illus. $7.50.
A practical, specialized work on pigeon shooting in flight, over decoys, how to make hideouts, decoys, etc.
The Police Shotgun Manual, by Robert H. Robinson, Charles C. Thomas, Springfield, IL 1973. 153 pp., illus. $10.50.
A complete study and analysis of the most versatile and effective weapon in the police arsenal.
Rough Shooting, by G. A. Gratten & R. Willett. Faber & Faber, London, Eng., 1968. 242 pp., illus. $6.75.
The art of shooting, dogs and their training, games, rearing and their diseases, proof marks, etc.
Score Better at Skeet, by Fred Missildine, with Nick Karas. Winchester Press, NY, 1972. 160 pp., illus. $5.95. In paper covers, $2.95.
The long-awaited companion volume to *Score Better at Trap.*
Score Better at Trap, by Fred Missildine. Winchester Press, NY, 1971. 192 pp., illus. $5.95.
Step-by-step instructions, fully illustrated, on mastering the game by one of the world's leading coaches. In paper covers, $2.95.
75 Years with the Shotgun, by C. T. (Buck) Buckman, Valley Publ., Fresno, CA, 1974. 141 pp., illus. $5.95.
An expert hunter and trapshooter shares experiences of a lifetime.

Shooting For Beginners, by E. N. Barclay. Percival Marshal & Co., London, 1963. 74 pp., illus. $1.75.
Concise introduction to British techniques and customs in shotgunning for game birds.
Shooting Preserve Management (The Nilo System), by E. L. Kozicky and John Madson, Winchester Press, New York, NY, 1969. 312 pp., photos., line drawings and diagrams. $10.00.
The new look in 13 chapters, a full account of American field shooting at Nilo Farms, the show-case of the shooting-preserve concept.
The Shotgun, by T. D. S. & J. A. Purdey. A. & C. Black, London, Eng., 1969. 144 pp., illus. with Photos and diagrams. $5.00.
Reprinted 4th ed. of a well-known British work by two members of the notable gunsmith family. Covers the gun and its use in the field, at traps, and for skeet.
The Shotgun Book, by Jack O'Connor. Alfred A. Knopf, NY, 1965. 332 pp., plus index, illus. with line and photos. $10.00.
The definitive, authoritative book with up-to-date chapters on wild-fowling, upland gunning, trap and Skeet shooting. It includes practical advice on shotgun makes, models and functions, as well as data on actions.
Shotgun Digest, by Robert Stack, Digest Books, Inc., Northfield, IL. 1974. 8½"x11", 288 pp. Profusely illus. Paperbound. $6.95.
Movie star Robert Stack is a National Skeet Shooting Hall of Famer and an outstanding shotgunner. He covers all aspects of shotguns and shotgun shooting.
Shotgun and Shooter, by G. Carlisle and P. Stanbury, Barrie & Jenkins, London, 1970. 217 pp., illus. $6.95.
On guns, wildfowling, dog training, decoys, safety, etc.
Shotgun Marksmanship, by P. Stanbury & G. L. Carlisle. A. S. Barnes & Co., NY, 1969. 224 pp., illus. $7.95.
A new and revised edition for beginners, veterans, skeet shooters, hunters, etc. Valuable tips on improving marksmanship, etc.
The Shotgun Stock, by Robt. Arthur. A. S. Barnes & Co., NY, 1971. 175 pp., illus. $15.00.
The first and only book about the shotgun stock. Its design, construction, and embellishment. A much-needed work.
The Shotgunner's Bible, by George Laycock. Doubleday & Co., Garden City, NY, 1969. 173 pp., illus., paper covers. $1.95.
Coverage of shotguns, ammunition, marksmanship, hunting of various types of game, care and safety, etc.
Shotguns & Cartridges, by Gough Thomas. A. & C. Black, London, Eng., 1970. 136 pp., illus. $7.50.
An excellent work on the choice and use of guns and loads, by the gun editor of *The Shooting Times* (England).
Shotguns by Keith, by Elmer Keith, Bonanza Books, NY, 1973. 340 pp., illus. $1.98.
A new edition, with a complete rundown on new product development.
Shotguns and Shooting, by A. J. Barker, Paladin Press, Boulder, CO., 1973. 84 pp., illus., paper covers. $2.50.
All about shotguns and their use in shooting and hunting.
Skeet Shooting with D. Lee Braun, Robt. Campbell, ed. Grosset & Dunlap, NY, 1967. 160 pp., illus. Paper covers $2.95.
Thorough instructions on the fine points of Skeet shooting.
Successful Shotgun Shooting, by A. A. Montague. Winchester Press, NY, 1970. 160 pp., illus. $5.95.
The work of a superb shot and a great teacher; even the experts can read with profit.
Trapshooting with D. Lee Braun and the Remington Pros., ed. by R. Campbell. Remington Arms Co., Bridgeport, CT, 1969. 157 pp., well illus., $5.95. Also in paper covers. $2.95.
America's masters of the scattergun give the secrets of professional marksmanship.
Wing & Shot, by R. G. Wehle, Country Press, Scottsville, NY, 1967. 190 pp., illus. $8.50.
Step-by-step account on how to train a fine shooting dog.

Lightner Reprints

The following titles come from the Lightner Library Coll., Cocoa Beach, Fla. All have paper covers, all were publ. in 1973.
Baker Gun Catalog, 1915. 7 pp., illus. $2.00.
Facsimile showing all grades including deluxe.
Browning Arms Co. Catalog, 1935. 188 pp., illus. $4.00.
Facsimile reprint showing first superposed models and grades.
Charles Daly (Prussian) Catalog, ca. 1930. 24 pp., illus. $4.00.
Facsimile catalog showing Regent and Diamond grades, over-unders, 3-barrel trap models.
A. H. Fox (Original factory) Catalog, ca. 1910. 20 pp., illus. $4.00.
Facsimile of the first Fox catalog.
A. H. Fox Gun Co. Catalog, 1923. 40 pp., illus. $4.00.
Facsimile of the 1923 catalog. All models and grades including single barrel trap models, and information on the Fox-Kautsky single trigger.
A. H. Fox Gun Catalog, ca. 1936. 24 pp., illus. $4.95.
Facsimile showing all models and prices.
Ithaca Gun Co. Catalog, 1915. 25 pp., illus. $4.00.
Facsimile reprint of a large format catalog. Shows hammerless models.
Ithaca Gun Co. Catalog 51-F, 1930. 22 pp., illus. $4.00.
Facsimile of a large format catalog. Shows new lock models, gives prices.
D. M. Lefever (Bowling Green, Ohio) Catalog, 1905. 20 pp., illus. $4.00.
Facsimile of probably the rarest of all shotgun catalogs.
Lefever Arms Catalog, 1892. 32 pp., illus. $4.00.
Facsimile of a very rare catalog.
Lefever Arms Catalog, 1913. 32 pp., illus. $5.95.
Facsimile giving details on "Thousand Dollar Grade."
The Parker Gun Catalog, 1908. 32 pp., illus. $5.95.
Facsimile showing models A-1 Special through PH grades.
The Parker Gun Catalog, 1926. 32 pp., illus. $6.00.
Facsimile showing Invincible to Trojan, including P grades.
The Parker Gun Catalog, 1934. 15 pp., illus. $3.00.
Facsimile of the last catalog issued by the original Parker Bros. Company.
The Parker Gun Catalog, 1937. 34 pp., illus. $12.95.
Facsimile of the 1937 catalog, publ. by the Parker Gun Works, Remington Arms Co., Inc. Their largest, most beautiful and last regular catalog issued. The only one displaying all Parker trap and Skeet models.
The Parker Gun Dealer's Illustrated Price Catalog, 1940. 8 pp., illus. $2.00.
Last wholesale and retail price catalog issued by Parker Gun Works.
Remington Arms Co. Catalog, 1910. 62 pp., illus. $4.00.
Facsimile showing all double barreled models, including special 750 grade, autos, rifles, parts.
Remington Arms Co. Catalog, 1932. 32 pp., illus. $3.00.
Facsimile of first catalog showing the Model 32 over/under shotgun.
L.C. Smith (Hunter Arms Co.) Catalog, 1892. 24 pp., illus. $5.00.
Facsimile showing first hammerless models.
L.C. Smith (Hunter Arms Co.) Catalog, 1907. 34 pp., $5.95.
Facsimile of a large, beautifully illus. catalog. Shows early hammerless models, parts and prices.
L.C. Smith (Hunter Arms Co.) Catalog, 1918. 24 pp., illus. $4.95.
Facsimile reprint showing all hammerless models and prices.
L.C. Smith (Hunter Arms Co.) Catalog, 1928. 28 pp., illus. $4.00.
Facsimile reprint showing all models—trap, Skeet, eagle, etc.
L.C. Smith (Hunter Arms Co.) Catalog, 1939. 24 pp., illus. $4.50.
Facsimile of the Golden Anniversary Issue. Separate anniversary brochure included.
L.C. Smith (Hunter Arms Co.) Catalog, 1945. 24 pp., illus. $4.00.
Facsimile of the last L.C.S. catalog. Shows most modern models.
Winchester Firearms Co. Catalog, 1933. 61 pp., illus. $3.00.
Facsimile showing first Model 21 double barrel shotguns, including Skeet and tournament trap grader.
Winchester Model 21 Catalog. 33 pp., illus. $4.95.
Facsimile of a special post-war catalog.

Firearms Registration Proven Worthless Again!

Evidence that firearms legislation is not a deterrent to the criminal continues to mount. Yet crime abatement had been one of the chief arguments voiced by proponents of gun legislation.

Another theory held by anti-firearms people is that gun registration would also be a deterrent. The reasoning is that a registered gun complete with serial number makes it a simple task for police to track down a criminal.

Not so, according to police, and they ought to know. A survey of 50 state law enforcement agencies conducted by Alan S. Krug, research director for the National Shooting Sports Foundation, has exploded the theory.

Only six homicides and six robbery cases resulting in convictions were attributed to the tracing of firearms, the survey revealed, and that's over a period of 10 years! What's more, not a single case of aggravated assault has been solved as the result of tracing a firearm by its serial number.

All of which doesn't speak too well for the registration of firearms.

Savage Arms of Westfield, Mass., conducted a survey of its own on a smaller scale in 1968. Five police departments were polled in Massachusetts' five largest cities. Four responded.

All four said there had been no need to trace a gun involved in a criminal act. In each case the gun was apprehended with the suspect, or easily located by other means.

These two studies show how useless registration is. Yet, if it were ever passed into law, the administration cost would be tremendous. The taxpayer would probably bear the burden, and all for nothing.

PERIODICAL PUBLICATIONS

ALASKA Magazine
Alaska Northwest Pub. Co., Box 4-EEE, Anchorage, Ak 99509. $9.00 yr. Hunting and fishing articles.
The American Blade*
Beinfeld Publishing, Inc., 13222 Saticoy St., No. Hollywood, CA 91605. $7.50 yr. Add $1 f. foreign subscription. A magazine for all enthusiasts of the edged blade.
American Field†
222 W. Adams St., Chicago, IL. 60606. $10.00 yr. Field dogs and trials, occasional gun and hunting articles.
American Firearms Industry
Nat'l. Assn. of Federally Licensed Firearms Dealers, 7001 No. Clark St., Chicago, IL 60626. $10 yr. Est. 1972 for firearms dealers & distributors. Oriented to the gun trade.
The American Hunter (M)
Natl. Rifle Assn., 1600 Rhode Island Ave. N.W., Washington, DC 20036. $7.50 yr. NRA members only.
The American Rifleman (M)
National Rifle Assn., 1600 Rhode Island Ave., N.W., Wash., DC 20036. $10.00 yr. Firearms articles of all kinds.
The American Shotgunner
P.O. Box 3351, Reno, NV 89505. $6.50 yr. Shotgun articles of all kinds.
The American West*
American West Publ. Co., 599 College Ave., Palo Alto, CA 94306. $12.00 yr.
Argosy
Popular Publ., Inc., 420 Lexington Ave., N.Y., NY 10017. $7.90 yr.
Arms Gazette
Beinfield Publ., Inc., 13222 Saticoy St., No. Hollywood, CA 91605. $10.00 yr. Excellent brief articles for the collector of antique and modern firearms.
Army (M)
Assn of the U.S. Army, 1529 18th St. N.W., Wash., DC 20036. $10.00 yr. Occasional articles on small arms.
Australian Shooters' Journal
P.O. Box 12, Elizabeth, South Australia 5112, Australia. $7.50 yr. locally; $9.50 yr. overseas. Hunting and shooting articles.
Canadian Journal of Arms Collecting (Q)
Museums Restoration Service P.O. Box 2140, Picton, ont., Canada.KOK 2TO. $4.00 yr.
Deutsches Waffen Journal
Journal-Verlag Schwend GmbH, Postfach 340, D7170 Schwabisch Hall, Germany. $21.85 yr. Antique and modern arms, their history, technical aspects, etc. German text.
Ducks Unlimited, Inc. (M)
P.O. Box 66300, Chicago, IL 60666.
Enforcement Journal (Q)
Natl. Police Officers Assn., 14600 S. Tamiami Trail, N.P., Venice, FL 33595. $6.00 yr.
The Field†
The Harmsworth Press Ltd., 8 Stratton St., London W.I., England. $33.80 yr. Hunting and shooting articles.
Field & Stream
CBS Publications, 383 Madison Ave., New York, N.Y. 10017. $5.95 yr. Articles on firearms plus hunting and fishing.
Fur-Fish-Game
A. R. Harding Pub. Co., 2878 E. Main St., Columbus, OH 43209. $4.00 yr. "Gun Rack" column by M. H. Decker.
The Gun Report
World Wide Gun Report, Inc., Box 111, Aledo, IL 61231. $10.00 yr. For the gun collector.
Gun Week†
Amos Press, Inc., P.O. Box 150, Sidney, OH 45365. $6.00 yr. U.S. and possessions; $8.50 yr. other countries. Tabloid paper on guns, hunting, shooting.
Gun World
Gallant Publishing Co., 34249 Camino Capistrano, Capistrano Beach, CA 92624. $7.50 yr. For the hunting, reloading and shooting enthusiast.
Guns & Ammo
Petersen Pub. Co., 8490 Sunset Blvd., Los Angeles, CA 90069. $9.00 yr. Guns, shooting, and technical articles.
Guns
Guns Magazine, 8150 N. Central Park Ave., Skokie, IL 60076. $9.00 yr. Articles for gun collectors, hunters and shooters.
Guns Review
Ravenhill Pub. Co. Ltd., Standard House, Bonhill St., London E.C. 2A 4DA, England. $10.50 USA & Canada yr. For collectors and shooters.
The Handgunner (M)
U.S. Revolver Assn., 59 Alvin St., Springfield, MA 01104. $5.00 yr. General handgun and competition articles.
Handloader*
Wolfe Pub. Co. Inc., Box 3030, Prescott, AZ 86301 $6.50 yr. The journal of ammunition reloading.
Hobbies
Lightner Pub. Co., 1006 S. Michigan Ave., Chicago, IL 60605. $6.00 yr.; Canada $7.00; foreign $7.50. Collectors departments.
International Shooting Sport*
Union Internationale de Tir, 62 Wiesbaden-Klarenthal, Klarenthalerstr., Germany. $7.20 yr., p.p. For the International target shooter.
The Journal of the Arms & Armour Society (M)
F. Wilkinson (Secy.), 40 Great James St., Holborn, London WC1, N 3HB, England. $4.00 yr. Articles for the collector.
Journal of the Historial Breechloading Smallarms Assn.
Publ. annually, Imperial War Museum, Lambeth Road, London SE1 6HZ, England. $7 yr. Articles for the collector plus mailings of lecture transcripts, short articles on specific arms, reprints, etc.
Law and Order
Law and Order Magazine, 37 W. 38th St., New York, NY 10018. $7.00 yr. Articles on weapons for law enforcement.
The Luger Journal
Robt. B. Marvin, Publ., P.O. Box 326, Jasper, FL 32052. $6.00 yr.
Muzzle Blasts (M)
National Muzzle Loading Rifle Assn. P.O. Box 67, Friendship, IN 47021. $8.00 yr. For the black powder shooter.
The Muzzleloader
Rebel Publishing Co., Inc., P.O. Box 6072, Texarkana, TX 75501. $6.00 yr. The publication for black powder shooters.
National Rifle Assn. Journal (British)
Natl. Rifle Assn. (BR.), Bisley Camp, Brookwood, Woking, Surrey, England. Gu24 OPB.
National Wildlife*
Natl. Wildlife Fed., 1412 16th St. N.W., Washington, DC 20036. $7.50 yr. World/Assoc. membership *includes Intl. Wildlife;* 12 issues $12.50.
New Zealand Wildlife (Q)
New Zealand Deerstalkers Assoc. Inc., P.O. Box 263, Wellington, N.Z. $2.00 U.S. and Canada, elsewhere on application. Hunting and shooting articles.
National Defense (M)
American Defense Preparedness Assn., 819 Union Trust Bldg., Wash., DC 20005. $12.00 yr. Articles on small arms, military equipment, and related subjects.
Outdoor Life
Times Mirror Magazines, Inc., 380 Madison Ave., New York, NY 10017. $6.00 yr. Shooting column by Jim Carmichel, Trap and Skeet by Bob Rodale.
Outdoor World (Q)
Country Beautiful Corp., 24198 W. Bluemound Rd., Waukesha, WI 53186. $5.00 yr. Conservation and wildlife articles.
Point Blank
Citizens Committee for the Right to Keep and Bear Arms (sent to contributors) 1601 114th S.E., Suite 151, Bellevue, WA 98004.
Police Times (M)
1100 N.E. 125th St., No. Miami, Fla. 33161.
Popular Mechanics
Hearst Corp., 224 W. 57th St., New York, NY 10019. $7.00 yr., $9.00 Canada, $12.00 foreign. Hunting and shooting articles.
Precision Shooting
Precision Shooting, Inc., Box 6, Athens, PA 18810. $6.00 yr. Journal of the International Benchrest Shooters and target shooting in general.
Rifle*
Wolfe Publishing Co. Inc., Box 3030, Prescott, AZ 86301. $6.50 yr. Journal of the NBRSA. The magazine for shooters.
Saga
Gambi Public., 333 Johnson Ave., Brooklyn, N.Y. 11026. $7.50 yr. U.S., $8.00 Canada.
Scoreboard West
2222 So. Barrington Ave., Los Angeles, CA 900640. Trap and Skeet shooting , plus hunting in the West articles. Write for price.
The Shooting Industry
Publisher's Dev. Corp., 8150 N. Central Pk., Skokie, IL 60076. $9.00 yr.
The Shooting Times & Country Magazine (England) †
Cordwallis Estate, Clivemont Rd., Maidenhead, Berksh., England. $27.50 yr. Game shooting, wild fowling, hunting and firearms articles.
Shooting Times
PJS Publications, News Plaza, Peoria, IL 61601 $7.50 yr. Guns, shooting, reloading; articles on every gun activity.
The Shotgun News‡
Snell Publishing Co., Box 1147, Hastings, NB 68901. $5.00 yr. Sample copy 75¢. Gun ads of all kinds.
The Skeet Shooting Review
National Skeet Shooting Assn., P.O. Box 28188, San Antonio, TX 78228. $9.00 yr. (Assn. membership of $10.00 includes mag.) Scores, averages, skeet articles.
Sporting Goods Business
Gralla Publications, 1515 Broadway, New York, NY 10036, Trade journal.
The Sporting Goods Dealer
1212 No. Lindbergh Blvd., St. Louis, Mo. 63166. $6.00 yr. The sporting goods trade journal.
Sports Afield with Rod & Gun
The Hearst Corp., 250 W. 55th St., New York, N.Y. 10019. $5.97 yr. Pete Brown and Grits Gresham on firearms plus hunting and fishing articles.
Sports Illustrated†
Time, Inc., 541 N. Fairbanks Court, Chicago, IL 60611. $14.00 yr. U.S. Poss. and Canada; $18.00 yr. all other countries. Articles on the current sporting scene.
Trap & Field
1100 Waterway Blvd., Indianapolis, IN 46202. $10.00 yr. Official publ. Amateur Trapshooting Assn. Scores, averages, trapshooting articles.
True
Peterson Publ. Co., P.O. Box 9555, Greenwich, CT 06830. $7.00 yr. U.S. Poss., and Canada; $10.00 yr. all other countries.
Wildlife Review (Q)
Dep't of Rec. and Conservation, Parliament Bldgs., Victoria, B.C., Canada $1.00 yr.

* Published bi-monthly.
‡ Published twice per month. † Published weekly Q Published Quarterly.
M Membership requirements; write for details. All others are published monthly.

ARMS ASSOCIATIONS IN AMERICA AND ABROAD

UNITED STATES

ALABAMA

Alabama Gun Collectors Assn.
P.O. Box 2131, Birmingham, AL 35201
North Alabama Gun Coll. Assn.
P.O. Box 564, Huntsville, Ala. 35804

ARIZONA

Arizona Gun Collectors Assn., Inc.
Miles S. Vaughn, 1129 S. 6th Ave., Tucson, Ariz. 85701

CALIFORNIA

Calif. Hunters & Gun Owners Assoc.
V. H. Wacker, 2309 Cipriani Blvd., Belmont, Cal. 94002
Greater Calif. Arms & Collectors Assn.
Donald L. Bullock, 8291 Carburton St., Long Beach, Cal. 90808
Los Angeles Gun & Ctg. Collectors Assn.
F. H. Ruffra, 20810 Amie Ave., Torrance, CA 90503
Northern California Historical Arms Coll. Assn.
Julia Lundwall, 25 Mizpah St., San Francisco Ca. 94131
San Bernardino Valley Arms Collectors, Inc.
Harold R. F. Thrasher 1970 Mesa St., San Bernadino, Cal. 92405
Santa Barbara Antique Arms Coll. Assn., Inc.
P.O. Box 6291, Santa Barbara, CA. 93111
Southern California Arms Collectors Assn.
Frank E. Barnyak, 4204 Elmer Ave., No. Hollywood, Cal. 91602

COLORADO

Arapahoe Gun Collectors
Bill Rutherford, 2968 S. Broadway, Englewood, Colo. 80110
Pikes Peak Gun Collectors Guild
Charles Cell, 406 E. Uintah St., Colorado Springs, Colo. 80903

CONNECTICUT

Antique Arms Coll. Assn. of Conn.
T. N. Reiley, 17 Philip Rd., Manchester, Conn. 06040
Stratford Gun Collectors Assn., Inc.
P.O. Box 721, Stratford, CT 06497
Ye Conn. Gun Guild, Inc.
Rob. L. Harris, P.O. Box 67, Cornwall Bridge, Conn. 06754

DELAWARE

Delaware Antique Arms Collectors
C. Landis, 2408 Duncan Rd., Wilmington, Del. 19808

FLORIDA

Florida Gun Collectors Assn.
Bob Marvin, P.O. Box 470, Jasper, Fla. 32052

GEORGIA

Georgia Arms Collectors
Cecil W. Anderson, P.O. Box 218, Conley, GA 30027

IDAHO

Idaho State Rifle and Pistol Assn.
Fritz Dixon, 1621 Los Ave., Coeur d'Alene, ID 83814

ILLINOIS

Central Illinois Gun Collectors Assn., Inc.
Donald E. Bryan, 20 Book Lane, Jacksonville, Ill. 62650
Fox Valley Arms Fellowship, Inc.
P.O. Box 301, Palatine, Ill. 60067
Illinois State Rifle Assn.
224 S. Michigan Ave., Chicago, IL 60604
Illinois Gun Collectors Assn.
P. E. Pitts, P.O. Box 1524, Chicago, Ill. 60690
Little Fort Gun Collectors Assn.
Ernie Robinson, P.O. Box 194, Gurnee, IL 60031
Mississippi Valley Gun & Cartridge Coll. Assn.
Harold S. Parsons, Route Z, Alexis, IL 61412
Sauk Trail Gun Collectors
Gordon Matson, P.O. Box 645, Milan, IL 61264
Wabash Valley Gun Collectors Assn., Inc.
Mrs. Betty Baer, 1002 Lincoln Pk. Ave., Danville, Ill. 61832

INDIANA

Crawfordsville Gun Club, Inc.
Rob. J. K. Edmonds, R.R. 2, Crawfordsville, Ind. 47933
Indiana Sportsmans Council—Legislative
Maurice Latimer, P.O. Box 93, Bloomington, IN 47401
Indiana State Rifle & Pistol Assn.
Thomas E. Graham, 1321 Fletcher St., Anderson, IN 46016
Midwest Gun Traders Inc.
c/o Glen Whittenberger, 4609 Oliver St., Ft. Wayne, IN 46806
Northern Indiana Gun Collectors Assn.
Joe Katona, 16150 Ireland Rd., Mishawaka, IN 46544
Southern Indiana Gun Collectors Assn., Inc.
Harold M. McClary, 509 N. 3rd St., Boonville, Ind. 47601

IOWA

Central States Gun Collectors Assn.
Avery Giles, 1104 S. 1st Ave., Marshtown, IA 50158

KANSAS

Four State Collectors Assn.
M. G. Wilkinson, 915 E. 10th, Pittsburgh, Kan. 66762
Kansas Cartridge Coll. Assn.
Bob Linder, Box 84, Plainville, Kans. 67663
Missouri Valley Arms Collectors Assn.
Chas. F. Samuel, Jr., Box 8204, Shawnee Mission, Kans. 66208

KENTUCKY

John Hunt Morgan Gun Coll. Inc.
P.O. Box 525, Paris, Ky. 40361
Kentuckiana Arms Coll. Assn.
Charles R. Phelps, Box 1776, Louisville, Ky. 40201
Kentucky Gun Collectors Assn., Inc.
J. A. Smith, Box 64, Owensboro, Ky. 42301

LOUISIANA

Ark-La-Tex Gun Collectors Assn.
Ray Franks, 1521 Earl St., Shreveport, La. 71108
Bayou Gun Club
David J. Seibert, Jr., 2820 Ramsey Dr., New Orleans, LA 70114
Pelican Arms Collectors
8681 Sharon Hills Blvd., Baton Rouge, LA 70811

MARYLAND

Baltimore Antique Arms Assn.
Stanley I. Kellert, R.D. 1, Box 256, Lutherville, MD 21093

MASSACHUSETTS

Bay Colony Weapons Collectors Inc.
Ronald B. Santurjian, 47 Homer Rd., Belmont, Mass. 02178
Massachusetts Arms Collectors
John J. Callan, Jr., P.O. Box 1001, Worcester, Mass. 01613

MICHIGAN

Michigan Antique Arms Coll., Inc.
W. H. Heid, 8914 Borgman Ave., Huntington Woods, Mich. 48070
Michigan Rifle & Pistol Assn.
Betty Swarthout, 8384 Perrin, Westland, Mich. 48185
Royal Oak Historical Arms Collectors, Inc.
Nancy Stein, 25487 Hereford, Huntington Woods, Mich. 48070

MINNESOTA

Dakota Territory Gun Coll. Assn., Inc.
Jim Jasken, 1022 1st St., So., Moorhead, MN. 56560
Minnesota Weapons Coll. Assn., Inc.
Box 662, Hopkins, MN 55343
Twin Ports Weapons Collectors
Jack Puglisi, 6504 Lexington St., Duluth, MN. 55807

MISSOURI

Edwardsville, Ill. Gun Collectors
A. W. Stephensmeier, 1055 Warson Woods Dr., St. Louis, MO 63122
Mineral Belt Gun Coll. Assn.
G. W. Gunter, 1110 E. Cleveland Ave., Monett, Mo. 65708

MONTANA

Montana Arms Collectors Assn.
Lewis E. Yearout, 308 Riverview Dr. East, Great Falls, MT 59404

NEBRASKA

Nebraska Gun & Cartridge Collectors
E. M. Zalud, 710 West 6th St., North Platte, Neb. 69101
Pine Ridge Gun Coll.
Loren Pickering, 509 Elm St., Crawford, NB 69339

NEW MEXICO

New Mexico Gun Collectors Assn.
P.O. Box 14145, Albuquerque, NM. 87111

NEW HAMPSHIRE

Maple Tree Gun Coll. Assn.
E. P. Hector, Meriden Rd., Lebanon, N.H. 03766
New Hampshire Arms Collectors Inc.
Frank H. Galeucia, Rt. 3, Windham, N.H. 03087

NEW JERSEY

Experimental Ballistics Associates
Ed Yard, 110 Kensington, Trenton, N.J. 08618
Jersey Shore Antique Arms Collectors
Joe Sisia, P.O. Box 100, Bayville, NJ 08721
New Jersey Arms Collectors Club, Inc.
Joseph S. Rixon, 1 Towns End Rd., Mendham, NJ 07945

NEW YORK

Hudson-Mohawk Arms Collectors Assn., Inc.
Bennie S. Pisarz, 108 W. Main St., Frankfort, N.Y. 13340
Iroquois Arms Collectors Assn.
Dennis Freeman, 12144 McNeeley Rd., Akron, N.Y. 14001
Mid-State Arms Coll. & Shooters Club
Bennie S. Pisarz, 108 W. Main St., Frankfort, N.Y. 13340
New York State Arms Collectors Assn., Inc.
Marvin Salls, R. D. 1,Ilion, N.Y. 13357
Westchester Arms Collectors Club, Inc.
F. E. Falkenbury, Secy., 79 Hillcrest Rd., Hartsdale, N.Y. 10530

NORTH CAROLINA

Carolina Gun Collectors Assn.
Morris Lawing, 1020 Central Ave., Charlotte, NC 28204

OHIO

Barberton Gun Collectors Assn.
R. N. Watters, 1108 Bevan St., Barberton, O. 44203
Central Ohio Gun and Indian Relic Coll. Assn.
Coyt Stookey, 134 E. Ohio Ave., Washington C.H., O. 43160
Maumee Valley Gun Collectors Assn.
A. Kowalka, 3203 Woodville Rd., Northwood, OH 43619
National Bench Rest Shooters Assn., Inc.
Bernice McMullen, 607 W. Line St., Minerva, O. 44657
Ohio Gun Collectors, Assn., Inc.
Mrs. C. D. Rickey, 130 S. Main St., Prospect, O. 43342
The Stark Gun Collectors, Inc.
Russ McNary, 147 Miles Ave., N.W., Canton, O. 44708
Tri-State Gun Collectors
Doyt S. Gamble, 1115 N. Main St., Lima, OH 45801

OKLAHOMA

Indian Territory Gun Collectors Assn.
P.O. Box 4491, Tulsa, Okla. 74104

OREGON

Oregon Cartridge Coll. Assn.
John L. Heyman, 1410 Main St., Springfield, OR 97477
Oregon Arms Coll. Assn., Inc.
Ted Dowd, P.O. Box 25103, Portland, OR 97225
Willamette Valley Arms Coll. Assn.
K. Gardner, Rt. 3, Box 283, Springfield, OR 97477

PENNSYLVANIA

Central Penn Antique Arms Assn.
Geo. Smithgall, 549 W. Lemon St., Lancaster, PA 17603
Forks of the Delaware Weapons Assn., Inc.
John F. Scheid, 348 Bushkill St., Easton, Pa. 18042
Lancaster Muzzle Loading Assn.
James H. Frederick, RD 1, Box 447, Columbia, PA 17512
Pennsylvania Gun Collectors Assn.
Arch Waugh, 37 Woodside Dr., Washington, PA 15301
Presque Isle Gun Coll. Assn.
James Welch, 156 E. 37 St., Erie, PA 16506
Somerset Sportsmen & Rifle Club
Clifford Dunmyer, Rt. 1, Somerset, PA 15501

SOUTH CAROLINA

Belton Gun Club Inc.
J. K. Phillips, P.O. Box 605, Belton S.C. 29627
South Carolina Arms Coll. Assn.
J. W. McNelley, 3215 Lincoln St., Columbia, S.C. 29201

SOUTH DAKOTA

Dakota Territory Gun Coll. Assn., Inc.
Jim Jasken, 1022 1st St., So., Moorhead, MN 56560

TENNESSEE

Memphis Antique Weapons Assn.
Nelson T. Powers, 4672 Barfield Rd., TN 38117
Tennessee Gun Collectors Assn., Inc.
M. H. Parks, 3556 Pleasant Valley Rd., Nashville, Tenn. 37204

TEXAS

Alamo Arms Collectors
Bill Brookshire, 410 Rector, San Antonio, Tex. 78216
Houston Gun Collectors Assn.
P.O. Box 53435, Houston, TX 77052
Paso Del Norte Gun Collectors Inc.
Robert L. Bullard, 5910 Falcon St., El Paso, Tex. 79924
Permian Basin Rifle & Pistol Club, Inc.
E. L. Good, Box 459, Midland, Tex. 79701
Sabine Gun Collectors Club
Mrs. Irene Vivier, 1042 Iowa, Beaumont, Tex. 77705
Texas Gun Collectors Assn.
Mrs. Taska Clark, 3119 Produce Row, Houston, TX 77023
Texas State Rifle Assn.
Lafe R. Pfeifer, P.O. Drawer 34809, Dallas TX 75234
Waco Gun Collectors
C. V. Pruitt, 4021 N. 26th, Waco, Tex. 76708

UTAH

Utah Gun Collectors Assn.
S. Gerald Keogh, 875 20th St., Ogden, Utah 84401

VIRGINIA

Shenandoah Valley Gun Coll. Assn.
Daniel E. Blye, P.O. Box 926, Winchester, Va. 22601
Virginia Arms Collectors & Assn.
W. H. Bacon, 4601 Sylvan Rd., Richmond, Va. 23225

WASHINGTON

Washington Arms Collectors, Inc.
Don Zwicker, 446 Pelly Ave., Renton, WA 98055

WISCONSIN

Chippewa Valley Weapons Collectors
J. M. Sullivan, 504 Ferry St., Eau Claire, Wis. 54701
Great Lakes Arms Coll. Assn., Inc.
E. Warnke, 1811 N. 73rd St. Wauwatosa, WI 53213
Wisconsin Gun Collectors Assn., Inc.
Rob. Zellmer, W180N8996 Leona Lane, Menomonee Falls, WI. 53051

WYOMING

Wyoming Gun Collectors
Bob Funk, Box 1805, Riverton, Wyo. 82501

NATIONAL ORGANIZATIONS

Amateur Trap Shooting Assn.
P.O. Box 246, Vandalia, OH 45377
American Defense Preparedness Assn.
819 Union Trust Bldg., Washington, DC 20005
American Military Inst.
Box 568, Washington, DC 20044
American Police Pistol & Rifle Assn.
Law enforcement members only.
1100 N.E. 125th St., No. Miami, FL 33161
American Single Shot Rifle Assn.
Dennis Hrusosky, 411 David Ave., Joliet, IL 60433
American Society of Arms Collectors, Inc.
Robt. F. Rubendunst, 6550 Baywood Lane, Cincinnati, OH 45224
Armor & Arms Club
J. K. Watson, Jr., 25 Broadway, New York, NY 10004
Association of Firearm and Tool Mark Examiners
Invest. John S. Bates, N.Y. State Police, Scientific Lab., State Campus, Albany, NY 12226
Boone & Crockett Club
c/o Carnegie Museum, 4400 Forbes Ave., Pittsburgh, PA 15213
Citizen's Committee for the Right to Keep and Bear Arms
Natl. Hq.: Bellefield Office Park, 1601 114, S.E., Suite 151, Bellevue, WA 98004
Ducks Unlimited
P.O. Box 66300, Chicago, IL 60666
Experimental Ballistics Assoc.
Ed Yard, 110 Kensington, Trenton, NJ 08618
International Benchrest Shooters
Donalee Stekl, RD 1, Robinson Rd., Mowhawk, NY 13407
International Cartridge Coll. Assn., Inc.
A. D. Amesbury, 4065 Montecito Ave., Tucson, AZ 85711
Miniature Arms Collectors/Makers Society Ltd.
Joseph J. Macewicz, 104 White Sand Lane, Racine, WI 53402
National Assn. of Federally Lic'd. Firearms Dealers
Andrew Molchan, 7001 N. Clark St., Chicago, IL 60625
National Automatic Pistol Collectors Assn.
Ernie Lang, P.O. Box 272, Cayce, SC 29033
National Bench Rest Shooters Assn., Inc.
Bernice McMullen, 607 W. Line St., Minerva, OH 44657
National Muzzle Loading Rifle Assn.
Box 67, Friendship, IN 47021
National Police Officers Assn. of America
National Police Hall of Fame Bldg., 14600 S. Trail, N.P., Venice, FL 33595
National Reloading Mfgrs. Assn., Inc.
1220 Morrison St., S.W., Portland, OR 97205
National Rifle Assn.
1600 Rhode Island Ave., N.W., Washington, DC 20036
National Shooting Sports Fdtn., Inc.
Warren Page, President, 1075 Post Rd., Riverside, CT 06878
National Skeet Shooting Assn.
Carroll E. Bobo, P.O. Box 28188, San Antonio, TX 78228
North-South Skirmish Assn., Inc.
John L. Rawls, Rt. 2, Box 245A, Winchester, VA 22601
Sporting Arms and Ammunition Mfgrs. Inst., Inc.
420 Lexington Ave., New York, NY 10017
U.S. Revolver Assn.
Stanley A. Sprague, 59 Alvin St., Springfield, MA 01104

AUSTRALIA

Nat'l. Sporting Shooters' Assn. of Australia
Mrs. O. H. Francis, Box 1064, G.P.O., S.A. 5001 Australia

CANADA

ALBERTA

Canadian Historical Arms Society
P.O. Box 901, Edmonton, Alb., Canada T5J 2L8

ONTARIO

Oshawa Antique Gun Coll. Inc.
Gordon J. Dignem, 613 Rosmere St., Oshawa, Ont., Canada

QUEBEC

Lower Canada Arms Collectors Assn.
Secretary, P.O. Box 1162, St. B. Montreal 101, Quebec, Can.

EUROPE

ENGLAND

Arms and Armour Society of London
F. Wilkinson, 40 Great James St., Holborn, London, N. 3HB W.C.1.
Historical Breechloading Smallarms Assn.
D. J. Penn, M.A., Imperial War Museum, Lambeth Rd., London SE1 6HZ, England. Journal is $7 a yr.
Muzzle Loaders' Assn. of Great Britain
Membership Records, 12 Francis Rd., Baginton, Coventry, England
National Rifle Assn. (British)
Bisley Camp, Brookwood, Woking, Surrey, England

FRANCE

Les Arquebusiers de France,
Mme, Marckmann, 70 Rue des Chantiers, 78-Versailles, France

GERMANY (WEST)

Deutscher Schützenbund
62 Wiesbaden-Klarenthal, West Germany

NEW ZEALAND

New Zealand Deerstalkers Assn.
J. M. Murphy, P.O. Box 263, Wellington, New Zealand

SOUTH AFRICA

Historical Firearms Soc. of South Africa
"Minden" 11 Buchan Rd., Newlands, 7700 Cape Town, South Africa

Union Internationale de Tir
Wiesbaden-Klarenthal, West Germany
(member countries 1974)

ALBANIA
Federation Albanaise de Tir
Rruga Kongresi i Permetit Nr. 41, Tirana

ARGENTINA
Federacion Argentina de Tiro
Moreno 1270-P.1-Of. 109, Buenos Aires

AUSTRALIA
Australian Shooting Association
P.O. Box 4842, Melbourne, Victoria 3001

AUSTRIA
Osterreichischer Schutzenbund
A-4181 Oberneukirchen
Verband der Jagd- und Wurftaubenschutzen Osterreichs
Haus des Sportes, Prinz-Eugen-Str. 12, A-1040 Wien

BAHAMAS
Yellowbirds Gun Club of the Bahamas

BARBADOS
The Barbados Rifle Association
P.O. Box 437, Barbados, W.I.

BELGIUM
Union Royale des Societes de Tir de Belgique
p. a. M. O. Peeters, 22, Bromeliastraat, B-9110 Sint Amandsberg
Federation Belge de Tir aux Claybirds
268, Avenue d'Auderghem, Bruxelles

BERMUDA
Bermuda Rifle Association
P.O. Box 1620, Hamilton

BOLIVIA
Federacion Boliviana de Tiro
Deportivo, Casilla No. 3048, La Paz

BRAZIL
Confederacao Brasileira de Caca e Tiro
Avenida Nilo Pecanha 155, s/227, Rio de Janeiro
Confederacao Brasileira de Tiro ao Alvo
Avenida Pasteur, 120, Apart. 703, Rio de Janeiro

BULGARIA
Bulgarischer Schutzenverband
Boul. Tolbuchin 18, Sofia
Bulgarischer Jager—und Fischerverband
Gawril Genov Str. 12, Sofia

BURMA
Burma Shooting Federation
Aungsan Memorial Stadium, Rangoon

CANADA
Shooting Federation of Canada
333 River Rd., Vanier City, Ontario K1L 8B9

CHILE
Federacion Nacional de Tiro al Blanco de Chile
Vicuna Mackenna 44, Casilla 9055, Santiago de Chile
Federacion de Tiro al Vuelo de Chile
Casilla 14.861 Sucursal 21, Santiago de Chile

CHINA (Republic of)
Republic of China Shooting Association
P.O. Box 7400-16, Lungtang 325, Taiwan, Republic of China

COLUMBIA
Federacion Colombiana de Tiro y caza
Calle 18 No. 43-B-65, Apartado Aereo No. 10803 Bogota D.E.

COSTA RICA
Federacion Nacional de Tiro
Apartado 3955, San Jose

CUBA
Federacion Cubana de Tiro
c/o Comite Olimpico Cubano, Hotel Habana Libre, Habana

CZECHOSLOVAKIA
Ceskoslovensky Strelecky Svaz
Opletalova 29, Praha 1

DDR
Deutscher Schutzenverband der Deutschen Demokratischen Republik
DDR-1272 Neuenhaben b. Berlin

DENMARK
Dansk Skytte Union
21, Brondbyvester Boulevard, DK-2600 Glostrup

DOMINICAN REPUBLIC
Federacion Dominicana de Tiro
Ramon Matias Mella, Villa Duarte, D.N. Santa Domingo
Federacion Dominicana de Tiro
Apartado Correos 445, San Pedro de Macoris

ECUADOR
Federacion Deportiva Nacional del Ecuador
Apartado 3409, Guayaquil

ARABIC REPUBLIC OF EGYPT
The Egyptian Shooting Federation
37, Abdel Khalek Sarwat St., P.O. Box 290, Cairo

FINLAND
Suomen Ampujainliitto
Aurorankatu 9 B 10, SF-00100 Helsinki 10

FRANCE
Federation Francaise de Tir
8, Place de la Concorde, F-75008 Paris

GERMANY
Deutscher Schützenband e. V.
Klarenthaler StraBe, D-62 Wiesbaden-Klarenthal

GREAT BRITAIN
Joint Shooting Committee for Great Britain
Codrington House, 113, Southwark Street, London, S.E. 1 OJW
National Small-bore Rifle Association
Codrington House, 113, Southwark Street, London, S.E. 1 OJW
The Clay Pigeon Shooting Association
Angel Road, London, N18 3BH

GREECE
Federation Hellenique de Tir
10 Rue Stadiou, Athens (133)

GUATEMALA
Federacion Nacional de Tiro de Guatamala
Palacio de los Deportes, Ciudad Olimpica, Guatamala, C.A.

HOLLAND
Koninklijke Nederlandse Schutters Associatie
Bondsbureau, Joz. Israelslaan 20, P.O. Box 2665, Den Haag

HONDURAS
The National Shooters' Association of British Honduras
P.O. Box 163, Belize

HONG KONG
Hong Kong Rifle Association
Architectural Office, P.W.D., Hong Kong

HUNGARY

Magyar Sportlovo Szovetseg
Dozsa Gyorgy u. 1-3, Nepstadion, H-1143 Budapest

ICELAND

Icelandic Sport Federation
Postholf 864, Reykjavik

INDIA

The National Rifle Association of India
82-83 Theatre Communication Building, Connaught Circus, New Delhi-1

INDONESIA

Indonesian Shooting and Hunting Association
Lapangan Menembak, Komplek Gelora Senayan, Jakarta Selatan

IRAN

Iranian Shooting Federation
Meidan Jaleh Farah-Abad Street, Stadium Varzeshi Farahnaz Pahlavi, Teheran

IRELAND

National Rifle and Pistol Association of Ireland
51 Parnell Square, Dublin-1
Irish Clay Pigeon Shooting Association
c/o Mr. Arthur E. MacMahon, Nass, Co. Kildare

ISRAEL

Sports Federation of Israel
P.O. Box 4575, Tel-Aviv

ITALY

Unione Italiana di Tiro a Segno
Palazzo delle Federazioni, Viale Tiziano, 70, I-00100 Roma
Federazione Italiana Tiro a Volo
Palazzo delle Federazioni, Viale Tiziano, 70, 1-00100 Roma

JAMAICA

Jamaica Rifle Association
P.O. Box 64, 148 Mountain View Avenue, Kingston 6
The Jamaica Skeet Club
P.O. Box 190, Kingston 11

JAPAN

National Rifle Association of Japan
c/o Kishi Memorial Hall, Kannami 1-1-1, Shibuya-ku, Tokyo
Japan Clay Pigeon Shooting Association

JORDAN

Jordan Shooting Federation
P.O. Box 413, Amman

KENYA

The Kenya Rifle Association
P.O. Box 45526, Nairobi

KHMER

Federation Khmere du Tir au Fusil et au Pistolet
Complexe Sportif National Khmer Phnom-Penh

KOREA

Korea Shooting Federation
Room 810, Korea Athletics Association Building, 19 Mukyodong, Choonggu, Seoul

DEMOCRATIC PEOPLE'S REPUBLIC OF KOREA

Shooting Association of the Democratic People's Republic of Korea
Moonsin-dong 2, Dongdaiwon District, Pyongyang/DPRK

LAOS

Association Nationale de Tir du Laos

LEBANON

Federation Libanaise de Tir
P.O. Box 2030, Beyrouth

LIECHTENSTEIN

Liechtensteiner Schützenverein
Vaduz

LUXEMBURG

Federation Luxembourgeoise de Tir aux Armes Sportives
Case Postale 184, Luxembourg-Ville

MALAYSIA

National Shooting Association of Malaysia
No. 15, Jalan Alor, Kuala Lumpur

MALTA

Malta Shooting Club
P.O. Box 310, Valletta

SAN MARINO

Federazione Sammarinese Tiro Volo
Palazzo del Turismo, RSM-47031 Repubblica di San Marino

MEXICO

Federacion Mexicana de Tiro Olimpico e Internacional, A.C.
Aldama y Moctezuma, Mexico—3, D.F.

MONACO

Federation Monegasque de Tir
32, Boulevard des Moulins, Monaco

MONGOLIA

Federation de Tir de la RPM
PF n/a 46-209, Oulan-Bator

NETHERLANDS-ANTILLES

Schietbond Nederlandse Antillen
c/o Dienst Openbare, Werken Parera, Curacao

NEW ZEALAND

National Shooting Federation of New Zealand
P.O. Box 7059, Wellington

NORWAY

Norges Skytterforbund
Torggt, 3, Oslo 1

PAKISTAN

National Rifle Association of Pakistan
Parvez Abbasi, Secy., NRA of Pakistan, 338 No. Circular Ave., Defence Hsg. Soc., Karachi, Pakistan

PANAMA

Comision Nacional de Tiro de Panama
P.O. Box 868, Panama 1

PAPUA NEW GUINEA

Shooting Association of Papua New Guinea
P.O. Box 4120, Badili

PARAGUAY

Federacion Deportiva Militar Paraguaya

PERU

Directorio de las Sociedades de Tiro del Peru
Apartado No. 1214, Lima

PHILIPPINES

Philippine Shooting Association
P.O. Box 2272, Rizal Memorial Field, Manila

POLAND

Polski Zwiazek Strzelectwa Sportowego
Chocimska 14 pok. 304, Warszawa 12

PORTUGAL

Fedaracao Portuguesa de Tiro
Avenida de Liberdade, 18-4. E., Lisboa-2
Federacao Portuguesa de Tiro com Armas de Caca (Seccao de Tiro aos Pratos)
Av. Julio Dinis, 10-4-Letra E, Lisboa-1

PUERTO RICO

Puerto Rico Shooting Association
Apartado 22981, Estacion de la Universidad, Rio Piedras, P.R. 00931
Federacion de Tiro de Puerto Rico
c/o Mr. Jaime L. Loyola, "G" St. 1168 Urb. Munoz Rivera, Guaynabo, P.R. 00657

RHODESIA

The Rhodesia National Small-Bore Shooting Association
P.O. Box HG 141, Highlands, Salisbury
The Rhodesian Clay Pigeon Shooting Association
P.O. Box 803, Salisbury

ROUMANIA

Federatia Romana de Tir
Str. Vasile Conta, 16, Bukarest

EL SALVADOR

Federacion Nacional de Tiro
Apartado Postal 1823, San Salvador

SINGAPORE

Singapore Shooting Association
59-B, Robinson Road, Singapore 1

SOUTH AFRICA

South Africa Shooting Union
P.O. Box 3959, Pretoria, 0001
South African Small-Bore Rifle Association
P.O. Box 3959, Pretoria, 0001
South African Pistol Association
MacKay Chambers, MacKay Avenue, Blairgowrie, Randburg, Tvl. 2001
The Clay Pigeon Shooting Association of Southern Africa
P.O. Box 707, Durban

SOVIET UNION

The Shooting Federation of the USSR
Skatertnyi pereulok 4, Moscow 69

SPAIN

Federacion Nacional del Tiro Olimpico Espanol
Alberto Aguilera, 3, Madrid-15

SRI LANKA

The Ceylon Rifle Association
"Molaguthotam", Angampitiya, Waikkala

SWAZILAND

Swaziland National Shooting Association
P.O. Box 177, Mbabane

SWEDEN

Svenska Sportskytteforbundet
Grev Turegatan 13 A, S-114 46 Stockholm

SWITZERLAND

Societe Suisse des Carabiniers
c/o Herrn Oberst Jos. Burkhard, Gruneggstrasse 36, CH-6005 Luzern

SYRIA

Federation Syrienne de Tir Maison des Federations Sportives
Mohagerine-Damas

THAILAND

The National Shooting Sport Association of Thailand
Sunandha Palace, Bangkok 3
Skeet and Trap Shooting Association of Thailand
c/o Asoke Motors Ltd., 211-213 Asoke Road, Bangkok

TONGA

Tonga Rifle Association
P.O. Box 72, Nuku'alofa

TRINIDAD

Trinidad Rifle Association
P.O. Box 451, Port of Spain

TUNISIA

Federation Tunisienne de Tir Stand National de Tir et d'Equitation
Sidi Belhassen el Ouardia, Tunis

TURKEY

Turkiye Aticilik ve Avcilik Federasyonu
Ulus is Hani, A Blok, Ankara

UNITED STATES OF AMERICA

National Rifle Association of America
1600 Rhode Island Avenue, N.W., Washington, D.C. 20036

URAGUAY

Comision Nacional de Tiro
Canelones 982, Montevideo

VENEZUELA

Federacion Venezolana de Tiro
Apartado 3970, Caracas

VIETNAM

Vietnam Shooting Federation
284 Thanh-Thai, Saigon

VIRGIN ISLANDS

Virgin Islands Shooting Federation
P.O. Box 2842, Christiansted, St. Croix, U.S. Virgin Islands 00820

YUGOSLAVIA

Streljacki savez Jugoslavije
Kosovska br. 9, Beograd

ZAMBIA

Zambia Small-Bore Rifle Association
P.O. Box 41, Mulfulira

Shooting Publications

A Joint Resolution—A 4-page statement by the National Police Officers Assn. and the National Shooting Sports Foundation, outlining the role of firearms in U.S. history and voicing their stand against ill-planned restrictive gun laws. Free.[1]

Basic Pistol Marksmanship—Textbook for basic pistol courses. 25¢[2]

Basic Rifle Marksmanship—Textbook for basic rifle courses. 25¢ ea.[2]

The Elk—125-page report on the hunting and management of this game animal, more properly called *wapiti*. Extensive biblio. $1.00.[4]

Free Films—Brochure listing outdoor movies available to sportsmen's clubs. Free.[1]

The Gun Law Problem—Information about firearms legislation. Free.[2]

How to be a Crack Shot—A 14-page booklet detailing everything necessary to becoming an outstanding shot. Free.[3]

Fundamentals of Claybird Shooting—A 39-page booklet explaining the basics of Skeet and trap in non-technical terms. Many diagrams. 25¢ ea.[4]

Hunter Safety Instructor's Guide—How to conduct an NRA Hunter Safety Course. 25¢ ea.[2]

Hunting and Shooting Sportsmanship—A 4-page brochure defining the "true sportsman" and giving information on the outdoor field. Free.[1]

Junior Rifle Handbook—Information about the NRA junior program with short instruction course. (25 copies issued to each new affiliated junior club without charge.) 25¢ ea.[2]

NRA Hunter Safety Handbook—Textbook for students. 10¢ ea.[2]

National Shooting Preserve Directory—Up-to-date listing of small game preserves in the U.S. and Canada. Free.[1]

Game, Gunners and Biology—A thumbnail history of American wildlife conservation. 50¢ ea.[4]

Shooting's Fun for Everyone—The why, when, where, and how of riflery for boys and girls. 20 pp. 5¢ ea.[1]

Trap or Skeet Fundamentals—Handbooks explaining fundamentals of these two sports, complete with explicit diagrams to start beginners off right. Free.[3]

25 Foot Shooting Program—Complete information on a short range shooting program with CO[2] and pneumatic rifles and pistols. 35¢[2]

What Every Parent Should Know When a Boy or Girl Wants a Gun—Straightforward answers to the 15 questions most frequently asked by parents. 8 pp. 5¢ ea.[1]

The Cottontail Rabbit—56-page rundown on America's most popular hunting target. Where to find him, how to hunt him, how to help him. Bibliography included. $1.00 ea.[4]

For the Young Hunter—A 32-page booklet giving fundamental information on the sport. Single copies free, 15¢ each in bulk.[4]

Gray and Fox Squirrels—112-page paperbound illustrated book giving full rundown on the squirrel families named. Extensive bibliography. $1.00 ea.[4]

How to Have More Pheasant Hunting—A 16-page booklet on low cost hunting, including data on in-season stocking and how to start a small preserve. 25¢.[1]

The Mallard—80-page semi-technical report on this popular duck. Life cycle, laws and management, hunting—even politics as they affect this bird—are covered. Bibliography. $1.00 ea.[4]

NRA Booklets—Ranging from 12 to 36 pages, these are articles on specific arms or arms types. Titles available are: Sighting In; The 45 Automatic; The M1 Rifle; Telescopic Sights; Metallic Sights; Duck Hunting; U.S. Cal. 30 Carbine; Remodeling the 03A3; Remodeling the 303 Lee-Enfield; Remodeling the U.S. 1917 Rifle; M1903 Springfield Rifle; Military Rifles and Civil War Small Arms, 50¢ ea. Gun Cabinets, Racks, Cases & Pistol Boxes, 75¢. Deer Hunting, $1.00.[2]

Under the heading of "Range Plans" are 15 booklets priced from 10¢ to $1.00. All are described in an order form pamphlet available from the NRA.

NRA Digest of the Federal Gun Control Act of 1968—A 12-page booklet clearly explaining the new law and its provisions. Free to NRA members.[2]

NRA Federal Firearms Laws—A 28-page booklet digesting the several U.S. gun laws affecting the citizen today. Free to NRA members.[2]

NRA Firearms & Ammunition Fact Book—352-page book of questions and answers, ballistic charts and tables, descriptions of firearms and ammunition. NRA, Washington, D.C., 1964. $2.00 ea. ($1.75 to NRA members).

NRA Firearms Assembly Handbook, Volumes I and II—Articles describing the assembly and disassembly of various arms. Vol. I, 160 pp., covers 77 guns, Vol. II, 176 pp., 87 guns. Illustrated with exploded-view and supplementary drawings. NRA, Washington, D.C., 1960 and 1964. $3.50 ea. (2.50 to NRA members).

NRA Firearms Handling Handbook—21 major articles on the proper useage of most types of small arms available to civilians. Illus. NRA, Washington, D.C., 1962, 80 pp. $2.75 ($1.75 to NRA members).

NRA Gun Collectors Handbook—20 feature articles on all phases of gun collecting, plus a listing of all important museums. NRA, Washington, D.C., 1959. 48 pp., illus. $2.50 ($1.50 to NRA members).

NRA Handloader's Guide—Enlarged & Revised. A successor to the *NRA Illustrated Reloading Handbook*, this excellent new work covers all aspects of metallic-case and shotshell reloading. Washington, D. C., 1969, fully illus. $5.00 (NRA members, $4.00).

NRA Hunters Handbook—51 major pieces, 18 shorter ones. NRA, Washington, D.C., 1960. 72 pp., illus. $3.00 ($2.00 to NRA members).

NRA Illustrated International Shooting Handbook—18 major articles detailing shooting under ISU rules, training methods, etc. NRA, Washington, D.C., 1964. $2.50 ea. ($1.50 to NRA members).

NRA Illustrated Shotgun Handbook—50 articles covering every phase of smoothbore shooting, including exploded views of many shotguns. NRA, Washington, D.C. 1964. 128 pp. $3.00 ea. ($2.00 to NRA members).

NRA Questions and Answers Handbook—150 queries and replies on guns and shooting. NRA, Washington, D.C., 1959. 46 pp. with index, illus. $2.50 ($1.50 to NRA members).

NRA Shooters Guide—40 articles of high interest to shooters of all kinds. Over 340 illus. NRA, Washington, D.C., 1959. 72 pp., $3.00 ($2.00 to NRA members).

NRA Shooting Handbook—83 major articles plus 35 shorts on every phase of shooting. NRA, Washington, D.C., 1961. 224 pp., illus. $4.50 ($3.50 to NRA members).

Principles of Game Management—A 25-page booklet surveying in popular manner such subjects as hunting regulations, predator control, game refuges and habitat restoration. Single copies free, 15¢ each in bulk.[4]

The Ring-Necked Pheasant—Popular distillation of much of the technical literature on the "ringneck." 104-page paperbound book, appropriately illustrated. Bibliography included. $1.00 ea.[4]

Ruffed Grouse, by John Madson—108-page booklet on the life history, management and hunting of *Bonasa umbellus* in its numerous variations. Extensive biblio. $1.00.[4]

Start A Gun Club—All of the basic information needed to establish a club with clay bird shooting facilities. 24 pp. 50¢[1]

Where To Shoot Muzzle Loaders In The U.S.A.—Publ. for black powder burners, and lists more than 100 muzzle loading clubs. 10¢.[1]

The White-Tailed Deer—History, management, hunting—a complete survey in this 108-page paperbound book. Full bibliography. $1.00 ea.[4]

You and Your Lawmaker—A 22-page citizenship manual for sportsmen, showing how they can support or combat legislation affecting shooting and outdoor sports. 10¢ ea.[1]

[1]National Shooting Sports Foundation, Inc. 1075 Post Road, Riverside, Conn. 06878

[2]National Rifle Association of America, 1600 Rhode Island Ave., Washington, D. C. 20036

[3]Remington Arms Company, Dept. C—Bridgeport, Conn. 06602

[4]Olin Mathieson Conservation Dept., East Alton, Ill. 62024

Directory of the Arms Trade

AMMUNITION (Commercial)

Alcan Shells, (See: Smith & Wesson Ammunition Co.)
Cascade Cartridge Inc., (See Omark)
DWM (see RWS)
Dynamit Nobel of America, Inc., 910, 17 St. NW, Suite 709, Washington DC 20006
Federal Cartridge Co., 2700 Foshay Tower, Minneapolis, Minn. 55402
Frontier Cartridge Co., Inc., Box 1848, Grand Island, Neb. 68801
Lee E. Jurras & Assoc., Inc., P.O. Box 846, Roswell, NM 88201 (Auto Mag only)
Omark-CCI, Inc., Box 856, Lewiston, Ida. 83501
RWS (see Dynamit Nobel)
Remington Arms Co., Bridgeport, Conn. 06602
Service Armament, 689 Bergen Blvd., Ridgefield, N.J. 07657
Smith & Wesson Ammunition Co., 2399 Forman Rd., Rock Creek, OH 44084
Weatherby's, 2781 E. Firestone Blvd., South Gate, Calif. 90280
Winchester-Western, East Alton, Ill. 62024

AMMUNITION (Custom)

Ed Agramonte, Inc., 41 Riverdale Ave., Yonkers, NY 10701
Bill Ballard, P.O. Box 656, Billings, MT 59103 (ctlg. 25¢)
Beal's Bullets, 170 W. Marshall Rd., Lansdowne, PA 19050
Bell's Gun & Sport Shop, 3309-19 Mannheim Rd., Franklin Park, IL 60131
Brass Extrusion Labs. Ltd. (see Bell's)
Russell Campbell, 219 Leisure Dr., San Antonio, Tex. 78201
Collectors Shotshell Arsenal, 365 S. Moore, Lakewood, CO 80226
Crown City Arms, P.O. Box 1126, Cortland, NY 13045
Cumberland Arms, 1222 Oak Dr., Manchester, Tenn. 37355
E. W. Ellis Sport Shop, RFD 1, Box 139, Corinth, N.Y. 12822
Ellwood Epps (Orillia) Ltd., Hwy. 11 North, Orillia, Ont., Canada
David J. Gaida, 1109 S. Millwood, Wichita, KS 67203
Gussert Bullet & Cartridge Co., 1868 Lenwood Ave., Green Bay, WI 54303
Hutton Rifle Ranch, 619 San Lorenzo St., Santa Monica, CA 90402
J-4, Inc., 1700 Via Burton, Anaheim, CA 92806 (custom bullets)
R. H. Keeler, 1304 S. Oak, Port Angeles, Wash. 98362
KTW Inc., 710 Foster Park Rd., Lorain, OH 44053 (bullets)
Dean Lincoln, P.O. Box 1886, Farmington, NM 87401
Lomont Precision Bullets, 4421 S. Wayne Ave., Ft. Wayne, IN 46807 (custom bullets)
Pat B. McMillan, 1828 E. Campo Bello Dr., Phoenix, Ariz. 85022
Mansfield Gunshop, Box 83, New Boston, N.H. 03070
Numrich Arms Corp., 203 Broadway, W. Hurley, N.Y. 12491
The Outrider, Inc., 3288 LaVenture Dr., Chamblee, GA 30341
Robert Pomeroy, Morison Ave., Corinth, ME 04427 (custom shells)
A. F. Sailer, P.O. Box L, Owen, WI 54460
Sanders Cust. Gun Serv., 2358 Tyler Lane, Louisville, Ky. 40205
Shotshell Components, 365 S. Moore, Lakewood, CO 80226
Geo. Spence, P.O. Box 222, Steele, MO 63877 (box-primed cartridges)
H. Winter Cast Bullets, 422 Circle Dr., Clarksville, TN 37040

AMMUNITION (Foreign)

Abercrombie & Fitch, Madison at 45th St., New York, N.Y. 10017
Canadian Ind. Ltd. (C.I.L.), Ammo Div., Howard House, Brownsburg, Que., Canada, J0V 1A0
Colonial Ammunition Co., Box 8511, Auckland, New Zealand
Dynamit Nobel of America, Inc., 910, 17 St. NW, Suite 709, Washington, DC 20006
Eastern Sports Distributors Co., Inc., P.O. Box 28, Milford, NH 03055 (RWS; Geco)
Gevelot of Canada, Box 1593, Saskatoon, Sask., Canada
Hirtenberger Patronen-, Zündhütchen- & Metallwarenfabrik, A.G., Leobersdorfer Str. 33, A2552 Hirtenberg, Austria
Hy-Score Arms Co., 200 Tillary, Brooklyn, N.Y. 11201
Paul Jaeger Inc., 211 Leedom St., Jenkintown, Pa. 19046
S. E. Laszlo, 200 Tillary, Brooklyn, N.Y. 11201
NORMA-Precision, Lansing, NY 14882
Oregon Ammo Service, Box 19341, Portland, Ore. 97219
The Outrider, Inc., 3288 LaVenture Dr., Chamblee, GA 30341
RWS (Rheinische-Westfälische Sprengstoff) see: Eastern

AMMUNITION COMPONENTS—BULLETS, POWDER, PRIMERS

Alcan, (see: Smith & Wesson Ammunition Co.)
Ammo-O-Mart, P.O. Box 66, Hawkesbury, Ont., Canada (Curry bullets)
Austin Powder Co. (see Red Diamond Dist. Co.)
Bahler Die Shop, Rte. 1, Box 412 Hemlock, Florence, OR 97439 (17 cal. bull.)
Joe J. Balickie, 6108 Deerwood Pl., Raleigh, NC 27607
Ballistic Research Industries, see: S & W(12 ga. Sabot bullets)
B.E.L.L., Bell's Gun & Sport Shop, 3309-19 Mannheim Rd., Franklin Pk., IL 60131
Bitterroot Bullet Co., Box 412, Lewiston, Ida. 83501
The Bullet Boys, Box 367, Jaffrey, NH 03452 (cast bullets)
Centrix, 2116 N. 10th Ave., Tucson, Ariz. 85705
Kenneth E. Clark, 18738 Highway 99, Madera, CA 93637 (Bullets)
Colorado Custom Bullets, Rt. 1, Box 507-B, Montrose, Colo. 81401
Curry Bullets Canada, P.O. Box 66, Hawkesbury, Ont., Canada
Division Lead, 7742 W. 61 Pl., Summit, Ill. 60502
DuPont, Explosives Dept., Wilmington, Del. 19898
Eastern Sports Distributors Co., Inc., P.O. Box 28, Milford, NH 03055 (RWS percussion caps)
Elk Mountain Shooters Supply, 1719 Marie, Pasco, WA 99301 (Alaskan bullets)
Farmer Bros., see: Lage Uniwad
Federal Cartridge Co., 2700 Foshay Tower, Minneapolis, MN 55402 (nickel cases)
Forty Five Ranch Enterprises, 119 S. Main, Miami, Okla. 74354
Godfrey Reloading Supply, R.R. 1, Box 688, Brighton, Ill. 62012 (cast bullets)
Lynn Godfrey, see: Elk Mtn. Shooters Supply
Green Bay Bullets, 233 No. Ashland, Green Bay, Wis. 54303 (lead)
Gussert Bullet & Cartridge Co., 1868 Lenwood Ave., Green Bay, WI 54303
Hercules Powder Co., 910 Market St., Wilmington, Del. 19899
Herter's Inc., Waseca, Minn. 56093
Hodgdon Powder Co. Inc., 7710 W. 50th Hwy., Shawnee Mission, KS 66202
Hornady Mfg. Co., Box 1848, Grand Island, Neb. 68801
N. E. House Co., Middletown Rd., E. Hampton, Conn. 06424 (zinc bases only)
J-4, Inc., 1700 Via Burton, Anaheim, CA 92806 (custom bullets)
L. L. F. Die Shop, 1281 Highway 99 North, Eugene, Ore. 97402
Lage Uniwad Co., 1102 Washington St., Eldora, IA 50627
Ljutic Ind., Inc., Box 2117, Yakima, WA 98902 (Mono-wads)
Lomont Precision Bullets, 4421 S. Wayne Ave., Ft. Wayne, IN 46807
Lyman Gun Sight Products, Middlefield, Conn. 06455
Markell, Inc., 4115 Judah St., San Francisco, Calif. 94112
Meyer Bros. Mfgrs., Wabasha, Minn. 55981 (shotgun slugs)
Michael's Antiques, Box 233, Copiague, L.I., NY 11726 (Balle Blondeau)
Miller Trading Co., 20 S. Front St., Wilmington, N.C. 28401
Norma-Precision, Lansing, NY 14882
Northridge Bullet Co., P.O. Box 1208, Vista, Ca. 92083
Nosler Bullets, P.O. Box 688, Beaverton, OR 97005
Old West Gun Room, 3509 Carlson Rd., El Cerrito, CA 94530 (RWS)
Oregon Ammo Service, Box 19341, Portland, Ore. 97219
Robert Pomeroy, Morison Ave., East Corinth, ME 04427
Red Diamond Distributing Co., 1304 Snowdon Dr., Knoxville, TN 37912 (black powder)
Remington-Peters, Bridgeport, Conn. 06602
Sanderson's, 724 W. Edgewater, Portage, Wis. 53901 (cork wad)
Sierra Bullets Inc., 10532 Painter Ave., Santa Fe Springs, CA 90670
Sisk Bullet Co., Box 874, Iowa Park, TX 76367
Smith & Wesson Ammunition Co., 2399 Forman Rd., Rock Creek, OH 44084
Speedy Bullets, Box 1262, Lincoln, Neb. 68501
Speer Products Inc., Box 896, Lewiston, Ida. 83501
C. H. Stocking, Rte. 3, Box 195, Hutchinson, Minn. 55350 (17 cal. bullet jackets)
Taylor Bullets, P.O. Box 21254, San Antonio, Tex. 78221
Vitt & Boos, 11 Sugarloaf Dr., Wilton, CT 06897 (shotgun slugs)
Winchester-Western, New Haven, Conn. 06504
F. Wood, Box 386, Florence, Ore. 97439 (17 cal.)
Xelex Ltd., Hawksbury, Ont., Canada (powder, Curry bullets)
Zero Bullet Co., P.O. Box 1012, Cullman, AL 35055

ANTIQUE ARMS DEALERS

Robert Abels, P.O. Box 428, Hopewell Junction, NY 12533 (Catalog $1.00)
Ed Agramonte, Inc., 41 Riverdale Ave., Yonkers, NY 10701
F. Bannerman Sons, Inc., Box 126, L.I., Blue Point, NY 11715
Wm. Boggs, 1243 Grandview Ave., Columbus, Ohio 43212
Ed's Gun House, 1626 W. 9th St., Winona, MN 55987
Ellwood Epps (Orillia) Ltd., Hwy. 11 North, Orillia, Ont., Canada
Farris Muzzle Guns, 1610 Gallia St., Portsmouth, Ohio 45662
A. A. Fidd, Diamond Pt. Rd., Diamond Pt., N.Y. 12824
N. Flayderman & Co., Squash Hollow, New Milford, Conn. 06776
Fulmer's Antique Firearms, P.O. Box 792, Detroit Lakes, MN 56501
Herb Glass, Bullville, N.Y. 10915
Goergen's Gun Shop, 707 8th St. S.E., Box 499, Austin, MN 55912
Goodman's for Guns, 1101 Olive St., St. Louis, Mo. 63101
Griffin's Guns & Antiques, R.R. 4, Peterboro, Ont., Canada K9J 6X5
The Gun Shop, 6497 Pearl Rd., Cleveland, O. 44130
Hansen & Company, 244 Old Post Rd., Southport, CT 06490
Heritage Firearms Co., P.O. Box 69, Rte. 7, Wilton, CN 06897
Holbrook Arms Museum, 12953 Biscayne Blvd., N. Miami, Fla. 33161
Jackson Arms, 6209 Hillcrest Ave., Dallas, Tex. 75205
Jerry's Gun Shop, 9220 Ogden Ave., Brookfield, Ill. 60513
Kenfix Co., 3500 E. Hillsborough Ave., Tampa, FL 33610
Lever Arms Serv. Ltd., 771 Dunsmuir St., Vancouver, B.C., Canada V6C 1M9
John J. Malloy, Briar Ridge Rd., Danbury, CT 06810
Charles W. Moore, R.D. 2, Schenevus, N.Y. 12155
Museum of Historical Arms, 1038 Alton Rd., Miami Beach, Fla. 33139
National Gun Traders, Inc., 225 S.W. 22nd Ave., Miami, Fla. 33135
New Orleans Arms Co., Inc., P.O. Box 26087, New Orleans, LA 70186
Old West Gun Room, 3509 Carlson Blvd., El Cerrito, Cal. 94530 (write for list)
The Outrider, Inc., 3288 LaVenture Dr., Chamblee, GA 30341
Pioneer Guns, 5228 Montgomery, Cincinnati (Norwood), OH 45212
Powell & Clements Sporting Arms, 210 E. 6th St., Cincinnati, O. 45202
Martin B. Retting Inc., 11029 Washington, Culver City, Calif. 90230
Ridge Guncraft, Inc., 234 N. Tulane Ave., Oak Ridge, Tenn. 37830
S.G. Intl., P.O. Box 702, Hermosa Beach, CA. 90254
Safari Outfitters Ltd., 71 Ethan Allen Highway, Ridgefield, CT 06877
San Francisco Gun Exch., 124 Second St., San Francisco, Calif. 94105
Santa Ana Gunroom, P.O. Box 1777, Santa Ana, Calif. 92702
Ward & Van Valkenburg, 402-30th Ave. No., Fargo, N. Dak. 58102
M. C. Wiest, 234 N. Tulane Ave., Oak Ridge, Tenn. 37830
Yale's Gun Shop, 2618 Conowingo Rd., Bel Air, MD 21014
Lewis Yearout, 308 Riverview Dr. E., Great Falls, MT 59404
Yeck Antique Firearms, 579 Tecumseh, Dundee, Mich. 48131

BOOKS (ARMS), Publishers and Dealers

CB Press, Box 4087, Bartonville, IL 61607
DBI Books, Inc., 540 Frontage Rd., Northfield, IL 60093
Norm Flayderman, RFD 2, Squash Hollow, New Milford, CT 06776
Fortress Publications Inc., P.O. Box 241, Stoney Creek, Ont. L8G 3X9, Canada
Handgun Press, 5832 S. Green, Chicago, IL 60621
Normount Technical Publications, P.O. Drawer N-2, Wickenburg, AZ 85358
Personal Firearms Record Book, Box 201, Park Ridge, IL 60068
Ray Riling Arms Books Co., 6844 Gorsten St., Philadelphia, PA 19119
Rutgers Book Center, Mark Aziz, 127 Raritan Ave., Highland Park, NJ 08904
James C. Tillinghast, Box 568, Marlow, NH 03456

BULLET & CASE LUBRICANTS

Birchwood-Casey Co., Inc., 7900 Fuller Rd., Eden Prairie, Minn. 55343 (Anderol)
Chopie Mfg. Inc., 531 Copeland, La Crosse, Wis. 54601 (Black-Solve)
Cooper-Woodward, Box 972, Riverside, Cal. 92502 (Perfect Lube)
D. R. Corbin, P.O. Box 44, North Bend, OR 97459
Green Bay Bullets, 233 N. Ashland, Green Bay, Wis. 54303 (EZE-Size case lube)
Gussert Bullet & Cartridge Co., 1868 Lenwood Ave., Green Bay, WI 54303 (Super Lube)
Herter's, Inc., Waseca, Minn. 56903 (Perfect Lubricant)
IPCO (Industrial Products Co.), Box 14, Bedford, MA 01730
Javelina Products, Box 337, San Bernardino, Cal. 92402 (Alox beeswax)
Jet-Aer Corp., 100 Sixth Ave., Paterson, N.J. 07524
Lenz Prod. Co., Box 1226, Sta. C, Canton, O. 44708 (Clenzoil)
Lyman Gun Sight Products, Middlefield, Conn. 06455 (Size-Ezy)
Marmel Prods., P.O. Box 97, Utica, MI 48087 (Marvelube, Marvelux)
Micro Shooter's Supply, Box 213, Las Cruces, N. Mex. 88001 (Micro-Lube)
Mirror Lube, P.O. Box 693, San Juan Capistrano, CA 92675
Pacific Tool Co., P.O. Drawer 2048, Ordnance Plant Rd., Grand Island, NB 68801
Phelps Rel. Inc., Box 4004, E. Orange, N.J. 07019
RCBS, Inc., Box 1919, Oroville, Calif. 95965
SAECO Rel. Inc., P.O. Box 778, Carpinteria, CA 93103
Scientific Lubricants Co., 3753 Lawrence Ave., Chicago, Ill. 60625
Shooters Accessory Supply (SAS), see D. R. Corbin
Testing Systems, Inc., 2832 Mt. Carmel, Glenside, PA 19038

BULLET SWAGE DIES AND TOOLS

Bahler Die Shop, Box 386/412 Hemlock St., Florence, OR 97439
Belmont Products, Rte. #1, Friendsville, TN 37737
C-H Tool & Die Corp., P.O. Box L, Owen, WI 54460
Clymer Mfg. Co., 14241 W. 11 Mile Rd., Oak Park, MI 48237
Lester Coats, 416 Simpson St., North Bend, OR 97459 (lead wire cutter)
D. R. Corbin, P.O. Box 44, North Bend, OR 97459
Herter's Inc., Waseca, MN 56093
Hollywood, Whitney Sales Inc., P.O. Box 875, Reseda, CA 91335
Independent Machine & Gun Shop, 1416 N. Hayes, Pocatello, ID 83201 (TNT)
L.L.F. Die Shop, 1281 Highway 99 North, Eugene, OR 97402
Rorschach Precision Products, P.O. Box 1613, Irving, TX 75060
SAS Dies, see: D. R. Corbin
Robert B. Simonson, Rte. 2, 2129 Vanderbilt Rd., Kalamazoo, MI 49002
TNT (see Ind. Mach. & Gun Shop)

CARTRIDGES FOR COLLECTORS

J. A. Belton, 52 Sauve Rd., Mercier, Chateauguay Cty, Quebec, Canada
Peter Bigler, 291 Crestwood Dr., Milltown, N.J. 08850 (ctlg. $1.50)
Geo. Blakeslee, 3135 W. 28th St., Denver, CO 80211
Cameron's, 16690 W. 11th Ave., Golden, Colo. 80401
Carter Gun Works, 2211 Jefferson Pk. Ave., Charlottesville, Va. 22903
Collectors Shotshell Arsenal, 365 S. Moore St., Lakewood, CO 80226
Chas. E. Duffy, Williams Lane, West Hurley, N.Y. 12419
Tom M. Dunn, 1342 So. Poplar, Casper, Wyo. 82601
Ellwood Epps (Orillia) Ltd., Hwy. 11 North, Orillia, Ont., Canada
George Kass, 30 Ivy Circle, West Haven, CT 06516 (ctlg. $1; rimfire cartridges)
Oregon Ammo Service, Box 19341, Portland, Ore. 97219 (catlg. $2.00)
The Outrider, Inc., 3288 LaVenture Dr., Chamblee, GA 30341
Powder Horn, 3135 W. 28th, Denver, CO 80211
Martin B. Retting Inc., 11029 Washington, Culver City, Calif. 90230
San Francisco Gun Exchange, 124 Second St., San Francisco, CA 94105
Perry Spangler, 519 So. Lynch, Flint, Mich. 48503 (list 50¢)
Ernest Tichy, 365 S. Moore, Lakewood, Colo. 80226
James C. Tillinghast, Box 568, Marlow, N.H. 03456 (list 50¢)
Lewis Yearout, 308 Riverview Dr. E., Great Falls, MT 59404

CASES, CABINETS AND RACKS—GUN

Alco Carrying Cases, 601 W. 26th St., New York, N.Y. 10001
Artistic Wood Specialties, 923-29 W. Chicago Ave., Chicago, Ill. 60622
Morton Booth Co., Box 123, Joplin, Mo. 64801
Boyt Co., Div. of Welsh Sportg. Gds., Box 1108, Iowa Falls, Ia. 50126
Browning, Rt. 4, Box 624-B, Arnold, MO 63010
Cap-Lex Gun Cases, Capitol Plastics of Ohio, Inc., 333 Van Camp Rd., Bowling Green, OH 43402
Castle Westchester Prods. Co., Inc., 498 Nepperhan Ave., Yonkers, N.Y. 10701
Challanger Mfg. Co., 118 Pearl St., Mt. Vernon, NY 10550
E & C Enterprises, 9582 Bickley Dr., Huntington Beach, CA 92646 (gun socks)
East-Tenn Mills, Inc., Box 1030, Johnson City, TN 37601 (gun socks)
Ellwood Epps (Orillia) Ltd., Hwy. 11 North, Orillia, Ont., Canada
Flambeau Plastics Corp., 801 Lynn, Baraboo, Wis. 53913
Gun-Ho Case Mfg. Co., 110 East 10th St., St. Paul, Minn. 55101
Harbor House Gun Cabinets, 12508 Center St., South Gate, CA 90280
B. E. Hodgdon, Inc., 7710 W. 50 Hiway, Shawnee-Mission, Kans. 66202
Ithaca Gun Co., Terrace Hill, Ithaca, N.Y. 14850
J-K Imports, Box 403, Novato, Cal. 94947 (leg 'o mutton case)
Jumbo Sports Prods., P.O. Box 280-Airport Rd., Frederick, MD 21701
Kolpin Mfg., Inc., Box 231, Berlin, WI 54923
Marble Arms Corp., 420 Industrial Park, Gladstone, Mich. 49837
Bill McGuire, Inc., 10324 Valmay Ave., NW, Seattle, WA 98177 (custom cases)
W. A. Miller Co., Inc. (Wamco), Mingo Loop, Oguossoc, ME 04964 (wooden handgun cases)
National Sports Div., 19 E. McWilliams St., Fond du Lac, Wis. 54935
Nortex Co., 2821 Main St., Dallas, Tex. 75226 (automobile gun rack)
North Star Devices, Inc., P.O. Box 2095, North St., Paul, MN 55109 (Gun-Slinger portable rack)
Paul-Reed, Inc., P.O. Box 227, Charlevoix, Mich. 49720
Penguin Industries, Inc., Box 97, Parkesburg, Pa. 19365
Pistolsafe, Dr. L., N. Chili, NY 14514 (handgun safe)
Precise Imp. Corp., 3 Chestnut, Suffern, N.Y. 10901
Protecto Plastics, Inc., 201 Alpha Rd., Wind Gap, Pa. 18091 (carrying cases)
Richland Arms Co., 321 W. Adrian, Blissfield, Mich. 49228
San Angelo Die Castings, Box 984, San Angelo, Tex. 76901
Buddy Schoellkopf, 4100 Platinum Way, Dallas, Tex. 75237
Security Gun Chest, Div. of Tread Corp., P.O. Box 5497, Roanoke, VA 24012
Sile Distr., 7 Centre Market Pl., New York, N.Y. 10013 (leg o'mutton case)
Stearn Mfg. Co., Div. & 30th St., St. Cloud, Minn. 56301
Sundance Prods., 255 W. 200 S., Salt Lake City, UT 84101
Tread Corp., P.O. Box 5497, Roanoke, VA 24012 (security gun chest)
Woodstream Corp., Box 327, Lititz, Pa. 17543
Yield House, Inc., RFD, No. Conway, N.H. 03860

CHOKE DEVICES & RECOIL ABSORBERS

Arms Ingenuity Co., Box 1, Weatogue, Conn. 06089 (Jet-Away)
Contra-Jet, 7920 49th Ave. So., Seattle, Wash. 98118
Dahl's Gun Shop, 6947 King Ave., Route 4, Billings, MT 59102
Diverter Arms, Inc., 6520 Rampart St., Houston, TX 77036 (shotgun diverter)
Edwards Recoil Reducer, 269 Herbert St., Alton, Ill. 62002
Emsco Chokes, 101 Second Ave., S.E., Waseca, Minn. 56093
Herter's Inc., Waseca, Minn. 56093. (Vari-Choke)
Lyman Gun Sight Products, Middlefield, Conn. 60455 (Cutts Comp.)
Mag-Na-Port Arms, Inc., 30016 S. River Rd., Mt. Clemens, MI 48043 (muzzle-brake system)
Pendleton Dekickers, 1210 S. W. Hailey Ave., Pendleton, Ore. 97801
Poly-Choke Co., Inc., Box 296, Hartford, Conn. 06101

CHRONOGRAPHS AND PRESSURE TOOLS

B-Square Co., Box 11281, Ft. Worth, Tex. 76110
Chronograph Specialists, P.O. Box 5005, Santa Ana, Calif. 92704
Delta Technology, Inc., Lewisburg, TN 37091
Display Electronics, Box 1044, Littleton, CO 80120
Diverter Arms, Inc., 6520 Rampart St., Houston, TX 77036 (press. tool)
Herter's, Waseca, Minn. 56093
Micro-Sight Co., 242 Harbor Blvd., Belmont, Calif. 94002 (Techsonic)
Oehler Research, P.O. Box 9135, Austin, Tex. 78756
Scharon Fabricators, 2145 East Dr., St. Louis, MO 63131
Schmidt-Weston Co., Box 9, West Islip, NY 11795
Sundtek Co., P.O. Box 744, Springfield, Ore. 97477
Telepacific Electronics Co., Inc., P.O. Box 2210, Escondido, CA 92025
M. York, 19381 Keymar Way, Gaithersburg, MD 20760 (press. tool)

CLEANING & REFINISHING SUPPLIES

ADSCO, Box 191, Ft. Kent, Me. 04743 (stock finish)
A 'n A Co., Box 571, King of Prussia, PA 19406 (Valet shotgun cleaner)
Allied Products Co., 734 N. Leavitt, Chicago, Ill. 60612 (Cor-O-Dex)
Armite Labs., 1845 Randolph St., Los Angeles, CA 90001 (pen oiler)
Armoloy, 206 E. Daggett St., Ft. Worth, TX 76104
Ber Big Enterprises, P.O. Box 291, Huntington, CA 90255 (gunsoap)
Birchwood-Casey Chem. Co., 7900 Fuller Rd., Eden Prairie, Minn. 55343 (Anderol, etc.)
Bisonite Co., Inc., P.O. Box 84, Kenmore Station, Buffalo, NY 14217
Blue and Gray Prods., Inc., 817 E. Main St., Bradford, PA 16701
Jim Brobst, 299 Poplar St., Hamburg, Pa. 19526 (J-B Compound)
GB Prods. Dept., H & R, Inc., Industrial Rowe, Gardner, MA 01440
Browning Arms, Rt. 4, Box 624-B, Arnold, Mo. 63010
J. M. Bucheimer Co., Airport Rd., Frederick, MD 21701
Burnishine Prod. Co., 8140 N. Ridgeway, Skokie, Ill. 60076 (Stock Glaze)

Caddie Products Corp., Div. of Jet-Aer, Paterson, NJ 07524 (the Cloth)
Cherry Corners Mfg. Co., 11136 Congress Rd., Lodi, Ohio 44254 (buffing compound)
Chopie Mfg. Inc., 531 Copeland, La Crosse, Wis. 54601 (Black-Solve)
Clenzoil Co., Box 1226, Sta. C, Canton, O. 44708
Clover Mfg. Co., 139 Woodward Ave., Norwalk, CT 06856 (Clover compound)
Craftsman Wood Serv. Co., 2729 S. Mary, Chicago, Ill. 60608 (ctlg. 50¢)
Dri-Slide, Inc., Industrial Park, Fremont, Mich. 49412
Forty-Five Ranch Enterpr., 119 S. Main St., Miami, Okla. 74354
Garcia Sptg. Arms Corp., 329 Alfred Ave., Teaneck, N.J. 07666
Gun-All Products, Box 244, Dowagiac, Mich. 49047
Frank C. Hoppe Div., P.O. Box 97, Parkesburg, Pa. 19365
J & G Rifle Ranch, Box S 80, Turner, MT 59542
Jet-Aer Corp., 100 Sixth Ave., Paterson, N.J. 07524 (blues & oils)
Kellog's Professional Prods., Inc., Sandusky, OH 44870
K.W. Kleinendorst, 48 Taylortown Rd., Montville, N.J. 07045 (rifle clg. cables)
LPS Res. Labs. Inc., 2050 Cotner Ave., Los Angeles, Calif. 90025
LEM Gun Spec., Box 31, College Park, Ga 30337 (Lewis Lead Remover)
Liquid Wrench, Box 10628, Charlotte, N.C. 28201 (pen. oil)
Lynx Line Gun Prods. Div., Protective Coatings, Inc., 20626 Fenkell Ave., Detroit, MI 48223
Marble Arms Co., 420 Industrial Pk., Gladstone, Mich. 49837
Micro Sight Co., 242 Harbor Blvd., Belmont, Ca. 94002 (bedding)
Mill Run Prod., 1360 W. 9th, Cleveland, O. 44113 (Brite-Bore Kits)
Mirror-Lube, P.O. Box 693, San Juan Capistrano, CA 92675
Mistic Metal Mover, Inc., R.R. 2, P.O. Box 336, Princeton, Ill. 61356
Mitchell Chemical Co., Wampus Lane, Milford, CT 06460 (Gun Guard)
New Method Mfg. Co., Box 175, Bradford, Pa. 16701 (gun blue)
Northern Instruments, Inc., 4643 No. Chatsworth St., St. Paul, MN 55112 (Stor-Safe rust preventer)
Numrich Arms Co., West Hurley, N.Y. 12491 (44-40 gun blue)
Ordnance Parkerizing, 1511 Waverly Ave., Florence, SC 29501
Outers Laboratories, Box 37, Onalaska, Wis. 54650 (Gunslick kits)
Radiator Spec. Co., 1400 Independence Blvd., Charlotte, N.C. 28201 (liquid wrench)
Realist Inc., N. 93 W. 16288 Megal Dr., Menomonee Falls, Wis. 53051
Reardon Prod., 103 W. Market St., Morrison, IL 61270 (Dry-Lube)
Rice Gun Coatings, 1521-43rd St., West Palm Beach, FL 33407
Riel & Fuller, 423 Woodrow Ave., Dunkirk, N.Y. 14048 (anti-rust oil)
Rig Products Co., Box 279, Oregon, Ill. 61061 (Rig Grease)
Rocket Chemical Co., Inc., 5390 Napa St., San Diego, Calif. 92110 (WD-40)
Rusteprufe Labs., 605 Wolcott St., Sparta, Wis. 54656
Saunders Sptg. Gds., 338 Somerset, No. Plainfield, NJ 07060 (Sav-Bore)
Schultea's Gun String, 67 Burress, Houston, TX 77022 (pocket-size rifle cleaning kit)
Service Armament, 689 Bergen Blvd., Ridgefield, N. J. 07657 (Parker-Hale)
Silicote Corp., Box 359, Oshkosh, Wis. 54901 (Silicone cloths)
Silver Dollar Guns, P.O. Box 489, Franklin, NH 03235 (Silicone oil)
A. D. Soucy, Box 191, Ft. Kent, Me. 04743 (ADSCO stock finish)
Southeastern Coatings, Ind., (SECOA), Bldg. 132, P.B.I. Airport, W. Palm Beach, Fla. 33406 (Teflon Coatings)
Sportsmen's Labs., Inc., Box 732, Anoka, Minn. 55303 (Gun Life lube)
Surcon, Inc., P.O. Box 277, Zieglerville, Pa. 19492
Taylor & Robbins, Box 164, Rixford, Pa. 16745 (Throat Saver)
Testing Systems, Inc., 2832 Mt. Carmel, Glenside, PA 19038 (gun lube)
Texas Platers Supply Co., 2453 W. Five Mile Parkway, Dallas, TX 75233 (plating kit)
C. S. Van Gorden, 120 Tenth Ave., Eau Claire, Wis. 54701 (Instant Blue)
WD-40 Co., 1061 Cudahy Pl., San Diego, CA 92110
West Coast Secoa, Inc., Rt. 5, Box 138, Lakeland, FL 33801 (Teflon coatings)
Williams Gun Sight, 7389 Lapeer Rd., Davison, Mich. 48423 (finish kit)
Winslow Arms Co., P.O. Box 578, Osprey, Fla. 33595 (refinishing kit)
Wisconsin Platers Supply Co., see: Texas Platers Supply Co.
Woodstream Corp., P.O. Box 327, Lititz, Pa. 17543 (Mask)

CUSTOM GUNSMITHS

Abe and Van Horn, 5124 Huntington Dr., Los Angeles, CA 90032
P. O. Ackley, 2235 Arbor Lane, Salt Lake City, UT 84117
Ed Agramonte, Inc., 41 Riverdale Ave., Yonkers, NY 10701
Ahlman Cust. Gun Shop, R.R. 1, Box 20, Morristown, Minn. 55052
Anderson's Guns, Jim Jares, 706 S. 23rd St., Laramie, WY 82070
Dale P. Andrews, 3572 E. Davies, Littleton, CO 80122
Antique Arms, D. F. Saunders, 1110 Cleveland Ave., Monett, MO 65708 (Hawken copies)
R. J. Anton, 874 Olympic Dr., Waterloo, IA 50701
Atkinson Gun Co., P.O. Box 512, Prescott, AZ 86301
Bacon Creek Gun Shop, Cumberland Falls Rd., Corbin, Ky. 40701
Bain and Davis Sptg. Gds., 599 W. Las Tunas Dr., San Gabriel, Calif. 41776
Joe J. Balickie, 6108 Deerwood Pl., Raleigh, N.C. 27607
Wm. G. Bankard, 4211 Thorncliff Rd., Baltimore, MD 21236 (Kentuckys)
Barta's, Rte. 1, Box 129-A, Cato, Wis. 54206
Bayer's Gun Shop, 213 S. 2nd, Walla Walla, Wash. 99362
Bennett Gun Works, 561 Delaware Ave., Delmar, N.Y. 12054
Irvin L. Benson, Saganaga Lake, Pine Island Camp, Ontario, Canada
Fred M. Bergen, 6 Longview Rd., High Crest Lake, Butler, NJ 07405
Gordon Bess, 708 River St., Canon City, Colo. 81212
Bruce Betts Gunsmith Co., 100 W. Highway 72, Rolla, MO 65401
John Bivins, Jr., 200 Wicklow Rd., Winston-Salem, NC 27106
Edwin T. Blackburn, Jr., 474 E. McKinley, Sunnyvale, CA 94086 (precision metal work)
Ralph Bone, 806 Ave. J, Lubbock, TX 79401
Boone Mountain Trading Post, Averyville Rd., St. Marys, Pa. 15857
T. H. Boughton, 410 Stone Rd., Rochester, N.Y. 14616
Kay H. Bowles, Pinedale, Wyo. 82941
Breckheimers, Rte. 69-A, Parish, NY 13131
L. H. Brown, Rte. 2, Airport Rd., Kalispell, Mont. 59901
Lenard M. Brownell, Box 25, Wyarno, WY 82845
David Budin, Margaretville, NY 12455
George Bunch, 7735 Garrison Rd., Hyattsville, Md. 20784
Samuel W. Burgess, 25 Squam Rd., Rockport, MA 01966 (bluing repairs)
Tom Burgess, 180 McMannamy Draw, Kalispell, MT 59901 (metalsmithing only)
Leo Bustani, P.O. Box 8125, W. Palm Beach, Fla. 33407
Gus Butterowe, 10121 Shoreview Rd., Dallas, TX 75238
Cameron's Guns, 16690 W. 11th Ave., Golden, Colo. 80401
Carpenter's Gun Works, Gunshop Rd., Plattekill, N.Y. 12568
Carter Gun Works, 2211 Jefferson Pk. Ave., Charlottesville, VA 22903
Cassell Gun Shop, 403 West Lane, Worland, Wyo. 82401
Ray Chalmers, 18 White Clay Dr., Newark, Del. 19711
N. C. Christakos, 2832 N. Austin, Chicago, IL 60634
Gene Clark, P.O. Box 26087, New Orleans, LA 70186
Jim Clark, Custom Gun Shop, 5367 S. 1950 West, Roy, UT 84067
Kenneth E. Clark, 18738 Highway 99, Madera, Calif. 93637
Cloward's Gun Shop, J. K. Cloward, 4023 Aurora Ave. N., Seattle, WA 98102
Crest Carving Co., 14849 Dillow St., Westminster, Ca. 92683
Philip R. Crouthamel, 513 E. Baltimore, E. Lansdowne, PA 19050
Custom Rifle Shop, 4550 E. Colfax Ave., Denver, Colo. 80220
Jim Cuthbert, 715 S. 5th St., Coos Bay, Ore. 97420
Dahl's Gunshop, 6947 King Ave., Billings, MT 59102
Davis Gun Shop, 7213 Lee Highway, Falls Church, VA 22046
Dee Davis, 5658 So. Mayfield, Chicago, Ill. 60638
Jack Dever, 8520 N.W. 90, Okla. City, OK 73132 (S. S. Work)
Dominic DiStefano, 4303 Friar Lane, Colorado Springs, CO 80907
Drumbore Gun Shop, 119 Center St., Lehigton, PA 18235
Charles Duffy, Williams Lane, W. Hurley, N.Y. 12491
Gerald D. Eisenhauer, Rte. #3, Twin Falls, Ida. 83301
Bill English, 4411 S. W. 100th, Seattle, Wash. 98146
Ken Eyster, Heritage Gunsmiths Inc., 6441 Bishop Rd., Centerburg, O. 43011
N. B. Fashingbauer, Box 366, Lac Du Flambeau, Wis. 54538
Ted Fellowes, Beaver Lodge, 9245-16th Ave., S.W., Seattle, Wa. 98106 (muzzle loaders)
The Fergusons, R.F.D. #1, Box 143, Hillsboro, NH 03244
H. J. and L. A. Finn, 12565 Gratiot Ave., Detroit, MI 48205
Loxley Firth Firearms, 8563 Oswego Rd., R. D. 4, Baldwinsville, N.Y. 13027
Marshall F. Fish, Westport, N.Y. 12993
Jerry Fisher, 1244—4th Ave. West, Kalispell, Mont. 59901
Flagler Gun Clinic, Box 8125, West Palm Beach, Fla. 33407 (Win. 92 & 94 Conv.)
Flynn's Cust. Gunsmithing, 3309 Elliott, Apt. B, Alexandria, LA 71301
Frazier's Custom Guns, Box 3, Tyler, WA 99035
Clark K. Frazier/Matchmate, RFD 1, Rawson, OH 45881
Freeland's Scope Stands, 3737—14th Ave., Rock Island, Ill. 61201
Fred's Gun Shop, Box 725, Juneau, Alaska 99801
Frederick Gun Shop, 10 Elson Drive, Riverside, R.I. 02915
Frontier Arms, Inc., 420 E. Riding Club Rd., Cheyenne, Wyo. 82001
Fuller Gunshop, Cooper Landing, Alas. 99572
Geo. M. Fullmer, 2499 Mavis St., Oakland, Cal. 94501 (metal work, precision chambering only)
Georgia Gun & Smith, 5170 Thistle Rd., Smyrna, GA 30080
Ed Gillman, 116 Upper High Crest Rd., Butler, NJ 07405
Dale Goens, Box 224, Cedar Crest, NM 87008
A. R. Goode, R.D. 1, Box 84, Thurmont, MD 21788
G. T. Gregory, P.O. Box 162, Plymouth, CA 95669 (saddle rifles)
Griffin & Howe, 589-8th Ave., New York, N.Y. 10017
H. L. Grisel, Rte. 1, Box 925, Bend, OR 97701 (rifles)
Dale M. Guise, Rt. 2, Box 239, Gardners, Pa. 17324 (Rem. left-hand conversions)
The Gunshop, Inc., Jack First, 44633 Sierra Highway, Lancaster, CA 93534
H & R Custom Gun Serv., 68 Passaic Dr., Hewitt, N.J. 07421
Paul Haberly, 2364 N. Neva, Chicago, IL 60635
Chas. E. Hammans, Box 788, Stuttgart, AR 72160
Harkrader's Cust. Gun Shop, 111 No. Franklin St., Christiansburg, Va. 24073
Rob't W. Hart & Son, 401 Montgomery St., Nescopeck, Pa. 18635 (actions, stocks)
Hal Hartley, 147 Blairs Fork Rd., Lenoir, NC 28654
Hubert J. Hecht, 55 Rose Mead Circle, Sacramento, CA 95831
Edw. O. Hefti, 300 Fairview, College Sta., Tex. 77840
Iver Henriksen, 1211 So. 2nd, Missoula, Mont. 59801
Wm. Hobaugh, Box 657, Philipsburg, Mont. 59858
Richard Hodgson, 9081 Tahoe Lane, Boulder, Colo. 80301
Hoenig-Rodman, 853 So. Curtis Rd., Boise, ID 83705
Hollis Gun Shop, 917 Rex St., Carlsbad, N.M. 88220
Hurt's Specialty Gunsmithing, Box 1033, Muskogee, Okla. 74401
Hyper-Single Precision SS Rifles, 520 E. Beaver, Jenks, OK 74037
Independent Machine & Gun Shop, 1416 N. Hayes, Pocatello, Ida. 83201
Jackson's, Box 416, Selman City, TX 75689
Paul Jaeger, 211 Leedom, Jenkintown, Pa. 19046
J. J. Jenkins, 462 Stanford Pl., Santa Barbara, CA 93105
Jerry's Gun Shop, 9220 Ogden Ave., Brookfield, Ill. 60513
Johnson's Gun Shop, 1316 N. Blackstone, Fresno, Calif. 93703

John Kaufield Small Arms Eng. Co., P.O. Box 306, Des Plaines, IL 60018 (restorations)
Kennedy Gun Shop, Rt. 6, Clarksville, Tenn. 37040
Monte Kennedy, P.O. Box 214, Kalispell, MT 59901
Kennon's Custom Rifles, 5408 Biffle, Stone Mtn., Ga. 30083
Kerr Sport Shop, Inc., 9584 Wilshire Blvd., Beverly Hills, Calif. 90212
Kess Arms Co., 12515 W. Lisbon Rd., Brookfield, Wis. 53005
Kesselring Gun Shop, 400 Pacific Hiway 99 No., Burlington, Wash. 98233
Vern Kitzrow, 2504 N. Grant Blvd., Milwaukee, WI 53210 (single shots)
K. W. Kleinendorst, 48 Taylortown Rd., Montville, NJ 07045
Knights Gun Store, Inc., 103 So. Jennings, Ft. Worth, Tex. 76104
Ward Koozer, Box 18, Walterville, Ore. 97489
Lacy's Gun Service, 1518A West Blvd., Charlotte, N.C. 28208
Sam Lair, 520 E. Beaver, Jenks, OK 74037
R. H. Lampert, Rt. 1, Box 61, Guthrie, MN 56451 (metalsmithing only)
LanDav Custom Guns, 7213 Lee Highway, Falls Church, VA 22046
Harry Lawson Co., 3328 N. Richey Blvd., Tucson, Ariz. 85716
John G. Lawson, 1802 E. Columbia, Tacoma, Wa. 98404
Gene Lechner, 636 Jane N.E., Albuquerque, NM 87123
LeDel, Inc., Main and Commerce Sts., Cheswold, Del. 19936
Art LeFeuvre, 1003 Hazel Ave., Deerfield, Ill. 60015
LeFever Arms Co., R.D. 1, Lee Center, N.Y. 13363
Max J. Lindauer, R.R. 1, Box 114, Washington, Mo. 63090
Robt. L. Lindsay, 9416 Emory Grove Rd., Gaithersburg, Md. 20760 (services only)
Ljutic Ind., Box 2117, Yakima, WA 98902 (Mono-Wads)
Llanerch Gun Shop, 2800 Township Line, Upper Darby, Pa. 19083
Ned McCandless, Box 126, Meriden Rte., Cheyenne, WY 82001
McCormick's Gun Bluing Service, 4936 E. Rosecrans Ave., Compton, Calif. 90221
Bill McGuire, Inc., 10324 Valmay Ave., Seattle, WA 98177
Pat B. McMillan, 1828 E. Campo Bello Dr., Phoenix, Ariz. 85022
R. J. Maberry, 511 So. K, Midland, Tex. 79701
Harold E. MacFarland, Star Route, Box 84, Cottonwood, Ariz. 86326
Marquart Precision Co., Box 1740, Prescott, AZ 86301
Martel's Custom Guns, 4038 S. Wisteria Way, Denver, CO 80237
E. H. Martin's Gun Shop, 937 S. Sheridan Blvd., Denver, CO 80226
Maryland Gun Exchange, RD 5, Rt. 40 W., Frederick, MD 21701
Mashburn Arms Co., 1020 N.W. 6th St., Oklahoma City, OK 73102
Seely Masker, 261 Washington Ave., Pleasantville, NY 10570
Mathews & Son, 10224 S. Paramount Blvd., Downey, Calif. 90241
Maurer Arms, 2366 Frederick Dr., Cuyahoga Falls, Ohio 44221 (muzzleloaders)
Maxson's Gun Shop, 122 E. Franklin, Box 145, Clinton, MO 64735
Middaugh's Nodak, 318 2nd St., Bismarck, N.D. 58501
Miller Gun Works, P.O. Box 7326, Tamuning, Guam 96911
C.D. Miller Guns, St. Onge, SD 57779
Earl Milliron, 1249 N.E. 166th Ave., Portland, Ore. 97230
Mills (D.H.) Custom Stocks, 401 N. Ellsworth, San Mateo, Calif. 94401
Mitchell's Gun Repair, Rt. 1, Perryville, Ark. 72126
Thurman Nation, Rte. 1, Box 236, Hiway 60 & 84, Clovis, NM 88101
Natl. Gun Traders, Inc., 225 S.W. 22nd Ave., Miami, Fla. 33135
Clayton N. Nelson, R.R. #3, Box 119, Enid, OK 73701
Newman Gunshop, 119 Miller Rd., Agency, Ia. 52530
Nu-Line Guns, Inc., 3727 Jennings Rd., St. Louis, Mo. 63121
Oak Lawn Gun Shop, Inc., 9618 Southwest Hwy., Oak Lawn, Ill. 60453
O'Brien Rifle Co., 324 Tropicana No. 128, Las Vegas, Nev. 89109
The Outrider, Inc., 3288 LaVenture Dr., Chamblee, GA 30341
Pachmayr Gun Works, 1220 S. Grand Ave., Los Angeles, Calif. 90015
Charles J. Parkinson, 116 Wharncliffe Rd. So., London, Ont., Canada N6J2K3
Pendleton Gunshop, 1210 S. W. Haley Ave., Pendleton, Ore. 97801
C. R. Pedersen & Son, Ludington, Mich. 49431
Al Petersen, Box 8, Riverhurst, Sask., Canada S0H3P0
A. W. Peterson Gun Shop, 1693 Old Hwy. 441 No., Mt. Dora, FL 32757 (ML rifles, also)
Ready Eddie's Gun Shop, 501 Van Spanje Ave., Michigan City, IN 46360
Marion Reed Gun Shop, 1522 Colorado, Bartlesville, Okla. 74003
R. Neal Rice, Box 12172, Denver, CO 80212
Ridge Guncraft, Inc., 234 N. Tulane, Oak Ridge, Tenn. 37830
Riedl Rifles, 15124 Weststate St., Westminster, CA 92683
Rifle Shop, Box 657, Philipsburg, Mont. 59858
Riflemen's Hdqs., Rte. 3, RD 550-E, Kendallville, IN 46755
W. Rodman, 6521 Morton Dr., Boise, ID 83705
Carl Roth, P.O. Box 2593, Cheyenne, WY 82001
Royal Arms, Inc., 10064 Bert Acosta, Santee, Calif. 92071
Murray F. Ruffino, Rt. 2, Milford, ME 04461
Rush's Old Colonial Forge, 106 Wiltshire Rd., Baltimore, MD 21221 (Ky.-Pa. rifles)
Sanders Custom Gun Serv., 2358 Tyler Lane, Louisville, Ky. 40205
Sandy's Custom Gunshop, Rockport, Ill. 62370
Saratoga Arms Co., R.D. 3, Box 387, Pottstown, Pa. 19464
Roy V. Schaefer, 965 W. Hilliard Lane, Eugene, Ore. 97402
N.H. Schiffman Cust. Gun Serv., 963 Malibu, Pocatello, ID 83201
Schuetzen Gun Works, 1226 Prairie Rd., Colorado Springs, Colo. 80909
Schumaker's Gun Shop, 208 W. 5th Ave., Colville, Wash 99114
Schwab Gun Shop, 1103 E. Bigelow, Findlay, O. 45840
Schwartz Custom Guns, 9621 Coleman Rd., Haslett, Mich. 48840
Schwarz's Gun Shop, 41-15th St., Wellsburg, W. Va. 26070
Jim Scott, Hiway 2-East, Leon, IA 50144
Scotty's Gun Shop, 534 E. Hwy. 190, Harker Heights, TX 76541 (ML)
Joseph M. Sellner, 1010 Stelton Rd., Piscataway, N.J. 08854
Shaw's, Rt. 4, Box 407-L, Escondido, CA 92025
Shell Shack, 113 E. Main, Laurel, MT 59044
George H. Sheldon, P.O. Box 489, Franklin, NH 03235 (45 autos & M-1 carbines only)
Shilen Rifles, Inc., 205 Metropark Blvd., Ennis, TX 75119
Harold H. Shockley, Box 355, Hanna City, Ill. 65126 (hot bluing & plating)
Walter Shultz, R.D. 3, Pottstown, Pa. 19464
The Sight Shop, 1802 E. Columbia Ave., Tacoma, Wa. 98404
Silver Dollar Guns, P.O. Box 489, Franklin, NH 03235 (45 autos & M-1 carbines only)
Simmons Gun Spec., 700 Rogers Rd., Olathe, Kans. 66061
Simms Hardward Co., 2801 J St., Sacramento, Calif. 95816
Skinner's Gun Shop, Box 30, Juneau, Alaska 98801
Markus Skosples, c/o Ziffren Sptg. Gds., 124 E. Third St., Davenport, IA 52801
Jerome F. Slezak, 1290 Marlowe, Lakewood (Cleveland), OH 44107
Small Arms Eng., P.O. Box 306, Des Plaines, IL 60018 (restorations)
John Smith, 912 Lincoln, Carpentersville, Ill. 60110
Smitty's Gunshop, 308 S. Washington, Lake City, Minn. 55041
Snapp's Gunshop, 6911 E. Washington Rd., Clare, Mich. 48617
R. Southgate, Rt. 2, Franklin, Tenn. 37064 (new Kentucky rifles)
Sport Service Center, 2364 N. Neva, Chicago, IL 60635
Sportsman's Den, 1010 Stelton Rd., Piscataway, N.J. 08854
Sportsmens Equip. Co., 915 W. Washington, San Diego, Calif. 92103
Sportsmen's Exchange & Western Gun Traders, Inc., P.O. Box 603, Oxnard, CA 93030
Jess L. Stark, 12051 Stroud, Houston, TX 77072
Keith Stegall, Box 696, Gunnison, Colo. 81230
Victor W. Strawbridge, 6 Pineview Dr., Dover Point, Dover, NH 03820
W. C. Strutz, Rte. 1, Eagle River, WI 54521
Suter's House of Guns, 332 N. Tejon, Colorado Springs, Colo. 80902
Swanson Custom Firearms, 1051 Broadway, Denver, Colo. 80203
A. D. Swenson's 45 Shop, P.O. Box 606, Fallbrook, CA 92028
T-P Shop, 212 E. Houghton, West Branch, Mich. 48661
Talmage Ent., 43197 E. Whittier, Hemet, CA 92343
Taylor & Robbins, Box 164, Rixford, Pa. 16745
Daniel Titus, 119 Morlyn Ave., Bryn Mawr, PA 19010
Tom's Gunshop, 600 Albert Pike, Hot Springs, Ark. 71901
Dave Trevallion, 3442 S. Post Rd., Indianapolis, IN 46239
Trinko's Gun Serv., 1406 E. Main, Watertown, Wis. 53094
Herb. G. Troester's Accurizing Serv., Cayuga, ND 58013
Doc Ulrich, 2511 S. 57th Ave., Cicero, IL 60650
Brent Umberger, Sportsman's Haven, R.R. 4, Cambridge, OH 43725
Upper Missouri Trading Co., Inc., Box 181, Crofton, MO 68730
Roy Vail, R. 1, Box 8, Warwick, N.Y. 10990
VanHorn-Abe, 5124 Huntington Dr., Los Angeles, CA 90032
J. W. Van Patten, Box 145, Foster Hill, Milford, Pa. 18337
Herman Waldron, Box 475, Pomeroy, WA 99347 (metalsmithing)
Walker Arms Co., R. 2, Box 73, Selma, AL 36701
Harold Waller, 1288 Camillo Way, El Cajon, CA 92021
R. A. Wardrop, Box 245, Mechanicsburg, Pa. 17055
Weatherby's, 2781 Firestone Blvd., South Gate, Calif. 90280
Wells Sport Store, 110 N. Summit St., Prescott, Ariz. 86301
R. A. Wells, 3452 N. 1st, Racine, Wis. 53402
Robert G. West, Rte. 1, Box 941, Eugene, OR 97402 (L.H. conversions)
Western Gunstocks Mfg. Co., 550 Valencia School Rd., Aptos, CA 95003
Duane Wiebe, 426 Creekside Dr., Pleasant Hill, CA 94563
M. C. Wiest, 234 N. Tulane Ave., Oak Ridge, Tenn. 37830
W. C. Wilber, 400 Lucerne Dr., Spartanburg, SC 29302
Williams Gun Sight Co., 7389 Lapeer Rd., Davison, Mich. 48423
Williams Gunsmithing, 1706 E. Rosslynn, Fullerton, CA 92631
Bob Williams, c/o Hermans-Atlas Custom Guns, 800 E St. N.W., Washington, DC 20004
Williamson-Pate Gunsmith Service, 6021 Camp Bowie Blvd., Ft. Worth, TX 76116
Wilson Gun Store Inc., R.D. 1, Rte. 225, Dauphin, Pa. 17018
Robert M. Winter, Box 484, Menno, SD 57045
Lester Womack, Box 17210, Tucson, AZ 85710
Yale's Gun Shop, 2618 Conowingo Rd., Bel Air, MD 21014 (ML work)
York County Gun Works, RR 4, Tottenham, Ont., Canada (muzzleloaders)
G. A. Yorks, Rte. 3, Box 135, Newaygo, MI 49337
Russ Zeeryp, 1601 Foard Dr., Lynn Ross Manor, Morristown, TN 37814
R. E. Zellmer, W180 N8996 Leona Ln., Menomonee Falls, WI 53051

DECOYS

Carry-Lite, Inc., 3000 W. Clarke, Milwaukee, WI 53245
Deeks, Inc., P.O. Box 2309, Salt Lake City, UT 84114
G & H Decoy Mfg. Co., P.O. Box 937, Henryetta, OK 74437
Tex Wirtz Ent., Inc., 1925 Hubbard St., Chicago, IL 60622
Woodstream Corp., P.O. Box 327, Lititz, PA 17543

ENGRAVERS, ENGRAVING, TOOLS

Alpen Engraving Service, 39 Horseshoe Rd., Gilford, CT 06437
Austrian Gunworks Reg'd., P.O. Box 136, Eastman, Que., Canada, J0E 1P0
E. Averill, 60 Chestnut St., Cooperstown, NY 13326
Joseph Bayer, Sunset Ave., Sunset Hill, RD 1, Princeton, N.J. 08540
Sid Bell Originals, R.D. 2, Tully, NY 13159
Weldon Bledsoe, 6812 Park Place Dr., Fort Worth, Tex. 76118
Henry D. Bonham, Box 656 (Main St.), Brownville, Me. 04414
Burgess Vibrocrafters (BVI), Rt. 83, Grayslake, Ill. 60030
Winston Churchill, 55 High St., Ludlow, VT 05149
Joe Condon, 2983 E. Fremont, Las Vegas, NV 89104
Carl E. Courts, 2421 E. Anaheim St., Long Beach, Cal. 90804
James R. DeMunck, 3012 English Rd., Rochester, NY 14616
Bill Dyer, P.O. Box 75255, Oklahoma City, Okla. 73107

Ken Eyster, Heritage Gunsmiths Inc., 6441 Bishop Rd., Centerburg, O. 43011
John Fanzoi, P.O. Box 25, Ferlach, Austria 9170
Ken Flood, 63 Homestead, Stratford, Conn. 06497
H. H. Frank, Route #1, Mountain Meadows, Whitefish, MT 59937
Ed F. Giles, 3 Arnold St., Attleboro, MA 02703
Donald Glaser, 1520 West St., Emporia, Kans. 66801
Howard V. Grant, P.O. Box 396, Lac Du Flambeau, WI 54538
Griffin & Howe, 589-8th Ave., N.Y., N.Y. 10017
F. R. Gurney, Engraving Methods Ltd., #205 Birks Building, Edmonton, Alberta, Can.
Bryson J. Gwinnell, 2895 Seneca St., Buffalo, NY 14224
Neil Hartliep, Box 733, Fairmont, Minn. 56031
Frank E. Hendricks, Rt. 2, Box 189J, San Antonio, Tex. 78228
Heide Hiptmayer, P.O. Box 136, Eastman, Que., Canada
Ken Hunt, c/o Trevallion, 3442 S. Post Rd., Indianapolis, IN 46239
Ken Hurst, Box 21, Warrentown, VA 22186
Bob Izenstark, 101 Wolpers Rd., Park Forest, IL 60466
Paul Jaeger, 211 Leedom, Jenkintown, Pa. 19046
Robert C. Kain, R.F.D. Rte. #30, Newfane, Vermont 05345
T. J. Kaye, 4745 Dellwood, Beaumont, TX 77706
Lance Kelly, 4548 N. Andrews Ave., Ft. Lauderdale, FL 33309
Kleinguenther's, P.O. Box 1261, Seguin, TX 78155
E. J. Koevenig, Keystone, SD 57751
John Kudlas, 622 14th St. S.E., Rochester, MN 55901
N. Lewis, Rt. 1, Mikon Rd., Palmetto, GA 30268
Lynton S.M. McKenzie, P.O. Box 26087, New Orleans, LA 70186 (booklet $3.00)
Wm. H. Mains, 5780 W. Del Rey Ave., Las Vegas, NV 89102
Rudy Marek, Rt. 1, Box 1A, Banks, Ore. 97106
Franz Marktl, c/o Davis Gun Shop, 7211 Lee Hwy., Falls Church, VA 22046
James B. Meek, 405 E. 10th St. S., Newton, IA 50208
S. A. Miller, Miller Gun Works, P.O. Box 7326, Tamuning, Guam 96911
Frank Mittermeier, 3577 E. Tremont Ave., New York, N.Y. 10465
New Orleans Jewelers Supply, 206 Chartres St., New Orleans, LA 70130
Hans Obiltschnig, Ferlach, Austria
Tom Overbey, 612 Azalea Ave., Richmond, VA 23227
Pachmayr Gun Works, Inc., 1220 S. Grand Ave., Los Angeles, Calif. 90015
Hans Pfeiffer, 286 Illinois St., Elmhurst, IL 60126
Wayne E. Potts, 912 Poplar St., Denver, CO 80220
E. C. Prudhomme, 302 Ward Bldg., Shreveport, La. 71101
John R. Rohner, Sunshine Canyon, Boulder, Colo. 80302
Robert P. Runge, 94 Grove St., Ilion, N.Y. 13357
Shaw-Leibowitz, Rt. 1, Box 421, New Cumberland, W.Va. 26047 (etchers)
Russell J. Smith, 231 Springdale Rd., Westfield, Mass. 01085
Robt. Swartley, 2800 Pine St., Napa, Calif. 94559
Ray Viramontez, 4348 Newberry Ct., Dayton, OH 45432
Floyd E. Warren, 1273 St. Rt. 305 N.E. Rt. #3, Cortland, OH 44410
John E. Warren, P.O. Box 72, Eastham, Mass. 02642
A. A. White Engr., Inc., P.O. Box 68, Manchester, Conn. 06040

GAME CALLS

Black Duck, 1737 Davis, Whiting, Ind. 46394
Burnham Bros., Box 100-C, Marble Falls, Tex. 78654
Faulk's, 616 18th St., Lake Charles, La. 70601
Lohman Mfg. Co., 320 E. Spring, Neosho, Mo. 64850
Mallardtone, 2901 16th St., Moline, Ill. 61265
Edward J. Mehok, 1737 Davis Ave., Whiting, IN 46394
Phil. S. Olt Co., Box 550, Pekin, Ill. 61554
Penn's Woods Products, Inc., 19 W. Pittsburgh St., Delmont, Pa. 15626
Sport-Lore, Inc., 1757 Cherry St., Denver, Colo. 80220
Johnny Stewart Wildlife Calls, Box 7954, Waco, Tex. 76710
Thomas Game Calls, P.O. Box 336, Winnsboro, TX 75494
Weems Wild Calls, 500 S. 7th, Fort Smith, AR 72901
Wightman Electronics, Box 989, Easton, Md. 21601
Tex Wirtz Ent., Inc., 1925 W. Hubbard St., Chicago, Ill. 60622

GUNS (Foreign)

Abercrombie & Fitch, Madison at 45th, New York, N.Y. 10017
Alaskan Rifles, Box 30, Juneau, Alaska 99801
American Import Co., 1167 Mission St., San Francisco, Calif. 94103
American International, 103 Social Hall Ave., Salt Lake City, UT 84111
Armi Fabbri, Casella 206, Brescia, Italy 25100
Armi Famars, Via Cinelli 33, Gardone V.T. (Brescia), Italy 25063
AYA (Aguirre y Aranzabal) see: Ventura Imports (Spanish shotguns)
Armoury Inc., Rte. 25, New Preston, Ct. 06777
Bretton, Soc. Gen. de Mecanque, 21 Rue Clement Forissier, 42-St. Etienne, France
Browning, Rt. 4, Box 624-B, Arnold, Mo. 63010
Centennial Arms Corp., 3318 W. Devon, Chicago, (Lincolnwood) Ill. 60645
Century Arms Co., 3-5 Federal St., St. Albans, Vt. 05478
Champlin Firearms, Inc., Box 3191, Enid, OK 73701 (Gebruder Merkel)
Connecticut Valley Arms Co., Saybrook Rd., Haddam, CT 06438 (CVA)
Continental Arms Corp., 697 Fifth Ave., New York, N.Y. 10022
W. H. Craig, Box 927, Selma, Ala. 36701
Creighton & Warren, P.O. Box 15723, Nashville, TN 37215 (Krieghoff combination guns)
Morton Cundy & Son, Ltd., 413 6th Ave. E., Kalispell, MT 59901
Daiwa, 14011 Normandie Ave., Gardena, CA 90247
Charles Daly (see: Sloan's Sptg. Gds.)
Davidson Firearms Co., 2703 High Pt. Rd., Greensboro, N.C. 27403 (shotguns)
Davis Gun Shop, 7213 Lee Highway, Falls Church, VA 22046 (Fanzoj, Ferlach; Spanish guns)
Diana Co., 842 Vallejo St., San Francisco, CA 94133 (Benelli, Breda shotguns)
Dixie Gun Works, Inc., Hwy 51, South, Union City, Tenn. 38261 ("Kentucky" rifles)
Eastern Sports Distributors Co., Inc., P.O. Box 28, Milford, NH 03055 (Rottweil; Geco)
Euroarms, Via Solferino 13/A, 25100 Brescia, Italy
J. Fanzoj, P.O. Box 25, Ferlach, Austria 9170
Ferlach (Austria) of North America, P.O. Box 143435, S. Miami, FL 33143
R. C. Fessler & Co., 1634 Colorado Blvd., Los Angeles, Calif. 90041
Firearms Center Inc. (FCI), 113 Spokane, Victoria, TX 77901
Firearms Imp. & Exp. Co., 2470 N.W. 21st St., Miami, Fla. 33142
Firearms International Corp., 515 Kerby Hill Rd., Washington, DC 20022
Flaig's Lodge, Millvale, Pa. 15209
Florida Firearms Corp., 5555 N.W. 36th Ave., Hialeah, FL 33142
Freeland's Scope Stands, Inc., 3737 14th Ave., Rock Island, Ill. 61201
J. L. Galef & Son, Inc., 85 Chambers, New York, N.Y. 10007
Renato Gamba, Fabbrica d'Armi, via Metteotti, 81-ang. via Castelli, 29, 25063 GardoneV.T. (Brescia), Italy
Armas Garbi, Fundidores 4, Eibar, Spain (shotguns)
Garcia Sptg. Arms Corp., 329 Alfred Ave., Teaneck, N.J. 07666
Gevelot of Can. Ltd., Box 1593, Saskatoon, Sask., Canada
Georges Granger, 66 Cours Fauriel, 42 St. Etienne, France
Hawes Firearms Co., 8224 Sunset Blvd., Los Angeles, Calif. 90046
Healthways, Box 45055, Los Angeles, Calif. 90061
Gil Hebard Guns, Box 1, Knoxville, IL 61448 (Hammerli)
A. D. Heller, Inc., Box 268, 2322 Grand Ave., Baldwin, NY 11510
Herter's, Waseca, Minn. 56093
Husqvarna, see FFV Sports Inc.
Interarmco, see: Interarms (Walther)
Interarms Ltd., 10 Prince St., Alexandria, Va. 22313 (Mauser, Valmet M-62/S)
Intercontinental Arms, 2222 Barry Ave., Los Angeles, Calif. 90064
International Distr., Inc., 7290 S.W. 42nd St., Miami, FL 33155 (Taurus rev.)
Ithaca Gun Co., Terrace Hill, Ithaca, N.Y. 14850 (Perazzi)
Italguns, Via Leonardo da Vinci 36, 20090 Zingoni Di Trezzano, Milano, Italy
JBL Arms Co., 156 Terrace Way, Camillus, NY 13031 (AYA)
J-K Imports, Box 403, Novato, Cal. 94947 (Italian)
Paul Jaeger Inc., 211 Leedom St., Jenkintown, Pa. 19046
Jana Intl. Co., Box 1107, Denver, Colo. 80201 (Parker-Hale)
J. J. Jenkins, 462 Stanford Pl., Santa Barbara, CA 93105
Guy T. Jones Import Co., 905 Gervais St., Columbia, S. Car. 29201
Kanematsu-Gosho USA Inc., 543 W. Algonquin Rd., Arlington Heights, IL 60005 (Nikko)
Kassnar Imports, P.O. Box 3895, Harrisburg, PA 17105
Kerr's Sport Shop, Inc., 9584 Wilshire Blvd., Beverly Hills, CA 90212
Kimel Industries, P.O. Box 335, Matthews, NC 28105
Kleinguenther's, P.O. Box 1261, Seguin, TX 78155
Knight & Knight, 5930 S.W. 48 St., Miami, FL 33155 (made-to-order only)
Krieghoff Gun Co., P.O. Box 48-1367, Miami, FL 33148
L. A. Distributors, 4 Centre Market Pl., New York, N.Y. 10013
L.E.S., 3640 Dempster, Skokie, IL 60076 (Steyr, Mannlicher-Schonauer
S. E. Laszlo, 200 Tillary St., Brooklyn, N.Y. 11201
Lever Arms Serv. Ltd., 771 Dunsmuir, Vancouver, B.C., Canada V6C 1M9
Liberty Arms Organization, Box 306, Montrose, Calif. 91020
McKeown's Guns, R.R. 1, Pekin, Ill. 61554
McQueen Sales Co. Ltd., 1760 W. 3rd Ave., Vancouver, B.C., Canada V6J 1K5
Mandall Shooting Supplies Corp., 7150 E. 4th St., Scottsdale, AZ 85252
Manu-Arm, St. Etienne, France
Manufrance, 100-Cours Fauriel, 42 St. Etienne, France
Marietta Replica Arms Co., 706½ Mongomery St., Marietta, OH 45750
Mars Equipment Corp., 3318 W. Devon, Chicago, Ill. 60645
Mauser Amerika, 1721 Crooks Rd., Troy, MI 48084
Navy Arms Co., 689 Bergen Blvd., Ridgefield, N.J. 07657
Nikko Sporting Firearms, 543 W. Algonquin Rd., Arlington Heights, IL 60005
Omnipol, Washingtonova 11, Praha 1, Czechoslovakia
Harry Owen, P.O. Box 774, Sunnyvale, Ca. 94088.
Pachmayr Gun Works, 1220 S. Grand Ave., Los Angeles, CA 90015
Pacific Intl. Merch. Corp., P.O. Box 8022, Sacramento, CA 95818
Parker-Hale, Bisleyworks, Golden Hillock Rd., Sparbrook, Birmingham 11, England
Ed Paul Sptg. Goods, 172 Flatbush Ave., Brooklyn, N.Y. 11217 (Premier)
Picard-Fayolle, 42-rue du Vernay, 4200 Saint Etienne, France
Precise Imp. Corp. (PIC), 3 Chestnut, Suffern, N.Y. 10901
Premier Shotguns, 172 Flatbush Ave., Brooklyn N.Y. 11217
RG Industries, Inc., 2485 N.W. 20th St., Miami, FL 33142 (Erma)
Richland Arms Co., 321 W. Adrian St., Blissfield, Mich. 49228
Rottweil, see: Eastern
Sanderson's, 724 W. Edgewater, Portage, Wis. 53901
Savage Arms Corp., Westfield, Mass. 01085 (Anschutz)
Security Arms Co., 1815 No. Ft. Myer Dr., Arlington, VA 22209 (Heckler & Koch)
Service Armament, 689 Bergen Blvd., Ridgefield, N.J. 07657 (Greener Harpoon Gun)
Sherwood Dist., Inc., 18714 Parthenia St., Northridge, CA 91324
Simmons Spec., Inc., 700 Rogers Rd., Olathe, Kans. 66061
Skinner's Gun Shop (see Alaskan Rifles)
Sloan's Sprtg. Goods, Inc., 10 South St., Ridgefield, CT 06877
Franz Sodia Jagdgewehrfabrik, 9170 Ferlach, Austria
Steyr, A4400 Steyr, Austria
Stoeger Arms Co., 55 Ruta Ct., S. Hackensack, N.J. 07606
Tradewinds, Inc., P.O. Box 1191, Tacoma, Wash. 98401
Twin City Sptg. Gds., 217 Ehrman Ave., Cincinnati, OH 45220
Uberti, Aldo & Co., Via G. Carducci 41 or 39, Ponte Zanano (Brescia), Italy

Ignacio Ugartechea, Eibar, Spain
Universal Sporting Goods Co., Inc., 3746 E. 10th Ct., Hialeah, FL 33013
Valor Imp. Corp., 5555 N.W. 36th Ave., Miami, FL 33142
Ventura Imports, P.O. Box 2782, Seal Beach, CA 90740 (Spanish shotguns)
Verney-Carron, 17 Cours Fauriel, 42010 St. Etienne Cedex, France
Waffen-Frankonia, Box 380, 87 Wurzburg, W. Germany
Weatherby's, 2781 Firestone Blvd., So. Gate, Calif. 90280 (Sauer)
Dan Wesson Arms, 293 So. Main, Monson, Mass. 01057
Zavodi Crvena Zastava, 29 Novembra St., No. 12, Belgrade, Yugosl.

GUNS & GUN PARTS, REPLICA AND ANTIQUE

Antique Gun Parts, Inc., 1118 S. Braddock Ave., Pittsburgh, PA 15218 (ML)
Armoury Inc., Rte. 25, New Preston, Conn. 06777
Artistic Arms, Inc., Box 23, Hoagland, IN 46745 (Sharps-Borchardt replica)
Bannerman, F., Box 126, Blue Point, Long Island, N.Y. 11715
Shelley Braverman, Athens, N.Y. 12015 (obsolete parts)
Carter Gun Works, 2211 Jefferson Pk. Ave., Charlottesville, Va. 22903
R. MacDonald Champlin, P.O. Box 74, Wentworth, NH 03282 (replicas)
Cornwall Bridge Gun Shop, P.O. Box 67, Cornwall Bridge, CT 06754 (parts)
R. MacDonald Champlin, P.O. Box 74, Stanyan Hill, Wentworth, NH 03282 (replicas)
David E. Cumberland, 3509 Carlson Blvd., El Cerrito, CA 94530 (Replica Gatling guns)
Darr's Rifle Shop, 2309 Black Rd., Joliet, Ill. 60435 (S.S. items)
Dixie Gun Works, Inc., Hwy 51, South, Union City, Tenn. 38261
Federal Ordnance Inc., 9643 Alpaca St., So. El Monte, CA 91733
Kindig's Log Cabin Sport Shop, R.D. 1, P.O. Box 275, Lodi, Ohio 44254
Lever Arms Service Ltd., 771 Dunsmuir, Vancouver, B.C., Canada V6C 1M9
Edw. E. Lucas, 32 Garfield Ave., Old Bridge, N.J. 08857 (45-70)
Lyman Gun Sight Products, Middlefield, CT 06455
Markwell Arms Co., 2413 W. Devon, Chicago, IL 60645
Numrich Arms Co., West Hurley, N.Y. 12491
The Outrider, Inc., 3288 LaVenture Dr., Chamblee, GA 30341
Replica Models, Inc., 610 Franklin St., Alexandria, VA 22314
Riflemen's Hdqs., Rt. 3, RD 550-E, Kendallville, IN 46755
S&S Firearms, 88-21 Aubrey Ave., Glendale, N.Y. 11227
C. H. Stoppler, 1426 Walton Ave., New York, NY 10452 (miniature guns)
C. H. Weisz, Box 311-D, Arlington, Va. 22210
W. H. Wescombe, P.O. Box 488, Glencoe, CA 95232 (Rem. R.B. parts)

GUN PARTS, U. S. AND FOREIGN

Badger Shooter's Supply, Box 397, Owen, WI 54460
Shelley Braverman, Athens, N.Y. 12015
Philip R. Crouthamel, 513 E. Baltimore, E. Lansdowne, Pa. 19050
Charles E. Duffy, Williams Lane, West Hurley, N.Y. 12491
Federal Ordnance Inc., 9634 Alpaca St., So. El Monte, CA 91733
Greg's Winchester Parts, P.O. Box 8125, W. Palm Beach, FL 33407
The Gunshop, Inc., 44633 Sierra Highway, Lancaster, CA 93534
Hunter's Haven, Zero Prince St., Alexandria, Va. 22314
International Sportsmen's Supply Co., Inc., Arapaho-Central Park, Suite 311, Richardson, TX 75080 (bbld. actions)
Numrich Arms Co., West Hurley, N.Y. 12491
The Outrider, Inc., 3288 LaVenture Dr., Chamblee, GA 30341
Pacific Intl. Merch. Corp., P.O. Box 8022, Sacramento, CA 95818
Potomac Arms Corp. (see Hunter's Haven)
Martin B. Retting, Inc., 11029 Washington, Culver City, Cal. 90230
Ruvel & Co., 3037 N. Clark, Chicago, IL 60614
Sarco, Inc., 192 Central, Stirling, N.J. 07980
Sherwood Distr. Inc., 18714 Parthenia St., Northridge, CA 91324
Simms, 2801 J St., Sacramento, CA 95816
Clifford L. Smires, R.D., Box 39, Columbus, NJ 08022 (Mauser rifles)
N. F. Strebe, 4926 Marlboro Pike, S.E., Washington, D.C. 20027
Triple-K Mfg. Co., 568-6th Ave., San Diego, CA 92101

GUNS (Pellet)

Air Rifle Hq., 247 Court St., Grantsville, W. Va. 26147
Beeman's Precision Airguns, P.O. Box 278, San Anselmo, CA 94960
Benjamin Air Rifle Co., 1525 So. 8th St., Louis, Mo. 63104
Continental Arms Corp., 697 5th Ave., New York, N.Y. 10022
Crosman Arms, a Coleman Co. Div., Fairport, NY 14450
Daisy Mfg. Co., Rogers, Ark. 72756 (also Feinwerkbau)
Fanta Air Rifles, Box 8122, La Crescenta, Calif, 91214
J. L. Galef & Son, Inc., 85 Chambers St., New York, N.Y. 10007 (B.S.A.)
Harrington & Richardson Arms Co., Industrial Rowe, Gardner, MA 01440 (Webley)
Healthways, Box 45055, Los Angeles, Calif. 90061
Gil Hebard Guns, Box 1, Knoxville, Ill. 61448
Hy-Score Arms Co., 200 Tillary St., Brooklyn, N.Y. 11201
Interarms, 10 Prince, Alexandria, Va. 22313 (Walther)
Marksman Products, P.O. Box 2983, Torrance, CA 90509
Power Line (see: Daisy Mfg. Co.)
Precise Imports Corp. (PIC), 3 Chestnut, Suffern, N.Y. 10901
Sears, Roebuck & Co., 825 S. St. Louis, Chicago, Ill. 60607
Service Armament, 689 Bergen Blvd., Ridgefield, N.J. 07657 (Webley, Jaguar)
Sheridan Products, Inc., 3205 Sheridan, Racine, Wis. 53403
Smith & Wesson, Inc., 7710 No. 30th St., Tampa, FL 33610
Stoeger Arms Corp., 55 Ruta Ct., S. Hackensack, N.J. 07606 (Peerless)
Dan Wesson Arms, 293 S. Main, Monson, Mass. 01057

GUNS, SURPLUS PARTS AND AMMUNITION

Century Arms, Inc., 3-5 Federal St., St. Albans, Vt. 05478
W. H. Craig, Box 927, Selma, Ala. 36701
Cummings Intl. Inc., 41 Riverside Ave., Yonkers, N.Y. 10701
Eastern Firearms Co., 790 S. Arroyo Pkwy., Pasadena, Calif. 91105
Hunter's Lodge, 200 S. Union, Alexandria, Va. 22313
Lever Arms Serv. Ltd., 771 Dunsmuir St., Vancouver, B.C., Canada V6C IM9
Mars Equipment Corp., 3318 W. Devon, Chicago, Ill. 60645
National Gun Traders, 225 S.W. 22nd, Miami, Fla. 33135
The Outrider, Inc., 3288 LaVenture Dr., Chamblee, GA 30341
Pacific Intl. Merch. Corp., P.O. Box 8022, Sacramento, CA 95818
Plainfield Ordnance Co., Box 447, Dunellen, N.J. 08812
Potomac Arms Corp., Box 35, Alexandria, Va. 22313
Ruvel & Co., 3037 N. Clark St., Chicago, Ill. 60614
Service Armament Co., 689 Bergen Blvd., Ridgefield, N.J. 07657
Sherwood Distrib. Inc., 18714 Parthenia St., Northridge, CA 91324

GUNS, U.S.-made

ArmaLite, 118 E. 16th St., Costa Mesa, Calif. 92627
Apollo Custom Rifles, Inc., 1235 Cowles St., Long Beach, CA 90813
Artistic Arms, Inc., Box 23, Hoagland, IN 46745 (Sharps-Borchardt)
Bauer Firearms, 34750 Klein Ave., Fraser, MI 48026
Bortmess Gun Co., Inc., RD #1, Box 199A, Scenery Hill, PA 15360
Challanger Mfg. Corp., 118 Pearl St., Mt. Vernon, NY 10550 (Hopkins & Allen)
Champlin Firearms, Inc., Box 3191, Enid, Okla. 73701
Charter Arms Corp., 430 Sniffens Ln., Stratford, CT 06497
Clerke Products, 2219 Main St., Santa Monica, Ca. 90405
Colt, 150 Huyshope Ave., Hartford, CT 06102
Commando Arms, Inc., Box 10214, Knoxville, Tenn. 37919
Cumberland Arms, 1222 Oak Dr., Manchester, Tenn 37355
Day Arms Corp., 7515 Stagecoach Ln., San Antonio, Tex. 78227
Falling Block Works, P.O. Box 22, Troy, MI 48084
Firearms Imp. & Exp. Co., 2470 N.W. 21st St., Miami, FL 33142 (FIE)
Firearms Intl. Corp., (see: Garcia)
4 Ace Mfg. Inc., P.O. Box 3820, Brownsville, TX 78520
Golden Age Arms Co., 14 W. Winter St., Delaware, OH 43015
Greyhawk Arms Corp., 1900 Tyler Ave., Unit 15, South El Monte, CA 91733
H & N Minicraft, Inc., 1066 E. Edna Pl., Covina, CA 91722 (Thomas auto pistol)
Gyrojet (see Intercontinental Arms)
Harrington & Richardson, Industrial Rowe, Gardner, MA 01440
A. D. Heller, Inc., Box 268, Grand Ave., Baldwin, NY 11510
Hi-Shear Corp., 2600 Skypark Dr., Torrance, CA 90509 (Omega rifle)
High Standard Mfg. Co., 1817 Dixwell Ave., Hamden, Conn. 06514
Hopkins & Allen, see: High Standard
Hyper-Single Precision SS Rifles, 520 E. Beaver, Jenks, OK 74037
Indian Arms Corp., 13503 Joseph Campar, Detroit, MI 48212
Intercontinental Arms, Inc., 2222 Barry Ave., Los Angeles, Ca. 90064
Int'l. Sportsmen's Supply Co., Inc., Arapaho-Central Park, Suite 311, Richardson, TX 75080 (Santa Barbara bbld. actions)
Ithaca Gun Co., Ithaca, N.Y. 14850
Iver Johnson Arms & Cycle Works, Fitchburg, Mass. 01420
J & R carbine, (see: PJK Inc.)
Lee E. Jurras & Assoc., Inc., P.O. Box 846, Roswell, NM 88201 (Auto Mag)
Ljutic Ind., Inc., P.O. Box 2117, Yakima, WA 98902 (Mono-Gun)
MBAssociates (see Intercontinental Arms)
Manchester Arms, Inc., 6858 Manchester Rd., Rt. 2, Clinton, OH 44216
Marlin Firearms Co., 100 Kenna Dr., New Haven, Conn. 06473
Merrill Co. Inc., Box 187, Rockwell City, IA 50579
O. F. Mossberg & Sons, Inc., 7 Grasso St., No. Haven, Conn. 06473
W. L. Mowrey Gun Works, Inc., Box 28, Iowa Park TX 76367
Natl. Ordance Inc., 9643 Alpaca, S. El Monte, CA 91733
Navy Arms Co., 689 Bergen Blvd., Ridgefield, N.J. 07657
Norarmco, 41471 Irwin, Mt. Clemens, MI 48043 (D.A. 25 auto)
North American Arms Co., 3303 Old Conejo Rd., Newbury Park, CA 91320
North Star Arms, R.2, Box 74A, Ortonville, MN 56278 (The Plainsman)
Numrich Arms Corp., W. Hurley, N.Y. 12491
Omega (see Hi-Shear Corp.)
PJK, Inc., 1527 Royal Oak Dr., Bradbury, Ca 91010 (J&R Carbine)
Pedersen Custom Guns, Div. of O. F. Mossberg & Sons, Inc., 7 Grasso Ave., North Haven, CT 06473
Plainfield Machine Co., Inc., Box 447, Dunellen, N.J. 08812
Plainfield Ordnance Co., P.O. Box 251, Middlesex, NJ 08846
Potomac Arms Corp., P.O. Box 35, Alexandria, Va. 22313 (ML replicas)
R G Industries, 2485 N.W. 20th SE., Miami, FL 33142
Remington Arms Co., Bridgeport, Conn. 06602
Riedl Rifles, 15124 Weststate St., Westminster, CA 92683 (S.S.)
Ruger (see Sturm, Ruger & Co.)
Savage Arms Corp., Westfield, Mass. 01085
Sears, Roebuck & Co., 825 S. St. Louis, Chicago, Ill. 60607
Security Industries of America, Inc., 31 Bergen Turnpike, Little Ferry, NJ 07643
Seventrees Ltd., 315 W. 39th St., New York, N.Y. 10018
Smith & Wesson, Inc., 2100 Roosevelt Ave., Springfield, MA 01101
Sporting Arms, Inc., 9643 Alpaca St., So. El Monte, CA 91733 (M-1 carbine)

Springfield Armory, Div. of RSI, 218 N. State St., Geneseo, IL 61254
Sterling Arms Corp., 4436 Prospect St., Gasport, NY 14067
Sturm, Ruger & Co., Southport, Conn. 06490
Thompson-Center Arms, Box 2405, Rochester, N.H. 03867
Tingle, 1125 Smithland Pike, Shelbyville, Ind. 46176 (muzzleloader)
Trail Guns Armory, 2115 Lexington, Houston, TX 77006 (muzzleloaders)
Universal Firearms Corp., 3746 E. 10th Ct., Hialeah, Fla. 33013
Unordco, P.O. Box 15723, Nashville, TN 37215
Ward's, 619 W. Chicago, Chicago, Ill. 60607 (Western Field brand)
Weatherby's, 2781 E. Firestone Blvd., South Gate, Calif. 90280
Dan Wesson Arms, 293 So. Main St., Monson, Mass. 01057
Winchester Repeating Arms Co., New Haven, Conn. 06504
Winslow Arms Co., P.O. Box 578, Osprey, Fla. 33595

GUNSMITHS, CUSTOM (see Custom Gunsmiths)

GUNSMITHS, HANDGUN (see PISTOLSMITHS)

GUNSMITH SCHOOLS

Colorado School of Trades, 1545 Hoyt, Lakewood, CO 80215
Lassen Community College, P.O. Box 3000, Susanville, CA 96130
Oregon Institute of Technology, Klamath Falls, OR 97601
Penn. Gunsmith School, 812 Ohio River Blvd., Avalon, Pittsburgh, Pa. 15202
Trinidad State Junior College, Trinidad, Colo. 81082

GUNSMITH SUPPLIES, TOOLS, SERVICES

Alamo Heat Treating Co., Box 55345, Houston, Tex. 77055
Albright Prod. Co., P.O. Box 1027, Winnemucca, NV 89445 (trap buttplates)
Alley Supply Co., Carson Valley Industrial Park, Gardnerville, NV 89410
Ames Precision Machine Works, 5270 Geddes Rd., Ann Arbor, MI 48105 (portable hardness tester)
Anderson & Co., 1203 Broadway, Yakima, Wash. 98902 (tang safe)
Armite Labs., 1845 Randolph St., Los Angeles, Cal. 90001 (pen oiler)
B-Square Co., Box 11281, Ft. Worth, Tex. 76110
Jim Baiar, Rt. 1-B, Box 352, Columbia Falls, Mont. 59912 (hex screws)
Al Biesen, W. 2039 Sinto Ave., Spokane, WA 99201 (grip caps, buttplates)
Bonanza Sports Mfg. Co., 412 Western Ave., Faribault, Minn. 55021
Brookstone Co., 16 Brookstone Bldg., Vose Farm Rd., Peterborough, NH 03458
Brown & Sharpe Mfg. Co., Precision Pk., No. Kingston, R.I. 02852
Bob Brownell's, Main & Third, Montezuma, Ia. 50171
W. E. Brownell, 1852 Alessandro Trail, Vista, Calif. 92083 (checkering tools)
Maynard P. Buehler, Inc., 17 Orinda Hwy., Orinda, Calif. 94563 (Rocol lube)
Burgess Vibrocrafters, Inc. (BVI), Rte. 83, Grayslake, Ill. 60030
M. H. Canjar, 500 E. 45th, Denver, Colo. 80216 (triggers, etc.)
Chapman Mfg. Co., Rte. 17, Durham, CT 06422
Chase Chemical Corp., 3527 Smallman St., Pittsburgh, PA 15201 (Chubb Multigauge)
Chubb (see Chase Chem. Corp.)
Chicago Wheel & Mfg. Co., 1101 W. Monroe St., Chicago, Ill. 60607 (Handee grinders)
Christy Gun Works, 875-57th St., Sacramento, Calif. 95819
Clover Mfg. Co., 139 Woodward Ave., Norwalk, CT 06856 (Clover compound)
Clymer Mfg. Co., 14241 W. 11 Mile Rd., Oak Park, Mich. 48237 (reamers)
Colbert Industries, 10107 Adella, South Gate, Calif. 90280 (Panavise)
A. Constantine & Son, Inc., 2050 Eastchester Rd., Bronx, N.Y. 10461 (wood)
Cougar & Hunter, G 6398 W. Pierson Rd., Flushing, Mich. 48433 (scope jigs)
Alvin L. Davidson, 1215 Branson, Las Cruces, NM 88001 (action sleeves)
Dayton-Traister Co., P.O. Box 593, Oak Harbor, Wa. 98277 (triggers)
Dem-Bart Hand Tool Co., 6807 Hwy 2, Snohomish, WA 98290 (checkering tools)
Ditto Industries, 527 N. Alexandria, Los Angeles, Cal. 90004 (clamp tool)
Dixie Diamond Tool Co., Inc., 6875 S.W. 81st St., Miami, Fla. 33143 (marking pencils)
Dremel Mfg. Co., 4915-21st St., Racine, WI 53406 (grinders)
Chas. E. Duffy, Williams Lane, West Hurley, N.Y. 12491
E-Z Tool Co., P.O. Box 3186, 25 N.W. 44th Ave., Des Moines, Ia. 50313 (lathe taper attachment)
Edmund Scientific Co., 101 E. Glouster Pike, Barrington, N.J. 08007
F. K. Elliott, Box 785, Ramona, Calif. 92065 (reamers)
Forster Products, Inc., 82 E. Lanark Ave., Lanark, Ill. 61046
Keith Francis, 8515 Wagner Creek Rd., Talent, Ore. 97540 (reamers)
G. R. S. Corp., Box 1157, Boulder, Colo. 80302 (Gravermeister)
Gager Gage and Tool Co., 27509 Industrial Blvd., Hayward, CA 94545 (speedlock triggers f. Rem. 1100 & 870 pumps)
Gilmore Pattern Works, 1164 N. Utica, Tulsa, Okla. 74110
Gold Lode, Inc., 181 Gary Ave., Wheaton, IL 60187 (gold inlay kit)
Grace Metal Prod., 115 Ames St., Elk Rapids, MI 49629 (screw drivers, drifts)
Gopher Shooter's Supply, Box 246, Faribault, Minn. 55021 (screwdrivers, etc.)
Gunline Tools Inc., 719 No. East St., Anaheim, CA 92805
H. & M. 24062 Orchard Lake Rd., Farmington, Mich. 48024 (reamers)
Half Moon Rifle Shop, Rt. 1B, Box 352, Columbia Falls, MT 59912 (hex screws)
Hartford Reamer Co., Box 134, Lathrup Village, Mich. 48075
O. Iber Co., 626 W. Randolph, Chicago, Ill. 60606
Paul Jaeger Inc., 211 Leedom St., Jenkintown, PA. 19046
Jeffredo Gunsight Co., 1629 Via Monserate, Fallbrook, CA 92028 (trap buttplate)
Kasenite Co., Inc., 3 King St., Mahwah, N.J. 07430 (surface hrdng. comp.)
LanDav Custom Guns, 7213 Lee Highway, Falls Church, VA 22046
John G. Lawson, 1802 E. Columbia Ave., Tacoma, WA 98404
Lea Mfg. Co., 237 E. Aurora St., Waterbury, Conn. 06720
Lock's Phila. Gun Exch., 6700 Rowland Ave., Philadelphia, Pa. 19149
Marker Machine Co., Box 426, Charleston, Ill. 61920
Michaels of Oregon Co., P.O. Box 13010, Portland, Ore. 97213
Viggo Miller, P.O. Box 4181, Omaha, Neb. 68104 (trigger attachment)
Miller Single Trigger Mfg. Co., RD1, Box 69, Millersburg, PA 17061
Frank Mittermeier, 3577 E. Tremont, N.Y., N.Y. 10465
Moderntools Corp, Box 407, Dept. GD, Woodside, N.Y. 11377
N&J Sales, Lime Kiln Rd., Northford, Conn. 06472 (screwdrivers)
Karl A. Neise, Inc., 5602 Roosevelt Ave., Woodside, N.Y. 11377
Palmgren, 8383 South Chicago Ave., Chicago, Ill. 60167 (vises, etc.)
Panavise, Colbert Industries, 10107 Adelia Ave., South Gate, CA 90280
C. R. Pedersen & Son, Ludington, Mich. 49431
Ponderay Lab., 210 W. Prasch, Yakima, Wash. 98902 (epoxy glass bedding)
Redford Reamer Co., Box 40604, Redford Hts. Sta, Detroit, MI 48240
Richland Arms Co., 321 W. Adrian St., Blissfield, Mich. 49228
Riley's Supply Co., 121 No. Main St., Avilla, Ind. 46710 (Niedner buttplates, caps)
Ruhr-American Corp., So. Hwy #5, Glenwood, Minn. 56334
A. G. Russell, 1705 Hiway 71N, Springdale, AR 72764 (Arkansas oilstones)
Schaffner Mfg. Co., Emsworth, Pittsburgh, Pa. 15202 (polishing kits)
Schuetzen Gun Works, 1226 Prarie Rd., Colo. Springs, Colo. 80909
Shaw's, Rt. 4, Box 407-L, Escondido, CA 92025
A. D. Soucy Co., Box 191, Fort Kent, Me. 04743 (ADSCO stock finish)
L. S. Starrett Co., Athol, Mass. 01331
Texas Platers Supply Co., 2453 W. Five Mile Parkway, Dallas, TX 75233 (plating kit)
Timney Mfg. Co., 5624 Imperial Hwy., So. Gate, Calif. 90280 (triggers)
Stan de Treville, Box 33021, San Diego, Calif. 92103 (checkering patterns)
Twin City Steel Treating Co., Inc., 1114 S. 3rd, Minneapolis, Minn. 55415 (heat treating)
Ward Mfg. Co., 500 Ford Blvd., Hamilton, O. 45011
Will-Burt Co., P.O. Box 160, Orrville, O. 44667 (vises)
Williams Gun Sight Co., 7389 Lapeer Rd., Davison, Mich. 48423
Wilson Arms Co., 63 Leetes Island Rd., Branford, CT 06405
Wilton Tool Corp., 9525 W. Irving Pk. Rd., Schiller Park, Ill. 60176 (vises)
Wisconsin Platers Supply Co., see: Texas Platers
W. C. Wolff Co., Box 232, Ardmore, PA 19003 (springs)
Woodcraft Supply Corp., 313 Montvale, Woburn, MA 01801

HANDGUN ACCESSORIES

A. R. Sales Co., 9624 Alpaca St., South El Monte, CA 91733
Baramie Corp., 6250 E. 7 Mile Rd., Detroit, MI 48234 (Hip-Grip)
Bar-Sto Precision Machine, 633 S. Victory Blvd., Burbank, CA 91502
B. L. Broadway, Rte. 1, Box 381, Alpine, CA 92001 (machine rest)
C'Arco, P.O. Box 2043, San Bernardino, CA 92406 (Ransom Rest)
Case Master, 4675 E. 10 Ave., Miami, Fla. 33013
Central Specialties Co., 6030 Northwest Hwy., Chicago, Ill. 60631
John Dangelzer, 3056 Frontier Pl., N.E., Albuquerque, N.M. 87106 (flasks)
Bill Dyer, 503 Midwest Bldg., Oklahoma City, Okla. 73102 (grip caps)
R. S. Frielich, 396 Broome St., New York, N.Y. 10013 (cases)
R. G. Jensen, 16153½ Parthenia, Sepulveda, Calif. 91343 (auxiliary chambers)
Lee E. Jurras & Assoc., Inc., P.O. Box 846, Roswell, NM 88201 (Auto Mag only)
Lee Prec. Mfg., 46 E. Jackson, Hartford, WI 53027 (pistol rest holders)
Los Gatos Grip & Specialty Co., P.O. Box 1850, Los Gatos, CA 95030 (custom-made)
Marcon, 1720 Marina Ct., Suite D, San Mateo, CA 94403 (Mellmark pistol safe)
Matich Loader, Box 958, So. Pasadena, Calif. 91030 (Quick Load)
W. A. Miller Co., Inc., Mingo Loop, Oguossoc, ME 04964 (cases)
No-Sho Mfg. Co., 10727 Glenfield Ct., Houston, TX 77035
Pachmayr, 1220 S. Grand, Los Angeles, Calif. 90015 (cases)
Pistolsafe, Dr. L., N. Chili, NY 14514 (handgun safe)
Platt Luggage, Inc., 2301 S. Prairie, Chicago, Ill. 60616 (cases)
Sportsmen's Equipment Co., 415 W. Washington, San Diego, Calif. 92103
M. Tyler, 1326 W. Britton, Oklahoma City, Okla. 73114 (grip adaptor)

HANDGUN GRIPS

Beckelhymer's, Hidalgo & San Bernardo, Laredo, Tex. 78040
Belmont Prods., Rte. #1, Friendsville, TN 37737
Cloyce's Gun Stocks, Box 1133, Twin Falls, Ida. 83301
Crest Carving Co., 8091 Bolsa Ave., Midway City, CA 92655
Custom Combat Grips, 148 Shepherd Ave., Brooklyn, N.Y. 11208
Fitz, Box 49697, Los Angeles, Calif. 90049
Herrett's, Box 741, Twin Falls, Ida. 83301
Hogue Custom Combat Grips, c/o Gateway Shooters' Supply, Inc., 991 Gun Club Dr., Jacksonville, FL 32218
J. R. Grips, 1601 Wilt Rd., Fallbrook, CA 92028
Mershon Co., Inc., 1230 S. Grand Ave., Los Angeles, Calif. 90015

Mustang Custom Pistol Grips, 28030 Del Rio Rd., Temecula, CA 92390
Safety Grip Corp., Box 456, Riverside St., Miami, Fla. 33135
Sanderson Custom Pistol Stocks, 17695 Fenton, Detroit, Mich. 48219
Jay Scott, 81 Sherman Place, Garfield, N.J. 07026
Sile Dist., 7 Centre Market Pl., New York, N.Y. 10013
Sports Inc., P.O. Box 683, Park Ridge, IL 60068 (Franzite)

HEARING PROTECTORS

AO Safety Prods., Div. of American Optical Corp., 14 Mechanic St., Southbridge, MA 01550 (ear valve)
Bausch & Lomb, 635 St. Paul St., Rochester, N.Y. 14602
David Clark Co., 360 Franklin St., Worcester, Mass. 01604
Curtis Safety Prod. Co., Box 61, Webster Sq. Sta., Worcester, Mass. 01603 (ear valve)
EAR Corp., Concord Rd., Billerica, MA 01821
Hodgdon, 7710 W. 50 Hiway, Shawnee Mission, Kans. 66202
Sigma Eng. Co., 11320 Burbank Blvd., No. Hollywood, Ca. 91601 (Lee-Sonic ear valve)
Safety Direct, P.O. Box 8907, Reno, NV 89507 (Silencio)
Smith & Wesson, 2100 Roosevelt Ave., Springfield, MA 01101
Vector Scientific, P.O. Box 21106, Ft. Lauderdale, FL 33316
Willson Prods Div., P.O. Box 622, Reading, Pa. 19603 (Ray-O-Vac)

HOLSTERS & LEATHER GOODS

American Sales & Mfg. Co., P.O. Box 677, Laredo, Tex. 78040
Andy Anderson, P.O. Box 225, North Hollywood, CA 91603 (Gunfighter Custom Holsters)
Bianchi Holster Co., 100 Calle Cortez, Temecula, CA 92390
Boyt Co., Div. of Welch Sptg., Box 1108, Iowa Falls, Ia. 51026
Brauer Bros. Mfg. Co., 817 N. 17th, St. Louis, Mo. 63106
Browning, Rt. 4, Box 624-B, Arnold, MO 63010
J. M. Bucheimer Co., Airport Rd., Frederick, Md. 21701
Cathey Enterprises, P.O. Box 3545, Chula Vista, CA 92011
Clements Custom Leathercraft, 1245 S. Pennsylvania St., Denver, CO 80203 (Custom-made holsters)
Cole's Acku-Rite, Box 25, Kennedy, N.Y. 14747
Colt's, 150 Huyshope Ave., Hartford, Conn. 06102
Daisy Mfg. Co., Rogers, Ark. 72756
Eugene DeMayo & Sons, Inc., 2795 Third Ave., Bronx, N.Y. 10455
Ellwood Epps (Orillia) Ltd., Hwy. 11 North, Orillia, Ont., Canada
Filmat Enterpr., Inc., 200 Market St., East Paterson, N.J. 07407
Goerg Ent., 3009 S. Laurel, Port Angeles, Wash. 98362
Gunfighter (See Anderson)
Hoyt Holster Co., P.O. Box 1783, Costa Mesa, Cal. 92626
Don Hume, Box 351, Miami, Okla. 74354
The Hunter Co., 3300 W. 71st Ave., Westminster, CO 80030
Jet Sports Corp., 4 Centre Market Pl., New York, N.Y. 10013
Jumbo Sports Prods., P.O. Box 280, Airport Rd., Frederick, MD 21701
George Lawrence Co., 306 S. W. First Ave., Portland, Ore. 97221
Leathercrafters, 710 S. Washington, Alexandria, VA 22314
MMGR Corp., 5710 12th Ave., Brooklyn, N.Y. 11219
S. D. Myres Saddle Co., Box 9776, El Paso, Tex. 79988
Pancake Holsters, Roy Baker, Box 245, Magnolia, AR 71753
Pony Express Sport Shop, 17460 Ventura Blvd., Encino, Calif. 91316
Red Head Brand Co., 4100 Platinum Way, Dallas, Tex. 75237
Rickenbacker's, P.O. Box 532, State Ave., Holly Hill, SC 29059
R. E. Roseberry, 810 W. 38th, Anderson, Ind. 46014
Roy's Custom Leather Goods, Hwy. 132, Rt. 1, Box 245, Magnolia, AR 71753
Safariland Leather Products, 1941 Walker Ave., Monrovia, Calif. 91016
Safety Speed Holster, Inc., 910 So. Vail, Montebello, Calif. 90640
Saguaro Holsters, 1508 Del Carlo Circle, Seagoville, TX 75159 (custom)
Buddy Schoellkopf Products, Inc., 4100 Platinum Way, Dallas, Tex. 75237
Seventrees, Ltd., 315 W. 39 St., New York, N.Y. 10018
Sile Distr., 7 Centre Market Pl., New York, N.Y. 10013
Smith & Wesson Leather Co., 2100 Roosevelt, Springfield, Mass. 01101
Stein Holsters & Accessories, Inc., Drawer B, Wakefield Sta., Bronx, NY 10466
Swiss-Craft Co., Inc., 33 Arctic St., Worcester, MA 01604
Tandy Leather Co., 1001 Foch, Fort Worth, Texas 76107
Tayra Corp., 1529-19th St. N.W., Canton, O. 44709
Torel, Inc., 1053 N. South St., Yoakum, TX 77995 (gun slings)
Triple-K Mfg. Co., 568 Sixth Ave., San Diego, CA 92101
Whitco, Box 1712, Brownsville, Tex. 78520 (Hide-A-Way)

HUNTING AND CAMP GEAR, CLOTHING, ETC.

Abercrombie & Fitch, 45th & Madison Ave., N.Y., N.Y. 10017
Eddie Bauer, 1737 Airport Way So., Seattle, Wash. 98134
L. L. Bean, Freeport, Me. 04032
Bear Archery Co., R.R. 1, Grayling, Mich. 49738 (Himalayan backpack)
Bernzomatic Corp., 740 Driving Pk. Ave., Rochester, N.Y. 14613 (stoves & lanterns)
Big Beam, Teledyne Co., 290 E. Prairie St., Crystal Lake, Ill. 60014 (lamp)
Bill Boatman & Co., So. Maple St., Bainbridge, OH 45612
Browning, Rte. 1, Morgan, Utah 84050
Camouflage Mfg. Co., P.O. Box 5437, Pine Bluff, AR 71601
Camp Trails, P.O. Box 14500, Phoenix, Ariz. 85031 (packs only)
Camp Ways, 415 Molino St., Los Angeles, CA 90013
Challanger Mfg. Co., Box 550, Jamaica, N.Y. 11431 (glow safe)
Coleman Co., Inc., 250 N. St. Francis, Wichita, Kans. 67201
Colorado Outdoor Sports Co., 5450 N. Valley Hwy., Denver, Colo. 80216
Converse Rubber Co., 1200 Kirk St., Elk Grove Village, IL 60007 (boots)
Corcoran, Inc., 2 Canton Street, Stoughton, Mass, 02072
Dana Safety Heater, J. L. Galef & Son, Inc., 85 Chamber St., N.Y. N.Y. 10007
DEER-ME Prod. Co., Box 345, Anoka, Minn. 55303 (tree steps)
Dunham's Footwear, RFD 3, Brattleboro, Vt. 05301 (boots)
Filmat Enterpr., Inc., 200 Market St., East Paterson, N.J. 07407 (field dressing kit)
Freeman Ind., Inc., 100 Marblehead Rd., Tuckahoe, N.Y. 10707 (Trak-Kit)
Game-Winner, Inc., 515 Candler Bldg., Atlanta, GA 30303 (camouflage suits)
Gander Mountain, Inc., Box 248, Wilmot, Wis. 53192
Gerry Mountain Sports, Inc. (see Colorado Sports)
Gokey, 94 E. 4th St., St. Paul, Minn. 55101
Gun Club Sportswear, Box 477, Des Moines, Ia. 50302
Gun-Ho Case Mfg. Co., 110 E. 10th St., St. Paul, Minn. 55101
Herter's Inc., Waseca, Minn. 56093
Himalayan Back Packs, P.O. Box 5668, Pine Bluff, AR 71601
Bob Hinman, 1217 W. Glen, Peoria, Ill. 61614
Holubar Mountaineering, Box 7, Boulder, Colo. 80302
Kelty Pack, Inc., Box 3645, Glendale, Calif. 91201
Peter Limmer & Sons, Box 66, Intervale, N.H. 03845 (boots)
Marathon Rubber Prods. Co., 510 Sherman St., Wausau, WI 54401 (rain gear)
Marble Arms Corp., 420 Industrial Park, Gladstone, Mich. 49837
National Sports Div., 19 E. McWilliams St., Fond du Lac, Wis. 54935
Nimrod & Wayfarer Trailers, 500 Ford Blvd., Hamilton, O. 45011
Charles F. Orvis Co., Manchester, Vt. 05254 (fishing gear)
Palco Prods., 15 Hope Ave., Worcester, MA 01603
Paulin Infra-Red Prod. Co., 30520 Lakeland Blvd., Willowick, OH 44094
Primus-Sievert, 354 Sackett Pt. Rd., No. Haven, CT 06473 (stoves)
Ranger Mfg. Co., Inc., P.O. Box 3676, Augusta, GA 30904
Red Head Brand Co., 4100 Platinum Way, Dallas Tex. 75237
Red Wing Shoe Co., Rte. 2, Red Wing, Minn. 55066
Refrigiwear, Inc., 71 Inip Dr., Inwood, L.I., N.Y. 11696
Reliance Prod. Ltd., 1830 Dublin Ave., Winnipeg 21, Man., Can. (tent peg)
W. R. Russell Moccasin Co., 285 S.W. Franklin, Berlin, WI 54923
Buddy Schoellkopf, Inc., 4100 Platinum Way, Dallas, Tex. 75237
Servus Rubber Co., 1136 2nd St., Rock Island, Ill. 61201 (footwear)
The Ski Hut-Trailwise, 1615 University Ave., P.O. Box 309, Berkeley, CA 94701
Snow Lion Corp., P.O. Box 9056, Berkeley, CA 94709 (sleeping bags and parkas)
Stearns Mfg. Co., Division & 30th St., St. Cloud, Minn. 56301
Sterno Inc., 105 Hudson St., Jersey City, N.J. 07302 (camp stoves)
Teledyne Co., Big Beam, 290 E. Prairie St., Crystal Lake, IL 60014
10-X Mfg. Co., 6185 Arapahoe, Boulder, CO 80303
Thermos Div., KST Co., Norwich, Conn. 06361 (Pop Tent)
Norm Thompson, 1805 N.W. Thurman St., Portland, Ore. 97209
Ute Mountain Corp., Box 3602, Englewood, Colo. 80110 (Metal Match)
Utica Duxbak Corp., 815 Noyes St., Utica, N.Y. 13502
Visa-Therm Prod., Inc., P.O. Box 486, Bridgeport, Conn. 06601 (Astro/Electr. vest)
Waffen-Frankonia, Box 380, 87 Wurzburg, W. Germany
Ward Mfg. Co., 500 Ford Blvd., Hamilton, O. 45015 (trailers)
Weinbrenner Shoe Corp., Polk St., Merrill, WI 54452
Wenzel Co., 1280 Research Blvd., St. Louis, MO 63132
Woods Bag & Canvas Co., Ltd., 16 Lake St., Ogdensburg, N.Y. 13669
Woodstream Corp., Box 327, Lititz, Pa. 17543 (Hunter Seat)
Woolrich Woolen Mills, Woolrich, Pa. 17779
Yankee Mechanics, Lacey Place, Southport, CT 06490 (hand winches)

KNIVES, AXES, HATCHETS, KNIFEMAKER'S SUPPLIES—HUNTING

Baker Forged Knives, P.O. Box 514, Hinsdale, IL 60521 (custom-made, folder $1)
L. L. Bean, Freeport, Maine 04032
Bear Archery Co., R.R. 1, Grayling, MI 49738
Lee Biggs, 3816 Via La Silva, Palo Verde, CA 92266 (custom-knives)
Ralph Bone Knife Co., 806 Avenue J, Lubbock, Tex. 79401
H. Gardner Bourne, 1252 Hope Ave., Columbus, O. 43212 (custom-knives)
Bowen Knife Co., P.O. Box 14028, Atlanta, GA 30324
L. E. "Red" Brown, 3203 Del Amo Blvd., Lakewood, CA 90712 (custom-knives)
Buck Knives, Inc., P.O. Box 1267, El Cajon, CA 92022
Busch Custom Knives, 418 Depre St., Mandeville, LA 70448
Pete Callan, 17 Sherline Ave., New Orleans, LA 70124 (custom-knives)
Camillus Cutlery Co., Main St., Camillus, NY 13031
W. R. Case Knives, 20 Russell Blvd., Bradford, Pa. 16701
Challanger Mfg. Co., 118 Pearl St., Mt. Vernon, NY 10550
Clements Custom Leathercraft, 1245 S. Pennsylvania St., Denver, CO 80203 (supplies)
Collins Brothers Div. (belt-buckle knife), see: Bowen Knife Co.
Michael Collins, Rte. 4, Batesville Rd., Woodstock, GA 30188 (custom-knives, scrimshander)
Cooper Knives, P.O. Box 1423, Burbank, CA 91505 (custom, ctlg. 50¢)
Custom Cutlery, 907 Greenwood Pl., Dalton, GA 30720
Custom Knifemaker's Supply, P.O. Box 11448, Dallas, TX 75223 (ctlg. 50¢)
Dan-D Custom Knives, Box 4479, Yuma, AZ 85364
Davis Custom Knives, North 1405 Ash, Spokane, WA 99201
Philip Day, Rte. 1, Box 465T, Bay Minetter, AL 36507 (custom-knives)
J. R. Dennard, 907 Greenwood Pl., Dalton, GA 30720 (custom-knives)
D'Holder Custom Knives, 6808 N. 30th Dr., Phoenix, AZ 85017
Chas. E. Dickey, 803 N.E. A St., Bentonville, AR 72712 (custom-knives)
T. M. Dowell, 139 St. Helen's Pl., Bend, OR 97701 (TMD custom-knives, ctlg. $1)
Rob. Dozier, P.O. Box 58, Palmetto, LA 71358 (custom-knives, ctlg. $1)
John Ek, 1547 NW 119th St., No. Miami, FL 33167

Eze-Lap Diamond Prods., Box 2229, Westminster, CA 92683 (knife sharpeners)
Fischer Custom Knives, Rt. 1, Box 170-M, Victoria, TX 77901
H. H. Frank, Rte. #1 Mountain Meadows, Whitefish, MT 59937 (custom-knives)
Franklin Hand-Made Knives, R.R. #2, Columbus, IN 47201
James Furlow, 2499 Brookdale Dr. N.E., Atlanta, GA 30345 (custom-knives)
Garcia Sptg. Arms Corp., 329 Alfred Ave., Teaneck, NJ 07666
Gault Present. Knives, 1626 Palma Plaza, Austin, TX 78703 (ctlg. 50¢)
Gerber Legendary Blades, 14200 S.W. 72nd St., Portland, OR 99223
Gutman Cutlery Co., Inc., 900 S. Columbus Ave., Mt. Vernon, NY 10550
H & B Forge Co., Rte. 2, Box 24, Shiloh, OH 44837 (tomahawks)
Hale Handmade Knives, 609 Henryetta St., Springdale, AR 72764
C. M. (Pete) Heath, 119 Grant St., Winnecone, WI 54986 (custom-knives)
J. A. Henckels Twinworks, 1 Westchester Plaza, Elmsford, NY 10523
Heritage Custom Knives, 2895 Seneca St., Buffalo, NY 14224
G. H. Herron, 920 Murrah Ave., Aiken, SC 29801 (custom-knives)
Hibben Knives, Box 207, Star Rte. A, Anchorage, AK 99502 (custom, ctlg. $1)
Chubby Hueske, 4808 Tamarisk Dr., Bellaire, TX 77401 (custom-knives)
Imel Custom Knives, 945 Jameson Ct., New Castle, IN 47362
Imperial Knife Assn. Co., Inc., 1776 Broadway, New York, NY 10019
Indian Ridge Traders, P.O. Box X-50, Ferndale, MI 48220
Jet-Aer Corp., 100 Sixth Ave., Paterson, NJ 07524 (G96 knives)
LaDow (Doc) Johnston, 2322 W. Country Club Parkway, Toledo, OH 43614 (custom-knives)
KA-BAR Cutlery, Inc., 5777 Grant Ave., Cleveland, OH 44105
Jon W. Kirk, 800 N. Olive, Fayetteville, AR 72701 (custom-knives)
W. Kneubuhler, P.O. Box 327, Pioneer, OH 43554 (custom-knives)
Kustom Made Knives, 418 Jolee, Richardson, TX 75080
Lile Handmade Knives, Rte. 1, Box 56, Russellville, AR 72801
LocKnife, Inc., 11717 E. 23rd St., Independence, MO 64050
R. W. Loveless, P.O. Box 7836, Arlington Sta., Riverside, CA 92503 (custom-knives, ctlg. $1)
Bob Ludwig, 1028 Pecos Ave., Port Arthur, TX 77640 (custom-knives)
Marble Arms Corp., 420 Industrial Park, Gladstone, MI 49837
H. O. McBurnette, Jr., Rte. 4, Box 337, Piedmont, AL 36272 (custom knives)
John T. Mims, 620 S. 28th Ave., Apt. 327, Hattiesburg, MS 39401 (custom-knives)
Mitchell Knives, 511 Ave. B, So. Houston, TX 77587 (custom)
W. F. Moran, Jr., Rt. 5, Frederick, MD 21701 (custom-knives, ctlg. 50¢)
Morseth Sports Equip. Co., 1705 Hiway 71N, Springdale, AR 72764 (custom-knives)
Naifeh Knives, Rte. 13, Box 380, Tulsa, OK 74107
Nolen Knives, Box 6216, Corpus Christi, TX 78411 (custom-made, ctlg. 50¢)
Normark Corp., 1710 E. 78th St., Minneapolis, MN 55423
Ogg Custom Knives, Rt. 1, Box 230, Paris, AR 72855
Olsen Knife Co., Inc., 7 Joy St., Howard City, MI 49329
Ramrod Knife & Gun Shop, Route 5, State Road 3 North, Newcastle, IN 47362 (custom-knives)
Randall-Made Knives, Box 1988, Orlando, FL 32802 (ctlg. 25¢)
Razor Edge, Box 203, Butler, WI 53007 (knife sharpener)
F. J. Richtig, Clarkson, NB 68629 (custom-knives)
Rigid Knives, P.O. Box 460, Santee, CA 92071 (custom-made)
Ruana Knife Works, Box 574, Bonner, MT 59823 (ctlg. 50¢)
A. G. Russell, 1705 Hiwy. 71 N., Springdale, AR 72764
Sanders, 2358 Tyler Lane, Louisville, KY 40205 (Bahco)
Jack D. Schmier, 16787 Mulberry Ct., Fountain Valley, CA 92708 (custom-knives)
Bob Schrimsher, Custom Knifemaker's Supply, P.O. Box 11448, Dallas, TX 75223
John J. Schwarz, 41 Fifteenth St., Wellsburg, WV 26070 (custom-knives)
N. H. Schiffman Custom Knives, 963 Malibu, Pocatello, ID 83201
Shaw-Leibowitz, Rt. 1, Box 421, New Cumberland, WV 26047 (blade etchings)
C. R. Sigman, Star Rte., Box 3, Red House, WV 25168
Silver Fox Knives, 4714-44th St., Dickinson, TX 77539 (custom)
Skachet, (see: Gyrfalcon Inc.)
Smith & Wesson, 2100 Roosevelt Ave., Springfield, MA 01101
John T. Smith, 6048 Cedar Crest Dr., So. Haven, MS 38671 (custom-knives)
W. J. Sonneville, 1050 Chalet Dr. W., Mobile, AL 36608 (custom-knives)
Bernard Sparks, Box 32, Dingle, ID 83233 (custom-knives)
Stone Knives, 703 Floyd Rd., Richardson, TX 75080
Thompson/Center, P.O. Box 2405, Rochester, NH 03867
Dwight L. Towell, Rt. 1, Midvale, ID 83645 (custom knives)
Track Knives, 1313 2nd St., Whitefish, MT 59937
Tru-Balance Knife Co., 2115 Tremont Blvd., Grand Rapids, MI 49504
True-Temper, 1623 Euclid, Cleveland, OH 44100 (handaxes and hatchets only)
Unique Inventions, Inc., 3727 W. Alabama St., Houston, TX 77027 (throwing knife)
W-K Knives, P.O. Box 327, Pioneer, OH 43554
Western Cutlery Co., 5311 Western Ave., Boulder, CO 80302
W. C. Wilber, 400 Lucerne Dr., Spartanburg, SC 29302 (custom knives)
Ronnie Wilson, P.O. Box 2012, Weirton, WV 26062 (custom-knives)
Don Zaccagnino, P.O. Box Zack, Pahokee, FL 33476 (custom-knives)

LABELS, BOXES, CARTRIDGE HOLDERS

Milton Brynin, Box 162, Fleetwood Station, Mount Vernon, NY 10552 (cartridge box labels)
E-Z Loader, Del Rey Products, P.O. Box 91561, Los Angeles, CA 90009
Jasco, J. A. Somers Co., P.O. Box 49751, Los Angeles, CA 90049 (cartridge box labels)
Peterson Label Co., P.O. Box 186, Redding Ridge, CT 06876 (cartridge box labels; Targ-Dots)
N. H. Schiffman, 963 Malibu, Pocatello, ID 83201 (cartridge carrier)
Shooters Supplies, 1251 Blair Ave., St. Paul, MN 55104 (cartridge and shotshell boxes)

LOAD TESTING & CHRONOGRAPHING

Carter Gun Works, 2211 Jefferson Pk. Ave., Charlottesville, Va. 22903
Custom Ballistics' Lab., 3354 Cumberland Dr., San Angelo, Tex. 76901
Horton Ballistics, North Waterford, Me. 04267
Hutton Rifle Ranch, Box 898, Topanga, CA 90290
Jurras Co., Box 163, Shelbyville, Ind. 46176
Kennon's, 5408 Biffle, Stone Mountain, Ga. 30083
NeSal Enterprises, Box 126, Meriden Rte., Cheyenne, WY 82001
Plum City Ballistics Range, Rte. 1, Box 29A, Plum City, Wis. 54761
H. P. White Lab., Box 331, Bel Air, Md. 21014

MISCELLANEOUS

Accurizing Service, Herbert G. Troester, Cayuaga, ND 58013
Action Sleeves, Alvin L. Davidson, 1215 Branson, Las Cruces, NM 88001
Adhesive Flannel, Forest City Prod., 722 Bolivar, Cleveland, OH 44115
Archery, Bear Co., R.R. 1, Grayling, Mich. 49738
Arms Restoration, J. J. Jenkins, 462 Stanford Pl., Santa Barbara, CA 93105
Barrel Band Swivels, Phil Judd, 83 E. Park St., Butte, Mont. 59701
Bedding Kit, Bisonite Co., P.O. Box 84, Kenmore Station, Buffalo, NY 14217
Bedding Kit, Fenwal, Inc., Resin Systems Div., 400 Main St., Ashland, Mass. 01721
Bootdryers, Baekgaard Ltd., 1855 Janke Dr., Northbrook, Ill. 60062
Breech Plug Wrench, Swaine Machine, 195 O'Connell, Providence, R.I. 02905
Cannons, South Bend Replicas Inc., 61650 Oak Rd., S. Bend, IN 46614 (ctlg. $1.50)
Case Gauge, Plum City Ballistics Range, Rte. 1, Box 29A, Plum City, Wis. 54761
Chrome Brl. Lining, Marker Mach. Co., Box 426, Charleston, Ill. 61920
Color Hardening, Alamo Heat Treating Co., Box 55345, Houston, Tex. 77055
Crow Caller, Wightman Elec. Inc., Box 989, Easton, Md. 21601
Distress Flares, Marsh Coulter Co., P.O. Box 333, Tecumseh, MI 49286
Dog House, Canine Pal Sales, 421 E. 39th Ave., Gary, Ind. 46409 (portable)
Dryer, Thermo-Electric, Golden-Rod, Phinney-Hale, Inc., Box 5286, Oxnard, CA 93030
E-Z Loader, Del Rey Prod., P.O. Box 91561, Los Angeles, CA 90009
Ear-Valv, Sigma Eng. Co., 11320 Burbank Blvd., N. Hollywood, Cal. 91601 (Lee-Sonic)
Emergency Food, Chuck Wagon, Micro Dr., Woburn, Mass. 01801
Fill N'File, Apsco Packaging Co., 9325 W. Bryon St., Schiller Park, IL 60176
Flares, Colt Industries, Huyshope Ave., Hartford, Conn. 06102
Flares, Intercontinental Arms, 2222 Barry Ave., Los Angeles, Ca. 90064 (MBA)
Flares, Smith & Wesson Chemical Co., 2399 Forman Rd., Rock Creek, OH 44084
Flat Springs, Alamo Heat Treating Co., Box 55345, Houston, Tex. 77055
Game Hoist, Cam Gear Ind., P.O. Box 1002, Kalispell, MT 59901 (Sportsmaster 500 pocket hoist)
Game Hoist, PIC, 3 Chestnut, Suffern, N.Y. 10901
Game Scent, Buck Stop, Inc., 3015 Grow Rd., Stanton, Mi 48888
Game Scent, Pete Rickard, Box 1250, Cobleskill, NY 12043 (Indian Buck lure)
Gas Pistol, Penguin Ind., Inc., Box 97, Parkesburg, Pa. 19365
Golden-Rod, Phinney-Hale, Inc., P.O. Box 5286, Oxnard, CA 93030 (Thermo-Electric Dryers)
Gun Bedding Kit, Resin Systems Div., Fenwal, Inc., 400 Main St., Ashland, Mass. 01721
Gun Jewelry, Sid Bell Originals, R.D. 2, Tully, NY 13159
Gun Jewelry, Al Popper, 614 Turnpike St., Stoughton, Mass. 02072
Gun Lock, E & C Enterprises, 9582 Bickley Dr., Huntington Beach, CA 92646
Gun Sling, Kwikfire, Wayne Prods. Co., P.O. Box 247, Camp Hill, PA 17011
Gun Slings, Torel, Inc., 1053 N. South St., Yoakum, TX 77995
Hand-Plucks f. game birds, Hageman Corp., 102 5th St., Arbuckle, CA 95912
Hat Saver Co., Inc., P.O. Box 307, Rosenberg, TX 77471
Hollow Pointer, Goerg Ent., 3009 S. Laurel St., Port Angeles, Wash. 98362
Hugger Hooks, Roman Products, Box 860, Golden, Colo. 80401
Insect Repellent, Armor, Div. of Buck Stop, Inc., 3015 Grow Rd., Stanton, Mich. 48888
Insert Barrels, (22 RF), H. Owen, P.O. Box 774, Sunnyvale, Calif. 94088
Lightnin-Loader, Hunter Mfg. Co., Box 2882, Van Nuys, Cal. 91404
Locks, Gun, Bor-Lok Prods., 105 5th St., Arbuckle, CA 95912
Locks, Gun, Master Lock Co., 2600 N. 32nd St., Milwaukee, WI 53245
Military Museum, Lt. Col. E.H. Hoffman, 768 So. Main St., Woodstock, Va. 22664

Miniature Cannons, A & K Mfg. Co., 5146 E. Pima, Tucson, AZ 85712
Miniature Guns, C. H. Stoppler, 1426 Walton Ave., N.Y., N.Y. 10452
Monte Carlo Pad, Frank A. Hoppe Div., P.O. Box 97, Parkesburg, Pa. 19365
Muzzle-Top, Allen Assoc., 7502 Limekiln, Philadelphia, PA 19150 (plastic gun muzzle cap)
Pell Remover, A. Edw. Terpening, 838 E. Darlington Rd., Tarpon Springs, FL 33589
Pockethoist, Cam-Gear Industries, Inc., P.O. Box 1002, Kalispell, MT 59901 (Sportsmaster 500)
Powder Storage Magazine, C & M Gunworks, 2603 41st St., Moline, IL 61265
Pressure Testg. Machine, M. York, 19381 Keymar Way, Gaithersburg, MD 20760
Ransom Handgun Rests, C'Arco, P.O. Box 2043, San Bernardino, CA 92406
Retriev-R-Trainer, Scientific Prods. Corp., 426 Swann Ave., Alexandria, VA 22301
Rifle Slings, Bianchi, 212 W. Foothill Blvd., Monrovia, Cal. 91016
Rifle Sling, Ready Sling Co., P.O. Box 536, Delano, CA 93215
RIG, NRA Scoring Plug, Rig Prod. Co., Box 279, Oregon, Ill. 60161
Rubber Cheekpiece, W. H. Lodewick, 2816 N. E. Halsey, Portland, Ore. 97232
Safeties, Williams Gun Sight Co., 7389 Lapeer Rd., Davison, Mich. 48423
Salute Cannons, Naval Co., R.D. 2, Doylestown, PA 18901
Sav-Bore, Saunders Sptg. Gds., 338 Somerset St., N. Plainfield, NJ 07060
Scrimshaw Engraving, C. Milton Barringer, 217-2nd Isle N., Port Richey, FL 33568
Scrimshaw Engraving, A. Douglas Jacobs, Box 1236, Cutchogue, NY 11935
Sharpening Stones, Russell's Arkansas Oilstones, 1705 Hiway 71N., Springdale, AR 72764
Shell Shrinker Mfg. Co., Box 6143, Lubbock, Tex. 79413
Shok-Baton Co., 440 W. Nixon St., Savage, MN 55378
Shooting Bench/Porto, Seyferth's, Inc., 926 N. Memorial Dr., Racine, WI 53404
Shooting Coats, 10-X Mfg. Co., 6185 Arapahoe, Boulder, CO 80303
Shooting Ranges, Shooting Equip. Inc., 10 S. LaSalle, Chicago, IL 60603
Shotgun Sight, bi-ocular, Trius Prod., Box 25, Cleves, O. 45002
Silver Grip Caps, Bill Dyer, P.O. Box 75255, Oklahoma City, Okla. 73107
Snap Caps, Filmat, 200 Market, East Paterson, N.J. 07407
Snap Caps, Frank's Mach. Shop, 11529 Tecumseh-Clinton Rd., Clinton, MI 49236
Snowshoes, Sportsmen Prod. Inc., Box 1082, Boulder, Colo. 80302
Springfield Safety Pin, B-Square Co., P.O. Box 11281, Ft. Worth, Tex. 76110
Springs, W. Wolff Co., Box 232, Ardmore, Pa. 19003
Supersound, Edmund Scientific Co., 101 E. Gloucester Pike, Barrington, NJ 08007 (safety device)
Swivels, Michaels, P.O. Box 13010, Portland, Ore. 97213
Swivels, Sile Dist., 7 Centre Market Pl., New York, N.Y. 10013
Swivels, Williams Gun Sight Co., 7389 Lapeer Rd., Davison, Mich. 48423
Targ-It Stamp Co., Box G, Emlenton, PA 16373 (rubber stamp target makers)
Trophies, L. G. Balfour Co., Attleboro, Mass. 02703
Trophies, Blackinton & Co., 140 Commonwealth, Attleboro Falls, Mass. 02763
Trophies, F. H. Noble & Co., 559 W. 59th St., Chicago, Ill. 60621
Universal 3-shot Shotgun Plug, LanDav Custom Guns, 7213 Lee Highway, Falls Church, VA 22046
World Hunting Info., Jack Atcheson & Sons, Inc., 3210 Ottawa St., Butte, MT 59701
World Hunting Info., Denver Jonas Bros., 1037 Broadway, Denver, CO 80203
World Hunting Info., Wayne Preston, Inc., 3444 Northhaven Rd., Dallas, TX 75229

MUZZLE-LOADING GUNS, BARRELS OR EQUIPMENT

Luther Adkins, Box 281, Shelbyville, Ind. 47176 (breech plugs)
Anderson & Co., 1203 Broadway, Yakima, WA 98902
Armoury, Inc., Rte. 25, New Preston, Conn. 06777
Beaver Lodge, 9245 16th Ave. S.W., Seattle, WA 98106
John Bivins, Jr., 200 Wicklow Rd., Winston-Salem, NC 27106
Blue and Gray Prods., Inc., 817 E. Main St., Bradford, PA 16701
G. S. Bunch, 7735 Garrison, Hyattsville, Md. 20784 (flask repair)
Caution Tool Co., Scout Rd., Southbury, CT 06488
Challanger Mfg. Co., 118 Pearl St., Mt. Vernon, NY 10550
Cherry Corners Mfg. Co., 11136 Congress Rd., Lodi, Ohio 44254
Chopie Mfg. Inc., 531 Copeland Ave., LaCrosse, WI 54601 (nipple wrenches)
Cornwall Bridge Gun Shop, P.O. Box 67, Cornwall Bridge, CT 06745
Earl T. Cureton, Rte. 6, 7017 Pine Grove Rd., Knoxville, Tenn. 37914 (powder horns)
John N. Dangelzer, 3056 Frontier Pl. N.E., Albuquerque, N. Mex. 87106 (powder flasks)
Dixie Gun Works, Inc., P.O. Box 130, Union City, TN 38261
Ted Fellowes, Beaver Lodge, 9245 16th Ave. S.W., Seattle, Wash. 98106
Firearms Imp. & Exp. Corp., 2470 N.W. 21st St., Miami, Fla. 33142
Clark K. Frazier/Matchmate, RFD. 1, Rawson, OH 45881
Golden Age Arms Co., 14 W. Winter St., Delaware, OH 43015 (ctlg. $1.50)
Golden Strip Enterprises, Box 457, Simpsonville, SC 29681 (powder horns)
A. R. Goode, R.D. 1, Box 84, Thurmont, MD 21788
Green River Forge, 4326 120th Ave. S.E., Bellevue, WA 98006 (Forge-Fire flints)
House of Muzzle Loading, Box 4099, Downey, CA 90241
International M. L. Parts Co., 19453 Forrer, Detroit, MI 48235 (flint and percussion parts)
JJJJ Ranch, Wm. Large, Rte. 1, Ironton, Ohio 45638
K & W Cap and Ball Dispenser, Rte. 2, 5073 Townsley Rd., Cedarville, OH 45314
Kindig's Log Cabin Sport Shop, R.D. 1, Box 275, Lodi, OH 44254
Art LeFeuvre, 1003 Hazel Ave., Deerfield, Ill. 60015 (antique gun restoring)
Les' Gun Shop (Les Bauska), Box 511, Kalispell, Mont. 59901
Lever Arms Serv. Ltd., 771 Dunsmuir, Vancouver 1, B.C., Canada
McKeown's Guns, R.R. 1, Pekin, IL 61554 (E-Z load rev. stand)
Judson E. Mariotti, Beauty Hill Rd., Barrington, NH 03825 (brass bullet mould)
Maryland Gun Exchange Inc., Rt. 40 West, RD 5, Frederick, MD 21701
Maurer Arms, 2366 Frederick Dr., Cuyahoga Falls, OH 44221 (cust. muzzleloaders)
Jos. W. Mellott, 334 Rockhill Rd., Pittsburgh, Pa. 15243 (barrel blanks)
W. L. Mowrey Gun Works, Inc., Box 28, Iowa Park, TX 76367
Numrich Corp., W. Hurley, N.Y. 12491 (powder flasks)
R. Paris & Son, R.D. 5, Box 61, Gettysburg, Pa. 17325 (barrels)
Penna. Rifle Works, 319 E. Main St., Ligonier, Pa. 15658 (ML guns, parts)
A. W. Peterson Gun Shop, 1693 Old Hwy. 441 N., Mt. Dora, FL 32757 (ML guns)
Richland Arms, 321 W. Adrian St., Blissfield, MI 49228
Rush's Old Colonial Forge, 106 Wiltshire Rd., Baltimore, MD 21221
H. M. Schoeller, 569 So. Braddock Ave., Pittsburgh, Pa. 15221
Scott and Sons, P.O. Drawer "C", Nolanville, TX 76559
Sharon Rifle Barrel Co., P.O. Box 106, Kalispell, MT 59901
Shilo Products, 37 Potter St., Farmingdale, NY 11735 (4-cavity mould)
C. E. Siler, 181 Sandhill School, Asheville, N.C., 28806 (flint locks)
Ken Steggles, 77 Lower Eastern Green Lane, Coventry, CV5 7DT, England (accessories)
Upper Missouri Trading Co., Box 191, 2nd Harold St., Crofton, NB 68730
R. Watts, 826 Springdale Rd., Atlanta, GA 30306 (ML rifles)
Thos. F. White, 5801 Westchester Ct., Worthington, O. 43085 (powder horn)
Williamson-Pate Gunsmith Serv., 6021 Camp Bowie Blvd., Ft. Worth, TX 76116
York County Gun Works, R.R. #4, Tottenham, Ont., Canada (locks)
R. E. Zellmer, W180 N8996 Leona Ln., Menomonee Falls, WI 53051 (Kentucky Fullstocks)

PISTOLSMITHS

Alamo Heat Treating, Box 55345, Houston, Tex. 77055
Allen Assoc., 7448 Limekiln Pike, Philadelphia, Pa. 19138 (speed-cock lever for 45 ACP)
Bain and Davis Sptg. Gds., 559 W. Las Tunas Dr., San Gabriel, Cal. 91776
Bar-Sto Precision Machine, 633 So. Victory Blvd., Burbank, CA 91502 (S.S. bbls. f. 45 Acp)
Behlert & Freed, Inc., 33 Herning Ave., Cranford. N.J. 07016 (short actions)
F. Bob Chow, Gun Shop, 3185 Mission, San Francisco, Calif. 94110
J.E. Clark, Rte. 2, Box 22A, Keithville, LA 71047
Custom Gunshop, 33 Herning Ave., Cranford, N.J. 07016
Day Arms Corp., 7515 Stagecoach Lane, San Antonio, Tex. 78227
Alton S. Dinan, Jr., P.O. Box 6674, Canaan, Conn. 06018
Dominic DiStefano, 4303 Friar Lane, Colorado Springs, CO 80907 (accurizing)
Dan Dwyer, 915 W. Washington, San Diego, Calif. 92103
Giles' 45 Shop, Rt. 1, Box 47, Odessa, Fla. 33556
H. H. Harris, 1237 So. State, Chicago, Ill. 60605
Gil Hebard Guns, Box 1, Knoxville, Ill. 61448
Lee E. Jurras & Assoc., Inc., P.O. Box 846, Roswell, NM 88201 (Auto Mag only)
Rudolf Marent, 9711 Tiltree, Houston, Tex. 77034 (Hammerli)
Maryland Gun Exchange, Inc., Rte. 40 W., RD 5, Frederick, MD 21701
Match Arms Co., 831 Mary St., Springdale, Pa. 15144
Pachmayr Gun Works, 1220 S. Grand Ave., Los Angeles, Calif. 90015
L. W. Seecamp, Box 255, New Haven, CT 06502 (DA Colt auto conversions)
R. L. Shockey Guns, Inc., 1614 S. Choctaw, E. Reno, Okla. 73036
Silver Dollar Guns, 7 Balsam St., Keene, N.H. 03431 (45 auto only)
Sportsmens Equipmt. Co., 915 W. Washington, San Diego, Calif. 92103
A. D. Swenson's 45 Shop, P.O. Box 606, Fallbrook, CA 92028
Doc Ulrich, 2511 S. 57th Ave., Cicero, IL 60650
Dave Woodruff, Box 5, Bear, DE 19701

REBORING AND RERIFLING

P.O. Ackley, 2235 Arbor Lane, Salt Lake City, UT 84117
Atkinson Gun Co., P.O. Box 512, Prescott, AZ 86301
Bain & Davis Sptg. Gds., 559 W. Las Tunas Dr., San Gabriel, Calif. 91776
Carpenter's Gun Works, Gunshop Rd., Plattekill, N.Y. 12568
Fuller Gun Shop, Cooper Landing, Alaska 99572
John Kaufield Small Arms Eng. Co., P.O. Box 306, Des Plaines, IL 60018
Ward Koozer, Box 18, Walterville, Ore. 97489
Les' Gun Shop, Box 511, Kalispell, Mont. 59901
Morgan's Cust. Reboring, 707 Union Ave., Grants Pass, OR 97526
Nu-Line Guns, 3727 Jennings Rd., St. Louis, Mo. 63121
Al Petersen, Box 8, Riverhurst, Saskatchewan, Canada S0H3P0
Schuetzen Gun Works, 1226 Prairie Rd., Colorado Springs, Colo. 80909
Siegrist Gun Shop, 2689 McLean Rd., Whittemore, MI 48770
Small Arms Eng., P.O. Box 306, Des Plaines, IL 60018
Snapp's Gunshop, 6911 E. Washington Rd., Clare, Mich. 48617

R. Southgate, Rt. 2, Franklin, Tenn. 37064 (Muzzleloaders)
J. W. Van Patten, Box 145, Foster Hill, Milford, Pa. 18337
Robt. G. West, Rte. 1, Box 941, Eugene, OR 97402

RELOADING TOOLS AND ACCESSORIES

Advanced Mfg. Co., Inc., 18619 W. 7 Mile Rd., Detroit, MI 48219 (super filler primer tube)
Alcan, (See: Smith & Wesson Arms Co.)
Anderson Mfg. Co., Royal, Ia. 51357 (Shotshell Trimmers)
Aurands, 229 E. 3rd St., Lewistown, Pa. 17044
B-Square Eng. Co., Box 11281, Ft. Worth, Tex. 76110
B & W Enterprises, 1206 11th Ave. N.E., Rochester, MN 55901 (Meyer shotgun slugs)
Bahler Die Shop, Rte. 1, Box 412, Hemlock, Florence, OR 97439
Bair Co., 4555 N. 48th St., Lincoln, NB 68504
Bill Ballard, P.O. Box 656, Billings, MT 59103 (ctlg. 25¢)
Belding & Mull, P.O. Box 428, Philipsburg, Pa. 16866
Belmont Prods., Rte. 1, Friendsville, TN 37737 (lead cutter)
Blackhawk SAA East, K2274 POB, Loves Park, Ill. 61111
Blackhawk SAA West, Box 285, Hiawatha, KS 66434
Bonanza Sports, Inc., 412 Western Ave., Faribault, Minn. 55021
Gene Bowlin, 3602 Hill Ave., Snyder, Tex. 79549 (arbor press)
Brown Precision Co., 5869 Indian Ave., San Jose, Calif. 95123 (Little Wiggler)
A. V. Bryant, 72 Whiting Rd., E. Hartford, CT 06118 (Nutmeg Universal Press)
C-H Tool & Die Corp., Box L, Owen, Wis. 54460
Camdex, Inc., 23880 Hoover Rd., Warren, MI 48089
Carbide Die & Mfg. Co., Box 226, Covina, CA 91724
Carter Gun Works, 2211 Jefferson Pk. Ave., Charlottesville, Va. 22903
Cascade Cartridge, Inc., (See Omark)
Clymer Mfg. Co., 14241 W. 11 Mile Rd., Oak Park, MI 48237 (½-jack. swaging dies)
Lester Coats, 416 Simpson St., No. Bend, Ore. 97459 (core cutter)
Conevera's Reloading Supplies, 5064 Dialette Dr., Rockford, IL 61102
Container Development Corp., 424 Montgomery St., Watertown, WI 53094
Continental Kite & Key Co., Box 40, Broomall, PA 19008 (primer pocket cleaner)
Cooper-Woodward, Box 972, Riverside, Calif. 92502 (Perfect Lube)
D. R. Corbin, P.O. Box 44, North Bend, OR 97459
Corey Enterprises, Inc., 4838 N. 29th St., Phoenix, AZ 85016 (Tap-It bullet puller)
Diverter Arms, Inc., 6520 Rampart St., Houston, TX 77036 (bullet puller)
Division Lead Co., 7742 W. 61st Pl., Summit, Ill. 60502
Eagle Products Co., 1520 Adelia Ave., So. El Monte, Cal. 91733
W. H. English, 4411 S. W. 100th, Seattle, Wash. 98146 (Paktool)
Farmer Bros., See: Lage
The Fergusons, R.F.D. #1, Box 143, Hillsboro, NH 03244
Fitz, Box 49697, Los Angeles, Calif. 90049 (Fitz Flipper)
Flambeau Plastics, 801 Lynn, Baraboo, Wis. 53913
Forster Products Inc., 82 E. Lanark Ave., Lanark, Ill. 61046
Gene's Gun Shop, 3602 Hill Ave., Snyder, Tex. 79549 (arbor press)
John R. Gillette, 4514 W. 123d Place, Alsip, IL 60658
Goerg Enterprises, 3009 S. Laurel, Port Angeles, WA 98362 (hollow pointer)
Gopher Shooter's Supply, Box 246, Faribault, Minn. 55021
The Gun Clinic, 81 Kale St., Mahtomedi, Minn. 55115
Hart Products, Rob. W. Hart & Son, 401 Montgomery St., Nescopeck, PA 18635
Ed Hart's Gun Supply, U.S. Rte. 15 No., Bath, NY 14810 (Meyer shotgun slugs)
Hensley & Gibbs, Box 10, Murphy, Ore. 97533
Herter's Inc., RR1, Waseca, Minn. 56093
B. E. Hodgdon, Inc., 7710 W. 50 Hiway, Shawnee Mission, Kans. 66202
Hollywood Reloading, see: Whitney Sales, Inc.
Hornady (see: Pacific)
Hulme Firearm Serv., Box 83, Millbrae, Calif. 94030 (Star case feeder)
Hunter Bradlee Co., 2800 Routh St., Dallas, TX 75201 (powder measure)
Independent Mach. & Gun Shop, 1416 N. Hayes, Pocatello, Ida. 83201
Ivy Armament, P.O. Box 10, Greendale, WI 53129 (shell case dispenser for Star and Phelps machines)
JASCO, Box 49751, Los Angeles, Calif. 90049
J & G Rifle Ranch, Box S80, Turner, MT 59542 (case tumblers)
Javelina Products, Box 337, San Bernardino, Cal. 92402 (Alox beeswax)
Kexplore, Box 22084, Houston, Tex. 77027
Kuharsky Bros. (see Modern Industries)
Lachmiller Eng. Co., 11273 Goss St., Sun Valley, CA 91352
Lac-Cum Bullet Puller, Star Route, Box 242, Apollo, PA 15613
Lage Uniwad Co., 1102 N. Washington St., Eldora, IA 50627 (Universal Shotshell Wad)
LanDav, 7213 Lee Highway, Falls Church, VA 22046 (X-15 bullet puller)
Lee Engineering, 46 E. Jackson, Hartford, Wis. 53027
Leon's Reloading Service, 3945 No. 11 St., Lincoln, Neb. 68521
Lewisystems, Container Dev. Corp., 426 Montgomery St., Watertown, WI 53094
L. L. F. Die Shop, 1281 Highway 99 N., Eugene, Ore. 97402
Dean Lincoln, P.O. Box 1886, Farmington, NM 87401 (mould)
Ljutic Industries, 918 N. 5th Ave., Yakima, Wash. 98902
Lock's Phila. Gun Exch., 6700 Rowland, Philadelphia, Pa. 19149
Lyman Gun Sight Products, Middlefield, Conn. 06455
McKillen & Heyer, Box 627, Willoughby, O. 44094 (case gauge)
Paul McLean, 2670 Lakeshore Blvd., W., Toronto 14, Ont., Canada (Universal Cartridge Holder)
Pat B. McMillan, 1828 E. Campo Bello Dr., Phoenix, Ariz. 85022
MTM Molded Prod., 5680 Webster St., Dayton, OH 45414
Magma Eng. Co., P.O. Box 881, Chandler, AZ 85224
Judson E. Mariotti, Beauty Hill Rd., Barrington, NH 03825 (brass bullet mould)
Marmel Prods., P.O. Box 97, Utica, MI 48087 (Marvelube, Marvelux)
Marquart Precision Co., Box 1740, Prescott, AZ 86301 (precision caseneck turning tool)
Mayville Eng. Co., 715 South St., Mayville, Wis. 53050 (shotshell loader)
Merit Gun Sight Co., P.O. Box 995, Sequim, Wash. 98382
Modern Industries, Inc., 613 W-11, Erie, PA 16501 (primer pocket cleaner)
Murdock Lead/RSR Corp., P.O. Box 1695, Dallas, TX 75222
National Lead Co., Box 831, Perth Amboy, N.J. 08861
Normington Co., Box 6, Rathdrum, ID 83858 (powder baffles)
Ohaus Scale Corp., 29 Hanover Rd., Florham Park, N.J. 07932
Omark-CCI, Inc., Box 856, Lewiston, Ida. 83501
Pacific Tool Co., P.O. Drawer 2048, Ordnance Plant Rd., Grand Island, NB 68801
Pak-Tool Co., 4411 S.W. 100th, Seattle, WA 98146
John Palmer, Box 35797, Houston, TX 77035
Perfection Die Co., 1614 S. Choctaw, El Reno, Okla. 73036
Personal Firearms Record Book, Box 201, Park Ridge, Ill. 60068
Ferris Pindell, R.R. 3, Box 205, Connersville, IN 47331 (bullet spinner)
Plum City Ballistics Range, Rte. 1, Box 29A, Plum City, Wis. 54761
Ponsness-Warren, Inc., P.O. Box 861, Eugene, OR 97401
Potter Eng. Co., 1410 Santa Ana Dr., Dunedin, FL 33528 (electric pots only)
Marian Powley, 19 Sugarplum Rd., Levittown, Pa. 10956
Precise Alloys Inc., 69 Kinkel St., Westbury, NY 11590 (chilled lead shot; bullet wire)
Quaco Industries Ltd., St. Martins, St. John Co., New Brunswick, Canada E0G 2Z0 (Echo dies, etc.)
Quinetics Corp., Box 13237, San Antonio, TX 78213 (kinetic bullet puller)
RCBS, Inc., Box 1919, Oroville, Calif. 95965
Redding Inc., 114 Starr Rd., Cortland, NY 13045
Remco, 1404 Whitesboro St., Utica, N.Y. 13502 (shot caps)
Rifle Ranch, Rte. 5, Prescott, Ariz. 86301
Rochester Lead Works, Rochester, N.Y. 14608 (leadwire)
Rorschach Precision Prods., P.O. Box 1613, Irving, Tex. 75060
Rotex Mfg. Co. (see Texan)
Ruhr-American Corp., So. East Hwy. 55, Glenwood, Minn. 56334
SAECO Rel. Inc., P.O. Box 778, Carpinteria, Calif. 93013
Sandia Die & Cartridge Co., Rte. 5, Box 5400, Albuquerque, NM 87123
Saunders Gun & Machine Shop, 145 Delhi Rd., Manchester, IA 52057 (primer feed tray)
Scientific Lubricants Co., 3753 Lawrence Ave., Chicago, Ill. 60625
Shilo Products, 37 Potter St., Farmingdale, NY 11735 (4-cavity bullet mould)
Shooters Accessory Supply, see: D. R. Corbin
Shooters Specialties, 8371 W. Virginia Ave., Denver, CO 80226
Sil's Gun Prod., 490 Sylvan Dr., Washington, Pa. 15301 (K-spinner)
Jerry Simmons, 713 Middlebury St., Goshen, Ind. 46526 (Pope de- & recapper)
Rob. B. Simonson, Rte. 7, 2129 Vanderbilt Rd., Kalamazoo, Mich. 49002
Smith & Wesson Ammunition Co., Inc., 2399 Forman Rd., Rock Creek, OH 44084
J. A. Somers Co., P.O. Box 49751, Los Angeles, CA 90049 (Jasco)
D. E. Stanley, P.O. Box 323, Arvin, CA 93203 (Kake-Kutter)
Star Machine Works, 418 10th Ave., San Diego, Calif. 92101
Texan Reloaders, Inc., P.O. Box 5355, Dallas, Tex. 75222
W. S. Vickerman, 505 W. 3rd Ave., Ellensburg, Wash. 98926
WAMADET, Silver Springs, Goodleigh, Barnstaple, Devon, England
Walker Mfg. Inc., 8296 So. Channel, Harsen's Island, MI 48028 (Berdan decapper)
Weatherby, Inc., 2781 Firestone Blvd., South Gate, Calif. 90280
Webster Scale Mfg. Co., Box 188, Sebring, Fla. 33870
Whits Shooting Stuff, P.O. Box 1340, Cody, WY 82414
Whitney Sales, Inc., P.O. 875, Reseda, CA 91335 (Hollywood)
L. E. Wilson, Inc., Box 324, Cashmere, Wash. 98815
Xelex, Ltd., Hawksbury, Ont., Canada (powder)
Zenith Ent., 361 Flagler Rd., Nordland, WA 98358

RESTS—BENCH, PORTABLE, ETC.

Bill Anderson, 551 Fletcher, Wayne, PA 19087
Bausch & Lomb, 635 St. Paul St., Rochester, NY 14602 (rifle rest)
Gene Beecher Prods., 2155 Demington Dr., Cleveland Hghts., OH 44106
Jim Brobst, 299 Poplar St., Hamburg, PA 19526 (bench rest pedestal)
C'Arco, P.O. Box 2043, San Bernardino, CA 92401 (Ransom handgun rest)
Central Specialties Co., 630 Northwest Hwy., Chicago, IL 60631 (portable gun rest)
Cole's Acku-Rite Prod., Box 25, Kennedy, N.Y. 14747
Decker Shooting Products, 1729 Laguna Ave., Schofield, WI 54476 (rifle rests)
F & H Machining, 4645 Cambio Ct., Fremont, CA 94536
The Fergusons, R.F.D. #1, Box 143, Hillsboro, NH 03244 (rifle rests)
Frontier Arms, Inc., 420 E. Riding Club Rd., Cheyenne, Wyo. 82001
The Gun Case, 11035 Maplefield, El Monte, Cal. 91733
GVA Enterprises, P.O. Box 725, Garland, TX 75040 (Rif-L-Vise)
Harris Engr., Inc., Box 305, Fraser, Mich. 48026 (bipods)
Rob. W. Hart & Son, 401 Montgomery St., Nescopeck, Pa. 18635
North Star Devices, Inc., P.O. Box 2095, North St. Paul, MN 55109 (Gun Slinger)
Porto/Shooting bench, Seyferth's Inc., 926 N. Memorial, Racine, WI 53404
Rec. Prods, Res., Inc., 158 Franklin Ave., Ridgewood, N.J. 07450 (Butts Pipod)

D. E. Stanley, P.O. Box 323, Arvin, CA 93203 (portable shooting rest)
Suter's, 332 Tejon, Colorado Springs, CO 80902
Basil Tuller, 29 Germania, Galeton, PA 16922 (Protector sandbags)

RIFLE BARREL MAKERS

P.O. Ackley, 2235 Arbor Lane, Salt Lake City, UT 84117
Apex Rifle Co., 7628 San Fernando, Sun Valley, Calif. 91352
Atkinson Gun Co., P.O. Box 512, Prescott, AZ 86301
Christy Gun Works, 875 57th St., Sacramento, Calif. 95819
Clerke Prods., 2219 Main St., Santa Monica, Calif. 90405
Cuthbert Gun Shop, 715 So. 5th, Coos Bay, Ore. 97420
Darr's Rifle Shop, 2309 Black Rd., Joliet, IL 60435
Douglas Barrels, Inc., 5504 Big Tyler Rd., Charleston, W. Va. 25312
Douglas Jackalope Gun & Sport Shop, Inc., 1205 E. Richards St., Douglas, WY 82633
Federal Firearms Co., Inc., Box 145, Oakdale, Pa. 15071 (Star bbls., actions)
A. R. Goode, R.D. 1, Box 84, Thurmont, MD 21788
Hart Rifle Barrels, Inc., RD 2, Lafayette, N.Y. 13084
Wm. H. Hobaugh, Box 657, Philipsburg, Mont. 59858
Intern'l Casting Co., 19453 Forrer, Detroit, Mich. 48235
Gene Lechner, 636 Jane N.E., Albuquerque, NM 87123
Les' Gun Shop, Box 511, Kalispell, Mont. 59901
McGowen Rifle Barrels, Rte. 3, St. Anne, Ill. 60964
D. M. Manley, 295 Main St., Brookville, PA 15825
Marquart Precision Co., Box 1740, Prescott, AZ 86301
Nu-Line Guns, Inc., 3727 Jennings Rd., St. Louis, Mo. 63121
Numrich Arms, W. Hurley, N.Y. 12491
R. Paris & Son, R.D. 5, Box 61, Gettysburg, Pa. 17325
Al Petersen, The Rifle Ranch, Box 8, Riverhurst, Sask., Canada SOH3PO
Rheinmetall (see John Weir)
Sanders Cust. Gun Serv., 2358 Tyler Lane, Louisville, Ky. 40205
Scotty's Gun Shop, 534 E. Hwy 190, Harker Heights, TX 76541
Sharon Rifle Barrel Co., P.O. Box 106, Kalispell, MT 59901
Ed Shilen Rifles, Inc., 205 Metropark Blvd., Ennis, TX 75119
W. C. Strutz, Rte. 1, Eagle River, WI 54521
Titus Barrel & Gun Co., R.F.D. #1, Box 23, Heber City, UT 84032
John E. Weir, 3304 Norton Ave., Independence, Mo. 64052
Wilson Arms, 63 Leetes Island Rd., Branford, CT 06405

SCOPES, MOUNTS, ACCESSORIES, OPTICAL EQUIPMENT

Alley Supply Co., Carson Valley Industrial Park, Gardnerville, NV 89410 (Scope collimator)
American Import Co., 1167 Mission, San Francisco, Calif. 94103
Anderson & Co., 1203 Broadway, Yakima, Wash. 98902 (lens cap)
Avery Corp., P.O. Box 99, Electra, TX 76360 (Mini-Light)
Ball-One Buck Scope Lens Cover, Box 426, Midway City, CA 92655
Bausch & Lomb Inc., 635 St. Paul St., Rochester, N.Y. 14602
Bennett, 561 Delaware, Delmar, N.Y. 12054 (mounting wrench)
Bridge Mount Co., Box 3344, Lubbock, Tex. 79410 (one-piece target mts.)
Browning Arms, Rt. 4, Box 624-B, Arnold, Mo. 63010
Maynard P. Buehler, Inc., 17 Orinda Highway, Orinda, Calif. 94563
Burris Co., 351 E. 8th St., Greeley, CO 80631
Bushnell Optical Co., 2828 E. Foothill Blvd., Pasadena, Calif. 91107
Kenneth Clark, 18738 Highway 99, Madera, Calif. 93637
Clearview Mfg. Co., Inc., 23702 Crossley, Hazel Park, MI 48030 (mounts)
Clear View Sports Shields, P.O. Box 255, Wethersfield, CT 06107 (shooting/testing glasses)
Colt's, Hartford, Conn. 06102
Compass Instr. & Optical Co., Inc., 104 E 25th St., New York, N.Y. 10010
Conetrol, Hwy 123 South, Seguin, Tex. 78155
Continental Arms Corp., 697-5th Ave., New York, N.Y. 10022 (Nickel)
Davis Optical Co., P.O. Box 6, Winchester, Ind. 47934
Del-Sports Inc., Main St., Margaretville, NY 12455 (Habicht)
M. B. Dinsmore, Box 21, Wyomissing, PA 19610 (shooting glasses)
Eder Instrument Co., 5115 N. Ravenswood, Chicago, IL 60640 (borescope)
Flaig's, Babcock Blvd., Millvale, Pa. 15209
Freeland's Scope Stands, Inc. 3734 14th, Rock Island, Ill. 61201
Griffin & Howe, Inc., 589-8th Ave., New York, N.Y. 10017
Herter's Inc., Waseca, Minn. 56093
J. B. Holden Co., Box 393, 603 Aurelia, Plymouth, MI 48170
The Hutson Corp., P.O. 1127, Arlington, Tex. 76010
Hy-Score Arms Corp., 200 Tillary St., Brooklyn, N.Y. 11201
Paul Jaeger, 211 Leedom St., Jenkintown, Pa. 19046 (Nickel)
Jana Intl. Co., Box 1107, Denver, Colo. 80201
Jason Empire Inc., 9200 Cody, Overland Park, KS 66214
Jeffredo Gunsight Co., 1629 Via Monserate, Fallbrook, CA 92028
Kesselring Gun Shop, 400 Pacific Hiway 99 No, Burlington, Wash. 98283
Kris Mounts, 108 Lehigh St., Johnstown, PA 15905
Kuharsky Bros. (see Modern Industries)
Kwik-Site, 27367 Michigan Ave., Inkster, MI 48141 (rings, mounts only)
LanDav, 7213 Lee Highway, Falls Church, VA 22046 (steel leverlock side mt.)
T. K. Lee, Box 2123, Birmingham, Ala. 35201 (reticles)
E. Leitz, Inc., Rockleigh, N.J. 07647
Leupold & Stevens Inc., P.O. Box 688, Beaverton, Ore. 97005
Jake Levin and Son, Inc., 9200 Cody, Overland Park, KS 66214
W. H. Lodewick, 2816 N.E. Halsey, Portland, OR 97232 (scope safeties)
Lyman Gun Sight Products, Middlefield, Conn. 06455
Marble Arms Co., 420 Industrial Park, Gladstone, MI 49837
Marlin Firearms Co., 100 Kenna Dr., New Haven, Conn. 06473
Mitchell's Shooting Glasses, Box 539, Waynesville, MO 65583
Modern Industries, Inc., 613 W-11, Erie, PA 16501
O. F. Mossberg & Sons, Inc., 7 Grasso Ave., North Haven, Conn. 06473
Normark Corp., 1710 E. 78th St., Minneapolis, Minn. 55423 (Singlepoint)
Numrich Arms, West Hurley, N.Y. 12491
Nydar Div., Swain Nelson Co., Box 45, Glenview, Ill. 60025 (shotgun sight)
PGS, Peters' Inc., 622 Gratiot Ave., Saginaw, Mich. 48602 (scope shields)
Pachmayr Gun Works, 1220 S. Grand Ave., Los Angeles, Calif. 90015
Pacific Tool Co., P.O. Drawer 2048, Ordnance Plant Rd., Grand Island, NB 68801
Ed Paul's Sptg. Goods, Inc., 172 Flatbush Ave., Brooklyn, N.Y. 11217 (Tops)
Precise Imports Corp., 3 Chestnut, Suffern, N.Y. 10901 (PIC)
Ranging Inc., P.O. Box 9106, Rochester, N.Y. 14625
Ray-O-Vac, Willson Prod. Div., P.O. Box 622, Reading, PA 19603 (shooting glasses)
Realist, Inc., N. 93 W. 16288, Megal Dr., Menomonee Falls, Wis. 53051
Redfield Gun Sight Co., 5800 E. Jewell Ave., Denver, Colo. 80222
S & K Mfg. Co., Box 247, Pittsfield, Pa. 16340 (Insta-mount)
Sanders Cust. Gun Serv., 2358 Tyler Lane, Louisville, Ky. 40205 (MSW)
Saunders Gun & Machine Shop, 145 Delhi Rd., Manchester, IA 52057 (lens caps)
Savage Arms, Westfield, Mass. 01085
Sears, Roebuck & Co., 825 S. St. Louis, Chicago, Ill. 60607
Sherwood Distr., Inc., 18714 Parthenia St., Northridge, CA 91324 (mounts)
W. H. Siebert, 22720 S.E. 56th Pl., Issaquah, WA 98027
Singlepoint (see Normark)
Southern Precision Inst. Co., 3419 E. Commerce St., San Antonio, TX 78219
Spacetron Inc., Box 84, Broadview, IL 60155 (bore lamp)
Stoeger Arms Co., 55 Ruta Ct., S. Hackensack, N.J. 07606
Supreme Lens Covers, Box GG, Jackson Hole, WY 83001 (lens caps)
Swift Instruments, Inc., 952 Dorchester Ave., Boston, Mass. 02125
Tasco, 1075 N.W. 71st, Miami, Fla. 33138
Thompson-Center Arms, P.O. Box 2405, Rochester, N.H. 03867 (handgun scope)
Tradewinds, Inc., Box 1191, Tacoma, Wash. 98401
John Unertl Optical Co., 3551-5 East St., Pittsburgh, Pa. 15214
United Binocular Co., 9043 S. Western Ave., Chicago, Ill. 60620
Universal Firearms Corp., 3746 E. 10th Ct., Hialeah, Fla. 33013
Vissing (see: Supreme Lens Covers)
H. P. Wasson, P.O. Box 1286, Homestead, FL 33030 (eyeglass apertures)
Weatherby's, 2781 Firestone, South Gate, Calif. 90280
W. R. Weaver Co., 7125 Industrial Ave., El Paso, Tex. 79915
Wein Prods. Inc., 115 W. 25th St., Los Angeles, CA 90007 (Cronoscope)
Williams Gun Sight Co., 7389 Lapeer Rd., Davison, Mich. 48423
Willrich Precision Instrument Co., 37-13 Broadway, Rte. 4, Fair Lawn, NJ 07410 (borescope)
Carl Zeiss Inc., 444 Fifth Ave., New York, N.Y. 10018 (Hensoldt)

SIGHTS, METALLIC

B-Square Eng. Co., Box 11281, Ft. Worth, Tex. 76110
Bo-Mar Tool & Mfg. Co., Box 168, Carthage, Tex. 75633
Maynard P. Buehler, Inc., 17 Orinda Highway, Orinda, Calif. 94563
Christy Gun Works, 875 57th St., Sacramento, Calif. 95819
Cornwall Bridge Gun Shop, P.O. Box 67, Cornwall Bridge, CT 06754 (vernier)
E-Z Mount, Ruelle Bros., P.O. Box 114, Ferndale, MT 48220
Firearms Dev. Lab., 360 Mt. Ida Rd., Oroville, CA 95965 (F. D. L. Wondersight)
Freeland's Scope Stands, Inc., 3734-14th Ave., Rock Island, Ill. 61201
Paul T. Haberly, 2364 N. Neva, Chicago, IL 60635
Paul Jaeger, Inc., 211 Leedom St., Jenkintown, PA 19046
Lyman Gun Sight Products, Middlefield, Conn. 06455
Marble Arms Corp., 420 Industrial Park, Gladstone, Mich. 49837
Merit Gunsight Co., P.O. Box 995, Sequim, Wash. 98382
Micro Sight Co., 242 Harbor Blvd., Belmont, Calif. 94002
Miniature Machine Co., 212 E. Spruce, Deming, N.M. 88030
Modern Industries, Inc., 613 W-11, Erie, PA 16501
C. R. Pedersen & Son, Ludington, Mich. 49431
Poly Choke Co., Inc., P.O. Box 296, Hartford, CT 06101
Redfield Gun Sight Co., 5800 E. Jewell St., Denver, Colo. 80222
Schwarz's Gun Shop, 41 - 15th St., Wellsburg, W. Va. 26070
Simmons Gun Specialties, Inc., 700 Rodgers Rd., Olathe, Kans. 66061
Slug Site Co., Box 268, Nesswa, MN 56468
Sport Service Center, 2364 N. Neva, Chicago, IL 60635
Tradewinds, Inc., Box 1191, Tacoma, WA 98401
Williams Gun Sight Co., 7389 Lapeer Rd., Davison, Mich. 48423

STOCKS (Commercial and Custom)

Abe and VanHorn, 5124 Huntington Dr., Los Angeles, CA 90032
Adams Custom Gun Stocks, 13461 Quito Rd., Saratoga, CA 95070
Ahlman's Inc., R.R. 1, Box 20, Morristown, MN 55052
Anderson's Guns, Jim Jares, 706 S. 23rd St., Laramie, WY 82070
Dale P. Andrews, 3572 E. Davies, Littleton, CO 80122
R. J. Anton, 874 Olympic Dr., Waterloo, IA 50701
Austrian Gunworks Reg'd., P.O. Box 136, Eastman, Que., Canada, J0E 1P0
Jim Baiar, Rt. 1-B, Box 352, Columbia Falls, Mont. 59912
Joe J. Balickie, Custom Stocks, 6108 Deerwood Pl., Raleigh, N.C. 27607
Bartas, Rte. 1, Box 129-A, Cato, Wis. 54206
John Bianchi, 212 W. Foothill Blvd., Monrovia, Calif. 91016 (U. S. carbines)

Al Biesen, West 2039 Sinto Ave., Spokane, Wash. 99201
Stephen L. Billeb, Rte. 3, Box 163, Bozeman, MT 59715
E. C. Bishop & Son Inc., Box 7, Warsaw, Mo. 65355
Nate Bishop, Box 334, Minturn, CO 81645
Kay H. Bowles, Pinedale, Wyo. 82941
Brown Precision Co., 5869 Indian Ave., San Jose, CA 95123
Lenard M. Brownell, Box 25, Wyarno, WY 82845
Calico Hardwoods, Inc., 1648 Airport Blvd., Windsor, Calif. 95492 (blanks)
Dick Campbell, 1445 So. Meade, Denver, Colo. 80219
Winston Churchill, 55 High St., Ludlow, VT 05149
Cloward's Gun Shop, 4023 Aurora Ave. N., Seattle, WA 98102
Mike Conner, Box 2383, Juneau, AK 99803
Crane Creek Gun Stock Co., 25 Shephard Terr., Madison, WI 53705
Crest Carving Co., 8091 Bolsa Ave., Midway City, CA 92655
Charles De Veto, 1087 Irene Rd., Lyndhurst, O. 44124
Custom Gunstocks, 1445 So. Meade, Denver, Colo. 80219
Reinhart Fajen, Box 338, Warsaw, Mo. 65355
N. B. Fashingbauer, Box 366, Lac Du Flambeau, Wis. 54538
Ted Fellowes, Beaver Lodge, 9245 16th Ave. S. W., Seattle, Wash. 98106
Clyde E. Fischer, Rt. 1, Box 170-M, Victoria, Tex. 77901
Jerry Fisher, 1244-4th Ave. W., Kalispell, MT 59901
Flaig's Lodge, Millvale, Pa. 15209
Donald E. Folks, 205 W. Lincoln St., Pontiac, IL 61764
Horace M. Frantz, Box 128, Farmingdale, N.J. 07727
Freeland's Scope Stands, Inc., 3734 14th Ave., Rock Island, Ill. 61201
Aaron T. Gates, 3229 Felton St., San Diego, Calif. 92104
Dale Goens, Box 224, Cedar Crest, N.M. 87008
Gary Goudy, 263 Hedge Rd., Menlo Park, CA 44025
Gould's Myrtlewood, 1692 N. Dogwood, Coquille, Ore. 97423 (gun blanks)
Rolf R. Gruning, 315 Busby Dr., San Antonio, Tex. 78209
Gunwoods (N.Z.) Ltd., Box 18505, New Brighton, Christchurch, New Zealand (blanks)
Half Moon Rifle Shop, Rte. 1B, Box 352, Columbia Falls, MT 59912
Harper's Custom Stocks, 928 Lombrano St., San Antonio, Tex. 78207
Harris Gun Stocks, Inc., 12 Lake St., Richfield Springs, N.Y. 13439
Hal Hartley, 147 Blairsfork Rd., Lenoir, NC 28654
Hayes Gunstock Service Co., 914 E. Turner St., Clearwater, Fla. 33516
Hubert J. Hecht, 55 Rose Mead Circle, Sacramento, CA 95831
Edward O. Hefti, 300 Fairview, College Sta., Tex. 77840
Herter's Inc., Waseca, Minn. 56093
Klaus Hiptmayer, P.O. Box 136, Eastman, Que., Canada
Richard Hodgson, 9081 Tahoe Lane, Boulder, CO 80301
Hollis Gun Shop, 917 Rex St., Carlsbad, N.M. 88220
Jack's Walnut Woods, 10333 San Fernando Rd., Pacoima, CA 91331 (English and Claro blanks)
Jackson's, Box 416, Selman City, Tex. 75689 (blanks)
Paul Jaeger, 211 Leedom St., Jenkintown, Pa. 19046
I. D. Johnson, Rt. 1, Strawberry Point, Ia. 52076 (blanks)
Johnson's Gun Shop, 1316 N. Blackstone, Fresno, CA 93703
Monte Kennedy, P.O. Box 214, Kalispell, MT 59901
Leer's Gun Barn, Rt. 3, Sycamore Hills, Elwood, Ind. 46036
LeFever Arms Co., Inc., R.D. 1, Lee Center, N.Y. 13363
Bill McGuire, Inc., 10324 Valmay Ave., N.W., Seattle, WA 98177
Maryland Gun Exchange, Rd., 5, Rt. 40 W., Frederick MD 21701
Maurer Arms, 2366 Frederick Dr., Cuyahoga Falls, O. 44221
Leonard Mews, Spring Rd., Box 242, Hortonville, WI 54944
Robt. U. Milhoan & Son, Rt. 3, Elizabeth, W. Va. 26143
C. D. Miller Guns, St. Onge, S.D. 57779
Mills (D.H.) Custom Stocks, 401 N. Ellsworth Ave., San Mateo, Calif. 94401
Nelsen's Gun Shop, 501 S. Wilson, Olympia, Wash. 98501
Oakley and Merkley, Box 2446, Sacramento, CA 95811 (blanks)
Maurice Ottmar, Box 657, Coulee City, WA 99115
Pachmayr Gun Works, 1220 S. Grand Ave., Los Angeles, CA 90015 (blanks and custom jobs)
Ernest O. Paulsen, Rte. 71, Box 11, Chinook, MT 59523 (blanks)
Peterson Mach. Carving, Box 1065, Sun Valley, Calif. 91352
Andrew Redmond, Inc., No. Anson, Me. 04958 (birchwood blanks)
R. Neal Rice, Box 12172, Denver, CO 80212
Richards Micro-Fit Stocks, P.O. Box 1066, Sun Valley, CA. 91352 (thumbhole)
Roberts Gunstocks, 1400 Melody Rd., Marysville, Calif. 95901
Carl Roth, Jr., P.O. Box 2593, Cheyenne, Wy. 82001
Royal Arms, Inc., 10064 Bert Acosta Ct., Santee, Calif. 92071
Sanders Cust. Gun Serv., 2358 Tyler Lane, Louisville, Ky. 40205 (blanks)
Saratoga Arms Co., R.D. 3, Box 387, Pottstown, Pa. 19464
Roy Schaefer, 965 W. Hilliard Lane, Eugene, Ore. 97402 (blanks)
Shaw's, Rt. 4, Box 407-L, Escondido, CA 92025
Hank Shows, The Best, 1202 N. State, Ukaih, CA 95482
Walter Shultz, R.D. 3, Pottstown, Pa. 19464
Sile Dist., 7 Centre Market Pl., New York, N.Y. 10013
Ed Sowers, 8331 DeCelis Pl., Sepulveda, Calif. 91343
Sportsmen's Equip. Co., 915 W. Washington, San Diego, Calif. 92103 (carbine conversions)
Keith Stegall, Box 696, Gunnison, Colo. 81230
Stinehour Rifles, Box 84, Cragsmoor, N.Y. 12420
Surf N' Sea, Inc., 62-595 Kam Hwy., Box 268, Haleiwa, HI 96712 (custom gunstocks blanks)
Swanson Cust. Firearms, 1051 Broadway, Denver, Colo. 80203
Talmage Enterpr., 43197 E. Whittier, Hemet, CA 92343
Trevallion Gunstocks, 3442 S. Post Rd., Indianapolis, IN 46239
Brent L. Umberger, Sportsman's Haven, R.R. 4, Cambridge, OH 43725
Roy Vail, Rt. 1, Box 8, Warwick, N.Y. 10990
Harold Waller, 1288 Camillo Way, El Cajon, CA 92021
Weatherby's, 2781 Firestone, South Gate, Calif. 90280
Frank R. Wells, 2832 W. Milton Rd., Tucson, AZ 85706 (custom stocks)
Western Gunstocks Mfg. Co., 550 Valencia School Rd., Aptos, CA 95003
Joe White, Box 8505, New Brighton, Christchurch, N.Z. (blanks)
Duane Wibe, 426 Creekside Dr., Pleasant Hill, CA 94563
Bob Williams, c/o Hermans-Atlas Custom Guns, 800 E St. N.W., Washington, DC 20004
Williamson-Pate Gunsmith Service, 6021 Camp Bowie Blvd., Ft. Worth, TX 76116
Robert M. Winter, Box 484, Menno, S.D. 57045
Fred Wranic, 6919 Santa Fe, Huntington Park, Calif. 90255 (mesquite)

TARGETS, BULLET & CLAYBIRD TRAPS

Black Products Co., 13513 Calumet Ave., Chicago, Ill. 60627
Caswell Equipment Co., Inc., 1215 Second Ave. N., Minneapolis, MN 55405
Cole's Acku-Rite Prod., Box 25, Kennedy, N.Y. 14747 (Site Rite targets)
Detroit Bullet Trap Co., 2233 N. Palmer Dr., Schaumburg, Ill. 60172
Duncan Prods., P.O. Box 19036, Diamond Lake Sta., Minneapolis, MN 55419 (target holders)
Electro Ballistic Lab., P.O. Box 5876, Stanford, CA 94305 (Electronic Trap Boy)
Ellwood Epps (Orillia) Ltd., Hwy. 11 North, Orillia, Ont., Canada (hand traps)
Gopher Shooter's Supply, Box 246, Faribault, Minn. 55021 (Lok-A-Leg target holders)
Laporte S.A., B.P. 212, 06 Antibes, France (claybird traps)
Millard F. Lerch, Box 163, 10842 Front St., Mokena, Ill. 60448 (bullet target)
National Target Co., 4960 Wyaconda Rd., Rockville, MD 20852
Outers Laboratories, Inc., Onalaska, Wis. 54650 (claybird traps)
Peterson Label Co., P.O. Box 186, Redding Ridge, CT 06876 (paste-ons)
Professional Tape Co., 355 E. Burlington Rd., Riverside, Ill. 60546 (Time Labels)
Recreation Prods. Res. Inc., 158 Franklin Ave., Ridgewood, NJ 07450 (Butts bullet trap)
Remington Arms Co., Bridgeport, Conn. 06602 (claybird traps)
Scientific Prod. Corp., 426 Swann Ave., Alexandria, VA 22301 (Targeteer)
Sheridan Products, Inc., 3205 Sheridan, Racine, Wis. 53403 (traps)
Shooting Equip. Inc., 2001 N. Parkside Ave., Chicago, Ill. 60639 (electric range)
Targ-It Stamp Co., Box G, Emlenton, PA 16373 (rubber stamp targets)
Time Products Co. (See Prof. Tape Co.)
Trius Prod., Box 25, Cleves, O. 45002 (claybird, can thrower)
Winchester-Western, New Haven, Conn. 06504 (claybird traps)

TAXIDERMY

Jack Atcheson & Sons, Inc., 3210 Ottawa St., Butte, MT 59701
Clearfield Taxidermy, 603 Hanna St., Clearfield, PA 16830
Jonas Bros., Inc., 1037 Broadway, Denver, CO 80203 (catlg. $2)
Knopp Bros., N. 6715 Division St., Spokane, WA 99208
Mac's Taxidermy, 1316 West Ave., Waukesha, WI 53186

TRAP & SKEET SHOOTERS EQUIP.

Creed Enterprises, P.O. Box 159, Coevr D'Alene, ID 83814 (ammo pouch)
Filmat Ent., Inc., 200 Market St., East Paterson, NJ 07407 (shotshell pouches)
Laporte S.A., B.P. 212, Pont de la Brague, 06 Antibes, France (traps, claybird)
Outers Laboratories, Inc., P.O. Box 37, Onalaska, WI 54650 (trap, claybird)
Remington Arms Co., Bridgeport, CT 06602 (trap, claybird)
Super Pigeon Corp., P.O. Box 428, Princeton, MN 55371 (claybird target)
Trius Products, Box 25, Cleves, OH 45002 (can thrower; trap, claybird)
Daniel Titus, 119 Morlyn Ave., Bryn Mawr, PA 19010 (hull bag)
Winchester-Western, New Haven, CT 06504 (trap, claybird)

TRIGGERS, RELATED EQUIP.

M. H. Canjar Co., 500 E. 45th Ave., Denver, CO 80216 (triggers)
Dayton-Traister Co., P.O. Box 593, Oak Harbor, WA 98277 (triggers)
Flaig's, Babcock Blvd. & Thompson Run Rd., Millvale, PA 15209 (trigger shoe)
Gager Gage & Tool Co., 27509 Industrial Blvd., Hayward, CA 94545 (speedlock triggers f. Rem. 1100 and 870 shotguns)
Michaels of Oregon Co., P.O. Box 13010, Portland, OR 97213 (trigger guards)
Viggo Miller, P.O. Box 4181, Omaha, NB 68104 (trigger attachment)
Ohaus Corp., 29 Hanover Rd., Florham Park, NJ 07932 (trigger pull gauge)
Pachmayr Gun Works, 1220 S. Grand Ave., Los Angeles, CA 90015 (trigger shoe)
Pacific Tool Co., P.O. Drawer 2048, Ordnance Plant Rd., Grand Island, NB 68801 (trigger shoe)
Richland Arms Co., 321 W. Adrian St., Blissfield, MI 49228 (trigger pull gauge)
Schwab Gun Shop, 1103 E. Bigelow, Findlay, OH 45840 (trigger release)
Sport Service Center, 2364 N. Neva, Chicago, IL 60635 (release triggers)
Melvin Tyler, 1326 W. Britton Ave., Oklahoma City, OK 73114 (trigger shoe)
L. H. Waltersdorf, 29 Freier Rd., Quakertown, PA 18951 (release trigger)
Williams Gun Sight Co., 7389 Lapeer Rd., Davison, MI 48423 (trigger shoe)

INDEX

to the departmental and display pages of the GUN DIGEST – 30th Edition